Chapter

EMPLOYEE BENEFITS HANDBOOK

Editor

FRED K. FOULKES

Professor of Management Policy
Boston University

WARREN, GORHAM & LAMONT
Boston • New York

By WARREN, GORHAM & LAMONT, INC.
210 South Street
Boston, Massachusetts 02111

ISBN 0-88262-705-8

Library of Congress Catalog Card No. 82-70718

PRINTED IN THE UNITED STATES OF AMERICA

Contributing Authors

Ronald L. Adler
Vice-President, Reed, Roberts Associates

Paul S. Berger
Arnold & Porter

Robert A. Bildersee
Morgan, Lewis & Bockius

Thomas Brown
Policy Analyst, U.S. Department of Labor

G. Ashley Cooper
Actuary, The Wyatt Company

Barry I. Cosloy
Coopers & Lybrand

Nicholas P. Damico
Attorney, Washington, D.C.

Harold Dankner
Coopers & Lybrand

Jack M. Elkin
Consultant, Martin E. Segal Company

Fred K. Foulkes
Professor of Management Policy, Boston University

Geoffrey M. Gilbert
Ernst & Whinney

Paul A. Guerin
Administrative Director, Benefits Administration, Services, and Risk Management, Touche Ross & Co.

Howard Hensley
Chief, Division of Pension Plan Exemptions, U.S. Department of Labor

Leon E. Irish
Caplin & Drysdale, Chartered

Michael F. Klein, Jr.
Price Waterhouse

Andrew Lawlor
Coopers & Lybrand

Jeffrey D. Mamorsky
Shea & Gould

Mark Manin
Coopers & Lybrand

Rodney N. Mara
Vice-President, Towers, Perrin, Forster & Crosby

Michael J. McGee
Manager, Mass Merchandising Department, Kemper Insurance

Bruce Alan Miller
Legal Division, W.R. Grace & Co.

Thomas S. Monfried
Willkie Farr & Gallagher

Leslie J. Obus
Legal Division, W.R. Grace & Co.

Christopher O'Flinn
Manager, Domestic Benefits, Mobil Oil Corporation

Oscar Ornati
Professor of Manpower Management, Graduate School of Business Administration, New York University

Thomas H. Paine
Hewitt Associates

Robert D. Paul
Vice-Chairman, Martin E. Segal Company

Jeffrey Perlmuter
Coopers & Lybrand

Richard Reichler
Ernst & Whinney

Daniel Rosenberg
Marketing Analyst, Blue Cross and Blue Shield of Greater New York

K. Peter Schmidt
Arnold & Porter

Russell F. Schuck
Manager, Employee Benefits Planning, International Business Machines Corporation

Michael W. Sculnick
Vedder, Price, Kaufman, Kammolz & Day

Richard P. Seiden
Vice-President, Frank B. Hall Consulting Company

Steven Sieverts
Vice-President, Blue Cross and Blue Shield of Greater New York

Diana Chapman Walsh
Director of Program Evaluation, Boston University Health Policy Institute

Preface

During the past decade of remarkable growth in employee benefits, many organizations have been forced to make significant decisions relating to coverages, provisions, and funding methods on an ad hoc basis, with "bottom-line" costs often the single deciding factor. Unions have frequently adopted positions without full familiarity with the employee benefits universe and the real needs of the work force they represent. It is against this background of rapid expansion in plans and programs and the need for definitive guidance that the *Employee Benefits Handbook* has been conceived and developed.

The aim from the outset has been to provide the most complete array of reference materials possible for enlightened decision-making.

The contents of the *Handbook* follow a careful analysis of the needs of its audience—benefits administrators, personnel directors, top management, and the representatives of organized labor and government agencies, as well as the various groups of benefit professionals—attorneys, actuaries, accountants, and independent consultants. With all these groups in mind, we have tried to combine comprehensiveness with utmost practicality. More importantly, the *Handbook* has been structured to provide a truly functional approach to employee benefits, rather than a sequence of plans and options.

Thus, the volume focuses on three broad areas of fundamental importance: replacement income in the event of retirement, disability, unemployment, and death; financial protection against health-related and other extraordinary expenses incidental to daily living; and the expanding group of innovative benefits and amenities that are becoming part of the corporate environment. The *Handbook* also breaks new ground by reflecting, in the composition of its editorial board and the choice of the individual authors, the diversity of disciplines that contribute to employee benefits decision-making. It introduces the reader to the work of experts in accounting, tax planning and compliance, law, finance, employee relations, and plan design—integrated by a team of skilled editors in a unified volume that is fully cross-referenced and indexed.

Each chapter, as appropriate, examines the benefit plan's advantages and disadvantages in terms of design complexity, implementation factors, tax and legal considerations, actuarial procedures and problems, and costs to the company. A separate chapter explores various health care cost containment strategies. Early chapters deal with collective bargaining, accounting, administration, communications, and employers' reporting and fiduciary responsibilities.

Most of the discussion is descriptive. Quick-reference use is facilitated through many illustrative examples, charts, forms, and tables. In keeping with the consistent emphasis on practicality, there is a minimum of encumbering documentation. However, statutory and regulatory citations are provided in the several chapters devoted to legal and tax problems as an aid to readers concerned with compliance and regulation.

Finally, the usefulness of the *Handbook* over time has been assured through the publisher's commitment to make cumulative updates regularly available.

As editor-in-chief of this volume, it has been my privilege to work with an extraordinarily talented group of individuals. To my distinguished colleagues on the editorial board who helped and gave useful advice; to the contributing authors who drew upon their invaluable experience and expertise to provide information and analysis heretofore inaccessible in print; and to the fine staff at Warren, Gorham & Lamont, my sincere thanks and appreciation for jobs well done.

Special thanks, however, must go to the following individuals: Robert Paul, who devoted an extraordinary amount of time to this project and contributed many fine ideas both to its substance and organization; Jeffrey Mamorsky, who coordinated and edited the complex legal material; Jack Elkin, whose expert professional review helped to assure the technical quality of the *Handbook*; and Naomi Weinberg, the project book editor who edited the chapters, conformed its style, and coordinated the preparation of the volume. I am deeply grateful to all those who helped to make this *Handbook* possible.

FRED K. FOULKES

Boston, Massachusetts
February 1982

Contents

Part IV Protection Against Extraordinary or Catastrophic Costs

Part V Specialized Plans

Part I

Benefits Principles and Administration

1

Benefit Objectives and Issues

FRED K. FOULKES
Professor of Management Policy, Boston University

OVERVIEW

Benefit Classifications

In the past when benefit costs comprised a small fraction of payroll, some employers tended to view various benefit plans in a separate, piecemeal fashion. But with the cost of benefits approaching almost half of total payroll, it becomes increasingly necessary to view benefits in an integrated, coordinated way. Benefit plans today must not only be considered in terms of a package, but they must also be regarded in terms of company objectives.

Management and its professional advisors must understand the various functions of benefit plans.

If benefit plans are viewed from an employee-needs standpoint, a sensible point of view, they have three functions: they can replace income in certain situations; they provide increased security through financial protection; and they are a source of opportunities and services for the work force.

Replacement of Income. As Social Security and pensions replace earned income at the time of retirement, salary continuation and short- and long-term disability plans replace income lost through sickness or disability. Retirement benefits, which include both pension (*defined benefit*) and capital accumulation- (*defined contribution*) type plans, are generally integrated with Social Security by directly or indirectly offsetting part of the Social Security benefits. They generally are noncontributory, utilize cliff vesting (as opposed to graduated vesting), and, in the case of pensions, use a final/high-average pay benefit formula.

Companies also may offer separate benefit plans that provide income in the event of unemployment or death. Some companies provide *supplemental unemployment benefits* (SUB) in addition to unemployment compensation. Death benefits usually come from group life insurance plans. SUB was pioneered by the Ford Motor Company and the United Automobile Workers in 1955. Today it is primarily found in the automobile, steel, and rubber industries. In the automobile industry in 1981 it provided approximately 95 percent of after-tax take-home pay. With respect to death benefits provided by group life insurance plans, most are related to employee pay. The benefit typically amounts to 1 to 1.5 times annual pay. Most plans specify a dollar maximum, such as $150,000. Some employers also provide post-retirement lump-sum death benefits.

Providing Increased Security. Other benefits, such as health, dental, vision, and hearing care benefit plans, provide increased security to employees by paying for the extra or extraordinary expenses that employees may unexpectedly incur. Although employees do not wish to need such benefits, they are glad to have them available during times of emergency and need.

Employee Services and Special Services. Numerous benefits can be viewed as employee services or special services. These can range from tuition reimbursement plans to vacations and holidays. The employer may provide, for example, eleven paid holidays, three weeks of paid vacation after five years, tuition assistance after six months on the job, and substantial discounts on the products it manufactures.

Types of Benefits

As Figure 1.1 indicates, many different types of benefits are offered to employees. A traditional way to classify them is to distinguish between those that are legally required and those that are either privately offered or collectively bargained for.

Legally Required. Benefits required by law include Social Security, unemployment insurance, and workers' compensation. In 1981, for example, the Social Security tax amounted to 6.65 percent of all wages and salaries up to a base of $29,700 for both the individual and the employer. The federal-state unemployment insurance system provides benefits for those eligible workers who are temporarily unemployed. Workers' compensation insurance provides payment for adequate and reasonable hospital, medical, and surgical bills resulting from work-connected injuries or illnesses and weekly benefits, with the maximums set by state law, if the injury or illness causes the employee to be absent from work for more than a set period.

Privately Offered or Negotiated. There are, in addition, and unlike the custom in most foreign countries, those benefits which are either privately negotiated in collective bargaining or offered voluntarily by the employer such as pensions, profit sharing, tuition reimbursement, paid vacations and holidays, group medical and life insurance plans, short- and long-term disability plans, and savings and thrift plans. Private benefits of more recent vintage of this type include dental, optical, prepaid legal insurance plans, floating holidays, and coverage for second surgical opinions. Because of high inflation, there is also much current union interest in pension increases for retirees as well as establishment of pension benefits which would be adjusted automatically for the rising cost of living.

As one notes from Figure 1.1, the Chamber of Commerce includes several other types of employee benefits. These include suggestion awards, service awards, subsidized meals, and discounts on company products. Though relatively small in terms of cost, these benefits can be extremely important from an employee relations point of view.

Growth of Employee Benefits

At one time the term "fringe benefits," as applied to employees generally, was appropriate since virtually all compensation was in the form of pay for time worked. Total benefit payments as a percentage of wages and salaries were less than one percent in 1929. But over the years, the term "fringe" has become a misnomer. According to the most recent Chamber of Commerce survey, the costs of benefits averaged 36.6 percent of payroll in 1979, or $5,560 per employee. By contrast, in 1975 benefits averaged 35.4 percent of payroll, and only $3,984 per employee. Furthermore, based on a survey conducted by the Council on Employee Benefits, concerned with the expectations of companies, benefit costs could rise to 56 percent or more of payroll by 1990.

Type of benefit	***Total, all companies***	***Total, all manufacturing***	***Total, all nonmanufacturing***
Total employee benefits as percent of payroll	36.6	37.2	35.7
1. Legally required payments (employer's share only)	9.0	10.1	7.6
a. Old-Age, Survivors, Disability, and Health Insurance (FICA taxes)	5.8	5.9	5.6
b. Unemployment Compensation	1.5	1.9	1.0
c. Workers' compensation (including estimated cost of self-insured)	1.7	2.3	0.9
d. Railroad Retirement Tax, Railroad Unemployment and Cash Sickness Insurance, state sickness benefits insurance, etc.**	*	*	0.1
2. Pension, insurance, and other agreed-upon payments (employer's share only)	12.1	12.1	12.1
a. Pension plan premiums and pension payments not covered by insurance-type plan (net)	5.4	4.7	6.4
b. Life insurance premiums; death benefits; hospital, surgical, medical, and major medical insurance premiums, etc. (net)	5.7	6.6	4.4
c. Salary continuation or long-term disability	0.3	0.3	0.3
d. Dental insurance premiums	0.3	0.3	0.2
e. Discounts on goods and services purchased from company by employees	0.1	*	0.2
f. Employee meals furnished by company	0.1	*	0.3
g. Miscellaneous payments (compensation payments in excess of legal requirements, separation or termination pay allowances, moving expenses, etc.)	0.2	0.2	0.3
3. Paid rest periods, lunch periods, wash-up time, travel time, clothes-change time, get-ready time, etc.	3.5	3.6	3.4

4. Payments for time not worked	9.5	8.8	10.2
a. Paid vacations and payments in lieu of vacation	4.7	4.5	4.8
b. Payments for holidays not worked	3.2	3.2	3.1
c. Paid sick leave	1.2	0.8	1.8
d. Payments for State or National Guard duty; jury, witness, and voting pay allowances; payments for time lost due to death in family or other personal reasons, etc.	0.4	0.3	0.5
5. Other items	2.5	2.6	2.4
a. Profit-sharing payments	1.4	1.6	1.2
b. Contributions to employee thrift plans	0.3	0.2	0.4
c. Christmas or other special bonuses, service awards, suggestion awards, etc.	0.4	0.5	0.3
d. Employee education expenditures (tuition refunds, etc.)	0.2	0.1	0.3
e. Special wage payments ordered by courts, payments to union stewards, etc.	0.2	0.2	0.2
Total employee benefits as cents per payroll hour	267.6	267.1	268.2
Total employee benefits as dollars per year per employee	5,560	5,605	5,501

* Less than 0.05 percent.
** Figure shown is considerably less than legal rate, because most reporting companies had only a small proportion of employees covered by tax.
Source: Employee Benefits 1979, U.S. Chamber of Commerce.

Fig. 1.1 Employee Benefits, by Type of Payment, 1979

Industry payments vary widely. The Chamber survey reported benefits paid by hospitals averaged 28.2 percent of payroll in 1979; chemicals and allied products payments averaged 43.1 percent of payroll. Traditionally those companies in the P-industries—pharmaceutical, petroleum, and photography—have offered their employees outstanding benefit packages. As a consequence, many employees today seem to view benefits not as special privileges but rather as employee rights.

There are five major reasons that explain both the growth and the widespread prevalence of significant benefit programs.

Employer Paternalism and Concern. Many employers have felt an obligation to take care of those who worked for them. It was thought that employees should simply have, for instance, adequate medical and pension plans. These companies also viewed these expenditures as good for business. Workers freed from worrying about family medical expenses are more productive workers because they have greater peace of mind.

Nearly 300 years ago, Dr. Bernardino Ramazzini, considered the father of occupational medicine, said, "Tis a sordid profit that's accomplished by the destruction of health." Many industrial leaders have wanted to take care of their employees. In years past it was through improved working conditions and health and welfare plans. Today it may be through physical fitness centers and stress reduction programs.

Union Pressures. In the late 1930s and 1940s after key industries were unionized and pensions and insurance were held to be bargainable issues under the National Labor Relations Act, there was intense union interest, responding to perceived member desires, in benefits and benefit improvements. Benefits also increased during World War II, when wages were frozen and companies were seeking incentives to attract and retain workers. The success of major unions in negotiating generous specific benefit plans created pressure for other unionized as well as non-union companies either to match or to exceed such programs. Unions also viewed increased time-off benefits such as longer vacations and more holidays as ways to increase employment by spreading the available work during periods of high unemployment. Major unions have been particularly interested in various employment and income security programs. The United Auto Workers' past interest in SUBs and current interest in the four-day workweek are two such examples.

International staffs of major unions include among their members many technicians, such as lawyers, accountants, and actuaries who usually want to bargain not only benefits but costs as well. They may also display interest in how the company is managing the pension fund.

Competitive Pressures. Companies may have to improve or add benefit programs simply to remain reasonably competitive in the labor markets in which they compete for employees. For instance, a company without a dental plan in a geographic area where most employers have such plans may, unless its other benefit programs are unusually generous, find it difficult to continue to resist either employee or union pressures for such plans. This is a particularly difficult issue for the large national employer that, by design, offers the same benefit package to all of its employees regardless of where in the United States they work. While a vision care plan in West Coast plants may be necessary to compete in that area, the national adoption of such a plan may be both unduly expensive for the employer and unnecessary for competitive purposes in other parts of the country.

A company may design and offer benefit plans that give it a competitive advantage in the attraction and/or retention of employees. For example, the First National Bank of Chicago offered outstanding college graduates a special "Scholars" program which allowed them to receive an MBA from the University of Chicago at bank expense and, in part, on bank time. Trainees selected for this program were given jobs related to the courses they were taking either in the late afternoon or the evening. Some companies have also been unusually effective in recruiting outstanding engineering undergraduates by giving them an opportunity to earn a master's degree by taking courses on company premises offered by professors from cooperating universities. Offering childcare facilities, van pools, flexible working hours or the four-day workweek are other ways some companies have been able to recruit and retain some employees.

Tax Considerations. U.S. tax laws encourage the growth and development of substantial private benefit programs. In most cases the benefit purchased is not taxable to the individual but its cost is fully deductible for tax purposes to the corporation. Company contributions to employee benefits, such as pension and deferred profit-sharing plans, health insurance, and other comparable coverages, are exempted from employee taxation by existing law. For example, a company deducts its pension costs but the value of that benefit is not taxable to the individual until he actually retires and begins receiving retirement income. Also, when the employee buys life insurance, it is purchased with after-tax dollars. Company-provided life insurance, on the other hand, is bought with pre-tax dollars. With inflation-type wage increases pushing the average individual into higher tax brackets, the argument for company-provided benefits becomes increasingly compelling. With the so-called bracket-creep, more and more families are being pushed into the 40 and 50 percent tax brackets.

Savings and thrift plans, which permit employees to contribute a percentage of their annual salaries to a managed fund, are particularly attractive because the regular employee contribution is generally matched by a company contribution. While the most common match is 50 percent, some companies match 75 percent or even dollar for dollar. The employee also reaps the advantages of a professionally managed fund. In addition, if employees are able to keep their savings intact, contributions earn interest and dividends on a tax-deferred basis. The net effect of these plans is that long-service employees, at the time of retirement, can have a nest egg or pool of cash of as much or more than twice their final salaries.

Consider also the attractiveness of a group legal service plan. Under such plans, employer contributions as well as plan benefits are excluded from the worker's taxable income. Given the tax structure, it is easy to understand the attractiveness of qualified benefits.

Other types of employee benefits which have been exempted from taxation by Internal Revenue Service regulations, include price discounts enjoyed by department store employees, reduced air fares for airline employees, free or subsidized meals in company cafeterias, and supper money for employees who work overtime. At various times the IRS has considered the taxation of certain of these benefits. While such benefits cause some obvious inequities, their taxation would result in bookkeeping difficulties as well as economic, social, and political costs.

Economies of Scale. Benefits purchased by the company can be obtained more cheaply than those purchased individually. In addition to the convenience and tax aspects, group insurance rates are simply lower than individual rates. Many employees are pleased to be able to participate through payroll deductions in company-sponsored benefits in which the entire cost is passed over to the participating employees, because the cost through the group is considerably less than the amount employees would have to pay on their own for comparable benefits. Some examples of these "no or low cost" to the company benefits are: family and dependent life insurance, group automobile insurance, homeowners' and tenants' insurance, extra disability income and additional life insurance.

Role of the Benefits Director

With the growing importance of employee benefits throughout the business and industrial community, increasing recognition has been awarded to those charged with benefits planning and administration. Frequently the person in charge of benefits is also responsible for wage and salary administration. The title *Director of Compensation and Employee Benefits* is found in larger corporations, with this individual frequently accorded vice-presidential rank. For obvious reasons, the benefits director has earned his position in the top councils of management where vital contributions are made to short-term and strategic planning.

Escalation of Benefit Costs

Benefit costs are escalating not only because of the costs of new programs and improvements, but also because of the spiraling costs of maintaining existing benefit plans. This is, in part, because so many benefits are payroll-related. With salaries rising rapidly because of inflation, benefit costs, too, increase sharply. Company-provided life insurance related to salary level increases as pay rises. A pension plan designed to provide a person with 50 percent of his final five-year's average pay upon retirement requires greater employer contributions during periods of high inflation, rapidly rising salaries, and poor investment results. Then, too, insurance premiums for health care have soared. Health insurance costs, over which the employer has little or no control, are the fastest increasing benefit cost. At some companies the health insurance carrier has become a very large outside supplier. As Figure 1.1 shows, the high-cost benefits are pension and medical plans.

ESTABLISHING CORPORATE OBJECTIVES

Individual Company Philosophy and Motivation

It is important for companies to develop philosophies and objectives with respect to benefits. Such goals function as both a framework and a standard by which potential benefit changes can be evaluated. Some large companies wishing to remain non-union attempt to maintain leadership positions with respect to benefits. Some of these companies, moreover, operate on the principle of egalitarian treatment All employees, from janitors to vice-presidents, receive the same benefit package. One such company is Hewlett-Packard, whose corporate benefits objective is expressed as follows:

> OBJECTIVE: To help HP [Hewlett-Packard] people share in the company's success, which they make possible; to provide job security based on their performance; to recognize their individual achievements; and to help people gain a sense of personal satisfaction and accomplishment from their work.

Under this umbrella objective, one better understands the company's benefit plans. Commenting on the company's approach, William Hewlett, co-founder of the company, writes in an employee publication the following:

> There are a number of corollaries to this policy. One is that employees should be in a position to benefit directly from the success of the organization. This led to the early introduction of a profit-sharing plan, and eventually to the employee stock purchase plan. A second corollary was that if an employee was worried about pressing problems at home, he could not be expected to concentrate fully on the job. This, and the fact that in the early days Dave [Packard] and I were very closely associated with people throughout the company and thus had a chance to see firsthand the devastating effect of domestic tragedy, led, amongst other things, to the very early introduction of medical insurance for catastrophic illness.

On the other hand, companies with different attitudes and values provide more attractive benefit packages and many additional perquisites for executives, a practice which the founders of Hewlett-Packard would not tolerate.

Formulating Basic Guidelines

Rather than approaching benefits in a piecemeal and uncoordinated fashion, management should establish benefit objectives that relate to business goals. What, for example, is the retirement income plan to accomplish? Unless realistic goals are established, it is impossible to evaluate benefit changes intelligently.

In addition to being responsive to top management values, the benefits a company offers must respond to its business needs and the economics of the industry in which a company competes. Some companies have experienced competitive problems when they have imposed their benefit plans on acquired divisions. Even though there are advantages to uniformity, frequently it is appropriate for a highly diverse company to offer different benefit plans.

More and more companies are adopting an objective of cost containment with respect to benefits. One company which seeks to "lead in pay and lag in benefits" only tries to stay even with competition for the so-called visible benefits, such as health care.

POLICY AND ADMINISTRATIVE ISSUES

As the cost of benefits has escalated, so has the attention which is paid to both the methods of planning, designing, administering, and communicating benefit programs. Benefit objectives that take into account both the needs of the company and of the employees have to be articulated well so that benefit plans will be well designed, coordinated, and cost effective. Effective communications programs with employees, with insurers outside the company, and with various government agencies become increasingly important as does keeping abreast and complying with state and federal legislation such as the federal Employee Retirement Income and Security Act of 1974 (ERISA). As various sections of this handbook make clear, the accounting, financial, legal, and tax considerations with respect to employee benefit plans are extremely important.

Design

Designing benefit plans that respond to employee needs is not easy when there is much diversity within the work force. In addition to the basic trade-off between pay and benefits, younger workers may be interested in longer vacations and more holidays while older employees will favor higher pension benefits. Designing benefit plans for "the average employee" is becoming increasingly complex. Attitude surveys and other forms of employee input are frequently used to determine employee preferences. It may be that to employees the perceived value of a lower cost benefit is higher than the perceived value of a higher cost benefit. If so, such employee preference analysis is invaluable to the company desiring to minimize benefit costs while maximizing employee satisfaction. At one company it was discovered through such analysis that employees preferred two additional holidays over an additional week of vacation. Another company substituted a dental plan in exchange for the cancellation of its annual Christmas party. The increased diversity in the work force, including more two-career couples, as well as recent changes in the tax laws, results in more companies considering flexible benefits, or the so-called cafeteria approach to compensation. In a cafeteria plan, employees participate in a basic decision-making process by electing certain benefits from a package of company-provided benefit options.

Many benefit problems that companies experience are the result of poor initial design. Such designs may result from an early expedient decision to copy another company's plan rather than to tailor one to the needs of a particular company and its employees. Since it is probably impossible to reduce benefits, initial poor designing can be very costly to correct. Personnel and finance staffs need to plan and coordinate effectively up front rather than after the fact.

Communication

Few employees know very much about employee benefits. Since most employees do not understand what they have nor appreciate either their benefits or the costs, company benefit communication programs are becoming common. Delta Airlines presents an annual slide show to its employees which, among other purposes, depicts Delta's benefits in relation to those of its competitors. Companies also frequently send an annual benefit statement to employees at home which educates and informs employees and their spouses. A spouse, for example, might learn that the company gives $25,000 of free life insurance. Other companies have developed other means of communicating benefits. Included in such methods are meetings, publications, and contests requiring employees to use their benefit handbooks. Through such communications programs, companies hope to create more awareness of benefit programs, to help employees understand changes in such programs, and to foster greater appreciation of the company.

Benefit plans need to be communicated in easy-to-understand language; short sentences with active verbs are best. Increasingly, companies are also using other technologies in addition to print to communicate benefits. Pictures, films, or videotapes can effectively communicate the benefit message.

Cost Containment

With benefit costs rising so rapidly, even to simply maintain existing benefit levels, it is not surprising that cost containment strategies are being developed rapidly. Cost control associated with employee benefits, as has been indicated, is receiving top management priority. Many different approaches are being tried.

Increased Emphasis on Management. Talented benefits managers and consultants are recommending a variety of ways to contain costs. More insured plans are being put out for competitive bids. Increased pressure is being put on investment managers to perform with respect to the management of pension or profit-sharing funds. Those investment managers who do not perform better than the average may lose the account. A variety of ways is being discovered to share financing and administrative costs.

Exploring Alternative Methods. Self-insurance, too, is being tried in some areas as are administrative service contracts. For large companies the establishment of special tax-exempt trusts for funding employee benefits, such as health, accident, and disability insurance, can also result in substantial reductions in costs as compared with conventional insurance plans. The coordination of benefits can also result in some savings.

Health Care Cost Containment. With health costs soaring, company managers are also taking keen interest in the inefficiencies of the nation's health care delivery system. Some companies are training their executives, who are also hospital board members, to ask the hard questions at trustee meetings. Why, for instance, can't more tests be done on an outpatient basis? In 1979, Health Maintenance Organizations (HMOs), whose aim is preventive medicine, had close to 8 million Americans covered. Top management interest and action as well as location and perceived quality has a great impact on whether many company employees enroll in an HMO.

Companies are also using claims data to contain health care costs. When health services data is used for utilization review purposes, a company can manage its medical costs more effectively. Companies, in addition, are reviewing claims for compliance with coverage rules, for appropriateness of service, fees and charges, and for possible fraud and abuse.

Many companies are encouraging the development of HMOs and health education. If the real solution is prevention, then it makes sense to offer physical fitness, weight reduction, and smoking cessation courses as well as hypertension screening and employee assistance programs. The savings can be in reduced insurance premiums and increased productivity. A few companies have even tried cost-reduction programs whereby some of the savings are shared with the employee. This feature helps obtain necessary employee involvement. In such medical rebate plans, employees who do not spend over a specified sum on medical expenses get the difference.

Contributory Programs. Another suggested way to contain costs and to increase employee awareness of benefits and costs is to have a benefit package that is contributory rather than noncontributory. In noncontributory programs the company pays 100 percent of the costs. If the employee must contribute toward, for instance, his health care and pension plans, he, some think, better appreciates what the company is providing. Employee contributions also reduce the company's costs. Union leaders generally find such company arguments unpersuasive. They favor noncontributory benefit programs. Tax laws also work against employee contributions. It does not make good economic sense for the employee to purchase with after-tax income what the company can buy for him more economically with pre-tax income.

Government Regulations

Objectives. Prior to ERISA, the IRS had a rule that if a plan were to be qualified its essential features had to be communicated. But compliance with current federal and state legislation now requires an increasingly larger share of company resources. Administered by both the Labor and Treasury Departments, ERISA established, among other objectives, new standards with respect to eligibility and vesting, funding, reporting and disclosure, and fiduciary responsibilities. Pension plans had to be amended to comply with this law. Greater employee communications programs as well as reports to the government were required. In addition to a summary plan description, the plan administrator or sponsor must furnish certain material upon written request from employees and must make certain material available at a designated place, usually the principal office of the plan administrator.

Impact of ERISA and Anti-Discrimination Laws. Besides legal considerations with respect to benefit communications, federal and state government regulations also affect the substance of private employee benefit plans. For example, in 1978 Congress passed a law which prohibited employment discrimination on the basis of pregnancy. Pregnancy, therefore, had to be treated like any other disability under the company's health, temporary disability, or sick leave plan. Similarly, in 1978 federal law (the Age Discrimination in Employment Act—as amended in 1978), postponed the age of mandatory retirement from age 65 to age 70. Some states, however, have passed laws that outlaw mandatory retirement at any age. These laws, however, permit employers to modify some of their benefits for older workers.

Benefit Staffs and Consultants

Talented employee benefit managers and employee benefit consultants have been much in demand due to increased costs and complexity of employee benefits. Benefit managers at large companies command high salaries today. In addition, the expertise of benefit consultants is often called upon in both small and large companies. The use of experienced consultants can be very cost effective from the employer's point of view. Through their expertise and experience they can help with questions concerning design, funding, and communications. Their data banks and surveys can also be invaluable.

FUTURE DEVELOPMENTS

It is unlikely that the 1980s will see the introduction of new benefits characteristic of earlier times. This is because the cost of maintaining present benefit levels is becoming prohibitively expensive. Cost containment will almost assuredly be the order of the day for the 1980s. Low-cost changes, however, that respond to worker needs will be looked upon with favor.

Flexible benefits will probably grow dramatically in the next decade. As several large companies pioneer and new policies and attitudes gain exposure, other companies will probably follow. A flexible benefits program may represent another cost containment approach if management can get something back in exchange for its introduction.

Benefit staffs, to be sure, will become even more professional. Armed with lessons from economics, statistics, psychology, sociology, and corporate strategy, their advice and recommendations will be increasingly sought and respected. Their contributions will be recognized and rewarded as they find new managerial approaches to contain or reduce costs.

2

Principles of Plan Design

ROBERT D. PAUL
Vice-Chairman, Martin E. Segal Company

JACK M. ELKIN
Consultant, Martin E. Segal Company

HISTORICAL ROOTS OF BENEFIT DESIGN

As pointed out in Chapter 1, employee benefits are clearly a major component of the economic life of both employers and employees today. The panoply of benefits provided through government-mandated plans, privately initiated plans, or as a result of collective bargaining, was not created all at once. Benefits have grown over a long period, with most of the growth dating from the Great Depression and the government's entry into the field of social insurance in the 1930s. Their development, moreover, at least in the earlier stages, was more haphazard than systematic.

The Railroad Pensions

The earliest private pensions go back just over 100 years, but only in the railroad industry, where they eventually covered over 90 percent of the employees, did they become at all widespread until after World War II. They were unilaterally employer-sponsored and generally unfunded, that is, pay-as-you-go plans. When they were hit by the Depression, the railroads first reduced benefits then discontinued paying them altogether and rescue came only when Congress created in 1935 a federal retirement system for railroad workers. Significant growth in the private pension field took place beginning with the 1940s. Employers during World War II were encouraged to adopt pension and other employee benefit programs because of the tax deductibility of their costs at a time when corporate tax rates were at historic heights and because such costs were not subject to wage controls. Originally these plans were viewed as completely at the discretion of the employer, putting him under no legal obligation to continue payments and conferring on the employee no legal rights to demand them. In 1948, as the result of a National Labor Relations Board ruling, pension plans became subject to collective bargaining. Although some plans had been negotiated earlier, it was the years that followed that witnessed the rapid growth of negotiated pension and other employee benefit plans.

Pension Momentum and the Insurance Industry

Momentum was maintained after the war into the 1950s and 1960s—in both the unionized and non-unionized sectors of the economy—by growing public interest in pensions as an essential supplement to Social Security, by the need of employers to remain competitive in the labor market, and by favorable tax legislation. An important factor encouraging the establishment of pension plans, especially for smaller employers, was the insurance industry, which marketed a variety of products to meet the needs of employers who wished to provide the benefits but with instruments that suited their specific situations. Today, with the growth rate now substantially leveled off, about half of all the workers in industry and commerce—nearly two-thirds of those who have reached age 25 and have spent at least a year with their employer—are covered by private pension plans.

Expanding Benefits

Group insurance to protect employees against the economic hazards resulting from death, sickness, and disability developed along lines roughly parallel to those of pensions and under similar economic and historical influences. The first employer-sponsored funds providing such benefits were created in the latter part of the last century. They were generally mutual benefit funds financed by the employees themselves. The first major group life insurance plan written by a standard insurance company and financed by the employer was in 1912. Group sickness and accident insurance, to provide payments for disability due to sickness or accident not compensable by workers' compensation laws, was a by-product of group life insurance and began to be written in the 1920s. The earliest Blue Cross plans provided hospital benefits on a group basis, and later the Blue Shield plans, providing surgical benefits, followed in the 1930s.

Although a few health and welfare plans had been established through collective bargaining in previous years, a major impetus to their proliferation was provided, as in the case of pensions, by the wartime restrictions on wage increases and by the expanded scope of collective bargaining during and in the years following World War II.

Major medical insurance dates from around 1950 and dental insurance followed. Later, the enactment of the Medicare program made it feasible to provide supplemental major medical protection to retired employees. By 1978, about 181 million persons had insurance protection against hospital expense, 172 million against surgical expense, 142 million against major medical expense, and 60 million against dental expense. In addition, 70 million had short-term and 19 million long-term disability income insurance. The majority of these benefits were provided under group benefit plans.

Unemployment Compensation

Insurance against unemployment is a more recent development. Except for a few scattered guaranteed annual wage plans and plans guaranteeing a minimum number of days of employment, there was no protection against unemployment in the form of cash benefits before the enactment in the 1930s of the state unemployment insurance laws. After some years of working to liberalize these laws, labor unions began to direct their efforts towards supplementing them by means of Supplemental Unemployment Benefit (SUB) plans. The first SUB plan was negotiated in 1955 and today there are about 1,000 such plans registered with the Department of Labor, primarily in the automobile, steel, rubber, and glass industries.

Evolving Design Criteria

In the earlier stages of the various benefit programs, benefit design was, of course, relatively simple and the level of benefits relatively low. Efforts were at first concentrated only on the most pressing needs, and there were limitations on the availability of money, on the variety of suitable insurance arrangements, and on administrative experience. Eventually, more and more hazards were insured against, patterns of comprehensive protection were gradually developed and became widespread, and higher and higher levels of benefit adequacy were attained.

Pension Liberalization. Early pension plans generally provided benefits only at age 65 or 70, sometimes on disability at a relatively advanced age, but in any event, only after a long period of uninterrupted service. Early retirement on reduced pensions came later, as well as age retirement for employees with shorter periods of service and, in some cases, disability retirement at younger ages. Still later developments were deferred, that is, vested, pensions for those leaving employment with substantial service but before retirement age; full retirement benefits for those with many (twenty-five to thirty-five) years of service, regardless of age; supplementary benefits for those retiring on reduced early retirement pensions to bridge the period until Social Security benefits became payable; and various forms of pre-retirement death benefits.

Group deferred annuity contracts, which were widely used from the 1940s into the 1960s, were compatible only with the simplest of plans that provided nothing more than age retirement benefits. Only with the growth of self-insured arrangements and the development by the insurance industry of deposit administration and immediate participation guarantee contracts did plans acquire the flexibility that made it possible to provide a wide variety of benefits.

Decline of Contributory Plans. Although the very early pension plans were mainly final-pay plans, those funded by group deferred annuity contracts were of necessity career-average plans. As these contracts were abandoned in favor of self-insurance or as they were supplemented by the newer, more flexible, forms of insurance contract, final-pay plans again became the predominant form. At the same time there took place a gradual reduction in the proportion of contributory plans and today these account for a small minority of the total.

Indemnity Health Care. Employee welfare or health benefit plans of twenty and twenty-five years ago, like the early pension plans, were simple and uncomplicated by today's standards. They provided relatively few benefits and, with the notable exception of Blue Cross or Blue Shield, these were usually indemnity benefits. Blue Cross provides a service benefit—namely semi-private room accommodation and most other expenses, regardless of cost. Indemnity programs pay a stated number of dollars for each day of hospital stay or each surgical procedure.

In addition to life insurance, accidental death and dismemberment and weekly accident or sickness benefits, the benefit plans included hospitalization, a surgical scheduled benefit, and perhaps an in-hospital medical visit and diagnostic x-ray and laboratory benefit. Dependent coverages were frequently optional. Major Medical benefits were not yet developed; dental and drug expenses were considered uninsurable; and service benefits and reasonable and customary reimbursement were uncommon.

Modern Health Benefits. Today, drugs, vision care, and dental care are common coverages. There are very few health benefit programs written that do not provide some form of major or comprehensive medical coverage. The variation in co-insurance, deductibles, and maximums that are today available under major medical plans are far different from those of fifteen or twenty years ago. New types of health delivery systems have been introduced. In such programs as prepaid group Health Maintenance Organizations (HMOs) and individual practice association HMOs, the insurer and provider of care are the same.

Not too many years ago employers were limited in the way they could fund these benefit programs. They had a choice of insurance or self-insurance. If insured, it was either community rated or experience rated. Today there is a choice of insurance alternatives including Administrative Services Only contracts, minimum premium contracts, retrospective experience rating, and prospective experience rating. With interest rates going up, insurance companies have agreed to alternative methods of collecting premiums, maintaining reserves, and paying dividends. These alternative methods are geared to the needs and interests of the policyholder.

The past thirty years have seen many changes in the population covered, the benefits provided, the way these benefits are provided, and the way they are paid for. The changes in the coming years may be even greater and further developments in the provision of welfare benefits can be expected.

BENEFIT GOALS

The development of employee benefit plans and the particular forms they took were the result of efforts by employers and employees to achieve their respective goals, as these goals were modified by the restraints imposed by a government that had its own interests to pursue.

Employer Objectives

Employer objectives, which originally may have been limited to a desire to extend a humanitarian helping hand to economically depressed present and former employees, gradually expanded to include the improvement in efficiency and productivity that could be achieved by satisfied personnel, reduced turnover, and the orderly retirement of employees no longer productive. The more widespread benefit programs became, the more important it became for employers without programs to adopt them in order to remain competitive in the recruitment and retention of valuable employees. Sometimes they adopted them as a means of inhibiting a drive toward unionization with pensions or other benefits as the objective. Finally, among the employer's considerations is the constant need to keep costs down without doing undue violence to the objectives. Hence, the emphasis on such areas as cost containment of medical programs and investment return of pension assets.

Employee Objectives

The employee's goals can, by and large, be put under the heading of security—against excess inroads into current income because of the extra expenses resulting from sickness or accident and against loss of income because of disability, unemployment, retirement, or death. The employee also wants to enjoy this protection at no expense to himself if possible or, at least, with a minimum personal contribution. Among the goals of a unionized employee group must be included the goals of the union: increasing its membership, influence, and bargaining power. Not all employees require the same elements or the same degree of a security package. Some see more need for life insurance, others for more medical insurance, and still others find their greatest reward in longer vacations and in contributions to a capital accumulation account. An employer that can meet such diverse objectives can naturally count on a greater degree of employee satisfaction. We are consequently seeing the development—still in only scattered situations, however—of flexible benefit programs, under which all employees are covered by a basic core of benefits and each is given a list, cafeteria-style, from which to select the rest of his benefit package.

Government Influence

The government has its own goals in the area of employee benefits and sometimes exercises a restraining influence on those pursued by employers and employees. Government influence is exerted through labor laws that attempt to balance the interests of labor and management and through tax laws that, on the one hand, encourage the establishment of benefit programs and, on the other, protect the public against discriminatory use of tax advantages.

Benefit Trends

The programs are probably now approaching maturity. Further growth is likely to be mainly horizontal, that is, in the extent of employer coverage for benefits already provided by the larger employers. More employers, for example, are recognizing the need for post-retirement cost-of-living adjustments in pension plans. Dental benefits are now spreading rapidly and group legal plans are more frequently part of collective bargaining settlements. Day care centers, tuition refund payments, child adoption allowances, and other types of benefits recently developed to cater to the changing nature of the work force and environment—more women, more two-worker families, more flexible work hours, longer vacations—are among the more significant trends in the early 1980s. There is still, however, apparently some room for new forms of benefit. Group automobile insurance is being experimented with in some companies, and group homeowners' insurance may be just over the horizon.

CONTEMPORARY DESIGN PRINCIPLES

Elements of Compensation

Because pay and the various types of benefits are all forms of compensation, they have come to be classified by plan designers in four major categories:

Direct Compensation. Money payments which provide the employee and his dependents with a certain standard of living while he is employed.

Protective Compensation. Protection for the income of an employee against certain risks entailing extraordinary, infrequent, and not easily budgeted expenses that would otherwise reduce his standard of living, such as accident, sickness, dental treatment, and legal emergency. These are programs providing hospital, surgical, major medical, dental, prepaid legal, and other types of insurance.

Replacement Compensation. Replaces income from employment when it is cut off for one reason or another. Loss of income may be permanent because of death, retirement, or permanent disability. It may be temporary because of unemployment, sickness, or accident. Replacement of income is provided by pensions, life insurance, and sickness and accident benefits, unemployment insurance and supplementary unemployment benefits, and long-term disability benefits.

Capital Compensation. This allows the employee to accumulate capital for various purposes—for example, to supplement retirement income, to finance children's education, to purchase a home, or to pass on to the next generation. Plans which meet these needs in whole or in part are thrift and savings plans, profit-sharing plans, Employee Stock Ownership Plans (ESOPs) and Tax Reduction Act Stock Ownership Plans (TRASOPs), and a wide variety of plans providing executives with stock options, restricted stock, stock appreciation rights, and other forms of deferred compensation.

A more detailed description of these four kinds of compensation, together with their tax consequences to employer and employee, is presented in Appendix 2-1 found at the end of this chapter.

Determining Benefit Adequacy

Retirement Income. Using this analytic framework, the designer then needs to establish objectives to be met by all government and private plans available to a particular employee population. For example, at retirement an employee typically has Social Security benefits and a private pension to replace his preretirement take-home pay. The ratio of the employee's benefit to his preretirement earnings is usually called the replacement ratio.

Replacement ratio. Because taxes in retirement are lower and work-related expenses such as commuting and outside lunches are eliminated, preretirement income may not need to be fully replaced after retirement. But no single replacement ratio can be used as the benchmark for measuring adequacy of retirement income for employees at all income levels. And within each income level, individuals or family units have different needs and expenditures. To compensate for these variables, retirement income needs may best be considered as a range of replacement ratios for each preretirement earnings category rather than a single point at which retirement income is considered adequate.

Little information is currently available on income needs after retirement. However, from statistics compiled by the Bureau of Labor Statistics, it can be estimated that retired couples' expenditure needs are approximately 75 percent of expenditures immediately prior to retirement. This relationship is derived by comparing the expenditures of married couples age 65 and over with those of married couples between ages 55 and 65. Obviously, since these are two different groups of people, their expenditure patterns do not depict the changes that one group is likely to experience as it moves through different life cycle periods. Moreover, the statistics do not show how many of the under age 65 group are retired and how many of the over age 65 group are still in the work force. Also, the fact that expenditures are lower does not necessarily mean that income needs have declined. Some may hold that expenditures decline as a result of a decrease in income. Based on these considerations, a replacement ratio target of between 75 percent and 90 percent of preretirement take-home pay might be taken as a reasonable objective.

Disposable income goals. Figure 2.1 illustrates the retirement income amounts necessary to replace 75 percent and 90 percent of preretirement disposable income at various earnings levels for a single employee retiring at age 65. At $15,000, for example, disposable preretirement income is $11,400. To replace 90 percent of that amount, together with Social Security of $5,500, the retirement plan needs to provide $4,900. At the $100,000 level, $61,500 is needed from the retirement plan to replace 90 percent of preretirement disposable income. However, at the higher income levels, a 90 percent objective is probably too high and it is more reasonable to focus on the lower end of the target range.

Single-person basis. The single wage earner is considered because the economic factors relating to his group closely approximate those applicable to a married employee with a working spouse. Census statistics for 1970 show that more than 50 percent of couples nearing retirement were dual wage earner families. It is likely that the current percentage is well above that level and will increase further still in future years.

Since the single-person and two-worker households are the predominant

Source of Income	*Amount*				
Before Retirement:					
Final Earnings	$15,000	$25,000	$40,000	$70,000	$100,000
(Taxes & OASDI)	—3,616 *	—6,844 **	—12,414 **	—27,166 **	—44,554 **
Disposal Income	11,384	18,156	27,586	42,834	55,446
Post-Retirement Objective I:					
75% Preretirement Disposable Income	$ 8,538	$13,617	$20,690	$32,126	$41,585
From:					
Social Security	5,480	7,715	7,846	7,846	7,846
Retirement Plan	3,058	6,127	14,523	30,220	45,592
(Taxes)	0	—225	—1,679	—5,940	—11,853
Post-Retirement Objective II:					
90% Preretirement Disposable Income	$10,246	$16,340	$24,827	$38,551	$49,901
From:					
Social Security	5,480	7,715	7,846	7,846	7,846
Retirement Plan	4,855	9,370	19,863	40,389	61,547
(Taxes)	—89	—745	—2,882	—9,684	—19,492

* Standard deduction: state and local taxes = 15 percent of federal taxes.

** Itemized deduction = 20 percent of gross income; state and local taxes = 15 percent of federal taxes.

Note: Based on single worker

Fig. 2.1 Disposable Income Goals for Age 65 at Retirement on December 31, 1980

family units, most designers suggest the use of the single-worker criterion. This approach requires higher benefits than would result from taking into account the tax treatment and Social Security benefits applicable when there is a dependent spouse. In addition, such a design assumes that the employer's responsibility for retirement income adequacy is based only on the income paid by the employer. Taking dependent spouse income into account would not provide adequate replacement income for single workers or for dual-worker couples.

Replacement level objectives. Figure 2.2 translates the dollar requirements developed in Figure 2.1 to provide between 75 percent and 90 percent of preretirement disposable income into income needs as a percentage of gross earnings. Primary Social Security provides a portion of these needs. Income is needed from other sources, including the pension plan, to provide the remaining portion.

For employees at the $15,000 income level, to replace 75 percent to 90 percent of preretirement disposable income requires a retirement benefit of from 20 percent to 32 percent of gross earnings. At the lower income levels, the target should probably be at the upper end of the 75 percent to 90 percent range. At $40,000, the retirement plan needs to provide from 36 percent to 50 percent of gross earnings to fall within the objective. Here the focus can be at the lower end of the range.

These ratios were developed on the basis of 1980 dollars, but because Social Security is indexed, they hold for low, median, and high income categories in the future. However, the relationships will change if there are substantial changes in the levels of Social Security benefits. As this illustration demonstrates, the primary task of the designer of replacement income programs is to help the plan sponsor decide on the appropriate level of replacement ratio. The designer then assists the sponsor in identifying all sources of income after retirement and then designs, for example, a pension plan to fill whatever gap remains. The material in Appendix 2-1 will be of help in identifying all sources of post-retirement income.

Cost considerations may force an employer to postpone implementation of a pension plan as generous as might be needed to meet his objectives. If so, he can go part way at first and by periodic changes bring the pension plan benefit level up to the objective.

Unemployment, Disability, and Death. A similar process of determining benefit adequacy can be used to set objectives for replacing income in the event of unemployment, disability, and death. The designer would undertake to determine what amounts are payable to an employee in the event, for example, of a permanent and total disability. A tabulation would be made of income from Social Security and all other benefit programs now provided by the employer. The total would then be compared with the objective the employer feels is appropriate.

	$15,000		$25,000		$40,000		$70,000		$100,000	
	Replacement Level Objective		*Replacement Level Objective*		*Replacement Level Objective*		*Replacement Level Objective*		*Replacement Level Objective*	
	75%	90%	75%	90%	75%	90%	75%	90%	75%	90%
Total gross income from retirement plan and Social Security: Amount*	$8,538	$10,335	$13,842	$17,085	$22,369	$27,709	$38,066	$48,235	$53,438	$69,393
Percent of final earnings	57%	69%	55%	68%	56%	69%	54%	69%	53%	69%
Social Security, as a percentage of final earnings	37%	37%	31%	31%	20%	20%	11%	11%	8%	8%
Gross income needed from retirement plan, as a percentage of final earnings	20%	32%	24%	37%	36%	50%	43%	58%	46%	62%

* Disposable Income plus taxes from Figure 2.1.

Fig. 2.2 Replacement Level Objectives at Age 65 Retirement by Final Earnings

For benefits in the event of death, account should be taken of the needs of a family left without all or part of its income. Identifying all sources of income payable by governmentally mandated and employee benefit programs is extremely important. Typical corporations provide life insurance as a multiple of salary. These amounts will provide very different replacement rates for two equally paid employees at different ages. Rarely are life insurance programs thought of as replacements for the stream of earnings cut off by early death. Designers can, therefore, be of considerable help in assisting employers to make the translation from lump-sum payments that are a multiple of salary to their equivalent value as lifetime income. Once all sources of death benefit protection have been translated into annual lifetime payments, objectives can be set and plans designed or amended to meet the objectives.

Replacing income during periods of unemployment requires a determination of how long benefits should be payable. Since unemployment is expected to be for a short period of time, most benefit programs that supplement state unemployment insurance benefits do so for periods of up to a year or slightly longer.

Benefit programs that replace income are particularly subject to the ravages of inflation. A person totally disabled at age 45 may have a thirty-year life ahead. A program that replaced 90 percent take-home pay at age 45 will buy very little thirty years later, if inflation continues. To the extent that his benefits are partially provided by Social Security which is indexed to the CPI, he will be protected. But the part paid for under a typical employer-sponsored long-term disability program is not indexed. Employers are increasingly examining this issue for both pension plans and long-term disability programs. To a designer the issue has to do with maintaining the purchasing power set at retirement, for example. For the sponsoring employer the costs can be enormous. Accordingly, most employers have so far dealt with the issue only by providing periodic increases on an ad hoc basis.

Health Care. The design of benefit plans that protect the employee from having to use his regular stream of income to pay the extraordinary expenses of hospitalization, surgery, dental care, and the like, has evolved slowly. Initially, the argument arose between those who preferred to provide benefits that covered expenses beginning with the first dollar of cost as opposed to those who preferred that benefit payments should only be made after a certain level of costs were paid by the employee and thereafter the plan should only pay, say, 80 percent of the remainder. A second argument grew out of the issue of whether there should be reimbursement of hospital, medical, and related expenses in accordance with a schedule of allowances or, alternatively, provision of a certain amount of service—like semi-private hospital accommodations regardless of cost.

To some extent these debates arose because the suppliers of coverage came from two camps. The Blue Cross-Blue Shield and other nonprofit providers believed in providing first-dollar benefits on a service basis. The insurance companies originally advocated indemnity or reimbursement benefits in accordance with a schedule of allowances and when they introduced major medical benefits in 1950, they began to urge deductibles and coinsurance, thereby moving away from first-dollar benefits.

Over the years the distinctions have blurred; the adoption of Medicare in the mid 1960s has institutionalized reasonable and customary charges instead of scheduled allowances. Today service benefits can be obtained from insurance companies and nonprofit plans alike. Nonprofit carriers will write major medical coverage, and self-insurance has become so widespread that large plan sponsors can get underwriters to tailor-make whatever they want. The attention of designers has, as a result, shifted to the more fundamental question of how much out-of-pocket cost employees should bear when they or their family members incur medical, hospital, and related expenses. Should the amount they bear vary with their income level? Answers to these questions are useful in deciding whether to underwrite or to buy a product offered by an insurance company or nonprofit plan.

The Design Cycle

The design cycle for replacement income and protective compensation can therefore be visualized as a circular one, with the following sequential steps:

- Select an objective of replacement income to be provided or out-of-pocket cost to be met by employees
- Design a plan to meet those objectives
- Determine the short- and long-range costs of the plan
- Revise objectives and design if costs are excessive
- Decide on insurance or self-insurance or a combination
- Take competitive proposals from underwriters, investment managers, administrators as needed, and select service supplier
- Communicate the plan to participants
- Monitor performance of the plan and the suppliers of services to the plan
- Sense employee attitudes
- Repeat the whole process periodically

Relevance to Thrift Plans. This circular design cycle is now coming into greater use not only for replacement and protective compensation but also for capital accumulation compensation. The most common such plan is a thrift and savings plan. Under its terms an employee agrees to contribute 2, 4, or 6 percent of his pay and his employer matches the contributions at a 50 percent rate. The employee's money can usually be invested in stocks, bonds, an insurance contract with a guaranteed rate of interest, or company stock. The company's contribution is normally invested in company stock.

Originally, little thought was given to how much capital might be accumulated under such a plan in a career with a company. Withdrawals during employment, fluctuations in the value of company stock, the newness of such plans shifted attention away from how much might be there at retirement.

As these plans mature, more attention is being devoted to what they might buy at retirement by way of cost-of-living adjustments in retirement income, as a replacement for group life insurance no longer available after retirement, and to pay for medical bills not covered by Medicare. The growth of these plans in recent years attests to their popularity. Employers are now considering with more care what their objectives should be and their designs are taking on a more needs-oriented look.

Meeting Design Challenges

The process by which individual plans are designed has pretty well been established. Even more difficult questions arise when employers have to consider questions like:

- In what order do I adopt benefit plans? Health insurance before life insurance; profit-sharing plan before pension?
- How do I relate adoption of benefit programs to my overall business strategy?
- How can I adopt a benefit program that gives me some identity in the marketplace so I am not simply copying what others are doing?
- How valuable is employee participation in developing plans and priorities?

These are challenges faced by benefit designers in the last decades of the twentieth century. This handbook is intended to help find the answers to deal with these problems in day-to-day work.

APPENDIX 2-1 Forms and Tax Effects of Various Types of Compensation *

Type of Compensation	*Description or Remarks*	*Tax Effect for Employer*	*Tax Effect for Employee*	*Contribution by Employee*
DIRECT COMPENSATION				
1. Wages or salary	Hourly or salaried	Deductible expense	Taxed as ordinary income.	None
2. Bonus	Annual or more frequent; can be arbitrary, uniform as a percent of pay for all employees. May be paid either in cash, stock, or combination. Can be based on individual or corporate performance.	Deductible expense	Taxed as ordinary income.	None
3. Vacation		Compensation paid while employee is out is a deductible expense.	Taxed as ordinary income.	None
PROTECTIVE COMPENSATION				
1. Health insurance	Includes: (a) Hospital coverage (b) Doctor's care (c) Major Medical (d) Dental	Deductible expense	Benefits paid to employee for covered expenses for both the employee and his covered dependents are not taxable to the employee.	Optional

(*Continued*)

* Adapted with permission from *A Summary of Types of Compensation* © 1981, Martin E. Segal & Company, Inc. Revised 1982.

Type of Compensation	*Description or Remarks*	*Tax Effect for Employer*	*Tax Effect for Employee*	*Contribution by Employee*
	(e) Prescription drugs (f) Vision care (g) Maternity Can be both group and individual policies.			
2. Accidental death and dismemberment	Can also be considered replacement compensation because it provides death benefits.	Deductible expense	Both the premiums paid by the employer and the proceeds are tax-exempt.	Optional
3. Travel accident insurance	Covers the employee for injuries sustained while travelling on business for the employer. Can also be considered replacement compensation because it provides death benefits.	Deductible expense	Both the premiums paid by the employer and the proceeds are tax-exempt.	Optional
4. Group legal insurance	Protects the employee against large legal fees.	Deductible expense	Both the premiums paid by the employer and the proceeds are tax-exempt if through a qualified plan. .	Optional
5. Educational assistance	Tuition refund	Deductible expense	If the courses improve the employee's skills on the job, the refund is tax-exempt income.	None
6. Payment for relocation expenses		Deductible expense	Tax-exempt if certain tests are met (e.g., new job must be more than fifty miles from old house).	None

7. Day care		Deductible expense	Excludable from income within limits if provided under a qualified, nondiscriminatory plan.	None
8. Perquisites	Expense accounts, cars, country club memberships, travel expenses, etc. Protects the employee's earnings by paying for higher standard of living required by his business.	Deductible expense	At present, not taxed for the most part if demonstrably job-related, but there are indications that the IRS will consider certain perquisites ordinary income for the employee and they will be taxed as such.	None
	REPLACEMENT COMPENSATION			
1. Unemployment insurance	Provided through specific state and federal requirements	Deductible expense	Tax-exempt income if wages of household are below specified minimum.	None
2. Supplementary unemployment benefits	Provided while employee is temporarily unemployed to maintain income at a level comparable to income received while employed.	Deductible expense	Taxed as ordinary income	None
3. Workers' compensation	For on-the-job injuries. Compulsory statutory coverage.	Deductible expense	Both premiums paid by the employer and the proceeds from the coverage are tax-exempt.	None
4. Short-term disability (nonoccupational)	Coverage is typically for up to six months but can be longer. This coverage is	Deductible expense	Taxed as ordinary income	Optional

(*Continued*)

Type of Compensation	*Description or Remarks*	*Tax Effect for Employer*	*Tax Effect for Employee*	*Contribution by Employee*
	compulsory by statute in some states. A salary continuation plan can maintain an employee's salary while disabled for up to six months.			
5. Long-term disability: Social Security	With medical evidence of permanent disability, payable beginning with six months of disablement for life or recovery.	Social Security payroll tax		Social Security payroll tax
6. Long-term disability: group or individual	Either through a pension plan or a separate LTD insurance contract. Provides coverage from six months after disablement to (generally) age 65. Some cover only five or ten years of disability, some can continue coverage for life.	Deductible expense	Tax-exempt up to $100/week until the employee reaches age 65; taxable as ordinary income thereafter. Benefits attributable to employee contributions are exempt. Also gross income over $15,000 reduces dollar for dollar the $100 a week exemption	Optional
7. Group life insurance	Can provide coverage for both before and after retirement.	Deductible expense	Taxed on the premium paid by the company for coverage in excess of $50,000. If the employee contributes, he can subtract the amount of his contribution from the taxable amount. Proceeds to the	Optional

			survivor are tax-exempt income.	
8. Additional life insurance for key executives		Deductible expense	Taxed on the premium paid by the company for coverage in excess of $50,000. Proceeds to the survivor are tax-exempt income.	None
9. Social Security retirement income		Social Security payroll tax		Social Security payroll tax
10. Qualified pension plans	A pension plan that meets the requirements established under the Internal Revenue Code and the Employee Retirement Income Security Act of 1974.	Annual contributions are deductible expenses. The investment income on contributed funds is tax-exempt.	Not taxed when contributions by the employer are made in the employee's behalf. The pension, when received, is taxed as ordinary income. Special tax rules apply for lump-sum distributions at retirement. The portion of the retirement benefit attributable to the employee's nondeductible contributions is not taxable income. The portion attributable to deductible employee contributions is taxed as ordinary income when received.	Optional
(a) Defined benefit	A retirement plan with a fixed benefit, generally based upon salary and years of service. Employer contributions are			

(Continued)

Type of Compensation	*Description or Remarks*	*Tax Effect for Employer*	*Tax Effect for Employee*	*Contribution by Employee*
	variable, depending, in part, upon investment experience, employee turnover, and salary levels. Years of past service with the company are generally recognized.			
(b) Defined contribution	A retirement plan with a fixed contribution by the employer, generally defined as a percentage of each employee's salary. Employee benefits at retirement are variable, depending upon employer contributions plus investment experience. Past service with the company is generally not recognized.			
11. Executive nonqualified pension plans	Usually pay as you go; a fund is not established.	Pension payments to retired executives are deductible expenses.	Pension payments received are taxed as ordinary income.	None
12. Profit-sharing plans	An individual account plan where the employer contribution is related to the amount of profit produced by the company. Individual distributions are generally	Annual contributions are deductible expenses as long as the contributions are made from current	Not taxed when contributions by the employer are made in the employee's behalf. The payments, when received upon retirement or earlier, are taxed as ordinary income.	Optional

	related to salary. Employee benefits at retirement are variable, depending upon the employer's contributions plus investment experience. Funds in an employee's account can often be withdrawn, under certain defined circumstances, before retirement.	or accumulated profits. The investment income on contributed funds is tax-exempt.	Special tax rules apply for lump-sum distributions.	
13. Thrift and savings plans	Generally employee's contributions are matched by employer contributions; can also be considered capital compensation. Employee can generally withdraw his contributions at any time.	Employer contributions are tax-deductible.	Contributions are from after-tax income. The pension payments, when received upon retirement or earlier, are taxed as ordinary income. Special tax rules apply for lump-sum distributions. Interest earned on savings is tax-exempt.	Always
14. Severance pay	Generally related to some proportion of preseverance base compensation.	Deductible expense	Taxed as ordinary income.	None
15. Employee Stock Ownership Plan (ESOP) and Tax Reduction Act Stock Ownership Plan (TRASOP)	Can also be considered capital compensation.	Deductible expense. (Additional investment tax credit for contributions to TRASOP through	Not taxed when contributions by employer made in the employee's behalf. The payments, when received, are taxed as ordinary income. Pass-through dividends may be taxed as ordinary income.	None

(*Continued*)

Type of Compensation	*Description or Remarks*	*Tax Effect for Employer*	*Tax Effect for Employee*	*Contribution by Employee*
		1982; replaced by income tax credit in 1983–1987.)		
		CAPITAL COMPENSATION		
1. Stock options: (a) Incentive stock options (b) Nonqualified stock options	An option granted to the employee by the company to purchase shares of company stock at a price fixed at the date the option is granted. Usually, the option must be exercised within a specified number of years from the date of the grant. The introduction of a stock option plan requires shareholders' approval.	Incentive stock options: No deductible expense to employer unless specific conditions are not met by the employee after the exercise of the option. Nonqualified stock options: Deductible expense for the excess of the exercise price of the option over the grant price of the option.	Incentive stock options: Capital gains tax treatment on the difference between the sale price of the stock and grant price of the option, provided employees hold the stock for specified period of time. Nonqualified stock options: Ordinary income tax on the excess of the exercise price of the option over the grant price of the option.	None
2. Stock appreciation right	A right attached to a stock option entitling the employee, in lieu of exercising his option, to receive a payment equal to the amount by which the fair market value of the stock, on the	Tax deductible expense at the time of exercise or payment equal to recipient's taxable income.	Tax, as ordinary income, on amount received from company.	None

	date the option otherwise would have been exercised, exceeds the option price.			
3. Performance unit plan	An award of contingent units earned upon the attainment of certain pre-established goals. The units are given an arbitrary value at the beginning of the plan. Units are generally awarded by position and salary level. The pre-established goals may be company-related (e.g., growth in earnings per share), or individual-related (e.g., meeting a budget), or a combination of both.	Tax-deductible expense at the time of payment equal to the recipient's taxable income.	Taxed as ordinary income on amount received from company.	None
4. Performance share plan	Similar to a performance unit plan (see above) with the exception that the units, when earned, are converted into shares of common stock. The value of the award is variable depending on the market value of the stock at the time the award is made.	Deductible expense for the fair market value of the stock on the day it is received from the company.	Taxed as ordinary income equal to or the fair market value of the stock on the day it is received from the company.	None
5. Dividend unit plan	The employee is assigned units equivalent to shares of the company's stock. As	Deductible expense at the time of the payment equal to	Taxed as ordinary income on amount received from company.	None

(Continued)

Type of Compensation	*Description or Remarks*	*Tax Effect for Employer*	*Tax Effect for Employee*	*Contribution by Employee*
	dividends are paid to stockholders on outstanding issued shares, awards equivalent to such dividends can be paid currently to employee or can be deferred.	the recipient's taxable income.		
6. Phantom stock plan	Actual shares of common stock are neither actually issued by the company nor received by the employee. Rather, the employee is granted stock units entitling him to receive, at intervals of time, only the appreciation in market value and the dividends declared on the units granted.	Tax-deductible expense at the time of payment equal to the recipient's taxable income.	Taxed as ordinary income on amount received from company.	None
7. Restricted stock grant	An award of shares of stock either a) subject to restrictions covering voluntary resignation, but not future performance, or b) deferred until the employee has remained with the company for a specified period of time, with no standard for future performance.	Deductible expense for the fair market value of the stock in the year that the grant is not subject to a substantial risk of of forfeiture.	Taxed as ordinary income in the year that the grant is not subject to a substantial risk of forfeiture. Tax is on the fair market value of the stock.	None

3

Accounting for Employee Benefit Plans

GEOFFREY M. GILBERT[1]

Ernst & Whinney

INTRODUCTION

When the Employee Retirement Income Security Act (ERISA), was passed in 1974 there was little available guidance for implementing its requirements for financial statements prepared in conformity with Generally

---

[1] The author acknowledges with thanks the contribution to this chapter of Gregory Lachowicz of Ernst & Whinney.

Accepted Accounting Principles (GAAP). Accordingly, the Financial Accounting Standards Board (FASB) placed the entire subject of accounting and reporting for employee benefit plans on its technical agenda.

After reviewing the many responses to the Exposure Draft of a statement on "Accounting and Reporting for Defined Benefit Pension Plans," the FASB worked with the U.S. Department of Labor (DOL) and the actuarial profession in an attempt to avoid conflicts, duplication, and confusion in determining meaningful financial reporting. During early 1979, the FASB exposed a staff draft of standards to certain interested parties for their comments. Because of the complexities of the issues involved, the significant length of time since the issuance of the initial Exposure Draft, and the limited exposure of the staff draft, the FASB decided to revise and reissue the Exposure Draft ("Revised Exposure Draft") for comments, in lieu of issuing a final statement. In March 1980, the FASB issued Statement of Financial Accounting Standards No. 35 (SFAS 35), "Accounting and Reporting by Defined Benefit Pension Plans." The Statement is effective for plan years beginning after December 15, 1980.

Defined contributions or health and welfare benefit plans are not covered by this statement. The American Institute of Certified Public Accountants (AICPA) Employee Benefit Plans and ERISA Committee has prepared two issue papers, "Accounting and Reporting by Defined Contribution Plans" and "Accounting and Reporting by Health and Welfare Benefit Plans" and has submitted them to the FASB for their consideration. The accounting and reporting principles recommended in the issues papers are generally consistent with those of SFAS 35; however, the ultimate form and content of any accounting guidance are yet to be determined.

ACCOUNTING AND REPORTING BY DEFINED BENEFIT PENSION PLANS—SFAS 35

Covered Plans

SFAS 35 establishes financial accounting and reporting standards for the annual financial statements of defined benefit pension plans, including those of state and local governments. The Board believes the Statement is consistent with the views of the DOL and the American Academy of Actuaries (Academy). This means that most private pension plans will be able to prepare one set of financial statements—in accordance with this Statement—for filings under ERISA and for distribution to other users. All pension plans, including those with fewer than 100 participants, that issue financial statements in conformity with GAAP are covered by SFAS 35.

Summary of Accounting and Reporting Requirements

The accounting and reporting requirements of SFAS 35 are summarized below:

- The plan's financial statements should be prepared on the accrual basis of accounting, and include statements of net assets available for benefits and changes in net assets.
- Plan investments should be presented at their fair value, except for insurance contracts, which should be presented in the same manner as required for filing under ERISA (i.e., fair value or contract value).
- Information should be included about the actuarial present value of accumulated plan benefits, measured either as of the beginning or end of the plan year, and significant changes therein. If measured as of the beginning of the year, statements of net assets available for benefits and changes in net assets should be presented for the prior year as well as the current year.
- Accumulated plan benefit information may be disclosed on the face of the statements of net assets available for benefits and changes therein, in separate statements, or in the notes to the financial statements.
- The actuarial present value of accumulated plan benefits should be based on employees' earnings and service rendered before the measurement date. Plan actuaries should not consider future salary increases and benefit improvements.

Objective of Plan Financial Statements

Plan participants are considered the primary users of pension plan financial statements because pension plans exist primarily for their benefit. However, a plan's financial statements should also be useful to other users (e.g., individuals who advise or represent participants, present or potential investors or creditors of the employer, and government authorities) as well.

The primary objective of a pension plan's financial statements is to provide information that will help users assess the plan's present and future ability to pay benefits when they are due. To accomplish that objective, the plan's financial statements should provide information about:

1. Plan resources and how the stewardship responsibility for them has been discharged.
2. The accumulated plan benefits of participants.
3. The results of transactions and events that affect the information about those resources and benefits.
4. Other factors necessary for users to understand the information provided.

It was recognized by the FASB that for a plan to meet this broad objective, users need information beyond that required by the Statement. One important consideration, for example, is the continued ability of the plan sponsor to fund the plan properly. Although financial statements for several years can provide information more useful in assessing the plan's future ability to pay benefits than can the financial statements for a single year, comparative financial statements are not required by SFAS 35. It recommends, but does not require, supplementing the financial statements with voluntary disclosures of matters deemed important, including a summary of financial information. Some suggestions on how this may be accomplished are covered later in this chapter.

Content of Plan Financial Statements

Plans must present the following elements, prepared on the accrual basis of accounting:

- Statement of net assets available for benefits.
- Statement of changes in net assets available for benefits.
- Information about the actuarial present value of accumulated plan benefits as of the benefit information date (which must be either the beginning or end of the plan year), categorized as follows:
  —Vested benefits of participants currently receiving payments
  —Other vested benefits
  —Nonvested benefits
- Information about certain significant changes in the actuarial present value of accumulated plan benefits.

Information about net assets and accumulated plan benefits must be as of the same date (either the beginning or end of the plan year). The information about the changes in plan assets and accumulated benefits must be presented for the same annual period. Therefore, if the most recent accumulated plan benefit information is as of the *beginning* of the plan year, the plan would present a statement of net assets as of the end of the current plan year and as of the end of the prior plan year. It also would present a statement of changes in the net assets for both the current and prior plan years.

For example, assume a calendar year plan's most recently determined accumulated plan benefit information is determined as of the *beginning* of the plan year. The plan would present the following financial information for 1981:

- Statements of net assets available for benefits as of December 31, 1981 and 1980.
- Statements of changes in net assets available for benefits for the years ended December 31, 1981 and 1980.
- Information about the actuarial present value of accumulated plan benefits as of December 31, 1980.
- Information about certain significant changes in the actuarial value of accumulated plan benefits for the year ended December 31, 1980.

Statement of Net Assets Available for Benefits

Plans must present their net assets in enough detail for users to identify (1) the types of investments held (e.g., marketable securities, common stocks, corporate bonds) and (2) other assets and liabilities (e.g., cash, receivables, operating assets, and liabilities arising from operations).

Investments. Investments, except for insuring contracts, must be presented at their fair value as of the financial statement date. *Fair value* is defined as the amount that the plan could reasonably expect to receive in a *current sale* between a willing buyer and a willing seller. Because it also applies to bonds, mortgages, and other fixed-term investments, the fair value requirement is particularly significant. Even if the plan has the ability and intention to hold such investments to maturity, it must establish a fair value as of the reporting date.

Insurance contracts should be recognized and measured according to Form 5500 instructions as required under ERISA. Even plans not subject to ERISA reporting requirements should follow this approach. According to the current instructions to Form 5500, in general, allocated insurance contracts are not included in plan assets and unallocated insurance contracts *are* included in plan assets.

Reporting basis. The accrual method of accounting requires that purchases and sales of securities be reported on a trade-date basis. However, accounting on a settlement-date basis is acceptable if (1) the fair value of securities purchased or sold just before the reporting date does not change significantly from the trade date to the reporting date, and (2) the purchases or sales do not significantly affect the composition of the plan's assets available for benefits.

Disclosure of the historical cost of significant types of investments is not required. However, such disclosure is not proscribed.

Reporting on Form 5500. The FASB's illustrative statement of net assets available for benefits is very similar to the requirements of Item 13 of Form 5500 (plan assets and liabilities). Principal differences between the two presentations are that Item 13 contains more captions and follows the traditional commercial balance sheet presentation (e.g., cash, receivables, investments). The Statement's illustrative statement follows the traditional investment company balance sheet presentation (e.g., investments, receivables, cash).

When financial statements, prepared in accordance with GAAP, are attached to Form 5500, the DOL regulations permit variance from the aggregation of the information presented in Item 13. This means the style and format of the GAAP statements need not conform to the Item 13 format. However, according to DOL regulations, significant differences, which are not readily apparent, in the presentation of net assets should be explained in a note to the GAAP financial statements submitted with Form 5500.

Contributions Receivable. Contributions receivable are amounts due to the plan as of the reporting date from the employer(s), participants, and other funding sources such as state subsidies or federal grants. Amounts due include those under both formal commitments and legal or contractual requirements. A plan sponsor would be contractually required to contribute to a pension plan if such a requirement, for example, were included in a labor contract. Also, ERISA legally obligates a sponsor to annually fund a minimum amount unless the Internal Revenue Service grants a waiver. Generally, when a waiver is obtained, the plan sponsor must fund the waived amount over a period not to exceed fifteen years. Plans generally should not recognize any amounts waived as receivables unless events after the reporting date support that recognition. For example, subsequent remittance of a portion of the amount would justify reporting that installment as an asset.

Evidence of commitment. Formal commitments of the employer also are receivables. SFAS 35 includes these examples that "may" provide evidence of a formal commitment:

- A resolution by the employer's board of directors approving a specified contribution.
- A consistent pattern of making payments after the plan's years end under an established funding policy that attributes such subsequent payments to the preceding plan year.
- A deduction of a contribution for federal tax purposes for periods ending on or before the reporting date.
- The employer's recognition as of the reporting date of a contribution payable to the plan.

If the plan receives payment soon after its year end, this would provide additional evidence supporting recognition of the receivable. On the other hand, in certain situations the plan sponsor's recognition of a contribution payable to the plan might not support the corresponding accrual of a receivable. The following example demonstrates a situation in which the plan sponsor's payable would not be equal to the plan's receivable:

> The plan sponsor consistently measures pension expense under APB Opinion No. 8 ("Accounting for the Cost of Pension Plans"). However, the sponsor bases its contributions to the plan on a yearly analysis of its tax situation, and the amount funded varies between the IRS minimum and maximum amounts. The difference between the amount funded after year end, for which a tax deduction is recognized, and pension expense recognized in the sponsor's financial statements is reflected by the sponsor either as a deferred charge or an accrued pension cost. In this example, the plan's contribution receivable should

equal the amount of the tax deduction taken; that is, the amount expected to be funded between the plan's current year end and the filing date of the sponsor's tax return.

In some situations, the plan sponsor's recognition of a deduction for federal income tax purposes might not support the corresponding accrual of a receivable. The following example demonstrates such a situation:

> The plan sponsor consistently funds the pension plan based on the amount accrued for pension expense. The contribution to the plan is funded on a monthly basis during the year; by year end no contribution is due the plan. After issuing the sponsor's financial statements, however, the sponsor decides to take advantage of the IRS regulations that permit a portion of the next year's funding amounts to be deducted in the current year's tax return. In this situation, the plan sponsor has not recognized a contribution payable and does not intend to change its funding policy. Pursuant to the Statement, we believe that the plan should not recognize a receivable for this additional amount. If the funding policy was changed or a contribution payable were recorded, the additional contribution could be recognized.

As is true for other areas of accounting and reporting, substance is more important than form in determining the existence of a formal commitment. If the plan's financial statements are prepared after the sponsor's tax return has been filed, the plan will be able to benefit from hindsight in assessing the amount of contribution receivable, if any, to be recognized.

Plans should separately disclose contributions due from the employer(s), employees, and other sources, and they should adequately provide for estimated uncollectible amounts.

Operating Assets. SFAS 35 requires plans to report assets used in their operations at historical cost, less accumulated depreciation or amortization. This differs from DOL regulations for financial data filed under ERISA which require the use of current value in measuring operating assets.

When operating assets are not significant to the plan's financial position (which is the case for most plans) and the financial statements are submitted with Form 5500, the plan should consider disclosing that depreciated historical cost is not materially different (in relation to net assets) from fair value to satisfy DOL requirement.

In unusual circumstances when operating assets are significant and the plan is subject to DOL requirements, plans should consider estimating the assets' fair value, using some form of indexing. If the difference between historical cost and fair value is material to the net assets available for benefits, Form 5500 can reflect fair value of these operating assets, and the financial statements submitted with Form 5500 can reflect these assets at depreciated historical cost. Such statements should contain a note explaining the difference between the value reported in Form 5500 and in the financial statements prepared according to the GAAP.

Operating Liabilities. While plan liabilities are not specifically addressed by SFAS 35, the Statement's illustrative statement of net assets includes "accounts payable" and "accrued expenses." Under the accrual method of accounting, plans should record liabilities for unpaid expenses and securities purchases if they were incurred before the financial statement date.

The vested benefit category of the actuarial value of accumulated plan benefits must include those benefits due and payable as of the benefit information date. This means, for example, that any benefit payments due for month(s) prior to the plan's year end should not be considered plan liabilities in the statement of net assets available for benefits.

This assures that all benefit information is presented together. The financial statements' usefulness for assessing benefit security might be impaired if the user had to extract portions of the benefit information from various locations.

Statement of Changes in Net Assets Available for Benefits

Plans should present information about changes in net assets available for benefits in enough detail to identify the significant changes during the year. The following are the minimum items that should be disclosed separately:

1. The net appreciation or depreciation in fair value of investments including realized gains or losses. Plans should disclose in a note, for each significant class of investments, the net appreciation or depreciation of investments whose fair values have been measured by quoted prices in an active market and those whose fair values have been determined in another manner.
2. Investment income.
3. Contributions from the employer(s), segregated between cash and non-cash contributions (recorded at fair value and described either parenthetically or in a note).
4. Contributions from participants, including those transmitted by the sponsor.
5. Contributions from other identified sources (e.g., state subsidies or federal grants).
6. Benefits paid to participants.
7. Payments to insurance companies to purchase contracts that are excluded from plan assets. Plans may net dividend income related to excluded contracts against payments, in which case the amount of the dividend should be disclosed.
8. Administrative expenses.

Realized gains or losses on security transactions and *unrealized appreciation or depreciation* of investments may be combined in the statement of changes in net assets. However, realized gains or losses (i.e., the difference between the selling price and original cost) may be (1) separately presented in the statement or (2) separately disclosed parenthetically or in a footnote.

Unrealized appreciation or depreciation and the realized gains or losses should be calculated as follows:

Assumptions regarding the plan's investments and investment activity for 19X0:

Investments held at the beginning of the year (January 1, 19X0) had a fair value of $1 million and a cost of $800,000.

Investment purchases during 19X0 aggregated $100,000 and had a fair value at year end of $120,000.

Investments sold during 19X0 had a selling price of $90,000, a fair value of $85,000 on January 1, 19X0 and an original cost of $50,000.

Investments held at the end of the year (December 31, 19X0) had a fair value of $1,200,000 and a cost of $850,000.

The net realized and unrealized appreciation reported in the statement of changes in net assets would be computed as follows:

	January 1, 19X0	*December 31, 19X0*	
Fair Value	$1,000,000	$1,200,000	
Cost	800,000	850,000	
	$ 200,000	$ 350,000	$150,000
Gain on Sale			
Selling Price		$ 90,000	
Cost		50,000	40,000
			$190,000

The net change in the fair value of assets as reported in this statement would be $190,000. If realized gains and losses are disclosed or presented separately ($40,000 in this example), the significant accounting policies footnote should state the method of determining cost (e.g., specific identification, average cost).

Accumulated Benefits

Accumulated plan benefits are defined in SFAS 35 as "those future benefit payments that are attributable under the plan's provisions to employees' service rendered to the benefit information date." When the plan provisions specify or clearly imply the benefit attributed to each year of service, these provisions should be used to determine the benefits accumulated as of the current benefit information date. In other cases, such as a flat benefit after a defined length of service, a pro rata allocation of the benefits provided by the plan should be imputed. This means that accumulated benefits for each participant should include:

1. All plan benefits earned as of the measurement date by the participant that are attributed to service rendered as defined by the plan's benefit provisions. For example, assume a plan provides a basic retirement benefit of $20 per month for each year of service and the participant has completed six years of service. The accumulated plan benefit relating to the basic retirement benefit would be $120 per month.

2. Pro rata allocation of plan benefits that will become vested once the participant satisfies minimum service requirements These benefits should be considered to accrue in proportion to the ratio of completed years of service to total projected years of service when they become fully vested. For example, assume a plan provides a $200 per month supplemental retirement benefit payable to age 62 when the participant retires before age 62 with thirty years of service. A participant age 26 who has completed six years of service would be assumed to have accumulated a $40 per month (six years divided by thirty years times $200 per month) supplemental retirement benefit.
3. Pro rata allocation of other plan benefits that are not the type that become vested. These benefits will be considered to accrue in proportion to the ratio of completed years of service to total projected years of service upon anticipated separation from covered service. For example, assume a plan provides a $500 per month supplemental disability benefit payable to age 62 when the participant becomes fully disabled before age 62 with twenty years of service. A participant age 26 whom we assume will become disabled after twenty-five years of service and has completed six years of service would have accumulated a $120 per month (six years divided by twenty-five years times $500 per month) supplemental disability benefit.

The definition of accumulated plan benefits includes both the retirement benefits and the ancillary benefits, such as death, disability, and early retirement, provided by the plan and includes both vested and unvested benefits.

Even though benefits should be based on participants' history of pay and service and other appropriate factors as of the benefit information date, projected years of service may be a factor in determining a participant's expected eligibility for particular benefits. For example, assume the plan provides a preretirement disability benefit once the participant has completed twenty years of service. A participant hired at age 50 *would not* be eligible for this ancillary benefit because only fifteen years of service will be rendered prior to expected retirement at age 65.

Automatic benefit increases specified by the plan (for example, automatic cost-of-living increases) that are expected to occur after the benefit information date should be recognized in measuring benefits. However, SFAS 35 requires that plan amendments adopted after the benefit information date which retroactively increase accumulated benefits should not be recognized.

When the plan provisions are integrated with Social Security benefits, the offset to accumulated plan benefits should be based on the employee's current compensation and the current provisions in the Social Security law.

Determining the accumulated benefits "earned" by each participant is a complicated process because of the trend in pension plans to provide subsidized early retirement benefits, ancillary benefits after a specified number of years of covered service, and supplemental retirement allowances. Previously, many actuaries approximated the cost of these various features to simplify the calculations performed. Now, both the FASB and the Academy place more emphasis on individually valuing each type of benefit provided.

Presenting Information on Plan Benefits. Several alternatives are provided by SFAS 35 for presenting accumulated plan benefit information:

- As separate statements (one of accumulated plan benefits and one of changes in accumulated plan benefits).
- As a note to the financial statements.
- As part of the statement of net assets if the asset and accumulated plan benefit information are presented as of the same date (statement of accumulated plan benefits and net assets available for benefits); and as part of the statement of changes in net assets if the information is for the same period (statement of changes in accumulated plan benefits and net assets available for benefits).

Whichever alternative is employed, the plan must present the required accumulated plan benefit information (i.e., vested benefits for participants currently receiving payments, vested benefits for other participants, and nonvested benefits) in its entirety in the same location. Likewise, the plan must present the significant changes in accumulated plan benefits during the year that are required to be disclosed by the SFAS 35 in the same location. However, the accumulated plan benefit information and the changes in accumulated plan benefit information do not have to be presented in the same place (i.e., one may be in a statement and the other in a note).

Disclosing Changes. SFAS 35 provides two alternatives for disclosing changes in accumulated plan benefits: a reconciliation format that accounts for the changes between the two valuation dates, or a narrative format. Under either presentation style, the *minimum required disclosures* should include the significant effects of (1) plan amendments that retroactively increase accumulated benefits earned; (2) changes in the nature of the plan that affect comparability (e.g., plan spinoff or merger); and (3) changes in actuarial assumptions. Disclosure of the actuarial value of accumulated plan benefits as of the *preceding* benefit valuation date also is required under either presentation style.

Other recurring changes may be, but are not required to be, separately disclosed, including increases caused by the passage of time, such as interest accretion and additional benefits accrued, and decreases caused by payment of benefits. When the reconciliation format is used, the significant effects of these recurring changes may be aggregated in an "other" category.

Other Financial Statement Disclosures

Plans should describe all significant accounting policies, including the method(s) and significant assumptions used to determine:

- The fair value of investments and the reported value of contracts with insurance companies.

- The actuarial present value of accumulated plan benefits and any significant changes in the method or assumptions. (Significant actuarial assumptions illustrated in the Statement are the interest, retirement, and inflation rate assumptions.)

The following disclosures, if applicable, are also required:

1. A brief, general description of the plan agreement, including, but not limited to, vesting and benefit provisions. Plans may omit this information if it is provided in other published sources, such as a summary plan description, but they must then refer to the other source.
2. A description of significant plan amendments made during the year ended on the latest benefit information date. If significant amendments were adopted between the latest benefit information date and the plan's year end, the plan should disclose that the actuarial present value of accumulated plan benefits does not reflect those amendments.
3. A brief, general description of the priority order of participants' claims to the assets of the plan upon plan termination (first, employee contributions; second, vested benefits of retired participants; etc.) and benefits guaranteed by the Pension Benefit Guaranty Corporation (PBGC). (However, the Board does not require the plan to group assets by priority class.) If material providing this information is otherwise published and made available to participants, the descriptions required by this paragraph may be omitted provided that (1) reference to such other source is made and (2) disclosure similar to the following (taken from SFAS 35) is made in the financial statements:

   > Should the plan terminate at some future time, its net assets generally will not be available on a pro rata basis to provide participants' benefits. Whether a particular participant's accumulated plan benefits will be paid depends on both the priority of those benefits and the level of benefits guaranteed by the PBGC at that time. Some benefits may be fully or partially provided for by the then existing assets and the PBGC guarantee while other benefits may not be provided for at all.

4. The funding policy and any changes in it during the plan year. Contributory plans should disclose the method of determining participants' contributions and the amount of accumulated contributions of present employees as of the benefit information date, including interest, if any, and the applicable interest rate(s). Plans subject to ERISA should disclose whether the plan has met ERISA's minimum funding requirements. If a minimum funding waiver from the IRS has been granted or is pending, the plan should disclose that fact.
5. The policy for purchasing contracts with insurance companies if the contracts are excluded from plan assets, and the dividend income received on these contracts.
6. The federal income tax status of the plan, if a favorable letter of determination has not been obtained or maintained. DOL requires this disclosure regardless of the plan's tax status.

7. Identification of individual investments that represent 5 percent or more of the fair value of net assets available for benefits. Also, the plan must show investments in enough detail to identify the types of investments, and categorize them as follows: (1) securities for which fair values have been measured by quoted prices in an active market and (2) securities for which fair values have been determined another way. Although a plan need not disclose the cost of investments, it may do so if it wishes.
8. Significant real estate or other transactions in which the plan and any of the following parties are jointly involved: (1) the sponsor, (2) the employer(s), or (3) the employee organization(s) (e.g., the plan owns a building and leases it to the sponsor).
9. Unusual or infrequent events or transactions occurring after the latest benefit information date but before the financial statements are issued if they might significantly affect the statements' usefulness for assessing the plan's present and future ability to pay benefits. If reasonably determinable, plans should disclose the effects of such events or transactions. If such effects are not quantified, plans should explain why they are not reasonably determinable.
10. The percentage reduction in the interest assumption for future administrative expenses associated with paying accumulated benefits if these costs are accounted for in this manner (versus the acceptable alternative of estimating future administrative expenses and discounting them to present value). If the plan sponsor pays significant administrative costs, the plan must disclose that fact.

Voluntary Disclosures

Many users of the plan's financial statements may need to be educated about the financial information presented. Accordingly, plan administrators may wish to include a brief explanation that highlights those matters expected to be of most interest and usefulness to users. For example, some plan administrators have included information concerning investment strategy, investment performance, and rates of return on existing assets with the distributed financial statements to assist users in their assessment of the discharge of the plan administrator's stewardship responsibility.

Such voluntary disclosures also could address any inappropriate inferences that users might draw as they assess the plan at a given point in time. For example, a plan heavily invested in high-grade mortgage loans with the intention and ability of holding them to maturity may wish to address any significant short-term market decline from the perspective of benefit security. Otherwise, participants who are not aware of the plan's investment policies may fear that their benefit security has been impaired by poor investment decisions.

Also, a summary of financial information, including ratios, for a period of years may be helpful to assist users in assessing trends in the plan's ability to pay benefits when they are due. Even though there are no requirements or standards governing the preparation of summary financial information, plan administrators who wish to follow the FASB's recommendation may consider presenting the following:

- Net assets available for benefits
- Accumulated plan benefits by major category
- Contributions, both employer and employee
- Benefits paid (possibly categorized by type, such as retirement, disability, and death)
- Net unrealized appreciation or depreciation
- Number of retired participants
- Number of active participants

Presenting certain ratios also may help the users understand trends in the plan's financial status over a period of years. When presenting ratio comparisons, the plan administrator should carefully select relationships that are important for understanding current developments and trends in plan operations. Although there are many types of ratios, the following are some which may be helpful in reviewing pension plans:

- Ratio of net assets available for benefits to accumulated plan benefits
- Ratio of net assets available for benefits to benefits paid during the year
- Ratio of retired participants to active participants

Plan administrators could make other important comparisons between the contributions made to the plan and the sponsor's financial results—that is, the financial impact the plan has had on the sponsor's profitability and cash flow.

These voluntary disclosures, if made, could be presented as a "Financial Highlights" section to the plan's financial statements. If the plan administrator distributes a transmittal letter with the financial statements, the voluntary disclosures could be incorporated within the body of the letter.

Illustrative Plan Financial Statements

Because SFAS 35 and the DOL have very similar accounting requirements for measuring and presenting plan assets, most pension plans should be able to prepare a single set of financial statements for filing under ERISA and for distribution to other users.

The financial statements in the Appendix to this chapter are prepared in conformity with SFAS 35 and illustrate many of the disclosure requirements previously discussed. This format, when combined with the additional DOL schedule and note requirements discussed below, should conform to the financial statement requirements of Form 5500.

When the financial statements are used in filings under ERISA, the following information must be presented, if applicable, in addition to that required by SFAS 35:

- Disclosure of tax status. SFAS 35 requires this disclosure only if plans have not obtained or maintained a favorable determination letter.
- An explanation of the differences, if any, between the information contained in the GAAP financial statements and the information contained in Items 13 and 14 of Form 5500.
- A description of any agreements and transactions with persons known to be parties-in-interest.
- Schedule of Assets Held for Investment. This schedule requires a detailed listing of investments held at year end. SFAS 35 requires disclosure only of investments in excess of 5 percent of net assets available for benefits.
- Schedule of Loans or Fixed-Income Obligations in Default or Classified as Uncollectible.
- Schedule of Transactions Involving Plan Assets and a Party Known to Be a Party-in-Interest.
- Schedule of Leases in Default or Classified as Uncollectible.
- Schedule of Transactions or Series of Transactions in Excess of 3 Percent of the Current Value of Plan Assets.

Only current-year financial statements are required if the accumulated plan benefit information is presented as of the end of the current plan year. However, under the DOL guidelines, plans are required to include comparative statements of assets and liabilities as of the beginning and end of the current plan year.

ACCOUNTING FOR STOCK PURCHASE, SAVINGS, AND SIMILAR PLANS

As previously noted, SFAS 35 does not cover defined contribution plans; however the form and content of financial statements of employee stock purchase, savings, and similar plans required to be filed with the SEC are governed by Article 6C of Regulation S-X. The specific requirements of Article 6C are in addition to the general requirements of Articles 1, 2, 3, and 4; however, the specific rules take precedence over the general rules if there are conflicts. The financial statements prescribed by Article 6C are statements of financial condition, and income and changes in plan equity.

Statement of Financial Condition

The statement of financial condition should include separate sections for each class of securities of participating employers, investments in securities or unaffiliated issuers, U.S. Government bonds and other direct obligations of the U.S. Government, other securities, investments other than securities, dividends and interest receivable, cash, and other assets.

Each major class of investment other than securities should be separately stated, and other securities should be segregated between marketable and other securities. Other assets should state separately amounts due from participating employers or their director, officers, and principal holders of equity securities, amounts due from trustees or managers of the plan, and any other significant amounts.

Liabilities and plan equity should be broken down by amounts payable to participating employers, amounts payable to participating employees, reserves and other credits, other significant liabilities, and plan equity. Reserves and other credits should be appropriately described, either in the caption or in a footnote.

Statement of Income and Changes in Plan Equity

Net investment income should be broken down by source—cash dividends, interest, and other. Separate aggregation should be made of income from securities of participating employers. Any significant expenses should be stated separately.

Realized gains and losses on investment transactions should be stated separately for investments in securities of participating employers, other security investments, and other investments. Footnote disclosure should be made of how the cost of securities sold was determined (e.g., first in-first out, average cost). Also, the aggregate cost, proceeds, and gain or loss from transactions in each separate category of investments should be given.

Unrealized appreciation or depreciation of investments should be disclosed at the beginning and end of the period. The increase or decrease during the period should be stated separately if investments are accounted for at fair value, or disclosed if investments are accounted for at cost.

Contributions and deposits to the fund should be segregated between employers and employees. Footnote disclosure should be made of employer and employee contributions by participating employer if more than one employer participates in the plan. Withdrawals, lapses, and forfeitures of employees' accounts should be separately stated as well as amounts disbursed in settlement of such accounts and the disposition of balances remaining after settlement.

Other Accounting and Disclosure Requirements

Article 6C provides that all assets may be valued at either cost or market, provided cost or market, whichever is not used for the primary valuation, is shown parenthetically. For plans providing investment options to participants, footnote disclosure of the various investment programs and the number of employees in each program is required. For plans which measure participant's equity in terms of units, the number of units and net asset value per unit should be disclosed.

Income taxes should be provided if the plan is not exempt from federal income taxes, including appropriate taxes on recognized unrealized appreciation on investments. If the plan is not subject to federal income taxes, a brief statement as to why should be included. In addition, the federal income tax status of the employee with respect to the plan should be disclosed.

Schedule Requirements

A detailed schedule of investments is required for each statement of condition. Information to be included in the schedule is as follows: (1) name of issuer and title of issue, (2) balance held at close of period, number of shares, principal amount of bonds and notes, (3) cost of each item, and (4) value of each item at close of period.

For plans providing separate investment programs with separate funds, a schedule allocating all assets and plan income and changes in plan equity to the applicable funds should be filed unless this information is shown in the basic financial statements.

ACCOUNTING FOR WELFARE BENEFIT PLANS

The status of accounting for welfare benefit plans is similar to that of accounting for defined contribution plans in that neither is covered by SFAS 35. Until the FASB takes further action, the AICPA audit guide, *Audits of Employer Health and Welfare Benefit Funds* continues to represent the most authoritative literature on accounting for these plans.

Accounting and Reporting Principles

The accounting principles included in the guide may be summarized as follows:

- *Basis and form of financial statements.* The guide concludes that the accrual basis is the most appropriate. Changes to adopt the accrual basis should be made retroactively in accordance with paragraphs 27 and 28 of Accounting Principles Board (APB) Opinion No. 20.

  The illustrative financial statements presented in the guide include a balance sheet, a statement of operations and fund balance, and a statement of changes in financial position.
- *Investments.* Investments of welfare benefit plans are generally short term in nature; accordingly, the audit guide concluded that cost is the appropriate basis for carrying all investments. However, market is also probably now

acceptable because of ERISA's requirements, the FASB position with respect to defined benefit plans, and the generally insignificant difference for short-term investments.

- *Contributions receivable.* Contributions are generally paid on a self-assessment basis and are received by the plan the month after they accrue. Such contributions should be accrued by the plan.
- *Premium deposits.* Premium deposits should be reported as assets of the plan until applied against future premiums.
- *Accrued experience-rating adjustments.* Any excess of premiums paid over claims paid, reserves required by the insurance company, and the insurance company's retention (fee) should be accrued. These experience-rating refunds may have to be estimated. Experience-rating deficits for which the plan has a liability should also be accrued.
- *Property and equipment.* Buildings, equipment, furniture and fixtures, and leasehold improvements used in operations should be carried at cost and depreciated or amortized over their estimated useful lives.
- *Claims reported but not paid and claims incurred but not reported.* Benefit claims in fully insured plans are liabilities of the insurance company and not the plan. Self-insured funds should accrue estimated liabilities for claims reported but not paid and claims incurred but not reported. In addition, the financial statements of a self-insured plan that provides death benefits should reflect an estimated liability for such benefits based upon determinations by the funds' insurance consultants or actuaries.
- *Insurance premiums payable.* Insurance premiums due but not paid as well as any estimated contingent premiums (usually based on excess loss ratios) should be accrued.
- *Liability for accumulated eligibility credits.* Some welfare benefit plans provide for continued eligibility for benefits during periods of unemployment based on accumulated eligibility credits or hours. The guide requires that a liability for such future benefits based on past service be provided in the financial statements.
- *Fund balance.* The fund balance is represented by the excess of assets over liabilities. Consideration should be given to segregating amounts applicable to specific plans if the fund consists of more than one plan.
- *Other financial statement disclosures.* The guide lists the following three items as recommended disclosures:

  —The nature of the plan's activities and any changes in the plan;
  —The tax status of the fund;
  —Any other matters necessary to fairly present the financial statements of a particular fund. Examples given are lease commitments and transactions which may involve conflicts of interest.

APPENDIX 3-1 Financial Statements

Statement of Net Assets Available for Benefits
Employer Company Pension Plan

	December 31 19X2	December 31 19X1
Assets:		
Investments, at fair value—Note D:		
U.S. Government securities	$ 3,888,740	$ 1,606,214
Corporate bonds and notes	8,815,701	8,458,329
Common stock		
Employer company	1,775,000	1,498,000
Other	9,341,668	5,608,171
Common trust fund	2,500,000	2,450,000
Insurance company separate account	2,450,000	2,600,000
	28,771,109	22,220,714
Unallocated insurance contract, at contract value —Note E	5,050,000	4,950,000
Total investments	33,821,109	27,170,714
Receivables		
Contribution receivable from employer company	238,305	216,145
Contributions receivable from employees	25,000	23,000
Accrued income	136,202	171,295
Total receivables	399,507	410,440
Cash	187,439	95,813
Total assets	34,408,055	27,676,967
Liabilities:		
Accounts payable and accrued expenses	99,145	67,968
NET ASSETS AVAILABLE FOR BENEFITS	$34,308,910	$27,608,999

See notes to financial statements.

Reader note: The statements of net assets available for benefits and changes therein for 19X1 are not required by SFAS 35 because the accumulated plan benefit information is presented at the end of the year. The 19X1 statements are included to illustrate comparative presentation.

Statement of Changes in Net Assets Available for Benefits
Employer Company Pension Plan

	Year Ended December 31 19X2	19X1
Additions:		
Investment income		
Interest	$ 955,100	$ 929,832
Dividends	602,012	467,175
	1,557,112	1,397,007
Contributions		
Employer Company	4,700,000	3,900,000
Employees	209,855	144,264
	6,466,967	5,441,271
Deductions:		
Benefits paid directly to participants	1,395,821	1,122,467
Administrative expenses	215,972	174,558
	1,611,793	1,297,025
	4,855,174	4,144,246
Net realized and unrealized appreciation (depreciation) in fair value of investments—Note D *	1,844,737	(1,363,363)
NET INCREASES	6,699,911	2,780,883
Net assets available for benefits at beginning of year	27,608,999	24,828,116
NET ASSETS AVAILABLE FOR BENEFITS AT END OF YEAR	$34,308,910	$27,608,999

See notes to financial statements.

Notes to Financial Statements
Employer Company Pension Plan
December 31, 19X2

NOTE A—SIGNIFICANT ACCOUNTING POLICIES

Valuation of Investments. Marketable securities are stated at fair value. Securities traded on a national securities exchange are valued at the last reported sales price on the last business day of the plan year; investments traded in the over-the-counter market and listed securities for which no sale was

* *Reader note:* Alternatively, "Net realized and unrealized appreciation (depreciation) in fair value of investments" could be presented as a component of investment income (consistent with the FASB's illustrative presentation) or realized gains (losses) may be separately presented with "Additions" (consistent with Item 14 of Form 5500).

reported on that date are valued at the average of the last reported bid and ask prices.

For certain investments consisting of corporate bonds and notes that do not have an established fair value, the Employer Company Pension Administration Committee has established a fair value based on yields currently available on comparable securities of issuers with similar credit ratings.

The fair value of the participation units owned by the Plan in the common trust fund and separate account were based on quoted redemption value on the last business day of the plan year.

The unallocated insurance contract is valued at contract value as estimated by The Insurance Company (Insurer). Contract value represents contributions made under the contract, plus interest at the contract rate, less funds used to pay retirement benefits and to pay for the insurance company's administrative expenses.

Actuarial Present Value of Accumulated Plan Benefits. Accumulated plan benefits (see Note C) are those estimated future periodic payments, including lump-sum distributions, that are attributable under the Plan's provisions to services rendered by the employees to the valuation date. Accumulated plan benefits include benefits expected to be paid to (a) retired or terminated employees or their beneficiaries, and (b) present employees or their beneficiaries. Benefits for retired or terminated employees or their beneficiaries are based on employees' compensation during their last five years of credited service. The accumulated plan benefits for active employees are based on their average compensation during the five years preceding the valuation date. Benefits payable under all circumstances—retirement, death, disability, and termination of employment—are included, to the extent they are deemed attributable to employee service rendered to the valuation date.

NOTE B—DESCRIPTION OF THE PLAN

The pension plan of the Employer Company ("Company") is a contributory defined benefit plan that covers substantially all employees and provides for retirement, death, and disability benefits. Covered employees may contribute 2 percent of their annual compensation. Present employees' accumulated contributions are $3,420,000 and $3,147,000 as of December 31, 19X2 and 19X1, respectively, including interest at 8 percent compounded annually.

The Company has agreed to voluntarily contribute such additional amounts as are necessary to provide assets sufficient to meet the benefits to be paid to Plan members. The Company's present intention is to make contributions in amounts sufficient to annually fund the Plan's current service cost and the initial past service cost plus interest over a period of thirty years. The Plan has met the ERISA minimum funding requirements.

Should the Plan terminate at some future time, its net assets will generally not be available on a pro rata basis to provide participants' benefits. Whether a particular participant's accumulated plan benefits will be paid depends on both the priority of those benefits and the level of benefits guaranteed by the Pension Benefit Guaranty Corporation (PBGC) at that time. Some benefits may be fully or partially provided for by the then existing assets and the PBGC's benefit guarantee, while other benefits may not be provided for at all.

Information about the Plan agreement, the vesting and benefit provisions, and the PBGC's benefit guarantee is contained in the pamphlet *Description of Employee Benefits*. Copies of this pamphlet are available from the Pension Administration Committee.

NOTE C—ACCUMULATED PLAN BENEFITS

An actuary from the AAA Company* estimates the actuarial present value of accumulated plan benefits, which is the amount that results from applying actuarial assumptions to adjust the accumulated plan benefits earned by the participants to reflect the time value of money (through discounts for interest) and the probability of payment (by means of decrements such as for death, disability, withdrawal or retirement) between the valuation date and the expected date of payment.

The accumulated plan benefit information as of the end of each plan year is as follows:

	December 31	
	19X2	*19X1*
Actuarial present value of accumulated plan benefits		
Vested benefits		
Participants currently receiving payments	$ 4,960,414	$ 4,108,207
Other participants	19,790,421	19,542,036
	24,750,835	23,650,243
Nonvested benefits	7,351,800	6,925,400
	$32,102,635	$30,575,643

The actuarial present value of accumulated plan benefits was $28,816,421 as of December 31, 19X0. There were no factors significantly affecting the comparability of accumulated plan benefits during the two years ended December 31, 19X2.

---

* *Reader note:* Even though not required by the Statement, the FASB's illustrative financial statements identify the actuarial firm. Considering the extensive participation of the plan's actuary, this disclosure is desirable.

Significant assumptions underlying the actuarial computations are:

Assumed rate of return on investments:	8 percent, including a reduction of 0.2 percent to reflect anticipated administrative expenses associated with providing benefits
Retirement:	At normal retirement age (65)

These actuarial assumptions are based on the presumption that the Plan will continue. Were the Plan to terminate, different actuarial assumptions and other factors might be applicable in determining the actuarial present value of accumulated plan benefits.

NOTE D—INVESTMENTS

The Plan's investments are held by a bank-administered trust fund, except for its separate account and unallocated insurance contract with The Insurance Company (see Note E). During 19X2 and 19X1 the Plan's investments (including investments bought, sold, as well as held during the year) appreciated (depreciated) in fair value by $1,844,737 and ($1,363,363), as follows:

	Net Appreciation (Depreciation) in Fair Value During Year	*Fair Value at End of Year*
Year ended December 31, 19X2		
Fair value as determined by quoted market price:		
U.S. Government securities	$ 97,000	$ 3,888,740
Corporate bonds and notes	12,413	7,814,826
Common stock		
Employer Company	277,000	1,775,000
Other	1,064,174	9,341,668
Common trust fund	275,000	2,500,000
Insurance company separate account	236,150	2,450,000
	1,961,737	27,770,234
Fair value estimated by the Pension Administration Committee:		
Corporate bonds and notes	(117,000)	1,000,875
	$ 1,844,737	$28,771,109
Year ended December 31, 19X1		
Fair value as determined by quoted market price:		
U.S. Government securities	$ 28,000	$ 1,606,214

Corporate bonds and notes	207,586	7,475,000
Common stock		
Employer Company	(102,000)	1,498,000
Other	(1,433,000)	5,608,171
Common trust fund	(35,000)	2,450,000
Insurance company separate account	(41,949)	2,600,000
	(1,376,363)	21,237,385
Fair value estimated by the Pension Administration Committee:		
Corporate bonds and notes	13,000	983,329
	$(1,363,363)	$22,220,714

The fair value of individual investments that represent 5 percent or more of the Plan's net assets are as follows:

	December 31	
	19X2	*19X1*
ABC Company, 8 percent debenture due 1995 ($2,500,000 face amount)	$ 1,950,000	$ 2,000,000
XYZ Company Common stock (30,000 shares)	1,875,000	1,925,000
Eureka Corporation Common stock (25,000 shares and 24,500 shares)	2,125,000	1,860,000
Employer Company Common Stock (15,000 shares)	1,775,000	1,498,000
First City Bank Fixed-Income Common Trust Fund (27,000 and 26,000 units)	2,500,000	2,450,000
The Insurance Company Pooled Separate Account No. 1 (24,000 and 25,000 units)	2,450,000	2,600,000

NOTE E—CONTRACT WITH INSURANCE COMPANY

In 19X0, the Company entered into an insurance contract with The Insurance Company under which the Plan deposits a minimum of $100,000 a year. The Insurer maintains the Plan's deposits in a fund to which it adds interest at a rate of 7 percent per annum. The interest rate is guaranteed through 19X4 but is subject to change for each succeeding five-year period. When changed, the new rate applies only to funds deposited from the date of change. At the direction of the Plan's administrator, a portion of the fund can be used to purchase units in The Insurance Company Pooled Separate Account. The Separate Account's portfolio is primarily invested in high-grade corporate bonds and notes. The Insurer does not guarantee the monies invested in the Separate Account as to principal or income. Benefit payments to participants or their beneficiaries are made directly by the Insurer from the funds accumulated under the contract.

NOTE F—INCOME TAX STATUS *

The Internal Revenue Service has ruled (January 15, 1978) that the Plan qualifies under Section 401(a) of the Internal Revenue Code (IRC) and is, therefore, not subject to tax under present income tax law. Once qualified, the Plan is required to operate in conformity with the IRC to maintain its qualification. The Pension Administration Committee is not aware of any course of action or series of events that have occurred that might adversely affect the Plan's qualified status.

NOTE G—TRANSACTIONS WITH PARTIES-IN-INTEREST **

During 19X2 the Plan received $133,000 in common stock dividends from the Employer Company. Fees paid during the year for legal, accounting, and other services rendered by parties-in-interest were based on customary and reasonable rates for such services.

---

* *Reader note:* Required under GAAP only when the plan has not obtained or maintained a favorable letter of determination from the IRS. This disclosure is included because disclosure of the plan's current tax status is required in financial statements submitted to DOL.

** *Reader note:* Required under ERISA in the notes to the financial statements even though the Plan may be exempt from reporting the transactions on the schedule of transactions involving parties-in-interest. Under GAAP, similar disclosure in the notes to the financial statements only is required when such transactions are related party transactions as defined by Statement on Auditing Standards No. 6, "Related Party Transactions."

4

Organization for Benefits

PAUL A. GUERIN

Administrative Director, Benefits Administration, Services and Risk Management, Touche Ross & Co.

MANAGEMENT RESPONSIBILITY FOR BENEFITS

Primary Responsibility

In most large and medium-size companies, the *employee benefits manager* has primary responsibility for the management, operation, and administration of employee benefit programs. In small companies, the management of the employee benefit function may be delegated to the personnel manager, office manager, or controller with assistance from outside vendors such as insurance companies, brokers, or consultants.

Typical Structure

The benefits department is normally found in the personnel or human resource function with the employee benefits manager reporting to the vice-president, personnel, or human resources departments. Reporting structures differ from organization to organization, but a typical one is shown in Figure 4.1.

In addition, an Administrative Committee or Retirement Committee may set broad policy guidelines and be responsible for the overall management of the plans. These committees generally report to the Board of Directors.

Decentralized Approach

Since organization and management of the employee benefits function are closely interrelated, it is not unusual for large companies to separate different parts of the benefits function across departmental lines. In this type of organization, different departments may exercise various degrees of planning, operational, or administrative responsibility for specific aspects of the benefits program. Figure 4.2 demonstrates how financial, legal, data processing personnel, employee relations, labor relations, or payroll personnel may be involved in different ways in the overall management of the employee benefits function.

However, under such a decentralized approach, it is vital that the employee benefits manager coordinate the decision-making and implementation process. The total day-to-day management responsibility should rest with the employee benefits manager.

The Benefits Manager

The successful benefits manager must be able to apply sound business ad-

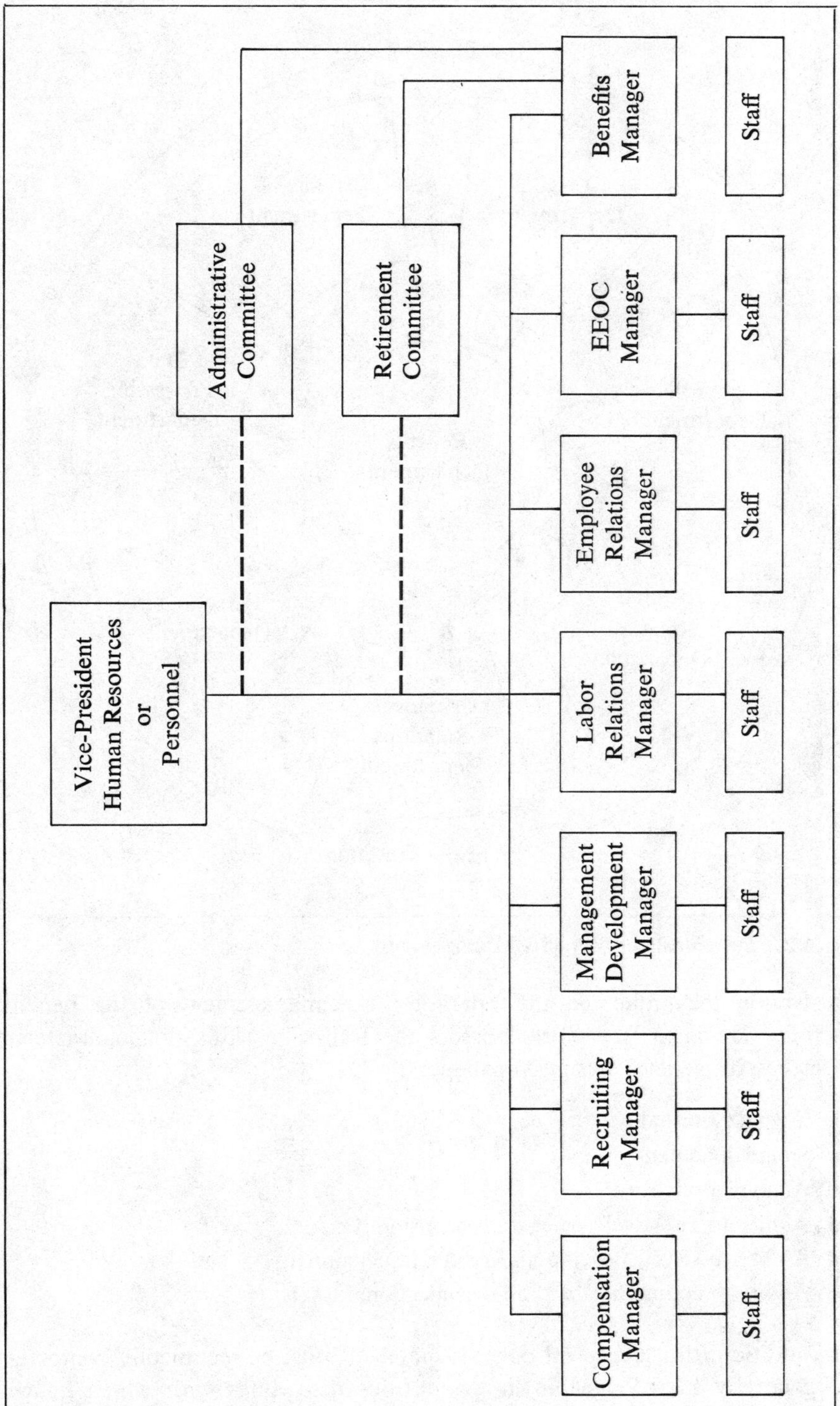

Fig. 4.1 Organization Chart—Macro

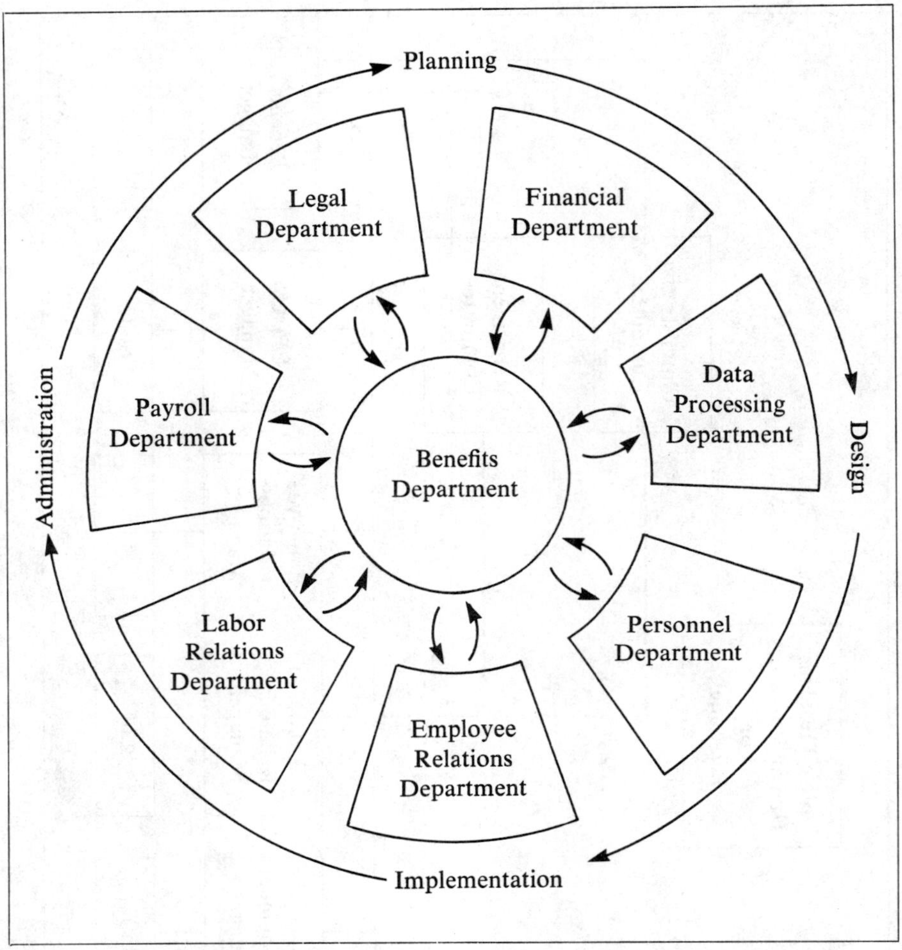

Fig. 4.2 Decentralized Benefits Management

ministration techniques to the operation and management of the benefits function. He must, therefore, possess the following skills that characterize the successful general business manager:

- Organization talent
- Sound judgment
- Analytical ability
- Ability to effectively delegate responsibility
- Ability to select, develop and motivate personnel
- Ability to communicate at all organizational levels

In addition, the successful benefits manager must be technically competent and generally knowledgeable in the various disciplines with which he will be concerned:

- Investments
- Finance
- Law
- Taxation
- Data processing
- Insurance underwriting
- Pensions and actuarial sciences
- Communications
- Administration

The job description provided in Figure 4.3 illustrates the varied functions that an employee benefits manager must perform.

1. Develops, implements, and administers non-cash compensation programs
2. Prepares annual benefits budget
3. Prepares annual cost analyses of benefit programs, and future cost projections
4. Evaluates benefit programs against stated objectives
5. Monitors government regulations, developments and trends
6. Represents the company with outside vendors and regulatory agencies
7. Conducts management studies, including internal and external surveys
8. Keeps necessary records, and develops appropriate administrative systems and controls
9. Communicates to management and employees

Fig. 4.3 Job Description—Employee Benefits Manager

ROLE AND FUNCTIONS OF THE BENEFITS DEPARTMENT

Although the scope of the benefits department's activity is determined by the internal and external parameters discussed below, the role of the benefits department is essentially the same in most companies:

- Planning
- Plan design/funding
- Implementation
- Administration
- Monitoring
- Communications

Stated another way, the role of the benefits department is to deliver promised benefits to employees efficiently, accurately, and in the most cost-effective manner.

Organization and Staffing

Scope of Activities. The role and size of the benefits department depends on the following company (internal) characteristics:

1. Company structure
   —Domestic or multinational
2. Company size
   —Number of divisions, subsidiaries, and locations
3. Number of employees
4. Employee mix
   —Non-union or collective bargaining
5. Capital intensive or labor intensive
6. Management style
   —Centralized or decentralized
7. Management philosophy

External characteristics also influence the scope of the benefits department's activity:

1. Number and types of plans
   —Single plan or multiplan
2. Plan design and funding
   —Insured or self-insured
   —Conventional or flexible
3. Systems capability
4. Use of outside vendors
5. Definition of "employee benefits"
6. Functional/departmental responsibilities

Choice of Organizational Model. Figure 4.4 illustrates how a benefits staff may be structured. It may be organized on either a functional responsibility, or a total-plan-basis model. The structure itself does not change the department's role previously described.

The *total-plan model* invests complete responsibility in a single staff. Under a *functional responsibility model,* planning and administrative responsibilities are split between separate staffs. Regardless of the model chosen, the benefits manager has the responsibility for hiring, training, and developing the professional capabilities of his staff.

Staffing Requirements. Opinion and practice vary when it comes to the use of *specialists* or *generalists* in meeting professional staffing requirements. Whether a department should staff according to specialization depends on the degree of functional responsibility delegated to the department, budget considerations over staff size, use of outside consultants, and funding vehicles. Use of the benefits generalist, who is adequately cross-trained, affords greater

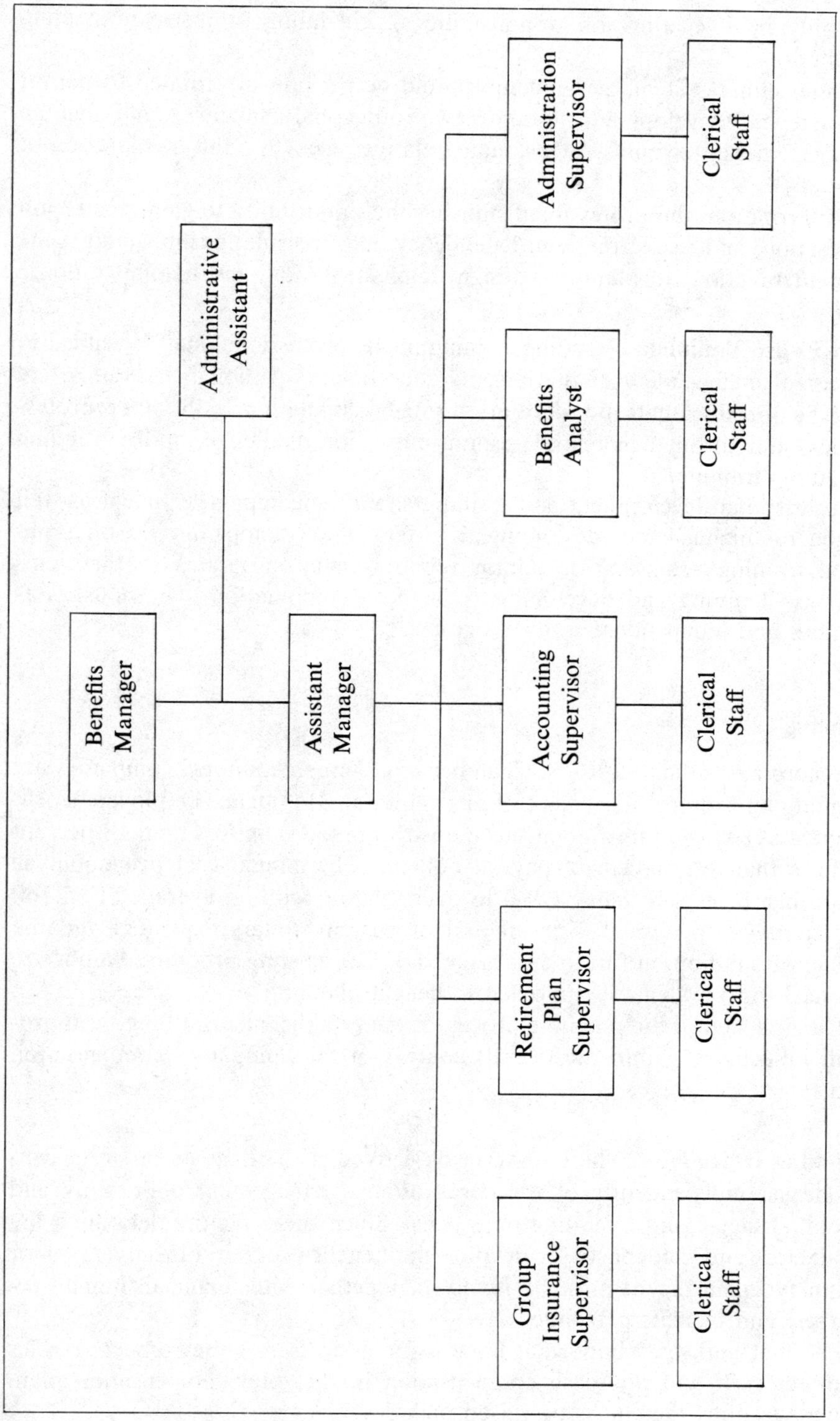

Fig. 4.4 Organization Chart—Benefits Staff

flexibility in delegating job responsibilities, scheduling projects, or meeting deadlines.

Under either system, assignments should be periodically rotated to permit adequate staff development, present new professional challenges, and give the manager the opportunity to evaluate relative strengths and weaknesses of his staff.

With rotation, the professional staff has the opportunity to gain greater job satisfaction, and to see the interdependency and interrelationships among the different functions of planning, design, implementation, and administration.

In-House Training. On-going training of the professional staff is critical to successful management of the benefits department. Although it sounds like a cliché, professionals do develop through association with other professionals, and through increased responsibility, job challenge, and continuing education/training.

Professional development and training should encompass technical as well as general management development. Many large companies do offer national training programs or tuition reimbursement programs to their employees. Training and development can be a combination of in-house, off-premise, and independent study programs.

Planning

According to the 1979 U.S. Chamber of Commerce Survey, companies are spending an average 36 percent of payroll dollars to finance employee benefit programs. Expenditures in various industries range from less than 18 percent to more than 65 percent of payroll dollars. The annual cost per employee may range from less than $2,400 to over $9,500, with an average of $5,560 per employee, per year. The amount of current dollars expended and the impact of inflation on future cost projections for existing programs emphasize the need for a systematic approach to benefit planning.

The first step in the planning process is the establishment of long-term program objectives, within the overall context of the company's compensation plan.

Setting Objectives. The long-term objectives of the benefits program cannot be set independently of the corporation's management philosophy and overall strategic and operating objectives. Since these factors determine the parameters and guideposts for defining the benefit program objectives, senior company management must be involved, together with financial, human resources, and benefits personnel.

The first and most important issue to be addressed is the respective roles of direct cash and non-cash compensation in the total compensation plan. Other questions that must be raised include:

- What is the firm trying to accomplish through its benefit programs?
- How are benefit programs related to its total compensation policy?
- To what extent must these programs be measured against related industry competition?
- Should basic or optional benefit programs be related to profitability?
- Should employees be required to contribute? To what degree?
- How will the benefit programs reflect or contribute to overall company goals and objectives?
- Should all employees be treated alike?
- What is management's perception of employees' needs?
- How will labor negotiations affect non-union employees?
- To what extent will the company be influenced by employee attitudes?
- Are these programs realistic?
- Can management afford them?
- What is the company's attitude towards retirees?

The end result of this exercise is to produce a written statement of objectives and general principles. It should provide realistic guidelines to assist in the development, management, and review of benefit programs. A representative list of objectives is shown in Figure 4.5.

1. Protect against catastrophic loss
2. Enhance employee security
3. Maximize tax advantage to company and employees
4. Provide a reasonable level of retirement benefits
5. Encourage personal savings for retirement
6. Attract, retain, and reward employees
7. Maintain a favorable competitive position within the industry
8. Prevent unionization
9. Reduce benefits as a source of discontent
10. Address the changing needs of the work force

Fig. 4.5 Statement of Benefits Objectives

Surveying Employees. Another important benefit planning tool is determining employee attitudes and preferences.

Formal methods. There are several techniques that can be used to inform management of employee perceptions:

- Climate review
- Focus group interviews
- Opinion surveys

The selection of a suitable technique depends upon the type of information desired. For example, the choice would be determined by management's concern with gathering general perceptions on the one hand, or precise statistical data to evaluate attitudes on specific issues. Regardless of the technique selected, the end result should be the same—to collect, quantify, and utilize the data. It is also highly desirable to have a feedback mechanism in place. Employees surveyed should be informed of their contributions and to what end the data results have been used.

There are two major potential pitfalls in any employee surveying program. Management must be constantly alert to avoid raising expectations unnecessarily, and also must be prepared to act upon discovery of dissatisfaction or discontent. Failure to take appropriate corrective action will not only damage relations with employees but will also cause management to lose credibility.

It is important to note that each of these formal techniques requires specific expertise that may or may not be present in the benefits department. It may be advisable to use outside consultants, or other in-house personnel with demonstrated competency in this area.

Other survey techniques. There are other less formal methods of gathering employee attitude data that can be used in lieu of, or as a supplement to, the formal approaches:

- Regular staff meetings
- Suggestion programs
- Exit interviews with terminated employees
- Informal management-employee meetings
- Supervisory feedback

External Surveys. Another useful way to gather benefits data is to survey competitor practices. This can be done on an industrywide or geographic basis. The survey data can be collected by participating in formal industry surveys, or by informally exchanging information with competitors.

Competitive practices should not be the benchmark or catalyst for making changes. Knowledge of the benefits program in competing companies is obviously important information for quantitative analysis, but it is not a substitute for effective planning and internal analysis of employee needs. Emerging trends and developments that may create competitive disadvantage should also be known and evaluated—but the evaluation must be made on a total compensation basis.

Included in other external sources that publish useful data on a wide range of employee benefit issues are the following groups:

- U.S. Chamber of Commerce, Washington, D.C.
- The Conference Board, New York, N.Y.
- American Management Associates, New York, N.Y.

- Council on Employee Benefits, Chicago, Ill.
- Council on Life Insurance, New York, N.Y.
- Bankers Trust Company—*Corporate Pension Study,* New York, N.Y.
- Major accounting and benefit consulting firms

Demographics. Employee surveys are important in that they measure employee attitudes and feelings, but they do not provide suitable identification of the group's demographic characteristics. The collection of personal and job-related data then becomes an important planning ingredient. The company's Management Information System is the logical source for this information. The information may be available from one file source such as the personnel file, or a combination of file sources.

Distribution analysis of employees within the following criteria provides useful benefit planning information by creating a composite profile of the work force.

Personal Data	*Management Data*
Age	Length of Service
Sex	Job Position—Status
Marital Status	Compensation
Number of Dependents	Full Time—Part Time
Education	Location

In addition to profile information, the following supplementary data should also be collected and analyzed:

- Turnover statistics
- Recruiting results
- Attendance
- Sick leave—disability
- Retirement patterns
- Enrollment or program participation patterns

Careful analyses of employee attitudes and needs, coupled with a factual work force profile, avoid the danger of making benefit plan improvements solely based on a reaction to what the "competition" is doing.

Plan Design/Funding

Plan design and funding vehicle selection highlight the interrelationships between the benefits manager and other functional departments within the company. (Chapter 2 covers the principles of general plan design in detail, so only a brief overview will be included here.)

The compilation of planning data from both internal and external sources is the first step in analyzing how current plans correlate with company objectives. If the current plans are not satisfying those objectives, management must then decide whether plan improvements should be made, or new plans adopted. Existing plans should be thoroughly examined on a provision-by-provision basis.

Cost Analyses. Detailed cost analyses should also be prepared on the same basis to see what the true cost of plan provision changes would be. These analyses should be a joint responsibility of the benefits department and the finance department. Improvements must be analyzed from both the employee relations (people) and cash management (money) perspectives. The finance department (or company controller) can provide important input on the impact of the changes on cash flow, as well as their impact on earnings, budget, and profitability.

Costs must also be measured in terms of their future impact. This is particularly true in retirement plans where improvements must be amortized over a long period of time, up to thirty years. It is equally true with respect to health insurance costs, where inflation has a dramatic effect on escalating costs.

Compensation and Compliance Review. Plans that are compensation sensitive such as life insurance, disability, retirement plans, and savings/thrift plans also require additional review of compensation planning and strategy. The following questions should be posed and answered:

- What will be the cost impact of a 10 percent salary increase?
- What is the budgeted bonus?
- What salary increase assumptions should be used next year?
- What are the projected salary increases for new employees entering the work force?

Tax and legal compliance is another critical review step:

- Does the plan or improvement satisfy current or proposed IRS regulations?
- Have discrimination, ADEA (Age Discrimination in Employment Act), and EEOC guidelines been reviewed?
- What will be the impact of anticipated legislation?
- Could the improvement jeopardize the plan's current tax-exempt status?
- Should the plan file for an advanced determination of continued tax exemption?
- What government agencies have jurisdiction?
- Are the regulations clear, or have conflicting regulations been issued by agencies with overlapping jurisdiction?

Funding Alternatives. The benefits manager must be thoroughly familiar with various funding vehicles and cash-flow arrangements. The choice of the funding vehicle is a primary determinant of cost. (See Chapter 11 for a detailed discussion of this topic.)

For retirement plans, management may choose among various funding alternatives depending upon the size and resources of the company:

- Individual retirement or annuity contracts
- Group permanent policies
- Group deferred annuities
- Group deposit administration contracts
- Immediate participation guarantee contracts
- Trust-funded arrangements
- Investment-only contracts with insurance companies
- Guaranteed investment contracts

For group insurance plans, benefits can be provided through *self-insurance* or *conventional insurance*. Several questions then arise. If self-insured, will the plan be self-administered? If self-insured, should a 501(c)(9) trust be established? Should the plan process its own claims, or would an Administrative Services Only (ASO) contract with an insurance company be more practical? Of the following cash-flow arrangements, which would be most advantageous?

- Minimum premium plan
- Retrospective rating agreement
- Premium deferral or delay arrangement
- Flexible life funding

The benefits manager must be aware of the advantages and disadvantages of these alternatives in order to recommend the appropriate funding vehicle to finance the benefit plan or improvements.

The choice of the funding vehicle and plan design have a significant effect on plan administration.

The inherent administrative differences between a self-insured, self-administered health insurance plan and a conventionally (fully) insured plan best illustrate this concept. Under a conventional insurance plan, the insurance company would provide administrative, claim processing, legal, actuarial, and underwriting services. Under a self-insured/self-administered plan, staff must be hired to perform these necessary services, and an entire administration system must be installed to operate the plan.

Plan Design Features. As discussed in Chapter 2, plan design features also have a direct impact on plan administration. The following questions indicate the important issues that should be raised:

- Have benefits been designed according to an events-oriented grid, or are there overlapping coverages spread out over several plans?
- How many employee classifications are there? Are there different waiting periods or benefit levels according to classification?
- How frequently has the plan been amended? How many endorsements and riders have been added to the plan?

There is a critical mass point in terms of amending a plan that makes it virtually impossible to administer or interpret the plan document.

Flexible Plan Approach. Finally, the ultimate impact of plan design on administration can be seen in the choice of a flexible (cafeteria) plan approach vis-à-vis a traditional approach. (See Chapter 25.) Flexible or cafeteria plans can impose substantially different administrative and record-keeping systems.

The adoption of a flexible planning approach will almost certainly require sophisticated systems capability and development for the large or medium-size company. Existing systems will have to be radically modified or scrapped entirely.

Implementation

Once the decisions concerning plan design, funding, and compliance have been determined, the program must be implemented. Implementation requires careful planning and execution and can involve other functional departments within the company, as well as outside sources.

There must be a high degree of cooperation between the parties involved. The benefits manager must coordinate the efforts of those engaged in the implementation process both to promote efficiency and to insure employee acceptance of the program, whether it involves an amended, supplemental, or new program.

Implementing Changes. Suitable lead time must be allowed in planning changes. Trying to implement changes without adequate lead time will only make the task more complicated, increase the margin for errors, and often result in poor acceptance by employees. Retroactive changes should be avoided because they create confusion and administrative overload.

Internal record-keeping and administration systems must be updated to accept and properly record necessary changes. This process may involve accounting, payroll, data processing, and personnel departments.

Implementation often involves the participation of external sources—the insurance company, broker, or consultant. The benefits manager must determine who can do the job most efficiently and economically, and must assign responsibility between in-house and outside resources.

Regardless of the change adopted, the program must be communicated, descriptive material must be distributed, and the employees must be enrolled. Whether in-house or outside assistance is used, the benefits manager should review and approve all material that is prepared for distribution. Strict budget controls should be established to prevent the project from running off the track.

Monitoring for Compliance. Implementation does not end when the last employee has been enrolled. The entire administration system must be monitored for compliance. Are policy instructions being followed? Are claims being processed accurately? Have the proper premiums been withheld from payroll? Are the correct premiums being reported to the insurance company? Have there been any unanticipated problems? System breakdowns?

Employee Feedback. Implementation should also include appropriate employee feedback. Has there been a high level of participation and enrollment? Are the employees enthusiastic or excited about the change? Has there been an adequate level of understanding, or has the change precipitated an avalanche of telephone and written inquiries?

Finally, negative comment or feedback must be taken into account. It can function as a barometer of a program's success or failure, and should provide useful insight for future changes.

ADMINISTRATION THROUGH EDP

Regardless of company size, systems capability, or number of benefit programs, the benefits manager must take responsibility for basic administrative functions, such as record-keeping, claims processing, report generation, and communication.

However, in the 1980s, benefits managers must be especially aware of the application of new technology to these basic administrative functions, and must learn to plan or update their systems' capability to manage, process, use, and store information. Word processing, intelligent copiers, telecommunications, data processing, electronic mail, and data storage/retrieval systems will all play an increasingly critical role in shaping the administrative function.

Role of the Computer

Advantages of Automation. The need to collect, analyze, store, and retrieve information for benefit planning and administration is the major reason to consider automating systems capability. A computer can do these essential functions more accurately, quickly, consistently, and cost effectively.

In terms of systems development, benefit administration systems have been built around the payroll and personnel functions. The payroll and personnel files feed data into other specified systems on sub-routines such as those required to maintain benefit records for pension, health care, salary continuation, or other programs. Under this operating mode, there is no single source where all information is captured for review, analysis, or costing.

If a company adopts a flexible or "cafeteria" approach to benefit planning, additional complications and needs arise. The system must not only maintain records, but also:

- Determine eligibility of elective and basic benefits
- Track compensation ingredients
- Track basic and elective benefits chosen
- Determine the amount of compensation or "credit points" set aside to purchase electives
- Allow calculation of the cost of elective benefits to determine how much of the credits have been used
- Compute various benefit levels at any given time

The system might also be designed to incorporate features that permit:

- Updating of employee records to generate pension valuations
- Calculation of retirement benefits
- Production of an annual benefits statement

The design of a benefits administration system is a highly complex task. To be successful, careful planning and coordination of professional skills in such diverse areas as finance, accounting, payroll, legal, actuarial, and data processing, will be required. A systems checklist appears in Figure 4.6.

1. Project management
2. Quality assurance
3. Planning
4. Documentation of existing system
5. User requirements
6. System design
7. Program documentation
8. Test and training documentation
9. Implementation documentation
10. Maintenance of discrepancy reports

Fig. 4.6 Systems Checklist

Factors Influencing System Design. The very first question to be asked in designing a system is, "What do we expect the system to accomplish?" In addition, a number of other external and internal factors must be addressed:

- Financial resources of the firm
- Number of plan participants
- Integration with existing systems
- Number of plans
- Plan design considerations
- Functional requirements
- Applications
- Performance
- Turnaround time
- Information flow and interrelationships
- Costs
  —Hardware
  —Programming
  —Development
  —Operating
- Staffing requirements
  —Operations
  —Input/output
  —File maintenance/update
- Conversion requirements
- Flexibility
- Leasing vs. purchasing
- In-house development vs. outside development

Unless a company has substantial in-house systems capability, a feasibility study should be conducted with the assistance of outside specialists.

The successful administration system must be flexible in design, and be responsive to future changes—government regulation, changing needs of the work force and changing plan objectives. (See Figure 4.7).

EDP UTILIZATION IN SPECIFIC FUNCTIONS

As described earlier, the computer is an extremely valuable administrative tool. Some of the routine administrative and record-keeping functions that can be performed by an automated system include:

- Record-keeping
  —Employee
  —Management
  —Eligibility
  —Financial and general
- Records retention
- Claims processing and control
- Retirement plan administration

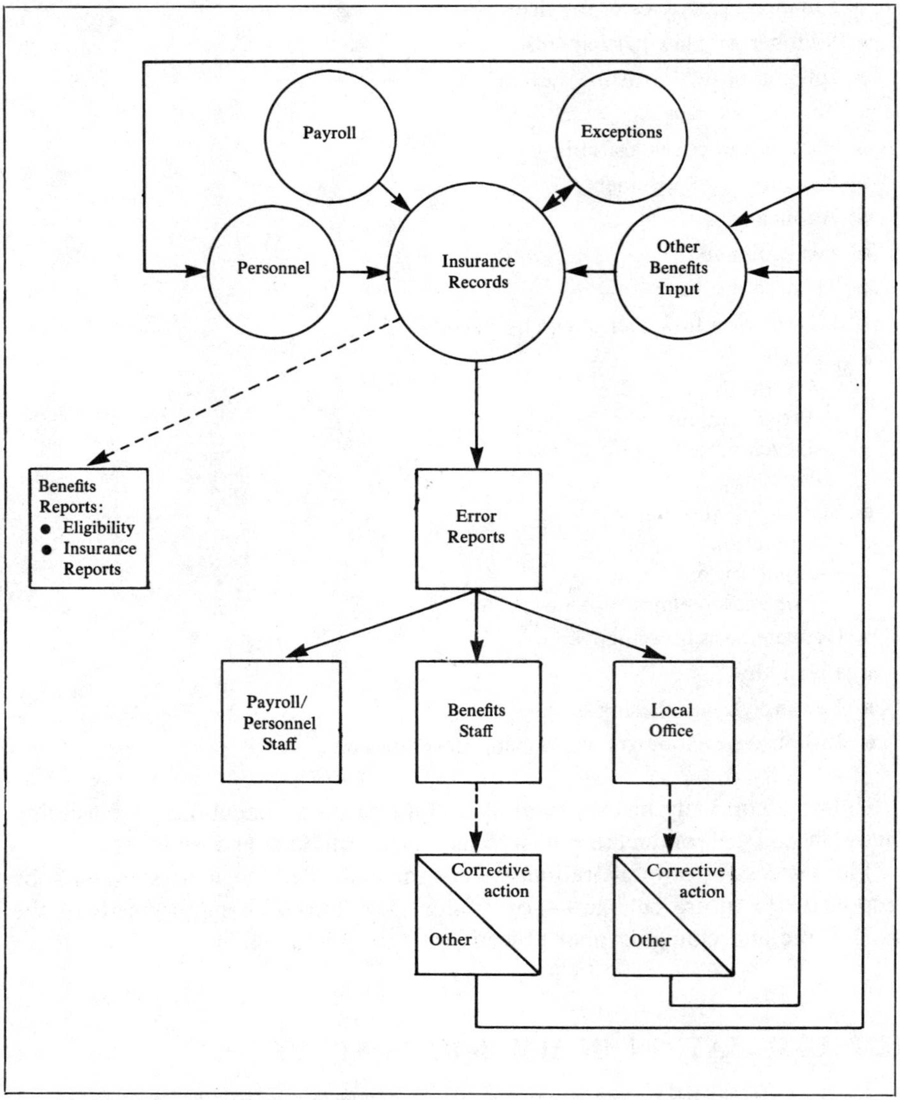

Fig. 4.7 Systems Design Flow Chart

- Report generation
- Cost analysis
- Communication

Record-keeping

Although significant differences may exist as to the type of information required on a plan-by-plan basis, the fundamental objective of any record-keeping system is to provide information that is:

- Complete
- Accurate
- Accessible
- Confidential

Employee (Personal) Data. This is the basic personal data for all employees. Information is usually updated daily, monthly, or on an event basis (i.e., hire, termination, marriage), etc.

This data generally includes:

- Permanent mailing address
- Date of birth
- Sex
- Marital status
- Number of dependents
- Education
- Social Security number

Management (Employer) Data. Management data is usually entered by the personnel or payroll function and includes:

- Employee identification number
- Date of hire
- Compensation history
- Job classification (position)
- Job status—exempt, non-exempt, union
- Promotion date
- Leave of absence
- Full time/part time
- Plant, office, or location

This data may also be updated on a daily, monthly, or event basis.

Eligibility (Participation) Records. Eligibility records are usually maintained on a plan-by-plan basis due to wide variations in eligibility rules, waiting periods, and employee contribution requirements. The basic data source for this information is usually the group insurance enrollment card. Eligibility data may include:

- Plan identification
- Eligibility date or effective date of coverage
- Birth date and sex
- Job classification
- Salary

- Required contribution
- Benefit level chosen, if options exist
- Designated beneficiary(ies)
- Dependent coverage
  —Names and dates of birth for dependents
- Effective dates of change
  —Coverage added
  —Coverage terminated
- Special arrangements (exceptions)

The method of storing and retrieving eligibility data ranges from hard copy computer printouts, terminal access, or CRT direct inquiry on a case-by-case basis. Eligibility data must be current, up-to-date, and readily accessible information.

The system should also have a flag or signal mechanism to alert the system's user of circumstances that can lead to a loss of benefits.

In addition to the general eligibility information indicated above, pension plans have specific additional requirements:

- Merger data, if appropriate
- Past-service credit records or history
- Frozen accrued benefits under prior plan
- Suitable work history or employment data to identify:
  —Current participation, vesting and accrual
  —Breaks in service
  —Leaves of absence
  —Disability
- Track active, retired, terminated, and deferred vested plan participants

Financial and General Records. One of the most important aspects of any administration system is to provide accurate records of income and expenses. Furthermore, the plan records should produce information necessary for financial reporting, as well as provide detailed information for effective management.

The basic accounting records for employee benefit plans are similar to those applicable to other entities. For single-employer plans, the plan's daily administration (collection of contributions, payments of benefits, control of cash and investments, maintenance of records and preparation of reports) may be delegated to one or more of the following:

1. The sponsoring employer
2. Bank trust department
3. Corporate trustee
4. An insurance company

Meeting ERISA requirements. ERISA focused attention on the financial reporting and auditing of pension and welfare benefit plans.

ERISA requires the plan administrator to engage, on behalf of all plan participants, an independent qualified public accountant to review the plan's financial statements, unless the plan qualifies for exemption because:

1. It has fewer than 100 participants, or
2. Is fully insured, or
3. Is unfunded.

The accountant is required to conduct an examination of the financial statements of the plan and express an opinion on whether the financial statements and required schedules are presented fairly in conformity with Generally Accepted Accounting Principles (GAAP).

Basic records. The following basic records are common to most employee benefit plans:

Welfare Benefit Plans

1. Insurance contracts and agreements
2. Contribution records
   —Employer
   —Employee, if contributory
3. Chart of accounts
4. Claims register
   —All claims paid during a reporting period (type and amount paid)
   —Summary record
5. Participant eligibility records

Retirement Benefit Plans

1. Trust agreement and plan documents
2. Investment/custodian agreements
3. Committee minutes
4. Actuarial valuation reports
5. Benefit calculations
6. Chart of accounts
7. Insurance contracts (if all or part of benefits are insured)
8. List of parties-in-interest
9. Contribution record
   —Employer
   —Employee, if contributory
10. Participant eligibility records
11. Investment accounts

12. Trusteed assets
    —Cash receipts and disbursements transactions (benefits)
    —Investment transactions (purchase and sale)
    —Statement of assets (cost and current values)
    —Broker-dealer transactions statements
    —Realized and unrealized changes in value of investments
    —Transactions in excess of 3 percent of plan assets
13. Administrative expenses

In addition, defined contribution plans require individual participant account files, showing the transactions and net assets which have been allocated to individual participant accounts. Such transactions might include employer and employee contributions, allocated portions of forfeited amounts, income, gain or loss in value of investments held and sold, and administrative expenses.

Records Retention

Basic documents as defined in ERISA must be kept in their original form for a minimum six-year period. To facilitate compliance with this requirement, the benefits department should systematically review its records management procedures. Records should be kept and stored in the most economical fashion possible. This might involve a combination of offsite storage and use of microfilm-microfiche technology. It may be advisable to keep duplicate sets of important records at a secure offsite facility to guard against loss or destruction.

Claims Processing and Control

The claims processing activity is a highly specialized task, requiring trained personnel, careful system design and planning, and ongoing commitment to quality assurance and cost monitoring.

Its design depends on the following variables:

- Type of plan
- Funding arrangement
- Number of participants
- Volume of claims
- Eligibility rules

Types of Systems. For fully insured plans, the claims processing function is essentially limited to *verification of eligibility*. This can be done on a claim-by-claim basis, either manually or using a computerized eligibility record. It may save considerable administrative time and expense to furnish the insurance carried with a monthly listing of eligible employees and dependents. Such a listing could be hard copy printout, but more appropriately would be magnetic tape. If the eligibility records are up-to-date and accurately maintained, this opportunity for direct claim processing should be given careful consideration.

For self-insured and self-administered plans, there are only three claims processing systems available:

- Manual
- Partially automated
- Fully automated

Manual system. A manual system may be appropriate for the small employer with a few employees and small claims volume. For medium-size and large companies, however, either the partially automated or fully automated claims processing systems are the only viable options.

Partially automated. A partially automated system actually combines manual claims processing and record-keeping with data processing for check issuance. Statistical data compilation may be included in the check register system. The partially automated system requires considerable storage space for maintaining and updating historical and detailed claim processing records.

Fully automated. A fully automated claims processing system is illustrated in Figure 4.8. It requires a substantial capital expenditure for development and testing, but should offer significant offsetting savings in the following areas:

- Compilation and retrieval of statistical information
- Quicker claims turnaround time
- Improved service
- Claims control by analyzing cost and utilization data
- Reduced clerical error
- Improved productivity

A fully automated system has three hardware components:

1. Entry device or video terminal
2. Computer
3. Printer

How the Automated System Works. Although there is considerable latitude in system design flexibility, an automated system should incorporate the following basic procedural steps:

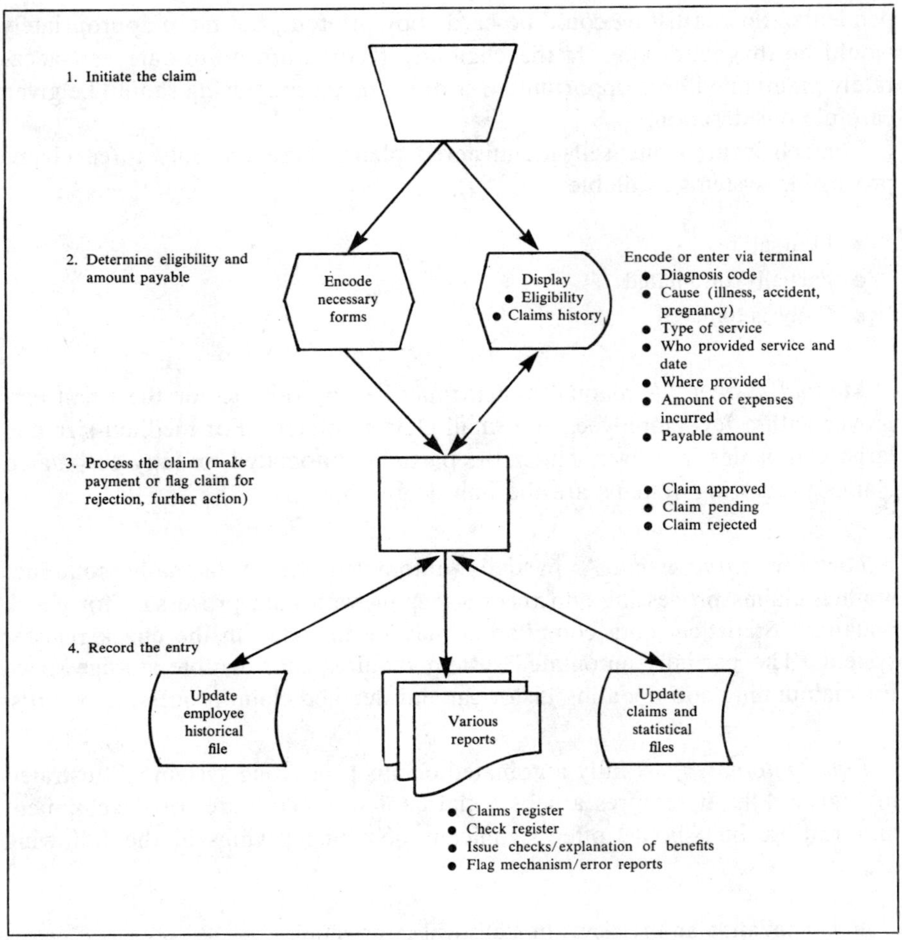

Fig. 4.8 Automated Claims System

Historical Information:

- Eligibility data or enrollment information
  —Employee name, address, date of birth, effective date of coverage, Social Security number
  —Coverage type—individual or family
  —Names, dates of birth, relationship, and effective dates of coverage for eligible dependents
  —Status—active or retired
  —Coordination of Benefits (COB) history
  —Medicare eligibility
- Prior claims history
- Record of annual deductibles and totals paid to date

Claim Preparation:

- Date-stamp claim form and supporting data
- Enter into claim control log
- Assign claim or batch number
- Establish eligibility

Claim Processing:

- Claim form
  —Patient data
  —Provider data
  —Assignment of benefits
- Coding hierarchy—identify diagnosis
  —ICDA codes (International Classification of Diseases as Adopted)
  or
  —Specific codes developed by the user
- Indicative information
  —Date of loss or service
  —Cause (illness, accident, pregnancy)
  —Type of service (surgery, anesthesia, office visit)
  —Place services rendered (hospital, doctor's office)

Determining Amount Payable:

- RVS scale (Relative Value Scale)—for allowances based on fixed fee schedules
  or
- UCR scale (Usual, Customary and Reasonable)—for allowances based on reasonable and customary charges
- Enter amount billed
- Enter amount payable
- Enter name of payee

System Acceptance:

- Issue check
- Issue explanation of benefits form
- Update claims history
- Update statistical file
- Update financial file
- Prepare check register
- Prepare claims register

Additional controls: Apart from those touched upon above, there are other controls that must be built into a fully automated claims system:

- Claim denial procedures
- Review procedures for claims denied

- Partial payment procedures
- Pending claims log
- Claim review and audit
- Quality control
- Method for establishing and updating UCR schedules
- Security over blank checks
- Security over facsimile signatures and checkwriters
- Strict accounting for checks issued, voided and destroyed
- Separation of claims processing and check issuance procedures
- Procedures against theft or fraudulent claims
- Written claim procedures
- Cost controls

Retirement Plan Administration

Computerization greatly facilitates the management and administration of retirement plan programs. Two essential functions that should be considered for automation are:

1. Data generation for the actuarial valuation
2. Retirement calculations

Data Generation. Most retirement plans perform an annual actuarial valuation. The plan sponsor should collect the census data and edit it before submitting it to the actuary. This data usually consists of the participant's name, Social Security number, birth date, sex, credited service (plan entry), hours worked or pension credits, compensation (current and historical), date of termination, disability, or leave of absence, break in service, and past service credits.

The census data is usually arranged according to specific categories:

1. Active participants
2. Active participants over age 65
3. Active participants on leaves of absence
4. Terminated participants
5. Terminated vested participants who received lump-sum payments
6. Terminated vested participants with deferred benefits
7. Deceased retired participants
8. Deceased terminated vested participants who had deferred payments
9. Retired participants
10. New plan entrants

In addition to the standard census information mentioned above, the categories for retirees and terminated vested participants with deferred benefits (including the respective sections for deceased participants) should include:

amount of pension, type of annuity, and contingent annuitant's date of birth (if applicable).

The plan sponsor may also want to generate additional control reports showing:

1. Active employees not in the plan
2. Error listing
3. Distribution analysis for discrimination testing
4. Emerging retirees

Retirement Calculations. A good deal of administrative time is also spent doing retirement calculations. Incorrect calculations could result not only in employee dissatisfaction, but also in legal or financial liability to the plan.

Advantages of computerization. A computer program, run from an inexpensive time-sharing terminal, can provide calculations on demand in a fraction of the time required for manual calculations. Benefit personnel can enter data in response to simple English questions. Additional calculations with different estimated retirement dates or future salaries can be easily generated. The computer printed forms can be photocopied for distribution to participants. Uniformity and accuracy of computations are assured.

The calculation program can also generate ERISA-required statements showing accrued benefit amounts, degree of vesting, or when vesting will be attained and facilitate identification of and communication to vested and non-vested terminated participants. In addition, updates to the program for plan amendments, changes to Social Security benefits and IRS benefit limitations can be easily generated.

Feasibility. Whether an automated retirement calculation program is economically feasible depends on several factors:

- Volume of calculations and estimates
- Complexity of plan provisions
- Frequency of plan amendment

CARRIER ADMINISTRATION

Selection Process

Selecting the right insurance carrier to provide benefits is a primary function of the benefits manager. The task is complicated by the fact that there are literally thousands of licensed insurance companies from which to choose.

Depending on staffing depth, level of staffing, and the benefits manager's own experience level, it may be useful to engage the services of a benefits consulting firm or insurance broker to assist in the selection process.

Factors to Consider. Group insurance marketing is highly specialized and keenly competitive, but there are objective factors that should be evaluated:

- Contract and underwriting flexibility
- Projection of gross costs and net costs
- Setting premium rates
- Method of determining reserves
- How interest is credited on reserves held
- Types of reserves to be established
- Itemization of retention components
- Premium deferral arrangements
- Conversion options/charges
- Claims runout procedures on policy termination
- Pooling levels/catastrophic loss protection
- Administrative/claims processing capability and facilities
- Claims payment philosophy
- Cost control procedures
- Administrative services provided
- Reports furnished
- Carrier reputation
- Financial solvency
- Location of administrative and claims processing facilities

When all factors have been considered, the final judgment on selection will probably be made on the basis of the carrier's ability to provide services. Competition and marketplace factors should neutralize or narrow pricing and underwriting factors.

Services Provided by Carrier

Once a carrier has been selected, let us look at some of the services that should be provided.

Claims Processing. The carrier's ability to pay claims promptly and accurately is the single most important factor to be considered.

Promptness. Claims processing is a highly specialized task, but assuming that a claim is fully documented and complete, the turnaround time should not exceed three weeks. Naturally, claims that require further investigation, or that are missing necessary data, will take longer. The amount of time required to process a claim is in inverse ratio to the carrier's experience, staffing, and systems capability. Claims volume, plan provisions, and number of plan participants are also controlling factors.

Other considerations. A major consideration is the location and organization structure of the claims payment facility. For a multi-office or plant employer, will claims be handled at a central processing station, or in regional claim offices? If claims are handled at local or regional claim offices, what safeguards are in place to assure uniform policy interpretation?

Another consideration is the carrier's procedures for paying a claim. What is the carrier's claim payment philosophy? What cost control features are built into its system, and how does this affect processing turnaround time? What review procedures are followed?

If the plan provides for payment in accordance with UCR allowances, how does the carrier determine these allowances, and how is the UCR schedule updated and maintained?

Administrative Services. In addition to claims processing, many carriers perform various types of administrative services:

- Assistance in enrollment
- Availability for employee presentations
- Employee communication
- Form design and report generation

Cost Control. Another extremely important service rendered by the insurance carrier is establishing cost control program measures to identify:

- Overcharges
- Unnecessary medical treatments
- Excessive hospital confinements
- Overutilization
- Abuse or fraud
- Excessive hospital charges

The methodology used by insurance carriers to establish cost control programs involves:

- Claims review
- Developing patient profiles
- Analyzing hospital confinement by attending physician, showing average length of each provider's confinements
- Analyzing hospital confinement by geographic area, showing average confinement by hospital
- Comparing medical procedures of one provider to another for similar diagnoses
- Comparing hospital confinement by diagnosis against norms
- Use of peer review

Claims Audit

Every policyholder should establish internal audit review programs to verify that claims are being paid accurately and in accordance with plan provisions.

Insurance carriers should submit monthly claims payment registers to the policyholder. These registers should be closely reviewed to assure that only authorized and eligible claims have been charged against the group's experience.

Claims auditing may be done on an all-claim-review basis, random-sample basis, or establishment of an audit threshold (i.e., all medical claims over $1,000, all hospital claims in excess of $5,000).

Carrier Reports

Each policyholder should request and receive the following reports from the insurance carrier:

1. Monthly claims payment register/year-to-date payment register
2. Monthly claims processed/pending report
3. Statistical claims studies
4. Monthly report of conversions and charges
5. Monthly status report on pending late enrollment applications
6. Reporting and disclosure documents (Schedule A Form 5500)
7. Monthly premium and claims comparison report
8. Special reports showing savings to the plan from:
   —Coordination of Benefits (COB)
   —Reasonable and customary allowances
   —Second surgical opinions

Contract Compliance

The insurance contract is a legal document. Various statutory language provisions, in addition to general contract law provisions, are contained within the contract.

Jurisdictional Factors. Insurance companies are regulated by individual state insurance departments; therefore, state law and regulations govern a particular contract. Considerable variation exists from state to state that can influence the design of group benefits and contractual provisions.

In plans that cover employees residing in several states, the law of the state where the contract is delivered usually governs. Delivery is usually interpreted to take place in the state where the policyholder is incorporated, or where the policyholder's principal office is located, or where the greatest number of employees is located.

If several of these conditions exist, the policyholder should request that delivery take place in the state that offers the most flexibility.

Role of the Benefits Manager. The group insurance contract defines in detail all the governing terms and conditions. The benefits manager should be familiar with contract definitions and terminology.

It is extremely important for the benefits manager to carefully examine the master contract on delivery. A broker or consultant who provides placement assistance should also review the contract. In addition, good business practice dictates that all contracts be seen by the in-house legal department.

The master contract should be reviewed against the underwriting specifications to make sure that all agreed-to benefits, as well as any special arrangements, have been included.

It is also important to fully understand the insurance carrier's interpretation of specific policy provisions. Contract ambiguities or unclear interpretations should be resolved in writing before a claim arises.

COORDINATING SERVICES WITH OUTSIDE VENDORS

The benefits manager must deal with a wide range of outside vendors in obtaining professional assistance, advice, or support. The number of outside experts that must be engaged depends upon in-house expertise available, special or ad hoc situations requiring specific assistance, or is mandated by regulation or agreement.

A partial list of professionals that are frequently engaged includes:

- Accountants
- Actuaries
- Insurance brokers
- Attorneys
- Money managers
- Benefit consultants
- Management consultants
- Bankers

Selection Considerations

Criteria. The overriding criteria in the selection of consultants and other professionals are competency, independence, and reputation for quality service. Other qualities to look for during the selection process include an organization's:

- Experience
- Approach

- Innovative techniques
- Skill, background, competency
- Administration/implementation ability
- Depth of management/management turnover
- Assignments of day-to-day responsibility
- Quality control

On an individual basis, the following characteristics should be sought:

- Flexibility
- Ability to understand specific needs
- Ability to communicate
- Enthusiasm
- Ability to listen
- Personal relationships

Interviews. Initial screening or selection interviews with outside vendors should take place at the benefits manager's office. But, in order to accurately measure the vendor's ability to provide promised services, follow-up interviews should be conducted at his place of business.

Initial contact with the prospective vendor is normally made with marketing or sales personnel. Their description of their organization's capabilities should not pass unchallenged or untested. Accordingly, it is critical for the benefits managers to meet, interview, and assess the firm's technical and operations people.

Prospective vendors should be required to furnish a client list or selected references. The vendor's reputation and financial solvency should be checked with other professionals, members in the business community, financial institutions, or professional societies.

Formal Agreement

Finally, after the selection process has been completed, a formal contract, letter of understanding, or scope and engagement letter should be executed.

The document should be specific in defining the exact responsibilities of the respective parties, how fees or charges will be determined and billed, the exact nature of the services to be rendered and completion date for submitting the report or study.

If the project or assignment is sensitive, a letter of confidentiality describing internal security procedures should also be furnished. Also, management may limit or prohibit use of the findings or conclusions without specific authorization.

Fees

There is considerable variation in the fee structure and method of calculating fees for services performed.

Attorneys may charge on an hourly basis, retainer basis, or some combination thereof. Actuaries usually charge an annual fee for valuations, but may submit hourly charges for special projects or reports outside the scope of the valuation. Large accounting firms generally charge fees based on hourly billing rates.

Insurance brokers are generally compensated through earned commissions on policies issued. Other consultants usually bill for their services on an hourly basis.

Investment managers usually set their fees based upon a percentage of the market value of the portfolio. Banks that act as corporate trustee or custodian may charge for their services on a percentage basis based on portfolio size, flat dollar service-fee basis, or some variation thereof.

Fees are negotiable and should be set in accordance with the level, type, and complexity of services rendered. Requests for additional fees or increased fees should always be documented and supported in detail by the vendors. Fees should also be tested against the marketplace to determine their adequacy and competitiveness.

Relationships With Outside Vendors

The benefits manager must assume the role of coordinator among the various professionals rendering service. All the professionals involved must work in harmony and on a cooperative basis, and their roles must be subordinated to fulfilling the objectives and needs of the benefit function.

Successful working relationships with outside vendors are based on:

- Frequency of contact
- Clearly defined needs and objectives
- Frequent communication
- Division of responsibility
- Understanding the interrelationships and mutual reliance between outside vendors and the benefits manager

Services must be monitored and audited to assure quality control. Reports should be generated on a timely basis in accordance with previously established guidelines. The outside professional must clearly understand his role vis-à-vis other professionals and the benefits manager.

COMMUNICATIONS

Communication of plan information to participants and regulatory agencies is another important aspect of benefits administration. Chapters 5 and 6 provide detailed information on reporting and disclosure requirements to regulatory agencies and participants, as well as general communication techniques.

Although the legal responsibility to furnish detailed information to regulatory agencies and plan participants is delegated to the plan administrator, as a practical matter the benefits manager usually is the individual charged with this responsibility. (See Appendix 4-1 for a calendar of reporting and disclosure requirements.)

The benefits manager should also play a central role in the planning process of developing the communications strategy, and has the responsibility to see that the communications program is implemented, and that its primary objectives are attained—increasing employee awareness and understanding of the benefits program.

APPENDIX 4-1 Reporting and Disclosure Requirements

File With	*Item*	*Description*	*Who Files*	*When Due*
Internal Revenue Service	1. Form 5500	Annual report	All benefit plans covering more than 100 participants	Within seven months after end of plan year
	* 2. Form 5500-C	Annual report	All benefit plans covering fewer than 100 participants, *except* unfunded or insured welfare plan	Same as Form 5500
	3. Form 5500-G	Annual report	Government and church plans not electing coverage under Section 401(d)	Same as Form 5500
	* 4. Form 5500-K	Annual report (Keogh pension plans)	Sole proprietor or partnership with no employees; or at least one owner-employee and from one to ninety-nine employees	Same as Form 5500
	* 5. Form 5500-R	Registration statement	Employee benefit plans with fewer than 100 participants	Same as Form 5500

* For plan years starting in 1980, Form 5500-C and Form 5500-K are filed once every three years. For alternate years, Form 5500-R is required.

(*Continued*)

File With	*Item*	*Description*	*Who Files*	*When Due*
	6. Schedule A	Insurance information	All insured plans filing Form 5500 Series	Attachment to Form 5500 Series
	7. Schedule B	Actuarial information	Defined benefit plans subject to minimum funding	Attachment to Form 5500 Series
	8. Schedule SSA	Registration statement	Pension benefit plans (report separated vested participants)	Attachment to Form 5500 Series
	9. Form 5558	Annual report extension request	All benefit plans	Prior to Form 5500 Series filing deadline
	10. Form 5300	Application for determination	Defined benefit plans	N/A
	11. Form 5301	Application for determination	Defined contribution plans	N/A
	12. 1099R and 1096 transmittal	Report of lump-sum distribution	Pension benefit plans	2/28
	13. W-2P and W-3 transmittal	Report of periodic annuities, pensions, and retired pay	Pension benefit plans	2/28
Department of Labor	1. Summary plan description	Summary of plan provisions including statement of ERISA rights	All benefit plans	120 days after effective date or adoption of plan

	2. Summary of material modification	Summary of material plan changes	All benefit plans	210 days after close of plan year in which modification is adopted
	3. Terminal report	Plan termination information	Pension benefit plans	To be determined by regulation
Pension Benefit Guaranty Corporation	1. Form PBGC-1	Premium payment	Defined benefit plans	Within seven months after beginning of plan year
	2. Notice of reportable event	Description of event	Defined benefit plans	Thirty days after knowledge that a reportable event has occurred
	3. Notice of intent to terminate	—	Defined benefit plans	At least ten days before proposed termination date
File With	*Item*	*Distributed*	*Who Files*	*When Due*
Participants and beneficiaries	1. Summary plan description	Automatically	All benefit plans	Within ninety days after becoming a participant

(Continued)

File With	*Item*	*Distributed*	*Who Files*	*When Due*
	2. Summary of material modification	Automatically	All benefit plans	Within 210 days after close of plan year in which modification occurred
	3. Summary annual report	Automatically	All benefit plans	Within nine months after end of plan year
	4. Notice of claim denial	Automatically	All benefit plans	Within ninety days after a claim is filed
	5. Deferred vested pension statement	Automatically	All benefit plans	No later than filing date of Schedule SSA
	6. Notice to interested parties of application for amendment to plan	Automatically	All benefit plans	Between seven and twenty-one days before application is made
	7. Accrued and vested pension statement	On written request	All benefit plans	Not more than once every twelve months, within thirty days after request
	8. Latest annual report	On written request	All benefit plans	Within thirty days after request
	9. Plan documents	On written request	All benefit plans	Within thirty days after request

5

Reporting to Regulatory Agencies

JEFFREY D. MAMORSKY[1]

Shea & Gould

---

[1] The material in this chapter is based on chapters written by the author in *Employee Benefits Law: ERISA and Beyond* copyright 1981 Law Journal Seminars-Press, Inc. The material herein is reproduced with the permission of the publisher.

EMPLOYEE RETIREMENT INCOME SECURITY ACT OF 1974 (ERISA) REPORTING REQUIREMENTS

Under ERISA, reporting of pension and welfare plan information must be made to three separate governmental agencies: Internal Revenue Service, Department of Labor (DOL), and Pension Benefit Guaranty Corporation (PBGC). (ERISA's disclosure requirements are discussed in Chapter 6 on Communication of Benefits.)

FILINGS WITH THE INTERNAL REVENUE SERVICE

The IRS requires that four separate forms be filed with it in order to qualify pension, profit-sharing, and thrift plans under the Internal Revenue Code and assure that contributions to such plans are tax deductible to employers and tax exempt to employees. Form 5300 is used to qualify pension plans; Form 5301 for profit-sharing, savings, or thrift plans; Form 5302 (which is attached to Form 5300 or 5301) is a special Employee Census form requiring compensation data on the twenty-five highest paid participants; and Form 5303 is used to qualify collectively bargained plans involving one or more employers. Form 6406 is used to secure a determination letter as to the continued qualification of a plan as the result of an amendment.

These forms reflect the *controlled group* concept introduced by ERISA. For example, basic coverage information that must be included in Forms 5300 and 5301, such as total employed, number of employees covered by the plan, and the number excluded, is based on an employer's entire controlled group of corporations rather than on each employer in the plan. Moreover, the forms require the submission of a schedule of all employees of the controlled group, broken down into compensation brackets and indicating the number of employees who are by virtue of collective bargaining and other statutory exclusions ineligible to participate in the plan.

The Annual Report (Form 5500)

Form 5500 is the annual financial report for both pension and welfare plans. It is to be filed with the IRS only on or before the last day of the seventh month following the end of the plan year (an extension of up to two and a half months may be granted by the filing of Form 5558 with the IRS). Generally, Form 5500 consists of information regarding the plan's financial condition, coverage, source of funding, and any changes made in the plan during the year.

Plans with fewer than 100 participants at the beginning of the plan year may complete and file Form 5500-C or Form 5500-K for sole proprietorship and partnerships, which is significantly shorter and less complicated than the regular 5500 form. For plan years beginning on and after January 1, 1980, the regular Form 5500-C or 5500-K is filed only once every three years and a Form 5500-R registration statement is filed the other two years. Plans are cycled into the reporting system according to the last digit of their plan sponsor's employer identification numbers (EINs) in accordance with the following rules:

If the EIN ends in	*File Form 5500-C or K for*
4, 5, or 6	1981
7, 8, 9, or 0	1982
1, 2, or 3	1983

If the EIN ends in	*File Form 5500-R for*
1, 2, 3, 7, 8, 9, or 0	1981
1, 2, 3, 4, 5, or 6	1982
4, 5, 6, 7, 8, 9, or 0	1983

There are three exceptions to this timetable:

1. The regular Form 5500-C or 5500-K is filed for the first year of the plan's operation and for the last year.
2. If a plan has between eighty and 120 participants (inclusive) at the beginning of the plan year, the plan may file the same category of form (Form 5500 or Forms 5500-C, 5500-K or 5500-R, whichever is applicable) that was filed the previous year.
3. The cycle may, from time to time, be changed by filing Form 5500-C or 5500-K before the year it is otherwise due. If this is done, then Form 5500-R will be filed for the next two years of the new cycle.

ERISA is very detailed concerning the matters to be included in the annual report. The following items, required by ERISA, must be filed with the IRS:

Plan Administrator's Statement. As part of the annual report, the plan administrator (in most cases, the employer) must provide the following information:

1. The number of employees covered by the plan.
2. The name and address of each fiduciary.
3. The name of each person who, directly or indirectly, received compensation from the plan for services rendered to the plan or its participants. In addition, the statement must indicate the amount paid, the nature of the service rendered, the relationship of the performer of the services to the employer or union, and any other office, position, or employment such person holds with any party-in-interest. Persons whose compensation is "minimal" and who perform "solely ministerial duties" (as those terms are defined in regulations) do not need to be included in this list.
4. An explanation of the reason for any change in the plan's trustee, accountant, insurance carrier, enrolled actuary, administrator, investment manager, or custodian.

Actuarial Statement and Opinion (Schedule B). This schedule contains detailed actuarial information regarding any defined benefit plan subject to ERISA's minimum funding standards. This schedule, which must be signed by an enrolled actuary, must be filed for the first year to which the minimum funding standards apply and every year thereafter. Except as noted below, the administrator of each defined benefit pension plan that is subject to the annual reporting requirement must engage an enrolled actuary to prepare the actuarial statement required as part of the annual report. The enrolled actuary is to utilize such assumptions and techniques as necessary to enable him to form an opinion of whether the contents of the actuarial statement are in the aggregate reasonably related to the experience of the plan and to reasonable expectations, and represent the actuary's best estimate of anticipated experience under the plan. The opinion of the enrolled actuary must be part of the annual report. In giving this opinion, the actuary is entitled to rely on the correctness of any accounting matter as to which a qualified public accountant has expressed an opinion.

The actuarial statement should include the following:

1. The date of the plan year and the date of the actuarial evaluation applicable to the plan year for which the report is filed.
2. The date and the amount of the contribution or contributions received for the plan year for which the report is filed, and a report of contributions for prior years which may not have been previously reported.
3. The normal costs applicable to the plan year for which the report is filed, plus the accrued liabilities, an identification of benefits not included in the calculation, a statement of the other facts and actuarial assumptions and methods used to determine costs, a justification for any change in actuarial assumptions or cost methods, and the minimum contribution required under Section 302 of ERISA.
4. The number of participants and beneficiaries, both retired and nonretired, covered by the plan.
5. The current value of the assets accumulated in the plan, and the present value of the assets of the plan used by the actuary in any computation of the amount of contributions to the plan required to meet ERISA's minimum funding standards, plus a statement explaining the basis of such valuation of the present value of assets.
6. The present value of all of the plan's liabilities for nonforfeitable pension benefits allocated by the termination priority categories set forth in Section 4044 of ERISA, and the actuarial assumptions used in these computations.
7. A certification of the contribution necessary to reduce the accumulated funding deficiency to zero.
8. A statement by the enrolled actuary that: (i) to the best of his knowledge the report is complete and accurate, and (ii) the requirements of Section 302(c)(3) of ERISA (relating to reasonable actuarial assumptions and methods) have been complied with.
9. A copy of the actuary's opinion that the materials comprising the actuarial

statement are, in the aggregate, reasonably related to the experience of the plan and to reasonable expectations, and whether they represent his best estimate of anticipated experience under the plan.

10. Such other information regarding the plan as the Secretary of the Treasury may, by regulations, require.
11. Such other information as may be necessary to disclose fully and fairly the actuarial position of the plan.

The following types of plans are not required to include an actuarial statement in their annual reports:

1. Welfare benefit plans;
2. Profit-sharing, savings, or other individual account plans as defined in Section 3(34) of ERISA;
3. A plan that, at no time after September 2, 1974, has provided for employer contributions;
4. An insurance contract plan;
5. Any other plan not subject to ERISA's funding requirements or the termination provisions.

A plan is an *insurance contract plan* within the meaning of Item (4) above if it has the following characteristics:

- The plan is funded exclusively by the purchase of individual insurance contracts;
- The contracts provide for level annual premiums commencing when the individual becomes a participant and ending no later than the retirement age of each participant;
- Benefits provided by the plan are equal to the benefits provided under each contract at normal retirement age, and are guaranteed to the extent premiums have been paid;
- All premiums for the plan year and prior years are paid before lapse or the policy has been reinstated;
- No rights under the contracts have been subject to a security interest during the plan year; and
- No policy loans are outstanding at any time during the plan year.

In addition, plans funded through group insurance contracts that are determined under regulations to have the same characteristics as described above will be regarded as insurance contract plans.

Financial Statement. The financial statement, in the case of a welfare benefit plan, must include a statement of assets and liabilities, changes in fund balance, and changes in financial position. In the case of a pension plan, it must include a statement of assets and liabilities and a statement of changes in net assets available for plan benefits (including details of revenues, expenses, and other changes aggregated by general source and application).

Separate Schedules. The financial statements must have the following information contained in attached separate schedules:

1. Assets and liabilities aggregated by categories, valued at current value, and comparative data for the plan's previous fiscal year.
2. Receipts and disbursements for the preceding twelve months, aggregated by general sources and applications.
3. A schedule of all assets held for investment, aggregated and identified by issuer, borrower or similar party to the transaction (with a notation as to whether such party is known to be a party-in-interest), maturity date, rate of interest, collateral, par or maturity value, cost, and current value.
4. A schedule of each transaction involving a person known to be a party-in-interest, identifying the party and his relationship or that of any other party-in-interest to the plan. The schedule must describe the asset involved in each such transaction, and, as appropriate, the purchase or selling price, the rental, the interest rate and maturity date, expenses incurred in the transaction, the cost and current value of the asset, and the net gain or loss on each such transaction.
5. A schedule of all loans or fixed-income obligations in default or uncollectible at the close of the fiscal year, noting whether the parties involved are known to be parties-in-interest. The schedule must also include the original principal amount of the loan, the amount of principal and interest received during the year, the unpaid balance, and the identity and address of the obligor. There must also be provided a detailed description of the loan, including the date it was made, maturity date, interest rate, type and value of collateral, and other material terms. The amount of principal and interest overdue must be stated, with an explanation for the default.
6. A schedule of all leases in default or uncollectible at the end of the year, noting whether the parties involved are known to be parties-in-interest. The schedule must set forth the type of property leased, its location, the identity of the lessor or lessee and relationship to the plan or any party-in-interest, the terms of the lease, the date the leased property was purchased and its costs, the date of the lease and approximate value as of such date, the gross rental received and expenses paid during the reporting period, the net receipts from the lease, the amounts in arrears, and the steps taken to remedy the default.
7. If assets of the plan are held in a common or collective trust maintained by a bank or similar institution, the most recent annual statement of assets and liabilities of such common or collective trust, and, in the case of a separate account or separate trust maintained by an insurance company or a bank, such other information as may be required. This information must be transmitted, along with a certificate of accuracy from the bank or insurance company, within 120 days after the end of the plan year. (If the pertinent statements and other information are filed by the bank or insurance company directly with the Secretary of Labor, the Secretary, by regulation, has relieved the plan administrator from filing the information described in this paragraph.)
8. A schedule of each "reportable transaction," including the name of each

party to the transaction (unless it was a transaction in the securities market), a description of each asset involved, and, as appropriate, the purchase or selling price, the rental, or the interest rate and maturity date. In addition, the schedule must state any expenses connected with the transaction, the cost and current value of the asset, and the net gain or loss on the transaction. A "reportable transaction" is any of the following: (i) a transaction involving an amount in excess of 3 percent of the current value of the plan's assets; (ii) any transaction (other than a security transaction) that is part of a series of transactions with the same person where the aggregate amount during the year exceeds 3 percent of the plan's assets; (iii) a transaction that is part of a series of transactions involving securities of the same issuer, where the aggregate amount during the year exceeds 3 percent of the plan's assets; or (iv) a transaction involving a security if any other transaction involving a security with the same person during the same year exceeds 3 percent of the assets of the plan.

Accountant's Statement and Opinion. The administrator of each employee benefit plan that has 100 or more participants at the beginning of the plan year and is subject to the annual report requirement is required to engage an independent qualified public accountant to examine the plan's financial statements, and such books and records as the accountant may deem necessary, to form an opinion of whether the financial statements and schedules required to be included in the annual report are presented fairly "in conformity with generally accepted accounting principles applied on a basis consistent with that of the preceding years." The accountant must also offer his opinion of whether the separate schedules and summaries required to be furnished to participants fairly present the information contained therein. The opinion of the independent qualified public accountant must be made part of the annual report.

In giving his opinion, the accountant is entitled to rely on the correctness of any actuarial matter certified by an enrolled actuary. Moreover, his opinion need not be expressed as to any statements prepared and certified by a regulated bank or insurance carrier that are part of the annual report.

The accountant is directed to consider, in notes to the financial statements, the following items:

1. The description of the plan, including any significant changes in the plan made during the reporting period and the impact of such changes on benefits.
2. The funding policy, if a pension plan, and any changes in such policy during the reporting period.
3. If a pension plan, a description of any significant changes in plan benefits made during the reporting period.
4. A description of material lease commitments, other commitments, and contingent liabilities.
5. A description of agreements and transactions with persons known to be parties-in-interest.

6. A general description of priorities upon termination of the plan.
7. Information as to whether a tax ruling or determination letter has been obtained.
8. Any other matters necessary to present fully and fairly the financial statements of the plan.

Schedule A (Insurance Information). If some or all of the benefits under the plan are purchased from and guaranteed by an insurance carrier, the annual report must include a statement from such carrier enumerating the following information for the plan year:

1. The premium rate or subscription charge and the total premium or subscription charges paid to each such carrier, plus the approximate number of persons covered by each class of such benefits.
2. The total amount of premiums received, the approximate number of persons covered by each class of such benefits.
3. The dividends or retroactive rate adjustments, commissions, and administrative service or other fees or other acquisition costs paid by such carrier.
4. Any amounts held to provide benefits after retirement and the remainder of any premiums received by such carrier.
5. The names and addresses of brokers, agents, or other persons to whom commissions were paid, and the amount paid to each and for what purposes.

If the insurance carrier does not maintain separate experience records covering the specific groups it serves, in lieu of the information specified in Items (2) through (5), it must state the basis of its premium rate or subscription charge, and the total premium or charges received from the plan, and provide a copy of the carrier's financial report. If the carrier incurs specific costs in connection with the acquisition or retention of any particular plan, it must provide a detailed statement of such costs.

Annual Registration Statement (Schedule SSA). The plan administrator must file information about each separated participant entitled to but not yet receiving deferred vested benefits under the plan on Schedule SSA attached to the Annual Report Form 5500 series. A deferred benefit is considered vested if vested under the terms of the plan. It need not be nonforfeitable within the meaning of I.R.C. § 411.

The information required by Schedule SSA includes name, Social Security number, and a description of the nature, form, and amount of the deferred vested retirement benefit the participant is entitled to.

The time for reporting the deferred vested benefit is no later than the plan year after the participant separates.

No information is required, however, if before the end of the plan year after the plan year of separation the participant:

1. Is paid benefits under the plan;
2. Returns to service covered under the plan; or
3. Forfeits deferred retirement benefits under the plan.

This statement is filed with the IRS but will be forwarded to the Secretary of Health and Human Services for inclusion in the Social Security Records.

Termination or Curtailment of Plan (Forms 5500 and 5310)

The IRS asks to be notified of any plan terminations on Form 5500. A procedure for obtaining IRS approval of the termination of any plan is also available. This is highly desirable, since the plan administrator may be held liable for any distributions made upon plan termination if the plan is later deemed to have been disqualified. Moreover, a determination on termination is necessary for defined benefit plans, since the PBGC guarantees benefits paid only from qualified plans.

If IRS approval is sought for termination of a plan, a separate filing similar to an application for qualification is required on Form 5310, with an appropriate notice to all interested parties.

Notice of Change in Plan Status (Form 5500)

As part of the annual filing of the Form 5500 series, the plan administrator must notify the IRS of any:

1. Change in name of plan
2. Change in name or address of plan administrator
3. Termination of plan
4. Merger or consolidation
5. Division of a plan into more than one plan

Notice of Merger, Consolidation, or Transfer of Plan Assets or Liabilities

Form 5310 (with only Parts I and II completed) must be filed at least thirty days prior to the date of any plan merger, consolidation, or transfer of plan assets or liabilities to another plan. In the case of a defined benefit plan, the employer must also attach an actuarial statement of valuation evidencing compliance with the requirements of I.R.C. § 401(a)(12) (i.e., that each participant in the plan will receive a benefit immediately after the merger, consolidation, or transfer, if the plan were to then terminate, which is equal to or greater than the benefit he would have been entitled to receive immediately before the merger, consolidation, or transfer if the plan were to then terminate). This costly calculation can be avoided if the actuary certifies that pertinent records will be maintained for five years so that the calculation can be performed if it becomes necessary in the event of a termination following the merger, consolidation, or transfer.

If the plan administrator wishes to obtain a determination regarding the qualification of a plan after a merger, consolidation, or transfer of assets or liabilities, he must file with the IRS on Form 5300, 5301, or 5303 (whichever is applicable).

Statements of Distribution

No later than February 1 of each year, a participant who terminated or received a benefit from the plan during the prior year must be supplied with a Form 1099-R covering any lump-sum distributions, or a Form W-2P covering installment payments made during the year. Copies of these forms must be filed with the IRS no later than March 1 of each year, along with a transmittal form, Form W-3.

FILINGS WITH THE DEPARTMENT OF LABOR

Summary Plan Description

Prior to June 1, 1979, a Form EBS-1 Plan Description had to be filed with the DOL within 120 days after the plan became subject to the reporting and disclosure provisions of ERISA. This requirement is now satisfied by filing a copy of the summary plan description with the DOL.

A summary plan description of each employee benefit plan must be filed by the employer with the DOL at the time the summary plan description is to be furnished to plan participants and beneficiaries. It is to be written in a manner designed to be understood by the average plan participant, and must be accurate and comprehensive enough to reasonably inform the participants and beneficiaries of their rights and obligations under the plan. Essentially, the summary plan description is comparable to the booklets that many plans have used in the past to inform participants of plan benefits. However, ERISA sets forth a number of requirements as to the specific content of the summary plan description (considered in detail below). In addition, the DOL has prescribed certain standards as to style and format to insure that layout, typesize, and the like do not render a summary plan description misleading.

Contents of the Summary Plan Description. DOL regulations contain a list of items that must be included in the summary plan description. These content provisions apply to both pension and welfare plans and must reflect the plan provisions in effect at least 120 days before the summary is disclosed to employees. The matters required to be included are as follows:

1. The name of the plan, and, if different, the name by which the plan is commonly known to its participants and beneficiaries.

2. The name and address of the employer whose employees are covered by the plan, and the name and address of the labor organization whose members are covered by the plan. If the plan is established or maintained by two or more employers, or jointly by one or more employers and one or more labor organizations, the summary plan description must provide the name and address of the employer association, committee, or joint board of trustees, the parent or most significant employer of the group of employers, or other similar representative of the parties maintaining the plan. It must also contain a statement that a complete list of the employers and/or employee organizations sponsoring the plan may be obtained upon written request and is available for examination or that the plan administrator will, upon request, answer queries as to whether any specific employer or employee organization is a sponsor of the plan.
3. The EIN assigned by the IRS to the plan sponsor, and the plan number assigned by the plan sponsor pursuant to IRS instructions.
4. The type of pension or welfare plan involved. For example, a pension plan might be described as defined benefit, money purchase, profit-sharing, etc. A welfare plan might be described by the services it covers: hospitalization, disability, prepaid legal services, etc.
5. The type of administration of the plan—e.g., contract administration, insurer administration, joint board of trustees, etc.
6. The name, business address, and business telephone number of the plan administrator.
7. The name of the person designated as agent for service of process and the address at which process may be served on such persons, and, in addition, a statement that service of legal process may be made upon a plan trustee or plan administrator.
8. The name, title, and address of the principal place of business of each trustee of the plan.
9. If a plan is maintained pursuant to one or more collective bargaining agreements, a statement that the plan is so maintained and that a copy of any such agreement is available for examination and may be obtained by participants and beneficiaries upon written request to the plan administrator.
10. The plan's requirements respecting eligibility for participation and benefits. This should include a description of any age or service requirements for participation. In the case of a pension plan it should also include a description of the plan's normal retirement age and a statement describing any other conditions that must be met before a participant will be eligible to receive benefits. Plan benefits should also be described. For welfare benefit plans, there must be included an explanation of any conditions for eligibility to receive benefits, and a description of the benefits. Where the plan provides an extensive schedule of benefits (as in the case of a medical care plan), only a general description is required if it is stated that detailed schedules of benefits are available without cost to any participant or beneficiary who so requests.
11. In the case of pension plans, a statement describing any joint and survivor

benefits provided under the plan, including any requirement that an election be made as a condition for accepting or rejecting the joint and survivor annuity.

12. An explanation of circumstances that may result in disqualification or ineligibility, or denial, loss, forfeiture, or suspension of any benefits. In the case of a pension plan, this should include a description of any plan provision relating to forfeiture of benefits, breaks in service, and eligibility for participation and benefits.
13. If a pension plan is not covered by the termination insurance program under Title IV of ERISA (because, for example, it is a profit-sharing or other type of defined contribution plan), a statement of this fact and the reason for the lack of insurance. If a pension plan is covered by ERISA's termination insurance program, this fact must be stated, along with a summary of the pension benefit guarantee provisions of Title IV. There should also be a statement concerning any limitations on such coverage, and if these limitations are not set forth in detail a statement that the plan administrator will provide further information concerning such insurance upon request. Such limitations would exist, for example, because the plan or some of its benefits had been in effect less than five years, because benefits under the plan exceed the maximum that the termination insurance program will cover or because the plan includes "nonbasic" benefits not yet covered by the termination insurance program. The summary plan description must also include a statement indicating that further information on ERISA's termination insurance program can be obtained from the plan administrator or the PBGC. Suggested language for this required provision is included in the regulations.
14. In the case of pension plans, a description and explanation of the plan provisions for determining years of service for eligibility to participate, vesting, breaks in service, and years of participation for benefit accrual. The description must state the number of years of service required to accrue full benefits and the manner in which accrual of benefits is prorated for partial years of service.
15. In the case of pension plans that use the IRS "cutback" rule to make retroactive changes in the vesting or accrual provisions, the summary plan description must include a statement that certain provisions of the plan are subject to amendments that may modify certain plan rights and benefits, the nature of such modification, the identification of such plan provisions, and the portions of the summary plan description where such provisions are described.
16. The sources of contributions to the plan—for example, employer, union, employees—and the method by which the amount of contribution from each source is calculated. Defined benefit pension plans may state without further explanation that the contribution is actuarially determined.
17. The identity of any funding medium used for the accumulation of assets through which benefits are provided. Any insurance company, trust fund, or any other institution or entity that maintains a fund on behalf of the plan or through which the plan is funded or benefits are provided must be named.

18. The date of the end of the plan's fiscal year.
19. Every summary plan description must contain a description of the plan's claims procedure. These are the steps that a participant must take to file a claim for benefits, the steps that a plan must take to handle the claim, and the rules concerning how a participant may make an appeal if his claim is denied. The DOL has issued detailed regulations on claims procedures for employee benefit plans. These regulations require a plan to establish the following claims procedure rules that must be described in the summary plan description:

   i *Filing a claim for benefits.* A claim or request for plan benefits is filed when the requirements of a reasonable claim-filing procedure have been met. If such a procedure has not been established by the plan, a claim is considered filed when a written or oral communication is made by the claimant to the person or organization unit that handles claims for benefits under the plan.

   ii *Processing the claim.* The plan administrator must process the claim within ninety days after the claim is filed. If an extension of time for processing is required, written notice must be furnished to the claimant prior to the termination of the initial ninety-day period. The extension notice must indicate the special circumstances requiring an extension of time and the date by which the plan expects to render its final decision. In no event can the extension period exceed a period of ninety days from the end of the initial ninety-day period.

   iii *Denial of claim.* If a claim is wholly or partially denied, the plan administrator must notify the claimant within ninety days following receipt of the claim—or up to 180 days in the case of an extension for special circumstances—setting forth the specific reason or reasons for the denial, specific reference to pertinent plan provisions on which the denial is based, a description of any additional material or information necessary to perfect the claim, and appropriate information as to the steps to be taken if the claimant wishes to submit his claim for review. If notice of the denial of a claim is not furnished within the 90/180-day period, the claim is considered denied and the claimant must be permitted to proceed to the review stage.

   iv *Review procedure.* Every plan must establish and maintain a procedure by which a claimant or his duly authorized representative has at least sixty days after receipt of a claim denial to appeal the denied claim to an appropriate named fiduciary or to a person designated by such fiduciary and to receive a full and fair review of the claim. As part of the review the participant must be allowed to see all plan documents and other papers that affect the claim and must be allowed to submit issues and comments and argue against the denial in writing.

   v *Decision on review.* The plan must conduct the review and decide on the appeal within sixty days after the request for review is made.

If special circumstances require an extension of time for processing (such as the need to hold a hearing if the plan procedure provides for such a hearing), the claimant must be furnished with written notice of the extension, which can be no later than 120 days after receipt of a request for review. The decision on review must be written in clear and understandable language and must include specific reasons for the decision as well as specific references to the pertinent plan provisions on which the decision is based. In the case of a plan with a committee or board of trustees designated as the appropriate named fiduciary, a decision does not have to be made within the sixty-day limit if the committee or board meets at least four times a year (about every ninety days). Instead, it must be made at the first meeting after the request is filed, except that when a request is made less than thirty days before a meeting the decision can wait until the date of the second meeting following the plan's receipt of request for review. If a hearing must be held, the committee can wait to make its decision until the first meeting after the hearing. However, it must notify the participant and explain the delay, which can be no later than the third meeting of the committee or board following the plan's receipt of the request for review. If the decision on review is not made within the time limits specified above, the appeal will be considered denied. If appeal is denied, in whole or in part, the claimant has a right to file suit in a state or federal court.

20. A statement of the rights of a participant or beneficiary under ERISA must be included in the summary plan description. This statement must describe the right to get more information about the plan, the right to review of a claim denial, the right to be free from any retaliation for exercising legal rights, and the right to bring lawsuits to remedy violations of the disclosure, fiduciary, or anti-discrimination provisions of ERISA and to obtain benefits that have been denied improperly. This information must be presented in language the average plan participant can understand, and must state that the participant can contact the local office of the DOL for further information. DOL regulations include a standard statement that plans may use to satisfy this requirement.

When to File. As discussed above, a copy of each summary plan description must be filed with the DOL by the date when the summary plan description is required to be furnished to participants and beneficiaries.

ERISA requires each plan administrator to provide a summary plan description to participants and beneficiaries under the plan within 120 days after the plan becomes subject to ERISA's reporting and disclosure provisions. Normally this 120-day period will run from the date the plan is established.

General Format. The design of the summary plan description is generally left to the discretion of the employer. However, the format must not have the effect of misleading, misinforming, or failing to inform participants and beneficiaries. Accordingly, any description of exceptions, limitations, reductions, and other restrictions of plan benefits cannot be minimized, or rendered obscure, or otherwise made to appear unimportant. Such exceptions, limitations, reductions, or restrictions of plan benefits must be described or summarized in a manner not less prominent than the style, captions, typeface, and format used to describe or summarize plan benefits. The advantages and disadvantages of the plan should be presented without either exaggerating the benefits or minimizing the limitations. The description or summary of restrictive plan provisions need not be disclosed in the summary plan description in close conjunction with the description or summary of benefits, provided that the page on which the restrictions are described is noted adjacent to the benefit description.

To make the summary plan description both comprehensive and understandable to the average plan participant, the employer must exercise his best judgment and discretion regarding such factors as the level of comprehension and level of education of typical participants in the plan and the complexity of the plan's provisions. In particular, DOL regulations suggest that the employer do the following:

- Minimize or eliminate technical jargon and long complex sentences
- Use clarifying examples and illustrations
- Be clear in use of cross-references
- Provide a table of contents

If plan participants do not speak English, the summary plan description must prominently display a notice "offering assistance" in the language best understood by the foreign-language participants if the following conditions exist:

1. In the case of plans covering fewer than 100 employees at the beginning of the plan year, if 25 percent or more of all plan participants are literate only in the same non-English language, or
2. In the case of plans covering 100 or more employees at the beginning of the plan year, if either 500 or more participants or 10 percent or more of all plan participants are literate only in the same non-English language.

The notice should advise such participants that assistance is available from the plan administrator to help them become informed as to their rights and obligations under the plan, and describe the procedures to follow in obtaining such assistance. The assistance itself need not involve written materials, but may consist of oral explanations given in the language best understood by participants who are not literate in English.

Multiple Classes of Participants. A plan may provide different benefits for various categories of participants and beneficiaries. For example, an amendment changing the benefit formula of a pension plan may apply only to those participants who are employed after the amendment is adopted, and not to those no longer employed at the time of adoption. Similarly, a plan may provide different benefits for participants employed at different plants of the employer, or even for different classes of participants working in the same plant.

In such cases DOL regulations say that the employer may prepare a single summary plan description that presents the required information together with an explanation of its different application to various classes of participants and beneficiaries. Each separate summary plan description must include all the information previously discussed, but may omit matters that do not apply to the class of participants or beneficiaries to which it is furnished. If separate summary plan descriptions are prepared in accordance with the option, each description should clearly identify on the first page of text "the class of participants and beneficiaries for which it has been prepared and the plan's coverage of other classes." If the classes the plan covers are too numerous to be listed adequately on the first page of the text, they may be listed elsewhere in the text containing this information. If more than one summary plan description is prepared, a copy of each must be filed with the DOL.

Merged Former Plans. When participants retain rights to benefits under the terms of a former pension plan, the employer does not have to describe relevant portions of the old plan in summary plan descriptions furnished after the merger into the successor plan, since the information would be useless and perhaps confusing to many participants of the merged plan. To use this alternative, the plan administrator must, within ninety days after the merger's effective date, furnish participants and beneficiaries covered by the predecessor plan with:

1. A copy of the most recent summary plan description of the successor plan;
2. A copy of any summaries of material modifications to the successor plan not incorporated in the most recent summary plan description; and
3. A separate statement containing a brief description of the merger, the provisions and benefits of both predecessor and successor plans that are applicable to participants in the predecessor plan, and a notice that the predecessor plan, successor plan, and merger documents are available for inspection or can be obtained on written request.

The plan administrator must also be sure that a new, complete, up-to-date summary plan description on the successor plan is furnished to all participants and beneficiaries and filed with the DOL within 120 days after the plan becomes subject to Part I of ERISA. These summary plan descriptions must include a "clear and conspicuous" notice identifying the classes of participants to which the old plan provisions apply and a statement of the rights of participants and beneficiaries to inspect and copy the predecessor plan, successor plan, and merger documents.

Form 5500

Prior to plan years beginning in 1977, DOL also required the filing of a Form 5500 annual financial report. To reduce duplication of reporting and the burden of compliance with ERISA by plan administrators and employers, IRS, DOL, and PBGC have designed a single annual return/report Form 5500 series that is to be filed *with IRS only* on or before the last day of the seventh month following the end of the plan year (an extension of up to two and a half months may be granted by the filing of Form 5558 with IRS).

Updated Plan Description. DOL must be furnished with an updated plan description not more frequently than once every five years and receive updated summary plan description booklets every fifth year if any amendments have been made. A completely restated summary plan description is due every tenth year regardless of amendments.

Material Modifications. A plan administrator must file any material modification in the plan or any change in information required under ERISA § 102(b) within sixty days after such modification or change is adopted or occurs. Prior to April 10, 1978 an amended EBS-1 Plan Description Form had to be filed with DOL within sixty days of a material modification or change. Specifically, the following items in the EBS-1 were categorized as "material":

- Name and address of sponsor/employer
- Name and address of plan administrator
- Structure of plan
- Name of plan
- Type of plan
- Agent for service of process
- Persons performing functions for the plan
- Sources and method of determining contributions
- Method of asset accumulation
- Procedure for representing claims
- Eligibility requirements
- Vesting provisions
- Features of portability or reciprocity
- Length of service in determining participation, vesting, or benefit accrual
- Break-in-service rules
- Requirements for pension benefits
- Basis for computing retirement benefits

- Circumstances causing loss of pension benefits
- Joint and survivor annuity
- Disposition of employee's contributions
- Requirements for welfare benefits
- Circumstances causing loss of welfare benefits
- Fiduciaries' names and addresses

The following items that appear on the Form 5500 Annual Report *did not require* the filing of an amended EBS-1:

- DOL WP file number
- Effective date of plan
- Plan's fiscal year
- Number of participants and beneficiaries
- Collective bargaining agreements
- Type of plan documents
- Types of participants

Although the EBS-1 Form is no longer required, the above listing is helpful in determining what constitutes a "material" modification.

A plan now meets the requirements by filing with DOL the summary of material modifications (SMM) that employers are required to furnish to each participant and beneficiary, within 210 days after the close of the year in which any change or modification occurs. The SMM must be written in a style and manner calculated to be understood by the average plan participant.

FILINGS WITH THE PENSION BENEFIT GUARANTY CORPORATION

Form PBGC-1

Plan sponsors must file on Form PBGC-1 a premium declaration for all defined benefit plans that are subject to ERISA's termination insurance provisions. The filing and premium payment for a year are due the last day of the seventh month after the close of the prior plan year. For any plan newly covered by ERISA's termination insurance provisions, they are due by the latest of:

- Seven months after the beginning of the plan year;
- Thirty days after the date of the plan's adoption;
- Thirty days after the date on which the plan became effective for benefit accruals for future service; or
- Thirty days after the date on which the plan became covered by the termination insurance provisions.

The premium rate for non-multiemployer plans is $2.60 for participants in the plan on the last day of the preceding plan year. The premium for multiemployer plans is $1.40 for each participant for the first, second, third, and fourth plan years beginning after September 26, 1980 (the date of enactment of the Multiemployer Pension Plan Amendments Act of 1980 (MPPAA)), $1.80 for each participant for the fifth and sixth plan years, $2.20 for each participant for the seventh and eighth plan years and $2.60 for each participant for the ninth plan year and each succeeding year.

Reportable Event Notice

Within thirty days after a plan administrator knows, or has reason to know, that a "reportable event" has occurred, he must notify the PBGC. Notice of reportable event is not required when expressly waived by the PBGC. However, in any case, a reportable event must be included in the Form 5500 annual return. When an employer who contributes to a plan covered by the plan termination insurance provisions knows, or has reason to know, that a "reportable event" has occurred, he must notify the plan administrator immediately.

Definition of Reportable Event. A "reportable event" is defined as any of the following:

1. Loss of tax qualification;
2. Any amendment reducing benefits;
3. Reduction in number of participants to less than 80 percent of participation at the beginning of the plan year;
4. IRS determination of any termination or partial termination of the plan;
5. Failure to meet minimum funding standards;
6. Inability to pay benefits when due;
7. Any distribution to "a substantial owner";
8. The filing of an actuarial statement with the IRS preliminary to a plan merger, consolidation, or transfer of assets or the granting of an alternate method of ERISA compliance by the Secretary of Labor; or
9. Any other event as determined by the PBGC. The PBGC has determined that "other events" include bankruptcy, insolvency, liquidation, dissolution, or a change in plan sponsor of a single-employer plan with unfunded nonforfeitable benefits and 100 or more participants.

Applicability of Thirty-Day Notice Requirement. The PBGC has exercised its authority to waive the thirty-day notice requirement in the following instances:

1. IRS issuance of a determination letter that the plan does not meet the requirements of a pension plan under Section 401(a) or 404(a)(2) of the Internal Revenue Code;

2. DOL determination of noncompliance with Title I of ERISA;
3. IRS determination of termination or partial termination within the meaning of Section 411(d)(3) of the Internal Revenue Code;
4. Plan merger, consolidation or transfer; and
5. Alternative method of compliance prescribed by the DOL as set forth in Title I of ERISA.

Conversely, PBGC regulations provide that there are five reportable events the occurrence of which always render the thirty-day notice requirements applicable:

1. A plan's failure to meet ERISA's minimum funding standards;
2. A plan's inability to pay benefits when due;
3. The bankruptcy, insolvency or similar settlement with respect to a contributing sponsor;
4. The liquidation or dissolution of a contributing sponsor; and
5. A transaction involving change of employer.

The three remaining reportable events require filing a thirty-day notice with the PBGC *under certain circumstances.* A plan administrator, for example, must file such a notice regarding an amendment decreasing benefits payable *only if* the plan has at least 100 participants at the end of the prior plan year, the amendment is not adopted to effect compliance with any federal law *and* it either: (1) decreases any participant's accrued normal retirement benefit; or (2) reduces by more than 50 percent the normal retirement benefit that would accrue in the future for more than 50 percent of the active participants as of the end of the prior plan year. Even then, a thirty-day notice is not required if, as a result of the amendment in question and any other amendments incident thereto, each participant for whom there was a decrease receives, at least, an offsetting increase in his projected normal retirement benefit under a second plan maintained by the same employer if it is a money purchase plan or a plan covered by the plan termination insurance provisions of ERISA.

The second reportable event to which the thirty-day notice requirements apply only under limited circumstances is an active participant reduction. Specifically, such notice is waived if either: (1) the plan has less than 100 participants as of the beginning of either the current or prior plan year; or (2) as of the date of the reportable event, a participant reduction would not occur if all single-employer plans maintained by the employer and covered by Title IV are considered in the aggregate. Consequently, administrators of plans with at least 100 participants must comply with ERISA's thirty-day notice requirements if this reportable event occurs *unless* the employer maintains more than one, covered single-employer plan and the active participation level for all these plans taken in the aggregate has not decreased by more than 20 percent in the current plan year or more than 25 percent from the beginning of the previous plan year.

Finally, the thirty-day notice requirement concerning certain distributions to substantial owners is waived *unless* all distributions to that substantial owner equal at least $10,000 in a twelve-month period and the amount of all such distributions exceed the amount of the maximum guaranteeable benefit for the substantial owner, for the year in which the distribution or the last distribution in a series was made.

Thirty-Day Notice Filing and Content. The thirty-day time period commences on the day following the occurrence of the reportable event, and ends thirty days later unless the thirtieth day is a Saturday, Sunday, or federal holiday. A notice is considered filed on the day it is postmarked if the postmark was made by the U.S. Postal Service and the document was properly mailed (postage prepaid), packaged and addressed; otherwise, it is not considered filed until the PBGC receives it.

Each thirty-day notice must contain the following data:

- The name of the plan;
- Name, address, and telephone number of both the plan sponsor and plan administrator (if the latter is a corporation, an individual must be designated);
- Both the employer identification number assigned by the IRS to the plan sponsor and the plan identification number assigned by the plan sponsor to the plan itself;
- A brief statement of the pertinent facts related to the reportable event;
- A copy of the current plan document including any subsequent amendments;
- A copy of the most recent actuarial statement and opinion as well as a statement of any subsequent material changes in plan assets or liabilities; and
- A copy of the most recent IRS determination letter.

Additional material is required with respect to certain reportable events. Finally, as it deems appropriate, the PBGC may determine that still further information is necessary.

Also, specific reportable events require the following additional information:

1. An amendment decreasing benefits payable: The percentage decrease in normal retirement benefits and percentage of participants affected.
2. An active participant reduction: The total number of:
    - Participants currently accruing benefits or retaining or earning credited service for vesting purposes;
    - Participants with partially vested rights;
    - Participants without vested rights;

- Retired participants receiving benefits;
- Former employees with vested rights;
- Deceased participants whose beneficiaries are either entitled to or receiving benefits.

3. A failure to meet minimum funding standards: Statement of the current funding standard account (or its alternative) showing the balance at the beginning of the plan year and charges and credits to the account for the plan year.
4. The inability to pay benefits when due:
   - The reason why;
   - Amount of benefits due;
   - Normal date of benefit payment;
   - Amount and date of last payment;
   - Value of plan assets determined consistent with the evaluation standard set forth in PBGC Reg. §§ 2620.1 et seq.
5. A distribution to a substantial owner:
   - The amount and form of the distribution;
   - Total amount of nonforfeitable benefits which are not funded;
   - Actuarial assumptions used to value benefits;
   - Whether an indemnity agreement has been entered between the participant receiving distribution and trustee concerning lump-sum distributions to twenty-five highest paid employees subject to early termination restrictions.
6. A plan merger, consolidation or transfer: A copy of Form 5310 and actuarial data submitted to IRS.
7. Bankruptcy, insolvency or similar settlements: A copy of papers filed in relevant proceedings showing:
   - Name of court;
   - Date of filing;
   - Docket number;
   - Type of proceeding;
   - Names, addresses, and telephone numbers of attorneys;
   - Last date for filing claims;
   - Name, address, and telephone number of any trustee or receiver.
8. A change in employer-sponsor of single-employer plan:
   - Name, address, telephone number, and EIN of new plan sponsor;
   - Name, address, telephone number, and EIN of each member of commonly controlled group of former plan sponsor and new plan sponsor.
9. If no change of plan sponsor but plan sponsor is no longer a member of same commonly controlled group:
   - Name, address, and telephone number of each member of the plan sponsor's former group and the new group;
   - Total value of nonforfeitable benefits unfunded;
   - Actuarial assumptions used to value benefits.

Plan Termination

In general, defined benefit pension plans can be terminated either by the plan administrator or by the PBGC. If the administrator terminates the plan, he must supply a Notice of Intent to Terminate to the PBGC at least ten days prior to the effective date of such termination. There follows a ninety-day waiting period, which can be extended by the PBGC, during which the PBGC determines whether the plan's assets are sufficient to discharge its obligations, i.e., to pay accrued vested benefits. If the assets are sufficient, the plan administrator may proceed to terminate the plan and to distribute the assets. If the assets are not sufficient, or if it cannot be determined that they are sufficient, the plan will, in effect, be terminated by the PBGC.

Content of Notice of Intent to Terminate. An extensive itemized list of information must be included in the Notice of Intent to Terminate filed by the plan administrator. Duplication of information is not necessary, and any requested information that has already been included in a submission to the IRS requesting approval of the plan termination need not be repeated in the PBGC Notice. Instead, it is sufficient to attach the IRS form to the Notice of Intent to Terminate. The information will then be incorporated by reference. The Notice of Intent includes such items as the following:

1. The name, address, zip code, and telephone number of the plan administrator;
2. The name of the plan;
3. The name and address of the plan sponsor or sponsors;
4. The nine-digit IRS employer identification number assigned to each employer identified above;
5. The name, address, and telephone number of every person, including a trust, holding or managing any plan assets;
6. The proposed date of termination of the plan (which may not be earlier than ten days after the date of delivery of the Notice);
7. A copy of the documents establishing the plan;
8. Copies of all amendments to the plan adopted or effective within the most recent five-year period;
9. A copy or copies of any group annuity or group insurance contract or trust agreement or agreements providing for the management of the plan assets, if contract administration, or the payment of benefits under the plan;
10. A complete copy of any collective bargaining agreement that contains provisions relating to the plan;
11. A copy of the most recent actuarial statement and opinion (if any) relating to the plan;
12. A statement of any material change in the assets or liabilities of the plan occurring after the date of the actuarial and financial statements referred to above;

13. A copy of any request for a determination from the IRS with respect to the plan's termination;
14. Information as of the proposed date of termination concerning the number of participants and, for retired and disabled participants, the aggregate monthly dollar amount of the benefits such participants are currently receiving from the plan, completed in the following tabular format:
    (a) Active participants without vested rights;
    (b) Active participants with deferred vested rights;
    (c) Separated participants with deferred vested rights;
    (d) Retired and disabled participants and beneficiaries receiving payments from the plan;
    (e) Total;
15. The number of active participants who, if the plan were not terminated as of the proposed date of termination, would reasonably be expected to attain a vested benefit within thirty, sixty, ninety, or 120 days following the proposed date of termination, shown separately for each such period;
16. A statement of the reason for terminating the plan;
17. A brief description of the proposed method of distributing the plan assets, e.g., purchase of single premium annuities;
18. A statement of whether the plan assets are believed to be sufficient to satisfy all vested benefits;
19. A certification that all information and documents submitted are true and correct to the best of the plan administrator's knowledge and belief.

Proposed Use of Form 5310. Under a "one-stop service" proposal issued jointly by IRS and PBGC, the filing of revised IRS/PBGC Form 5310 with the PBGC at least ten days prior to the proposed date of termination will satisfy the notice of intent to terminate requirement. If the plan also wished to obtain a determination from IRS on its tax-qualification status upon termination, it need only submit a duplicate of completed Form 5310 and the PBGC will send the duplicate to IRS. Thus if this proposal is adopted, a plan need not make separate filings with both agencies.

Notice to Employees by Plan Administrators

When a plan administrator or his duly authorized representative files a notification of voluntary termination with the PBGC, he must immediately give written notification to the employees covered by the plan that is to be terminated. The notice must be in writing and must state: (a) the date upon which the notification of voluntary termination was filed with the PBGC and (b) the proposed termination date of the plan.

If the employees covered by the plan are represented by a union, notification is accomplished by delivering the notice to the union representative. If the employees are not represented by a union, the notice must be posted in the location or locations normally used by the employer to post notifications to the employees.

Notice to Interested Parties by Trustee

If a trustee has been appointed to administer a plan in connection with the PBGC's procedures under the termination insurance provisions, as soon as practicable after his appointment he must give notice to interested parties that a proceeding will be instituted to determine whether the plan should be terminated or to terminate the plan, whichever is applicable. "Interested parties" include the plan administrator, each participant in the plan, each beneficiary of a deceased participant, and each employer and former employer who may be subject to liability under the law's termination insurance provisions.

Reports to Trustee

The plan administrator and the PBGC are required to furnish to the trustee all information they have or can practicably obtain regarding the following:

1. Amount of benefits payable with respect to each participant under the plan;
2. Amount of benefits guaranteed by the PBGC with respect to each participant;
3. As of the time of termination, the aggregate amount of the present value of benefits guaranteed by the PBGC, ignoring the limitations on payments;
4. The fair market value of the assets of the plan at the time of termination;
5. All actuarial assumptions under which Items (1) through (4) were computed, and computations to make required allocations of plan assets to various categories of benefits;
6. Any other information needed by the trustee to terminate the plan.

Notice of Inability to Pay Basic Benefits

If, after having begun to terminate a plan covered by the termination insurance provisions of ERISA, the plan administrator finds that the plan is, or will be, unable to pay basic benefits when due, the plan administrator must notify the PBGC of that finding as soon as practicable thereafter and furnish such reports to the PBGC as it may require.

Notice of Termination of Multiemployer Plan

The PBGC has issued procedures to be used by multiemployer pension plans in notifying the PBGC of their intent to terminate. (See Chapter 26 for a detailed discussion of the special rules governing termination insurance provisions as they apply to multiemployer plans.) Such plans are required to comply with the following procedures:

1. For multiemployer plans terminating as a result of plan amendment, the plan sponsor must file a Notice of Termination thirty days after the date the amendment is adopted or thirty days after its effective date, whichever is later. The notice must contain (a) the name of the plan; (b) name, address, and telephone number of the plan sponsor and his duly authorized representative, if any; (c) name, address, and telephone number of the person who will administer the plan after the date of termination if other than the plan sponsor; (d) a copy of the plan's most recent Form 5500 including schedules; and (e) the date of termination of the plan.

2. For multiemployer plans terminating as a result of a mass employer withdrawal, the plan sponsor must file a Notice of Termination thirty days after the date on which the last employer withdraws or thirty days after the beginning of the plan year in which no employer contributions are required, whichever is earlier. In addition to the information specified in Item (1) above, the notice must contain (a) a copy of the plan document in effect five years prior to the date of termination and copies of any amendments adopted after that date; (b) copy of the trust agreement; (c) most recent actuarial statement and opinion; (d) statement of any material change in the assets or liabilities of the plan occurring after either the date of the actuarial statement or Form 5500 submitted as part of the Notice; (e) copies of any letters of determination issued by the IRS; (f) a statement whether the plan will be able to pay all benefits in pay status during the twelve-month period following the date of termination; (g) if plan assets are sufficient to satisfy all nonforfeitable benefits and if the plan sponsor intends to distribute such assets, a brief description of the proposed method of distributing the plan assets; and (h) if plan assets are not sufficient to satisfy all nonforfeitable benefits, the name and address of any employer who contributed to the plan within three plan years prior to the date of termination.

Information specified in Items (1) and (2) above need not be supplied if it duplicates information contained in Form 5500 or a schedule thereof which a plan submits as part of the notice.

6

Communication of Benefits

RODNEY N. MARA

Vice-President, Towers, Perrin, Forster & Crosby

MANAGEMENT OBJECTIVES

The passage of the Employee Retirement Income Security Act of 1974 (ERISA), with its stringent requirements for pension plan reporting, the rise in benefit costs, and competitive pressures that encouraged the addition of new plans have all caused a shift in thinking about what benefit communications should accomplish. Management now identifies three primary communications goals, namely to:

- Comply with the complexities of the law;
- Enhance employees' understanding of benefits and appreciation of their value; and
- Facilitate administration of the benefit program.

Compliance With the Law

Management must explain to employees in a clear and simple way the following technical concepts, particularly with regard to pension plans, that were introduced by ERISA.

- New eligibility requirements for coverage
- Breaks in service
- Restoration of service following a break
- Plan payment methods
- New vesting requirements

The law requires that management communicate these concepts at the level of understanding held by the "average plan participant." These explanations must be easily understood because these concepts determine in large measure just what the plan will or will not do for the individual. In addition, the employer must provide a laundry list of "administrative" information in each *summary plan description,*[1] the document that must be furnished to all plan participants. ERISA reporting and disclosure requirements are described in detail later in this chapter.

ERISA clearly describes the penalties for noncompliance. For any willful violation of any of ERISA's reporting and disclosure requirements, a corporation can be fined up to $100,000; an individual up to $5,000 plus one year in jail.

Communicating the Nature and Value of Benefits

Companies have long been aware of the cost for benefits—costs which, in the early 1980s, are approaching 35 percent to 40 percent of payroll. The payoff for management for this enormous investment rests in how well the firm's employees recognize what is being done for them. Employees, however, are not nearly as impressed with the cost of benefits as they are with the answer to the question: "What's in it for me?"

Answering that question is the challenge of benefit communications. Answering it well can help enhance employees' appreciation of their financial association with the company. Do they have good jobs? Do they work for

---

[1] DOL Reg. § 2520.102-3.

a company that cares? Do they have reasons for caring about the company? Does the company have credibility? Is its total compensation package—benefits and salary—competitive?

Establishing Credibility

One organization—a major drug company—was faced with employee unrest at a large and critically important manufacturing facility in the Midwest. In reviewing the situation and developing its communications strategy, the company elected not to take a position on pay. Its pay levels, though adequate for the area, were not outstanding. Its benefit program, however, was solid. Compared to the plans offered by local industry, most of the plans in the benefit program were clearly superior and the program included plans that no local company—and only a few companies anywhere in the drug industry—then offered. So the company communicated its benefits—"sold" them to employees—in group meetings. The fundamental objective, of course, was to sell the credibility of the company—to regain the loyalty and commitment of the work force. And the communications program enabled them to do just that. Companies that seriously commit themselves to building employee understanding of the value of their benefits are reducing the risk of poor employee attitude based on ignorance of work-related values that are already in place. They are highlighting these values by consciously attempting to help their employees understand what they have going for them.

Facilitating Administration

Under ERISA, the following administrative information must be included in each summary plan description.

Legally Required Administrative Information

- The official plan name;
- The plan administrator (address and telephone number);
- The plan trustee or insurance carrier (address and telephone number);
- Plan funding (who pays for the plan and where this money goes);
- Procedure to obtain benefits (whom to contact and where to obtain appropriate forms);
- Payment of benefits (who pays the benefits provided by the plan);
- Claim appeal (procedures and timing for processing a request for reconsideration of a denied claim);
- Legal service (the individual—including the trustee for plans that have a trust agreement—on whom legal process may be served);
- Plan records (the basis on which plan records are kept—i.e., calendar or fiscal year and the beginning and end dates of the annual record-keeping cycle);

- Type of plan (welfare, defined benefit, or defined contribution pension plan as those terms are defined under ERISA);
- Plan identification numbers (the employer identification number assigned by the Internal Revenue Service; the plan identification number assigned by the company);
- Availability of plan documents (the right to review all supportive plan documents during normal working hours at the employee's work site within ten days after the request for review is received by the plan administrator; the right to purchase these documents at reasonable cost);
- Listing of applicable union contracts (the bargaining units covered by the plan);
- Government insurance (notification that the plan is or is not insured by the Pension Benefit Guaranty Corporation (PBGC) and a description of the limitations of this insurance); and
- ERISA Rights Statement.

Administrative Manuals. Personnel who administer benefit plans obviously need a clear understanding of all the provisions of the various plans. They must also understand the rationale behind the plans. Very often they are the only ones who are in close contact with employees on benefit matters. Their knowledge of the benefits and their attitude about them can greatly influence how employees view the program itself. They are the "in-house" communicators, and what they say and what they do can greatly affect the value-perception employees have of their benefits.

Well-written administrative manuals are essential to the communications process. If they are not well organized and properly updated, administrative clerks may misinterpret certain provisions and inconsistencies in administration may occur. The serious consequences that may develop were experienced by a company in which one clerk had been incorrectly processing disability claims on the basis of gross earnings while another clerk properly calculated such claims on base wages. Ultimately, the company was forced to adhere to the higher payment basis for all employees to avoid disturbing delicate union negotiations. All companies need clearly presented, current information related to the administration of benefit programs. For companies that have adopted flexible compensation programs—or are thinking about doing so—the communications-administrative link is even more critical. (See Chapter 25 on flexible/cafeteria plans.)

Role of Supervisors. It is critically important to enlist the aid of supervisors who are in daily contact with employees. If they are given special supervisory training both in benefits and communications, they can help answer questions about benefits, assist in the proper filing of claims, and thereby eliminate or reduce claim processing difficulties and delays in payment. This training can be tied directly to a major benefit change. Some companies select supervisory personnel to participate in special training sessions in which all aspects of the new benefit program are thoroughly discussed. The supervisors are then given an opportunity to rehearse—under direction and before their peers—the presentation they will make to their employees. Typically, these training sessions last about two days. Their value in building a benefit dialogue between the supervisor and his people can last a long time.

EMPLOYEE COMPREHENSION OF BENEFITS

Importance of Employee Orientation

In an effort to determine the effectiveness of its benefit communications efforts, a major U.S. corporation commissioned a special study. To provide a representative view of its entire system, two operating companies were selected as the study sites. Both were large organizations employing more than 35,000 employees each. One was located in New England, the other in the Midwest.

Each company's business area included at least one major city and a number of small, rural communities. The benefits covering the employees of both companies were essentially the same. The study methodology involved interviews with senior-level *management* to determine how well they thought they were communicating benefit information to their employees; with the in-house *communications specialists* to determine how the benefit communications program was being carried out; with *supervisors* to assess how well they thought the process was working; and with *employees* to determine their understanding, interest, and appreciation of the benefits they had.

The study produced a number of findings concerning the effectiveness of each company's communications efforts. The two key findings were:

- The company that built periodic employee benefit orientation meetings into its communications program had clearly achieved a much higher level of employee appreciation of the value of the benefit program; and
- Employees in both companies were very interested in benefits and highly receptive to information about them.

Selectivity of Employee Response

Attitude surveys and communications audits conducted by companies clearly demonstrate that the benefits program, if communicated properly, is a subject that can capture employee interest. However, employees are highly selective about the type of communications to which they will respond.

Older employees, for example, are clearly interested in retirement policy and respond with attention to communications on this subject. The Age Discrimination in Employment Act (ADEA), which eliminates mandatory retirement at age 65 for most employees—and for all employees at any age in some states—is also of major interest to this age group.

Although many companies are reluctant to influence an individual's decision to retire, they may provide valuable assistance to the individual by furnishing information that clearly explains the consequences of whatever decision is made. One company proved that this can be done without establishing a formal, time-consuming, and costly preretirement counseling program.

The company developed a special packet designed specifically for employees about to reach age 65. It contained information showing which benefits would remain in force if the employee elected to stay on and those that would be paid if a retirement decision was made. Included was a personalized benefit statement providing a dollar display of this same information. The "bottom line" was a computation of net income payable during continued employment or during retirement. The packet and the statement were personally delivered to the employee by a field personnel representative.

This communications approach provides an excellent formula to match effective benefit communications to the needs of employees of all ages:

- Keep it brief
- Make it personalized
- Create an opportunity for dialogue between the individual and the company's "information" representative

Benefit communications that are not sensitive to these basic employee communications needs will prove ineffective, not because employees lack an interest in benefits, but because the communications efforts will go largely unnoticed.

ERISA DISCLOSURE

Required Reports to Employees

ERISA establishes three categories of disclosure materials that must be:

1. Furnished as a matter of course
2. Provided if requested by the employee
3. Made available for review during normal working hours at the employee's work location

Materials Required for All Employees. The following reports must be furnished to *all* employees:

- Plan payment notification
- Summary plan descriptions

- Plan amendments (material modifications)
- Summary annual reports
- Pension benefit statement for terminating vested employees
- Notice to interested parties
- Written explanation of claims denied

Plan payment notification. This notice requirement applies to all plans providing retirement benefits—including thrift and profit-sharing plans—if benefits are payable, or available, in the form of a life annuity. Profit-sharing and thrift plans that do not provide for lifetime annuity payments are exempt. The notice informs employees who are in the "retirement zone" how their retirement benefit can be paid and what the financial consequences of the various payment methods are. Employees are also told about the availability of the preretirement spouse's benefit and, if the benefit is not fully paid for by the company, how they can elect it.

There are actually *two* notices here—*an initial notice* and a *detailed notice*. The initial notice must be sent 180 days before the earliest date on which the employee can retire—or becomes eligible for the preretirement spouse's benefit if the employee has to elect that benefit to obtain the protection it provides. If the preretirement spouse's benefit is "automatic," the notice must be distributed at least nine months prior to early retirement age.

The initial notice need not contain specific information about the employee's accrued benefit. It need only list the various payment methods available and the relative financial impact of electing any one of them. Mathematical examples or percentages reflecting the alternate choices are all that is required. However, this notice must inform the employee that more detailed information is available upon request. If and when the employee responds to the initial notice and requests more information, then a second, more detailed notice must be furnished. This notice must show the employee's accrued benefit and the adjustments that will be made to it based on whatever payment method the employee selects.

Summary plan descriptions (SPDs). SPDs must be furnished to all plan participants within 120 days after a plan has been adopted—or within ninety days after the employee becomes a plan participant or his beneficiary begins to receive benefits. Updated SPDs must be distributed every five years if there have been major changes in the plan; every ten years whether there have been any changes or not.

SPDs are to be written in "clear" language capable of being understood by the "average plan participant." ERISA, however, has never defined specifically what "clear" language means. Consequently, companies have rather wide latitude in structuring the language for these booklets. However, the high degree of legal visibility attached to these booklets requires careful preparation of copy.

Severe consequences can attach to inferred promises which the plan is incapable of meeting. The case of *Hurd v. Hutnik* [2] underscores the importance of the SPD as the legal conveyor of a promise that having been made must be kept—regardless of what the plan document itself says. In this case, a multiemployer plan was terminated, threatening a substantial reduction in the pension benefits of employees who had already retired. The employees sued, citing the plan booklet as stating "Pensions awarded by the Board of Trustees . . . are payable for the lifetime of the Pensioner." The employees won the case—even though the plan document stated that pensions would be paid *from the plan only as long as the plan continued in existence.* Interestingly enough, the plan document was included in the very copy of the booklet that the employees used to mount their legal action. It is for this reason that "disclaimer clauses" are always found in SPDs. A case that emphasizes their importance—*O'Brien, et al. v. Sperry Univac & Sperry Rand* [3]—denied a claim for pension benefits based on a seeming conflict between the SPD and the actual wording of the plan. The court, in effect, ruled that the individual must also look to the plan for relief—if indeed any relief is to be found there—since the booklet, as stated in the disclaimer, is only a "summary description of the plan" itself. However, decisions such as this do not represent the weight of judicial authority. For example, the plan booklet which was involved in *Hurd v. Hutnik* not only contained the full text of the plan but also such a disclaimer.

Plan amendments (material modifications). Employees must be notified if a major change is made in the plan—i.e., if the name is changed; if eligibility, vesting, and benefit calculation provisions are altered; if the plan administrator or the individual on whom legal process can be served is replaced, etc.[4] The notification must be made no later than 210 days after the end of the plan year in which the change occurs. However, if the change is incorporated into a new SPD, a separate notice is not required.

Summary annual reports. These reports must be sent to plan participants and beneficiaries nine months after the end of the plan year—i.e., two months after Form 5500, on which the summary is based, is filed with the Internal Revenue Service. These reports have never been looked upon as an effective benefit communications vehicle by management. Although the language used in them is now mandated by the government and is simpler than required in the initial version, the copy is still complex and uninteresting. They are a compliance item that many would prefer to have eliminated—and legislation has been introduced to accomplish that.

---

[2] 419 F. Supp. 630 (D.N.J. 1976).
[3] 458 F. Supp. 1179 (D.D.C. 1978).
[4] ERISA § 104(B)(1).

Pension benefit statement for terminating vested employees. This statement shows the employee's accrued and vested benefits under any applicable plan. It must be given to each terminated employee who has vested rights.

Notice to interested parties. This notice must be furnished to prospective plan participants prior to the approval of a qualified plan by the IRS. The government has developed model language for it. The notice can be posted and need not be sent to anyone. This is another compliance item with doubtful communications value.

Written explanation of claims denial. If anyone is denied a claim under any pension or welfare plan, that person is entitled to a clearly written statement giving the reasons for the denial. The explanation must also include a description of any material or information necessary for the claimant to improve the claim and the reason why the additional material is needed.

Materials Provided on Request. Materials that must be furnished after they are requested by the plan participant or beneficiary include the following:

- Form 5500s (the plan's full annual report)
- Supportive plan documents *and*
- Personalized benefit statements

The company can impose a "reasonable" charge for reproducing these documents—up to 25¢ a page.

If the material is not furnished within thirty days, the plan administrator may be personally liable to the participant for up to $100 a day.

Materials Available in the Workplace. Materials that must be made available for review by plan participants or beneficiaries include the following:

- Form 5500s
- Plan texts and other supportive documents—i.e., insurance contracts, union agreements, etc.

Impact of ERISA on Employees

ERISA disclosure requirements have worked to the definite advantage of employees. For some, perhaps for many, ERISA meant obtaining plan descriptions in a form other than a plan document or insurance certificate. But employees—*all* employees—got more than just a description of their various coverages. They also received information about plan numbers, plan records, plan insurers, and trustees. They were given their ERISA Rights Statement and a description of the protection provided by the PBGC. They learned who they could sue, which courts to sue in, and for what reason to sue if they felt they had a case.

Communications Problems

The critical communications problem associated with ERISA is the "bottom line" of effective communications—i.e., the employee's need for information that is easy to understand. Management must not only fully disclose the employee's rights but must describe these rights in a manner that attracts the attention of the reader and maintains that attention through clear, easy-to-read copy and creative graphics.

As previously noted, it is possible to comply with the law and still do a poor job of communicating. Communicating effectively requires rising above the challenge of compliance. Companies who communicate benefits clearly, consistently, and through a wide variety of media comply too. How they are doing it is described in the remainder of this chapter.

COMMUNICATIONS TRENDS AND OPPORTUNITIES

Phaseout of Plan Documents

A number of companies are reexamining the need for—and the advisability of—including plan documents or insurance certificates in their booklets. Prior to ERISA, most booklets included the plan text or the insurance certificate in their closing pages. Many companies are now eliminating these items because the SPD has proven to be the document that may force a company into court. In most instances, the "extra baggage" (the plan text or insurance certificate) will not serve as sufficient defense if a company is challenged on the accuracy of its communications. If benefit payment promises are made or implied in the SPD, the company runs the strong risk of being forced to pay these benefits no matter what the plan document has to say on the subject.

Restructuring of Summary Plan Descriptions

Some companies have also elected to rewrite and restructure their SPDs, recognizing that they had focused their initial energies on compliance rather than communications. In restructuring the SPD, they built a "highlight" plan description into the introduction and isolated the ERISA information from the description of the plan's benefit values. This approach is simple, but highly effective.

Highlight Plan Descriptions. A highlight plan description summarizes all the key provisions of the plan. It does so with minimum use of language and with maximum emphasis on what the plan can do for the individual. It gives the employee a capsule view of the plan's value—and sets the stage for further reading about the plan if the employee so desires.

These highlights can be written in several ways and can be developed for every type of plan in most benefit programs found in industry today. Figure 6.1 shows the highlight description taken from the retirement plan SPD prepared for salaried employees of a major corporation.

ERISA Inserts and Spread Sheets. To communicate benefit values, many companies have separated the ERISA administrative information from the basic body of the text. One company added a pocket on the last page of each of its SPDs. All the ERISA-required information was placed in that pocket.

Other companies—those that include all their benefit plan descriptions in one booklet or binder—have developed spread sheets that display most of the ERISA information in a single-sheet matrix similar to the one shown in Figure 6.2.

Flexible Compensation

Several companies have begun to explore the possibilities of installing *flexible compensation*—or *cafeteria*—benefit programs (see Chapter 25). A few organizations, including Educational Testing Service, American Can, a division of TRW located in California, PepsiCo, and Morgan Stanley, have instituted such plans covering part or all of their employees. Flexible compensation has captured considerable industry interest since it links benefits with a growing desire on the part of employees to participate more directly in shaping the policies and programs that affect them directly. The Revenue Act of 1978, which eliminated the problem of constructive receipt for certain types of employee elections within the benefit program, sparked that interest even further. Although companies have been cautious about introducing such programs, the concept appears to be more than a passing fad. It is an idea to be reckoned with and, in terms of benefit communications, dealt with because flexible compensation programs present an entirely new and challenging mission for the benefit communications function.

Need for Active Employee Participation. A flexible compensation program must be supported by effective benefit communications. Certainly, in examining the feasibility of installing such a program, a company should build the communications element into the planning process right from the start.

Flexible compensation requires a much more interpersonal, highly interactive communications mode. The company is confronted with a pressing need to inform employees about their various benefit coverages to enable them to make intelligent choices among the combination of coverages available to them. And this need to inform—to educate—increases the importance of the employee in the communications process.

HERE'S HOW THE PLAN WORKS FOR YOU	AND WHEN
You automatically become a plan member if you were hired before age 60	On the next January 1 or July 1 after you: • reach age 25 and complete one year of eligibility service or • complete 5 years of eligibility service
You retire with your highest possible income under the plan	At age 65
You can retire early with the full benefits you have earned to date	When you reach age 62 and complete 10 years of continuous service
You can retire even earlier with less income from the plan	When you reach age 55 and complete 10 years of continuous service
You will earn credit towards retirement benefits if you become disabled	If you become totally and permanently disabled after you complete 10 years of continuous service and qualify for Social Security disability benefits
You get non-forfeitable (vested) rights to plan income even if you leave before retirement	When you complete 10 years of continuous service
You can elect a plan option that pays an income to a survivor if you die before retirement	When you reach age 55 and complete 10 years of continuous service
You can choose the benefit payment method best suited to your situation and needs when you retire	As you approach the date on which you are first eligible to receive retirement income from the plan

Fig. 6.1 Highlight Plan Description

ERISA SPREAD SHEET

OTHER IMPORTANT INFORMATION

The following information is provided to comply with the Employee Retirement Income Security Act of 1974 (ERISA). If you would like any additional information about your Benefit Program, contact the Benefits Section of the Personnel Department.

PLAN NAME	PLAN TYPE	PLAN YEAR	PLAN ADMINISTRATOR	AGENT FOR SERVICE OR LEGAL PROCESS	PLAN TRUSTEE(S) AND/OR INSURER(S)	PAYMENT OF BENEFITS	IDENTIFICATION NUMBERS COMPANY	IDENTIFICATION NUMBERS PLAN
Hospital Insurance Plan								
Medical-Surgical Insurance Plan								
Major Medical Benefits Plan								
Major Dental Expense Benefits Plan								
Long Term Disability Plan								
Group Life Insurance Plan								
Group Accident Insurance Plan								
Group Travel Accident Insurance Plan								
Retirement Plan								
Profit Sharing Plan								

Fig. 6.2 ERISA Spread Sheet

In a flexible compensation environment, the employee needs to act on the information that is provided—every year and across the entire benefit program.[5] In addition, the employee must communicate his response—i.e., the benefit elections that are made—to the program administrators both clearly and accurately. The employee is not only a receiver of information, he becomes a communicator too.

It comes as no surprise, therefore, that among those companies that have installed flexible compensation programs, there has been a marked increase in one-on-one communications. This form of communications, though time-consuming and costly, is a highly effective way to share information.

Use of Single Benefit Booklet. In companies utilizing flexible programs, multiple benefit booklets have given way to just one SPD that describes all the benefit plans. The text attempts to show how the different coverages can be linked into varying patterns of personal protection. Such a booklet is extremely hard to write—much more so than a traditional SPD. It is organized on a "functional" basis—i.e., around the various coverages that are available within the program to help in given situations such as disability, retirement, or death. The challenge in writing such a booklet is to avoid redundancy, not an easy challenge to meet.

Development of Special Benefit Graphics

Many companies pride themselves on their corporate identities—symbols and/or letters which are often created at great cost and once purchased are presented consistently in every message directed to their many publics. Building on this corporate approach, a number of companies have created distinctive symbols or logos that portray a graphic representation of their entire benefit program. These logos are most always purchased at relatively low cost. However, in their own selective way they have as much value in immediately identifying for the employee the benefit message in whatever format it appears, as the corporate symbol does for the public messages to which it is attached.

Caution must be exercised here. Logos, symbols, attractive graphics—i.e., photographs, illustrations, use of type, paper, and bindings—are never a substitute for good content. What is written or spoken—and how it comes across to employees—is the most important factor in the communications package. Nonetheless, creative graphics can greatly enhance the message, invite reading, and can even help clarify some difficult concepts. Good graphics show the employee that the company cares enough to do it right. The benefit booklet, announcement folder, benefit statement, or audiovisual presentation are certainly not greeting cards, but it's hard to contest the

---

[5] At TRW and PepsiCo, employees have choices only with respect to their welfare plans.

success of a demonstration of "caring enough" as every greeting card purchaser only too well knows.

New Uses for Benefit Statements

Other companies have explored ways to capitalize on the high readership results achieved by personalized employee benefit statements. No other form of printed media is as effective in reaching employees. When they are first introduced, employees invariably, almost universally, respond favorably, and subsequent editions are anxiously awaited. The popularity of statements clearly suggests that they can be used to "market" other benefit messages that are built into them.

A few companies are now using their annual benefit statement to market their SPDs. The SPD and the statement are combined in one presentation. The employee is encouraged to review his SPD each year since the employee's personal stake in the company's benefit program is also contained in that booklet.

Other companies, not yet ready to go that far, are using the annual benefit statement to communicate current and important benefit messages to employees. They are putting the statement to work to carry the rationale behind various plans in the benefit program. The main text of the statement shows the employee what benefits he has; the supportive text explains why these benefits are there in that form and why they provide the dollars of protection they do.

Benefit Statement Messages. For example, here is a list of the important questions that a major New York bank includes in its employee benefit statement:

- Why does the bank provide health care coverage?
- Why does the health care program pay some costs and not others?
- Can the program help me avoid unnecessary hospital stays and unnecessary surgery?
- Why are the bank's benefit plans coordinated with government benefits?
- How do the bank's disability and pension plans work together?
- Why does the bank offer a choice of life insurance plans?
- How do my life insurance, pension plan, and government benefits work together?
- How does my salary affect my pension plan benefits?
- What is the purpose of vesting—and how does it work?

The list of issues that can be addressed in any annual statement is limited by the size of the statement. The answers provided to these issues are, however, deliberately brief so the list itself can be fairly complete. The list, of course, can and will change each year, so there is no limit to the number of messages that can be communicated through the statement over time. Since the statement is generally well received, these messages may be expected to get close employee attention. It is advisable to take full advantage of repetitive presentation of benefit values; in communications, nothing succeeds better than repetition.

Employee Feedback

Many companies that have designed their benefit communications efforts to achieve greater employee understanding and appreciation of the coverages they have, are now regularly surveying their "market." Companies that are committed to effective benefit communications are adopting devices long used by those in marketing and research—techniques that provide insight into what the audience wants and the ways to best meet those needs.

Some companies have developed rather simple but highly effective survey cards to obtain a better sense of this benefit communications market. These cards (one is shown below in Figure 6.3) provide more than statistical data. Through write-in comments, they can provide a wealth of subjects for future communications efforts. The company can focus its follow-up communications on specific items of interest as identified by its benefits "market."

A survey card does more than help sell. It responds directly to the issue of ERISA compliance. Where the benefit communications get solid employee "ratings," the company has tangible affirmative evidence if asked by the Department of Labor whether its SPDs comply with ERISA on the very hard and elusive test of clarity.

Expanded Use of Audiovisual Media

A number of companies are supporting their printed benefit communications materials with highly creative audiovisual presentations. The best of these are brief, with sharp focus on the "whys" rather than the "whats" of the benefit program. Multiple projector shows are being used more (even two projectors running in tandem are significantly more effective than one). And video, if used properly, is an even better medium than slides.

A milestone in audiovisual benefit communications has been achieved by United Technologies Corporation through the use of video. The company offered new employees a highlight overview of their entire benefit program. Every plan was covered. No item of information relating to the *value* of the various plans was overlooked. Technical benefit details were ignored and the program used real employees as part of the cast. It also featured comedian Jonathan Winters, incorporating his talents for humor and communications in what proved to be a tremendously effective benefits presentation. It was a costly program to produce—about $100,000 in all. However, compared with the total cost of the company's benefit program, the price was relatively inexpensive. According to Robert Morrissey, Manager of Employee Com-

Your comments, please . . .

A special effort has been made to make your new benefit book informative and understandable. Would you please take a moment after reading the book to answer the questions below? Your comments and suggestions are most welcome.

It is not necessary to sign your name, and no postage is required if mailed in the U.S.

A. How do you feel about the amount of information in the booklet?

□ Complete □ Generally complete

□ Not enough

B. What subjects would you like to know more about?

C. How would you describe the text of the book?

□ Clear and easy to understand

□ Generally clear □ Difficult to understand

D. Which section did you understand least?

Section title: ______

E. Which section was the easiest to understand?

Section title: ______

F. Please check whichever of the following applies to you:

Your Age	Length of Service	
□ Under 25	□ Under one year	□ Man
□ 25 - 34	□ 1 - 4 years	□ Woman
□ 35 - 44	□ 5 - 9 years	
□ 45 - 54	□ 10 - 19 years	□ Hourly Paid
□ 55 or over	□ 20 or more	□ Salaried

G. What schools have you attended?

□ high school □ college

□ technical school □ graduate school

H. Any additional comments?

Please fold, seal, and place in the company mail or any U. S. Postal Service box. Thank you for your help.

Fig. 6.3 Survey Card

munications at United Technologies: "It gave our new employees, who are very important to us, an immediate, good feeling about their benefits and about the company. It piqued their interest in the SPDs which they later received and gave them a favorable frame of reference for future benefit communications efforts to which they'll be exposed."

Limitations. There are limitations, of course, to the use of audiovisual media in communicating benefits. The cost of the equipment and the availability of proper facilities in which to make the presentations may be limiting factors. But the major hurdle is employee time off the job. Companies still are reluctant to move a communications program through their organization, particularly one involving hourly employees, if participation requires these employees to come off the line. Some companies believe the lost time is never made up. Other forward-looking companies take the opposite view. They believe that the cost of time in terms of the value gained is largely recaptured, particularly if employees' feelings about the company are enhanced by the messages they receive.

Each company has to address the time issue in this form of benefit communications on its own. Nevertheless, it is clear that a benefit communications program cannot be supported with full effectiveness through print alone. Today there is not a single new employee under age 30 entering any company in America who can remember any period of his life in which television was not a major source of information and news.

NEW COMMUNICATIONS TECHNOLOGY

The commitment to communicate well, to provide the people and financial resources sufficient to accomplish this goal, is the key to any company's success in making employees aware of the benefits they enjoy.

Many companies have effectively repositioned their benefit communications practices since the passage of ERISA. Much has been achieved by linking creativity to technology. The computer and "in-house" use of television have provided new opportunities for communications creativity. Both will continue to do so in the future—and their impact should be even more powerful than it has been up to now.

Computer Statements on Demand

The computer has dramatically changed the way benefits are communicated through *annual* benefit statements. In the future, computers may be put to use to provide statements *on demand.* One company already has in place on its computer a complete, current record of every salaried employee's pension status. This large company has people and locations all across the United States and abroad; yet in twenty-four hours or less, it can produce a pension status report for any of these employees anywhere in the United States.

In the future, companies may give employees direct access to the computer to obtain instant information about their benefit status. An employee could be given a special, personal code that would provide access to his file. To reduce or eliminate frivolous calls, employees could be told the computer will respond to a request made on any employee's personal code only once in a given period—each quarter or every six months.

Another promising possibility is the interim statement issued by a company whenever an employee's service or earnings change the individual's benefit status. These statements can call attention to the achievement of vested status and its significance, eligibility for the preretirement spouse's benefit, and any and all increases in life or disability insurance based on a change in pay. They can focus employee attention on the viability of the benefit program—demonstrate how the values it provides change in step with the individual's career progress.

Computers are also moving into the home—thousands are being purchased and put to work by individuals all across the country.[6] These computers offer interesting possibilities for benefit communications. Companies, for example, could provide data and programs with which employees—on their own—could calculate their own benefits. And these calculations could include future earnings and service scenarios (or investment fund returns for thrift and profit-sharing plans) which the company itself would perhaps be most reluctant to provide in printed form.

Bringing the Message Home

When technology reduces the cost of home playback video units and these units begin to appear in large numbers in the homes of employees, a new threshold of benefit communications opportunities will arrive. Companies will be able to produce programs on various benefit subjects for home viewing. The audience will be more than just the employee—it will include the spouse and other interested family members. The messages that are brought home can demonstrate, in ways unique to this medium, just how valuable the company's benefit program is to the entire family. The programs can focus attention on the care and commitment that underlie the design, funding, and administration of the various plans. They can build and reinforce the employee's appreciation of just what these benefits can do, as well as what the company has done, and is doing, to make these benefits available. Since viewing time will be off-the-job, one major hurdle to the use of audio-visual presentations will be overcome.

THE COMMUNICATIONS ACTION PLAN

An effective benefit communications effort must be supported by a sound communications plan. This plan should reflect a careful blending of management's communication goals and employees' needs for information packaged in a manner best-suited to the employee's attention span. The action plan should provide ongoing messages as highly personalized as possible across a broad array of media. The plan should also reflect the varying information interests of different employee groups based on age, position, education, and, in the case of large multiemployer companies, the industry and location in which these employees work.

---

[6] According to an article published in *The New York Times* in early July 1980, there were some 300,000 to 500,000 home computers then in use in the United States; anticipated growth by the end of the decade is that one out of every four families will have one.

Objectives

The objectives of the communications effort should be clearly stated and in writing. They should reflect those values important to *management,* for example:

- Better appreciation of the company
- Higher employee productivity
- Lower turnover
- Reduced absenteeism
- Strong community image
- Legal compliance

These objectives will vary from company to company, and their importance for any given company will change over time. The key is to tie these objectives to the overall mission of the organization as it relates to the human resource input so critical to corporate success.

To assure that these objectives are current, it is important to seek and obtain senior management input on a periodic basis. This can be achieved through interviews with selected executives and through careful review by senior management of the annual action plan. One way to assure such a review is to build the budget for the next year's efforts into the plan.

The action plan should reflect a sound understanding of the following information needs, important to the employee audience:

- Clearly written reference materials; administrative manuals for supervisors; summary plan descriptions for all
- Timely and brief written announcements on all important benefit changes or additions; letters to the home; payroll stuffers; bulletin board notices; special folders
- Audiovisual presentations on all important benefit changes plus overview presentations on the entire benefit program; slide and script presentations delivered by company personnel or by use of a slide/cassette "controlled" format; television—either on the company's closed circuit TV network or on cassettes prepared for home playback
- Personalized benefit status reports; annual or interim benefit statements
- Special programs—including both written and audiovisual materials—for new employees and for those approaching retirement

One way to gain and maintain an effective perception of employees' benefit information needs is to build a feedback system into the action plan. That system can involve simple survey cards or a complete communications audit. Both are useful—particularly a complete communications audit conducted every two or three years.

Media

Whatever the media, and there are, as noted, many to select from, they should be appropriate to the message. For example, a slide presentation cannot be expected to carry all the reference material that can be placed in an administrative manual or an SPD. An announcement of a benefit program change should be brief—just touching on the highlights.

To introduce new information, the following media work best:

- Announcement letters or folders, bulletin board notices including posters
- Audiovisual presentations—in the case of major changes—first with supervisors and plan administrators followed by meetings with employees

To document the changes, the following media work best:

- Administrative manuals
- Summary plan descriptions and/or employee handbooks
- Highlight folders

To keep the benefit program highly visible to employees, the following media work best:

- Personalized benefit statements
- Audiovisual presentations
- Telephone "hot-lines"
- Special programs—orientation for new employees; preretirement counseling for older members of the staff and their families

Budgeting

The budget included in the action plan should encompass payroll costs (pay plus benefits) for all personnel directly involved in the communications effort plus all anticipated media to be used the following year.

The size of the budget should reflect the overall annual costs for the entire benefit package. A good rule of thumb is to budget at least one percent of the total costs for benefit communications less the cost of payroll for staff.

Timing

Communicating benefits requires an ongoing effort. Companies that exert great effort to introduce new benefits—or improvements—and do little to follow up this initial activity generally realize a poor return on their budgeted investment. Employee benefits—as any other product—must be sold and resold to the audience if management wishes to achieve an effective return on the funds being spent each year on the benefit program.

Fortunately, new technology has increased the opportunity for ongoing benefit communications. The challenge is to use this technology plus personal creativity to the fullest advantage.

7

Fiduciary Responsibility

JEFFREY D. MAMORSKY[1]
Shea & Gould

INTRODUCTION

New and stricter standards of fiduciary responsibility were introduced by the Employee Retirement Income Security Act (ERISA). It also imposed new requirements for plan investments and prohibited specified transactions.

Employee benefit plans are required to name one or more fiduciaries to control, manage, operate, and administer each plan. Also, with certain exceptions, employee benefit plans are required to have their assets held in trust by one or more named trustees. The establishment of plans and pension trusts are governed by specific rules and exceptions geared to protect plan participants and to insure responsible management.

General standards of conduct are provided for plan fiduciaries. In addi-

[1] The material in this chapter is based on chapters written by the author in *Employee Benefits Law: ERISA and Beyond,* copyright 1981 Law Journal Seminars-Press, Inc. The material herein is reproduced with permission of the publisher.

tion, there are very specific rules relating to prohibited transactions which plan fiduciaries must not engage in. A breach of fiduciary duty can result in personal liability for losses and nondeductible excise taxes on prohibited transactions.

APPLICABILITY OF FIDUCIARY RULES

The fiduciary responsibility rules apply to every employee benefit plan (including employee welfare benefit plans) that is established or maintained (1) by any employer engaged in interstate commerce, or in any industry or activity affecting interstate commerce, or (2) by any labor union, or similar organization, representing employees engaged in interstate commerce, or (3) by a combination of those employers and labor unions. However, the rules do not apply to governmental plans, certain church plans, plans established to comply with workers' compensation laws or unemployment compensation or disability insurance laws, or plans maintained outside the United States primarily for the benefit of persons substantially all of whom are nonresident aliens, or unfunded excess benefit plans.

In addition, the fiduciary rules do not apply to unfunded plans maintained by an employer primarily for the purpose of providing deferred compensation for a select group of management or highly compensated employees. For example, if a plan were established solely for the officers of a corporation, it would not be covered by the fiduciary rules. Moreover, the fiduciary rules do not apply to a deferred compensation arrangement solely for retiring or deceased partners or a deceased partner's successor in interest.

Identifying the ERISA Fiduciary

ERISA conveniently divides the definition of "fiduciary" into three parts.

First, a person is a fiduciary of a plan to the extent he exercises any discretionary authority or responsibility in the administration of the plan. The key word is "discretionary." Thus, a person performing only ministerial functions, such as mere mathematical computation of a participant's benefit, would not be a fiduciary.

Second, a person is a fiduciary to the extent he exercises any authority or control concerning management and disposition of plan assets. In this regard, ERISA does not expressly make "discretion" a condition of fiduciary status, but the requirement of "authority or control" implies at least some degree of discretion. For example, it is unlikely that a mere custodian of plan assets would be regarded as a fiduciary.

Third, a person is a fiduciary to the extent he renders investment advice with respect to plan assets (or has any authority or responsibility to do so) for a fee or other compensation, other than regular compensation received as an employee of the plan sponsor. Regulations issued by the Department of Labor (DOL) and the Treasury Department indicate that a person will be deemed to have rendered investment advice only in the following circumstances: (1) the person renders advice to the plan concerning the value of securities or property, or makes recommendations about the advisability of investing in, purchasing, or selling securities or other property; and (2) the person either directly or indirectly (a) has discretionary authority or control with regard to purchasing or selling securities or other property, or (b) renders any advice with the understanding that such advice will serve as a primary basis for investment decisions and that the person will render individualized investment advice to the plan based on the plan's particular needs regarding such things as investment policies or strategy, overall portfolio composition, or plan investment diversification.

Plainly, a person's status as a fiduciary depends on his function, authority, and responsibility rather than his title or label. It is clear, however, that some people become fiduciaries merely because they hold certain positions in a plan's operations. For example, an investment manager is a fiduciary by definition under ERISA. Trustees and members of an administrative or investment committee are inherently vested with discretionary authority in the administration of a plan or management of plan assets in virtually all cases. The company maintaining the plan is a fiduciary, since it has such discretionary authority (at least in a single-employer plan) and any officer or employee who exercises discretionary authority on behalf of such a company is also a fiduciary. Attorneys, accountants, actuaries, and consultants are not fiduciaries when performing their usual professional functions. But they too will be fiduciaries if, in a particular case, they fall within the standards set forth above. Attorneys, for example, may become fiduciaries to the extent they advise on matters of plan policy. Moreover, an attorney, pension consultant, accountant, or insurance salesman who is contacted by the plan trustee or administrator on a regular basis to determine the advisability of certain investments may be considered a fiduciary. If this occurs, the advisor may become involved in a prohibited transaction because of the receipt of compensation for services rendered.

Fiduciaries who are responsible for management and investment of plan assets must also take care to identify the potentially long list of persons who are parties-in-interest or disqualified persons with respect to the plan. This is normally an essential step in avoiding prohibited transactions between the plan and such persons.

Parties-in-Interest and Disqualified Persons

A plan fiduciary is prohibited from engaging in certain specific transactions with a party-in-interest. A party-in-interest may be:

- Any fiduciary, counsel or employee of the plan;
- A person providing services to the plan;

- An employer whose employees are covered by the plan;
- Any owner of a 50 percent interest in such employer; or
- A union whose members are covered by the plan.

Other persons and entities are parties-in-interest by reason of their relationship to those mentioned above. Thus, any corporation, partnership, trust, or estate in which the above-described parties-in-interest hold a 50 percent interest would also be a party-in-interest. Certain relatives of the above parties-in-interest, including spouses, parents, grandparents, children, grandchildren, and the spouses of children and grandchildren are themselves parties-in-interest. An employee, officer, director, 10 percent shareholder or 10 percent partner of a firm or company which is a party-in-interest may also be a party-in-interest.

Most parties-in-interest will also fall within the Internal Revenue Code's definition of "disqualified person." However, an employee of the employer whose employees are covered by the plan would not automatically be a disqualified person unless he earns at least 10 percent of the aggregate yearly wages paid by the employer. The Code's "disqualified person" definition and ERISA's "party-in-interest" definition also appear to differ in a few other minor respects.

FIDUCIARY STANDARDS

Except in certain specified circumstances where assets may revert to an employer, there is imposed upon each fiduciary the broad responsibility of discharging his duties with respect to a plan:

1. Solely in the interest of plan participants and beneficiaries;
2. For the exclusive purpose of providing benefits to participants and their beneficiaries and defraying reasonable plan expenses;
3. With the care, skill, prudence, and diligence under the circumstances then prevailing that a prudent man acting in a like capacity and familiar with such matters would use in the conduct of an enterprise of a like character and with like aims;
4. By diversifying the investments of the plan so as to minimize the risk of large losses, unless under the circumstances it is clearly prudent not to do so;
5. In accordance with the governing plan documents and instruments, insofar as they are consistent with the provisions of Title I.

Prudent Man Rule

ERISA states that a fiduciary shall act:

> With the care, skill, prudence, and diligence under the circumstances then prevailing that a prudent man acting in a like capacity and familiar with such

matters would use in the conduct of an enterprise of a like character and with like aims. . . .

A federal fiduciary standard is embodied in ERISA so as to bring a measure of uniformity in an area where decisions under the same set of facts may differ from state to state. Congress incorporated into the Act a version of the prudent man rule generally consistent with the rule applied by the courts (and some statutes) to trustees and corporate directors.

While basic trust law concepts relating to the prudent man rule will form a starting point from which a federal common law may be developed, it will be some time before the courts provide a clear picture of the new prudence standard. In the meantime, the DOL has issued regulations relating to the investment duties of a fiduciary of an employee benefit plan under ERISA. According to the regulations, the factors to be considered by a fiduciary in making an investment decision are (1) the composition of the portfolio with regard to diversification, (2) the liquidity and current return of the portfolio relative to the anticipated cash-flow requirements of the plan, and (3) the projected return of the portfolio relative to the funding objectives of the plan. The regulations include a "safe harbor" provision which states that fiduciaries who comply with the provisions of the regulation will have satisfied the prudence requirements. It does not mean, however, that those who do not comply necessarily do not meet the prudence rule.

On the other hand, it should be noted that under the Internal Revenue Code requirement that plans must be for the exclusive benefit of the employees and their beneficiaries, the IRS has developed investment rules which require that the cost of plan assets must not exceed fair market value at the time of purchase, that there must be a fair return commensurate with prevailing rates, that sufficient liquidity must be maintained to permit distributions, and that the safeguards and diversity that would be followed by a prudent investor must be present. It is intended that if a fiduciary meets ERISA's "prudent man" rule, he will meet the IRS requirements.

Diversification of Plan Investments

ERISA imposes upon a fiduciary the duty of diversifying plan investments to minimize the risk of large losses, unless under the circumstances it is clearly prudent not to do so.

Under the diversification rule, a fiduciary usually should not invest the entire trust fund, or an unreasonably large portion of it, in a single security, nor in one type of security or various types dependent upon the success of one enterprise or upon conditions in one locality, since such investments would increase the risk of large losses. Accordingly, a fiduciary should not invest, for example, a disproportionate amount of the trust fund in stock of corporations engaged in a particular industry, or in mortgages upon real estate in a particular district, or upon a particular class of property lest a decline in property values in that district or that class cause a large loss. The ERISA Conference Committee Report indicates that the degree of investment concentration necessary to violate the diversification requirement could not be stated as a fixed percentage because a prudent fiduciary has to consider the facts and circumstances in each case, including:

- The purposes of the plan;
- The amount of the plan assets;
- Financial and industrial conditions;
- The type of investment, whether mortgages, bonds, shares of stock, or otherwise;
- Geographic dispersion;
- Distribution as to industries; and
- The date of maturity.

Adherence to Plan Documents

ERISA provides that a fiduciary shall discharge his duties with respect to a plan "in accordance with the documents and instruments governing the plan insofar as such documents and instruments are consistent with the provisions of this title." The significance of this provision lies in its departure from the common-law rule of trusts under which the trustee was charged with carrying out the intent of the settlor as specified in the trust instrument. The provisions of the trust instrument were binding upon the trustee unless compliance was impossible, or illegal, or there has been a change of circumstances. A fiduciary may disregard the plan document if compliance with the document would be inconsistent with any of the provisions of ERISA, including the prudent man standard.

PROHIBITED TRANSACTIONS

A fiduciary may not cause a plan to engage in a transaction if he knows or should know that the transaction constitutes a direct or indirect:

- Sale, exchange, or leasing of property between the plan and a party-in-interest;
- Lending of money or other extension of credit between the plan and a party-in-interest;
- Furnishing of goods, services, or facilities between the plan and a party-in-interest;
- Transfer to, or use by or for the benefit of, a party-in-interest of any plan assets; or
- Acquisition or retention of any qualifying employer security or employer real property in excess of 10 percent of plan assets.

All but the last of these prohibitions has a counterpart in the Internal Revenue Code which imposes on the disqualified person (the Code's counterpart to the party-in-interest) who participates in such a transaction, an excise tax of 5 percent of the amount involved for each year involved regardless of whether the disqualified person knew or should have known that the transaction was prohibited. The Code also imposes an additional 100 percent tax if the prohibited transaction remains uncorrected for ninety days after the mailing of the notice of deficiency for the initial tax. If a plan is not subject to the Code's excise tax provisions (e.g., a nonqualified plan), ERISA subjects the plan to a civil penalty equal to the excise tax. In addition, a fiduciary who has engaged in a prohibited transaction will be personally liable for any losses the plan has sustained as a result of the violation.

Sale, Exchange, or Lease

It is a prohibited transaction for a fiduciary to permit a plan and a party-in-interest to engage, directly or indirectly, in a sale, exchange, or leasing transaction. Under this rule, the transaction is prohibited whether or not the property involved is owned by the plan or the party-in-interest or disqualified person. The prohibition includes sales from the party-in-interest or disqualified person to the plan and vice versa. Since this prohibition applies to indirect sales, a prohibited transaction would occur, for example, where a mutual fund acquired property from a party-in-interest or disqualified person as part of an arrangement under which the plan would invest or retain its investment in the mutual fund.

Mortgaged Property. An additional statutory provision prevents the circumvention of the prohibition of sales by mortgage of the property before transfer to the plan. Both the Code and ERISA provide that a transaction will be treated as a prohibited sale or exchange if a party-in-interest or disqualified person transfers to a plan real or personal property that is subject to a mortgage or similar lien which the plan assumes, or if the transferred property is subject to a mortgage or a similar lien which a party-in-interest or disqualified person has placed on the property within ten years prior to transfer.

Transitional Provisions. Transitional rules provide that the prohibition does not apply to a lease between a plan and disqualified person or a party-in-interest pursuant to a binding contract in effect on July 1, 1974 (or pursuant to renewals thereof) until June 30, 1984. The prohibition does not apply to a sale, exchange, or other disposition of property between a plan and a disqualified person before June 30, 1984, provided that, if the plan disposes of property, the plan must receive at least fair market value for the property; if the plan acquires property, it must not pay more than fair market value for the property.

Exemptions. Limited exemption for the prohibition on the leasing of property between a plan and a party-in-interest is provided by both ERISA and the Code. Under these provisions, contracting or making reasonable arrangements with a party-in-interest or disqualified person for office space necessary for the establishment or operation of the plan is not a prohibited transaction if no more than reasonable compensation is paid. In determining what is a reasonable contract or arrangement, the regulations state that the contract must permit the plan to terminate without penalty on a reasonably short notice. For example, a long-term office lease will not be unreasonable merely because of its long term if it provides that the plan may terminate without penalty on short notice under the circumstances. Reasonable compensation is defined as compensation reasonable under the facts and circumstances, a clearly unhelpful definition. Significantly, the exemption allowing the leasing of office space is not an exemption from the self-dealing prohibition. Thus, one who is a fiduciary with respect to the plan may not provide office space and receive consideration for it unless such a provision is arranged and approved on behalf of the plan by a fiduciary who is independent of and unrelated to the fiduciary providing the service.

Another possible exemption with regard to the leasing of property is the exemption allowed for qualifying employer real property. The definition of qualifying employer real property means real property (and related personal property) that is leased to the employer whose employees are covered by a plan or to an affiliate of such an employer and consists of a substantial number of parcels that are geographically dispersed and suitable for more than one use.

Complete exemption is provided by ERISA for the purchase of qualifying employer real property or qualifying employer securities from an eligible individual account plan and a limited exemption for other plans. An eligible individual account plan (a profit-sharing, stock bonus, thrift or savings plan, employee stock ownership plan (ESOP), or money purchase plan in existence on September 2, 1974 that at the time invested primarily in employer securities) may purchase qualifying employer securities or qualifying employer real property. Qualifying employer securities are stock or marketable obligations of the employer.

All other plans are subject to a limitation on the acquisition or holding of qualifying employer securities or qualifying employer real property. The limitation is expressed as 10 percent of the fair market value of the assets of the plan. Transitional rules are provided for plans to comply with this ruling with the requirements to be effective fully in 1985.

Loans

It is a prohibited transaction if any direct or indirect lending of money or other extension of credit occurs between a plan and party-in-interest or disqualified person. The mere guarantee by a disqualified person or party-in-

interest of a loan to a plan will generally constitute a prohibited transaction, unless it comes within the special exemption for employee stock ownership plans. The Conference Report states that prohibited loans include acquisition by the plan of a debt instrument (such as a bond or note) which is an obligation of a party-in-interest or a disqualified person. Similarly, the funding of employer contributions by employer debt obligations is a prohibited transaction since, in effect, it constitutes a loan by the plan to the employer.

Exemptions. There are two basic statutory exemptions to this prohibition. Loans from a plan to a party-in-interest or disqualified person who is a participant or beneficiary of a plan will not be considered a prohibited transaction if certain requirements are met. The loans must be available to all participants on a reasonably equivalent basis, must bear a reasonable rate of interest, must be adequately secured and must be paid pursuant to specific provisions of the plan authorizing such loans. The loans may be secured by a first mortgage or the vested interest of the participant in the plan. Such collateral will not constitute an alienation of the participant's benefit that would disqualify the plan under the provisions of the Code.

Another statutory exemption to the prohibited transaction rules with regard to loans or extensions of credit concerns loans to an employee stock ownership plan. The exemption indicates that as long as a loan is primarily for the benefit of participants and beneficiaries and has a reasonable rate of interest, an exemption will be granted from the prohibited transaction rules. This section also requires that collateral, if any, consist only of employer securities. The Conference Committee Report indicates that this exemption is intended to cover not only the extension of credit in the form of a loan, but also the guarantee of the loan by a party-in-interest.

The transition rule applicable to this prohibition provides that if certain conditions are met, loans or other extensions of credit between a plan and a party-in-interest or disqualified person pursuant to a binding contract in effect on July 1, 1974 (or renewals thereof) may remain in effect until June 30, 1984.

Furnishing of Goods, Services, or Facilities

The direct or indirect furnishing of goods, services, or facilities between a plan and a party-in-interest or a disqualified person is prohibited. For example, the furnishing of personal living quarters to a party-in-interest or disqualified person is prohibited.

Exemptions. There are three separate exemptions from this prohibition. First, ERISA and the Internal Revenue Code permit a party-in-interest or disqualified person to furnish a plan with office space, legal or accounting services, or other similar services necessary for the establishment of or operation of the plan, if no more than reasonable compensation is paid for the services. However, the contract or arrangement for such services must allow the plan to terminate the services on reasonably short notice so that the plan will not become locked into an arrangement that could become disadvantageous.

Second, a plan can pay a fiduciary or other party-in-interest or a disqualified person reasonable compensation (or reimbursement of expenses) for services rendered to the plan if the services are reasonable and necessary. However, the Conference Report indicates that, to prevent double payment, this exemption does not apply to persons receiving full-time pay from an employer or association of employers (with employees covered by the plan) or from a union (with members covered by the plan), except for the reimbursement of expenses properly and actually incurred.

Third, a bank or similar financial institution which is a fiduciary of the plan and which is supervised by the United States or a state, may provide multiple ancillary services (such as non-interest-bearing checking accounts) to a plan, subject to several limitations:

- The institution may not charge more than reasonable compensation for services;
- The institution must have adopted adequate internal safeguards to assure that its provision of ancillary services is consistent with sound banking and financial practice, as determined by federal or state banking authorities; and
- The institution's action must be in accordance with specific guidelines which the institution itself has issued.

Adherence to such guidelines will prevent the institution from providing ancillary services in a manner that would be unreasonable, excessive, or inconsistent with the best interests of the plan's participants and beneficiaries. These guidelines must be reported to each plan for which multiple services are provided.

The general rule, which provides that a fiduciary cannot provide "multiple services" to a plan, was adopted because of the potential problems inherent in situations where persons who can act on behalf of a plan may also be in a position to personally benefit at the expense of the plan. In addition to the limited statutory exemptions from this general rule, the Conference Report suggests that administrative exemptions will be granted for sound commercial and financial practices where there are adequate safeguards.

Transfers of Plan Assets

ERISA prohibits the transfer to, or use of, any of the plan's assets by or for a party-in-interest. The Internal Revenue Code prohibits transfers to, or use of, the plan's income or assets by a disqualified person. The ERISA Conference Committee Report indicates that it was the intention of Congress that these two provisions be interpreted in the same way and that both provisions are to apply to income and assets.

Exemptions. Statutory exemptions are found in the following provisions: The ERISA provision which covers the exercise of privileges for conversions of securities; the section dealing with distributions of plan assets in accordance with the terms of the plan; and the section concerning the receipt of benefits by a participant who is a party-in-interest or disqualified person. The Conference Committee Report notes that since a plan legally can acquire and hold employer securities that may be convertible in nature, the plan to convert the securities will not be a prohibited transaction as long as fair market value is received. Similarly, the distribution of plan assets or benefits in accordance with the terms of the plan will not be prohibited transactions. This might include a return of contributions or assets to the employer under certain conditions, as well as the normal payment of benefits to a party-in-interest who is also a plan participant or beneficiary.

Certain Acquisitions of Employer Securities or Realty

Acquisition on behalf of a plan of any employer security or employer real property is in violation of Section 407(a) of ERISA. In addition, a fiduciary who has authority or discretion to control or manage plan assets is prohibited from permitting the plan to hold any employer security or employer real property if he knows or should know that holding such security or real property violates Section 407(a). Such a violation will occur if the plan acquires or holds any employer security or employer real property not qualifying under Section 407(d)(4) or 407(d)(5) of ERISA, or if the acquisition of qualified property results in the aggregate value of such property exceeding 10 percent of the value of the assets of the plan.

Exemptions. ERISA exempts from the scope of the prohibited transaction rules those transactions in qualifying employer securities and real property which meet the following conditions:

1. The acquisition, sale, or lease must be for adequate consideration (or in the case of a marketable obligation, at a price not less favorable to the plan than the price determined under Section 401(e)(1));
2. No commission may be charged for the transaction; and
3. Either the plan must be an eligible individual account plan (as defined in Section 407(b)(3)) or the transaction must not violate the 10 percent rule of Section 407(a).

This exemption is incorporated into the tax law provisions by I.R.C. Section 4975(d)(13), which provides that any transaction which is exempt from the prohibited transaction provisions in Section 406 of ERISA by reason of Section 408(e) of ERISA shall also be exempt from the prohibited transactions provisions of I.R.C. Section 4975(c).

The transitional rules in ERISA provide that the prohibited transaction rules will not apply to property owned by a plan on June 30, 1974, and all times thereafter, which is transferred to a party-in-interest or disqualified person, if the plan is required to dispose of the property in order to comply with the prohibition against holding excess employer securities and employer real property under Section 407(a) of ERISA. However, the plan must receive at least adequate consideration.

FIDUCIARY SELF-DEALING TRANSACTIONS

In addition to prohibiting the transactions enumerated above, ERISA and the Internal Revenue Code also impose penalties upon fiduciaries who engage in specific acts of self-dealing. ERISA provides that a fiduciary may not deal with the assets of the plan in his own interest; receive any consideration for his personal account from a party dealing with the plan in any transaction involving plan assets; nor act in a transaction involving the plan on behalf of a party whose interests are adverse to those of the plan participants or beneficiaries. The first two prohibitions are also contained in the Code and therefore a fiduciary who violates either of these two rules may subject himself to an excise tax as well as civil liability under the labor provisions.

Exemptions. ERISA and the Code contain the exemptions to the prohibited transaction rules that apply to fiduciary self-dealing transactions. A fiduciary may be reimbursed for expenses properly incurred and may receive reasonable compensation for services rendered, as long as the fiduciary is not a full-time employee of the employer maintaining the plan. An officer, employee, agent, or other representative of a party-in-interest or disqualified person is expressly permitted to serve as a plan fiduciary.

A fiduciary is permitted to receive any benefit to which he is entitled as a participant or beneficiary in a plan, as long as the benefit is computed and paid on a basis which is consistent with the terms of the plan that are applicable to all other participants and beneficiaries. But for this exemption, any payment of benefits under a plan to a fiduciary would be a prohibited transaction under ERISA, since a fiduciary is a party-in-interest, and the payment would amount to a transfer to a party-in-interest of plan assets. The definition of a party-in-interest under ERISA also includes employees of the employer maintaining the plan. Thus, since ERISA contains no exemption for employees, a strict reading of that section could lead to the conclusion that benefits provided to participants who are employees of the employer maintaining the plan are prohibited—a reduction to the absurd. This problem does not exist under the exemption contained in the Code, since that exemption applies to disqualified persons, the definition of which does not include employees.

8

Collective Bargaining Considerations

OSCAR ORNATI

Professor of Manpower Management, Graduate School of Business Administration, New York University

COLLECTIVE BARGAINING IN THE UNITED STATES

The present-day structure of private sector employee benefits—their level, composition, cost impact, variations among economic sectors, industries, size of firms and geographic region—was, to a very large degree, shaped through the collective bargaining process. The impact of collective bargaining in the United States was most marked between 1947 and 1973, with government playing a larger role thereafter. This chapter highlights the underlying causes of the existing patterns of employee benefits, as these affect the total compensation of nonmanagement employees.

The varied and multifaceted process of collective bargaining was captured early in its history in a description of how individual bargaining (still the way in which employment benefits of senior managers are set) became transformed into collective bargaining: "In unorganized trade the individual workman, . . . accepts or refuses the terms offered by the employer without communication with his fellow workmen. . . . But if a group of workmen concert together, and send representatives to conduct bargaining on behalf of the whole body, the position is at once changed." [1] The collective bargaining framework, process, and outcomes in the United States are to a large degree determined by the framework of laws, primarily federal, that structures the relationship of employers and employees and limits the conflicts between labor and capital.

Differences Between American and European Patterns

The difference between the private sector employee benefit picture in the United States and in the rest of the world, is, to a large extent, traceable to the particularism of American collective bargaining. American workers have a long history of self-help through negotiations and through their influence on legislation. Indeed, many of the fringe benefits negotiated with employers can be seen as a successful effort to offset, through the workings of the labor market, the long-term governmental tendency to react slowly to unemployment, inflation, or other social changes affecting workers. European governments, on the other hand, have tended to be more responsive to the changing social and economic needs of workers, setting employee benefits through legislation with the consequent provision of various benefits, health, child care, unemployment insurance, etc., directly through governmental agencies. Obviously the total employment and benefit picture in the United States and abroad is influenced also by other factors—the history, economic development, etc., of each country. In turn, the collectively agreed-upon benefit structures of the United States also reflect changing social values. Thus while employer initiatives in devising and making available employee benefits have always been important, one can well describe U.S. labor history—often unfortunately characterized primarily by strikes or other job actions—in terms of negotiated and litigated fringe benefit victories by workers.

A Brief Historical Perspective

Early Union Role in Providing Benefits. Labor's interest in non-wage benefits is of long standing. By the 1820s, workers' organizations had set out to provide many benefits directly. The earliest examples involved the payment of cash benefits to the needy unemployed, later to those affected by injury, illness, or widowhood.

---

[1] Webb & Webb, *Industrial Democracy* 173 (1914).

Early labor history is filled also with concerns with health programs—a subject to which collective bargaining turned only in the 1960s when the costs of medical care escalated.

Union efforts to provide protection against sickness goes back to 1877, when the Granite Cutters began providing sick benefits from union dues. By 1904, 107 national unions had such programs. A few organizations went beyond financial support, with the Printers' Union building a home for the sick by 1892 and the Ladies' Garment Workers Union opening a diagnostic clinic in 1913.

At various points in history, union leaders and members supported and rejected the idea of playing a large role in providing social benefits to employees. At times, various cooperative and union stores, even union banks, were used to provide members with benefits. Some of these ventures were successful, but most failed because of undercapitalization, poor management, and, in a few cases, corruption.

All union ventures in the direct provision of benefits were eventually adjusted by changing conditions; in later years they were modified to supplement governmental programs and to become financed primarily by employer contributions rather than union dues.[2] Still the history of unions' own efforts to structure and provide employee benefits is important enough to have led former Labor Secretary Dunlop to the conclusion that "In fact, so many labor organizations began as benefit societies that it is hardly an exaggeration to say that trade unionism in America arose almost as much from a desire to band together for mutual insurance as from a desire to bargain collectively."[3]

Not all early employee benefits initiatives originated with unions; between 1910 and 1920 a few employers launched pension plans on their own and as early as 1928 Congress rescued the faltering railroad retirement funds through legislation that made them a permanent part of the national pension scene.

The Current Setting. As the contractually established provision of private sector employee benefits expanded in the 1960s and 1970s, more and more of the unions' efforts were directed toward administration of benefit funds and education of workers about and organization of the provisions of services rather than the concern with its financing. As a result, the range of current benefit activities varies enormously among different areas and organizations. The breadth of services currently available can be gleaned by listing those provided by several locals of Los Angeles:

- Credit unions to make loans to members on reasonable terms.
- Health services, including medical clinics, convalescent homes, psychiatric

---

[2] See generally Kennedy, *Beneficiary Features of American Trade Unions* (1908) and Boeckel, *Labor's Money* (1923).

[3] Bok & Dunlop, *Labor and the American Community* 363 (1970).

counseling, dental clinics, and plans for purchasing drugs, eyeglasses, hearing aids, and the like, at reduced costs.

- Legal services and representation before accident commissions and unemployment compensation boards, or aid with assorted private legal problems.
- Retirement facilities, including clubs, nursing homes, recreational facilities, and pensions.
- Purchasing programs to allow members to buy consumer goods at lower prices.[4]

The Evolving Legislative Framework

The legal environment and the tax code are at the heart of the distinction between required and voluntary benefits. Unions and employers, through lobbying and the marshaling of technical arguments, contributed to the shaping of the legal requirements. These are not amenable to changes through agreements between employers and employees whether acting as individuals or when represented by organizations. Voluntary payments, on the other hand, are more directly influenced by employee preferences. Subsequent to the famous *Inland Steel Co. v. N.L.R.B.*[5] decision in 1948 in which the U.S. Supreme Court ruled that pensions were covered by the National Labor Relations Act's (NLRA) "duty to negotiate on wages and working conditions," unions bargained with vigor to expand voluntary payments or fringes.

Legally Required Benefits. Benefits required by law include Social Security, unemployment compensation, and workers' compensation. (See Chapters 9, 18, 19, and 20 for detailed discussions of these programs.)

- *Social Security* provides retirement pay, disability insurance (which provides pay to those who cannot work because of disability), survivors benefits (paid to an employee's aged parents, spouse, or children after he dies), and Medicare (which provides hospital and medical insurance for retired workers or those who have become disabled). Both employers and employees contribute to Social Security payments.
- *Unemployment compensation,* which is administered by local states with federal guidelines, provides payments for up to twenty-six weeks or more for workers who have been laid off. Taxes paid by the employer provide the funds for this.
- *Workers' compensation* provides money to employees who have had job-related accidents or illnesses, and have incurred related expenses, e.g., medical expenses. The money for this comes, in most states, directly from employer contributions to insurance carriers.

Since 1939, the AFL-CIO and some of the major international unions

---

[4] *Id.* at 364.
[5] 170 F.2d 247 (7th Cir. 1948).

have lobbied with mixed success for the liberalization of legally required benefits; most employers opposed these programs because of the continually increasing labor costs that accompanied them. Indeed, increases in legally mandated benefits have been so rapid that their costs represent a larger and larger proportion of all employer benefit costs. This is particularly true of smaller employers for whom changes in the level of legally required benefits is important. In the 1970s increases in benefits grew at an even larger rate than before. (See Figure 8.1.)

Period	*Increase in Total Benefit as a Percentage of Total Payroll*	*Increase in Employer Share of Required Benefits as a Percentage*
1959 to 1961	5.73	14.20
1961 to 1963	3.87	11.00
1963 to 1965	1.11	(4.76)
1965 to 1967	7.38	16.42
1967 to 1969	6.53	8.16
1969 to 1971	6.41	5.66
1961 to 1971	**5.06**	**7.29**
1971 to 1973	6.36	17.85
1973 to 1975	7.12	6.06
1975 to 1977	6.12	8.57
1977 to 1979	3.26	7.89
1979 to 1981 *	5.00	14.50
1971 to 1981 *	**5.57**	**10.97**

* Estimated
Source: Based on a sample of 182 continually reporting companies. See Table 19 of U.S. Chamber of Commerce, *Employee Benefits 1979,* at 27.

Fig. 8.1 Increases in the Employer Share of Legally Required Benefits

Government Wage Regulations. The development of various fringe benefits is also associated with sporadic federal attempts at controlling the upward movement of wages. For example, during World War II, the War Labor Board, to provide a channel for union pressures in the face of agreed-upon wage constraints, permitted the introduction of a variety of new fringe benefit packages. Later the Wage Stabilization Board employed the same strategy. Even the Nixon Pay Board contributed, albeit indirectly, to the systemization of insurance and pension programs by pulling together and coordinating the bargaining interests of rival trade unions to make their competition less inflationary.

Voluntary Payments and the Duty to Bargain. There are four major classifications of voluntary benefits:

1. Payment for time not worked. This benefit includes paid vacations, sick leaves, holidays, coffee breaks, rest periods, jury duty service, voting time, clean-up time, and bereavement time. In different degrees this category of payment is available to all kinds of employees. (See Chapter 28.)
2. Employee welfare. The first of four types, *health insurance,* involves contributory and noncontributory systems that help the employee pay for hospital rooms and medical expenses, which often include dental plans. (See Chapters 22 and 23.) *Group life insurance,* paid for by the employer, is another. (See Chapters 20 and 21.) *Private retirement plans* and *pension* schemes are a third kind of voluntary benefit. These are intended to supplement the Social Security payments which covered retired employees receive. (See Chapter 9–17.) *Supplemental unemployment benefits,* (SUBs), usually financed by the employer, provide supplementary payments for those who are receiving unemployment compensation. They are typically part of large collectively bargained agreements. (See Chapter 19.)
3. Employee services, including benefits such as company subsidized food services, credit unions, legal and income tax aid, and athletic and recreational programs. These are typical of employer-originated benefits, rarely covered by collective bargaining agreements. (See Chapter 28.)
4. Premium pay—money paid to some employees for working overtime, undesirable hours, or under hazardous conditions when such payments are not required by state or federal legislation.

Voluntary benefit payments—as the very term suggests—have traditionally been perceived by employers as the means to exemplify their interest in their employees' well-being and to heighten employee allegiance. Employers try to attract potential quality employees by structuring a total compensation approach rich in the variety of its benefits. Thus, employers with sophisticated human resource managements currently provide a very large variety of voluntary benefits, some of which are now available only to managers, but can be expected to be part of future employee benefit packages. (See Figure 8.2.)

Industrial relations practitioners, aware of the long history of employer-originated voluntary benefit systems, contend that the judicial interpretation of the meaning of "the duty to bargain collectively over wages and working conditions" of Section 8(2)5 of the NLRA has fundamentally transformed the level and nature of voluntary benefit payments. Originally intended as an independent and flexible addition to base pay, benefits have become a permanent supplement varying with base pay.

The turning point, as discussed earlier in this chapter, is generally associated with the *Inland Steel*[6] decision. In this case the employer maintained that it had the right to unilaterally change the conditions of the pension plan established before the arrival of the union. The court ruled to the contrary;

---

[6] *Id.*

it found that pensions were in fact covered by the phrase "working conditions" and therefore part of the mandatory duty to bargain. Other later court decisions followed the *Inland Steel* precedent in ruling that a large number

Accidental death, dismemberment insurance	Loans of company equipment
Birthdays (vacation)	Long-term disability benefit
Bonus eligibility	Matching educational donations
Business and professional memberships	Nurseries
Cash profit sharing	Nursing home care
Club memberships	Outside medical services
Commissions	Paid attendance at business, professional, and other outside meetings
Company medical assistance	Parking facilities
Company-provided automobile	Pension
Company-provided housing	Personal accident insurance
Company-provided or subsidized travel	Personal counseling
Day care centers	Physical examinations
Deferred bonus	Political activities (time off)
Deferred compensation plan	Price discount plan
Deferred profit sharing	Psychiatric services
Dental and eye care insurance	Resort facilities
Discount on company products	Retirement gratuity
Education costs	Sabbatical leaves
Educational activities (time off)	Salary
Employment contract	Salary continuation
Executive dining room	Savings plan
Free checking account	Scholarships for dependents
Free or subsidized lunches	Severance pay
Group automobile insurance	Shorter or flexible workweek
Group homeowners' insurance	Sickness and accident insurance
Group life insurance	Social service sabbaticals
Health maintenance organization fees	Split-dollar life insurance
Holidays (extra)	Stock appreciation rights
Home health care	Stock bonus plan
Hospital-surgical-medical insurance	Stock purchase plan
Incentive growth fund	Survivors' benefits
Interest-free loans	Tax assistance
Layoff pay (SUB)	Title
Legal, estate-planning, and other professional assistance	Training programs
	Vacations
	Wages
	Weekly indemnity insurance

Fig. 8.2 Employee Compensation Vehicles Utilized in a Cafeteria Compensation Approach

of other kinds of voluntary benefits were similarly covered.[7] Those who have observed how frequently and how intensively union and management representatives conflict over pensions and other types of voluntary benefits give this interpretation much credence.

The influence of the legal environment on the level, composition, and even administration of employee benefits was further expanded in the 1960s and 1970s, first by cases establishing the employer's and unions' detailed responsibility over multiemployer jointly managed pension and welfare funds and then by the passage of ERISA.

COLLECTIVE BARGAINING PATTERNS AND THE SPREAD OF BENEFITS

The existing structure of *all* employee benefits in the United States (except for the compensation of senior executives) was determined by developments in the major industries—steel, automobile, rubber, construction, etc.—that, until the last decade, dominated the economic scene. Here we find large and sophisticated employers dealing on a continuing basis with large and representative unions during a period of significant economic growth. The collective bargaining system and the technical experts that surround it functioned as an ideal channel for the establishment of a rich package of employee benefits (exemplified in Figure 8.3) that at first imposed only a small unit cost burden on large and profitable firms. Where such conditions did not exist—except for the employees of a few non-unionized industry leaders such as Mobil or IBM—employee benefits either did not expand or remained the prerogative of managerial and professional employees.

Different Industrial Settings

Collective bargaining in the United States takes place in a wide variety of settings. It covers workers in occupations ranging from actors and airline pilots to police officers and word processors. It involves public and private, large and small employers, and old-fashioned as well as high technology industries. Industrial structures, the nature of competition in the product market, and past practices have all contributed to the process of collective bargaining. To understand how the specific impact of collective bargaining affects employee benefits, one needs to look at the setting in which it takes place. The industrial and craft groups establish reasonably clear and different patterns in the area of employee benefits. Other groups fall somewhere in between.

---

[7] For a more detailed analysis of the broadening of the meaning of the "duty to bargain" see Cox & Dunlop, "Regulation of Collective Bargaining by the National Labor Relations Board," in 63 Harv. L. Rev. 389-397 (1950).

The Industrial Pattern. The industrial pattern is exemplified by the results of negotiations between the International Association of Machinists (IAM) and Boeing Corporation. These negotiations are national in scope, involve several national unions and set the pattern for the industry. Over the years the Boeing-IAM agreements have steadily improved the fringe benefit package. Although Boeing Corporation was first organized in 1916, it was twenty years later that its employees joined the IAM and obtained their first agreement. By today's standards, the fringe benefits of these early agreements were meager. Seven holidays were granted in 1936, compared to thirteen in 1981. However, in 1936, the holidays were not paid days off; rather, workers were paid double time if they had to work. At present, all holidays are paid time off, and triple time is paid if work is required. The first week of vacation, as it is now understood, was negotiated in 1943. By contrast, in 1981, a worker with twenty-five years of service is entitled to five weeks paid vacation, while a worker with five years of service is entitled to three.

A health insurance plan was first included in 1952. The plan covered life insurance of $4,500, accidental death and dismemberment benefits up to $4,000, sickness and accident benefits up to $31.50 per week for thirteen weeks, and a medical and surgical package. The plan was a contributory one, with management paying $8.68 and the employee paying $.57. Today's basic plan is paid for by Boeing entirely. It includes a $15,000 life insurance policy, an accidental death and dismemberment policy of $15,000, and sickness and accident benefits of $150 per week for up to twenty-six weeks. The basic medical package is, of course, much broader and includes hearing aids, eye care, a prescription drug plan, home care and second opinions on surgery.

Coordinated efforts. Between 1937 and 1953 the contractual improvements gained by the IAM were in part the result of the competition that this older and more stable AFL union faced from the rapidly expanding United Automobile Workers (UAW). In 1949, the UAW and IAM dealt with their rivalry by establishing a union "no-raid" pact. Since 1953, collective bargaining in the air frame industry has been highly coordinated, at first primarily through the exchange of information. In 1962, all union representatives from the industry worked out coordinated bargaining goals covering general wage issues, employment security, and insurance. Since many aspects of the insurance and pension programs are companywide, these bargaining issues become a natural platform for coordinated collective bargaining for the two national unions.

Today's aerospace negotiations are highly coordinated, as they are in most industries dominated by a few large employers such as automobile or electrical equipment.

The Craft Pattern. The pattern of fringe benefits of most craft workers is exemplified by the collectively bargained fringe benefits in the construction industry. In construction, collective bargaining is characterized by strong and fiercely autonomous local unions only loosely affiliated with national unions. On the other side of the table, employers usually bargain through local associations of like contractors. Construction workers are employed in one of many trades ranging in skill from laborer to carpenter to electrician. They may be involved in building highways, electrical transmissions, pipe lines, buildings, or homes. The worker may be with one employer for a full year or only a few weeks. The contractor may be headquartered in the area or be from another part of the country. Or, the worker may be a *traveler* from another part of the country, i.e., a member of one local union who is covered by that local's benefit program but is temporarily working under the terms and conditions of another local union's agreement.

Use of trust funds. From the perspective of labor negotiations on fringe benefits, the major difference between the industrial and craft pattern is the latter's use of jointly administered trust funds. Negotiations in industrial situations concentrate on the nature of the benefit and then the cost is considered. In the construction industry and in most other craft settings, the emphasis is on the amount of money per hour that employers can pay into the trust fund and then on what benefits these funds will buy.

Multiemployer, jointly administered trust funds are used for almost all construction industry benefits: vacation funds, health insurance, life insurance, and pensions. Most of these funds are locally negotiated and locally administered. In recent years, due to the development of large contractors and because of problems associated with the traveler, a trend is developing toward more regional trust funds and toward making national trust funds more prevalent. The employer pays into the trust fund where the worker is working but the traveler's benefit rights are predominately determined by conditions in his union of origin. The equity problem associated with the traveler can most easily be resolved through broader regional and national trust funds, exemplified by the growth in reciprocal agreements among these funds.

Effect of employment irregularity. There are other issues particular to employment in construction that shape the craft pattern of benefits. The construction worker usually works about 1,300 hours per year depending upon weather and the availability of work. Often construction workers take their vacations during layoffs aware that upon returning they may have to go to the hiring hall for referral to another job, probably with a different employer. The industrial worker on the other hand has a scheduled work year of approximately 2,000 hours.

Treatment of seniority rights. In the construction industry, as well as in most craft unions, with the exception of the Teamsters, seniority with a local union does not apply to employment opportunity rights. On the other hand, industrial employment seniority controls almost all employment rights including the guarantee that after a vacation the worker comes back to his job.

The vacation issue. The whole vacation issue in the crafts was further complicated some years ago by a series of court decisions that in effect treated the vacation trust funds distribution as a wage payment with all the associated tax obligations. Vacation fringe benefits in construction are thus distinctly different from fringe benefits in other industries in that they may be viewed by the union as a form of employee savings from wages rather than an employer-provided benefit while the employers see them as their contribution and as an addition to labor costs.

Employer contributions. Overall employer contributions to the jointly administered fringe benefit trust funds are 24 percent of wages. However, there are substantial variations between trades and geographic regions. Wages on the West Coast tend to be higher and there is a higher percentage (36 percent) of compensation allocated to the benefit trust. In 1979 the average construction rate on the West Coast was $14.06 per hour with an additional $5.05 going to voluntary benefits. At the other extreme, lower wages and fringes that are a lower percentage (13 percent) of compensation are prevalent in the southeastern states. 1979 construction wages in St. Petersburg, Florida averaged $9.51 per hour with another $1.20 going to voluntary benefits. The various construction crafts differ also. The boilermakers' national average wage rate was $12.63 in 1979 with another $3.40, or 27 percent of nonlegally required compensation, going to fringes ($1.10 to the hospitalization and life insurance funds, $1.30 to the pension fund, and $1.00 to the vacation fund). By contrast, the glaziers' national average wage rate in 1979 was $11.35 with another $2.22, or 19 percent of nonlegally required compensation, going to fringes.

Responses to Changing Social Pressures

A survey of the various unions' thrusts in increasing employee benefits over the last thirty-five years suggests that unions regularly pressure private employers to offset broad social system failures. A survey of employer initiatives in companies that have no trade union organization suggests that employers are also interested in providing for their employees services that are either hard to find or expensive in the private market.

Organized Labor's View. The AFL-CIO leadership argues that bargaining settlements represent a reaction to the government's failure to meet the needs of the American work force; thus, when the statutory promise of a full employment economy did not materialize, the unions responded by negotiating for SUBs. Labor leadership maintains that the federal government failed to adopt a national health care program; therefore most unions had to protect employee health needs through negotiated settlements. In labor's view, local and national negotiations fill the void of governmental inaction by enhancing job security and income security provisions while avoiding national statutes having direct ties to negotiated fringes.[8]

Labor leadership looks with a jaundiced eye at the ups and downs of the growth of government Social Security benefits. The Social Security retirement program, for example, was, for a time, fully integrated into many of the negotiated pension programs. Integrated private pension programs in effect provided a benefit level based upon the Social Security benefit to which the employee was entitled, with the employer's negotiated benefit plan making up the difference between this benefit level and a higher contractual level. As a result, when labor lobbied in support of an increased Social Security benefit level many of its members received no additional benefit while management's pension costs were decreased. These plans were fairly prevalent in the 1950s and early 1960s but have long been negotiated out of existence in all labor agreements; in fact, the old fully integrated plans are no longer legal. A greater part of the employee pension burden has thus been shifted back onto the various companies concerned.

In essence, organized labor believes that its greatest achievement lies in providing the rank and file with a level of security and benefits not otherwise available to American workers. It regards its task as incomplete and believes employees need further protection, particularly from inflationary pressures that are eliminating the protection that was built into pensions over the years.

The Managerial View. Management does not agree that unions are the main defenders of employee interests. To the extent that management speaks with a united voice, management argues that it is also concerned with employee welfare, for both humanitarian and practical business reasons. "The fact that we have such a high proportion of men who stay here long enough to earn pensions," a U.S. steel company spokesman once said, "is proof that our men are pretty well satisfied. Our company was first to recognize the union and when Andrew Carnegie was still living it was the first to institute pensions. We anticipated a lot of social security, years before the Government or most industries got around to it."[9] Employers argue further that they have initiated the purchase of a variety of social insurance schemes because (1) there are considerable savings associated with such group purchases; (2) such schemes enhance employment stability, with the consequent reduction in labor costs; and (3) employers believe it is the right thing to do.

Employers, as a group, believe that the primary effect of union pressures in negotiations of employee benefits has been an increase in labor costs, and that union lobbying for governmental social programs has been a significant

---

[8] Based on data provided by J.L. Zalusky, Economist, Department of Economic Research, AFL-CIO (April 1981).

[9] See, e.g., *American Labor Since the New Deal* 200 (M. Dubofsky, Ed., 1970).

factor affecting increases. In addition, employers argue that including voluntary benefits in the collective bargaining contract had reduced their flexibility in rewarding meritorious employees and in developing motivational systems. Organized labor's desire to enlarge negotiated and legislated benefits is viewed with much distress by a vocal minority of employers who argue that the current level of nonmanagerial employee protection saps individual initiative, weakens employee loyalty to the employer, and is a contributory factor, if not a primary cause, of the country's unwarranted movement to a welfare state.

SCIENTIFIC ANALYSES OF UNION IMPACT

Definitive scientific analyses evaluating the impact of trade unions on both the level (in dollar or percentage) and the composition of benefits received by employees have been limited by the lack of data. Except for the Social Security Administration's compilation and publication of data on pension benefits received, almost no data exists on the benefits actually received by employees; almost all data currently available relates to employer costs of benefits. That which is available is limited and is not easily comparable. This is true for both the benefit cost side and the union penetration side of the relationship. Indeed the U.S. Chamber of Commerce's yearly survey of employee benefits, although the best available resource, necessarily suffers from the biases typical of surveys based on voluntary submissions: the larger, more structured companies are over-represented; nor is it possible to know which of the survey's respondents, or what proportion of their employees, is organized. Similarly, the Bureau of Labor Statistics of the U.S. Department of Labor—the major source of reliable industrial relations statistics—does not issue data on the extent of union organization by industry or by size of firm. Only rough estimates of the degree of union penetration for thirty-four broad industrial classifications are available, grouped in terms of industries with less than 25 percent, between 25 and 49 percent etc., penetration. In part because of such data shortages, empirical analyses of the determination of fringes, as late as 1966, found little quantifiable evidence of union impact.[10] This finding reenforced the conventional wisdom that "much of the increase in employee benefits, particularly in areas such as pensions or insurances, can probably be attributed to voluntary employer action." [11] This commonly held position was reenforced by the generally available data that revealed that about 70 percent of the variance in benefits was related to the level of direct pay and the size of the company.

Such conclusions did not sit well with employers that negotiated with unions and with union leadership, all of whom refused to accept that all

---

[10] Rice, "Skill, Earnings and the Growth of Wage Supplements," Am. Econ. Rev. Proc. 583–593 (May 1966).

[11] Reynolds, *Labor Economics and Labor Relations* 200 (1978).

their efforts were for naught. The following section describes a major recent econometric study by the National Bureau of Economic Research (NBER) that significantly affected knowledge in terms of union impact in this area.

The NBER Study

In 1978 Professor R.B. Freeman completed an extensive analysis of data pooled from the 1967–1972 Bureau of Labor Standards census-type establishment survey of Expenditures of Employee Compensation (EEC).[12] The EEC survey contains industry-identified establishment data on the component parts of compensations separately for nonoffice and office (nonmanagerial) employees and permits distinguishing between firms whose employee groups are organized and those whose employees are not. The data thus permits a measure of union effect on pay, fringe level, and fringe composition within and across establishments as well as "spillover effects" of unionism on office workers.

By adding to the EEC data comparable information as to the average age and tenure of union and non-union employees in each industry and crude indications of skill levels by enterprise, Freeman was able to factor in the personal characteristics, and therefore the presumed desires of different groups of employees.

Freeman attempted to examine differences in terms of *"the supply price of fringes,"* which he defined as the amount of direct wages that workers would forego to obtain a given benefit. The supply price of fringes construct recognized that (1) there is some form of trade-off between level and composition of total compensation; (2) how the trade is made must depend on the preferences as to wages and fringes of each company's employees; and (3) some fringes are bought more cheaply than others when group buying is involved. Observation of the collective bargaining process, as well as of the decision-making process of the nonorganized employer, shows that all the above considerations are in fact involved. Consequently, if differences in the supply price of fringes that employers face in unionized and non-unionized situations can be identified, they will show the magnitude of the union impact.

Freeman's data analyses and their econometric manipulations, without in any way denying the strong effect on fringes of the level of pay and of the size of firms, led to several conclusions that hold when the level of compensation is held constant.

1. Unionism does, in fact, raise the voluntary fringe share of the wage bill by about 42 cents for each dollar in pay in industry in general, and by about 80 cents for each dollar of pay in manufacturing.

---

[12] Freeman, "The Effect of Trade Unionism on Fringe Benefits," NBER Working Paper No. 292 (Oct. 1978).

2. Unions also influence the composition of the voluntary fringe package so that organized employers contribute 11 cents an hour more to pensions and between 13.5 and 17.4 cents an hour more to vacation and holiday pay than their counterparts that are not organized. On the other hand unionism decreases the overtime premium, sick leave and bonus part of the fringe package payments of organized compared with that of nonorganized employers.
3. Unionism's impact is most marked on small, low-wage firms.
4. The presence of unions in the plant probably has a small effect (14 cents an hour in all industries and 10 cents in manufacturing) in raising the level of fringes among office workers without influencing their pay levels.

Freeman's assumptions—in particular the assumption that the length of employment with a firm is the major determinant of the employee's preferences as to the make-up of the fringe package, as well as the econometric complexity of the study—expose it to various challenges on substantive grounds. In addition, it is hard to read, and therefore not well known among practitioners. Nevertheless, this NBER paper must be given weight not only because of its findings but because of the large number of observations (over 10,000 contrasted to about 900 respondents in the 1979 Chamber of Commerce survey) and because it brings the findings of impartial scientific analyses more in line with the beliefs of industrial relations practitioners, on both the management and union side.

Cost Implications

The Freeman analysis traced both the direct and the indirect (spillover effects) influence of collective bargaining on fringe benefits. To the individual employer these considerations often appear theoretical. Such an employer wants to know the dollars involved in terms of his particular location and industry. Unfortunately, such data is not available. However, we here provide a so far unpublished calculation for average union and non-union employers.

Figure 8.3 shows the differences in the cost of the 1977 "nonlegally required" total compensation between union employees and non-union employees for a sample of 1,900 firms participating in the EEC survey. The data indicates *net* amount of employer contributions towards Social Security, workers' compensation and unemployment insurance, and shows clearly that the level of pay, the proportion of fringe benefits and the level of almost every separate benefit is higher for union than for non-union employees. The only exception involves bonus payments that are a component of total compensation which are, on the average, more than twice as high for non-unionized employees.

	1977					
		Union Employees			*Non-Union Employees*	
		Percent of Pay	*Percent of Compensation*		*Percent of Pay*	*Percent of Compensation*
Total, nonlegally required compensation	$8.51			$5.04		
Pay for time worked:						
Straight-time pay	$6.45		75.8	$4.38		86.9
Premium pay	.33	5.1	3.9	.12	2.7	2.4
Overtime, et al.	.27	3.7	3.2	.11	2.5	2.2
Shift differentials	.06	0.9	0.7	.01	0.2	0.2
Paid leave	.63	9.8	7.4	.23	5.3	4.6
Employer expenditures for private retirement plans	.47	7.3	5.5	.10	2.3	2.0
Employer expenditures for health insurance, benefit plans, and life insurance	.52	8.1	6.1	.16	3.6	3.2
Sick leave	.05	0.8	0.8	.03	0.7	0.6
Employer unemployment plans:						
Severance plans	.005	0.1	0.1	.005	0.1	0.1
Severance plans and SUBs	.01	0.2	0.1	.005	0.1	0.1
Bonuses	.02	0.3	0.3	.03	0.7	0.6
Savings and thrift plans	.01	0.2	0.1	.005	0.1	0.1

Source: Calculated by J.L. Zalusky, from unpublished data derived from the Bureau of Labor Statistics "employment costs index."

Fig. 8.3 Nonlegally Required Hourly Pay and Fringe Benefits as a Percent of Pay and Compensation: Union Verus Non-Union

FUTURE GOALS AND CHALLENGES

Most analyses of the expected employment picture of the next decade stress the multiplicity of factors that will affect it. The consensus is that inflation, productivity, energy, and shifts in the country's economic structure will set the matrix of future changes. According to the authors of a 1979 position paper by the Work in America Institute, Inc., the critical issues that need to be tracked also include pay, job security, and employee benefit(s).[13]

Inflation, estimated to average 8.5 percent to 10 percent per year through the decade, is bound to set the context of the trade-off between direct pay and employee benefits. The pressure to raise the level of productivity will most probably create continuing tensions between labor demands for employee benefits that increase workers' protection against social changes and employers' advocacy of benefits that reward employees' dedication, hard work, and performance.

Changes in the relative costs of labor and of energy, as well as changes in the organizational, geographic, and industrial structure of the economy, will probably create conflicts between workers in declining industries and workers in expanding areas. The former are primarily interested in increasing job security and pension benefits; employees in expanding industries seek broader participation in decision-making and "a piece of the action."

The future goals of unions and managements will thus differ on many aspects of employee benefits, while in other areas unions and managements will be moving in parallel directions. Although neither union nor management goals will probably be achieved in their entirety, it is possible to foresee a decade devoid of major collective bargaining conflicts about employee benefits. Except for a limited number of cases involving major financial employer commitments to maintain the integrity of large pension systems, future conflicts over employee benefits will probably be resolved by creative benefit technicians. Instead, it is fair to assume that conflicts between unions and managements will center on job security issues, exacerbated by changes in the industrial structure of the United States.

Management Goals for Pay and Benefits

Managements with a significant number of organized employees will turn their attention to the following goals in the compensation area:

1. Pay systems that reward individuals, over and above their basic pay, for increased job responsibility and superior performance. Direct pay will undoubtedly remain at the core of such pay systems, but four factors will tend to weaken the incentive value of pay raises:

---

[13] *Work in America: The Decade Ahead* (C. Kerr & J. Rossow, Eds., 1980).

- The inflated costs of goods and services, especially housing, education, energy, and health care.
- The growing Social Security tax, if proposals to freeze the tax base are not enacted, which will triple the maximum tax by 1987.
- The steady rise in federal and state income taxes linked to progressive tax brackets (unless indexing modifications take hold).
- Rising property and sales taxes.

Because of these factors, indirect pay will probably continue to be a major part of total compensation; pay managers will, in all likelihood, increase their efforts to determine if the compensation package produces the intended incentive effects.

2. Methods to convert wage-and-hour pay systems to annual salary plans in order to eliminate economic differences among employee groups, to confirm the continuity of income, to reduce periodic variations in pay, and to underline the economic security provided by the pay plan.

With this thrust, according to Work in America Institute, Inc., there will probably come:

> Increased experimentation with the "executive type" incentives for technical and professional personnel, including stock appreciation rights, performance bonuses, deferred pay, stock awards, and other extra incentives tailored to individual performance and motivation with year-to-year discretion. These provide flexibility and high opportunity for individual selectivity. They are one-time payments, impose no benefit-plan costs, and provide greater management involvement in the decision process.[14]

3. Expansion of company-sponsored thrift and savings plans. These plans combine a number of attractive multipurpose features at low cost, such as voluntary participation; tax-sheltered income; long-term employee savings encouraged by employer-matching formulas; investment options, including company stock; withdrawal and loan provisions to finance education, housing, and the capital needs of workers; and the long-term achievement of a second layer of pension protection resulting from these savings.

4. The continued and probable heightened drive to limit, if not exclude, collective bargaining's role in establishing the make-up of voluntary benefits. Because of inflation's effect on existing pension systems, employers can be expected (1) to resist labor's drive to expend pension coverage; (2) to encourage the integration of private pensions with Social Security benefits; and (3) to encourage workers' voluntary participation in IRA-type plans.

Union Goals for Fringe Benefits

While the coming decade may see the organization of workers in industries previously not involved with trade unions—banking, insurance and

---

[14] Rossow, "Quality of Work Life Issues of the 1980s," 14 Training and Dev. J. 36 (March 1981).

office employees, EDP and health technicians, etc., most of organized labor will be primarily engaged in defending previously won gains. The major goals of organized labor in the coming decade can be expected to be:

1. The defense of the real value of established pension systems. While unions will meet considerable employer sympathy in the pursuit of this broad goal, managements' needs to contain labor costs will create formidable resistance. Furthermore, the union role in maintaining the integrity of existing pension plans was restricted in the 1971 *Pittsburgh Plate Glass v. N.L.R.B.*[15] case in which the Court ruled that "retirees" were not to be considered "employees" and that therefore the condition of those receiving benefits was not a mandatory collective bargaining topic.

2. The careful analysis of certain trade-offs between increases in direct pay to employees and the provision of specialized voluntary benefits, such as prepaid legal services or maximum benefit for catastrophic illnesses, that can be purchased for groups with minimal employer outlays. In such proposed trade-offs, unions must do extensive missionary work with the rank and file concerned with infrequent but potentially troublesome events.

3. The turn of attention to the "two worlds" reality of employee benefits. This refers to a situation in which major employers provide a most attractive total benefit package, while a great number of companies, especially small and medium-size, labor intensive, marginally efficient employers (many non-unionized) provide few if any benefits. The dichotomy that has developed in the structure of the fringe benefit package is reinforced by the fact that some employers see no real advantage in trying to retain workers through adequate pay and fringe benefits. This employer philosophy (found, for example, in the fast-food industry and in some retail establishments) is reflected in the fact that many workers in such industries are not covered by accidental death and dismemberment insurance, paid sick leave, hospitalization, and other desirable benefits. Organized labor will, to some degree, have to address this issue to maintain its credibility as a spokesman for all labor.

The Future of Health Care Benefits

Employers and unions will probably move almost in parallel directions with regard to provision of health care benefits to employees, for the following reasons:

1. Although health care costs are likely to continue to increase, most of the increases are behind us.

2. The next decade will see the impact of federal and state efforts to restore consumer control over health services. In addition, the very size of

---

[15] 404 U.S. 157 (1971).

the health care industry has created opportunities for investments and for competition that may improve quality and productivity and reduce prices.

3. The interests and goals of organized, of nonorganized employers, and of their employees and unions do not seem to differ significantly in this area. The "supply price of health care fringes" can be assumed to vary little among employee groups; also, executives, managers, and professional employees are as interested and concerned with health care protection as are production and clerical workers.

A look at the future of health care benefits, therefore, includes the following predictions:

1. Employers, whether ideologically in favor or opposed to the provision of health benefits to their employees, will probably play a bigger role in the provision of employee health services or insurance.

2. Health insurance coverage will continue to expand to embrace psychiatric, dental, vision and other comprehensive services, with the drive for expansion coming from employers in new industries in which a large proportion of workers possess a relatively high level of skill.

3. In many instances employers and unions will work together to reduce insurance costs through more careful monitoring of services, and by encouraging employees to shop for competitively priced insurance arrangements.

4. In order to reduce health-related absenteeism and to control health care costs, employers will increase in-house health-related counseling services and forge links to community-based programs that deal with alcoholism, drug addiction and work-related stress.

5. To deal with a mobile work force or employment fluctuations, a number of industries will try to develop forms of portability for medical care catastrophe insurance that might be available at reasonable rates.

Part II

Replacement Income—Retirement

9

Social Security Replacement Rates

JACK M. ELKIN
Consultant, Martin E. Segal Company

INTRODUCTION

A plan sponsor deciding on the pension formula to be incorporated in the plan judges its effectiveness by the replacement rate it produces at various compensation levels (i.e., by the benefit as a percentage of earnings just before retirement). In doing so, he takes into account the replacement rate of the Social Security benefit and combines the two rates to evaluate the adequacy of the total retirement income.

Most pension plans in which benefits are related to earnings are integrated with Social Security, that is, the Social Security benefit enters directly or indirectly into the pension formula. In an integrated plan, therefore, its replacement rate is in part dependent on the Social Security replacement rate.

ELIGIBILITY REQUIREMENTS

Eligibility for Social Security old-age benefits is relatively easy to achieve. It consists of an earnings requirement expressed in terms of *quarters of coverage.* Before 1978, a worker earned a quarter of coverage, generally, for each calendar quarter he was paid $50 or more in wages. For 1978 he received a quarter of coverage up to a maximum of four for each $250 of wages paid in that year. The amount was increased to $260, $290, $310, and $340 for 1979, 1980, 1981, and 1982, respectively, and will continue to be increased annually in proportion to average wages. Workers born in 1929 or later will need forty quarters of coverage, roughly ten years of service, to qualify. For each year of birth before 1929, one quarter is subtracted from forty, except that the rule was somewhat stricter for men born before 1913. A man or woman who attains age 62 in 1982 needs thirty-one quarters of coverage; a man age 70 in 1982 needs twenty-four and a woman only twenty-three. Over 90 percent of persons in paid employment are currently under Social Security coverage, the chief exceptions being almost all civilian employees of the federal government and about 30 percent of the employees of state and local governments. Many of these government employees, however, have worked or will work in covered employment long enough to qualify for Social Security benefits in addition to their government benefits. It is expected that, by the year 2000, 97 percent of the aged population will be eligible for Social Security—if not as retired workers, then as eligible wives and husbands, widows and widowers, or parents.

BENEFIT FORMULA

The amount of retirement depends, first, on the worker's year of birth. If he was born in 1922 or later, it is calculated in accordance with the new formula adopted by Congress in 1977; if he was born in 1916 or earlier, it is calculated under the formula in effect before the 1977 amendments. A five-year transitional period from the old to the new formula is allowed for persons born in 1917-1921; for them, the new formula is applied but the benefit is guaranteed to be no less than it would have been under the old (but somewhat modified) procedure.

The benefit is related, depending on the age at retirement, to the primary insurance amount, which is in turn a function of the employee's wage history.

Wage Indexing

The new benefit formula involves the calculation of the covered employee's *average indexed monthly earnings* (AIME). The employee's covered wages in each year beginning with 1951 and ending with the year in which he attained age 59 are indexed; that is, they are multiplied by the ratio of

the average wage for all workers in the year in which he attained age 60
to
the average wage for all workers in the year in question.

For example, if he was 60 in 1980, his covered wages in 1965 (up to the then maximum of $4,800) are multiplied for benefit calculation purposes by 2.6860, because that is the ratio of the national average wage in 1980 to the average in 1965. His covered wages in each year beginning with the one in which he attained age 60 are not indexed but are taken at their actual value. The AIME is then calculated by totaling the indexed and unindexed earnings for the prescribed number of so-called computation years which yield the highest total and dividing the result by twelve times the number of computation years. The prescribed number is thirty-five if he was born in 1929 or later, thirty-four if in 1928, thirty-three if in 1927, down to twenty-three if he was born in 1917. The number is reduced by one for each year the employee was under a qualifying disability.

Covered Wages

The wage base, i.e., the maximum covered wages taken into account in benefit calculations, had risen from $3,600 in 1951 to $17,700 in 1978. At first the changes came about by ad-hoc congressional action but under the 1972 amendments, increases in the wage base were automatically triggered by increases in the Consumer Price Index (CPI) and were in proportion to increases in the national average wage. The 1977 amendments set the wage base arbitrarily at $22,900 for 1979, $25,900 for 1980, and $29,700 for 1981. Thereafter, changes are automatically tied to changes in the national average wage; for 1982, the base is $32,400. In January 1981 the National Commission on Social Security recommended that the level reached in 1984 (expected to be about $39,000) remain fixed for the next two years and then automatically adjusted thereafter.

Primary Insurance Amount

The AIME yields the *primary insurance amount* (PIA), which, for persons reaching age 62 in 1982, is calculated in the first instance as follows:

90 percent of the AIME up to $230
plus
32 percent of the AIME over $211 but not over $1,388
plus
15 percent of the AIME over $1,388

The PIA so calculated is adjusted in June of each year according to increases in the CPI beginning with the year of attainment of age 62. Adjustments are upward only and are made when the CPI for the first quarter of a year is at least 3 percent above the first quarter of a year that last triggered an increase. Thus, a worker who reaches age 62 in 1982 but retires in January 1985 will have his PIA determined in accordance with the above formula, including the cost-of-living adjustments for 1982, 1983, and 1984. In June 1985, and each June thereafter, he will become eligible for successive further adjustments.

The maximum AIME for a person retiring at age 62 in 1982 is $1,493 (somewhat higher if earnings in 1982 are high enough to warrant using it as one of the computation years). For that AIME, the formula yields a PIA of $593.60 for January–May 1982 and appropriately CPI-adjusted amounts effective each June thereafter.

If the employee reached age 62 in period 1979–1981 and retires in 1982 or a later year, his PIA is calculated under the formula applicable to the year in which he reached age 62 and then adjusted for the cost-of-living increases effective for that and subsequent years. In 1979, 1980, and 1981, these increases were 9.9 percent, 14.3 percent, and 11.2 percent, respectively. The resulting maximum PIA for retirement at age 65 early in 1982 is $666.88. (Under the transitional guarantee referred to above, the actual PIA amounts are slightly higher than those shown in this and the preceding paragraph.)

For persons reaching age 62 in 1983 and subsequent years, the *bendpoints,* $230 and $1,388, will be adjusted to correspond with changes in the average wage. The original bendpoints, applicable to persons who were 62 in 1979, were $180 and $1,085; for those age 62 in 1980, they were $194 and $1,171; and for those age 62 in 1981, they were $211 and $1,274.

There is a special minimum benefit for low-paid workers with many "years of coverage," i.e., years before 1979 in which earnings were at least 25 percent of the prevailing wage base and years after 1978 in which they were at least 25 percent of what the prevailing base would have been if it had merely kept pace with increases in the national average wage without reflecting specially legislated increases. If the wage bases for 1979–1981 had not been arbitrarily set by the 1977 amendments, the $17,700 base in 1978 would have increased to $22,200 in 1981. The PIA under this special minimum, effective June 1981, is $16.07 for each year of coverage over ten but not over thirty—thus, $321.40 for someone with thirty years of coverage. The minimum per year of coverage, which started at $11.50 in January 1979, will be increased automatically by future increases in CPI. The PIA is rounded down to the next lower multiple of 10 cents.

Benefit Amount

An individual retiring at or after age 65 receives the primary insurance amount as calculated above, increased 3 percent for each year (prorated monthly) he does not receive a benefit between ages 65 and 72. (After age 72—age 70 beginning in 1982—full benefits are payable regardless of earnings.) If he retires at age 62, the primary insurance amount is reduced by

20 percent. Prorated reductions are made for retirements between ages 62 and 65. The benefit is rounded down to the next lower multiple of $1.

Family Benefits

The spouse of a retired worker is entitled to a benefit equal to 50 percent of the latter's primary insurance amount if the spouse is age 65. At age 62, this is reduced to 37.5 percent. The spouse's benefit is offset by any Social Security benefit (and in some cases by a government pension) the spouse is entitled to receive in his or her own right. A minor child receives 50 percent and the wife, where there is a child, also 50 percent regardless of her age. There is a maximum amount payable to a family, however, varying from 150 percent to 188 percent of the worker's primary insurance amount.

Weighting Toward Low-Paid Workers

The benefit formula is heavily weighted to favor low-paid workers since lower segments of the AIME contribute relatively heavily to the PIA, and additional favor is shown through the special minimum benefit.

Old Benefit Formula

The benefit formula in effect before the 1977 amendments—still applicable to persons born before 1917 and, in modified form, to some born in 1917–1921—involved the calculation of an *average monthly wage* (AMW). The AMW was determined in the same way as the AIME, except that it was based on actual rather than indexed covered earnings. The number of computation years used was twenty-two for a person born in 1916 down to nineteen for one born in 1913. Progressively fewer years were used for older workers, with the requirement for women from one to three years fewer than for men.

The primary insurance amount was determined from the AMW in accordance with a schedule which, until 1971, was periodically revised by Congress in response to increases in the cost of living and, since then, was adjusted each year for changes in the CPI under the "automatic escalator" provision enacted in 1972. The same adjustment formula was and continues to be applied to the benefit after retirement. The delayed retirement credit under the old formula was only one percent for each year the worker did not receive a benefit between ages 65 and 72. The maximum PIA under the old formula, for an employee retiring at age 66 at the beginning of 1982, is $789.20, and this becomes subject to CPI increases beginning June 1982.

PROJECTED REPLACEMENT RATES

Automatic Escalator Formula

The automatic escalator of the 1972 amendments was designed to accomplish what Congress had previously done by ad-hoc benefit increases, namely, to maintain a relatively constant relationship between benefits and wage levels. With a continuation of the then prevailing trends in prices and wages it was a fair assumption that this objective would have been met. By 1977, however, it had become obvious that with higher rates of inflation, benefit increases under the formula would outstrip wages and the resulting replacement rates would be far higher than the system had ever been intended to provide.

Present Method

The present method of computing Social Security benefits was intended to correct this flaw in the 1972 automatic escalator formula. The indexing of wages insures that the benefit payable at retirement will keep pace with the rise in wages up to retirement and with rising prices thereafter. (More precisely, as described above, indexing is through the year of attainment of age 60 and, regardless of the age of actual retirement, CPI adjustments are made for each year after attainment of age 62.)

The replacement rates resulting from the 1977 amendments were stabilized at roughly where they were before the adoption of the 1972 automatic escalator formula—about 5 percent to 10 percent below those that would have been payable under the escalator formula in 1979 (the year the amendments became effective) and considerably more than that below the rates the formula would have produced after years of continued inflation.

For someone with average earnings, the new formula was intended to produce a benefit at age 65 equivalent to a replacement rate of about 43 percent, a figure that would be only moderately influenced by alternative assumptions as to future wage levels. Under the old formula, certain possible combinations of wage and price trends could in time have produced benefits in excess of preretirement earnings.

Figures 9.1 and 9.2 illustrate, under alternative sets of assumptions, the projected replacement rates for workers at various earnings levels in 1981 who will be retiring in the future at age 62 or 65.[1] Model A is based on the ("intermediate," as opposed to "optimistic" and "pessimistic") assumptions made by the board of trustees of the Social Security system in their 1980 report: The average wage will increase by amounts ranging from 9.9 percent in 1981 down to 6.1 percent in 2005 and the CPI by amounts ranging from 9.7 percent down to 4.0 percent. The figures shown therefore apply to a worker whose yearly earnings progression follows the national average. The

---

[1] The calculations were performed by Edward Greene, Vice-President and Associate Actuary, Martin E. Segal Company.

National average wage and individual's earnings assumed to increase in accordance with Social Security projection*

1981 Earnings	Retirement at age 62 in — 1985	1990	1995	2000	2005	Retirement at age 65** in — 1985	1990	1995	2000	2005
$10,000	36	37	37	37	38	45	45	44	45	45
12,500	34	34	34	35	35	42	41	41	42	42
15,000	32	32	33	33	33	40	39	39	39	40
17,500	30	31	31	32	32	38	38	37	38	38
20,000	28	28	29	29	30	34	34	34	35	35
25,000	23	24	24	25	26	28	29	29	30	31
30,000	20	20	21	22	23	24	25	25	26	27
35,000	17	17	18	19	20	21	21	22	23	23
40,000	15	15	16	17	17	18	19	19	20	21
45,000	13	13	14	15	15	16	16	17	18	18
50,000	12	12	13	13	14	15	15	15	16	16

* Increases as assumed in 1980 OASDHI Trustees' Report for purpose of "intermediate" projection: from 9.9 percent in 1981 down to 6.1 percent in 2005.

** Cost-of-living increases, applied to formula benefit beginning with year of attainment of age 62, assumed to range from 9.7 percent in 1981 to 4.0 percent in 2005.

Note: Retirement is assumed to occur early in the year, before the individual has earned enough to make it one of the computation years and before the CPI adjustment for the year has become effective.

Fig. 9.1 Social Security Benefits as Percentage of Earnings in Year Preceding Retirement—Model A

increases assumed by the trustees can be thought of as resulting from the combined effect of increases in the CPI and increases in real wages from improved productivity. An individual, however, may experience a salary progression representing the national average wage increase superimposed on an underlying progression reflecting promotions to higher paid jobs. Model B, therefore, is based on the same economic assumptions except that it represents a person whose earnings progression is at an annual rate one percent above the national average. For years before 1981, the worker is assumed to have had earnings moving with the national average in Model A and one percent a year above the average in Model B. The assumption as to the CPI, of course, affects only the figures for retirement at age 65. Retirement is assumed to occur early in the year, before the individual has earned enough to make it one of the computation years and before the cost-of-living adjustment for the year has become effective.

A Model A worker whose earnings in 1981 were $12,500 (the approximate national average in 1980), and who has always had and will continue to have the same earnings relative to the average, will retire at age 62 with a replacement rate of 34 percent–35 percent. If he continues working to age 65 under

National average wage assumed to increase in accordance with Social Security projection,* individual's earnings 1 percent faster

	Retirement at age 62 in —					*Retirement at age 65** in —*				
1981 Earnings	*1985*	*1990*	*1995*	*2000*	*2005*	*1985*	*1990*	*1995*	*2000*	*2005*
$10,000	33	33	32	32	32	41	40	39	38	38
12,500	31	30	30	30	29	38	37	36	36	35
15,000	29	28	28	28	28	36	35	34	34	34
17,500	28	27	27	27	27	35	34	33	33	32
20,000	27	26	26	25	25	33	32	31	30	29
25,000	22	22	22	21	21	28	27	26	26	26
30,000	19	19	19	19	19	23	23	22	22	22
35,000	16	16	16	16	16	20	20	19	19	19
40,000	14	14	14	14	14	18	17	17	17	17
45,000	13	12	12	12	12	16	15	15	15	15
50,000	11	11	11	11	11	14	14	13	13	13

* Increases as assumed in 1980 OASDHI Trustees' Report for purpose of "intermediate" projection: from 9.9 percent in 1981 down to 6.1 percent in 2005.

** Cost-of-living increases, applied to formula benefit beginning with year of attainment of age 62, assumed to range from 9.7 percent in 1981 to 4.0 percent in 2005.

Note: Retirement is assumed to occur early in the year, before the individual has earned enough to make it one of the computation years and before the CPI adjustment for the year has become effective.

Fig. 9.2 Social Security Benefit as Percentage of Earnings in Year Preceding Retirement—Model B

conditions of a projected annual increase in the CPI, he will retire with a replacement rate of 41 percent–42 percent. An individual earning $20,000 in 1981—a more representative figure for participants in private pension plans—whose earnings have progressed and will continue to do so at the same rate as the national average wage will retire at 62 with a replacement rate of 28 percent–30 percent or at age 65 with a replacement rate of 34 percent–35 percent.

A Model B worker whose 1981 earnings were $12,500 as in the first example, but who had reached that level with a progression of earnings one percent a year faster than the average and whose earnings will continue to progress at that faster rate will retire with a lower replacement rate—29 percent–31 percent at age 62 or 35 percent–38 percent at age 65. The $20,000 employee, on the same assumption as to a rate of salary advancement that is one percent greater than the increase in the average wage, will retire with a replacement rate of 25 percent–27 percent at age 62 or 29 percent–30 percent at age 65. By the same token, if the levels of $12,500 and $20,000 had been reached by a slower than average progression and will continue to advance more slowly, the replacement rates will be higher.

It will be noted that, under Model A, replacement rates are fairly stable with a slight tendency to rise in future years. Under Model B, as one would expect, the rates decline for later retirements.

A table constructed on the assumption that the national average wage pattern followed the pattern assumed for a worker in Model B would have been only negligibly different from the Model A table.

EFFECT OF 1977 AMENDMENTS ON PENSION PLANS

The fact that replacement rates under the 1977 amendments are substantially lower than they would have been under the previous law has the effect of raising the emerging costs of those pension plans that had previously been integrated with Social Security by means of a Social Security offset provision. About three out of four earnings-related pension plans provide a benefit based on final pay and, of these, three out of five offset it by a specified percentage of the Social Security benefit. Under a given pension formula, therefore, a reduction in the offset means a correspondingly higher benefit to be paid by the pension plan at a higher cost to the employer. From the standpoint of the employee, the higher pension partially compensates for the lower Social Security benefit.

Most of the final-pay plans that do not provide for a Social Security offset, as well as the great majority of the plans based on career-average pay, recognize Social Security indirectly by assigning a higher benefit-accrual rate to compensation above a specified amount and a lower accrual rate to compensation below that amount. Frequently, the specified amount in these step-rate plans is the Social Security wage base. Under the 1972 automatic escalator provision, the wage base in 1979, 1980, and 1981 would have increased over 1978 in proportion to the increase in the national average wage. The wage bases of $22,900, $25,900, and $29,700 mandated by the 1977 legislation were much higher than would have been obtained under the 1972 law. The effect of the 1977 law on step-rate plans tied to the wage base was therefore to reduce benefits and, consequently, employer costs.

WINDFALL BENEFITS

Reference has been made to the favorable treatment accorded low wage earners through the weighting of the benefit formula. Ironically, as this works out in practice, many people qualify for high benefits relative to their earnings not so much because they were low paid but because they were in noncovered employment in government or in nonprofit organizations for the major part of their career, or women out of the labor market for most of their working-life years, yet managed to obtain just enough covered employment to gain Social Security insurance status.

An employee reaching age 62 in 1982 needs only thirty-one quarters of coverage to qualify for a Social Security benefit and can meet the requirement on the basis of nominal employment of less than eight years. His average indexed earnings over eight calendar years of employment might have been, say, $450 a month, producing an AIME (because of sixteen zero years entering into the calculation) of $150 and a PIA also of $150.

A number of proposals have been made to eliminate such windfalls with their attendant disproportionate replacement rates: Mandatory coverage of presently excluded groups, reduction of Social Security benefits by some percentage of a pension earned in noncovered employment, and reduction of Social Security benefits in proportion to time spent in noncovered employment.

A solution, although urgently needed, is probably far off. None of the proposals mentioned will be accomplished without extensive public education and the overcoming of strong political objections.

PROPOSALS TO REDUCE BENEFITS

The financial difficulties of the Social Security system have prompted proposals to reduce benefits and it is unlikely that the 1977 amendments will remain the last word on either the basic formula or the indexing procedure. The National Commission on Social Security, for example, in January 1981 recommended that when over a two-year period the CPI has risen more rapidly than wages, the automatic benefit increase be equal to the two-year average rise in wages, with later "catch-up" increases when wages rise faster than prices. (Historically, wage increases have exceeded price increases, but in 1979, 1980, and 1981 the reverse was true.) At the same time it recommended that the Bureau of Labor Statistics evaluate a special price index for the elderly for this purpose and that the windfall portion of benefits arising from periods of noncovered government employment in the future be eliminated.

On a different level, the Commission also proposed that the range of eligibility ages for old-age benefits be raised—over a twelve-year period beginning in 2001—from ages 62–65 to ages 65–68. That is, 100 percent of the PIA would be payable at age 68 and only 80 percent at age 65. A similar proposal, but with the twelve-year phase-in period to begin in 1990, was made in February 1981 by the President's Commission on Pension Policy.

The Advisory Council on Social Security, in its 1979 report, recommended a new benefit formula that would increase benefits for long-term, low-wage workers and for high-wage workers. Its objectives are to guarantee long-service workers with average earnings at or somewhat below the federal minimum wage a benefit at least equal to the official poverty threshold, and at the same time to assure high-wage workers a benefit more in keeping with the value of their payroll taxes accumulated with interest. Benefits for workers with low average indexed earnings resulting from intermittent employment, on the other hand, would be sharply reduced. There would also be small reductions in benefits for career workers with AIME's falling within a band ranging from somewhat above the average to below the maximum.

EFFECT OF PROPOSED CHANGES IN FAMILY BENEFITS

In recent years a number of proposals have been made to restructure the Social Security system so as to eliminate certain perceived inequities in the treatment of men and women. A 1979 report by the then Department of Health, Education, and Welfare, "Social Security and the Changing Role of Men and Women," suggested certain fundamental changes that might be made in the law. Such changes would dramatically alter the pattern of individual (if not family) replacement rates and would therefore have a significant impact on private pension plans whose benefit formulas contain a Social Security offset.

The report is one of a series dealing with Social Security issues that has arisen because of changes in work patterns and family relationships since the law was passed, particularly, the increased labor-force participation of women and the increased rates of divorce and remarriage.

These changes in American society have given rise to questions about how women are treated under the Social Security programs. The programs were originally designed to meet the economic needs of the typical woman, namely, a lifetime homemaker dependent for her support on her breadwinner husband. Today, half the married women are in the labor market; many who are not will be when their children are older. Increased participation by women in the labor force, along with the growth in the divorce rate—from one in six then to one in two now—has created problems with which the Social Security system was not designed to deal.

The HEW report, without making a specific recommendation, suggested two new possible approaches for Congress to consider: The sharing of earnings and a double-decker benefit structure. The President's Commission on Pension Policy, in May 1980, recommended earnings sharing, contingent on further study.

Sharing of Earnings

Under earnings sharing, half of a couple's combined earnings would be credited separately to each spouse's individual earnings record. The benefits for each spouse would then be based on his or her own earnings while unmarried, combined with half of the couple's earnings while married. Among the many implications of the approach, one is noteworthy in any consideration of individual replacement rates: Retirement benefits to an employee who is or has been married will be reduced if he or she was the only earner or the higher earner of the couple. To take one example: Suppose a worker retires in 1982 at age 65 with average indexed monthly earnings of $1,200. If he was the only earner and his spouse is the same age, his benefit under the present law, before the June 1982 CPI increase, is $563 and the spouse's benefit $281, for a total of $844. Under the earnings-sharing approach, each partner (assuming they had been married throughout the wage earner's working career) would be credited with an AIME of $600 and receive a benefit of $349, for a total of $698. Thus, the Social Security benefit entering into an offset formula would be reduced, in this example, by 38 percent—from $563 to $349.

In the example given, the reduction in the employee's Social Security benefit would not be quite as large if his spouse had earnings; in fact his benefit would be increased if he was the lower earner. Thus, depending on whether they are or have ever been married and on the earnings contribution of their spouse(s), Social Security benefits will be different for different people with identical wage records.

Double-Decker Benefit Structure

Under the second approach suggested by HEW—a double-decker plan—there would be a flat dollar benefit payable regardless of earnings plus an earnings-related benefit, with certain features of earnings sharing incorporated in the second benefit component. The effect on the sole earner or the higher earner of a married couple would be the same as in the earnings-sharing approach—a reduction in his own Social Security benefit, the amount of the reduction depending on the earnings of his spouse. For the lower earner, the Social Security benefit would be increased.

Although it is not yet clear whether or how Congress will deal with these suggested approaches or their possible variations, it is clear that the adoption of any one of them will have an important effect on Social Security offset plans. If such a plan remains unchanged, it will find itself paying different benefits to employees with similar earnings histories. More important, its cost will rise because offsets will generally be smaller. If it is to be changed to permit approximately the same *amount* of offset as before, it may have a problem, among other things, with the IRS rulings on Social Security integration. Changes in these rulings will probably have to be made and individual employers will have to take them into account in redesigning their pension formulas.

CURRENT PROPOSALS

Proposals made by the administration in March (as part of the budget) and in May of 1981 and under consideration in Fall 1981 would affect the calculation of Social Security benefits, and therefore replacement rates, in a number of important ways:

- Reduction in the rate of increase of bendpoints—The bendpoints entering into the calculation of the PIA, currently scheduled to increase each year by 100 percent of the increase in the national wage, would increase by only 50 percent for the five-year period 1982-1987, after which the 100 percent factor would be restored. Under this change, benefits for persons retiring at age 65 in 1987 or later would be reduced by an average of 9.5 percent.
- Reduction of early retirement benefits—The proportion of the PIA payable at age 62 would be reduced from the current 80 percent to 55 percent. That is, the reduction factors for retirement before age 65 would be increased from an annual rate of 6⅔ percent of the PIA to 15 percent.
- Increase in the number of computation years—The number of computation years entering into the determination of the AIME would be increased by three. Thus, for a person reaching age 62 in 1982, the AIME would be averaged over twenty-nine years instead of twenty-six as at present; for one reaching 62 in 1991 or later it would be averaged over a maximum of thirty-eight years instead of the present maximum of thirty-five. All beneficiaries would incur a benefit reduction since their work histories would be extended to include three additional years of lower earnings or no earnings. Naturally, those retiring before age 65 would suffer a larger cut than those retiring at 65 or later. For a person who has always had maximum covered earnings and retires at age 62 at the beginning of 1982, the PIA is $593.60. Under the proposal, it would have been $587. For those whose earnings were less than maximum or who had been out of the labor market one or more years, the reduction can be substantially greater.

10

Defined Benefit Pension Plans

G. Ashley Cooper

Actuary, The Wyatt Company

BASIC PRINCIPLES

Characteristics of a Pension Plan

In simple terms, the main characteristics of a pension plan may be summarized as follows:

- It consists of a more or less formal program providing benefits to employees or a group of employees.
- It is established by an employer or an employee organization or, as part of the collective bargaining process, by a joint board of representatives of a union and a group of employers. This implies that a pension plan is part of the conditions of employment.
- Its main objective is to provide retirement income to employees, with emphasis on benefits after retirement and on some form of income payable periodically. Many pension plans contain other forms of benefits, such as lump sums, but they are usually offered as alternatives to the primary *pension* benefit.
- In addition, it may contain what are usually referred to as *ancillary benefits* payable on death, disability, or other types of termination of employment apart from retirement. However, Internal Revenue Service regulations require that these ancillary benefits be no more than incidental to the prime purpose of providing retirement income.

Defined Benefits vs. Defined Contributions

An important distinction should be made between a *defined benefit* pension plan and a *defined contribution* plan, which is often referred to as a *money purchase* plan. Two key elements differentiate the two types of plans:

As its name implies, the defined benefit plan promises specific benefits in specific circumstances, such as an employee's retirement.

Note that benefits are not necessarily the same for all employees. Typically, these plans provide benefits related to service, and perhaps salary, under a formula that determines how much an employee or his beneficiary will receive. By contrast, the defined contribution plan promises that certain contributions will be credited to the employee's account and that he will be entitled to all or a part of the value of this account should he, for example, retire.

The defined contribution plan requires the establishment of individual accounts for each employee participating in the plan because it is funded through the accumulation (with interest and capital appreciation) of the contributions made on behalf of each employee.

Neither type of plan is clearly superior in all circumstances, and in practice many employers operate both types concurrently. Each has its own advantages which are summarized below.

Advantages of Defined Benefit Plans. The principal advantages of the defined benefit plan are:

- It concentrates on ends rather than means; that is to say it emphasizes the resulting benefit to the employee or beneficiary. An employer can set benefit targets and design the plan to achieve those targets with relative accuracy.
- Benefit targets may be attained more easily because benefits may be based on salary close to retirement (the so-called final-average-pay formula, which will be described later in this section).
- It can recognize past service of the employee, when the plan is first established. A defined contribution plan, on the other hand, does little for employees already past the middle of their working lives when the plan is adopted.
- Likewise, the employee can budget expecting to receive a determinable benefit. (However, as the illustration shows, the benefit from a defined contribution plan will vary, especially in accordance with the investment performance of the account. This drawback to the defined contribution plan is particularly significant if an employee retires at a time when the stock or bond market is depressed.)
- Most employers find a defined benefit plan easier to administer mainly because contributions and investment income do not have to be allocated to individual accounts.

Advantages of Defined Contribution Plans. The defined contribution plan has its corresponding advantages:

- The employer's cost, as a percentage of profits or a percentage of payroll, is predictable. In a defined benefit plan, it must be estimated on the basis of actuarial assumptions, and experience may depart widely from the estimates.

- Some employees can relate more easily to an account that is growing each year than to a pension payable many years in the future.
- Defined contribution plans are controlled less rigorously under ERISA than defined benefit plans.
- In some ways, defined contribution plans are more flexible in meeting employee needs since they can be structured to allow withdrawals or loans for house purchase, children's education and other medium-term objectives.

Setting Benefit Targets

Under a defined benefit plan, the benefit target refers to the amount of pension the employer believes should be provided for his employees. Setting quantitative targets is not a simple matter and involves considering such questions as:

- The general level of pension in relation to pay just before retirement.
- Whether Social Security benefits should be considered as providing part of the target pension.
- Whether any other plans, such as savings or thrift, should be considered as part of, or supplemental to, the target pension.
- Whether the employee should bear part of the responsibility of providing for his own pension, and if so, how much.
- How the target pension should be influenced by the employee's service. Most employers believe that the target should be achieved only after a full career of, say, thirty or thirty-five years. The question then arises whether the benefit should be proportionately reduced for shorter periods of service.
- The degree to which the target should vary with pay. There is a general feeling that pensions (as a percentage of pay before retirement) should be higher for lower paid employees than for higher paid employees.

Maintenance of Standard of Living. A question often posed is whether or not it would be possible to provide a pension which, after allowance for taxes, would give the retired employee the same standard of living that he enjoyed before retirement. There are no definitive studies on this subject, or on such specific questions as whether allowance should be made for work-related expenses, personal savings, family status, completion of house purchase, and children's education. In general terms, it appears that a total pension of about 80 percent of preretirement income would be required to preserve the standard of living of most retired employees. Interestingly, this percentage does not vary widely by income level.

Prevalent Targets. In practice, a pension of 80 percent of pay immediately before retirement is rather more generous than most plans provide in the United States, even allowing for Social Security benefits. At this time at least, typical pension targets are as shown in Figure 10.1.

	Pension Target		
Category	*Meager*	*Average*	*Generous*
Low-paid	50%	65%	80%
Medium-paid	40%	55%	65%
Executives	30%	40%	50%

Fig. 10.1 Pension Targets As Percent of Final Pay

Collective Bargaining

For many years, input as to employee desires on pension and other employee benefits came almost exclusively through collective bargaining. This process essentially began with the *Inland Steel* decision in 1948, when the U.S. Supreme Court upheld that benefits were a mandatory subject for bargaining. Since then, unions have come a long way in developing pensions for their members and have been pioneers in other benefit areas. As an illustration, Figure 10.2 shows the pension benefit formulas negotiated between the United Auto Workers (UAW) and General Motors Corporation since 1950, when the first UAW pension plan was adopted.

Pattern Plans. Well-known "pattern plans" of the major unions, such as UAW and United Steelworkers, have emerged from these negotiations. These plans are first negotiated with leading firms in the industry and then copied, perhaps with modifications, by other companies in the same and related industries.

An interesting feature has been the prevalence of union-negotiated pension plans with benefits expressed as a certain number of fixed dollars per month

Year	*Benefit Formula—Monthly Pension For Each Year of Service*
1950	$ 1.50 (maximum 30 years)
1952	1.75 (maximum 30 years)
1955	2.25
1958	2.40 to 2.50
1961	2.40 to 2.50
1964	4.25
1967	5.50 to 6.00
1970	7.25 to 7.75
1973	8.00 to 8.50
1979	15.75 to 16.50

Fig. 10.2 Pension Benefit Formulas Negotiated Between UAW and General Motors Corp.

for each year of service. Employers have favored adoption of a pension benefit that does not increase automatically as salaries increase. At the same time, union negotiators are eager to show that bargaining has produced a concrete increase in pension benefits. Thus, there is a curious common interest between company and union negotiators.

Legislative Constraints

Legislation has a major impact on the design of both defined benefit and defined contribution plans; it even affects the decision of whether or not to adopt a plan. The major legislation affecting employee benefits, described in detail elsewhere in this handbook, include the following.

Social Security. Pension plan designers must take into account the significant benefits paid by Social Security (see Chapters 9 and 14).

Internal Revenue Code. The Internal Revenue Code introduced the concept of regulating or supervising private pension plans by a governmental agency. The current code was enacted in 1954 but has since been amended and supplemented by a vast number of regulations, revenue rulings, technical information releases, and other official material, which together form a massive and complex set of requirements (see Chapter 14.) The Code is an important factor in benefit plan design for the following reasons:

- In general terms, employers do not receive a tax deduction for their contributions to a pension plan unless it is "qualified" or approved under the terms of the Code. Since tax deductibility means a reduction in cost of about 50 percent, the importance of qualification is evident.
- The Code is basically written to limit tax deductions and to prevent abuse, e.g., a plan should not discriminate in favor of stockholders, supervisors, and more highly compensated employees. To prevent discrimination, requirements affecting eligibility and benefit formulas have been imposed; many control plan design in a direct manner.
- The Code also specifies how benefits will be taxed in the hands of employees or their beneficiaries, which has an indirect bearing on how benefits are structured.
- Finally, it is worth noting that the Internal Revenue Code affects areas other than plan design such as reporting, plan documentation, and financing.

Employee Retirement Income Security Act. Title I of ERISA spells out a substantial number of standards that pension plans must satisfy and most of them are reproduced (in Title II) as amendments to the Internal Revenue Code.

ERISA requires that pension plans comply with specific requirements as to:

- Participation clauses
- Vesting
- Pension benefit formulas
- Death benefits
- Maximum pensions

In addition, ERISA introduced termination provisions, plan reinsurance, and minimum funding standards, all of which have an indirect effect on pension plan design. (See Chapter 14 for a detailed discussion of ERISA provisions.) Another, but unintended, result due largely to increases in paper work and in fiduciary liabilities, has been the reluctance to adopt new plans and to favor defined contribution rather than defined benefit plans.

Age Discrimination. The 1978 Amendment to the Age Discrimination in Employment Act (ADEA) prohibits mandatory or unilateral retirement of employees before age 70, and requires equal employment conditions for older and younger employees. An Interpretative Bulletin on employee benefit plans allows benefits to be reduced with increasing age if costs increase with age, and includes special exceptions for retirement plans. However, in the long run these exceptions may disappear and benefit plans may be required to treat an employee, e.g., age 66 in exactly the same manner as an employee age 46.

Sex Discrimination. Sex discrimination is another area where future developments are expected. It is illegal to discriminate in conditions of employment between men and women but the application to benefit plans has been unclear. In view of recent court decisions, including the U.S. Supreme Court in the *Manhart* [1] case, the pace of events is quickening. It is now relatively clear that benefits and contributions under pension plans must be the same for both sexes. The next step is probably more detailed rules on optional benefits such as early retirement and elective forms of pension. These admittedly somewhat minor points present difficult technical questions.

Cost Considerations

The Nature of Pension Costs. The "cost" of pension payable from age 65 for an employee, e.g., age 40 is not intuitively apparent. In fact, the whole subject of pension plan costs is complex and depends on the employment of actuarial techniques. A description of the process is given in considerable detail in Chapter 11, but a relevant point is that a defined benefit pension plan carries, not a single cost, but a *range* of possible costs depending on the degree of optimism or pessimism involved in predictions of future events. If

---

[1] Manhart v. City of Los Angeles, 553 F.2d 581 (9th Cir. 1976).

predictions (especially of inflation, investment return, and other economic factors) are pessimistic, plan costs will tend to be higher, or more "conservative," than if the predictions are optimistic. This leads to the somewhat confusing result that "costs" can vary, often within wide limitations, for plans that have quite similar provisions.

Typical Cost Levels. Ignoring for the moment the issues of actuarial methodology, it may be instructive to review some statistics that give an idea of average levels of pension plan costs. The data shown in Figure 10.3 below covers the funds of companies in the Fortune 1000 ranking of large U.S. corporations.

Fortune Rank	*Total Wage and Salary Payroll*	*Contributions as Percent of Payroll*			
		Total EBF Plans	*Pension Plans*	*Profit-Sharing Plans*	*Savings and Thrift Plans*
001–100	$ 95,697	14%	9%	1%	6%
101–200	$ 32,359	11%	5%	1%	2%
201–300	$ 12,173	7%	5%	1%	2%
301–400	$ 10,979	6%	5%	1%	1%
401–500	$ 8,561	6%	5%	1%	1%
501–600	$ 4,288	6%	6%	3%	1%
601–700	$ 2,549	7%	4%	1%	2%
701–800	$ 3,462	6%	4%	1%	2%
801–900	$ 1,783	5%	3%	2%	1%
901–1000	$ 1,397	6%	5%	2%	1%
Total Utilities	$ 25,878	12%	10%	1%	4%
Large Utilities	$ 20,694	15%	12%	0%	5%
Medium Utilities	$ 4,431	11%	8%	0%	3%
Small Utilities	$ 752	7%	6%	1%	2%
Retailers	$ 10,624	8%	5%	2%	4%
Transportation	$ 4,257	5%	4%	0%	0%
Total Companies	$224,959	8%	6%	2%	2%

Source: 1979 Report of Large Corporate Pension Funds, prepared by Greenwich Research Associates.

Fig. 10.3 Average Levels of Pension Plan Costs of U.S. Corporations

Pension plan contributions for all companies in the survey average 6 percent of payroll, a substantial cost for most employers.

The Importance of Plan Costs. Naturally, the extent to which pension costs are a matter of concern will vary from one employer to another. Major factors are the nature of the industry, particularly whether it is labor intensive or capital intensive, and the employer's profit margin.

Another issue which interests employees but which is seldom voiced, is the manner in which costs are determined. There is an interesting question whether employees would prefer a good plan which is poorly (that is, less conservatively) funded or a less generous plan which is more conservatively funded.

Impact of ERISA. Legislative restraints are also tied into cost considerations, primarily through the provisions of ERISA. This Act contains specific minimum funding standards (described in Chapter 14) and allows for regulations to be published to describe which actuarial methodology will be acceptable.

NORMAL RETIREMENT PENSION

The Concept of Normal Retirement

The formal document detailing the provisions of a defined benefit pension plan will almost invariably contain a definition of "Normal Retirement Date." A very large percentage (probably 90 percent or more) of U.S. pension plans are built around the concept of "normal retirement" at age 65. This high degree of uniformity has almost certainly come from the Social Security Act, under which no benefit was payable before age 65 until this Act was amended in 1956. Age 65 has also been considered the proper normal retirement age under many foreign social security programs, especially in Europe.

Perhaps the best known exceptions are that of airline pilots where "normal" retirement is set at age 55 or age 60, or plans for police officers and firemen that often set no retirement age but provide pensions after a specified period of service. Exceptions to the rule also include pension plans that provide that normal retirement date be no earlier than ten years from the time a participant joined the plan. Thus, an employee entering at age 57 would have normal retirement deferred until age 67. The objective of this rule was to control costs, since the contribution to fund over a period of less than ten years could become unduly high.

The traditional concept of a fixed normal retirement age has become weakened, and many plans provide just as good a benefit (in relation to pay and service) at e.g., age 60 or age 62, as they do at age 65. Also, a number of plans, notably those for large groups of union employees, now regard retirement at any age after thirty or thirty-five years of service as "normal" and entitling the employee to a full pension. In other words, the concept of a *normal retirement range,* extending from age 55 to age 70 is replacing that of one normal retirement age. Within this range, any retirement will be considered "normal," depending on the individual's desires, health, and other circumstances.

Despite this changing practice, defining a normal retirement date provides a convenient frame of reference in plan design and documentation. This convention has also been reinforced by the provisions of ERISA that stipulate that a plan may not set the normal retirement age later than age 65 (except with respect to individuals who become participants after age 55).

The Benefit Formula

Every defined benefit pension plan includes a description of how the benefit will be calculated. That is often referred to as the *benefit formula.* The formula defines the pension that will be paid at normal retirement, while some derivative of the formula generally defines benefits payable at other times, such as death or disability.

Key Parameters. The benefit formula typically contains one or more of the following parameters:

A service factor. Most employers and employees believe it is only fair for the participant with, say, forty years of service to receive a larger pension than the participant with only ten years of service. However, under varying circumstances the formula may be weighted to give more or less emphasis to longer or shorter service.

A salary relationship. A large number of pension plans base pensions on salary level so that the higher paid employee receives a larger pension. The rationale is that, inasmuch as at retirement the pension replaces pay, the higher paid employee needs a higher pension to maintain all or a portion of his previous standard of living. On the other hand, an important category of benefit formulas is not pay related (see dollar-per-month benefit formulas described later in this chapter).

Social Security recognition. Social Security provides old-age benefits which constitute a significant replacement of pay, as high as 50 percent for lower paid employees. Although the wage base, or ceiling on salary for Social Security purposes, and deliberate weighting of the benefit formula in favor of the lower paid, causes the percentage of pay replacement to be much lower for higher paid employees, it is generally recognized that Social Security benefits are too large to be ignored.

Recognition of Social Security may be indirect; for example the benefit formula may be set at a lower level than it would have been if no Social

Security existed. Or recognition may be direct by adjusting the benefit formula to coordinate it with the government pension. Those formulas that are directly coordinated with Social Security are typically referred to as *"integrated" benefit formulas.*

Types of Benefit Formulas. Most of the hundreds, if not thousands, of different benefit formulas are based on the following three basic types of formula, together with their variations and combinations. (Set aside for the moment the complication of integration with Social Security.)

Dollar-per-month benefit formulas. In these formulas, the benefit is not related to pay, but normally to service, for example a benefit at retirement of $10 per month for each year of service.

A common variant is for the plan to specify a maximum period of service, e.g., thirty-five years, to be credited for benefit purposes. In this event, participants would receive the same $350 per month for thirty-five years of service, or for thirty-six years, or forty years. Another modification introduces a variation in benefit according to pay level, e.g.:

Pay Per Year	*Benefit Per Year of Service*
Up to $12,000	$10.00 per month
$12,000 to $18,000	$12.50 per month
Over $18,000	$15.00 per month

These dollar-per-month benefit formulas are the norm under multiemployer plans. In addition, they are common under union-negotiated plans, with the United Auto Workers' (UAW) plan as a prime example. The structure of this type of plan fits the pattern of collective bargaining which usually calls for contract negotiations every two or three years. When benefits are increased, the higher level of pension usually applies to all service of presently active employees, whether the service is before or after the effective date of the increase. Benefit increases for employees who have already retired are usually negotiated separately.

Union agreements, especially those that extend for three years or more, also commonly specify benefit increases in the later years of the contract. For example, the agreement might provide for benefits of:

- $12.00 per month per year of service for employees retiring in 1979.
- $13.00 per month per year of service for employees retiring in 1980.
- $14.00 per month per year of service for employees retiring in 1981, and later.

Career-average-pay formula (or career pay). As the name implies, the benefit is based on the employee's pay throughout his career, or more normally, his career as a plan participant. The formula is usually expressed as a percentage (say 2 percent) of each year's pay while a participant in the plan. If pay in a given year is $15,000, then the benefit credit for that year of service would be $300, and the final benefit at retirement would be the sum of 2 percent times pay for each of the participating years. Nonparticipation years (i.e., years before the plan was adopted) are commonly recognized by imputing to them the salary at the time of adoption. When the benefit credited for a particular year of service is known and fixed, administration is simplified. However, promotions to higher paying jobs and the impact of inflation cause benefits to be inadequate. When an employee retires, part of his benefit credit will be based on pay many years before, when his pay may have been a half or a third of his final pay. This inflation impact can be countered by using a larger benefit accrual rate, say 3 percent of each year's pay instead of 2 percent. However, this change could cause benefits to be unduly generous if inflation turns out to be less than expected.

Another solution to the problem of erosion by inflation is known as *updating*. Under this procedure, illustrated below, the benefit accrued up to a specified date (which will have been based on pay up to that date) is increased according to a formula related to more current pay.

Assume that a participant has twenty years of service under a plan and that his salary has increased from $10,000 per year to $29,000 per year with equal annual increases of $1,000 per year. Under a benefit formula of 2 percent of each year's salary, the participant will have accrued a total pension of $7,800. If the benefit is now "updated" on the basis of the same 2 percent formula being applied to the average of the last five years salary, the accrued benefit would be $10,800 (2 percent for twenty years on $27,000 of salary).

There is considerable flexibility to this updating procedure. For instance, it could be based on 1.5 percent of the last three years annual salary, in which case the accrued benefit would be $8,400 (1.5 percent for twenty years on a salary of $28,000). In no event, though, may the updating ever decrease the amount of the accrued pension. Accruals after the updating procedure would be calculated according to the regular benefit formula (2 percent of each year's salary for the example considered). This process could continue until another updating is made.

Final-average-pay formula (or final pay). In this type of formula, the benefit for all years of service is based on salary close to the time of retirement, for example 1.5 percent per year of the average salary during the last five years of service.

The use of real "final pay," in the sense of pay immediately prior to retirement, is not common. In the first place it would probably not be acceptable under current IRS regulations. And secondly, benefits would tend to fluctuate abnormally since they would be affected by salary increases (or possibly decreases) occurring just before the time of retirement.

The wide variety of ways in which "final average salary" has been defined in private salary related plans is illustrated below:

- The average salary over the last three years
- The average salary over the last five years
- The average salary over the last ten years
- The average salary over the highest three (or five) consecutive years in the last ten years
- The average salary over the highest three (or five) consecutive years in the participant's career

Final-average-pay plans have become increasingly common over the last ten to fifteen years. Although adoption of a final-average-pay benefit formula was formerly considered to represent a "blank check" signed by the employer, employers, in increasing numbers, have come to realize that only a final-average-pay plan will achieve pension targets that are based on the concept of pay replacement and will automatically compensate for inflation that occurs up to the time of the employee's retirement. (An important counter-argument holds that a career-average-pay plan with frequent updating will achieve the same objectives, and that moreover, each updating is under the control of the employer and carries a relatively fixed cost, which need not be assumed if the employer cannot afford to meet it.)

Final-average-pay plans provide flexibility in other areas. First, there can be a maximum on service, for example 1.5 percent of final average salary per year of service up to forty years. Secondly, the formula can be *"front-loaded"* to provide a higher rate of benefit accrual during, e.g., the first twenty years. This will give a proportionately higher benefit to an employee, who may be a key member of management, hired at age 40 or 45. An example of a frontloaded formula is as follows: 2 percent of final average salary for each year of service up to twenty years plus one percent of final average salary for each year of service over twenty years. Note that front-loading can also be applied to career-average-pay formulas. Theoretically, it is possible to have a benefit formula that is "backloaded," e.g., one percent for the first twenty years and 2 percent thereafter. However, ERISA restricts the ability to backload and this particular formula would not be acceptable. In practice, few companies feel there is any strong reason for backloading.

Advantages and Disadvantages. The principal advantages and disadvantages of the three basic types of benefit formula are summarized in Figure 10.4.

Combinations of Formulas. A number of employers have attempted to combine the advantages of two or more formulas. For example, it is possible to have part of the benefit based on career-average-pay and part on final-average-pay. Another device is to adopt a career-average-pay formula, with

Advantages	*Disadvantages*
Dollar-Per-Month-Formula	
Stable cost until benefit level revised	Cannot pre-fund future benefit increases
Credit to employer when benefits increased	No allowance for inflation before retirement
Simple to understand and administer	No distinction by salary level
Career-Average-Pay Formula	
Cost is more predictable	Benefits eroded by inflation unless updated
Concept simple to understand	Tends to penalize employees with rapid salary increases
Final-Average-Pay Formula	
Direct achievement of benefit targets	Costs unstable and likely to escalate under inflation
Automatic allowance for inflation before retirement	Can become complex and difficult to administer, especially if integrated

Fig. 10.4 Advantages and Disadvantages of the Three Basic Types of Benefit Formula

a final-average-pay minimum benefit. In this case, the plan would pay whichever benefit proves to be the larger of, say:

- 2 percent of each year's salary (career-average-pay).
- 1.5 percent per year of service of final-average-pay.

Obviously, combinations such as these increase the complexity of the plan, making it harder for employees to understand and for the employer to administer. Moreover, the formulas considered so far have ignored the complications introduced by integration with Social Security.

Integration With Social Security

Integration implies that the pension plan's benefit formula should allow in some way for the existence of a Social Security benefit. This benefit is significant at lower pay levels (around 40 percent to 50 percent of final salary for salaries up to about $20,000) but is far smaller, in terms of pay replacement, at the higher pay levels. Another important feature of Social Security is that it is dynamic: both the wage base and benefit level increase automatically with the rise in the national average wage, while the whole system is frequently revised by congressional action. (See Chapter 9 for a detailed discussion of Social Security Replacement Rates.)

Basically, the idea behind integration is that, since Social Security provides a proportionately larger benefit for lower paid employees, the private pension plan should counter this bias by providing a relatively larger benefit for higher paid employees.

IRS Restrictions. To prevent pension plans from using integration as a device to discriminate unduly in favor of the higher-paid executives, the Internal Revenue Service lays down a set of *integration rules* which must be satisfied by all qualified plans. These rules are extremely complicated but, in essence, they set a maximum degree of bias in favor of higher-paid employees. In addition, there are special adjustments for plans that include death, disability, or early retirement benefits, or provide for employee contributions. (Chapter 14 discusses in detail the legal implications of integration.)

Methods of Integration. The three generally recognized methods of integration are discussed below. However, there is no standard terminology and it is not uncommon to find these methods described differently. Another point to be noted is that, with few exceptions, dollar-per-month benefit formulas are not integrated. (One exception, in the form of a "cap" on the combined pension and Social Security benefit, is a form of integration on which the IRS has not yet ruled.)

Excess method. The excess method is sometimes referred to as the *salary deduction* or *franchise* method. The rationale is that Social Security provides an adequate benefit on a certain slice of an employee's salary, so the private plan can base its benefit only on salary above that slice. A typical benefit formula under this method might be:

> 50 percent of final average earnings in excess of $10,000 per year, after thirty years of service. For service of less than thirty years, the benefit is proportionately reduced.

Note that no benefit at all is provided on earnings up to $10,000 per year, which is usually referred to as the *breakpoint*. (Typically, the breakpoint is set at the Social Security wage base, for career-average plans, and almost always quite a bit lower in final-pay plans. However, subject to the IRS integration rules, it could be set at any figure.) If the plan provides for a fixed-dollar breakpoint, it can easily, and quite quickly, become outdated because of changes in Social Security. Amending the plan to bring the breakpoint into line with current conditions might be resisted since it involves decreasing the prospective benefits from the plan. The solution to this problem, common to all integration formulas that are based on fixed-dollar amounts, is to select a breakpoint, such as the Social Security wage base, which moves automatically over time. If the breakpoint is set equal to or some percentage of the Social Security wage base, the benefit formula will be relatively meager since it provides no benefit for employees earning less than the wage base and the integration rules limit the benefit on earnings above the wage base. For this reason, the excess method is becoming less common than in the past.

This method ties in to the structure of final-average-pay benefit formulas, and is primarily used with that type of plan. However, it can be used with a career-average formula.

Formula method. The formula method has a variety of other names, such as the *step-formula* or *two-formula* method. It is really a modification of the excess method, with a smaller benefit payable on salary up to the breakpoint and a larger benefit payable on salary above the breakpoint. Here are two examples:

- A career-average-pay formula of one percent of each year's salary up to the Social Security wage base for that year *plus* 2 percent of each year's salary above that wage base.
- A final-average-pay formula providing, for each year of credited service, a benefit of one percent of final average earnings up to $9,000 *plus* 1½ percent of final average earnings in excess of $9,000.

As in the case of the excess method, the breakpoint may be fixed in dollars or may float automatically with the Social Security wage base. There are also the same problems if a fixed breakpoint is selected and there are material changes in Social Security benefits. The formula method is subject to essentially the same integration rules as the excess method. In fact, the IRS views a formula-type plan (such as in the second example above) as a combination of a flat unintegrated plan (providing one percent of final average earnings) and an excess plan (of one-half percent of final average earnings above $9,000).

This type of integration is suitable for both career-average and final-average types of benefit formulas, subject to the complications of using the Social Security wage base as the breakpoint under final-average-pay plans.

Offset method. The offset method of integration uses a totally different principle, namely that of direct deduction of a part of the Social Security benefit. In each case, a portion of the Social Security benefit is deducted from a "gross" benefit formula to determine the "net" pension. Some examples are as follows:

- 60 percent of final average earnings *less* 75 percent of primary Social Security benefit, after thirty years of service. Benefit is reduced proportionately for lesser service.
- 1½ percent of final average earnings per year of credited service *minus* 50 percent of the Social Security benefit.

- For each year of credited service up to forty years, 1½ percent of final average earnings minus 1¼ percent of primary Social Security benefit.

One major question facing the plan designer is how much Social Security should be offset. The integration rules essentially allow a maximum offset of 83⅓ percent of the primary Social Security benefit, provided there are no special death, disability, or early retirement benefits. In practice, some ancillary benefits usually serve to reduce the integration limit. Inasmuch as there are logical reasons for using a 50 percent offset since employees pay half the total FICA contribution, many, but not all, plans point toward a 50 percent Social Security offset.

A special category of plans, usually known as *100 percent offset plans,* provides for a deduction of *all* of the Social Security benefit. Satisfaction of the integration rules is accomplished by giving a larger "gross pension" to lower paid employees. The result is a benefit formula which can be described in tabular form, as in the following example.

Final Average Earnings		*Total Benefit Percentage*
From	*To*	*Including Social Security*
—0—	$10,000	85%
$10,000	12,000	80%
12,000	15,000	75%
15,000	20,000	70%
20,000	30,000	65%
30,000	and over	60%

In practice, arrangements are made to prevent a discontinuity as salary changes from one bracket to another and to allow for proportionate reduction of benefits for service of less than a full career.

A second major question is whether the offset, at, e.g., 50 percent, should apply regardless of service (as in the second example above) or whether it should be prorated according to service at retirement. Prorating is generally considered to be more equitable; otherwise an employee could have a double (or even triple) offset of 50 percent if he participated in two (or three) different plans that did not prorate the offset.

The key characteristic of the offset method is that it integrates adequately no matter what happens to the wage base or benefit formula under Social Security. However, this advantage carries with it two potential problems. First there is a tendency for the system to be unpopular with employees, since an increase in Social Security is accompanied by a decrease in the private pension. This problem can, however, be resolved by good employee communications. Secondly, if Social Security benefits decrease (as they did in 1977), employer costs will increase.

Another feature is that the offset method does not work well with career-average-pay benefit formulas, unless they are frequently updated. Resulting pensions tend to be severely depressed because the gross benefit is based on earnings over the whole career while the offset is based on conditions at the time of retirement.

Advantages and Disadvantages. The principal advantages and disadvantages of the three integration methods are summarized in Figure 10.5.

Advantages	*Disadvantages*
	Excess and Formula Methods
Simple to understand	May be meager benefits for lower paid
Relatively simple to administer	Restricted benefits for higher paid
Some benefit to all participants	No allowance for changes in Social Security benefits
Works with career-average and final-average plans	Problems with changing fixed-dollar breakpoint
Stable costs	
	Offset Method
Automatic allowance for all Social Security changes	Requires good employee communications
Ties in closely to benefit objectives	Costs increase if Social Security decreases

Fig. 10.5 Advantages and Disadvantages of the Three Types of Integration Methods

Pay for Pension Purposes

As already indicated, a large proportion of defined benefit pension plans have pay-related benefit formulas. A necessary question is: What is pay?

In the early development of pension plans, *pay* (or *compensation*) was typically defined as *base* salary or wages. Objections have been raised that the use of base pay discriminates against lower paid employees since important elements of compensation such as overtime and shift differentials are omitted, and penalizes higher paid employees as much or more since it omits bonuses and similar payments.

There has also been a growing realization that, for significant numbers of employees, compensation above base salary represents an important part of take-home pay. Clearly this is true for many salesmen who are remunerated to a large extent by commissions, but it is also increasingly true for middle and upper levels of management who receive bonuses and other types of incentive compensation, and to hourly employees for whom overtime pay is significant.

There is, therefore, a general movement toward including commission, bonuses, and other special payments in the definition of "pay." If they are included as part of the qualified plan, the anti-discrimination regulations will virtually force inclusion of overtime and other payments to lower paid employees as well. The result of this trend may be widespread acceptance of a definition of pay which includes virtually all compensation, or all taxable compensation, a definition, incidentally, that is acceptable to the IRS.

Credited Service

Another parameter in the majority of benefit formulas is *service* and this too needs to be defined with precision.

Different Kinds of Service. As Chapter 14 of this handbook describes, ERISA has introduced a number of complexities in the area of service definitions. As a result many plans now include definitions of three kinds of service:

- *Service* in the general sense, which often encompasses service for purposes of participation in the plan.
- *Credited service,* which is service for calculation of benefit amounts.
- *Vesting service,* which is a different period specifically for determining the extent to which benefits are vested.

Service for Benefit Accrual. Credited service, or service for purposes of the benefit formula, is usually defined in one of two ways:

1. It includes all service (as that term is defined) starting from the date of employment.
2. It comprises service only while the employee is actually participating in the plan. This latter definition is particularly common in plans that require participants to contribute, since it would be somewhat illogical to give credit for periods of service when the employee did not contribute.

Service for Time Worked. Another important distinction between plans is whether credited service merely depends on continued service as an employee or whether it depends on the actual period (usually measured in hours) that the employee worked. ERISA allows, and many plans covering hourly or part-time employees so provide, that the benefit credit be reduced for employees who do not work a full year. A typical provision along these lines might provide for credited service to be accumulated as follows:

Hours Worked in Year	*Credited Service Counted*
Up to 500	One-Quarter Year
501 to 1,000	One-Half Year
1,001 to 1,500	Three-Quarters Year
1,501 and over	One Year

The Accrued Benefit

In the discussion so far, the benefit formula has been considered as it applies to normal retirement, usually at age 65. However, many employees retire at other ages and separation from service may occur at much younger ages. A defined benefit pension plan must, therefore, specify how the benefit formula will operate in cases where the participant leaves service before normal retirement age. The benefit to be credited at that point in time is referred to as the *accrued benefit*. In fact, ERISA requires that every plan define the accrued benefit. There are, moreover, a series of requirements (see Chapter 14) that the accrued benefit of every plan covered by ERISA must meet.

Methods of Definition. Most plans defined the "accrued benefit" in one of two ways. For ease of understanding, the two procedures are described in relation to a benefit formula that provides, at normal retirement age, $10 per month per year of service, up to a maximum of twenty years. Assume that the participant involved was hired (and entered the plan) at age 25 and is terminating service at age 45. The two basic methods of calculating his accrued benefit are as follows:

1. Merely apply the benefit formula to service (and, if relevant, salary) up to the date of termination. In the example, the employee has completed twenty years of service and will, therefore, have accrued the maximum pension of $200 per month.
2. Assume that normal retirement benefits are accrued evenly over the years from entry (or hire) up to normal retirement age. The procedure therefore, involves projecting the pension expected to be payable at normal retirement age, on the basis of continued service and, if relevant, continued salary. The accrued benefit is then the projected benefit multiplied by the ratio of actual service to date of termination to prospective service at normal retirement age. In the example noted, the participant would have forty years of service at age 65, which would give a prospective benefit of $200 per month. However, actual completed service at age 45 is only twenty years which is half the amount of prospective service. In this event, the accrued benefit would be half the prospective benefit or only $100 per month.

ERISA does allow other methods but they are used infrequently.

Details of Calculation. The accrued benefit definition must, of course, give full and complete details of the method of calculation, whichever of these two procedures is adopted. One area that needs special handling is the definition of the Social Security benefit when an employee terminates before age 62, which is the earliest age from which Social Security is payable. The plan must provide for an *estimate* of Social Security and specify the basis on which the estimate will be made. Some plans make the calculation assuming no future earnings while others assume that earnings would have continued unchanged.

PENSION AT OTHER AGES

Early Retirement

Under conventional practice, a defined benefit pension plan will set a normal retirement age (typically at age 65), and any retirement before that age will be designated as an *early retirement.*

Actuarial Reduction. For many years it has been common to allow for early retirement between the ages of 55 and 65. In order to provide a benefit requiring no additional cost, the early retirement benefit consists of the accrued benefit with an *actuarial reduction.* This reduction allows for benefit payments that start earlier (with consequential loss of interest) and are paid for a longer period of time. Generally, the participant is required to have ten or fifteen years of service before being eligible for early retirement. The actuarial reduction is sizeable. If normal retirement age is 65, retirement at age 60 would cause a reduction of 35 percent to 40 percent and retirement at age 55 would reduce benefits about 60 percent. Because most actuarial tables anticipate lighter mortality for women than for men, the actuarial reduction has been somewhat less for women than it is for men (see discussion of sex discrimination below).

In practice, relatively few employees elect to take early retirement under these conditions, unless forced to do so because of poor health or employer pressure. The resulting benefits, especially at ages between 55 and 60 are too low to encourage retirement, because they contain two, or possibly three, reduction factors. First, early retirement means shorter service so the accrued benefit is smaller for that reason. Second, there is no possibility of future salary increases and this itself causes a benefit reduction, especially under final-average-pay formulas. Finally, the actuarial reduction cuts a considerable percentage from the accrued benefit.

Employer Encouragement of Early Retirement. Employers who wish to encourage early retirement may provide "better than actuarial" early retirement benefits. The improvements follow no fixed pattern but usually involve percentage reductions lower than the actuarial equivalents and unreduced benefits at ages below 65, typically at age 62 or age 60. These changes bring material additions to pension costs but frequently the added cost is offset by increased efficiency as the less productive employees retire.

Union Pressures. Unions often press for improved early retirement benefits, for somewhat different reasons. They argue that many jobs are so laborious and monotonous that an employee has a right to retire after a long period of service. Moreover, early retirement leaves vacancies for younger workers and relieves unemployment. A prime example of this union pressure is the "thirty and out" early retirement provision negotiated by the United Auto Workers, which gives unreduced benefits after thirty years of service.

Sex Discrimination. Another recent development is the move toward eliminating sex discrimination in employment practices. Recent court cases brought under Title VII of the Civil Rights Act of 1964 and under the Equal Pay Act appear to confirm that differences in benefits between men and women are unlawful. Thus, the use of actuarial reductions that differ by sex appears to be prohibited, although in fact a number of plans still retain this type of early retirement provision.

Current Trends. All these factors have produced a strong trend toward more generous early retirement benefits, although there are now some signs of a slackening in this trend or even a counter-trend. Recent changes in age discrimination legislation point toward some proportion of employees remaining in service beyond age 65. In times of high inflation, people are frightened of retiring on what is often a fixed income. And in the future, the demographics of the population are expected to change so that there will be a shortage, rather than a surplus, of people of working age.

Meanwhile, the early retirement provisions of today's pension plans vary considerably, partly as a result of widely differing corporate objectives. Some employers place a high value on experienced workers and want to keep them, while others feel burdened by an unproductive group of older workers. Also, some employers want to handle early retirement entirely through their qualified plans and others prefer to take care of special cases by supplementary payments outside the qualified plan.

Costs. Costs of early retirement are also important. If in a given situation the "no-cost" actuarial reduction is 30 percent and full accrued benefit is actually provided, the additional cost to the employer is over 40 percent. In addition, the more generous an early retirement provision is, the more likely it is to be used by employees. Thus, a particularly generous (but not uncommon) early retirement provision could add as much as 40 percent to 50 percent to pension costs if a large majority of employees each year took advantage of the opportunity.

Integration Rules. One other factor deserves mention. The IRS rules regarding integration with Social Security reduce the amount of integration allowed the more early retirement benefits are improved. This presents a dilemma to the employer who wants both full integration and generous early retirement benefits. One solution is for the plan to pay an additional benefit from the time of early retirement up to age 62 or age 65, so that in effect the benefit is not integrated until a Social Security benefit is actually payable. This procedure also provides the retired employee with a more constant benefit.

Typical Early Retirement Provisions. The wide variety of early retirement provisions currently in force is summarized below. In each case, the reduction or adjustment shown is applied to the accrued benefit.

- Actuarial reduction.
- Reduction of one-fifteenth for each of the first five years and one-thirtieth for each of the next five years that early retirement precedes normal retirement date. These factors are specified by the IRS in the integration rules as acceptable.
- Reduction of one-half percent for each month early (6 percent per year).
- Full accrued pension payable on retirement at or after age 62 (or age 60). Benefits reduced 5 percent for each year before that age.
- Reduction of 2 percent per year below age 65 down to age 62, and 4 percent for each year below age 62.
- Full accrued pension payable if age plus service totals ninety or more. Otherwise benefit is reduced 3 percent for each "point" (age plus service) below 90.
- Full accrued pension payable if service is thirty years or more. Otherwise benefits are reduced 4 percent for each year below age 65.

Late Retirement

Under the conventional structure of pension plans, *late retirement* usually means retirement after age 65. Some plans use *postponed* or *deferred* retirement to describe late retirement.

Impact of the Age Discrimination in Employment Act. Late retirement has received attention in the last year or two because of the 1978 amendments to the Age Discrimination in Employment Act (ADEA). ADEA prohibits mandatory retirement before age 70, and some states have legislated against mandatory retirement at any age. ADEA may be amended again to follow this lead.

It is still too early to determine the full impact of ADEA on employment patterns. Some employers are reporting that, despite ADEA, very few employees elect to work beyond age 65. Other employers indicate that, of employees reaching age 65, a majority are choosing *not* to retire. In any event, there is increased interest in the subject of late-retirement provisions.

The general impact of ADEA on employee benefit plans is to require continued coverage for employees working beyond age 65. However, the regulations provide that pension plans need not provide additional benefits for service after age 65. It is widely believed that the exemption will soon disappear through further amendments to ADEA or possibly through court decisions. Thus far, ADEA's direct impact on pension plans has been relatively slight.

Current Practice. Currently there are three types of late-retirement provisions:

1. The most common provision is a *frozen benefit* at normal retirement date. After that date, there is no credit for additional service and any salary increases are not counted (even under final-average-pay plans). This approach is so common because many employers wish to discourage employees from working beyond age 65.
2. The second type of provision provides for *continued credit* after normal retirement date. This credit may apply to credited service, calculation of "pay" for plan purposes, or both.
3. A third approach provides for an *actuarial increase* to the benefit calculated at normal retirement date. This increase allows actuarially for the facts that the benefit is paid from a later starting date (and thus the reserve earns more interest) and that it will eventually be payable for a shorter time (since the participant will be older when the benefit begins). The combined effect of these adjustments is quite substantial: The actuarial increase is often as much as 12 percent for each year of deferment, or a total increase of 60 percent to 70 percent if retirement is at age 70 instead of age 65. These increases represent a strong encouragement for some employees to postpone retirement.

It is sometimes felt that granting continued credit is the most equitable treatment for employees over normal retirement age, because it treats service beyond that age exactly the same as service before it. Some practitioners believe that, in the long run, ADEA will require this type of equal treatment.

For most employees, who have, e.g., thirty years of service at normal retirement, counting an extra year of service will mean a benefit increase of only 3.3 percent. Counting an extra year's salary increase might raise the benefit more, but the total increase is likely to be less than under the actuarial increase approach.

Costs. Cost considerations for late retirement do not appear important. Late retirement generally causes a cost *decrease,* mainly because benefits will be paid over a shorter period of time. Obviously, the decrease is most significant if the frozen benefit provision applies, but there is also a decrease when continued credit is given. In principle, the actuarial increase approach is neutral, resulting in neither a decrease nor an increase in plan costs. Note, however, that the actuarial increase provision is more costly than giving continued credit or a frozen benefit.

DEATH BENEFITS IN PENSION PLANS

It is only natural that a pension plan should place major emphasis on retirement benefits. However, nearly all these plans include some form of benefit payable on the death of the participant both before and after retirement. (See Chapter 20 for a detailed discussion of replacement income in the event of death.)

Death Benefits Before Retirement

Legislative and Other Aspects. The 1954 Internal Revenue Code allows qualified pension plans to include death benefits, as long as they are "incidental" to the main purpose of providing retirement benefits. (A number of revenue rulings have defined the IRS interpretation of *incidental.*)

Since 1974, ERISA has required that pension plans include what is known as a *qualified joint and survivor annuity,* which is described under Common Practices below. Thus, death benefits must be included in virtually all pension plans.

Over and above this requirement, death benefits are payable under Social Security and are almost universally provided under separate life insurance plans. Coordination of death benefits from these three sources, therefore, becomes important. In addition, in providing death benefit protection, employers are faced with a choice between using life insurance or the pension plan as the vehicle for coverage. Frequently, the choice is made on the basis of the relative tax advantages, since group life insurance is paid free of income tax but is generally subject to estate tax, while death benefits from qualified plans are, except for the $5,000 exclusion, subject to income tax but not estate tax. Also, group life insurance in excess of $50,000 is subject to imputed income tax as described in Chapter 21 of this handbook. Another potential issue in this decision is that death benefits (other than those required by ERISA) in a pension plan reduce the degree of integration allowed under IRS regulations.

Common Practices. In today's practice, three types of benefits on death before retirement are commonly found in pension plans.

1. For many years, plans that require employees to contribute have provided for a *refund of employee contributions* on death before retirement. Typically, the refund includes accumulated interest and is payable to a

beneficiary nominated by the participant. Historically, the rate of interest credited has been somewhat below market returns, and a 5 percent rate is currently prevalent. This refund is based on the concept of equity. Participants joining the plan can be told that even if they do not live to draw a pension, the money they put in will be paid back.

2. *Other lump-sum death benefits* are not common under the plans of larger employers. However, many smaller plans are funded through insurance arrangements known as *individual policy pension trusts* or *retirement annuities*. These funding vehicles are described in more detail in Chapter 12 of this handbook, but the point to note here is that both arrangements use insurance policies containing substantial lump-sum life insurance.

3. As already indicated, ERISA requires that all qualified pension plans that permit early retirement include a *qualified joint and survivor annuity* benefit on death before retirement. The specific requirements are complex and are described in detail in Chapter 20. Essentially, the plan must provide an option that if a participant dies after the date when he (or she) becomes eligible for early retirement, his (or her) spouse will receive a pension for life equal to what would have been paid if the participant had retired immediately before the date of death with a 50 percent joint and survivor annuity in effect. Under a 50 percent joint and survivor annuity, the participant receives a reduced pension for as long as he lives and his spouse, if she is alive, then receives 50 percent of the participant's benefit for as long as she lives. The way this option works is described below, but basically the participant trades in his regular benefit form for a pension in the joint and survivor annuity form of equal actuarial value.

This qualified joint and survivor annuity is calculated in steps:

- First, the accrued benefit up to the date of death is determined.
- Next, the early retirement reduction (if any) is applied.
- Then, the resulting benefit is converted to the 50 percent joint and survivor form.
- Finally, the spouse gets 50 percent of the benefit the participant would have received.

ERISA allows the benefit to be larger than the 50 percent described above. It also allows the *participants* to be charged for the cost of this death benefit coverage. A typical charge is a reduction of one-half percent in the final pension for each year of coverage.

Although ERISA only requires the joint and survivor annuity to be an *option* that participants can elect, many employers have preferred to include automatic coverage in the plan without any charge to the participants. This causes a slight additional cost to the employer (typically about 3 percent to 5 percent of pension costs) but relieves the plan of the considerable administrative burden of operating the option under the procedures prescribed by ERISA. It should be noted that ERISA requires the qualified joint and survivor annuity coverage to be provided automatically to active employees over age 65. The joint and survivor provisions apply also to the participant who terminates after eligibility for normal or early retirement and dies before he has begun to receive a pension. For example, an employee who leaves at age 55 but chooses to wait until age 65 in order to receive a full rather than reduced pension must be offered the same optional (or automatic) coverage as active employees at the same age.

More Extensive Coverage. The qualified joint and survivor annuity, under the prescribed conditions, is the minimum benefit mandated by ERISA. Some pension plans provide more extensive survivor annuity coverage in terms of both broader eligibility and larger benefits. For example, a plan may give coverage after five or ten years of service, at ages well below 55 when the employee is eligible for early retirement. The benefit is sometimes 50 percent of the full accrued pension (without reduction for early retirement and conversion to joint and survivor annuity form) and is sometimes as large as 50 percent of the prospective pension at normal retirement date.

If the employee is at least age 50 when he dies, the spouse benefit may be equal to 100 percent of the employee's accrued benefit and still be deemed incidental. If he is age 55, a spouse benefit equal to 100 percent of the employee's anticipated benefit at age 65 is permissible. For younger ages, the permissible spouse benefit scales down to 75 percent of the accrued benefit or to 45 percent of the anticipated benefit, depending on his age.

Death Benefits After Retirement

Most pension plans contain some kind of arrangement for benefits to be payable on death of the participant after retirement. This practice has been reinforced by ERISA, which requires that qualified pension plans provide for a joint and survivor annuity (along the lines already described) as the normal form of benefit for participants who are married at the time of retirement.

There are other similarities between death benefits before and after retirement. The IRS requirement that death benefits be "incidental" also applies to post-retirement death benefits other than the qualified joint and survivor annuity. In addition, these post-retirement death benefits reduce the extent to which a qualified plan may integrate with Social Security, in much the same way as preretirement death benefits do.

Forms of Benefit. With benefits payable after retirement, it is much more important to make a distinction between three *forms* of benefit:

1. The *unreduced* form is the type of benefit that is payable when the benefit formula (including early retirement adjustments) is applied without any modification.

2. The *normal* form is the type of benefit that is paid if the participant takes no action or, more specifically, fails to elect any other type of benefit. It may be the same as the unreduced form, or it may be derived by the application of some factor.
3. *Optional* forms are different types of benefits that may be elected by the participant, usually just before retirement, and are typically of equal actuarial value to the benefit payable under the unreduced form.

Typical Practices. The distinction between these forms of benefit may become clearer after a discussion of the common types of benefit:

1. Most plans that require employees to contribute provide for a *refund of employee contributions* on death after retirement to match the similar benefit on death before retirement. This feature is often called *modified cash refund* and pays a lump-sum death benefit equal to employee contributions accumulated with interest *minus* the total of pension benefits actually received by the participant. Under these kinds of plans, the modified cash refund benefit is normally unreduced. This means that no adjustment is made to the amount produced by the benefit formula (and relevant early retirement provisions).

2. Other *lump sums* payable on death after retirement are not common, at least under pension plans. They may, of course, be a part of some post-retirement life insurance coverage.

3. *Joint and survivor annuity* benefits are not only common but, since the enactment of ERISA, are mandatory. This type of annuity pays a benefit to the participant and, after his death, continues a payment to the specified joint annuitant at the rate of 100 percent or some lesser percentage of the benefit previously paid to the participant.

ERISA requires that a 50 percent joint and survivor annuity (continuing half of the benefit to the participant's spouse) be the *normal* form of pension for married participants. However, participants must be given the opportunity to elect another type of benefit if they wish. Moreover, ERISA does not require that the joint and survivor annuity be the unreduced form produced by direct application of the benefit formula. The unreduced form may be an annuity merely for the life of the participant, with no benefit payable after death. In this case, the joint and survivor annuity would pay a reduced benefit to the participant such that the total value of this annuity is equal in actuarial value to the benefit on the unreduced form (i.e., the life annuity). Effectively, the participant is paying for the death benefit coverage with a reduction in his own benefit.

Naturally, ERISA will permit a pension plan to provide more generous benefits. For example, the normal form may be a 100 percent joint and survivor annuity (with 100 percent continuation to the spouse), but since the death benefit is more valuable, it would "cost" the participant an even larger reduction in his own benefit. Alternatively, the plan may provide for the joint and survivor annuity, on, for example, the 50 percent basis, to be the unreduced form, as well as the normal form, for married participants. If this were the case, the participant's benefit resulting from direct application of the benefit formula would not be reduced to provide the survivor annuity coverage. The cost of the coverage is borne not by the participant but by the plan and, therefore, effectively by the employer.

There is a definite trend toward employer-paid joint and survivor annuities, usually at the 50 percent level. The main drawback to this type of provision is its cost: a rough rule of thumb is that it adds about 15 percent to pension costs.

4. Another common type of benefit is the *period certain and life annuity*. This arrangement pays a pension for a given period (say five or ten years) whether or not the participant lives. After that period, the pension continues to be paid as long as the participant lives.

The period certain and life annuity is sometimes the unreduced form of benefit and may be offered as the normal form of benefit for single participants. The death coverage is less expensive than the joint and survivor benefit. A five-year certain form adds roughly 2 percent to 3 percent to pension costs, and a ten-year certain period adds about 9 percent to 10 percent.

5. A number of plans provide a *cash option,* under which the participant can elect a lump sum in place of a pension. Opponents believe this can lead to the benefit being dissipated, and the participant could then apply to the employer for hardship assistance. On the other hand, proponents claim that a cash option merely adds flexibility and that to deny it smacks of paternalism.

Optional Forms. All these types of plan benefits may be offered as options that may be elected by the participant. Conversion from one type to another is usually based on option factors so calculated that all the options have an actuarial value equal to the value of the benefit on the unreduced form. The normal pension plan might offer a choice to the participant among the following benefit types:

- A life annuity (providing the largest benefit to the participant).
- Modified cash-refund benefits (if the plan includes employee contributions).
- 50 percent and 100 percent joint and survivor annuities, sometimes with an even wider selection of percentages.
- Contingent annuitant options. These are similar to the qualified joint and survivor annuities introduced by ERISA with the same choice of percentages, except that the survivor is not the participant's spouse but an annuitant of the participant's selection, for example a parent, brother, or child.
- Period certain and life annuities, typically for five- and ten-year periods.
- A provision allowing the participant to choose any form of benefit of equal actuarial value that the administrative committee may permit. It is not uncommon for the cash option to be included in this clause.

ERISA Requirements. Plans must follow the procedure specified by ERISA for informing participants of the options available to them and for making the elections. It is also usual practice to provide for periods of time between the date an election is made and the date the option becomes effective. Otherwise, participants could select against the plan. For example, a participant in very bad health could make a deathbed election of the annuity type that would provide the largest amount of death benefit coverage.

Actuarial Factors. To provide this full range of options requires extensive actuarial factors, to be able to convert from one form to another. Normally, each set of factors varies according to the age and sex of the participant (and, if relevant, of the beneficiary). Mortality tables traditionally distinguish between males and females, since experience has shown that, on the average, women live longer than men. However, there are strong indications that sex-differentiated option factors may soon be ruled unlawful under the terms of the Civil Rights Act and/or Equal Pay Act.

DISABILITY BENEFITS IN PENSION PLANS

In much the same way as a pension plan may include death benefits, it may also include disability benefits. In fact, there are a number of similarities between these two kinds of ancillary benefits. In the first place, benefits from different sources need to be coordinated. Benefits payable in the event of disability may come from Social Security and from separate disability plans, as well as from the pension plan. (See Chapter 18.) Another similarity is that inclusion of death or disability benefits reduces the extent to which the qualified pension plan may be integrated with Social Security. However, ERISA lays down no special rules or requirements regarding disability benefits, as it does for death benefits. Nor are any specific limitations on disability benefits contained in the Internal Revenue Code.

A distinguishing characteristic of disability benefits is that most employers maintain a separate Short-Term Disability (or Salary Continuation) plan. Typically, this plan continues a portion of the employee's salary during periods of sickness or disability, usually to a maximum of twenty-six weeks. For disabilities that extend beyond twenty-six weeks, a different type of plan takes over. This may be the disability benefit under the pension plan, or it may be a separate Long-Term Disability (LTD) plan. A choice must be made between these two methods of providing the longer-term disability coverage. Recent trends have been toward using the separate LTD plan, since it affords somewhat greater flexibility and imposes fewer restrictions under ERISA and IRS regulations. Moreover, the degree of integration allowed under the pension plan is not reduced.

Typical Pension Plan Disability Provisions

Nevertheless, there are large numbers of pension plans that do include disability pensions. Many of these plans are union-negotiated. When disability pensions are included in defined benefit pension plans, provisions are frequently designed along the following lines.

1. Disability pension coverage often does not begin until the employee has completed a specified period of service, such as five or ten years. Sometimes a minimum age, e.g., 45 or 50, is also required.
2. There are a number of definitions of disability for purposes of qualification for a pension. Perhaps the most common is built on the concepts that the disability be *total* (preventing the participant from engaging in gainful employment) and *permanent* (or likely to be permanent). Plans usually include arrangements for submission of medical evidence, and they exclude disabilities that are self-inflicted or that arise from alcohol or drugs.
3. Many plans provide for a disability pension equal to the accrued benefit under the normal benefit formula. However, since this provision may provide a totally inadequate pension if disability occurs after a relatively short period of service, some plans provide a larger benefit per year of service in the event of disability. Other plans set the disability pension equal to the prospective regular pension at normal retirement date, assuming continued service at the salary earned immediately prior to disability.
4. The disability pension usually begins after the salary continuation payments cease; that is, after twenty-six weeks for most employers. Note, however, that this may cause a slight discontinuity, since Social Security disability benefits begin after the invalidism has lasted five months.
5. A pension plan normally pays the disability pension either for the life of the participant or until he recovers. There are often specific provisions for periodic medical examinations up to age 65 to determine continued disability.

Continuing Pension Credit

As mentioned, many employers have decided that there are advantages in providing disability pensions by means of a separate LTD plan rather than through the pension plan. In most cases, the LTD plan is insured, and the disability pension ceases at age 65 or earlier death or recovery. Quite frequently, the disabled participant will have an inadequate pension when he reaches age 65 if the LTD benefit stops, especially if he was disabled at a relatively early age and has, therefore, built up only a small accrued pension.

To fill this gap, it is now common for the pension plan to count continuing credited service while the participant is receiving LTD benefits. For those pension plans that have a pay-related benefit formula, this additional credit is usually based on the participant's salary (or final average earnings) just before disability occurred. For pension plan purposes, the disabled participant is treated as an active employee with unchanged salary.

BENEFITS ON TERMINATION OF SERVICE

Earlier sections have discussed customary pension plan provisions relating to an employee's retirement, death, or disability. Of course, employees separate from service for other causes, such as resignation or dismissal. Collectively, these other causes are often referred to as *termination of service.*

Vesting

Providing a pension for employees who terminate is known as *vesting.* The Internal Revenue Code refers to a *nonforfeitable* benefit, which means the same thing, although in fact the benefit may not be payable if the employee dies before benefits are due to start.

Central to the concept of vesting is the practice of giving the terminating participant the right to a pension payable not immediately but from normal retirement date. This *deferred vested pension,* as it is usually called, is all or a part of the accrued benefit previously described. Since the enactment of ERISA, vesting is a requirement for all qualified pension plans. Moreover, a vested pension must be provided for both voluntary and involuntary terminations. No distinction can be made as to the type of termination, and ERISA banned the use of "bad boy clauses," which would deny a pension if the employee leaves to work for a competitor or in some other way harms the original employer's interests.

The requirements are especially important because, although they are minimum standards that must be met, they are also viewed as maximum provisions: employers prefer to spend, out of limited resources, as little as possible on employees who are no longer working and who have relatively short service. Minimum vesting standards under ERISA are discussed in depth in Chapter 14.

Vested Benefits

Modern pension plans almost always append some additional provisions to the basic vested benefit.

1. *Lump sums.* Many plans allow for payment, at the time of termination, of a cash lump sum of equivalent value in lieu of the deferred vested pension. ERISA allows the plan (usually at the discretion of the administrative committee) to elect unilaterally to pay this lump sum if it is $1,750 or less. Subject to the agreement of the participant, larger lump sums may be paid.
2. *Death benefits.* In the event of death after termination but before retirement, most plans pay no death benefit associated with the deferred vested pension. However, it is almost universal practice for the plan to refund any employee contributions.

   ERISA allows this practice and specifically provides that cancellation of the benefit on death before payment begins is not considered a breach of the nonforfeitable requirement. The logic from the employer's point of view is that the participant will probably have taken another job and will therefore be covered under the death benefit programs of his new employer.

3. *Early payment.* ERISA requires that the participant be allowed to elect early payment of his deferred vested pension, provided of course that the plan includes an early retirement provision and that the participant has satisfied any age and service qualifications for early retirement.

   It is, though, quite common for the early retirement reduction applicable to the deferred vested pensions to be larger than that applicable to early retirements from active service. That is to say, the terminated employee gets a smaller benefit than the active employee who is retiring with a "better-than-actuarial" reduction.

4. *Optional forms.* The range of optional forms of benefit payment that are available for terminated vested employees are usually the same as for active employees who are retiring.

PENSION PLAN CONTRIBUTIONS

A category of pension plans, usually known as *contributory plans,* requires participants to bear a part of the cost. By contrast, under *noncontributory plans,* the employer pays the whole cost.

Employee Contributions

Under contributory plans, membership is normally voluntary; employees must elect to join, at the same time authorizing the employer to deduct contributions from the employee's paycheck. In these types of plans, credited service for purposes of determining the amount of benefit the participant will receive will include only the period of service during which an employee actually contributed.

Advantages and Disadvantages. Clearly, whether a plan should be contributory or noncontributory is an important factor in plan design. The *advantages* of a contributory plan are:

- A better plan can be provided for the same employer cost, or alternatively the same plan can be provided at lower employer cost.
- Employees tend to appreciate a plan more if they support it financially. It is hard to measure the strength of this argument, but some employers believe in it so strongly that as a matter of policy all their benefit plans are contributory.

There are, however, some crucial *disadvantages*:

- Employee contributions, even to a qualified pension plan, are *not* tax deductible, while employer contributions are. Thus there is a tax advantage if the employer meets the full plan cost while paying slightly lower salaries.
- Contributory plans are not popular with most employee groups, particularly

unions. This aspect is complicated by the fact that under plans that are heavily contributory, young participants may be paying more than the total cost of the benefits they are accruing. In effect, these younger employees are subsidizing the employer.

- Contributory plans are intrinsically more complicated than noncontributory plans. Additional records have to be kept, and refunds with interest may have to be made on termination and death. Additionally, it may be necessary to make separate calculations of the employee-purchased and employer-purchased benefits on terminations of service.

Recent Trends. In recent years, the disadvantages of a contributory plan appear to have outweighed the advantages, since there has been a steady trend toward noncontributory plans. The Bankers Trust Company *1980 Study of Corporate Pension Plans* showed that in 1970, 28 percent of the plans were contributory, while by 1980 only 8 percent were contributory. This trend has been accelerated by the growing prevalence of thrift and savings plans, which are analyzed in Chapter 12 of this handbook. Many major employers have converted their pension plans to a noncontributory basis, while at the same time instituting a savings plan toward which employees have contributed with enthusiasm.

It is interesting to note that in Canada, Britain, Western Europe, and indeed most other countries where pension plans are prevalent, employee contributions are tax deductible (up to certain limits). There are indications that the United States may follow suit in the near future, since a number of bills in Congress would allow for tax deductions, to some extent, on employee contributions to qualified plans.

Employee Contribution Formula. The employee contribution formula for contributory plans most often matches the benefit formula. For example, if the benefit formula is integrated with Social Security, the employee contributions will be likewise integrated.

Most contributory plans cover salaried employees and are pay related. In addition, benefits and contributions are usually integrated with Social Security in the same way. These practices are illustrated in the typical formulas shown below:

Benefit Formula	*Employee Contribution Formula*
1.5 percent of each year's pay up to $20,000 plus 2 percent of each year's pay above $20,000.	2 percent of pay up to $20,000 plus 4 percent of pay above $20,000.
1.75 percent of final average earnings minus 1.67 percent of primary Social Security per year of credited service.	1 percent of pay up to the Social Security wage base plus 5 percent of pay above the base.
1.5 percent of final average earnings minus 1.25 percent of primary Social Security per year of credited service.	3 percent of pay in excess of the Social Security wage base.

Partial Contributions. Because employees have to contribute to Social Security a relatively high percentage (6.65 percent in 1981) of earnings up to the Social Security wage base, it may be a real hardship for lower paid employees to contribute to the employer-sponsored pension plan as well. It is therefore becoming common for the pension plan to require employee contributions (if any) only on pay above the Social Security wage base (as in the third example above). Effectively, this kind of plan is noncontributory for lower paid employees and partially contributory for higher paid employees.

Employer Contributions

The essence of a defined benefit pension plan is that benefits are fixed by the plan's formula while costs are the amounts required to provide those benefits. Moreover, the real cost for a benefit to be paid many years in the future, and perhaps dependent on the level of pay in the future, is not known and can only be estimated using actuarial techniques.

The key element in plan design is that the employer will bear the whole cost of a noncontributory plan and, for a contributory plan, will bear the balance of the cost not met by employee contributions. It is important to note that since the employee contributions are almost universally made according to a fixed formula while employer contributions equal the balance of the actuarial cost, the employer bears the risk of adverse experience.

The technical aspects of funding and pension plan contributions are discussed at greater length in Chapter 14.

OTHER KEY PROVISIONS

Eligibility for Participation

Almost all pension plans contain an eligibility provision, which defines who may participate in the plan and when they may join. The provision may also spell out the steps that are required for membership, such as completing an application form and authorizing the deduction of employee contributions. The question of eligibility is discussed in detail in Chapter 14.

Cost-of-Living Adjustments

The term *cost-of-living adjustments* is used here to cover any kind of arrangement intended to protect pensions against erosion by inflation. Understandably, with inflation at its present high levels and with general pessimism about bringing it under control, cost-of-living adjustments are expected to be one of the major pension issues of the 1980s. As an example, a number of large unions, such as the autoworkers and steelworkers, have put this subject on the priority list for bargaining.

However, because inflation is often accompanied by poor stock market performance and by decreases in profit margins, it is difficult for employers to afford the increased benefits that employees and pensioners feel they need. There is no doubt that a pension plan that is fully indexed against inflation and that is also fully funded carries a price that most employers are not willing to pay.

It is important to distinguish between cost-of-living adjustments that operate before retirement and those that apply to benefits after retirement. The problems are quite different and employers view their responsibilities as quite different.

Adjustments After Retirement. The current controversy over cost-of-living adjustments relates to the adjustment of pensions after retirement, that is to say, once they are being paid. There is a major conflict here between employee and employer. On the one hand, the retired employee feels that a pension that declines in value each year because of inflation is totally inadequate. On the other hand, the employer is unwilling to take on the added cost and significant added risk of adjusting the pension automatically as the cost of living increases.

Technical problems. The situation is complicated by other technical factors:

- The only cost-of-living index that is available in the United States and that is widely accepted is the Consumer Price Index (CPI). However, the CPI is based on the buying patterns of the average family and probably does not reflect accurately the habits of pensioners. There has been discussion of a separate "Pensioner CPI," but it has not yet been constructed.
- There is even criticism of the CPI as it relates to the nonretired population, on the grounds that it overemphasizes some expenses, particularly house purchase.
- Even an accurate "Pensioner CPI" might not recognize the possibility of a pensioner's needs (and living expenses) changing significantly with advancing age. There is even a school of thought claiming that pensioners do not need increases as the cost of living goes up, because their needs decrease at about the same rate, especially if medical expenses are reimbursed through Medicare and group insurance. The problem here is that there are no reliable statistics to support or refute this argument.
- A further source of controversy is whether adjustments should keep pace with increases in the *standard* as well as the *cost* of living. If the working population is enjoying a higher standard (e.g., color television instead of black and white), should pensioners also be able to enjoy this higher standard?
- Since 1972, Social Security has been automatically indexed, to keep pace with the cost of living after retirement. Most employers feel these changes should be allowed for in measuring how much pensioners have lost through inflation.

- Another issue, although more political than technical, is how the burden of inflation should be shared. Employers argue that they cannot bear the whole cost and that pensioners should perhaps bear a part, possibly by having pensions adjusted for only a part of the cost-of-living increase. There are also suggestions that the government (or indirectly the public) should meet at least a part of the cost. One way this could be done is by the issue of government bonds with an interest rate varying with the rate of inflation.

Actual practices. It can be seen that cost-of-living adjustments, as they relate to pensions in payment, are still at the developmental stage. Consequently, there is no standard practice, and a wide variety of approaches has been followed:

- ☐ *No adjustment.* At one end of the spectrum, there are many thousands of plans under which benefits have never been adjusted after retirement. The employer's rationale is that these employees are no longer productive and, therefore, additional pension expense cannot be justified. Moreover, employers believe they should not be held responsible for the impact of inflation.
- ☐ *Automatic adjustment.* At the other end of the spectrum, there are plans that include automatic adjustments to pensions, usually according to the CPI, as an advance commitment. As already indicated, Social Security includes this kind of provision, as does the federal civil service retirement program. A large number of state and municipal pension plans have this same feature, but it is very uncommon in corporate plans. Where a commitment for pension adjustments is built into a nongovernmental plan, it is almost always subject to a *cap.* Typically, this cap will limit increases to 3 percent or possibly 4 percent per year, in order to control the cost involved.
- ☐ *Variable annuity.* Another solution, which was devised more than twenty years ago, is the variable annuity. The concept behind the variable annuity is that common stocks will, in the long run, provide a hedge against inflation. It follows that if a pension is geared to the performance of a common stock portfolio it will keep pace with the cost of living. Note that under this system, the pensioner bears the risk of the equity performance failing to match inflation: the employer has given up potential investment gains on this part of the pension fund.

  In actual operation, the basic problem has been one of timing. During some periods the equity portfolio has appreciated at a much faster rate than inflation, while in other periods, particularly 1973 to 1979, inflation has moved at a far higher rate. There have also been years when the performance of the common stock portfolio has caused a decrease in pensions while the cost of living has increased substantially. Nevertheless, there are some major variable annuity plans in operation. The best known is the College Retirement Equity Fund (CREF), which is available, actually as an option, to many thousands of faculty members of colleges and universities.
- ☐ *Variable annuity options.* A few plans offer variable annuity options; that

is, one of the participant's options at retirement is to elect a variable annuity in place of the fixed pension that is the normal form of payout. Naturally, the popularity of these options increases or decreases according to the relationship between stock market performance of equities and the rate of inflation. In some quarters it is believed that the philosophy behind an option may provide a solution to the problem of cost-of-living adjustments after retirement. One variation suggests that employers should start adding some kind of adjustment in place of benefit improvements or even accompanied by a benefit reduction. The thinking is that employees would prefer the security of an automatically indexed pension, although it might mean a lower initial pension. The same result could be achieved by giving the employee a choice between a higher fixed pension or a lower indexed pension. Another variant of this philosophy would allow employees to contribute additional amounts, or apply their savings plan accounts, toward "purchasing" cost-of-living adjustments for their pensions. However, at this point in time, these are largely subjects for discussion, rather than actual practices.

☐ *Ad hoc adjustments.* Ad hoc adjustments are, at this time, by far the most common solution to the cost-of-living problem. Two recent surveys showed that over 80 percent of major U.S. corporations had granted at least one benefit increase to pensioners in the previous five years. Typically, these were "one-shot" increases, with no commitment to future increases.

There is wide diversity in the types of formulas used for ad hoc increases. However, it is common for one or more of the following factors to enter into the calculation:

—The amount of increase usually varies according to the period since retirement or since the last ad hoc increase.

—A percentage increase is common, although many formulas include maximum and minimum increases.

—Usually the adjustment does not compensate completely for CPI increases. One reason is to allow for Social Security changes; another is to leave part of the inflation burden on the pensioners. An additional pragmatic reason is the cost involved in full indexing.

From the employer's point of view, the major advantage of ad hoc adjustments is their reasonably accurate known cost. When the increase is being considered, the plan's actuary can calculate the additional liability based on realistic assumptions without having to predict future rates of inflation.

Future Prospects. It is difficult to tell what will happen in the area of cost-of-living adjustments, especially since a great deal will depend on future economic events. However, many practitioners believe that in the long run automatic adjustments will become as common as final-average-pay benefit formulas are today. After all, final-average-pay formulas allow for inflation over periods for as long as forty years (from age 25 to age 65, for example), while the average pensioner only lives for fifteen or twenty years.

BASIC ADMINISTRATIVE ARRANGEMENTS

For persons not familiar with the operation of a pension plan, it is difficult to appreciate the great administrative effort involved. There is, therefore, a tendency to overlook the need for provisions defining the administrative arrangements and coordinating the activities of the various parties involved.

Under ERISA, the need is even greater. Not only does the statute impose administrative tasks (especially in the areas of reporting and disclosure), but it also emphasizes fiduciary responsibilities.

These legal aspects are described in detail in Chapters 5 and 7 of the handbook. This section describes the parties involved in the administration of a typical defined benefit pension plan and outlines their principal duties. In most plans, these parties and their responsibilities will be set out in the plan itself.

1. The *plan sponsor* is typically the employer, as an entity (for example, a company).
2. In a corporate plan, the *board of directors* plays an important part. The board is ultimately responsible for insuring that the plan is properly run and in compliance with relevant laws. Quite frequently, some of these tasks are delegated to a committee of the board, possibly the Compensation Committee. Alternatively, a board committee will be responsible for considering action and making recommendations to the full board.
3. It is virtually standard practice for a *committee* to be responsible for most aspects of regular plan administration. The committee is typically referred to as the Administrative Committee or Retirement Plan Committee and consists of three to seven members. The members are usually appointed by the board and might be officers from the company's personnel, financial, legal, and tax departments.
4. Some plans provide for the appointment of a separate *Investment Committee.* Generally, the idea is to lighten the load on the Administrative Committee and to appoint persons having special financial expertise to supervise the investment aspects of the pension fund.
5. ERISA requires that a *plan administrator* be named or, failing such an appointment, that the plan sponsor will be the plan administrator for purposes of ERISA. Quite frequently the company is named the plan administrator, although it is equally common to nominate the Administrative Committee to this post. Alternatively, the Director of Personnel or a vice-president could be plan administrator. The major duties are reporting to government agencies and disclosure to plan participants, both required by ERISA.
6. Under many pension plans, there is a *trustee* (or possibly more than one), in which event there will be a separate trust agreement. The most common procedure is for a bank or trust company to act as trustee, although individuals could be appointed. The trustee's main duties are to act as custodian of the plan's assets and to provide an accounting for the pension fund. The trustee may also act as investment manager, as described below,

but in recent years there has been a trend toward the appointment of separate investment managers.

7. *Investment managers* are responsible for decisions about the purchase and sale of securities making up the pension fund. For the larger pension funds, there may be several investment managers, either to obtain diversification or to take advantage of specialized services.
8. Instead of a trust fund, ERISA allows a plan to be funded through an *insurance company* under some form of insurance contract. In this event, the insurance company will have a role in the administrative arrangements. The basic functions of the insurer are to invest assets, to provide guarantees, and probably to pay benefits. In some cases, the insurance company provides more extensive services, such as calculation of benefits and actuarial advice.
9. ERISA requires that every defined benefit pension plan engage an *enrolled actuary*. In this sense, enrolled means that the actuary has been accepted by the Joint Board for Enrollment of Actuaries as having the necessary knowledge and experience to practice under ERISA.
10. Finally, ERISA demands (for many plans) the appointment of an *accountant* to undertake audits of the pension fund. The advice of an accountant may also be sought on other matters.

PLAN DOCUMENTATION

A pension plan depends on extensive legal documentation which must be prepared with great precision in order to define exactly what the provisions are and to comply with governmental requirements. This section refers briefly to the key documents required under most pension plans and explains the purpose of each.

The Plan Document

The *plan document* contains the rules, descriptions, and provisions that define the plan and how it is to be operated. It is, in effect, the controlling document, since it establishes the plan itself, subject of course to formal adoption by the sponsor's management, such as the board of directors of a corporation.

Trust Agreement

Plans that are financed through a trust fund require a *trust agreement*. This document is essentially a contract between the employer and the trustee and normally becomes part of the plan's basic documentation. However, the agreement would not normally be construed as interfering in any way with the plan's provisions delineated in the plan document.

Insurance Contract

An insurance contract is needed only if the plan is to be financed through some kind of insurance arrangement. Note, however, that a plan may be funded through insurance only in part, in which case there is likely to be a trust agreement *and* an insurance contract.

The usual procedure is for the insurance contract to be subordinate to the plan document. The contract merely allows for contributions to be invested in insurance policies and for the insurance company to pay the benefits. However, there are many different forms of insurance contract; there is therefore no standard practice in this area. Moreover, it is possible for the insurance contract to contain all the plan provisions and, in effect, represent the plan document as well.

Summary Plan Description

The last item of plan documentation that deserves mention here is referred to as the *summary plan description* (SPD). This is the new name for what used to be called the "employee booklet" that, under larger plans, has been distributed to participants for many years.

ERISA made distribution of a summary plan description a mandatory part of the reporting and disclosure rules. The SPD must be written "in a manner designed to be understood by the average participant." Revisions to the SPD must be issued within 210 days of the end of the plan year in which there is a substantive plan amendment and a completely new SPD must be distributed at least every five years if the plan has changed or every ten years in any event. Moreover, the regulations under ERISA specify certain standard items that must be included in every SPD, such as a statement of the participant's rights and the circumstances in which benefits could be forfeited or delayed. (See Chapter 5.)

11

Financing Defined Benefit Pension Plans

G. Ashley Cooper

Actuary, The Wyatt Company

ADVANCE FUNDING

General Principles of Funding

The fundamental cost of a pension plan is obviously related to the amount of benefits that are going to be paid or that have been paid. It is equally clear that expenses required to pay those benefits or in general to administer the plan must be considered an additional cost. Finally, if the plan has any accumulated assets, the investment return on those assets will help pay benefits, so investment income must be considered a form of *negative cost.*

Basic Cost Equation. This reasoning leads to the basic cost equation, which may be expressed as:

Long-Range Costs *equal* Benefits Paid *plus* Expenses Incurred
minus Return on Assets

This equation holds true no matter how the plan is financed. However, *outlay* in terms of contributions to the plan may be quite different.

The conceptual difficulty with pension plan costs is that they relate to *future* payments. If a pension plan has only one participant, who is currently age 45 and is not expected to retire until age 65, the basic cost equation would result in a present cost of zero, since no benefits are presently being paid. This is typically referred to as *pay-as-you-go* financing, since no costs are recognized and no payments are made until actual benefits are due.

Advance Funding. Under most pension plans (especially those that meet the requirements for tax qualification of the Internal Revenue Service), a system of *advance funding* is used. Under this procedure, assets are set aside and costs are recognized *before* a participant retires. The usual pattern is for assets to be accumulated during each employee's career or during the period of participation in the plan, so that there is enough accumulation at the time of retirement to pay the benefits that then become due.

Advance funding is the technique used in most pension plans for the following reasons:

1. It is legally required under minimum funding standards established by the Employee Retirement Income Security Act of 1974 (ERISA), subject to some exceptions.
2. Pay-as-you-go financing provides virtually no benefit security to employees. They are totally dependent on the continued existence of the employer and his ability to pay future benefits. This lack of security led to the imposition of minimum funding standards by ERISA.
3. From the accounting point of view, pay-as-you-go financing does not recognize costs until after the employee has left service. To reflect the proper cost of doing business, it would be more appropriate for the employer's

financial statements to show an expense charge as the benefits are being accrued. The advance funding system accomplishes this goal but, for accounting purposes, actual payments need not be made until benefits are due. The accounting objectives could be reached by a system of book entries without cash payments to a pension fund.

4. The investment return on assets accumulated in advance of the time when they are needed to pay benefits helps to meet part of the plan's long-range cost. However, it is important to bear in mind that cash (or property) paid into a pension fund is no longer available to the employer. Thus, his working capital is decreased or his need for borrowing is increased.

Pay-As-You-Go Plans. Despite powerful arguments, and in some cases legal requirements, for advance funding, there are some types of plans that operate on the pay-as-you-go principle. The most important category comprises governmental programs, such as Social Security and some civil service pension plans. These programs are not subject to ERISA's minimum funding standards.

Supplemental executive plans. Another important category of unfunded pension plans includes "excess" and "top-hat" plans established as supplemental arrangements for executives. As long as those plans merely provide benefits above the maximum limitations of ERISA or provide "deferred compensation for a select group of management or highly compensated employees," they are not subject to the minimum funding standards. Moreover, if the plans were to be funded in advance of benefits being payable, there would probably be either no tax deduction on the employer contributions or a current tax liability to the participants. These types of plans are, therefore, operated on the pay-as-you-go basis as far as outlay is concerned, although it is common for book reserves to be built up and a charge made to expense (if the amount is material) just as if the plans were advance funded.

Payment vs. recognition. It will be seen that there are two important, and sometimes quite distinct, techniques of advance funding. Under one method, contributions are paid to a pension fund before benefits are payable. These payments build up a pool of assets separate from the assets of the employer. Under the other, pension costs are recognized, especially in the employer's financial statements, while the participant is employed and benefits are accruing, rather than after service has been completed.

Employer's Funding Objectives

There is no single level of contribution that is required either by law or by generally accepted actuarial principles. Instead there is a *range* of contribution levels within which the employer may set his annual outlay. The employer, working with his accountant and the plan's actuary, is free to choose a contribution level within the acceptable range that will best meet the employer's funding objectives.

The development of these funding objectives will differ from one employer to another and must take into account the characteristics of the plan concerned. However, in most instances, the following factors will be considered:

1. *ERISA compliance.* It can be assumed that the employer, and the actuary involved, will be anxious to comply with the relevant ERISA requirements. As already mentioned, the key provisions are the minimum funding standards (which are described in more detail in Chapter 14). An additional reason for compliance, if one were required, is the substantial excise tax that would be levied if a funding deficiency came to light.
2. *Tax deductibility.* The Internal Revenue Code and regulations define a maximum contribution that the employer can pay and claim as a tax deduction. Although amounts in excess of this tax-deductible limit may be carried forward and deducted in future years, most employers are looking for contributions to be deductible in the year they are paid.
3. *Reasonable pension expense.* Typically, the employer will want to charge to expense a pension cost that is "reasonable." Otherwise, in the long run, one generation of stockholders will be gaining at the expense of another, because unduly low (or high) expense today will cause higher (or lower) expense in the future.

   The definition of "reasonable" will, however, vary from one employer to another, depending on such factors as:

   —The type of industry and degree of competition

   —The expected future work force

   —The type of plan involved

   —The importance of stability in expense from year to year

   —The desirability of matching pension expense to actual contributions
4. *Cash-flow considerations.* For many employers, cash flow is even more important than the amount of pension expense. In industries that are labor-intensive, the amounts paid in wages, salaries, and benefit costs may spell the difference between success and failure. For other employers, the stability or predictability of cash contributions is vital, perhaps even more important than the actual level. Another key element in deciding the appropriate level of employer contribution is the comparison between internal and external rate of return. If the pension fund is showing a return of 6 percent per annum while the employer is obtaining 20 percent on capital invested in his business, there is a strong incentive to set pension contributions at the lower end of the range of acceptable levels. The same would be the case if pension contributions had to be sustained by borrowing a higher rate of interest, e.g., 12 percent or 15 percent.
5. *Accumulation targets.* Many employers set a target as to how much they would like to accumulate in the pension fund and how quickly this target should be attained, subject of course to ERISA compliance. A number of different targets can be considered logical; for example:

—Assets sufficient to cover the benefits insured by the Pension Benefit Guaranty Corporation (PBGC) under Title IV of ERISA. There would be no residual employer liability if the plan were terminated.

—Assets sufficient to cover the value of all accrued vested benefits. In recent years, auditors have insisted on a footnote to the employer's financial statements indicating the extent to which the value of vested benefits is larger than the assets on hand. To many employers, there are important public relations advantages in being able to state that vested benefits are fully covered by pension fund assets.

—Assets at least equal to the value of all accrued benefits, whether or not vested. This target appeals to many employers because it is the amount necessary to show that benefits are being funded as they accrue. If this can be demonstrated, it is then believed that all moral commitments toward employee security have been met. It may be that this target (the value of all accrued benefits) will become more common in the future, because a recent accounting standard (No. 36) of the Financial Accounting Standards Board (FASB) requires that the value of all accrued benefits be shown in the employer's financial statements.

6. *Employer philosophy*. Frequently, other aspects of employer philosophy will affect the development of funding objectives. Some employers, for example, prefer to be "conservative," that is, to contribute more than is really required. They might be motivated by the desire to tell employees that their pensions are particularly secure. Alternatively, upward fluctuations in cost would be embarrassing, whereas downward fluctuations can easily be accommodated.

Major Funding Decisions

If a pension plan is to be funded, there are two basic types of decisions to be made. First, there are those relating to *how much* should be contributed, which are determined on the basis of actuarial principles. The other major decision is *where and how* the pension fund should be invested. The remainder of this chapter concentrates on the principles and factors that influence these major funding decisions, and the practices that are common today.

ACTUARIAL PRINCIPLES

Advance Funding

As discussed earlier in this chapter, the basic cost equation states that the costs of any pension plan over the long-term will equal:

Benefits Paid *plus* Expenses *minus* Any Investment Income

The concept of advance funding is based on the principle that these "costs" will not be met as they occur but, instead, will be spread over a participant's working career. In other words, the costs will be recognized and paid as the benefit is *earned,* not when it is received, by the participant. Obviously, if the contributions made during the active employment of each participant are to support the benefits expected to be paid (with proper allowance for expenses and investment income), contributions and benefits must in the long run be equal in value.

Thus, the basic actuarial principle for advance funding of a pension plan is to balance contributions and benefits. As later paragraphs will describe, this balancing process can become complex, principally for four reasons:

1. Since contributions are paid in advance of retirement whereas benefits are payable after retirement (and possibly after death or disability), the time value of money must be considered.
2. Under most pension plans, the amount of the benefit is not known until the participant actually retires. The amount may depend on future rates of salary and is likely to be influenced by whether retirement is early or normal.
3. The pension may be payable only if certain conditions are satisfied. For instance, no benefit at all may be due if the participant terminates before becoming vested or dies without being eligible for death benefit coverage.
4. Even assuming that contributions for a given employee are spread over his period of plan participation, there are a number of different contribution patterns that might be appropriate. To give a hypothetical, for example, contributions could be set as constant annual payments in dollars or could be arranged as a fixed percentage of the participant's salary.

The actuary's task, then, is to predict long-range costs according to the fundamental cost equation and to redistribute those costs into a contribution pattern that meets the funding objectives of both employer and employee.

Purposes of Actuarial Valuations

The process used to redistribute long-range costs within the desired contribution pattern will be described in the following sections. At this stage, it may be helpful to introduce the concept of an *actuarial valuation,* the set of calculations and their results made as of a given valuation date. As of that date, the actuary is given information about all the participants in the plan and about the assets accumulated in the pension fund. Using the techniques that will be described later, the actuary predicts the long-range costs and the consequential actuarial liabilities under the contribution pattern that has been selected. This valuation has a number of different purposes.

Setting Proper Contribution Levels. As of the valuation date, the actuary calculates, on the basis of employee data and asset information on hand, suitable contribution levels to be paid until the next valuation. Under most pension plans, employee contributions will be fixed by the terms of the plan provisions. What the actuary calculates, therefore, is the appropriate level of employer contributions, after allowing for what employees might contribute.

Measuring Funding Progress. In accordance with the chosen contribution pattern and the results of the previous valuation, the plan should have reached a scheduled funding level. The current valuation will measure the degree of actual funding and, therefore, the extent to which the plan is ahead of (or behind) its expected schedule.

Determining Benefit Security. One of the main purposes of funding is to provide benefit security to employees in the event (however unlikely) the plan is terminated or the employer is unable to meet contribution requirements. Frequently, the actuarial valuation will measure the amount of benefit security on the valuation date.

Considering Plan Revisions. Concurrent with the cost calculations under the existing pension plan, the valuation may be used to determine the impact on contributions of plan revisions that may be under consideration. The same valuation process would also be used for determining contribution levels for a new plan.

Producing Governmental Filing Information. Increasing governmental supervision, under IRS and other ERISA regulations, brings more voluminous reporting requirements. Some of the governmental filings (especially Form 5500, which must be submitted annually) include actuarial information that will normally be produced as a by-product of the actuarial valuation.

The Concept of Present Value

The *present value* concept is central to almost all actuarial calculations. Its basic principle is that the present value of a future payment is (1) × (2) × (3), where:

(1) is the amount of the future payment,
(2) is the probability of the payment being made, and
(3) is the interest discount to allow for the time period between the present and the expected date of future payment.

To take a simple example, assume that $100 will be paid a year from now if a tossed coin shows "heads" and that the current market rate of interest is 10 percent. The amount of payment is, of course, $100. The probability of it being paid is .50, since half the time the coin will show "heads" and half the time it will show "tails." Finally, the payment must be discounted for a year at 10 percent, since, if the payment is made, it will not be paid until a year from now. The present value is therefore $100 \times .50 \times \frac{1}{1.10}$ which equals $45.45.

Present value is very similar to the notion of discounted cash flow; the additional factor is the idea of probability of payment.

Compound Probabilities. Under a pension plan, the probabilities can be complex and usually involve compound events. To take a common example, it is often necessary to estimate the probability of a participant staying in service to a specific age and then electing to retire. This may also need to be related to the probability of the participant having a spouse at the time of retirement. These types of probabilities are all built up from sets of *actuarial assumptions* (such as mortality tables), which are discussed below.

Typical Present Values. Setting aside these complexities, it is apparent that an actuary can calculate an array of present values. Specific examples that occur frequently are:

1. *Immediate annuity.* The present value of a fixed annuity payable for life, starting at, e.g., age 65, for a participant who is now at that age involves the probability of whether the participant lives or dies.
2. *Deferred annuity.* The present value of an annuity payable for life from age 65 for a participant who is currently younger (e.g., age 40) involves the consideration of dual probabilities: First, whether the participant survives to age 65 and secondly, how long he draws his annuity beyond age 65.
3. *Temporary annuity.* The present value of an annuity starting now (at, e.g., age 40) and payable until age 65 or earlier death is based on the probabilities of surviving each year until age 65. A temporary annuity would be used to obtain the present value of future employee contributions, for instance. In that case, the probabilities of terminating or becoming disabled must also be incorporated, and it might be necessary to build in increasing amounts of contributions as an employee's salary increases.

The actuary will be concerned with a large number of present values. In the typical actuarial valuation there will be two key end products, the *present value of future benefits* and the *present value of future contributions.* Together with assets already accumulated, the present value of future contributions must be equal to the present value of future benefits for the plan to be in sound actuarial balance.

The Basis of Actuarial Costs

The typical actuarial valuation of a conventional funded pension plan consists of a number of steps:

1. *The selection of actuarial assumptions.* The actuarial assumptions form the basis for prediction of future benefits, expenses, and investment return, which are the three elements of the *fundamental cost equation.* Most of the

assumptions are, in fact, probabilities that will be used to determine present values of future benefits and contributions. The other key factor is the rate of interest to be used in the discounting process included in the concept of present value.

2. *Choosing an appropriate contribution pattern.* As already indicated, pension costs may be spread over an employee's working career in a number of different patterns. The generally recognized patterns are usually referred to as *valuation methods* or *actuarial cost methods.*
3. *Calculating actuarial liabilities.* The actual calculation process takes the employee data and the plan's provisions and produces present value results, based on the actuarial assumptions and valuation method.
4. *Comparing the liabilities with the assets.* In particular, the accrued actuarial liability is measured against the assets in the pension fund. If the accrued actuarial liability is larger, the balance will be the *unfunded accrued liability,* whereas if the assets are larger, the balance will normally be called an *actuarial surplus.* These terms will be explained in more detail later in this chapter. For actuarial purposes, assets may be valued in a number of ways, not merely at their market values. The various procedures commonly used are discussed later in this chapter.
5. *Determining level of contribution.* The final step is determination of suitable levels of contribution. Typically these will include the normal cost plus some amount of annual payment toward paying off the unfunded actuarial liability. As noted earlier, it is common to find a *range* of suitable contributions, rather than a single required level. The range is defined largely by IRS regulations that specify a minimum contribution required under ERISA's funding standards and a maximum contribution for which the employer may claim a tax deduction.

Each of these steps will be discussed in more detail in the sections that follow.

Legislative Aspects

Since ERISA was enacted, a number of aspects of the actuarial process have been regulated by law. The most important legislative requirements are:

1. Each defined benefit pension plan must engage an *enrolled actuary,* an actuary who has been accepted by the Joint Board for the Enrollment of Actuaries. Special standards relate to education, training, and experience.
2. An actuarial valuation must be made at least once every three years.
3. ERISA has defined minimum funding standards, which are controlled through a Funding Standard Account. Details of these minimum funding standards will be found in Chapter 14.
4. The actuarial assumptions used must be reasonable in the aggregate and must "offer the actuary's best estimate of anticipated experience under the plan."
5. The actuarial cost method must be acceptable, and any change must receive prior approval from the Internal Revenue Service.

6. Special rules concerning the valuation of assets must be followed. These are discussed in detail later in this chapter.
7. There are limits, set by the Code and regulations, as to the maximum employer contribution that can be claimed as a tax deduction.

Accounting Aspects

The activities of accountants and auditors also have an impact on the actuarial process. There are essentially two aspects to be borne in mind:

1. Opinion No. 8 of the Accounting Principles Board of the American Institute of Certified Public Accountants (AICPA) has for many years governed how pension expense will be reflected in the *employer's* financial statements. The opinion also refers to additional information that should be provided in the footnotes.

   This opinion has now been revised by Statement of Financial Accounting Standards No. 36 of the FASB, and there is the possibility that there will be other significant changes.
2. In 1980, Statement of Financial Accounting Standards No. 35 was issued by the FASB. This describes how financial statements for the *plans themselves* should be constructed. An important feature is that these statements must (with certain exceptions) show the present value of accrued benefits and vested accrued benefits.

See Chapter 3 for a comprehensive description of these accounting aspects and issues.

ACTUARIAL ASSUMPTIONS

The Need for Assumptions

As described, the actuarial assumptions play a key part in the process of predicting a plan's ultimate costs (benefits paid plus expenses minus investment income) and in redistributing those costs into a more appropriate funding pattern. In this process, one of the actuary's principal tools is the concept of *present value.* The calculation of present value requires knowledge of:

1. The amount to be paid (or received),
2. The probability of payment,
3. The expected time of payment, and
4. A suitable rate of discount to be applied.

All the actuarial assumptions have some part to play in determining any one of these four items. To assist in understanding the role of each assumption, it may be helpful to consider a very simple model:

- The participant is currently age 40 and has five years of service
- Normal retirement age is 65, but the plan allows for early retirement
- The benefit formula is 2 percent of final average earnings for each year of service *less* 2.5 percent of primary Social Security per year of service up to twenty years.

In the paragraphs that follow, each of the usual assumptions will be examined in the context of determining the present value of the benefit expected to be paid in this example.

The Nature of Actuarial Assumptions

Before getting into specific assumptions, it is important to realize the extended time frame involved. In the example chosen, the participant has twenty-five more years of service to complete before being eligible for normal retirement. He might live as long as forty years while on retirement. In total, therefore, the present value calculation includes possible payments sixty-five years or more into the future.

The long-range nature of actuarial calculations causes a number of problems. In the first place, it is obviously more difficult to predict events over a long period than over a short one. Secondly, it is necessary to avoid undue weight to recent, short-term experience, which naturally tends to influence current thinking. And thirdly, there is an acute difference between the viewpoints of the actuary who is trying to look 65 years into the future and the investment manager who has a time horizon of perhaps one year or at the most five years.

Mortality

Mortality is a specific actuarial assumption that comes immediately to mind. In the determination of present value for the example being used, some predictions of mortality are clearly required in order to determine:

1. The probability of the participant living until retirement in order to be able to draw a pension.
2. The probability of his living each year (or month) beyond retirement to receive the periodic pension. (Another way of looking at this is the need to predict how long the participant will live after retirement.)
3. The probability of dying before retirement in circumstances that will trigger the payment of a survivor's pension or some other form of death benefit (assuming the plan includes this type of benefit).

All these items are probabilities; in fact, a mortality table is merely a schedule of the probability of dying at each age shown. From this can be derived the probability of living (or not dying). Then, by linking these probabilities together, the actuary can determine compound probabilities such as that of living to age 65 and dying at that age.

In actual practice, most actuarial valuations are based on published mortality tables derived from the experience of insurance companies under group annuity contracts. Typical examples are the GA-51 and GA-71 tables. Very few pension plans are large enough to provide reliable experience on which to base the plan's own mortality table.

An important characteristic of mortality is that it has tended to decrease over time, due to improved medical care, sanitation, and nutrition. For most pension plans, lower mortality means higher costs since the probability of living to receive a pension is increased and so is the life expectancy after retirement. For this reason, it is common to find actuaries using mortality tables that include "projections" allowing for future decreases in mortality.

Withdrawal or Turnover

The hypothetical participant, currently age 40, could also terminate service before retirement. The present value calculation should, therefore, include the probability of remaining in service until retirement or, put another way, of not terminating service.

Since virtually all pension plans include a vesting provision, the present value calculation must also allow for the possibility of the participant terminating service with a vested benefit. There will be no present value related to the probability of terminating without a vested benefit, since, in those circumstances, no benefit would be payable.

It is, therefore, common practice for the actuarial assumptions to include a *turnover table*. This table comprises a set of probabilities of withdrawal from service. Conventional practice has tended toward rates (or probabilities) of withdrawal that vary by age and perhaps sex. This is because younger employees tend to have higher mobility than older employees. Withdrawal rates may also vary by length of service. The experience of most employers is that the probability of withdrawal is much higher for short-service than for long-service employees.

Rates of withdrawal vary widely from one employer to another and may fluctuate significantly according to prevailing economic conditions. There are, therefore, very few published turnover tables. Instead, most actuaries will have a set of tables, ranging from very low to very high turnover, and will select the table that appears to fit a particular plan. In following years, the actual experience will be compared with the table, and adjustments made if necessary.

It is important to note that higher rates of turnover lead to a lower probability of the participant staying in service until retirement. In turn, this means a smaller present value of anticipated benefits, or a lower "pension cost."

Disability

It is also possible that the participant will become disabled before reaching normal or early retirement age. If the plan contains no specific disability benefit, disability can be viewed as another kind of termination of service. In that event, the actuary may decide to include allowance for disability in the turnover table.

However, if the plan does provide for a disability benefit, the probabilities of becoming disabled must then be incorporated into the calculation of present value of future benefits. If a disability pension becomes payable, it may be necessary to build in a special mortality table to predict how long the disability pension will be payable. This is usually appropriate, since the mortality experience of disabled participants is likely to be much higher than that of healthy retired participants. It is common practice to use published tables that are available from the experience of insurance companies and from the Railroad Retirement Board actuarial studies.

Retirement Age

The assumptions discussed above (mortality, turnover, and disability) have been principally concerned with the probability of *whether* or not a benefit will become payable. In the determination of present value it is also important to predict *when* the benefit will be payable. For a pension plan, the key determinant of benefit timing is when the participant retires.

For many years it was common practice to assume that all employees would retire at normal retirement date (or at age 65 in the model). This remains satisfactory if the early retirement pension is based on the actuarial equivalent of the accrued pension at normal retirement age, since the present value of the future benefit would not be affected by the employee's decision to retire early.

However, in recent years there has been a trend toward adoption of early retirement benefits that are substantially more generous than the actuarial equivalent. This means that the present value would be much larger if the employee decided to retire at age 60 instead of at age 65.

This trend has led to more sophisticated assumptions as to retirement age. The following approaches are quite common:

1. To assume an average retirement age, of, e.g., 62, to allow, on a reasonably accurate basis, for actual retirement at a variety of different ages.
2. To assume that a certain percentage (e.g., 40 percent) of employees retire at a chosen early retirement age (e.g., 60) and the balance retire at normal retirement age.
3. To construct a complete table of probabilities of retirement at each age. For example:

Age	*Probability of Retirement*
55	10%
56	5%
57	5%
58	6%
59	6%
60	10%
61	10%
62	50%
63	10%
64	10%
65	100%

Note that the probabilities refer to the chances of retirement of employees reaching that age. For example, 50 percent at age 62 means that of the employees attaining age 62, 50 percent will retire before attaining age 63.

Retirement age experience varies materially from one employer and one plan to another, which is why published tables are essentially nonexistent. Obviously, one important determinant is the level of early retirement benefit provided.

Salary Increases

The present value of a future pension benefit is directly related to the expected amount of the benefit. If the plan has a pension benefit related to salary, it may be necessary to estimate future salaries in order to determine the expected benefit payable at retirement. This is particularly true of a benefit formula based on final average earnings, as in the example. If final average earnings are based on salary between age 60 and age 65, and the participant is currently only age 40, it follows that some assumption is required to predict future salaries.

Salary Scale. This is normally accomplished by means of a *salary scale* that states the expected increases for each year of age. The scale may actually be expressed in a number of different ways (for example, the ratio of final salary to current salary), but the principle is usually the same, namely to allow calculation of expected future salaries if current salary is known. As indicated, the scale normally shows the salary progression by age. It is expected, therefore, to include the effect of promotions, merit, seniority, etc. It is also common to allow, to some extent, for anticipated general salary increases that might come about as a result of inflation. This is a complex subject and will be explored in more depth when the general question of setting assumptions is considered.

Productivity. There is some controversy whether salary increases arising from greater productivity should be included in the actuarial assumptions.

From the point of view of realistic determination of the present value of future benefits, it would appear that allowance should be made for all types of salary increases. However, many employers are naturally reluctant to contribute today for benefits arising from tomorrow's productivity gains. They would much prefer to fund those additional benefits out of the increased income that should also result from productivity gains.

As a result, the salary scale is typically considered as combining two elements: age increases and inflationary increases. The two elements may be described separately (e.g., 2 percent for age and 4 percent for inflation) or combined into one rate of increase (e.g., 6 percent per year).

Shape of Scale. It is very common for the salary increase assumption to be a single compound rate of increase, such as 6 percent per year. However, many actuaries believe it is more realistic to expect more rapid salary increases at the younger ages and less rapid increases at older ages. In fact, many studies have shown that at ages above 50 or 55, average salary increases are frequently *less* than the overall rate of inflationary salary increase. This means that, at these ages, the age component, if taken alone, is producing salary decreases.

Investment Return

Investment income appears directly in the fundamental cost equation. Moreover, the rate of interest, or discount, plays an important part in the concept of present value.

Valuation Rate of Interest. All sets of actuarial assumptions, therefore, include an investment return assumption or, as it is more frequently called, a *valuation rate of interest*. This rate is, of course, based on the investment expectation over the long-term horizon of the typical pension plan. In this context it is usual to consider total return including interest, dividends, and capital appreciation (or depreciation). Despite the fact that investment return may come from different sources, the valuation rate of interest is ordinarily expressed as a single rate (e.g., 7 percent). In some instances, different rates may apply before and after retirement, especially if the fund's assets for retired participants are invested differently.

Effect of Changes. Relatively small changes in the assumed rate of interest can have a substantial impact on present values, so the choice of proper rate is the single most important decision in setting assumptions. This aspect, and the relationship between interest rate and the other assumptions, will be explored more thoroughly in later paragraphs.

Additional Assumptions

Many pension plans require additional assumptions for determination of the probability of payment, amount, and timing of benefits. The following are the most frequently encountered:

Social Security Increases. If the benefit formula includes an offset for Social Security or provides different benefits for salary below and above the Social Security wage base, some assumptions as to the future progress of Social Security should be included. These assumptions are normally closely related to the inflationary element in the salary scale. Typical examples might be increases of 4 percent per year in the wage base and 3 percent per year in the Consumer Price Index (CPI) factor included in the Social Security benefit formula.

Family Status. In connection with joint and survivor annuities or other kinds of death benefits, the actuary frequently needs to make some assumptions as to family status. For example, in obtaining the present value of a preretirement joint and survivor annuity provision, an assumption would be needed about the probability of a participant being married at the time of death and the relative ages of the participant and spouse.

Expenses. Expenses of administration are an item of cost entering directly into the fundamental cost equation. For most pension plans, however, the administrative cost is small relative to the cost of actual benefits. In addition, many employers prefer to pay expenses directly instead of considering them as part of the present value of future benefits.

Where expenses are paid out of the pension fund, it is common to add a small loading (of, e.g., 2 percent of benefits) to cover this feature. Another approach is merely to add to this year's contribution an amount sufficient to cover last year's expenses.

Cost of Living. Very few pension plans in the private sector provide for cost-of-living adjustments to pensions in payment. However, for those plans that do include this feature, the assumption as to future adjustments has an important impact on the present value of future benefits.

Relative Importance of Assumptions

The diagram in Figure 11.1 illustrates the approximate effect of changes in assumptions. The results are based on a typical plan and show approximate orders of magnitude, although the percentage changes will not hold true under all conditions.

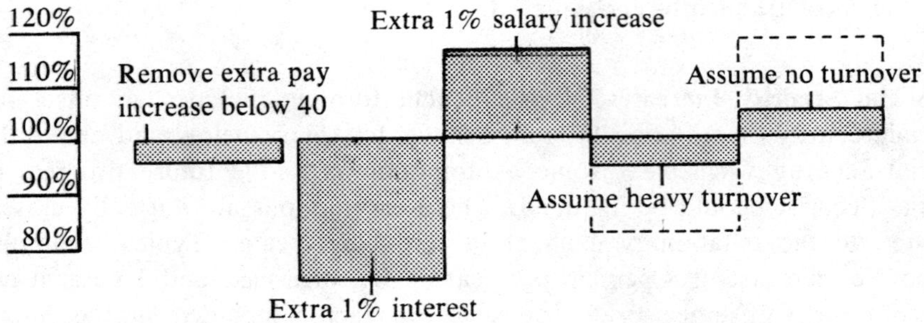

Note: Solid blocks are based on company with average age 43 and average service of twelve years. Dotted lines are based on company with average age 34 and average service of three years.

Fig. 11.1 Approximate Effects of Changes in Assumptions

The key features to be noted are:

1. The assumption having the most dramatic impact on pension plan liabilities is the assumed rate of interest. The often-quoted rule of thumb is that an increase of one percent per year in the valuation rate of interest will decrease contribution levels by 20 percent.
2. For final-average-pay plans, the next most important assumption is the salary scale. An increase of one percent per year in the rate of salary increase typically increases the contribution rate by about 15 percent. Note that the salary scale has less impact than the interest rate, largely because the salary scale operates only up to the time of retirement whereas the interest rate is used to discount the benefit payments throughout the period of retirement.
3. The other assumptions normally have a less significant impact, with the possible exception of the retirement age. If early retirement benefits are particularly generous (for example, no reduction down to age 60 or 62), the assumed age at retirement can then affect pension liabilities almost as much as the salary scale does.

Setting Actuarial Assumptions

Setting appropriate actuarial assumptions calls for skill and judgment. The process also requires input from the employer in terms of both funding policy and information on turnover, salary increases, retirement ages, and other personnel data.

Range of Reasonable Assumptions. Although ERISA requires the actuary to provide his single best estimate as to likely future experience, there is no one "correct" set of assumptions. Since the future is being predicted, the most that can really be expected is a range of what might be termed *reasonable* assumptions. At one end of this range are *conservative* assumptions, which produce a relatively high contribution level. At the other end are *liberal* assumptions, which produce lower contributions.

Although the notion of conservatism is still widely used, the conservative/liberal terminology is often replaced with *optimistic/pessimistic*. Assumptions that anticipate relatively high investment return and relatively low salary increases are considered optimistic. Conversely, pessimistic assumptions anticipate a low rate of return and high salary increases.

Guidelines. Although the choice of assumptions must, in the last resort, be based on judgment, there are guidelines that are widely accepted and can be of assistance:

1. Actuarial assumptions always operate over a long time span.
2. The assumptions must be mutually consistent. To take a simple example, if the valuation rate of interest is set at a level that implies continuing inflation, then it would be only reasonable to incorporate the same level of inflation in the salary increase assumption.
3. The package is more important than any individual assumption. This is the key to the ERISA requirement that assumptions be reasonable *in the aggregate*.
4. It is dangerous to deliberately understate some assumptions and overstate others to obtain a reasonable balance. This practice used to be common and is known as using *implicit* assumptions. The trend today is toward *explicit* assumptions, in which each individual element is reasonably realistic when viewed over the long term.
5. Some employers prefer to allow for a margin of conservatism on grounds of policy or on the theory that, if the assumptions are proved incorrect in practice, they would prefer a correction toward lower rather than higher costs.
6. One widely used measure of the degree of conservatism is the *difference* between the investment return and salary increase assumptions. A very small (or negative) difference would indicate a conservative, or pessimistic, set of assumptions, whereas a large difference of e.g., 3 percent or more would indicate liberal, or optimistic, assumptions.

   This yardstick is not entirely accurate, since the interest rate has a greater impact on contributions than the salary scale does. A more sophisticated measure of conservatism is *weighted spread,* which is defined as the interest rate minus 70 percent of the rate of salary increase anticipated.
7. An important decision is the extent to which inflation should be anticipated in the actuarial assumptions, especially the key elements of interest and salary increases. The usual compromise is to incorporate a moderate degree

of inflation, since anticipating very low rates could be unduly optimistic and anticipating very high rates leads to conclusions that most employers cannot accept. (For example, the minimum wage could be $50 an hour in twenty or thirty years under 10 percent to 15 percent inflation.)

8. There are dangers in accepting the *concept of symmetry* that was espoused at one time. This concept held that inflation would cause equal percentage changes in salary increases and investment return. Experience in the recent past has shown that, at least for relatively short periods, investment return may actually be lower (or even negative) during periods of quite high inflation.

Actuarial Costs As Estimates. In view of these taxing problems, it is comforting to bear in mind that all actuarial costs are *estimates.* Although the estimates are seldom exactly matched by actual experience, pension plans operate on a long time frame, and there is ample opportunity to correct errors in estimating. Actuarial assumptions can easily be changed at the next valuation; indeed, the whole process of setting assumptions can be viewed as one of successive approximation.

ACTUARIAL COST METHODS

General Principles

As described earlier, the concept of advance funding is based on the payment of contributions during an employee's working career in order to accumulate assets sufficient to support the payment of benefits once they become due. The function of the actuarial cost method, or valuation method as it is frequently called, is to determine the pattern into which annual contributions should fall. Put another way, the actuarial cost method is used to allocate to given years the portion of the total cost of the benefit to be provided.

At one extreme, it would be possible to devise a funding system that would provide for a single payment, equal to the value of all future benefits, to be made the day after each employee joins the plan. At the other extreme would be a pattern in which a single payment is made to the plan the day before each employee retires. Needless to say, neither of these patterns is normally used. They would not satisfy most employers' funding objectives and would not be acceptable under ERISA's minimum funding standards. The actuarial cost methods, which are acceptable under ERISA, all aim to produce a reasonably stable pattern of costs from one year to the next. In this context, stability is usually measured in terms of the percentage of payroll of active plan participants, under a pay-related benefit formula, or (for a benefit formula that is not pay related) as dollars per active participant.

If contributions are expected to support the benefits, then:

1. When an employee first joins the plan, or in actuarial terminology becomes a *new entrant*, the present value of future contributions must equal the present value of future benefits.
2. At any later date, when actual assets have been accumulated, the value of those assets plus the present value of future contributions must equal the present value of future benefits.

These equations must hold or the plan will eventually be overfunded or underfunded. Moreover, the equations must balance for the whole group of participants in a specific plan and do not depend on the pattern of future contributions—that is, on the actuarial cost method selected.

Families of Actuarial Cost Methods

The widely used actuarial cost methods fall into two categories:

1. Methods that focus on *accrued benefits.* The rationale here is that if a system can be devised for allocating to each year the amount of benefit deemed to be accrued in that year, an acceptable pattern of contributions will then be developed by calculating the total present value of the benefits being accrued each year. Then, if the value of each year's accrual is contributed (and the actuarial assumptions are matched by actual experience), by the time each employee retires his total benefit will have been financed. Thus the fundamental equation described above will have been satisfied.
2. Methods that focus on *projected benefits.* In the simplest case of a retirement benefit payable from a fixed retirement age (e.g., 65), the projected benefit will be a pension payable from age 65, allowing for service and salary increases, if relevant, up to that time. Using the present value concept, and appropriate actuarial assumptions, a value can be placed on the projected benefit. The actuary then calculates a future stream of contributions that will have the same present value as that of the benefits, after allowing for any assets that may have accumulated. In effect, the procedure is based on the fundamental equation that future contributions plus any assets on hand must meet future benefits.

Elements of Actuarial Cost

Virtually all the actuarial cost methods produce two elements, or components:

1. *Normal cost.* This is the current cost, or running cost, for the plan as if: (1) it had always been in effect; (2) all previous normal costs had been contributed; and (3) actual experience occurred exactly according to the assumptions. Typically, it represents the contribution due if the plan's funding were exactly on target and the accrued actuarial liability (see below) were exactly covered by accumulated assets.

2. *Accrued actuarial liability.* The accrued actuarial liability is the "reserve" that should have been accumulated at any given point in time if the funding pattern were precisely on target. Viewed retroactively, it is the amount that would have been accumulated if all prior normal costs had been paid and assumptions had been matched by experience. Viewed prospectively, it is the present value of all future benefits less the present value of future normal costs.

The paragraphs that follow examine each of the common actuarial cost methods and describe, in general terms, how normal cost and accrued actuarial liability are determined. In order to illustrate the principles involved, the various methods are applied to a hypothetical employee who is currently age 62 but who entered the plan at age 60. For this simple example, the following data represents his past and future salary.

Age	*Annual Salary*
60	$10,000
61	11,000
62	12,000
63	13,000
64	14,000

Upon retirement at age 65, this employee's final three-year average earnings would be $13,000 per year. If he is participating in a plan that provides a benefit of one percent per year of final three-year average earnings, his pension from age 65 would be $650 (5 percent of $13,000). If the plan had a career-average-pay benefit formula of one percent, the pension at age 65 would be $600 (sum of one percent of each year's salary).

Accrued Benefit Cost Methods

As described, the accrued benefit cost methods attach a present value to the pension being accrued in a particular year or to the total pension that has accrued in the past. Generally speaking:

- *Normal cost* for a specific year (e.g., 1980) is the present value of the pension deemed accrued in 1980.
- *Accrued actuarial liability* is the present value of all benefits accrued to date, that is to say accrued up to January 1, 1980, if that is the valuation date.

The same procedure would be applied year after year, so that, at retirement, the total benefit for each participant would be fully purchased.

Conceptually, there is another advantage, since the accrued actuarial liability is, by definition, the total value of accrued benefits. This means that if assets are accumulated to cover the accrued actuarial liability, the plan can then be considered fully funded in the sense that all pension obligations to date have been covered. This also meets a funding target that is commonly adopted by employers, namely to accumulate assets equal to the value of accrued benefits.

In practice, the manner in which the accrued benefit cost method is applied depends on the benefit formula (and other characteristics) of the plan.

Career-Average-Pay Plan. Under a career-average-pay plan, the cost method can be used directly, since the plan itself specifies how benefits are accrued. This application is usually referred to as the *unit credit* or *single premium* method. In the hypothetical example described above, for the year in which the employee is age 62:

- Normal cost would be the present value of a pension of $120 per year. Note that this pension would be payable from age 65 (omitting allowance for any early retirement provisions) but the present value would be determined as of age 62.
- Accrued actuarial liability, as of the beginning of the year, would be the present value of a pension of $210 per year (one percent of pay in each of the prior years). Again, the pension would be deferred to age 65, but the value would be calculated as of age 62.

The accrued benefit cost method fits particularly well with a career-average-pay benefit formula, because each year's accrued benefit is known and fixed unless the plan is changed in some way. The same applies to benefits that are a fixed number of dollars per year of service, although there can be complications if, for example, there is a maximum period of credited service.

Final-Average-Pay Plan. Under final-average-pay plans, the application is more complex. In the first place, it would be unrealistic to exclude allowance for future salary increases, since the plan bases benefits not on current pay but on some average of pay in the future. Secondly, if future salary increases are to be incorporated, some device must be used to determine how much benefit is being accrued in a given year or has been accrued in past years. This problem is compounded if the benefit formula includes a Social Security offset, a minimum benefit, or other complexities.

One common solution, known as the *service prorate procedure,* is to calculate the prospective benefit expected to be paid at retirement, including future salary increases, and to allocate that prospective benefit in equal proportions to each year of credited service. For the hypothetical employee, the prospective pension under the final-average-pay formula is $650 per year, including allowance for future salary increases. At age 65, he will have completed five years of service, so the procedure assumes that the benefit accrued each year is $130 ($650 divided by five). In this case, at age 62:

- Normal cost will be the present value of a pension of $130
- The accrued actuarial liability at the beginning of the year will be the present value of a pension of $260

Salary Prorate Procedure. In this variant, the starting point is the same, namely calculation of the prospective pension, but in determining accrued benefits it is assumed that the prospective pension is allocated evenly to each dollar of *salary* instead of each year of service.

To return to the hypothetical example, the final-average-pay pension of $650 is earned over five years during which the participant has received a total of $60,000 in salary. The salary prorate procedure assumes that the $650 of pension accrues at the rate of 1.083 percent ($650 divided by $60,000) of each dollar of salary earned. In effect, the final-average-pay pension is being converted to a career-pay equivalent. The calculation at age 62 would then give:

- Normal cost equal to the present value of a pension (at age 65) of $130, which is 1.083 percent of $12,000. Coincidentally, this is equal to normal cost on the service prorate procedure.
- Accrued actuarial liability equal to the present value of a deferred pension of $227.50 per year.

The IRS has recently published regulations under ERISA intended to define acceptable actuarial cost methods. These regulations would rule the unit credit cost method with a salary prorate procedure as *unacceptable* for purposes of ERISA's minimum funding standards.

Parenthetically, it should be noted that the regular unit credit cost method and the associated service prorate procedure are acceptable.

Projected Benefit Methods

As the name implies, the family of projected benefit actuarial cost methods focuses attention on the projected, or prospective, benefit anticipated to be payable at retirement. Where benefits are pay related, it is normal practice to incorporate assumptions as to future salary increases in the calculation of the prospective pension.

Two points should be noted here. First, every defined benefit pension plan contains a benefit formula by which the prospective pension may be calculated, although some are, of course, more complicated than others. It follows that, provided adequate assumptions are made, the prospective benefit can always be determined. Secondly, projected benefit cost methods generally ignore how much of the prospective benefit is accrued at any given point in time.

Projected benefit methods are concerned exclusively with satisfying the fundamental formula that assets on hand plus future contributions must equal the value of future benefits. Satisfaction of this formula is handled in a number of different ways according to the details of the cost method being used. Each specific method also has a slightly different objective.

Entry Age Normal Cost (EANC) Method. This method attempts to maintain a normal cost, payable from entry into the plan until retirement, that is a level percentage of payroll (or level in dollars if the plan is not pay related). This is normally achieved by valuing each employee separately and calculating a level normal cost from his entry age. Under this system:

- *Normal cost* is the level percentage of pay (or level dollar amount) that if paid from entry age to retirement age will fund the prospective benefits. At the entry age, the present value of future normal costs equals the present value of projected benefits. At later ages, normal cost merely goes up with salary, under a pay-related benefit formula. Another important characteristic is that entry age may occur at a date before the effective date of the plan, which effectively saddles the plan with a *past-service liability* consisting of prior normal costs that should have been paid but actually were not.
- *Accrued actuarial liability* is basically a balancing item. It consists of the present value of future benefits minus the present value of future normal costs. Typically it is calculated separately for each individual participant. Note that this liability is not in any way related to the value of accrued benefits. It is really just a hypothetical funding target equal to the amount that should have been accumulated if the current plan had always been in effect, if the assumptions had been matched by prior experience, and if past normal costs had been paid exactly.

Frozen Initial Liability Method. This method is essentially a modification of the EANC method. In fact, it is normal practice for the first valuation under the frozen initial liability system to be performed according to the EANC method. The differences appear only in subsequent valuations.

Under the EANC method, variations of actual from expected experience (e.g., salary increases larger than assumed) will affect the accrued actuarial liability at the next valuation. This is usually referred to as an actuarial gain or loss. Similarly, a gain or loss on the asset side as a result of larger or smaller investment return than predicted in the assumed rate of interest will cause the unfunded actuarial liability to be smaller or larger than expected at the next actuarial valuation.

Under the frozen initial liability method, these gains and losses are not allowed to affect the unfunded actuarial liability. Instead, the gains and losses are spread over the future working careers of active participants by being incorporated into normal cost. Normally, the spreading process is applied to the active participant population as a group, not individually. The objective, of course, is to produce an unfunded actuarial liability which remains stable. This method also considerably simplifies the second and subsequent valuations.

Attained Age Normal Cost Method. This method is another modification of the EANC method, and combines some features of the unit credit method.

The basic difference lies in the handling of past-service benefits—that is, benefits applying to service before the plan (or revision) became effective. Under the attained age normal cost method, these past-service benefits are calculated separately (with salary increase allowance, if appropriate) and the present value of those benefits is assumed to be the past-service liability. Benefits accruing after the effective date of the plan are valued on the EANC method, except that the minimum entry age for each participant is the age on the plan's effective date. What this really means is that past-service benefits are valued on the unit credit method and future-service benefits are valued on the EANC method.

Aggregate Cost Method. This method is yet another variant of the projected benefit methods. Its basic objective is to allow for *no* unfunded actuarial liability. It achieves this by setting the accrued actuarial liability at an amount equal to the accumulated pension fund assets. On the effective date of the plan there are no assets; therefore the accrued actuarial liability is set at zero. To satisfy the fundamental funding equation, normal cost is calculated so that the value of future normal costs plus assets (if any) equals the value of future benefits.

This objective is achieved at the expense of stability in normal cost. When the plan is first instituted, older employees have a relatively short period over which benefits can be funded; therefore normal cost will be relatively high in relation to its long-term level. In addition, as under the frozen initial liability method, actuarial gains and losses will be incorporated into normal cost, which may result in other fluctuations.

Ancillary Benefits

The discussion so far has concentrated on pension benefits payable from normal retirement age. In fact, most pension plans contain ancillary benefits payable on early retirement, death, disability, and termination of service. Generally, the plan's actuary will recommend that these ancillary benefits be valued by the same cost method as is used for normal retirement benefits. However, this may cause complications. For example, a plan may pay disability benefits equal to the full accrued pension, in which event the unit credit cost method that operates with regard to each year's accrual of benefits is not theoretically applicable. For this reason, ancillary benefits are quite frequently valued in a different manner:

1. Death and disability benefits may be valued on what amounts to the EANC method, even when the basic retirement benefits are valued by one of the accrued benefit methods.
2. Alternatively, death and disability benefits may be valued by a *term cost method* analogous to insurance company practices. This term cost method calculates, for each participant, the probability of a claim occurring in the year and the value of the claim if it did occur. The danger is that costs will be understated if an unusually small number of participants are eligible or if the age and service makeup of the group is biased. For example, a disability benefit requiring five years of service for eligibility would have no

cost under the term cost method if no employees had five or more years of service.

3. The value of vested benefits on termination is sometimes approximated by assuming no withdrawal above the age when most participants will be vested, e.g., age 40. The rationale is that participants who actually terminate at higher ages will retain a vested interest, so no release of liability will take place. In fact, there may be a significant change in liability because of the valuation method and because future salary increases are no longer relevant after termination.

All these devices should be viewed as approximations, introduced to simplify the actuarial procedure. Frequently, the approximation is justified, since all the actuarial liabilities are only *estimates* based on assumptions as to future experience, and because ancillary benefits typically cost little in relation to the cost of basic pensions.

Comparison of Contribution Patterns

The accrued benefit and projected benefit families of cost methods can produce quite different contribution patterns. This point is illustrated in the two graphs in Figures 11.2 and 11.3.

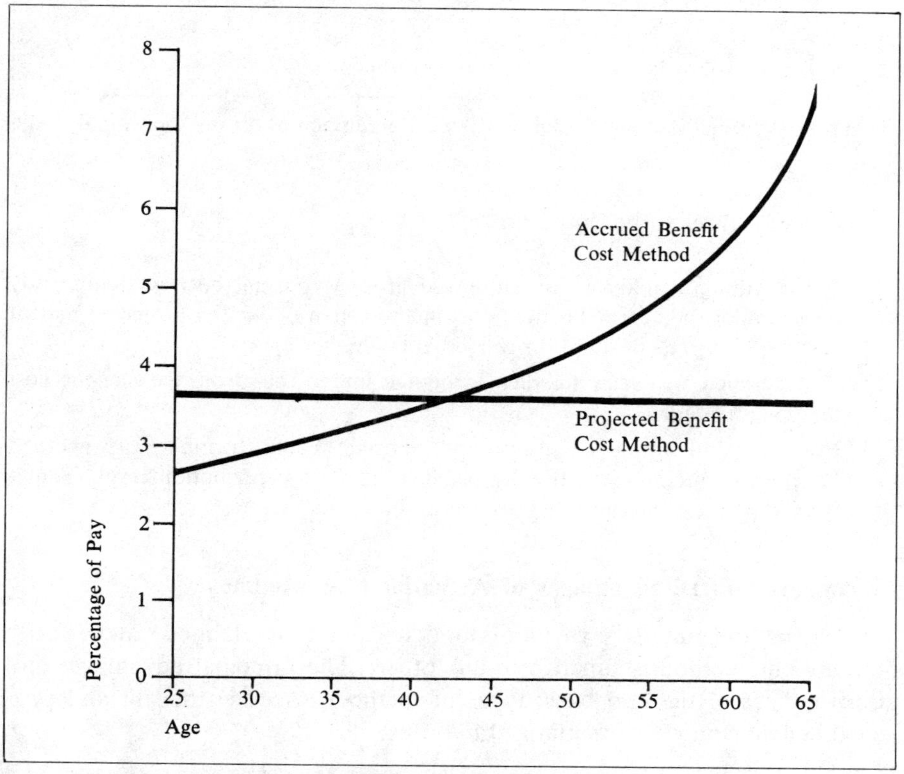

Fig. 11.2 Normal Cost As a Percentage of Pay—Varying By Age

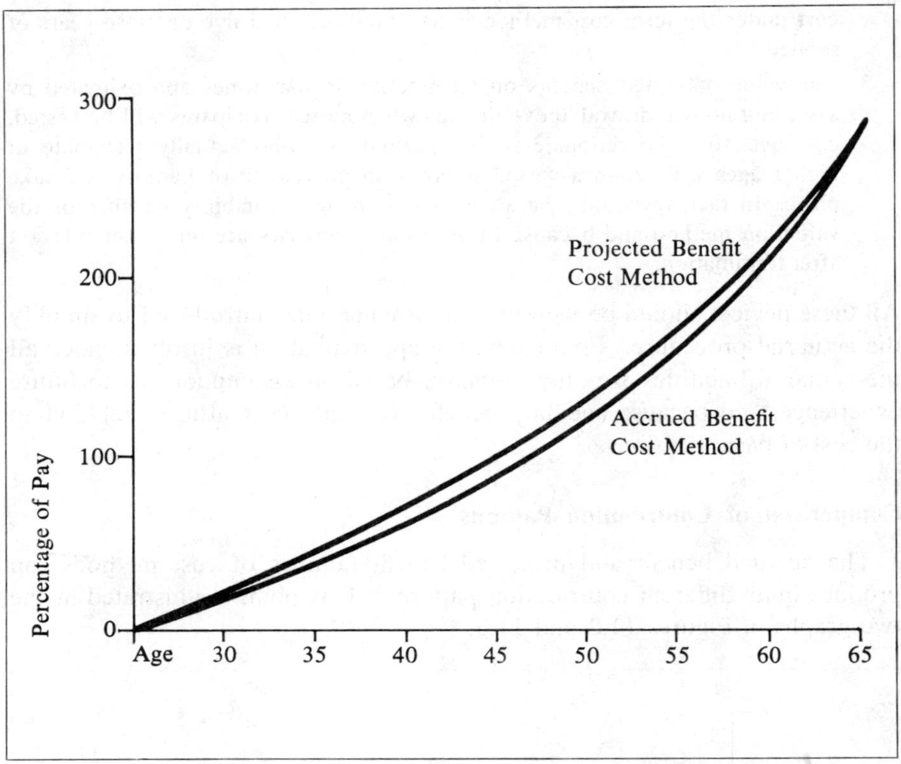

Fig. 11.3 Accrued Actuarial Liability As a Percentage of Pay—Varying By Age

The key features to be noted are:

1. For a young employee (or employee group), normal cost is significantly lower under the accrued benefit cost method than under the projected benefit cost method. The position is reversed at the higher ages.
2. The accrued actuarial liability is higher under the projected benefit cost method at all ages.
3. For a typical employee group and normal benefit formula, the accrued benefit cost method will usually produce a lower contribution level. Sometimes the difference can be as large as 50 percent.

Advantages and Disadvantages of Actuarial Cost Methods

Each method has its own merits and it cannot be claimed categorically that any one method is superior to any other. The principal advantages and disadvantages of the two basic types of methods (accrued benefit and projected benefit) may be summarized like this:

Method	*Advantages*	*Disadvantages*
Accrued Benefit	Costs generally lower for most employee groups	Costs tend to increase if average age of covered group increases
	Accrued actuarial liability consistent with target of funding value of accrued benefits	Some variants (e.g., salary pro rate procedure) not acceptable under ERISA
Projected Benefit	High degree of stability in normal cost	Tends to overfund accrued benefits
	Conservatism appeals to some employers	Costs generally higher than under accrued benefit method

Fig. 11.4 Advantages and Disadvantages of Actuarial Cost Methods

VALUATION OF ASSETS

Purposes of Valuation

Depending on the purpose, assets of a defined benefit pension plan may be valued in different ways. Normally, there will be a distinction between three different purposes.

Fund Accounting Purposes. Fund accounting covers the preparation of statements showing the fund's income, outgo, and balance at the end of the year. These statements are usually prepared by the trustee or insurance company and have historically accounted for assets on the basis of *book value,* or original cost.

However, more recently it has become the practice to present fund accounting on the basis of *fair market value,* with supplementary schedules giving a list of all securities held with both original cost and market values. This trend has been reinforced by the publication (in March 1980) of Statement of Financial Accounting Standards No. 35 of the FASB. This standard covers the preparation of financial statements for a defined benefit pension plan (the plan, not the sponsor) and mandates the valuation of assets at fair market value.

Investment Purposes. For investment purposes, especially the measurement of investment performance, it is almost universal practice to use market value. The principal reason is to obtain valid comparisons between one pension fund and another.

From the investment point of view, market value is obviously important, since it represents (at least approximately) the price at which specific securities could have been sold or bought on a given day.

Actuarial Purposes. Even within this limited area, there may be more than one purpose. For example, if a plan is about to be terminated, market value would be the most objective test of the plan's solvency. Market value can also be important in situations in which sponsoring organizations are being acquired, merged, or spun off. However, pension fund assets are routinely valued to determine appropriate contribution levels. This is the aspect that will be dealt with in more detail below.

Objectives of Asset Valuation

In a *regular actuarial valuation,* the value of the pension fund assets on the valuation date plays an important part in the setting of future contribution levels. The employer and the actuary will typically wish to choose an asset valuation procedure that satisfies, to the extent possible, the following objectives:

1. It would generally be desirable to have a contribution pattern that is relatively stable and that will not fluctuate unduly as the market rises and falls.
2. Assets should be valued in a manner consistent with the techniques used for determining actuarial liabilities. In particular, the asset valuation procedure should relate logically to the actuarial assumptions as to investment return, inflation, and salary progression.
3. The asset valuation procedure should also be consistent with the investment policy followed under the plan. For instance, assets might be valued differently if an active investment policy has been selected and securities are bought and sold frequently. Another example applies especially to the equity portfolio. If common stocks have been purchased primarily to obtain capital gains, it may be appropriate to recognize gains for actuarial purposes even before they are realized.
4. On the other hand, most employers believe it is important for the actuarial procedure for valuing assets to have no impact on the decisions of the investment manager. The general concept is that securities should be bought and sold for investment reasons, not to influence the actuarial valuation.

ERISA Requirements

In connection with the minimum funding standards, ERISA and subsequent regulations lay down certain rules for the valuation of assets for actuarial purposes.

Basically, the provisions in the statute allow for assets to be valued by any reasonable formula that "takes into account fair market value." Under a special option, the employer may elect to value bonds at cost together with amortization of the premium or discount over the period from purchase to earliest call or maturity.

Proposed regulations from the IRS have amplified these requirements without giving a comprehensive list of acceptable methods. Two specific provisions in these proposed regulations merit attention. The first is that the actuarial value of assets must lie within a "corridor" between 80 percent of market and 120 percent of market value. The second is that the asset valuation procedure is considered a part of the actuarial cost method, which means that *prior* approval from the IRS is required before a change can be made.

Typical Asset Valuation Procedures

Basically, there are four types of asset valuation procedures.

Original Cost Method. The original cost method consists of keeping a security valued at its original cost, or *book value,* until it is actually sold. At the time of sale, there would be a realized gain or loss comprising the difference between original cost and selling price.

For many years, the original cost method was widely used in actuarial valuations, largely because it is simple to use and it gives a very stable cost pattern unless there is heavy turnover in the portfolio. With the passage of ERISA, the method is now considered unacceptable, although it could be argued that if the 80 percent/120 percent corridor were superimposed, the method takes into account fair market value. In fact, the method was viewed with less favor even before ERISA was enacted. The main disadvantage is that capital gains are not recognized until they are realized, so that superior investment performance in times of appreciation would not be reflected in the determination of contributions.

Market Value Method. At the other end of the scale is the market value method, which merely values assets at market value on the valuation date. Obviously, this method is acceptable under ERISA, and it too is simple to use. The market value method satisfies most of the objectives for an asset valuation procedure, and it has the additional advantage of using the same asset values applied for accounting and investment purposes. On the other hand, it does tend to produce an unstable contribution pattern if the stock market is volatile.

Nevertheless, many actuaries use market values for actuarial purposes. The main argument is that actuarial gains and losses (as described below) can be spread over a period of up to fifteen years or absorbed into the normal cost, depending on the actuarial cost method. Generally, this means that a market value decline of 30 percent of assets will only increase annual contributions by about 3 percent of the asset value. Moreover, if the market rebounds the following year, there will be a gain that will reduce contributions again.

Earnings Power Method. The earnings power method operates on a completely different system. The theory is that if liabilities are valued by determining the present value of future benefit payments, assets could then be valued by calculating the present value of future interest, dividends, redemption values, and security sales. The method is widely used in the United Kingdom and a few other countries but has never become prevalent in the United States. The major disadvantage is that actuarial values can be vastly different from market values. In its pure form the method would not be acceptable under ERISA, but it could perhaps be modified to comply with the Act if the required corridor were incorporated.

Formula Methods. Finally, there are many formula methods that are commonly used. All of them have two characteristics:

- Actuarial values of assets are determined according to some kind of formula. To comply with ERISA, the formula is in some way based on market values.
- The basic objective is to follow the underlying trend of market values but not their fluctuations.

There are so many varieties of formula methods that it would be impossible to give a complete description. In addition the nomenclature used is far from standard, and the detailed application of each formula varies slightly between individual actuaries and firms of actuaries. A few examples of some of the approaches are briefly described below:

1. Actuarial value is related to current market value in the same ratio as the average over the previous five years.
2. An adjusted book value is used, and the previous year's value (together with income and outgo) is written up or down by 25 percent of the difference to current market value.
3. A variation of the formula in (2) would vary the percentage write-up (or write-down) according to the percentage difference between adjusted book value and market value.
4. A fixed write-up (of, e.g., 3 percent) is added provided market value exceeds adjusted book value by at least 15 percent.
5. The previous year's adjusted book value is brought forward at the assumed rate of interest, and the result is adjusted by 20 percent of the difference between the result and the current market value.

Each of these formulas has its advantages and disadvantages, but the final results often differ only to a minor degree.

CONTRIBUTION LEVELS

The three elements of actuarial cost, which have been discussed earlier, form the basis for determination of future contributions to the plan. These elements are:

1. The normal cost
2. The accrued actuarial liability
3. The actuarial value of assets

The excess of the accrued actuarial liability over the assets, that is to say (2) minus (3), is the unfunded actuarial liability, which is also an important element.

Actuarial Gain and Loss

A final element, which has not been discussed in detail, is the actuarial gain or loss for a particular year. Essentially, a gain (or loss) occurs if the unfunded actuarial liability at the end of the year is lower (or higher) than it would have been if actual experience in the year had exactly matched the assumptions. Typically, actuarial gains and losses arise in these situations:

- Investment return higher (lower) than the assumed rate of interest will produce an actuarial gain (loss)
- Salary increases higher (lower) than the assumed rates of increase will produce an actuarial loss (gain)
- Turnover higher (lower) than expected will produce an actuarial gain (loss)
- Sharp changes in the ages at which employees retire can produce gains or losses

Of course, a gain or loss can be associated with each of the actuarial assumptions, and indeed, it is unusual to find any assumption precisely reproduced by experience. Gains and losses can also arise from other sources, such as a change or correction in the employee data.

It will also be recalled that some actuarial cost methods, for example the frozen initial liability method, reveal no actuarial gains or losses. The effect of deviations from experience is spread back into normal cost.

Minimum Funding Standards

An important step in the determination of appropriate contribution levels is the calculation of the minimum contribution required. This must be determined according to the minimum funding standards of ERISA, as briefly described below. (The standards are discussed in detail in Chapter 14.)

1. Normal cost for the year, *plus*
2. Amortization over forty years of the initial unfunded liability when ERISA first applied, usually the beginning of the plan year in 1976. (This forty-year period is reduced to thirty years if the plan was not in existence on January 1, 1974.) *plus*
3. Amortization over thirty years of any additional liability arising after 1976 because of a change in the plan, actuarial cost method, or actuarial assumptions. (A negative amortization (reduction in contribution) applies if the accrued actuarial liability is decreased because of these changes.) *plus*
4. Amortization over fifteen years of any actuarial loss. (A gain would produce a contribution decrease, over fifteen years.)

Amortization. The amortization payments are equal annual amounts over the period involved that are equal in value to the liability or gain or loss that is being paid off. The process is almost identical to payments of capital and interest to redeem a mortgage.

Adjustment for Interest. All the payments due under the minimum funding standard must be adjusted for interest from the time they are due until the date the contribution is actually made. Interest does not have to be carried forward beyond the end of the year even if payments are made after that date. Since many employers do in fact delay their contributions until the latest date allowed (which may be as late as the following September 15, assuming a calendar-year tax year), it is normal practice for the minimum contribution to be adjusted for interest up to the end of the year.

Full Funding Limitation. It is also important to note that ERISA also contains a full funding limitation (requiring payment of no more than is needed to cover normal cost plus any unfunded actuarial liability) and provides for an alternative minimum calculation. These situations are seldom encountered and will not be described here.

Funding Standard Account

Calculation of the actual minimum required contribution follows the format of the funding standard account as laid down in ERISA. This account follows the outline given in the preceding paragraph but is laid out in the form of an accounting statement with debits and credits. The debits include normal cost and all the positive amortization amounts required to pay off liabilities. The credits comprise negative amortization amounts (arising from reduction in liabilities) and the actual employer contribution.

Compliance with ERISA demands that credits exceed debits on a *cumulative* basis, since the date the minimum funding standards were first effective for the plan (typically 1976 for older plans). This means that if in any year employer contributions are in excess of the minimum, a credit balance is created and is carried forward to the next year. The credit could then be used to permit contributions that are lower than the required minimum level. If a large enough credit is built up, the employer could conceivably skip contributions for a year (or more).

Tax-Deductible Limit

The Internal Revenue Code (as amended by ERISA) also provides for a maximum contribution for which a tax deduction may be claimed each year by the employer. This tax-deductible limit comprises:

1. Normal cost for the year, *plus*
2. Amortization over a ten-year period of the initial unfunded actuarial liability and any increases due to changes or actuarial losses. Once again, there is negative amortization in terms of decreases in liability or actuarial gains, in this case over ten years.

Technically, the tax-deductible limit is not a maximum contribution, since larger amounts could be contributed. Any excess would be carried forward and would be eligible for deduction in a later year, subject always to the tax-deductible limit for the year. In practice, employers are normally reluctant to contribute amounts for which an immediate tax deduction cannot be claimed; therefore the tax-deductible limit usually is viewed as a maximum.

Typical Contribution Practices

Employers are faced with a range of acceptable contributions between the minimum required contribution and the tax-deductible limit. The breadth of this range varies according to the history of the plan but is, broadly speaking, related to the amount of the unfunded actuarial liability. If the plan is well funded (that is, if the unfunded actuarial liability is relatively small), the percentage difference between minimum and maximum will also be small.

Within this range, the employer has flexibility to set his own contribution policy. This flexibility is, however, somewhat circumscribed by accounting rules. In particular, the auditors will probably demand a consistent charge to pension expense, which makes it difficult to contribute at the maximum deductible level one year and at the minimum level another year.

Common practice is to contribute on a basis slightly above the minimum level. This allows for the accumulation of a cushion in case an especially adverse year should be encountered and it becomes necessary to contribute at the absolute minimum level. Accordingly it is common to see employers setting contribution policy at:

1. The minimum level under ERISA without allowing for prior credit balances, *or*

2. Amortization over twenty or twenty-five years (instead of the thirty or forty years prescribed by ERISA), which results in contributions somewhat higher than the minimum funding standards.

Some employers are contributing at or near the maximum tax-deductible contribution, but this is relatively rare among large employers, especially in times of economic uncertainty.

THE ACTUARIAL VALUATION

For the plan sponsor, the *valuation*, often performed annually, is the most conspicuous part of the actuarial process. Basically, the valuation consists of a reporting of the actuarial liabilities, along the lines already discussed, and of the plan's assets so that the financial status of the plan can be evaluated.

Purposes of the Valuation

Determination of Contribution Levels. Employers consider the valuation's most important objective to be the determination of appropriate contribution levels for the following (or possibly preceding) year. Actuarial calculations under most cost techniques produce a range of acceptable contributions between the minimum ERISA requirement and the tax-deductible limit. Within this range, the employer may have decided on a funding policy, of, e.g., thirty-year amortization of unfunded actuarial liability.

Funding Status. In the typical modern valuation, the funding progress is tested in two ways:

1. The assets are compared with the accrued actuarial liability which represents the goal under the actuarial cost method (and assumptions) selected. Any excess of accrued actuarial liability over assets on hand is referred to as an *unfunded liability* and any excess of assets over accrued actuarial liability is considered a *surplus*. Most plans show an unfunded liability and this is normally no cause for concern. What is more important to the employer, and the actuary, is that his unfunded liability is decreasing over time, at a rate approximately in line with the employer's funding objectives.

2. The valuation will usually show the present value of both vested and accrued benefits as of the valuation date. These figures are required for accounting purposes but they also form important benchmarks for gauging funding progress. In fact, many employers have set their funding targets in relation to these two values, rather than to the accrued actuarial liability. In other words, the accumulation of assets equal to, e.g., the value of all accrued

benefits is judged to be more important than covering the accrued actuarial liability.

Reporting. The third most important purpose is to produce information needed to satisfy various reporting requirements. The key requirements are:

- The completion of the funding standard account, as mandated by ERISA
- Determination of the tax-deductible limits under IRS regulations
- Calculation of the values of vested and accrued benefits, required by the auditors

Analysis of Experience. A fourth purpose, sometimes of more significance to the actuary than to the employer, is to compare actual experience under the plan with that anticipated by the actuarial assumptions. This is often referred to as an analysis of actuarial gains and losses. Actuarial assumptions are merely predictions of expected future events, such as salary increases. As each year passes, the actual experience for that year (e.g., the actual increases in salary) will become known. For the plan, it is important to know the extent to which the predictions were right or wrong, and perhaps the financial effect of any deviations of actual from expected. By accumulating information about these deviations, the actuary will then be in a position to recommend changes in the actuarial assumptions.

Frequency of Valuations

ERISA requires that an actuarial valuation be made no less frequently than once every three years. In the United States, valuations are commonly made annually. Some employers have tried to economize on actuarial fees by arranging for valuations every two years. However, they often find that the savings are relatively small since the calculations are not routine. Moreover, in times of substantial economic variation, funding status and contribution adequacy should be investigated more frequently.

SPECIAL ACTUARIAL CALCULATIONS

Special calculations are required when the plan is being changed in some way or when a decision is required on some financial aspect of a defined benefit pension plan.

Plan Changes

The most common type of special calculation is made when consideration is being given to changes in a plan, or to the adoption of a new plan. The employer will want to know the cost of the revision or the new plan.

For this purpose, the actuary will go through almost exactly the same procedure as for a regular valuation, except that for a plan change, he will calculate the liabilities both before and after the change. These liabilities will, of course, include both normal cost and accrued actuarial liability so that the addition in each element due to the proposed change can be determined. A similar process would be followed to determine the cost impact of a change in actuarial assumptions or methods. In fact, it is common to find changes in the plan and changes in actuarial assumptions occurring simultaneously.

Plan Terminations

Special calculations are almost invariably required when a plan is terminated. In the first place, there may be a residual liability under Title IV of ERISA if assets do not cover the value of all insured benefits. Secondly, remaining assets may have to be allocated according to the priorities in Section 4044 of ERISA.

These "Section 4044" calculations are often complex, mainly because the PBGC does not insure all vested benefits. There are maximums on the insured benefits, as well as limitations on the basic benefit so that certain ancillary features (e.g., supplemental benefits on early retirement) are not covered. Moreover, a phase-in rule provides that the additional benefits arising from a substantive plan amendment become fully insured only after they are in effect for five years. For a plan that has been frequently changed, this phase-in rule alone can demand multiple calculations.

Mergers and Spinoffs

Mergers, spinoffs and other forms of corporate reorganization are enormously complex and frequently require additional calculations. Although each case has its own characteristics, a few points may prove helpful:

1. In many corporate acquisitions, a plan termination is involved. In this event, the comments in the preceding section will apply.
2. If a *plan* merger or spinoff is necessary, then Section 208 of ERISA must be followed. Basically, this section provides that all participants involved must be no worse off if the plan(s) were terminated immediately after the merger or spinoff than they would be if the plan(s) were terminated immediately before that event.
3. In the case of a spinoff, Section 208 leads to the conclusion that assets must be allocated to the two sets of plan participants exactly as if they were being allocated in the event of a plan termination. In other words, a "Section 4044 calculation" becomes necessary to allocate assets to each participant in the plan before spinoff.
4. If the plan before spinoff has enough assets to cover the value of all accrued benefits, a Section 4044 calculation is not needed, provided each plan after

the spinoff has enough assets to cover its accrued benefits. There can, however, be some argument as to how any excess of assets above the value of accrued benefits should be split among the two plans.

5. Section 4044 calculations can also be avoided if the group being spun off carries liabilities of no more than 3 percent of the liabilities for the whole plan, provided assets equal to the value of total accrued benefits are allocated to the spinoff group.
6. A literal interpretation of Section 208 would prevent the merger of two plans that are funded to a different extent. This is because if the merged plan were then terminated some assets that would have "belonged" to the better-funded group could be allocated to participants in the other group.

   Special regulations have been published to resolve this problem. These regulations allow the establishment of a "special schedule" which gives priority to the participants in the prior plan that was better funded. The regulations further provide that the special schedule need not be calculated provided data is maintained to allow for the calculation to be made if the plan is terminated within five years of the plan merger. The regulations specifically provide that the plan's actuary certify to the maintenance of the data and he will, of course, work closely with the employer to insure the data is in fact recorded and stored.
7. Another common arrangement in corporate acquisitions is for a special payment in the event that plan assets are either more or less than the value of accrued benefits on the date the acquisition becomes effective. The assumptions to be used are sometimes specified in the agreement of purchase and sale. These calculations will be processed in the same way as the determination of the value of accrued benefits in a regular valuation.
8. Finally, actuarial expertise may be important in the negotiation of an agreement of purchase and sale.

Projections

Reference should be made to projections of future events which might include:

- Benefit outgo
- Contributions
- Investment return
- Asset accumulation

In the last resort it is even possible to simulate future actuarial valuations. The concept works in the following manner:

1. Obviously the present work force is known. If assumptions about turnover, retirement, death, disability, and the hiring of new employees are applied, then a projected work force for each year in the future can be constructed. Assumptions as to future salary increases and salaries at the time of employment can then be combined to simulate complete employee census data for

each future year. It is then possible to complete "future valuations" on this census data.

2. Asset accumulation can be built up from the contributions derived from the future valuations and other assumptions as to investment return, appreciation, etc.
3. Thus, the simulation can produce a complete picture of the future experience of the plan. Note, however, that this picture is based on specific assumptions used, although it is quite possible to build a matrix of simulations based on a number of different sets of assumptions.

Advantages. The results of projections can prove very illuminating in a number of different ways:

1. These projections provide answers to questions such as: how large will the pension fund assets be in 1989? Furthermore, the year-by-year simulation allows the employer to see how the assets build up each year.
2. The projections can allow for experience to be different from the valuation assumptions. For example, future valuations could employ an assumed interest rate of, e.g., 6 percent but the asset accumulation could allow for a return of 10 percent or 2 percent. The simulation would then show the impact on the 1986 contribution (for example) of investment return 4 percent above or below what the valuation assumptions predict. It is even possible to test the effect of experience that varies over time, for example 10 percent return over the next three years, thereafter reducing one percent per year down to 5 percent per year after eight years.
3. The projection or simulation technique can be used for testing the impact of various investment strategies, such as variations in asset mix.

Potential Dangers. Although projections are a valuable tool and one that is popular with employers, the following dangers exist:

1. The calculations are relatively expensive to process if they are to produce exactly what the employer wants. Prepackaged programs are available at lower cost but they tend to be inflexible.
2. Too many variations of assumptions may be used, resulting in a positive avalanche of figures. To give a simple example, three assumptions of workforce growth plus three of investment return plus three of inflation, will produce twenty-seven sets of simulations.
3. It must always be borne in mind that the simulations are based on *assumptions*. Moreover, the longer the future time span, the more the assumptions swamp the facts of the present work force and assets. This is why it is usually unwise to project for more than a ten-year or fifteen-year period.

FUNDING VEHICLES

The actuarial assumptions and methods, together with the plan's provisions and participant demographics, determine how much should be contributed to the pension fund. It remains to be decided how the "pension fund" will be structured.

Types of Funding Vehicles

In order to make benefits as secure as possible, pension fund assets are separated from, and divorced from the control of, the employer. Otherwise, there is a risk that the pension fund will be used to meet the claims of general creditors if the employer becomes insolvent.

ERISA requires that all assets of a plan be held in trust, unless the assets "consist of insurance contracts or policies issued by an insurance company qualified to do business in a state." Thus a pension plan must invest its assets in either a trust or an insurance contract or both. These two types of financing vehicles, *insured* and *trusteed* are explored below. However, it may be useful to first explain two of the main ways in which financing vehicles are categorized.

Insured vs. Trusteed. For a number of years, especially in the 1950s and 1960s, there was intense competition between insurance companies and banks for investment of pension funds. This competition was often referred to as the "insured vs. trusteed" controversy. Basically, the two opposing sides were:

- The insurance companies offering products that guaranteed benefits and returns, but were relatively inflexible.
- The banks, operating as trustees, which would set up separate funds for each plan invested in common stocks, bonds, real estate, or whatever other security seemed appropriate.

The relative merits of each of these two approaches will be investigated but it should be noted that, in more recent times, the differences have become blurred. A trustee can invest part (or all) of the pension fund assets in an insurance policy. Thus, a plan can be both "trusteed" and "insured."

Moreover, some of the modern insurance contracts have all the characteristics of a "trusteed" vehicle, except that the assets are invested by an insurance company, instead of a bank or trustee company. Needless to say, however, there is still vigorous competition for pension fund business.

Allocated vs. Unallocated. It is also important to make a distinction between *allocated* and *unallocated* financing, especially under insured vehicles.

Under the allocated procedure, a separate contribution (or cost) is determined for each *individual* participant, and the total plan cost is the sum of the costs for all the individuals. Moreover, at any point in time, it is usually possible to determine how much of the total fund "belongs to" a given participant. The clearest example is a plan financed through individual policies.

Each participant has premiums and cash values which can be separately identified.

Unallocated funding is based on contributions, costs and assets being determined for the whole participant *group*. No specific part of the contribution, or of the pension fund, is identified as relating to any individual participant. Note, however, that although financing is considered "allocated" because individual costs are determined, this does not necessarily mean that specific assets, in terms of shares of IBM stock or U.S. Treasury bills, are held in the name of any employee. In fact, under most allocated insurance contracts, the assets are all part of the insurer's general reserves.

INSURED FUNDING ARRANGEMENTS

The Insurance Contract

The main types of insurance contract used for financing defined benefit pension plans are described below. Commonly accepted terminology is used generally but unfortunately, in this area there is little standardization, and different insurers use different names to describe their products. Four key characteristics distinguish one type of insurance contract from another:

1. *Guarantees.* Insurance companies can provide guarantees against fluctuations, especially of mortality and interest, while banks can provide no guarantees of this kind. Perhaps the easiest way to understand these guarantees is to examine an immediate annuity. Under this type of policy, a fixed purchase price of, e.g., $10,000 is used to purchase a fixed benefit of, e.g., $1,000 per year for the lifetime of the participant. Here are guarantees of interest and mortality of the simplest kind. Once the purchase is made, the insurance company will continue paying the annuity (of $1,000 per year) regardless of the current market rate of return. Whether interest rates go up or down, the insurer will pay the same benefit. Moreover, the benefit will be paid no matter how long the annuitant (or participant) lives, even up to age 100 or beyond.

   In this example, the purest form of insurance would provide for the same benefit ($1,000 per year for life) to be paid for the original purchase price ($10,000), without any consideration being given to actual experience after the original purchase was made. This is usually referred to as a *non-participating* policy.

2. *Experience rating.* It will be apparent that the insurance company makes a "gain" if the annuitant dies very soon after the purchase was made and takes a "loss" if the annuitant lives long after his life expectancy, as based on the mortality table used for setting the original purchase price. In addition, when the purchase price was set, the insurance company was anticipating a certain investment return on the $10,000 it received, after allowing for benefit payments. This might have been, e.g., 8 percent in which event the insurance company makes a gain if it earns more than 8 percent or a loss if it earns less than 8 percent.

Under the *participating* form of insurance contract, the insurance company shares its gains (in this case on both mortality and interest) with the policyholder. For example, if the annuitant died after only six months of payments, the resulting gain would eventually be passed back to the original policyholder.

The way in which gains are shared varies according to the type of contract:

- *Pooling.* Under some contracts, all experience is "pooled" which means that all policies of the same nature are considered together. The early death of one annuitant may be offset by abnormal longevity of another. Only if the pool as a whole shows a gain, will a "dividend" be paid to the policyholders and then each policyholder will receive a small dividend based on his share of the total pool's results, and not necessarily on the results of his policy.
- *Experience rating.* The opposite of "pooling" is "experience rating." Under the latter form, the policyholder receives a dividend if there is a gain under his policy, whether or not there are gains under similar policies held by other individuals.
- *Dividends.* The distribution, or recognition, of gains in some contracts is relatively immediate (typically in the same or following year); in others, dividends may emerge slowly as experience develops. Typically, insurance companies have dividend formulas, operated largely at their own discretion, under which dividends are distributed on the basis of actual experience over a period of time, while smoothing out fluctuations from one year to the next.
- *Losses.* The policyholder may share in losses, as well as gains. Under the older types of participating contracts, the policyholder could receive a dividend (in the event of a gain) but would not be charged any additional premium or other cost if experience showed a loss. Under some of the modern forms of insurance arrangements, the policyholder shares in the total experience of his contract, whether it be a gain or a loss, measured against original anticipations.

3. *Allocated vs. unallocated.* Types of insurance contracts differ in the extent to which costs are allocated to individuals or are unallocated. This feature was covered earlier in the discussion of types of funding vehicles.
4. *Flexibility.* Insurance arrangements also vary widely in the degree and kind of flexibility they afford to the plan sponsor. Flexibility can take many forms but the main ones that are of interest to the employer are:

   —*Flexibility in plan benefits.* Most employers want to design their plans first and then decide how to finance them. They are less enthusiastic about buying standard benefit packages that the insurance companies might offer.

   —*Flexibility in plan costs.* Reference has already been made to the relatively wide range of contributions allowed under ERISA and accepted actuarial practice. This flexibility can be severely limited if the insurance company charges a fixed contribution for a given benefit level.

   —*Flexibility in investment.* Some insurance contracts offer investment only in the general assets of the insurer which is typically a very large portfolio invested as the insurance company sees fit, subject to state insurance regulation. Other contracts offer, to each plan sponsor, the ability to vary the asset mix, especially as regards the percentage to be invested in common stocks.

—*Flexibility to change vehicles.* One of the major criticisms of insurance contracts, particularly the older versions, has been the difficulty and financial loss involved in cancelling the contract and switching to another type of vehicle. This is still a contentious issue but the newer forms of contract do provide far more flexible cash-out conditions.

New Insurance Products. As the various types of insurance contract are reviewed, it will be seen that the modern forms, as they are designed for the larger plans, tend to provide:

- Less extensive guarantees, except as regards interest
- More complete and more immediate participation in gains
- Unallocated funding
- Greater flexibility in virtually all areas

Insurance companies are continually developing new products, especially in the face of competition, both with other insurers and with other "trusteed" vehicles. Some of these new products contain virtually no "insurance" at all and resemble trust funds managed by an insurance company.

Individual Contracts

In the early days of pension plan development, the easiest way for an insurance company to handle the financing of these plans was to cover each participant with an individual policy. The type of policy might be one that had originally been designed for its individual ordinary business, such as a whole life or endowment insurance. Alternatively, it might be a pension policy, known variously as a *retirement annuity* or *retirement income* contract. All these policies have a common characteristic; a fixed benefit is purchased for a fixed annual premium.

When the plan first starts, or a new employee joins at a later date, the expected pension at normal retirement date is calculated and a policy is issued to cover that benefit. In the case of whole life insurance, the calculation is made so that the policy's cash value will be adequate to purchase an annuity at normal retirement. If a later salary increase occurs so that the expected benefit increases, a new policy is issued to cover the additional benefit, so that one individual could be covered by many policies, issued at different ages.

Another important feature is that most of these policy forms include substantial death benefits. For example, under endowment insurance, the death benefit equals the cash sum payable at maturity, i.e., at normal retirement.

The typical retirement income contract contains a death benefit of $1,000 for each $10 per month of insured pension.

Key Characteristics. In terms of the key characteristics enumerated earlier, these individual policies provide:

1. Relatively complete guarantees of interest and mortality. Once a contract is issued, the insurance company guarantees its benefits, in return for payment of fixed annual premiums.
2. Sharing of gains, but on a pooled basis subject to the insurer's dividend formula. Some plans have been financed through nonparticipating individual policies but it has been generally believed that participating policies are less costly.
3. Full allocation of costs. Policies are issued in the names of individuals and premiums are calculated separately for each policy. It is common also for dividends to be declared for each policy.
4. Virtually no flexibility. Except for the possibility of issuing new policies or surrendering old ones, benefits must be exactly as provided in the policies. There is no flexibility as regards contributions and investment mix.

Application. Although there have been relatively large plans insured through individual policies, nowadays this arrangement is used almost exclusively for small groups of, e.g., one to ten employees. In addition, because of the inflexibility of the benefit structure, only certain kinds of plans can be financed through conventional policy forms.

Individual Policy Pension Trust

The Individual Policy Pension Trust (IPPT) was developed from the individual policy funding arrangement, principally in order to give more flexibility and to solve the problem of inordinately large death benefits. Actually, the IPPT is only partly insured since it operates with a *side fund,* or *auxiliary fund* which is essentially a supplementary trust fund.

Usually, a whole life policy is issued to cover the amount of death benefit provided under the plan which might be, e.g., two times annual salary. A new policy would be issued if salary increases occur. The cash value of these policies provides a certain amount of lump sum at normal retirement, which effectively funds a part of the participant's prospective pension. The balance of the pension is financed through the side fund which may be invested with the insurance company or may be a separate portfolio of common stocks and/or bonds.

Key Characteristics. As far as the insurance policies are concerned, the characteristics of the IPPT are similar to those of individual policy arrangements. Insured benefits are guaranteed and the policies are usually participating, on a pooled basis. Obviously, the insured portion is also fully allocated. However, the side fund adds another dimension, especially as regards flexibility. It allows for investment in equities and other variations in asset mix, and it may allow for some flexibility in contribution levels.

Application. The IPPT is seldom used for plans of more than fifty or 100 participants. It is, however, a very common arrangement for smaller groups.

Group Permanent Insurance

Group permanent insurance is another variation on the use of individual policies for financing pension plans. It consists of a collection of policies, usually of the retirement annuity type, written under one overall contract, issued to the plan sponsors. Some of the administrative burden involved in issuing (and storing) a large number of individual contracts, including additional contracts for salary increases, is eased but benefits and premiums are calculated just as if individual policies were involved.

Key Characteristics. The key characteristics of group permanent insurance are almost identical to those of individual policies of the same type. Guarantees are provided for payment of the required annual premium and the contract is typically participating on a group basis. Costs are fully allocated and there is the same degree of inflexibility, especially as regards contributions and investment mix.

Application. Although group permanent insurance used to be quite prevalent, even for relatively large plans, it is no longer a common financing vehicle. The smaller plans are more likely to use IPPT funding and the larger plans tend to be financed through more flexible vehicles.

Deferred Group Annuity Contracts

Deferred group annuity contracts were developed many years ago, specifically for the funding of defined benefit pension plans. As the name implies, the one contract is issued to the employer to cover the whole participant group.

Despite the existence of a "group contract," calculations are normally made for each individual participant. For a given year, the current benefit being accrued for each participant is determined. Obviously, this is easier to do under a career-pay benefit formula than under a final-average-pay formula. The current benefit, payable from age 65 if that is the normal retirement date, is then "purchased" from the insurance company for a single premium based on a table of premium rates.

The following year, the next year's current benefit is purchased and so on each year, so that when a participant reaches retirement his benefit will be fully purchased. The insurance company then starts to pay the pension.

It is important to note that the typical deferred annuity purchased each year includes no death benefits, except possibly the return of employee contributions. Normal practice is to provide death benefits separately under a group insurance policy which gives added flexibility.

Key Characteristics. The characteristics of the deferred group annuity contract may be summarized as follows:

1. There are important guarantees of mortality and interest. Once a benefit is purchased it is fully guaranteed by the insurer, however long the participant may live.
2. The common form of contract participates in the insurance company's gains (but not losses). Typically, experience is pooled and subject to the insurer's dividend formula.
3. Since benefits and premiums are individually determined the contract is fully allocated.
4. Flexibility is mixed. The contract will theoretically accommodate any type of benefit formula but it does not operate as well for final-average-pay plans. Moreover, there are complications for plans that include modern features such as subsidized early retirement, preretirement joint and survivor annuities, and disability benefits.

   As far as current benefits are concerned, there is essentially no cost flexibility since fixed premiums will be charged for benefits purchased. However, it is possible to negotiate special amortization arrangements for past-service benefits when the plan is first adopted or later amended. This affords some flexibility in contribution levels.

   No investment flexibility is offered under the conventional deferred group annuity contract. As benefits are purchased, the premiums become part of the insurer's general assets, so the individual plan sponsor has no choice of asset mix.

   There tends to be relative inflexibility and the possibility of significant penalties in the cancellation and surrender terms.

Application. In the 1940s and 1950s, the deferred group annuity was probably the most common pension plan financing vehicle. Today, however, it is no longer considered flexible and most of these plans are now funded under a trusteed arrangement or one of the modern insurance contracts described below.

Deposit Administration

Deposit Administration (DA) represented a radical new form of contract for insurance companies. It marked the first step away from true "insurance," in the sense that insurance provides a fixed benefit for payment of a fixed premium. The system came to the forefront in the 1950s and is still popular today, even for plans with less than fifty participants.

The basic idea behind DA is that while an employee is still active (i.e., before he retires) there is no need to purchase or insure any pension. Instead, the plan's assets are kept in an *accumulation account,* merely an unallocated fund of money growing with interest. When an employee retires, his pension, then known in amount, is purchased from the insurance annuity account, and the purchase price is debited to the accumulation account. When an employee terminates with a vested pension, it may also be purchased or the purchase may be deferred until the participant's benefits are due to begin.

Credited Interest. The insurance company usually offers *interest guarantees* which take the form of *minimum* rates of interest that will be credited to the accumulation fund. These guarantees are of various types and insurers vigorously compete in offering interest guarantees. Typically the guarantees operate for a limited period only, either on money deposited during the first five years or on the first five years of operation of the contract.

Under the early DA contracts, the actual interest rate credited was set by each insurer based on the composite return on the insurance company's reserves. Thus, for all DA contracts with the same insurer, there was a uniform rate of credited interest. However, virtually all the major insurance companies have switched to an *investment year* or *new money* basis. This allows for the fact that new money invested this year will probably earn a different rate of return from new money deposited last year or the year before. Under this system, deposits are kept in *cells* for accounting purposes, each cell representing the year when the assets were deposited. Each year the insurance company will credit different rates of interest to each cell.

Purchase Rates. Another key feature is the table of rates to be used by the insurance company for the purchase of benefits as participants retire. Currently, the common practice is for the contract to contain a set of guaranteed rates which will not be exceeded, while rates actually being offered by the insurer based on prevailing rates of return will be used if they are more favorable to the plan.

Key Characteristics. The DA contract is characterized by the following features:

1. The guarantees are significant but much less extensive than under fully insured vehicles such as deferred group annuities or retirement income contracts. Some interest guarantees are provided by DA on the accumulation fund but they are usually limited over time. Interest and mortality are fully guaranteed for retired participants, since their benefits are "purchased."

2. Purchased benefits (i.e., for retired lives) are usually participating, determined according to the insurance company's dividend formula and the experience of all purchased annuities under pension business, not the experience of individual DA contracts. In a sense, the accumulation account is also participating since if the insurance company earns a higher rate of return, a higher rate of interest will be credited to the account.
3. The contract is unallocated for active participants and allocated for retired participants and possibly terminated participants with vested benefits.
4. Flexibility is much greater than under the types of insurance contracts discussed previously.
   —Almost any kind of benefit can be handled, since no purchase is made until a benefit is payable and known in amount.
   —As far as active lives are concerned, there is complete flexibility to use any actuarial methodology acceptable under ERISA. Because the insurance company is merely accumulating a pool of assets for active employees and has no interest in the size of the pool (beyond its adequacy for the purchase of eventual benefits), it is quite common for the plan to use an independent actuary, and not the insurance company, to determine appropriate contribution levels.
   —Under the conventional DA contract, investment flexibility is not offered, since all assets are pooled in the insurer's general asset account which cannot be invested to suit each contractholder. However, the development of "separate accounts," described below, can give each contractholder an opportunity to set the asset mix that suits his objectives.
   —In the older DA contracts, the flexibility to change to another medium was severely limited. The newer versions typically contain a surrender provision, although there may be a significant penalty imposed on contract cancellation, especially if rates of interest are higher at that time (with correspondingly lower market values) than at the time deposits were made to the contract.

Immediate Participation Guarantee

The Immediate Participation Guarantee (IPG) contract is a derivative of the DA moving further in the direction of more flexibility and less guarantee. In operation, the IPG contract is closely akin to a trust fund managed by an insurance company.

Differences From Deposit Administration. The main differences between an IPG and a DA contract may be summarized as follows:

1. Under IPG, benefits are *not* automatically purchased when a participant retires. Instead, the pension is paid out of the "accumulation fund" monthly, quarterly or however the plan may provide. However, payment of the pension is guaranteed by the insurer who earmarks a part of the total fund as covering the liability for these retired participants. If the

contract is terminated, the insurance company usually has the right to purchase the benefits from its annuity account.

It will be seen then that the IPG contract is, in normal operation, totally unallocated while the DA contract is allocated as far as retired participants are concerned.

2. The other major difference lies in flexibility of investment, although this distinction is becoming more vague. Most IPG contracts provide for the accumulation fund to be invested not only in the insurer's general asset account but also in a number of "separate accounts." These separate accounts are essentially investment pools established for qualified pension or profit-sharing plans. The original intent was to allow pension plans to hold a larger percentage of assets in common stocks than the insurance company was permitted, under state law, for its general assets. Thus, the traditional separate account is invested in common stocks.

   However, many of the major insurance companies have developed a variety of separate accounts which might, for example, be invested in venture capital stocks, special situations, real estate and so on. Individual plans can be invested in a number of these pools, for instance 50 percent in the insurer's general assets (essentially fixed interest securities), 40 percent in an equity separate account and 10 percent in a real estate separate account. This affords each plan the opportunity to set its own investment mix. For very large plans, some insurance companies are prepared to go one step further and set up a "separate separate account." This is a portfolio designed and invested solely for that plan.
3. As flexibility increases, guarantees decrease. Since the separate accounts are merely pools of investment, apart from the general assets of the insurance company, they carry no interest guarantees. However, there will typically be guarantees on the interest credited to general account assets.
4. It will be noted also that, unless an IPG contract terminates triggering the purchase of benefits for retired lives, there is no mortality guarantee. Benefits will be paid out of the accumulation fund for as long as the participant (and his survivor under some forms of pension) lives. The plan, therefore, receives immediate gain or loss in the case of abnormally heavy or light mortality.

Application. The absence of guarantees (except for interest on assets in the insurer's general account) has led to the normal practice of using IPG contracts only for the larger plans. What this really means is that IPG is in direct competition with the trust funds.

Investment-Only Contracts

Many insurance companies have gone one step further in the development of more flexible contracts. They offer what is usually referred to as an "investment only" contract, which is really a modification of the IPG vehicle.

Method of Operation. This is what might be termed the leading edge of insurance contract development. For that reason, practices vary from one insurance company to another and new refinements are frequently made. However, the typical investment-only contract, and the key points of difference from an IPG contract, may be described as follows:

1. The payment of benefits is not guaranteed by the insurer beyond the current year. This means that reserves for retired participants do not have to be earmarked, and assets can be transferred to and from the contract with greater flexibility.
2. Investment may be made in the insurer's general account or the variety of separate accounts, in just the same way as under an IPG contract.
3. However, it is common to find a Guaranteed Investment Contract (GIC) form offered as well. GIC is basically a fixed investment for a fixed period at a guaranteed rate of interest. At the end of the period, the amount deposited plus credited interest is available as a lump sum for investment in a new GIC or a different form of security.
4. Since an insurance contract must provide "insurance" in some form, an investment-only contract will normally contain options to purchase annuities. Since these options do not have to be elected, the contract is really an investment vehicle offered by an insurance company.

Application. The principal sphere of application for an investment-only contract is as *part* of the overall investment structure for a large plan. Advantage can be taken of the merits of a GIC or the ability of an insurer to guarantee interest on its general assets, within an overall structure that probably includes one or more forms of "trusteed" investment.

Summary of Insured Funding Vehicles

Figure 11.5 summarizes the main features of insured funding arrangements for defined benefit pension plans.

Some special aspects of insured funding arrangements become significant in the comparison of "insured" and "trusteed" funding vehicles.

Commissions. In the insurance business, agents and brokers traditionally are remunerated on the basis of commissions, usually expressed as a percentage of the premiums payable under the policy or contract. Problems consequently may arise since they have an incentive to *sell* insurance and to encourage the adoption of a more costly plan.

Rates of commission vary substantially from one type of contract to another. The rates are high for individual policies of the whole life and endowment insurance forms, usually running 50 percent or more of the first year's premium and 5 percent of the premium during the next nine years. Rates are considerably lower under group permanent and deferred group annuity contracts. Under DA, IPG, and investment-only contracts, commission rates are smaller still and can often be negotiated downwards to a token "finder's fee" or even to zero.

	Guarantees	Participation in Gains	Allocation	Flexibility			
				Plan Benefits	Costs	Investment	Cancellation
1. Individual Contracts	Complete as regards mortality	Usually available on pooled basis	Fully allocated	Restricted	Virtually none	None	Available but with significant penalties
2. Individual Policy	Complete on insured portion; Essentially none on side fund	Available on pooled basis on insured portion; Full experience on side fund	Partly allocated	Restricted to some extent	Considerable flexibility	On side fund only	Penalties on cancellation of policies
3. Group Permanent Insurance	Complete as regards mortality and interest	Usually available on pooled basis	Fully allocated	Restricted	Virtually none	None	May not be available and may involve penalties
4. Deferred Group Annuities	Complete as regards mortality and interest	Usually provided on pooled basis	Fully allocated	Some restrictions	Only available for past service benefits	None	May not be available and may involve penalties
5. Deposit Administration	For retired lives only	Automatic on active lives; Usual for retired life liability on pooled basis	Allocated for retired lives only	Very few restrictions	Fairly complete flexibility	None in conventional form of contract	Likely to be penalties
6. IPG Contract	Only for interest on general account assets	Automatically provided on plan's experience	Not allocated	Virtually no restrictions	Complete flexibility	Available through separate accounts	Penalty through market value adjustments
7. Investment Only Contract	Only for interest on general account assets	Automatically provided on plan's experience	Not allocated	Virtually no restrictions	Complete flexibility	Available through separate accounts	Penalty through market value adjustments

Fig. 11.5 Principal Characteristics of Insured Funding Arrangements

Liability to Participants. Under some forms of insured funding arrangements, the insurance company has a legal liability to the participants in the pension plan, as well as the plan sponsor or employer. This subject is complex, but can be summarized as follows:

- If there is a trust involved, as under IPPT, the participants will look to the trustees for payment of their benefits and will have no direct relationship with the insurance company. In effect, the insurance contract is merely an investment of the trust which can simply be sold (or surrendered) and invested in a different manner.
- If there is no trust, which is common under deferred group annuity and deposit administration contracts, the insurance company's guarantee of payment of benefits effectively extends directly to the participant. Any substantive change in this guarantee cannot be made unilaterally by the employer and may require the consent of the participants.

Changes in Funding Vehicle. This direct relationship between insurance company and plan participant may be particularly important if a change in financing vehicle is contemplated. For example, an employer cannot surrender a deferred group annuity contract and transfer the assets to a trust fund without the consent of the participants. This is because the change would involve cancellation of guarantees that had previously come into effect when benefits were purchased.

The same restriction applies when a deferred group annuity is converted to a DA or IPG contract. However, if the same insurance company is involved, it is possible to change the form of contract without cancelling the previous guarantees. The new contract will contain residual guarantees as regards benefits previously purchased and the insurance will retain the right to "repurchase" the benefits if the contract is suspended or terminated. To do this, the insurance company will write into the new contract minimum balance requirements which insure that there is always enough balance in the accumulation account to repurchase benefits for which there is a residual guarantee. Naturally, these minimum balance requirements further restrict flexibility under the contract to withdraw assets and invest them in a different funding vehicle.

NONINSURED FUNDING

Trust Funds

ERISA requires that pension plan assets be held in trust, if an insurance contract is not in force. Actually, trust funds have been used for funding defined benefit pension plans long before ERISA was enacted. In the late 1940s and 1950s "trusteed" pension plans became popular and employers began to change over from the insured vehicles that had previously been the dominant medium. Today, over 60 percent of pension fund assets are held in trust, although, because many smaller plans are insured, more plans are insured than trusteed. Note also that a plan may be financed through a trust fund and yet have assets invested partially (or totally) in insurance contracts.

Beneficiaries of Trust. The essence of a trust is that trustees are appointed to hold assets for the benefit of the beneficiaries. In the case of a pension plan, the beneficiaries are the plan's participants and their spouses and other beneficiaries. The disposition of the assets is regulated by the provisions of the plan, the trust agreement, and trust law.

Trust Investments. The trust fund itself is normally invested in various kinds of securities as allowed by the trust instrument. Typically, these are stock exchange securities such as government bonds, corporate bonds, and common stocks. Other kinds of investments are normally permitted, provided the qualification requirements of the Internal Revenue Code are met and the fiduciary standards of ERISA are satisfied. For example, real estate investment is quite common and foreign securities may be held. There is considerable discussion, although as yet little action, about pension fund investment in options and commodities.

Commingled Funds. A distinction needs to be made between investment in individual securities (such as 100 shares of IBM common stock) and participation in *commingled funds*. These commingled funds are established by many banks and some other financial institutions to provide a diversified pool of investments that can be offered to many pension and profit-sharing plans. Today, a wide variety of commingled funds is available, comprising common stocks, corporate bonds, foreign bonds, special situations, real estate and so on. The objective is, of course, to provide a spread of investments of various types to the smaller trust fund that could not obtain the same diversification in its own portfolio.

Separate Entity. Apart from any pooling in commingled funds, which is strictly for investment purposes, each trust fund is a separate entity. Contributions are received by the fund and invested, to produce investment income. The fund pays benefits when due and may also cover some administrative expenses. Each trust fund is supported by its own assets.

Key Characteristics. Although the nature of the pension trust fund is quite different from most forms of insurance contracts, it may be useful to view the trust fund in the light of the same characteristics used for examining insurance contracts.

1. There are *no guarantees* at all to the plan sponsor. Whatever investment income the fund earns, it will receive as credit, with no minimum return provisions. Moreover, since ERISA requires trust fund assets to be valued, according to a formula that takes into account fair market value, the net return on the trust fund can be negative.

   As far as mortality is concerned, the trust fund again offers no guarantees. The plan must carry its own liabilities in the event of abnormal longevity, for example.
2. The trust fund does, however, offer full *participation* in whatever profits there might be. If investment return is much larger than originally expected, the effect will be fully and immediately recognized in the performance of the fund. The opportunity to invest heavily in common stocks and to reflect immediately the gains obtained in so doing was the major reason why so many pension plans switched to the trusteed vehicle.
3. Pension trust funds are totally *unallocated,* as that term is used in discussing funding. All the assets of the fund stand behind all the benefits currently and prospectively payable, and no portion is specifically allocated to any individual participants.
4. *Flexibility* is almost complete in all areas:

   —Virtually any kind of plan benefit can be accommodated since all the trust fund has to do is pay the benefit when it becomes due.

   —Within the limits of ERISA requirements and actuarial practice, the trust fund can handle any contribution pattern that might be appropriate.

   —Apart from any legal restrictions, the asset mix of the trust fund can follow the objectives of the plan with almost total flexibility. To take an example, a pension trust fund could be invested 100 percent in common stock or 100 percent in fixed-income securities, although neither extreme might be considered entirely prudent.

   —Finally, a trust fund can easily be moved from one investment manager to another or from one trustee to another. It could also be cashed out and transferred to an insurance company, although this might involve realizing all the investments at their current market values.

It will be appreciated that the two fundamental characteristics of the trust fund are flexibility and the absence of guarantees.

Master Trusts

A special form of trust, known as a *master trust,* is offered as a service by a number of major banks. It has grown very rapidly in popularity in the last five years and is now utilized by about 60 percent of the country's largest 100 corporations. The master trust can operate a large number of different plans that are handled by several investment managers. Thus, it serves as the focal point for a variety of plans and a variety of investment managers. Assume, as a simple example, that a company has two pension plans, one for salaried and the other for hourly employees. Investment might be handled through two managers, one specializing in equities and the other in fixed-income securities. A master trust could act for both plans and coordinate the activities of both investment managers. Typically, the master trustee fulfills a number of different functions but most important are custodianship of the assets, allocation of moneys to be invested between the managers, and overall accounting.

Frequently the master trustee operates a Short-Term Investment Fund (STIF) into which contributions and other assets are deposited while they are awaiting investment at the direction of the respective investment managers. The STIF is usually handled directly by the master trustee and is invested in certificates of deposit, Treasury bills and other short-term "paper."

Advantages. The *advantages* of a master trust arrangement are typically considered to be:

- Control, on behalf of the plan sponsor, over the assets of a number of plans and the activities of several investment managers.
- Consistency in the application of investment guidelines.
- Coordination of the multiple manager setup.
- Consistency in accounting and reporting.
- Additional services provided by the master trustee. Many institutions offering the master trust facility offer as a by-product reports on investment performance, statistical analysis of the total portfolio and other diagnostic material, much of which is useful for determining whether investment objectives have been attained.

Disadvantages. The disadvantages of a master trust arrangement include the following:

- The additional cost of the master trust service.
- The loss of local autonomy over pension plan investment. Some companies have brought the pension funds of subsidiaries into one overall master trust controlled by the parent company and there have been complaints from the subsidiaries that they have lost their feeling of ownership and direction over the funds of their plans.

On balance, many large employers have felt that the advantages outweigh the disadvantages and, as mentioned, have adopted master trusts in recent years.

Investment Managers

The trustee (or trustees) generally is the custodian of the pension fund assets and is legally responsible for holding the assets on behalf of the plan and its participants. A function of almost equal importance is the investment of the assets to provide both security and investment income.

The party responsible for investment, including day-to-day decisions on which securities should be bought and sold, is usually referred to as the *investment manager*. (Note that deciding on investment policy and objectives is *not* normally handled by the investment manager. This task is usually performed by the employer himself or one of his delegates, such as an investment committee or subcommittee of the board of directors. The setting of investment objectives, policy and guidelines is discussed separately later in this chapter.)

Selection. The investment manager is usually selected by the employer, probably by the board of directors. Over the last ten years or so many larger plans have appointed several investment managers, to take advantage of specialized knowledge or expertise. Investment managers are usually chosen from among the following:

1. The *trustee* can also act as investment manager and this used to be the most common arrangement, especially if the trustee were a major bank. For many years, leading banks have handled a large volume of pension trust business and have built up investment, administrative, and accounting staff specifically to handle pension funds.
2. As discussed, *insurance companies* can act as investment managers for all or a part of a pension fund.
3. Firms of *investment advisers* (or perhaps even individuals) can also be investment managers. However, ERISA requires that they be registered as an investment adviser under the Investment Advisers Act of 1940.

   One of the reasons for the trend toward appointing multiple investment managers is that investment advisory firms often specialize, and establish a reputation, in a particular kind of investment expertise. For example, investment advisory firms may be experts in:

   —The active management of bonds
   —Investment in common stocks of "growth companies"
   —Selection of common stocks of smaller companies
   —"Market timing," which is essentially timing changes in investment between stocks, bonds and cash

4. *In-house* investment management is favored by some employers, especially for a part of the overall pension fund. The normal practice is to set up a separate "pension fund investment department" comprising investment professionals. Especially since the advent of ERISA, it is extremely uncommon to find investment management handled as a part-time duty of one of the company's officers.

Fiduciary Responsibilities. All investment managers are *fiduciaries* as described in ERISA. They are required to act "solely in the interest of the participants and beneficiaries" and to abide by what is known as the "prudent man rule." ERISA also includes a general provision regarding diversification of the plan's investments, which is yet another argument in favor of multiple investment managers.

Index Funds

The index fund is a subject much discussed and written about since the market collapse of 1973/1974, when it was found that very few investment managers were outperforming the major stock market indices, such as the Standard & Poor's 500 Stock Index. It followed that if a portfolio were invested in the stocks making up this index, it would perform better than most investment managers.

A number of banks have put together commingled common stock funds that closely match the makeup of the S&P 500 Index. For convenience and economy, the portfolio is not exactly the same as the stocks in the index. This commingled portfolio is then offered to pension funds who have appointed these banks as trustees or master trustees.

It is unusual for a pension fund to have its whole equity segment in an index fund, but many plans now invest a portion in such a fund. To date, performance has been satisfactory although quite a few investment managers did perform better than the index in 1979.

Market Inventory Funds

Some master trustees have used their index funds or a modified index fund to provide an additional service which, it is claimed, can show significant cost savings. The procedure is known as a *market inventory fund* and operates as follows:

1. Suppose one of the fund's investment managers wishes to buy or sell a stock held in the index fund.
2. If the purchase or sale can be made through the index fund, there would be a saving in brokerage fees and perhaps some financial advantage in not affecting the price in the open market.
3. The index fund would then be out of balance (as compared with the index) but necessary adjustments could be made on a planned basis after offsetting sales and purchases.

Experts conclude, after a great deal of research and many computer simulations, that a market inventory fund might be able to save one-half percent each year of the average stock portfolio.

To date only a handful of plans, all of them large, actually participate in a market inventory fund. The system is, therefore, in an early stage of development, and may even be legally challenged on the grounds that an unlawful "exchange" mechanism is created.

Immunized Bond Funds

An even newer investment device, known as the *immunized bond fund,* has recently been introduced by a few financial institutions. The intent is to lock in the current market rate of return on bonds for a given period of time, e.g., five or ten years.

Purchase of a normal bond, which yields, e.g., 10 percent to maturity, does not lock in the return of 10 percent because of the problem of reinvestment of interest payments. As interest is received (typically twice a year) it must be invested and the current market rate of return at that time could be much lower or higher than the return of 10 percent originally anticipated. The end result is that the 10 percent return may or may not be attained in total over the whole period.

An immunized bond fund achieves the "locking in" by balancing investment income against capital gains. If interest rates fall, the reinvestment of interest will be at a lower rate, but the market value of the original bond will have increased. Similarly, if interest rates rise, the higher return on reinvestment of interest will offset the loss in value of the original bond.

The results are actually achieved by a portfolio of bonds rather than a single security, and bonds are bought and sold each year. The final result is very close to a fixed total return over the five-year or ten-year period. It should be noted, however, that the return cannot be guaranteed.

SELECTION OF THE FINANCING STRUCTURE

To many pension plan sponsors, the variety of financing vehicles available is bewildering, and choosing among them is difficult. As discussed earlier in this chapter, there are many types of insurance contracts and the "trusteed" vehicle is more complex than it appears.

It is important to recognize that "cost," or outlay, quoted for a specific plan may be entirely misleading. Consider the situation of a plan sponsor who has obtained "quotations" from an insurance company and a leading bank. The insurance company might be quoting on the basis of individual policies which obviously do not allow for future salary increases. The actuary working with the bank may have allowed, in his cost estimate, for future increases in salary and *for this reason alone* might produce costs twice as high as the insurance company has quoted. Obviously, the difference lies in the way "costs" have been determined and does not reflect in any way the intrinsic merits of the two financing vehicles.

It would also be true to say that tax and regulatory (e.g., ERISA) aspects have little bearing on the selection of a financing vehicle. Apart from some minor subtleties, the tax treatment of a pension plan, its sponsor, and its beneficiaries are unaffected by the financing vehicle used, although this is not true of death benefits. In addition, the requirements of ERISA bear approximately equally on the various forms of insured and trusteed plans.

Criteria for Selection of the Vehicle

A set of logical criteria for the selection process will often be of assistance, although it does not necessarily simplify the choice. Moreover, assigning relative weights to each of the criteria almost always involves selective judgment rather than quantitative analysis.

Key Criteria. Bearing these factors in mind, the key criteria for selection of the financing vehicle are discussed briefly below:

1. There is almost unanimous agreement that *investment return* is the most important criterion. Because a pension plan operates over a long period of time and because investment return operates on a compounding basis, small differences in return can have a large impact on long-term costs.

   The common rule of thumb is that an increase of one-half percent in the rate of return, when compounded over a participant's lifetime, can reduce pension plan costs by about 10 percent.
2. For many plan sponsors, *flexibility* is the second most important criterion. This aspect has been developed as each type of vehicle was discussed and considered under four headings:

   —Benefit design

   —Contribution levels

   —Investment policy

   —Transfers to another vehicle
3. *Guarantees* may in some cases be more important than flexibility. Guarantees also have been discussed in some detail and were grouped under three headings:

   —Guarantees of interest (or return)

   —Guarantees of capital

   —Guarantees of mortality
4. *Administrative expense* is a criterion having a bearing on long-range cost but, almost invariably, it has a much smaller impact than investment return. Typical expenses might vary between 2 percent and 10 percent of annual contributions so that the difference between one vehicle and another will be completely outweighed (in the long run) by a difference of one-half percent or one percent in the rate of return.
5. *Convenience* can be a major factor, in practice. Under this heading, plan sponsors are typically interested in:

   —How the necessary services (investment, legal, actuarial, administrative, etc.) that a plan needs are provided.

   —The reporting needs that have to be met by the employer.

   —The extent to which the employer's officers will have to become involved in running the plan, possibly to the detriment of their other duties.
6. *Other criteria* often arise in specific cases, depending on the nature of the

employer, the employee group and the plan. One of the common examples is a business relationship between the employer and his bank, which needs to be respected.

Size of Employee Group. A specific factor that almost always comes into play is the size of the employee group. A small company is usually more interested in guarantees and convenience than a large company, and usually less interested in flexibility. Administrative expenses for a small plan tend to be lower under some of the insured vehicles than under the trusteed approach.

Investment Objectives

Especially since 1974 when ERISA was enacted, there has been increasing activity on the part of plan sponsors in setting investment objectives, together with guidelines for the fund's investment manager(s). Obviously, this exercise is only relevant if the financing vehicle allows for investment flexibility, for example, under the conventional trust fund.

The investment objectives and guidelines are, in effect, a distillation of the plan sponsor's funding philosophy. Frequently, they are recorded in a formal statement that will guide the trustee and each investment manager in the performance of their duties. The statement will typically record the employer's views on such subjects as:

- Risk vs. reward
- Asset mix
- Target return
- Quality of securities to be held
- Types of securities
- Diversification
- Active vs. passive management
- Management structure and responsibilities

Investment Performance

Investment performance is usually the most important criterion for selection of a financing vehicle and one of the key factors in selection of an investment manager.

There are essentially three issues involved in investment performance:

Measurement of Actual Performance. The measurement process has almost become standardized and is carried out on computers on a routine basis. The generally recognized system includes the following features:

- The calculation is made from market value to market value. This allows for direct comparison and, indirectly, accounts for the fact that if the portfolio had been changed at any time, the switch would have been made on market value.
- Calculations are normally made separately for each calendar quarter. It is normal practice to introduce some simplifying assumptions into the program, for example that benefit payments are made in the middle of the period being analyzed. If quarterly periods are used, those assumptions cause an insignificant distortion.
- The performance is usually measured separately for each sector of the fund, e.g., equities, fixed-income securities, short-term investments, etc.

Comparison of Funds. Comparison of one fund with another is more complex. In the first place, data on the other fund or funds must be available on a consistent basis. However, a number of firms offer a comparison service on the basis of a large enough "universe" for the results to be reliable and credible. Typically, the comparison will also be made with stock market indices as well.

A second problem is the possibility of significant distortions because of the timing of contributions to the fund. As a very simple example, consider two pension funds each with assets of $1 million at the beginning of the year. Assume also that each is invested to earn 10 percent return but each receives a contribution of $100,000. However Fund *A* receives the contribution on the first day of the year while Fund *B* receives it on the last day of the year.

At the end of the year, the two funds will have accumulated the following assets:

$$\text{Fund } A = (1.10) \times 1{,}000{,}000 + (1.10) \times 100{,}000 = \$1{,}210{,}000$$

$$\text{Fund } B = (1.10) \times 1{,}000{,}000 + 100{,}000 = \$1{,}200{,}000$$

It would appear that Fund *A* has performed better but, in fact, this is a result of the contribution pattern only. Both funds earned exactly 10 percent return.

Time-weighted rates of return. This potential problem is usually resolved by comparing "time-weighted" rates of return, which is essentially a compounding of each quarter's rate of return. This gives equal "credit" for each quarter's rate of return, regardless of the actual pattern of contribution to each pension fund.

When allowance is made for the actual date when contributions were made, the result is a "dollar-weighted" rate of return. However, direct comparison of dollar-weighted rates can be misleading.

Evaluation of Performance. When carried out in conjunction with the comparison process, evaluation will answer such questions as:

- Was the good (or bad) performance due to asset mix or security selection?
- How much did market timing add to (or subtract from) the overall fund performance?
- What "value added" did each investment manager bring?
- Why did the fund attain (or fail to attain) its target return?

Managing the Investment Function

ERISA imposes investment responsibilities on all plan fiduciaries. Although some of these are not entirely clear and have not been tested in the courts, there is little doubt that the Act demands ongoing supervision of the investment process. Over and above legal requirements, it would seem prudent for plan sponsors to monitor the investment manager(s) to determine whether objectives are being attained and guidelines followed. Consequently, many employers are setting up some of the following procedures for ongoing management of the investment function:

1. *Delegation of responsibilities.* Assigning responsibility for investment management to a specific party. Typically, this would be an investment committee or retirement plan committee.
2. *Monitoring compliance.* Setting up a system for monitoring compliance with investment policy and guidelines. As one example, if quality guidelines are established, it is important to check periodically that they are being followed. For this purpose, some employees are establishing control procedures, but this has not yet become a clear trend.
3. *Measuring performance.* Arranging for regular investment performance measurement, comparison, and evaluation. From the point of view of monitoring, the two key aspects appear to be:

   —The accumulation of statistics on a regular and consistent basis.

   —Determination whether objectives are being met.

4. *Arranging meetings.* Establishing a procedure for periodic meetings with trustees and investment managers. These are normally intended to be a dialogue in which:

   —Employers will communicate their needs and aims.

   —Investment managers will describe the market environment and the behavior of the funds they manage. As appropriate, they may also suggest changes in investment policy and strategy.

12

Defined Contribution Plans

BARRY I. COSLOY
Coopers & Lybrand

JEFFREY PERLMUTER
Coopers & Lybrand

INTRODUCTION

An employee retirement benefit plan can be characterized generally as either a *defined contribution plan* or a *defined benefit plan.*

The classification of retirement plans as either defined contribution or defined benefit is significant from the technical standpoint of tax-qualification requirements, because certain qualification requirements apply to one of the plans, but not to the other. From a broader perspective, the classification serves to describe the two fundamentally opposite approaches to providing retirement benefits under a qualified plan.

"Defined Contribution" vs. "Defined Benefit"

The Internal Revenue Code describes a defined contribution plan as a plan which "provides for an individual account for each participant and for benefits based solely on the amount contributed to the participant's account, and any income, expenses, gains and losses, and any forfeitures of accounts of other participants which may be allocated to such participant's account." Defined contribution plans include profit-sharing, stock bonus, money purchase pension, thrift-savings, target benefit, employee stock ownership, and tax credit employee stock ownership plans. The Code describes a defined benefit plan quite simply as any plan which is not a defined contribution plan (see Chapter 10).

A defined contribution plan does not guarantee an employee any fixed level of benefits at retirement. Rather, such plans generally require the employer to contribute a fixed or determinable amount to individual accounts for each participant. These accounts are then credited with their pro rata share of trust fund earnings, gains and losses, and in some plans, amounts forfeited by terminated, nonvested participants. The benefit provided under the plan, which is the variable in the defined contribution approach, will be whatever the employee's account can provide at retirement.

The defined benefit approach is distinguished by the *definitely determinable benefits* provided under such plans. In defined benefit plans, the level of retirement benefits is fixed, and the employer contributions necessary to provide such benefits are then determined on an actuarial basis.

This chapter examines the defined contribution approach to providing retirement benefits. At the outset, some common characteristics of the various defined contribution plans are identified. The rest of the chapter describes each type of defined contribution plan. Those plans designed to invest primarily in employer securities are discussed separately in recognition of their substantial differences.

Plan Characteristics

Risk of Trust Investment. Since the employer does not guarantee a particular level of benefits in a defined contribution plan, the employee's benefit depends on the value of his account at retirement. The trust's investment experience (with respect to the amounts allocated to an employee's account) will directly affect the employee's retirement benefit. If the trust's investments perform poorly, the employee's benefit suffers. If investment experience is favorable, the employee may receive a windfall.

A defined benefit plan, on the other hand, shifts the risk of investment experience to the employer. In such plans, the employer is obligated to contribute amounts sufficient to provide the promised retirement benefits without regard to the trust's investment experience. The employee's benefit is fixed; it does not suffer when investment experience is adverse and it does not increase when investment results are favorable.

Effective Communication. A defined contribution plan is generally more easily communicated to, and understood by, employees than a defined benefit plan. Employees can appreciate that the annual statement of their account balances represents the benefits they have accrued under the plan. This statement is more meaningful to employees, especially younger employees, than an accounting of their potential pension at retirement under a defined benefit plan. The employees' interest and involvement in a defined contribution plan can generally be maintained if the employer effectively communicates that benefits will be directly affected by the continuing investment experience of the plan. The employee would not become similarly involved in a defined benefit plan because the fixed benefit under those plans does not vary with investment results.

Cost Considerations. The employer's costs under a defined contribution plan can generally be estimated more accurately than under a defined benefit plan. In money purchase pension plans, the employer's cost can never exceed the predetermined percentage of payroll that the plan's contribution formula calls for. Since forfeitures must be used in a money purchase plan to reduce employer contributions, the employer's actual cost may be substantially less than the contribution formula calls for. In a profit-sharing plan, the employer can vary, reduce or even temporarily discontinue contributions. (The difference between money purchase and profit-sharing plans is explained in detail later in this chapter.) On the other hand, under a defined benefit plan, the estimated employer costs can be exceeded if the actuary's assumptions about mortality, interest, turnover, and salary increases are not borne out by plan experience.

Defined contribution plans also generally avoid some of the more costly expenses incurred in administering a defined benefit plan. Actuarial services, essential in a defined benefit plan to determine the employer contributions necessary to provide the promised benefit, are not needed in a defined contribution plan. (However, actuarial calculations are necessary in a target benefit plan. These simply involve the use of a present value table based on a designated interest rate and life expectancy. The full actuarial services and certification required under a defined benefit plan would not be necessary in a target benefit plan.)

Defined contribution plans are also not subject to the plan termination insurance provisions of the Employee Retirement Income Security Act (ERISA). Therefore, the employer maintaining such plans would avoid the expense of insurance premiums to the Pension Benefit Guaranty Corporation (PBGC), and the potential for corporate plan liability to the PBGC and/or the plan in the event of plan termination.

Motivational Value. Certain defined contribution plans (e.g., a profit-sharing plan, thrift plan, or a stock bonus plan) can provide an opportunity for employees to share in the profits of the employer. In such plans, the employer can increase his contributions to the plan when profits are up. This provides a strong incentive to the employees to increase productivity. A pension plan that cannot vary contributions with, or condition contributions on, profits would not provide such motivational value.

Age Considerations. Defined contribution plans tend to be relatively more favorable to employees who are younger when they first become plan participants. Figure 12.1 shows the accumulated contributions and annual benefit at age 65 for employees commencing participation at different ages in a defined contribution plan. Employees commencing participation at a younger age accumulate a proportionately greater benefit.

A defined benefit plan, on the other hand, may be more favorable for older employees. For example, if two employees ages 30 and 55 are to

Age at Commencement	*Annual Salary*	*Accumulated Contributions to Age 65*	*Annual Retirement Income at Age 65*	*Final Salary*	*Retirement Income as a Percent of Final Salary*
30	$10,000	$ 258,000	$ 31,000	$ 52,500	59.0%
40	10,000	102,000	12,000	32,000	37.5
50	10,000	34,000	4,000	20,000	20.0
60	10,000	6,000	750	12,000	6.3
30	$25,000	$ 645,000	$ 77,000	$131,000	59.0%
40	25,000	255,000	30,500	80,000	37.5
50	25,000	85,000	10,000	50,000	20.0
60	25,000	15,000	1,800	30,000	6.3
30	$40,000	$1,032,000	$123,000	$210,000	59.0%
40	40,000	408,000	49,000	128,000	37.5
50	40,000	136,000	16,000	80,000	20.0
60	40,000	24,000	3,000	48,000	6.3

Assumptions:

5 percent salary increase
7 percent annual interest
5 percent annual increase in dollar limitation under Section 415 of the Internal Revenue Code

Source: Based on 1951 Group Annuity Mortality Table with interest at 7 percent per annum.

Fig. 12.1 Projected Accumulated Contribution and Annual Retirement Income Under Money Purchase Pension Plan (Contribution Formula = 10 Percent of Annual Compensation)

receive the same pension at age 65, then the same amount of contributions must be accumulated to fund the benefit. However, since there is a much shorter time (until age 65) to accumulate the funds for the 55-year-old employee, the employer must contribute a much larger amount each year for him than for the 30-year-old. These larger contributions would be permitted in a defined benefit plan. The only defined contribution plan that permits more rapid funding for older employees is a target benefit plan.

Defined contribution plans are also relatively less favorable to older employees because such plans do not give credit for past service (i.e., service before the inception of the plan) as effectively as defined benefit plans. A defined benefit plan can give full credit for past service simply by incorporating past-service credits into the benefit formula. For example, the plan's benefit formula might multiply a specified percentage of compensation by service both prior to and after the inception of the plan.

Defined Contribution Plans in Tandem With Defined Benefit Plans

Defined contribution plans generally do have an inherent limitation: even liberal defined contribution plans cannot generate enough capital to provide an adequate retirement benefit to an employee nearing retirement age when the plan is established. Similarly, unless participants' accounts are invested in life insurance protection, they cannot provide substantial death benefits to the survivors of employees who die after a brief period of plan participation. However, these limitations are overcome if the employer maintains a defined contribution plan in tandem with a defined benefit plan.

Techniques. This can be done in different ways to achieve various purposes.

- A defined contribution plan may be designed merely to augment pension plan benefits.
- A defined contribution plan, such as a profit-sharing plan, may be presented to the employees as an incentive plan, while the pension plan is stressed as the basic retirement plan.
- A defined contribution plan can be used to provide future service benefits while a pension plan provides benefits for past service.
- A defined benefit pension plan might provide that the pension payable under the plan is the amount specified in the defined benefit formula, reduced by the amount in the employee's account at retirement in a separate defined contribution plan. (See a further discussion of this concept of "feeder plans" in the section on profit-sharing plans.)

TYPES OF DEFINED CONTRIBUTION PLANS

Money Purchase Pension Plan

A qualified pension plan is defined generally in the Treasury regulations as:

> a plan established and maintained by an employer primarily to provide systematically for payment of definitely determinable benefits to his employees over a period of years, usually for life, after retirement. . . .

Money purchase pension plans (money purchase plans) are distinguished from other pension plans by the manner in which such plans satisfy this "definitely determinable benefits" requirement. In defined benefit pension plans, the retirement benefits are fixed in advance by plan formula and the employer contributions necessary to provide such benefits are then determined actuarially. In a money purchase plan, as a defined contribution plan, the employer does not provide a specific retirement benefit in accordance with any predetermined formula. Rather, the employer's commitment is to contribute to the plan pursuant to a fixed formula. A typical formula might provide that the employer will contribute annually 10 percent of the employee's salary, or it might call for a contribution that is integrated with Social Security.

The employer's contribution is allocated to each participant's individual account, then credited with the account's pro rata share of trust fund earnings, gains, and losses. The employee's benefit at retirement under a money purchase plan will be whatever has accumulated in his account.

Because of the requirement that benefits be definitely determinable, the employer contributions to a money purchase plan may not depend on the existence of profits. Also, forfeitures in a money purchase plan must be used to reduce future employer contributions and not to increase the benefits of remaining participants.

Defined Contribution Characteristics. A money purchase plan is similar in many respects to a profit-sharing plan. Separate accounts must be maintained for each participant. Employer contributions, trust fund investment earnings and losses, expenses, etc., must generally be allocated to each participant (certain exceptions are permitted, such as the use of a suspense account in accordance with Section 415 of the Code).

Fixed Contribution Formula. While employer contributions to a profit-sharing plan may be made either pursuant to a formula specified in the plan or at the discretion of the employer, employer contributions to a money purchase plan must be specified in the plan. Thus, the employer maintaining a money purchase plan does not have the option of reducing or foregoing an annual contribution in a loss year, as he could in a profit-sharing plan. There is no flexibility with respect to his annual contribution. Even a defined benefit plan can be more flexible in this regard, since an employer may reduce or forego a contribution to a defined benefit plan in those years in which a surplus exists under the minimum funding standard. This could occur where contributions in previous years exceeded the minimum required contributions or where investment experience exceeded the actuarial assumptions.

Retirement Benefit Requirement. Regulations require that a pension plan provide primarily retirement benefits. Thus, a money purchase plan must not permit participants, prior to any severance of employment or termination of the plan, to withdraw employer contributions or the earnings thereon. However, the employee may withdraw his own contributions to the plan prior to retirement or separation from service. Also, an employee who works beyond normal retirement age may begin to receive benefits before terminating employment.

Incidental Benefits. Under a money purchase plan, certain nonretirement benefits may be provided as long as they are incidental to the plan's primary purpose of providing retirement benefits. Thus, a money purchase plan can provide for disability benefits and/or incidental death benefits through insurance or otherwise. It cannot, however, provide for accident and health benefits—except for *retired* employees. (This does not preclude an employer from establishing a separate, nonqualified accident and health plan for active employees.) Also, a money purchase plan cannot provide layoff benefits.

Distribution of Benefits. The requirement that pension benefits be paid over a period of years, usually for life, precludes a money purchase plan from qualifying if it provides for benefits only in the form of a lump-sum distribution. This rule does not prevent a pension plan from providing for a lump-sum distribution as an optional form of benefit, or for systematic payments after retirement for a period certain. Thus, a participant in a money purchase plan could receive a lump-sum distribution and obtain the favorable tax treatment for the distribution, as long as the lump-sum form was not the only mode of distribution under the plan.

Minimum Funding Requirements. Since money purchase plans are pension plans, they are subject to the minimum funding standard of ERISA. Failure to meet the requirements of the funding standard exposes the employer to a two-stage excise tax. The initial tax levied on a funding deficiency is 5 percent of the amount of the deficiency, with an additional 100 percent tax imposed if the deficiency is not made up within the statutory correction period.

Target Benefit Plan

A target benefit plan (target plan) is a hybrid. Contributions are determined as though the plan were a defined benefit plan, but the amount of retirement benefit actually received depends on the value of the assets in the participant's account, as in a defined contribution plan.

Internal Revenue Service Definition. Neither the Internal Revenue Code nor the Treasury regulations defines a target plan. However, the IRS has provided a definition of a target plan in Revenue Ruling 76-464.

A target plan is:

1. A money purchase pension plan,
2. Which describes a targeted benefit to begin at a designated normal retirement date,
3. With employer contributions necessary to fund the targeted benefit determined using "actuarial assumptions,"
4. With forfeitures used to reduce employer contributions,
5. With separate accounts maintained for each participant, to which employer contributions and trust earnings are allocated, and
6. From which account benefits are provided.

The target benefit described in the plan is not guaranteed as it would be in a defined benefit plan. It is merely a goal to be achieved. If trust earnings exceed the actuarial assumptions upon which the employer contributions are based, the benefit actually provided will exceed the targeted benefit. Conversely, if trust earnings lag behind the actuarial assumptions used, the benefit provided will be less than the target.

Employer Contributions. Revenue Ruling 76-464 indicates that the employer contributions necessary to fund the targeted benefit are determined using actuarial assumptions. These actuarial assumptions simply involve the use of a present value based upon a designated interest rate and life expectancy. The revenue ruling indicates that as long as the target benefit does not discriminate in favor of the prohibited group of officers, shareholders, and highly compensated, then the contributions to the plan will not discriminate where the interest rate used to determine the contributions is not less than 5 percent nor more than 6 percent.

Since a target plan is a form of a money purchase plan, the employer contributions determined in accordance with the actuarial assumptions become a fixed obligation of the employer. The employer does not have any discretion with regard to making a contribution as he might in certain profit-sharing plans.

Although the IRS has not provided guidance directly on the issue, it appears that a target plan may be integrated with Social Security under the rules that apply to defined benefit plans. A target plan also may exclude from participation on the basis of age, any employee who begins employment within five years of the plan's normal retirement age.

In all other respects, a target plan is treated as a money purchase plan, and would be subject to the rules pertaining to such plans.

Comparison With Defined Benefit Plan. A target plan offers many of the benefits available under a defined benefit plan while avoiding some of the requirements imposed on such plans, such as an actuarial certification, and PBGC insurance premiums and employer termination liability. Like a defined benefit plan, a target plan tends to favor older employees. Since there is less time to accumulate money to fund their retirement benefits, both types of plans would allow for larger contributions for older employees.

However, since a target plan is a defined contribution plan, the maximum annual addition to any participant's account may not exceed the lesser of 25 percent of compensation or $41,500 (as of 1981. This amount is adjusted annually to take into account increases in the cost of living). This limitation might not allow as large a contribution on behalf of older, highly compensated employees as would be possible under a defined benefit plan.

Profit-Sharing Plan

A qualified profit-sharing plan is described in the Treasury regulations as "primarily a plan of deferred compensation" which is "established and maintained by an employer to provide for the participation in his profits by his employees or their beneficiaries."

In order to meet qualification requirements, a profit-sharing plan must provide a definite predetermined formula for allocating the contributions made to the plan among the participants and for distributing the funds accumulated under the plan after a fixed number of years, the attainment of a stated age, or upon the prior occurrence of some other event such as layoff, illness, disability, retirement, death, or severance of employment.

Unlike a defined benefit plan, a profit-sharing plan does not guarantee any fixed level of benefits. In a profit-sharing plan, the employer contributes out of profits to individual accounts for each participant. These accounts are then credited with their pro rata share of trust fund earnings, gains, and losses, and in some plans, amounts forfeited by terminated, nonvested participants. The benefit provided by the plan after the period of deferment is whatever the account can provide.

For the employer whose primary objective is to provide a predictable level of retirement benefits, a pension plan is usually better suited than a profit-sharing plan because of the requirement that a pension plan provide definitely determined benefits. However, the incentive for employees is stronger under a profit-sharing plan than under a pension plan, because amounts allocated to participants' accounts will normally increase with the increased productivity and profitability of the employer.

Contributions Out of Profits. In order to qualify as a profit-sharing plan, the employer contributions must be made out of, and limited to, current and accumulated profits. A profit-sharing plan could provide, for example, that the employer's contribution will be a percentage of profits limited to 10 percent of the compensation of plan participants. However, if a plan provides that an employer contribution to the extent of 10 percent of compensation is to be made regardless of profits, the plan will not qualify as a profit-sharing plan. (Such a plan might, however, qualify as a money purchase plan or a stock bonus plan.)

Neither the Internal Revenue Code nor the Treasury regulations gives any guidance as to what constitutes earnings and profits for purposes of the qualification requirements. However, the IRS has ruled that earnings and profits can be determined under generally accepted accounting principles and practices without regard to whether the employer has current or accumulated earnings and profits for federal income tax purposes.

Contribution Flexibility. A profit-sharing plan provides an employer with great flexibility in determining his annual contribution to the plan. The employer's contribution may be determined by a formula in the plan calling for a specific contribution such as a percentage of the employer's annual net income. Alternatively, the plan may provide that the employer's contribution is to be determined at the employer's discretion. With a discretionary formula, it is not necessary that the employer contribute every year or that he contribute the same amount or in accordance with the same ratio every year. However, the employer contributions must be substantial and recurring in order for the plan to qualify.

Forfeitures. Forfeitures are amounts contributed by the employer to provide benefits for participants who terminated their employment before obtaining a vested right to the contributions. Under a profit-sharing plan, forfeitures may be used either to reduce employer contributions otherwise required or to increase the individual accounts of remaining participants, provided this does not result in prohibited discrimination. This flexibility is not available in pension plans, which must use forfeitures to reduce employer contributions.

Discretionary vs. nondiscretionary formulas. A profit-sharing plan that provides for employer contributions at the employer's discretion affords him the greatest latitude available under a qualified plan with respect to reducing or suspending contributions. This flexibility can be a tremendous advantage if other business needs for the same funds arise.

There are, however, some disadvantages to incorporating a discretionary formula into a profit-sharing plan. Such a plan is more susceptible to an attack from the IRS on the grounds that contributions are not recurring and substantial. Also, the amount and timing of the contributions that are made may result in prohibited discrimination. Finally, the plan has less motivational value to employees if there is no assurance that their efforts to increase profits will be rewarded.

A well-designed nondiscretionary contribution formula will often avoid the disadvantages inherent in a discretionary formula, while allowing sufficient flexibility to meet most needs of the business. The key here is to define the income from which a contribution can be made in a way which fits the employer's needs. For example, the plan might require a contribution of net income in excess of some specified dollar amount, which corresponds to the amount necessary to amortize a long-term debt. Another formula might require a contribution of net income in excess of a stated return on stockholder investment. This type of formula that calls for a fixed contribution reduces the likelihood of IRS attack on the plan, while allowing the employer to take care of the business' capital requirements.

Definite Allocation Formula. While a qualified profit-sharing plan does not have to provide for a fixed contribution formula, it must provide a definite predetermined formula for allocating the contributions made to the plan among the participants. It is not sufficient for the employer to make contributions for the benefit of the employees as a group. The contributions must be individually allocated. Suspense accounts for withholding allocations are generally not permitted.

Allocation related to compensation. The most common method of allocation is to allocate in proportion to the compensation of each participant. However, any method of allocation that does not discriminate in favor of the prohibited group of officers, shareholders or highly compensated employees is acceptable.

A number of plans relate the allocation of employer contributions to compensation, but give greater weight to annual compensation above the Social Security taxable wage base or some other specified level than to compensation below that level. Other formulas give no allocation for compensation below the taxable wage base or other specified level. These formulas must meet the complex requirements for integrating a profit-sharing plan with Social Security benefits.[1]

Allocation related to compensation and service. Some allocation formulas give credit for both compensation and years of service. However, if such a formula operates to favor the higher paid (who are often the long-service employees), then the plan's qualification would be threatened. Credit for past service is generally provided more effectively under a defined benefit plan,

---

[1] Section 15 of Rev. Rul. 71-446 permits a profit-sharing plan to allocate contributions first to employees whose compensation exceeds the integration level (which may be up to the maximum base wage covered by Social Security). Maximum integration will permit an allocation equal to 7 percent of such excess compensation before any contribution is allocated on the basis of compensation below the integration level.

because the years-of-service factor can be built into the benefit formula (e.g., a unit benefit, such as 2 percent of final compensation multiplied by years of service).

Allocation to participants' accounts. As in the case of other defined contribution plans, the trust fund investment income, gains and losses, and forfeitures (unless they are used to reduce employer contributions) must be allocated, at least annually, to participants' accounts. Typical formulas would allocate these amounts either in proportion to compensation, or in proportion to a participant's account balance. Once again, the allocation must not result in prohibited discrimination.

A profit-sharing plan can require that an employee still be employed on the allocation date in order for his account to share in the employer contribution.

Annual Valuation. All assets of the trust must also be valued, at least annually, at their market value if determinable, otherwise at some other reasonably determined value. The plan can provide for interim valuations, in addition to the annual valuation, provided that prohibited discrimination does not result.

Distribution. The primary purpose of a pension plan is to provide retirement benefits. The primary purpose of a profit-sharing plan is the deferral of compensation. Based upon this distinction, the rules regarding distributions from a profit-sharing plan are generally more flexible than those under a pension plan.

A profit-sharing plan can distribute funds accumulated from employer contributions after a fixed number of years (at least two), the attainment of a stated age, or upon the prior occurrence of some event such as layoff, illness, disability, retirement, death, or severance of employment. However, a plan that provides for current distributions of profits is not a plan of deferred compensation, and generally would not qualify as a profit-sharing plan. (See, however, "Qualified Cash or Deferred Arrangements.")

Provision may also be made in a profit-sharing plan for accelerated distributions due to hardship, provided that the term hardship is defined, the rules with respect thereto are uniformly and consistently applied, and the distributable portion does not exceed the employee's vested interest.

Unlike a pension plan, a profit-sharing plan can provide that benefits will be distributed only in the form of a lump sum. Benefits distributed in a lump sum may be eligible for favorable ten-year averaging and capital gains income tax treatment.

Vesting. A profit-sharing plan must provide for participants to vest in employer contributions at a rate which is at least as rapid as one of the statutory vesting alternatives. This requirement applies to qualified plans generally. However, because the emphasis in a profit-sharing plan is on deferred compensation rather than on retirement benefits, vesting is typically more rapid in a profit-sharing plan than in a pension plan.

Incidental Benefits. A portion of the employer contributions that are allocated to a participant's account under a profit-sharing plan may be applied to purchase *incidental* life, accident, or health insurance for the participant and his family. However, the incidental benefits rule does not apply to amounts that have been held in a profit-sharing plan for the period of deferment required by the plan. A profit-sharing plan may provide for the distribution of funds accumulated under the plan after a fixed number of years (as few as two). If life, accident, or health insurance may be purchased only with funds that have been accumulated for the period required by the plan for deferment of distributions, there is no limit on the amount that can be used to purchase such insurance.

Feeder Plans. A profit-sharing plan may be used to offset the benefit specified by a defined benefit plan. Use of this combination of pension and profit-sharing plans may be particularly useful in situations where key employees have too few years until retirement age to accumulate a significant benefit under a profit-sharing plan. Under this arrangement, the defined benefit plan will guarantee a level of retirement benefits for all employees, but the profit-sharing plan will finance these benefits for all but a few employees.

For example, assume that a company has an existing profit-sharing plan to which it has made substantial contributions for a period of years. To assure that key executives receive an adequate retirement income, the company establishes a pension plan that provides for a benefit at retirement of 50 percent of final-average salary offset by any benefit provided by the profit-sharing plan. One executive will retire in five years with a final-average salary of $4,000 a month. The executive's accumulated account balance under the profit-sharing plan will provide an equivalent annuity of $800 a month. The difference of $1,200 will be provided under the defined benefit plan. If his profit-sharing account balance provided an annuity greater than $2,000 a month, no amount would be provided under the defined benefit plan. Under most circumstances, rank-and-file employees will receive most, if not all, of their benefits from the profit-sharing plan.

IRS qualification. For several years, the IRS held that a *feeder* or *floor* arrangement could not qualify, since the defined benefit plan did not provide definitely determinable benefits, and the profit-sharing plan was used to fund the defined benefit plan and thus operated for the benefit of the employer and not the employees. However, ERISA's recognition of a combination defined benefit and defined contribution plan prompted the IRS to reverse its position.

Under Revenue Ruling 76-259, the IRS permits a feeder plan to qualify if it meets certain conditions:

- The plan must specify the actuarial factors used to convert the profit-sharing account balance to an equivalent annuity and the date for making the conversion.
- The defined benefit plan must satisfy one of ERISA's benefit accrual rules without regard to the profit-sharing offset.
- The offset cannot exceed the vested portion of an employee's account balance adjusted for any prior distributions.

Importance of investment strategy. One problem with feeder plans is that the cost of the defined benefit pension plan depends not only on the level of contributions to the profit-sharing plan, but also on its investment performance. Where the investment performance is poor, the pension costs will increase. Superior investment performance will reduce the cost of the pension plan. Thus, an investment strategy for the profit-sharing plan should reflect the plan's dual role as a capital accumulation device and a financing vehicle for the pension plan. In this regard, consideration should be given to the employer's liability under minimum funding standards. A highly volatile portfolio in the profit-sharing plan could result in dramatic losses and a resulting accumulated funding deficiency in the pension plan.

Makeup Contributions. As a general rule, an employer can only make deductible contributions to a plan that benefits his employees. An exception to this rule applies in the case of affiliated corporations that are eligible to file a consolidated return, and that participate in a profit-sharing plan. If a company in this group is required to contribute to the plan but cannot because of insufficient current and accumulated earnings and profits, the profitable companies in the group can contribute on behalf of the loss company.

If the affiliated companies file a consolidated return, it is immaterial how the makeup contribution is allocated among the profit-making companies. If the affiliated companies do not file a consolidated return, the makeup contribution must be allocated among the profit-making companies in proportion to their current and accumulated earnings and profits.

Qualified Cash or Deferred Arrangement. Generally, a profit-sharing plan may not permit distributions of employer contributions to plan participants until the funds have been held by the plan for at least two years unless the distribution is made on account of the contingencies discussed above (death, retirement, illness, etc.). However, the Revenue Act of 1978 added Section 401(k) to the Internal Revenue Code, which creates an exception to the general rule prohibiting the current distribution of profits.

Section 401(k) permits the establishment of a "qualified cash or deferred arrangement." This is defined as part of a qualified profit-sharing or stock bonus plan under which an employee may elect to have employer contributions paid to the qualified plan or paid directly to the employee in cash. The following additional requirements have to be met in order for the arrangement to qualify:

1. Amounts attributable to employer contributions made to the plan pursuant to the employee's election to defer must not be distributable before the participant's retirement, death, disability, separation from service, hardship, or attainment of age 59½. These amounts must not be distributable merely by reason of the completion of a stated period of participation or the lapse of a fixed number of years.
2. The employee's right to the accrued benefit derived from employer contributions made pursuant to the employee's election to defer must be nonforfeitable at all times.
3. The plan must meet special nondiscrimination tests. These tests effectively require that highly compensated employees do not defer a substantially greater percentage of compensation than non-highly compensated employees.

Thrift Plan

A qualified thrift plan (sometimes referred to as a "savings" or "thrift-savings" plan) is an employee benefit plan that requires employee contributions as a condition of plan participation and that bases employer contributions on the amount of employee contributions made. The plans are usually established to encourage employee savings, and so serve as both a retirement plan and a capital accumulation vehicle for employees.

Neither the Internal Revenue Code nor the Treasury regulations specifically provides for thrift plans. Therefore, such plans must be qualified as, and meet the requirements of, a profit-sharing, stock bonus, or money purchase pension plan. Most thrift plans are qualified as profit-sharing plans because of the flexibility provided to both employers and employees under such a plan. For example, if the plan is a stock bonus plan, distributions generally have to be made in employer securities. A profit-sharing plan could distribute cash or stock—or both. If the plan is a money purchase plan, then employees cannot be permitted to make withdrawals of employer contributions while active participants. A profit-sharing plan could permit in-service withdrawals. Furthermore, the employer would have some flexibility with regard to his contributions under a profit-sharing plan, but not under a money purchase plan.

Matching of Employee Contributions. In a typical thrift plan, the employee is permitted to contribute a certain percentage of his pay, or to contribute between some minimum and maximum percentage of pay, such as from 2 percent to 6 percent. Contributions are usually made through payroll deduction. The employee is generally permitted to discontinue contributions or change his contribution level periodically.

The employer contributions match the employee contribution, usually on a fractional basis. Common arrangements provide for employer matching contribution rates of one-third or one-half of employee contributions. Some formulas increase the employer match with the length of the employee's service.

Prohibited Discrimination. Employee contributions required under a thrift plan must not result in prohibited discrimination (i.e., discrimination in favor of officers, shareholders, or highly compensated employees) either with respect to coverage or with respect to contributions or benefits. Revenue Ruling 80-307 indicates that when required employee contributions are burdensome, some of the lower paid employees may not participate in the plan. This may result in discriminatory plan coverage. The revenue ruling also indicates that where the plan provides for optional rates of employee contributions, and employer contributions or the benefits are geared to employee contributions in such a way that a higher rate of employee contributions will result in larger benefits from employer contributions, the employee contributions may result in discrimination in contributions and benefits because the employer-derived benefits favor those who are highly compensated.[2]

Appeal to Employees. Thrift plans are attractive to employees because they offer the employee a degree of flexibility in determining their own deferred compensation arrangement. Many thrift plans permit a participant to choose between several alternative investment media for his contributions and/or the employer contributions. Typical investment choices might include an equity fund, a fixed-income fund, or investment in government securities or employer stock. The employee is usually permitted to change his investment mix periodically.

Since a thrift plan is a qualified plan, taxation of investment earnings are deferred until the employee actually receives benefits under the plan. Thus, a thrift plan provides employees with the ability to achieve an attractive rate of return on a tax-deferred basis.

Vesting. Like any other qualified plan, a thrift plan must provide that employees vest in employer contributions at least as rapidly as one of the minimum statutory vesting alternatives. Many thrift plans provide for vesting of employer contributions on a *class-year* basis. Class-year vesting means that each year's employer contribution vests separately. For example, a class-year plan may provide that a contribution will vest five years after the year in which the contribution is made. Thus, contributions made in 1981 will

---

[2] Rev. Rul. 80-307 specifically disapproves of the former IRS position that, generally, discrimination would not result from mandatory employee contributions if the rate of contributions did not exceed six percent of compensation.

vest at the end of 1986; contributions made in 1982 will vest at the end of 1987, etc. (This is in contrast to general vesting requirements that provide that accumulated employer contributions made on behalf of an employee will vest at the same time, that is, after the employee has attained a stated number of years of service, such as 10 percent vesting each year for ten years.) Class-year vesting is permitted if each class vests not later than five years after it is credited to the employee's account.

In-Service Withdrawals. Many thrift plans permit participants to withdraw their own contributions, and, part of the vested employer contribution, during employment (if the thrift plan is qualified as a money purchase plan, then in-service withdrawals of employer contributions or earnings on employer contributions would not be permitted). These withdrawal rights can be extremely attractive to young employees who see retirement as a remote event. The employer's decision whether to permit in-service withdrawals will depend on whether the plan is viewed as a retirement plan or a savings vehicle.

For tax years before 1982, the employee's right to make in-service withdrawals of employer contributions or earnings on employer or employee contributions must be subject to substantial conditions or restrictions in order to avoid constructive receipt. However, beginning in 1982, constructive receipt is no longer applicable to qualified plans. Thus, an employee can be given an unrestricted right to make in-service withdrawals without the mere right causing constructive receipt.

GENERAL DEFINED CONTRIBUTION RULES

Preretirement Death Benefits

A defined contribution plan often provides for life insurance protection for participants. There are two general approaches followed: either part of every participant's account is applied to the purchase of life insurance under a uniform procedure; or each participant is given the option to direct that part of his account be so applied.

Incidental Death Benefit Requirement. The death benefits provided by the life insurance must be "incidental" to the retirement benefits provided under a qualified plan.

25 percent test. Death benefits are considered incidental in any type of pension plan (including a money purchase plan) if the total cost of death benefits for any participant does not exceed 25 percent of the total cost of benefits for that participant. In the case of plans funded through the use of ordinary life insurance contracts, the 25 percent test is met if less than 50 percent of the employer contributions credited to the account of each participant is used to purchase ordinary life insurance on the participant's life. This is based on the fact that approximately one-half of each annual premium on an ordinary life insurance contract is required to pay the cost of current life insurance protection. Thus, a 50 percent ordinary life insurance premium is considered equivalent to a 25 percent pure insurance cost.

100-to-1 limitation. An alternative limitation provides that life insurance protection is incidental where the insurance protection is not greater than 100 times the monthly annuity (e.g., $1,000 of life insurance for each $10 of monthly annuity).

The 100-to-1 limitation can be exceeded in certain circumstances in which the plan trustee holds individual ordinary life insurance policies and additional amounts in a side or auxiliary fund. This is known as a *split-funded arrangement.* If the ordinary life insurance policy does not provide a death benefit in excess of the 100-to-1 limitation, the death benefit can equal the total of the *reserve* under the policy and the participant's account in the side fund, even if this death benefit is more than 100 times the anticipated monthly retirement benefit. However, the plan cannot provide a death benefit equal to the *face amount* of the insurance policy in addition to the side fund, unless it can be shown that the 50 percent rule, described above, is met.

"Incidental" purchases in profit-sharing plans. In a profit-sharing plan, the purchase of ordinary life insurance contracts will be considered "incidental" if (1) the aggregate premiums for life insurance in the case of each participant are less than one-half of the aggregate of the contributions and forfeitures allocated to him at any time, and (2) the plan requires the trustee either: (a) to convert the contract at or before retirement into cash or an annuity so that no portion of such value may be used to continue life insurance protection after retirement, or (b) to distribute the contract to the participant.

If the employee dies prior to retirement, the death benefit payable to his beneficiaries may consist of both the proceeds of the life insurance contract and the balance in his account in the profit-sharing plan.

If life insurance may be purchased only with funds that have been accumulated for the period required by the plan for deferment, there is no limit on the amount that can be used to purchase.

Tax considerations. It should be noted that the pure insurance cost of the life insurance purchased under a qualified plan with employer contributions is taxable to the employee annually.

Treatment of Employee Contributions. The above limitations, designed to insure incidental death benefits, apply only to employer contributions. There is no restriction on the amount of employee contributions that may be used to purchase life insurance. Furthermore, any payment of premiums with employee contributions will avoid the treatment of the pure insurance cost as a taxable distribution to the employee. Therefore, it is usually desirable to provide in the plan that employee contributions shall be applied first to the pure insurance cost of life insurance.

Post-Retirement Death Benefits

Post-retirement death benefits will be considered incidental in all defined contribution plans if the plan contains provisions that assure that the present value of the payments to be made to the participant is more than 50 percent of the present value of the total payments to be made to the participant and his beneficiaries. This rule prevents an employee from electing before his retirement to have all or part of his benefit retained in trust and paid to his beneficiary after his death.

Health and Accident Insurance

A money purchase pension plan cannot provide health and accident insurance, except for retired employees.

Profit-Sharing Plan Provisions. A profit-sharing plan may provide for the purchase of health and accident insurance under rules similar to those governing the purchase of life insurance. If accident and health insurance may be purchased only with funds that have been accumulated for the required period of deferment (at least two years), there is no limit on the amount of such insurance that may be purchased. But if the plan permits the use of funds that have not been so accumulated to purchase accident and health insurance, then the amount expended must be "incidental."

Meeting "Incidental" Test. The purchase of accident or health insurance will be considered incidental if the amount expended for premiums does not exceed 25 percent of the amount allocated to an employee.

If both ordinary life and accident and health insurance are purchased, the amount expended for the accident and health insurance plus one-half of the amount expended for ordinary life insurance may not exceed 25 percent of the amount allocated to an employee that has not been accumulated for the required period of deferment.

Integration

The contribution formula in a defined contribution plan may allow for the integration of employer contributions with Social Security. In an integrated plan, the proportionate benefits provided to employees earning above a specified level of compensation may exceed the proportionate benefit provided employees below the specified compensation level to the extent that the difference is offset by Social Security benefits. The total retirement benefit provided by Social Security and the integrated plan when viewed as a whole are uniformly proportionate to salary at all levels.

Employee Contributions

Qualified plans may require or permit employee contributions in addition to employer contributions. If the plan requires employee contributions, the level of contributions must not result in prohibited discrimination either with respect to coverage or with respect to contributions or benefits.

Defined contribution plans generally do not require employee contributions. Those plans that do require such contributions are generally "thrift plans" that relate employer contributions to employee contributions.

It is not unusual for a defined contribution plan to permit voluntary contributions. These contributions serve to augment the retirement benefits provided by the plans. All qualified plans may permit voluntary employee contributions up to a maximum of 10 percent of an employee's aggregate compensation for all years since he became a participant. If an employee is covered by more than one plan of the same employer, the combined voluntary contributions under all plans cannot exceed 10 percent of compensation. The Economic Recovery Tax Act of 1981 allows a participant in a qualified plan to deduct up to $2,000 of his voluntary contributions if the plan provides for such deductible contributions. These contributions are subject to the same restrictions on individual contributions to an individual retirement account (IRA).

The employee's interest in his own contributions must be nonforfeitable at all times.

Loans

Loans may be made by a qualified plan to participants if the loans are granted in a uniform and nondiscriminatory manner. Loans are usually limited to an employee's vested interest, but they may exceed this amount if there is a provision for a reasonable rate of interest and adequate security. However, a loan will be considered a distribution if there is a tacit understanding that collection is not intended, or if, for some other reason, the transaction does not create a debtor-creditor relationship. If such a distribution is deemed to have been made prior to the recipient's retirement or severance, the deemed distribution will be includable in the recipient's income. Also, the qualified status of a money purchase plan may be jeopardized because of the distribution before retirement or severance.

Plan Investments

Defined contribution plans, in a sense, consist of individual capital accumulation programs for each participant. Under a defined contribution plan, individual participant accounts that will receive allocations of employer contributions and will share in investment gains and losses must be established. The ultimate benefit derived from a defined contribution plan is the amount of contributions, plus net earnings and appreciation, which have accumulated in the participant's account up to the date of distribution.

Valuation of Assets. The IRS requires a valuation at least annually of plan assets to determine the gains or losses that are to be allocated among the accounts of participants. Many plans provide for this valuation on a year-end basis, and participants share in the investment experience of the plan in the same proportion as their respective account balances. More frequent valuations are permitted. However, the employer must balance the value of providing employees with current information regarding their accounts against the greater administrative burdens and costs associated with this undertaking.

Role of Trustee. Plan investments are the responsibility of a trustee appointed by the sponsoring employer. Under some plans, the trustee has sole discretion with respect to investments. Under other plans, the trustee follows instructions of the employer or an investment advisor appointed by the employer. Under many profit-sharing and thrift plans that accept employee contributions, a trustee may follow the investment instructions of participants.

Selection Criteria. The key characteristic of a defined contribution plan is that participants bear the risk of investment. Although ERISA provides various minimum standards and detailed requirements regarding the form and operation of qualified plans, the choice among plan investments is not specifically addressed by statute or regulations.[3] Rather, plan investments must satisfy the broad requirements that they be prudent and be for the exclusive benefit of employees. Generally, prudence requires that a particular investment be reasonable within the context of a plan's entire investment portfolio. Significant criteria include whether the plan will realize a fair rate of return, whether assets are sufficiently liquid to satisfy distribution requirements, and whether investments are sufficiently diverse to protect the value of the portfolio.

Performance Objectives. Within these general constraints, a plan's assets will be invested pursuant to a philosophy that attempts to balance risk with performance objectives. In developing an investment philosophy, consideration will include an analysis of the plan's objectives. These may include:

---

[3] Treas. Reg. § 1.401-1(b)(5)(i) states "No specific limitations are provided in section 401(a) with respect to investments which may be made by the trustees of a trust qualifying under section 401(a). Generally, the contributions may be used by the trustees to purchase any investment permitted by the trust agreement to the extent allowed by local law."

- Safety of principal
- Long-term growth
- Stable income
- Liquidity of assets
- Large current income

Types of Investment Vehicles. Defined contribution plans utilize a variety of investments to satisfy one or more of these objectives:

- *Common stocks.* Common stocks offer potential growth in earnings. However, as a result of their volatility, common stocks cannot assure the protection of principal and the stability of income. Defined contribution plans often use common stock funds that temper volatility by weighting investments in favor of relatively stable equities.
- *Fixed-income investments.* Fixed-income securities, such as bonds and mortgages, sacrifice growth potential for high current income and marketability. Fixed-income funds provide this high income and offer lower risk than equity funds.
- *Money market funds.* As a result of increases in short-term interest rates, participants under defined contribution plans have requested higher yields on their accounts. In response to this pressure, plans began to offer investments in money market funds. These funds, consisting of short-term money instruments with a maximum maturity of one year, closely parallel short-term interest rates. Of course, as short-term rates decline, money market rates will follow suit. Thus, these funds cannot assure long-term yields.
- *Guaranteed investment contracts (GICs).* In response to the movement by defined contribution plans away from equities and towards fixed-income investments, the insurance industry created a contract that resembles a fixed-income fund. Unlike a fixed-income fund, however, GICs guarantee both principal and a specified rate of return. Because they offer safety of principal as well as an attractive short-term rate of return, these contracts have become extremely popular, particularly with profit-sharing and thrift plans.[4]

  There are a variety of GICs on the market, and a plan sponsor should carefully examine and compare the provisions of several contracts before committing to any particular one. Among the provisions that may differ, are the following:

  - ☐ The guaranteed rate of return
  - ☐ The application of this rate to both current and future contributions
  - ☐ The length of the guarantee

---

[4] See "Pensionforum Survey, How Profit-Sharing and Savings Plans Invest Their Money," Institutional Investor 125 (May 1980) which indicates that common stocks and GICs are the most popular investments for these plans. But, 77 percent of those employees who were given a choice of investments for their own contributions moved out of equities and 65 percent of these employees moved into a GIC.

- ☐ Whether the contract provides for participation in the insurer's investment performance with a specified minimum rate of return
- ☐ Penalties in the event of early withdrawal
- ☐ Annual fees

Directed Investments

Since participants shoulder the risk of investment, many defined contribution plans, particularly profit-sharing and thrift plans, give participants discretion over plan investments. A number of programs allow participants to direct their own contributions to one of several investment vehicles. For example, a participant may have the option to have his contributions invested in an equity fund, a fixed-income fund, employer stock, etc., in whatever proportion he chooses.[5] Plans vary as to the frequency with which a participant may change from one investment to another. Some plans provide the same participant investment authority over employer contributions.

Participants may also be given complete discretion to invest the funds in their account attributable to employee or employer contributions or both. The advantage of complete participant discretion and control is that it relieves the plan sponsor and trustee from fiduciary liability for investment losses. The disadvantage is that, in large plans, additional administration would result.

To the extent that employees direct the investment of their accounts in collectibles (i.e., art, antiques, etc.), the amount invested will be treated as a taxable distribution.

EMPLOYEE STOCK OWNERSHIP PROGRAMS

Employee stock ownership programs are not new; stock bonus plans were among the first deferred compensation plans to be afforded favorable tax status. Until ERISA, however, companies that sought to provide a benefit program to their employees paid little attention to employee stock ownership programs.

In an effort to promote employee stock ownership, ERISA and subsequent legislation expanded the tax benefits and utility of these programs. But to assure that they operate for the benefit of participating employees, employee stock ownership programs are subject to various restrictions and standards in addition to the minimum standards that apply to other tax-qualified plans.

---

[5] Most qualified plans that invest their assets in company stock will be exempt from the registration requirements of the Securities Act of 1933. Section 3(a)(2) requires no registration where assets are held in a single trust maintained by a bank and no amount in excess of the employer's contributions is allocated to purchase company stock. Thus, except for TRASOP matching employee contributions, plans generally will not permit employees to invest their contributions in company stock. See SEC Interpretative Release 33-6281, 46 Fed. Reg. 8446 (1981).

Types of Programs

Any defined contribution plan may be used to transfer employer stock to employees. Certain plans, however, are expressly intended to provide equity ownership to employees. They are:

- Stock bonus plans
- Employee Stock Ownership Plans (ESOPs)
- Tax Credit Employee Stock Ownership Plans (established as TRASOPs under the Tax Reduction Act of 1975)

Different rules and restrictions apply to each of these plans. It is important, therefore, to distinguish each plan from the general description of "employee stock ownership program." In recent years, the phrase ESOP has been used interchangeably for any of the plans. The Technical Corrections Act of 1979 [6] resolved the confusion by ascribing a name to each of these unique programs.

The term *stock bonus plan* refers to the traditional profit-sharing-type program which has existed since 1921. Under a stock bonus plan, investment in company stock is not required except to make distributions to participants. An *ESOP* is a stock bonus plan or a combination stock bonus and money purchase pension plan designed to invest *primarily* in employer securities. While there is no statutory or regulatory standard by which to judge the degree of investment in employer securities, a substantially greater investment will be made by an ESOP than a stock bonus plan. The most significant difference between these programs though is the ability of an ESOP to utilize its sponsor's guarantee to borrow for the purpose of acquiring employer securities from the sponsor or its shareholders.

A TRASOP can be any type of defined contribution plan. Thus, it may be a profit-sharing, stock bonus plan, or a combination stock bonus and money purchase pension plan. It too is unique among qualified plans. In exchange for a contribution of employer securities to the plan, the sponsoring company receives an additional income tax credit.

Program Considerations

A company considering the adoption of an employee stock ownership program should apply the same cost-benefit analysis that it would to its consideration of a pension or profit-sharing plan. The analysis is somewhat more complex, and perhaps more critical, since the company is parting with stock, not cash.

---

[6] Section 101(a)(7)(L) of Public Law 96-222, enacted April 1, 1980, amended Section 409A to change the name of an "ESOP" to a "Tax Credit Employee Stock Ownership Plan" (commonly referred to as a TRASOP) and amended Section 4975(e)(7) to change the name of a "Leveraged Employee Stock Ownership Plan" to an "Employee Stock Ownership Plan" (commonly referred to as an ESOP).

There are certain positive and negative factors to consider that are common to all employee stock ownership programs. Frequently cited benefits stock, not cash.

Broad-Based Employee Ownership. Employee stock ownership programs are tax-qualified plans. As such, they must satisfy the broad coverage and nondiscriminatory contribution and benefit requirements of ERISA. An employee stock ownership program, therefore, may be an effective vehicle to transfer equity interest to employees on a companywide basis. Conversely, in large companies, these programs are not appropriate where the object is to concentrate ownership in only a few key employees.

Under an employee stock ownership program, stock is acquired and held for the benefit of employees under favorable tax provisions. Absent are financing problems associated with other broad-based stock acquisition programs, such as employee stock purchase plans and thrift plans, both of which require an employee investment.

Supplementary Benefits. Usually, a company would establish an employee stock ownership program to supplement the benefits under its basic pension plan. As a defined contribution plan, an employee stock ownership program does not specify a level of benefits at retirement. Rather, benefits are based solely on the value of company stock and other assets held in a participant's account at retirement. Thus, employee stock ownership programs share the same weakness with other defined contribution plans as a retirement planning device. A further source of weakness is the concentration of investments in company stock. Under a pension or profit-sharing plan, a business setback may result in an employer's cessation of future contributions. Under an employee stock ownership plan, a downturn in the financial health of a company may also diminish the value of past contributions.

Motivational Value. An employee stock ownership program can effectively motivate employees to improve productivity, particularly where the plan's contribution formula is geared to a profit goal. As an incentive device, an employee stock ownership program holds an advantage over an ordinary profit-sharing plan. Under such a program, employees become shareholders. Thus, they share a common interest with other shareholders to contribute to the overall success of their company.

Market for Stock. An employee stock ownership program offers a ready market for equity financing. Purchases by the plan must be for no more than fair market value. However, it may be easier and less costly for a company to sell large blocks of stock to its plan than to the public.

Tax Benefits Without Cash Outlay. As an alternative to a sale of stock to its plan, a company may contribute stock. In this case, the contribution generates a tax deduction equal to the fair market value of the stock on the date of contribution. In the case of a TRASOP, a limited tax credit is provided.[7] Thus, a contribution will result in an increased cash flow to the company which it then may use for investment purposes. For example, Company *A* contributes stock valued at $100,000 to its stock bonus plan. Through its reduction of the company's tax liability, the contribution increases capital by approximately $50,000. This generates only half the capital as would a sale of its stock. However, it provides a far more favorable cash position than a cash contribution to a profit-sharing or similar plan.

Tax Treatment of Distribution. Similar to other defined contribution plans, employee stock ownership programs often make distributions in a lump sum. While lump-sum treatment may be advantageous under all plans, plans that distribute employer stock offer an added benefit—net unrealized appreciation in employer stock distributed in a lump sum is not taxed until the recipient disposes of the stock. Upon disposition, the net unrealized appreciation is taxed as long-term capital gain. Any subsequent gain from the date of distribution to the date of disposition will be long- or short-term capital gain depending on the recipient's holding period.

Net unrealized appreciation is the difference in the fair market value of the securities at the time they were acquired by the plan and the fair market value at the time of distribution. Thus, if stock was contributed when it was valued at $10 a share and is distributed at a value of $20 a share, the recipient would be taxed only on the first $10. The $10 appreciation would be taxed as long-term capital gain when the stock is sold by the recipient.

In considering an employee stock ownership program, there are a number of potential drawbacks which should be addressed.

Dilution of Ownership. Contributions of newly issued stock to an employee stock ownership program or purchase of stock from the company by such a plan results in a dilution of the equity interest of outstanding shareholders. This dilution will continue until the shares are redeemed by the company. Dilution of ownership carries with it the loss, to existing shareholders, of the potential economic benefit arising from future growth of the company.

Where stock is purchased by the plan from existing shareholders, no dilution will occur. However, remaining shareholders will not enjoy the proportionate increase in their equity positions that would have resulted from a corporate redemption of those shares.

Dilution of Control. A defined contribution plan may acquire *qualifying employer securities*. Under ERISA, qualifying employer securities include

---

[7] I.R.C. § 46(a)(2)(F). A one percent tax credit was provided under Public Law 94-12 (Tax Reduction Act of 1975). An additional one-half of one percent credit was provided under Public Law 94-455 (Tax Reform Act of 1976). These additional credits shall be available until Dec. 31, 1983 (Revenue Act of 1978).

stock or other equity security, or a bond, debenture, note, or other evidence of indebtedness. Until recently, shares contributed to defined contribution plans, including employee stock ownership plans, could be nonvoting shares. Shares that did provide voting power could be voted by the plan administrator.

Pressure to require that stock held in a qualified plan be voting stock and that voting rights pass through to participants created a new definition of qualifying employer securities for ESOPs and TRASOPs. These plans are now limited in their investment to common stock of the employer (or member of its controlled group) that is readily tradeable on an established securities exchange. If there is no readily tradeable common stock, employer securities must be common stock of the employer (or member of its controlled group) that has a combination of voting power and dividend rights equal to classes of stock having the greatest voting power and the greatest dividend rights. In addition, noncallable preferred stock may be acquired by an ESOP or TRASOP if it is convertible to readily tradeable common stock at any time.

In addition to the restrictions on the type of security that may be acquired by certain employee stock ownership programs, participants must now be permitted to vote their shares under any TRASOP, ESOP, or other defined contribution plan (other than a profit-sharing plan) that holds stock, which is not publicly traded, having a value of more than 10 percent of the plan's total assets. The voting requirements provide that

- Where the employer has a registration class of securities, participants must have the same voting rights as other shareholders
- Where the company has unregistered securities, participants must have the right to vote on any issue which, by law or charter, must be voted by a majority of outstanding shares. These issues would include corporate mergers, acquisitions, and liquidations.

Under these rules, voting power is diluted, and corporate control may be affected if participants exercise their right to vote.

Valuation of Securities. A company that adopts an employee stock ownership program should expect the IRS and the Department of Labor to scrutinize closely the value ascribed to company stock contributed to or purchased by the plan. The fair market value of company stock is significant for two reasons. First, stock contributed to a plan is deductible to the extent of its fair market value. Second, any purchase of stock by a plan from the sponsoring employer or a major shareholder must be for no more than fair market value.[8] Payment of more than market value will result in a prohibited transaction and the imposition of a penalty tax.

---

[8] Section 4975(c)(1) of the Code provides that any sale of property between a plan and a party-in-interest (which includes the plan sponsor or major shareholder) will be a

Where securities are publicly traded, a measure of value is readily available. Companies maintaining a stock bonus or similar employee stock ownership program may look to the quoted price on a national securities exchange to sustain its deduction for contributions of stock or to satisfy the prohibited transaction rules that apply to stock acquisitions by the plan.

The problem of stock valuation is more acute in the case of a closely held corporation.[9] Since acquisition of securities by the plan from the employer or a major shareholder for more than fair market value will result in severe penalties, determining value prior to such acquisition is critical. This generally will require the services of an independent third party such as a professional appraiser.

Start-Up and Maintenance Costs. A company that establishes an employee stock ownership program will incur the same start-up expenses associated with any other qualified plan. These expenses may include the drafting of a plan document, submission of the document to the IRS for approval, annual allocation of contributions, as well as investment gains or losses, and the annual reporting and disclosure required by the IRS and the Department of Labor.

The expense of the company's stock appraisal is an additional cost of these programs. Professional appraisals, particularly the first one, can be costly. An appraisal is required on each valuation date, as well as on each date on which there is a securities transaction between the plan and the employer, or the plan and a major shareholder of the employer.

---

prohibited transaction subject to a six percent excise tax. Section 4975(b)(13) of the Code exempts from the prohibited transaction provision any "acquisition or sale by an eligible individual account plan of qualifying employer securities if such acquisition or sale is for adequate consideration." The term "adequate consideration" is defined in Section 3(18) of ERISA to mean the price established on a national securities exchange, or if not traded, the fair market value as determined in good faith and in accordance with regulations issued by the Department of Labor.

[9] Neither the IRS nor the Department of Labor has issued guidelines on the appropriate method for valuing the stock of a closely held company. Rev. Rul. 59-60, 1951-1 C.B. 237, relating to valuations for estate and gift tax purposes cites several factors that should be considered:

(a) The nature of the business, its history, and economic condition
(b) The economic condition of the industry
(c) The book value of the stock
(d) The earning and dividend-paying capacity of the company
(e) Goodwill and other intangible values
(f) Prior sales of the stock and the size of the block to be valued
(g) The market price of similar stocks traded on an exchange or over the counter

See also, Report to the Senate Comm. on Finance, *Employee Stock Ownership Plans: Who Benefits Most in Closely Held Companies?*, U.S. General Accounting Office (June 20, 1980), in which Comptroller General cites the need for guidance in this area.

Stock Bonus Plan

A stock bonus plan is established by an employer to provide benefits similar to those of a profit-sharing plan, except that the contributions by the employer are not necessarily dependent on profits and the benefits are distributable in stock of the employer. Until recently, the requirement that distributions be in stock was the most significant distinction between stock bonus and profit-sharing plans. Legislation now permits a stock bonus plan to make cash distributions subject to the employees' right to elect to receive stock.

Employer's Contribution. The employer's contribution to a stock bonus plan may be made in the form of cash or stock. There is no requirement as to the minimum amount of stock that must be held by stock bonus plans. Thus, not all contributions need be used to purchase company stock. Rather, cash may be contributed and used to purchase company stock from existing stockholders as it is needed to satisfy distribution requirements. Direct contributions of treasury stock or authorized but unissued stock will result in a tax deduction to the employer equal to the fair market value of the stock on the date it is contributed. With the cash distribution option now available under these plans, very little stock may actually be needed in a stock bonus plan to satisfy distributions to terminating participants.

In view of the cash distribution option and the requirement for voting rights under a stock bonus plan, unless a company intends to use the plan to promote employee stock ownership, there is no advantage to adopting a stock bonus plan in lieu of a profit-sharing plan.

As with a profit-sharing plan, there is no requirement that a stock bonus plan contain a definite formula for making plan contributions. It is not even necessary that contributions be made every year. To maintain its qualified status, there must be recurring and substantial contributions to the plan. Contributions may depend on the existence of profits. In such a case, the plan is essentially a profit-sharing plan except that distributions may be made in stock either under the terms of the plan or at the request of participants.

Allocation of Benefits. Employer contributions to a stock bonus plan must be for the exclusive benefit of employees. Amounts contributed are allocated among participant's accounts in accordance with a definite plan allocation formula. An example of such a formula would be allocations in the proportion that a participant's basic compensation bears to the compensation of all participants. A stock bonus plan may be integrated with Social Security under the same rules that apply to profit-sharing and money purchase pension plans.

Stock bonus plans are usually designed much like a profit-sharing plan with respect to vesting and events which give rise to a distribution. Thus forfeitures arising from a participant's termination of employment before he has fully vested in his account balance may be reallocated to remaining participants. Participants' accounts will reflect investment gains and losses, including dividends received on stock allocated to the accounts.

Since a stock bonus plan is a plan of deferred compensation, distributions to participants must be deferred for at least two years. Thereafter, distributions will be made in accordance with the terms of the plan, usually upon the attainment of a stated age or the occurrence of some event such as illness, disability, death or termination of employment. As in the case of other defined contribution plans, distributions at termination are often made in the form of a lump sum.

ESOP

The essential difference between an ESOP and a stock bonus plan is that a sponsoring company may guarantee an ESOP loan made for the purpose of acquiring employer securities. ERISA specifically prohibits employee plans from entering into any transaction involving the lending of money or other extension of credit between the plan and the employer or a major shareholder. ESOPs are exempted from this loan prohibition provided that

- The loan is primarily for the benefit of employees
- The interest rate is not unreasonable
- The only collateral used to secure the loan is the employer stock that is acquired with the proceeds of the loan

To qualify as an ESOP a number of additional requirements must be satisfied:

- The plan must be designated as an employee stock ownership plan in the plan document
- The plan may not be integrated with Social Security [10]
- There must be restrictions on the use of loan proceeds [11]
- Where employer securities held by the plan are not publicly traded, or, if publicly traded are subject to trading restrictions, there must be a put option allowing employees to require the company to repurchase their distributed shares

An ESOP may be a stock bonus plan or it may be a combination stock bonus plan and money purchase pension plan. The Tax Act of 1981 increased the deduction limitation for an ESOP from 15 percent of compensa-

---

[10] Treas. Reg. § 54.4975-11(a)(7)(ii) effective for ESOPs established after November 1, 1977. An ESOP established before that date may be integrated but may not be amended to increase the integration level or integration percentage. (Increases tied to increases in the Social Security wage base or other external factors are permitted.)

[11] Treas. Reg. § 54.4975-7(b)(4) provides that loan proceeds may be used only to acquire employer securities or to repay the loan or a prior exempt loan.

tion to 25 percent of compensation. Plan contributions representing interest payments on ESOP debt are deductible without limit. This will be particularly useful where the sponsor wishes to provide more substantial cash contributions to the plan for the purpose of acquiring employer securities.

ESOP Financing. ESOPs are as much a financing tool as an employee benefit plan. Leveraged plans offer substantially the same benefit to participants as traditional stock bonus plans.[12] Thus, employers who only wish to provide equity ownership to employees might avoid the complexity of a leveraged plan and adopt a traditional stock bonus plan.

The financing transaction of an ESOP works as follows:

- The ESOP trust borrows from a lending institution
- The sponsoring employer guarantees the repayment of the loan in the event of a default
- The trust uses proceeds of the loan to purchase stock from the sponsoring employer or from existing shareholders
- Stock purchased by the trust is given as collateral for the loan
- The sponsoring employer makes tax-deductible contributions to the trust that are used to repay the loan
- Stock held by the trust and representing collateral is released to individual participant accounts as the loan is retired [13]
- Stock held in a participant's account is distributed when the participant terminates employment (if vested), becomes disabled, or dies
- Stock may be resold to the employer or to the trust by the participant pursuant to a put option attached to the stock

Comparison With Conventional Financing. Early enthusiasts of the leveraged plan cited the advantage of borrowing through the plan as opposed to conventional financing. They argued that ESOP financing allows a company to retire its debt entirely on a tax-deductible basis, whereas conventional financing only permits a deduction for interest payments on a loan. The result is an increased cash flow to the company.

In utilizing leveraging to create cash flow, a company should recognize that deductions are not derived from its payoff of principal and interest under the loan. Deductions are the direct result of contributions the company makes

---

[12] Section 415(c)(6) of the Code, under certain circumstances, permits ESOP and TRASOP allocations that are twice the normal limitation on allocations to a defined contribution plan.

[13] Treas. Reg. § 54.4975-7(b)(8) and DOL Reg. § 2550.408(b)-3(h) provide two methods for releasing securities for allocation to participants' accounts. The most common method releases stock for allocation based on the repayment of principal and interest. The second method releases stock on the basis of principal payments only. This latter method is available only where the loan does not extend for a duration of more than ten years, and where certain other conditions are satisfied.

to the plan, just as it would receive a deduction of contributions made to any qualified plan.

Therefore, the company could accomplish the same result through the use of conventional financing combined with the adoption of a qualified stock bonus plan. Conventional financing could provide the company with the capital needed and a deduction for interest payments. Since the interest payments are separate from the qualified plan, they are not included within the deduction limitation applicable to such a plan. Contributions to such a plan, however, would be subject to a 15 percent of compensation limitation. Only a combination of a stock bonus and money purchase plan could duplicate the more generous deduction limits available under an ESOP.

A company also must recognize its continuing obligation to make contributions to the plan to meet the debt obligation. If payroll should drop as a result of a downturn in business, the company will be hardpressed to make sufficient contributions that will satisfy the ESOP loan and still will meet the limitations on deductions. The result may be that contributions will be required but will not be deductible, or that the company will be required to pay the debt directly to the lender, again with after-tax dollars. This potential difficulty would not be present if the company had adopted a profit-sharing plan. Under such a plan, contributions may vary in accordance with fluctuations in the company's profitability.

In summary, the decision whether to finance through an ESOP or through conventional financing or traditional equity financing must involve a careful cash-flow analysis, in addition to an analysis of the impact on the company's earnings per share.[14] The expense of establishing the plan and securing an independent appraisal of the securities should be included in the analysis.

ESOP Uses. While the ESOP may not be the most advantageous vehicle to raise capital, it may be a valuable device in several situations:

- *Estate planning.* An ESOP may purchase the stock of a major stockholder of a closely held company. Purchase of stock directly from the shareholder or his estate generally will not be treated as a redemption by the company since the plan is a separate entity.[15]

---

[14] Financial analyses generally conclude that ESOP financing does not provide more favorable results than debt or equity financing. While ESOP financing may provide a short-run cash-flow advantage over debt financing, ESOP financing, in the long run, will generally result in a lower net income, lower earnings per share, and less favorable cash flow than either of the two alternatives. See Profit-Sharing Council of America, prepared by Hewitt Assocs., *ESOP: An Analytical Report,* reprinted in *Employee Stock Ownership Plans and General Stock Ownership Trusts*; Hearings on S. 3241, S. 3223, and H.R. 13882 Before the Senate Comm. on Finance, 95th Cong., 2d Sess. (July 19, 20, 1978); Kaplan & Cowan, "ESOPs and TRASOPs," Tax Mngm't (BNA) No. 354 (1979).

[15] Rev. Proc. 77-30, 1977-2 C.B. 539, establishes conditions to receive an IRS advance ruling that a proposed sale of an employer's stock to a related plan will be a sale of

- *Conversion of public company.* An ESOP may be used to acquire stock held publicly. By concentrating ownership in the plan and a few shareholders, control of the company can be transferred to a small group of individuals. The requirement that voting rights pass through to participants on their allocated shares dilutes this control in the case of major issues such as mergers, etc.
- *Divestiture of division or subsidiary.* To divest itself of a division, a company could establish a new subsidiary that would adopt an ESOP. Where the subsidiary already exists, an ESOP would similarly be adopted. Through these plans, shares of the subsidiary could be acquired from the company, thereby transferring ownership out of the parent.

TRASOP

A TRASOP is a program created by the Tax Reduction Act of 1975 to encourage employee stock ownership. It provides an additional tax credit where an employer contributes its securities or cash that is invested in its securities to the plan. The term TRASOP was formally adopted by the Technical Corrections Act of 1979 to describe this type of program. The additional tax credit allowable under a TRASOP is available through December 31, 1987. Through 1982, the tax credit is based on qualifying investments; thereafter, the credit is payroll-based.

Investment Tax Credit. Currently, a TRASOP can be a valuable program for companies with large investments in property that qualifies for the investment tax credit. Since contributions to a TRASOP generate a tax credit rather than a tax deduction, TRASOPs are viewed as a no-cost program for the employer. For this reason, many airlines, utilities, mining companies, and oil companies utilize a TRASOP and take advantage of the additional tax credit.

A TRASOP must be a tax-qualified defined contribution plan that satisfies the same minimum standards as other tax-qualified plans. One advantage of the TRASOP is that it may be established anytime before the employer's due date for filing its tax return for the first year. Other qualified plans must be established before year-end. However, a TRASOP is subject to a number of more stringent qualification rules than other plans:

- The allocation of contributions to participants' accounts must be in the same

---

stock rather than a taxable dividend distribution under Section 301 of the Code. These conditions are:

(a) The beneficial interest in the plan of the selling shareholder and related parties does not exceed 20 percent
(b) Any restrictions on the stock are no more onerous than for employees generally
(c) There is no intention for the employer to redeem stock from the plan

See also Rev. Proc. 78-23, 1978-2 C.B. 503.

proportion as the compensation of participants. But, only compensation up to $100,000 may be taken into account.

- Participants must be fully vested in any securities or cash allocated to their accounts.
- Integration of employer contributions with Social Security is not permitted.
- No employer security allocated to a participant's account may be distributed before the earlier of eighty-four months after allocation, death, disability, or separation from service of the participant.

One Percent Tax Credit. A company that establishes a TRASOP must attach a statement to its income tax return in which the additional investment tax credit is claimed. This statement must be filed for each year's qualified investment and must indicate that the company agrees to implement or continue a TRASOP and claim the additional credit.

A company that elects the additional tax credit must transfer employer securities or cash equal to the one percent tax credit not later than thirty days after the due date, including extensions, for filing its tax return. Cash contributions must be used to acquire employer securities within thirty days. The value of securities transferred to the plan are determined by their average closing price on a national exchange over the twenty-day period preceding the contribution. Where securities are not publicly traded, or where they are acquired with a cash contribution, their value must be determined in good faith and in accordance with regulations to be issued by the Department of Treasury.

If, by reason of recapture or readjustment of the credit claimed, a contribution exceeds the amount required to qualify for the additional investment credit, the contribution may not be returned to the employer. Instead, the employer may apply the excess amount to claim the credit in a succeeding year, or may claim a tax deduction in the amount of the excess if it meets the applicable deduction limitations.

One-Half Percent Matching Credit. The Tax Reform Act of 1976 expanded the benefits of a TRASOP by allowing an additional one-half percent investment tax credit for contributions of securities to the plan that match employee contributions. To receive this additional credit, the company must be eligible for the one percent credit and must also file a statement with its tax return agreeing to match employee contributions.

Although this additional one-half percent tax credit has been available for some time, few TRASOPs have utilized this opportunity. Reluctance on the part of TRASOP sponsors stemmed from confusion regarding the timing requirements for employee and employer contributions.

The matching contribution operates as follows:

- Employees have twenty-four months to make contributions that will be matched by the employer.

- To the extent employees make contributions or pledge to make contributions prior to the employer's tax-return due date, including extensions, the employer may claim the credit for the year the tax return is filed, provided it contributes securities, within thirty days after filing its return, that are equal in value to employee contributions and pledges.
- Any employee contributions and pledges received after the tax-return due date must also be matched, but the company would claim the credit on its succeeding year's return.

Start-Up and Administrative Costs. To further encourage the establishment of TRASOPs, employers are permitted to recover a portion of their expenses relating to the implementation and maintenance of such a plan. With respect to start-up expenses, the company may withhold from its initial contribution an amount not exceeding 10 percent of the first $100,000 required to be transferred, plus 5 percent of any additional amount in excess of $100,000.

With respect to on-going expenses, the company may withhold from dividends paid on securities held by the plan an amount not exceeding the lesser of $100,000 or 10 percent of the first $100,000 of dividends, plus 5 percent of the amount of dividends in excess of $100,000.

Payroll-Based Credit. The 1981 Tax Act replaces the investment-related tax credit with a tax credit based on the compensation of participants covered under the plan. The payroll-based credit will equal .5 percent of payroll in 1983 and 1984, and, beginning in 1985, .75 percent of payroll until the credit terminates on December 31, 1987. The payroll-based TRASOP will be subject to the various requirements that apply to investment credit TRASOPS.

The payroll-based TRASOP should be attractive to publicly owned companies with large payrolls. However, the 5 percent of payroll cap may limit the ability to provide a substantial retirement benefit under the plan.

Distribution From ESOPs—Some Problems and Choices

Where a company's stock is publicly traded, distribution of that stock to a participant poses no problems for either the company or the recipient. In such a case, the participant holds marketable securities, which may be disposed of at any time. The company is not concerned with a disposition of the shares since the former participant is no different than thousands of other shareholders of the company.

A closely held company presents certain problems. First, the company may not want its shares held by a former employee or sold by that employee to a third party. Shares distributed are likely to create a greater threat to control of the company than in a publicly held situation. Thus, the company may want a mechanism to retain or repurchase the shares.

The employee may not be pleased with the form of his distribution as well.

Securities he receives may have no market and cash may meet his retirement needs better than the benefits that flow from stock ownership.

There are several mechanisms to alleviate the concerns of both the company and the employee in these situations. In each case, however, an additional investment by the company is involved.

Cash Distribution. Stock bonus plans, ESOPs, and TRASOPs all can provide that, in lieu of a stock distribution, participants will receive the value of their accounts in cash. However, before a cash distribution is made, a participant must be advised in writing of his right to receive the distribution in stock. Because of the limited marketability of nontraded securities, few plans of closely held companies are likely to receive a significant number of such requests.

Put Option. Both ESOPs and TRASOPs must provide a put option with respect to any unregistered stock, or if registered, is subject to trading restrictions. Thus, a participant who receives a distribution of stock that has no ready market may require the company to buy back the securities. Alternatively, the plan may repurchase the stock, but it cannot be forced to do so.

The put option must run for a period of at least sixty days from the date of the distribution of the stock and, if it is not exercised within this sixty-day period, for an additional period of at least sixty days in the next plan year.

Right of First Refusal. In instances where the plan distributes stock that an employee chooses not to sell back, or where the employee elects to receive stock in lieu of a cash distribution, the company may wish to avoid any transfer of those shares to a third party. ESOP and TRASOP rules prohibit a plan from imposing a call on its shares. However, while a plan or company may not force a participant to resell his shares, it can require that those shares be offered first to the company or plan. The selling price must be no less favorable to the participant than the greater of the fair market value of the stock or a good-faith offer made by a third party. The right of first refusal must terminate no later than fourteen days after the participant gives the company or plan written notice of a third-party offer.

Need for Cash Contributions. In adopting an ESOP or TRASOP, consideration should be given not only to the short-term benefits of the plan, but also to the long-range obligations. Distributions to participants present a further financial liability which may not be evident in the early years of the plan. At some point, however, a company must decide what is to be done with distributions. One alternative, cash distributions, will require substantial cash contributions to "free up" the shares in the accounts of the distributees. These shares will be reallocated to remaining participants on the next allocation date. The cost of this alternative is eased by the tax deduction received for the contribution of cash.

The second alternative, a put option to the plan or the plan's exercise of a right of first refusal, will similarly require an infusion of cash into the plan to finance these purchases.

The third alternative, a put option back to the company or the company's exercise of the right of first refusal, will involve a redemption of the distributed shares. In this case, the company will expend the same amount of cash, but will receive no deduction for its expense. At some future time, these shares may again be contributed or sold to the plan, perhaps after they have appreciated in value.

Flexible Disposition of Dividends. A company will also have certain options available with respect to the disposition of dividends paid on company stock held by the plan. Under an employee stock ownership plan, dividends paid on company stock must similarly be paid on stock held in the plan. Such dividends may be allocated to each participant based on the number of shares in his account. These dividends may be added to the account to accumulate until distribution, or may be passed through the plan and paid directly to participants.[16] Under an ESOP, dividends may be used to amortize the ESOP's debt. In this case, additional shares held as collateral will be released and allocated to participants' accounts. Under a TRASOP, the sponsor may withhold a portion of the dividends to defray ongoing plan expenses.

Dividends allocated to an account will result in no tax liability until they are distributed. Upon distribution, they will be taxed as ordinary income. Ordinary income treatment is also provided where dividends are passed through directly to participants.

---

[16] Section 803(h) of the Tax Reform Act of 1976 authorized the current pass-through of dividends to participants under an ESOP. Treas. Reg. § 54.4975-11(f)(3), however, provides that, in the case of a stock bonus plan, any income held in the plan for two years or more must be distributed in stock. In light of Section 401(a)(23) of the Code, a stock bonus plan may now pass through dividends held in the plan for more than two years, subject to a participant's right to receive a stock distribution.

13

Nonqualified Deferred Compensation for Key Executives

ANDREW LAWLOR
Coopers & Lybrand

MARK MANIN
Coopers & Lybrand

DEFERRED COMPENSATION IN RETIREMENT PLANNING

The term *deferred compensation,* as used in this chapter, refers to specific "nonqualified" arrangements designed and implemented to postpone the income of either a selected employee or a group of employees to some future period.[1] Deferred compensation may be, but need not be, based upon a contractual agreement entered into by an employer and selected employees. Such plans may take the form of a salary reduction or may involve deferring a salary increase or bonus payment. Deferred compensation arrangements are generally established prior to, or at the time of, the performance of service to which the compensation relates. Certain arrangements, especially those providing supplemental retirement income benefits, can be adopted after the service has been rendered.

Although tax planning and cash-flow planning have motivated the adoption of many deferred compensation plans, their use as retirement income vehicles is widespread. For many executives, nonqualified deferred compensation arrangements have become important elements of their post-retirement income package.

Advantages of Nonqualified Deferred Compensation Plans

The major advantages generally associated with nonqualified deferred compensation arrangements are that such plans are not covered by many of the requirements of the Employee Retirement Income Security Act of 1974 (ERISA). For example, the funding requirements of ERISA are not applicable to "a plan which is unfunded and is maintained by an employer primarily for the purpose of providing deferred compensation for a select group of management or highly compensated employees."[2] In addition,

---

[1] Nonqualified plans are distinguished from qualified plans (such as pension or profit-sharing plans). The latter group must adhere to certain requirements as established by Section 401(a) of the Internal Revenue Code of 1954, as amended. Such requirements include nondiscrimination, eligibility, funding, and vesting. In exchange for satisfying these requirements, qualified plans enable an employer to defer an employee's compensation without having to simultaneously defer the employer's deduction.

[2] It should be noted that Title I of ERISA makes a clear distinction between excess benefit plans and plans providing deferred compensation for a select management group or a group of highly compensated employees. Excess benefit plans are those plans

because such plans are nonqualified they are not subject to certain nondiscrimination, participation, or vesting requirements set forth in ERISA.

The advantages identified below provide a brief overview of how an employer may utilize a nonqualified deferred compensation arrangement to tailor an executive's retirement benefit to meet the specific objectives of either the employer or the executive. Each of these points will be discussed in greater detail later in this chapter.

Supplementary Retirement Income. Nonqualified deferred compensation plans may be used to supplement an executive's retirement income that might otherwise be inadequate because of benefit limitations associated with qualified retirement plans.

Improved Compensation Efficiency. In instances where an executive has no immediate need for additional income or seeks to reduce his annual tax liability, a nonqualified deferred compensation plan can be used to defer income taxes. In addition, interest income on tax-deferred dollars will accumulate tax free and the compounding effect on pre-tax dollars will produce a substantial net return.

Use in Early Retirement. Nonqualified deferred compensation arrangements can be used by the employer to encourage an executive to retire early or to protect an executive against lost benefits resulting from early retirement.

Executive Recruiting and/or Retention. As a recruiting tool, nonqualified deferred compensation plans may be necessary to persuade an individual to leave his present position. With regard to executive retention, such plans may reduce turnover through mandatory deferral provisions. Under such provisions, the executive would have to remain an employee of the employer for a specified period in order to become entitled to the deferred income.

A nonqualified deferred compensation plan can therefore be an effective executive compensation tool that has a variety of uses to both the employer

---

"maintained by an employer solely for the purpose of providing benefits for certain employees in excess of the limitations on contributions and benefits imposed by § 415 of the Internal Revenue Code of 1954 on plans to which that section applies, without regard to whether the plan is funded" (§ 3(36) of ERISA). The distinction between the deferred compensation plans for key executives and excess benefit plans is important because of the different treatment each receives.

An unfunded excess benefit plan, for example, is exempt from all of Title I of ERISA; whereas an unfunded executive deferred compensation plan is exempt only from Pts. 2, 3, and 4 of Title I of ERISA. Thus, unfunded executive deferred compensation plans, other than excess benefit plans, are subject to specified disclosure requirements including the need to file with the Department of Labor a statement that a plan exists for highly compensated executives, and the number of executives covered. In addition, a copy of the plan must be furnished to the Department of Labor upon request. A funded excess benefit plan is exempt from Pts. 2 and 3 of ERISA's Title I yet other funded executive deferred compensation plans are subject to all of ERISA's Title I.

and executive. Traditionally, such plans have been viewed as a means of reducing an executive's tax liability. However, in recent years nonqualified deferred compensation arrangements have evolved into versatile compensation arrangements designed in response to special corporate or executive needs.

Executive Retirement Income Needs

In considering deferred compensation plans as retirement income vehicles, it is important to distinguish the particular retirement income needs of executives.

Understanding Retirement Income Objectives. It is generally agreed that a reasonable retirement income objective is to maintain a standard of living consistent with that which an executive enjoyed prior to retirement.[3]

Establishing needed dollar amounts. Spendable income tables (see Figure 13.1) are presently used to establish dollar amounts commensurate with this objective. As this figure shows, the technique is to estimate the pre-retirement (after-tax) spendable income and let that amount equal the post-retirement (after-tax) income required. For example, a married individual earning $150,000 at the time of retirement would require an approximate yearly retirement income, in addition to Social Security, of approximately $71,700. This income would have to be provided by the employer and/or personal sources.

The underlying theory of spendable income tables is that the employee's income need after retirement will generally be significantly lower than his net disposable income prior to retirement. The lower need, as illustrated in Figure 13.1, is due to a reduction in income taxes, the elimination of Social Security taxes, lower personal savings requirements, and the elimination of certain work-related expenses.

Adjustments for Inflation. The figures calculated in Figure 13.1 are general benchmarks. Depending upon an individual's situation, other factors such as inflation must be considered when estimating the retirement income replacement needs of key executives. These needs differ both in degree and kind from the needs of lower paid employees. While inflation-adjusted Social Security benefits will, for example, cover a significant part of lower paid employees' retirement income needs, most of a key executive's retirement income must be an add-on to Social Security benefits. In establishing a retirement income goal for key executives, the problem of income reduction through inflation can be avoided by providing for automatic cost-of-living

[3] For a detailed discussion of retirement income objectives, see McGill, *Fundamentals of Private Pensions* 92–95 (4th ed. 1979).

Estimated 1980 Preretirement Spendable Income

	(1) *Gross Earnings Before Retirement*	(2) *Federal Income Tax Assuming Two Exemption*	(3) *Estimated Work-Connected Expenses*	(4) *Social Security Tax*	(5) *Estimated Personal Savings Life Insurance Premiums and Miscellaneous*	(6) *Spendable Income = Estimated After-Tax Retirement Income Required* (1) – [(2) through (5)]
A	$ 50,000	$ 12,452	$2,650	$1,588	$ 5,650	$ 27,660
B	75,000	23,435	3,050	1,588	9,700	37,227
C	100,000	34,935	3,350	1,588	14,200	45,927
D	150,000	57,935	3,650	1,588	26,700	60,127
E	300,000	126,935	4,550	1,588	64,200	102,727

Estimated Retirement Income Required From Employer and Personal Sources to Maintain Preretirement Living Standard (Retirement in 1980 at Age 65)

	(7) *After-Tax Retirement Income Required Column (6)*	(8) *Social Security Income for Retired Couple (Both Age 65)*	(9) *Estimated Tax*	(10) *Pre-Tax Retirement Income Required From Employer and Personal Sources* [(7) – (8)] + (9)	(11) *Pre-Tax Retirement Income Required From Employer and Personal Sources As a Percentage of Final Earnings (10) ÷ (1)*
A	$ 27,660	$9,208	$ 2,692	$ 21,144	42%
B	37,227	9,208	5,890	33,909	45
C	45,927	9,208	10,273	46,992	47
D	60,127	9,208	20,823	71,742	48
E	102,727	9,208	57,043	150,562	50

Assumptions:
Married employee retiring at age 65
Two exemptions of $1,000 before age 65
Deductions equal to the greater of $3,400 or itemized deductions of 20 percent of gross earnings
Maximum incremental tax rate of 50 percent
Income tax shown includes 15 percent additional for state taxes
Source: Coopers & Lybrand (April 30, 1980)

Fig. 13.1 Spendable Income for Couple

adjustments or by periodically updating the retirement benefits that are in pay status.

Sources of Executive Retirement Income

When assessing an individual's need for replacement income upon retirement, it is important to remember that the employer's qualified or nonqualified arrangements provide only part of the individual's total retirement income. Social Security and the executive's personal savings are additional factors to be considered when estimating retirement income needs.

Social Security provides a minimal part of an executive's retirement income. Other retirement sources are generally considered when an employer is establishing a goal for executive retirement income to be provided from a nonqualified deferred compensation plan. Such retirement income sources include benefits that will be provided by his current and any former employers from:

- Defined benefit pension plans
- Defined contribution plans (e.g., profit-sharing, stock bonus, employee stock ownership, or savings and thrift plans)
- Existing nonqualified arrangements

Allowing for Potential Shortfalls. In projecting benefits that will be available under qualified retirement programs, the employer must focus on potential shortfalls between an executive's retirement income needs and the income that will actually be available. One such benefit cutback may be required by Section 415 of the Internal Revenue Code of 1954, as amended, which establishes the maximum allowable benefit under qualified retirement plans. A defined benefit plan in 1981 imposes a maximum limit of the lesser of $124,500 or 100 percent of the average highest three consecutive years of annual compensation. A defined contribution plan in 1981 imposes a maximum benefit of the lesser $41,500 or 25 percent of compensation. Furthermore, additional limitations will apply where an individual is covered under both a defined benefit and defined contribution plan. To the extent that an executive's retirement income goals exceed these Section 415 limits, nonqualified plan benefits may be required to provide supplemental income.

Benefits may also be lost because of early retirement. When an individual retires early, there is frequently a reduction in pension income resulting from an actuarial reduction of the benefit. In addition, where a plan's benefit formula is based upon final-average pay and years of credited service, there will be a loss of retirement income because the individual's salary and credited service will be less than it would have been had he continued employment.

These problems illustrate the need for an employer to establish retirement income objectives for key executives. If undertaken at an early enough date, the identification of potential retirement income shortfalls will enable an executive to plan an investment or savings strategy and to manage his current cash flow to defer current income taxes. Such actions should provide an executive with additional retirement income through personal resources.

Of course, during a changing economic period, this retirement-income planning process requires periodic evaluations and adjustments to insure that the established objectives are likely to be attained.

Classification of Nonqualified Deferred Compensation Arrangements

Funded vs. Unfunded Arrangements. Nonqualified deferred compensation plans are sometimes categorized according to whether they are "funded" or "unfunded" arrangements. Although such reference can be helpful in a sales presentation for deferred compensation financing vehicles, it is generally inappropriate and misleading to think of nonqualified deferred compensation plans as funded.

In order to achieve the desired income tax deferral objectives, the vast majority of nonqualified deferred compensation arrangements are unfunded for all practical purposes. Employers provide benefits on a pay-as-you-go basis. The executive's interests in the plan are unsecured and any assets that might be associated with an executive's deferral agreement must not be set aside for him in a way that would result in a restricted allocation on his behalf. In short, the executive's interests in the plan are secured only insofar as there is a contractual obligation or a promise by the employer to pay specified benefits at some future time.

Although funded nonqualified deferred compensation arrangements have been developed, their use is quite limited. Such programs can have unsatisfactory results for the key executive as well as the employer. Under funded arrangements a nonqualified trust would generally need to be established. To accomplish income deferral, the executive's interest in the assets of the trust would have to be subject to a substantial risk of forfeiture until payments were made.

When the executive's interest becomes nonforfeitable (i.e., vested), he would be deemed to be in receipt of taxable income even though he may not actually have the assets for his use. Employers utilizing funded plans forgo the use of any assets paid into the trust even though the employer would not be entitled to a tax deduction until the executive was deemed to be in receipt of income.

Mandatory vs. Negotiated Deferral. A more meaningful way to distinguish nonqualified deferred compensation arrangements is by the type of deferral. Deferrals are generally mandatory or negotiated. A mandatory deferral is required by the employer. Frequently the mandatory deferral period is for an interval as short as three to five years. Provided that the deferred compensation has not already been made available or distributed, the executive may, prior to the end of this period, elect to continue deferring this income to some future point in time—usually retirement. Mandatory deferrals are most often associated with bonus or incentive awards and are viewed by the employer as a means of executive retention. Plans that require deferrals frequently credit interest on the deferred amount. The interest rate used is typically linked to a well-published rate that, in some measure, reflects market rates of return. In addition, such plans generally include provisions dealing with payments in the event of pre or post-retirement death, disability, and separation from employment.

Negotiated deferrals differ greatly from mandatory deferrals in that a negotiated deferral is usually tailored to meet specific employer and employee objectives and is frequently part of an executive's employment contract. Negotiated deferrals are generally used where the executive's goal is to defer part of his present income to a time when he expects to be in a lower income tax bracket.

In addition, negotiated deferral arrangements are often utilized to replace retirement benefits that a newly recruited executive forfeited under his former employer's retirement plan. Because these arrangements are developed as part of the recruiting process, they tend to be more flexible than mandatory deferral arrangements. Usually the deferral is long-term and provides for the crediting of interest on the deferred sum and payment in event of death, disability, or separation from employment. The executive's interest is usually credited to a "phantom" account from which payments are made either in installments, a lump sum, or as a defined benefit annuity.

It should be noted that because deferred compensation plus any accumulated interest is subject to the 50 percent maximum tax on personal service income it may, in certain circumstances, still be advantageous for an executive to defer current income even though he does not expect to be in a lower income bracket after retirement. This is due to the fact that each year interest is being compounded on a greater amount of money since taxes are not being deducted until the end of the deferral period.

Disadvantages of Nonqualified Deferred Compensation Plans

Most of the disadvantages identified below can be avoided or minimized through careful design at the time a nonqualified deferred compensation plan is adopted or amended.

Reduced Employee Benefits. A critical disadvantage of deferring compensation is that it may, depending upon the definition of compensation in the employer's other employee benefit plans, result in a reduction of pension, life insurance or disability benefits to the executive. Since the definition of compensation will vary by employer and by employee benefit plan, it is important to determine what the effect, if any, will be when an executive's compensation is deferred. Should the situation arise where deferrals result in a reduction of other benefits, the employer should generally consider how such benefits can be restored under other nonqualified supplemental plans.

Deferral to a Higher Tax Bracket. Nonqualified deferred compensation plans are often used for the purpose of deferring earnings from a year in which an executive is in a high income tax bracket to a year in which he is in a lower tax bracket.

However, on occasion such plans are used inappropriately and result in the deferral of income to an even higher tax bracket year. Before electing to enter into a voluntary deferred compensation arrangement, an executive must carefully analyze his tax status to affirm that the favorable tax results generally associated with such plans are reasonably likely in his particular situation.

Reduction of Social Security Benefits. A retired executive's Social Security benefits may be reduced if his deferred compensation payments are deemed to be attributable to services rendered during the period in which he is receiving payments. Furthermore, it is possible that the deferred compensation payments themselves could be subject to employment taxes when they are received by the executive. Thus, care must be exercised in planning and designing the deferred compensation agreement to insure that the plan's payouts are deemed to be associated with services rendered prior to retirement.[4] Otherwise, efforts to defer taxes could unintentionally result in significant economic losses to the executive.

Employment Taxes. In certain situations, a deferred compensation payment from a nonqualified plan may be considered by the Internal Revenue Service to be subject to employment taxes under the Federal Insurance Contributions Act (FICA) and the Federal Unemployment Tax Act (FUTA). The IRS, however, has implied that such payouts will not constitute wages for FICA and FUTA purposes provided that (1) payments are made only to former employees; (2) there is no rendering of services throughout the payment period; and (3) payments are made pursuant to a plan that provides deferred compensation to either a specific class of employees or employees in general.

Constructive Receipt. The tax deferral objectives of the plan will fail if the executive is deemed to be in "constructive receipt" of his deferred earnings. The concept of constructive receipt is addressed in more detail later in this chapter. At this point however, one should be aware that Treas. Reg. § 1.451-2(a) provides that

---

[4] Under Social Security law a retiree may lose one dollar of his Social Security benefit for every two dollars of earned income above the maximum earning level. The maximum earning level is $5,500 for an individual between age 65 and age 72: in 1982 the maximum earning level is $6,000 for an individual between age 65 and age 70. For further information see 42 U.S.C.A. § 403(f).

> Income although not actually reduced to a taxpayer's possession is constructively received by him in the taxable year during which it is credited to his account, set apart for him, or otherwise made available so that he may draw upon it at any time. . . .

If the IRS successfully contends that there is constructive receipt, the executive will be taxed on assets which are not in his possession.

Frequently, deferred compensation arrangements "informally funded" with insurance contracts or other financing vehicles are promoted to and adopted by an employer without either party giving sufficient consideration to the constructive receipt issue. Care must always be taken to avoid having an "informal funding" arrangement trigger constructive receipt (see discussion later in this chapter).

Excessive Benefits. Nonqualified deferred compensation plans like all compensation and benefit arrangements should be designed to meet specific objectives or needs. Unless the plan is designed independently of the vehicle that may be used to finance the program, an employer could adopt a plan that provides benefits that exceed some of an executive's needs but yet, are not responsive to other financial needs. This is particularly true when insurance contracts are used in conjunction with a plan and the death benefits are not coordinated with group term life insurance protection provided by the employer.

FINANCING DEFERRED COMPENSATION ARRANGEMENTS

Inasmuch as most nonqualified retirement income and deferred compensation plans are unfunded and employers disburse benefits on a pay-as-you-go basis, participating executives may not perceive their deferred compensation as adequately secured. In order to offset that perception and to provide a systematic method of accumulating assets to pay benefits, many employers consider "informally funding" their deferred obligations. Proposals to accomplish this objective frequently include the use of insurance contracts that are issued to and owned by the employer. Alternative arrangements not involving the use of insurance must also be evaluated in deciding whether a plan should be "informally funded."

Care must be exercised in adopting and maintaining such financing arrangements in order to satisfy IRS requirements concerning the avoidance of constructive receipt. Although the executive may perceive that he has more security under an "informally funded" arrangement, the assets of the plan must remain as an unsegregated part of the employer's general assets. These assets, therefore, would be subject to the creditors of the corporation in the event of bankruptcy, and as with a pay-as-you-go plan, the executive's only security is the employer's promise to pay.

Alternative Vehicles for "Informal Funding"

As previously discussed, an employer who desires to informally fund a nonqualified deferred compensation arrangement may utilize one of several different financing vehicles.

Investment Account. Allocated investment accounts, savings accounts, mutual fund, or stock holdings are sometimes used in connection with deferred compensation. When such vehicles are used the deferred compensation is informally invested on behalf of the executive. Thus interest and investment appreciation accumulate throughout the deferral period.

In these cases where interest or investment appreciation is credited by the employer the additional income will accumulate under the same "tax-deferred" status as the deferred compensation thus permitting the executive to enjoy the equivalent of a "tax-free" accumulation. It should be recognized however that in such circumstances the employer will pay taxes on the investment income.

Insurance. Life insurance or annuity contracts may be an integral part of the deferral arrangement depending upon how the plan is constructed. For example, plans that have death or disability provisions may use insurance to shift the risk of death or disability. Frequently, insurance policies that create cash reserves are marketed as a convenient and effective way to fund future obligations arising from nonqualified deferred compensation arrangements. Several advantages attributed to insurance arrangements are listed below.

- Insurance contracts provide a tax shelter for accumulated interest on the deferred compensation;
- Insurance contracts provide an employer with cost stability through scheduled premium payments;
- Insurance contracts may be used to give an executive some added confidence that funds will be available in the future.

When a life insurance contract is corporate-owned with the company as beneficiary, the premium payments made by the employer are not tax deductible.[5] However, if the executive dies prior to the end of the deferral period, the employer as beneficiary will receive the death benefit proceeds tax free.[6] If the executive survives the deferral period, then depending on the policy type, the employer may surrender the insurance contract and pay the deferred compensation out of the cash surrender value.

If the employer surrenders an insurance policy in order to meet the deferred obligation, he will then be taxed on the excess amount of the policy's

[5] See I.R.C. § 264(a)(1).
[6] See I.R.C. § 101(a)(1).

cash value (including the cash value of insurance purchased with policy dividends) over the total premiums paid less any dividends he has received in cash.

When the policy is kept in force after the deferral period and until the executive's death, the employer, as beneficiary, will receive the proceeds tax free.

Types of Insurance Arrangements

There are many types of life insurance contracts that may be used by an employer to finance a nonqualified deferred compensation plan. This section describes the major life insurance product variations frequently used with deferred compensation plans.

Virtually all such financing vehicles are a form of permanent life insurance (e.g., cash value or whole life policies). Depending on the design of the policy itself, these contracts may vary greatly in terms of commission and administrative charges, dividend payments, incidence of cash surrender buildup, policy loan provisions, underlying interest assumptions, and ultimate long-term cost. This diversity contributes to the difficulty employers have in evaluating alternative insurance proposals from a business viewpoint.

Insurance contracts with various characteristics can be packaged and applied to achieve different tax and financial results. This creative planning adds to the difficulty of understanding various proposals because fundamentally different ways to use an insurance contract may be proposed to respond to an identical financing need. Although many insurance companies have associated their own name with specific contractual arrangements, these insurance agreements are typically variations of basic applications such as: *Section 79; key-man; split-dollar;* and *minimum deposit plans.* This discussion is limited to the general characteristics of these arrangements.

Section 79 Plans. These arrangements generally provide a basic death benefit under a group term insurance policy and, for specified employees, supplement this coverage with additional permanent protection. The employer pays the premium for both the term and permanent coverage. Under Section 79 of the Code, the employee receives the first $50,000 of term insurance coverage tax free. The additional term insurance in excess of $50,000 will result in imputed income and will be taxed to the employee in accordance with the Uniform Premium Table (see Treas. Reg. § 1.79-3). The employer may deduct the entire premium payment associated with the term insurance. Contracts used in these arrangements must be carefully structured by the insurance company in order to achieve their desired tax results. In general terms, such results are described below.

Assuming the contracts are properly designed, the taxation of the permanent insurance generally depends upon the ownership of the cash surrender value. If the executive owns it, then he will realize taxable income to the extent there is a current economic benefit as measured by a formula delineated in regulations under Section 79 of the Code. This formula determines how much of the employer-paid premium is associated with the permanent insurance portion and hence is currently taxable (see Figure 13.2). In such cases, the premium payments made by the employer are tax deductible. However, in most instances, the employer (not the employee) is the owner and named beneficiary of the cash surrender value. The employer's premium associated with the permanent insurance coverage is not deductible and the employee realizes no taxable benefit (see Figure 13.3). These plans are sometimes referred to as *Split-Dollar—Section 79 Plans*.

At retirement, the employer can either borrow against the policy's cash value or surrender the cash value to meet the employer's promise of deferred compensation. When payments are made to the executive, he realizes income and the employer is entitled to a tax deduction. If the executive dies, then the proceeds from the permanent coverage are received tax free by the employer who can then pay the executive's beneficiary any death benefit due under the deferred compensation agreement. The employer is then entitled to a tax deduction and the executive's beneficiary is in receipt of income. It should be noted that the death benefit arising from the term insurance coverage is received by the beneficiary free of income taxes.

Key-Man Insurance. For purposes of this discussion, key-man insurance is distinguished from corporate-owned life insurance described below. Key-man insurance policies can serve dual purposes. A key-man policy can be combined with a nonqualified deferred compensation arrangement when the employer desires financial protection in the event of a key employee's death and also desires to provide the covered executive with additional retirement income in the event he survives and retires. The employer owns and is the named beneficiary of the policy. If the executive dies prior to retirement, the employer uses the tax-free proceeds to financially bolster the organization. If the key-man retires, the cash value of the policy is either borrowed against or surrendered in order to meet the employer's deferred compensation commitments. Since the key-man realizes no economic benefit until retirement payments are made, there is no taxable income until such time. As deferred income payments are made to the key-man, the employer will be entitled to a tax deduction and the executive will be in receipt of income.

Split-Dollar Insurance. This arrangement generally involves an agreement between the employer and the executive to split or to share either the cost of the insurance premium, the benefits available under the plan, or both.

Allocating the premium. There are four basic ways to allocate the premium of a split-dollar plan:

$100,000 Permanent Policy Owned by Employee Age 45

Year	Total Premium Paid by Corp.	After-Tax Cost to Corp.	Designated Group Term Benefit [1]	Employee's Taxes: On Group Term Benefit [2]	Employee's Taxes: On Permanent Benefit [3]	Total Taxes	Employee's Cash Value
1	$ 2,412	$ 1,206	$96,600	$112	$ 861	$ 973	$ –0–
2	2,412	1,206	92,800	103	851	954	500
3	2,412	1,206	87,600	91	841	932	2,600
4	2,412	1,206	82,600	78	831	909	4,700
5	2,412	1,206	78,300	68	820	888	6,800
6	2,412	1,206	74,500	100	808	908	9,000
7	2,412	1,206	70,800	85	795	880	11,200
8	2,412	1,206	67,300	71	783	854	13,400
9	2,412	1,206	64,000	57	771	828	15,700
10	2,412	1,206	60,800	44	758	802	17,900
11	2,412	1,206	57,700	51	745	796	20,200
12	2,412	1,206	54,800	32	731	763	22,500
13	2,412	1,206	52,000	13	718	731	24,800
14	2,412	1,206	49,300	0	703	703	27,200
15	2,412	1,206	46,500	0	751	751	29,500
16	2,412	1,206	43,700	0	778	778	31,800
17	2,412	1,206	40,800	0	810	810	34,200
18	2,412	1,206	38,200	0	744	744	36,500
19	2,412	1,206	35,600	0	778	778	38,900
20	2,412	1,206	33,200	0	715	715	41,200
	$48,240	$24,120		$905	$15,592	$16,497	

[1] Represents $100,000 minus the "Deemed Death Benefit" of the permanent policy according to Treas. Reg. § 1.79-1(d)(3).
[2] Based on the Uniform Premium Table (Table 1) of Treas. Reg. § 1.79-3 and assuming a $50,000 exemption.
[3] Based on the formula of Treas. Reg. § 1.79-1(d)(2).

Source: Weinberg, "Opportunities and Methods for Insurance Purchases Using Corporate Dollars—An Overview," XXXIV CLU J. 14 (April 1980).

Fig. 13.2 Section 79—Term and Permanent Insurance

$100,000 Permanent Policy Owned by Corporation
Increasing Term Rider Added to Term Policy to Maintain Level Benefit for Executive Age 45

Year	*Deductible Premium for Term Policy*	*Nondeduct Premium for Permanent Policy*	*After-Tax Cost to Company @ 50%*	*Annual Cash Value Increase Owned by Company*	*Annual Net Cost to Company*	*For Company*	*For Executive*	*Executive's Taxes @**
1	$ 1,233	$ 1,179	$ 1,796	$ –0–	$ 1,796	$ –0–	$100,000	$ 120
2	1,236	1,179	1,797	500	1,297	500	100,000	120
3	1,250	1,179	1,804	2,100	–296	2,600	100,000	120
4	1,266	1,179	1,812	2,100	–288	4,700	100,000	120
5	1,286	1,179	1,822	2,100	–278	6,800	100,000	120
6	1,309	1,179	1,834	2,200	–366	9,000	100,000	204
7	1,337	1,179	1,848	2,200	–352	11,200	100,000	204
8	1,369	1,179	1,864	2,200	–336	13,400	100,000	204
9	1,407	1,179	1,883	2,300	–417	15,700	100,000	204
10	1,450	1,179	1,904	2,200	–296	17,900	100,000	204
11	1,501	1,179	1,930	2,300	–370	20,200	100,000	330
12	1,559	1,179	1,959	2,300	–341	22,500	100,000	330
13	1,626	1,179	1,992	2,300	–308	24,800	100,000	330
14	1,704	1,179	2,031	2,400	–369	27,200	100,000	330
15	1,792	1,179	2,075	2,300	–225	29,500	100,000	330
16	1,893	1,179	2,126	2,300	–174	31,800	100,000	489
17	2,008	1,179	2,183	2,400	–217	34,200	100,000	489
18	2,137	1,179	2,248	2,300	–52	36,500	100,000	489
19	2,287	1,179	2,323	2,400	–77	38,900	100,000	489
20	2,453	1,179	2,466	2,300	106	41,200	100,000	489
	$32,103	$23,580	$39,637	$41,200	$–1,563			$5,715

* Tax is based on $100,000 face amount—$50,000 exemption.

Source: Weinberg, "Opportunities and Methods for Insurance Purchases Using Corporate Dollars—An Overview," XXXIV, No. 2 CLU J. 15 (April 1980).

Fig. 13.3 Dual Policy Split-Dollar Section 79

- Under a "classic" split-dollar plan, the employer contributes that portion of the premium equal to the yearly increase in the policy's cash surrender value with the employee contributing the balance;
- If a "level-basis" split-dollar arrangement is used, the employer's cost is a level amount for a specified number of years. The executive pays the balance of the annual premium. This method is used because cash surrender values in a policy's early years frequently represent a very small portion of the premium. Thus, under the "classic" approach in the early years, the executive will pay a large portion of the premium while the employer will pay a smaller portion of the premium;
- "Employer-pay-all" split-dollar plans are provided by employers who elect to pay the entire premium but desire to recover premium payments in the event of the executive's death;
- "P.S.-58 offset" split-dollar plans were designed to eliminate the executive's current tax liability. This is accomplished by having the executive pay a premium equal to the P.S.-58 economic benefit and the employer pay the remaining premium.

Under any split-dollar plan, the employee will be deemed to be in receipt of taxable income on the amount of the annual insurance protection for which he does not pay. This taxable income is derived from the P.S.-58 table.[7] Under certain arrangements, a lower term life insurance rate may be used to compute the executive's imputed taxable income.

Allocating death proceeds. There are two basic ways to allocate the death proceeds under split-dollar arrangements. The first is called the *endorsement method.* Under this approach, the policy is owned by the employer and the death proceeds are split in accordance with an endorsement to the policy. Typically, the employer receives the cash value of the policy or an amount equal to premiums paid plus, in many policies, the imputed interest. Under such policies, the beneficiary receives the balance. With the second method, the *collateral assignment method,* the executive is generally the owner of the policy; however, the policy is assigned to the employer, as collateral, for the employer's designated interest.

A split-dollar insurance policy will typically be used to fund a nonqualified deferred compensation arrangement in the following manner. Throughout the deferral period the executive will designate a beneficiary to receive the policy's insurance proceeds; the employer will receive the investment proceeds or the cash value of the policy to reimburse him for the premium payments. When the employee retires, the employer may surrender the policy and use the cash value to meet its deferred income obligation or borrow against the cash value of the policy in order to meet such obligations. Al-

---

[7] P.S.-58 rates generally are used to calculate the value of the life insurance coverage to an employee under qualified retirement plans, tax-sheltered annuities, and split-dollar insurance policies (see Figure 13.4).

P.S.-58 Rates

Age	*Premium*	*Age*	*Premium*	*Age*	*Premium*
15	$1.27	37	$ 3.63	59	$ 19.08
16	1.38	38	3.87	60	20.73
17	1.48	39	4.14	61	22.53
18	1.52	40	4.42	62	24.50
19	1.52	41	4.73	63	26.63
20	1.61	42	5.07	64	28.98
21	1.67	43	5.44	65	31.51
22	1.73	44	5.85	66	34.28
23	1.79	45	6.30	67	37.31
24	1.86	46	6.78	68	40.59
25	1.93	47	7.32	69	44.17
26	2.02	48	7.89	70	48.06
27	2.11	49	8.53	71	52.29
28	2.20	50	9.22	72	56.89
29	2.31	51	9.97	73	61.89
30	2.43	52	10.79	74	67.33
31	2.57	53	11.69	75	73.23
32	2.70	54	12.67	76	79.63
33	2.86	55	13.74	77	86.57
34	3.02	56	14.91	78	94.09
35	3.21	57	16.18	79	102.23
36	3.41	58	17.56	80	111.04

Source: Weinberg, "Opportunities and Methods for Insurance Purchases Using Corporate Dollars—An Overview," XXXIV No. 2 CLU J. 16 (April 1980).

Fig. 13.4 One-Year Term Premiums for $1,000 of Life Insurance Protection

ternatively, the executive could transfer the policy back to the employer. The executive would then receive retirement income payments and the employer would receive the policy proceeds upon the executive's death.

Corporate-Owned Life Insurance. The concept behind corporate-owned life insurance (COLI) is very similar to the concept of key-man life insurance. COLIs can be used to provide replacement income upon retirement, and they provide preretirement life insurance protection. COLIs, however, are always owned by the employer who is also always the beneficiary of the policy.

Employer as beneficiary. COLIs are generally used only as a financing arrangement for a formal executive benefit such as a nonqualified deferred compensation plan. The foundation of a COLI is the death proceeds payable to the employer. Such policies are kept in force until the executive dies and the proceeds are assumed to reimburse the employer for all deferred compensation payments, plus interest that had been paid to the executive.

What happens when the executive dies? Such proceeds may be used to:

- Pay the executive's beneficiary an amount promised under the deferred compensation agreement;
- Recoup or cover any deferred compensation payments already made by the employer to the executive; or
- Defray the cost of the employer's liability arising from its obligation to pay another executive's deferred compensation.

Minimum deposit approach. Since the cash reserves accumulated under a COLI are not utilized in the same way as under key-man insurance contracts, a COLI's cash value is frequently borrowed against and used to minimize future premium payments. This minimum deposit approach is a key component to the COLI funding arrangement.

The minimum-deposit concept appears to provide an employer with a number of advantages. Permanent insurance policies entitle the contractholder to borrow at contractual interest rates (recently this rate was 6 percent to 8 percent). Therefore, the employer may, by borrowing up to the maximum limit, reduce all cash outflows after the seventh policy year, and not realize tax on any monies borrowed. In addition, the employer may be able to deduct interest payments associated with the loan.[8]

Dividends. COLIs are frequently participating insurance policies. This means that the insurance carrier may issue dividends based upon the experience of the policy. Dividends can be used to purchase additional amounts of insurance that generate additional death benefits and to create an increase in the cash value of the policy thereby allowing the employer to borrow against a larger cash reserve.

If the employer takes the policy dividend in cash, there is no taxable income to the employer, except where such dividends exceed total premiums paid. Whereas cash dividends are usually treated as reducing the cost basis of a policy, dividends if reinvested in the policy, have no impact on the policy's basis, and therefore create no taxable income.

Evaluating Insurance Arrangements

As previously indicated, the pros and cons of using insurance contracts as "informal funding" vehicles for nonqualified retirement or deferred com-

---

[8] In order to satisfy the IRS requirements on the deductibility of an insurance policy loan (i.e., in order to be able to deduct the interest of the loan) the employer must pay the full premium amount in four of the first seven years.

pensation plans must be weighed against other investment alternatives available to the employer. Employers who are considering the use of insurance contracts for such purposes must be careful to analyze the long- and short-term financial characteristics of the contracts. Issues that should be addressed are:

- What is the real investment return on the contract, and how does it compare with alternative investment opportunities available to the employer?
- What will the return be if the plan is terminated and the policies are cancelled?
- How will future plan costs be affected by significant increases in the number of covered executives or in the compensation of the covered group?
- Do the costs associated with the contracts anticipate funding of the projected deferred compensation liability?
- What Security and Exchange Commission or shareholder disclosure will be required?
- Will the program create a corporate cash flow drain?
- How will the employer's financial statements be affected by the proposed arrangement?
- What will the cash flow be to the executive and his beneficiary after income and estate taxes?

In evaluating the use of insurance contracts to "informally fund" deferred compensation plans, care must be taken to insure that the death benefit proceeds being provided to beneficiaries of covered executives are actually needed. If the executive's death benefit protection can be provided through alternative vehicles the evaluation of whether or not to use an insurance contract as a funding vehicle can be reduced to a basic financial and actuarial analysis.

Tax Issues. The issues of estate taxes and income taxes with respect to a decedent are frequently overlooked in both the design and evaluation of "informally funded" deferred compensation agreements. These taxes can radically change the apparent economics of such programs and must be considered in their analysis.

Pre-Adoption Issues. If an employer is considering the use of insurance contracts to "informally fund" deferred compensation arrangements the employer should carefully review the proposed underwriting standards, the transferability of the policy after issuance, and the possibility that future policies will automatically be issued under the program.

Underwriting Considerations. When insurance contracts are proposed for use with a group of executives, the employer should strive to obtain favorable underwriting guarantees as well as a guarantee of issuance. With a group obtaining a guarantee of policy, issuance can be virtually assured in most instances. However, similar assurances that the contract's rating will be favorable is not so readily offered and is therefore a significant issue to negotiate. To the degree possible, the employer should strive to have all insurance policies issued on a preferred basis. The ability to accomplish this objective is likely to result in significant long-term cost savings.

Contract Transferability. A sizable portion of a contract's premiums in the early years is allocated to commissions, acquisition costs, and administrative costs. If such contracts are surrendered before the cash reserves have accumulated, the sponsoring employer will not recover his premium payments. Furthermore, if the policy is surrendered because an executive has terminated his employment, a new policy will need to be purchased for the executive hired as his replacement.

Significant cost savings can be realized if the arrangement with the insurance carrier allows for the transfer of the originally issued contract to newly hired executives. Although this arrangement will usually result in some premium adjustment, it will nonetheless avoid the loss that would otherwise be associated with surrendering the policy.

Automatic Issuance of Additional Contracts. The design of deferred compensation programs frequently anticipates automatic increases in the projected deferred compensation benefit. If the insurance contracts to be issued are tied to such a program, new contracts may have to be issued for each executive as his salary increases in the future. This can result in both unanticipated and uncontrolled increases in the cost of the plan. To avoid such a situation, the plan design could be changed or a limit could be established on the insurance to be purchased for each executive. This would eliminate the costs associated with the automatic issuance of future contracts.

Accounting Issues for Deferred Compensation

This discussion of the accounting treatment is confined to nonqualified retirement and deferred compensation arrangements. Although qualified pension and profit-sharing plans are admittedly types of deferred compensation arrangements, their accounting treatment differs substantially from the individual deferred compensation plans discussed here.

In Opinions of the Accounting Principles Board 8 (APB 8) *Accounting for the Cost of Pension Plans* (1966), the annual provision for pension or retirement plan costs (see paragraph 17) should be not less than

1. The normal cost of the plan, *plus*
2. An amount equal to the interest on any unfunded prior-service cost, *plus*
3. The additional amount, if any, necessary to reduce the vested unfunded liability by 5 percent during the period

and not greater than

1. The normal cost of the plan, *plus*
2. 10 percent of the plan's past-service costs, *plus*
3. 10 percent of any increases (or decreases) in the plan's prior-service costs, *plus*
4. The interest equivalent on any difference between the provision and the amounts funded.[9]

In the case of most nonqualified deferred compensation arrangements, APB 12 entitled *Omnibus Opinion—Deferred Compensation Contracts* generally describes the proper accounting treatment. Under APB 12, the cost of a deferred compensation plan is to be accrued in a "systematic and rational manner" over the period of the executive's active employment.[10] An executive's active employment is generally measured from the time the deferral contract is entered into until the anticipated date of his retirement. In cases where the deferral arrangement provides for payment prior to the executive's normal retirement date then the costs should be accrued over the contract period.

The annual charge against earnings for certain executive deferred compensation arrangements may be determined under either APB 8 or APB 12. If the plan provides defined retirement benefits and can be deemed to cover a group or classification of employees it is possible that either APB 8 or APB 12 would be applicable. In such instances, the disclosure requirements described in the Statement of Financial Accounting Standards (SFAS) No. 36 would also apply to these arrangements. Otherwise, APB 12 is likely to be applicable.

Since the payments to the executive will be tax deductible when they are made, deferred income taxes will generally be accrued in an asset account over the deferral period.

Accounting Treatment Where Insurance Is Utilized. Under some whole life insurance proposals, it is indicated that where an insurance policy is used to provide deferred compensation no accounting charges are required because the total cash outlays will be recovered from the insurance proceeds upon the executive's death. Such a proposed accounting is not in accordance with generally accepted accounting principles. The deferred compensation arrangement is separate from the financing arrangement and should be accounted for under APB 8 or APB 12. The accounting treatment for the insurance contract should be to record expense equal to the premiums paid, less an amount equal to the increase in the cash value of the policy. In some

---

[9] For further information see Mortimer, *Accounting for Pensions By Employers—A Background Paper* (FASB 1980).

[10] AICPA, *Omnibus Opinion—Deferred Compensation Contracts,* Accounting Principles Board Opinion No. 12, Para. 6 (1967).

instances, the accounting treatment proposed by certain insurance companies has been utilized due to a lack of materiality to the financial statements.

Since the cash value created during the first few policy years is generally quite small there is likely to be a substantial charge against income in the early years of the policy. However, in later years the cash value may increase each year by more than the annual premium. At that time, the employer will show a reduction in expense. During certain periods, income may actually result from the plan. The emergence of high first-year cash surrender policies will serve to reduce expense for financial reporting purposes.

A second major accounting consideration is whether or not the liability for deferred compensation should be offset against the cash value of the insurance policies. Under prevalent accounting practices the employer's deferred compensation liability and the cash value of insurance contracts are shown separately. This is done because the liability to pay the benefits is independent of the existence of the policies and the cash value of the life insurance constitutes a corporate asset available to pay the claims of creditors.

The final accounting issue relates to balance sheet presentation of the borrowings against an insurance contract's cash value. Under customary accounting practice, the cash value and the loan payable to the insurance company are offset against one another. This is an exception to the general rule stating that assets and liabilities are to be accounted for separately because (1) the cash value of the policy secures the borrowing and is not available to satisfy the claims of general creditors of the employer, and (2) the employer does not intend to repay the loan except upon surrender of the policy or payment of the death proceeds.

The significance of the nonqualified retirement and deferred compensation plan will influence the nature of any footnote disclosure required in the financial statements.

Securities and Exchange Commission Issues

The Securities and Exchange Commission has recently amended the management remuneration disclosure requirements found in Item 4 of Regulation S-K. Employers should be aware of SEC disclosure requirements and should recognize how nonqualified deferred compensation plans interface with such regulations.

Disclosure of Management Remuneration. Any SEC document filed after January 1, 1981 will be required to provide certain information on management remuneration. The necessary information is to be furnished in the "Remuneration Table" (see Figure 13.5) or by disclosure.

Each of the five highest paid executives (provided their total remuneration Columns (C1) and (C2) will exceed $50,000) are to be listed in Column (A). In addition, all officers and directors are to be listed as a group in Column (A).

(A)	(B)	(C)		(D)
Name of individual or number of officers and directors	Capacities served	Cash and cash-equivalent forms of remuneration		Aggregate of contingent forms of remuneration
		(C1) Salaries; fees; commissions; bonuses	(C2) Securities or property; insurance benefits or reimbursements; and personal benefits	

Fig. 13.5 Remuneration Table

Column (C) is to contain all "remuneration for services rendered during the fiscal year distributed to or for the account of the specified individual or group, or which is accrued and the measurement of benefits thereunder and the distribution or unconditional vesting thereof are not subject to future events." [11]

Therefore, any deferred compensation subject to a substantial risk of forfeiture will not be included in Column (C). However, where nonqualified retirement benefits are attributable to services already rendered, it is includable.

Instruction 3(a) to Item 4(a) of Regulation S-K stipulates that for the five named employees and for the group as a whole the disclosure must include any remuneration that has been expensed for financial reporting purposes. Any payment contribution or accrual that has been allocated to the account of a named executive (or if not individually allocated, then to the group as a whole) and which arises from the employer's obligation under a pension or retirement plan, annuity contract, deferred compensation plan, or any similar arrangement must be included in the remuneration table.

Plan Description. In deferred compensation arrangements where the remuneration is to be made in the future pursuant to a written agreement or contract, the employer must provide a description of the plan including:

- How the plan operates
- The plan's performance or benefit formula
- The time period over which the measurement of the benefits are to be calculated

---

[11] SEC Reg. S-K § 229.20.4, Item 4. (See Instruction 2 to Item 4(a).)

- Payment schedules
- Any recent amendments to the plan, if they are significant [12]

The above disclosure principles represent the basic guidelines established by the SEC for deferred compensation plans. Employers should, prior to filing SEC documents, confer with counsel on any additional requirements that pertain to their specific arrangement(s).

---

[12] SEC Reg. S-K, Item 4(b).

14

Legal Requirements for Plan Qualification

Crediting Service

LESLIE J. OBUS
Legal Division, W.R. Grace & Co.

YEAR OF SERVICE

Definition

Credited service is the yardstick for determining benefits under qualified retirement plans. Credited service must be computed to determine (1) whether or not an employee is eligible to participate in a qualified plan under Section 202 of the Employee Retirement Income Security Act of 1974 (ERISA) and under Section 410 of the Internal Revenue Code; (2) whether or not any portion of an employee's benefit is "vested," i.e., nonforfeitable, under Section 203 of ERISA and Section 411(a) of the Code; or (3) what benefit has actually accrued to a plan participant under Section 204 of ERISA and Section 411(b) of the Code.

The basic period used for determining credited service is the *year of service* for eligibility and vesting purposes and the *year of participation* for benefit accrual purposes. The units used in computing these periods of service are defined in terms of the number of *hours of service* credited to an employee during a specified *computation period,* generally a twelve-consecutive-month period.

Computation Periods

Eligibility Computation Period. For purposes of determining eligibility to participate in a qualified plan, a plan may require the completion of a *year of service*—a twelve-month period during which the employee has at least 1,000 hours of service. The initial computation period, required to be designated in the plan, is the twelve-consecutive-month period beginning on the employment commencement date, the first day the employee completes an hour of service.[1] If the employee completes 1,000 hours during this period, he has met the service requirement. If he does not, the plan may designate future computation periods to be subsequent twelve-month periods beginning on the anniversary of the employment commencement date (which means a separate computation period for each employee), or switch to a twelve-month period that coincides with the plan year. If the switch is made, the first plan year used must include the first anniversary of the employment commencement date. The two years must overlap so that an employee who completes

[1] I.R.C. § 410(a)(3).

1,000 hours of service during both the initial computation period and the overlapping plan year will be credited with two years of service for eligibility purposes.[2]

For example, consider an employee who commences employment on October 1, 1980. The plan year is the calendar year and the plan has designated a switch to the plan-year eligibility computation period after the initial computation period. If the employee completes 1,000 hours from October 1, 1980 until September 30, 1981, the anniversary of his employment commencement date, and also completes 1,000 hours from January 1, 1981 until December 31, 1981 (the overlapping plan year), he must be credited with two years of service for eligibility purposes.

Vesting Computation Period. Under Section 203 of ERISA and Section 411(a) of the Code, an employee's accrued benefit derived from employer contributions must be vested under certain statutory schedules, based generally on the employee's number of years of service. The vesting computation period used to determine whether or not an employee has a year of service for vesting purposes is required to be designated in the plan.[3] It may be any twelve-consecutive-month period, for example, plan year, calendar year or the twelve-consecutive-month periods beginning on the employee's employment commencement date and anniversaries of that date. If the computation period is based on the individual's employment anniversary date, the plan's vesting computation periods will not be the same for all employees and record-keeping will be somewhat complicated. Any designated computation period must apply equally to all employees so that no discrimination results.[4] Also, the plan may not use a period that artifically postpones vesting credit, such as a period that begins on a date four months after an employment commencement date.[5]

An employer may change a plan's vesting computation period as long as each employee's vested percentage derived from employer contributions under the new period is at least as great as it would have been if no change had taken place. According to the regulations, the new vesting computation period will have to be in effect before the end of the old period and each employee who is credited with 1,000 hours of service during both vesting computation periods will be credited with two years of service for vesting purposes.[6] This operates to credit service for vesting purposes in the same way as it does for a plan that changes from an initial eligibility computation period to a plan-year eligibility computation period. For example, a plan initially electing a calendar-year vesting computation period is amended to provide for a vesting computation period based on the employer's October

---

[2] Department of Labor (hereinafter cited as DOL) Reg. § 2530.202-2(b).
[3] DOL Reg. § 2530.200b-1(a).
[4] DOL Reg. § 2530.203-2(a).
[5] *Id.*
[6] DOL Reg. § 2530.203-2(c).

1–September 30 fiscal year beginning in 1980. An employee who completes 1,000 hours of service during the period from January 1, 1980 to December 31, 1980 and during the period from October 1, 1980 to September 30, 1981 is credited with two years of service for vesting purposes.

Accrual Computation Period. In determining the benefit that has accrued to a participant in a defined benefit plan under Section 204 of ERISA and Section 411(b) of the Code, it is necessary to measure an employee's *years of participation*. As with the selection of the vesting computation period, a plan may designate any twelve-consecutive-month period as the accrual computation period as long as the period selected applies equally to all participants.[7]

The important difference here is that a plan may require an employee to complete *more than* 1,000 hours of service during an accrual computation period to be credited with a full year of participation. However, any employee who completes at least 1,000 hours of service during the period must be credited with a partial year of participation equal to at least a ratable portion of a full year of participation. Also, the plan may credit the employee with a greater portion of a full year of participation than a ratable portion, provided that such crediting is reasonable and consistent with respect to all employees within the same job classifications.[8] For example, according to the regulations, a plan that requires 2,000 hours of service for a full year of participation may credit employees who have at least 1,000 hours of service with a partial year of participation according to the following table:

Hours of Service Credited	*Percentage of Full Year of Participation*
1,000	50
1,001–1,200	60
1,201–1,400	70
1,401–1,600	80
1,601–1,800	90
1,801 and above	100

When the accrual computation period differs from the eligibility computation period, an employee generally begins participation in a plan on a day other than the first day of an accrual computation period. In determining whether the employee has an initial 1,000 hours of service for benefit accrual purposes, the plan is required to credit the employee with the additional hours of service performed from the first day of the accrual computation period until the day he becomes a participant. However, once the employee has completed 1,000 hours of service, only hours after participation commences must be used to measure a partial year of participation.[9]

[7] DOL Reg. § 2530.204-2(a).
[8] DOL Reg. § 2530.204-2(c).
[9] DOL Reg. § 2530.204-2(c)(3).

For example, an employee is employed on July 1, 1980 by an employer whose retirement plan uses a calendar-year accrual computation period and requires 2,000 hours of service for a full year of participation. He completes 500 hours of service from July 1, 1980 to December 31, 1980 and 200 hours a month in each month of 1981. He becomes a participant on the anniversary of his employment commencement date, July 1, 1981. He is credited with at least 1,000 hours of service in 1981 and receives at least a partial year of participation in 1981 based on his service after he became a participant. Therefore, he is required to be credited with at least 60 percent of a year of participation (1,200 hours from July to December 1981/2,000 hours for a full year).

A defined benefit plan that provides benefits in such a way that they are prorated to reflect less than full-time employment or less than maximum compensation may not further prorate benefit accrual by crediting less than full years of participation unless it annualizes the compensation or adjusts the hours worked to reflect full-time compensation or hours.[10] Therefore, a plan with a benefit formula such as 3 percent times a participant's career-average compensation times his years of participation could not prorate the years of participation. The use of career-average compensation already takes into account any less than full-time employment. However, if the plan adjusts the average compensation during plan participation to reflect full compensation, it may then prorate years of participation.

A plan may eliminate the use of benefit accrual computation periods. Instead, it may use an alternative method for computing service for benefit accrual purposes which is reasonable and consistent provided that it gives credit for all service required under Section 410(a)(5) of the Code and that it meets the benefit accrual rules of Section 411(b)(1) of the Code. For example, a plan with a benefit formula based on a percentage of compensation earned during a participant's career or during participation, which does not take into account hours completed in given periods, is acceptable.[11]

A plan may be amended to change its accrual computation period only if the period from the beginning of the first accrual computation period until the beginning of the new accrual computation period is treated as a partial year and participants are given credit as described above.[12] Thus, a plan that utilized a calendar-year benefit accrual computation period may in 1980 change the period to a twelve-consecutive-month period beginning on October 1. However, if the plan requires 1,000 hours of service for a year of participation, it may require only 750 hours of service during the period from January 1, 1980 to September 30, 1980 for a participant to be credited with a year of participation (1,000 hours multiplied by the ratio of nine months to twelve months).

10 DOL Reg. § 2530.204-2(d).
11 DOL Reg. § 2530.204-3.
12 DOL Reg. § 2530.204-2(e).

HOURS OF SERVICE

Definition

Years of service or years of participation are determined based on the number of *hours of service* credited to an employee. Hours of service are divided into three basic categories: (1) hours for which an employee is paid, or entitled to payment for the performance of duties; (2) hours for which an employee is paid or entitled to payment for a period of time during which no duties are performed, such as vacation, illness, incapacity (including disability), layoffs, jury duty, military duty, and leave of absence; and (3) hours for which back pay is awarded or agreed to by the employer. The regulations qualify Item (2) above by providing that a plan need not credit an employee with more than 501 hours of service for any single continuous period of nonworking service. This number is critical for determining breaks in service (discussed below). In addition, an employee need not be credited with any hours if he is paid under a plan maintained to comply with workers' compensation, unemployment compensation or disability insurance laws, or if the payment is made to reimburse the employee for medical expenses. A payment may be made by an employer directly, or indirectly through, for example, a trust or insurer to which the employer contributes or pays premiums.[13]

If hours of service are to be the basis on which credited service will be measured, the plan document must state the basic "hours of service" definition. However, the specific rules for calculating hours when no duties are performed may be incorporated by reference to the Department of Labor regulations in which they are set forth.[14]

At times it may be difficult to determine how many hours must be credited if no service is actually performed. If payment is calculated on the basis of units of time, such as hours, days, weeks, or months, then the hours credited will be the number of regularly scheduled hours in the particular unit of time.[15] If there is no regular work schedule, then some reasonable, nondiscriminatory basis must be used to credit hours. If payment is not calculated on the basis of units of time, then the number of hours credited must equal the amount of payment divided by the employee's most recent hourly rate of compensation determined under the regulations.[16] For example, an employee who is disabled for five weeks because of an injury receives a lump-sum payment of $500. His pay rate is $160 per week and he regularly works forty hours per week. The employee's hourly rate of compensation is, therefore, $4.00 per hour ($160/40) and he must be credited with 125 hours of service for the period of absence ($500/$4.00).

---

[13] DOL Reg. § 2530.200b-2(a).
[14] DOL Reg. § 2530.200b-2(f).
[15] DOL Reg. § 2530.200b-2(b)(1).
[16] DOL Reg. § 2530.200b-2(b)(2).

Hours of service are generally credited to the computation period in which work is performed or for which payment is made (if no duties are performed), not to the period in which payment itself is made. If the period during which no duties are performed extends beyond one computation period, a reasonable allocation must be made between the two periods. If the hours to be credited relate to a period of no more than thirty-one days and extend beyond one computation period, all hours of service may be credited to one computation period provided that the same method is used consistently for all employees.[17]

Equivalencies

A plan can count the hours of service to be credited to each employee in one of two ways. It can either determine the hours from the employer records maintained which reflect the accurate number of hours to be credited, or it can use one of the simplified "equivalency" methods of computing hours. These equivalencies may be used even if accurate records are maintained. However, they must be set forth in the plan document. Different methods may be used for different classifications of employees as long as the classifications are reasonable and consistently applied. In addition, even though an equivalency may be permitted under the regulations, its use for some, but not all, purposes or employees may result in prohibited discrimination under Section 410(a)(4) of the Code.[18] Equivalencies are generally used to simplify the administration of a plan and the records that must be maintained. However, this simplification must be weighed against the added cost incurred when credit is given to employees for time not actually worked.

Basis of Hours Worked. A plan may credit service on the basis of hours actually worked or hours for which back pay is awarded if a period of 870 hours worked is treated as 1,000 hours of service and a period of 435 hours worked is treated as 500 hours of service. Under this equivalency method, an employee who works more than 435 hours during the year will not incur a break in service because he will have been credited with more than 500 hours of service (see discussion of breaks in service below).[19]

A plan may also determine credited service on the basis of "regular time" hours. These hours include all hours worked, except those hours in excess of the maximum workweek under Section 7(a) of the Fair Labor Standards Act of 1938 [20] or in excess of a bona fide standard workweek. If this method is used, 750 regular time hours must be treated as 1,000 hours of service and 375 regular time hours must be treated as 500 hours of ser-

---

17 DOL Reg. § 2530.200b-2(c).
18 DOL Reg. § 2530.200b-3(c)(3).
19 DOL Reg. § 2530.200b-3(d)(1).
20 29 U.S.C.A. § 207.

vice. Therefore, an employee with more than 375 hours of service will not incur a break in service.[21]

Basis of Periods of Employment. A plan may determine the number of hours of service to be credited to employees on the basis of (1) days of employment, if an employee is credited with ten hours of service for each day he is credited with one hour of service; (2) weeks of employment, if an employee is credited with forty-five hours of service for each week he is credited with one hour of service; (3) semi-monthly payroll periods, if an employee is credited with ninety-five hours of service for each semi-monthly payroll period for which he is credited with one hour of service; (4) months of employment, if an employee is credited with 190 hours of service for each month for which he is credited with one hour of service; and (5) shifts, if an employee is credited with the number of hours included in a shift for each shift for which he is credited with one hour of service.[22] Use of the equivalency based on weeks of employment, for example, requires that a plan credit an employee with forty-five hours of service if he works for only one hour on the first day of a week and then takes a leave of absence without pay for the rest of the week.

A plan may also combine an equivalency based on working time with an equivalency based on periods of employment if certain requirements are met.[23] For instance, a plan may use the weeks-of-employment equivalency method in conjunction with the hours-worked equivalency method. If an employee is paid for duties performed for at least one hour in each of twenty weeks during a vesting computation period, he will be credited with 900 hours of service (twenty weeks × forty-five hours per week). Based on the hours-worked equivalency method, he will then receive a year of service for vesting purposes because he has been credited with more than 870 hours during the computation period.

Basis of Earnings. A plan may determine the number of hours of service to be credited on the basis of earnings. For hourly employees, the calculation is made by dividing an employee's compensation in a given computation period by an amount representing his hourly rate, or the lowest hourly rate for a similar job classification, and by treating 870 hours as equivalent to 1,000 hours of service and 435 hours as equivalent to 500 hours of service. Hours of service for salaried employees are determined by dividing total compensation by the employee's lowest hourly rate and by treating 750 hours as 1,000 hours of service and 375 hours as 500 hours of service. The salaried employee's hourly rate of service is, in general, his salary for a specific period of time divided by the number of hours regularly scheduled

---

[21] DOL Reg. § 2530.200b-3(d)(2).
[22] DOL Reg. § 2530.200b-3(e).
[23] DOL Reg. § 2530.200b-3(e)(7).

for work during the period.[24] For employees whose compensation is not based on a fixed rate for a specified period of time, the employee's hourly rate will be considered to be the minimum wage under Section 6(a)(1) of the Fair Labor Standards Act of 1938. Again, 750 hours will be treated as 1,000 hours of service and 375 hours will be treated as 500 hours of service.

BREAK IN SERVICE

Definition

A plan may provide that for eligibility and vesting purposes an employee incurs a one-year *break in service* for a computation period in which he is credited with less than 500 hours of service, or the equivalent of 500 hours of service.[25] Under the elapsed-time method of determining credited service discussed below, a break in service occurs when an employee has a period of severance for one year.[26] A break in service may result in loss of years of credited service for participation and vesting.

Service Following a Break in Service

Participation. In general, all of an employee's years of service with an employer are taken into account for computing eligibility. However, under Section 410(a)(5)(C) of the Code, a plan is permitted to disregard service before a break in service until the employee completes a year of service after his return. In measuring breaks in service, the plan uses the same eligibility computation period as it uses in measuring service for eligibility purposes. If the plan switches to the plan year after the initial eligibility computation period, the same plan year is also used as the computation period for measuring breaks in service. After the employee completes a year of service upon his return, he is given credit, for eligibility purposes, retroactive to the date of his reemployment. To measure the employee's service after he returns, the plan uses the same computation period as used initially to determine year of service for eligibility purposes. The first period begins on the day the employee is credited with an hour of service upon his return and ends on the anniversary of that date. If the plan switches to the plan year, the next computation period used, if necessary, begins with the plan year that includes the first anniversary of an employee's reemployment date.[27] For example, if an employee has become a plan participant and then incurs a

---

24 DOL Reg. § 2530.200b-3(f).
25 I.R.C. §§ 410, 411.
26 DOL Reg. § 2530.200b-4(a).
27 DOL Reg. § 2530.200b-4(b)(1); Treas. Reg. § 1.410(a)-5(c)(3).

one-year break in service, he will not be considered a participant until he completes a year of service upon his return. He will then be considered a participant as of his reemployment date.

A plan that provides for 100 percent vesting after three years of service may require three years of service without a break in service as a condition of participation. However, such a plan cannot condition eligibility upon the performance of three *consecutive* years of service.[28] Under such a plan, an employee who has 1,000 hours of service in year one, 500 hours in year two (thus incurring a break in service), and 1,000 hours in years three, four, and five will satisfy the service requirements at the end of year five. His prebreak service in year one will be disregarded. However, an employee who has 1,000 hours of service in years one and two, 700 hours in year three, and 1,000 hours in years four and five will satisfy the plan's service requirements at the end of year four. His service in year one may not be disregarded because he did not incur a break in service.

The rule of parity is used in certain circumstances to determine whether service before a break in service must be considered in computing credited service. If a participant incurs a one-year break in service before he has any vested rights under the plan to an accrued benefit derived from employer contributions, the plan may disregard his prebreak years of service if the number of consecutive one-year breaks in service equals or exceeds the number of prebreak years.[29] To illustrate, an employee terminates his service with no vested benefit from employer-derived contributions after completing four years of service. He is reemployed after incurring five consecutive one-year breaks in service. Under Section 410(a)(5)(D) of the Code, the employee's four years of service may be disregarded. If the plan uses the elapsed-time method, the plan may disregard any prebreak years of service if the period of severance is at least one year and the period of severance equals or exceeds the prior period of prebreak service.[30]

Vesting. In general, all years of service with an employer are considered in determining vesting service. However, Section 411(a)(4) of the Code provides certain instances where vesting service may be disregarded if the plan so designates. In measuring both breaks in service and service after a break, a plan uses the vesting computation period that is set forth in the plan document.[31] If the plan uses a vesting computation period that relates to each employee's commencement of employment date, the plan may change the employee's vesting computation period to a new computation period after a break in service as long as the plan follows the rules for changing the vesting computation period set forth in DOL Reg. § 2530.203-2(c)(1).

[28] Treas. Reg. § 1.410(a)-5(c)(2).
[29] I.R.C. § 410(a)(5)(D).
[30] Treas. Reg. § 1.410(a)-5(c)(4).
[31] DOL Reg. §§ 2530.200b-4(b)(2), 2530.200b-4(b)(3).

This new computation period begins with the employee's first hour of service upon reemployment.[32]

If an employee incurs a one-year break in service, prebreak service is not required to be taken into account for vesting purposes until the employee completes a year of service upon his return. Once the employee completes the year of service, however, he must be given credit retroactive to the date of his reemployment.[33]

If a participant in a defined contribution plan (or an insured defined benefit plan) incurs a one-year break in service, his post-break years of service need not be taken into account in determining his vested percentage in his prebreak employer-derived benefits whether or not he has any vested rights under the plan. However, his prebreak years of service cannot be disregarded in determining his vested percentage in his post-break employer-derived accrued benefits (unless the rule of parity applies).[34]

If an employee incurs one or more breaks in service before he is vested in any employer-derived benefits, the rule of parity may be applied. If the plan so provides, years of service before any breaks in service need not be taken into account for vesting purposes if the number of consecutive breaks in service equals or exceeds the aggregate number of years of service before the break.[35] In an elapsed-time plan, vesting service before a period of severance may be disregarded if the period of severance equals or exceeds the prior period of service completed before the period of severance.[36]

Accrual of Benefits. In calculating an employee's period of service for benefit accrual purposes, Section 204(b)(3) of ERISA and Section 411(b)(3) of the Code permit certain service to be disregarded, e.g., service before an employee becomes a participant in the plan, service not required to be taken into account for eligibility purposes under Section 410(b)(5) of the Code (relating to breaks in service) and service not required to be taken into account under Section 411(b)(3)(C) of the Code (relating to twelve-consecutive-month periods during which an employee's service is less than 1,000 hours). In addition, service that can be disregarded under the vesting rule of parity is not required to be taken into account for benefit accrual purposes.[37]

---

[32] DOL Reg. § 2530.200b-4(b)(2).
[33] I.R.C. § 411(a)(6)(B).
[34] I.R.C. § 411(a)(6)(C).
[35] I.R.C. § 411(a)(6)(D).
[36] Treas. Reg. § 1.411(a)-6(c)(1)(iii).
[37] DOL Reg. § 2530.204-1(b).

ELAPSED-TIME METHOD OF CREDITING SERVICE

Alternative to Hours of Service

The elapsed-time method is an alternative method for crediting service for eligibility, vesting, and benefit accrual purposes. The amount of service credited to an employee is not determined by the number of hours worked in a particular year, but instead by reference to the total period of time that elapses while the individual is employed by the employer maintaining the plan.

The elapsed-time method is generally used to ease administrative burdens. Because a specified number of hours is not required for service to be credited, the employer does not have to maintain detailed records. Only the employment date and severance date are needed.

General Rule

Under the elapsed-time method of crediting service, an employee's service is required to be taken into account for eligibility and vesting purposes for the "period of service" from the date he first performs an hour of service until the date he "severs from service" with the employer maintaining the plan. However, under the *service spanning* rules described below, an employee who resumes employment within a certain period of time may be entitled to have an additional period of up to one year taken into account. To understand the elapsed-time method of crediting time, certain general terms must be explained.

Severance From Service Date. An employee's severance date is the earlier of (1) the date the employee quits, is discharged, retires, or dies, or (2) the first anniversary of the date he is absent for any other reason (e.g., disability, vacation, leave of absence, or layoff). For example, an employee begins employment on February 15, 1981 and is laid off on August 10, 1981. On October 10, 1981, he quits. His severance from service date is October 10, 1981, the date he quit, not August 10, 1982, the first anniversary of his absence from service.[38]

Period of Service. Under the elapsed-time method, the term *period of service* is used rather than "year of service" to compute service for eligibility, vesting, and benefit accrual purposes.[39]

Period of Severance. A period of severance begins on the severance from service date and ends when an employee returns to service with the employer maintaining the plan. This period is used to apply the "break in service"

---

[38] Treas. Reg. § 1.410(a)-7(b)(2).
[39] Treas. Reg. § 1.410(a)-7(a)(3)(iv).

rules to the elapsed-time method. A one-year period of severance occurs if an employee does not complete an hour of service in the twelve-consecutive-month period beginning on the severance from service date.[40]

Service Spanning Rules. The service spanning rules provide that for purposes of eligibility and vesting, if an employee severs from service by reason of a quit, discharge, or retirement and then returns to service within twelve months, the plan must take into account the period of severance. However, if an employee severs from service for other reasons and then quits or is discharged, he must return within one year from the first date of his absence to get credit for the period of severance. An employee, therefore, will never receive more than twelve months of credit from the date he is first absent.[41]

Benefit Accrual. For benefit accrual purposes, an employee's service is taken into account for the period from the time he commences *participation* in the plan until his severance from service date. A plan is not required to credit an employee with periods of severance, as it is for eligibility and vesting purposes. Therefore, if a plan participant is discharged on December 14, 1981 and is rehired on February 14, 1982, the plan would not have to credit him with the two months of severance for benefit accrual purposes, although it would for vesting purposes.[42]

Break in Service and Rule of Parity. The same break-in-service rules discussed in the previous section apply under the elapsed-time method of crediting service, except that the term one-year period of severance is used instead of the term one-year break in service. If the rule of parity is used, a plan may disregard the periods of service before a period of severance if the severance period equals or exceeds the prior periods of service. The rule is not applied until the employee incurs a period of severance of at least one year. For example, an employee is hired on January 1, 1981; he quits on March 1, 1981 and is rehired on February 1, 1982. Because the period of severance was less than one year, the rule of parity is not invoked, even though the period of severance exceeded the period of service. Under the service spanning rules, the employee receives thirteen months of credit for eligibility and vesting purposes.[43]

Transfers Between Methods of Crediting Service

A plan may use the *hours-tracking* method of crediting service for certain classes of employees and the elapsed-time method for others as long as

---

[40] Treas. Reg. § 1.410(a)-7(c)(4).
[41] Treas. Reg. §§ 1.410(a)-7(c)(2)(iii), 1.410(a)-7(d)(1)(iii).
[42] Treas. Reg. § 1.410(a)-(7)(e).
[43] Treas. Reg. §§ 1.410(a)-7(c)(6), 1.410(a)-7(d)(7).

certain requirements set forth in the regulations are met.[44] These rules insure that an employee does not lose credit for any of the service he has accumulated if he transfers from one classification to another. With respect to plans in existence on June 17, 1980, these rules are effective for plan years beginning after December 31, 1983.[45]

A plan may be amended to change the method of crediting service if the amendment contains provisions similar to ones used when employees transfer from one class to another.[46]

---

[44] Treas. Reg. § 1.410(a)-7(f).
[45] Treas. Reg. § 1.410(a)-7(h).
[46] Treas. Reg. § 1.410(a)-7(g).

Minimum Participation Standards for Qualified Plans

ROBERT A. BILDERSEE
Morgan, Lewis & Bockius

PURPOSE OF THE MINIMUM PARTICIPATION STANDARDS

Requirements Prior to ERISA

Prior to enactment of the Employee Retirement Income Security Act of 1974 (ERISA), qualified plans frequently required long periods of continuous service as a precondition to plan participation. Plans requiring five years of continuous employment as a precondition to participation were not unusual. Even the slightest interruption in employment continuity prior to plan admission would cause the prospective plan participant to start again the entire eligibility qualification cycle.

Many plans permanently excluded from participation persons who had attained a specific age by the time they were first employed, by the time they first entered the class of employees eligible for coverage, or by the time they completed the preparticipation service period. Commonly, employees hired after age 50 or those who first satisfied the plan's other participation requirements after attaining age 55 were permanently excluded from coverage, regardless of the type of plan involved, and regardless of the normal retirement age under the plan or normal retirement date specified under the plan.

Prior to ERISA, most plans even required individuals who already were plan participants at the time of an interruption in covered service to be treated as new employees, without any prior employment or participation history for plan purposes, upon return to covered employment.

Changes in Standards

The minimum participation standards introduced to the Internal Revenue Code by ERISA are designed to assure prompt participation in retirement plans by eligible class employees, to restrict omission of employees from plan coverage by reason of advanced age, and to protect rehired employees so that short interruptions in covered service do not result in lengthy periods of plan participation disablement.[1] The minimum participation standards do not directly prescribe the content of the eligible class of employees to be

---

[1] I.R.C. § 410(a).

covered by any plan. However, nondiscrimination rules (discussed elsewhere in the handbook) may require inclusion in the eligible class of certain employees, and IRS regulations under the minimum participation standards are designed to preclude any definition of the eligible class that is primarily a subterfuge to avoid the minimum participation standards.[2]

MINIMUM AGE REQUIREMENTS UNDER THE ERISAFIED CODE

In general, a qualified plan cannot require attainment of an age in excess of age 25 as a precondition to plan participation.[3] There is no requirement that persons under age 25 be admitted to participation under the minimum participation standards, regardless of the length of service of such individuals. Any plan maintained exclusively for employees of an educational institution by an employer who is tax exempt under Section 501(a) of the Code may omit persons under age 30 from coverage if all employees covered under the plan are fully vested after completing one year of service.[4]

MAXIMUM AGE REQUIREMENTS UNDER THE ERISAFIED CODE

Most qualified plans may not exclude persons from participation on the grounds of advanced age.[5] However, as an exception to the general rule, defined benefit plans and target (assumed benefit) plans may permanently exclude from participation any individual who is within five years of the normal retirement age specified under the plan at the time his or her employment with the employer commences.[6] Thus, no one may be excluded if the normal retirement age is defined as 65 or, if later, the tenth anniversary of the date of participation.

For the purposes of the minimum participation standards, employment in an ineligible class of employees and employment with certain related employers (those that form, with the plan sponsor, a controlled group of corporations, a group of trades or businesses under common control, or an affiliated service group) are treated as employment by the plan sponsor.[7] Thus, if employment in the ineligible class or employment with a related

---

[2] See I.R.C. §§ 401(a)(4) and 410(b) as to nondiscrimination rules and Treas. Reg. § 1.410(a)-3(e), including examples thereunder as to eligibility categories deemed to be subterfuges.

[3] I.R.C. § 410(a)(1)(A)(i).

[4] I.R.C. § 410(a)(1)(B)(ii).

[5] I.R.C. § 410(a)(2).

[6] I.R.C. § 410(a)(2)(A).

[7] I.R.C. §§ 414(b), 414(c), 414(m).

employer started more than five years before the normal retirement age stated under the plan, coverage cannot be denied even under a defined benefit or target plan to an employee who first transfers to the eligible class (or, among related employers, from a nonsponsor to a sponsor of the plan) merely because the employee was within five years of normal retirement age under the plan at the time of the transfer and consequent entry into the eligible class.[8] With regard to new plans, existing eligible class employees cannot be omitted from coverage because of attained age at the time of plan installation. Reference must be made to the employee's age at the time of employment commencement, and omission from plan participation is permissible only if employment commenced within five years of normal retirement age under the plan.[9]

MINIMUM SERVICE REQUIREMENTS UNDER THE ERISAFIED CODE

Year of Service

Every plan may require one "year of service" as a precondition to plan participation.[10] Plans that provide each participant at all times with full and immediate vesting in his accrued benefit may require up to three years of service as a precondition to participation.[11]

For participation eligibility purposes, a "year of service" is the completion of 1,000 or more hours of service during an "eligibility computation period."[12] Every employee's *initial eligibility computation period* is the period of twelve consecutive months starting on the employee's personal employment commencement date (even if that employment was not in a class of employees eligible for coverage under the plan, and even if that employment was in the service of a related enterprise that does not sponsor the subject plan). Subsequent eligibility computation periods are either plan years (starting with the first plan year to commence after the employee's employment commencement date) or personal years, each of which commences on the anniversary of the employee's employment commencement date.[13] The employee's *employment commencement date* is the date on which the employee first is entitled to credit for an hour of service for service rendered.[14] For plans operating on an elapsed-time basis, a "year of service" is an eligibility computation period of twelve consecutive months of unin-

---

[8] Treas. Reg. § 1.410(a)-4(a).
[9] Treas. Reg. § 1.410(a)-4(a), Ex. (4).
[10] I.R.C. § 410(a)(1)(A)(ii).
[11] I.R.C. § 410(a)(1)(B)(i).
[12] I.R.C. § 410(a)(3)(A).
[13] I.R.C. § 410(a)(3)(A); 29 C.F.R. § 2530.202-2 (1976).
[14] 29 C.F.R. § 2530.202-2(a) (1976).

terrupted employment.[15] (These important basic concepts are explained in more detail in the section on "Crediting Service.")

Break in Service

Service prior to a one-year break in service need not be taken into account for participation eligibility computation until the returning participant has completed one year of service subsequent to his or her return to covered employment.[16] However, because readmission to active participation must be retroactive to the date of return to covered employment after the one year of service requirement has been met, the one-year holdback is not a practical minimum service requirement to impose on returned participants in some defined contribution plans.[17]

Service for Predecessor Employer

Where the plan sponsor maintains a plan of a predecessor employer (as often happens after an acquisition), service for the predecessor employer is considered service with the plan sponsor.[18]

TIME OF ADMISSION

There is no requirement that an individual be admitted to plan participation if he is no longer employed by the employer (including within the concept of employer those related companies that form, with the employer, a controlled group of corporations, a group of trades or businesses under common control, or an affiliated service group) on the date as of which plan participation would otherwise commence.[19]

While admission to plan participation is not required in the case of those who satisfied the requirements but who then separated from service prior to their respective entry dates, employees who are temporarily absent due to vacation, sickness, strike, personnel layoff, or similar cause must be admitted at the appropriate time.

Except as indicated in the preceding paragraph, once an employee is in the eligible class and has satisfied the statutory minimum age and service requirements (generally attainment of age 25 and completion of a year of service), admission to active plan participation must occur no later than the earlier of (1) the date which is six months after the employee first satisfied

---

[15] 29 C.F.R. § 2530.200b-9(a)(2) (1976).
[16] I.R.C. § 410(a)(5)(C).
[17] Treas. Reg. § 1.410(a)-4(b)(2), Ex. (3).
[18] I.R.C. § 414(a).
[19] I.R.C. § 410(a)(4).

such requirements or (2) the first day of the first plan year next following the date on which the employee first satisfies the requirements.[20]

Change of Status

Where an employee changes status from an ineligible class to an eligible class, the employee must be admitted to plan participation as of the date of the change in status if, at that time, he has satisfied the statutory minimum age and service requirements. Thus, any employee transferred from ineligible to eligible status must become a participant on the date of transfer if he would have become a participant under the statutory standards on or before that date, had all of his prior employment been in the eligible class.

BREAKS IN SERVICE

In general, all service with the employer or employers maintaining a plan must be taken into account in determining service for participation purposes.[21] However, there are several exceptions. First, service prior to a break in service need not be taken into consideration until the employee has completed a year of service subsequent to the break in service.[22] Second, if the plan provides for full and immediate vesting, service prior to a break in service may be permanently disregarded if, at the time of the break in service, the employee had not yet completed sufficient service to qualify to plan participation.[23] Finally, under the so-called "rule of parity," service prior to a break in service may be permanently disregarded if the participant had no vested interest in the plan by reason of prebreak service, and if the period of interruption in service (the number of consecutive one-year breaks in service) equals or exceeds the number of years of service creditable for service prior to the break in service.[24]

Unless a plan provides otherwise, a break in service is experienced (for participation determination purposes) in any eligibility computation period in which the participant completes fewer than 501 hours of service, whether or not there is an actual termination of the employer-employee relationship.[25] Service in an ineligible class or service with a related enterprise (controlled group, common control or affiliated service group) must be counted as participation service, and therefore may prevent a break in service from occurring, even though the employee is no longer in the class of employees eligible to participate actively in the plan. (A more detailed explanation of "breaks in service" can be found earlier in this chapter.)

---

[20] I.R.C. § 410(a)(4).
[21] I.R.C. § 410(a)(5); 29 C.F.R. § 2530.200b-3 (1976).
[22] I.R.C. § 410(a)(5)(C).
[23] I.R.C. § 410(a)(5)(B).
[24] I.R.C. § 410(a)(5)(D); Treas. Reg. § 1.410(a)-5(c)(4).
[25] I.R.C. § 411(a)(6)(A).

SPECIAL SITUATIONS

In the case of pension plans that are multiemployer plans within the meaning of Section 3(37) of ERISA, covered service with any employer maintaining the plan is considered covered service with each such employer for eligibility computation purposes under the plan. Service will therefore be deemed continuous where an employee leaves covered service with Employer *A* to immediately undertake covered service under the same multiemployer plan with Employer *B*.

Uncovered service with any employer is creditable as covered service with the same employer for participation eligibility determination purposes where the employee has remained with that one employer and has changed from an uncovered to covered status. However, noncovered employment with Plan Sponsor *A* is not combined with covered employment with Plan Sponsor *B* for the purpose of determining an individual's eligibility to participate while in the employ of Plan Sponsor *B*, even though both *A* and *B* are sponsors of the same multiemployer plan. For service to be carried forward, there must either be continuity of employment with a single employer or within a controlled group, or continuity of coverage under the same plan sponsored by several employers.[26]

---

[26] I.R.C. § 413(b)(1); 29 C.F.R. § 2530.210(c) (1976).

Minimum Coverage Requirements

ROBERT A. BILDERSEE
Morgan, Lewis & Bockius

THE CONCEPT

The minimum participation standards of the Employee Retirement Income Security Act of 1974 (ERISA) and the Internal Revenue Code protect the *individual* rights of *eligible class employees.* Those minimum participation standards assure eligible class employees of prompt and timely commencement of participation in employee pension benefit plans. The minimum participation standards do not prescribe the inclusion of any person or group of persons among the eligible class.

Quite apart from the minimum participation standards of ERISA and the Code, which address the protection of individual plan participants and prospective participants, the Code mandates the satisfaction of certain minimum coverage standards as a precondition of tax-qualified status for employee pension benefit plans (including profit-sharing, stock bonus, thrift, and other similar kinds of retirement and deferred compensation plans).

Special rules apply to most Keogh plans and to all simplified employee pensions. Keogh plans sponsored by proprietorships and Keogh plans sponsored by partnerships where at least one ten percent partner is a plan participant must cover all employees who have completed three or more years of service (except certain union employees and certain nonresident aliens).[1] Simplified employee pensions must cover all employees who have attained age 25 and who have performed service for the employer during at least three of the immediately preceding five calendar years.[2]

Except as noted in the preceding paragraph with respect to most Keogh and all simplified employee pension plans, the minimum coverage requirements of the Code applicable to the majority of employee pension benefit arrangements (those sponsored by corporations and by partnerships where the plan does not include any ten percent or greater partner) serve only one function: to prevent discrimination in favor of officers, shareholders, and other highly compensated employees (collectively referred to as *the prohibited group*).

---

1 I.R.C. § 401(d)(3).
2 I.R.C. § 408(k)(2).

SATISFYING MINIMUM COVERAGE STANDARDS

There are three ways a plan (other than the Keogh and simplified employee plans mentioned above) can satisfy the minimum coverage standards of the Code:

- The plan can satisfy either of two percentage tests prescribed in the Code. Satisfaction of either of the percentage tests puts the plan into a "safe harbor" as to adequacy of coverage.
- The plan can satisfy a classification test that demonstrates that coverage under the plan is such as to preclude discrimination in favor of the prohibited group.
- The plan may satisfy the coverage test even if it fails the percentage tests and fails the classification test if it can be shown that the combined coverage of the plan and one or more other comparable plans sponsored by the employer, when aggregated and considered as a single plan, will satisfy either the percentage test or the classification test.

The Percentage Test

The percentage test is automatically satisfied if 70 percent of all of the "countable employees" of the employer are participants in the plan.[3]

The percentage test is also met if 70 percent of all of the "countable employees" of the employer are eligible to participate in the plan, and if at least 80 percent of that group are actually participating in the plan.[4]

Except as described in the following sentence, the *countable employees* of a plan sponsor include the employees of all enterprises which, with the plan sponsor, form a controlled group of corporations under Section 414(b) of the Code, a group of trades or businesses under common control under Section 414(c), or an affiliated service group under Section 414(m).[5] Countable employees do *not* include any of the following: persons who may later become eligible for plan participation, but who have not yet met the minimum age or service requirements for plan participation; persons whose terms and conditions of employment are established through collective bargaining if the issue of retirement benefits was the subject of good-faith collective bargaining (unless the collective bargaining agreement provides that such persons shall be included in the plan); nonresident aliens who have no U.S.-source income from the employer; and, in the case of certain trusts established under agreements between air pilots and their employers, all persons not covered by such agreements.[6]

A special percentage test is applicable only to tax credit employee stock ownership plans. Such a plan satisfies the special percentage test if it is the

[3] I.R.C. § 410(b)(1)(A).
[4] I.R.C. § 410(b)(1)(A).
[5] I.R.C. §§ 414(b), 414(c), 414(m).
[6] I.R.C. §§ 410(b)(1)(A), 410(b)(3).

only plan sponsored by the employer that is intended to be a qualified plan, if it benefits 50 percent or more of all of the employees who are eligible under the plan (excluding those who have not satisfied the minimum age and service requirements of the plan, if any), and if the sum of the amounts allocated to each participant's account for the year does not exceed 2 percent of the participant's compensation for the year.[7]

The Classification Test

A plan that does not satisfy the percentage test may still qualify if it covers employees in a classification found by the IRS not to be discriminatory in favor of the prohibited group.[8] A plan that does not include among its participants any prohibited group of employees will satisfy the classification test, regardless of how small the plan census appears when compared to the plan sponsor's total employment rolls.

The classification test may also be met, even if the plan enrollment includes prohibited group members, as long as the plan covers a fair cross-section of the employer's payroll spectrum. In running the *fair cross-section* test, the countable employees include not only those who are "countable" for percentage test purposes, but also those who would be participants in the plan but for failure to meet the plan's minimum age and/or minimum service requirements.

In running the fair cross-section test, which is more a judgment test than a prescribed standard, the number of employees covered by the plan in each $1,000 pay bracket is compared with the number of countable employees in that pay bracket who are not covered. If, on the basis of such a comparison, it can be demonstrated that the plan covers a fair cross-section of the employer's countable employees, the plan will be deemed to satisfy the minimum coverage requirements of the Code for the period with respect to which the test was run.

WELFARE PLANS

While the minimum coverage standards of the Code were originally conceived and enacted solely for the purpose of determining the existence of prohibited discrimination in connection with pension benefit plans that sought the special tax advantages of qualified status, Congress has imposed certain somewhat parallel minimum coverage requirements in connection with self-insured medical expense reimbursement programs sponsored by corporate employers.[9] The Treasury, without specific statutory authority, has imposed

---

7 I.R.C. § 410(b)(2).
8 I.R.C. § 410(b)(1)(B).
9 I.R.C. § 105(h)(3).

minimum coverage requirements for voluntary employee beneficiary associations as a precondition of tax exemption under Section 501(c)(9) of the Code.[10]

---

[10] Treas. Reg. § 1.501(c)(9)-4(b).

Minimum Vesting Standards for Qualified Plans

ROBERT A. BILDERSEE
Morgan, Lewis & Bockius

PURPOSE OF THE MINIMUM VESTING STANDARDS

An employee's *accrued benefit* under an employee pension plan is the amount of benefit that the employee has earned. In a defined contribution plan, the accrued benefit is the employee's account balance. In a defined benefit plan, the accrued benefit is the employee's pension earned to the date of reference. The employee's vested interest is that portion of the employee's accrued benefit in which the employee has a nonforfeitable interest. Typically, an employee's vested interest is expressed as a percentage of his accrued benefit.

Vesting Before ERISA

Before the enactment of the Employee Retirement Income Security Act of 1974 (ERISA), most plans based vesting on the period of an employee's participation in the plan. Service other than as a plan participant was commonly disregarded. Some plans, particularly those that did not require the reallocation of forfeited benefits to persons who were officers, shareholders, supervisory persons, and highly compensated individuals, offered no vesting at all. Any person who terminated employment prior to retirement under such a plan might well lose his entire accrued pension benefit. Occasionally, plans to which employees contributed their own funds provided for the forfeiture of all accrued benefits (including those attributable to employee contributions) upon premature termination of employment.

Right to Accrued Benefits

Congress, through ERISA, amended the Internal Revenue Code with respect to vesting provisions. Under the amended Code, every participant's right to the accrued benefit under a pension plan derived from his own contributions must be nonforfeitable (vested) at all times.[1]

The right of each participant to accrued benefits derived from employer contributions is to be determined on the basis of service, whether or not

---

[1] I.R.C. § 411(a)(1).

that service is performed as a plan participant. The rate at which a plan participant achieves a vested interest in his accrued benefit must meet certain standards designed to assure each employee who spends a significant portion of his career with that employer of such a vested interest.[2]

VESTING IN BENEFITS ATTRIBUTABLE TO PARTICIPANT CONTRIBUTIONS

Defined Contribution Plans

In defined contribution plans (profit-sharing plans, money purchase pension plans, target or assumed benefit plans, stock bonus plans, employee stock ownership plans, and thrift or savings plans), one or more separate accounts are maintained for each participant.

If a separate account is maintained with respect to an employee's contributions, the balance in that account, including all income, expenses, gains, and losses attributable thereto, is treated as the "accrued benefit" derived from the employee's contributions to the plan. Thus, the entire separate account, including those gains and losses, must be fully vested in the participant at all times.[3]

If the plan does not require that employee contributions and assets attributable thereto be maintained as a separate account, then the accrued benefit deemed to be attributable to employee contributions is the employee's total accrued benefit (account balance) multiplied by a fraction, the numerator of which is the total amount of the employee's contributions under the plan (less withdrawals of such amounts), and the denominator of which is the sum of the numerator plus total contributions made under the plan by the employer on behalf of the employee (less withdrawals, if any, of those amounts).[4]

Defined Benefit Plans

Where a defined benefit plan allows voluntary employee contributions, a separate account to which the employee's contributions are credited must be maintained. Earnings and accretions attributable to those contributions must be credited to that separate account. The employee must be fully vested in this separately maintained account at all times.[5]

Where a defined benefit plan requires employee contributions, the accrued benefit derived from employee contributions as of any date of reference is an annual benefit, in the form of a single life annuity (without ancillary

---

[2] I.R.C. § 411(a)(2).
[3] Treas. Reg. § 1.411(c)-1(b)(1).
[4] Treas. Reg. § 1.411(c)-1(b)(2).
[5] I.R.C. § 411(c)(2)(A); Treas. Reg. § 1.411(c)-1(b)(1).

benefits) commencing at normal retirement age, is equal to the amount of the employee's accumulated contributions (with interest thereon) multiplied by a *conversion factor* specified by the Secretary of the Treasury. The conversion factor is the factor necessary to convert an amount equal to the accumulated contributions (with interest) made by the employee to a single life annuity commencing at normal retirement age.[6] Interest on contributions made by participants must be credited at the rate specified in the plan for the period prior to the date on which the vesting requirements of ERISA first apply to the plan, and must be credited at the rate of 5 percent per annum, compounded annually, from the beginning of the first plan year with respect to which ERISA's vesting requirements apply to the plan. Interest must be credited to the date upon which the employee attains normal retirement age.[7] Contributions made by employees are considered *mandatory contributions* to the extent those contributions are required as a condition of employment, as a condition of participation in the plan, or as a condition of obtaining benefits under the plan attributable to employer contributions.[8] Tables of "conversion factors" for various retirement ages have been published by the Internal Revenue Service.[9] These tables permit calculation of the portion of an accrued benefit which is deemed derived from mandatory employee contributions to a defined benefit plan, and further provide those adjustment and conversion factors required where benefits are provided other than as single life annuities.

Benefits attributable to employee contributions, unlike vested benefits attributable to employer contributions, may not be forfeited by reason of the death of the participant. Section 411(a)(3)(A) of the Code, which permits forfeitures by reason of death to be nonviolative of the general vesting requirements, applies only to accrued benefits derived from employer contributions. However, once annuity payments commence, a forfeiture does not arise merely because payments cease upon the death of the participant, even if the participant has not yet recovered the full value of his accrued benefit attributable to his own contributions. A plan that requires employee contributions can provide for a benefit in the form of a single life annuity with no refund feature (or other actuarially equivalent benefit recovery guarantee).[10]

BENEFITS ATTRIBUTABLE TO EMPLOYER CONTRIBUTIONS

Benefits attributable to employer contributions must be fully vested upon attainment of normal retirement age.[11] Vesting prior to normal retirement

---

6 I.R.C. § 411(c)(2)(B); Treas. Reg. § 1.411(c)-1(c)(2).
7 I.R.C. § 411(c)(2)(C); Treas. Reg. § 1.411(c)-1(c)(3).
8 I.R.C. § 411(c)(2)(C); Treas. Reg. § 1.411(c)-1(c)(4).
9 Rev. Rul. 76-47, 1976-1 C.B. 109.
10 IRS Release 1589 (April 6, 1976).
11 I.R.C. § 411(a); Treas. Reg. §§ 1.411(a)-1(a)(1), 1.411(a)-7(b).

age must satisfy one of three alternative minimum vesting schedules, subject to the following exceptions:

1. Vesting must be full and immediate if the plan requires more than one year of service as a precondition of participation;
2. Class-year vesting is acceptable in connection with certain types of plans; and
3. In the case of qualified plans, the IRS may require vesting more rapid than the vesting provided by the alternative vesting schedules if there is an established pattern of abuse, or if there has been, or there is reason to believe there will be, an accrual of benefits or forfeitures tending to discriminate in favor of employees who are officers, shareholders, or highly compensated.[12]

Minimum Vesting Schedules

The following are the alternative rules for vesting prior to normal retirement age:

Alternative No. 1: The Ten-Year Rule. An employee's accrued benefit derived from employer contributions must be 100 percent vested after ten years of service.[13] While no interim vesting is required, election of the ten-year rule does not preclude offering earlier full or partial vesting if the plan sponsor is so inclined.

Alternative No. 2: Five to Fifteen-Year Graduated Vesting. A plan is deemed to satisfy the vesting requirements if an employee who has completed at least five years of service is at least 25 percent vested in his accrued benefit derived from employer contributions, and if his vested interest thereafter increases so that the vested percentage is not less than the percentage indicated in the following table.[14]

Years of Service	*Nonforfeitable Percentage*
5	25%
6	30%
7	35%
8	40%
9	45%
10	50%
11	60%
12	70%
13	80%
14	90%
15 or more	100%

[12] I.R.C. § 411(d)(1).
[13] I.R.C. § 411(a)(2)(A); Treas. Reg. § 1.411(a)-3(b).
[14] I.R.C. § 411(a)(2)(B); Treas. Reg. § 1.411(a)-3(c).

Alternative No. 3: "Rule of 45." Under the Rule of 45, any employee with five or more years of service and with respect to whom the sum of age and years of service equals or exceeds 45 must be at least 50 percent vested in his accrued benefit derived from employer contributions. The degree to which vesting must be granted is illustrated by the following table:

If Years of Service Equal or Exceed	*And the Sum of Age and Service Equals or Exceeds*	*Then the (Min.) Nonforfeitable Percentage Is:*
5	45	50%
6	47	60%
7	49	70%
8	51	80%
9	53	90%
10	55	100%

Notwithstanding the general requirement that the sum of age and service must equal or exceed 45 before vesting is required under the Rule of 45, no plan shall be treated as satisfying the Rule of 45 vesting requirements unless any participant who has completed ten years of service has a nonforfeitable right to at least 50 percent of his accrued benefit derived from employer contributions and to not less than an additional 10 percent for each additional year of service.[15] In applying the Rule of 45, "age" means the age attained by the participant as of his most recent birthday, regardless of the definition of "age" that might be used in the plan.[16]

SPECIAL RULES

Cash-or-Deferred Plans

Certain profit-sharing and stock bonus plans contain provisions permitting participants to take a portion (or all) of the current employer contributions allocable to their accounts in cash. To the extent that participants in such plans have the option to receive cash and elect to defer such amounts, rather than to receive them currently, the deferred amounts (and earnings and accretions attributable thereto) must at all times be fully vested. So much of the participant's account in any cash-or-deferred plan which was attributable to employer contributions and which was not subject to the current cash-withdrawal option may vest in accordance with the usual rules relating to the vesting of employer contributions.[17]

---

[15] I.R.C. § 411(a)(2)(C); Treas. Reg. § 1.411(a)-3(d)(2).
[16] Treas. Reg. § 1.411(a)-3(d)(3).
[17] I.R.C. § 401(k)(2)(C).

Class-Year Plans

In a class-year plan, each year's employer contribution (and the earnings and accretions attributable to that contribution) vests separately after the passage of a stipulated period. Such plans conform to the Code's vesting requirements if they provide for full vesting of each year's contributions (and attributable earnings and accretions thereto) not later than the end of the fifth plan year following the plan year for which the contribution was made.[18]

HR-10 (Keogh) Plans

The provisions of the pre-ERISA Code requiring 100 percent vesting in any plan including a sole proprietor or an owner-employee are continued.[19]

Certain Contributory Plans

A contributory plan may provide that benefits attributable to employer contributions shall be forfeited upon withdrawal of mandatory employee contributions if, at the time of that withdrawal, the participant had a less than 50 percent vested interest in so much of his benefit as was attributable to employer contributions and if the plan provides for restoration of the forfeited benefit accrual upon return to the plan, within prescribed time limits, of the withdrawn amount (and, in the case of defined benefit plans, interest on the withdrawn amount for the period of the withdrawal).[20]

TRASOPs. An employee must be fully vested in any employer security allocated to his or her account under a TRASOP.[21]

PERMITTED FORFEITURES

With limited enumerated exceptions, an employee's rights to benefits, once vested, are not to be forfeitable for any reason.[22] Accordingly, plans generally may not contain provisions requiring divestiture of interests by reason of violation of a restrictive covenant prohibiting (or placing the price of divestiture upon) competitive activities engaged in by a former employee, nor can a plan call for divestiture of an otherwise vested interest by reason of discharge for cause.[23]

---

[18] I.R.C. § 411(d)(4).

[19] I.R.C. § 401(d)(2)(A).

[20] I.R.C. §§ 401(a)(19), 411(a)(3)(D).

[21] I.R.C. § 409A(c).

[22] I.R.C. § 411(a)(3).

[23] If a plan offers vesting more generous than that required by statute, the excess vesting may be subject to divestiture under restrictive covenants and "bad boy" provisions. See Treas. Reg. §§ 1.411(a)-4(a), 1.411(a)-4(c), Ex. (1).

There are certain circumstances under which a plan may provide that an employee's vested rights to benefits attributable to employer contributions may be forfeited which will not be deemed violative of the vesting standards. For example, a plan may provide that the right to an accrued benefit derived from employer contributions may be forfeited in the event of the death of the participant (unless a "joint and survivor annuity" is to be provided).[24] Benefits shall not be treated as forfeited if a plan requires that payment of benefits be suspended for such period as the employee is reemployed by the plan sponsor after the commencement of benefit payments by the plan, or, in the case of a multiemployer plan, if the benefit payee is reemployed in the same industry, trade, or craft in the same geographic area covered by the plan.[25]

Plan Amendments

If a plan amendment reduces an employee's vested or nonvested accrued benefit attributable to employer contributions, that amendment will not be considered as creating a forfeiture if the amendment is adopted within two and one-half months after the close of the plan year in question (within two years after the close of the plan year in the case of multiemployer plans), does not reduce benefits accrued by any participant prior to the beginning of the first plan year to which the amendment applies, and is otherwise approved by the Secretary of Labor. With respect to any plan amendment that reduces accrued benefits, the Secretary of Labor must be given ninety days prior notice of the proposed amendment and must approve (or fail to disapprove) of it.[26] Approval is to be granted only to prevent substantial economic hardship, including a serious danger that the plan will be terminated unless the amendment is allowed. It must also be found by the Secretary that the economic hardship cannot be overcome by means of a variance.[27]

Participant Withdrawals

A plan shall not be deemed violative of the vesting requirements if it provides that, in the case of a participant who does not have a nonforfeitable right to at least 50 percent of his accrued benefit derived from employer contributions, such accrued benefit may be forfeited on account of the withdrawal by the participant of any amount attributable to the benefit derived from mandatory contributions made by that participant.[28] However, such a

---

24 I.R.C. § 411(a)(3)(A); Treas. Reg. § 1.411(a)-4(b)(1).
25 I.R.C. § 411(a)(3)(B); Treas. Reg. § 1.411(a)-4(b)(2).
26 Temp. Reg. § 11.412(c)-7.
27 I.R.C. §§ 411(a)(3)(C), 412(c)(8).
28 I.R.C. § 411(a)(3)(D)(i); Treas. Reg. § 1.411(a)-4(b)(4)(i).

plan must provide that any accrued benefit forfeited by reason of any such withdrawal will be restored upon repayment by the participant of the full amount of the withdrawal plus, in the case of defined benefit plans, interest at a prescribed rate.[29]

Plans will also be deemed to conform to the vesting requirements, even though they provide that an amount of accrued benefit may be forfeited on account of withdrawal by the participant of an amount attributable to the benefit derived from mandatory contributions made by such participant before the date of ERISA's enactment, if the benefit forfeited is proportional to the amount withdrawn. This last consideration does not apply to any plan to which mandatory contributions are made after September 2, 1974.[30] The right of a participant to restore prior benefit accruals forfeited through earlier withdrawal of mandatory contributions raises a particularly difficult problem in the case of defined contribution plans that allow reallocation of forfeitures. If the earlier forfeitures have been reallocated to the accounts of other participants (some of whom may have since received full benefit distributions) how it will be possible to effect a restoration of benefit accruals upon a return to the fund of withdrawn sums by the participant is problematical.

NONDISCRIMINATION REQUIREMENT

Section 401(a)(4) of the Code provides that a qualified plan may not discriminate in favor of the *prohibited group,* that group of employees consisting of officers, shareholders, and other relatively highly compensated individuals. A plan conforming to the statutory vesting standards (ten-year cliff, five to fifteen-year graduated, Rule of 45, class year) shall be treated as conforming to the nondiscrimination standards unless there has been a pattern of abuse under the plan (such as dismissals of employees before the accrued benefits become nonforfeitable) tending to make the plan discriminatory in favor of the prohibited group, or (in the opinion of the IRS) there has been or there is reason to believe that there will be an accrual of benefits or forfeitures tending to discriminate in favor of the prohibited group.[31]

While Congress intended, through the establishment of minimum vesting standards, to avoid the inconsistency of case-by-case application of vesting standards (such as characterized IRS handling of such matters prior to ERISA), there is substantial latitude for the IRS to continue to require more rapid vesting in circumstances in which it is perceived that the plan could become discriminatory in operation by reason of vesting in accordance with the minimum standards otherwise allowed by ERISA.

---

[29] I.R.C. § 411(a)(3)(D)(ii); Treas. Reg. § 1.411(a)-4(b)(4)(ii).
[30] I.R.C. § 411(a)(3)(D)(iii).
[31] I.R.C. § 411(d)(1).

4/40 Vesting

The Conference Committee Report "directs" the IRS "not to require a vesting schedule more stringent than 40 percent vesting after four years of employment with 5 percent additional vesting for each of the next two years, and 10 percent additional vesting for each of the following five years" except in cases of actual abuse.[32]

In the earliest days of ERISA, a standard procedure was followed by many IRS districts in which, as a precondition to the issuance of a favorable determination letter, it was "requested" that so-called committee or 4/40 vesting (as described in the preceding paragraph) be provided for in the plan under consideration.

Proposed "Testing" Procedures. In Revenue Procedure 75-49, the IRS set forth two tests that it intended to apply to determine if vesting as fast as "4/40" vesting would be required to prevent actual or potential abuse.[33]

- *Key-employee test.* The "key-employee" test examines the percentage of plan participants over time represented by officers, shareholders, and the five most highly compensated employees of the plan sponsor.[34]
- *Turnover test.* The "turnover" test relates the rank-and-file turnover rate to the "prohibited group" turnover rate over time.[35]

The nature of the tests suggests that the majority of plan sponsors, and virtually all small and recently established corporations, would be compelled to adopt "4/40" vesting to avoid receipt of adverse determination letters or to avoid the risk of an approved plan becoming "discriminatory in operation" by reason of circumstances beyond the control of the plan sponsor.

Alternative Proposals. Reaction from plan sponsors and elected representatives was swift and vocal. The IRS then announced that the original guidelines were "misunderstood." To resolve this "misunderstanding" and to allow additional time to restudy and reformulate the guidelines, the IRS issued Revenue Procedure 76-11.[36] This procedure states that, pending completion of reconsideration of Revenue Procedure 75-49, a plan's vesting would be adequate if it complied with either of the tests outlined in Revenue Procedure 75-49, or if it satisfied either of two other tests introduced with Revenue Procedure 76-11. The first alternative test applies only to plans in which a previous favorable letter of determination had been issued (and had not been revoked). That test is satisfied if the vesting under a plan

---

[32] Conf. Rep. on H.R. 2, *Joint Explanatory Statement of the Committee of Conference,* House Conf. Rep. No. 93-1280, 93d Cong., 2d Sess. 276 (1974).

[33] Rev. Proc. 75-49, 1975-2 C.B. 551.

[34] Rev. Proc. 75-49, 1975-2 C.B. 551, § 3.03(1).

[35] Rev. Proc. 75-49, 1975-2 C.B. 551, § 3.03(2).

[36] Rev. Proc. 76-11, 1976-1 C.B. 547.

revised to conform to ERISA is no less generous than the vesting under the plan upon which the prior letter of determination was based.[37] The second alternative test is a demonstration to the satisfaction of the IRS, on a "facts and circumstances" basis, that there is no reason to believe that a proposed vesting schedule will result in discrimination in favor of the prohibited group.[38] The IRS continues to reserve to itself the privilege of requiring vesting more rapid that "4/40" vesting if there has been a pattern of abuse or actual misuse of the plan in operation affecting qualified status.[39] When "4/40" vesting is required, it may not be possible to disregard service periods identified in Section 411(a)(4) of the Code.

VESTING ON PLAN TERMINATION

As under pre-ERISA law, all accrued benefits in a qualified retirement plan, to the extent funded, must become fully vested in the event of a plan termination, or the complete discontinuance of contributions under the plan. Complete discontinuance of contributions refers to the discontinuance of employer contributions under a defined contribution plan, but not the failure of employers to make required contributions to defined benefit plans, since other provisions of ERISA deal with the problems of underfunding of defined benefit plans, and since failure to contribute does not result in automatic termination of the benefit accrual process.[40] ERISA does not eliminate the ten-year and current funding limitations presently found in the regulations with respect to amounts payable to those with anticipated annual benefits of $1,500 or more who were among the twenty-five highest paid employees of the plan sponsor at the time of plan inception or the most recent substantial amendment increasing benefits.[41]

SERVICE FOR VESTING PURPOSES

Once an employee has become eligible to participate in a retirement plan, all of his "years of service" with the employer are taken into account for purposes of determining his vested interest pursuant to the plan's vesting schedule.[42] Service in an ineligible classification (such as, for example, service as a laborer in the case of a plan limited to office and clerical workers) and service for enterprises forming, with the plan sponsor, a controlled group of corporations, a group of trades or businesses under common control, or

---

[37] Rev. Proc. 76-11, 1976-1 C.B. 547 § 3.01(2).
[38] Rev. Proc. 76-11, 1976-1 C.B. 547 § 3.01(3).
[39] Rev. Proc. 76-11, 1976-1 C.B. 547 § 3.04.
[40] I.R.C. § 411(d)(3); Treas. Reg. § 1.411(d)-2(a)(2)(i).
[41] Treas. Reg. § 1.401-4(c).
[42] I.R.C. § 411(a)(4); Treas. Reg. § 1.411(a)-6.

an affiliated service group count as service for vesting purposes under the plan once the employee has qualified for participation.[43] Vesting service is measured in "years of service." Certain service may be disregarded, in certain circumstances, in computing a participant's vested interest in his accrued benefit.

Vesting Computation Period

A "year of service" must be credited for each *vesting computation period* within which the employee completes 1,000 "hours of service." A "vesting computation period" is a calendar year, a plan year, a personal year based on the date of employment commencement (or the anniversary thereof), or other twelve-consecutive-month period designated by the plan.[44] "Hours of service" are basically all hours for which the employee is compensated or entitled to compensation for services performed for the employer and for reasons other than the performance of service. If the employee completes the requisite number of hours of service during a vesting computation period, he must be credited with a year of service with respect to that computation period whether or not the employer-employee relationship continues to exist at the end of the computation period.

Elapsed-Time Method

Under the elapsed-time method, the amount of service to be credited to an individual is not determined by the number of hours worked in a particular year, but rather, with reference to the total period of time that elapses while that individual is employed by the employer or employers maintaining the plan. A "year of service" must be credited for each twelve-month period through which the employer/employee relationship continues from the employee's employment commencement date (the first day he is entitled to be credited with one hour of service) or reemployment commencement date (following a period of severance) to the date on which a severance of the employee-employer occurs.[45]

Although no credit need be given for periods during which the employer/employee relationship does not exist, interruptions in that relationship do not cause the loss of prior credit or otherwise interfere with the continuous crediting of service for periods during which the relationship exists unless there occurs a "break in service" and the prior service may be disregarded under the rule of parity. (These concepts are explained in greater depth earlier in this chapter under "Crediting Service.")

---

[43] I.R.C. §§ 414(b), 414(c), 414(m).

[44] I.R.C. § 411(a)(5); Treas. Reg. § 1.411(a)-5(b).

[45] Treas. Reg. §§ 1.410(a)-7(a)(3)(iv), 1.410(a)-7(b)(1), 1.410(a)-7(b)(3), 1.410(a)-7(b)(6), 1.410(a)-7(c)(2).

SERVICE WHICH MAY BE DISREGARDED UNDER THE GENERAL RULE

Certain periods of service identified by the statute may be disregarded, for vesting service computation purposes, if the plan provides for the exclusion of those periods. Exclusion of excludable service is not automatic as to those periods, and plans must be drafted to specifically identify those periods of service that are not to be included. The following service may be disregarded if the plan so provides: [46]

1. Years of service prior to the attainment of age 22, provided, however, that if a plan does not conform to either the ten-year vesting schedule or the graduated five to fifteen-year vesting schedule, service prior to age 22 may not be disregarded to the extent that the employee was a participant during such period of service;
2. Service during any period for which a participant declined to make contributions to a plan requiring employee contributions;
3. Service during any vesting computation period in which the employee fails to complete a year of service;
4. Service during any period with respect to which the employer did not maintain the plan or a predecessor plan;
5. Years of service prior to January 1, 1971, unless the employee had at least three years of service after December 31, 1970;
6. Years of service prior to the first plan year to which the vesting provisions of ERISA apply, if such service would have been disregarded under the rules of the plan with regard to "breaks in service" as in effect on the applicable date; and
7. Service performed prior to a "break in service" to the extent that such service may be ignored under the "break in service" rules discussed below.

A plan can provide different twelve-month periods for purposes of measuring compliance with the 1,000-hour rules for participation, vesting, and benefit accrual. The "vesting computation period" need not correspond to either the "eligibility computation period" or the "benefit accrual computation period."

For vesting purposes, special rules pertain to seasonal and maritime industries as to what constitutes a "year of service." [47]

BREAK-IN-SERVICE RULES

A break in service interrupts the accumulation of service credit for vesting purposes. In general, a one-year break in service is deemed to have occurred if, during the relevant measuring period set forth in the plan (i.e., a calendar

---

[46] I.R.C. § 411(a)(4); Treas. Reg. § 1.411(a)-5(b).

[47] ERISA §§ 203(b)(2)(C), 203(b)(2)(D).

year, plan year, or other twelve-consecutive-month period designated in the plan), the participant has not completed more than 500 hours of service.[48] The relevant measuring period for determining whether or not a break in service by a participant has occurred is the vesting computation period under the plan.[49]

For purposes of determining where an employee stands in the vesting schedule, in the case of any employee who has had a one-year break in service and who is thereafter reinstated, years of service prior to such break in service shall not be required to be taken into account until the employee has completed a year of service (not necessarily as a participant) after his or her return, after which time prior service must be reinstated unless excused by the "rule of parity."

Individual Account Plans

In the case of individual account plans (defined contribution plans, target or assumed benefit plans, and defined benefit plans funded solely by individual life insurance contracts), if any employee has a one-year break in service, there need be no increase in his vesting percentage in prebreak benefit accruals as a result of post-break service.[50] However, such prebreak service must be taken into account in determining the employee's percentage of vesting in post-break accruals (unless excused under the "rule of parity").

Where an employee experiences a break in service and then returns to covered employment, and where service prior to the break in service cannot be disregarded in computing the participant's vested interest in benefit accruals, the plan may provide, nonetheless, that prebreak service shall be disregarded until such time as the employee has completed a year of service subsequent to the break in service.[51]

Unless the plan provides otherwise, a break in service will be experienced by each employee failing to complete more than 500 hours of service during a computation period, whether or not the employment of the individual is terminated.

In maritime industry plans, sixty-two days of service is considered the equivalent of 500 hours of service.[52] In plans in which employees receive hours of service credit only for hours worked, 435 hours of service are considered equal to 500 hours of service.[53] Where employees receive credit only for regular time hours worked, 375 hours of service are considered the equivalent of 500 hours of service.[54]

---

48 I.R.C. § 411(a)(6)(A); Treas. Reg. § 1.411(a)-6(c).
49 29 C.F.R. § 2530.200b-4 (1976).
50 I.R.C. § 411(a)(6)(C); Treas. Reg. § 1.411(a)-6(c)(1)(ii).
51 I.R.C. § 411(a)(6)(B); Treas. Reg. § 1.411(a)-6(c)(1).
52 29 C.F.R. § 2530.200b-4 (1976).
53 29 C.F.R. § 2530.200b-3(d)(1) (1976).
54 29 C.F.R. § 2530.200b-3(d)(2) (1976).

Where a plan operates on the elapsed-time method, an employee is not considered to have experienced a one-year break in service until he has experienced a period of severance of employment extended, uninterrupted, over twelve consecutive months.[55] A period of severance commences on the effective date of an employee's severance from service, and ends on the date of employment recommencement.

"RULE OF PARITY"

Under the *rule of parity,* service prior to the occurrence of a break in service may be disregarded for the purposes of computing a participant's vested interest in a plan if (1) the participant has no vested interest under the plan by reason of a prior period of service, and (2) the number of consecutive one-year breaks in service experienced by the participant equals or exceeds the number of years of service that must be considered and that were completed prior to the occurrence of the break(s) in service to which reference is made.[56] For example, if an employee with two years of service experiences two or more consecutive one-year breaks in service and then reenters the service of the employer, his service prior to the breaks can be disregarded as long as the prebreak service did not result in any vested interest in the plan. However, if the employee had three years of service prior to experiencing two consecutive one-year breaks in service, or if the employee had a vested interest in the plan by reason of prior service, then, after fulfilling any applicable reentry requirement (not to exceed one year of service), he would have four years of service for vesting purposes when determining his vested interest in post-break benefit accruals because prebreak and post-break service must be aggregated in such case. Special rules apply where there have been multiple periods of service separated by multiple breaks in service.

SEPARATION FROM SERVICE

If a defined contribution plan permits distributions at a time when the participant is less than 100 percent vested in his accrued benefit and there has been no break in service prior to the distribution date (so that there remains the possibility of covered employment reinstatement without the occurrence of a break in service), the plan must provide that (1) a separate account is established for the participant's interest in the plan as of the date of the distribution, and (2) at any time, the participant's vested portion of the separate account maintained is not less than an amount determined by

---

[55] Treas. Reg. § 1.410(a)-7(d)(4).
[56] I.R.C. § 411(a)(6)(D); Treas. Reg. § 1.411(a)-6(c)(1)(iii).

a formula set forth in the regulations. The regulations offer alternate formulas for the determination of the vested interest of a participant who returns to plan participation prior to the occurrence of a break in service, but subsequent to a distribution of his vested interest.[57]

VESTING SCHEDULE AMENDMENTS

No amendment may divest an employee of benefits that are already vested. If a plan amendment is adopted that changes any vesting schedule under a plan, each participant having not less than five years of service is permitted to elect, within a reasonable period after the adoption of such amendment, to have his nonforfeitable percentage computed under the plan without regard to that amendment.[58]

The election period must begin no later than the date upon which the plan amendment is adopted and must end no earlier than the latest of the following dates:

1. Sixty days after the day the plan amendment is adopted;
2. Sixty days after the day when the plan amendment becomes effective; or
3. Sixty days after the day the participant is issued written notice of the plan amendment by the employer or plan administrator.

The five years of service requirement is to be computed in accordance with the manner in which years of service are computed for vesting purposes.[59] Any employee who has completed the requisite five years of service for vesting purposes by the end of the election period is entitled to file the election which, by its terms, may be irrevocable.[60] It would appear that an employee whose vesting service credit restoration privileges from a prior period of employment remain unexercised throughout the election period will be precluded from subsequently exercising the option to be governed by the former vesting schedule upon restoration of vesting service credit after the election period terminates.

SERVICE WITH OTHER EMPLOYERS

In a plan other than a multiemployer plan, the rules concerning service with predecessor employers are the same for the purposes of vesting as the rules stated in connection with participation standards. With respect to multiemployer plans, service with any employer under the plan during any

---

[57] Treas. Reg. § 1.411(a)-7(d)(5)(iii).
[58] I.R.C. § 411(a)(10); Treas. Reg. § 1.411(a)-8(b).
[59] Treas. Reg. § 1.411(a)-8(b)(3).
[60] Treas. Reg. § 1.411(a)-8(b)(5).

year in which that employee is a member of the plan shall be counted as though all employers who are parties to the plan were a single employer.[61] As stated above, employment with any entity constituting, with the employer sponsoring the plan, a controlled group of corporations, a group of trades or businesses under common control, or an affiliated service group shall be considered employment by the plan sponsor since it is considered employment by a single employer.[62]

RECORD-KEEPING REQUIREMENTS

Employers are required to keep records of the years of service of each employee and vested percentages earned so that employees who are reinstated are assured of assuming their proper places on the vesting scale. Failure to maintain such records without reasonable cause may subject the employer to a civil penalty of $10 for each employee with respect to whom records are deficient. In the case of a multiemployer plan, the records are to be maintained by the plan administrator.[63] Changes in the plan year or plan accounting period, if resulting in a change in the vesting computation period, may result in serious complications with respect to vesting service credit and may require partial double-crediting of participants.

---

[61] ERISA § 210; 29 C.F.R. § 2530.210(a)(1) (1976).
[62] I.R.C. §§ 414(b), 414(c), 414(m).
[63] ERISA § 209(a); I.R.C. § 6652(f).

Benefit Accrual Standards Under ERISA

ROBERT A. BILDERSEE
Morgan, Lewis & Bockius

PURPOSE OF THE MINIMUM ACCRUAL RULES

Since a participant's accrued benefit under a defined contribution plan is his account balance (or aggregate accounts balance in the case of plans that provide a participant with more than one account), it is not necessary to establish a minimum accrual rate for defined contribution plans. The Internal Revenue Code does, however, have some accrual rules that apply to defined contribution plans. These rules must be utilized to determine the portion of a participant's accrued benefit that is attributable to participant contributions and the portion that is attributable to employer contributions under a defined contribution plan to which both the participant and the employer contribute, but where the funds are commingled and not established as separate accounts by source.[1]

A more difficult concept is faced in connection with defined benefit plans. The Code, as amended by the Employee Retirement Income Security Act of 1974 (ERISA), establishes minimum benefit accrual rates that must be achieved by defined benefit pension plans. Since a participant's vested interest at any date of reference is a percentage of his benefit accrued to that date of reference, it is necessary to define the concept of accrued benefit. The minimum vesting standards of the Code would be rendered meaningless if the plan sponsor were free to "backload" the plan by providing minimal benefit accruals during the bulk of an employee's career, followed by a high rate of accrual in the final years, since a mandated large percentage of nothing is still nothing. Accordingly, the law now requires that defined benefit pension plans provide for benefit accruals to be spread in a reasonably even fashion (with limited backloading permitted) over an employee's entire period of participation under the plan. The accrual rate must satisfy one of three alternative rules.

---

[1] I.R.C. §§ 411(c)(1), 411(2).

ALLOCATION OF ACCRUED BENEFITS BY CONTRIBUTION SOURCE

Defined Contribution Plans

Where both the employer and the employee contribute to a defined contribution plan, it is necessary to determine which portion of the participant's accrued benefit is attributable to employee contributions and which portion is attributable to employer contributions (unless the plan provides for full and immediate vesting in all benefit accruals and does not differentiate between sources of funds in any other respect, such as in the existence of a withdrawal privilege or earmarking (investment direction) privileges). In general, the accrued benefit derived from employer contributions as of any date is the total accrued benefit for such employee to the extent that it exceeds the accrued benefit derived from employee contributions.[2] If employer and employee contributions (and the earnings, accretions, losses, and expenses attributable to each) are maintained in separate accounts, the accrued benefit derived from employee contributions as of any applicable date is the balance of the employee's separate account consisting only of his contributions, and the income, expenses, gains, and losses attributable thereto.[3] If separate accounts are not maintained for each source of funds, the accrued benefit in the single account maintained for the employee must be allocated between employee and employer contributions. The accrued benefit allocable to employee contributions, in plans where separate accounts are not maintained by sources of funds, is the amount in the single account that bears the same ratio to the employee's total accrued benefit (i.e., total account balance) as the total amount of that employee's contributions (less withdrawals) bears to the sum of employee contributions and contributions made on the employee's behalf by the employer (again reduced by withdrawals, if any).[4]

Defined Benefit Plans

If a defined benefit pension plan allows voluntary participant contributions, a separate account must be established under the plan to which such contributions shall be credited. All earnings, accretions, losses, and expenses attributable to each such separate account must be credited thereto.[5]

If a defined benefit plan requires employee contributions as a condition of employment, as a condition of plan participation, or as a condition of obtaining benefits (or increases in benefits) under the plan attributable to employer contributions, the accrued benefit derived from mandatory contributions as of any applicable date is an annual benefit in the form of a single life annuity (without ancillary benefits) and commencing at normal

---

2 I.R.C. § 411(c)(1); Treas. Reg. § 1.411(c)-1(a).
3 I.R.C. §§ 411(a)(7)(A)(ii), 411(c)(2)(A)(i).
4 I.R.C. § 411(c)(2)(A)(ii); Treas. Reg. § 1.411(c)-1(b)(2).
5 Pub. L. No. 93-406, 88 Stat. 829, 836 (1974), § 3(23)(A).

retirement age. The annuity attributed to participant contributions will be the annuity so described in the amount generated by the employee's contributions (with prescribed interest credited thereto), multiplied by an appropriate "conversion factor." [6]

DEFINED BENEFIT PLANS: THE ACCRUED BENEFIT

In the case of defined benefit pension plans, the term *accrued benefit* means the individual's accrued benefit determined under the plan.[7] The "accrued benefit" is expressed in the form of an annual benefit commencing at normal retirement age, except that if the plan does not provide such a benefit, it shall mean an annual benefit commencing at normal retirement age which is the actuarial equivalent of the accrued benefit determined under the plan.[8] The term "accrued benefit" does not apply to ancillary benefits, such as the payment of medical expenses (or insurance premiums for such expenses), or disability benefits that exceed the normal retirement benefit payable at age 65 to an employee with comparable service under the plan, or to life insurance benefits payable as a lump sum. Also, the "accrued benefit" does not include the value of the right to receive early retirement benefits, or the value of Social Security supplements, or other benefits under the plan that are not continued for any employee after he has attained normal retirement age.[9]

In computing a participant's "accrued benefit," a subsidized early retirement benefit provided by the plan is not taken into account, except to the extent of determining the normal retirement benefit under the plan. The "accrued benefit" includes any optional settlement at normal retirement age under actuarial assumptions no less favorable than those that would be applied if the employee were terminating his employment at normal retirement age. The "accrued benefit" does not include any subsidized value in a joint and survivor annuity to the extent that the annual benefit under the joint and survivor annuity does not exceed the annual benefit of a single life annuity.[10]

The accrued benefit is to be determined with reference to "normal retirement age" under the plan, provided that the normal retirement age may not be later than the later of attainment of age 65 or the tenth anniversary of the date that the participant commenced participation in the plan. If the plan document establishes an earlier "normal retirement age," the time specified in the plan prevails.[11]

---

[6] I.R.C. § 411(a)(7)(A)(i); Treas. Reg. § 1.411(a)-7(a)(1).

[7] Conf. Rep. on H.R. 2, *Joint Explanatory Statement of the Committee of Conference*, House Conf. Rep. No. 93-1280, 93d Cong., 2d Sess. 273 (1974).

[8] Treas. Reg. § 1.411(a)-7(a).

[9] I.R.C. § 411(a)(8); Treas. Reg. § 1.411(a)-7(b)(1).

[10] ERISA § 204(a).

[11] I.R.C. § 411(b)(1)(E); Treas. Reg. § 1.411(b)-1(d)(1).

Every defined benefit pension plan must generate benefit accruals at a rate no slower than that prescribed by one of the three alternative tests set forth in the statute.[12] However, it is permissible for a plan to provide a deferral of benefit accrual commencement for each participant until such time as the participant has completed two full years of continuous service.[13]

The 3 Percent Method

Under this benefit accrual rate alternative, the accrued benefit to which each participant is entitled upon separation from service must be computed as though the separation from service occurred at the end of the plan year, and the benefit accrual must be not less than 3 percent of the "3 percent method benefit," multiplied by the number of years (not in excess of 33⅓) of the participant's participation in the plan, including years after normal retirement age has been attained. The *3 percent method benefit* is the normal retirement benefit to which the participant would be entitled if he commenced participation at the earliest possible entry age for any individual who is or who could be a participant under the plan, and if he served continuously until the earlier of age 65 or the normal retirement age under the plan.[14] If the benefit under the plan is based upon compensation during any period, the normal retirement benefit to which a participant would be entitled is determined as if he continued to earn annually the average rate of compensation which he earned during consecutive years of service, not in excess of ten, for which his compensation was the highest. The number of consecutive years of service to be used in computing average compensation must be the number of years of service specified under the plan for computing normal retirement benefits, but may not, in any event, exceed ten years.[15] If the benefit under the plan is dependent upon Social Security benefits or other variables (such as the Consumer Price Index), these factors are treated as remaining constant as of the beginning of the current plan year for all subsequent plan years.[16]

The 133⅓ Percent Rule

If the benefit accrual rate for any participant for any subsequent year is not more than 133⅓ percent of his or her accrual rate for any earlier year, based on either a dollar or percentage rate, the plan will be deemed to satisfy the 133⅓ percent test. Frontloading (i.e., accruing benefits at a faster rate in earlier years than in later years) is allowed without limitation.[17]

---

[12] I.R.C. § 411(b)(1)(A); Treas. Reg. § 1.411(b)-1(b)(1)(i).
[13] Treas. Reg. § 1.411(b)-1(b)(1)(ii)(A).
[14] Treas. Reg. § 1.411(b)-1(b)(1)(ii)(B).
[15] I.R.C. § 411(b)(1)(B); Treas. Reg. § 1.411(b)-1(b)(2)(i)(B).
[16] Treas. Reg. § 1.411(b)-1(b)(2)(i)(A).
[17] Treas. Reg. § 1.411(b)-1(b)(2)(i)(E).

Under the plan, the accrued benefit payable at normal retirement age must equal the normal retirement benefit determined under the plan.[18] The plan may provide that no benefits shall accrue to a participant with respect to service with the employer after attainment of normal retirement age.[19] As in the case of the 3 percent method, Social Security benefits and all other relevant variable factors used to compute benefits are treated as remaining constant as of the beginning of the current plan year for all subsequent plan years.[20] An increase in accrual rates for current or future years does not necessitate an increase in prior service accrual rates to preserve compliance with the 133⅓ percent rule.

The Fractional Rule Benefit

Under this rule, a plan satisfies the requirements if the accrued benefit to which any participant is entitled is not less than the "fractional rule benefit" multiplied by a fraction (not exceeding one), the numerator of which is his total number of years of participation in the plan, and the denominator of which is the total number of years of participation he would have accumulated in the plan by remaining an active participant through normal retirement age.[21] The *fractional rule benefit* is the annual benefit commencing at normal retirement age under the plan to which a participant would be entitled if he continued to earn annually until such normal retirement age the same rate of compensation upon which his normal retirement benefit (to the date of the computation) would be computed. If the plan uses "average compensation," no more than ten years of service immediately preceding the date of termination can be taken into account in computing a participant's "average compensation" for benefit accrual projection purposes.[22] As with the 3 percent and the 133⅓ percent methods, Social Security benefits and other relevant variable factors that may be used to compute benefits under the subject plan must be treated as remaining constant as of the beginning of the current plan year for all subsequent plan years.[23] The plan need not provide for continued benefit accrual on account of continued service with the employer after normal retirement age has been attained.[24]

Notwithstanding the three alternatives outlined above, if a plan is funded exclusively by the purchase of insurance contracts, the accrued benefit is to be the cash surrender value of the contracts (determined as though the funding requirements with respect to the plan had been fully satisfied).[25]

---

[18] Treas. Reg. § 1.411(b)-1(b)(2)(i)(D).
[19] I.R.C. § 411(b)(1)(C); Treas. Reg. § 1.411(b)-1(b)(3)(i).
[20] Treas. Reg. § 1.411(b)-1(b)(3)(ii)(A).
[21] Treas. Reg. § 1.411(b)-1(b)(3)(ii)(B).
[22] Treas. Reg. § 1.411(b)-1(b)(3)(ii)(C).
[23] I.R.C. § 411(b)(1)(F); Treas. Reg. § 1.411(b)-1(d)(2).
[24] I.R.C. § 411(b)(1)(G); Treas. Reg. § 1.411(b)-1(d)(3).
[25] I.R.C. § 411(b)(1)(D); Treas. Reg. § 1.411(b)-1(c)(1).

Accrued benefits may not be decreased on account of increasing age or service.[26]

Accrued Benefit for Pre-ERISA Years

The accrued benefits for years prior to the effective date of ERISA's benefit accrual requirements may not be less than the greater of the participant's accrued benefit as determined under the plan (as it existed prior to the effective date of ERISA's benefit accrual requirements) or an accrued benefit not less than one-half of the accrued benefit to which the participant would have been entitled had one of the three alternatives set forth above been in effect.[27] In computing the benefit for years prior to the effective date, and in determining if the foregoing test of adequacy of accrual rate has been satisfied, the plan may use any of the alternative accrual methods, even if the method selected differs from the accrual method to be applied with respect to years of participation after the effective date of ERISA.[28] Finally, in the cases of participants and beneficiaries receiving benefits under a plan, and in the case of a participant who is separated from the service of the employer and who has a nonforfeitable right to benefits under a plan, there may be no reduction in the accrued or payable benefit by reason of increases in Social Security benefits after September 2, 1974, or, if later, the earlier of the date of first receipt of such benefits or the date of the participant's separation from service.[29]

BENEFIT ACCRUAL SERVICE

Benefit accrual requirements are couched in terms of "years of participation." Every employee pension benefit plan must designate a twelve-consecutive-month period as the "accrual computation period" under the plan. This does not necessarily mean that every participant has the same accrual computation period. For example, in defined benefit plans with multiple entry dates, it may be desirable to have each participant's accrual computation period commence on the anniversary date of his personal entry into plan participation.[30] Since ERISA requires that the period of service taken into account to determine a year of participation must begin at the earliest date on which the employee is a participant in the plan and which is included in a period of service required to be taken into account for participation eligibility computation purposes, an individual's accrual computa-

---

[26] Treas. Reg. § 1.411(b)-1(c)(2).
[27] I.R.C. § 401(a)(15); Treas. Reg. § 1.401(a)-15(a).
[28] I.R.C. § 411(c)(2); Treas. Reg. §§ 1.411(c)-1(a), 1.411(c)-1(b).
[29] I.R.C. § 411(c)(2)(B)(i); Treas. Reg. § 1.411(c)-1(c). Conversion factors are set forth in Rev. Rul. 76-47, 1976-1 C.B. 109.
[30] I.R.C. § 411(b)(3)(A); Treas. Reg. § 1.411(b)-1(f).

tion period must either begin on his date of entry or be treated as having commenced as of the beginning of the plan's current common accrual computation period, the commencement of which preceded the date of his entry into the plan.

Defined Contribution Plans

In the case of defined contribution plans, subject to the exception discussed below, a participant who completes 1,000 or more hours of service during an accrual computation period must be allowed to share in the employer contributions for that period. If the employee's participation commences on an entry date other than the first day of the accrual computation period, and if the plan has a minimum service requirement for benefit accrual expressed in terms of hours of service required for a "year of participation," the plan must provide for a partial accrual based upon the ratable portion of the accrual computation period during which the employee was a participant.[31] In a defined contribution plan, if the benefit accrual for a partial year of participation is based on compensation while a participant (disregarding compensation earned prior to plan entry), an automatic proration of benefit accrual occurs.

The Internal Revenue Service has ruled that a defined contribution plan will not violate minimum statutory requirements solely because it provides that no allocation of employer contributions will be made to the account of a participant who completes 1,000 or more hours of service in the accrual computation period involved, but who terminates employment prior to the allocation date under the plan. The IRS cautions, however, that if a departed plan participant who completed 1,000 or more hours of service during the accrual computation period prior to service termination is denied the opportunity to share in the allocation for that period, and if that denial results in discrimination in favor of employees who are officers, shareholders, or highly compensated employees, then the plan will fail to satisfy the qualification requirements of Section 401(a)(4) of the Code because the IRS continues to consider the departed employee as an active plan participant for the period in question.[32]

Defined Benefit Plans

In the case of a defined benefit plan, a "year of participation" is an accrual computation period during which the employee completes a sufficient number of hours of service to entitle him to a benefit accrual under the provisions of the plan. As to plan participation prior to the effective date of ERISA's benefit accrual requirements, all service from the date of participation in

[31] I.R.C. § 411(b)(3); Treas. Reg. § 1.411(b)-1(f).
[32] Rev. Rul. 76-250, 1976-2 C.B. 124.

the plan as determined in accordance with applicable plan provisions shall be considered in determining an employee's years of participation. If the plan documents do not provide a definite means of determining the date of commencement of participation, the date of commencement of employment covered by the plan during the period that the employer maintained the plan shall be presumed to be the date of commencement of participation. The presumption is rebuttable.[33]

Participation After Effective Date

With respect to participation after ERISA's benefit accrual requirement effective date, a benefit accrual must be allowed for any accrual computation period in which the participant completes 1,000 or more hours of service. However, completion of 1,000 hours of service does not assure the participant of a full benefit accrual for the accrual computation period. A plan must accrue benefits for less than full-time service on at least a pro rata basis. For example, a plan requiring 1,500 hours of service for a full benefit accrual for an accrual computation period would have to allow an accrual of at least 80 percent of the full benefit for a participant who completes 1,200 hours of service during that accrual computation period. Double proration of benefit accruals is not permissible.[34] That is, a participant's benefit accrual for a partial year of participation may be based on annualized compensation multiplied by a fraction representing the part of the year worked, or it may be based on actual compensation with a full year's accrual as to that compensation allowed. In no event is it permissible to double reduce the accrual for the partial year of participation in question by limiting the accrual to the benefit generated by actual compensation, further prorated for the fraction of the year of participation completed.

The IRS permits cessation of benefit accruals at normal retirement age in the case of plans using either the 133⅓ percent method or the fractional rule benefit method. However, benefit accrual may not cease under the 3 percent method in the case of persons deferring retirement beyond normal retirement age, unless the participant has accrued the full benefit under the plan (i.e., been credited with at least 33⅓ years of participation).[35]

---

[33] 29 C.F.R. § 2530.204-2(b) (1976).

[34] Treas. Reg. § 1.411(a)-7(c)(5).

[35] As to the 3 percent method requirement of continued benefit accruals for persons working beyond normal retirement age, see Treas. Reg. § 1.411(b)-1(b)(1)(i). As to the permissibility of benefit accrual cessation for those working beyond normal retirement age in plans using the 133⅓ percent method, see Treas. Reg. § 1.411(b)-1(b)(2)(ii)(E). As to the permissibility of benefit accrual cessation for those working beyond normal retirement age in plans using the fractional rule method, see Treas. Reg. § 1.411(b)-1(b)(3)(ii)(C). Query the effect, if any, on the IRS position with respect to plans providing for cessation of benefit accrual prior to actual retirement (or age 70, if earlier) which may flow from the Equal Employment Opportunity Commission or other interpretations of the Age Discrimination in Employment Act of 1967, as amended.

Special rules exist for determining a year of participation in seasonal and maritime industries.[36]

In recognition of the burden imposed on plan sponsors by reason of the accelerated eligibility provisions of ERISA, and in recognition of the front-end costs of insured plans, ERISA allows a deferral of benefit accruals until such time as the employee has completed two years of continuous service (as measured for participation purposes).[37] This permissible deferral is limited to defined benefit plans. Once benefit accrual commences, the first two years of continuous service, to the extent that they (or either of them) may also be years of participation, must be years for which benefits are accrued.

BREAKS IN SERVICE

Defined Contribution Plans

If a participant in a defined contribution plan leaves the employ of the plan sponsor and returns to covered employment before experiencing a one-year break in service, there can be no forfeiture of his accrued benefit. However, if the plan so provides, once there has been a one-year break in service, the forfeitable portion of the participant's accrued benefit with respect to service prior to the break in service is permanently forfeited, notwithstanding a return to covered employment subsequent to the break in service. Service subsequent to the break in service causing the forfeiture does not restore the forfeited portion of the previously accrued benefit attributable to employer contributions.

If, under the participation eligibility rules, service prior to a break in service has to be taken into account in determining the right of a former participant to reenter the plan, the participant must accrue benefits from the date of his return to covered service, even though the benefit accrual associated with the first year of resumed covered employment may be postponed until a year of service has been completed.[38]

Where a former participant who has not experienced a break in service receives a distribution of less than the full present value of his accrued benefit attributable to employer contributions by reason of termination of plan participation, if the plan is to disregard service prior to termination of plan participation upon recommencement of plan participation (i.e., if, after return to plan participation, a previous forfeiture is to stand), the plan must (subject to the exception noted below) contain a repayment provision pursuant to which the participant may repay the full amount of the distribution and by so doing restore the full amount of the accrued benefit. The plan may limit the time in which the repayment privilege can be exercised, and

---

[36] I.R.C. §§ 411(b)(3)(D), 411(b)(3)(E).

[37] I.R.C. § 411(b)(1)(E); Treas. Reg. § 1.411(b)-1(d).

[38] See Treas. Reg. § 1.410(a)-4(b), Ex. (3).

may provide that the employee must repay the full amount of his distribution before the close of the vesting computation period within which the participant has a one-year break in service. The plan may also require that such repayment be made within two years of the employee's resumption of employment covered by the plan.[39] The restoration contribution complication may be avoided by providing that no forfeiture will occur until the participant has experienced a one-year break in service.[40]

As with the participation and vesting rules, a break in service is not deemed to have occurred merely because an employee ceases to be in the classification of employees eligible to accrue benefits if the employee remains in the employ of the plan sponsor or is transferred to a controlled-group corporation, common control enterprise, or affiliated service group enterprise. However, unlike the participation and vesting rules, benefit accrual rules do not require service credit to be granted for service in the ineligible class or for service with controlled group, common control or affiliated service group enterprises.[41]

If a restoration contribution is made by the participant, the employer-derived accrued benefit that must be restored shall not be less than the amount in the account balance of the employee, both the amount distributed and the amount forfeited, unadjusted by any gains or losses subsequent to the distribution.[42] The regulations are silent as to what is to be done with gains attributable to the restored potential forfeiture and as to where the plan is supposed to get the funds to compensate for any losses attributable to the restored potential forfeiture.

Defined Benefit Plans

If a participant in a defined benefit plan leaves the employ of the plan sponsor and returns to covered employment before experiencing a one-year break in service, the separation from service is disregarded for benefit accrual purposes (except, of course, that no hours of service need to be credited for the period of absence in determining whether (or what portion of) a year of participation is to be credited). If a one-year break in service has been experienced by the reinstated participant, years of participation credited prior to the break in service cannot be disregarded except to the extent that the service represented by those years of participation can be ignored for purposes of determining eligibility to participate in the plan under Section 410(a)(5) of the Code (and Section 202(b) of ERISA).[43]

If a defined benefit plan participant receives, upon termination of plan participation, a distribution that is less than the present value of his full

---

39 I.R.C. § 411(a)(7)(C); Treas. Reg. § 1.411(a)-7(d)(2)(iv).
40 Treas. Reg. § 1.411(a)-7(d)(2)(iv).
41 29 C.F.R. § 2530.210(a)(2) (1976).
42 Treas. Reg. § 1.411(a)-7(d)(4)(iv).
43 I.R.C. § 411(b)(3)(A).

accrued benefit attributable to employer contributions, and if such participant subsequently resumes employment covered under the plan, the plan must provide an opportunity to repay the full amount of the distribution, with interest, within the time frame specified in the plan. Upon repayment of the distribution received, representing the value of the vested benefit at the time of earlier termination of plan participation, with interest, the participant's entire accrued benefit (including the portion thought to be forfeited) must be restored. A defined benefit plan may require that such repayment be made within two years of the employee's resumption of employment covered by the plan.[44]

"Cash-Outs"

A "cash-out" occurs when an employee receives a distribution of the present value of his entire nonforfeitable benefit due to termination of his participation in the plan. Such a distribution is due to termination of plan participation only if it is made no later than the close of the second plan year following the plan year in which such termination occurs.[45] For the purposes of determining an employee's accrued benefit under a plan, the plan may disregard service performed by the employee with respect to which he has received a "cash-out" only if the cash-out consisted of the present value of his entire accrued benefit, and was either (1) $1,750 or less, or (2) distributed in accordance with the participant's election.[46]

AMENDMENTS TO THE PLAN'S BENEFIT ACCRUAL PROVISIONS

Except with respect to amendments allowed within a limited period after the close of a plan year that may be retroactive to the beginning of that closed plan year, a participant's accrued benefit may not be decreased by plan amendment.[47] As with the vesting amendment rules, the IRS has recognized that benefit accrual provisions could be indirectly amended by changes in other provisions (such as those dealing with the crediting of years of service, hours of service, breaks in service, and actuarial factors). It has thus ruled that no such amendment will be acceptable if that amendment has the indirect effect of reducing accrued benefits.[48] Subject to limited exceptions, plan amendments may not be adopted that either directly or indirectly have the result of reducing previously accrued benefits.[49]

---

[44] I.R.C. § 411(a)(7)(C); Treas. Reg. § 1.411(a)-7(d)(2)(D).
[45] Treas. Reg. § 1.411(a)-7(d)(4).
[46] I.R.C. § 411(a)(7)(B); Treas. Reg. § 1.411(a)-7(d)(4)(B).
[47] I.R.C. § 411(d)(6).
[48] Rev. Rul. 76-378, 1976-2 C.B. 112, § 2.02.
[49] Pub. L. No. 93-406, §§ 204(g), 302(c)(8).

MERGERS, CONSOLIDATIONS, TRANSFERS OF ASSETS AND LIABILITIES

Every plan must provide that in the case of any merger or consolidation with, or transfer of assets or liabilities to, any other plan after September 2, 1974, each participant in the plan would (if the plan were then terminated) receive a benefit immediately after the merger, consolidation, or transfer that is equal to or greater than the benefit he would have been entitled to receive immediately before the merger, consolidation, or transfer, had the plan then been terminated.[50] (A detailed discussion of this subject is found elsewhere in this chapter under "Merger and Spinoff Requirements.")

CHANGES IN SOCIAL SECURITY BENEFITS

It is not permissible, under a qualified plan, to have changes in benefit levels payable under Title II of the Social Security Act reduce any benefit payable to a participant or beneficiary receiving benefits under a plan or any benefit which is nonforfeitable as to a participant who has separated from the service of the employer.[51] Apparently, changes in Social Security benefits occurring while the participant is still in service but after the participant has ceased accruing benefits under the plan may be reflected by the diminution of prospective plan benefits, as long as the participant has not already commenced receipt of benefits while in service.[52]

Record-keeping

Employers are required to keep records of the years of service of each employee and such other records as are necessary to make possible the determination of a participant's rights to benefits. Failure to maintain such records without reasonable cause may subject the employer to a civil penalty of $10 for each employee with respect to whom the records are deficient. In the case of a multiemployer plan, the records are to be maintained by the plan administrator.[53]

---

[50] I.R.C. § 401(a)(12); Treas. Reg. § 1.401(a)-12.
[51] I.R.C. § 401(a)(15); Treas. Reg. § 1.401(a)-15.
[52] Treas. Reg. § 1.401(a)-15(b).
[53] Pub. L. No. 93-406, § 209(b).

Joint and Survivor Annuities

THOMAS S. MONFRIED
Willkie Farr & Gallagher

INTRODUCTION

Section 401(a)(11) of the Internal Revenue Code, added by ERISA, provides protection for the spouses of participants in qualified defined benefit and defined contribution plans. This protection is afforded in the form of both a post-retirement and a preretirement benefit.

In general, the post-retirement spouse's benefit is payable in the event of the participant's death after retirement as well as in active service after attainment of normal retirement age. This benefit is payable automatically unless the participant elects otherwise. The preretirement spouse's benefit is payable in the event of the participant's death while in active service during the period the participant could have retired with an immediate pension. This benefit is payable only if the participant so elects it.[1]

POST-RETIREMENT SPOUSE'S BENEFIT

A qualified plan that provides for the payment of benefits in the form of a life annuity must provide for the payment of benefits in a form having the effect of a *qualified joint and survivor annuity* unless an election not to take such form of benefit is made. A qualified joint and survivor annuity is defined as an annuity payable for the life of the participant with a survivor annuity for the life of the participant's spouse that is at least 50 percent and not more than 100 percent of the annuity payable during the joint lives of the participant and his spouse and which is at least the actuarial equivalent of a single life annuity for the life of the participant. The survivor annuity may not be terminable upon the spouse's remarriage.

Assume a participant's accrued benefit under a defined benefit pension plan upon retirement at age 65 is $600 per month payable in the form of a life annuity. His spouse is also age 65. If the plan's qualified joint and survivor annuity provides a 50 percent survivor annuity, using typical actuarial factors, the participant would receive a benefit of $510 per month

---

[1] The sources of this discussion of joint and survivor annuities are I.R.C. § 401(a)(11) and Treas. Reg. § 1.401(a)-11.

for life and after his death the surviving spouse would receive one-half of such amount or $255 per month for life. If the plan's qualified joint and survivor annuity provides a 100 percent survivor annuity, the participant would receive a benefit of $450 per month for life and after his death the surviving spouse would receive the same $450 per month for life.

If a defined contribution plan provides that benefits may be paid only in the form of a lump sum or in installments for a period certain and does not offer a life annuity as an optional form of benefit, the plan is not required to provide a qualified joint and survivor annuity. Also, if the present value of a participant's benefit is not in excess of $1,750, a plan need not provide for payment in the form of a qualified joint and survivor annuity.

Required Benefits

A benefit in the form of a qualified joint and survivor annuity must be payable to a participant in the following situations:

1. If the participant begins to receive benefits after attainment of normal retirement age;
2. If the participant dies in active service after attainment of normal retirement age;
3. If the participant begins to receive benefits after attainment of the "qualified early retirement age" (which is defined as the earliest date the participant could elect to retire and receive an immediate benefit, but not earlier than ten years prior to attainment of normal retirement age); and
4. If the participant who had retired after normal or qualified early retirement age dies before beginning to receive benefits.

If Item (2) above applies, the survivor annuity payable to the spouse is calculated as if the participant had retired immediately prior to death; and if Item (4) above applies, the survivor annuity is calculated as if the participant's benefit had commenced immediately prior to death.

Election Provisions

The participant must be afforded the right to make a written election not to take the qualified joint and survivor annuity during a specified election period. This election period must include a period of at least ninety days following the furnishing of the applicable information described below. It must end prior to the commencement of benefits, but cannot end more than ninety days before the benefit begins. Benefit commencement may be delayed until the end of the election period because the amount of the participant's benefit payments cannot be determined until the end of the election period.

If a participant makes a request for additional information before the end of the election period, the election period is extended for ninety days following the furnishing of the requested additional information. However, if a plan so provides, the request for additional information must be made within sixty days after the beginning of the election period, in which case the election period is extended for sixty days following the furnishing of the additional information.

An election not to receive the qualified joint and survivor annuity may be revoked during the election period and, if the participant so wishes, another such election may be made before the end of the election period.

Disclosure Requirements

The information required to be furnished to the participant relating to the qualified joint and survivor annuity must be written in nontechnical language and must describe the qualified joint and survivor annuity, the circumstances in which it will be provided unless the participant has elected otherwise, the availability of such election, and a general explanation of the relative financial effect on the participant's benefit of making the election.

Following the furnishing of this general information, if the participant so requests within ninety days thereafter (unless the plan provides a sixty-day period), the plan administrator must within thirty days following the request furnish the participant with a written nontechnical explanation of the terms and conditions of the qualified joint and survivor annuity and the financial effect (in terms of dollars per annuity payment) upon the participant's particular annuity of making the election not to receive the qualified joint and survivor annuity.

The plan may provide that a participant's election not to receive the qualified joint and survivor annuity will be effective only if the spouse consents thereto. The plan may also provide that the qualified joint and survivor annuity is payable only if the participant and his spouse have been married for one year prior to the date the benefit commences.

PRERETIREMENT SPOUSE'S BENEFIT

Required Benefits

If a plan provides for the payment of benefits before normal retirement age in the form of a life annuity, it must permit each participant to elect to have a benefit in the form of a life annuity payable to the participant's spouse in the event the participant dies in active service with the employer after attainment of the qualified early retirement age (as described above) and prior to attainment of normal retirement age. No election of an early survivor annuity is required in the following situations:

1. If the plan provides that a life annuity to the spouse is the only death benefit payable upon a married participant's death in active service after the qualified early retirement age; or
2. Under a defined contribution plan, if the plan provides that the death benefit payable to the participant's designated beneficiary is at least equal to the participant's vested account balance.

In a typical defined benefit pension plan with a normal retirement age of 65 and where early retirement is permitted at age 55, the spouse's benefit must be made available at age 55. Even if under certain circumstances a participant could retire and receive an immediate benefit under the plan prior to age 55, the spouse's benefit need not be made available prior to age 55 (that is, ten years prior to normal retirement age).

Election Provisions

If a preretirement spouse's benefit is required to be made available under the plan, each participant must be afforded the right to make a written election to take the spouse's benefit during a specified election period. The election period must include a period of at least ninety days following the furnishing of the applicable information described below. It must begin at least ninety days before the plan's qualified early retirement age and end on termination of the participant's employment or normal retirement age, if earlier. A plan may, however, provide that an election of the spouse's benefit does not become effective if the participant dies within a period of two years (or a lesser period) following the date of the election. In such case, the election period must begin two years (or the lesser specified period) plus ninety days prior to the qualified early retirement age. It should be noted that even if a plan provides such a two-year waiting period, if the participant dies from accidental causes within two years of the election but after the qualified early retirement age, the spouse's benefit must be paid.

Disclosure Requirements

As in the case of the post-retirement spouse's benefit described above, the information required to be given to the participant relating to the preretirement spouse's benefit must be written in nontechnical terms and must describe the spouse's benefit, the circumstances in which it will be provided if elected, the availability of such election, and a general explanation of the relative financial effect on the participant's benefit if the election is made. If the participant so requests, the plan administrator must, within thirty days, furnish additional information relating to the participant's particular benefits.

Amount of Benefit

If the participant elects spouse's benefit coverage and then dies in active service after the qualified early retirement age and prior to normal retirement age, the amount of the spouse's benefit cannot be less than the survivor annuity the spouse would have received under the plan's qualified joint and survivor annuity if the participant had retired immediately prior to his death and his benefit was paid in the form of a qualified joint and survivor annuity. For example, assume the plan's qualified joint and survivor annuity provides a 50 percent survivor annuity; the participant elected spouse's benefit coverage and died in active service at age 60; and if the participant had retired immediately prior to his death and his benefit was payable in the form of a qualified joint and survivor annuity, his benefit would have been $500 per month for life and his spouse's survivor annuity would have been $250 per month for life. In this case, the amount of the spouse's benefit under the plan cannot be less than a life annuity of $250 per month.

Again, election of the preretirement spouse's benefit may be revoked and another election of the spouse's benefit may be made during the election period.

Permissible Restrictions

The plan may provide that the spouse's benefit is payable only if the participant and his spouse have been married for one year prior to the date of the participant's death. In addition, the plan may take into account the increased cost of providing the spouse's benefit and reduce the participant's benefit in an equitable manner consistent with acceptable actuarial principles consistently applied. In other words, a plan may provide that the participant's benefit will be reduced, for example, by 0.6 percent per month for each month the spouse's benefit protection is in effect. Thus, if a participant elects the coverage at age 55 and dies at age 60, the participant's benefit determined at age 60 on which the spouse's benefit will be based will be reduced by 3.6 percent (60 months × 0.6 percent); and if the participant lives and retires at age 65, the benefit determined at age 65 which he will receive will be reduced by 7.2 percent (120 months × 0.6 percent). However, if a plan provides an automatic spouse's benefit to all eligible participants upon a participant's death after qualified early retirement age, no actuarial reduction may be imposed on either the participant's or the spouse's benefit.

Limitations on Benefits and Contributions

THOMAS S. MONFRIED
Willkie Farr & Gallagher

INTRODUCTION

Prior to enactment of ERISA, there were no statutory limitations on the amount of benefits or contributions that could be provided for participants covered under qualified defined benefit and defined contribution plans. However, the Internal Revenue Service did rule that a defined benefit plan that provided a retirement benefit in excess of a participant's earnings while in active service did not qualify under Section 401(a) of the Internal Revenue Code of 1954.[1]

Section 415 was added to the Internal Revenue Code by ERISA and sets forth limitations on benefits and contributions that apply to participants covered under qualified plans. The effect of the new section is to disqualify the trust under such plans if the benefits or contributions under the plans exceed specified limits.

LIMITATIONS FOR DEFINED BENEFIT PLANS [2]

Basic Rule

Under Section 415(b), the annual benefit that may be paid to any participant by a defined benefit plan may not at any time during the applicable limitation year exceed the lesser of

- $75,000 (as adjusted for cost-of-living increases); or
- 100 percent of the participant's average total compensation for his high three consecutive years of service.

Annual benefit is defined as a benefit payable annually in the form of a straight life annuity, exclusive of benefits attributable to employee contributions and rollover contributions and benefits attributable to assets transferred to the plan from another plan.

Adjustments

Form of Benefit. If a defined benefit plan provides a benefit in a form other than a straight life annuity, the plan benefit must be adjusted to a

---

[1] Rev. Rul. 72-3, 1972-1 C.B. 105.

[2] The sources for this discussion are I.R.C. §§ 415(b) and 415(d) and Treas. Reg. §§ 1.415-3, 1.415-4 and 1.415-5.

straight life annuity of equivalent actuarial value. However, if the plan benefit is paid in the form of a qualified joint and survivor annuity, no such adjustment is required. Further, no adjustment is required for ancillary benefits that are not directly related to retirement benefits, such as pre-retirement death or disability benefits.

Assuming the 1981 maximum dollar limitation of $124,500 is applicable to a highly paid participant, the plan can pay the participant and his spouse a joint and 100 percent survivor annuity with payments to both the participant and the spouse equal to $124,500. However, the plan cannot, for example, provide a benefit payable in the form of a life annuity with ten years certain of $120,000 because the straight life annuity actuarial equivalent of such benefit exceeds $124,500.

Employee Contributions. If a defined benefit plan provides for mandatory contributions or permits voluntary contributions, the plan benefit based on such contributions is actuarially adjusted to eliminate the benefits attributable to such contributions. If a plan provides for either mandatory or voluntary contributions, these contributions are considered a separate defined contribution plan for the purpose of the Section 415 limitations (see below).

Benefit Commencement Prior to Age 55. No adjustment in the plan benefit is required if the benefit begins at or after age 55. Thus, a participant to whom the maximum dollar limitation is applicable could retire in 1981 at age 55 and receive an immediate straight life annuity of $124,500.

If a plan permits retirement prior to age 55 with an immediate benefit, the plan benefit payable prior to age 55 must be actuarially increased to a benefit commencing at age 55 for the purpose of determining compliance with the maximum dollar limitation but not for the purpose of determining compliance with the high-three compensation limitation. For a participant to whom the high-three compensation limitation is applicable and whose average compensation is $50,000, the participant could receive an annual benefit of $50,000 in the form of a straight life annuity commencing at age 50. If the maximum dollar limitation were applicable, the maximum annual benefit payable to a participant who retired early at age 50 in 1981 is $124,500 payable as a straight life annuity commencing at age 55, but actuarially reduced because of commencement at age 50.

Less Than Ten Years of Service. If a participant has less than ten years of service at the time the benefit begins, both the maximum dollar limitation and the high-three compensation limitation are reduced pro rata either on the basis of the ratio of years of service or months of service to ten or 120, respectively. Thus, if an individual has completed only seven years of service at retirement at age 65, the plan benefit may not exceed 70 percent of the applicable limitation.

$10,000 De Minimis Rule

Section 415(b) also contains a de minimis rule. Notwithstanding any of the above limitations, a participant may receive an annual benefit derived from employer contributions of $10,000 without regard to the age at which the benefit commences or the form of payment of the benefit provided the employer has not at any time maintained a defined contribution plan in which the individual participated. The only adjustment that must be made in the $10,000 limitation is for a participant who has completed less than ten years of service. If the defined benefit plan provides for mandatory or voluntary contributions, these contributions will not be deemed to be a separate defined contribution plan for the purpose of eliminating the applicability of the $10,000 limitation.

Transitional Rule

Section 2004(d)(2) of ERISA sets forth a transitional rule for active defined benefit plan participants immediately prior to October 3, 1973. For such a participant the annual benefit provided by the plan will be deemed not to exceed the Section 415(b) limitations if the following conditions are satisfied:

1. The annual benefit does not exceed 100 percent of the annual rate of compensation on October 2, 1973;
2. The annual benefit does not exceed the benefit payable on the basis of all terms and conditions of the plan as in effect on October 2, 1973 without change; and
3. The participant's compensation used to determine plan benefits for periods after October 2, 1973 does not exceed the annual rate of compensation on that date.

For a participant whose 1973 compensation was $300,000, upon retirement at age 65 in 1981, if the plan as in effect on October 2, 1973 provided the individual with an annual benefit of $180,000 payable in the form of a straight life annuity on the basis of such 1973 compensation, the full $180,000 may be paid under the transitional rule. However, any additional benefits under the plan due to compensation increases after 1973 and plan amendments after October 2, 1973 may not be paid to the participant under the plan.

Cost-of-Living Increases

The maximum dollar limitation under Section 415(b) is adjusted annually to take account of increases in the cost of living. The adjusted maximum dollar limitation is effective as of January 1 of each year for limitation years ending with or within the calendar year.

A provision may be included in a defined benefit plan that provides for automatic annual adjustments of the maximum dollar limitation in accordance with the cost-of-living adjustments. The plan may provide only that the annual increases in the maximum dollar limitation will become effective on the January 1 on which the adjustment becomes effective. The effect of this requirement is that projected annual increases in the maximum dollar limitation may not be funded for in advance.

LIMITATIONS FOR DEFINED CONTRIBUTION PLANS [3]

Basic Rule

Under Section 415(c), the annual additions made to a participant's account under a defined contribution plan for any limitation year may not exceed the lesser of

- $25,000 (as adjusted for cost-of-living increases); or
- 25 percent of the individual's total compensation for the limitation year.

The maximum dollar amount ($41,500 for 1981) is adjusted annually to take account of cost-of-living increases. The adjusted maximum dollar amount is effective as of January 1 of each year for limitation years ending with or within the calendar year. A defined contribution plan may provide for automatic annual adjustments of the maximum dollar amount in accordance with cost-of-living adjustments.

Annual Additions

Annual additions credited to a participant's account for a limitation year are defined as the sum of the following:

1. Employer contributions;
2. The lesser of (x) the amount of the participant's contributions in excess of 6 percent of compensation for the limitation year, or (y) one-half of the participant's contributions for the year; and
3. Forfeitures.

An annual addition is credited to a participant's account for a particular limitation year if under the plan it is allocated to the account as of any date within the limitation year. Employer contributions are not considered as annual additions for a particular limitation year unless the contributions are actually made within thirty days after the date the employer's federal in-

---

[3] The sources for this discussion are I.R.C. §§ 415(c) and 415(d) and Treas. Reg. § 1.415-6.

come tax return is due (including extensions) for the taxable year with or within which the limitation year ends. Mandatory or voluntary employee contributions are not considered as annual additions for a particular limitation year unless the contributions are actually made within thirty days after the end of the limitation year.

Treatment of Excess Annual Additions

If the annual additions under a plan for a particular participant would exceed the applicable Section 415(c) limitations because of a reasonable error in estimating the participant's compensation, allocation of forfeitures or under other limited facts and circumstances, the excess amount is not considered as an annual addition for the limitation year if it is treated in one of the following methods:

1. The excess must be allocated and reallocated to other participants.
2. The excess amount must be used to reduce the employer contributions for the next limitation year for that participant.
3. The excess amount must be held unallocated in a suspense account for the limitation year and then allocated and reallocated to all participants in the plan for the next limitation year.
4. Employee contributions may, if the plan so provides, be returned to the extent required to eliminate the excess amount.

LIMITATIONS FOR COMBINATIONS OF PLANS [4]

Basic Rule

Under Section 415(e), if an individual has at any time participated in a defined benefit plan and has also participated in a defined contribution plan maintained by the same employer, the sum of the defined benefit plan fraction and the defined contribution plan fraction for the individual for any limitation year cannot exceed 1.4.

Defined Benefit Plan Fraction

A participant's "defined benefit plan fraction" for a limitation year is a fraction—the numerator of which is the participant's projected annual benefit under the defined benefit plan determined as of the last day of the limitation year in question, and the denominator of which the maximum projected annual benefit allowable under Section 415(b) as of the last day of such year. A participant's projected annual benefit is the annual benefit (as described above) to which the participant is entitled under the plan provisions determined using the following assumptions:

---

[4] The sources for this discussion are I.R.C. § 415(e) and Treas. Reg. § 1.415-7.

- The participant will continue in employment until normal retirement age or current age, if later;
- The participant's compensation for the limitation year will remain the same until such age; and
- All other factors used in determining plan benefits will remain the same for future limitation years.

Defined Contribution Plan Fraction

A participant's "defined contribution plan fraction" for a limitation year is a fraction—the numerator of which is the sum of the annual additions (as described above) credited to the participant's account for the limitation year in question and for all prior limitation years, and the denominator of which is the maximum amount of annual additions which could have been credited to the participant's account for the limitation year in question and for all prior limitation years of the participant's service with the employer, without regard to whether the defined contribution plan was in existence during such years.

Special Rules

If the transitional rule described above, which allows a participant's annual benefit under a defined benefit plan to exceed the defined benefit plan maximum dollar limitation, is applicable, the participant's defined benefit plan fraction is deemed to be 1.0 for the limitation year in question.

In determining a participant's defined contribution plan fraction, in each pre-ERISA limitation year (that is, any limitation year that began prior to January 1, 1976), the maximum amount of annual additions used to determine the denominator of the fraction for each such year is the lesser of $25,000 or 25 percent of the participant's compensation for the year.

In determining the defined contribution plan fraction for any post-ERISA limitation year (that is, any limitation year beginning after December 31, 1975), the aggregate amount of annual additions constituting the numerator of the defined contribution plan fraction as of the end of the last pre-ERISA limitation year is deemed not to exceed the aggregate amount of annual additions constituting the denominator of such fraction as of such date.

For a defined contribution plan that provided for mandatory or voluntary contributions, in determining the numerator of the participant's defined contribution plan fraction for the pre-ERISA limitation years, the annual additions attributable to such employee contributions is the excess of the aggregate amount of the participant's contributions over 10 percent of the participant's aggregate compensation while a participant. Thus, if the participant's aggregate mandatory or voluntary contributions for the pre-ERISA limitation years did not exceed 10 percent of aggregate compensation for such years, no annual additions result for purposes of the defined contribution plan fraction numerator.

Rules for Controlled Groups

CHRISTOPHER O'FLINN
Manager, Domestic Benefits, Mobil Oil Corporation

BACKGROUND OF THE CONTROLLED-GROUP TEST

Under federal law prior to the Employee Retirement Income Security Act of 1974 (ERISA) the determination of whether a corporation's qualified plan illegally discriminated (in favor of highly paid employees, officers, or shareholders) was made with reference to the employees of *that corporation,* (and, generally, with no reference to the employee population of related businesses). It was possible, then, to legally provide higher paid employees in a business with greater qualified plan benefits than the lower paid group by placing the two groups in separate corporations and establishing a "richer" plan for the corporation with the higher paid employees. There were many variations of this practice, some of which used an unincorporated business in lieu of a corporation. Congress considered these practices an abuse and included the controlled-group rules in ERISA to stop it. The legislative history of that law simply states the reason for the new rules:

> The committee, by this provision, intends to make it clear that the coverage and anti-discrimination provisions cannot be avoided by operating through separate corporations instead of separate branches of one corporation.

The legislative history also describes what the new rules were *not* intended to do. If one corporation in a controlled group contains a fair cross-section of high- and low-paid employees (compared to the employees of the controlled group as a whole), its qualified plans are to be judged without regard to other companies in the controlled group, even if those other companies have a less favorable retirement plan or no plan at all. Accordingly, a key question in evaluating problems of a controlled group in the qualified plan area is: Does the plan in question cover, or benefit, in a nondiscriminatory fashion, a group that represents a fair cross-section of the entire controlled group? If the answer is yes (and if the legislative history is given deference by the Internal Revenue Service and the courts) the controlled-group test should not present a substantial problem. Gathering the information to prove that a fair cross-section exists, however, may not be an easy task.

THE CONTROLLED-GROUP RULES

The controlled-group rules require that the employees of *all* organizations in the group be taken into account in determining whether the qualified plan of any *one* company within the group illegally discriminates. The matter of illegal discrimination essentially breaks down to the following four questions:

1. Does the classification of employees covered by the plan discriminate in favor of officers, shareholders, or highly compensated employees?
2. Are the 70/80 percent coverage requirements met?
3. Do contributions or benefits under the plan discriminate in favor of officers, shareholders, or highly compensated employees?
4. How does service with members of the controlled group other than the plan sponsor affect the determination of years of service, for purposes of an employee's eligibility and vesting under the sponsor's plan? The answer to this question may be needed to answer questions (1), (2), and (3) above.

The controlled-group rules also affect the limitations on benefits and contributions and liability under Title IV, ERISA (PBGC insurance). These subjects are discussed elsewhere in this book.

Statutory Composition of a Controlled Group

The controlled-group rules are separate statutory provisions referring to the three types of groups listed in Figure 14.1. All three statutory provisions may apply to a particular group.

Controlled Corporate Groups	*Commonly Controlled Trades or Businesses*	*Affiliated Service Groups*
(a) Parent-subsidiary (b) Brother/sister (c) Combined group	Similar to controlled corporate group but applies to more than corporations—includes all trades or businesses	(a) Principal or "first" organization (b) Service organization

Fig. 14.1 Statutory Provisions

Commonly Controlled Trades or Businesses and Controlled Corporate Groups

These two sections of the controlled-group rules may be discussed together for our purposes. The *commonly controlled rule* applies to all trades or businesses, whether or not incorporated, whereas the *controlled corporate rule* applies only to corporations and is really a subdivision of the first rule.

Under these two rules, if any of the following principles apply, the company will be required to take into consideration the employee population of other members of the control group in which it finds itself in order to determine if its plan illegally discriminates.

Parent-Subsidiary. The answers to the following two questions should determine whether the company is part of a controlled parent-subsidiary group:

- Does the company own a controlling interest in any other company?
- Is a controlling interest in the company owned by any other company?

If the answer to either of these two questions is yes, the company is part of a parent-subsidiary controlled group. The members of that group are companies controlled jointly or singly by other members of the group; however, the group must have a common parent organization that alone owns a controlling interest in at least one of the other members of the group.

The term *controlling interest* essentially means at least an 80 percent ownership interest. Generally, an *80 percent controlling interest* can be defined, for various entities, as follows:

- *Corporation.* Ownership of stock possessing at least 80 percent of the combined voting power of all classes of outstanding stock or at least 80 percent of the total value of all shares of all classes of outstanding stock.
- *Partnership.* Ownership of at least 80 percent of the profit interest or the capital interest.
- *Trust or estate.* Ownership of an actuarial interest of at least 80 percent of the value of such trust or estate.
- *Sole proprietorship.* Ownership of the proprietorship.

A diagrammatic example of parent-subsidiary controlled group is provided in figure 14.2. Under this example, *A*, *X* Corporation and the *ABC* partnership are all members of a parent-subsidiary control group.[1] Similarly, *A* and *DEF* are also members of a parent-subsidiary group. Although there are two "chains" of ownership, the parent-subsidiary rule treats all chains with a common parent as a single entity.[2] Thus, *A*, *X* Corporation and both the *ABC* and *DEF* partnerships are members of the same parent-subsidiary control group.

Brother-Sister Controlled Group. These controlled-group rules apply here when a group of organizations is owned by five or fewer owners who are

---

[1] See I.R.C. § 414.
[2] Treas. Reg. § 11.414(c)-2 Ex. 1.

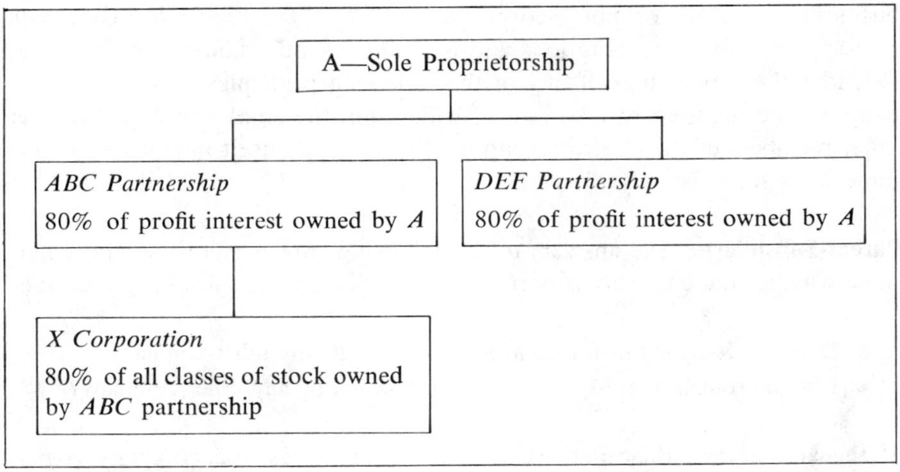

Fig. 14.2 Parent-Subsidiary Controlled Group

either individuals, estates, or trusts. (Note: a corporation is considered a person but not an individual). If five or fewer individuals, estates, or trusts own an 80 percent controlling interest (see the 80 percent test above) in an organization and they also own at least a 50 percent controlling interest taking into account the ownership of each individual or estate or trust only to the extent such ownership is identical with respect to each such organization, then all the organizations so controlled by the group are members of a brother-sister group. For example, in the illustration of the parent-subsidiary controlled-group test above, both the *ABC* partnership and the *DEF* partnership are members of a brother-sister controlled group since each is owned by *A,* a sole proprietor by an identical interest of 80 percent (of course, *ABC* and *DEF* are already part of the more inclusive parent-subsidiary chain discussed in that example). If *A*'s interest in *DEF* partnership were 90 percent, the level of his identical interest in both *DEF* and *ABC* would still be 80 percent, the level of control "identical" in both partnerships.

Figure 14.3 illustrates the broad scope of the brother-sister rule. In this example, the following brother-sister groups of trades or businesses under common control exist: *A*, *GHI*, *W*, *X* and *Y*; *A*, *GHI*, *W*, *X* and *Z*; *A*, *GHI*, *W*, *Y* and *Z*; *A*, *W*, *X*, *Y*, and *Z*; and *A*, *GHI*, *X*, *Y*, and *Z*. The brother-sister rule is characterized by organizations owned in common by five or fewer individuals. In the view of Treas. Reg. § 11.414(c)-2, this means that an organization can find itself a member of many brother-sister groups depending upon how many groups of five owners the IRS can identify. Also, if an organization has dozens of owners who, as a group, own an 80 percent controlling interest in it and these individuals also control other organizations, the problem of defining brother-sister controlled groups involves first identifying how many separate groups of five can be named and

Individuals		*Organizations*					*Identical Ownership*
	A	GHI	W	X	Y	Z	
A	100%	60%	60%	60%	60%	60%	60%
B	—	40%	—	—	—	—	—
C	—	—	40%	—	—	—	—
D	—	—	—	40%	—	—	—
E	—	—	—	—	40%	—	—
F	—	—	—	—	—	40%	—
Total	100%	100%	100%	100%	100%	100%	60%

Fig. 14.3 The Brother-Sister Rule

then determining what other organizations are controlled by each group of five (or fewer) owners identified. Thus, the first brother-sister group identified in the above example (*A, GHI, W, X,* and *Y*), consists of the organizations controlled by the first group of five individual owners identified: *A, B, C, D,* and *E.*

The second group identified (*A, GHI, W, X,* and *Z*) consists of those organizations owned by individuals *A, B, C, D,* and *F,* etc. The formidable tasks involved in identifying brother-sister controlled groups are compounded by a key Treasury interpretation of the rule, also illustrated by the above example; namely, that the five or fewer persons who must own the required 80 percent and 50 percent under the brother-sister rule may do so singly or in combination. In other words, under the above example, the first five organizations listed across are deemed to be owned by the first five individuals listed vertically even though some of the individual owners identified have *no interest whatsoever* in some of the organizations controlled by the group as a whole. As of this writing, the U.S. Supreme Court is scheduled to resolve the controversy surrounding this interpretation which has received a divided reception among the circuit court of appeals as well as the Court of Claims and the Tax Court. At present, the Court of Claims, the Fifth Circuit, and the Tax Court are in disagreement with the Treasury's interpretation and the Second, Fourth, and Eighth Circuits support the interpretation.

The Combined Group. A combined controlled group exists if each organization in the group is a member of either a parent-subsidiary group or a brother-sister group and at least one such organization is both a common parent and also a member of a brother-sister group. Essentially, the combined group rule serves to unite a parent-subsidiary chain or chains of businesses with an otherwise unrelated brother-sister group or groups of business. The only example provided by this rule is the one discussed above under the parent-subsidiary headnote.

Affiliated Service Group

Under ERISA and the controlled-group rules discussed above relating to corporations and other forms of businesses, it was possible for a professional corporation, for example, to become a 50 percent partner in a medical partnership with several low-paid employees and, under the (parent-subsidiary) controlled-group rules discussed above, which require more than a 50 percent controlling interest, not be obligated to extend the pension plan of the professional corporation to the employees of the medical partnership. The Miscellaneous Revenue Act of 1980, which established Section 414(m) of the Code, changes this result. In essence, the law now provides that a business organization must take into account the employees of an "affiliated service organization" in measuring compliance with the discrimination rules applicable to qualified plans. It authorizes the Secretary of the Treasury to prescribe regulations, as necessary, to prevent service organizations from avoiding the anti-discrimination requirements with respect to qualified plans. Since those regulations have not yet been issued, this section will only discuss what the statute indicates is an affiliated service group. It remains to be seen what obligations will be placed upon that service group with respect to qualified plan coverage requirements.

An *affiliated service group* (ASG) consists of (1) an organization, the principal business of which is the performance of services ("service organization") and (2) any other service organization that is a partner in or shareholder of the first organization and which is regularly associated with it in the performance of services. An organization whose principal business is not the performance of services (*third organizations*) can also be included in an ASG if a significant portion of its business is the performance of services for organizations within the ASG and 10 percent or more of the interest in the third organization is held by persons who are officers, highly compensated employees, or owners of the service organizations within the ASG. The IRS has announced that it will issue rulings and determination letters concerning affiliated service groups.[3]

SPECIAL REQUIREMENTS OF CONTROLLED-GROUP MEMBERS

Information Gathering

The first obligation is to determine the employee population in the controlled group in which the subject company participates. For a smaller organization, particularly one affected by the brother-sister rules discussed above, this can be a formidable task involving inquiry into the employee population of businesses unrelated to it, except for the relationship imposed

[3] Rev. Proc. 81-12, 1981-14 I.R.B. 42. See also Rev. Rul. 81-105, 1981-12 I.R.B. 27.

upon by the controlled-group rule. A larger organization, whose stock is publicly traded, may have the advantage of centralized data naming the other business organizations in which it participates. Gathering information on employees of those known organizations can raise other difficulties. For example, in the case of a multinational corporation, information must be gathered on U.S. citizens working abroad since foreign corporations are not excluded from the controlled-group rules.

The information gathering begins with the annual report (Form 5500), in which Question 17 requires information regarding all companies in the controlled group even if not all such companies are participating in the plan being reported. Thus, the total employees entered on Line 17(a), the breakdown of excluded employees shown in 17(b) and the ineligible employees shown in 17(d) must take into account all employees in the controlled group. (Question 17 does not apply to multiemployer collectively bargained plans). In addition, the report requires an explanation of how the plan meets the coverage requirements of the Code, if the 70/80 percentage tests of the Code (discussed in the section on "Participation") are not met.

The "Application for Determination" (Form 5300) for a qualified plan requires even more information about employees of the controlled group. Essentially, it asks for all of the information requested in the annual report, just discussed, but also indicates that if the 70/80 percentage tests are not met, comprehensive information regarding employees in all compensation ranges for the entire controlled group must be provided.

This comprehensive data is required not only at the time the Application for Determination is submitted but annually thereafter. In practice, many large corporations, particularly those in multiple lines of businesses, are unable to compile information on the compensation ranges of employees throughout the controlled group in which they participate. This inability does not necessarily result in a disqualified plan, since some district offices reviewing Applications for Determination may recognize the enormous burden imposed by the controlled-group rules and Question 15 of Form 5300 and accept applications without detailed information regarding employees in various compensation ranges.

If an organization finds itself within a controlled group, it is worthwhile to attempt to contact the reviewing agents at the district office to determine what information will be deemed sufficient for the purpose of accepting the applications. Once accepted, the district office may or may not request all of the information called for in Question 15.

Participation Standards

In determining whether a qualified plan sponsored by a member of a controlled group meets the percentage or classification anti-discrimination tests now found in Section 410(b)(1) of the Code, the employees of all of the other organizations within the controlled group must be considered, except for those who may be disregarded under the statute by class (such as those not meeting the minimum age and service requirements of the plan who may be excluded from the percentage test and collective bargaining unit employees who may be excluded from both the percentage and classification test). Unless the business organization in question employs a significant percentage of the employees in the controlled group of companies, its qualified plan would obviously not meet the 70/80 percentage test.

Qualification would therefore depend on meeting the requirements of the classification test. This will essentially involve a determination that the plan covers a "fair cross-section" of all employees of the controlled group. The ability of a large organization to quickly demonstrate that its plan covers employees in all conceivable compensation ranges is probably the reason why district offices do not require, in many such cases, the comprehensive compensation and participation data referred to above.

Vesting Standards

It is important to note here that service with any organization in the controlled group of enterprises to which the plan sponsor belongs must be considered service with the plan sponsor, for purposes of calculating a plan participant's vested interest in his accrued benefit. Thus, an individual transferred to an organization within a controlled group from another organization within the same group, will have his service with his former employer taken into account for purposes of determining his vested right to *future* accruals of benefits under his *new* employer's pension plan. Similarly, his service with his new employer will be taken into account by his former employer in determining his vested rights to any qualified plan benefits accrued prior to his transfer.

DEVELOPING CONCEPTS IN THE CONTROLLED-GROUP AREA

Since the controlled-group rules established under ERISA were intended to correct an abuse (see earlier discussion on the reasons for these rules), there was some expectation on the part of many lawyers and tax practitioners that either the IRS or the courts would interpret the new statutory rules to require a finding of "manipulative purpose," in order for the new rules to result in the denial of a plan's qualified status; particularly for those plans that would have satisfied the requirements of the law, as it stood prior to ERISA. The regulations discussed above impose no such limitation on the new rules. Indeed, the Commissioner has taken quite the opposite position, and has been sustained by the Tax Court, in *Fujinon Optical, Inc. v.*

Comm'r.[4] In that case, the Commissioner had determined that Fujinon's plan did not satisfy the coverage requirements of the Code because it discriminated in favor of highly compensated employees. The Tax Court noted that an appealing argument existed that the plan did not discriminate because, judged by the employee population of the sponsor, the plan met the qualification rules and the sponsor operated completely independently of the other members of the controlled group.

Nevertheless, the court found insufficient reason to overturn the Commissioner's determination noting that the petitioner's plan, "can never be said either to cover a representative cross-section of all the employees of the controlled group or to benefit the employees in general." In the absence of the manipulative purpose requirement, the "fair cross-section test" becomes extremely important for those plan sponsors who find themselves to be members of a controlled group.

---

[4] 76 T.C. 44 (1981).

Integration of Qualified Retirement Plans With Social Security

RICHARD P. SEIDEN
Vice-President, Frank B. Hall Consulting Company

INTRODUCTION

Integration of qualified pension and profit-sharing plans with old-age, survivors, and disability insurance benefits payable under the Social Security system is a widespread practice, and yet is often misunderstood. In many cases the rules for integration are applied mechanically (mathematically might be a better term) without any real understanding of what they are intended to do. This lack of understanding of the conceptual purposes of integration impairs the ability of some to take advantage fully of the cost savings and benefit planning advantages available in an "integrated" plan.

Statutory Basis of Integration

Integration with Social Security is not a qualification requirement in and of itself. Rather, it is a part of the general qualification requirement that a plan cannot discriminate in contributions or benefits in favor of highly paid employees, officers, or shareholders. This general nondiscrimination requirement is found in Section 401(a)(4) of the Internal Revenue Code. Section 401(a)(5) of the Code amplifies this general rule by stating that a plan will not be considered discriminatory merely because it excludes employees whose wages do not exceed the Social Security wage base or because contributions or benefits on wages above the Social Security wage base are greater than contributions or benefits on wages below the wage base.

While this statutory provision is not a blank check, it is certainly a recognition of the fact that Social Security benefits represent, at least in part, an employer-provided retirement pension. It is also the basis for taking that pension into account in determining whether employer-provided retirement benefits under a plan are discriminatory or not. The regulations under Section 401(a) of the Code tell us that a plan will not be viewed as discriminatory in contributions or benefits (nor for that matter with respect to eligibility, where employees are entirely excluded from participation because their wages do not exceed the Social Security wage base) if the benefits under the plan, together with the employer-provided Social Security benefits, "establish an integrated and correlated retirement system satisfying the tests of section 401(a)."

INTEGRATION AS A CONCEPT

The key to satisfying the tests of Section 401(a) of the Code is the general rule, set forth in Section 401(a)(5) of the Code, that benefits or contributions for a qualified plan will not be deemed discriminatory if they bear a uniform relationship to compensation. In a sense this is an oversimplification of the rule, but it is an accurate statement of the concept. What this means is that you can have a plan that provides a retirement benefit of one percent of compensation multiplied by years of service, even though the result is that higher paid people will get larger dollar benefits.

Once we understand that larger benefits can be paid to higher paid participants as long as the benefits for all participants bear a uniform relationship to compensation, the theory of integration begins to take form. If the employer-provided portion of the Social Security benefit can be stated as a percentage of the compensation that it is based on, (basically, wages subject to Social Security tax) that percentage can be compared to the percentage of compensation above that level that is represented by the plan benefit. As long as the percentage for the Social Security benefit is at least as high as the percentage for the plan benefit on "excess" compensation, the plan benefit will be deemed nondiscriminatory. Similarly, no discrimination will result if an otherwise nondiscriminatory benefit formula is reduced, or "offset" by a portion of the employee's Social Security benefit not exceeding the amount deemed provided by the employer-paid tax. In either case, the plan benefits, together with the employer-provided portion of the employee's Social Security benefits represent an integrated and correlated benefit satisfying the nondiscrimination rules of Section 401(a) of the Code.

TYPES OF INTEGRATED PLANS

Defined benefit plans, therefore, generally integrate on either an *excess basis* or on an *offset basis*. Simply put, an excess plan provides benefits only on compensation above a certain level (the "integration level") or provides greater benefits on compensation above the integration level than below (these are called *step-rate excess* plans). An offset plan, on the other hand, does not exclude employees earning below a specified level nor does it provide greater benefits on compensation above that level. Rather, it provides a uniform rate of benefit accrual on all compensation and then reduces (or "offsets") that amount by a specified percentage of the participant's old-age benefit under Social Security.

IMPLEMENTING THE INTEGRATION RULES

The extent to which greater benefits can be provided on compensation above the integration level or the extent to which old-age benefits under the Social Security system can be used to reduce plan benefits is what the integration rules are all about. For the most part, they are contained in Revenue Ruling 71-446.

Excess Plans

For excess plans, the limitations in Revenue Ruling 71-446 are based on a 1971 computation of the value of the employer-provided portion of old-age, survivors, and disability benefits under Social Security expressed as a percentage of the covered compensation upon which those benefits are based. This computation took the average of the maximum old-age benefit under Social Security payable at age 65 for someone ready to retire in 1971 and for someone whose Social Security covered employment was just then beginning (someone who would reach age 65 in the year 2010). The average of these benefits, as a percentage of the average monthly wage on which such benefits were based, was 43 percent. Since the total of old-age, survivors, and disability insurance benefits under Social Security was deemed to be worth 162 percent of the old-age benefit alone, the value of the entire old-age, survivors, and disability program, as a percentage of "covered compensation" was deemed to be 70 percent (162 percent × 43 percent). Since employers pay roughly half of the Social Security tax, the employer-provided portion was deemed to be 35 percent. In recognition of future changes in the Social Security Act that would increase the value of benefits, the 35 percent figure was raised to 37½ percent.

Offset Plans

For offset plans, the value of the employer-provided portion of the total old-age, survivors, and disability benefits package, expressed as a percentage of the old-age benefit alone, was based, again, on the given that the total old-age, survivors, and disability package under Social Security was deemed to be worth 162 percent of the old-age benefit alone. Since employer taxes pay at least half of that amount, the percentage of the old-age benefit that represents the employer-provided portion of the entire old-age, survivors, and disability package was deemed to be 81 percent. This figure was adjusted for future increases to 83⅓ percent. This represents the basic limitation, or the portion of the old-age benefit that can be used to offset the formula benefit.

Based on these general limitations, Revenue Ruling 71-446 sets forth specific limitations for the various types of integrated plans and provides for adjustments in the case of certain plan features that make a benefit more valuable than a life annuity beginning no earlier than age 65.

INTEGRATING AN EXCESS PLAN

Since excess and offset plans differ considerably in design, we will look at the rules for integrating these types of plans separately, starting with excess plans. As will be noted, however, many of the adjustments that have to be made to the maximum permitted level of integration are quite similar in both cases. Before examining the actual mechanics of determining the integration limits for excess plans, some relevant definitions should be considered.

Types of Excess Plans

Some excess plans provide a retirement benefit equal to a fixed percentage (e.g., 30 percent) of excess compensation as long as the participant has a minimum number of years of service. These plans are generally known as *flat benefit excess plans*. Some excess plans, on the other hand, credit a specified percentage of compensation for each year of service or participation (e.g., one percent of compensation multiplied by years of service at retirement). These plans are generally referred to as *unit benefit excess plans*. Unit benefit excess plans may base the benefit on some average compensation figure for a period (e.g., ten years) prior to retirement, in which case they will be referred to additionally as *final-pay plans*. On the other hand, if a unit benefit excess plan accrues its specified percentage for each year's service on the participant's compensation in that year of service, it will be referred to as a *career-average plan*. Most flat benefit plans use compensation averaged over less than an entire career.

Step-Rate Excess Plans. Some excess plans provide for a benefit on compensation below the integration level. These plans are known as "step-rate excess" plans. This approach can basically be accomplished under any of the excess plans described above. In the case of a step-rate excess plan, compliance with Revenue Ruling 71-446 is measured with respect to the difference between the two levels of benefit accrual. This difference is known as the *spread*. As an example of a step-rate excess plan, consider a plan that provides 10 percent of final-average pay up to covered compensation, and 40 percent of excess compensation. The limitations of Revenue Ruling 71-446 would be applied, not to the 40 percent rate on excess compensation, but to the 30 percent spread between the two rates. In effect this is like having two plans; one, an unintegrated plan providing a benefit of 10 percent of all compensation, and the other providing a benefit of 30 percent of compensation above the integration level. The first formula is nondiscriminatory in and of itself because it provides benefits that are a uniform percentage of all compensation. The second formula (the 30 percent spread) will be deemed nondiscriminatory if it can be shown that it properly integrates with Social Security.

EXCESS COMPENSATION

For excess plans, the integration rules involve several concepts relating to compensation. First, there is excess compensation itself, the portion of compensation on which benefits (or greater benefits in the case of a step-rate excess plan) are provided. The determination of excess compensation requires a determination of the integration level, or breakpoint, the level of compensation at which excess compensation begins. Finally, compensation itself is subject to certain limiting rules.

Excluded Compensation

The use of W-2 compensation in an excess plan benefit formula is acceptable. A more restrictive definition will only be acceptable if it does not discriminate in favor of highly compensated employees, officers, and shareholders. Compensation defined as base pay, excluding overtime and bonuses, will not be permitted, for instance, if overtime is a more significant component of rank-and-file compensation than bonuses are of highly paid employees' compensation. Put simply, if bonuses are not generally paid to upper- and middle-management employees, a definition of compensation excluding bonuses and overtime will have the effect of recognizing less than all of a rank-and-file worker's total compensation (his overtime pay) in computing his pension benefit, while taking into account all of the highly paid employee's compensation. On the other hand, if bonuses to highly paid employees were significant, the definition might be acceptable. Because of the variables involved, this issue can only be evaluated on a case-by-case basis. However, if the portion of compensation taken into account, as a percentage of total compensation, is generally uniform for employees in all compensation ranges, or is not higher for employees in higher compensation ranges, there should be no problem.

Average Compensation

As we have seen above, some excess plans use average compensation in the benefit formula (flat benefit and final-pay plans). In order to take full advantage of the integration rules, these plans must generally base average compensation on at least an average of five consecutive years. Such a plan can use a period of four consecutive years if it reduces the maximum allowable level of integration to 95 percent of that which is otherwise permitted, or three consecutive years if it only integrates at 90 percent of the maximum permitted level.

Excess Compensation—Integration Level

As noted above, excess compensation is the portion of the compensation used by the plan that is in excess of the integration level. In other words, the integration level under any excess plan is the level of compensation on which Social Security benefits are deemed to be based.

For excess plans that use average compensation (most flat benefit plans and unit benefit final-pay plans) the integration level can either be separately applied to each participant as that participant's covered compensation or can be a uniform dollar amount for all participants, which does not exceed the covered compensation of any individual who is or may become a participant. As we will see in more detail shortly, covered compensation is the average compensation upon which the participant's Social Security benefits are based, assuming the participant earns at least the Social Security taxable wage base up until age 65.

For career-average excess plans, which use each year's compensation as the basis for determining each year's benefit accrual, the integration level is generally the Social Security taxable wage base for the year. For plans with plan years other than the calendar year, the integration level for any plan year would be the taxable wage base for the calendar year in which the plan year begins.

Covered Compensation

As we saw above, the determination of the integration level for excess plans that use average compensation is generally dependent on a determination of *covered compensation.* To better understand the concept of covered compensation, a brief explanation of how Social Security benefits are determined for any individual may be helpful.

The amount of an individual's Social Security benefit is based on an average monthly wage determined under a complicated formula that averages the employee's wages for a selected group of years during his career. For any year selected for the average, only those wages up to the then current Social Security taxable wage base are taken into account. The maximum Social Security benefit is payable to an employee whose wages equaled or exceeded the taxable wage base in each of the selected years. For employees whose average monthly wage is less, a lower level of Social Security benefit is paid; the lower the average monthly wage, the lower the benefit.

For the purposes of the integration rules, an employee's covered compensation is the amount of compensation with respect to which Social Security benefits would be provided if his wages were at least equal to the taxable wage base for each year up through age 65.

MAXIMUM PERMITTED INTEGRATION—EXCESS PLANS

Maximum levels of integration are provided under Revenue Ruling 71-446 for the various types of excess plans described above, subject, in most cases, to reduction where benefits are payable before age 65 or in a form other than a straight life annuity or where preretirement death or disability benefits are provided. The maximum level, as adjusted, applies to the excess benefit, in the case of an excess-only plan, or the "spread" between the level of benefits on compensation above and below the integration level, in the case of a step-rate excess plan.

Flat Benefit Excess Plan

The maximum permitted rate of benefit accrual on excess compensation for a flat benefit excess plan is 37½ percent. If a participant has less than fifteen years of service, the maximum rate is 2½ percent per year of service. A plan could, therefore, provide a benefit of 37½ percent of compensation in excess of covered compensation and be properly integrated.

A step-rate plan, of course, could integrate as long as the rate of accrual on excess compensation did not exceed 37½ percent of the rate of accrual on compensation up to the integration level.

Career-Average Unit Benefit Excess Plan

A unit benefit excess plan that bases benefit accruals on actual compensation in each year (as opposed to averaged compensation) can provide an accrual for each year of up to 1.4 percent of excess compensation in that year. Thus a plan could provide, for example, for an accrual in each year of 1.4 percent of compensation in excess of that year's taxable wage base, or an accrual of 1.4 percent more on excess compensation in the case of a step-rate plan (e.g., one percent on compensation up to the taxable wage base and 2.4 percent on compensation in excess of the taxable wage base).

Final-Pay Unit Benefit Excess Plan

Unit benefit excess plans that use average compensation can provide a benefit accrual of up to one percent on excess compensation for each year of service.

Unit Benefit Plans Under Flat Benefit Rules

If a unit benefit excess plan does not satisfy the requirements applicable to such a plan, it may still integrate as a flat benefit plan. It must then continue to be considered as a flat benefit plan for the purpose of any necessary adjustments on account of early retirement or disability benefits.

Example. A plan provides a benefit of 1¼ percent of excess average compensation for each year of service up to a maximum of thirty. It does not qualify as a unit benefit excess plan because the benefit rate exceeds one percent. It does qualify as a flat benefit excess plan because the benefit rate does not exceed 37½ percent (1.25 × 30 = 37½) for an employee with fifteen or more years of service or 2 percent per year for an employee with less than fifteen years.

ADJUSTMENTS TO MAXIMUM LIMITATIONS—EXCESS PLANS

Certain plan features, such as a pre or post-retirement death benefit, make a plan's benefit more valuable. In effect, a pension equal to 37½ percent of excess compensation is really worth more than 37½ percent of excess compensation if it also provides in-service death benefit protection or certain other additional benefits. Accordingly, Revenue Ruling 71-446 provides for adjustment to the various maximum integration limits for certain pre and post-retirement death benefit features, early retirement, and disability benefits. These adjustments are cumulative. That is, you start off with the maximum limitation and keep adjusting it downward by applying each adjustment separately.

DEATH BENEFITS

Lump-Sum Preretirement Death Benefit

If the plan provides a preretirement death benefit in the form of a lump sum, the otherwise applicable limitation must be reduced as follows:

- If the lump sum is based on the reserve that would be required for the pension under a typical level annual premium method (or total prior contributions, if greater), the maximum limitation must be no more than 8/9 of the otherwise applicable limitation (e.g., 37½ percent of excess compensation becomes 33⅓ percent).
- If the lump sum is equal to 100 times the anticipated monthly pension the employee would have received if he had continued in employment until retirement at the same rate of compensation, the maximum limitation must be reduced to 8/10 of its otherwise applicable level (e.g., 37½ percent becomes 30 percent).
- If the lump sum is equal to the greater of the reserve or 100 times the anticipated monthly pension, the maximum limitation must be reduced to 7/9 of the otherwise applicable limit (e.g., 37½ percent becomes 29.16 percent).

Preretirement Spouse Annuity

If the plan provides a spouse's annuity upon death before retirement equal to a fraction (up to 100 percent) of the participant's accrued benefit, the integration limits must be reduced to a fraction equal to 7 ÷ (7 + 2 × the fraction of the participant's benefit payable to the spouse). So, if a plan provides a 50 percent spouse's benefit, the adjustment fraction would be 7 ÷ (7 + [2 × ½]) or ⅞.

However, plans that provide an in-service early survivor annuity under the qualified joint and survivor rules introduced by ERISA need not make any adjustment for that benefit.

Actuarial Value Alternative

Under certain circumstances, a smaller adjustment will be allowed based on the ratio of the actuarial value of the participant's benefit to the actuarial value of that benefit plus the death benefit.

NORMAL FORM OF PAYMENT OTHER THAN STRAIGHT LIFE ANNUITY

Since the value of the employer-provided portion of Social Security, when stated as a percentage of compensation, is based on an annuity payable for life only, the integration limitations must be applied against excess benefits payable in a similar form. If a plan's normal form contains any type of death benefit or continuation feature it will, of course, be more valuable than a straight life annuity. Thus, the integration limit must be actuarially reduced to reflect the more valuable form of payment. The actuarial reductions for most of the more common forms of payment are set forth in Revenue Ruling 71-446, as follows:

Normal Form	*Percentage of Otherwise Applicable Maximum*
Five year certain and life	97%
Ten year certain and life	90%
Fifteen year certain and life	80%
Twenty year certain and life	70%
Life annuity with installment refund	90%
Life annuity with full cash refund	85%
Life annuity with 50 percent continuation to surviving spouse	80%

You should remember that these reductions only apply if the benefit derived from the plan formula is paid in a form other than life-only without any actuarial adjustment.

As a rule, a plan's normal form is based on the benefit formula and is not actuarially reduced (or made equivalent to) a life annuity where different from that form. The one general exception to this statement is the statutorily required joint and survivor annuity form. The law generally requires that this form be the automatic normal form for married participants. However, it can be provided as an actuarially equivalent amount to the otherwise applicable normal form and in most cases is. Where this is true, no reduction need be made to the otherwise applicable integration limits for the statutory joint and survivor form.

EARLY RETIREMENT REDUCTIONS

Since benefits payable in the event of early retirement can be more valuable in certain instances than benefits beginning at age 65, reductions in the otherwise maximum permitted level of integration may have to be made.

Benefits Beginning at Age 65 or Later

For unit benefit plans (plans that credit a piece of retirement benefit for each year of service) no reduction in the maximum integration level is required for early retirement benefits that do not begin before age 65. For flat benefit plans, the benefit payable beginning at age 65 cannot exceed the benefit that could have been payable at age 65 if the employee remained employed, prorated by applying a fraction equal to the participant's years of service at early retirement over the years of service he would have had at age 65.

Benefits Payable Before Age 65

Most plans require some sort of actuarial or other reduction in the amount of benefit payable to an early retiree if benefits begin before age 65. The concept behind this is simple. A benefit payable beginning at age 55, for example, is expected to be payable longer than a benefit payable beginning at age 65, and is therefore more valuable to the participant, and more costly to provide. To defray this additional cost, the formula benefit otherwise payable beginning at age 65 is generally reduced. For this same reason, appropriate reductions in the otherwise maximum integration limitations must be made unless the benefit beginning before age 65 is reduced so that it is actuarially equivalent to the benefit beginning at age 65.

An early retirement reduction of $1/15$ for each of the first five years and $1/30$ for each of the next five years that payment precedes age 65 will be deemed actuarially equivalent. Therefore, no reduction in the maximum integration limitations will be required. However, many plans subsidize early retirement benefits by providing reductions that are not as severe as the $1/15$–$1/30$ reductions specified in Revenue Ruling 71-446, or that do not require a reduction at all after a certain age. In those situations, the maximum integration limitations must be adjusted to reflect the subsidy. This is done by comparing the subsidized reduction factors to the $\frac{1}{15}$–$\frac{1}{30}$ factors at each age and finding the age at which the largest discrepancy occurs in the ratio of the actuarial equivalent factors to the subsidized factors.

A look at two examples will be helpful. In the first example, the reduction for early commencement of benefits is 3 percent per year.

	A	B	
Age	*$\frac{1}{15}$–$\frac{1}{30}$ Reduction as a Percentage*	*3 Percent Reduction*	*A ÷ B*
64	.933	.97	.962
63	.867	.94	.922
62	.800	.91	.879
61	.733	.88	.833
60	.667	.85	.785
59	.633	.82	.772
58	.600	.79	.759
57	.567	.76	.746
56	.533	.73	.730
55	.500	.70	.714

Note that the worst discrepancy is at age 55, where the actuarial equivalent ($\frac{1}{15}$–$\frac{1}{30}$) benefit at age 55 is 71.4 percent of the benefit actually payable under the subsidized schedule. Thus if the otherwise maximum benefit allowable under the integration limits is reduced by a factor of .714, it will not exceed the benefit that would have resulted if the $\frac{1}{15}$–$\frac{1}{30}$ table were used (.70 × .714 = .500). The .714 factor thus becomes an additional adjustment to the maximum allowable integration level.

Assume that the subsidized early retirement reduction factors in the second example are the same as in the first for ages 59–55, but that no reduction is required from age 60 on. The comparison tables would look like this:

	A	B	
Age	*$\frac{1}{15}$–$\frac{1}{30}$ as a Percentage*	*Subsidized Factors*	*A ÷ B*
64	.933	1.000	.933
63	.867	1.000	.867
62	.800	1.000	.800
61	.733	1.000	.733
60	.667	1.000	.667
59	.633	.82	.772
58	.600	.79	.759
57	.567	.76	.746
56	.533	.73	.730
55	.500	.70	.714

Here, the worst case is age 60. The subsidized benefit would have to be reduced by a factor of .667, or ⅔, to be equivalent to the benefit provided under the $\frac{1}{15}$–$\frac{1}{30}$ reduction. Therefore, the otherwise maximum allowable integration limitation is subject to adjustment by a factor of .667.

For plans funded solely by typical individual level premium annuity or insurance contracts, no reduction is required for early commencement of benefits as long as the benefit does not exceed what can be provided by the reserve.

INTEGRATING DISABILITY BENEFITS

Immediate Payment Upon Disability

If the disability benefit begins immediately upon disability, the maximum integration limitation is reduced as follows:

Flat Benefit Plans. The maximum integration limitations must be reduced to 70 percent of the otherwise applicable limit. However, if the ratio of the participant's years of service at disability over his projected years of service to age 65 exceeds 70 percent, that higher percentage will be used as the adjustment.

Unit Benefit Plans. The maximum integration limitation must be reduced to 90 percent. In addition, the following rules apply:

- The term "disability" must be defined and the rules in respect thereof must be uniformly and consistently applied to all persons similarly situated;
- Disability benefits can only be payable during a period of eligibility for and receipt of Social Security disability benefits (not counting the waiting period, if the plan so provides).

Benefits at Age 65. No reduction is required if disability benefits begin at age 65 as long as:

- The benefit does not exceed the maximum normal retirement benefit that would have been paid to the participant if he remained in service until age 65 at the same rate of compensation;
- "Disability" is defined and is subject to uniform rules;
- No integrated benefits are payable before age 65. What this means is that you could provide an unintegrated benefit before age 65, say $10 per month for each year of service;
- The participant is *continuously* eligible for and receiving Social Security disability benefits (other than during the waiting period) up to age 65.

EMPLOYEE CONTRIBUTIONS UNDER AN EXCESS PLAN

In a contributory excess plan, the maximum integration limitations are increased to reflect the fact that part of the participant's benefits are provided by his own contributions.

Unit Benefit Career-Average Plan

In a plan that credits a piece of benefit in each year, based on that year's compensation, the increase is ⅙ of the employee contribution rate. If the employee contribution rate is 2 percent, for example, the maximum integration limitation (1.4 percent, before adjustments) would be increased by ⅓ of one percent (to 1.733 percent, before adjustments).

Unit Benefit Final-Pay Plan

A unit benefit plan that uses average compensation can increase the maximum limitation (one percent, before adjustments) by ⅛ of the employee contribution rate. Using our 2 percent example, the increase would be ¼ of one percent.

Flat Benefit Plan

The increase is either ⅙ or ⅛ of the employee's aggregate contributions over his career, as a percentage of aggregate compensation, depending upon whether the flat benefit plan is a career-average (use ⅙) or final-pay plan (use ⅛).

INTEGRATING AN OFFSET PLAN

Maximum Permitted Offset

The maximum permitted offset applicable to any participant under an offset plan is 83⅓ percent of the participant's old-age benefit under Social Security, determined under the Social Security Act in effect at the time the offset is first applied, disregarding any subsequent increases in Social Security benefits.

A higher percentage can be used if the offset is geared to the old-age benefit determined under the Social Security Act in effect prior to the 1971 amendments to the Act, but these provisions are generally no longer utilized.

Adjustments to Maximum Limitations

The adjustments required to be made to the otherwise applicable maximum limitations for death benefits and normal forms other than life annuity are the same for both excess and offset plans and are discussed above in the portion of this chapter dealing with excess plans. The discussion below deals with the adjustments required under offset plans for early retirement and disability benefits.

Early Retirement Benefits

The integration rules prevent an employer from taking credit for providing the entire employer-provided portion of a participant's Social Security old-age benefit where the participant leaves that employer before age 65. This is done in one of two ways. The old-age benefit is determined either by assuming no further earnings after early retirement or by assuming continued earnings until age 65, and then prorating the amount so determined by applying a fraction equal to the participant's service at early retirement over the years he would have had if he stayed until age 65.

Under either approach, if benefits commence before age 65, the offset must also be reduced actuarially to reflect early commencement. The rules for determining this reduction are the same as those discussed in the section on excess plans. An exception to this, which is not too common, is where benefits commence before age 65, but the offset is not applied to the benefit until age 65. In that case, the offset need not be actuarially reduced.

Disability Benefits

If disability benefits are payable under an offset plan, the term disability must be defined and subject to uniform rules. The maximum allowable offset is also subject to reduction as follows:

- The offset applied after age 65 cannot exceed 90 percent of the otherwise applicable maximum offset;
- If benefits are payable before age 65 and an offset is applied, it cannot exceed 64 percent of the actual Social Security disability benefits payable to participants at the time of disability.

Some Special Problems

Many offset plans utilize a unit benefit approach to determining the offset. Instead of a fixed offset of 50 percent, 75 percent or 83⅓ percent, the benefit formula might be 2 percent of final-average compensation less 2 percent of Social Security old-age benefit for each year of service. The problem arises in insuring that the total offset for any participant does not exceed the maximum allowable offset. One common approach to this problem has been to limit the years of service that determine the offset (e.g., 2 percent of Social Security benefit for each year of service not to exceed twenty-five years).

That approach solves the integration problem, but has a potential for violating the backloading prohibitions of ERISA and Section 411 of the Code (see discussion of benefit accrual standards under ERISA elsewhere in this chapter). Simply put, the cessation of the offset in a given year (in our example in the preceding paragraph, the twenty-sixth year) results in a larger accrual rate in that year and later years. Care, therefore, must be given to the impact of any "cap" on a unit benefit type offset to insure compliance with both the integration rules and the backloading rules.

INTEGRATING A DEFINED CONTRIBUTION PLAN

Money purchase and profit-sharing plans can be integrated with Social Security on an excess basis. The integration of these types of plans is less complicated than integration of defined benefit plans. What the integration rules measure is the rate of contribution on excess compensation. The various reductions or adjustments found in the rules for defined benefit plans are not involved. For the vast majority of these plans, excess compensation is measured by the Social Security wage base applicable to the year of contribution. Where the plan year is not on a calendar-year basis, the applicable wage basis for any plan year is the wage basis in effect at the beginning of the plan year.

For both money purchase and profit-sharing plans, the rate of contribution on excess compensation in any year can be 7 percent. This means that you can have an excess-only plan that only applies to employees with compensation in excess of that year's wage base, or you can cover employees whose compensation does not exceed the wage base, with a differential of rate of contribution on earnings above and below the wage base of up to 7 percent.

In a typical step-rate approach under a profit-sharing plan, the contribution is first allocated to all employees with excess compensation, until each has been credited with 7 percent of excess compensation; the balance, if any, of the contribution is then allocated to all participants on the basis of the ratio of each participant's total compensation to the total compensation of all participants. Let's assume that the second step of the allocation results in the crediting of 2 percent of each participant's total compensation. In that case, the result will be that all participants get an allocation equal to 2 percent of their total compensation, plus an additional 7 percent of their excess compensation, if any. *A word of caution:* Profit-sharing plans cannot take advantage of the integration rules unless they restrict distributions to retirement, death, or separation from service. Money purchase plans are prohibited from allowing preretirement withdrawals by the general qualification rules. However, these types of distributions are an attractive feature of most profit-sharing plans. The value of integrating a profit-sharing plan in any given situation should, therefore, be weighed against the loss of preretirement withdrawals.

Minimum Funding Requirements for Qualified Plans

RICHARD P. SEIDEN
Vice-President, Frank B. Hall Consulting Company

A BRIEF LOOK AT FUNDING CONCEPTS

A plan's costs cannot be exactly determined at any given point in time because a plan's costs depend on many variables relating to future events. For example, the number of current participants who leave before vesting, or die before becoming entitled to any statutory or other in-service death benefits will impact on the benefits paid, or not paid, under a plan. Annual costs, therefore, have to be determined by using certain assumptions. In addition, the benefit costs so determined must be allocated in some fashion over the period during which the benefits are earned. The actuary, therefore, determines a plan's annual costs with certain tools. The first is commonly referred to as *an actuarial cost* (or *funding*) *method.* The second is a set of *actuarial assumptions.*

An actuarial cost method is a means of allocating costs, when determined, over a period of years. Under most cost methods the cost of the benefits accrued under a plan with respect to a group of participants is determined by projecting benefit accruals for that group into the future. These projected costs are then discounted back to the present by using a set of actuarial assumptions, in order to arrive at a present value of benefits expected to be paid. The actuary then subtracts from this the value of the plan's assets. The remainder represents the plan's liability for benefits that remain to be funded. The portion of this unfunded liability that relates to future years' accruals is generally allocated to those years. This annual cost is commonly referred to as a plan's normal cost. The portion of the unfunded liability relating to benefits already accrued (the actuarial accrued liability, or, past-service liability, as it is sometimes referred to) is amortized over a specified period. Under one method, aggregate cost, no past-service liability is separately identified. Instead, the entire excess of expected benefits over assets is allocated to future service.

The costs themselves, whether projected or not, are in a sense estimates, based on the actuarial assumptions employed by the actuary. These assumptions relate to such factors as mortality, turnover, plan expenses, morbidity (in the case of disability benefits) interest, and assumed retirement age. Of these assumptions, preretirement, mortality, disability incidence, turnover, and retirement age, go directly to the issue of whether or not a liability will be incurred, while interest and post-retirement mortality are used to value the liability.

When we put a cost method and a set of actuarial assumptions together we get an estimate of annual costs. If the actuary's assumptions exactly coincide with future experience in all respects, the annual costs will meet future obligations. Of course, actual experience will always differ from a given set of actuarial assumptions, no matter how reasonable they are. To reflect this, a cost method has to reflect actuarial gains and losses. These gains and losses are either amortized over a specified period or are allocated to future years as part of the plan's annual cost, depending upon the cost method.

MINIMUM FUNDING STANDARDS

Background

The need for minimum funding standards stems from a number of concerns, some of which precede the Employee Retirement Income Security Act of 1974 (ERISA). For example, a qualified plan could have been deemed terminated under pre-ERISA rules if the employer did not contribute in each year at least the normal cost of the plan plus interest on any unfunded liabilities. There was, however, no requirement to actually amortize any unfunded liabilities nor was there any real control over how costs were determined.

The need for tighter control over funding and for the imposition of certain minimum levels of funding under ERISA was two-fold. First, the other protections being afforded to plan participants under ERISA in the areas of vesting, participation, and benefit accrual, among others, could be rendered less meaningful if a plan's assets were insufficient to provide the benefits generated by these new protections. Moreover, the government, through the Pension Benefit Guaranty Corporation (PBGC), was undertaking to guarantee certain benefits that could not be provided by a plan's assets upon plan termination. It was almost imperative, therefore, that the government limit its exposure as much as it could. Greater control over the level of funding and the determination of plan costs certainly offered a means of doing just that.

Minimum Funding—The Approach Under ERISA

The focus of ERISA's minimum funding standards involves both the rate of funding of a plan's costs and the method of determining those costs. A plan's costs must be funded at a rate that takes care of its normal cost for each year and that generally provides for amortization of unfunded actuarial liabilities and actuarial losses over a specified period of years. Failure to meet this required rate of funding can result in the imposition of severe penalties in the form of excise taxes imposed upon the employer.

As we will see in more detail later, ERISA's minimum funding standards also impose rules on certain aspects of the way a plan's costs are determined, including the reasonableness of the actuarial assumptions used and the valuation of a plan's assets.

Plans Subject to the Minimum Funding Requirements

The minimum funding requirements generally apply to all defined benefit pension plans except for certain such plans funded by individual insurance contracts, government plans, and church plans. Money purchase pension plans are technically subject to the minimum funding requirements, but the contribution level specified in the plan is deemed to be the required contribution. Profit-sharing and stock bonus plans are not subject to the minimum funding requirements.

The Funding Standard Account

Every plan subject to the minimum funding rules must establish a funding standard account. This account is charged annually with the annual components of the minimum annual rate of funding required by ERISA and credited with the employer's annual contribution and certain other credits. In effect, the minimum contribution required in any year is the amount necessary to bring the credit side of the account equal to the charges to the account. Thus, if the account has a surplus, resulting, for example, from amortization of unfunded actuarial liabilities at a rate faster than that required, the minimum contribution required may be less than that year's normal cost, or may be zero. On the other hand, if the account is ever in a deficit situation, a penalty tax results.

Charges to the Funding Standard Account. For each plan year, a plan's funding standard account is charged with the following:

- *Normal cost.* This is the portion of the plan's unfunded costs allocated to the plan year under the plan's actuarial cost method.
- *Amortizable amounts.* The amount necessary to amortize the following in equal annual installments over the period specified:
  - —Unfunded actuarial (or past-service) liabilities—over thirty years for new plans and forty years for plans in existence on January 1, 1974. A plan's actuarial cost method may allocate these liabilities over future years, in which case they will be reflected in the plan's normal cost each year and not as a separate amortizable amount.
  - —Increases in unfunded actuarial liabilities arising from plan amendments

adopted in the plan year. These increases must be amortized over thirty years.

—Net experience losses, where separately determined. These losses must be amortized over fifteen years. As discussed briefly, certain actuarial cost methods do not separately amortize experience gains and losses, but rather allocate them over future years and thereby reflect them in the plan's normal cost.

—Losses from changes in actuarial assumptions, where separately determined. These losses must be amortized over thirty years. Only the aggregate cost method reflects these losses in the plan's normal cost; all of the other cost methods amortize these losses separately.

—Waived funding deficiencies. These amounts must be amortized over fifteen years. As we will see later, amounts otherwise required to be contributed in any plan year can be waived under certain limited circumstances.

Credits to the Funding Standard Account. The following amounts are credited to a plan's funding standard account for each plan year:

- *Annual contribution.* The amount considered contributed to the plan by the employer for the plan year. For this purpose a contribution made within eight and a half months after the end of a plan year will be considered to have been made in that plan year. This rule is independent of the rules relating to the deductibility of contributions made to a plan after employer's taxable year-end. It is possible therefore, to have a contribution to a plan deductible in one year and credited for minimum funding purposes in another year.
- *Amortizable amounts.* The amount necessary to amortize the following in equal annual installments over the period specified:

  —Decrease in unfunded actuarial liabilities resulting from plan amendments adopted in the plan year. These decreases must be amortized over thirty years.

  —Net experience gains, where separately determined. These gains must be amortized over fifteen years.

  —Gains from changes in actuarial assumptions, where separately determined. These gains must be amortized over thirty years.

  —The amount of any waived funding deficiency.

Items charged or credited to the funding standard account have to be credited with interest. Also, charges can be combined or offset against one another.

The Alternative Minimum Funding Standard Account

The law provides an alternative to the minimum funding standard account described above for certain plans that utilize the Entry Age Normal Cost Method. The alternative can produce lower annual minimum funding requirements by permitting a plan near the end of its amortization schedule to slow down the accumulation of assets. This is true, in part, because it measures a given year's benefit accrual in relation to its expected date of payment, rather than as part of an overall amortization of a participant's benefit accrual over his career. If a participant accrues the same amount of benefit each year and the total cost is amortized in equal installments over his career, the annual cost will be greater than the actual cost of a year's accrual early in his career, due to the heavy discounting from the early year to the date of payment. Of course, an individual year's costs will begin to exceed the level of amortization with respect to the later years of a participant's career. Therefore, the alternative is generally considered a temporary advantage at best.

Moreover, use of the alternative requires maintaining both the regular and the alternative account and requires complicated adjustments when switching from one to the other.

Failure to Meet the Funding Requirements—Excise Tax

If a plan's funding standard account has a negative balance, an accumulated "funding deficiency" results. This deficiency must be reported to the Internal Revenue Service and is subject to a tax of 5 percent on the deficiency. If the tax is not paid within ninety days of a notice of deficiency from the IRS the tax becomes a prohibitive 100 percent of the deficiency.

SOME SPECIAL RULES IN DETERMINING MINIMUM FUNDING

In determining the credits and charges to a plan's funding standard account, certain special rules apply.

Valuation of Assets

The valuation of a plan's assets is an integral part of determining a plan's costs. Simply put, the costs that an actuarial cost method allocates are the excess of the value of the benefits over the value of the plan's assets. The minimum funding standards imposed by ERISA require that a plan's assets be valued on a basis that takes into account fair market value. The actuary may adopt a method of asset valuation that softens the impact of short-run fluctuations in fair market value as long as the "averaging" falls within certain specified parameters. It cannot be less than the lesser of 80 percent of current fair market value or 85 percent of a five-year average, nor more than the greater of 120 percent of current or 115 percent of five-year average fair market value. In addition, a plan may elect to value certain bonds on an amortized basis running from cost at purchase to amount payable at maturity, rather than on a basis that reflects fair market value. This election can be helpful where bonds are generally kept to maturity.

Reasonable Actuarial Assumptions

The actuarial assumptions used by an actuary in determining a plan's costs obviously have a significant impact on the amounts determined. Pre-ERISA, there were generally no legal constraints on the assumptions used by actuaries. We must keep in mind, however, that the actuarial profession is a highly structured profession with well-developed guidelines as to "sound actuarial practices," not dissimilar to those of the accounting profession relating to generally accepted accounting principles.

Nevertheless, the drafters of ERISA saw the unrestricted use of actuarial assumptions as a potential means of manipulating plan costs in a way that could evade the minimum funding requirements. To prevent this, the law requires that a plan's actuarial assumptions be reasonable, in the aggregate, and offer the actuary's best estimate, as certified by him, of the anticipated experience under the plan. Moreover, the reasonableness of the assumptions is to be measured to a certain extent against the experience of the plan and reasonable expectations.

The requirement of "best estimate" has, perhaps, made actuaries more sensitive to the impact of a given set of actuarial assumptions on plan costs, and the interplay between specific assumptions. In certain respects, the pre-ERISA ability to minimize or maximize costs over a short period by adjusting assumptions may have been lost. Generally, however, the vast majority of actuaries were probably determining plan costs within the parameters of "best estimate" all along.

Note that the reasonableness of the actuarial assumptions is measured in the aggregate. Remember that actuarial assumptions are really just that: assumptions as to future experience. In some cases, future experience is harder to anticipate than in others. Interest, for example, can be a volatile factor while mortality may not be. Actuaries often hedge their bets by using assumptions which, taken by themselves, may not be considered reasonable, but which may be used to balance the unpredictability of other factors, or which, taken in the aggregate, produce reasonable cost estimates. What is reasonable in the aggregate therefore is not always a quantitative judgment, but often times a qualitative one.

Changes in Actuarial Cost Method or Plan Year

To further eliminate the possibility of manipulation of the minimum funding standards, the law requires that changes in the actuarial cost method or plan year must be approved by the IRS. For this purpose a plan's actuarial cost method is deemed to include not only the actuarial cost method but the actuarial method of asset valuation, the valuation date itself, and certain other changes in computing the minimum contribution.

Full Funding Limitation

The minimum contribution required with respect to any plan year will not be more than the amount required to fully fund the benefits accrued under the plan. If the normal operation of the funding standard account would require a larger contribution, appropriate adjustments to the funding standard account will be made to limit the minimum contribution to the full funding amount.

Waiver of the Minimum Funding Standard

In certain cases of substantial business hardship, the minimum funding requirement for a given plan year can be waived. A waiver will only be granted if to do otherwise would be adverse to the interests of plan participants in the aggregate, as, for example, where a contribution could cause the insolvency of the employer. No more than five waivers in any fifteen-consecutive-year period may be granted.

In determining whether the minimum funding requirements will cause a substantial business hardship, the Secretary of the Treasury must consider, among other things, such factors as whether the employer is operating at an economic loss, the existence of unemployment or underemployment in the trade or business and the industry concerned, any decline or depression in the sales and profits of the industry involved, and whether a failure to grant a waiver could reasonably be expected to result in a discontinuance of the plan. A waived funding deficiency must be amortized over fifteen years.

Plan Termination

Bruce Alan Miller
Legal Division, W.R. Grace & Co.

PENSION BENEFIT GUARANTY CORPORATION CONSIDERATIONS

Overview

Title IV of the Employee Retirement Income Security Act of 1974 (ERISA) established a new form of guarantee of benefits to participants under covered defined benefit pension plans. Under Title IV, the Pension Benefit Guaranty Corporation (PBGC) will pay certain guaranteed vested benefits to plan participants in the event that the covered plan terminates and assets held to fund such benefits under the plan are not sufficient to fund such benefits. The PBGC will only guarantee a basic benefit up to a certain dollar amount. The PBGC insurance program is funded by premiums paid annually by plans covered by Title IV. Before making any distribution of plan benefits upon termination of a covered plan, the plan administrator must receive a Notice of Sufficiency from the PBGC. If the PBGC incurs a liability to plan participants because plan assets are insufficient, it can impose that liability upon the employer or employers formerly maintaining the plan, up to 30 percent of the employer's net worth.

The PBGC can also force a plan to terminate under certain circumstances. It learns about the financial condition of a plan through the occurrence of certain reportable events that must be reported to the PBGC by the plan administrator within thirty days of their occurrence. Withdrawal of a substantial employer from a covered multiple-employer plan triggers a requirement that the employer post a bond to secure its liability in the event of plan termination. The same rule applies to an employer's cessation of business at a facility if the cessation results in a greater than 20 percent reduction in the number of participants in a covered plan. Under the Multiemployer Pension Plan Amendments Act of 1980, the PBGC will insure benefits under a multiemployer plan only upon plan insolvency. Since withdrawing employers would continue to have funding duties, such insolvency would generally result only if the contributing employers became bankrupt. (See Chapter 28 for a detailed discussion of multiemployer plans.)

Plans Subject to Title IV Requirements

Title IV applies to a defined benefit pension plan which the Internal Revenue Service has classified as tax-qualified by means of a favorable determination letter or which has in practice satisfied IRS requirements during the preceding five plan years.[1] However, this law does not apply to a defined contribution plan, a governmental plan, an employee-funded plan using a trust under Section 501(c)(9) of the Code, an unfunded deferred compensation plan for highly compensated employees, a plan maintained outside the United States for nonresident aliens, a defined benefit plan with twenty-five or fewer participants which is maintained by a professional service employer (such as a doctor or law firm), and certain other types of plans.[2]

The provisions of Title IV became effective on September 2, 1974, except that the termination of a covered plan (other than a multiemployer plan) between July 1, 1974 and September 1, 1974, inclusive, triggered the payment of guaranteed vested benefits by the PBGC under certain circumstances.[3] The guaranteed benefit provisions of Title IV began to apply to multiemployer plans on August 1, 1980.

Nature of Termination

Termination of a plan (other than a multiemployer plan) for PBGC purposes involves the cessation of funding of the plan and is appropriate where the employer maintaining the plan is unable to continue funding the plan or does not desire to continue funding the plan. Termination ends the employer's obligation to fund the plan with respect to periods after the termination. However, in place of a funding obligation, the employer will have a financial obligation to the PBGC if plan assets are not sufficient to fund the plan's guaranteed vested benefits upon termination.

When a covered plan is merged into another covered plan or where a new employer assumes obligations under the plan as a result of a business reorganization, termination of a plan and consequent liability to the PBGC need not occur. Termination need not occur where a plant or facility is closed or shut down. The employer may continue to fund for benefits accrued before the closing. In effect, the trust relating to the plan continues to receive contributions from the employer, although no participants are accruing benefits under the plan after the closing. This is true even if there is a full or partial termination of the plan requiring full vesting of participants under regulations of the IRS as a result of the substantial decrease in the number of plan participants. Similarly, an ongoing plan can be amended to cease future benefit accruals under the plan, and this will not be considered a plan termination for PBGC purposes.

---

[1] ERISA § 4021(a).
[2] ERISA § 4021(b).
[3] ERISA §§ 4082(a), 4082(b).

However, the conversion of a defined benefit plan into a defined contribution plan is a plan termination for PBGC purposes.[4] But not if the defined contribution plan operates only prospectively after the conversion date.

Voluntary Termination of Single-Employer Plan

A single-employer plan is a plan covered under Title IV of ERISA that is maintained by one trade, business, or corporation or by a controlled group of trades, businesses, or corporations. Control is generally determined on the basis of an 80 percent ownership test.

Notice to Employees. The plan administrator of a covered plan that proposes to terminate must give written notification to the employees covered by the plan. If the plan is collectively bargained, the union representative gets the notice on behalf of the employees. If the plan is not collectively bargained, the notice is posted where employees work. Presumably, the notice may instead be mailed to employees.

The PBGC has proposed to allow satisfaction of the notice requirement by means of the Notice to Interested Parties which precedes an application for a determination letter from the IRS upon plan termination. This is regarded as "one-stop service."[5]

Notice to Pension Benefit Guaranty Corporation. At least ten days prior to the proposed date of plan termination, the plan administrator must submit to the PBGC a Notice of Intent to Terminate. The notice contains basic information about the employer, plan administrator, and participants and requires the attachment of the plan, the collective bargaining agreement, if any, the most recent plan actuarial report, and the most recent plan financial statement. The notice is deemed submitted when it is received by the PBGC. If the notice is incomplete, it is voidable by the PBGC. However, the plan administrator and the PBGC may sign an agreement to extend the period of time to complete the filing. If such an agreement is made, termination distributions of plan assets cannot be made during the ninety-day period after the extension date.

The PBGC has proposed to allow satisfaction of the notice requirement by means of a revised Form 5310 of the IRS that can be used to seek a determination letter from the IRS with respect to the plan termination, as well as to notify the PBGC of an intent to terminate a plan.

Period Before Issuance of Notice of Sufficiency. The plan administrator cannot make any termination distributions to participants during the ninety days after the proposed termination date unless a Notice of Sufficiency is

---

[4] ERISA § 4041(f).
[5] 44 Fed. Reg. 43,404 (1979).

received from the PBGC.[6] After receipt of the Notice of Intent to Terminate, the PBGC will issue a Notice of Inability to Determine Sufficiency if the plan clearly does not have sufficient assets to fund the plan's guaranteed vested benefits. If the PBGC determines that the plan is not clearly insufficient, the PBGC will issue instructions to the plan administrator for demonstrating sufficiency. The plan administrator has 120 days to make the demonstration.

Demonstration of Sufficiency. In order to demonstrate sufficiency, the plan administrator must submit asset valuation data, benefit valuation data, a statement relating to participants who have elected lump-sum payments instead of annuities, and the proposed date of asset distribution. The plan administrator must certify to the accuracy of the information submitted. However, no demonstration of sufficiency is necessary if the PBGC determines that a plan has no participants entitled to receive guaranteed benefits and a Notice of Sufficiency will be issued immediately. Based upon the data submitted, the PBGC must make a determination as to the sufficiency of plan assets to fund the guaranteed vested benefits.

Value of Assets. The valuation of plan assets is determined under PBGC rules set forth in PBGC Reg. §§ 2620.1 et seq. The plan administrator must estimate the value of plan assets as of the proposed date of distribution. The plan administrator may use the plan's financial statements and a projection of earnings based on a rate of return that does not exceed the PBGC interest rate for valuing immediate annuities. If the estimate of plan assets is based on inadequate information, the PBGC may require a current valuation. The amount of plan assets must be reduced for estimated expenses and benefit payments to be paid out of plan assets before the proposed date of distribution. Plan assets are deemed to include a legal commitment (in the form prescribed by the PBGC) made by the employer, and submitted to the PBGC, before the date of plan termination promising to pay any sum necessary on the date of distribution to make the plan sufficient (assuming the employer is solvent).

Value of Guaranteed Benefits. The value of guaranteed benefits to be provided in annuity form is determined by means of a qualifying bid from an insurance company. A qualifying bid is an insurer's bid for nonsurrenderable single premium nonparticipating annuities that may be exercised for a period that includes the proposed date of distribution. A plan administrator is only required to obtain one bid if that bid indicates that the plan is sufficient. If that bid indicates that the plan is not sufficient, the plan administrator must attempt to get one or two more bids to show that the plan is sufficient, or the PBGC may request a bid. The value of guaranteed benefits to be pro-

[6] ERISA § 4041(a).

vided in lump-sum form is determined as of the proposed date of distribution on the basis of actuarial assumptions. The actuarial assumptions must be reasonable and may consist of assumptions set forth in the plan, the plan's funding assumptions, the PBGC-prescribed assumptions, or an insurer's assumptions.

Value of Early Retirement Benefits. If a participant has a nonforfeitable right to an early retirement benefit before the date of plan termination but has not retired, the cost of such early retirement benefit is determined by a bid from an insurer as in the case of all other guaranteed benefits payable in annuity form. But if the plan administrator cannot get a bid from an insurer that reasonably reflects the probabilities that the participant might not retire until some future date, the PBGC will provide the early retirement benefit and the plan will be charged with the cost of the benefit determined under PBGC benefit valuation rules.

Guaranteed Benefits. Subject to certain limitations, a benefit guaranteed by the PBGC must satisfy three criteria: (1) it must be nonforfeitable; (2) it must qualify as a pension benefit; and (3) the participant must have an entitlement to the benefit. A benefit is considered nonforfeitable if the participant or beneficiary has satisfied, on the date of termination, all conditions required in order to establish entitlement to the benefit other than filing of an application, actual retirement, or completion of a waiting period. A benefit is considered to be a pension benefit if it is payable as an annuity to a participant who permanently leaves or has left covered employment, or to a surviving beneficiary. A disability benefit is regarded as a pension benefit in most cases. A lump-sum benefit is not a pension benefit, but an equivalent annuity is a pension benefit. In general, a participant or surviving beneficiary is entitled to a benefit if his benefit was in pay status on the date of plan termination or would be payable upon retirement.

Guaranteed benefits are subject to certain limitations. A guaranteed benefit may generally not exceed the dollar amount payable as a straight life annuity commencing at normal retirement age based on the accrued benefit at the date of plan termination. A guaranteed benefit may not exceed the actuarial value of a straight life annuity at age 65 equal to one-twelfth of a participant's average compensation during his highest paid five consecutive calendar years, or $1,261.36 per month in 1981, if less. Benefits under a new plan and benefit increases under an existing plan are subject to five-year phase-in rules in the determination of the portion of the benefit or benefit increase guaranteed. In the case of a substantial owner (generally, a more than 10 percent shareholder or partner or a sole proprietor), guaranteed benefits are subject to a thirty-year phase-in rule.

Distribution of Plan Assets. After receiving a Notice of Sufficiency, the plan administrator must complete the distribution of plan assets within ninety days after the date of the Notice of Sufficiency, subject to extension by the PBGC. This is accomplished by purchasing insurance contracts to provide benefits payable in annuity form, paying the PBGC for any early retirement benefits to be provided by it, and paying a lump-sum amount to those who have so elected.

Allocation of Assets. Plan assets must be allocated to the benefit categories applicable upon plan termination under Section 4044 of ERISA. These categories represent a rank-order scheme that determines where assets go first in order to fund particular benefits. Beginning with the benefit category that has the first claim on plan assets, the categories are as follows:

1. Benefits attributable to voluntary employee contributions;
2. Benefits attributable to mandatory employee contributions;
3. Benefits that are or could be in pay status to certain retirees;
4. Benefits generally that are guaranteed by the PBGC;
5. Benefits that are vested (other than by reason of plan termination);
6. All other benefits under the plan.

Assets must be allocated to the categories sequentially until assets run out. Assets are allocated as of the date plan assets are to be distributed in the case of sufficient plans and as of the date of plan termination in the case of insufficient plans. Benefits in each category are to be valued according to PBGC benefit valuation rules (discussed above under "Value of Guaranteed Benefits").

Surplus Assets. If assets remain after covering the actuarial present value of all accrued benefits of participants under the plan, the excess assets may be returned to the employer if the plan so provides, but any residual assets attributable to employee contributions must be allocated to plan participants.[7] However, a plan may not be retroactively amended after the date of plan termination to provide for the reversion of excess assets to the employer.[8] In cases where residual assets cannot be returned to the employer, such assets are allocated to participants based on the ratio of the present value of each participant's accrued benefit to the present value of all participants' accrued benefits (excluding any amount attributable to voluntary employee contributions).

Elections as to Benefits. If a plan provides for a form of benefit other than an annuity, a participant who desires a benefit other than an annuity (such as a lump sum) must so elect in writing. The plan administrator must

---

[7] ERISA § 4044(d).

[8] Audio Fidelity Corp. v. PBGC, 624 F.2d 513, (4th Cir. 1980); See also Pollack v. Castrovinci, 476 F. Supp. 606 (S.D.N.Y. July 23, 1979).

advise the participant of the available forms of benefit, the estimated amount payable as an annuity and as a lump sum, the risks involved in a lump sum, the fact that an election of a lump sum will not be effective unless the plan is sufficient, and the fact that the PBGC does not guarantee any benefit not payable in the form of an annuity. However, a participant may be forced to accept a lump sum if his monthly benefit is less than the amount normally paid by an insurer or the present value of his benefit does not exceed $1,750.

Distribution Statement. Within sixty days after completion of termination distributions of plan assets, the plan administrator must submit a certified statement to the PBGC. The statement must indicate various data about the participants in the plan and the form and amount of benefits provided to each of them.

Notice of Inability to Determine Sufficiency. If the PBGC cannot issue a Notice of Sufficiency to a plan administrator, it will issue a Notice of Inability to Determine Sufficiency. If a Notice of Sufficiency is issued based upon the estimated value of assets and benefits, but the plan administrator later discovers that the value of plan assets is less than the value of guaranteed vested benefits, the plan administrator must take no further action to close out the plan. Instead the plan administrator must notify the PBGC and the Notice of Sufficiency will be revoked. In either case, the PBGC must proceed to place the plan in trusteeship and the plan administrator may take no further action with regard to the plan termination.[9]

Employer Liability. If plan assets are not sufficient to fund guaranteed vested benefits under the plan, the PBGC will provide these benefits. The employer will have liability to the PBGC to the extent that the actuarial present value of the guaranteed vested benefits (determined on the basis of PBGC-prescribed actuarial assumptions) exceeds plan assets, as of the date of plan termination. However, this liability cannot exceed 30 percent of the net worth of the employer.[10] The "employer" is defined by the PBGC to include all trades or businesses, whether or not incorporated, which are under common control with the entity maintaining the plan. Common control is generally determined under an 80 percent control test. So if a parent corporation maintaining a plan owns 90 percent of the stock of a subsidiary, the assets of the subsidiary are aggregated with the assets of the parent in order to apply the 30 percent of net worth limitation. The 30 percent limitation must be affirmatively asserted by the employer in a notice to the PBGC within thirty days after the establishment of the date of plan termination.

The view of the PBGC on the definition of employer has some support in the legislative history, but is currently being litigated. Initially, one court

---

[9] ERISA §§ 4041(c), 4041(e).
[10] ERISA § 4062.

decision held that the broad definition of "employer" advocated by the PBGC would conflict with other provisions of Section 4062 of ERISA. However, this decision has been reversed on the basis that there is no conflict within the statutory language and that Section 4001(b) of ERISA states that "employer" includes other entities under common control with the employer.[11]

As soon as the PBGC determines the amount of employer liability, it will generally notify the employer and set a date for payment in the notification letter. If payment is not made, a demand letter will be issued. Upon a showing of hardship, an employer may be permitted to pay on an installment basis.

Lien. If payment is not made pursuant to a demand letter, the PBGC has a lien in the amount of the employer's liability, plus interest, arising as of the date of plan termination, on all property of the employer. The priority of a PBGC lien is determined in the same way as a federal tax lien.[12]

Voluntary Termination of Multiple-Employer Plan

A multiple-employer plan is a plan covered under Title IV of ERISA that is maintained by more than one trade, business, or corporation not under common control. For purposes of this discussion, *multi*employer plans are excluded.

Procedure. The procedures for voluntary termination are the same as those for single-employer plans. However, employer liability is treated differently.

Employer Liability. When a multiple-employer plan terminates and plan assets are not sufficient to cover the actuarial present value of guaranteed vested benefits, the total plan liability is apportioned among the employers who have maintained the plan during the five plan years ending before plan termination. Each employer's share of the liability is as follows:

$$\text{Total Liability} \times \frac{\text{Employer's required contributions during the five plan years ending before termination}}{\text{All required contributions during such period}}$$

The 30 percent of net worth limitation is applied to each employer separately.[13]

---

[11] PBGC v. Avon Sole Co., 138 Pens. Rep. (BNA) D-3 (D. Mass. (Bankr.) 1977), *rev'd sub nom.* PBGC v. Ouimet Corp., 470 F. Supp. 945, 233 Pens. Rep. (BNA) D-1 (D. Mass. 1979), *aff'd* 630 F.2d 4 (1st Cir. 1980), *cert. denied* 101 S. Ct. 1356 (1981).

[12] ERISA § 4068(c).

[13] ERISA § 4064.

Voluntary Termination of Multiemployer Plan

Under the Multiemployer Pension Plan Amendments Act of 1980, a multiemployer plan is defined as a collectively bargained plan to which more than one employer is required to contribute and which satisfies other regulatory requirements of the Department of Labor.[14]

Procedure. Under the Multiemployer Pension Plan Amendments Act of 1980, a multiemployer plan will terminate if a plan amendment ceases crediting service for all purposes or changes the plan into a defined contribution plan, or if all employers withdraw from the plan.[15] The plan sponsor of a plan terminated by employer withdrawal must limit the payment of benefits to those that are vested as of the termination date and must generally pay benefits in the form of an annuity unless all vested benefits are to be cashed-out in the process of termination.[16] In the case of a plan terminated by employer withdrawal, vested benefits accrued under a plan or amendment adopted after March 26, 1980 which are not guaranteed by the PBGC because such benefits were not effective for at least five years must be reduced if their value exceeds assets.[17] If a plan is terminated by employer withdrawal, each employer must continue to make plan contributions under the withdrawal liability rules.[18] If a plan is terminated by amendment, each employer must also continue to make plan contributions.[19] The PBGC will pay benefits under a multiemployer plan only in the event of plan insolvency that occurs when a plan's available resources are not sufficient to pay benefits under the plan when due for the plan year.[20]

Guaranteed Benefits. In the case of an insolvent plan, the PBGC will guarantee a monthly benefit equal to 100 percent of the accrual rate (generally, a participant's monthly plan benefit divided by years of service for benefit accrual purposes) up to $5 plus 75 percent of the lesser of $15 or the accrual rate, if any, which exceeds $5, multiplied by a participant's years of service for benefit accrual purposes. If a plan has previously reduced or suspended benefits and is insolvent before the year 2000, the 75 percent multiplier above is replaced by a 65 percent multiplier unless certain funding standards have been satisfied.[21] A benefit or benefit increase must have been in effect for at least five years in order to be guaranteed.[22] Guaranteed benefits for substantial owners are subject to the same phase-in rules as are

---

[14] ERISA § 3(37).
[15] ERISA § 4041A.
[16] *Id.*
[17] ERISA § 4281.
[18] ERISA § 4201.
[19] ERISA § 4041A(e).
[20] ERISA § 4022A.
[21] ERISA § 4022A(c)(2).
[22] ERISA § 4022A(b).

applicable in the case of single-employer plans.[23] The actuarial value of benefits guaranteed on behalf of a person under all plans cannot exceed the actuarial value of a life annuity commencing at age 65 in an amount determined under a statutory formula which is currently $1,261.36 per month in 1981.[24]

In the case of a participant or beneficiary under a multiemployer plan who is in pay status on July 29, 1980 or who is within thirty-six months of normal retirement age and has a vested benefit as of that date, the PBGC will guarantee benefits under the single-employer plan rules, except where a plan has been terminated by a withdrawal of all employers.[25]

Involuntary Termination by the Pension Benefit Guaranty Corporation

The PBGC is authorized to seek a court order terminating a covered plan if the plan has not satisfied the minimum funding standards imposed by law, the plan is unable to pay benefits when due, certain distributions have been made to substantial owners by a plan with unfunded vested benefits, or the possible long-run loss to the PBGC under the plan can be expected to increase unreasonably.[26]

INTERNAL REVENUE SERVICE CONSIDERATIONS

Full Vesting

Upon termination of a tax-qualified pension, profit-sharing, or stock bonus plan, all accrued benefits under the plan, to the extent then funded, become fully vested and nonforfeitable.[27]

Permanency

The termination of a tax-qualified plan may indicate that from its inception it was not intended to be a permanent program required of all tax-qualified plans.[28] This would apply where a plan is terminated shortly after benefits for highly compensated employees are fully funded. This could result in the retroactive disqualification of the plan.

Prohibition Against Discrimination. A tax-qualified plan may not discriminate in favor of officers, shareholders, or highly compensated em-

---

23 ERISA § 4022A(e).
24 ERISA § 4022B.
25 ERISA § 4022A(h).
26 ERISA § 4042.
27 I.R.C. § 411(d)(3).
28 Treas. Reg. § 1.401-1(b)(2).

ployees.[29] This prohibition applies in connection with the termination of a plan.

Early Termination Rules. In order to mitigate possible discrimination, a tax-qualified defined benefit pension plan must include provisions restricting the use of employer contributions to provide benefits for any employee who is among the twenty-five highest paid employees (the "restricted employees") at the time the plan is established and whose annual pension exceeds $1,500.[30] The restrictions only apply if (1) the plan is terminated within ten years after its establishment, (2) the benefits of a restricted employee become payable within ten years after the plan is established, (this restriction continues until the plan has existed for ten years if full current costs for the ten years are funded, and if not, until such costs are funded), or (3) the benefits of a restricted employee become payable after the plan has been in effect for ten years and the full current costs of the plan for the first ten years have not been funded (this restriction continues until such costs are funded).

The restrictions must provide that employer contributions used to provide benefits for a restricted employee may not exceed the greater of (a) $20,000; or (b) 20 percent of the first $50,000 of annual compensation of the restricted employee multiplied by the number of years between the date that the plan was established and (corresponding to the numbers above) (1) the date of plan termination; (2) the date benefits became payable to the restricted employee; or (3) the date of the failure to meet the full current costs of the plan. If the condition in (3) exists on the date in (1) or (2), it will apply instead.

The restrictions do not apply to the payment of current retirement income in the form of a level amount annuity in the basic form or a lesser optional form under the plan.

The restrictions apply at the time of establishment of the plan and again at any date that the plan has been changed so as to substantially increase potential discrimination resulting from subsequent plan termination or cessation of contributions. This would apply to an amendment substantially increasing benefits.

Asset Allocation Rules. Upon plan termination, assets that would be allocated to fund benefits within priority categories lower than the category relating to benefits guaranteed by the PBGC can be reallocated in order to avoid discrimination.[31] If a plan terminates with assets less than the actuarial present value of accrued benefits, reallocation will be required where necessary in order for rank-and-file employees to receive the same proportion of the actuarial present value of their accrued benefits as officers, shareholders,

---

[29] I.R.C. § 401(a)(4).
[30] Treas. Reg. § 1.401-4(c).
[31] ERISA § 4044(b)(4).

or highly compensated employees. If a plan terminates with assets in excess of the actuarial present value of accrued benefits and the plan does not provide for a reversion of the surplus assets to the employer, the surplus assets must be applied to increase benefits in a manner that does not discriminate in favor of officers, shareholders, or highly compensated employees.

Determination Letters for Complete Termination

The IRS will issue a determination letter with respect to a plan that has terminated. This will insure that the termination does not retroactively disqualify the plan. As in the case of other determination letters, a Notice to Interested Parties must be distributed. An application for a determination letter is made on IRS Form 5310 and its accompanying Schedule A. Form 5310 requires information about the employer, the plan, plan participants, trust assets, and amounts to be distributed.

Partial Termination

A partial termination occurs when a group of employees who were once covered by a tax-qualified plan cease to be covered as a result of a plan amendment or termination of service by the employer. It also occurs when a plan amendment makes vesting more restrictive.[32] A partial termination occurs also where a defined benefit pension plan ceases or decreases future benefit accruals under the plan if a potential reversion to the employer is created or increased.[33] In the case of a partial termination, the full vesting rule applies to the benefits of each affected employee (but not other employees) accrued to the date of the partial termination, to the extent such benefits are then funded.[34] Benefits subject to the full vesting rule may be restricted to the portion of the benefits deemed terminated.[35] Thus, if a benefit accrual formula is prospectively reduced from $10 per year of credited service to $9 per year of credited service, the full vesting rule should apply only to $1 per year of credited service.

A determination letter with respect to a partial plan termination can be obtained in the same manner as other determination letters. Forms 5300, 5301, 5302, and 5303 should be used where applicable in the case of a partial termination.

If a defined benefit plan is partially terminated and distributes assets to certain participants in a "qualifying rollover distribution" (as defined in Section 402 of the Code) the PBGC must be notified.[36] Such a distribution may occur in connection with a business divestiture. The PBGC has not prescribed any form for the notification.

---

[32] Treas. Reg. § 1.411(d)-2(b)(1).
[33] Treas. Reg. § 1.411(d)-2(b)(2).
[34] Treas. Reg. § 1.411(d)-2(a)(1).
[35] Treas. Reg. § 1.411(d)-2(b)(3).
[36] I.R.C. § 401(a)(20).

OTHER DUTIES OF TERMINATED PLANS

Summary Plan Descriptions

The duty to file a summary plan description with the Department of Labor and distribute it to plan participants ends when there are no longer any plan participants. This occurs when the entire benefit rights of an individual are guaranteed by an insurance company that has issued a contract, policy, or certificate to the individual, or the individual has received a lump-sum distribution of cash or property representing the balance to the credit of the individual under the plan.

Annual Reports and Summary Annual Reports

The duty to file an annual report with the IRS and to distribute a summary annual report to plan participants ends when all assets have been distributed to participants after plan termination. The annual report for the plan year in which all assets are distributed is to be marked "Final Return" at the top.

Payment of Premiums to the Pension Benefit Guaranty Corporation

The duty to pay premiums to the PBGC with respect to a defined benefit pension plan covered by Title IV of ERISA continues until plan assets are distributed under a termination procedure.

Notification of Change in Status

A plan administrator of a tax-qualified plan that files Schedule SSA as an attachment to annual reports with the IRS must notify the IRS that the plan has terminated.[37] This is satisfied by the filing of an annual report on Form 5500 series indicating that the plan has been terminated.

---

[37] I.R.C. § 6057(b).

Merger and Spinoff Requirements

Bruce Alan Miller
Legal Division, W.R. Grace & Co.

INTRODUCTION

A merger of plan assets and liabilities involves the combination of the assets and liabilities (benefits owed to participants) of two or more single plans so that the assets which previously related to a single plan become available to pay benefit liabilities to all participants in the combined plan which results from the merger.

Conversely, spinoff of plan assets and liabilities involves the division of the assets and liabilities (benefits owed to participants) of an original single plan between such plan and one or more new single plans so that not all of the assets which previously related to an original single plan are available to pay benefit liabilities under such plan. Instead, the original single plan and each new single plan has its own separate assets to cover the benefits of participants in that plan only.

LEGAL BACKGROUND

Statutory Law

Section 414(*l*) of the Internal Revenue Code and Section 208 of ERISA are the statutory provisions governing mergers and spinoffs of plan assets and liabilities for tax-qualified pension, profit-sharing, and stock bonus plans and nonqualified plans of the same types. However, these statutory provisions do not apply to multiemployer plans, governmental plans, church plans that have not elected to be subject to the basic qualification requirements of the Code, plans for nonresident aliens, excess benefit plans, plans to comply with workers' compensation, unemployment compensation, and disability insurance laws, unfunded deferred compensation plans for highly compensated employees, and certain other plans.[1] Mergers and spinoffs of multiemployer plans are governed by Sections 4231–4235 of ERISA added by the Multiemployer Pension Plan Amendments Act of 1980.

Section 401(a)(12) of the Code requires that a provision be set forth in tax-qualified plans (other than multiemployer plans) referring to the principles of law that govern mergers.

---

[1] I.R.C. § 414(*l*); ERISA §§ 208, 4(b), 201.

Section 414(*l*) of the Code and Section 208 of ERISA apply to mergers and spinoffs of plan assets and liabilities occurring after September 2, 1974. Section 401(a)(12) applies to plan years beginning on or after January 1, 1976, unless the plan was not in existence on January 1, 1974. In that case, it applies to plan years beginning after September 2, 1974.[2] Sections 4231–4235 of ERISA apply to mergers and spinoffs of plan assets and liabilities of multiemployer plans occurring on or after September 26, 1980.[3]

Regulatory Law

On August 17, 1979, the Internal Revenue Service issued final regulations under Sections 414(*l*) and 401(a)(12) of the Code. The regulations, which are denominated Treas. Reg. §§ 1.414(1)-1 and 1.401(a)-12, set forth the governing legal principles for mergers and spinoffs of plan assets and liabilities. However, the rules that apply to multiemployer plans are different and will be discussed at the end of this chapter.

Governing Legal Rules

In connection with any merger or spinoff of plan assets or liabilities, each participant in any plan involved must be entitled to receive a benefit immediately after the merger or spinoff, under the assumption that such plan then terminated, which is equal to or greater than the benefit he would have been entitled to receive immediately before the merger or spinoff, under the assumption that such plan had then terminated. The assumption of plan termination is important because it means that plan vesting schedules are not relevant in determining the benefit to which a participant is entitled. In the case of a defined benefit plan, it also means that the termination priorities of Section 4044 of ERISA must be examined in order to determine the level of funding of a particular plan and the benefits of participants in the plan. The essence of the merger and spinoff requirements concerns dilution of assets held to fund accrued benefits. Merger and spinoff transactions must not dilute the plan assets held to fund benefits of participants to an extent that violates the regulations.

Single Plan

The legal rules governing a merger or spinoff of plan assets or liabilities are applicable only where assets held by one single plan are merged with the assets of another single plan. Therefore, it is important to determine whether a single plan exists. A plan is regarded as a single plan even though any of the following features or conditions exists:

---

[2] ERISA § 1017.
[3] ERISA § 4402(e)(1).

1. The plan has several documents;
2. The plan is funded wholly or partially by insurance contracts allocated to participants;
3. The plan has different benefit structures that apply to the same or different participants;
4. The plan has assets invested in several trusts or annuity contracts;
5. The plan is maintained by multiple employers, whether or not affiliated;
6. The plan is maintained using separate accounting for cost allocation but not for provision of benefits;
7. The employer maintaining the plan engages in a business reorganization such as a merger or stock or assets acquisition, whether or not taxable;
8. A successor employer assumes the plan and moves all the plan assets to a new trust;
9. The plan assets are commingled with those of other plans for investment purposes.[4]

The essential element of a single plan is that the assets of that plan are available to pay benefits to participants in that plan, and not to anyone else.

MERGER OF PLAN ASSETS AND LIABILITIES

Defined Benefit Plans

Step-by-Step Analysis. Various steps must be undertaken to analyze the level of funding of the single plans to be merged in order to determine whether the governing legal principles discussed above are satisfied with respect to a merger of plan assets and liabilities. Detailed analysis of an example given in the regulations of the IRS will help in understanding how this works.

1. The value of the assets available to pay benefits under each single plan must be calculated based on standards set by the Pension Benefit Guaranty Corporation (PBGC).[5] In the example, Single Plan *A* has $220,000 of assets and Single Plan *B* has $200,000 of assets.

2. The actuarial present value of accrued benefits, whether or not vested, that are owed to all participants in each single plan must be calculated as if the plan had terminated. The calculation of the actuarial present value of an accrued benefit must be based on reasonable actuarial assumptions. For this purpose, the assumptions used by the PBGC as of the date of the merger are deemed reasonable.[6] In the example, the actuarial present value of accrued benefits under Single Plan *A* is $271,000 and the actuarial present value of accrued benefits under Single Plan *B* is $325,000.

[4] Treas. Reg. §§ 1.414(1)-1(b)(1), 1.414(1)-1(b)(2), 1.414(1)-1(b)(3).
[5] Treas. Reg. § 1.414(1)-1(b)(10).
[6] Treas. Reg. § 1.414(1)-1(b)(9).

3. The sum of the value of the assets of the two single plans to be merged is compared with the sum of the actuarial present value of the accrued benefits under the two single plans to be merged. If the combined assets are greater than the combined actuarial present value of accrued benefits, the assets can be merged and each participant's accrued benefit will be preserved under the combined plan.[7] The focus on whether combined assets will suffice to cover combined accrued benefits means that an "overfunded" single plan (the plan whose assets exceed the actuarial present value of accrued benefits) may be "subsidizing" an "underfunded" single plan (the plan whose assets are less than the actuarial present value of accrued benefits). Thus, under the regulations, this dilution of the assets held to pay benefits under the overfunded single plan is permitted since the actuarial present value of accrued benefits under that single plan is still fully covered by plan assets after the merger. Nevertheless, all or part of the surplus of the overfunded single plan will have been siphoned off by the underfunded single plan. In the example, the combined plan assets are $420,000 and the combined actuarial present value of accrued benefits is $596,000.

Section 401(a)(2) of the Code sets forth the rule that the assets of a tax-qualified plan must not be diverted to any purpose other than for the exclusive benefit of employees prior to plan termination. This has been interpreted to prohibit the transfer of assets from an overfunded plan to an underfunded plan on the basis that the employees referred to in Section 401(a)(2) of the Code are those employees covered under a specific plan, not all employees in the aggregate. It is not clear whether this interpretation made under pre-ERISA law survives the enactment of Section 414(*l*) of the Code and the regulations thereunder. It is arguable that Section 414(*l*) of the Code fills the field of requirements regarding mergers and spinoffs of plan assets and liabilities. Therefore, Section 401(a)(2) of the Code may no longer have any role to play. Alternatively, it is possible that since Section 414(*l*) of the Code calculates plan benefits based on an assumption that each plan has terminated, such assumption may be carried over to Section 401(a)(2). Under this view, one pretends that the plans have terminated, and hence the disposition of any surplus in existence at the time of a merger of plan assets of two single plans can be determined by the employer (as would be the case if the plans really had terminated). Arguably, the surplus may be used for the benefit of participants in the combined plan who were formerly covered by the underfunded plan.

4. In the example, there is a deficiency since the combined plan assets are equal to $420,000 and the combined actuarial present value of accrued benefits is equal to $596,000. Where a deficiency exists, a special schedule of benefits must be prepared or data must be maintained so that such schedule can be prepared if necessary. The special schedule is necessary to prevent

---

[7] Treas. Reg. § 1.414(1)-1(e)(1).

improper dilution of the assets held to fund benefits under the better-funded single plan. If the special schedule were not used, the benefits provided on a termination basis under the combined plan after merger would be different from the benefits provided on a termination basis under the plans prior to merger. Some participants would receive greater benefits on a termination basis as a result of the merger and others would receive smaller benefits. The special schedule is designed to prevent this from happening upon any future plan termination or spinoff.

Special Schedule for Plan A. All of the assets held to pay benefits under Plan *A* ($220,000) must be allocated to the benefit categories applicable upon plan termination under Section 4044 of ERISA. These categories represent a rank-order scheme that determines where assets go first in order to fund particular benefits. Beginning with the benefit category that has the highest priority (that is, the first claim on plan assets), the categories are as follows:

1. Benefits attributable to voluntary employee contributions;
2. Benefits attributable to mandatory employee contributions;
3. Benefits that are or could be in payout status to certain retirees;
4. Benefits generally guaranteed by the PBGC;
5. Benefits that are vested (other than by reason of plan termination);
6. All other benefits under the plan.

Assets must be allocated to the highest category first and thereafter to each lower category until assets run out.

Plan *A* has three participants ("EE_1," "EE_2," and "EE_3"). The annual accrued benefit of EE_1 is $12,000 of which $10,000 falls into Category (3) above and $2,000 falls into Category (4) above. The annual accrued benefit of EE_2 is $7,000 of which $4,000 falls into Category (4) above and $3,000 falls into Category (5). The annual accrued benefit of EE_3 is $5,000 of which $4,000 falls into Category (5) above and $1,000 falls into Category (6). Each piece of the annual accrued benefit of each employee has an actuarial present value set forth below.

Plan *A*

Priority Category of Section 4044 of ERISA	*Annual Accrued Benefits*			*Present Value of Accrued Benefits*		
	EE_1	EE_2	EE_3	EE_1	EE_2	EE_3
3	$10,000			$120,000		
4	2,000	$4,000		24,000	$44,000	
5		3,000	$4,000		33,000	$40,000
6			1,000			10,000

Plan *A* has \$220,000 of assets to cover the actuarial present value of accrued benefits. \$120,000 is used to cover benefits in Category (3). \$68,000 is used to cover benefits in Category (4). But only \$32,000 is available (out of \$73,000 necessary) to cover benefits in Category (5). No assets are available (out of \$10,000 necessary) to cover benefits in Category (6). Because assets are exhausted in Category (5), EE_2 and EE_3 may receive only part of their Category (5) benefits. Assuming that the special rule of Section 4044(b)(3) of ERISA does not apply since it is not referred to in the regulations that govern the special schedule, the \$3,000 of EE_2 is multiplied by a fraction whose numerator is \$32,000 (the assets available for Category (5)) and whose denominator is \$73,000 (the assets necessary to satisfy Category (5)). Thus, EE_2 has a Category (5) benefit of \$1,315 and EE_3 has a Category (5) benefit of \$1,753. So under Plan *A*, each participant has the following accrued benefit computed on a termination basis:

Priority Category of Section 4044 of ERISA	*Benefits on a Termination Basis*		
	EE_1	EE_2	EE_3
3	\$10,000		
4	2,000	\$4,000	
5		1,315	\$1,753
6			
	\$12,000	\$5,315	\$1,753

Special Schedule for Plan *B*. All of the assets held to pay benefits under Plan *B* (\$200,000) must similarly be allocated to the benefit categories applicable upon plan termination. Plan *B* has two participants ("EE_4" and "EE_5"). The annual accrued benefit of EE_4 is \$15,000, all of which falls into Category (3) above. The annual accrued benefit of EE_5 is \$13,000 of which \$5,000 falls into Category (4) above and \$8,000 falls into Category (5) above. Each piece of the annual accrued benefit for each employee has an actuarial present value set forth below.

Plan *B*

Priority Category of Section 4044 of ERISA	*Annual Accrued Benefits*		*Present Value of Accrued Benefits*	
	EE_4	EE_5	EE_4	EE_5
3	\$15,000		\$195,000	
4		\$5,000		\$50,000
5		8,000		80,000
6				

Plan *B* has $200,000 of assets to cover the actuarial present value of accrued benefits. $195,000 is used to cover benefits in Category (3). But only $5,000 is available (out of $50,000 necessary) to cover benefits in Category (4). No assets are available (out of $80,000 necessary) to cover benefits in Category (5). Because assets are exhausted in Category (4), EE_5 may receive only part of his Category (4) benefit. The $5,000 of EE_5 is multiplied by a fraction of $5,000/$50,000, which is the ratio of assets available to assets necessary to satisfy benefits in Category (4). Thus, EE_5 has a Category (4) benefit of $500. So under Plan *B*, each participant has the following accrued benefit computed on a termination basis:

Priority Category of Section 4044 of ERISA	*Benefits on a Termination Basis*	
	EE_4	EE_5
3	$15,000	
4		$500
5		
6		
	$15,000	$500

The assets of Plan *A* run out in Category (5) and the assets of Plan *B* run out in Category (4). So Plan *A* is the better-funded plan, since assets cover more categories of benefits.

Special Schedule for Combined Plan After Merger. The assets of the combined plan after merger must be allocated first to the benefit categories fully satisfied by the less well-funded plan, Plan *B*. The only relevant category here is Category (3), and EE_1 is entitled to a $10,000 benefit in this category from Plan *A* on a termination basis before the merger and EE_4 is entitled to a $15,000 benefit in this category from Plan *B* on a termination basis before the merger.

As noted above, Plan *B*'s assets run out in Category (4) and within that category only 10 percent of the accrued benefits could be provided on a termination basis ($5,000 of assets available divided by $50,000 of assets necessary to satisfy Category (4)). Thus, each participant in the combined plan after merger is credited with 10 percent of his Category (4) benefits. So each participant is entitled to the accrued benefits indicated in Column (4) below. At this point, the funding of categories of benefits under the combined plan after merger is equal for the participants formerly covered by Plan *A* and Plan *B*. If the assets of the combined plan were further allocated without a special schedule, EE_1, EE_2, and EE_3 would be cheated because of the diversion of assets formerly held by Plan *A* from them to EE_4 and EE_5. So each participant formerly covered by Plan *A* is entitled to a special benefit equal to the benefit that would have been provided to him on a termination basis before the merger, minus the benefit provided to him through 10 percent of Category (4), the point of equal funding. This special benefit is indicated in Column (5) below.

EE	(1) *Benefits on a Termination Basis Before Merger*	(2) *Benefits Provided From Priority Categories Higher Than Category 4*	(3) *10% of Benefits Provided in Priority Category 4*	(4) *Benefits Provided Before Schedule (2) + (3)*	(5) *Schedule of Benefits (1) − (4)*
1	$12,000	$10,000	$200	$10,200	$1,800
2	5,315		400	400	4,915
3	1,753				1,753
4	15,000	15,000		15,000	
5	500		500	500	

If the combined plan terminates one year later with no change in accrued benefits (except that the $2,000 benefit of EE_1 which was originally in Category (4) has moved to Category (3)), assets of the combined plan would be allocated first to benefits up to the point of equal funding described above, then to the benefits on the special schedule for participants formerly covered by Plan *A* (separated by benefit category), then to the remaining benefits of all participants (separated by benefit category), until assets run out. The chart below illustrates the priority of allocation of assets to fund benefits for each participant under the combined plan upon termination. The first two rows go to the point of equal funding described above. The next three rows are the special schedule benefits, and the final three rows are all remaining benefits not subject to the special schedule. EE_1 is entitled to an annual accrued benefit of $12,000, all of which is in Category (3) at the time of plan termination. EE_2 is entitled to an annual accrued benefit of $7,000 of which $4,000 is in Category (4). Ten percent of that $4,000 goes to the point of equal funding and the balance of $3,600 is part of the benefit on the special schedule. $3,000 of the annual accrued benefit is in Category (5) and $1,315 is part of the benefit on the special schedule. The balance of $1,685 is the remaining accrued benefit. EE_3 is entitled to an annual accrued benefit of $5,000 of which $4,000 is in Category (5). $1,753 of that $4,000 is the benefit on the special schedule. $2,247 is the remaining accrued benefit in Category (5) and $1,000 is the remaining accrued benefit in Category (6).

Priority Termination Category	EE_1	EE_2	EE_3	EE_4	EE_5
3	$12,000			$15,000	
10% of 4		$ 400			$ 500
Schedule of benefits included in balance of Category (4)		3,600			
Schedule of benefits included in Category (5)		1,315	$1,753		
Schedule of benefits included in Category (6)					
Balance of Category (4) not included in schedule					4,500
Balance of Category (5) not included in schedule		1,685	2,247		8,000
Balance of Category (6) not included in schedule			1,000		

Data Maintenance. A special schedule need not be prepared if data is maintained so that it can be prepared if needed in the future.[8] An enrolled actuary must certify to the plan administrator that the necessary data is being maintained.[9]

Five-Year Limitation. A special schedule in a merger, or the data necessary to prepare such a schedule, can be disregarded after five years from the date of the merger.[10]

Small Mergers. A small defined benefit plan and a large defined benefit plan can be merged under a special rule. The special rule applies if the actuarial present value of accrued benefits under the small plan is less than 3 percent of the plan assets of the large plan determined on at least one day of the plan year in which the merger occurs. If applicable, the special rule requires that the benefits under the small plan that would be provided on a termination basis before the merger must be regarded as a priority category higher than any other category under Section 4044 of ERISA.[11] The special rule can be disregarded after five years.[12] All mergers occurring during a plan year are aggregated to determine if the 3 percent threshold above is exceeded.[13]

---

[8] Treas. Reg. § 1.414(1)-1(i)(1).
[9] Treas. Reg. § 1.414(1)-1(i)(2).
[10] Treas. Reg. § 1.414(1)-1(j)(1).
[11] Treas. Reg. § 1.414(1)-1(h)(1).
[12] Treas. Reg. § 1.414(1)-1(j)(1).
[13] Treas. Reg. § 1.414(1)-1(h)(2).

Defined Contribution Plans

Consider two defined contribution plans to be merged. The account balances of participants in Plan *C* and Plan *D* are as follows:

Plan *C*			Plan *D*		
EE_6	EE_7	EE_8	EE_8	EE_9	EE_{10}
$5,000	$4,000	$8,000	$2,000	$2,500	$4,000

Step-by-Step Analysis. (1) The sum of the account balances in Plan *C* must equal the fair market value of all the plan assets on the date of the merger.[14] Thus, the assets of Plan *C* must be worth $17,000. Similarly, the assets of Plan *D* must be worth $8,500. If any plan assets are not allocated to an account (as where a suspense account is maintained to hold excess contributions under Section 415 of the Code), the applicable rule cannot be satisfied. However, the preamble to Treas. Reg. § 1.414(1)-1 states that the rules contained in the regulations are intended to be a safe harbor. Therefore, a merger should still be possible even if the rule above is not satisfied.

(2) The assets of Plan *C* and Plan *D* must be combined to form the assets of the combined plan after merger.[15]

(3) After the merger, each participant in the combined plan must have an account balance equal to his balance in Plan *C* and/or Plan *D* before the merger. Therefore, EE_6 must have a balance of $5,000; EE_7, $4,000; EE_8, $10,000 (since he had a balance in both Plan *C* and Plan *D*); EE_9, $2,500; EE_{10}, $4,000. This requirement prevents improper dilution of the assets in a participant's account due to the merger.[16]

SPINOFF OF PLAN ASSETS AND LIABILITIES

Defined Benefit Plans

Consider a defined benefit plan prior to a spinoff. The participants, their annual accrued benefits, and the actuarial present value of their accrued benefits (divided by benefit category) are set forth below. It is desired to separate a new plan (Plan *F*) from the original plan (Plan *E*). Plan *E* will continue to cover EE_{11} and EE_{13} and their accrued benefits. Plan *F* will cover EE_{12} and his accrued benefit.

---

[14] Treas. Reg. § 1.414(1)-1(d)(1).
[15] Treas. Reg. § 1.414(1)-1(d)(2).
[16] Treas. Reg. § 1.414(1)-1(d)(3).

Priority Category of Section 4044 of ERISA	*Annual Accrued Benefits*			*Present Value of Accrued Benefits*		
	EE_{11}	EE_{12}	EE_{13}	EE_{11}	EE_{12}	EE_{13}
3	$6,000			$72,000		
4		$5,000			$55,000	
5		$4,000			$44,000	
6		$1,000	$2,000		$11,000	$20,000

Step-by-Step Analysis. (1) The accrued benefit of each participant must be allocated to either Plan *E* or Plan *F*.[17] As noted above, the accrued benefits of EE_{11} and EE_{13} will be allocated to Plan *E*, and the accrued benefit of EE_{12} will be allocated to Plan *F*.

(2) The assets allocated to Plan *E* must be not less than the actuarial present value of the accrued benefits of EE_{11} and EE_{13} on a termination basis before the spinoff. The assets allocated to Plan *F* must be not less than the actuarial present value of the accrued benefit of EE_{12} on a termination basis before the spinoff.[18]

(3) To calculate the actuarial present value of an accrued benefit on a termination basis before the spinoff, the value of plan assets must be determined. If the original plan prior to the spinoff has assets greater than $202,000, there will be sufficient assets to cover the actuarial present value of the accrued benefits of all participants. Under such circumstances, Plan *E* should receive assets equal to $92,000 (the actuarial present value of the accrued benefits of EE_{11} and EE_{13}) and Plan *F* should receive assets equal to $110,000 (the actuarial present value of the accrued benefit of EE_{12}). If assets exceed $202,000, there is a surplus that presumably remains with the original plan. The regulations make no reference to the disposition of the surplus. The rules for determining the value of plan assets and the actuarial present value of accrued benefits are the same as those described above with reference to the merger of plan assets and liabilities of defined benefit plans.

(4) If the value of plan assets is only $150,000, which is less than the actuarial present value of the accrued benefits of all participants in the original plan, there is a deficiency and it is necessary to allocate the assets to fund the accrued benefits of participants according to the benefit categories applicable upon plan termination under Section 4044 of ERISA. These categories have been described above in connection with the special schedule required upon the merger of defined benefit plans. As noted above, these categories represent a rank-order scheme that determines where assets go first in order to fund particular benefits. The $150,000 of plan assets can cover $72,000 of the Category (3) accrued benefit of EE_{11}; $55,000 of

[17] Treas. Reg. § 1.414(1)-1(n)(1)(i).
[18] Treas. Reg. § 1.414(1)-1(n)(1)(ii).

the Category (4) accrued benefit of EE_{12}; and \$23,000 (out of \$44,000) of the Category (5) accrued benefit of EE_{12}. At this point, the \$150,000 is exhausted. No assets are available to be allocated to fund the remainder of the Category (5) accrued benefit of EE_{12}, or the Category (6) accrued benefits of EE_{12} and EE_{13}. Since EE_{11} and EE_{13} and their accrued benefits will be covered by Plan *E* after the spinoff, Plan *E* must receive \$72,000 relating to the accrued benefit of EE_{11} and \$0 relating to the accrued benefit of EE_{13}. Plan *F* must receive \$78,000 relating to the accrued benefit of EE_{12}.

Small Spinoffs. A small spinoff from a large defined benefit plan can occur under a special rule. The special rule applies if all assets transferred in spinoffs by a single plan during the plan year in which a particular spinoff occurs are less than 3 percent of total plan assets determined on at least one day of the plan year.[19] If applicable, the special rule requires that the assets transferred must equal the actuarial present value of the accrued benefits (whether or not vested) transferred in the spinoff.[20] The IRS has determined that small spinoffs do not improperly dilute the assets held to fund the benefits of participants who remain behind in the original plan.

Defined Contribution Plans

Consider a defined contribution plan prior to a spinoff. The account balances of participants are set forth below. It is desired to separate a new plan (Plan *H*) from the original plan (Plan *G*). Plan *G* will continue to cover EE_{14} and EE_{15}. Plan *H* will cover EE_{16} and EE_{17}.

Account Balances Under Original Plan

EE_{14}	EE_{15}	EE_{16}	EE_{17}
\$4,000	\$6,000	\$10,000	\$2,000

Step-by-Step Analysis. (1) The account balance of each participant in Plan *G* and Plan *H* must equal his existing account balance under the original plan.[21] Thus, EE_{14} must have an account balance under Plan *G* or Plan *H*, or both, equal to his existing account balance of \$4,000. This requirement prevents improper dilution of the assets in a participant's account as a result of a spinoff.

(2) The assets held by Plan *G* after the spinoff must equal the sum of the account balances for all participants in Plan *G* after the spinoff. The same rule applies to Plan *H*.[22] Thus, the assets held by Plan *G* must be \$10,000, the sum of the account balances of EE_{14} and EE_{15} and the assets held by Plan *H* must be \$12,000, the sum of the account balances of EE_{16} and EE_{17}.

---

19 Treas. Reg. § 1.414(1)-1(n)(2).
20 Treas. Reg. § 1.414(1)-1(n)(2).
21 Treas. Reg. § 1.414(1)-1(m)(1).
22 Treas. Reg. § 1.414(1)-1(m)(2).

NOTICE TO INTERNAL REVENUE SERVICE

A notice on IRS Form 5310 must be given to the IRS at least thirty days before a merger or spinoff of plan assets or liabilities.[23] The notice is sent to the Office of the District Director, not the Service Center. An actuary's certificate must accompany any notice relating to a defined benefit plan. The certificate, for which no special form is prescribed, must state that the legal requirements relating to mergers and spinoffs have been satisfied. A penalty of $10 per day, up to $5,000, is imposed for failure to file a timely notice on Form 5310, unless the failure was due to reasonable cause.[24]

MULTIEMPLOYER PLANS

Mergers

Under the provisions of ERISA added by the Multiemployer Pension Plan Amendments Act of 1980, two or more multiemployer plans may merge or engage in a transfer of assets and liabilities only if the following conditions are satisfied:

1. There is no reduction of any participant's or beneficiary's accrued benefit as a result of the merger or transfer;
2. No reduction of any accrued benefit due to plan insolvency is reasonably expected;
3. The plan sponsor has notified the PBGC of the merger or transfer at least 120 days before the merger or transfer;
4. An actuarial valuation of each plan has been performed for the plan year preceding the merger based on the most recent data available;
5. There is compliance with rules established by the multiemployer plan which must not unreasonably restrict the transfer of assets to accompany a transfer of liabilities, although variations in financial impact of various transfers may be taken into account.[25]

A merger or transfer of assets and liabilities between a multiemployer plan and a single-employer plan is subject to special rules.[26] The same is true of a transfer of assets resulting from a change in the employees' collective bargaining representative.[27]

Spinoffs

A spinoff from a multiemployer plan is permitted where the plan sponsor makes application to the PBGC for an order partitioning the plan and the

---

[23] I.R.C. § 6058(b).
[24] I.R.C. § 6652(f).
[25] ERISA §§ 4231, 4234.
[26] ERISA § 4232.
[27] ERISA § 4235.

PBGC finds that there has been or will be a substantial decrease in contributions to a plan due to employer bankruptcy, that the plan is likely to become insolvent, that a contribution increase will be necessary to prevent plan insolvency, and that partition would significantly decrease the risk of plan insolvency. The PBGC must notify the plan sponsor and affected participants of the proposed partition. Thereafter, the PBGC may permit a transfer of nonforfeitable benefits attributable to service with the bankrupt employer and an equitable share of plan assets.[28]

A spinoff from a multiemployer plan to a single-employer plan is also permitted under the following conditions:

1. There is no reduction of any participant's or beneficiary's accrued benefit as a result of the spinoff;
2. The multiemployer plan will have residual liability in certain cases if the single-employer plan terminates within five years;
3. The multiemployer plan is not in reorganization except where the PBGC has approved the transfer;
4. The plan sponsor of the single-employer plan agrees to the transfer;
5. There is compliance with the asset transfer rules described above in Paragraph (5) under "Mergers" of "Multiemployer Plans." [29]

---

[28] ERISA § 4233.
[29] ERISA §§ 4232, 4234.

15

Procedural Laws for Qualified Plans

NICHOLAS P. DAMICO
Attorney, Washington, D.C.

PROCEDURES FOR QUALIFICATION OF PLANS

Overview

The unique tax benefits of a qualified plan are best secured by obtaining a favorable determination letter from the Internal Revenue Service. Such a letter is also an important indication that the Department of Labor requirements (Title I of the Employee Retirement Income Security Act of 1974 (ERISA)) have been complied with.

An employer is not obligated by law or regulations to secure a determination letter from the IRS. However, several factors require the letter as a practical matter, including:

1. The IRS places great emphasis on the letter in any audit of the plan;
2. Other government agencies and the company's accountants may demand that the letter be obtained;
3. Any unanticipated amendments required by the IRS can be made retroactively during a "remedial amendment period" if the plan is submitted to the IRS; and
4. Both the employer and the employee can suffer severe adverse tax consequences from a disqualified plan.

A determination letter can be requested with respect to a proposed plan. The normal approach, however, is to adopt the plan first but to include a provision allowing for a return of contributions if the plan should fail to qualify.

What a Determination Letter Means

It should be noted that there are important limitations to the effectiveness of the determination letter. In general, a determination letter is valid evidence of the plan's qualified status. This is true as long as the facts upon which the letter was issued do not materially change and the applicable law remains the same. The continued qualification of the plan, however, will depend upon its actual operation.

Prior to ERISA, almost all questions presented to the IRS involved qualification (particularly discrimination) issues. The favorable determination letter was a seal of approval for most purposes. Later audits of the plan by the IRS, or complaints by participants, generally stopped at the production of the letter.

A favorable determination letter creates a presumption of compliance with similar rules in Title I (the Labor provisions) of ERISA.[1] However, the determination letter is not a full guarantee that all aspects of ERISA have been complied with. This fact puts a premium on independent close examination of ERISA requirements, as opposed to reliance on the skills of IRS examiners. For example, where a clear violation of ERISA occurs, a favorable determination letter by the IRS will not preclude a lawsuit by an affected participant.

At the same time, audits of qualified plans, by skilled technicians of the IRS, are becoming more prevalent. These audits are expected to place increased emphasis on a plan's actual operation and on its compliance with changes in regulations and rulings.

Procedural Aspects

The basic rules applicable to rulings and determination letters are contained in a series of revenue procedures, most of which have been recently re-

---

[1] ERISA § 3001(d), as amended.

stated.[2] One principal effect of these rulings has been to distinguish between those areas in which determination letters are to be sought from the district director and those areas in which rulings are to be requested from the national office. For example, under Revenue Procedure 80-24,[3] dealing with general procedures for obtaining rulings in the employee plan and exempt organization areas, taxability issues (i.e., issues of how and when a participant in a qualified plan is taxed) are handled by the national office.

The IRS rules also provide that the principal area of the district director's authority in the pension area relate to qualification of the plan, including amendments to the plan, and qualification on termination of the plan. Under Revenue Procedure 80-30, which provides the specific rules for issuing determination letters in the employee plan area [4] new rules are provided for issuing determination letters on "individually designed" plans. The principal difference from the prior rules are as follows:

1. Determination letters are now handled *only* by seventeen key districts;
2. A request for a determination letter will not be processed unless proper "notice to interested parties" has been given prior to the filing of the application; and
3. Applications for initial approval of defined contribution plans must be made on IRS Form 5301, accompanied by Form 5302. Applications for initial approval of defined benefit plans must be made on Form 5300, accompanied by Form 5302. Requests for approval of plan amendments can be made on Form 6406. If the request relates to an employee stock ownership plan, the applicant should also file Form 5309. Applications for approval of plan terminations must be made on Form 5310.

What and Where to File

A request for a determination letter should be filed with the key district director in which the employer's principal place of business is located. Revenue Procedure 80-30 contains a list of seventeen key district directors who handle all requests for determination letters on employee plans and exempt organizations. Special rules apply if all the employers are not in the same key district.[5]

Forms 5300 and 5301 contain checklists of various plan provisions and their location in the plan documents. These forms give the pension plan examiners a reference point for reviewing the plan. Form 5302 is a detailed employee census with information as to all participants, but individually as to the twenty-five highest paid participants.

The IRS has also developed (and periodically revises) a booklet entitled

---

[2] Rev. Proc. 80-20 through 80-30, 1980-1 C.B. 633 et seq.
[3] See Rev. Proc. 80-24, § 3, 1980-1 C.B. 658.
[4] 1980-1 C.B. 685.
[5] Rev. Proc. 80-30, § 4.16, 1980-1 C.B. 685.

Alert Guidelines Package to assist the IRS specialist in reviewing substantive issues.[6] The booklet contains a series of questions as well as explanations in various substantive areas including participation, vesting, and joint and survivor annuity requirements. The alert guidelines can also be used as a checklist to the practitioner who is developing a plan document. In some cases, practitioners have submitted completed alert guidelines as part of their submission as a means of accelerating the approval process.

Notice to Interested Parties

Section 3001 of ERISA requires a notice to interested parties and opportunity to comment before issuing a determination letter. Section 4.02 of Revenue Procedure 80-30 [7] provides that the notice to interested parties is a prerequisite to any application for a determination letter. Notice to interested parties is also a prerequisite for any Tax Court declaratory judgment. The regulations under Section 7476 of the Internal Revenue Code, dealing with Tax Court declaratory judgments, provide rules for determining who is an interested party for purposes of determination letter requests. The rules are discussed under "Tax Court Declaratory Judgment Proceedings," below.

Sections 6–8 of Revenue Procedure 80-30 provide specific rules for the form of the notice and the time frame in which it is to be provided. The notice must be given not less than seven nor more than twenty-one days prior to submission of the determination letter request to the IRS (ten days and twenty-four days are substituted for seven and twenty-one in the case of mailings). Revenue Procedure 80-30 provides applicable dates within which comments may be made by interested parties and contains sample notices to interested parties.

A copy of the notice to interested parties is not required to be submitted with the application to the IRS. However, both Forms 5300 and 5301 contain a question inquiring as to whether or not the notice has been given, and an incorrect answer will subject the signer to perjury.

Of course, the application must also be accompanied by all relevant plan documents, including the trust agreement, in the case of a trusteed plan.

Other materials commonly submitted include a power of attorney form (e.g., IRS Form 2848) if a representative has been authorized to submit the application. Although copies of announcements to employees concerning the plan and/or the summary plan description are not required to be submitted to the IRS, Forms 5300 and 5301 do require information as to how and when the plan was communicated to employees.[8]

---

[6] See, e.g., *IRS Alert Guidelines Package*, Pens. Rep. (BNA) No. 281 (March 10, 1980).

[7] 1980-1 C.B. 685.

[8] For a sample determination letter request, See Hildebrandt & Goldberg, "ERISA—Qualified Plans—I.R.S. Determination Letter Procedures," Tax Mngm't Portfolio (BNA) No. 360 (1977).

When to File

In determining *when* an application for IRS approval should be made, one should keep in mind the difference between deadlines for *adoption* of a qualified plan and *submission* to the IRS.

In order for a qualified plan to be effective for a particular taxable year, the plan must be put into effect before the end of the year. According to the IRS, this means adoption and execution of all plan and trust documents.[9] Communication of the salient features of the plan to employees before the initial year-end should also be made.[10] According to another pre-ERISA ruling, no contribution to the plan is required before the filing of the employer's tax return (including extensions) in the case of an accrual-basis taxpayer.[11] This rule was extended by ERISA[12] to cash-basis taxpayers. Notwithstanding these rulings, it is still advisable to make a nominal contribution (e.g., $100) to the trust before the initial year-end.

Deadlines for Retroactive Amendments. Section 401(b) of the Code establishes deadlines for any retroactive amendments needed for approval of qualified plans. As amended by ERISA, Section 401(b) codifies and liberalizes certain administrative practices that existed prior to ERISA. Under the pre-ERISA version of Section 401(b), retroactive amendments necessary to qualify a plan could be made by the fifteenth day of the third month following the taxable year in which the plan was put into effect. This rule was extended under administrative practices of the IRS, which generally permitted such retroactive amendments at any time during the determination letter process, provided the plan was *submitted* to the IRS within the period specified in Section 401(b). A similar practice was invoked with respect to plan amendments. Under Section 401(b), as amended by ERISA, retroactive curative amendments are referred to as *remedial amendments,* and the period in which such amendments must be made is referred to as the *remedial amendment period.* Compliance with the remedial amendment rules is required for both initial and continued qualification of a plan.

Single-employer plans. Under Section 401(b), as amended, the remedial amendment period depends upon the type of plan. In the case of plans maintained by a single employer, the remedial amendment period begins on the date the plan is put into effect. Subject to certain extensions, the period

---

9 Rev. Rul. 76-28, 1976-1 C.B. 106, as modified by Rev. Rul. 76-77, 1976-1 C.B. 107.

10 Rev. Rul. 72-509, 1972-2 C.B. 221. There have been some indications that the summary plan description requirements (generally requiring the distribution of a summary plan description to participants within 120 days of adoption of the plan) have replaced Rev. Rul. 72-509. However, the IRS has yet to formally revoke Rev. Rul. 72-509, and most practitioners have continued to recommend some written announcement to employees before the initial year-end.

11 Rev. Rul. 57-419, 1957-2 C.B. 264.

12 I.R.C. § 404(a)(6), as amended by ERISA.

ends on (1) the due date (including extensions) for filing the employer's federal income tax return for the taxable year in which the plan was made effective, or (2) if later, the last day of the first plan year. Thus, if the plan year and the employer's taxable year were both a calendar year and the plan was adopted December 10, 1981, effective January 1, 1981, the remedial amendment period would not expire before the due date for the federal income tax return of the employer (i.e., March 15, 1982) or any extensions of the due date for filing the return if they are secured. If the employer requests a determination letter from the IRS within the above time frame, the period during which remedial amendments can be made is extended to ninety days following the final determination by the IRS on the determination letter request or a decision by the Tax Court is reached if a declaratory judgment is sought.

In practical terms, this means that in most cases the employer must submit his request to the IRS by the due date for his federal income tax return, plus extensions for the year in which he adopts the plan (unless the first plan year ends on a later date). Having done so, he must then make any amendments necessary to qualify the plan within ninety days following the issuance of the determination letter.

Multiemployer plans. The regulations under Section 401(b) also provide special rules for situations in which plans are maintained by more than one employer. In that case, the remedial amendment period does not expire until the end of the tenth month following the last day of the plan year in which the amendment is adopted (or effective).

Master, prototype, and pattern plans. A series of other special rules are applicable with respect to determination letters requested by sponsoring organizations of master and prototype plans and by law firm sponsors or district-approved pattern plans.[13]

Filing of ERISA-Mandated Amendments. The remedial amendment period has been particularly troublesome in connection with amendments required by ERISA. Revenue Procedure 76-31 [14] (the "Special Reliance Procedure"), permitted plans that filed ERISA amendments by December 31, 1976, special privileges in complying with final regulations under ERISA. In general, the Special Reliance Procedure was an unsuccessful attempt by the IRS to encourage early ERISA submission.

Under a series of extensions, plans that did not elect to use the Special Reliance Procedure were given until June 30, 1978 to file ERISA amendments, with provisions for further extensions in the case of hardship.[15] At

[13] Treas. Reg. § 1.401(b)-1(d).
[14] 1976-2 C.B. 649, as modified by I.R. 1963 (1978).
[15] T.I.R. 2002 (June 1, 1978).

the same time, the issuance of final regulations under ERISA necessitated further changes in plans that had been amended for ERISA. Revenue Procedure 79-28 [16] provided a special program for amending plans solely to comply with final regulations by June 30, 1979.

Finally in Notice 80-7 [17] the IRS issued a comprehensive relief procedure for certain plans that had not been timely amended for ERISA or the final regulations. With respect to plans with only a favorable pre-ERISA determination letter, the plan would have to have been in substantial compliance (as defined in the notice) with ERISA on June 4, 1980, and the sponsor must execute and implement any necessary retroactive amendments.

In the case of plans with post-ERISA determination letters, the sponsor would be allowed to make necessary amendments on a retroactive basis absent certain operational defects.

Relief will not be granted under the procedure if: (1) the plan was found to violate the exclusive benefit rule, or (2) after September 30, 1982, amendments required for complete compliance have not been executed or a request for a determination letter with proposed ERISA amendments has not been filed.

In order to use the relief procedure, necessary amendments must be made within ninety-one days after the issuance of (1) a final determination letter, or (2) a notice of amendments needed to effect compliance. Plans with pre-ERISA determination letters, but that were not in substantial compliance with ERISA on June 4, 1980, will be granted relief only with respect to taxability of certain employees.

Appeal Procedures

The statement of Procedural Rules [18] provides an appeal procedure for taxpayers who receive proposed adverse determination letters from the key districts. Under this procedure, a taxpayer may appeal a proposed adverse determination by the key district to the regional office for consideration. The request must be made within a thirty-day period following the issuance of the proposed adverse determination letter.

If the regional office agrees with the key district, or refuses to take the appeal, the taxpayer may request national office consideration. Failure of the taxpayer to request either regional office or national office consideration will be considered a failure to exhaust administrative remedies, thus precluding the taxpayer from seeking a declaratory judgment from the Tax Court.[19]

---

[16] 1979-1 C.B. 569.

[17] 1980-1 C.B. 578.

[18] See Rev. Proc. 80-30, § 2.11, 1980-1 C.B. 250 and IRS Statement of Procedural Rules, 26 C.F.R. § 601.201(o)(6) (1978).

[19] See also Rev. Proc. 78-3, 1978-1 C.B. 552 for special procedures applicable to appeals arising in connection with IRS examination of an ERISA return (e.g., IRS Form 5500) or a proposed revocation of a determination letter.

As an alternative, technical advice may be requested by the district director or regional office of the IRS. For example, the district director may request technical advice from the national office. The taxpayer may request that technical advice be requested, and may appeal a decision not to request technical advice. However, the final decision of whether or not to request technical advice is made by the IRS.[20] If technical advice is requested and the District Director issues a decision based on technical advice secured from the national office that is adverse to the taxpayer, the taxpayer may not appeal the issues covered in the technical advice, except by requesting a Tax Court declaratory judgment.

Amendments

The IRS has issued new procedural rules applicable to plan amendments.[21] Under the new rules, an employer may use a new short form (Form 6406) for approval of a plan amendment. Alternatively, the same type of detailed filing required in connection with an initial request can be made. This would include a fully completed Form 5300 or 5301, whichever is applicable, and Form 5302. If the short form (Form 6406) approach is used, the IRS will only rule on the effect of the amendment on plan qualification. However, if the applicable Form 5300 series is submitted, the employer may request an opinion as to the qualification of the entire plan, as amended.[22]

Plan amendments should be submitted to the same district director with whom the employer filed his request for initial approval (unless the employer has moved, etc.). Notice to interested parties is also required in connection with a request for approval of a plan amendment.

Similar rules apply in determining the remedial amendment period for plan amendments. In fact, the existence of a remedial amendment period in connection with the plan amendments lessens the need to submit plan amendments in proposed form. Thus, if the amendments are objectionable and have been timely filed, the employer may retroactively revoke them to maintain the qualified status of the plan. The computation of the remedial amendment period for plan amendments is specified in the regulations under Section 401(b) and is similar to the rules described above on initial qualifications.

Termination

Special procedural rules apply to plan terminations. Request for approval by IRS of the termination of a plan is made on Form 5310. Notice to interested parties must be given prior to the submission of the form. The same

---

[20] See Rev. Proc. 80-30, § 2.04, 1980-1 C.B. 250 and IRS Statement of Procedural Rules, 26 C.F.R. § 601.201(n)(9) (1978).

[21] Rev. Proc. 81-19, 1981-1 C.B. 689. See also, Rev. Rul. 81-105, 1981-1 C.B. 27, discussing substantive requirements of the new rules.

[22] Rev. Proc. 81-19, § 3.04, 1981-1 C.B. 689.

rules applicable to initial adoption and plan amendment apply in determining the district director to whom the form should be sent.

Form 5310 elicits detailed information as to turnover of employees within the five years preceding the date of termination and account balances of employees on termination. The IRS takes a close look at the history of the plan in examining a request for approval of a termination. Request for IRS approval on a plan termination (as on initial qualification or amendment) is elective; however, failure to secure such approval runs several risks. First, in the process of securing IRS approval a reallocation of accounts may be necessary to avoid discrimination and retain the plan's qualified status. Payments of amounts from the plan before IRS approval is secured may preclude the ability to reallocate. Moreover, important tax consequences, such as the ability to make tax-free rollover of lump-sum distributions hinges on the qualification of the plan upon termination.

In the case of defined benefit plans, approval by the Pension Benefit Guaranty Corporation (PBGC) must also be secured. Section 4041 of ERISA and the regulations thereunder provide the procedure for termination of a defined benefit plan by the plan administrator with the PBGC.[23]

In the case of any plan subject to PBGC jurisdiction, the Plan Administrator must file a detailed notice of intent to terminate with the PBGC at least ten days *prior* to the effective date of the termination. Upon filing the notice with the PBGC, the plan administrator must immediately notify employees of both the notice to the PBGC and the date of proposed termination of the plan. Notice to, and request for approval from, the PBGC is mandatory for plans subject to PBGC jurisdiction.

A number of complications and duplications with respect to defined benefit plans occur in obtaining clearance from two government agencies on plan terminations. In an effort to eliminate these complications and duplications the PBGC has proposed rules that would allow employers to file duplicate copies of a combined IRS/PBGC Form 5310 with the PBGC that would elicit all the information needed by both government agencies with respect to the plan termination. The PBGC would forward one copy to the IRS for their review. The employer could also file a single copy with the IRS in certain circumstances (e.g., where the PBGC is not involved or where an advance determination, prior to termination, is needed from the IRS).[24]

Special Rules

In Revenue Procedure 81-12,[25] the IRS issued special guidelines for applying the affiliated service organization rules of Section 414(m) of the Code

[23] See 29 C.F.R. Pt. 2604 (1975).

[24] 29 C.F.R. Pt. 2616, Revised Method of Filing Notice of Intent to Terminate, Proposed Rulemaking, 44 Fed. Reg. 43404 (1979).

[25] 1981-1 C.B. 652.

added in 1980. These rules require certain service organizations which are connected through services or ownership with another organization to be jointly treated as a single employer for pension and other purposes. Revenue Procedure 81-12 allows employers to obtain rulings from the national office as to whether or not an affiliated service group exists, and determination letters from key district directors as to the effect of the existence of an affiliated service group on the plan's qualified status.

The IRS procedural rules also provide a number of special rules for unique situations, such as the approval of *master* and *prototype plans.* All requests for approval of master and prototype plans are submitted under these procedures to the national office. Individual employers adopting master and prototype plans have varying requirements depending upon whether the plan is a corporate or Keogh plan.

Under Revenue Procedure 80-29,[26] approval of the master or prototype corporate or H.R. 10 plans are made at the national office level by a submission of the sponsoring organization. However, the employer who adopts a master or prototype H.R. 10 plan or an IRS model plan does not have to request a determination letter, but must give notice to interested parties.[27]

Individual employers who adopt a master or prototype *corporate* plan must request specific approval from the district director in much the same way as one would make such a request on the individually designed plan. However, short Form 5307 replaces the more elaborate Forms 5300 to 5302 in connection with an application for approval of the adoption of a master and prototype corporate plan. Form 5307 basically elicits information as to coverage and vesting and does not require the employer to provide detailed information as to the twenty-five highest paid employees or other burdensome details required by the other forms. Thus, the approval of the adoption of a master or prototype corporate plan is a much abbreviated process.

In Revenue Procedure 76-15,[28] the IRS provided special rules for so-called district-approved pattern plans under which law firms could receive accelerated approval of defined contribution plans in a particular IRS district office. The plan document, however, may not substantially differ from one employer to another. The district-approved pattern plan procedures have received limited acceptance, which may be due in large part to the need to continuously revise various plan documents as the ERISA rules and regulations have developed.

In hopes of streamlining the entire process further, the IRS issued its own prototype plans that allow employers wishing to adopt the plan to do so by filling in the blanks and giving notice to interested parties. These plans have had limited acceptance in part because of the restrictive provisions and in part because of the limited situations in which the IRS permits them to be

---

[26] 1980-1 C.B. 93.
[27] See Rev. Proc. 80-30, §§ 8, 15, 1980-1 C.B. 250.
[28] 1976-1 C.B. 553, as modified by Rev. Proc. 76-31, 1976-2 C.B. 647.

used. Serious practitioners of the art of designing pension plans have used the IRS model plans for limited purposes of determining acceptable IRS language or provisions in certain areas. Finally, the Revenue Act of 1978 introduced the concept of a *simplified employee pension.* Under this approach, an employer can contribute up to the lesser of $7,500 ($15,000 beginning in 1982) or 15 percent of compensation to Individual Retirement Accounts for employees that meet certain eligibility and other requirements.[29] Streamlined procedures for adoption of these plans are in the process of development.[30] Other approaches are sure to develop in the future.

ADMINISTRATION AND ENFORCEMENT OF TITLES I AND II OF ERISA

Jurisdictional Conflicts

Titles I and II of ERISA provide duplicative jurisdictional requirements in many areas. Title III of ERISA attempts to divide the jurisdictional aspects of these requirements between the Labor and Treasury Departments. However, a substantial overlap exists and the early administration of ERISA resulted in conflicts between the agencies. In many cases, it became necessary, for example, to obtain clearance from both agencies.

Against this background, Congress adopted White House Reorganization Plan No. 4, effective December 31, 1978.[31] The plan attempts to establish the jurisdictional aspects of both agencies. In essence, the plan consolidates in the Treasury Department most of the responsibility for applying the eligibility, vesting and funding requirements of both Titles I and II of ERISA, and consolidates in the Labor Department most of the fiduciary responsibility areas. There are exceptions to each. For example, in the fiduciary area, questions concerning the special exceptions for certain Employee Stock Ownership Plans transactions, and the application and enforcement of the excise tax on prohibited transactions, are consigned to the Treasury Department.

In the areas in which the Department of Labor now has jurisdiction, rules for issuing opinions and rulings are addressed in ERISA Procedure 76-1. Procedures for administrative exemptions are provided by ERISA Procedure 75-1.

---

[29] Section 152 of the Revenue Act of 1978 adding I.R.C. § 408(k) and amending I.R.C. §§ 219, 401, 404, 414, 415 and Section 312(c) of the Economic Recovery Tax Act of 1981 amending §§ 219, 401, 408. For a general discussion of the new rules, see Damico & Schachter, "An Analysis of the New Simplified Employee Pension Plan Alternative," 50 J. Taxation 322 (1979).

[30] See, e.g., IRS Form 5305—SEP.

[31] Reorg. Plan No. 4 of 1978, 43 Fed. Reg. 47713 (1978). See also: I.R. 2076 (1979) and Announcement 79-6, 1979-4 I.R.B. 43, for a further description of Reorg. Plan No. 4 and the jurisdictional breakdowns thereunder.

Advisory Opinions and Information Letters

ERISA Procedure 76-1[32] provides guidelines for requesting and obtaining advisory opinions and general information letters from the Labor Department. General information letters do no more than call attention to a well-established interpretation or principle of ERISA without applying it to a specific factual situation. Information letters are not binding on the Department of Labor. Advisory opinions, on the other hand, are formalized written statements that are binding on the Labor Department, but only as to the situation described in the opinion and only insofar as the material facts and representations are accurate.

The procedure for issuing advisory opinions is in many respects similar to those for rulings and determination letters issued by the IRS. Thus, advisory opinions are not issued in a number of areas, primarily factual in nature. Conferences on advisory opinions may be requested, but are granted only if the Labor Department thinks such a conference is necessary. Specific rules for obtaining an advisory opinion are contained in ERISA Procedure 76-1.

Exemptions From Prohibited Transaction Rules

Under Reorganization Plan No. 4, most requests for exemptions from the prohibited transaction rules are now handled by the Labor Department. Prior to Reorganization Plan No. 4, approval had to be secured from both the Labor Department and the IRS.

There is considerable activity in the area of requests for exemptions from prohibited transaction status. The prohibited transaction provisions of ERISA are extremely broad, and there are many areas in which a literal prohibited transaction may have occurred but in which the purpose of ERISA would not be defeated by an exemption. Moreover, the Labor Department has shown more leniency recently in granting exemptions for prohibited transactions and in granting them promptly.

The procedure for requesting an exemption from a prohibited transaction is similar to the procedure for requesting a ruling, with some important differences. ERISA Procedure 75-1 [33] provides detailed rules and informational requirements for securing an exemption. Announcement 79-6,[34] cited above, removes the requirements for simultaneous filings with the IRS in areas in which the Labor Department now has exclusive jurisdiction.

One of the unique aspects of the exemption procedure is the publication of a notice in the *Federal Register* concerning the pending of the exemption. It is the obligation of the requesting party to give adequate notice of the pending exemption, a copy of the *Federal Register* material, and advise an

---

[32] 41 Fed. Reg. 36281 (1976).
[33] 40 Fed. Reg. 18471 (1975).
[34] 1979-4 I.R.B. 43.

individual of his right to comment. Individuals who are considering requesting an exemption should be aware of the formalities and notoriety involved in the exemption process.

One of the difficulties involved in exemptions from prohibited transactions is the determination as to whether or not an individual or class exemption is appropriate. Where several requests are received with respect to a common problem, the Labor Department may invoke the class exemption procedure. Under this procedure, for example, if several exemptions are requested on the same question of law, the Labor Department may hold a hearing or joint conference in lieu of an individual conference.

Administration and Enforcement

Title I of ERISA provides for broad administrative and enforcement provisions. First, Section 501 of ERISA provides for criminal penalties for willful violation of any of the reporting and disclosure requirements of ERISA. The individual who willfully violates any of the reporting and disclosure requirements and is convicted can be fined not more than $5,000 for each violation (up to a limit of $100,000 in the case of a corporation) or imprisonment for not more than one year.

With respect to civil enforcement, broad relief is given for participants, beneficiaries, fiduciaries, and the Labor Department, in enforcing their respective rights under ERISA. For example, these provisions broaden the use of the U.S. district courts by permitting lawsuits without regard to the amount in controversy or the citizenship of the parties. Moreover, the suit may be brought "in the district where the plan is administered, where the breach took place, or where a defendant resides or may be found, and process may be served in any other district where a defendant resides or may be found." [35]

The ease of starting a lawsuit and the many questions unanswered under ERISA have already resulted in a proliferation of lawsuits by various parties. It is interesting to note that the suits are not restricted to suits brought by participants or beneficiaries, a number being lawsuits initiated by union funds against employers for nonpayment of contributions.

The Labor Department has also been given broad administrative and enforcement rights under these provisions. Possible relief includes injunctive relief and other equitable relief. Finally, the provisions allow the plan itself to sue or to be sued as an entity.

Beyond the scope of lawsuits, Section 504 of ERISA gives the Labor Department broad investigative power to determine whether or not ERISA violations have occurred. Sections 510 and 511 of ERISA specifically provide that certain discriminations against participants for exercising their rights under ERISA, or interference or coercion with respect to ERISA

---

[35] ERISA § 502(e)(2).

rights, are unlawful. Under Section 511 of ERISA, persons who willfully coerce a participant not to exercise a right under the plan or ERISA by "fraud, force, violence, or threat of the use of force or violence," are subject to a specific penalty of a fine of $10,000 or imprisonment for not more than one year, or both. Section 503 of ERISA provides a specific procedure for handling claims for benefits under any employee benefit plan subject to ERISA. In addition, administrators who fail to comply with requests for information required to be furnished from participants or beneficiaries for over thirty days can be held personally liable in the court's discretion for up to a $100 a day penalty.

TAX COURT DECLARATORY JUDGMENT PROCEDURES

Section 7476 of the Code, as added by ERISA, provides new procedures for securing Tax Court declaratory judgments in situations in which the IRS has acted adversely to a determination letter request.

Background

The Tax Court declaratory judgment procedure is in specific response to a pre-ERISA problem. Prior to ERISA, a taxpayer could not appeal an adverse determination by the IRS—beyond the national office level—without risking retroactive disqualification. To put a qualification issue before a court, the taxpayer had to put the plan into effect and await an IRS challenge to a claimed deduction on audit. Most employers were not willing to take this risk.

The Tax Court declaratory judgment procedure was instituted in an effort to give the taxpayer a higher level of review. It was also hoped that it would provide a greater degree of uniformity in application of the law.

Prerequisites to Review

There are several prerequisites to Tax Court review.

Notice to Interested Parties. The taxpayer must be able to demonstrate to the satisfaction of the court that he has given notice to interested parties. As discussed earlier, the notice to interested parties is also a prerequisite to seeking a determination letter. The regulations under Section 7476 describe the group to whom the notice must be given and the method of communication for the purposes of both requirements. Once the notice is given correctly in connection with the determination letter process, it need not be given again when a Tax Court declaratory judgment is sought in the same case.

With a variety of exceptions, the notice must be given to all employees, whether or not they are participants. As a general rule, the regulations require that all present employees "eligible to participate" in the plan and all other present employees in the same location as those eligible to participate, must receive the notice.[36] If the plan covers a "principal owner" and the employer has 100 or less employees, generally all employees, regardless of location, must be notified.[37]

It is important to keep in mind in this discussion that the term *eligible to participate* for this purpose includes those actually participating *plus* (1) those who would be a participant upon meeting the minimum age and service requirements of the plan or (2) who would be a participant upon making mandatory employee contributions.[38]

A number of adjustments are to be made to this group depending upon the type of submission and whether or not special rules for certain small employers are to be invoked. Generally, union employees would not have to be notified in the case of a non-union plan and vice versa. In some cases, (e.g., a plan amendment to an already qualified plan that does not affect participation) only employees who are eligible to participate need be notified.[39] If the application concerns a plan termination, the class is expanded to include former employees with vested benefits and beneficiaries of deceased former employees currently receiving benefits.[40]

Controlled-group situations. One of the principal problems with the notice to interested parties concerns controlled-group situations, since all members of the controlled group are considered as a single employer for purposes of the notice requirement. The final regulations offer some relief by eliminating notice requirements to individuals who are eligible to participate in another qualified plan. Thus, employees who are eligible to participate in Plan A would not have to be notified of a change in Plan B.[41]

In the case of doubt as to the application of a particular exemption, notice is generally recommended to avoid any question of a defective notice at a later time.

Methods of notification. Notice can be given to present employees in person, by mailing, by posting, or by printing it in a publication of the employer or an employee organization that is distributed in such a manner so as to be reasonably available to such employee. If notice is given by posting, the notice should be posted in all locations in which there are interested parties.[42] Where notice is required to be given to a former employee

---

[36] Treas. Reg. § 1.7476-1(b)(1).
[37] Treas. Reg. § 1.7476-1(b)(2).
[38] Treas. Reg. § 1.7476-1(d)(2).
[39] Treas. Reg. § 1.7476-1(b)(3).
[40] Treas. Reg. § 1.7476-1(b)(5).
[41] Treas. Reg. § 1.7476-1(b)(6)(iii).
[42] Treas. Reg. § 1.7476-2(c)(1).

or beneficiary, the notice must be given in person or by mail to the last known address of such former employee or beneficiary.[43] The determination of "present employees" must be made not earlier than five business days before the notice is given.[44]

Exhaustion of Administrative Remedies. Another prerequisite to a Tax Court declaratory judgment is that the applicant must have exhausted his administrative remedies. This generally requires that the applicant exhaust all levels of review within the IRS before seeking Tax Court review. As discussed above, exhaustion of administrative remedies would include appeal to the IRS regional office and a request for national office consideration.[45]

In general, a taxpayer will not be deemed to have exhausted his administrative remedies before 270 days after his request for determination has been made. At the same time, the mere expiration of 270 days does not give the taxpayer the right to be heard in the Tax Court. The taxpayer must show that the delay has been caused by lack of due diligence on the part of the IRS.[46]

The request for Tax Court review must be filed by the employer, the plan administrator, an interested party, or the PBGC.[47] The Tax Court request must be made within ninety days of a final adverse determination by the IRS. No time limits appear to be applicable where the 270-day period has expired and the IRS has not acted.[48]

Determination letters are issued by the IRS on either proposed or completed transactions. However, no proceeding can be maintained at the Tax Court level unless the plan or amendment with respect to which a Tax Court decision is sought has been put into effect before the filing of the pleading.[49] Consequently, an employer who seeks a determination letter on a proposed plan would have to place the plan into effect before seeking Tax Court review.

Determining Court's Jurisdiction

The Tax Court declaratory judgment provisions became effective on September 2, 1975, one year after the enactment of ERISA. Since that time most of the Tax Court declaratory judgment cases have dealt with the court's jurisdiction.

By statute,[50] the jurisdiction of the Tax Court to issue declaratory judg-

---

43 Treas. Reg. § 1.7476-2(c)(2).
44 Treas. Reg. § 1.7476-2(c)(1).
45 IRS Statement of Procedural Rules, § 601.201(o)(11).
46 Prince Corp. v. Comm'r, 67 T.C. 318 (1976).
47 I.R.C. § 7476(b)(1).
48 See Falk, *Tax Court Declaratory Judgment Proceeding*, 1 Pens. and Profit-Sharing Service (P-H) ¶ 1045 (1976).
49 I.R.C. § 7476(b)(4).
50 I.R.C. § 7476(a).

ments is limited to cases of actual controversy involving a determination by the IRS (or failure by the IRS to make a determination) with respect to the initial or continuing qualification of a retirement plan.

In the case of *Sheppard & Myers, Inv. v. Comm'r,*[51] the Tax Court held their declaratory judgment jurisdiction with regard to retirement plans was limited to a new plan, a plan amendment, or a plan termination. The Tax Court in this case refused to review a revocation of a previously obtained qualification. Apparently, there was some feeling that this decision did not meet with the legislative intent of the declaratory judgment rules. In any event, the Revenue Act of 1978 specially added revocations of qualified status to the court's declaratory judgment jurisdiction by amending Section 7476(a) of the Code to state:

> For purposes of this section, a determination with respect to a continuing qualification includes any revocation of or other change in a qualification.

In general, the Tax Court has also refused to decide pre-ERISA matters through the declaratory judgment proceedings.[52] As mentioned earlier, the Tax Court has permitted the IRS to delay a Tax Court petition beyond 270 days, at least where the IRS was not clearly to blame for the delay.[53]

In planning for an actual controversy, a close examination of the applicable Tax Court rules would be in order. Rule 217(a) provides that the controversy will be decided on the basis of the administrative record. Thus, the petitioner will be required to demonstrate that proper notice to interested parties was given and may wish to take certain precautions, such as a request that favorable oral communication by the IRS be reduced to writing. Under Rule 217(c), the petitioner will generally have the burden of proof.[54]

In time, the Tax Court declaratory judgment procedure should become a fertile source of substantive law on controversial provisions of ERISA. To date, however, the decisions have dealt primarily with procedural areas, and the procedure itself has been primarily used to hasten IRS pronouncements, rather than to define them.

---

[51] 67 T.C. 26 (1976).

[52] See, e.g., Miller S. Kearney, 36 T.C.M. 81 (1977), Metadure Corp., 36 T.C.M. 164 (1977).

[53] See note 43 *supra.*

[54] For a further discussion of these points, see Short, "Using Tax Court's Declaratory Judgment Procedure to Obtain Plan Determination," 43 J. Taxation 90 (1976).

16

Federal Securities, Labor, and Employment Laws

Federal Securities Laws

BRUCE ALAN MILLER
Legal Division, W.R. Grace & Co.

REGISTRATION UNDER THE SECURITIES ACT OF 1933

Requirement to Register

The sale of a security by means of interstate commerce facilities or the mails must be accomplished through a registration statement containing a prospectus conforming to the requirements of the Securities Act of 1933 (1933 Act) that has been filed with and made effective by the Securities and Exchange Commission, unless the security or the transaction is exempted under the 1933 Act. The offer of such a security (but not the sale) can be made if the registration statement has been filed, even though it is not yet effective. The statutory requirement to register can apply to securities connected with employee benefit plans. Therefore, it must be determined if there is an "offer" or "sale" of a "security" that is not an "exempted security" in a transaction that is not an "exempted transaction."

Types of Securities

In connection with an employee benefit plan, there can exist three types of securities: Type (1), the security represented by the employee's interest in the plan and its related trust, if any; Type (2), an employer security held as an asset of a trust for investment purposes; and Type (3), the security represented by the plan's participation interest in the collective investment vehicles in which the plan invests its assets. The definition of *security, offer or sale, exempted security,* and *exempted transaction* relative to each type of security will be examined.

Definition of Security Under the Securities Act of 1933

Type (1) Security. The term *security* includes a certificate of interest or participation in any profit-sharing agreement and an investment contract.[1]

Interest in profit-sharing plan. The definition of security clearly encompasses an interest in a profit-sharing plan and trust. However, a "certificate

[1] The Securities Act of 1933 (hereinafter cited as 1933 Act), § 2(1).

of interest or participation in any profit-sharing plan" has been held to be no broader than an "investment contract." [2]

Investment contract. An investment contract involves an investment in a common venture premised on a reasonable expectation of profits to be derived from the entrepreneurial or managerial efforts of others.[3] An interest in a retirement plan might be an investment contract if the plan is viewed as an investment vehicle designed to produce profits in the form of employee retirement benefits by means of the efforts of plan managers. In construing the term "security," the U.S. Supreme Court has held that an employee's interest in an involuntary, noncontributory pension plan is not a security because under the economic realities of the situation, the employee is not an investor who has chosen to give up a specific consideration in return for a separable financial interest with the characteristics of a security; an employee is merely selling his labor to make a living, not making an investment for the future.[4] Moreover, an employee is not looking primarily toward trust earnings for his pension, but to employer contributions. The employee's struggle is to vest in a pension, not to receive an investment return.[5]

The SEC has stated that the existence of a security does not depend on whether the plan is a defined benefit plan or a defined contribution plan, but rather depends on other factors such as whether the plan is voluntary or involuntary and contributory or noncontributory.[6] Based on *Daniel,* the SEC has agreed that an interest in an involuntary, noncontributory plan is not a security. The SEC has also stated that an interest in an involuntary, contributory plan is not a security because of the lack of investment choice on the part of the employee.[7] An interest in a voluntary, noncontributory plan is not a security because there is inadequate investment of money by the employee and the employee's profit motive in relation to the trust is too tangential.[8] The SEC regards an interest in a voluntary, contributory plan as a security because all the elements of an investment contract are present in its view. There is employee investment discretion whether or not to contribute. The employee pays cash or property into the trust. The employee has an economic interest in the plan that is separable from his employment compensation. The employee expects the plan managers to earn profits for him on his contributions, at least in a defined contribution plan.[9] Although *Daniel* suggests that an interest in a defined benefit plan can be a security only if the plan depends substantially on earnings, rather than employer con-

---

[2] International Bhd. of Teamsters v. Daniel, 439 U.S. 551, 558 n.11 (1979).
[3] SEC v. W.J. Howey Co., 328 U.S. 293 (1946).
[4] Note 2 *supra,* at 559–560.
[5] Note 2 *supra,* at 561–562.
[6] SEC Release 33-6188.
[7] *Id.*
[8] *Id.*
[9] *Id.*

tributions, the SEC has asserted that an employee in a voluntary, contributory plan is seeking an investment return in the form of promised benefits. Moreover, the SEC has found that many, if not most, defined benefit plans depend substantially on earnings. Moreover, under ERISA, vesting has been made easier than under the plan in *Daniel* so that the contemporary employee's struggle is to earn an investment return, not just to vest.[10]

There is much disagreement with the view of the SEC that an interest in a voluntary, contributory defined benefit plan is a security. It has been stated that an employee's interest in profits under such a plan is not primary or substantial.[11]

Other types of plans. In addition to an interest in a voluntary, contributory defined benefit or defined contribution plan maintained by a corporation, the SEC finds a security in a similar H.R. 10 plan and in an Individual Retirement Account (IRA).[12] However, registration may not be required as discussed below. In the SEC view, an interest in a stock purchase plan is a security where there are substantial differences between the manner of acquiring stock under the plan and the manner of acquiring it in ordinary brokerage transactions (such as limitations on the right to withdraw stock).[13] Voluntary, contributory participation interests in Code Section 405 bond purchase plans, Code Section 403(b) annuity plans, Employee Stock Ownership Plans (ESOPs), Tax Reduction Act stock ownership plans (TRASOPs), and stock appreciation right plans are securities, although registration may not be required as discussed below.[14]

Type (2) Security. Section 2(1) of the 1933 Act includes "stock" and clearly applies to employer stock transferred to a retirement plan.

Type (3) Security. The SEC has stated that the participation interests of plans in pools of assets such as bank collective trust funds or insurance-company pooled accounts are securities.[15] An investment contract exists in that there is an investment of money (the plan assets) in a common enterprise (the fund) with an expectation of profits (the fund earnings) from the efforts of others (the fund managers). In the language of *Daniel,* the plans give up a specific consideration in return for a separable financial interest with the characteristics of a security.

---

[10] *Id.*

[11] Tanuggi v. Grolier, Inc., 246 Pens. Rep. (BNA) D-1 (S.D.N.Y. 1979); Newkirk v. General Elec. Co., 261 Pens. Rep. (BNA) D-5 (N.D. Cal. 1979).

[12] SEC Release 33-6188.

[13] *Id.*

[14] *Id.*

[15] *Id.*

Definitions of Offer and Sale Under the Securities Act of 1933

Type (1) Security. The term *sale* includes every contract of sale or disposition of a security or interest in a security, for value.[16] The term *offer to sell* includes every attempt or offer to dispose of, or solicitation of an offer to buy, a security, or interest in a security, for value.

Value. The term *value* is not defined by the 1933 Act, but the SEC regards the term as including all ordinary forms of consideration such as cash, property, services, or the surrender of a legal right.[17]

Conversion of plans. The conversion of a pension or profit-sharing plan into an ESOP or other type of plan involves an exchange of an employee's interest in one plan for an interest in another plan. This is an exchange for value in the SEC view, but registration is not required as long as the conversion is mandatory and the employee has no investment choice.[18] Registration also may not be required under Section 3(a)(2) of the 1933 Act if none of the funds transferred is invested in employer stock.[19]

Investment elections in noncontributory plans. In many noncontributory plans, an employee may choose to invest his account in different funds, to accept cash or defer part of the employer contribution, or to receive cash or employer stock upon termination of employment. These choices involve investment choice and the transfer of value (often by means of surrender of a legal right). But in view of *Daniel,* the SEC has asserted that in a noncontributory plan, the presence of these investment choices will not necessitate registration of participation interests in the plan.[20] This is based upon the SEC view that the funds contributed by the employer are not made available to the employee and cannot be regarded as employee monies.[21]

Type (2) Security

Solicitiation of an offer to buy employer stock. Because the term sale includes a solicitation of an offer to buy, an employer may be deemed to be selling its stock in a stock purchase plan if the employer has substantial involvement in the plan, even though the employer stock is purchased on the open market. If the employer solicits employees to participate, this is substantial involvement. However, announcing the plan and making payroll deductions are not.[22] Moreover, if the stock is acquired directly from the

---

16 1933 Act, § 2(3).
17 SEC Release 33-6188.
18 *Id.*
19 SEC Release 33-6281.
20 SEC Release 33-6188.
21 SEC Release 33-6281.
22 SEC Release 33-4790.

employer, there is a sale of employer stock requiring registration, unless an exemption applies.[23]

In a contributory TRASOP, an employer makes certain contributions which may be matched by an employee, thus giving the employee an incentive to participate in the plan and buy employer stock.[24] The employer is soliciting an offer from the employee to buy employer stock.[25] But if the employer stock is acquired in the open market, and if the employer's contribution is the only form of substantial involvement by the employer in the plan, a registration requirement will not be triggered. This is because employer stock acquired in the open market pursuant to a completely employee-paid stock purchase plan is not required to be registered, and the real party paying the employer's share of the contribution is the federal government since the employer is entitled to a tax credit.[26] The registration exemption will also apply to other open market stock purchase plans under which employer contributions equal or exceed employee contributions.[27]

Acquisition of employer stock by plan. When a plan acquires employer stock in the open market, by contribution from or purchase from the employer, or by purchase from an affiliate of the employer (such as a controlling shareholder), there is no sale to the plan (as distinguished from the employees) of employer stock, or if there is a sale, the transaction will probably be exempted from registration under Section 4 of the 1933 Act, discussed below.[28] Thus, there was either no sale, or an exempted sale, to the plan where an employer sold stock to the plan,[29] or where an employer contributed stock to the plan,[30] or where an affiliate sold stock to the plan and the plan acquired the stock solely to hold for ultimate distribution to participants.[31] However, there is a sale of employer stock to an employee when an employee makes a contribution to a plan that is invested in employer stock transferred by the employer.[32] As discussed above, even where employee contributions are used to purchase employer stock only in the open market, the employer's involvement will generally be substantial so that the employer is soliciting an offer to buy employer stock.

The SEC has conspicuously failed to state that there is no sale to employees when employer stock is contributed by an employer to a voluntary, noncontributory plan. The consideration for the sale of stock is arguably the

---

[23] SEC Release 33-6188.
[24] SEC Release 33-4790.
[25] SEC Release 33-6188.
[26] *Id.*
[27] SEC Release 33-6281.
[28] SEC Release 33-6188.
[29] SEC No-Action letter, Finnigan Corporation, 86 Pens. Rep. (BNA) A-3 (1976).
[30] *Id.*
[31] SEC No-Action letter, Tracy-Locke Co., 94 Pens. Rep. (BNA) A-1 (1976).
[32] SEC No-Action letter, Public Service Co. of New Mexico, 4 Pens. & Profit Sharing (P-H) ¶ 120,107 (1978).

employee's services. This raises the possibility that, while an interest in such a plan is not a security that is sold to employees, the underlying employer stock is a security that is sold to employees, and such a security is not an exempted security.

Distribution of employer stock by plan. The distribution of employer stock by a plan to an employee does not require registration, presumably because no sale of employer stock is involved.[33]

Sale of employer stock by plan. If a plan sells employer stock (even stock previously acquired in the open market) to employees or third parties, there is a sale, and registration is required unless an exemption exists. If the plan is not an affiliate of the employer, Section 4(1) of the 1933 Act, will provide an exemption.[34] An affiliate is a person or entity that controls, is controlled by, or is under common control with the employer.[35] If the plan is an affiliate of the employer, the employer stock to be sold must be registered unless another exemption can be found. SEC Rule 144, discussed below, may also be used.[36]

Resale of employer stock by employee. An employee who receives a plan distribution of employer stock, which has already been registered, may resell such stock without registration unless the employee is an affiliate of the employer. A resale by an affiliate may be made pursuant to the provisions of SEC Rule 144 or may be exempt from registration as discussed below. An employee, whether an affiliate or a nonaffiliate of the employer, who receives a plan distribution of employer stock that has not already been registered may resell such stock, which is considered a "restricted security," if the stock is registered, or if he complies with the provisions of SEC Rule 144, or if another exemption is available. However, a nonaffiliate may resell without registration, compliance with Rule 144, or an exemption if the employer is subject to the reporting and disclosure provisions of the Securities Exchange Act of 1934 (1934 Act), the stock is actively traded in the open market, and the number of shares distributed is relatively small in relation to the number of shares issued and outstanding.[37] The number of shares distributed by the plan to participants during a fiscal year will be considered small if it does not exceed one percent of the outstanding securities of the class.[38] The requirement can also be satisfied by a showing that resales of the distributed shares will not have a measurable impact on the trading market.[39] More-

---

[33] SEC Release 33-6188.
[34] *Id.*
[35] SEC Rule 405.
[36] SEC Release 33-6281.
[37] SEC Releases 33-5750, 33-6188.
[38] SEC Release 33-6281.
[39] *Id.*

over, if the foregoing conditions are satisfied, the employer stock will no longer be considered a "restricted security" [40] and therefore an affiliate can make resales under Rule 144 without compliance with the two-year holding requirement of SEC Rule 144.[41]

Type (3) Security. When a sponsor of a collective investment vehicle transfers a participation interest in such vehicle to a plan, such sponsor is making an offer and sale of such interest within the meaning of the 1933 Act. However, the sale of the security represented by the participation interest may be exempt from registration because the security is an exempted security, as discussed below.

Exempted Security Under the Securities Act of 1933

Type (1) Security. Section 3(a)(2) of the 1933 Act exempts from registration the security represented by an interest or participation in a single trust fund which is issued in connection with a tax-qualified pension, profit-sharing, stock bonus, or annuity plan or certain governmental plans. Any security arising out of a contract issued by an insurance company in connection with the foregoing types of plans is also exempt from registration. However, an interest or participation in a single trust fund (or in an insurance company separate account) for a single employer, and relating to a plan that provides that an amount in excess of the employer's contribution is used to purchase Type (2) employer securities, is not an exempted security under Section 3(a)(2) of the 1933 Act; nor is an interest or participation in an H.R. 10 plan.

Single trust fund or separate account. A single trust fund is not collective and hence is not established by a financial intermediary for the use of separate employers. A single trust fund includes a trust fund for employees of a single employer, a trust fund for employees of closely related employers such as a parent and its subsidiaries, and a trust fund established and controlled by an employer and/or a union representing the employees.[42] A separate account of an insurance company is not part of the general assets of the insurance company and is maintained in a fashion similar to a single trust fund.

International Brotherhood of Teamsters v. Daniel. In the *Daniel* case discussed above, the U.S. Supreme Court stated that Section 3(a)(2) of the 1933 Act applies only to the interest or participation that a plan has in an investment vehicle maintained by a bank or an insurance company. In the Court's view, Section 3(a)(2) does not affect the registration status of the

---

[40] SEC Release 33-5750.
[41] SEC Release 33-6281.
[42] SEC Release 33-6188.

security represented by the employee's interest or participation in the underlying plan and trust because the section deals only with the relationship between a plan and its bank or insurance company.

SEC view. The SEC continues to believe, despite *Daniel,* that Section 3(a)(2) is intended to exempt the security represented by an employee's interest or participation in a plan and trust, as well as a plan's interest in investment vehicles. The basis for this view is that an employee's interest or participation in many plans might be subject to registration unless Section 3(a)(2) is broadly construed.[43] However, this assumes that such an interest or participation in a plan and trust is a security under the 1933 Act, an assumption that has largely been judicially demolished as even the SEC has recognized.

"Maintained by a bank" requirement. Before October 21, 1980, the technical language of Section 3(a)(2) of the 1933 Act appeared to require that a single trust fund must be maintained by a bank in order for an employee's interest therein to be an exempted security. However, although assuming that Section 3(a)(2) applies to a single trust fund, the SEC took the position that such a trust fund need not be maintained by a bank in order for an employee's interest therein to be an exempted security not subject to registration. The "maintained by a bank" requirement was held to apply only to a collective trust fund.[44] On October 21, 1980, a law was enacted that clarifies the statutory language of Section 3(a)(2) of the 1933 Act to indicate that the "maintained by a bank" requirement applies only to a collective trust fund.

Single employer. A single employer includes an employer and any entity controlling, controlled by, or under common control with, such employer. The exception to the Section 3(a)(2) of the 1933 Act exemption applies to interests in certain plans and trusts maintained for a single employer. The purpose of the exception is to deny exemption to interests in plans and trusts that invest employee contributions in Type (2) securities of the employer or related entities.[45] A parent and its subsidiaries are deemed a single employer for purposes of the exception to the exemption. Thus, if a tax-qualified plan is maintained by a parent alone, or a parent and its subsidiaries together, and employee contributions can be invested in Type (2) employer stock, registration is required.[46]

Employer contributions. Under the literal language of Section 3(a)(2) of the 1933 Act, the exception to the exemption applies to an interest in a

---

43 *Id.*
44 *Id.*
45 *Id.*
46 *Id.*

plan which invests "an amount in excess of the employer's contribution" in Type (2) stock of the employer or related entities. If this text were applied literally, any plan that provides that earnings on employer contributions are to be reinvested in employer stock (as is provided in most defined contribution plans that invest in employer stock) would be within the exception to the exemption and registration of the employee's interest in such a plan and its related trust would be required. The SEC apparently thinks that trust assets consist only of employee contributions and employer contributions. The SEC, for example, has asserted that the reference in the exception to

> amounts in excess of the employer's contributions simply means that *employee funds* may not be used to purchase securities of the employer or affiliated entities. . . . It is enough simply to demonstrate that the amount invested by the plan in employer securities is the same or less than the *amount contributed by the employer* to the plan.[47]

The quoted text does not indicate what happens if earnings on employer contributions are reinvested in employer stock. Despite the text of the statute, the better view appears to be that an employee's interest in the plan and its related trust is subject to registration only when employee contributions (or earnings thereon) may be invested in employer stock; in other cases, the exception to the exemption should not apply.

Despite the SEC position that the exemption under Section 3(a)(2) of the 1933 Act is available if the amount invested by the plan in employer stock is the same or less than the amount contributed by the employer, the SEC has also imposed a tracing rule. Under the tracing rule, the exemption under Section 3(a)(2) of the 1933 Act is only available if, under the terms of the plan, employee contributions cannot be directly invested in employer stock.[48]

H.R. 10 plans. Under a second exception to the exemption under Section 3(a)(2) of the 1933 Act, an employee's interest in an H.R. 10 plan is not exempted and hence is subject to registration. However, the statute provides that the SEC may exempt such an interest from registration where it is necessary or appropriate to do so. On December 1, 1981, the SEC issued a rule exempting from registration an employee's interest in any tax-qualified H.R. 10 plan.[49]

Individual retirement accounts. An employee's interest in an IRA is an investment in a security which is issued by a bank, and hence is exempt from registration under a clause of Section 3(a)(2) of the 1933 Act.[50]

---

[47] SEC Release 33-6188, n.152.
[48] SEC Release 33-6281.
[49] SEC Rule 180(b).
[50] SEC Release 33-6188.

Other types of plans. A voluntary, contributory participation interest in a Code Section 405 bond purchase plan is deemed exempt from registration under the 1933 Act because the underlying bonds are exempt under a clause of Section 3(a)(2) of the 1933 Act that exempts any security issued by the United States. A voluntary, contributory participation interest in a Code Section 403(b) annuity plan is not required to be registered due to SEC administrative practices.[51]

Type (2) Security. A Type (2) security is not exempted from the provisions of the 1933 Act. At one time, the SEC regarded the exemption under Section 3(a)(2) of the 1933 Act as applying to a Type (2) security contributed to a plan, if employees' interests in such plan were exempted by Section 3(a)(2) of the 1933 Act. However, the SEC has moved away from this position.[52]

Type (3) Security. Section 3(a)(2) of the 1933 Act exempts from registration the security represented by an interest or participation in any collective trust fund maintained by a bank that is issued in connection with a tax-qualified pension, profit-sharing, stock bonus, or annuity plan, or certain governmental plans other than H.R. 10 plans.

Collective trust fund. A collective trust fund is an investment vehicle maintained by a bank solely for the assets of tax-qualified plans or certain governmental plans. It may not be used for direct investment by members of the public. Initially the SEC held that assets of H.R. 10 plans must not be included in the collective trust fund or the exemption would be lost.[53] However, the SEC has now abandoned this position.[54]

"Maintained by a bank" requirement. In order for a plan's interest in a collective trust fund to be exempt, a bank must exercise substantial investment responsibility over the trust fund administered by it. A bank that functions in a mere custodial capacity will not satisfy the requirement, although the bank may hire an investment adviser to assist it as long as the adviser does not make a final decision regarding investments.[55]

H.R. 10 plans. The SEC has exempted from registration the security represented by an interest or participation in a single trust fund or in a collective trust fund maintained by a bank, or any security arising out of a contract issued by an insurance company, if these investment media are used in connection with a tax-qualified H.R. 10 plan and certain additional requirements

---

[51] *Id.*
[52] SEC No-Action letter, Champion Int'l Corp., (Dec. 19, 1977).
[53] SEC Release 33-6188.
[54] SEC Release 33-6281.
[55] SEC Release 33-6188.

are satisfied. The H.R. 10 plan must cover only employees of a single employer or interrelated partnerships and the employer must be a law firm, accounting firm, investment banking firm, pension consulting firm, or investment advisory firm which is sophisticated in financial matters, or the employer must obtain the advice of an expert who is sophisticated in financial matters and who is not related to the bank or insurance company providing the investment medium.[56]

Insurance company contracts. Some tax-qualified plans are funded by means of guaranteed investment contracts sold by insurance companies. Employer contributions are held as general assets of the insurance company. These contracts provide for guaranteed interest and annuity purchase rates. Some contracts provide for payment of interest (or dividends in the case of mutual companies) in excess of the guaranteed amount. An interest or participation in a guaranteed investment contract is a security. However, under certain amendments to Section 3(a)(2) of the 1933 Act enacted in 1980, any security arising out of a contract issued by an insurance company in connection with a tax-qualified plan (other than an H.R. 10 plan) or governmental plan is exempt from registration. Nevertheless, under the 1980 amendments, an annuity contract issued in connection with a Code Section 403(b) annuity plan is not exempt from registration under Section 3(a)(2) of the 1933 Act.[57]

Multiple-employer trusts. These trusts are formed by insurance companies and are funded by fixed and/or variable annuity contracts. An interest or participation in a multiple-employer trust is a security for which the 1933 Act provides no exemption. The impact of the 1980 amendments to Section 3(a)(2) of the 1933 Act on such a trust is unclear. However, registration is not required if participants in the trust tender consideration directly to, and receive annuity payments directly from, the insurance company; the insurance company performs all marketing, administrative, and investment functions; financial claims can be made directly against the insurance company; the insurance company names the trustee and has a right of removal; the sole responsibility of the trustee is to hold the contracts; and the trust has no financial interest in the contracts.

Exempted Transactions. The registration of a security that does not qualify as an exempted security is, nevertheless, not necessary if the transaction in which it is offered and sold is exempted. Exempted transactions are set forth in Sections 4 and 3(a)(11) of the 1933 Act.

Section 4(1) of the 1933 Act and SEC Rule 144. This provision exempts a transaction by any person other than an issuer, underwriter, or dealer. Be-

---

56 SEC Rule 180(a).

57 SEC Release 33-6281.

cause the offer and sale of a Type (1) and Type (3) security always involve an issuer (the employer/trust or the sponsor of the collective investment vehicle), this exemption will only apply to an offer or sale of a Type (2) security, and even then only when an employee who is not an affiiliate of the employer is reselling employer stock after distribution from a plan or when a plan that is not an affiiliate of the employer is selling employer stock. In order to avoid the status of an "underwriter" so that the exemption under Section 4(1) of the 1933 Act will apply, an employee who is an affiliate of the employer generally must comply with SEC Rule 144 in the resale of employer stock (unless another exemption is available or the stock is registered). Similarly, an employee who is not an affiliate of the employer who has received restricted securities must comply with SEC Rule 144 in the resale of the restricted employer stock unless the exception under SEC Release 33-5750 discussed above applies, another exemption is available, or the stock is registered.

Section 4(2) of the 1933 Act and SEC Rule 146. This provision exempts transactions by an issuer not involving any public offering. Similar transactions by an affiliate of the issuer are regarded as exempted under the "Section 4 (1½)" exemption. This private offering exemption is available for an offering made to a limited number of persons who are sophisticated in business matters and have access to the types of information that could be obtained through a registration statement. SEC Rule 146 provides a safe harbor under Section 4(2) if all the provisions of the rule are satisfied. This exemption will generally not apply to the offer and sale of a Type (1) or a Type (3) security because the sophistication and limited number requirements will not be satisfied. This exemption may apply to the offer or sale of a Type (2) security to a plan by a controlling shareholder of the employer or by an employee who has received a distribution of employer stock. This avoids the need for compliance with SEC Rule 144 discussed above.

Section 3(a)(11) of the 1933 Act and SEC Rule 147. Although placed in Section 3 of the 1933 Act with exempted securities, the intrastate offering exemption set forth in Section 3(a)(11) of the 1933 Act is really a transactional exemption. The exemption applies to offerings that are limited to residents of the state in which the issuer is organized and conducts business. SEC Rule 147 provides a safe harbor under Section 3(a)(11) if all the provisions of the rule are satisfied. It is unclear whether the issuer of a Type (1) security is the plan or the employer and whether the purchaser of a Type (2) security is the plan or the employee. The answers to these issues may change application of the exemption.

SEC Rule 240. This rule provides an exemption for the offer and sale of securities up to $100,000 in a twelve-month period by an issuer whose securities are held by 100 or fewer persons, if the conditions of the rule are satisfied.

SEC Rule 242. This rule provides an exemption for the offer and sale of securities up to $2 million to thirty-five or fewer purchasers in a single issue by certain qualified issuers, if the conditions of the rule are satisfied.

Registration. The following forms are used to register Types (1), (2), and (3) securities under varying circumstances.

Form S-8. Form S-8 is the principal form used to register Type (1) and Type (2) securities offered by an employer to employees in connection with a benefit plan. It may not be used for resales of Type (2) securities by employees. The information required on Form S-8 is less extensive than that required on other forms based on the theory that employees are more familiar with the employer than most other investors.[58] Effective June 1, 1980, Form S-8 is available to an issuer that has been subject to the periodic reporting requirements under Sections 13 or 15(d) of the 1934 Act for at least ninety days, that has filed all required reports during the preceding twelve months, and that has furnished or will furnish an annual report to security holders for its last fiscal year containing the information required by SEC Rule 14a-3.[59] The revised Form S-8 incorporates by reference much material concerning the plan and the issuer in order to avoid the necessity for regular updating. This is permitted based on the view that the information in the 1934 Act reports is widely available and sufficiently detailed to satisfy the disclosure requirements of the 1933 Act.[60] The prospectus relating to Form S-8 can be an "evergreen prospectus" which can be used over many years without change; where annual updating cannot be accomplished by means of the filing of the 1934 Act reports, a simple appendix may be used.[61]

An original registration statement on Form S-8 is effective automatically on the twentieth day after filing with the SEC.[62] Pre-effective amendments may be filed before the end of the twenty-day period and no new twenty-day period will begin. Post-effective amendments are effective on the date of filing.[63] Delaying amendments are not permitted. However, a registration statement may be withdrawn before it is effective.

Other forms. If Form S-8 is not available to an issuer, other forms are available such as Form S-1, S-18, S-7, and S-16. Form S-1 is the general

[58] SEC Release 33-6188.
[59] SEC Release 33-6202.
[60] SEC Release 33-6188.
[61] SEC Release 33-6281.
[62] SEC Rule 456; SEC Release 33-6190.
[63] SEC Rule 464; SEC Release 33-6190.

registration form available to an issuer when no other form is available for use. It requires detailed business information and financial disclosures. Form S-18 can be used by a U.S. or Canadian issuer not subject to the 1934 Act reporting requirements and that satisfies certain other criteria for an offering of securities up to $5 million for cash. Form S-7 can be used by an issuer that has had net income of at least $250,000 for three of its last four fiscal years, which is subject to, and has complied with, the 1934 Act reporting requirements for at least thirty-six months before the form is used, and that satisfies certain other criteria. This form is less burdensome than Form S-1. Form S-16 can be used by an issuer that qualifies to use Form S-7, at least $50 million of whose stock is held by nonaffiliates, and that satisfies certain other criteria. It is a simplified registration statement. However, no matter which of the forms is used, all the information concerning the plan which would be disclosed on Form S-8 must similarly be disclosed on whatever form is used.[64] In addition, Regulation A, which provides for more limited disclosure, can be relied upon for offerings of up to $1.5 million during a twelve-month period.[65]

Resale of Type (2) security. Form S-8 is not available for resales of Type (2) securities by affiliates who desire to resell securities distributed to them by the plan where no transactional exemption is available, or by nonaffiliates who desire to resell restricted securities distributed to them by the plan where no transactional exemption is available. Form S-16 may be used for this purpose by affiliates if the issuer meets the qualifications for use of the form and the affiliates have a present intention to sell their Type (2) securities within the next sixteen months.[66] If Form S-16 is not available, Form S-1 should be used.[67]

ANTI-FRAUD PROVISIONS OF THE SECURITIES ACT OF 1933 AND THE SECURITIES EXCHANGE ACT OF 1934

Section 10(b) of the Securities Exchange Act of 1934 and SEC Rule 10b-5

It is unlawful under Section 10(b) of the 1934 Act and SEC Rule 10b-5 for any person to use the facilities of interstate commerce or a stock exchange or the mails in order to employ a scheme to defraud, to make untrue statements of material fact, or to omit the statement of material facts necessary to avoid misleading impressions, in connection with the purchase and sale of a security. Rule 10b-5 applies to any security under the 1934 Act, including an exempted security. The definition of security under Section

[64] SEC Release 33-6188.
[65] *Id.*
[66] Form S-8, General Instruction E.
[67] SEC Release 33-6188.

3(a)(10) of the 1934 Act is virtually identical to the definition of security under Section 2(a)(1) of the 1933 Act. For purposes of a Type (1) security, the coverage of the 1933 Act and the 1934 Act is the same.[68] Thus, if a security was found to exist under the 1933 Act above, even if registration was not required because of the 1933 Act, Section 3(a)(2), Rule 10b-5 is potentially applicable. For example, securities law violations are alleged in *O'Neill v. Marriott Corp.*,[69] relating to an employee's interest in a voluntary, contributory defined contribution plan. But where a security does not exist, such as an employee's interest in an involuntary, noncontributory pension plan under *Daniel,* Rule 10b-5 cannot apply.

Section 17(a) of the Securities Act of 1933

It is unlawful under Section 17(a) of the 1933 Act for any person to use the facilities of interstate commerce or the mails in order to employ a scheme to defraud, or to obtain money or property by means of material misstatements or omissions, in connection with the offer or sale of a security. As in the case of Rule 10b-5, a private right of action under Section 17(a) of the 1933 Act has been held to exist,[70] although the courts are not unanimous on this point.[71] However, as in the case of Rule 10b-5, Section 17(a) is potentially applicable only if a security exists, even if registration of such security is not required because of the exemptions of Section 3 of the 1933 Act. If a security does not exist, as in *Daniel,* Section 17(a) cannot apply.

PROXY RULES UNDER THE SECURITIES EXCHANGE ACT OF 1934

The solicitation under Section 14(a) of the 1934 Act and SEC Regulation 14A by management of a proxy for a meeting of shareholders in respect of a security (other than an exempted security) registered under Section 12 of the 1934 Act, (for example, a security listed on a securities exchange or a security issued by a large entity with many security holders) must be accompanied or preceded by a proxy statement conforming to SEC Schedule 14A. Item 7 of Schedule 14A requires disclosure of information contained in Item 4 (as currently set forth in SEC Release 33-6261) and Instruction 4 to Item 5 of SEC Regulation S-K if action is taken at the shareholders' meeting to elect directors or if action is taken relating to a profit-sharing, pension, stock option, or other remuneration plan in which a director, nominee for director, or officer will participate. Regulation S-K requires

---

[68] International Bhd. of Teamsters v. Daniel, note 2, *supra,* at 556 n.7.
[69] 264 Pens. Rep. (BNA) D-3 (D. Md. 1979).
[70] Kirshner v. United States, [1979-1981 Transfer Binder] Pens. Plan Guide (CCH) ¶ 22,204 (2d Cir. 1979).
[71] Leonard v. Drug Fair, Inc., 266 Pens. Rep. (BNA) D-1 (D.D.C. 1979).

disclosures relating to plan contributions. In addition, if action is taken at the shareholders' meeting relating to a profit-sharing plan, a pension plan, or a stock option plan, additional disclosures relating to such plan are required by Items 9, 10, and 11 of Schedule 14A, respectively. Even if management does not solicit a proxy for a meeting of shareholders, it must furnish an information statement to shareholders which sets forth the information above.[72]

PLAN REPORTS UNDER THE SECURITIES EXCHANGE ACT OF 1934

Under Section 15(d) of the 1934 Act, every issuer of securities registered under the 1933 Act is required to file an annual report on the form prescribed by the SEC. Even though the employer maintaining an employee benefit plan may report to the SEC on Form 10-K, the plan is regarded as a separate issuer, and if employees' participation interests in such plan are registered under the 1933 Act, the plan must file an annual report with the SEC on Form 11-K. Effective June 1, 1980, Form 11-K requires disclosures concerning plan amendments, administration, investments, and financial condition.

INSIDER REPORTING AND TRADING PROVISIONS

Section 16 of the 1934 Act applies to "insiders" who consist of any person who beneficially owns more than 10 percent of any class of equity security (other than an exempted security) registered under Section 12 of the 1934 Act or an officer or director of the issuer of such security. In the context of an employee benefit plan, beneficial ownership includes the ownership of a vested beneficial interest in a trust.[73] Indications of beneficial ownership include the right to control voting and transfer; the right to receive or control the disposition of income; and the right to control disposition of proceeds upon liquidation. Not all of these characteristics need be present in order for beneficial ownership to exist.[74]

Reporting of Ownership

An insider report to the SEC is required by Section 16(a) of the 1934 Act. The amount of equity securities (as to which he is an insider) beneficially owned by him and any change in beneficial ownership is also required. An employee benefit plan and its related trust may be an insider

---

72 SEC Rule 14c-2; SEC Schedule 14C.
73 SEC Rule 16a-8(a)(2).
74 SEC Release 34-18114.

subject to reporting requirements if the trust holds more than 10 percent of any class of registered equity security.[75]

Plan Distributions. An insider who receives a distribution from a plan of an equity security as to which he is an insider must report such acquisition.[76]

Plan Allocations. An allocation of an equity security otherwise subject to Section 16(a) reporting to the vested account of an insider under a defined contribution plan is exempt from reporting requirements provided the market value of such equity securities allocated to all insiders in the aggregate is less than 20 percent of the market value of all securities owned by the trust. Similarly, the vested beneficial interest of an insider in portfolio equity securities held by a pension trust is exempt from reporting requirements provided the market value of the shares of a particular equity security held by the trust is less than 20 percent of the market value of all securities owned by the trust. These exemptions are not affected by plan provisions allowing participants to transfer their account balances among different investment funds.[77] An exemption also applies where the ownership, acquisition, or disposition of an equity security held in trust occurs without prior approval of the trust beneficiary.[78] However, this exemption does not apply where an employer, as settlor of a trust, has full control over the disposition of the securities held by the trust.[79]

Retirement Plans. The vested beneficial interest of an insider in employer securities held by a pension or retirement plan sponsored by the employer is not required to be reported.[80] However, provisions in a plan providing for withdrawal prior to retirement, death, or termination of service will prevent exemption as a retirement plan unless a participant is suspended from participation for at least a year as a result of a withdrawal.[81]

Short-Swing Trading Profit Recovery

An issuer may recover, under Section 16(b) of the 1934 Act, the profit made by an insider from a purchase and sale, or sale and purchase, of equity securities of the issuer within a period of less than six months. However, any transaction exempted from the reporting provisions of Section 16(a) of the 1934 Act is also exempt from the profit recovery provisions

---

75 SEC Rule 16a-8(c).
76 SEC No-Action letter, St. Regis Paper Co., (Nov. 10, 1977).
77 SEC Rule 16a-8(b); SEC Release 34-18114.
78 *Id.*
79 SEC Release 34-18114.
80 SEC Rule 16a-8(g)(3).
81 SEC No-Action letter, Flintkote Co., 201 Pens. Rep. (BNA) A-9 (1978); SEC Release 34-18114.

of Section 16(b).[82] The acquisition of shares of stock by an insider from a stock bonus, profit-sharing or similar plan is exempt from the operation of Section 16(b) if the plan is approved by a vote of shareholders, selection of plan participants is made by disinterested persons where selection is discretionary, and there is a limit on the dollar amount or number of shares allocated under the plan.[83] However, the subsequent disposition of such shares is not exempt. The receipt and exercise of a stock option are exempt if the foregoing conditions are satisfied but the acquisition of shares of stock for cash pursuant to the exercise of an option and the subsequent disposition of such shares are not exempt.[84]

PLAN AND TRUST AS ONE "PERSON" UNDER THE SECURITIES ACT OF 1933 AND THE SECURITIES EXCHANGE ACT OF 1934

Registration of Employer Under Section 12(g) of the Securities Exchange Act of 1934

Section 12(g) of the 1934 Act requires that an issuer with more than $1 million in assets and 500 or more shareholders of record of a class of equity securities at the end of a fiscal year must register such securities with the SEC. Registration under the 1934 Act means that the issuer becomes subject to the periodic reporting, ownership disclosure, proxy, and insider reporting and trading rules of the 1934 Act. For purposes of determining whether the 500 shareholder threshold has been reached, all securities held of record by a trust (including a trust relating to an employee benefit plan) are deemed to be held by one person.[85] If distributions of employer stock are made to current or former employees under the plan, each recipient will count as a shareholder.

Registration of Plan Under Section 12(g) of the Securities Exchange Act of 1934

Even if a large plan has more than 500 participants and $1 million in assets, participation interests in employee stock bonus, stock purchase, profit-sharing, pension, and similar plans are exempt from registration under Section 12(g) of the 1934 Act if such interests are not transferable except on account of death or incompetency.[86]

---

[82] SEC Rule 16a-10.
[83] SEC Rule 16b-3.
[84] SEC Release 34-18114.
[85] SEC Rule 12g5-1(a)(2).
[86] SEC Rule 12h-2(a).

Registration of Collective Investment Vehicle Under Section 12(g) of the Securities Exchange Act of 1934

Interests in a collective trust fund maintained by a bank or a separate account maintained by an insurance company are exempt from registration under Section 12(g) of the 1934 Act if such interests are issued in connection with a tax-qualified stock bonus, pension, or profit-sharing plan.[87]

Rule 240—Small Offering Exemption Under the Securities Act of 1933

An offering of securities under SEC Rule 240 is limited to an issuer whose securities are beneficially owned by 100 or fewer persons.[88] A noncontributory employee stock ownership plan, and presumably any other employee benefit plan and its related trust, that owns securities of the issuer is counted as a single person or beneficial owner.[89]

Rule 146—Private Offering Exemption Under the Securities Act of 1933

An offering of securities under SEC Rule 146 that provides a safe harbor under the private offering exemption set forth in Section 4(2) of the 1933 Act is limited to thirty-five purchasers. A trust is counted as one purchaser except that if it was organized for the specific purpose of acquiring the securities offered, each beneficial owner is counted as a separate purchaser.[90]

BENEFICIAL OWNERSHIP REPORTING REQUIREMENTS

Ownership by Plan and Trust

If an employee benefit plan and its related trust own, after an acquisition, more than 5 percent of any equity security registered under Section 12 of the 1934 Act (or certain insurance company and mutual fund securities), the plan and trust must publicly report their ownership within ten days after acquisition on SEC Schedule 13D, as required by Section 13(d) of the 1934 Act. However, an employee benefit plan subject to ERISA may elect instead to file a short form Schedule 13G within forty-five days after the end of the calendar year in which the acquisition occurs if the plan has acquired the securities in the ordinary course of business and not with the effect of changing or influencing the control of the issuer and has notified any plan beneficiary who might be required to report as a result of such acquisition.[91] Additional ownership changes of the same security trigger an accelerated filing

---

[87] 1934 Act, § 12(g)(2)(H).
[88] SEC Rule 240(f).
[89] 259 Pens. Rep. (BNA) A-13 (1979).
[90] SEC Rule 146(g)(2)(ii).
[91] SEC Rule 13d-1(b)(1).

requirement.[92] Material changes in the information disclosed on Schedules 13D and 13G must be reported by amendments.[93]

Under Section 13(g) of the 1934 Act, if an employee benefit plan and its related trust own, as of December 31, 1978 or the end of any later calendar year, more than 5 percent of any equity security described above, but are not required to file under the rules above (as, for example, where no recent acquisition of securities occurred), Form 13G must be filed within forty-five days after the end of the relevant calendar year.[94]

Ownership by Plan Participants

A person who has the power to vote or dispose of a security is deemed to be the beneficial owner of such security.[95] Thus, plan participants may, under certain circumstances, be considered beneficial owners of certain securities held in the trust. Moreover, such securities held in the trust are to be aggregated with securities beneficially owned by the participant in any other capacity in determining whether the 5 percent threshold has been reached.[96]

TENDER OFFER REQUIREMENTS

It is unlawful under Section 14(d) of the 1934 Act for any person to make a tender offer for any equity security registered under Section 12 of the 1934 Act (or certain insurance company and mutual fund securities) if such person would own more than 5 percent of such equity security after the tender offer, unless a tender offer statement on SEC Schedule 14D-1 has been filed with the SEC. In addition, a tender offeror must comply with substantive rules regarding withdrawal of tendered securities by shareholders, pro rata purchase of securities in the event of oversubscription, and payment of equal consideration to all shareholders who tender securities. However, the rules do not apply to the acquisition of 2 percent or less of the outstanding shares of a security in a period of twelve months. If the trust relating to an employee benefit plan cannot purchase sufficient employer stock on the open market to satisfy an annual purchase requirement, it must comply with Section 14(d) of the 1934 Act, in order to send a letter to shareholders announcing an interest in purchasing their securities.[97]

---

[92] SEC Rule 13d-1(b)(2).
[93] SEC Rule 13d-2.
[94] SEC Rule 13d-1(c).
[95] SEC Rule 13d-3(a).
[96] SEC Rule 13d-3(c).
[97] SEC No-Action letter, Schaevitz Eng'r, 257 Pens. Rep. (BNA) A-6 (1979).

RESTRICTIONS ON OPEN MARKET PURCHASES

SEC Rule 10b-6 forbids an employer to make purchases of employer stock in the open market at the same time that it is engaged in a distribution of such securities.

An employer is engaged in a distribution, for example, if it is making a public offering of its securities or is offering its stock upon conversion of other securities. However, Rule 10b-6, as amended on February 19, 1981, does not apply to a distribution by an employer or a subsidiary to an employee, a shareholder, or a plan trustee under any bonus, profit-sharing, pension, stock option, savings or stock purchase plan.[98]

APPLICATION OF INVESTMENT COMPANY ACT OF 1940

Section 3(c)(11) of the Investment Company Act of 1940 (1940 IC Act) excludes from the definition of an *investment company* to which the 1940 IC Act applies any stock bonus, pension or profit-sharing trust which is tax-qualified (including that of an H.R. 10 plan), any trust relating to certain governmental plans, any collective trust fund maintained by a bank consisting solely of assets of such trusts, and any insurance company separate account holding assets of a tax-qualified plan or certain governmental plans. If a plan and its related trust are not within the exemption above, the trust would probably constitute an "employees' securities company" under Section 2(a)(13) of the 1940 IC Act. The plan would then be authorized to file an application with the SEC under Section 6(b) of the 1940 IC Act seeking exemption from the provisions of the 1940 IC Act. An exemption under Sections 6(c) and 6(e) of the 1940 IC Act was sought by the Teamsters Central States, Southeast and Southwest Areas Pension Fund when it was notified by the IRS that its tax-qualified status would be revoked.[99] A temporary exemption was granted by the SEC.[100]

Section 3(c)(3) of the 1940 IC Act exempts from the definition of an "investment company" any common trust fund or similar fund maintained by a bank exclusively for the investment of funds contributed to it in a fiduciary capacity. Because funds contributed to an IRA are not held for fiduciary purposes beyond money management, a bank common trust fund consisting of IRA contributions is not exempt under Section 3(c)(3) of the 1940 IC Act.[101] Moreover, a bank common trust fund may not be maintained as a vehicle for direct investment by individual members of the public.[102] In addition, IRA contributions cannot be commingled with the

---

[98] SEC Rule 10b-6(e).

[99] 97 Pens. Rep. (BNA) A-7 (1976).

[100] 109 Pens. Rep. (BNA) A-2, R-6 (1976).

[101] SEC No-Action letter, Citytrust, 284 Pens. Rep. (BNA) A-24 (1980).

[102] SEC No-Action letter, First National Bank of Peoria, 272 Pens. Rep. (BNA) A-21 (1979).

assets of tax-qualified plans contained in a bank collective trust fund without endangering the latter's exemption under Section 3(c)(11) of the 1940 IC Act.[103]

APPLICATION OF INVESTMENT ADVISERS ACT OF 1940

The Investment Advisers Act of 1940 (1940 IA Act) provides for the registration of persons who advise others for compensation as to the advisability of buying or selling securities and are in the business of giving such advice. Persons who advise employee benefit plans in this regard may be investment advisers. However, Section 202(a)(11) of the 1940 IA Act excludes from the definition of investment adviser any lawyer whose performance of investment advisory services is solely incidental to the practice of his profession. Whether such services are solely incidental to law practice depends on the nature and extent of the advice and the basis of the attorney's compensation.[104]

Section 203(b)(3) of the 1940 IA Act exempts from registration any investment adviser who in the preceding twelve months has had fewer than fifteen clients and who neither holds himself out generally to the public as an investment adviser nor advises an investment company. A person is considered to be holding himself out to the public as an investment adviser if he uses terms such as "investment adviser" or "investment management" on his stationery, or if he lets it be known that he is willing to take on new advisory clients.[105]

Excluded from the definition of investment adviser by IA Act Rule 202-1 is any person who offers investment advice to an employee benefit plan as defined in ERISA which is sponsored by the employer of such person, if such person is not engaged in the business of providing investment advice to others and does not hold himself out generally to the public as an investment adviser. This rule is designed to exempt plan participants who make investment choices under a plan.

Anti-fraud provisions that apply to all investment advisers, whether or not exempt from registration, are set forth in Section 206 of the 1940 IA Act. Section 206 makes it unlawful for an investment adviser, directly or indirectly, to employ any device or scheme to defraud a client or prospective client or to engage in any transaction, practice or course of business which operates as a fraud or deceit upon such persons. Generally, an adviser must disclose to clients all material facts regarding any conflict of interest between the client and the adviser.[106]

---

[103] Note 101, *supra*.

[104] SEC No-Action letter, Peter H. Jacobs, 229 Pens. Rep. (BNA) A-1 (1979).

[105] *Id.*

[106] SEC Release IA-770.

MARGIN RULES

Section 7 of the 1934 Act confers power on the Board of Governors of the Federal Reserve System to adopt regulations governing the amount of credit which may be extended or maintained with respect to any security (other than an exempted security). The Board has adopted Regulation U, which applies to banks, Regulation T, which applies to broker-dealers, Regulation G, which applies to certain other lenders, and Regulation X, which applies to borrowers. Under these regulations, it is necessary to determine the type of lender covered, the purpose or use of the loan proceeds, and whether application of the regulation depends on direct or indirect collateral and, if so, whether such collateral exists. These regulations are potentially applicable to leveraged ESOPs.

Federal Labor and Employment Laws

MICHAEL W. SCULNICK
Vedder, Price, Kaufman, Kammolz & Day

LABOR LAWS

National Labor Relations Act

The National Labor Relations Act of 1935[1] (NLRA) was designed to promote collective bargaining between employers and representatives of their employees. Unlike the Internal Revenue Code and the other revenue laws discussed above, the NLRA does not contain specific provisions regulating employee benefit plan structure and content. The NLRA does have significant impact on the collective bargaining aspects of benefit plans, however, as it affects the process by which benefit plans covering unionized employees are established and maintained.

Mandatory Subjects of Bargaining. An early court decision interpreting the NRLA held that employee benefits were a mandatory subject of collective bargaining. Specifically, through the conjunction of Sections 8(a)(5) and 9(a) of the NLRA, employers in interstate commerce must "bargain collectively with representatives of (its) employees . . . with respect to . . . rates of pay, wages, hours of employment or other conditions of employment. . . ." In *Inland Steel Co. v. N.L.R.B.*[2], the Seventh Circuit Court of Appeals held that employee benefit plans were within the scope of the terms "wages" and "other conditions of employment." Consequently, an employer presented with a proper demand by a union must bargain with respect to the establishment and maintenance of an employee benefit plan for its unionized employees. In addition, employers are prohibited from making any unilateral changes in the terms of employee benefit plans, unless agreed to by the union involved.

The Supreme Court has held that retired employees, however, are not "employees" within the meaning of the NLRA and, therefore, the employer's duty to bargain does not extend to them.[3] Thus, an employer does not violate the NLRA by unilaterally changing the provisions of an employee benefit plan as it relates to retired employees, although such modifications may violate other laws, such as the Employee Retirement Income Security

---

1 29 U.S.C. §§ 151 et seq.
2 170 F.2d 247 (7th Cir. 1948), *cert. denied* 336 U.S. 960 (1949).
3 Allied Chemical Workers v. Pittsburgh Plate Glass Co., 404 U.S. 157 (1971).

Act of 1974 (ERISA). Of course, an employer may voluntarily bargain with its unions regarding benefits for retired employees.

Labor Management Relations Act

General Prohibitions. The Labor Management Relations Act of 1947 [4] (the Taft-Hartley Act), an amendment to the NLRA, has had enormous impact on the development of employee benefits law. Section 302 of the Taft-Hartley Act prohibits payments by employers in interstate commerce to representatives of its employees, such as unions; moreover, it is illegal for any person to request, demand, or receive any payment from an employer. The purpose of Section 302 is to preserve the integrity of the labor-management relationship by prohibiting bribery, extortion, and similar forms of dishonesty.

Section 302(c)(5) of the Taft-Hartley Act. Section 302(c) of the Taft-Hartley Act contains an exception to the broad prohibitions contained in Section 302. Section 302(c)(5) provides that

> The provisions of Section 302 shall not be applicable . . . (5) with respect to money or other things of value paid to a trust fund established by such representative, for the sole and exclusive benefit of the employees of such employer, and their families and dependents. . . .

For a payment by an employer to a union to be within the scope of Section 302(c)(5) a number of requirements must be satisfied. First, the basis on which payments are to be made by the employer must be specified in a written agreement between the employer and the union. Second, the payments must be held in trust for the purpose of providing certain benefits to employees, and pension trusts must be kept segregated from health and welfare trusts. Third, the trusts in which payments are held must be jointly administered by employers and unions, who must be equally represented. Joint administration, in many cases, means that the trustees are appointed in equal number by management (i.e., the employer contributing to the plan) and labor (i.e., the employee organization representing the employees of the contributing employers). Finally, trustees must act for the exclusive benefit of the employees and may not act in an arbitrary or capricious manner.

Although Section 302(c)(5) broadly affects the structure and content of collectively bargained employee benefit plans, the courts have had a great deal of difficulty defining the extent to which Section 302(c)(5) relates to the administration of the plan. Other than the "sole and exclusive benefit" language, the Taft-Hartley Act does not explicitly regulate the administration of the plan by its trustees. Some courts, however, have concluded that the

---

4 Note 1 *supra*.

Taft-Hartley Act implicitly governs such matters. The general rule is that trustees of a plan, as fiduciaries, are liable for breach of fiduciary duty if their conduct is arbitrary and capricious. Moreover, trustees of jointly administered plans may not actively represent the interests of the party that appointed them (i.e., labor or management); their exclusive duty is to the participants and beneficiaries of the plans.

Overlap and Conflict With ERISA. Since 1974, ERISA has governed in much greater detail all aspects of collectively bargained benefit plans, which are now subject to both Taft-Hartley and ERISA. In most cases, there is no conflict between the two laws; in the event of conflict, however, it is clear that ERISA governs the rights of participants and beneficiaries and the liabilities of trustees and the plan.

Labor Management Reporting and Disclosure Act

The Labor Management Reporting and Disclosure Act of 1959[5] (the LMRDA), like the Taft-Hartley Act, was intended to remedy certain deficiencies in labor-management relations. The LMRDA, however, does not contain provisions that determine the structure and content of employee plans or the administration of plans; rather, its provisions primarily affect employee organizations, such as unions, and their internal governance.

The LMRDA requires every employee organization to adopt a constitution and bylaws and to file copies of these documents with the Secretary of Labor. These documents must be accompanied by a report containing certain information. Section 431(a) provides that the report must contain:

> (5) Detailed statements, or references to specific provisions of documents filed under this subsection which contains such statements, showing the provisions made and procedures followed with respect to . . . (C) participation in insurance or other benefit plans. . . .

This provision is enforced by the requirement imposed on every employee organization to file an annual report with the Secretary of Labor indicating whether it has any employee benefit plans. If the employee organization has an unfunded dues financed plan, for example, or a plan that pays benefits out of the employee organization's general assets, the plan administrator must file an annual report for the trust formed as part of the plan.

Fair Labor Standards Act of 1938

The Fair Labor Standards Act of 1938[6] (FLSA), regulates the minimum wages and maximum hours applicable to the employees of private employers

[5] 29 U.S.C. §§ 401 et seq.
[6] 29 U.S.C. §§ 200 et seq.

in interstate commerce. In general, employers must pay specified minimum wages for all hours worked by covered employees; in addition, hours worked in excess of the specified maximum must be compensated at a rate not less than one and one-half times the employee's "regular rate."

Overtime Provisions. The overtime provisions of FLSA have an impact on the structure and content of employee benefit plans. Generally, "wages" paid to an employee include all payments made to or on behalf of an employee as remuneration for employment. Thus, Section 207(e) of the FLSA provides that an employee's *regular rate* (or wages) include "all remuneration for employment paid to, or on behalf of, the employee. . . ."

Sections 207(e)(3)(b) and 204(e)(4), however, provide that "remuneration" does not include payments to a "bona fide profit-sharing plan or trust or bona fide thrift or savings plan," or contributions to a "bona fide plan for providing old-age, retirement, life, accident, or health insurance or similar benefits."

Regulations promulgated by the Department of Labor's Employment Standards Administration delineate both the essential requirements for qualification under Sections 207(e)(3)(b) and 207(e)(4) and the disqualifying provisions.[7] Compliance with these regulations will assure that payments made for employee benefit plans will not be deemed part of an employee's "regular rate" upon which overtime compensation is calculated. Of course, qualifying benefit payments do not qualify as part of required overtime compensation; nor do they constitute part of the required minimum wage.

One of the essential requirements for qualifying a "bona fide" thrift or savings plan for FLSA purposes is that the plan must specifically set forth the category or categories of employees participating in the plan and the basis of their eligibility. The employer's contribution may not exceed 15 percent of the participating employee's total yearly earnings, and the contributions must be apportioned among employees in accordance with a definite formula. Disqualifying provisions include nonvoluntary participation in the plan or the requirement that the amounts contributed by the employer under the plan may not be based on the employee's hours of work, production, or efficiency.

Interpretive regulations promulgated under Section 207(e)(4) set forth several conditions for the exclusion of pension and health and welfare plan contributions from the definition of "remuneration" under this section. Plans satisfying the requirements for qualification delineated in Section 401(a) of the Code (i.e., tax-qualified plans) are deemed to have met some of these conditions. Tax-qualified plans must also satisfy other conditions, including a *primary purpose* requirement (i.e., the plan is primarily designed to provide systematic welfare benefits), and a requirement of specified and deter-

---

[7] See 29 C.F.R. Pts. 547, 549; 29 C.F.R. § 778.213-22.5 (1981).

minable contributions and benefits. In addition, the employer's contributions must be paid irrevocably to a trustee who assumes the usual fiduciary responsibilities imposed upon trustees under applicable law. In general, therefore, the requirements of the FLSA are at least as broad as the requirements under ERISA; compliance with ERISA, however, will not satisfy all of the requirements of the FLSA for a "bona fide" plan as that term relates to the calculation of overtime compensation.

Government Contract Laws

Several statutes [8] require the payment of minimum wages and overtime to employees who perform work in connection with government contracts. All of these statutes affect the structure, content, and administration of employee benefit plans in the same manner as the FLSA; on the one hand, payments made for *fringe benefits* (defined broadly to include all types of employee benefit plans) do not constitute wages for purposes of calculating minimum wages; on the other hand, such payments, if made to "bona fide" plans, are excluded from the calculation of an employee's "regular rate" for purposes of determining any overtime pay.

EQUAL EMPLOYMENT OPPORTUNITY LAWS

Numerous laws, at both the federal and state level, prohibit discrimination in employment on such bases as race, color, sex, religion, natural origin, age, handicap, or marital status. These laws apply to all aspects of the employment relationship and have significant impact upon the structure, content, and administration of employee benefit plans. Generally, benefit plans may not discriminate in their participation, contribution or benefit provisions against any protected group. The areas of greatest concern, however, have been the prohibitions against age and sex discrimination.

Age Discrimination in Employee Benefit Plans

Source of Law and Coverage. The Age Discrimination in Employment Act of 1967 (ADEA) originally prohibited discrimination because of age against persons 40 to 65 years of age.[9] Amendments passed in 1978, in addition to other substantive changes, have expanded the protected group to age 70 for private employers and have completely eliminated the upper-age limit for federal government employees. The ADEA applies to all private and public employers in the United States who employ at least twenty employees for each working day in each of twenty or more calendar weeks.

---

[8] See Walsh-Healy Public Contracts Act, 41 U.S.C. § 35; Davis-Bacon Act, 40 U.S.C. § 276a; Service Contract Act of 1965, 41 U.S.C. § 351.

[9] 29 U.S.C. §§ 621 et seq.

The Age Discrimination Act of 1975 prohibits "unreasonable discrimination on the basis of age in programs that receive federal financial assistance." Unlike ADEA, the 1975 Act is not limited in its application to employees between the ages of 40 and 70.

Executive Order 11246, as amended, provides that federal contractors may not discriminate "in connection with the terms, conditions, or privileges" of employment against employees on the basis of age "except on the basis of a bona fide occupational qualification, retirement plan, or statutory requirement."

Mandatory Retirement. Although the ADEA's prohibitions against age discrimination are broad, Section 623(f)(2) specifically provides that it is not unlawful for an employer:

> To observe the terms of a bona fide employee benefit plan such as a retirement, pension, or insurance plan, which is not a subterfuge to evade the purposes of this Act, except that no such employee benefit plan shall excuse the failure to hire any individual, and no such employee benefit plan shall require or permit the involuntary retirement of any individual because of the age of such individual.

In *United Airlines v. McMann*,[10] the U.S. Supreme Court held that the 1967 version of Section 623(f)(2) of ADEA permitted the mandatory retirement of an employee at age 60 pursuant to a pension plan's mandatory retirement provision as long as the plan was "bona fide" and was not a "subterfuge" to evade ADEA's purposes. It was conceded that United Airline's plan was bona fide because it actually existed and paid substantial benefits. The Supreme Court found that the pension plan and its mandatory retirement provision could not be regarded as a subterfuge because both were already in existence in 1967 when ADEA was passed. At the time of this case, several lower federal courts had ruled that forced early retirement based solely on age was lawful when it was permitted (although not required) by the terms of a bona fide employee benefit plan which antedated the Act. The Supreme Court never reached the question of whether such forced early retirement at the employer's option was sanctioned by ADEA, but it did conclude that Congress did not require employers to prove a business or economic purpose to justify involuntary retirements pursuant to a bona fide pension plan.

Congress overruled the *McMann* decision in the 1978 amendments to ADEA by adding to Section 623(f)(2) the provision that "no . . . employee benefit plan shall require or permit the involuntary retirement of any individual," with limited exceptions applicable to highly paid executives and tenured faculty.[11]

---

[10] 434 U.S. 192 (1977).

[11] Mandatory retirement prior to age 70 may still be valid if it constitutes a bona fide occupational qualification under Section 623(f)(i) of ADEA.

Effective dates of 1978 amendments. The prohibition on mandatory early retirement became effective April 6, 1978 (the date of enactment of the 1978 amendments to ADEA) for employees between ages 40 and 65. The ban on involuntary retirement prior to age 70 became effective January 1, 1979 when ADEA's other protections were extended to persons in the age 65 to 70 group. The 1978 amendments forbidding early retirement below age 70 do not have retroactive application to forced retirements which were permissible prior to 1979.[12] For employees between ages 65 and 70 who were covered by a collective bargaining agreement which was in effect on September 1, 1977, and which permitted mandatory retirement at age 65, the prohibition on early mandatory retirement did not take effect until the earlier of January 1, 1980, or the expiration of the collective bargaining agreement.

Exemptions to the prohibition against mandatory retirement. Limited exceptions to the prohibition against mandatory retirement apply to highly paid executives and tenured faculty.

1. *Executive exemption.* As noted above, an employee between the ages of 65 and 70 may be involuntarily retired if he or she held an "executive or high policymaking position," as "is entitled to an immediate nonforfeitable annual retirement benefit from a pension, profit-sharing, savings, or deferred compensation plan, or any combination of such plans, of the employee, which equals in the aggregate at least $27,000."

   Interpretive regulations issued by the Equal Employment Opportunity Commission (EEOC) state that the exemption will be narrowly construed, with the employer carrying the burden of demonstrating that the exemption applies. The EEOC interpretation states that to be considered an executive or high policymaking employee, the employee involved must be exempt from the overtime provisions of the FLSA under the so-called "long test." Not all FLSA-exempt employees, however, are covered by the exemption. It applies only to FLSA-exempt employees who exercise substantial executive authority over a significant number of employees and a large volume of business, are heads of major departments of divisions or a corporation or who, although having little or no line authority, "play a significant role in the development of corporate policy and effectively recommend its implementation," such as the chief economist or chief scientist of a corporation.

   Additionally, the EEOC interpretation provides that in determining whether the $27,000 test has been met, only retirement benefits from a pension, profit-sharing, savings, or deferred compensation plan may be counted; benefits from other plans, such as life or health insurance, may not. Amounts attributable to Social Security, employee contributions, contributions by prior employers and rollovers must be excluded. Moreover, the $27,000 benefit must be "immediately available," and nonforfeitable. Although the plan

---

[12] See Sikora v. American Can Co., 622 F.2d 1116, 22 FEP Cases 638 (3d Cir. 1980); Gonsalves v. Caterpillar Tractor Co., —— F. Supp. ——, 22 FEP Cases 967 (C.D. Ill. 1980).

need not be funded, there must be a "reasonable expectation" that the plan will pay the promised benefit.

2. *Faculty exemption.* A limited exemption to the mandatory retirement provisions of ADEA applies to faculty members between the ages of 65 and 70 who serve under a contract or system providing for unlimited tenure at institutions of higher education.

   The exemption expires July 1, 1982; according to the EEOC's Interpretive Bulletin, it too will be narrowly construed, with the employer carrying the burden of showing its applicability.

Plan Participation. It is a violation of ADEA to exclude an employee, hired prior to normal retirement age, from participation in a defined contribution plan. Although ADEA does not expressly so provide, the Department of Labor (DOL), in the "final" Interpretive Bulletin it issued on employee benefit plans before ADEA enforcement responsibility was shifted to the EEOC on July 1, 1979, stated that employees hired within five years of normal retirement age may be excluded from a defined benefit plan covered by ERISA, and employees hired after normal retirement age may also be excluded. Employees hired more than five years prior to normal retirement age may be excluded from a defined benefit plan not covered by ERISA only if the exclusion is justified by cost considerations, a subject discussed below.

Employee Contributions. It is a violation of ADEA to require an older employee, as a condition of employment, to contribute to a retirement plan when younger employees are not required to do so. In a contributory plan, an older employee may be required to make a greater contribution as long as he does not bear a greater share of the cost of providing benefits than younger employees. Additionally, older employees may be given the option of making greater contributions than younger employees to receive the same benefits as younger employees.

Plan Benefits. ADEA's exception for actions taken to observe the terms of a plan that is bona fide and not a subterfuge has been interpreted by the DOL's Interpretive Bulletin to permit benefit reductions based on age if the reduction is justified actuarially by "significant cost considerations." In general, a plan is in compliance with ADEA as long as the actual amount of payment made or cost incurred on behalf of the older worker is equal to that made or incurred for a younger worker, even though the older worker may, as a result, receive lower benefits. In order to justify paying lower benefits to the older worker, however, the employer bears the burden of showing that the plan is bona fide, that the reduction is made to observe the terms of the plan and that the plan is not a subterfuge.

For a plan to be bona fide, it must accurately describe its provisions in writing to all employees, and must actually provide benefits in accordance with its terms. Actions taken "to observe the terms of a plan" must actually be mandated, not merely permitted, by the terms of the plan. Finally, a plan is not a "subterfuge" only if any age-based benefit reductions are premised on valid and reasonable cost data. Retirement benefit costs must be made on a benefit-by-benefit basis, rather than on the "benefit package" approach permitted for other nonretirement benefits.

Benefits Treatment for Individuals Who Work Past Normal Retirement Age. The 1978 amendments to ADEA, as interpreted by the DOL Interpretive Bulletin, also provide for a variety of special rules applicable to the administration of benefit plans for individuals who work past normal age.

Defined contribution plans. It is not a violation of ADEA, according to the DOL Interpretive Bulletin, for an employer to cease contributions on behalf of any participant in a defined contribution plan (i.e., a profit-sharing, thrift, or money purchase plan) after the attainment of normal retirement age, if the plan is not *supplemental.* A defined contribution plan is deemed "supplemental" if the employee also participates in a defined benefit plan or in more than one defined contribution plans. In addition, the employer may exclude from participation any employee hired after normal retirement age.

Finally, even though the Interpretive Bulletin permits employers to cease contributions to nonsupplemental defined contribution plans after normal retirement age, allocation of investment gains and losses may not be done in a manner that treats older employees less favorably than younger employees. Since most defined contribution plans allocate such gains or losses on the same basis as contributions, such plans may be required to amend the method of allocation so as not to disadvantage older workers.

These provisions of the Interpretive Bulletin are potentially in conflict with ERISA, since ERISA only permits the exclusion of employees hired within five years of normal retirement from defined benefit plans. By negative inference, therefore, ERISA arguably prohibits the exclusion of any individual on the basis of age from defined contribution plans.

Defined benefit plans. The DOL Interpretive Bulletin permits employers to cease crediting years of service, for purposes of benefit accrual, that occur after attainment of normal retirement age. In addition, a defined benefit plan need not adjust actuarially the benefit accrued as of normal retirement age for an employee who continues to work beyond that age.

The DOL Interpretive Bulletin also permits defined benefit plans to commence payment of retirement benefits at the actual date of retirement rather than at normal retirement age. Employees receiving long-term disability benefits as a salary replacement may be deemed not to have "actually retired," thereby avoiding simultaneous receipt of benefits. Finally, the Interpretive Bulletin provides that if the pension benefit of an employee who works past normal retirement age is frozen, the amount of the offset for

Social Security must be frozen at normal retirement age. If the plan formula recognizes employment after normal retirement age by providing for accrual of full benefits to actual retirement, the Social Security offset may be based on the amount to which the employee is entitled at that time.

Sex Discrimination in Employee Benefit Plans

The courts and administrative agencies have struggled at great length with issues of discrimination on the basis of sex in plan coverage, contributions, and benefit payments.

Sources of Law and Coverage. Prohibitions against employment discrimination are covered on the federal, state, and local levels.

- *Civil Rights Act of 1964.* Discrimination with respect to the terms, conditions, or privileges of employment on the basis of race, color, religion, sex, or national origin is prohibited by Title VII of the Civil Rights Act of 1964, as amended by the Equal Employment Opportunity Act of 1972 (Title VII).[13] In 1978, Title VII was amended to provide that the ban on sex discrimination also prohibited discrimination in providing benefits or in the terms or conditions of employment on the basis of pregnancy, childbirth, and related medical conditions.[14]

  Title VII applies to all employers in the United States having fifteen or more employees on each working day in each of twenty or more calendar weeks in the current or preceding calendar year.
- *Equal Pay Act of 1963.* Wage differentials based on sex are generally prohibited by the Equal Pay Act of 1963 (the Equal Pay Act),[15] which amended the Fair Labor Standards Act of 1938. Section 206(d) makes it unlawful for an employer to discriminate between the sexes in the payment of wages:

  > for equal work on jobs the performance of which requires equal skill, effort, and responsibility, and which are performed under similar working conditions, except where such payment is made pursuant to (i) a seniority system; (ii) a merit system; (iii) a system which measures earnings by quantity or quality of production; or (iv) a differential based on any other factor other than sex. . . .

  Since the Equal Pay Act is part of the Fair Labor Standards Act, its jurisdictional coverage is identical with the FLSA, except that it covers exempt as well as nonexempt personnel.
- *Executive Order 11246.* Executive Order 11246 requires that contracts between the U.S. Government and private contractors and subcontractors contain an "Equal Opportunity Clause," providing that the contractor will not discriminate against any employee because of race, color, religion, sex, or

---

[13] 42 U.S.C. §§ 2000(e) et seq.
[14] 42 U.S.C. § 2000e(k).
[15] 29 U.S.C. § 206(d).

national origin. Executive Order 11246 also requires that contractors or subcontractors adopt written affirmative action plans designed to increase equal employment opportunities for women and minorities for each of its establishments if the employer has fifty or more employees and holds a contract or subcontract of $50,000 or more, or if it serves as a depository of federal funds or issues U.S. savings notes and savings bonds.

- *State and local fair employment practice laws.* Virtually every state, and many cities and counties, have statutes prohibiting employment discrimination. While state laws generally follow federal law in substantive content, in some areas state law goes even further than federal law in prohibiting various types of discrimination. For example, some states prohibit age discrimination regardless of the individual's age. A complete review of state law is beyond the scope of this text; state law must always be checked, however, to ascertain whether additional considerations affect any given issue.

Sex Discrimination in Coverage of Employee Benefit Plans. Title VII prohibits discrimination on the basis of sex in coverage or participation in employee benefit plans. Thus, it is illegal for an employer to provide dependents' benefits only to employees who are the "principal wage earner in the family unit" or the "head of the household," or to limit coverage to dependents of male employees or to provide benefits only to wives of male employees but not to female employees. At least one court has held, however, that an employer did not violate Title VII by covering the spouse of an employee only if the employee is the head of the household, finding that each employee's benefit entitlement was a function of income and not sex.[16]

Sex Discrimination in Pension Benefit Plans. A pension plan may not establish different optional or compulsory retirement ages for men and women without violating Title VII. Moreover, the EEOC interprets Title VII to require the provision of equal periodic pension benefits to men and women even if it costs more to fund equal benefits for women as a class due to their greater longevity. Thus, for example, the EEOC has ruled that a group life insurance plan that provides for sex-based differences in death benefits, based upon sex-segregated actuarial tables, also violates Title VII.

Unequal contributions. In *City of Los Angeles v. Manhart,*[17] the U.S. Supreme Court held that an employer violated Title VII by requiring female employees to make larger contributions to its pension fund than male employees, even though both received equal benefits. Even though women, as a class, live longer than men, the Court concluded that use of female class characteristics could not justify discrimination against individual women.

---

[16] Wambheim v. J.C. Penney Co., 20 FEP Cases 1286 (N.D. Cal. 1979). This case should be considered a minority view.

[17] 435 U.S. 702 (1978).

Similarly, the Court rejected the argument that the differential contributions were based on a factor other than sex, namely longevity, because the actuarial tables were based solely on sex. The guiding principle of Title VII enunciated by *Manhart* is that employees must be treated equally as individuals, and not according to class characteristics which, while generally true, are not true for each individual.

Unequal benefits. Lower federal courts have interpreted the Supreme Court's reasoning in *Manhart* to prohibit pension plans that require equal contributions but provide lower periodic benefits to women because of the use of sex-segregated mortality tables.[18] These decisions are consistent with the position of the EEOC. Prior to July 1, 1979, however, the DOL, not the EEOC, had enforcement responsibility under the Equal Pay Act: DOL had consistently taken the position that the Equal Pay Act was *not* violated if the employer made equal contributions even if this resulted in unequal benefits. The DOL has now adopted the EEOC's view by proposing to amend its regulations to require equal periodic retirement benefits under both the Equal Pay Act and Executive Order 11246 (covering government contractors). It therefore seems clear that the requirement of benefit equalization prohibits the use of sex-based factors (i.e., sex-segregated mortality tables, etc.) in determining benefit payments.

The implications for employee benefit plan administration are manifold and complex. For defined benefit plans, employers must either make the same male early retirement and option factors applicable to females (despite the expense) or develop and adopt unisex factors applicable to all employees. For defined contribution plans, employers must insure that annuity contracts purchased by the plan provide equal benefits for equal contributions, or drop the annuity option from a plan entirely.

Finally, adoption of a unisex table may result in violations of the Equal Pay Act or ERISA if accrued benefits are reduced (under ERISA) or if benefits payable to members of either sex are reduced (under the Equal Pay Act). ERISA prohibits a plan amendment "decreasing an accrued benefit." [19] This might occur if unisex tables were adopted based on average mortality experience for men and women combined, without guaranteeing the level of benefits accrued under the plan prior to the amendment. No courts have addressed this issue to date, but great care should be taken in amending plans to insure no reduction in previously accrued benefits.

Maternity Benefits. On October 31, 1978, Title VII was amended to expand the definition of "sex discrimination" to include discrimination be-

---

[18] EEOC v. Colby College, 589 F.2d 1139, 18 FEP Cases 1125 (1st Cir. 1978); Norris v. Arizona, 486 F. Supp. 645, 22 FEP Cases 1059 (D. Ariz. 1980); Spirt v. Teachers Ins. & Annuity Assoc., 475 F. Supp. 1298, 1306, 20 FEP Cases 738 (S.D.N.Y. 1979).

[19] I.R.C. § 411(d)(6); 26 U.S.C. § 411(d)(6); Treas. Reg. § 1.411(d)-3(b), 26 C.F.R. § 1.411(d)-3(b) (1981).

cause of pregnancy, childbirth, or related medical conditions. Thus, all fringe benefit programs, such as health insurance, sick pay and disability plans must include pregnancy benefits on the same basis as any other medical condition. The amendment does not require an employer to provide these benefits if it does not presently offer any such benefits.

Impact on employment practices related to benefit plans. The amendment provides, for example, that

1. Pregnancy and childbirth (but not abortion) must be treated the same as any other medical condition or disability;
2. Commencement of maternity leave must be based on actual disability of the individual, not the mere fact of pregnancy;
3. Employers may not discharge or refuse to hire or promote a woman solely because she is pregnant;
4. Employers must credit accumulated seniority after pregnancy, disability, or leave of absence on the same basis as for persons absent from work for other disabilities or leaves of absence, and must provide the same reinstatement rights.

Impact on medical and health insurance plans. Pregnancy and related conditions must be covered under a medical reimbursement plan on the same basis as other disabilities. For example, the same percentage of reasonable and customary charges (e.g., 80 percent must be reimbursed; if dollar amounts are provided by schedule, the amount must treat pregnancy as generously as the *most* generously treated medical condition). A plan need not provide coverage for pregnancy of spouses or other dependents as long as it excludes the pregnancy-related conditions of all spouses and dependents.

Impact on disability plans. Disability benefits for pregnancy and related conditions must be provided in the same manner as other disabilities. This is true even if applicable state law provides for lesser or limited benefits, as Title VII preempts state law in this regard. Of course, if state law provides greater benefits, it is not affected by Title VII.

Service Credit for Military Leave

The Vietnam Era Veterans Readjustment Assistance Act of 1974,[20] which is a recodification of the Military Selective Service Act, provides in part that any person who leaves employment in order to enter the armed forces and who subsequently makes an application for reemployment must be restored by such employer to a position of "like seniority, status, and pay." This section further provides that the employee must be entitled to participate in insurance or other benefits offered by the employer pursuant to the

---

[20] 38 U.S.C. §§ 2021, et seq.

established rules and practices relating to employees on furlough or leave of absence.

In *Alabama Power Co. v. Davis,*[21] the U.S. Supreme Court unanimously ruled that a pension plan that provides benefits based on final-average compensation must grant pension benefit accrual credit for employee's military service where the employee leaves employment to enter military service and subsequently resumes employment within ninety days of discharge, the period prescribed by the Military Selective Service Act for the protection of reemployment rights. This protection applies to all those involuntarily inducted into military service, and to those who voluntarily enlist only if the total time spent in the military does not exceed four years.

The pension plan at issue provided a benefit based on final-average compensation and years of credited service. The Court left open the question whether an employer must count military service for accrual of benefits under a defined contribution plan, or in a contributory defined benefit plan. Nor did the Court address the potential retroactive effect of its decisions, although generally such decisions, based on interpretations of existing laws, do have retroactive impact to the effective date of the statute. Thus, employers may be held liable for "improperly" withheld benefits based on their previous failure to include military service in credited service for accrual purposes in defined benefit final-average-pay plans.

The Supreme Court's decision also requires that noncontributory final-average-pay plans be amended prospectively so that future retirees and beneficiaries received full credit for military service, where required. Employers should also consider notifying all existing retirees that their pensions will be increased if they can demonstrate performance of military service while employed by the company.

---

21 431 U.S. 581 (1977).

17

Tax Considerations for Qualified Retirement Plans

HAROLD DANKNER
Coopers & Lybrand

TAX TREATMENT OF QUALIFIED PLAN DISTRIBUTIONS

Prior to the passage of the Employee Retirement Income Security Act of 1974 (ERISA), the types of plans eligible for qualified status included pension, profit-sharing, stock bonus, and annuity plans. (Savings or thrift plans qualify as either a profit-sharing or money purchase pension plan, depending upon their design.) ERISA and subsequent legislation have added the employee stock ownership plan (ESOP) and tax credit employer stock ownership plan (TRASOP) to the list of qualified plans.

Qualified retirement plans have a number of important tax benefits, including:

- The current deductibility of contributions by the employer, within certain limitations;
- The deferment of income to the participating employees until the benefits are distributed;
- The favorable tax treatment (e.g., long-term capital gain and ten-year income averaging) for certain lump-sum distributions;
- The exemption of the retirement trust from income tax, other than the tax on unrelated business taxable income; and
- The favorable estate and gift tax treatment to participating employees.

"Constructive Receipt"—Taxation of Benefits Before Actual Distribution

The Economic Recovery Tax Act of 1981 (ERTA) effectively eliminates the threat of "constructive receipt" of benefits under qualified plans for taxable years beginning after December 31, 1981. This new law change means that employees and their beneficiaries will now be taxed only when benefits are actually distributed from qualified plans and *not* when amounts are merely "made available." Sponsors of plans that contain provisions intended to prevent the constructive receipt of income prior to actual benefit distribution will be reconsidering their plan design in light of the more liberal rules available under the new law.

Background—Rules in Effect Through 1981. Under the rules governing the taxation of qualified plans in effect through 1981, an employee was taxed on benefits that were "made available" under the plan as well as on benefits that were actually distributed. This rule requiring the taxation of amounts "made available" is known as the doctrine of *constructive receipt*. In general, amounts were deemed to be constructively received, or "made available," if there were no substantial restrictions or limitations on the employee's right to receive benefits—these amounts were currently taxable to the employee even if he did not exercise his right to receive distributable benefits.

This principle most directly affected qualified plans that permitted employees to make in-service withdrawals of vested employer contributions and/or earnings attributable to employee contributions. It was generally necessary for such plans to incorporate IRS-sanctioned limitations and restrictions to prevent participants' withdrawal rights from resulting in current tax liability under the doctrine of constructive receipt. Among the limitations and restrictions incorporated in plans to prevent taxation of benefits prior to actual distribution have been the following:

- *Withdrawal penalties.* A substantial limitation exists (and, hence, constructive receipt was avoided) if withdrawals were penalized either (1) by the forfeiture of a portion of a participant's vested interest in the plan, or (2) by the suspension of participation and resulting loss of employer-derived benefits during the prescribed suspension period. (However, ERISA limits the availability of such restrictions.)
- *Administrative committee review.* Amounts were not generally "made available" to plan participants if withdrawals were permitted only with the express consent of an administrative committee on the basis of objective standards (such as established proof of financial hardship).

Constructive receipt was also a threat in those situations in which a plan participant wanted to defer the receipt of otherwise distributable amounts, or wanted to have his benefits transferred from one qualified plan to another. In these situations, immediate taxation was avoided where the participant made an irrevocable election prior to the time that his interest initially became withdrawable to defer distribution to some fixed or determinable future time.

Plan Design Under the New Law. As noted above, ERTA eliminates the "made available" basis for taxing benefits under qualified plans beginning in 1982. With constructive receipt no longer a threat, employers will have considerable latitude to remove limitations and restrictions on participants' withdrawal rights (e.g., participation suspension penalties and committee review of hardship withdrawal requests). Participants will also be able to defer distribution of benefits to a more favorable tax year without irrevocably sacrificing the privilege to receive such monies at an earlier date if needs or circumstances change. However, the new rules do not supersede established tax-qualification requirements, notably:

- Employer contributions to a pension plan may not be distributed prior to the employee's separation from service or the plan's termination; and
- Employer contributions to a profit-sharing plan may not be distributed prior to a fixed period of time (generally, at least two years), attainment of a stated age, or the prior occurrence of certain specified events.

In addition, the plan sponsor may want to continue to limit participants' withdrawal rights for various reasons relating to plan design and/or employer benefits philosophy. For example, the typical thrift or savings plan which requires an employee to contribute in order to receive a corresponding employer contribution might continue to restrict the withdrawal of employee contributions to prevent the manipulation of matching employer contributions. Similarly, unlimited withdrawal rights would not be appropriate in a plan that was intended as the primary source of retirement income for employees, but might be appropriate in a plan intended more as a capital accumulation vehicle.

Periodic Distributions

Generally, periodic distributions, whether in the form of a life annuity or fixed-installment payments, are taxable under the annuity rules of Section 72 of the Internal Revenue Code. Under these rules, periodic distributions are reduced by amounts representing the employee's cost (his contribution to the plan) and the balance is taxed at ordinary income rates. These payments qualify for the special 50 percent maximum tax rate available for "personal service income."

If only employer contributions have been made to the plan, the full amount of the distribution is taxable. An exception exists where employer contributions are used to purchase pure life insurance protection for the employee. In this case, the annual cost of life insurance protection is includable in the employee's income for each year of coverage. This taxable cost, the so-called *P.S. 58 cost,* is derived from a tax table developed by the Internal Revenue Service to determine the one-year premium cost of $1,000 of term insurance at various ages. The P.S. 58 cost, which is taxable to an employee, becomes part of his cost in the plan and will be returned to him tax free if the actual insurance contract is distributed to the employee.

If the employee contributed toward the cost of his benefit, plan payments will be taxed under one of two methods: the *three-year cost recovery rule* or the *general annuity rule.* Both methods are designed to return the employee's contributions, which were made with after-tax dollars, to the employee tax free. The method used will depend on the size of the employee's cost in relation to the total amount he will receive during the first three years of payment.

As its name implies, the three-year cost recovery rule will apply if the total payments receivable during the first three years after payments begin will equal or exceed the employee's cost. If total payments during this three-year period will be less than the employee's cost, the general annuity rules apply.

Three-Year Cost Recovery Rule. Under this rule, the employee excludes from gross income all payments received until they equal his cost; thereafter, all amounts received are taxed as ordinary income.

Example: An employee will receive $500 a month at retirement from an insurance contract purchased for him by his employer's pension plan. His total cost basis is $12,000, representing $10,000 in employee contributions and $2,000 pure life insurance protection that has been previously taxed to him. Since payments during the first three years ($500 × 12 months × 3 years = $18,000) will exceed his cost, the three-year rule applies. Thus, the employee will exclude $6,000 a year from his income for the first two years and, thereafter, all amounts received by him will be includable in gross income.

General Annuity Rules—The Exclusion Ratio. Under this method, payments are taxed on the basis of an exclusion ratio determined as of the benefit commencement date. The exclusion ratio is determined by dividing the employee's cost by the total amount expected to be distributed under the plan. Where benefits are payable only for the life of a participant or a beneficiary, the expected return is determined by multiplying the total amount that will be distributed each year by the number of years in the individual's life expectancy according to IRS tables of expected return multiples. Adjustments are required where benefits are payable in a form other than a straight life annuity. For example, where distributions will be made under a qualified joint and survivor annuity, the exclusion ratio must reflect the life expectancies of both annuitants as well as any difference in the amount of payment that will be made to the employee and his survivor. The exclusion ratio is the percentage of each payment that may be excluded from gross income.

Example: An employee retires at age 65 and is entitled to retirement benefits of $250 a month for the remainder of his life. According to the applicable annuity table, his life expectancy is fifteen years. Therefore, the expected return under the plan is $45,000 ($250 × 12 months × 15 years) and the employee's cost is $10,000 which exceeds the total payments receivable over the first three years. The employee's exclusion ratio is $\frac{\$10{,}000}{\$45{,}000} = 22\%$. Thus, the employee may exclude from gross income $55.50 of each $250 payment received under the plan.

Lump-Sum Distributions

The Code provides special tax treatment for "lump-sum distributions" from qualified plans. A lump-sum distribution made on or after January 1, 1974 is divided into two parts. The portion of the payment attributable to years of active participation prior to January 1, 1974 is taxed as long-term capital gain, while the portion attributable to plan participation on or after January 1, 1974 is taxed as ordinary income, subject to an election to apply ten-year forward income averaging. In addition, the Tax Reform Act of

1976 extended this ten-year forward averaging treatment to the entire distribution under certain circumstances.

Lump-Sum Distribution Defined. The term *lump-sum distribution* refers to a distribution from a qualified plan of the total balance to the credit of an employee. In order to qualify for special tax treatment, the distribution must also meet the following requirements:

1. The payment must be completed within one taxable year of the recipient;
2. It must be payable on account of the employee's death, on or after his attainment of age 59½, on account of his separation from service, or upon becoming disabled.

Total Balance. The distribution must represent the employee's total interest in all plans of the same type which are maintained by a single employer. All pension plans (defined benefit and money purchase) are classified as one type of plan; all profit-sharing plans are classified as another type of plan; and all stock bonus plans are classified as another. For example, if in one year an employee received a total distribution from his defined benefit but not from his money purchase plan (maintained by the same employer), his defined benefit distribution would not qualify for special tax treatment (but see the special rule for rollovers, below). An employee would not be required to receive the balance to his credit in any profit-sharing, stock bonus, or nonqualified plan maintained by the same employer in order to receive favorable tax treatment on his qualified pension plan distribution.

Sometimes an employee will receive an additional payment from his plan in a taxable year after the year in which he has received his total plan balance. This could occur when there has been an actuarial error in computing a lump-sum benefit or when the employee is entitled to a profit-sharing amount for his last year of service which could not be computed at the time his account balance was initially distributed. In such cases, the employee generally does not lose favorable tax treatment on his initial lump-sum distribution but will be taxed on the later payment at ordinary rates.[1]

ERISA created a problem in this area by prohibiting the forfeiture of a nonvested account balance before a "break in service" occurs. Since it may not be known whether a break in service will have occurred until a year or more after the employee has terminated service, the employee will be uncertain whether the payment he receives upon termination will be considered the "total balance to his credit." Temporary regulations clarify this issue by providing that such a payment will be considered the total balance if a forfeiture occurs within twenty-five months of termination and upon the close of the break-in-service year. If no break occurs, and therefore no forfeiture, the employee must amend his tax return accordingly and "undo" any previous IRA rollover transaction.[2]

---

[1] Ltr. Rul. 7829033 (April 19, 1978).
[2] Temp. Reg. § 11.402(e)(4)(A)-1.

Beginning in 1982, participants in qualified plans will be entitled to a tax deduction for voluntary contributions to the plan. Although the accumulated employee contributions are not eligible for lump-sum distribution treatment these amounts will not taint an otherwise valid lump-sum distribution. (See the section below on deductibility of employee contributions.)

One Taxable Year. Even though payment must be completed within one taxable year, there is no requirement that the total balance be paid all at once; installment payments may be made as long as the total balance is distributed within one taxable year of the recipient. Payment need not be made during the year in which service was terminated; in fact, it may be to the employee's advantage if the receipt of benefits is delayed, as long as lump-sum distribution treatment can be retained.[3] It should be noted, however, that the distribution must not be contingent upon some other event or be deferred so far into the future that the amount would no longer be considered "on account of separation from service."

If the balance to the credit of an employee is paid within one taxable year to his beneficiary upon the employee's death, the amount will qualify for favorable tax treatment even though the employee received one or more payments from the plan before his death.

Events Triggering Lump-Sum Distribution. Lump-sum distribution is permitted under certain specified conditions.

Separation from service. Lump-sum tax treatment is available when the employee leaves for any reason including layoff, voluntary separation, retirement, or disability.

When a corporate merger or acquisition takes place, an employee who starts working for a "new" employer is generally considered not to have "terminated" his employment with his "former" company. As a general rule, such an employee is not considered "terminated" for lump-sum tax treatment purposes,[4] however, he may be able to roll over his benefit from the acquired employer's plan tax free.

A distribution from an H.R. 10 plan to a self-employed individual will generally not receive favorable lump-sum tax treatment if it is only made as a result of "separation from service," although this is a legitimate "triggering" event for common-law employees covered by H.R. 10 plans.

Age 59½. A distribution may be accorded capital gains/ten-year averaging treatment if the employee had attained at least age 59½. The IRS has taken the position with regard to pension plans that favorable tax treatment will be available for active employees if an individual receives a lump-sum distribution after reaching both age 59½ and the pension plan's normal retire-

[3] Rev. Rul. 60-292, 1960-2 C.B. 153.
[4] Rev. Rul. 79-336, 1979-2 C.B. 187.

ment age.[5] As a general rule, qualified pension plans may not distribute benefits before normal retirement age since they must be maintained primarily for the purpose of providing benefits after retirement.

It is noted that not more than one election for special ten-year forward averaging may be made with respect to an individual after he has attained age 59½.

Disability. Lump-sum tax treatment may be elected by a self-employed individual when the distribution is made on account of total disability. The disability must render the person unable to engage in any substantial gainful activity and can be expected to result in death, or to be of long-continued and indefinite duration.[6]

Determination of Tax. The calculation of the tax due on a lump-sum distribution involves several separate computations. First it is necessary to determine how much of the lump-sum distribution will be taxable. Of that amount, a certain portion may be taxed as a long-term capital gain; the balance will be taxed at ordinary income rates. If ten-year averaging is elected for the ordinary income portion, an initial separate tax is computed. Where there are multiple distributions or where an annuity contract is distributed, additional computations may be necessary to determine the appropriate tax.

The maximum tax rate (50 percent) for "personal service income" which has been in effect through 1981 does not apply to lump-sum distributions receiving special tax treatment.

Total Taxable Amount. Amounts representing employee contributions are not included in the taxable portion of a lump-sum distribution. This is because the employee would have paid taxes on these amounts before contributing them to the plan. Generally, employer contributions on which the employee had previously paid tax (such as those used for providing pure life insurance protection where the contract is distributed) are likewise excluded. Of course, earnings attributable to employee contributions are generally considered taxable.

Where employer securities[7] are part of a lump-sum distribution,[8] any "net unrealized appreciation" on those securities is not immediately taxed.[9] In effect, the total value standing to the employee's credit is reduced by the

---

[5] IRS Special Rul. (Oct. 29, 1976).

[6] I.R.C. § 72m(7).

[7] Employer securities consist of shares of stock, bonds, or debentures of the employer corporation, its parent, or subsidiary.

[8] Regardless of whether they are attributable to employer or employee contributions or earnings thereon.

[9] The five-year requirement of relating to ten-year averaging does not apply for the exclusion of unrealized net appreciation.

dollar amount of this appreciation. The dollar amount of net unrealized appreciation on employer securities is the excess of the market value of the securities at the time of the distribution over the cost or other basis of the securities to the trust. When the recipient sells the securities, the net unrealized appreciation is taxed as a long-term capital gain regardless of how long the securities were actually held. However, any gain realized in excess of that appreciation will be taxed as either a long- or short-term capital gain, depending on how long the securities were held after they were distributed to the recipient.

Where the lump-sum distribution includes property, other than employer securities, the recipient will be taxed immediately on the market value of the property as of the date of distribution over the amount of employee contributions.

Example: The total balance to the credit of an employee has the following elements:

Contributions by employee:	$ 10,000
Contributions by employer for life insurance protection on which the employee previously paid tax. The life insurance contract will be distributed to the employee at the time his account is disbursed:	5,000
Current market value of employer securities attributable to employer contributions. The basis of these securities to the trust is $5,000, their value at the time contributed:	20,000
Cash representing employer contributions:	65,000
Total	$100,000

The total taxable amount equals:

Cash, employer contributions:	$ 65,000
The basis of the employer securities to the trust:	$ 5,000
Total	$ 70,000

The net unrealized appreciation of $15,000 ($20,000 − $5,000) on employer securities is not taxed at the time of distribution. Employee contributions and, if the same insurance contract is distributed to the employee, previously taxed employer contributions, are also excluded.

Capital Gain Portion. To determine the portion of the lump-sum distribution to be taxed as a long-term capital gain (attributable to pre-1974 participation), the total taxable amount is multiplied by the following fraction:

$$\text{Total taxable amount} \times \frac{\text{months of active participation before 1974}}{\text{total months of active participation}}$$

The fraction is weighted in favor of the capital gain element such that in computing months of active participation before 1974, any part of a calendar year in which the employee was an active participant is counted as twelve months; in determining the number of months after 1973, any part of a calendar month of active participation is counted as only one month. The number of months of active participation begins with the first month an employee becomes a participant and ends with the earliest of the month in which he:

- Received the distribution;
- Separated from service;
- Died; or
- Became disabled, in the case of a self-employed individual.

Example: An employee participated from December 1, 1971 to September 15, 1978. The employee's participation during part of 1971 entitles him to credit for the full year. The employee's participation during part of September 1978 entitles him to credit for the full month, thus total months of participation equal ninety-three (seven full years, 1971 through 1977, and nine months in 1978).

$$\frac{\text{36 months before 1974}}{\text{93 total months}} \times \$50{,}000 = \$19{,}355 \text{ capital gain portion}$$

Once the long-term capital gain portion has been determined, it is added to other gross income and will be taxed in the same manner as would any other long-term capital gain for the taxable year.

If the employee does not elect ten-year averaging for the balance of the taxable distribution, it is taxed separately as ordinary income.

Ordinary Income Portion. To determine the portion of the lump-sum distribution that is ordinary income, the total taxable amount is multiplied by the following fraction:

$$\text{Total taxable amount} \times \frac{\text{months of active participation after 1973}}{\text{total months of active participation}}$$

Example: Total months of active participation = 93
Active months after 1973 = 57

$$\text{Ordinary income portion} = \frac{57}{93} \times \$50{,}000 = \$30{,}645$$

Electing Ten-Year Averaging for Ordinary Income Portion. In order to receive ten-year averaging tax treatment on the ordinary income portion of the lump-sum distribution, the following conditions must be satisfied:

1. The employee must have been a plan participant for *five or more taxable years* before the taxable year of the distribution. This rule does not apply,

however, with respect to a distribution made to the employee's beneficiary on account of the employee's death.

2. The recipient must elect ten-year averaging on *all* lump-sum distributions received during a single taxable year. For example, if an employee who receives lump-sum distributions from both his profit-sharing and pension plan rolls over one distribution into an IRA, he will lose his chance to elect ten-year averaging on the remaining distribution. However, capital gain treatment for the applicable portion of the remaining distribution would be available.
3. Once an employee reaches age 59½, *only one election* may be made with respect to that employee. For example, if an employee age 61 receives a lump-sum distribution from his profit-sharing plan for which he elected ten-year averaging, his beneficiary, upon his death, would not be eligible to make the ten-year averaging election for a lump-sum distribution received from the employee's pension plan, even though the death beneficiary, upon receiving the lump sum, was younger than age 59½.
4. A lump-sum distribution may be made to an individual, a trust, or an estate; it may not be made to a corporation or to a partnership. In the case of a distribution to more than one recipient, each recipient may elect individually to use ten-year averaging. Each recipient will pay a proportionate part of the tax calculated on the entire ordinary income portion.
5. The election must be filed on IRS Form 4972.

Minimum Distribution Allowance. Small lump-sum distributions receive a special tax benefit. The total taxable amount of a small distribution is reduced by a minimum distribution allowance. The minimum distribution allowance is the lesser of $10,000 or one-half of the total taxable amount. This figure is reduced by 20 percent of the amount of the total amount that exceeds $20,000, so that there is no minimum distribution allowance for taxable amounts of $70,000 or more.

Initial Separate Tax. The "initial separate tax" on the amount subject to ten-year income averaging is computed on one-tenth of the total taxable amount of the distribution after reduction by the minimum distribution allowance, plus $2,300. The tax is determined without regard to the employee's other taxable income and at single taxpayer rates. The tax is then multiplied by ten to arrive at the initial separate tax.

Example: Initial separate tax for 1978 is computed as follows:

Total taxable amount:		$50,000
Less minimum distribution allowance (lesser of $10,000 or one-half of total taxable amount:	$10,000	
Reduced by 20 percent of total taxable amount over $20,000 ($30,000 × 20%)	6,000	4,000
Distribution less minimum:		46,000

$2,300 + one-tenth distribution less allowance	6,900
Tax on $6,900 at single taxpayer rates	768
Multiplied by 10	7,680
Initial separate tax	$ 7,680

To determine the tax on the ordinary income portion, the initial separate tax is multiplied by the following fraction:

$$\frac{\text{Ordinary income portion}}{\text{Total taxable amount}} \times \text{initial separate tax} = \text{tax on ordinary income portion}$$

Example:

$$\frac{\$30{,}645 \text{ ordinary income portion}}{\$50{,}000 \text{ total taxable amount}} \times \$7{,}680 = \$4{,}707 \text{ tax on ordinary income portion}$$

The Lookback Rule for Multiple Distributions. For the purpose of determining the tax rate on a lump-sum distribution where the recipient has elected ten-year averaging, all lump-sum distributions made during the current year and the five preceding taxable years (beginning after December 31, 1973) which were subject to ten-year forward averaging, are combined. (As discussed below, the distribution of annuity contracts is included in this aggregation.) The lookback rule is applied only where multiple lump-sum distributions are received by *the same recipient.* Thus, where a plan participant receives a lump-sum distribution from his profit-sharing plan and later dies, a subsequent pension plan distribution made to his death beneficiary would not be aggregated with the earlier distribution.

Application of the lookback rule results in the taxation of the last lump-sum distribution at a higher rate. Once the initial separate tax on the combined distributions is determined under the regular ten-year averaging rules, the portion of the tax that is attributable to prior distributions is subtracted to arrive at the tax on the most recent distribution. This amount is then multiplied by the fraction:

$$\frac{\text{Ordinary income portion of the most recent distribution}}{\text{Total taxable amount for the most recent distribution}}$$

to determine the tax on the ordinary income portion.

Taxation of Annuity Contract. An individual who receives a nontransferable annuity contract from a qualified plan will not be taxed on it until he begins to receive payments under that contract. However, the value of a distributed annuity contract is taken into account for purposes of determining the taxation of lump-sum distributions, including the application of the lookback rule. The effect of including the value of the annuity contract in the determination of the tax on the taxable portion of the distribution is to tax the nonannuity elements of the distribution at a higher rate.

Election of Ten-Year Averaging for Entire Distribution. A recipient of a lump-sum distribution may elect to have his entire lump-sum distribution, including the portion attributable to pre-1974 participation, taxed as ordinary income subject to ten-year averaging. The election to waive capital gain treatment is irrevocable. Proposed IRS regulations [10] clarify the following points:

1. The election must be for the first lump-sum distribution made on behalf of a particular employee. A taxpayer may not elect to waive capital gain treatment for a distribution if a prior distribution made on behalf of the same employee received capital gain treatment.
2. This special election will apply to all lump-sum distributions made *on account of a particular employee.* In other words, after the initial election is made for a particular employee's distribution, subsequent lump-sum distributions made on behalf of that employee will continue to be subject to that election and will not receive capital gain treatment. But an election made by one recipient for a distribution relating to a particular employee will not automatically apply to distributions made to that recipient with respect to a different employee.
3. In order to waive capital gain treatment, all conditions for ten-year averaging discussed earlier must be met. For example, no portion of a lump-sum distribution will receive ten-year averaging treatment unless the employee had completed five years of plan participation.[11]

Treatment of Employer Securities in a Non-Lump-Sum Distribution

As indicated earlier, if a payment does not qualify as a lump-sum distribution, it will generally be taxed as ordinary income. However, even if *not* part of a qualifying lump-sum distribution, the net unrealized appreciation on employer stock purchased with *employee contributions* will not be taxed at the time of distribution. When such securities are sold, the amount of appreciation which is excluded at the time of distribution will be treated as a long-term capital gain regardless of how long the securities were held. Any net gain realized in a subsequent sale of the securities, which exceeds the appreciation that was excludable at the time of distribution, will be treated as either long-term or short-term capital gain depending on the period that the recipient held the securities.

Employer securities purchased with employer contributions or with dividends earned on stock purchased with employee contributions (or with

---

[10] Prop. Reg. § 1.402(e)-14.

[11] The five-year rule does not apply to receipt by a beneficiary in the event of the employee's death.

earnings on such contributions), and which are distributed in a manner that does not qualify as a lump-sum distribution, will be taxable at market value.[12]

Whenever an employee receives (employer or nonemployer) stock with a fair market value that is less than the contributions he made for that stock, the employee may not claim a deductible loss,[13] but a capital loss would generally result when the recipient sells the stock. However, where a retired participant receives a *cash* distribution of his entire account balance which is less than his total contributions made to the trust, the difference is deductible as an ordinary loss if he itemizes deductions for the year of distribution.[14]

Tax-Free Rollover Treatment of Certain Plan Distributions

By transferring all or a part of a plan distribution to an IRA or to another tax-qualified retirement plan, an individual can postpone his taxes on that distribution until he later receives the transferred amounts. Interest on the transferred amount also accrues tax free until it is distributed.

Two types of distributions are eligible for such a transfer:

1. A "lump-sum distribution" that would otherwise be eligible for ten-year averaging/capital gain treatment.
2. The balance to an employee's credit paid in one or more distributions within a single year of the employee *on account of a plan termination* or, in the case of a profit-sharing and stock bonus plan, a complete discontinuance of contributions.

Lump-Sum Distribution. To qualify for a rollover as a "lump-sum distribution," the payment must comply with all of the basic lump-sum requirements (be on account of separation from service, or age 59½, be the "full balance," etc.) except that the employee is not required to have completed five or more years of plan participation. Generally, the aggregation of plan rules apply (see earlier discussion of "Total Balance"). However, a money purchase pension plan does not have to be aggregated with a defined benefit pension plan for purposes of determining whether a distribution from the money purchase plan is eligible for a rollover.[15] This may be particularly helpful for certain thrift plan lump-sum distributions where employees also participate in defined benefit plans.

---

[12] I.R.C. § 72; Rev. Rul. 67-165, 1967-1 C.B. 89.

[13] Rev. Rul. 71-251, 1971-1 C.B. 129; Rev. Rul. 72-15, 1972-1 C.B. 114.

[14] Rev. Rul. 72-305, 1972-1 C.B. 116.

[15] This rule does have a potential drawback for employees participating in both a money purchase pension plan and a defined benefit pension plan of the same employer. If the employee rolls over a total distribution from the money purchase plan, then a total distribution in a subsequent year from the defined benefit plan would only be eligible for rollover treatment and would not be eligible for capital gain or ten-year averaging treatment. I.R.C. § 402(a)(6)(E).

Plan Termination Distribution. Payments on account of plan termination may be rolled over if the full balance to the employee's credit in the plan is distributed in one or more payments within a single taxable year of the employee. The tax-free rollover for this type of payment applies without regard to whether the employee had been a plan participant for five or more tax years; in addition, this payment need not otherwise qualify for lump-sum tax treatment.[16] For example, a rollover may generally be made even if the employee does not receive his total interest in all of the same type of plans maintained by his employer during the year the termination distribution is made.

When a distribution is made to an employee in connection with the liquidation or sale of the employer-corporation, a tax-free rollover may be available even though the employee's plan had not actually terminated during the reorganization process. Under the following circumstances, such a distribution will be considered "on account of a plan termination" for the purpose of obtaining rollover treatment:

1. When the payment is made in connection with a liquidation, sale, or other event that causes termination of the employer corporation's parent-subsidiary or controlled-group relationship.[17]

or

2. When the payment is made in connection with a sale or transfer of substantially all of the assets of an employer, where the employee, as a result of the sale, is employed by the company which acquired the previous employer's assets.

Note that the special treatment for employees of terminated plans only permits tax-free rollovers; it does not automatically provide for capital gain/forward averaging treatment. However, a termination distribution will often qualify for treatment as a "lump sum" where the recipient has left the company or has reached at least age 59½.

If the employee dies, a lump-sum distribution to the employee's spouse may also be rolled over into an IRA.

Timing and Eligibility. Transfer must occur within sixty days after receiving payment. Rollover transactions are not subject to the general eligibility requirements for IRAs; for example, the recipient may be an active participant in a qualified plan other than the one from which a payout was received. It may also be possible for a person age 70½ or older to open an IRA for rollover purposes even though the general IRA rules would require the distribution of benefits to commence by age 70½. In such a case, distribution would have to begin as soon as the IRA is established.

---

16 I.R. 1676 (Oct. 1, 1976).

17 A company is generally considered "controlled" for this purpose if 50 percent or more of its stock is owned by another entity.

Amounts Eligible for Rollover. The recipient may roll over all or a part of his entire plan distribution, excluding employee contributions. Property other than money that is part of a lump-sum distribution may be sold and the proceeds transferred to the IRA. To the extent the proceeds are transferred, no gain or loss on such a sale will be recognized. Amounts not transferred to the IRA are taxed currently as ordinary income without the special ten-year averaging treatment afforded lump-sum distributions. However, regular five-year income averaging may be available.

If a payment is made from the plan after the initial plan distribution is received and rolled over, the additional amount will not qualify for rollover treatment and will generally be taxed as ordinary income in the year received. This additional payout will generally not invalidate the employee's tax-free rollover.

Conduit Individual Retirement Accounts. Once the employee transfers his qualified plan distribution to an IRA he may roll that IRA amount back into his new qualified plan, if the new plan accepts such rollovers. The primary advantage of such a transfer is that the rollover amount may become eligible for lump-sum tax treatment when it is finally distributed from the new plan. In order to successfully make this tax-free rollover, the employee may not have made any additions to or withdrawals from his IRA. The entire account must be transferred to the qualified plan, including accrued earnings.

It is noted that rollover transfers must be made within sixty days after the distribution from the conduit IRA is received.

Taxation of Rollover Amounts. The earliest age at which an individual can begin receiving benefits from an IRA without tax penalty is age 59½, unless he is disabled. He must begin to receive his interest in an IRA by the close of the year in which he reaches age 70½. Amounts distributed from the IRA are taxed at ordinary rates. No special lump-sum tax treatment is available.

Tax Planning for Distributions

The foregoing material has included a discussion of some important tax planning considerations. Without attempting to review all of the available options, some of the basic planning techniques are summarized here. It is important to note that not all of the options will be available to every participant, and that what is good for one person might not fit the needs and goals of another person.

Tax and financial planning can be very important at the time an employee receives a payout of his interest from a qualified plan. If a plan allows a participant to receive his benefits in a lump sum, consideration should be given to whether the payout qualifies for the special ten-year averaging and long-term capital gain treatment available for lump-sum distributions. This special tax treatment will reduce the income tax burden on the payout in the year that it is received from the plan. Certain recipients of lump-sum distributions may also find it advantageous to elect to waive the available long-term capital gain treatment in favor of ten-year averaging for the entire distribution.

An alternative planning technique is to roll over a plan distribution. The rollover postpones tax on the payout. By transferring all or any part of a lump-sum distribution or plan termination distribution to an IRA, the recipient can postpone taxes on the payout until he withdraws amounts from the IRA. Amounts can be withdrawn from the IRA at the discretion of the participant. (However, penalties are imposed if amounts are withdrawn before age 59½ or are accumulated beyond age 70½ in more than prescribed amounts.) If amounts are withdrawn from the IRA over a period of years, the income tax liability is spread over those years and thereby reduced.

Amounts distributed from the IRA are not eligible for either the special ten-year averaging or long-term capital gain treatment. However, if the IRA is maintained separately (i.e., there are no contributions to the IRA other than the original amount rolled over) the funds can be rolled back into a qualified plan to generate the special tax treatment.

Some of the considerations involved in deciding whether to pay taxes immediately on a distribution or to roll over the payout to an IRA are:

- How much will the income tax be if taxes are paid immediately?
- Does the payout qualify for any special tax treatment that will reduce the immediate tax cost?
- Is the payout needed as a source of ready cash?
- Are there any investment opportunities for the payout that can earn as much or more than an IRA?

This highlights general tax planning techniques for recipients of qualified plan payouts. However, it is generally advisable for the recipient of a payout to consult with his tax advisor to identify a course of action that best fits the recipient's situation.

Employees who receive a distribution from a qualified retirement plan should discuss their personal situation with a CPA, attorney, or other tax advisor. Benefits managers and other corporate employees should exercise caution in offering tax advice to employees who will be receiving retirement plan distributions. A number of companies provide a general description of the tax treatment for retirement plan distributions. However, when an employee asks specific tax questions, it is nearly always suggested that the employee consult with his own tax advisor.

Estate and Gift Tax Considerations

In addition to the income tax considerations discussed above, there are various estate and gift tax concerns involving qualified retirement plans.

A special estate tax exclusion is available for certain benefits paid by qualified plans to beneficiaries of a deceased employee.[18] Generally, that portion of the death benefit paid by a qualified plan which is attributable to the employer's contribution to the plan is excluded from the employee's gross estate. Any portion of the death benefit which is attributable to the employee's own contribution to the plan is not eligible for the estate tax exclusion.

Under this general rule, if a qualified plan is noncontributory, that is, there are no employee contributions to the plan, then any death benefits paid over a period of years by the plan will generally be excludable from the deceased employee's estate. For contributory plans, the amount of the death benefit attributable to the employee's own contribution is determined by multiplying the amount of the death benefit by the ratio of employee contributions to total contributions. This amount, which represents the benefit attributable to the employee's contribution, is not excludable from the employee's estate.

This special estate tax exclusion may not be available, however, if the death benefit is paid to, or for the benefit of, the employee's estate. The exclusion may also not be available if the death benefits are paid in the form of a lump-sum distribution, unless the recipient of the death benefit irrevocably elects to forego the special capital gain and ten-year averaging income tax treatment that might otherwise be available. This trade-off of income and estate tax advantages for a lump-sum death benefit should be considered in tax planning for the recipient of such a benefit. Moreover, the unlimited marital deduction allowed under ERTA must also be considered since it may eliminate estate taxes in many situations.

Gift tax considerations with respect to qualified retirement plans arise in those situations in which a plan participant irrevocably designates a beneficiary to receive some portion of his benefit under the plan. This typically occurs when the participant elects to receive his benefits in the form of a joint and survivor annuity. Under the general gift tax rules, a taxable gift occurs at the time that such an irrevocable designation is made.

Paralleling the estate tax exclusion discussed above, a gift tax exclusion is available for the gift made by an irrevocable [19] designation under a qualified plan to the extent that the value of the annuity or other payment elected for the survivor is attributable to employer contributions to the plan. As with the estate tax exclusion, the gift tax exclusion is not available to the extent that the designated survivor benefits are attributable to employee contributions.

---

18 I.R.C. § 2039(c).
19 I.R.C. § 2517(a).

DEDUCTIBILITY OF EMPLOYER CONTRIBUTIONS TO QUALIFIED PLANS

Section 404(a) of the Internal Revenue Code governs the deductibility of contributions to any plan that defers compensation for services rendered. This includes all qualified pension, annuity, profit-sharing, and stock bonus plans as well as nonqualified deferred compensation arrangements. The initial test for deductibility is that amounts contributed constitute "ordinary and necessary business expenses" under Sections 162 and 212 of the Code.

Compensation for services rendered is an ordinary and necessary business expense only to the extent that it is reasonable. In determining the reasonableness of compensation, the contribution made to a plan on behalf of any employee plus other compensation for his services is considered. To the extent that compensation is unreasonable, a pro rata portion of the plan contribution will not be deductible.

In addition, compensation must be for services actually rendered to the employer by the end of the taxable year; compensation for future services or for services rendered to another employer may not be considered. However, contributions to pension or annuity plans may be made for services rendered in a prior year. Also, under certain circumstances, deductible contributions may be made with respect to past service rendered for a predecessor employer. Finally, under a special rule, members of an affiliated group of employers that maintain a profit-sharing plan or a stock bonus plan that is dependent on profits may contribute on behalf of other members of the group that are unable to contribute due to the absence of profits.[20]

Generally, an employer contribution is deductible if it is made during the taxable year or after the taxable year but before the tax return for that year is filed. Under Section 404(a)(6) of the Code both cash- and accrual-basis taxpayers are deemed to have made a contribution in the preceding tax year if the payment is on account of that year and is made no later than the date the employer's tax return is due, including extensions. The payment will be considered made on account of the preceding tax year if the plan treats it as if received on the last day of the tax year and the employer either designates the payment in writing as on account of the previous year, or claims it as a deduction on his tax return for the previous year.[21]

Limitations on Pension and Annuity Plans

Section 404(a)(1)(A) of the Code, as amended by ERISA, provides three basic methods for computing the maximum allowable deduction in any year for contributions to a defined benefit plan. Each of these methods is subject to an overall limitation—the amount deductible in any year cannot

---

[20] I.R.C. § 404(a)(3)(B).

[21] Rev. Rul. 76-28, 1976-1 C.B. 106.

exceed the full funding limitation for that year. The three basic methods, and the respective circumstances under which they are applicable, are as follows:

- *Minimum funding standard.* The employer may deduct the amount necessary to satisfy the minimum funding requirement for the plan year, if greater than the amount determined under the otherwise applicable method.
- *Level funding.* The employer may deduct the amount necessary to provide the remaining unfunded cost of past and current service credits distributed as a level amount, or a level percentage of compensation, over the remaining future service of each participant. However, if more than one-half of the remaining unfunded cost is attributable to three or fewer participants, the deduction of such unfunded cost for them must be spread over at least five years. This method combines all supplementary costs, of whatever type, without separately identifying them, with the "regular" annual costs of the plan; the method was not changed by ERISA.
- *Normal cost plus ten-year amortization.* The employer may deduct an amount equal to the normal cost of the plan, plus any supplementary cost amortized in equal annual payments over ten years. Prior to ERISA, this method was based on normal cost plus 10 percent of past-service and other supplementary costs. ERISA thus provides for faster amortization, because of the operation of interest.

Contributions in excess of the deduction limits, but otherwise deductible, may be carried over to succeeding tax years and deducted if within the annual limitation applicable to the succeeding year.

Deductibility and Minimum Funding [22]

The cost of funding a pension plan is based upon the so-called "normal cost" and (depending upon the funding method used) various amortizable segments. These amortizable segments relate specifically to:

- Experience gains and losses of the plan that arise from the departure of actual experience from actuarial assumptions;
- Changes in actuarial assumptions that increase or decrease the plan's accrued liability;
- Past-service or supplementary credits attributable to the establishment or amendment of the plan.

The most significant change in the deductibility rules from pre-ERISA practices is that both experience gains and losses are amortized. Prior to ERISA, only losses were amortized, while gains were generally used to immediately reduce costs.

---

[22] For a detailed discussion of minimum funding standards see Chapter 14.

The deduction limits are a function of the actuarial-cost method used by the plan for minimum funding purposes. (ERISA, in turn, provides that the same method must be used by the plan for determining the maximum deductible amount and for minimum funding purposes.) Some actuarial-cost methods recognize certain amortizable segments, while others compute all cost on the basis of normal cost.

Example 1: A plan uses the aggregate-cost method to determine minimum funding requirements. The aggregate-cost method computes all cost on the basis of normal cost. Consequently, in determining deduction limits only normal cost will be recognized.

Example 2: Under the frozen initial liability and attained age normal cost methods, amortizable segments are recognized for minimum funding purposes for past-service and supplementary credits and changes in accrued liability attributable to changes in actuarial assumptions. However, experience gains or losses are not separately recognized but, rather, are included in normal costs. Deductions are similarly based upon the recognition or nonrecognition of these amortizable segments.

Example 3: Under the entry age normal, unit credit, and individual level premium cost methods, all amortizable segments are recognized for minimum funding purposes and also, for deduction purposes.

Limitations on Profit-Sharing and Stock Bonus Plans

In general, under Section 404(a)(3) of the Code the amount that can be deducted in any year for contributions to a qualified profit-sharing or stock bonus plan is 15 percent of compensation in respect to all participants in the plan. Compensation means all of the compensation paid or accrued except for amounts deducted under a qualified plan. In the case of a profit-sharing plan, deductible contributions may be made only in a year the employer has current or accumulated profits.

As in the case of a pension or annuity plan, if more than the annual limitation is contributed in a year, the excess may be carried over and deducted in succeeding tax years. However, for any succeeding year, the deduction for current contributions and contribution carry-overs cannot exceed 15 percent of participant compensation for the year.

Furthermore, in any year in which the full 15 percent deduction is not taken, the amount of the unused deduction can be carried forward as a credit to increase the deduction limits in succeeding tax years. However, the amount deductible under the credit carry-over provisions in any succeeding year is subject to certain limitations. First, the credit carry-over cannot exceed 15 percent of compensation for the year. Second, the deduction limit for the combination of current contributions and credit carry-over contributions cannot exceed 25 percent of compensation paid in the current year.

For example, if an employer contributed $5,000 to a profit-sharing plan in prior years, although the maximum deductible amount for those years was $9,800, the employer has a credit carry-over of $4,800. In the current year, if the employer has a covered payroll of $50,000, and thus, may make a maximum current contribution of $7,500, the amount of credit carry-over that may be deducted in the current year is computed as follows:

Primary limitation =

$7,500 ($50,000 × 15%) which exceeds the $4,800 credit carry-over

Secondary limitation = lessor of

(a) $12,000 ($7,500 current contribution plus $4,800 credit carry-over), or
(b) $12,500 (25% × $50,000)

Thus, the full credit carry-over could be deductible in the current year.

Combined Limitation for Pension and Profit-Sharing or Stock Bonus Plans

Section 404(a)(7) of the Code provides that where one or more employees are covered under a pension or annuity plan and are also covered under a profit-sharing or stock bonus plan of the same employer, the total deduction for contributions to all plans is limited to 25 percent of compensation paid or accrued to all plan participants during the taxable year or, if greater, the amount of contribution necessary to satisfy the minimum funding standard for the plan year. Under this combined limitation, the employer is assured of receiving a deduction for the full contribution to his pension or annuity plan necessary to avoid a funding deficiency. However, if the amount necessary to satisfy the minimum funding standard equals or exceeds 25 percent of compensation, contributions to the profit-sharing or stock bonus plan will not be deductible, but may be carried over to succeeding tax years. Under the combined limitation, the deduction for current contributions and contribution carry-overs in a taxable year cannot exceed the overall 25 percent of compensation limit.

ESOPS

An ESOP is a stock bonus plan or a combination stock bonus and money purchase pension plan that allows a sponsoring employer to guarantee a loan incurred by the plan for the purpose of acquiring employer securities. Contributions by the employer to the plan are used to retire the ESOP debt. Limitations on the amount of employer securities that may be allocated to a participant's account were generally more liberal than allocation limitations that apply to other defined contribution plans. Deductions, however, were generally limited to 15 percent of participants' compensation, the basic limitation for profit-sharing and stock bonus plans.

To accommodate contributions that may be required to repay an ESOP loan, ERTA provides more generous deduction and allocation limits for these plans beginning in 1982.

Annual contributions to an ESOP, which are applied to repay principal on a loan, are deductible in an amount up to 25 percent of the compensation paid or accrued to participants of the ESOP. A deduction carry-over is provided for contributions that exceed this limit. An unlimited deduction is provided for contributions that are applied to repay interest on a loan.

Increased allocations to participants are also allowed under ERTA. ESOPs must adhere to limitations on amounts that may be added to a participant's account in any year. Generally, in 1981, a participant may not receive contributions and forfeitures that exceed the lesser of $41,500 or 25 percent of his compensation. In measuring a participant's allocation against this limitation, the new law disregards the allocation of contributions applied to pay loan interest and forfeited securities which were acquired with loan proceeds.

Observations. These provisions reflect a strong, congressional effort to promote ESOPs. There are also a number of other technical changes that are favorable to ESOPs and TRASOPs. The changes discussed above generally make it easier to accomplish financing through an ESOP. Although financing may be easier because of less IRS restrictions, it is noted that many companies in the past have not found ESOPs to be more effective than alternative arrangements.

In determining whether or not an ESOP is a feasible financing vehicle, a company should first focus on its financial needs and goals. Apart from this effort, the company should identify the types and levels of benefits it wishes to provide employees. After making these independent determinations, alternative financing and benefit plans can be better analyzed and compared.

TRASOPs

A tax credit ESOP (TRASOP) is a form of an employee stock ownership plan initially created by the Tax Reduction Act of 1975 which entitles an employer to an additional investment tax credit in exchange for its contribution of employer stock to the plan. Under old law, an employer that established a TRASOP could elect an additional one percent investment tax credit if it transferred employer securities (or cash used to acquire employer securities) to the plan equal in value to one percent of its qualified capital investment for the year. An additional one-half percent credit was available based on matching employee contributions. This maximum 1½ percent additional annual investment tax credit for TRASOP contributions is available through December 31, 1983.

ERTA replaces the investment-related tax credit with a tax credit based on the compensation of participants covered under the plan. The investment-related tax credit expires on December 31, 1982. The payroll-based credit is scheduled to begin in 1983 and will terminate on December 31, 1987. The payroll-based credit will be effective according to the following schedule:

Year	*Payroll Credit Percentage*
1983	.50
1984	.50
1985	.75
1986	.75
1987	.75

It is noted that allocations to officers, shareholders, and highly paid employees are restricted under a special set of rules.

Observations. Capital-intensive companies generally found TRASOPs to be an attractive plan from a financial standpoint. Many publicly held labor-intensive companies may find the new payroll-based TRASOP attractive and may make this new benefit plan part of their overall compensation package.

DEDUCTIBILITY OF EMPLOYEE CONTRIBUTIONS AND INCREASED INDIVIDUAL RETIREMENT ACCOUNT LIMITS

Background

Prior to 1982, a tax deduction was not available to employees for their mandatory or voluntary contributions to a qualified employer-sponsored pension or thrift plan. In addition, an active participant in a qualified plan was expressly prohibited from making tax-deductible contributions to an IRA. The deduction limit for contributions to an IRA had been the lesser of 15 percent of compensation or $1,500 ($1,750 for a spousal IRA).

New Law Provisions

In order to encourage retirement savings, ERTA entitles an active participant in an employer's qualified plan to a tax deduction with respect to either (1) *voluntary* contributions to that plan or (2) contributions to an IRA. *Mandatory* employee contributions to a qualified plan, i.e., contributions made as a condition of participation or entitlement to company-provided benefits, are not tax deductible.

The limit on this new deduction for active plan participants corresponds to the general IRA deduction limit, which the new law raised to the lesser of $2,000 or 100 percent of compensation. This limit applies to the aggregate of an employee's IRA and deductible voluntary contributions. An employee can allocate deductible contributions to all plans (IRAs and employer-sponsored) as long as the total amount deducted does not exceed the lesser of $2,000 or 100 percent of compensation. The limit for spousal IRAs has been raised to $2,250.

An employer maintaining a qualified plan is *not* required to allow deductible employee contributions to that plan. If the employer-sponsored plan does not permit such contributions, the deduction would still be available to a plan participant who established an IRA. If the employer wants to permit deductible employee contributions to its qualified plan, the plan must be amended to specifically allow for such contributions.

In general, deductible employee contributions to a qualified plan are subject to many of the restrictions applicable to a conventional IRA. For example, a tax penalty is imposed on distributions that commence prior to age 59½, except in the case of death or disability.

All distributions of accumulated deductible employee contributions are includable in gross income as ordinary income, except for amounts that are "rolled over" tax free to an IRA or to another retirement plan that holds the amounts as accumulated deductible employee contributions. Accumulated deductible employee contributions are not eligible for the ten-year averaging and capital gain treatment that is available for certain lump-sum distributions from qualified retirement plans.

These new provisions apply to tax years beginning in 1982.

Deduction Limits for H.R. 10 Plans, SEPs, and Plans of Subchapter S Corporations

Beginning in 1982, larger deductions will be available under H.R. 10 plans, SEPs, and plans of Subchapter S corporations. The deduction limit for contributions to defined contribution H.R. 10 plans, SEPs, and Subchapter S plans has been raised from $7,500 to $15,000. The 15 percent of earnings limit remains in effect. The amount of compensation that may be taken into account to test for discrimination under these plans has been increased to $200,000.

To provide a similar increase in the level of benefits permitted, the amount of compensation that may be taken into account for purposes of determining benefit accruals under defined benefit H.R. 10 and Subchapter S corporation plans has been increased to $100,000.

Observations. The increased deduction limits provide self-employed individuals with a much greater opportunity to accumulate retirement income on a tax-favored basis. As a result, a new dimension is added to the question of whether to incorporate to take advantage of greater tax deductions for qualified plan contributions. Moreover, self-employed individuals, who are participating in H.R. 10 plans, are also eligible for the additional deduction for retirement savings discussed above.

Part III

Replacement Income—Disability, Unemployment, and Death

18

Disability Benefit Plans

THOMAS BROWN

Policy Analyst, U.S. Department of Labor

HOWARD HENSLEY

Chief, Division of Pension Plan Exemptions, U.S. Department of Labor

INTRODUCTION

According to surveys conducted by the U.S. Department of Health and Human Services, American workers miss an average of five days work per year because of sickness. About 15 percent of working-age adults consider that they suffer some degree of long-term disability and about 5 percent report themselves to be so disabled they cannot work at all. Three percent have actually met the disability test for Social Security Disability Insurance (SSDI). (The test determines inability to engage in gainful employment in the U.S. economy due to injury or illness.) This means that between 3 million and 5 million working-age adults were totally disabled from working in 1981.

This chapter discusses benefits for private sector workers whose ability to earn a living is interrupted or terminated by disability, with particular emphasis on cash payments that replace part of earnings lost on account of disability. More than ten categories of public and private programs furnish income replacement to the disabled work force, but, unfortunately, these programs are not well coordinated and do not always assure income security or avoid unintended duplication. Medical services for the disabled are mentioned here, but are discussed in greater detail in Part VI. Rehabilitation and reemployment assistance for the disabled are also covered.

Concepts and Definitions

Disability. *Disability,* as the term is used here, is the inability to work for pay because of an injury or illness. Disability may be partial if some kinds of work, such as lifting, cannot be done while less strenuous work can be done. *Occupational disability,* a sub-category of partial disability, means the inability to perform one's usual work. Or, disability may be total, if no remunerative work can be done. On another dimension, disability may be temporary, if it is caused by a problem that will pass, or it may be permanent.

Each benefit program contains its own definition of disability, which is included among eligibility requirements for that particular benefit. In general these definitions become more stringent as the duration of benefit payments increases. Sick pay and other short-term benefits are ordinarily available when a worker is unable to do his or her customary job, while most long-term disability benefits are reserved for those who are unable to hold any substantial employment for which they are qualified.

Although it is easy to define disability, it is quite another thing to evaluate cases and to decide into which category they fit. The occurrence of disability, is seldom a tidy event with an unmistakable onset and defined degree of severity. Ambiguity in these matters coupled with the large sums of money at stake cause considerable controversy about benefit eligibility. The distinction between disability and impairment explains another aspect of the ambiguity.

Impairment. As the term is used here, *impairment* means diminished bodily function resulting from illness or injury. A given impairment may or may not cause disability—i.e., partial or total inability to work for pay—depending on outside factors. The most notable outside factor is the kind of work usually done by the impaired person. To illustrate, a piano mover would be considerably disabled by a broken ankle throughout his recovery, while most office workers would suffer little or no disability after the bone was set and the cast was in place. Other factors besides occupation also affect the disabling effects of impairments. Age, education, attitudes toward work, job availability, and the ratio of benefits to usual earnings are among them.

Attempts to differentiate between these factors and to measure their effects have not been very successful, but the direction of many effects and incentives are obvious. Advanced age and low levels of education make it harder for impaired persons to retain employment, for instance. Low benefit levels increase incentives for impaired persons to continue working despite the fact that it may be medically inadvisable to do so. Conversely, high benefits may discourage persons who could and should be employed, from working. It is generally considered prudent to design disability benefit programs so that no more than 70 percent of pre-tax or 80 percent of after-tax earnings are replaced from all available sources.

Disability Benefits Among Working-Age Adults

In 1977, totally disabled men, on average, had about 68 percent of lost earnings replaced by benefits. The average varied widely. Men who qualified for Social Security had about 74 percent replaced, reflecting the increased adequacy of benefits available to workers with stronger attachment to the labor force. On the other hand, for one-fourth of totally disabled men, benefits replaced less than 40 percent of lost earnings.

Social Security Administration surveys of disabled working-age adults show sources of benefits for persons who report that they cannot work at all. Figure 18.1 shows that in 1977, Social Security was by far the most frequently utilized source, followed at a considerable distance by veterans' benefits, welfare, workers' compensation, and employer- or union-sponsored disability benefits.

Fifty-four percent of totally disabled men reported that they received payments from two or more sources. Conversely, 11 percent reported that they

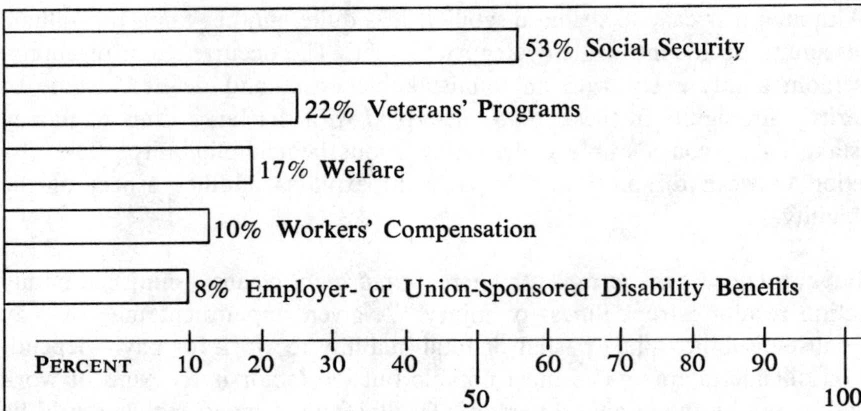

Source: Social Security Administration, *1978 Survey of Disabled and Non-Disabled Adults.*

Fig. 18.1 Percentage of Long-Term Disabled Men Under Age 65 Reporting Receipt of Benefit (1977)

received no disability payments at all. Multiple sources of benefits do not necessarily translate into large dollar amounts, however. The average amount received by totally disabled men from all benefit sources in 1977 was between $5,000 and $6,000, and 70 percent received less than $8,000.

Gaps and Overlaps in Coverage. The U.S. retirement income system is diverse, but in general, it is designed to include two or more tiers. Social Security provides basic benefits and employment-based pensions furnish a second tier. Similarly, most workers who suffer long-term total disability receive benefits from SSDI at a basic level. Another 20 to 40 percent who are vested in a pension plan or who qualify for employment-based, long-term disability benefits have a second tier of disability protection. For those without either tier because of insufficient covered employment, and for those whose total income is very low, the Supplemental Security Income (SSI) program (supplemented in some states by Aid for the Totally and Permanently Disabled) makes payments to disabled persons with demonstrable financial need. Among the severely disabled who are veterans of wartime service, there is also a need-tested veterans' pension program. Coverage for long-term severe disabilities appears to be nearly comprehensive, yet in 1978, about one of each ten severely disabled men reported receipt of no benefits at all.

Privately funded employment-related benefit plans furnish most of the payments to replace short-term disability income losses, in the form of sick pay and accident and sickness benefits. In five states, in Puerto Rico and in the railroad industry, accident and sickness benefits are required by law.

In all, about 60 to 70 percent of workers have accident and sickness, and/or sick-pay coverage.

Unintended overlaps beyond the normal tiers may occur when certain combinations of eligibility criteria are met. They often involve workers with both public and private employment experience, as benefits in one sector are infrequently offset against benefits earned in the other. Careful design of voluntary benefit plans offers the best opportunity to avoid unintended overlaps.

Trends. Disability payments in the private sector, as a percentage of the gross national product, almost tripled between 1960 and 1977, from 0.6 percent to 1.5 percent. During this period, the relative share of privately funded and publicly funded payments reversed itself, as shown in Figure 18.2.

In 1960, the five-year-old SSDI program paid out about a half billion dollars—only 16 percent of disability benefits paid that year to private sector workers. By 1977, the program expended $11.5 billion, representing about 40 percent of the total. During the same period, welfare payments to the disabled grew from about 9 percent of the total in 1960 to about 13 percent in 1977.

As seen in Figure 18.2, privately funded disability payments have grown considerably since 1960, though their proportionate share has decreased.

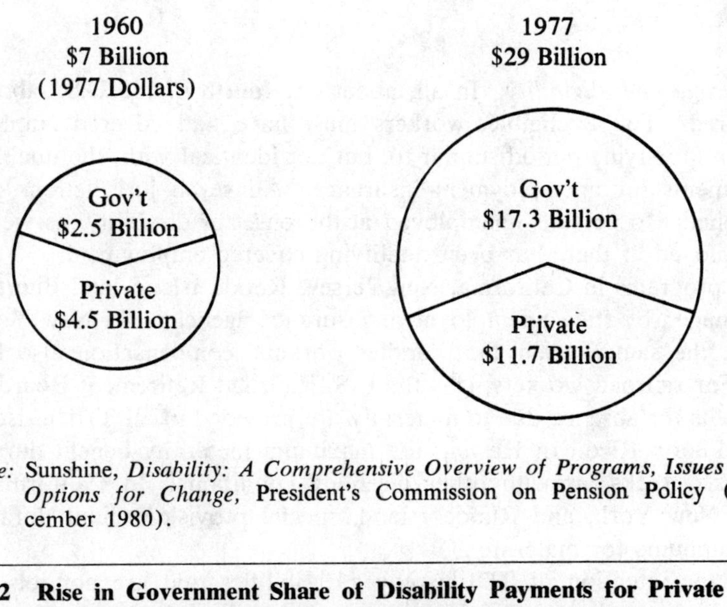

Source: Sunshine, *Disability: A Comprehensive Overview of Programs, Issues and Options for Change,* President's Commission on Pension Policy (December 1980).

Fig. 18.2 Rise in Government Share of Disability Payments for Private Sector Workers From 36 Percent in 1960 to 60 Percent in 1977

SOURCES OF DISABILITY PAYMENTS FOR PRIVATE SECTOR WORKERS

The still-evolving set of disability programs available to private sector workers in the United States has grown from many origins. Private measures to minimize economic risks were the first in the field. They have developed alongside governmental programs designed to reduce hardship and provide for the common good. Private and public disability income systems coexist with legal liability of wrongdoers to pay damages to persons they have disabled. The entire structure is influenced by tax law, as it affects benefit payers and recipients.

Because of their varied origins and different purposes, benefit programs do not fit neatly into a pattern. Avoiding gaps in coverage and unintended overlaps requires close attention by plan designers. Figure 18.3 shows the major sources of disability income replacement for private sector workers.

The disability benefit planner builds on a foundation of governmentally required programs to fill gaps and to avoid excesses. This section describes the underlying mandatory sources of disability income payments and then discusses the factors that planners must consider in designing a voluntary plan for disability income replacement.

Mandatory Benefits for Short-Term Disability

Temporary Disability Insurance (TDI) Required by Law. Most workers in California, Hawaii, New Jersey, New York, Rhode Island, Puerto Rico, and in the railroad industry, are covered by short-term disability insurance under rules set by law.

Coverage and eligibility. In all, about one-fourth of the U.S. labor force is covered. To be eligible, workers must have had covered employment during a qualifying period similar to, but not identical with, the qualification requirements for unemployment insurance. All seven jurisdictions provide TDI benefits to persons unemployed at the onset of disability, as well as to the employed, if there has been qualifying covered employment.

TDI programs in California, New Jersey, Rhode Island, and Puerto Rico are managed by state unemployment insurance agencies. In New York and Hawaii, the same agency that handles workers' compensation also handles TDI. For railroad workers, it is the U.S. Railroad Retirement Board.

Benefits for absence due to maternity are provided in all TDI jurisdictions except Puerto Rico. In Hawaii, the maximum maternity benefit duration is twenty-six weeks, as with other disabling conditions. In California, New Jersey, New York, and Rhode Island, special provisions limit duration or dollar amounts for maternity.

It is the intention of TDI to cover disabilities that are not job-caused. Most, however, allow payments to be made pending resolution of contested

Sources of Payments	*Required by Law?*	*Privately Funded*	*Funded by Taxes*	*Notes*
Short-term disability (usually under six months)				
Accident and sickness	Yes, in five states; no in others	X		Cal., Haw., N.J., N.Y., R.I. require accident and sickness coverage
Sick pay	No	X		
Long-term disability				
Social Security Disability Insurance	Yes		X	
Supplemental Security Income for the disabled and state supplements in some states	Yes		X	For low-income, only
Veterans' pensions	Yes		X	For low-income, veterans of wartime service, only
Black lung benefits	Yes	Some	Most	For coal workers with coal miners pneumoconiosis only
Long-term disability benefits	No	X		
Disability pensions	No	X		
Short- and long-term				
Workers' compensation	Yes	X		For job-caused disabilities, only
Tort liability	Yes	X		Only where there is a legally liable wrongdoer

Fig. 18.3 Major Sources of Disability Income Replacement for Private Sector Workers

workers' compensation claims with provision for repayment if workers' compensation is ultimately paid.

Disability criteria. Generally, TDI benefits are paid after a one-week waiting period to workers whose attending physicians certify their inability to perform their usual duties. In New Jersey, New York, and Puerto Rico, there is a more stringent definition of disability for unemployed claimants. They must be unable to perform work for which they are reasonably qualified.

Benefits. Weekly benefit amounts in each jurisdiction are a function of earnings during the base of coverage, subject to maximum and minimum weekly amounts. Usually the benefit amount is between one-half to two-thirds of base period earnings, subject to ceilings between $100 and $150 per week. In New Jersey, California, and Rhode Island, maximum benefit duration is related to duration of employment during the base period. In other jurisdictions, the maximum is a flat twenty-six weeks. Only California and the railroad board provide TDI benefits for more than twenty-six weeks, as Californians who had a full fifty-two weeks of employment during the base year are eligible for up to thirty-nine weeks of benefits. Railroad workers may qualify for fifty-two weeks.

There is a week-long waiting period in all jurisdictions except the railroads, where it is four days. If disability continues long enough in California and New Jersey, benefits are paid retroactively for the waiting period.

Death benefits are payable to survivors of disabled workers in California, New Jersey, and Puerto Rico.

Financing of benefits. Employers and workers share the cost of TDI in all jurisdictions except Rhode Island, where workers pay the entire cost, and the railroads, where employers pay the cost. In Rhode Island and for railroad workers, all assessments are paid into, and benefits are paid out of a government-managed fund. All other jurisdictions allow employers choices as to how to meet TDI funding obligations.

New York employers may provide the plan defined in the law or its actuarial equivalent in any of three ways:

1. By self-insurance;
2. By a contract with a private insurance carrier; or
3. By purchasing insurance from a state-operated insurance fund.

In Hawaii, employers may provide coverage at least as favorable as that defined in the law, whether by self-funding or with a private insurer. In California, employers may substitute a private plan for the statutory plan if benefits are more favorable to workers. In New Jersey and Puerto Rico, employers may substitute a privately funded plan for the state plan if it is at least as favorable for workers.

Payments to the disabled unemployed are made from state government-managed funds with authority to make assessments against employers, workers, and private insurance companies so that sufficient funds are available.

Mandatory Benefits for Long-Term Disability

Social Security Disability Insurance. SSDI pays monthly benefits to eligible workers so disabled that they are unable to hold substantial employment. Workers with sufficient recent employment in Social Security-covered jobs are eligible regardless of demonstrated economic need. Disabled workers' benefit amounts averaged about $415 per month in 1981, plus supplements for dependents averaging $120 per month. Payments are made from the SSDI trust fund which receives equal contributions from workers and employers, collected by the Internal Revenue Service from employers as payroll taxes.

Coverage and eligibility. In the private sector, an individual earns one quarter of coverage (to a maximum of four) for each $310 of earnings in a year, so that $1,240 in a single quarter counts as four quarters of coverage for the year. For eligibility, he needs twenty quarters of coverage in the forty-quarter period ending with the quarter in which disability begins, but he must also be fully insured. (A blind person need only be fully insured.) For workers under age 24, the requirement is six quarters of coverage in the twelve quarters ending when disability begins; for those ages 24 through 30, it is half the quarters from age 21 to the onset of disability.

Disability criteria. To meet the disability criteria, one must have a physical or mental impairment that precludes substantial gainful employment in the U.S. economy, for an anticipated period of one year or more, or which is expected to result in death. There is a five-month waiting period after onset of the disability. Benefits are payable on the first day of the next month after the end of the five-month wait.

Disability determinations are made by state rehabilitation agencies under supervision from the Social Security Administration. There are published medical criteria for several types of disabilities, such as those caused by musculoskeletal, respiratory, and heart conditions. For applicants who do not meet these criteria, other factors, such as age, education, and work experience may be taken into consideration. These factors are more often applied to older applicants, recognizing that it is harder for them to regain employment after becoming unable to continue in their normal occupation. But, in any event, physical or mental impairment must be the cause of disability.

Although the statutory definition explicitly excludes from eligibility persons who can perform gainful work anywhere in the U.S. economy, judicial interpretations require consideration to be given to realistic chances for employment in the locality of the applicant.

Kinds of benefits. The basic SSDI benefit is a monthly cash payment, with separate payments to spouses and dependent children. There is also a payment to the surviving spouse of a deceased SSDI recipient if he or she is disabled.

After twenty-four continuous months of SSDI payments, or earlier if age 65 is reached, the beneficiary becomes eligible for *medicare* health and hospitalization insurance.

Disabled beneficiaries receive special consideration for *rehabilitative* services through the state/federal vocational rehabilitation program. The costs of rehabilitation for selected SSDI beneficiaries are paid in their entirety from the SSDI trust fund. When an SSDI recipient turns age 65, benefits convert automatically to old-age benefits.

Amounts of benefits. Social Security benefits are a complicated function of taxable monthly earnings. Unlike nondisabled persons who retire before age 65, a full benefit is paid regardless of age. A spouse, age 62 or caring for a minor child, or a child, receives, in addition, one-half the full benefit. (The spouse's benefit is reduced, however, by any benefit she receives in her own right and by earnings in excess of the limitation.) If there are two or more dependents, the maximum family benefit is 150 percent of the disabled worker's benefit, or, if less, 85 percent of his average earnings before becoming disabled.

The benefit formula is progressive in that beneficiaries with low predisability incomes receive a higher percentage of lost income than those with higher incomes. In 1978, a worker with an average annual income, adjusted for inflation, of $5,000 would have received 57 percent of lost wages. If he had, in addition, one dependent, the combined total would have been about 86 percent. Comparable figures for an adjusted average income of $15,000 would have been 38 percent replacement for the disabled worker alone and 57 percent for the worker and one dependent. Since 1979, replacement ratios have been slightly lower. Benefits are adjusted each year, proportional to the Consumer Price Index in years when the increase exceeds 3 percent. Social Security benefits are tax free.

Supplemental Security Income. In 1972, a federal benefit program was established to provide uniform payments for the aged, blind, and disabled who have a clear financial need. For the disabled, SSI provided a uniform federal payment in place of welfare state payments for the permanently and totally disabled. States, however, are allowed to supplement SSI payments, and initially they were required to continue payments to active beneficiaries at levels of state payments prior to the federal programs. In 1981, all states supplemented some benefits, and overall, about 74 percent of SSI benefits are federal and 21 percent are state supplements.

To qualify, an individual must not have assets other than a home and automobile worth more than $1,500, and an income less than the benefit level. For a couple, the asset limit is $2,250. In 1981, the monthly benefit amount for an individual was $238, and for a couple living in their own home, it was $357. The first $65 of earnings per calendar quarter are not counted, but half of income above that is deducted from the benefit. The disability criterion for new applicants is the same as for SSDI. SSI recipients are eligible for medicaid health and hospitalization insurance from the start of their eligibility.

Payments are made by the Social Security Administration from general tax revenue funds. In addition to the disabled, blind and aged persons who meet the financial-need test may also receive SSI.

Veterans' Pensions. Veterans of wartime service who are in financial need and who are totally disabled or over age 65 are entitled to monthly pensions from the Veterans Administration. Unlike veterans' service-connected disability compensation, disabilities for pensions may arise from any cause. The 1981 income limit for pension eligibility for a veteran alone was $5,073, and for a veteran with dependents was $6,822. Pension amounts were $4,460 for an individual and $5,844 with one dependent. Wartime service includes service during the Vietnam War, the Korean War, World War II, World War I, and the Mexican Border period.

Railroad Retirement Act Disability Benefits. The Railroad Retirement Act provides disability as well as retirement pensions for persons who work for railroads, railroad associations, and railroad unions. Benefits are funded by employer and worker payroll deductions. If an individual meets eligibility requirements for both SSDI and railroad disability, both benefits are payable. If a worker has insufficient railroad employment to qualify for the railroad benefit, the credits are combined with Social Security credits toward Social Security eligibility.

A worker with twenty years of railroad service or a worker over age 60 with ten years of service qualifies for a disability annuity if disabled from performance of usual duties. A worker with ten years of railroad service under age 60 is eligible for a disability annuity if disabled from all substantial work. (Any railroad service within a twelve-month period is creditable as a year of service.)

Amounts of railroad disability annuities depend on years of service and average monthly compensation. Additional amounts are paid to the dependents of disabled workers. Railroad pensions and disability benefits are administered by the Railroad Retirement Board.

Black Lung Benefits. Coal miners and certain others who are exposed to coal dust and who are disabled by coal miners pneumoconiosis (black lung disease) are eligible for compensation under the Coal Mine Health and Safety Act. The law was passed in 1969, amended in 1972, 1978, and again in 1981. Criteria for identifying compensable cases are defined in the law. These criteria were liberalized in 1972 and 1978 and were tightened in 1981.

Eligible miners who applied for benefits before December 31, 1973 receive benefits funded by the U.S. Treasury as long as they are eligible. This provision was intended to free mine operators from liability under the Act until they could benefit from the better health experience expected after the new dust level limits that were enacted in 1969. During this initial period, the accumulated damage of years of exposure was to be compensated at public expense, and, after that, mine operators were to be responsible under a more conventional workers' compensation law.

Eligible claimants who filed after December 31, 1973, receive benefits through workers' compensation arrangements made by their employers if a responsible employer is identified by the U.S. Department of Labor, or from a fund established by a tonnage tax on mined coal if no responsible employer can be linked to the disease. The fund is also the source of payment for cases where the last exposure to coal dust occurred before the law was enacted. Receipts in the fund have proven to be far less than benefit payments, but the 1981 amendments increased the tax to a level designed to enable the fund to repay Treasury loans by the mid-1990s.

The amount of benefits for total disability from black lung disease in 1981 was $293.20 per month for a claimant alone and $439.80 for a claimant and one dependent. The benefit amount is tied to the salary scale for federal employees, so it changes each time federal salaries are changed.

Benefits resulting from applications filed before the end of 1973 are paid in addition to any SSDI benefit that may be paid. Benefits resulting from applications after 1973 are considered workers' compensation, so the offset that limits combined SSDI and workers' compensation benefits to 80 percent of adjusted predisability earnings is in effect.

Other Sources of Payments

Workers' Compensation. The workers' compensation program covers job-caused injuries and illnesses. Income replacement benefits are provided—at the employer's expense—for disabilities that are temporary or permanent, partial or total, and to surviving dependents in the case of job-caused deaths. In addition, full medical care is provided and, to a limited extent, vocational rehabilitation is furnished.

The system was adapted from western European experience in the early twentieth century to replace unpredictable employer liability awards. An implicit trade-off underlies the system. Employers are responsible for payment of fair but modest benefits to workers without regard to who was at fault. In turn, employers are substantially freed from common-law liability for the safety and health of their workers. The objective is for disabled workers to have accessible benefits and for employers to have predictable limits on their liability. In seventy years of practice, workers' compensation has strayed from these objectives but periodic reform movements bring it back into line.

Fifty state and three federal workers' compensation laws govern the system. Each one is different in important ways, but there are common threads.

Types of benefits. There are income replacement benefits for temporary disabilities, permanent disabilities, and death. Unlike most other U.S. disability programs, workers' compensation provides benefits for partial as well as total disabilities. Medical care needed to treat job injuries and illnesses is included, even if no compensable income loss occurs. For the relatively few cases with identified rehabilitation potential, services aimed at restoring employability are provided.

Amount of benefits. The starting point for total disability benefits is usually two-thirds of predisability earnings. This amount is constrained by maximum weekly benefits that average about ninety percent of state average-weekly wages. The 1980 average embraced a range from just over half to twice the state's average. In most states, there is also a minimum benefit which is the lesser of a set figure or actual earnings. There is a waiting period for workers' compensation disability payments in every state; most often, from three to seven days.

Death benefits for surviving dependents are ordinarily set at one-half to two-thirds the deceased workers' wage up to maximum limits similar to those for total disability.

Partial disability benefits are less standardized, both in amount and method of calculation. Nearly all states have a schedule of impairments that can be clearly defined, such as loss of an arm, or sight of one eye for which predetermined numbers of weekly payments are allowed. In addition, all states have a separate arrangement for compensating partial disabilities that do not fit on a schedule.

Back injuries are a common and troublesome example of nonscheduled injuries. Payments may be based on:

1. An evaluation of the worker's overall impairment as a percentage of total impairment;
2. An evaluation of the worker's predicted wage-earning capacity as compared to predisability earning capacity; or
3. A record of actual wage losses due to the disability.

Partial disability evaluation is inherently complex, and there is no wholly satisfactory and generally accepted way to compensate partial disabilities.

Workers' compensation benefits are not subjected to state or federal taxation, so actual replacement rates are higher than nominal rates, especially at higher income levels.

Inflation. Long-term benefits are eroded by inflation unless adjustments are made. Twelve states make annual adjustments of permanent total disability benefits based on either a price or wage index. Some other states make ad hoc adjustments as deemed appropriate by their legislatures. Permanent partial disability benefits are rarely adjusted for inflation.

Administration. Employers may cover their workers' compensation liability in three different ways:

1. Insurance with private carriers;
2. Insurance with state-operated insurance funds; and
3. Self-insurance.

Not all options are available in all states. Six states with exclusive state insurance funds do not allow private insurance carriers to write workers' compensation policies (Ohio, North Dakota, Nevada, Washington, West Virginia and Wyoming). Three states do not allow self-insurance (North Dakota, Texas, and Wyoming). In all, nineteen states operate workers' compensation insurance funds. Thirteen are operated competitively, alongside private carriers. Self-insured employers frequently carry reinsurance to cover excess risks.

Most states have a commission or board that oversees administration of the workers' compensation law, though in three states only the state courts are involved (Alabama, Louisiana, and New Mexico). The commissions and boards are quasi-judicial bodies. Their decisions may be appealed to state courts.

The amount of governmental oversight is modest and private parties—employers, insurance carriers, and claimants—resolve most claims informally. Thus, the private parties and their lawyers are the principal administrators, with exceptional cases resolved in adversarial, court-like proceedings. If a claim is complicated or expensive, the chances are that the claimant will have to retain counsel and fight a contest with the insurer.

As in any adversarial process, a high proportion of contested cases are settled by compromise. Frequently, settlements take the form of a lump sum for part of the amount claimed, accompanied by a release from future liability. In some states, over half of the permanent disability claims are settled this way. Compromise settlements simplify administration and reduce costs. They are attractive to attorneys working for contingency fees and they appeal to claimants, tired of waiting for benefits. However, they damage the income replacement objective of workers' compensation and they encourage defendants to contest claims as a strategy for strengthening their negotiating position. Some states have taken steps to control compromise settlements. Washington, for instance, prohibits release of future liability along with a settlement, and New York has stringent standards for approval of each compromise by a member of the Workers' Compensation Board.

Employer costs. Workers' compensation insurance is priced according to loss payment experience in up to 700 different industry classifications. Manual rates are set for each industry classification by an insurance industry rating bureau and approved or modified by state insurance commissioners. In several ways, the manual rates may be modified up or down for individual clients:

- Very small policies are subject to an extra charge and conversely, large policies may be discounted to adjust for economies of scale.
- In most states, if the cost of a policy exceeds $500 the premium is "experience rated" upward or downward based on prior loss experience. The percentage impact of experience varies directly with the size of the policy so, as the experience base grows larger, the price impact of the firm's experience grows and the impact of industrywide experience diminishes.
- Very large employers may elect retrospective rating, which allows the employer to pay actual losses plus an amount for services performed by the insurer.
- Mutual insurance companies, participating stock companies and most state insurance funds return a dividend to policyholders at the end of each successful year.

Employer costs, before adjustment, for dividends averaged $1.93 per $100 of payroll in 1979. This average embraces very low-hazard white collar occupations that cost less than 25¢ per $100 and highly dangerous occupations, such as steel erection, that can cost over $30 per $100 of payroll.

Occupational diseases. Though workers' compensation began with coverage of accidental injuries only, every state now purports to cover job-caused diseases as well. By their nature, slowly developing chronic diseases are more difficult to relate to their cause than are injuries. At the same time, chronic diseases tend to have serious and costly disabling effects. The ambiguity of disease causes and the high expense of disease claims combine to encourage insurers to contest claims. The resulting litigation encourages compromise settlements and discourages future claims for similar conditions.

Most studies indicate that only a small percentage of disabilities and deaths from job-related chronic diseases results in workers' compensation payments. Losses from these diseases are borne largely by other benefit programs and the families of disabled workers.

Common-Law Indemnity. If one person's disability is caused by the fault of another, the disabled person has a common-law right to sue in court for damages. Compensatory damages may be ordered to repay the disabled person for losses caused by the disability, disfigurement, and pain and suffering. In addition, for cases involving extreme negligence, punitive damages may be ordered. In practice, a large majority of damage suits are settled by attorneys for the parties before they reach trial.

The most prevalent types of personal injury damage suits are from motor vehicle accidents, product liability, and medical malpractice. Most persons and institutions who risk liability purchase insurance: although most governments and many large corporations with liability self-insure.

Privately insured personal injury liability payments in 1977 totaled about $11 billion. This amount includes amounts paid for deaths as well as for disabilities, medical costs, and legal fees for successful plaintiffs, so it is not strictly comparable to amounts cited in Figure 18.2.

State laws and judicial decisions modify the common-law recovery rights of injured parties in ways that may enhance or limit liability. Every state, for instance, has a statute that sets time limits for filing suits after the occurrence of an injury. No-fault auto insurance laws in a number of states protect faulty drivers from suits up to a specified limit, and workers' compensation laws protect employers against most personal injury suits filed by their employees. Conversely, employer liability laws applicable to merchant seamen (the Jones Act) and railroad workers (the Federal Employers' Liability Act) enable disabled workers to prevail against certain common-law defenses that would otherwise be available to the employer.

Insurance contracts that cover liability commonly give the right to recover all or part of amounts paid from third parties, who may have contributed to the incident causing the loss, through subrogation. The extent and limits of subrogation rights are defined by insurance contracts and by law.

Wrongful damages for which a business is liable are not deductible as business expenses. Neither are contingency reserves set aside by a company to provide for possible future liability. Premiums paid to an insurance company for liability insurance are, however, tax deductible as business expenses.

Interrelationships Between Disability Income Payment Sources

As will be explained in the discussion on plan design, voluntary disability plans should be written to provide the desired overlaps and offsets, as these plans offer more flexibility than programs defined by law. In order to achieve plan design goals, one must consider the interrelationships among governmentally defined programs that are discussed in this section.

Short-Term Disability Benefits. In California, Hawaii, New Jersey, New York, Rhode Island, Puerto Rico, and in the railroad industry, most workers must be covered by TDI benefits. They are for disabilities that are not job-caused, but, while workers' compensation benefits are in dispute, TDI benefits may be paid subject to reimbursement if workers' compensation is ultimately paid. In California, if TDI benefits are greater than workers' compensation, the difference is paid from TDI. In all states, claimants may receive workers' compensation from a prior partial disability, along with TDI for a new disability, not caused by the job.

In Rhode Island, full benefits are paid regardless of whether private disability benefits are paid, and in New York, collectively bargained benefits may be paid in full, concurrent with TDI. In other state jurisdictions, TDI benefits are reduced by the amount necessary to assure that total benefits do not exceed predisability earnings.

Long-Term Disability Benefits. SSDI benefits are reduced by the amount necessary to preclude combined SSDI and workers' compensation disability payments that exceed 80 percent of predisability earnings after adjustment of the earnings figure to reflect average wage inflation. The law has allowed states to reduce workers' compensation payments in lieu of the SSDI reduction. Although in accord with 1981 amendments, no further states will be allowed to enact this reduction; the following twelve states now have such laws in effect:

- Alaska
- Colorado
- Florida
- Louisiana
- Minnesota
- Montana
- North Dakota
- Ohio
- Oregon
- Utah
- Washington
- Wisconsin

The offset does not apply to workers' compensation payments for medical care.

The Employee Retirement Income Security Act of 1974 (ERISA) precludes reduction of disability benefits classified as pensions in response to cost-of-living increases in SSDI benefits. This restriction does not apply to disability benefits classified as welfare plans.

At age 65, SSDI benefits are converted automatically to retirement benefits, which are not subject to the federal offset rule.

SSI, Aid for the Permanently and Totally Disabled, and Veterans' Disability Pensions all require a showing of financial need. As income increases above the threshold levels for benefit eligibility, including income from other benefit sources, benefits are reduced, thus providing an automatic offset.

With increasing frequency, product suppliers are being found liable under common law for injuries and illnesses that occur in the workplace. In general, workers' compensation insurers can recover amounts paid for workers' compensation claims in such cases from the product suppliers, but product manufacturers cannot recover from employers who may share responsibility for the disability beyond the liability limits set for employers by the workers' compensation law. This pattern has been altered by law in some states.

DESIGNING DISABILITY BENEFIT PLANS

Lawmakers have defined a set of disability income benefits available to all, or nearly all, in the work force if they meet certain conditions: if the disability is job-caused, they are covered by workers' compensation, and if the disability is long-lasting and severe, they are covered by Social Security or SSI. For most workers, coverage for other kinds of disabilities and adequate levels of income replacement are dependent on the fringe benefit bargain they, or their union, make with their employer. Employers, in turn, want to provide attractive yet practical benefits plans.

A complete disability income program should address both short- and long-term disabilities. Though there is some variation, the most frequent practice is to address disabilities of less than six months in a manner separate from those that extend beyond that period. Within the first six months, the first week or so may be treated differently than the remaining time, in order to screen out disabilities with modest impact on the worker, and to discourage excessive use.

Short-Term Disability Plans

Sick-pay plans and accident and sickness plans (A&S) are the principal ways of providing for the shorter periods of disability. Sick pay is most commonly provided for salaried workers and A&S is most commonly provided for wage earners. Some plans combine the use of both.

Sick Pay. Sick pay may be granted informally as needed, simply by retaining the disabled worker on full pay. While this might work well for small and highly responsible groups, it is less likely to be satisfactory for larger groups where there is a greater need for consistency in administration. Formal sick-pay plans usually provide for accrual of credit days for use as needed. A common arrangement is for employees to earn ten days per year and to allow accumulation of unused days up to a maximum of three to six months. An alternative is to provide a schedule of available days, based on length of service. Most frequently, sick-pay days may be used at full pay from the first day of disability, without any waiting period. Some plans, however, provide a schedule of days, some of which may be used at full pay, while the remainder if needed, may be used at half pay.

Formal sick-pay plans should spell out whether available days may be used to cover waiting periods for workers' compensation and A&S benefits, and whether they may be used to supplement partial pay benefits from these or other sources. It is the nature of most sick-pay plans that only long-service employees have sufficient credit available to cover the entire waiting period for long-term disability benefits.

Accident and Sickness Plans. A&S plans provide partial pay replacement for up to a stipulated number of weeks, after a waiting period. Most commonly, they replace from 60 to 67 percent of pay after a one-week waiting period, for up to twenty-six weeks. A few are designed for different durations —between thirteen and fifty-two weeks—and some offer a shorter waiting period for accidental injuries than for illnesses, as beneficiaries have less discretion about absence from work in the case of injuries. A&S plans ordinarily have carefully structured incentives to discourage excessive use, and they are most frequently used for wage earners and for large groups.

Most A&S plans are insured. Underwriters try to assure that waiting periods and benefit maximums discourage adverse selection of participants and improper use. Benefit schedules in excess of 70 percent of gross earnings are seldom allowed, and flat dollar maximums are usually included, as well.

A choice should be made whether to allow receipt of A&S benefits concurrent with workers' compensation and other mandatory benefits; in any case, offsets should be included to avoid duplication that would increase total benefits above the 70 percent level. Consideration should also be given to curtailing benefits in the event of a common-law recovery from a third party, such as a product supplier or a vehicle operator.

Most plans allow full benefits for each occurrence of disability provided that there is one or two weeks of full-time work between them. Federal law requires that disability in the event of pregnancy must be treated the same as other disabilities, under benefit plans.

Since most sick-pay plans fail to cover the full waiting period for longer term benefits and since A&S waiting periods preclude beneficiaries from recovering any benefit for short periods of illness (the most common type of disability), some plans offer a combination of the two.

Plans for Long-Term Disability

For disabilities that last more than six months, employers frequently use either of two arrangements or, as is becoming increasingly common, a combination of the two. The first is to make provision for long-term disabilities in the pension plan and the second is to provide an insured or self-insured Long Term Disability plan (LTD). In order to protect pension funds from erosion due to adverse disability experience among its members, it may be desirable to provide separately for beneficiary income during the period between onset of disability and age 65. This section discusses factors to be considered in designing such a plan.

Waiting Periods and Maximum Terms. Benefits most commonly begin twenty-six weeks after the beginning of disability, though some prefer shorter or longer waiting periods. Plans written with shorter waiting periods are substantially more expensive and there are usually less costly ways to cover the first six months of longer disability periods.

If a beneficiary is able to return to work after receiving LTD benefits there is usually a three- to six-month period during which recurrence may be compensated immediately without requiring a new waiting period. Some plans offer trial work periods of up to two years during which benefits are reduced by only 70 percent to 80 percent of earnings, in order to encourage rehabilitation.

Some LTD plans fix a maximum benefit term for all disabilities, or for disabilities due to illnesses rather than injuries, but most pay benefits from the end of the waiting period until attainment of age 65. Many plans limit payments for nervous disorders and drug or alcohol abuse to a fixed term of two years.

Many plans allow payments for up to two years if disabled from performance of one's usual occupation; in the long run, however, almost all LTD plans require that a person be totally disabled from performance of any gainful work for which qualified. Plans do not ordinarily preclude benefits for job-caused disabilities, but reductions of the benefits in the amount of workers' compensation payments are usually made.

Studies by the health insurance industry have shown that the number of applications filed for LTD benefits is sensitive to the ratio of benefits to predisability earnings, as shown in Figure 18.4.

Benefits as Percentage of Gross Pay	*Application Frequency as Percentage of Average*
50%	91%
51% to 60%	100%
61% to 70%	106%
Over 70%	119%

Source: Health Insurance Assoc. of America, *Compensation Systems Available to Disabled Persons in the United States* (1979).

Fig. 18.4 Application Frequency for Long-Term Disability Benefits

It should be noted that the above data contains no measure of "true" disability; it may be that low benefits motivate disabled people to work when they shouldn't, or that high benefits motivate people to claim benefits when they should be working. In any event, it is generally considered imprudent to allow benefits from all sources to exceed 70 percent of gross pay.

Integration With Social Security. Integration of LTD benefits with Social Security is complicated by the fact that not all who qualify for LTD will necessarily qualify for SSDI, and by the fact that SSDI pays a higher percentage of predisability earnings to persons with low incomes than to persons with higher incomes. In some cases, reduction of LTD benefits by the full amount of SSDI would result in no LTD benefit. To comply with the laws of some states and to avoid misunderstandings, many plans provide for payment of a minimum benefit in such cases.

To keep benefits somewhat abreast of inflation, some LTD plans provide automatic increases. Most, however have a 2 percent to 3 percent per year cap which prevents them from keeping up with recent rates of inflation. A more common provision is to freeze the SSDI offset at the beginning of the eligibility period, thereby allowing total benefits for those who receive both SSDI and privately funded benefits to increase by the amount of Social Security cost-of-living increases. A freeze of this kind is required in several states and by federal law in the case of disability benefits classified as pensions.

Pension Accrual. In some cases, LTD provides funds for pension accrual in addition to cash benefits. Other plans provide that the pension itself accrues a deferred benefit payable at normal retirement age, while the disabled worker is receiving LTD benefits.

Minimizing Costs. Insurance carriers are reluctant to write LTD plans for companies with workers exposed to high risks. Likewise, they avoid companies and industries with unstable employment. Experience has shown a strong correlation between high unemployment and high rates of application for disability benefits.

Many plans exclude benefits for self-inflicted disabilities and for disabilities arising from war, riot or felony, and preexisting conditions that have been treated within three months before coverage of the group.

LTD benefits can be costly and unpredictable. For these reasons, self-funding is risky, especially for small groups. On the other hand, insurers must establish relatively high reserves for LTD claims, thus tying up considerable amounts of the employers' money, at low rates of interest. Thus, plan designers may want to look into financing methods that minimize the cost of insurance.

Rehabilitation and Reemployment Assistance

Rehabilitation. For some workers with permanent impairments, disability is overcome by successful reemployment. Most, fortunately, return to former employers and do jobs much like the ones they left. Others need more help and rehabilitation is a term that includes related available services.

Rehabilitation, in the disability context, is restoration of impaired workers to regular employment for adequate pay. It involves counseling, testing, medical treatment, therapy, training, and education. It begins with primary medical care, as therapy is prescribed to maintain and restore various body functions. Specific efforts to establish and move toward new vocational goals begin when someone—usually a rehabilitation counselor—identifies an elusive thing called *rehabilitation potential*. Regrettably, not every impaired person has the potential to make rehabilitation succeed. Some are too badly impaired or too near retirement. Some have too little aptitude for jobs within their reduced capacity and some may have lost their will to overcome adversity.

Public policy encourages a wide range of restorative services for a broadly defined category of rehabilitation potential, while private benefit payers understandably recommend employment-focused rehabilitation for a narrower band of potential, when they can anticipate short-run benefit savings. Rehabilitation agencies are expected to show a clear margin of return on their investment.

However rehabilitation potential is defined, there are numerous public and private groups available to design and carry out rehabilitation plans.

Federal-State Vocational Rehabilitation. Governmental efforts to restore the disabled to employability center on fifty state vocational rehabilitation agencies. Each state operates facilities for delivering therapeutic services and in addition has counselors in major cities. Counselors may prescribe services to be given at state rehabilitation centers or, more often, at hospitals and other health care institutions in the community. Public monies pay for much of the service, but the rehabilitation agencies also recover a substantial share of costs from clients and insurance carriers. Federal grants to states carry about 80 percent of the public costs while states and localities pay the remainder.

Disabled persons are accepted for services if potential is identified for improved vocational opportunities or for increased independent living. If rehabilitation potential is unclear, applicants may be accepted for evaluation. In recent years, over one million persons per year have been served at an annual cost of about $1 billion.

An extra effort is made to restore employability to SSDI and SSI recipients. State rehabilitation agencies are reimbursed in full by the federal government for services to these groups.

Insurance Company Rehabilitation Services. A few large casualty insurance companies are leaders in the development of rehabilitation techniques and devices. In line with their interest in minimizing disability, most large casualty companies have professional rehabilitation staffs. Some companies maintain their own rehabilitation centers where services are provided directly to selected clients but, as with state agencies, most prescribed services are purchased from over 900 certified rehabilitation providers throughout the country.

Insurance carrier rehabilitation interest has increased in recent years for several reasons; among them:

- Disability benefits are higher and maximum durations are longer;
- Some workers' compensation laws have added strong client entitlements to rehabilitation;
- Some workers' compensation laws provide for a reduction or termination of benefits if clients decline reasonable offers of rehabilitation services.

Private Rehabilitation Service Vendors. Motivation plays a large role in rehabilitation. Public and private payers of disability benefits encourage the disabled to return to work with both carrots and sticks. Most of the disabled want to work also, but self-doubt and reliance on cash benefits causes some reluctance to cooperate with rehabilitation plans. Private vendors of rehabilitation services have stepped into this relationship to work as agents of benefit payers. Their service package includes consultation, evaluation, and placement assistance. No comprehensive measure of their effectiveness is yet available to evaluate reports of successes or complaints that some vendors cross the line between motivation and coercion.

The Economics of Rehabilitation. The dollar benefits of rehabilitation are much analyzed and debated. Not surprisingly, the rehabilitation community presents an impressive argument that their programs are worthwhile and cost beneficial. The case for rehabilitation can be studied in the form of elaborate statistical analyses or through a series of well-presented success stories, depending on one's preference. The largest program (state vocational rehabilitation) reports successful case closings for about one-third of their clients and a comfortable margin dollar savings over costs. But survey responses of formerly disabled people deflate some of these conclusions by attributing successes to factors other than rehabilitation services. In 1972, only 17 percent felt that rehabilitation had increased employability.[1]

Clearly, rehabilitation yields benefits. The important unresolved question is whether more rehabilitation dollars would yield their value in more benefits.

Reemployment Assistance. Amendment of the Vocational Rehabilitation Act in 1973 requires employers with government contracts to take affirmative action to aid employment of handicapped people, defined as people with physical or mental impairments that substantially limit one or more major life activities.

All contractors with contracts exceeding $2,500 are obliged to take affirmative action. Larger contractors, those with fifty or more employees or contracts exceeding $50,000, must establish and carry out a formalized affirmative action program that includes:

- Assuring that job qualification requirements do not arbitrarily screen out handicapped people;

---

[1] Levitan & Taggart, *Jobs for the Disabled* 82 (1977).

- Making reasonable accommodations in the workplace for impaired workers;
- Setting pay without deductions because of benefits or services received from an outside source; and
- Reaching out to find handicapped candidates for suitable jobs.

SPECIAL LEGAL CONSIDERATIONS

The Taft-Hartley Act

Section 302(a) of the Labor Management Relations Act of 1947, as amended, (Taft-Hartley Act) generally makes it unlawful for any employer or association of employers or any person who acts as a labor relations expert, advisor, or consultant to an employer or who acts in the interest of an employer to pay, lend, deliver, or agree to the same, any money or other thing of value to the following:

1. Any representative of any of his employees;
2. Any labor organization, or any officer or employee thereof, that represents, seeks to represent, or would admit to membership, any of his employees;
3. Any employee or group of employees in excess of their normal compensation for the purpose of causing them directly or indirectly to influence any other employees in their right to organize and bargain collectively through representation by their own choosing;
4. Any officer or employee of a labor organization with intent to influence him in respect to any of his actions, decisions, or duties as a representative of employees or as an officer or employee of such organization.

Section 302(b)(1) also makes it unlawful for any person to request, demand, receive, or accept or agree to the same of any money or other thing of value prohibited by Section 302(a).

However, Section 302(c)(5) provides an exception to the prohibitions if the money or other thing of value is for the purpose of providing certain types of employee benefit plans (including, disability plans) provided specified conditions are met.

Therefore, it is lawful to establish a disability benefits plan if payment is made to a trust fund established by the representative, for the sole and exclusive benefit of the employees and their families and dependents, if the following conditions are met:

1. The money must be held in trust for the purpose of paying disability benefits either from principal or income or both, for the benefit of employees, their families, and dependents;

2. Details regarding such payments must be specified in a written agreement with the employer. Employees and employers must be equally represented in the administration of the fund, together with such neutral persons

as the representatives of the employees and the representatives the employers may agree upon. In the event the employer and employee groups deadlock on the administration of the fund and there are no neutral persons empowered to break the deadlock, the agreement will provide that the two groups shall agree on an impartial umpire to decide the dispute. In the event of their failure to agree within a reasonable length of time, an impartial umpire to decide the dispute shall, on petition of either group, be appointed by the U.S. district court for the district where the trust fund has its principal office. Finally, the plan must contain provisions for an annual audit of the trust fund, a statement of the results of which shall be made available for inspection by interested persons at the principal office of the trust fund and at other places as may be designated by the parties.

3. The payments that are intended to be used for the purpose of providing pensions (including disability provisions) or annuities must be made to a separate trust and must provide that the funds held in the trust cannot be used for any purpose other than paying such pensions and annuities.

Employee Retirement Income Security Act of 1974 (ERISA)

Section 3(1) of ERISA defines "employee welfare benefit plan" and "welfare plan" as any plan, fund, or program established or maintained by an employer or by an employee organization for the purpose of providing for its participants or their beneficiaries, through the purchase of insurance or otherwise, inter alia, benefits in the event of disability. The ERISA definition of "employee pension benefit plan" and "pension plan" in Section 3(2) includes disability provisions in such pension plans.

Thus, employers have the option of providing for disability provisions in either an employee welfare benefit plan or an employee pension benefit plan. The possibility also exists, of course for providing for two separate disability plans that would overlap if careful planning is not observed. As pointed out below, employee welfare benefit plans and employee pension benefit plans are subject to different rules that must be considered when determining how a disability program should be provided.

Coverage Under Title I. Title I of ERISA is administered by the U.S. Department of Labor. Title I generally covers all employee welfare benefit plans and all employee pension benefit plans with the exception, among others, of plans maintained solely for the purpose of complying with applicable workers' compensation laws, unemployment compensation laws, or disability insurance laws.

The Department of Labor has by regulation also excluded certain other plans from coverage. For example, payment of an employee's normal compensation, out of the employer's general assets, for periods of time the employee is physically or mentally unable to perform his or her duties, or is otherwise absent for medical reasons (such as pregnancy, a physical examination, or psychiatric treatment) is excluded from coverage.[2]

Also excluded are group or group-type insurance programs offered by an insurer to employers or members of an employee organization, under which:

1. No contributions are made by an employer or employee organization;
2. Participation in the program is completely voluntary for employees or members;
3. The sole functions of the employer or employee organization with respect to the program are, without endorsing the program, to permit the insurer to publicize the program to employees or members, to collect premiums through payroll deductions or dues checkoffs and to remit them to the insurer; and
4. The employee or employee organization receives no consideration in the form of cash or otherwise in connection with the program, other than reasonable compensation, excluding any profit, for administrative services actually rendered in connection with payroll deductions or dues checkoffs.[3]

Reporting and Disclosure. Section 101(a) of ERISA requires the administrator of each employee benefit plan to submit certain reports to the Department of Labor and to furnish certain information to plan participants. (See Chapter 5.)

Also, the plan administrator must provide each plan participant with a summary annual report within nine months after each plan year, as well as make the full annual report available for inspection by plan participants and to provide copies if requested. Finally, the plan administrator must provide a summary plan description in plain, understandable language to plan participants within either ninety days after becoming a plan participant or 120 days after the plan is established. The summary plan description must also be filed with the Department of Labor. When a plan is modified in a major way, both the plan participants and the Department of Labor must be notified. (See Chapter 6.)

There is a limited exemption for certain small welfare plans from reporting and disclosure requirements for welfare plans that cover fewer than 100 participants at the beginning of the plan year. The benefits are paid as needed solely from the general assets of the employer or employee organization maintaining the plan or are provided exclusively through an insurance contract issued by a company qualified to do business in any state.[4]

There is also a limited exemption for certain group insurance arrangements for welfare plans covering fewer than 100 participants at the beginning of the plan year. The welfare plans must be part of a group insurance arrangement that

---

[2] 29 C.F.R. § 2510.3-1(b)(2) (1975).
[3] 29 C.F.R. § 2510.3-1(j) (1975).
[4] 29 C.F.R. § 2520.104-20 (1978).

1. Provides benefits to the employees of two or more unaffiliated employers;
2. Fully insures one or more welfare plans of each participating employer through insurance contracts purchased solely by the employers or purchased partly by the employers and partly by their participating employees, with all benefit payments made by the insurance company; or
3. Uses a trust or other entity such as a trade association as the holder of the insurance contracts and the conduit for payment of premiums to the insurance company.[5]

ERISA provides serious penalties for not complying with the reporting and disclosure requirements. Section 501 provides that any person who willfully violates any of the provisions of the reporting and disclosure requirements or any order or any regulation issued pursuant to the provisions shall, if convicted, be fined not more than $5,000 or imprisoned not more than one year, or both. In the case of such a violation by a person not an individual, i.e., a corporation, the fine shall not exceed $100,000.

Further, Section 502(c) provides that any administrator who fails or refuses to comply with a request for information required to be furnished may, in the court's discretion, be personally liable to such participant or beneficiary up to $100 per day from the date of failure or refusal to comply. The court may, in its discretion, order other relief as it deems appropriate.

Fiduciary Responsibility. The fiduciary responsibility provisions contained in Part 4 of ERISA cover both employee benefit pension plans and employee benefit welfare plans, and should be looked at carefully. (See Chapter 7.)

Trust requirement. Section 403 of ERISA requires, with certain exceptions, that all assets of an employee benefit plan be held in trust by one or more trustees which shall be either named in the trust instrument or in the plan document or appointed by a named fiduciary. Two exceptions to this trust requirement are that it does not apply to:

1. Any assets of a plan that consist of insurance contracts or policies issued by an insurance company qualified to do business in a state; or
2. Any assets of such an insurance company or any assets of a plan which are held by such an insurance company.

It is also important to note that Section 403 provides, with certain exceptions, that the assets of a plan shall never inure to the benefit of any employer and shall be held for the exclusive purposes of providing benefits to participants in the plan and their beneficiaries and defraying reasonable expenses of administering the plan.

---

[5] 29 C.F.R. § 2520.104-21 (1978).

Liability of Employers Beyond Workers' Compensation

By and large, the liability of employers for their workers' job-caused injuries and illnesses is limited to the amounts set forth in workers' compensation laws. This is not true, however, for merchant seamen or railroad workers who are covered by employer liability laws rather than workers' compensation. These laws restrict the common-law defenses available to maritime and railroad employers so that it is easier for injured workers to recover damages in court. For most other employers, assumption of no-fault liability within a workers' compensation statute is a trade-off for freedom from common-law tort liability. This freedom, however, is not complete. Exceptional cases have broken through the protection afforded by workers' compensation. They are still rare, but some believe they are on the rise.

Third-Party Liability. Before examining the bases of some of the successful attacks on workers' compensation exclusivity, note that third parties, outside the employer-employee relationship, are generally not protected from tort liability should they cause injury or illness in the workplace. A simple case of third-party liability would be an automobile accident caused by a private party that injures a delivery man engaged in his work. The delivery man could recover damages from the driver who caused the accident without constraint by the limits set by any workers' compensation law. A more complicated case, and one that is currently common, involves diseases caused by substances used in the workplace that were furnished to the employer by third parties, whose performance is alleged to have been at fault for the resulting disease. Cases like this involving asbestos-related cancer are numerous and increasing. Other disease-causing substances may follow the same pattern.

Employer Liability. Employers themselves may be held liable beyond workers' compensation limits if:

1. They are acting in a dual capacity that has characteristics of a third party and an employer. In one court, for instance, the safety inspection responsibility of a self-insured employer was found to be separate from the same corporation's role as employer of the injured worker. In others, the employer's role as medical examiner was found to be separate from the employer role; or
2. They have intentionally caused injury; or
3. The employer's behavior has caused damage to the worker in addition to injury or illness, such as deceit that caused economic damage or defamation that caused social damage.

In general, these are matters for state courts to decide. Judicial precedents vary greatly from state to state as do outcomes. That these kinds of decisions have been rendered in specific cases should not be taken to indicate that the liability limits of workers' compensation are becoming ineffectual.

SPECIAL TAX CONSIDERATIONS

Compensation for Injuries or Sickness

Section 104 of the Internal Revenue Code governs compensation for injuries or sickness. In general, gross income for tax purposes does not include:

1. Amounts received under workers' compensation acts as compensation for personal injuries or sickness;
2. The amount of any damages received either by suit or agreement as a result of personal injuries or sickness;
3. Amounts received through accident or health insurance for personal injuries or sickness other than amounts received by an employee, to the extent such amounts:

   a. Are attributable to contributions by the employer, which were not includable in the gross income of the employee; or

   b. Are paid by the employer;

4. Amounts received as a pension, annuity, or similar allowance for personal injuries or sickness resulting from military and other specified services; and
5. Amounts received by an individual as disability income attributable to injuries incurred as a result of terrorist attacks while the individual was a U.S. employee outside the United States.

Compensation Under Accident and Health Plans. Section 105 concerns amounts received under accident and health plans. This section was added to insure that the tax treatment of amounts received under noninsured employee accident and health plans would be similar to that of amounts received under accident and health insurance. The general rule is that amounts received by an employee for personal injuries or sickness through accident and health insurance are taxable if paid by the employer or attributable to employer contributions not included in the gross income of the employee.

However, Section 105(d) provides that in the case of a taxpayer who (1) has not attained age 65 before the close of the taxable year, and (2) retired on disability, and when retired, was permanently and totally disabled, gross income does not include amounts referred to in Section 105(a) if such amounts constitute wages or payments in lieu of wages for a period during which the employee is absent from work due to permanent and total disability. Permanent and total disability is defined as an individual who is unable to engage in any substantial gainful activity by reason of any medically determinable physical or mental impairment that can be expected to result in death or that has lasted or can be expected to last for a continuous period of not less than twelve months.

Self-Insured Medical Reimbursement Plans

Section 105(h) sets forth certain standards that must be met with regard to highly compensated individuals under a discriminatory self-insured medical expense plan. In general, the amounts paid to a highly compensated individual under a self-insured medical reimbursement plan that does not satisfy certain requirements will not be excludable from gross income to the extent that they constitute an excess reimbursement of such highly compensated individual.

A self-insured medical reimbursement plan meets the requirements only if (1) the plan does not discriminate in favor of highly compensated individuals as to eligibility to participate, and (2) the benefits provided under the plan do not discriminate in favor of participants who are highly compensated individuals. Also, a self-insured medical reimbursement plan will not meet the requirements unless the plan benefits:

1. Seventy percent or more of all employees, or 80 percent or more of all the employees who are eligible to benefit under the plan if 70 percent or more of all the employees are eligible to benefit under the plan; or
2. Such employees who qualify under a classification set up by the employer and found not to be discriminatory in favor of highly compensated participants.

Certain employees may be legitimately excluded from the plan, such as:

1. Employees who have not completed three years of service;
2. Employees who have not reached the age of 25;
3. Employees not included in the plan who are included in a unit of employees covered by an agreement between employee representatives and one or more employees which the Secretary of Labor finds to be a collective bargaining agreement, if accident and health benefits were the subject of good-faith bargaining between the employee representatives and the employer;
4. Part-time or seasonal employees; and
5. Certain nonresident alien employees.

The term *highly compensated individual* is defined as an individual who is

1. One of the five highest paid officers;
2. A 10 percent or more shareholder of the stock of the employer; or
3. Among the highest paid 25 percent of all employees, with minor exceptions.

Tax Effect on Employees of Employer Contributions

Section 106 deals with the tax consequences to employees of contributions by an employer to pay for sickness and injury benefits. The general rule is that contributions by an employer to an accident or health plan to provide the employee with benefits in the event of personal injury or sickness are not taxable as income to the employee.

Cafeteria Plans

Section 125 of the Code enables the employer to establish what are called *cafeteria plans*. This concept allows the employer to create a welfare benefit plan that gives participants a choice among one or more nontaxable benefits and one or more taxable benefits. It should be noted that there are substantial differences in the anti-discrimination rules between Sections 105 and 125.

Tax Treatment of Pension Plan Disability Benefits

Section 162(a) of the Code generally provides that amounts paid by an employer to finance sickness and injury benefits for employees generally constitute ordinary and necessary business expenses and are therefore deductible. However, contributions to qualified pension, profit-sharing and stock bonus plans are deductible only under the provisions of Section 404, even if those plans provide benefits for sickness or injury (i.e., temporary or permanent disability).

If an employer wanted to provide disability benefits as a part of a pension plan, the employer should make sure that the plan is qualified under Section 401 of the Code. This would insure that the beneficiaries of the plan will receive favorable tax treatment pursuant to Sections 402 and 403 and that the employer would receive favorable tax treatment from the contributions to the plan pursuant to Section 404.

19

Unemployment Benefit Plans

RONALD L. ADLER
Vice-President, Reed, Roberts Associates

NATURE OF UNEMPLOYMENT BENEFITS

Benefits provided in the event of unemployment, while countercyclical, are generally more curative than preventative, attempt to guarantee income maintenance and independence, and are paid irrespective of personal wealth. These benefits attempt to redress the effects of general economic instability caused by "normal" business cycles—changes in the demand for goods and services; fluctuations in weather and other seasonal conditions; the liquidation of products and firms; turnover caused by changes in employment patterns; the effect of changing technologies; and general inadequacies of the American economy. Whether unemployment results from seasonal, cyclical, or structural factors, an attempt is made to maintain the unemployed worker's purchasing power and standard of living.

Programs providing these benefits are often fragmented, sometimes inconsistent, and, to a large extent, uncoordinated. Generally, however, these programs meet the income maintenance needs of the unemployed work force. This chapter discusses the most important benefit program for the unemployed, the regular federal-state unemployment insurance program, as well as those programs directly related and supplemental to the federal-state unemployment insurance program and other nongovernmental monetary and nonmonetary programs.

THE FEDERAL-STATE UNEMPLOYMENT INSURANCE PROGRAM

General Description of Federal-State System

Born in an era of great economic distress, the current federal-state unemployment insurance program was designed to alleviate the economic chaos caused by massive unemployment. At the time, more than 20 percent of the work force was unemployed; the typical unemployed worker had been unemployed for a year or more and had lost his savings when financial institutions collapsed in 1929. President Roosevelt, as part of his economic recovery proposals, requested an unemployment compensation program that promoted employment stabilization, maintained some purchasing power for those temporarily out of work, and retarded the further downward spiral of the then economic crisis.

Enacting Legislation. In 1935 Congress incorporated, as part of the Social Security Act, the framework for the federal-state unemployment insurance system. This system provided income maintenance for those temporarily unemployed through no fault of their own, and determined eligibility irrespective of the individual's personal wealth. Subsequently, Congress passed the Federal Unemployment Tax Act (FUTA).

Two points about this legislation should be noted: First, unlike other pieces of social legislation emanating from the Roosevelt New Deal era, unemployment insurance is not a totally federalized program. Within broad boundaries, each state is allowed to develop a program that best serves its citizens. Second, a "means test" is not used for determining eligibility. The receipt of unemployment insurance benefits is based, instead, on a retrospective review of a claimant's past attachment to the labor market.

Since federal unemployment legislation's original inception, a number of amendments and other changes have been made:

- The Railroad Unemployment Insurance Act of 1938 removed railroad workers from the regular federal-state unemployment insurance system and created a separate program.
- Amendments to the Social Security Act in 1939 broadened the coverage of the unemployment insurance laws and changed the tax base from "all wages" to a $3,000 ceiling.
- In the post-World War II period, veterans and federal civilian employees were added to the list of covered employment.
- In the 1960s, additional amendments:
  - —Temporarily extended the duration of benefits for individuals who exhausted their normal benefits;
  - —Paid for occupational, vocational, and on-the-job training;
  - —Provided assistance for workers adversely affected by trade agreements; and
  - —Provided aid for families with dependent children and individuals unemployed as a result of a major disaster.
- In 1970 the Employment Security Amendments extended coverage to employees of nonprofit organizations, state hospitals, and state institutions of higher education. Additionally, the FUTA tax rate was increased from 3.1 percent to 3.2 percent on an increased taxable wage base of $4,200 (from the previous $3,000). These amendments also provided for a permanent extended benefits program.
- During the remainder of the 1970s, amendments were passed that temporarily provided additional weeks of benefits; first, increasing the maximum duration from thirty-nine weeks to fifty-two weeks, and later to sixty-five weeks of benefits. Additionally, under the Special Unemployment Assistance Program, temporary coverage was provided to unemployed individuals not covered by the regular federal-state unemployment insurance program.
- The 1976 Unemployment Compensation Amendments included an increase in the taxable wage base to $6,000 from $4,200 and the extension of cov-

erage to nearly all employees of state and local governments, nonprofit schools, and some farm and domestic workers. As a result of these amendments, approximately 97 percent of the American work force is now in "covered" employment.

State Participation. The provisions of the 1935 Social Security Act and, subsequently, FUTA strongly encouraged state participation. By 1937, all states had enacted legislation. The constitutionality of this program has since been upheld by the U.S. Supreme Court.

Prior to 1935, attempts to establish independent state unemployment insurance programs met with little success. The proponents of a national unemployment insurance program were eager to leave the "hard decisions" concerning duration and benefit amount to the states and were very much concerned about the constitutionality of a centralized federal program. They recognized, however, that the causes of unemployment were national in scope and that uniform protection of unemployed workers was economically and administratively advantageous for a mobile society that was involved in interstate commerce. This program is, then, a unique blend of federal engineering, state administration and control, and employer funding. Since the states are more familiar with the geographic, demographic, climatic, and economic factors affecting their constituents, they were left to develop and administer, within the federal guidelines programs that were sensitive and responsive to the needs of their citizens.

Enforcing Compliance With Federal Laws. Compliance with federal unemployment insurance laws is obtained by imposing a federal tax on employers within a state, then by allowing an offsetting tax credit for state taxes paid. The current FUTA tax is 3.4 percent on the first $6,000 earned by each employee in a calendar year. A credit of 2.7 percent is subsequently given to all employers in a state that conforms with federal standards. A ruling of nonconformity and concomitant decertification by the Secretary of Labor results in the loss of the 2.7 percent credit against the Federal Unemployment Insurance tax obligation. A ruling of nonconformity also means the loss of funds to the state for administration of its unemployment insurance program.

Sanctions for nonconformity with the provisions of the Social Security Act and FUTA fall into four categories:

Sanction I. Federal tax credit and administrative grants are forfeited if the state:

- Fails to pay unemployment benefits through public employment offices or other agencies.
- Fails to use funds from the State Unemployment Trust Fund for the payment of unemployment benefits and certain refunds.

- Denies benefits to an individual because he refuses to accept new work when the position offered is vacant due to a labor dispute, is at less favorable wages, hours or conditions than those prevailing in the area, or when he would be required to join a company union or resign or refrain from joining a bona fide labor union.
- Fails to provide coverage to employees of nonprofit organizations.
- Fails to cover employees of state and local governments.
- Denies certain nonprofit organizations and state and local governments the election of the method of financing their unemployment insurance costs by either taxation or reimbursement methods.
- Allows benefits to professional employees who work in schools and who have contracts or reasonable assurance of employment for the succeeding term or period.
- Allows an unemployed individual, who has received unemployment benefits in one benefit year, to qualify for benefits in the succeeding benefit year without an earnings requirement.
- Denies benefits to an individual who is in an approved training program offered by a state agency or denies benefits because of the individual's application for such training program.
- Cancels wage credits or totally reduces benefit rights for any cause other than misconduct, fraud, or disqualifying income.
- Fails to provide extended benefits under the federal-state extended benefits program, when the state trigger is "on."
- Denies benefits on the basis of pregnancy or termination of pregnancy.
- Pays benefits to professional athletes during the "off season" when there is reasonable assurance that the athlete will play in the next season.
- Pays benefits on the basis of services performed by illegal aliens.

Sanction II. Administrative grants are withheld or suspended if the state:

- Fails to design methods of administration that insure full payment of benefits when due.
- Fails to provide an opportunity for a fair hearing before an impartial tribunal before a claim is denied.
- Denies benefits to a substantial number of individuals who should have been entitled under the state law.
- Fails to cooperate with the Railroad Retirement Board or *every* federal agency administering *any* unemployment insurance law.

Sanction III. The 2.7 percent federal tax-offset credit is forfeited if the state:

- Fails to provide for a pooled fund system with experience rating, which is directly related to the unemployment insurance risk experienced by the employer during the previous three consecutive years as of the computation date.

- Provides a reduction of rates below one percent for newly subject employers prior to the establishment of sufficient experience to be rated under the regular state experience rating system.

Sanction IV. The tax credit is reduced if the state:

- Fails to repay loans made to its state fund from the Federal Unemployment ment Insurance Trust Fund under Title XII of the Social Security Act.
- Fails to have an approved Trade Act agreement with the Secretary of Labor under which the state agency pays trade adjustment assistance.

Operation of State Programs

The present federal-state unemployment insurance system, through the network of individual state programs, pays weekly benefits to partially replace lost wages during periods of temporary unemployment. The delivery channels for this program are the separate state unemployment insurance programs. As noted earlier, each state is allowed to determine within certain federal guidelines the eligibility, weekly benefit amount, duration, disqualification, and administrative procedures regarding the payment of unemployment benefits to its unemployed workers. Because socioeconomic conditions vary in each state, eligibility and benefit provisions differ greatly. Thus a detailed discussion of each state's eligibility and benefit provisions would be lengthy and complex. Therefore, individual reference sheets for each state are found in Appendixes 19-3 and 19-4.

Eligibility Requirements. The issue of "eligibility" requires a determination of a claimant's past and current attachment to the labor market. A claimant ruled ineligible is prevented by an open-ended postponement from receipt of benefits. The removal of an ineligibility determination requires the claimant to demonstrate (through positive action) that he has satisfied his state's eligibility requirements.

Generally, each state requires that a claimant be able and available for work; be actively seeking work; demonstrate a past attachment to the labor market; be partially or totally unemployed through no fault of his own; and file a valid claim for benefits. Each state also provides an administrative adjudication process that allows each claimant or his employer(s) the right to appeal any determination regarding eligibility and qualification for benefits.[1]

---

[1] In the case of an interstate claim, the unemployment insurance laws of the state in which the claimant's wages were reported govern the eligibility and benefit rights of the claimant. The Employment Security Amendments of 1970 (Public Law 91-373) require all states to participate in an interstate plan for the payment of benefits. The purpose of this agreement is to encourage a claimant to move to an area where work is available and where he may best utilize his skills.

The requirement that a claimant *be able to work* is most often satisfied by the claimant's registration with the job service at the time he files for unemployment insurance benefits. While most states have very general definitions of the term "able to work," a few specifically require that the claimant be physically and mentally able to work. In some states, once a claimant is determined eligible for benefits he will not be considered ineligible for benefits during his "benefit year" [2] even if he becomes ill or disabled, as long as he is not offered or does not refuse suitable work.

Availability for work requires that the claimant be ready, willing, and able to work. He must not place any undue restrictions on the work he will accept. In some states, the law provides that the claimant be available for "suitable work," while in others he must be available for work in his usual occupation, or work for which he has been trained or has prior work experience. Some states require that a claimant be available for "full-time work," while other states require that a claimant be available for work in the geographic area where he has earned his base period wages, or in a similar geographic area where such work is normally performed. Arizona requires that the claimant be a resident of Arizona or of a state or foreign country that has entered into a reciprocal agreement with Arizona.

In order to be eligible for benefits, a claimant must also be *"actively seeking work."* The intensity of the state's investigation of a claimant's activity in this area varies significantly among the states. Pennsylvania considers it is prima facie evidence that a claimant is able, available, and actively seeking work when he applies for benefits, since he also must register with the state job service. In some states, the question of whether or not the claimant is able, available, and actively seeking work is not an issue that the employer can challenge. In other states, the employer can actively participate in the process that tests the claimant's "genuine" attachment to the labor market.

Benefit Amount and Duration. The determination of weekly benefit amount and the duration of benefits depend on a complex interrelationship of various factors. Unlike a determination of the claimant's attachment to the labor market, which is a test of current weekly benefit eligibility, the determination of the claimant's weekly benefit amount and the calculation of benefit duration is a retrospective test. Benefit rights are determined by a claimant's work experience during a prior period referred to as the *base period*.[3] Depending on the state, the claimant's weekly benefit amount is

---

[2] A fifty-two-week period during which a claimant may receive his unemployment insurance benefit entitlement. The benefit year usually begins when a claimant files an application for benefits.

[3] Generally a fifty-two-week or four-quarter period that is defined in terms of the first four of the last five completed calendar quarters, the last four quarters, or a fifty-two-week period preceding the benefit year.

determined by: the number of weeks worked in covered employment; the number of weeks worked with some minimum earnings amount; the total amount earned during the base period; or the amount of high-quarter earnings. A premium is generally placed on long-time, stable employment.

In all states, the determined weekly benefit amount is determined for a week of *total unemployment* as defined by the state law. Total unemployment is usually defined as a week in which the claimant has provided no services for which remuneration is paid or payable.

States generally use one of three benefit formulas to determine the claimant's weekly benefit amount:

- A fraction of high-quarter earnings in the base period;
- A percentage of weekly average wage in the base period; or
- A percentage of annual wage in the base period.

Originally, the weekly benefit amount was based primarily on the number of weeks of full-time employment, with benefits representing a fraction of the amount of weekly earnings in this employment. This method, however, necessitated the reporting of full-time earnings on a weekly basis. When this method proved administratively difficult, the alternative procedures were developed.

The *high-quarter earnings* formula is used by thirty-four states plus the District of Columbia and Puerto Rico. This formula multiplies, generally, one-twenty-sixth times the claimant's high-quarter earnings. In this method of computation, the claimant is required to have earnings in at least two calendar quarters. The second most common benefit formula is the *average weekly wage* formula used by nine states. This method computes the weekly benefit amount on the basis of wages earned in weeks worked during the base period. Generally, a minimum weekly earnings requirement must be satisfied for the week to be counted. The third method is the *average wage* formula used by four states. This method multiplies the state factor by the wage credits earned during the base period.

The actual total benefit amount payable to an individual is limited by the state's minimum and maximum benefit rates and by the benefit duration provision.

Figure 19.1 indicates, for each state, the current minimum and maximum weekly benefit amount, the maximum duration of benefits, and the maximum potential benefit amount.

Dependents' Allowance. In addition to the basic benefit amount, thirteen states provide dependents' allowance. The amount and the eligibility for this varies with each state. Generally, a dependent is defined as someone receiving substantial and regular support from the claimant. All states, except Maine and Massachusetts, that pay dependents' allowance include stepchildren in the statutory definition of dependent.

State	*Min. Weekly Benefit Amount*	*Max. Weekly Benefit Amount*	*Duration (Weeks)*	*Max. Potential Benefit Amount*
Alabama	$15	$ 90	26	$2,340
Alaska	34	150	28	4,200
Arizona	25	95	26	2,470
Arkansas	31	136	26	3,536
California	30	136	26	3,536
Colorado	25	176	26	4,576
Connecticut	15	146	26	3,796
Delaware	20	150	26	3,900
District of Columbia	14	206	34	7,004
Florida	10	125	26	3,250
Georgia	27	115	26	2,990
Hawaii	5	169	26	4,394
Idaho	36	145	26	3,770
Illinois	45	148	26	3,848
Indiana	40	84	26	2,184
Iowa	17	146	26	3,796
Kansas	37	149	26	3,874
Kentucky	22	140	26	3,640
Louisiana	10	183	28	5,124
Maine	12	115	26	2,990
Maryland	25	140	26	3,640
Massachusetts	12	156	30	4,680
Michigan	16	197	26	5,122
Minnesota	30	177	26	4,602
Mississippi	10	90	26	2,340
Missouri	14	105	26	2,730
Montana	36	145	26	3,770
Nebraska	12	106	26	2,756
Nevada	16	136	26	3,536
New Hampshire	26	132	26	3,432
New Jersey	10	145	26	3,770
New Mexico	26	130	26	3,380
New York	25	125	26	3,250
North Carolina	15	152	26	3,952
North Dakota	42	156	26	4,056
Ohio	10	147	26	3.822
Oklahoma	16	176	26	4,576
Oregon	41	158	26	4,108
Pennsylvania	35	190	30	5,700
Puerto Rico	7	84	20	1,680
Rhode Island	35	143	26	3,718
South Carolina	10	118	26	3,068
South Dakota	28	129	26	3,354
Tennessee	20	110	26	2,860
Texas	24	147	26	3,822
Utah	10	166	36	5,976
Vermont	15	135	26	3,510
Virginia	44	138	26	3,588
Washington	45	163	30	4,890
West Virginia	18	194	28	5,432
Wisconsin	34	179	34	6,086
Wyoming	24	165	26	4,290

Fig. 19.1 Current Minimum and Maximum Weekly Benefit Amount, by State

All states limit the amount of weekly dependents' allowance. Generally, this is a fixed sum determined by the number of dependents and, except in the state of Connecticut, does not change during the benefit year. It should be noted that Indiana, Iowa, Michigan, and Ohio also use an earnings factor in determining the dependents' allowance. In most states only one parent will be allowed to collect dependents' allowance when both parents are receiving regular unemployment insurance benefits.

Partial Benefits. The weekly benefit amounts discussed so far have been based on total unemployment. Unemployment benefits are also paid for partial unemployment. In most states, partial unemployment occurs in any week in which the claimant works less than full time and earns less than his determined weekly benefit amount. In determining the partial weekly benefit amount, each state will reduce the benefit amount by a portion of the claimant's earnings or employment in the given week.

Benefit Duration. Most states provide regular unemployment insurance benefits for a maximum duration of twenty-six weeks. Currently only eight states and the District of Columbia have benefit durations longer than twenty-six weeks: Alaska, Louisiana, and West Virginia—twenty-eight weeks; Massachusetts, Pennsylvania, Washington—thirty weeks; the District of Columbia and Wisconsin—thirty-four weeks; and Utah—thirty-six weeks. Puerto Rico is the only jurisdiction that provides benefits for less than twenty-six weeks, i.e., twenty weeks of benefits.

Potential duration of benefits is determined for each eligible claimant under either a uniform duration formula or a variable duration formula. In either case the duration of benefits is based on the relationship between the duration fraction, the qualifying requirements, and the benefit formula. Eight states and Puerto Rico currently use a *uniform duration* formula. Under this method, eligible claimants receive a fixed duration of benefits irrespective of their previous attachment to the labor market. The following states provide a uniform duration of benefits of twenty-six weeks:

- Connecticut
- Hawaii
- Illinois
- Maryland
- New Hampshire
- New York
- Vermont

West Virginia, which also has a uniform duration, provides claimants with twenty-eight weeks of benefits.

In other states, the potential duration varies with the earnings or the number of weeks of employment in the base period. Thirty states have a variable duration based on high-quarter wages. In the remaining states, benefit duration is a function of either weeks of work, the ratio of base-period wages to high-quarter wages, or, as in Ohio, twenty times the weekly benefit amount for the first twenty weeks credited, plus one times each credit week in excess of twenty to a maximum of twenty-six weeks.

After serving a waiting period in all but eleven states—Alabama, Connecticut, Delaware, Iowa, Kentucky, Maryland, Michigan, Nevada, New Hampshire, Virginia, and Wisconsin—a claimant may collect his benefits at any time during the benefit year. Receipt of partial benefits during any week will cause the number of weeks to exceed the claimant's assigned duration of benefits. The total maximum benefits received, however, may not exceed the claimant's total potential benefit allowance.

Public Law 91-373, Federal-State Extended Benefit Program, established a permanent plan to provide benefits exceeding the normal state duration during periods of high unemployment. Under the extended benefit program up to thirty-nine weeks of benefits can be collected; thus, in those states paying a maximum duration of twenty-six weeks, thirteen weeks of additional benefits are available at the same benefit rate.

In addition to the Federal-State Extended Benefit Program, California, Connecticut, Hawaii, and Puerto Rico have independent state-extended benefit programs.

Seasonal Unemployment Benefits. Seasonal unemployment results from many factors, including changes in climate, market demand, and the availability of raw material. Seasonal unemployment usually refers to an industry that operates less than a specific number of weeks or lays off a certain percentage of its employees for a specific number of weeks in any consecutive fifty-two-week period. Examples of seasonal industries are the canning industry, agriculture, baseball and other professional athletics, carnivals and resort facilities, lumber and logging industries, and educational institutions. Claimants in these industries are subject to the same eligibility and benefit right provisions as claimants in nonseasonal employment. In some cases, specific statutory provisions prevent employees in these industries from collecting benefits. Professional athletes and professional employees of educational institutions are statutorily prevented from collecting benefits during the off-season or between terms, if they have reasonable assurance of returning to work.

Only ten states have specific benefit provisions concerning claimants in seasonal employment. Arkansas, Colorado, Maine, North Carolina, Ohio, and South Dakota make a distinction between wage credits earned in seasonal employment and wage credits earned in nonseasonal employment. The payment of benefits based on seasonal wage credits is restricted to that period during the year when seasonal employment exists. Benefits based on nonseasonal wage credits are payable at any time during the remainder of the year. Delaware and South Carolina combine the wage credits for both seasonal and nonseasonal employment but pay benefits only during periods of seasonal employment. In West Virginia and Wisconsin, claimants are not entitled to benefits unless they have worked a specific length of time and earned a specified amount of nonseasonal wage credits.

Benefit Disqualification

To qualify for benefits, a claimant must satisfy the "eligibility requirements" of the state law, i.e., be able, available, and actively seeking work and have sufficient wage credits. He must also demonstrate that he has lost his job through "no fault" of his own. Because wholesale layoffs were prevalent during the depression years, the "no fault" concept became the guiding principle in the determination of benefit entitlement. The reason for unemployment, whether a voluntary quit, a discharge, the refusal of suitable work, or involvement in a labor dispute, is examined for adherence to this canon.

During the intervening years since the original enactment of the unemployment insurance laws, statutory provisions, administrative rules, and judicial rulings concerning the "no fault" concept have resulted in a great diversity in the various states' unemployment insurance laws. Variations in the severity of the disqualification exist. A voluntary quit in one state may result in a six-week postponement of benefits, while the same separation would result in a denial of benefits for the duration of unemployment in another state. This lack of uniformity is due to each state's administrative and judicial interpretations of "no fault" and its attitude concerning the theory that the longer an individual is unemployed, the more his unemployment can be attributed to general economic conditions, rather than the individual's reason for separation.

Disqualification vs. Ineligibility. A disqualification for receipt of benefits differs significantly from a ruling of *ineligibility*. A ruling of "ineligibility" is a penalty based on current conditions and ends as soon as those conditions are removed. The disqualification, on the other hand, is based on the reason for separation and specifies and defines the period of time or the activity necessary to purge the penalty. A disqualification may be a postponement of benefits for a specified period of time, a reduction of benefits otherwise payable, a cancellation of benefit rights, or a combination of these penalties. The disqualification imposed varies with the type of separation. As previously noted, the 1970 amendments to the FUTA prohibit the state from cancelling an individual's wage credits or totally reducing benefit rights for any reason other than a discharge for misconduct connected with his employment, fraudulent claims, or the receipt of disqualifying income. In most states the disqualification imposed is based on the separation from the last employer and commences with the week of the disqualifying act. In states that provide for a postponement of benefits, a claimant may self-serve the disqualification by not filing a claim immediately. In such cases, a claimant will be allowed to collect benefits immediately upon filing his claim, even though he has been separated for a disqualifying act.

Voluntary Quits. The unemployment insurance program pays benefits to individuals "who have lost their job through no fault of their own." A voluntary quit results from a volitional act by the claimant. It therefore may appear contrary to the "no fault" principle to grant benefits in cases of a voluntary quit. In fact, all states disqualify claimants for voluntary quits depending upon whether or not the claimant had "good cause" for quitting, and in some states, whether or not the "good cause" was attributable to the employer. More precisely, the issue is whether or not the claimant had a "necessitous and compelling reason" to quit his job. Perhaps the most precise definition of "necessitous and compelling reason" is found in a case decided by the Pennsylvania Superior Court:

> "Voluntarily" and "involuntarily" are antonymous and therefore irreconcilable words, but the words are merely symbols of ideas, and the ideas can be readily reconciled. Willingness, wilfulness, volition, intention reside in "voluntarily," but the mere fact that a worker wills and intends to leave a job does not necessarily and always mean that the leaving is voluntary. Extraneous factors, the surrounding circumstances, must be taken into the account, and when they are examined it may be found that the seemingly voluntary, the apparently intentional, act was in fact involuntary. A worker's physical and mental condition, his personal and family problems, the authoritative demand of legal duties—these are circumstances that exert pressure upon him and imperiously call for decision and action.
>
> When therefore the pressure of real not imaginary, substantial not trifling, reasonable not whimsical, circumstances *compel* the decision to leave employment, the decision is voluntary in the sense that the worker has willed it, but involuntary because outward pressures have compelled it. Or to state it differently, if a worker leaves his employment when he is compelled to do so by necessitous circumstances or because of legal or family obligations, his leaving is voluntary with good cause, and under the act he is entitled to benefits. The pressure of necessity, or legal duty, or family obligations, or other overpowering circumstances and his capitulation to them transform what is ostensibly voluntary unemployment into involuntary unemployment.[4]

Misconduct Discharges. All states provide for a disqualification in cases of misconduct discharges. Similar to the criterion used in voluntary quits, the dischargeable offense must be work-related or have a direct influence on the employer's best interest. Unlike the voluntary quit, however, the discharge is initiated by the employer and the burden of proof rests with the employer to prove any alleged misconduct.

Misconduct, while not specifically defined, has generally been interpreted by the courts to include a willful or wanton disregard of the employer's best

---

[4] Bliley Elec. Co. v. Board of Review (*In re* Sturdevant), 158 Pa. Super. 548, 45 A.2d 898 (1946) (footnote omitted).

interests, a deliberate violation or disregard of standards of behavior which the employer has a right to expect, carelessness or negligence of such degree or recurrence as to manifest culpability, wrongful intent or evil interests, or an intentional breach of an employee's duties or obligations to the employer. Note the use of the words "intentional" or "willful." Activities that might be considered misconduct, without the presence of willfulness, will not be disqualifying. It is also important to note that a causal relationship must exist between the alleged misconduct and discharge. Generally, discharges that are not immediate or approximate to the alleged misconduct will not be disqualifying.

In most states the disqualification penalty for misconduct discharges is more severe than for other types of separation. Many states also differentiate between "misconduct" and "gross misconduct" and apply a more severe penalty in a case of gross misconduct. As a guiding principle, the states impose the least severe penalty available; only increasing the severity of the penalty with the severity of the alleged misconduct. Thus, aggravating rather than mitigating circumstances generally control the severity of the disqualification penalty.

Refusal of Suitable Job Offer. All states disqualify a claimant when he fails to accept a job offer, fails to apply for available work, or fails to return to his customary self-employment. Before imposing a disqualification, most states determine the suitability of the job offer and whether or not the claimant has good cause in refusing or not applying for suitable work. The definition of suitability varies among the states, however, Section 3304(a)(5) of the Federal Unemployment Tax Act requires that a state not disqualify an individual from receipt of benefits if:

- There is a strike, lockout or other labor dispute at the location which offers a job;
- The wages, hours, or other working conditions offered are substantially less favorable to the claimant than those prevailing for similar work in the same geographic area;
- Conditions of employment include the requirement that the claimant join a company union or resign or refrain from joining a bona fide labor organization.

Other factors that determine suitability include:

1. The degree of risk to the worker's health, safety and morals;
2. The physical fitness of the claimant;
3. Prior training;
4. Experience and earnings;
5. The availability of similar work in the local geographic area;
6. The duration of his unemployment.

As a general rule, the longer an individual is unemployed, the less restrictive the factors become for refusing a job offer.

Participation in Labor Disputes. All states specifically deny unemployment benefits to individuals unemployed due to participation in a labor dispute. The imposition of a disqualification is not determined by the "no fault principle," but rather by the state's desire to maintain a neutral position and not be a causal or inhibiting factor in the labor dispute. Additionally, participants in a labor dispute are denied benefits because of the unpredictability and drain on the state unemployment insurance trust funds.

Alabama, Arizona, and Minnesota specifically define labor disputes in their statutes. The remaining states use such general terms as "trade disputes," "strikes," "lockouts," or "other bona fide labor disputes."

The imposition of the disqualification is based on:

1. The determination that a work stoppage exists;
2. That the unemployment of the claimant was caused by the work stoppage;
3. That the claimant is participating in, or directly interested in, the outcome of the labor dispute;
4. That the claimant is a member of a grade or class of worker affected by the labor dispute; and
5. That the labor dispute is at the factory, establishment, or other premises of the employer.

The period of disqualification varies in each state. Most states do not set a time limit for the period of disqualification and will deny benefits as long as the labor dispute exists or the employer's operations have been curtailed. Only New York and Rhode Island specify the duration of disqualification. In New York, a claimant unemployed because of a strike or a lockout will be denied benefits for seven weeks plus the waiting week. In Rhode Island, a claimant unemployed because of a strike is denied benefits for a six-week period plus a one-week waiting period. Seventeen states allow benefits if a labor dispute is caused by a "lockout."

The constitutionality of the New York unemployment insurance laws granting the payment of benefits to strikers after the specified period, and more recently Hawaii's unemployment insurance laws granting benefits to strikers after a determination that "substantial curtailment" does not exist, has recently been tested. In both cases, the courts have ruled that while the payment of benefits to strikers violated the doctrine of neutrality and perhaps was unwise, such laws were not preempted by the federal labor laws and were not unconstitutional.

Receipt of Certain Income. Public Law 94-566, enacted in October 1976, provides for an offset against a claimant's unemployment insurance weekly benefit amount by the amount of all governmental or other pension, retirement pay, annuity, or other payments received. Congress has since amended the pension provisions of Public Law 94-566. Public Law 96-364, Multiemployer Pension Plan Amendments Act of 1980, provides for a reduction of a claimant's weekly benefit amount by the allocated pension, retirement or retired pay, annuity, or other similar periodic payment only if such payment is made by a base-period employer or chargeable employer. The state may limit the amount of reduction to that portion contributed by the employer.

In an attempt to prevent duplicate payment of benefits for the same week, all states deny benefits to a claimant for any week in which he is receiving or seeking benefits under any other federal or state unemployment insurance law. This disqualification applies only to the week in which, or for which, other unemployment insurance benefits are actually received.

Other disqualifying income affecting a claimant's weekly benefit amount includes:

- Receipt of workers' compensation (twenty-three states).
- Receipt of wages in lieu of notice (thirty-two states).
- Receipt of dismissal or severance pay (twenty-three states).

Members of Special Groups. All states have specific provisions in their unemployment insurance laws that disqualify or find ineligible members of certain groups. Generally, students are considered unavailable for work while attending school. Individuals who quit their job for marital or filial obligations are not available for work.

Public Law 94-566 specifically denies benefits to employees of governmental entities including instructional, research, or principal administrative employees of educational institutions between successive academic years or terms, when an individual has performed services preceding the recess period and has either a contract or reasonable assurance of performing such service in the successive term. This law also allows the state to deny benefits to other employees of educational institutions between successive academic years or terms.

Additionally, Public Law 94-566 specifically denies benefits to professional athletes between two successive sport seasons when there is reasonable assurance that the athlete would report in the second season. Aliens are to be denied benefits unless they have been lawfully admitted for permanent residence at the time the services were performed, were lawfully present to perform the work upon which wage credits were established, or were lawfully residing in the United States as a result of the provisions of Sections 203(a)(7) or 212(d)(5) of the Immigration and Naturalization Act.

Requalification for Benefits

In an effort to prevent claimants from receiving benefits in two successive benefit years as a result of a single separation, all states require that a claimant earn wages prior to the beginning of the second benefit year. Thus, a claimant who has exhausted his benefits before the end of his first benefit year must not only wait until a new benefit year begins in order to draw benefits, but must also meet the state's earnings requirement for requalification.

PRIVATE PROGRAMS—SUPPLEMENTAL UNEMPLOYMENT BENEFIT PLANS

In a further attempt to mitigate the financial impact of unemployment, private plans have been established. These private plans, Supplemental Unemployment Benefit Plans (SUBs), pay benefits as a supplement to regular state unemployment insurance benefits. Designed to replace a specified percentage of the workers' average weekly wage, SUB benefits are calculated by determining the difference between the percentage of weekly wage to be replaced and the receipt of any regular state unemployment insurance benefits and trade assistance benefits (where applicable). Additionally, the duration of SUB benefits often exceeds the duration of regular state unemployment insurance benefits, thus providing the unemployed worker with increased protection against long-term unemployment.

Common Features

SUB plans include the following common features:

- A contractual agreement. SUBs are typically an element of automobile, rubber, and steel industry collective bargaining agreements.
- An employer-financed program. Generally, this type of program is based on a specific amount contributed for each man-hour worked; e.g., 15 cents is paid by the employer into a separate trust fund.
- Administration of the trust fund by an independent trustee.
- Employer contributions are required until the fund balance reaches the specified maximum level.
- SUB payments are a function of the fund balance. As the fund balance decreases, individual weekly SUB payments decrease.
- Individual SUB benefit entitlement is a function of seniority. The benefit amount is paid in accordance with a schedule that considers the worker's average earnings during a specified period of time—usually the last year.
- Eligibility for benefits generally include:
  —A qualifying separation;
  —Eligibility under the regular state unemployment insurance;

—Compliance with state registration and reporting requirements;
—Benefits not being paid under another SUB plan
—Sufficient seniority and earnings.

Types of SUB Plans

The most common SUB plan is generally referred to as the "Ford-General Motors" plan. Under this plan, the employer makes contributions into a pooled fund. Payments are made to individuals from this fund. Under this plan, an individual worker does not acquire a vested interest in future benefits and benefits are forfeitable. Generally, SUB benefits are payable only when the individual has been laid off.

The second major type of SUB is that used in the "glass industry." Under this plan the employer is required to make payments into individual employee accounts or "security benefit funds" and is required to maintain a specified fund balance. After this specified level has been reached, the employer makes payment at the same rate into a "vacation pay account" established for each employee. Unlike the Ford-General Motors plan, individuals have vested rights and each "security benefit fund" is nonforfeitable. Thus, upon retirement, separation, or death, previously unpaid benefits are payable in a lump-sum payment to either the employee or his beneficiary or estate.

The third type is referred to as the "Inco Plan" (developed by the International Nickel Company) which provides for voluntary participation by the employee. Under this plan, both the employer and employee contribute a specified amount into a security benefit fund. Once made, the employer cannot recover his contributions. Benefits are paid from the security benefits fund in case of retirement, separation—including layoff—death, or withdrawal from participation in the plan. As in the glass industry plan, benefits are vested and nonforfeitable.

Effect on Receipt of Regular State Unemployment Insurance Benefits

As noted earlier, regular state weekly benefits will be reduced when "disqualifying income" is received by a claimant. The determination by the state of whether or not SUB payments are wages, and thus serve to reduce or deny regular state unemployment insurance benefits, is critical. While only nine states (Alaska, California, Colorado, Georgia, Hawaii, Indiana, Maryland, Ohio, and Virginia) have specific amendments in their unemployment insurance statutes concerning the treatment of SUBs, all states except New Hampshire, New Mexico, Puerto Rico, South Carolina, and South Dakota have addressed this issue. Benefits paid under the Ford-General Motors-type plan are not considered disqualifying income and have no effect on receipt of unemployment insurance benefits. Benefits paid under the glass industry and Inco-type plans, however, do not enjoy such treatment. The disqualifying aspects of SUBs paid under the glass industry and Inco-type plans vary from state to state. In Arkansas, Colorado, Florida, Hawaii, Indiana, Iowa, North Carolina, Ohio, Oregon, Tennessee, Utah, Vermont, Wisconsin, and Washington, SUBs paid as either "security benefit account" and/or "vacation pay account" reduce the regular state weekly unemployment insurance benefit amount and thus may make a claimant ineligible for regular state unemployment insurance benefits.

ADDITIONAL INCOME SUPPORT PROGRAMS

Trade Adjustment Assistance (TAA)

Under the Trade Act of 1974, Public Law 93-618, monetary and non-monetary assistance is provided to workers separated or on reduced work schedules due to the impact of foreign imports. This federal program, funded from general revenues, is administered by the local state unemployment insurance offices.

Eligibility requirements for this program include:

- Certification by the U.S. Department of Labor that increased imports contribute substantially to the reduction of jobs in the claimant's company;
- That the individual claimant has either been laid off or assigned to a reduced work schedule resulting in employment of the 80 percent or less of the individual's average weekly hours or the receipt of 80 percent or less of the individual's weekly wage;
- That the individual claimant has worked in the affected plant or location for at least twenty-six of the fifty-two-week period preceding the layoff date;
- That the individual claimant has earned at least an average of $30 a week;
- That the claimant has up to one year after the loss of his job or since the reduced schedule has begun to file for benefits.

The maximum duration of benefits is a total of fifty-two weeks during a two-year period. If the claimant is over age 60 or in training, the maximum duration is increased to seventy-eight weeks during a three-year period.

Monetary benefits include that

- Seventy percent of the individual's average weekly wage with the maximum benefit amount (currently $269) equal the national average weekly manufacturing wage;
- The TAA benefit amount will be reduced by 50 percent of wages earned during the week and by the amount of unemployment insurance benefits received during the week.

Other benefits include a relocation allowance of 80 percent of moving expenses plus a maximum $500 transportation and living expense, assistance in finding a new job, and training and vocational instruction.

The TAA program is currently scheduled to end on October 1, 1982.

Disaster Unemployment Assistance

The Disaster Relief Act of 1974 (Public Law 93-288) provides unemployment assistance to individuals whose employment has been interrupted as the result of a major disaster. Disaster Unemployment Assistance (DUA) will be provided in those states where the governor of the state has entered into an agreement with the Secretary of Labor pursuant to Section 407 of this Act.

DUA is a permanent program, which is financed by funding from general revenue. Availability of DUA is based on a request by the governor to the President for declaration of a major disaster. Upon such presidential declaration, federal assistance will be provided to defined areas in the state.

Eligibility for DUA will be made to individuals unemployed if such unemployment, whether total or partial, is a direct result of a major disaster and the individual:

- No longer has a job;
- Is unable to reach his place of work;
- Was to begin work but no longer has a job or is unable to reach such job;
- Has become the breadwinner as the result of the death of the head of household;
- Cannot work due to a disaster-incurred injury.

The DUA weekly benefit amount will be determined by the applicable state unemployment insurance laws and will be based on wages earned in all employment. Generally the DUA weekly benefit amount will be equal to the regular state weekly unemployment benefit entitlement, including any dependents' allowance. The weekly DUA amount payable to an individual will be reduced by the amount of:

- Any regular state unemployment insurance benefits;
- Any benefits paid under a SUB program;
- Any benefit or insurance proceeds from any source for loss of wages due to illness or disability;
- Any income received under a private income protection insurance program;
- The amount of workers' compensation received by virtue of the death of the head of household which was directly caused by the disaster;
- The amount of pension or governmental or private retirement pay.

A disqualification will be imposed for any week after the individual becomes reemployed in a suitable job or the individual refuses to accept, without good cause, a bona fide offer of employment. DUA benefits will be paid as long as the individual's unemployment continues as a result of a major disaster, with a maximum duration of fifty-two weeks.

Claimants are required to apply for benefits within thirty days after the governor of the state announces availability of DUA assistance. Exception to this timeliness rule will be made if the claimant can show good cause for his untimely appeal. However, all claimants must file their application for benefits within the fifty-two-week period from the date of the governor's announcement of availability of DUA assistance.

Industry-Specific Programs

A number of federally established, industry-specific benefit programs have been established that remove workers from the provisions of federal-state regular unemployment insurance programs. These special programs generally provide benefits for a longer duration and provide other assistance not available to regular state unemployment insurance claimants. Industry-specific programs differ also in that:

- Unlike the regular state unemployment insurance program, which tests a claimant's substantial and continuing attachment to the work force, *all* workers adversely affected in the specific industry, regardless of work force attachment, receive benefits.
- Unlike the regular state unemployment insurance program, which limits benefit payments to individuals unemployed through no fault of their own and who are genuinely attached to the labor market, eligibility for industry-specific benefits is made on the basis of employment in the "affected" industry. Under some industry-specific programs, individuals reemployed in lower paying jobs receive benefits equal to the difference between the new job and the old job. Additionally, the claimant need not be totally or partially unemployed to receive benefits, and in some cases, lump-sum payments are available.
- Unlike the regular state unemployment insurance program, which recognizes the trade-off between wage replacement and the need to maintain incentives for the claimant to return to work, these special programs seek to restore the affected worker to his former status with little regard for maintaining reemployment incentives.
- Unlike the regular state unemployment insurance program, which protects the worker during periods of temporary unemployment, benefits paid under industry-specific programs are considered compensation for not only loss of employment, but also, for the loss of the investment that a worker has in the particular industry. This investment includes: accumulated years of service, acquired skills and training, and the probability that older workers will have difficulty in obtaining reemployment.

As noted above, the original purpose of these special programs was to provide indemnification to workers affected by governmental activity. In many cases, industries were impacted by the government's attempt to promote the public interest through industry consolidation or deregulation. In the case of the railroad industry, government intervention began as early as 1888. In 1938, the Railroad Unemployment Insurance Act was passed. The purpose of this legislation was to protect labor from the dislocation that occurred as a result of railroad consolidation. Since then, the Rail Passenger Service Act of 1970 (Amtrak), Public Law 91-518; the Regional Railroad Reorganization Act of 1973 (Conrail), Public Law 93-236; and the Milwaukee Railroad Restructuring Act (1979), Public Law 96-101 have been passed. The purpose of these laws was to provide benefits to railroad workers adversely affected by railroad reorganization.

Following precedent legislation enacted to protect railroad employees, Congress has subsequently passed legislation to protect airline, transit, and public institution employees. Under the Airline Deregulation Act of 1978, Public Law 95-504, eligible employees can receive benefits for a maximum of six years. Under the Urban Mass Transit Act of 1964, Public Law 88-365; the High Speed Ground Transportation Act of 1965, Public Law 89-220; the Demonstration Cities and Metropolitan Development Act of 1966, Public Law 89-754; and the Federal-Aid Highway Act of 1973, Public Law 93-87 employees affected by the federal government's support of mass transit receive benefits similar to the benefits provided under the Rail Passenger Act of 1970. In an effort to protect the employees of public institutions, Congress passed the Juvenile Justice and Delinquency Prevention Act of 1974, Public Law 93-415; the Special Health Revenue Sharing Act 1975, Public Law 94-63; and the Developmental Disabilities Services and Facilities Construction Act of 1975, Public Law 95-103 for employees affected by the government's activities in the treatment of delinquency, mental illness, and developmentally disturbed individuals.

Under the Federal Communications Act Amendments of 1943, Public Law 78-4, benefits are provided to individuals earning less than $5,000 annually who are affected by industry consolidation or mergers. The amendment to the Act establishing the National Park (1978), Public Law 95-250, also known as the Redwoods Act, provides benefits to individuals laid off because of the expansion of the Redwood National Park. The Health Planning and Resources Development Amendments of 1979, Public Law 96-79, provides benefits to employees laid off because of discontinuation of hospital services.

OTHER SOCIAL INSURANCE BENEFITS

CETA Amendments of 1973

Under the provisions of Public Law 93-203 and subsequent legislation, Public Law 93-567 (Dec. 31, 1974), Public Law 94-444 (Oct. 1, 1976), and Public Law 95-524 (Oct. 27, 1978), benefits are provided to economically disadvantaged, unemployed, and underemployed. The program's purpose is to enhance self-sufficiency and maximize job opportunity through training and other services. The program is administered by a "flexible and decentralized system of Federal, state, and local programs," and is federally funded through reimbursement of "prime sponsors."

While in training, benefits include:

1. Basic allowances equal to the number of hours in training multiplied by the highest of the federal, state, or local minimum wage. This amount may be adjusted upwards in cases where the local cost of living exceeds the national norm or in cases where an incentive program exists. Cash benefits supplement any regular state unemployment insurance benefits up to minimum wage.
2. Dependents' allowance equal to $5 a week per dependent in excess of two dependents up to a maximum of $20. No adjustment is made for the receipt of regular state unemployment insurance benefits.
3. Additional allowance (at the option of the prime sponsor) for out-of-pocket expenditures for travel, meals, and lodging.
4. Relocation loans or grants and job search assistance. These may be provided.

Work Incentive Program (WIN)

Established by Parts IV(A) and IV(C) of the 1967 amendments to the Social Security Act, WIN attempts to restore independence and more meaningful roles to the families of applicants for Aid to Families with Dependent Children (AFDC). By utilizing all available manpower services, incentives, opportunities, and support services, the program furnishes training and employment for WIN recipients.

Administered locally under the direction of the Unemployment Insurance Service, Employment and Training Administration, the program provides various benefits. Benefits paid under the WIN program to individuals registered in both WIN and AFDC include:

- Incentive allowance up to $15 per training period not to exceed $30 per month.
- Training-related expense allowances as compensation for daily transportation costs and lunches equal to a basic allowance of $3 per day plus the amount of transportation costs exceeding $1 (a reduction of $1 occurs when transportation is provided for the WIN recipient).
- Temporary residence allowances are paid for special transportation and living expenses when a WIN participant receives an assignment beyond the normal commuting distance. In addition to travel allowance at the rate of 14 cents per mile for use of a private vehicle or the fare of the most economical public transportation to and from the assignment, a reasonable stipend, established by the sponsor, is paid for meals and lodging.
- Automobile repair allowances are paid for repairs and replacement parts for the purpose of restoring the WIN participant's automobile to a condition that makes it roadworthy or able to meet a state's safety inspection. The purpose of this allowance is to make the participant able to accept or retain employment.

- Special clothing allowances are paid for the purchase of special clothing or protective equipment necessary for the job or training program.
- Food and equipment allowances are paid, up to $300, for tools and equipment necessary for employment or training.
- Relocation assistance is paid for unemployment interviews—not covered by prospective employers—and relocation when employment is not available in current locale, when the participant agrees to relocate, and when a bona fide job offer has been made.

Plant Closing Legislation

Recent plant closings in the steel, automobile, and other industries in the Northeast and Midwest have again focused attention on legislation that protects the employee and the community. This legislation, commonly referred to as Plant Closing Laws or Industrial Hostage Laws, attempts to promote employment stabilization, to mitigate the economic impact upon the community and employee, and to attempt to assign the cost of the economic disruption on the responsible party—the employer. More specifically, Plant Closing Legislation addresses:

- The flight of industries from the northeastern and central states to the sunbelt states;
- The flight of industries from the United States to foreign countries;
- The closing of firms due to business failure;
- The closing of a location due to intrastate consolidation;
- The maintenance of the economic well-being of community and the employees affected by work force reductions;
- The purchase of the affected plant or company by its employees or other interested parties.

While the specific provisions of federal and state legislation vary, a number of common features can be identified:

- Prenotification by the company to its employees, its employees' representatives, the community, and the state of the employer's intention to close a plant or "substantially" reduce the work force. Under some legislation, the employer must notify these parties a year in advance.
- The employer is required to publicly disclose confidential and operational data.
- The imposition of civil and criminal penalties for noncompliance with the prenotification disclosure and other provisions of the statutes.
- Increased investigatory powers are given to the Department of Labor and other agencies to intervene and act on behalf of the state, the community, or the employees.

The proposed legislation generally does not affect the receipt of regular state unemployment insurance benefits. The assistance provided to affected employees includes:

- Severance payments equal to the number of years worked multiplied by the average weekly wage;
- Continuation of health insurance for a specified period of time;
- An offer of reemployment, transfer, training, and, if applicable, relocation;
- In some cases, plant closing laws require that the individual become fully vested in any pension plan.

CONTROLLING WORK FORCE REDUCTION

As societal pressures increase for the employer to protect its employees and the community from the economic consequences of lost wages and to cushion the blow of work force reduction on minorities and women, it is becoming increasingly obvious that optimal tactics in response to economic downturns or temporary business declines may not be "layoffs." Thus, in addition to federal and state unemployment benefit programs and the programs designed to supplement unemployment insurance benefits, employers are now paying greater attention to managing human resources, controlling work force reduction, and reducing the impact of unemployment.

As employers reassess the real cost of unemployment, new employment stabilization approaches are being tested. These include:

- Implementation of tighter operational, administrative, and financial controls to improve cash flow;
- Improvement in human resource deployment resulting in more effective resource allocation;
- Use of natural and accelerated attrition to obtain staff reduction;
- Utilization of flexible work schedules;
- Assignment of employees for work on special projects, such as maintenance work, previously postponed;
- Coordination of vacations and plant shutdowns.

Work-Sharing Programs

Particular attention is being focused on the use of work sharing as an alternative to layoffs. Currently, California and Arizona have shared-work programs and similar legislation is being considered on a federal level. As noted previously, an individual may collect unemployment insurance benefits when partially unemployed. In all states, weekly earnings (in New York, the number of days worked) above an earnings disregard will be used to reduce a claimant's weekly unemployment insurance benefit amount. Thus, the partial benefit amount is a function of the state program, the weekly earnings, the earnings disregard, and the determined weekly benefit amount.

Example: An employee earns $40 a day or $200 a week. Because of a temporary business decline, the employer reduces the employee's work schedule and places the employee on a four-day workweek. The employee files for regular unemployment insurance benefits. Assume his determined weekly benefit amount, if totally unemployed, is $100 and this state has a $25 earnings disregard. Based on these factors, the employee is eligible for benefits as shown below:

Weekly benefit amount (if totally unemployed)	$100
Less: Earnings in excess of earning disregard ($40/day × four days − $25)	135
Partial benefit	$ 0

In the example cited above, the employee, although partially unemployed, would be ineligible for unemployment insurance benefits. If this employee had worked only three days, however, he would be eligible for $5:

Weekly benefit amount (if totally unemployed)	$100
Less: Earnings in excess of earnings disregard ($40/day × three days − $25)	95
Partial benefit	$ 5

Under the provisions of the shared-work program, an employee's earnings are not used as a benefit offset. Employees under a shared-work program receive their earnings plus the percentage of the reduction in wages multiplied by their determined weekly benefit amount. Using the above-cited example of an employee with a reduced workweek of 20 percent (one day), the employee would receive in unemployment insurance benefits under the shared-work program $20 ($100 × 20 percent). Obviously, from the employee's standpoint, the shared-work program provides him with greater weekly income. For example, he would receive $180 ($160 in earnings and $20 in unemployment insurance benefits) under the shared-work program compared with $160 under normal partial benefit calculation.

It should be noted that "labor" has been less than enthusiastic about work-sharing programs. Union leadership generally opposes work sharing on the basis that it disrupts the seniority system, affects, most significantly, senior employees, and that because employers may be able to get the same productivity from their employees after work sharing has been introduced, employers will be less likely to return to pre-work-sharing schedules when business improves.

Other Employer-Initiated Programs

When work force reduction cannot be prevented, many employers in recognition of their obligation to mitigate the detrimental effect of layoffs provide additional monetary and nonmonetary benefits to their employees. These include:

- Severance pay
- Wages in lieu of notice
- Benefit plan buyouts
- Employer-sponsored retraining, reassignment, and relocation programs
- Out-placement counseling

Effect on Receipt of Regular Unemployment Insurance Benefits

As a general rule, these employer-initiated programs or activities do not affect the receipt of regular state unemployment insurance. Certain exceptions, however, exist to this rule. Twenty-two states either reduce or deny unemployment insurance benefits when a claimant receives severance pay. Thirty-three states reduce or deny benefits when a claimant receives wages in lieu of notice.

SPECIAL TAX CONSIDERATIONS

As a general rule, benefits paid to the unemployed under federally sponsored programs are not taxable to the employees. Effective January 1, 1979, however, Section 85 of the Internal Revenue Code requires that a claimant pay federal income tax if the sum for the taxable year of the adjusted gross income of the claimant and the amount of unemployment compensation exceeds the base amount. Gross income for the taxable year includes unemployment compensation in the amount equal to the lesser of: one-half of the amount of the excess of such sum over the base amount, or the amount of unemployment compensation. The base amount is defined as $20,000 for single taxpayers, $25,000 for married taxpayers filing jointly, and zero for married taxpayers filing separately.

Benefits received under SUBs are subject to federal income tax. Benefits such as severance pay and wages in lieu of notice are also considered wages subject to federal income tax.

FINANCING THE FEDERAL-STATE UNEMPLOYMENT INSURANCE SYSTEM

This discussion concentrates on the employer's cost of financing unemployment benefit programs, specifically, on the financing of that program which is funded almost exclusively by the employer—the federal-state unemployment insurance system.

Section 3301 of the Internal Revenue Code imposes a tax on employers as defined in Section 3306(a). This annual excise tax is currently 3.4 percent of taxable wages reported less a credit of 2.7 percent for taxes paid by an employer under a state unemployment insurance program in conformity with the requirements of the FUTA. Taxable wages for federal purposes are currently defined as the first $6,000 earned by each employee in covered employment.

A report prepared by the staff members of the U.S. Senate Budget Committee in 1977 noted that unemployment and other "social insurance taxes" provided 33 percent of the federal revenue in 1975, an increase of 13 percent since 1965. Additionally, although social insurance taxes were roughly equal to the federal revenues generated by corporate income taxes in 1967, by 1975 these taxes had increased so rapidly that they provided twice as much revenue to federal coffers.[5]

Whether unemployment insurance payments are considered as social insurance taxes or payroll taxes, the trend is clear. As wages reflect the upward pressures of inflation, as taxable wage bases and tax rate structures reflect the results of statutory increases, and as an individual employer's experience rates reflect the impact of past and present business conditions, the financial impact of unemployment insurance taxes is becoming increasingly significant in reducing profits.

Taxable Wages

Originally, unemployment insurance taxes were paid on all wages. In an effort to achieve simplicity in reporting, the law was changed in 1940 to equate the wage base for unemployment insurance with the Social Security wage base: $3,000. This amount represented 93 percent of the average *total* wages earned. From 1940 through 1971, the federal unemployment insurance taxable wage base remained at the first $3,000 earned by each employee in covered employment—obviously not keeping pace with either the Social Security taxable wage base or with average total wages. By 1971, the Social Security taxable wage base had reached $7,800 and the average total wages covered at $3,000 had decreased to 45 percent.

Upward Trend of Taxable Wage Base. Effective January 1, 1972, the federal taxable wage base was increased to $4,200, an increase of 40 percent. Because FUTA requires that the states have taxable wage bases equal to or greater than the federal taxable wage base, all states and the District of Columbia, then below the new federal base, raised their taxable wage base effective January 1, 1972 to comply with the federal standard.

---

[5] U.S. Gov't Printing Office, *Economic Recovery and the Financing of Social Insurance* (1977).

Effective January 1, 1978, the federal taxable wage base was increased to the current $6,000. Although this represented a 43 percent increase, by 1978 the federal unemployment insurance taxable wage base fell further behind the Social Security taxable wage base of $17,700 and now represents only 56 percent of the average total wage.

Figure 19.2 shows the upward trend of federal and state taxable wage bases. Future increases in unemployment insurance taxable wage bases are inextricably tied to economic conditions and sociopolitical pressures.

Economic conditions. From the economic standpoint, the present and future solvency of the federal and individual state trust funds is a cause for concern. Figure 19.3 shows the total outstanding debt of states borrowing funds from the Federal Unemployment Insurance Trust Fund. With a $6.2 billion debt and the improbability of repayment of this debt under current economic conditions and the existing repayment requirements, future increases in the taxable wage base are predictable. A number of states have already had to raise their taxable wage bases above the federally established minimum. The net result is increased unemployment insurance taxes for employers.

Sociopolitical pressures. Sociopolitical pressures to protect the solvency of the unemployment insurance system and to improve benefit entitlement are also likely to produce future increases in the taxable wage base. The National Commission on Unemployment Compensation recommended that the federal taxable wage base approximate 65 percent of the national average annual wage in covered employment. The 65 percent requirement would be phased in in accordance with Figure 19.4.[6]

If the recommendations of the National Commission are adopted, the federal taxable wage base in 1990 would increase by 168 percent over its current level. While it is unlikely that the Commission's recommendation will be approved in its present form, pressures to increase the taxable wage bases are expected to continue. Labor and some economists have long advocated such increases. In the last few years the concept of one taxable wage base, i.e., a federal unemployment insurance taxable wage base equal to that of the Social Security taxable wage base, has received greater attention.

At the state level, pressure to increase the taxable wage base continues unabated. As of January 1, 1982, twenty-two states, the District of Columbia, and Puerto Rico had raised their taxable wage bases above the federal standard. Unless some other revenue source is found, it is obvious that with or without changes in federal requirements, the various states will be forced to raise their taxable wage bases further, and employers will have to pay higher unemployment insurance taxes.

---

[6] U.S. Gov't Printing Office, Nat'l Comm'n on Unemployment Compensation, *Unemployment Compensation: Final Report* 80–86 (July 1980).

State	1977	1978	1979	1980	1981
Federal	$ 4,200	$ 6,000	$ 6,000	$ 6,000	$ 6,000
Alabama	4,800	6,600	6,600	6,600	6,600
Alaska	10,000	10,000	10,000	10,000	13,300
Arizona	6,000	6,000	6,000	6,000	6,000
Arkansas	5,400	6,000	6,000	6,000	6,900
California	7,000	6,000	6,000	6,000	6,000
Colorado	4,200	6,000	6,000	6,000	6,000
Connecticut	6,000	6,000	6,000	6,000	6,000
Delaware	4,200	6,000	6,000	6,000	6,000
District of Columbia	4,200	6,000	6,000	6,000	6,000
Florida	4,200	6,000	6,000	6,000	6,000
Georgia	6,000	6,000	6,000	6,000	6,000
Hawaii	9,300	9,800	10,400	11,200	12,200
Idaho	8,400	9,600	10,200	10,800	12,000
Illinois	4,200	6,000	6,000	6,500	6,500
Indiana	4,200	6,000	6,000	6,000	6,000
Iowa	6,000	6,500	6,900	7,400	8,000
Kansas	4,200	6,000	6,000	6,000	6,000
Kentucky	4,200	6,000	6,000	6,000	6,000
Louisiana	4,200	6,000	6,000	6,000	6,000
Maine	4,200	6,000	6,000	6,000	6,000
Maryland	4,200	6,000	6,000	6,000	6,000
Massachusetts	4,200	6,000	6,000	6,000	6,000
Michigan	5,400	6,000	6,000	6,000	6,000
Minnesota	7,000	7,500	8,000	8,000	8,000

Fig. 19.2 Taxable Wage Base Trends

Factors Governing Covered Employment

Effective January 1, 1978 virtually all employers and most types of employment became subject to federal and state unemployment insurance tax liability. With the passage of the 1976 amendments, 97 percent of all employees now work in "covered employment" as defined by the Federal-State Unemployment Insurance Laws.

The coverage provisions of federal and state unemployment insurance laws are generally defined in terms of the size of employing unit, the size of payroll, the employer-employee relationship, and the location that wages are earned. The coverage provisions also determine which employers are liable for unemployment insurance taxes, which types of employment are subject or excluded under coverage, and individual benefit rights.

State	*1977*	*1978*	*1979*	*1980*	*1981*
Mississippi	$ 4,200	$ 6,000	$ 6,000	$ 6,000	$ 6,000
Missouri	4,500	6,000	6,000	6,000	6,000
Montana	4,800	6,000	7,400	7,600	7,800
Nebraska	4,200	6,000	6,000	6,000	6,000
Nevada	6,500	6,900	7,400	7,900	8,400
New Hampshire	4,200	6,000	6,000	6,000	6,000
New Jersey	5,800	6,200	6,600	6,900	7,500
New Mexico	6,000	6,100	6,600	7,200	8,000
New York	4,200	6,000	6,000	6,000	6,000
North Carolina	4,200	6,000	6,000	6,000	6,000
North Dakota	4,300	6,000	7,000	7,600	8,400
Ohio	4,200	6,000	6,000	6,000	6,000
Oklahoma	4,200	6,000	6,000	6,000	6,000
Oregon	8,000	8,000	9,000	10,000	10,000
Pennsylvania	4,200	6,000	6,000	6,300	6,300
Puerto Rico		GROSS WAGES			
Rhode Island	4,800	6,000	6,000	7,200	7,800
South Carolina	4,200	6,000	6,000	6,000	6,000
South Dakota	4,200	6,000	6,000	6,000	6,000
Tennessee	4,200	6,000	6,000	6,000	6,000
Texas	4,200	6,000	6,000	6,000	6,000
Utah	8,800	9,600	10,300	10,900	12,000
Vermont	6,000	6,000	6,000	6,000	6,000
Virginia	4,200	6,000	6,000	6,000	6,000
Washington	7,800	8,400	9,000	9,600	10,200
West Virginia	4,200	6,000	6,000	6,000	8,000
Wisconsin	6,000	6,000	6,000	6,000	6,000
Wyoming	4,200	6,000	6,000	6,000	6,000

Types of Eligible Employment. Over the years, the coverage provisions have been redefined to include larger and larger segments of the work force. Originally, an employing unit subject to the provisions of federal and state unemployment insurance laws was defined as any employer, whether person or entity, employing eight or more employees in each of twenty weeks. In 1956, coverage was extended to employing units with four or more employees in each of twenty weeks. Effective January 1, 1972, coverage was extended to employing units of *one* or more employees in each of twenty weeks or more during a calendar year or an employer who pays $1,500 or more during any calendar quarter in the calendar year or the preceding calendar year.

The coverage provisions of the unemployment insurance laws have also been expanded over the years to include employment in previously excluded

State	($ Millions) Total Outstanding Debt
Pennsylvania	$1,566.3
Illinois	1,405.4
Michigan	1,075.0
New Jersey	612.4
Ohio	599.9
Connecticut	320.9
Minnesota	114.0
Rhode Island	112.0
West Virginia	99.8
Puerto Rico	80.8
Arkansas	64.0
Kentucky	52.1
District of Columbia	51.1
Delaware	46.4
Vermont	36.2
Maine	31.4
Virgin Islands	4.2
	$6,199.9

Source: U.S. Department of Labor/ETA/UIS Office of Research, Legislation and Program Policies Division of Actuarial Services (Dec. 31, 1981).

Fig. 19.3 Total Outstanding Debt (Estimated) to the Federal Unemployment Insurance Trust Fund as of December 31, 1981

Year	*Percentage of Average Annual Wage*	*Taxable Wage Base*
1981	—	$ 6,000
1982	—	6,000
1983	50%	8,000 *
1984	50%	8,000 *
1985	55%	10,400 *
1986	55%	10,400 *
1987	60%	13,000 *
1988	60%	13,000 *
1989	65%	16,100 *
1990	65%	16,100 *

* Estimated

Fig. 19.4 National Commission on Unemployment Compensation's Recommendations for Increases in the Federal Taxable Wage Base

areas. Under recently enacted federal coverage provisions, the following types of employment became covered under the unemployment insurance laws:

1. *Agricultural labor.* An employer is defined in terms of wages of $20,000 or more for agricultural work during any calendar quarter or if ten or more employees are employed in agricultural labor in each of twenty days.[7]
2. *Domestic service.* An employer is defined in terms of cash wages of $1,000 or more paid to one or more workers in any calendar quarter for domestic service in a private home, local college club, or local chapter of a college fraternity or sorority.[8]
3. *Nonprofit organizations.* Effective January 1, 1972 nonprofit organizations employing four or more persons for each of twenty weeks became subject to the unemployment insurance laws. Note that while FUTA requires coverage of such nonprofits under the various state unemployment insurance laws, nonprofits classified as Section 501(c)(3) employers and exempt from federal income tax under Section 501(a) of the Internal Revenue Code are also exempt from federal unemployment insurance tax liability. FUTA also provides that nonprofit organizations must be given the option of electing the method of financing benefit costs, i.e., reimbursement or taxation method.
4. *Government entities.* Public Law 94-566 extended coverage effective January 1, 1978 to the employees of state and local governmental entities and political subdivisions.
5. *Self-employment.* Generally the coverage provisions do not contemplate wages earned in self-employment. The notable exception is California's unemployment insurance laws which provide for the election of voluntary self-coverage. If approved by the state, the subject employer will pay taxes at the fixed rate of 1.25 percent of wages.
6. *Some other employment exclusions*
   - Employees of church school
   - Insurance agents on commission

---

[7] The following states and jurisdictions extend coverage to agricultural workers beyond the federal requirement:

- *California.* One or more employees or wages of $101 or more at any time in a calendar quarter.
- *District of Columbia.* Does not apply special exclusion provisions to agricultural workers.
- *Minnesota.* Four or more employees in each of twenty weeks or $20,000 or more in a calendar quarter.
- *Puerto Rico.* One or more workers at any time.
- *Rhode Island.* One or more workers at any time.

[8] Coverage in Arkansas, District of Columbia, and New York has extended to employers paying quarterly wages in excess of $500; in Hawaii $225. Additionally, in Arkansas employers with three or more workers in domestic service irrespective of quarterly earnings are subject to coverage.

- Real estate agents on commission
- Part-time service (remuneration does not exceed $45 per calendar quarter; $250 in Alaska) for Section 501(c)(3) nonprofit organizations
- Student nurses and interns employed by a hospital
- Students working for schools, college, or university at which they are regularly enrolled
- Service for relatives

Employer-employee relationship. As a general rule, unless the type of employment is specifically exempted, all services performed by an employee for his employer are covered and thus subject to unemployment taxes—up to the taxable wage limit. Unanswered is the question: are the services provided by casual labor or an independent contractor subject to the coverage provisions? Section 3306(c)(3) of the FUTA specifically exempts from coverage: services performed that are not in the course of the employer's trade or business if the individual earns less than $50 during any calendar quarter. Additionally, the common-law test of a master-servant relationship is also used in determining whether or not an employer-employee relationship exists. Unfortunately, the determination of an employer-employee relationship can be arbitrary and capricious. As a result, this area has been the subject of much litigation and the target of IRS review. Currently, while Congress tries to resolve this matter, it has given employers a reprieve from the IRS's enforcement of the broad interpretation of the meaning of the employer-employee relationship. At least for the present, the best test (and the one found in many states' regulations) to determine whether or not an employer-employee relationship exists is shown below. Note that all factors must be met to be exempted from coverage.

1. Is the worker free from direction or control in the performance of his work?
2. Is the service performed outside the employer's usual course of business?
3. Is the individual customarily engaged for other employers in an independent trade, occupation, profession, or business?

Interstate Employment. Since each state, the District of Columbia, and Puerto Rico has its own unemployment insurance laws, jurisdictional questions arise for employees working in more than one state. In an effort to protect the individual and at the same time prevent a duplication of taxes on the wages earned by the individual, the states have agreed on a uniform definition of employment in terms of "localization" of work. This agreement attempts to establish benefit rights in the state where the individual is most likely to look for work should he become unemployed. Therefore, all wages earned in multistate employment are treated as if earned exclusively in one state, with the benefit eligibility calculation based on the unemployment insurance laws of that state.

Coverage determination factors. In determining in which state the individual's employment should be reported, the following factors are used. (Note that these coverage determination factors are listed in controlling order, i.e., if the conditions of the first factor are met, no further test is made; if not, a test of the conditions of the second factor is made, if satisfied, no further test is made and so on.)

1. *Place where employment is localized.* If an individual's employment is performed exclusively within one state or if any employment outside the state is temporary or incidental to such work within the state, the individual's employment is localized and wages must be reported to that state. Example: if an individual lives in Maryland, but works only in the District of Columbia, his wages must be reported to the District of Columbia.

2. *Place of "base of operations."* If services are not performed exclusively in one state, but are normally and regularly performed in two or more states, the individual's employment cannot be considered localized, and the location of the individual's *base of operation* will be controlling. This factor requires that the individual perform some part of his service in the state where the base of operation is located. The base of operation is the place from which the individual normally starts his work, receives direction and instructions, receives mail and obtains supplies and equipment, maintains files and records, and usually returns to. Example: if an individual lives in Maryland, has an office in Virginia, and performs services on a regular and routine basis in Maryland, the District of Columbia, and Virginia, his service is not "localized," and the location of his base of operation is considered. In this case, the office (base of operation) to which he reports is in Virginia, and therefore, wages should be reported to Virginia.

3. *Place from which operations are directed or controlled.* When an employee's employment is not "localized" in any state and a base of operation cannot be established or he does not work in the state where the base of operation is located, the place from which the employee receives direction or control is the determining factor. This situation is most typical of traveling salespersons and construction workers. Example: an individual lives in Maryland, is employed by a company headquartered in New York, reports to a sales office in Pennsylvania, and has a sales territory that includes Maryland, the District of Columbia, Virginia, Delaware, West Virginia, and Pennsylvania. Because the salesperson services are not "localized," and because no services are performed in New York, the place of direction is the state from which the salesperson receives direction and instructions and performs some service. In this case, Pennsylvania is the state where the sales office, the place of direction, is located.

4. *Place of the employee's residence.* Note that the previous coverage determination factors do not consider the residence of the employee. Only when the other factors are not controlling is the individual's place of residence used in determining coverage and reporting requirements.

Foreign Employment. Effective January 1, 1972 coverage was extended to U.S. citizens working for an American employer outside the U.S. "except in a contiguous country with which the United States has an agreement relating to unemployment compensation"—Canada.

The state coverage determination of U.S. employees working abroad is based on the following factors:

1. The state of the employer's principal office
2. The state in which the employer resides
3. The state in which the employer elects coverage
4. The state in which the individual files a claim

Wages. As previously noted, federal and state unemployment insurance taxes are paid on taxable wages up to the federal wage base limit of $6,000 or the wage base limit established under state law. The general definition of the term wage includes all remuneration for services provided including the cash value of non-cash remuneration. Under the unemployment insurance laws, the designation of the remuneration, i.e., wages, salary, commission, hours, etc., the frequency, i.e., daily, hourly, weekly, etc., and the medium of remuneration, i.e., clothing or goods, is immaterial.

Exceptions. Obviously, exceptions and limitations exist. For instance, while other than cash remuneration is considered wages, facilities and privileges, e.g., entertainment, medical services, or other services, when of relatively little value and provided to promote goodwill or health, are not considered wages.

Meals and lodging. Sections 119(a) and 119(b) of the Internal Revenue Code excludes from the definition of gross income for federal income tax withholding purposes "the value of any meals or lodging furnished to an employee, his spouse or any of his dependents by or on behalf of his employer. . . ." Sections 3121(a) and 3306(b) of the Federal Insurance Contribution Act (Social Security) and the FUTA, respectively, include meals and lodging in the definition of wages.

This double standard was invalidated by the U.S. Supreme Court on June 8, 1981 by excluding the value of meals and lodging from the calculation of wages for FUTA and FICA purposes.[9] In light of the IRS's previous position regarding the taxability of meals and lodging for FUTA purposes, most states promulgated regulations concerning the value of meals and lodging in calculating state taxable wages. In accordance with the recent Supreme Court decision and considering the significant difference in the various state provisions for specific application, reference should be made to the current and future provisions promulgated by each state.

---

[9] Rowan Cos. v. United States, 101 S. Ct. 2288 (1981).

"Sick Pay." Another major exception in the definition of wages is "sick pay" paid under a qualified sick-pay plan. Sections 3306(b)(2) and 3306(b)(4) of the FUTA exclude from the definition of wages:

> the amount of any payment (including any amount paid by an employer for insurance or annuities, or into a fund, to provide for any such payment) made to, or on behalf of, an employee or any of his dependents under a plan or system established by an employer which makes provision for his employees generally (or for his employees generally and their dependents) or for a class or classes of his employees (or for a class or classes of his employees and their dependents), on account of—
>
> A. retirement, or
>
> B. sickness or accident disability, or
>
> C. medical or hospitalization expenses in connection with sickness or accident disability, or
>
> D. death. . . .; and
>
> any payment on account of sickness or accident disability, or medical or hospitalization expenses in connection with sickness or accident disability, made by an employer to, or on behalf of, an employee after the expiration of 6 calendar months following the last calendar month in which the employee worked for such employer;

In order that the sick-pay plan be "qualified" for exclusion, it should be definite rather than capricious, applicable to a class or classes of employees rather than discretionary, and notice be given to the participants. While the plan need not be in writing or directly communicated to the employees, such factors lend credibility to the existence of a qualified sick-pay plan.

It should be noted that any payment made to the employee for unused sick leave is considered to be wages and therefore taxable.

Tax Treatment of Other Remuneration

Figure 19.5 shows on a state-by-state basis the taxability treatment of other types of remuneration paid to employees. For specific application, reference should be made to the respective state laws.

1. *Tips and gratuities.* Tips and gratuities are not taxable for FUTA purposes except when tips are used in meeting the federal and state minimum wage provisions or when the employment agreement between a hotel and a waiter guarantees a fixed remuneration and tips are used in meeting this income requirement.[10] Since states must comply with the taxing requirements of FUTA, Figure 19.5 indicates those states that have additional taxing provisions in their laws or regulations.

2. *Vacation pay.* Vacation pay is taxable for FUTA purposes when paid for periods the employee is on vacation or is given to the employee at the

[10] I.R.C. § 3306(b)(1).

	Tips	Vacation Pay	Severance Dismissal Pay	Wages in Lieu of Notice
Federal	—	yes	yes	yes
Alabama	yes	yes	yes	yes
Alaska	yes	yes	yes	yes
Arizona	—	yes	yes	yes
Arkansas	—	yes	yes	yes
California	yes	yes	—	—
Colorado	yes	yes	yes	yes
Connecticut	yes	yes	yes	yes
Delaware	yes	yes	yes	yes
District of Columbia	yes	yes	yes	yes
Florida	—	yes	yes	yes
Georgia	—	yes	yes	yes
Hawaii	—	yes	yes	yes
Idaho	yes	yes	yes	yes
Illinois	—	yes	yes	yes
Indiana	—	yes	yes	yes
Iowa	yes	yes	—	—
Kansas	—	yes	yes	yes
Kentucky	—	yes	yes	yes
Louisiana	—	yes	yes	yes
Maine	yes	yes	yes	yes
Maryland	—	—	yes	yes
Massachusetts	—	yes	yes	yes
Michigan	—	yes	yes	yes
Minnesota	—	yes	yes	yes
Mississippi	—	yes	yes	yes

Fig. 19.5 Taxability of Miscellaneous Remuneration

time of separation for vacation previously not taken. Vacation pay is also taxable for state unemployment insurance purposes except in California and Oklahoma where unused vacation payments are not taxable.

3. *Dismissal and severance pay*. Payment made to an employee at the time of discharge, whether paid voluntarily or because of a contract, statutory agreement, or custom is taxable for federal unemployment insurance purposes. Dismissal pay is also considered taxable for state unemployment insurance purposes except in California, Iowa, and Puerto Rico. In New Jersey, separation pay is not taxable if discretionary, i.e., the employer is not required to pay severance pay as a result of a management-labor agreement, an employment contract, or established customs and procedures. Note,

	Tips	*Vacation Pay*	*Severance Dismissal Pay*	*Wages in Lieu of Notice*
Missouri	yes	yes	yes	yes
Montana	yes	yes	yes	yes
Nebraska	—	yes	yes	yes
Nevada	—	yes	yes	yes
New Hampshire	yes	yes	yes	yes
New Jersey	yes	yes	—	yes
New Mexico	yes	yes	yes	yes
New York	yes	yes	yes	yes
North Carolina	—	yes	yes	yes
North Dakota	yes	yes	yes	yes
Ohio	yes	yes	yes	yes
Oklahoma	yes	yes	yes	yes
Oregon	—	yes	yes	yes
Pennsylvania	—	yes	yes	yes
Puerto Rico	yes	yes	—	—
Rhode Island	yes	yes	yes	yes
South Carolina	—	yes	yes	yes
South Dakota	yes	yes	yes	yes
Tennessee	yes	yes	yes	yes
Texas	—	yes	yes	yes
Utah	yes	yes	yes	yes
Vermont	yes	yes	yes	yes
Washington	—	yes	yes	yes
West Virginia	—	yes	yes	yes
Virginia	yes	yes	yes	yes
Wisconsin	yes	yes	yes	yes
Wyoming	—	yes	yes	yes

that the maximum tax rate in New York for wages classified as "severance" or "dismissal" pay is 2.7 percent.

4. *Wages in lieu of notice.* For federal and most state unemployment insurance tax purposes, "wages in lieu of notice" as a type of dismissal pay is taxable. Only California, Iowa, and Puerto Rico consider "wages in lieu of notice" to be nontaxable. New Jersey, which considers "dismissal pay" nontaxable, treats "wages in lieu of notice" as taxable wages.

Calculation and Methods of Financing Unemployment Insurance Costs

As noted previously, the cost of financing unemployment insurance has been rising at an increasing rate. The total cost to the employer is influenced by such factors as:

- National and statewide economic conditions
- Adequacy of federal and state trust funds
- Past, current, and future levels of unemployment
- Special federal programs that extend coverage or benefit duration
- The taxing revenue base

While these factors may not determine the individual employer's successes or failures in stabilizing his employment and in minimizing his unemployment insurance tax liability, they do produce microeconomic pressures, in the form of lower profits or, in the case of reimbursing nonprofits, higher direct benefit cost that cause the employer to reduce total wages, pass along increased unemployment insurance costs in the form of higher prices, or both. Thus, more attention is being given to the calculation and methods of controlling the individual employer's unemployment insurance costs.

Federal Unemployment Insurance Tax Calculation. An employer's total unemployment insurance tax liability consists of the federal unemployment insurance tax component (except Section 501(c)(3) nonprofits), paid annually, and the state unemployment insurance tax components, paid quarterly. The federal unemployment insurance tax liability equation is:

$$\text{FTL} = \text{FTP} \times \text{EFTR}:$$

Where: *FTL* is the Federal unemployment insurance Tax Liability; *FTP* is the Federal Taxable Payroll; and *EFTR* is the Effective Federal Tax Rate or 3.4 percent less (2.7 percent minus any credit reduction imposed due to the failure of a state to repay any outstanding trust fund loans).

Note, that the per employee federal unemployment tax liability has increased from \$9.00 per employee in 1940, to \$12.00 in 1961, to \$15.00 in 1971, and to \$42.00 per employee for 1982 (assuming no credit reduction).

State Unemployment Insurance Tax Calculation. The second component of the total cost equation is the state unemployment insurance tax liability, calculated as follows:

$$\text{STL} = \text{STP} \times \text{ER}$$

Where: *STL* is the State unemployment insurance Tax Liability; *STP* is the State Taxable Payroll; *ER* is an employer's state experience rate. See Figure 19.2 for current state taxable wage bases.

Appendix 19-3 shows on a state-by-state basis the 1982 minimum and maximum rates, the 1982 new employer tax rate, and the estimated 1981 average tax rates based on state taxable and total wages.

Total Tax Liability. An employer's annual total unemployment insurance tax liability is then the sum of the two tax liability components, i.e., FTL + STL. Thus, TTL = FTP × EFTR + STP × ER where TTL is the total unemployment insurance tax liability.

Appendix 19-2 shows the calculation of an employer's 1981 total unemployment insurance tax liability by state on a per-employee basis. In calculating the effective federal tax rates, 1981 credit reduction penalties were used. Federal law requires that outstanding loans be repaid by November 10. A state's failure to repay these loans results in a partial loss of the 2.7 percent credit against FUTA taxes. Additionally, it should be noted that Section 3302(c)(2)(B) of the Internal Revenue Code of 1954 provides for an additional loss of credit during the third and fourth consecutive taxable years of outstanding debt by the amount that 2.7 percent exceeds the state average employer tax rate. Thus, based on Connecticut's 1981 average employer tax rate of 2.6 percent, the total credit reduction for taxable year 1981 is 0.7 percent.

A review of the data in Appendix 19-2 indicates that the average total tax liability on a per-employee basis ranges from a low of $78 in Texas to a high of $480.90 in Alaska. With such vast differences in the per-employee cost, long- and short-term strategies are needed to minimize a total tax unemployment insurance tax liability. Long-term strategies are primarily concerned with more effective deployment and utilization of human resources. Short-term strategies involve controlling an employer's rate and, in the case of reimbursable nonprofits, the direct benefit cost.

Experience Rating. While the use of experience rating has historical justification for its existence and it is used by all states and the District of Columbia (Puerto Rico does not experience rate employers) as the method of equating benefit requirements with funding, it is not universally accepted as the best method for assigning unemployment insurance cost on an equitable basis. Experience rating, by assigning unemployment insurance costs on the basis of risk or the exposure to risk, attempts to provide the necessary incentives to cause the employer to stabilize his employment and participate in the unemployment insurance benefit process.

Opponents of experience rating argue that appropriate measures of performance are difficult to establish, that the proper relationship between past experience and current liability is difficult to achieve, and that the balance between inflow (taxes) and outflow (benefits) is difficult to maintain. Some states have suspended experience rating in recent years and New York has a "sunset" provision in its unemployment insurance laws that automatically terminates the experience rating schedule and requires a uniform rate of 2.7 percent.

Proponents argue that experience rating, although it is imperfect, motivates the employer to stablize his work force and to interact at the functional level with the state agency and the claimant. This functional interaction helps insure the integrity of the program. Thus, it is argued that experience rating should be strengthened rather than eliminated.

While the pros and cons of experience rating are debated in national and local forums, FUTA provides a basis and an inducement for the various states to establish experience rating systems. Interestingly, very little is said in the federal statutes about experience rating. The federal statutes specifically establish only the minimum time an employer must have "experience" in the unemployment insurance system before being allowed to become experience rated [11] and the amount of credit (2.7 percent) that an employer may claim against the employer's federal tax liability for taxes paid to the state. Since the difference between 2.7 percent and the employer's actual experience rate creates an additional credit, experience rating provides an additional encouragement to stabilize employment.

There are four basic formulas used by the states in experience rating:

1. *Reserve ratio method.* This method is used by thirty-three states [12] plus the District of Columbia either exclusively or in combination with other formulas. Employing the principles of cost accounting, this method attempts to equate long-term benefit cost requirements with adequate tax receipts and attempts to accumulate reserves adequate to cover fund outflow contingencies. The taxes paid under this formula are a function of the relationship between the excess of all taxes paid and all benefits charged to taxable payroll.[13] Such that the:

$$\text{Reserve Ratio} = \frac{(\text{PB} + \text{C}) - \text{BC}}{\text{TP}}$$

Where: *PB* is the Previous Balance

C is Contributions for the current period. This includes not only quarterly taxes paid but also any voluntary contributions.[14]

BC is current Benefit Charges

TP is the Taxable Payroll—generally the average of the last three years

---

[11] Originally an employer was required to have three years of "experience" before a state could allow an employer to become experience rated; this was changed to the current minimal requirement of one year of experience with enactment of the 1954 amendments.

[12] Reserve ratio states: Ariz., Ark., Cal., Colo., D.C., Ga., Hawaii, Ind., Iowa, Kan., Ky., La., Me., Mass., Mo., Neb., Nev., N.H., N.J., N.M., N.Y., N.C., N.D., Ohio, R.I., S.C., S.D., Tenn., W. Va., Wis. Additionally, Mich. and Pa. use a combination of reserve ratio and benefit ratio; Idaho and Mont. use a combination of reserve ratio and payroll variation.

[13] Except for Ga., Idaho, La., Mo., Mont., N.H., and R.I., reserve ratio formula states consider all taxes paid and all benefits charged in previous years. Ga. uses only benefits since July 1, 1939; Idaho since January 1, 1940; La. since October 1, 1941; Mont. since July 1, 1976; and R.I. since October 1, 1958. Mo. uses either all taxes and benefits or the data for the last five years, whichever is more beneficial to the employer. N.H. uses either all taxes and benefits or the data for the last five years, in certain situations.

[14] In the following states, employers are permitted to voluntarily increase on an annual

Under the reserve ratio formula, the higher the reserve balance the lower the tax rate. Thus, as the excess of contributions to taxable payroll increases, the tax rate decreases. Note that the reserve ratio method of calculating tax rates may act as a disincentive to increases in employment. As the taxable payroll increases because of additional hiring at a faster rate than the reserve balance, the employer is assigned a higher tax rate.

2. *Benefit ratio method.* This method is used by fourteen states either exclusively or in combination with other formulas.[15] The benefit ratio calculates taxes as a function of the relationships between benefits charged and taxable payroll. Because this method considers only the experience in the last three years (five years in Michigan) it is more sensitive and responsive to the vagaries of economic trends and individual employer activities than the reserve ratio method. Additionally, because this formula reflects only the most recent short-term relationship between benefit charges and payroll, the impact of a significant change in benefit charges in a given year is more pronounced and not diluted by past experience. Fortunately, while the impact of a "bad" year is more dramatic, its effect is confined to a short period of time. Under the benefit ratio method, as the average taxable payroll increases in respect to benefit charges, the tax rate decreases. The benefit ratio is:

$$\text{Benefit Ratio} = \frac{\text{ABC}}{\text{ATP}}$$

Where: *ABC* is the Average Benefits Charged (usually a three-year average)
ATP is the Average Taxable Payroll (usually a three-year average)

Note that the amount of taxes paid by the employer is not considered in the rate calculation, thus unlike the reserve ratio method, a voluntary contribution cannot be used to lower the experience rate (except in Minnesota where a voluntary contribution may be used to lower the benefit charge component, thus producing a more favorable rate).

3. *Benefit-wage ratio method.* This method, used by five states,[16] differs from the reserve ratio and benefit ratio methods in that it does not measure the total benefits collected by claimants, but rather the number of separations that result in benefit payments. Neither the weekly benefit amounts nor the duration of benefits are factors. Under this method, separations are weighed with respect to wages from each base-period employer.

---

basis the balance in their reserve in an amount that will effect a lower rate—subject to certain state limitations. In effect, the voluntary contribution allows the employer to buy a lower rate. Ariz., Colo., Conn., Fla., Ind., Iowa, Kan., Ky., La., Me., Mich., Minn., Mo., Neb., N.J., N.M., N.Y., N.C., N.D., Ohio, Pa., S.C., S.D., W. Va., and Wis.

[15] Benefit ratio states: Alaska, Conn., Fla., Md., Minn., Miss., Ore., Tex., Va., Vt., and Wyo. Additionally, Mich. and Pa. use a combination of benefit ratio and reserve ratios. Wash. uses a combination of benefit ratios and payroll variation.

[16] Benefit wage ratio states: Ala., Del., Ill., and Okla.

Benefit-wage charges are assessed for each claimant in each benefit year against each base-period employer's account.

$$\text{Benefit-Wage Ratio} = \frac{\text{ABWC}}{\text{ATP}}$$

Where: *ABWC* is the three-year Average of Benefit-Wage Charges
ATP is the three-year Average Taxable Payroll

4. *Payroll variation method.* This method, used by five states either exclusively or in combination with other formulas,[17] attempts to relate experience with business fluctuation as expressed by declines in payroll. Over specific periods of time (quarter-to-quarter or year-to-year) payroll declines are measured as a percent of payroll. Stability in employment patterns is rewarded by lower tax rates. Neither the amount of benefits, the duration of benefits, nor the relationship of benefits to wages is considered.

Reimbursement Method of Financing. In extending coverage to nonprofit organizations (the 1970 amendments) and to state and local governments (the 1976 amendments), Congress also included provisions that allow nonprofit organizations and state and local governments the option of electing the financing of their unemployment insurance cost through the taxation (experience rating) method or through direct reimbursement. As an historical footnote, prior to the enactment of the 1970 amendments the states were prevented from allowing direct reimbursement of benefits inasmuch as the federal provisions required that an employer's unemployment insurance taxes be based on experience.

As a general rule, direct reimbursement is the less costly method of financing unemployment insurance and most nonprofit organizations have elected this method either individually or as a member of a pooled or joint account. As reimbursers, nonprofit organizations are self-insured, i.e., they do not pay the state and, indirectly, other employers to assume a portion of their unemployment risk. This sole assumption of risk by the reimburser has financial benefits, but it also has some potential disadvantages:

- Under the taxation method, an employer receives a tax rate at the beginning of the year and since the employer can predict with some degree of certainty its taxable payroll for the year, it can also predict its annual unemployment insurance cost. The reimbursement method does not provide the employer with such predictive accuracy. Additionally, the timing of cash flow can less accurately be predicted under the reimbursement method.
- Generally, the reimbursing employer cannot recoup erroneous payments made by the state agency. A taxation-method employer will have its account

[17] Payroll variation states: Alaska and Utah. Mont. and Idaho use a combination of payroll variation and reserve ratio; Wash. uses a combination of payroll variation and benefit ratio.

credited for erroneous payments without regard to whether or not the state obtains repayment of benefits already paid to the claimant. A reimbursing employer will only get credit if, and when, the state obtains repayment from the claimant.

- Noncharging provisions (see the decision of noncharging below) usually do not apply to reimbursing employers.
- Reimbursing employers are subject to unlimited liability. Taxation-method employers are protected by the tax rate structures in the various states, and while high, these rate structures limit exposure. While the probabilities are low that a catastrophe might befall a reimbursing employer, the potential exists.

Benefit Charging Method. Under the reserve ratio, benefit ratio, and benefit-wage ratio formulas, the amount of benefits, the benefit derivatives, and the amount of benefit wages are fundamental components in the determination of an employer's experience rate. When an unemployed worker has a long history of employment with only one employer, the assignment of cost is simple and predictable. But when employment history is short or there are a number of employers, the answer to the question which employer or employers should be charged is less easily determined. To answer this question, the state must decide whether the unemployment is directly related to and controlled by an employer's activities or by general business conditions. If the former, benefit costs are most closely assigned to risk when the most recent employer is charged; if the latter, the conflict is best resolved by charging base-period employers proportionately.

Alternative charging methods are described below:

1. *Charging most recent employer.* This method attaches primary responsibility for unemployment on the most recent employer. If the employment history is brief with the last employer, the most recent previous employer is charged.

2. *Charging base-period employers in reverse chronological order.* The underlying premise in this method is that both the payment of wages and the proximity of employment to the separation determines the incident of risk (unemployment) and, concomitantly, the cost (charging of benefits). The more remote the employment period becomes to the period of benefit compensability, the less an employer is responsible for the incident of benefits. Under this method, the maximum chargeability is limited by a specified amount of earnings in the base period or quarter, by a fraction of earnings attributable to an employer, or both. If this limit is reached before the claimant has exhausted his benefits eligibility, the next previous employer is charged.

3. *Charges in proportion to base-period wages.* This method is used by the majority of states and is based on the theory that unemployment is more a function of general economic conditions than it is of an employer's separation activities. Assignment of chargeability is determined by comparing the

wages paid to an employee during the base period—usually the first four of the last five completed calendar quarters—to total wages paid by all employers.

In reserve ratio and benefit ratio states, the maximum charge is based on the maximum entitlement of the claimant. Some states provide for an additional charge in the form of a multiple of the maximum when the employer is guilty of a deliberate false submission of information for the purposes of evading or preventing benefit charging.

Noncharging of Benefits. In most nonpayroll variation states, certain types of benefits are socialized, i.e., the state relieves a specific employer account from direct benefit charging in favor of indirect charging of all employers by charging the state account. Types of benefits noncharged are:

- Benefits paid on the basis of short-term employment with the last employer. In this case, charging is passed backward to previous employers.
- Dependents' allowance.
- Benefits paid during the pendency of an employer's appeal, which later disqualifies or results in a finding of ineligibility.
- Benefits based on seasonal employment.
- Benefits paid when a separation is caused by a national disaster or severe inclement weather.

Internalized Experience Rating. As noted earlier, one of the primary goals of the federal-state unemployment insurance system is employment stabilization. It is an accepted principle that achievement of this goal requires employer participation. Experience rating attempts to provide the necessary motivation and incentive to achieve this objective. But experience rating need not be limited to the employer level. The benefits derived from experience rating, e.g., employer participation, can be extended to employing units, i.e., division, location, plant, and department levels.

Improving an employer's ability to identify separations, claims, and benefit charges directly attributable to an employing unit improves his ability to discern employment trends, assign costs, and control tax liability.

The purpose of internalized experience rating is to accurately assign financial responsibility to employing units. Rather than allocate unemployment insurance taxes as overhead or as administrative costs and rather than assign cost on the basis of taxable payroll or number of employees, internalized experience rating determines the extent to which each employing unit contributes to the company's unemployment insurance liability. *Example:* rather than assign five divisions, which have equal employment numbers, on a 20 percent of total unemployment insurance-cost basis, the employer might weigh the experience in the form of benefit charges of each division to the total benefits charged to the company. Thus, if Division *A* were responsible for 40 percent of the benefits charged while the remaining divisions were each responsible for only 15 percent, Division *A* would be internally charged for 40 percent of the company's total unemployment insurance tax liability. This amount would be deducted from the profits of Division *A*. An incentive to stabilize employment and participate in the company's unemployment insurance-cost control program has now been established.

TRENDS IN FEDERAL-STATE PROGRAMS

The election of President Reagan and the trend towards conservatism would seem to portend a reduced role for the federal-state unemployment insurance program as an income support system. Legislation has been passed which redefines the "insured rate of unemployment," alters the "trigger" for extended benefits, and requires greater evidence of labor force attachment for benefit eligibility. Parenthetically, a review of recent history reveals that liberalization of benefits and increases in employer-financing requirements occurred during Republican rather than Democratic administrations.

Further demonstration of this trend is evinced by the recent political viability of equating "workfare" and "welfare" and the more restricted definition of "safety net" by the administration's lexicographers. It appears that the benefit diet for the unemployed will, in the future, be leaner—or at least comprised of fewer federally sponsored calories.

At the same time, there is consternation and solicitude about the continuing effects of double-digit inflation, high unemployment rates, increased competition from abroad, decreasing productivity, and labor shortages in certain professions. Answers for these problems are being found in supply-side economics, trade quotas and tariffs, increased use of robots, and the deregulation of industries and the concomitant fragmentation of the regular state unemployment insurance system, i.e., industry-specific unemployment insurance programs.

Pressures in the form of recommendations from national commissions also exist. In its "Final Report," the National Commission on Unemployment Compensation presented a number of recommendations including:

1. The repeal of federal standards concerning the eligibility treatment of undocumented alien workers, professional athletes, and professional employees of schools.
2. The establishment of federal basic minimum benefit standards including a maximum weekly benefit amount for 1982 equal to 55 percent of the state's average weekly wage; for 1984—60 percent, and for 1986—66.7 percent.
3. An increase in the definition in taxable wages from the current $6,000 to 50 percent of national average total wage in covered employment beginning in 1983, 55 percent in 1985, 60 percent in 1987, and 65 percent in 1989.

Another national commission recently recommended a change in national policy and advanced the position that the government should promote a redeployment of resources from the "frostbelt" to the "sunbelt." Assistance to employees unemployed due to this redeployment will require extensive study.

While national attention is focused on the solvency of the Social Security fund, concern also exists for the future solvency of the federal and individual state unemployment insurance trust funds. As of December 31, 1981, seventeen jurisdictions had outstanding loans from the Federal Unemployment Insurance Trust Fund with Pennsylvania leading the pack with an outstanding debt of $1.6 billion.

It is obvious that the future shape of benefit programs for the unemployed will certainly be affected by these political, economic, and social crosscurrents. Based on these factors, benefits for the unemployed (both monetary and nonmonetary) will continue to be a mixed bag of federal, state, and private plans.

APPENDIX 19-1 1982 State Tax Rates

State	*1982 State Min. Rate (%)*	*1982 State Max.* Rate (%)*		*1982 New Employer Rate (%)*	*Estimated 1981 ** Average Tax Rates (%)*	
		Pos.	*Neg.*		*Taxable*	*Total*
Alabama	0.50	4.00		2.70	1.80	1.00
Alaska	1.22	4.86		average industry rate	3.30	2.10
Arizona	0.10	1.92	2.90	2.70	1.60	0.60
Arkansas	0.70	3.30	6.10	3.30	2.40	1.30
California	0.70	3.60	4.00	2.70	2.60	1.00
Colorado	0.00	4.50		2.70	0.80	0.40
Connecticut	1.50	6.00		2.90	2.20	0.80
Delaware	1.60	6.50		4.20	3.00	0.90
District of Columbia	1.00	5.40		2.60	2.60	1.00
Florida	0.10	4.50		2.70	1.10	0.50
Georgia	0.06	3.46	5.38	2.70	1.40	0.70
Hawaii		4.50		4.50	1.60	1.10
Idaho	0.09	2.70	4.00	2.90	1.90	1.30
Illinois	0.60	5.70		3.10	3.30	1.30

(Continued)

<table>
<tr><th rowspan="2">State</th><th rowspan="2">1982 State Min. Rate (%)</th><th colspan="2">1982 State Max.* Rate (%)</th><th rowspan="2">1982 New Employer Rate (%)</th><th colspan="2">Estimated 1981 ** Average Tax Rates (%)</th></tr>
<tr><th>Pos.</th><th>Neg.</th><th>Taxable</th><th>Total</th></tr>
<tr><td>Indiana</td><td>2.70</td><td>3.00</td><td>3.30</td><td>2.70</td><td>1.70</td><td>0.70</td></tr>
<tr><td>Iowa</td><td>0.00</td><td colspan="2">6.00</td><td>construction 6.00
all other 1.80</td><td>2.40</td><td>1.30</td></tr>
<tr><td>Kansas</td><td>0.06</td><td colspan="2">4.30</td><td>1.94 to 2.91</td><td>2.10</td><td>1.00</td></tr>
<tr><td>Kentucky</td><td>1.30</td><td>3.00</td><td>6.70</td><td>3.00</td><td>3.20</td><td>1.40</td></tr>
<tr><td>Louisiana</td><td>0.10276</td><td>2.77452</td><td>3.39108</td><td>3.39108</td><td>2.00</td><td>1.00</td></tr>
<tr><td>Maine</td><td>2.40</td><td>4.70</td><td>5.00</td><td>3.00</td><td>3.10</td><td>1.50</td></tr>
<tr><td>Maryland</td><td>0.10</td><td colspan="2">5.00</td><td>2.30</td><td>2.80</td><td>1.00</td></tr>
<tr><td>Massachusetts</td><td>2.90</td><td>5.40</td><td>6.70</td><td>3.00 or 3.70</td><td>3.30</td><td>1.50</td></tr>
<tr><td>Michigan</td><td>1.00</td><td colspan="2">9.00</td><td>construction 4.00
all other 2.70</td><td>4.00</td><td>1.70</td></tr>
<tr><td>Minnesota</td><td>1.00</td><td colspan="2">7.50</td><td>2.10</td><td>1.90</td><td>0.90</td></tr>
<tr><td>Mississippi</td><td>1.70</td><td colspan="2">4.00</td><td>1.70</td><td>2.10</td><td>1.00</td></tr>
<tr><td>Missouri</td><td>0.50</td><td>3.20</td><td>4.90</td><td>construction 2.80
all other 2.70</td><td>1.60</td><td>0.60</td></tr>
<tr><td>Montana</td><td>1.70</td><td>3.50</td><td>4.40</td><td>3.70</td><td>2.90</td><td>1.60</td></tr>
<tr><td>Nebraska</td><td>0.10</td><td>2.70</td><td>3.70</td><td>2.70</td><td>1.70</td><td>0.70</td></tr>
<tr><td>Nevada</td><td>0.30</td><td colspan="2">3.60</td><td>3.00</td><td>2.40</td><td>1.40</td></tr>
</table>

State	1982 State Min. Rate (%)	1982 State Max.* Rate (%)		1982 New Employer Rate (%)	Estimated 1981 ** Average Tax Rates (%)	
		Pos.	Neg.		Taxable	Total
New Hampshire	0.01	2.00	6.50	2.70	1.30	0.60
New Jersey	1.20	4.10	6.20	3.40	3.40	1.60
New Mexico	0.60	3.60	4.20	2.70	1.80	1.00
New York	1.50	4.10	5.20	3.70	3.20	1.20
North Carolina	0.10	2.70	5.70	2.70	1.70	0.90
North Dakota	0.50	4.30	5.00	average industry 1.00 min. 5.00 max.	2.60	1.50
Ohio	1.10	4.60	4.80	3.00	2.80	1.10
Oklahoma	0.10	3.10		3.10	0.90	0.40
Oregon	2.00	3.80		3.40	3.00	1.80
Pennsylvania	2.35	5.75	6.45	all other 6.50 construction 3.50	3.60	1.50
Puerto Rico ***	2.95	2.95		2.95	2.95	2.95
Rhode Island	2.80	4.80	6.00	4.20	4.20	2.30
South Carolina	1.30	2.70	4.10	2.70	2.10	1.10
South Dakota	first quarter 0.60	3.30	6.10	2.90	1.70	0.90

(Continued)

State	1982 State Min. Rate (%)	1982 State Max.* Rate (%)		1982 New Employer Rate (%)	Estimated 1981 ** Average Tax Rate (%)	
		Pos.	Neg.		Taxable	Total
	second—fourth quarter 0.20	2.90	5.70	3.30		
Tennessee	0.75	3.30	4.40	2.70	2.40	0.90
Texas	0.10	4.00		2.70	0.60	0.20
Utah	1.30	2.80		2.70	1.70	1.20
Vermont	1.70	6.00		3.20	3.20	1.50
Virginia	0.80	6.90		6.20	1.90	0.80
Washington	3.00	3.00		3.00	3.00	1.70
West Virginia	2.50	5.50	8.50	construction & foreign corporations 8.50 all other 3.70	2.80	1.10
Wisconsin	0.00	4.50	7.40	3.60	2.60	1.10
Wyoming	0.38	3.08		3.08	0.90	0.40

* Where tax rate schedules assign separate rates for negative balance employers, the first figure indicated is the maximum rate for positive balance employers; the second figure negative balance employers.

** *Source:* U.S. Department of Labor/ETA/UIS Office of Research, Legislation and Program Policies, Division of Actuarial Services (May 5, 1981).

*** Puerto Rico's unemployment insurance laws do not provide for experience rating.

APPENDIX 19-2 1981 Total Unemployment Insurance Tax Liability on Per-Employee Basis

State	*FTP* × *EFTR* (%) = *FTL*	*STP* × *Avg. ER* (%) = *Avg. STL*	*TTL* = *FTR* + *STL*
Alabama	($6,000 × 0.7) = $42	($6,000 × 1.8) = $118.80	$160.80
Alaska	($6,000 × 0.7) = 42	($13,300 × 3.3) = 438.90	480.90
Arizona	($6,000 × 0.7) = 42	($6,000 × 1.6) = 96.00	138.00
Arkansas	($6,000 × 0.7) = 42	($6,900 × 2.4) = 165.00	207.60
California	($6,000 × 0.7) = 42	($6,000 × 2.6) = 156.00	198.00
Colorado	($6,000 × 0.7) = 42	($6,000 × 0.8) = 48.00	90.00
Connecticut	($6,000 × 1.4) = 84	($6,000 × 2.2) = 132.00	216.00
Delaware	($6,000 × 1.3) = 78	($6,000 × 3.0) = 180.00	258.00
District of Columbia	($6,000 × 1.3) = 78	($6,000 × 2.6) = 156.00	234.00
Florida	($6,000 × 0.7) = 42	($6,000 × 1.1) = 66.00	108.00
Georgia	($6,000 × 0.7) = 42	($6,000 × 1.4) = 84.00	126.00
Hawaii	($6,000 × 0.7) = 42	($12,200 × 1.6) = 195.20	237.20
Idaho	($6,000 × 0.7) = 42	($12,000 × 1.9) = 228.00	270.00
Illinois	($6,000 × 1.3) = 78	($6,500 × 3.3) = 214.50	392.50
Indiana	($6,000 × 0.7) = 42	($6,000 × 1.7) = 102.00	144.00
Iowa	($6,000 × 0.7) = 42	($8,000 × 2.4) = 192.00	234.00
Kansas	($6,000 × 0.7) = 42	($6,000 × 2.1) = 126.00	168.00

State	*FTP* × *EFTR* (%) = *FTL*	*STP* × *Avg. ER* (%) = *Avg. STL*	*TTL* = *FTR* + *STL*
Kentucky	($6,000 × 0.7) = $42	($6,000 × 3.2) = $192.00	$234.00
Louisiana	($6,000 × 0.7) = 42	($6,000 × 2.0) = 120.00	162.00
Maine	($6,000 × 1.3) = 78	($6,000 × 3.1) = 186.00	264.00
Maryland	($6,000 × 0.7) = 42	($6,000 × 2.8) = 168.00	210.00
Massachusetts	($6,000 × 0.7) = 42	($6,000 × 3.3) = 198.00	240.00
Michigan	($6,000 × 0.7) = 42	($6,000 × 4.0) = 240.00	282.00
Minnesota	($6,000 × 0.7) = 42	($8,000 × 1.9) = 152.00	194.00
Mississippi	($6,000 × 0.7) = 42	($6,000 × 2.1) = 126.00	168.00
Missouri	($6,000 × 0.7) = 42	($6,000 × 1.6) = 96.00	138.00
Montana	($6,000 × 0.7) = 42	($7,800 × 2.9) = 226.20	268.20
Nebraska	($6,000 × 0.7) = 42	($6,000 × 1.7) = 102.00	144.00
Nevada	($6,000 × 0.7) = 42	($8,400 × 2.4) = 201.60	243.60
New Hampshire	($6,000 × 0.7) = 42	($6,000 × 1.3) = 78.00	120.00
New Jersey	($6,000 × 1.3) = 78	($7,500 × 3.4) = 255.00	333.00
New Mexico	($6,000 × 0.7) = 42	($8,000 × 1.8) = 144.00	186.00
New York	($6,000 × 0.7) = 42	($6,000 × 3.2) = 192.00	234.00
North Carolina	($6,000 × 0.7) = 42	($6,000 × 1.7) = 102.00	144.00
North Dakota	($6,000 × 0.7) = 42	($8,400 × 2.6) = 218.40	260.40

(Continued)

State	*FTP* × *EFTR* (%) = *FTL*	*STP* × *Avg. ER* (%) = *Avg. STL*	*TTL* = *FTR* + *STL*
Ohio	($6,000 × 0.7) = $42	($6,000 × 2.8) = $168.00	$210.00
Oklahoma	($6,000 × 0.7) = 42	($6,000 × 0.9) = 54.00	96.00
Oregon	($6,000 × 0.7) = 42	($10,000 × 3.0) = 300,00	342.00
Pennsylvania	($6,000 × 1.3) = 78	($6,300 × 3.6) = 226.80	304.80
Puerto Rico	($6,000 × 1.3) = 78	State Tax Liability Based on Total Wages	
Rhode Island	($6,000 × 1.3) = 78	($7,000 × 4.2) = 327.60	405.60
South Carolina	($6,000 × 0.7) = 42	($6,000 × 2.1) = 126.00	168.00
South Dakota	($6,000 × 0.7) = 42	($6,000 × 1.7) = 102.00	144.00
Tennessee	($6,000 × 0.7) = 42	($6,000 × 2.4) = 144.00	186.00
Texas	($6,000 × 0.7) = 42	($6,000 × 0.6) = 36.00	78.00
Utah	($6,000 × 0.7) = 42	($12,200 × 1.7) = 204.00	246.00
Vermont	($6,000 × 1.3) = 78	($6,000 × 3.2) = 192.00	270.00
Virginia	($6,000 × 0.7) = 42	($6,000 × 1.9) = 114.00	156.00
Washington	($6,000 × 0.7) = 42	($10,200 × 3.0) = 306.00	348.00
West Virginia	($6,000 × 0.7) = 42	($8,000 × 2.8) = 224.00	266.00
Wisconsin	($6,000 × 0.7) = 42	($6,000 × 2.6) = 156.00	198.00
Wyoming	($6,000 × 0.7) = 42	($6,000 × 0.9) = 54.00	96.00

APPENDIX 19-3 State Benefit Fact Tables

ALABAMA

Benefit Eligibility Requirements

Qualifying wages: At least $522 and 1½ times high-quarter earnings with over $350 in one quarter

Able and available for: Work in usual occupation

Actively looking for work: No

Qualification requirement in successive benefit years: Wages equal to 8 times WBA* in insured work

Benefit Determination

Base period: First 4 of last 5 completed calendar quarters

Benefit year: 52-week period beginning week of valid claim

Initial waiting week period for total unemployment: 0

Benefit formula: High-quarter

Minimum WBA: $15

Maximum WBA: $90

Initial waiting week period for partial unemployment: 1

Partially unemployed if: Earnings less than WBA

Earnings disregard: $6

Dependent allowance: No

Normal minimum duration of benefits: 11+

Normal maximum duration of benefits: 26

ALASKA

Benefit Eligibility Requirements

Qualifying wages: $1,000 paid in at least 2 quarters of base period

Able and available for: Suitable work

Actively looking for work: No

Qualification requirement in successive benefit years: Wages equal to 8 times WBA

Benefit Determination

Base period: First 4 of last 5 completed calendar quarters

Benefit year: 52-week period beginning week of valid claim

Initial waiting week period for total unemployment: 1

Benefit formula: Annual-wage

Minimum WBA: $34

Maximum WBA: $150

Initial waiting week period for partial unemployment: 1

Partially unemployed if: Earnings less than basic WBA plus one-half basic WBA

Earnings disregard: One-half WBA

Dependent allowance: Yes

Normal minimum duration of benefits: 16

Normal maximum duration of benefits: 28

ARIZONA

Benefit Eligibility Requirements

Qualifying wages: At least 1½ times high-quarter earnings and $725 in high quarter

Able and available for: Work

Actively looking for work: No

Qualification requirement in successive benefit years: Wages equal to 8 times WBA

Benefit Determination

Base period: First 4 or last 5 completed calendar quarters

Benefit year: 52-week period beginning week of valid claim

---

* Weekly benefit amount

Initial waiting week period for total unemployment: 1

Benefit formula: High-quarter

Minimum WBA: $25

Maximum WBA: $95

Initial waiting week period for partial unemployment: 1

Partially unemployed if: Earning less than WBA

Earnings disregard: $15

Dependent allowance: No

Normal minimum duration of benefits: 12+

Normal maximum duration of benefits: 26

ARKANSAS

Benefit Eligibility Requirements

Qualifying wages: At least 30 times WBA earned in two quarters

Able and available for: Suitable work

Actively looking for work: Yes

Qualification requirement in successive benefit years: Wages equal to 10 times WBA in insured work subsequent to date of last valid claim

Benefit Determination

Base period: First 4 of last 5 completed calendar quarters

Benefit year: 52-week period beginning calendar quarter valid claim filed

Initial waiting week period for total unemployment: 1

Benefit formula: High-quarter

Minimum WBA: $31

Maximum WBA: $136

Initial waiting week period for partial unemployment: 1

Partially unemployed if: Earnings less than WBA plus 40% WBA

Earnings disregard: 40% WBA

Dependent allowance: No

Normal minimum duration of benefits: 10

Normal maximum duration of benefits: 26

CALIFORNIA

Benefit Eligibility Requirements

Qualifying wages: At least $1,200 in base-period earnings, or $20 in each of 8 weeks or more with total base-period wages of at least $900

Able and available for: Work

Actively looking for work: Yes

Qualification requirement in successive benefit years: Wages equal to qualifying wages within preceding benefit year

Benefit Determination

Base period: 4 calendar quarters ending 4 to 7 months before benefit year

Benefit year: 52-week period beginning week of valid claim

Initial waiting week period for total unemployment: 1

Benefit formula: High-quarter

Minimum WBA: $30

Maximum WBA: $136

Initial waiting week period for partial unemployment: 1

Partially unemployed if: Less than full-time work and wages payable are less than WBA and are earned from other than individual's regular employing unit

Earnings disregard: Lesser of $25 and one-quarter of wages

Dependent allowance: No

Normal minimum duration of benefits: 12+

Normal maximum duration of benefits: 26

COLORADO

Benefit Eligibility Requirements

Qualifying wages: 30 times WBA. WBA equals: (1) 60% of 1/13 of high-quarter wages or (2) 50% of 1/52 of total base-period wages

Able and available for: Suitable work

Actively looking for work: Yes

Qualification requirement in successive benefit years: Wages equal to $750

Benefit Determination

Base period: First 4 of last 5 completed calendar quarters

Benefit year: 52-week period beginning week of valid claim

Initial waiting week period for total unemployment: 1

Benefit formula: High-quarter

Minimum WBA: $25

Maximum WBA: $176

Initial waiting week period for partial unemployment: 1

Partially unemployed if: Earnings less than WBA

Earnings disregard: One-quarter WBA

Dependent allowance: No

Normal minimum duration of benefits: 7 +

Normal maximum duration of benefits: 26

CONNECTICUT

Benefit Eligibility Requirements

Qualifying wages: At least 40 times WBA in the base period

Able and available for: Work

Actively look for work: Yes

Qualification requirement in successive benefit years: Wages equal to the greater of $300 or 5 times WBA in insured work

Benefit Determination

Base period: First 4 of last 5 completed calendar quarters

Benefit year: 52-week period beginning week of valid claim

Initial waiting week period for total unemployment: 0

Benefit formula: High-quarter

Minimum WBA: $15

Maximum WBA: $146

Initial waiting week period for partial unemployment: 0

Partially unemployed if: Earnings less than 1½ times basic WBA

Earnings disregard: One-third wages

Dependent allowance: Yes

Normal minimum duration of benefits: 26

Normal maximum duration of benefits: 26

DELAWARE

Benefit Eligibility Requirements

Qualifying wages: At least 36 times WBA

Able and available for: Work

Actively looking for work: Yes

Qualification requirement in successive benefit years: Wages equal to 10 times WBA in insured work subsequent to date of last valid claim

Benefit Determination

Base period: First 4 of last 5 completed calendar quarters

Benefit year: 52-week period beginning week of valid claim

Initial waiting week period for total unemployment: 0

Benefit formula: Base-period wages

Minimum WBA: $20

Maximum WBA: $150

Initial waiting week period for partial unemployment: 0

Partially unemployed if: Earnings less than WBA plus 30% of WBA

Earnings disregard: 30% of WBA or $10, whichever is greater

Dependent allowance: No

Normal minimum duration of benefits: 11–18

Normal maximum duration of benefits: 26

DISTRICT OF COLUMBIA

Benefit Eligibility Requirements

Qualifying wages: 1½ times high-quarter earnings, but not less than $450 in 2 quarters, at least $300 in one quarter

Able and available for: Work

Actively looking for work: Yes

Qualification requirement in successive benefit years: Wages equal to 10 times WBA

Benefit Determination

Base period: First 4 of last 5 completed calendar quarters

Benefit year: 52-week period beginning week of valid claim

Initial waiting week period for total unemployment: 1

Benefit formula: High-quarter

Minimum WBA: $14

Maximum WBA: $206

Initial waiting week period for partial unemployment: 1

Partially unemployed if: Earnings less than WBA plus $20

Earnings disregard: 20% wages

Dependent allowance: Yes

Normal minimum duration of benefits: 17+

Normal maximum duration of benefits: 34

FLORIDA

Benefit Eligibility Requirements

Qualifying wages: 20 weeks of employment at average wage of at least $20

Able and available for: Work

Actively looking for work: No

Qualification requirement in successive benefit years: Wages equal to 3 times WBA

Benefit Determination

Base period: First 4 of last 5 completed calendar quarters

Benefit year: 52-week period beginning week of valid claim

Initial waiting week period for total unemployment: 1

Benefit formula: Average weekly wage

Minimum WBA: $10

Maximum WBA: $125

Initial waiting week period for partial unemployment: 1

Partially unemployed if: Earnings less than WBA

Earnings disregard: $5

Dependent allowance: No

Normal minimum duration of benefits: 10

Normal maximum duration of benefits: 26

GEORGIA

Benefit Eligibility Requirements

Qualifying wages: At least 36 times WBA with $175 or more in one quarter and $432 in two quarters

Able and available for: Work

Actively looking for work: Yes

Qualification requirement in successive benefit years: Wages equal to 8 times WBA

Benefit Determination

Base period: First 4 of last 5 completed calendar quarters

Benefit year: 52-week period beginning week of valid claim

Initial waiting week period for total unemployment: 1

Benefit formula: High-quarter

Minimum WBA: $27

Maximum WBA: $115

Initial waiting week period for partial unemployment: 1

Partially unemployed if: Earnings less than WBA plus $8

Earnings disregard: $8

Dependent allowance: No

Normal minimum duration of benefits: 4

Normal maximum duration of benefits: 26

HAWAII

Benefit Eligibility Requirements

Qualifying wages: At least 30 times WBA and 14 weeks of employment

Able and available for: Work

Actively looking for work: Yes

Qualification requirement in successive benefit years: A one-year waiting period

Benefit Determination

Base period: Last 4 calendar quarters

Benefit year: 52-week period beginning week of valid claim

Initial waiting week period for total unemployment: 1

Benefit formula: High-quarter

Minimum WBA: $5

Maximum WBA: $169

Initial waiting week period for partial unemployment: 1

Partially unemployed if: Earnings less than WBA

Earnings disregard: $2

Dependent allowance: No

Normal minimum duration of benefits: 26

Normal maximum duration of benefits: 26

IDAHO

Benefit Eligibility Requirements

Qualifying wages: 1¼ high-quarter wage but not less than $1,137.51

Able and available for: Suitable work

Actively looking for work: Yes

Qualification requirement in successive benefit years: Wages equal to 3 times WBA

Benefit Determination

Base period: First 4 of last 5 completed calendar quarters

Benefit year: 52-week period beginning week of valid claim

Initial waiting week period for total unemployment: 1

Benefit formula: High-quarter

Minimum WBA: $36

Maximum WBA: $145

Initial waiting week period for partial unemployment: 1

Partially unemployed if: Earnings less than WBA plus one-half WBA

Earnings disregard: One-half WBA

Dependent allowance: No

Normal minimum duration of benefits: 10

Normal maximum duration of benefits: 26

ILLINOIS

Benefit Eligibility Requirements

Qualifying wages: At least $1,600 in base period with $440 earnings other than the high quarter

Able and available for: Work
Actively looking for work: Yes
Qualification requirement in successive benefit years: Wages equal to 4 times WBA

Benefit Determination

Base period: First 4 of last 5 completed calendar quarters
Benefit year: 52-week period beginning week of valid claim
Initial waiting week period for total unemployment: 1
Benefit formula: Average weekly wage
Minimum WBA: $45
Maximum WBA: $148
Initial waiting week period for partial unemployment: 1
Partially unemployed if: Earnings less than WBA
Earnings disregard: 50% WBA
Dependent allowance: Yes
Normal minimum duration of benefits: 26
Normal maximum duration of benefits: 26

INDIANA

Benefit Eligibility Requirements

Qualifying wages: $1,500 total with $900 in the last 2 quarters and 1¼ times high-quarter earnings
Able and available for: Work
Actively looking for work: Yes
Qualification requirement in successive benefit years: Wages equal to $900 in the last two quarters of base period and $1,500 total since the end of the last base period

Benefit Determination

Base period: First 4 of last 5 completed calendar quarters
Benefit year: 52-week period beginning week of valid claim
Initial waiting week period for total unemployment: 1
Benefit formula: High-quarter
Minimum WBA: $40
Maximum WBA: $84
Initial waiting week period for partial unemployment: 1
Partially unemployed if: Earnings less than WBA
Earnings disregard: 20% of WBA
Dependent allowance: Yes
Normal minimum duration of benefits: 3+
Normal maximum duration of benefits: 26

IOWA

Benefit Eligibility Requirements

Qualifying wages: $400 in one quarter and at least $200 in any other quarter and must earn total wages of at least 1¼ times the high quarter
Able and available for: Work
Actively looking for work: Yes
Qualification requirement in successive benefit years: Wages equal to $200

Benefit Determination

Base period: First 4 of last 5 completed calendar quarters
Benefit year: 52-week period beginning week of valid claim
Initial waiting week period for total unemployment: 0
Benefit formula: High-quarter
Minimum WBA: $17
Maximum WBA: $146
Initial waiting week period for partial unemployment: 0
Partially unemployed if: Works less than regular full-time week and earns less than WBA plus $15

Earnings disregard: 25% of WBA

Dependent allowance: Yes

Normal minimum duration of benefits: 15

Normal maximum duration of benefits: 26

KANSAS

Benefit Eligibility Requirements

Qualifying wages: At least 30 times WBA earned in two quarters

Able and available for: Work in usual occupation

Actively looking for work: Yes

Qualification requirement in successive benefit years: Wages equal to 8 times WBA in insured work subsequent to date of last valid claim

Benefit Determination

Base period: First 4 of last 5 completed calendar quarters

Benefit year: 52-week period beginning week of valid claim

Initial waiting week period for total unemployment: 1

Benefit formula: High-quarter

Minimum WBA: $37

Maximum WBA: $149

Initial waiting week period for partial unemployment: 1

Partially unemployed if: Earnings less than WBA

Earnings disregard: $8

Dependent allowance: No

Normal minimum duration of benefits: 10

Normal maximum duration of benefits: 26

KENTUCKY

Benefit Eligibility Requirements

Qualifying wages: High-quarter base-period wages of at least $500, base-period wages of at least 1⅜ times high-quarter wages, and in last six months of base period, wages equal to at least $500 earned outside the high quarter.

Able and available for: Suitable work

Actively looking for work: Yes

Qualification requirement in successive benefit years: Wages equal to 8 times WBA in last 2 quarters of base period

Benefit Determination

Base period: First 4 of last 5 completed calendar quarters

Benefit year: 52-week period beginning week of valid claim

Initial waiting week period for total unemployment: 0

Benefit formula: High-quarter

Minimum WBA: $22

Maximum WBA: $140

Initial waiting week period for partial unemployment: 0

Partially unemployed if: Earnings less than 1¼ times WBA

Earnings disregard: 20% of WBA

Dependent allowance: No

Normal minimum duration of benefits: 15

Normal maximum duration of benefits: 26

LOUISIANA

Benefit Eligibility Requirements

Qualifying wages: 30 times WBA, where WBA equals: (1) 5% of high-quarter wages if base-period wages are $875 or less; (2) 4% of high-quarter earnings if base-period wages exceed $875

Able and available for: Work

Actively looking for work: Yes

Qualification requirement in successive

benefit years: Wages equal to the lesser of 6 times WBA or 3/13 of the wages paid in high quarter of current base period

Benefit Determination

Base period: First 4 of last 5 completed calendar quarters

Benefit year: 52-week period beginning week of valid claim

Initial waiting week period for total unemployment: 1

Benefit formula: High-quarter

Minimum WBA: $10

Maximum WBA: $183

Initial waiting week period for partial unemployment: 1

Partially unemployed if: Earnings less than WBA

Earnings disregard: 50% of WBA

Dependent allowance: No

Normal minimum duration of benefits: 12

Normal maximum duration of benefits: 28

MAINE

Benefit Eligibility Requirements

Qualifying wages: At least 2 times annual average weekly wage in two quarters and total base-period wages equal to 6 times annual average weekly wage

Able and available for: Work in usual occupation

Actively looking for work: Yes

Qualification requirement in successive benefit years: Wages equal to 8 times WBA

Benefit Determination

Base period: First 4 of last 5 completed calendar quarters

Benefit year: 52-week period beginning week of valid claim

Initial waiting week period for total unemployment: 1

Benefit formula: High-quarter

Minimum WBA: $12

Maximum WBA: $115

Initial waiting week period for partial unemployment: 1

Partially unemployed if: Earnings less than WBA plus $5

Earnings disregard: $10

Dependent allowance: Yes

Normal minimum duration of benefits: 7

Normal maximum duration of benefits: 26

MARYLAND

Benefit Eligibility Requirements

Qualifying wages: 1½ times high-quarter wages with $576.01 in one quarter and wages in at least two quarters

Able and available for: Work

Actively looking for work: Yes

Qualification requirement in successive benefit years: Wages equal to 10 times WBA

Benefit Determination

Base period: First 4 of last 5 completed calendar quarters

Benefit year: 52-week period beginning week of valid claim

Initial waiting week period for total unemployment: 0

Benefit formula: High-quarter

Minimum WBA: $25

Maximum WBA: $140

Initial waiting week period for partial unemployment: 0

Partially unemployed if: Earnings less than augmented WBA

Earnings disregard: $10

Dependent allowance: Yes

Normal minimum duration of benefits: 26

Normal maximum duration of benefits: 26

MASSACHUSETTS

Benefit Eligibility Requirements

Qualifying wages: 30 times WBA and not less than $1,200

Able and available for: Work in usual occupation

Actively looking for work: No

Qualification requirement in successive benefit years: Wages of at least $900

Benefit Determination

Base period: 52-week period preceding benefit year

Benefit year: 52-week period beginning Sunday preceding filing of claim

Initial waiting week period for total unemployment: 1

Benefit formula: High-quarter

Minimum WBA: $12

Maximum WBA: $156

Initial waiting week period for partial unemployment: 1

Partially unemployed if: Earnings less than basic WBA

Earnings disregard: 40% of weekly benefit amount but not less than $10 nor more than $30

Dependent allowance: Yes

Normal minimum duration of benefits: 9

Normal maximum duration of benefits: 30

MICHIGAN

Benefit Eligibility Requirements

Qualifying wages: At least $25.01 in each of 14 weeks within the past 52 weeks

Able and available for: Work in usual occupation

Actively looking for work: Yes

Qualification requirement in successive benefit years: No additional requirements

Benefit Determination

Base period: 52-week period preceding benefit year

Benefit year: 52-week period beginning week of valid claim

Initial waiting week period for total unemployment: 0

Benefit formula: Average weekly wage

Minimum WBA: $16

Maximum WBA: $197

Initial waiting week period for partial unemployment: 0

Partially unemployed if: Earnings less than WBA

Earnings disregard: Up to 50% WBA

Dependent allowance: Yes

Normal minimum duration of benefits: 13.5

Normal maximum duration of benefits: 26

MINNESOTA

Benefit Eligibility Requirements

Qualifying wages: At least $750 and $50 in 15 or more weeks

Able and available for: Work

Actively looking for work: Yes

Qualification requirement in successive benefit years: No additional requirements

Benefit Determination

Base period: 52-week period preceding benefit year

Benefit year: 52-week period beginning week of valid claim

Initial waiting week period for total unemployment: 1

Benefit formula: Average weekly wage

Minimum WBA: $30

Maximum WBA: $177

Initial waiting week period for partial unemployment: 1

Partially unemployed if: Earnings less than weekly benefit amount

Earnings disregard: $25

Dependent allowance: No

Normal minimum duration of benefits: 11

Normal maximum duration of benefits: 26

MISSISSIPPI

Benefit Eligibility Requirements

Qualifying wages: At least 36 times WBA and $160 in one quarter, and wages in two quarters

Able and available for: Work

Actively looking for work: No

Qualification requirement in successive benefit years: Wages equal to 8 times WBA

Benefit Determination

Base period: First 4 of last 5 completed calendar quarters

Benefit year: 52-week period beginning week of valid claim

Initial waiting week period for total unemployment: 1

Benefit formula: High-quarter

Minimum WBA: $10

Maximum WBA: $90

Initial waiting week period for partial unemployment: 1

Partially unemployed if: Earnings less than WBA

Earnings disregard: $5

Dependent allowance: No

Normal minimum duration of benefits: 12

Normal maximum duration of benefits: 26

MISSOURI

Benefit Eligibility Requirements

Qualifying wages: Wages of $300 or more in at least one quarter of base period, total base-period wages of at least 30 times claimant's WBA, wages in at least two quarters of base period

Able and available for: Work

Actively looking for work: Yes

Qualification requirement in successive benefit years: Wages equal to 5 times WBA in insured work or 10 times WBA in noncovered work

Benefit Determination

Base period: First 4 of last 5 completed calendar quarters

Benefit year: 52-week period beginning week of valid claim

Initial waiting week period for total unemployment: 1

Benefit formula: High-quarter

Minimum WBA: $14

Maximum WBA: $105

Initial waiting week period for partial unemployment: 1

Partially unemployed if: Earnings less than WBA plus $10

Earnings disregard: $10

Dependent allowance: No

Normal minimum duration of benefits: 10

Normal maximum duration of benefits: 26

MONTANA

Benefit Eligibility Requirements

Qualifying wages: At least $1,000 with wages in separate weeks

Able and available for: Work

Actively looking for work: Yes

Qualification requirement in successive benefit years: Wages equal to 6 times WBA or 3/13 of high-quarter wages, whichever is lesser

Benefit Determination

Base period: First 4 of last 5 completed calendar quarters

Benefit year: 52-week period beginning week of valid claim

Initial waiting week period for total unemployment: 1

Benefit formula : High-quarter

Minimum WBA: $36

Maximum WBA: $145

Initial waiting week period for partial unemployment: 1

Partially unemployed if: Earnings less than 2 times WBA

Earnings disregard: One-half wages over 25% of WBA

Dependent allowance: No

Normal minimum duration of benefits: 8

Normal maximum duration of benefits: 26

NEBRASKA

Benefit Eligibility Requirements

Qualifying wages: At least $600 in base-period earnings with $200 in each of two quarters

Able and available for: Work

Actively looking for work: No

Qualification requirement in successive benefit years: No additional requirements

Benefit Determination

Base period: Last 4 completed quarters immediately preceding benefit year

Benefit year: 52-week period beginning week of valid claim

Initial waiting week period for total unemployment: 1

Benefit formula: High-quarter

Minimum WBA: $12

Maximum WBA: $106

Initial waiting week period for partial unemployment: 1

Partially unemployed if: Earnings less than WBA

Earnings disregard: Up to 50% WBA

Dependent allowance: No

Normal minimum duration of benefits: 17

Normal maximum duration of benefits: 26

NEVADA

Benefit Eligibility Requirements

Qualifying wages: 1½ times high-quarter wages

Able and available for: Work

Actively looking for work: No

Qualification requirement in successive benefit years: Wages equal to 3 times WBA

Benefit Determination

Base period: First 4 of last 5 completed calendar quarters

Benefit year: 52-week period beginning week of valid claim

Initial waiting week period for total unemployment: 0

Benefit formula: High-quarter

Minimum WBA: $16

Maximum WBA: $136

Initial waiting week period for partial unemployment: 0

Partially unemployed if: Earnings less than WBA

Earnings disregard: 25% wages

Dependent allowance: No

Normal minimum duration of benefits: 11+

Normal maximum duration of benefits: 26

NEW HAMPSHIRE

Benefit Eligibility Requirements

Qualifying wages: At least $1,700 in base period, with $800 in each of two quarters

Able and available for: Suitable work

Actively looking for work: Yes

Qualification requirement in successive benefit years: No additional requirements

Benefit Determination

Base period: Calendar year preceding benefit year

Benefit year: April 1 to March 31

Initial waiting week period for total unemployment: 0

Benefit formula: Annual wage

Minimum WBA: $26

Maximum WBA: $132

Initial waiting week period for partial unemployment: 0

Partially unemployed if: Earnings less than WBA

Earnings disregard: 20% of WBA

Dependent allowance: No

Normal minimum duration of benefits: 26

Normal maximum duration of benefits: 26

NEW JERSEY

Benefit Eligibility Requirements

Qualifying wages: At least $30 in each of 20 weeks or $2,200 in base year

Able and available for: Work

Actively looking for work: Yes

Qualification requirement in successive benefit years: No additional requirements

Benefit Determination

Base period: 52-week period ending with second week preceding benefit year

Benefit year: 364 days beginning week of valid claim

Initial waiting week period for total unemployment: 1

Benefit formula: Average weekly wage

Minimum WBA: $10

Maximum WBA: $145

Initial waiting week period for partial unemployment: 1

Partially unemployed if: Earnings less than WBA plus 20% of WBA

Earnings disregard: 20% of WBA

Dependent allowance: No

Normal minimum duration of benefits: 15

Normal maximum duration of benefits: 26

NEW MEXICO

Benefit Eligibility Requirements

Qualifying wages: 1¼ times high-quarter wages

Able and available for: Work

Actively looking for work: Yes

Qualification requirement in successive benefit years: Wages equal to 6 times WBA or 3/13 of high-quarter wages, whichever is lesser

Benefit Determination

Base period: First 4 of last 5 completed calendar quarters

Benefit year: 52-week period beginning week of valid claim

Initial waiting week period for total unemployment: 1

Benefit formula: High-quarter

Minimum WBA: $26

Maximum WBA: $130

Initial waiting week period for partial unemployment: 1

Partially unemployed if: Earnings less than WBA

Earnings disregard: 20% of WBA

Dependent allowance: No

Normal minimum duration of benefits: 18+

Normal maximum duration of benefits: 26

NEW YORK

Benefit Eligibility Requirements

Qualifying wages: Average weekly wage of at least $40 in each of 20 weeks during last year or in each of 15 in the last 52 weeks and a total of 40 in the last 104 weeks

Able and available for: Work in usual occupation

Actively looking for work: No

Qualification requirement in successive benefit years: No additional requirements

Benefit Determination

Base period: 52-week period ending on Sunday immediately preceding filing of valid original claim

Benefit year: 52-week period beginning first Monday after filing valid claim

Initial waiting week period for total unemployment: 1

Benefit formula: Average weekly wage

Minimum WBA: $25

Maximum WBA: $125

Initial waiting week period for partial unemployment: 2

Partially unemployed if: At least 4 days of total unemployment within the week and not paid compensation aggregating more than the claimant's highest benefit rate for any week of total unemployment

Earnings disregard: 25% of WBA per day worked

Dependent allowance: No

Normal minimum duration of benefits: 26

Normal maximum duration of benefits: 26

NORTH CAROLINA

Benefit Eligibility Requirements

Qualifying wages: At least $565.50 in base-period earnings which must equal 1½ times high-quarter earnings

Able and available for: Work

Actively looking for work: Yes

Qualification requirement in successive benefit years: Wages equal to 10 times WBA and at least $550 in base period

Benefit Determination

Base period: First 4 of last 5 completed calendar quarters

Benefit year: 52-week period beginning week of valid claim

Initially waiting week period for total unemployment: 1

Benefit formula: High-quarter

Minimum WBA: $15

Maximum WBA: $152

Initial waiting week period for partial unemployment: 1

Partially unemployed if: Week of less than 3 customary scheduled full-time days

Earnings disregard: 10% of average weekly wage in high-quarter of base period

Dependent allowance: No

Normal minimum duration of benefits: 13

Normal maximum duration of benefits: 26

NORTH DAKOTA

Benefit Eligibility Requirements

Qualifying wages: Paid wages in at least 2 calendar quarters of base period totaling not less than 40 times minimum WBA and not less than $600

Able and available for: Suitable work

Actively looking for work: Yes

Qualification requirement in successive benefit years: Wages equal to 10 times WBA in insured wages subsequent to date of last valid claim

Benefit Determination

Base period: First 4 of last 5 completed calendar quarters

Benefit year: 52-week period beginning week of valid claim

Initial waiting week period for total unemployment: 1

Benefit formula: High-quarter

Minimum WBA: $42

Maximum WBA: $156

Initial waiting week period for partial unemployment: 1

Partially unemployed if: Earnings less than WBA

Earnings disregard: 50% of WBA

Dependent allowance: No

Normal minimum duration of benefits: 12

Normal maximum duration of benefits: 26

OHIO

Benefit Eligibility Requirements

Qualifying wages: At least $20 in each of 20 weeks

Able and available for: Suitable work

Actively looking for work: Yes

Qualification requirement in successive benefit years: No additional requirements

Benefit Determination

Base period: 52 weeks preceding benefit year

Benefit year: 52-week period beginning week of valid claim

Initial waiting week period for total unemployment: 1

Benefit formula: Average weekly wage

Minimum WBA: $10

Maximum WBA: $147

Initial waiting week period for partial unemployment: 1

Partially unemployed if: Earnings less than WBA

Earnings disregard: 20% of WBA

Dependent allowance: Yes

Normal minimum duration of benefits: 20

Normal maximum duration of benefits: 26

OKLAHOMA

Benefit Eligibility Requirements

Qualifying wages: At least $1,000 and 1½ times high-quarter wages in the base period

Able and available for: Work

Actively look for work: Yes

Qualification requirement in successive benefit years: Wages equal to 10 times WBA

Benefit Determination

Base period: First 4 of last 5 completed calendar quarters

Benefit year: 52-week period beginning week of valid claim

Initial waiting week period for total unemployment: 1

Benefit formula: High-quarter

Minimum WBA: $16

Maximum WBA: $176

Initial waiting week period for partial unemployment: 1

Partially unemployed if: Earnings less than $7 plus WBA

Earnings disregard: $7

Dependent allowance: No

Normal minimum duration of benefits: 20+

Normal maximum duration of benefits: 26

OREGON

Benefit Eligibility Requirements

Qualifying wages: At least $1,000 and 18 weeks employment

Able and available for: Suitable work

Actively looking for work: Yes

Qualification requirement in successive benefit years: Wages equal to 6 times WBA

Benefit Determination

Base period: First 4 of last 5 completed calendar quarters

Benefit year: 52-week period beginning week of valid claim

Initial waiting week period for total unemployment: 1

Benefit formula: Annual wage

Minimum WBA: $41

Maximum WBA: $158

Initial waiting week period for partial unemployment: 1

Partially unemployed if: Earnings less than WBA

Earnings disregard: One-third of WBA

Dependent allowance: No

Normal minimum duration of benefits: 6+

Normal maximum duration of benefits: 26

PENNSYLVANIA

Benefit Eligibility Requirements

Qualifying wages: At least $1,320 in base-period earnings including $800 in high quarter and 20% in other than high quarter. If base-period earnings are less than $600, must be earned in 18 different weeks

Able and available for: Suitable work

Actively looking for work: Yes

Qualification requirement in successive benefit years: Wages equal to 6 times WBA

Benefit Determination

Base period: First 4 of last 5 completed calendar quarters

Benefit year: 52-week period beginning week of valid claim

Initial waiting week period for total unemployment: 1

Benefit formula: High-quarter

Minimum WBA: $35

Maximum WBA: $175

Initial waiting week period for partial unemployment: 1

Partially unemployed if: Earnings less than 1⅖ times WBA

Earnings disregard: 40% of WBA

Dependent allowance: Yes

Normal minimum duration of benefits: 26

Normal maximum duration of benefits: 30

PUERTO RICO

Benefit Eligibility Requirements

Qualifying wages: At least $280 earned in at least 2 quarters and at least $75 in one quarter

Able and available for: Suitable work

Actively looking for work: No

Qualification requirement in successive benefit years: Wages equal to at least 3 times WBA, but not less than $50

Benefit Determination

Base period: First 4 of last 5 completed calendar quarters

Benefit year: 52-week period beginning week of valid claim

Initial waiting week period for total unemployment: 1

Benefit formula: High-quarter

Minimum WBA: $7

Maximum WBA: $84

Initial waiting week period for partial unemployment: 1

Partially unemployed if: Earnings less than 1½ times WBA

Earnings disregard: WBA

Dependent allowance: No

Normal minimum duration of benefits: 20

Normal maximum duration of benefits: 20

RHODE ISLAND

Benefit Eligibility Requirements

Qualifying wages: At least $3,720 in base-period earnings or $62 per week for 20 weeks

Able and available for: Work

Actively looking for work: Yes

Qualification requirement in successive benefit years: No additional requirements

Benefit Determination

Base period: 52-week period ending with second week preceding benefit year

Benefit year: 52-week period beginning week of valid claim

Initial waiting week period for total unemployment: 1

Benefit formula: Average weekly wage

Minimum WBA: $35

Maximum WBA: $143

Initial waiting week period for partial unemployment: 1

Partially unemployed if: Earnings less than WBA plus $5

Earnings disregard: $5

Dependent allowance: Yes

Normal minimum duration of benefits: 12

Normal maximum duration of benefits: 26

SOUTH CAROLINA

Benefit Eligibility Requirements

Qualifying wages: At least $300 in base-period earnings with $180 in high quarter and total base-period earnings of at least 1½ times high quarter

Able and available for: Work in usual occupation

Actively looking for work: Yes

Qualification requirement in successive benefit years: Wages equal to 8 times WBA in insured work with a single employer

Benefit Determination

Base period: First 4 of last 5 completed calendar quarters

Benefit year: 52-week period beginning week of valid claim

Initial waiting week period for total unemployment: 1

Beneficial formula: High-quarter

Minimum WBA: $10

Maximum WBA: $118

Initial waiting week period for partial unemployment: 1

Partially unemployed if: Earnings less than WBA

Earnings disregard: 25% of WBA

Dependent allowance: No

Normal minimum duration of benefits: 10

Normal maximum duration of benefits: 26

SOUTH DAKOTA

Benefit Eligibility Requirements

Qualifying wages: $728 in high quarter and 30 times WBA outside high quarter

Able and available for: Work

Actively looking for work: No

Qualification requirement in successive benefit years: Wages equal to 4 times WBA

Benefit Determination

Base period: First 4 of last 5 completed calendar quarters

Benefit year: 52-week period beginning week of valid claim

Initial waiting week period for total unemployment: 1

Benefit formula: High-quarter

Minimum WBA: $28

Maximum WBA: $129

Initial waiting week period for partial unemployment: 1

Partially unemployed if: Earnings less than 50% of WBA

Earnings disregard: 25% up to 50% of WBA

Dependent allowance: No

Normal minimum duration of benefits: 13

Normal maximum duration of benefits: 26

TENNESSEE

Benefit Eligibility Requirements

Qualifying wages: Earnings at least 36 times WBA. For minimum benefit, the high-quarter base-period wage requirement is $494.01. Claimants who are otherwise entitled to maximum WBA must have base-period wages in some quarter other than their high quarter of 6 times WBA.

Able and available for: Work

Actively looking for work: No

Qualification requirement in succesive benefit years: Wages equal to 5 times WBA in insured work

Benefit Determination

Base period: First 4 of last 5 completed calendar quarters

Benefit year: 52-week period beginning week of valid claim

Initial waiting week period for total unemployment: 1

Benefit formula: High-quarter

Minimum WBA: $20

Maximum WBA: $110

Initial waiting week period for partial unemployment: 1

Partially unemployed if: Earnings less than WBA

Earnings disregard: $30

Dependent allowance: No

Normal minimum duration of benefits: 12

Normal maximum duration of benefits: 26

TEXAS

Benefit Eligibility Requirements

Qualifying wages: At least $500 base-period earnings and 1½ times high quarter; or two-thirds FICA tax base in one quarter

Able and available for: Work

Actively looking for work: No

Qualification requirement in successive benefit years: Wages equal to $250

Benefit Determination

Base period: First 4 of last 5 completed calendar quarters

Benefit year: 52-week period beginning week of valid claim

Initial waiting week period for total unemployment: 1

Benefit formula: High-quarter

Minimum WBA: $24

Maximum WBA: $147

Initial waiting week period for partial unemployment: 1

Partially unemployed if: Earnings less than 1¼ times WBA

Earnings disregard: Greater of $5 or 25% of WBA

Dependent allowance: No

Normal minimum duration of benefits: 9

Normal maximum duration of benefits: 26

UTAH

Benefit Eligibility Requirements

Qualifying wages: 19 weeks of employment at $20 or more but not less than $700 base-period wages

Able and available for: Work

Actively looking for work: Yes

Qualification requirement in successive benefit years: No additional requirement

Benefit Determination

Base period: Last 4 quarters

Benefit year: 52-week period beginning week of valid claim

Initial waiting week period for total unemployment: 1

Benefit formula: High-quarter

Minimum WBA: $10

Maximum WBA: $166

Initial waiting week period for partial unemployment: 1

Partially unemployed if: Earnings less than WBA

Earnings disregard: 30% of WBA

Dependent allowance: No

Normal minimum duration of benefits: 10

Normal maximum duration of benefits: 36

VERMONT

Benefit Eligibility Requirements

Qualifying wages: At least $35 in each of 20 weeks

Able and available for: Work

Actively looking for work: Yes

Qualification requirement in successive benefit years: No additional requirement

Benefit Determination

Base period: 52-week period preceding benefit year

Benefit year: 52-week period beginning week of valid claim

Initial waiting week period for total unemployment: 1

Benefit formula: Average weekly wage

Minimum WBA: $15

Maximum WBA: $135

Initial waiting week period for partial unemployment: 1

Partially unemployed if: Earnings less than WBA plus $15

Earnings disregard: $15 plus $3 per dependent up to 5 dependents

Dependent allowance: No

Normal minimum duration of benefits: 26

Normal maximum duration of benefits: 26

VIRGINIA

Benefit Eligibility Requirements

Qualifying wages: $2,200 in the highest two quarters of base-period WBA earned in at least 2 quarters

Able and available for: Work

Actively looking for work: No

Qualification requirement in successive benefit years: 30 days work

Benefit Determination

Base period: First 4 of last 5 completed calendar quarters

Benefit year: 52-week period beginning week of valid claim

Initial waiting week period for total unemployment: None

Benefit formula: High-quarter

Minimum WBA: $44

Maximum WBA: $138

Initial waiting week period for partial unemployment: None

Partially unemployed if: Earnings less than WBA

Earnings disregard: Greater of $10 or one-third of WBA

Dependent allowance: No

Normal minimum duration of benefits: 12

Normal maximum duration of benefits: 26

WASHINGTON

Benefit Eligibility Requirements

Qualifying wages: 15% of statewide average weekly wage for 16 weeks or 680 hours of employment and total earnings at least 15% of average annual wage

Able and available for: Work in usual occupation

Actively looking for work: Yes

Qualification requirement in successive benefit years: Wages equal to 6 times WBA in last 6 months

Benefit Determination

Base period: First 4 of last 5 completed calendar quarters

Benefit year: 52-week period beginning week of valid claim

Initial waiting week period for total unemployment: 1

Benefit formula: High-quarter

Minimum WBA: $45

Maximum WBA: $163

Initial waiting week period for partial unemployment: 1

Partially unemployed if: Earnings less than 1⅓ times WBA plus $5

Earnings disregard: 25% of wages over $5

Dependent allowance: No

Normal minimum duration of benefits: 30

Normal maximum duration of benefits: 30

WEST VIRGINA

Benefit Eligibility Requirements

Qualifying wages: At least $1,150 base-period earnings in more than one quarter

Able and available for: Work in usual occupation

Actively looking for work: Yes

Qualification requirement in successive benefit years: Wages equal to 8 times WBA in insured work

Benefit Determination

Base period: First 4 of last 5 completed calendar quarters

Benefit year: 52-week period beginning week of valid claim

Initial waiting week period for total unemployment: 1

Benefit formula: Annual wage

Minimum WBA: $18

Maximum WBA: $194

Initial waiting week period for partial unemployment: 0

Partially unemployed if: Earnings less than WBA plus $25

Earnings disregard: $25

Dependent allowance: No

Normal minimum duration of benefits: 28

Normal maximum duration of benefits: 28

WISCONSIN

Benefit Eligibility Requirements

Qualifying wages: An average weekly wage of at least $66.01 in at least 15 base-period weeks

Able and available for: Work

Actively looking for work: Yes

Qualification requirement in successive benefit years: No additional requirement

Benefit Determination

Base period: 52 weeks preceding benefit year

Benefit year: 52-week period beginning week of valid claim

Initial waiting week period for total unemployment: 0

Benefit formula: Average weekly wage

Minimum WBA: $33

Maximum WBA: $175

Initial waiting week period for partial unemployment: 0

Partially unemployed if: Earnings less than WBA

Earnings disregard: Up to 50% of WBA

Dependent allowance: No

Normal minimum duration of benefits: 1

Normal maximum duration of benefits: 34

WYOMING

Benefit Eligibility Requirements

Qualifying wages: At least $960 base-period earnings and $600 in high quarter

Able and available for: Work

Actively looking for work: Yes

Qualification requirement in successive benefit years: Wages equal to 8 times WBA in insured work

Benefit Determination

Base period: Last 4 completed calendar quarters

Benefit year: 52-week period beginning week of valid claim

Initial waiting week period for total unemployment: 1

Benefit formula: High-quarter

Minimum WBA: $24

Maximum WBA: $165

Initial waiting week period for partial unemployment: 1

Partially unemployed if: Earnings less than basic WBA

Earnings disregard: Greater of $15 or 25% of WBA

Dependent allowance: No

Normal minimum duration of benefits: 12

Normal maximum duration of benefits: 26

APPENDIX 19-4 State Unemployment Insurance Financing Tables

ALABAMA

Coverage

Employers with one employee working: 20 weeks

Alternative conditions: Quarterly payroll of $1,500

Exclusions

Insurance agents on commission: Yes

Real estate agents on commission: No

Casual labor: Yes

Student nurses and interns in employ of a hospital: Yes

Students working for schools: Yes

Contributions

Taxable wage base: $6,600

Standard tax rate: 2.7%

Minimum tax rate: 0.5%

Maximum tax rate: 4.0%

Tax year: Calendar year

Qualification for experience rating: Benefits chargeable for 12 months ending Sept. 30

Experience Rating Provisions

Method: Benefit-wage ratio formula

Voluntary contributions: No

Transfer of experience—total: Mandatory

Transfer of experience—partial: Mandatory

ALASKA

Coverage

Employers with one employee working: Any time

Alternative conditions: Quarterly payroll of $1,500

Exclusions

Insurance agents on commission: Yes

Real estate agents on commission: Yes

Casual labor: Yes

Student nurses and interns in employ of a hospital: No

Students working for schools: Yes

Contributions

Taxable wage base: $14,600

Standard tax rate: Average rate for industry

Minimum tax rate: 1.22%

Maximum tax rate: 4.86%

Tax year: Calendar year

Qualification for experience rating: Contributions payable for 4 quarters ending June 30

Experience Rating Provisions

Method: Payroll-variation plus benefit ratio formulas

Voluntary contributions: No

Transfer of experience—total: Mandatory

Transfer of experience—partial: Mandatory

ARIZONA

Coverage

Employers with one employee working: 20 weeks

Alternative conditions: Quarterly payroll of $1,500

Exclusions

Insurance agents on commission: Yes

Real estate agents on commission: Yes

Casual labor: Yes

Student nurses and interns in employ of a hospital: Yes

Students working for schools: Yes

Contributions

Taxable wage base: $6,000

Standard tax rate: 2.7%

Minimum tax rate: 0.1%

Maximum tax rate: 2.9%

Tax year: Calendar year

Qualification for experience rating: Benefits chargeable for 12 months ending June 30

Experience Rating Provisions

Method: Reserve ratio formula

Voluntary contributions: Yes

Transfer of experience—total: Mandatory

Transfer of experience—partial: Optional

ARKANSAS

Coverage

Employers with one employee working: 10 days

Alternative conditions: None

Exclusions

Insurance agents on commission: Yes

Real estate agents on commission: Yes

Casual labor: Yes

Student nurses and interns in employ of a hospital: Yes

Students working for schools: Yes

Contributions

Taxable wage base: $6,900

Standard tax rate: 3.3%

Minimum tax rate: 0.7%

Maximum tax rate: 6.1%

Tax year: Calendar year

Qualification for experience rating: Benefits chargeable for three years ending June 30

Experience Rating Provisions

Method: Reserve ratio formula

Voluntary contributions: Yes

Transfer of experience—total: Mandatory

Transfer of experience—partial: Optional

CALIFORNIA

Coverage

Employers with payroll of: Over $100 in quarter

Alternative conditions: Quarterly payroll of $1,500

Exclusions

Insurance agents on commission: No

Real estate agents on commission: Yes

Casual labor: Yes

Student nurses and interns in employ of a hospital: Yes

Students working for schools: Yes

Contributions

Taxable wage base: $6,000

Standard tax rate: 2.7%

Minimum tax rate: 0.7%

Maximum tax rate: 4.0%

Tax year: Calendar year

Qualification for experience rating: Benefits chargeable for 12 quarters ending June 30. New employers qualify if subject for 12 months ending June 30.

Experience Rating Provisions

Method: Reserve ratio formula

Voluntary contributions: No

Transfer of experience—total: Optional

Transfer of experience—partial: Optional

COLORADO

Coverage

Employers with one employee working: 13 weeks

Alternative conditions: $500 in quarter

Exclusions

Insurance agents on commission: Yes

Real estate agents on commission: Yes

Casual labor: Yes

Student nurses and interns in employ of a hospital: No

Students working for schools: Yes

Contributions

Taxable wage base: $6,000

Standard tax rate: 2.7%

Minimum tax rate: 0.0%

Maximum tax rate: 4.5%

Tax year: Calendar year

Qualification for experience rating: Benefits chargeable for 12 months ending June 30

Experience Rating Provisions

Method: Reserve ratio formula

Voluntary contributions: Yes

Transfer of experience—total: Mandatory only if successor corporation controls 50% or more of predecessor's business

Transfer of experience—partial: No provision

CONNECTICUT

Coverage

Employers with one employee working: 20 weeks

Alternative conditions: Quarterly payroll of $1,500

Exclusions

Insurance agents on commission: Yes

Real estate agents on commission: Yes

Casual labor: Yes

Student nurses and interns in employ of a hospital: Yes

Students working for schools: Yes

Contributions

Taxable wage base: $6,000

Standard tax rate: 2.9%

Minimum tax rate: 1.5%

Maximum tax rate: 6.0%

Tax year: Calendar year

Qualification for experience rating: Subject to the law for at least 12 months ending June 30

Experience Rating Provisions

Method: Benefit ratio formula

Voluntary contributions: No

Transfer of experience—total: Mandatory

Transfer of experience—partial: Optional

DELAWARE

Coverage

Employers with one employee working: 20 weeks

Alternative conditions: Quarterly payroll of $1,500

Exclusions

Insurance agents on commission: Yes

Real estate agents on commission: Yes

Casual labor: No

Student nurses and interns in employ of a hospital: No

Students working for schools: Yes

Contributions

Taxable wage base: $6,600

Standard tax rate: 4.2%

Minimum tax rate: 1.6%

Maximum tax rate: 6.5%

Tax year: Calendar year

Qualification for experience rating: Contributions payable for 3 years ending Sept. 30

Experience Rating Provisions

Method: Benefit-wage ratio formula

Voluntary contributions: No

Transfer of experience—total: Optional

Transfer of experience—partial: Not permitted

DISTRICT OF COLUMBIA

Coverage

Employers with one employee working: Any time

Alternative conditions: Quarterly payroll of $1,500

Exclusions

Insurance agents on commission: Yes

Real estate agents on commission: No

Casual labor: Yes

Student nurses and interns in employ of a hospital: Yes

Students working for schools: Yes

Contributions

Taxable wage base: $7,500

Standard tax rate: 2.6%

Minimum tax rate: 1.0%

Maximum tax rate: 5.4%

Tax year: Calendar year

Qualification for experience rating: Benefits chargeable for 36 months ending June 30

Experience Rating Provisions

Method: Reserve ratio formula

Voluntary contributions: No

Transfer of experience—total: Mandatory

Transfer of experience—partial: Mandatory

FLORIDA

Coverage

Employers with one employee working: 20 weeks

Alternative conditions: Quarterly payroll of $1,500

Exclusions

Insurance agents on commission: Yes

Real estate agents on commission: Yes

Casual labor: Yes

Student nurses and interns in employ of a hospital: Yes

Students working for schools: Yes

Contributions

Taxable wage base: $6,000

Standard tax rate: 2.7%

Minimum tax rate: 0.1%

Maximum tax rate: 4.5%

Tax year: Calendar year

Qualification for experience rating: Benefits chargeable for 8 quarters ending Dec. 31

Experience Rating Provisions

Method: Benefit ratio formula

Voluntary contributions: No

Transfer of experience—total: Optional

Transfer of experience—partial: Optional

GEORGIA

Coverage

Employers with one employee working: 20 weeks

Alternative conditions: Quarterly payroll of $1,500

Exclusions

Insurance agents on commission: Yes

Real estate agents on commission: Yes

Casual labor: Yes

Student nurses and interns in employ of a hospital: Yes

Students working for schools: Yes

Contributions

Taxable wage base: $6,000

Standard tax rate: 2.7%

Minimum tax rate: 0.06%

Maximum tax rate: 5.38%

Tax year: Calendar year

Qualification for experience rating: Benefits chargeable for 4 calendar quarters ending June 30

Experience Rating Provisions

Method: Reserve ratio formula

Voluntary contributions: No

Transfer of experience—total: Mandatory

Transfer of experience—partial: Optional

HAWAII

Coverage

Employers with one employee working: Any time

Alternative conditions: Quarterly payroll of $1,500

Exclusions

Insurance agents on commission: Yes

Real estate agents on commission: Yes

Casual labor: Yes

Student nurses and interns in employ of a hospital: Yes

Students working for schools: Yes

Contributions

Taxable wage base: $13,100

Standard tax rate: 4.5%

Minimum tax rate: 0.6%

Maximum tax rate: 4.5%

Tax year: Calendar year

Qualification for experience rating: Benefits chargeable for 12 months ending Dec. 31

Experience Rating Provisions

Method: Reserve ratio formula

Voluntary contributions: No

Transfer of experience—total: Optional

Transfer of experience—partial: Not permitted

IDAHO

Coverage

Employers with one employee working: 20 weeks

Alternative conditions: $300 in quarter

Exclusions

Insurance agents on commission: Yes

Real estate agents on commission: Yes

Casual labor: No

Student nurses and interns in employ of a hospital: Yes

Students working for schools: Yes

Contributions

Taxable wage base: $13,200

Standard tax rate: 2.9%

Minimum tax rate: 0.9%

Maximum tax rate: 4.0%

Tax year: Calendar year

Qualification for experience rating: Benefits chargeable for 1 fiscal year ending June 30

Experience Rating Provisions

Method: Reserve ratio formula

Voluntary contributions: No

Transfer of experience—total: Optional; mandatory if predecessor had a negative experience rating on last computation date

Transfer of experience—partial: Optional; mandatory if predecessor had a negative experience rating on last computation date

ILLINOIS

Coverage

Employers with one employee working: 20 weeks

Alternative conditions: Quarterly payroll of $1,500

Exclusions

Insurance agents on commission: Yes

Real estate agents on commission: Yes

Casual labor: No

Student nurses and interns in employ of a hospital: Yes

Students working for schools: No

Contributions

Taxable wage base: $7,000

Standard tax rate: 3.1%

Minimum tax rate: 0.6%

Maximum tax rate: 5.7%

Tax year: Calendar year

Qualification for experience rating: Contributions payable for 3 years ending Dec. 31

Experience Rating Provisions

Method: Benefit-wage ratio formula

Voluntary contributions: No

Transfer of experience—total: Mandatory

Transfer of experience—partial: Optional

INDIANA

Coverage

Employers with one employee working: 20 weeks

Alternative conditions: Quarterly payroll of $1,500

Exclusions

Insurance agents on commission: Yes

Real estate agents on commission: No

Casual labor: Yes

Student nurses and interns in employ of a hospital: Yes

Students working for schools: Yes

Contributions

Taxable wage base: $6,000

Standard tax rate: 2.7%

Minimum tax rate: 2.7%

Maximum tax rate: 3.3%

Tax year: Calendar year

Qualification for experience rating: Contributions payable for 36 months preceding June 30

Experience Rating Provisions

Method: Reserve ratio formula

Voluntary contributions: Yes

Transfer of experience—total: Mandatory

Transfer of experience—partial: Optional

IOWA

Coverage

Employers with one employee working: 20 weeks

Alternative conditions: Quarterly payroll of $1,500

Exclusions

Insurance agents on commission: No

Real estate agents on commission: No

Casual labor: No

Student nurses and interns in employ of a hospital: No

Students working for schools: Yes

Contributions

Taxable wage base: $8,700

Standard tax rate: 1.8% (6.0% for construction industry)

Minimum tax rate: 0.0%

Maximum tax rate: 6.0%

Tax year: Calendar year

Qualification for experience rating: Benefits chargeable for 20 calendar quarters ending June 30

Experience Rating Provisions

Method: Reserve ratio formula

Voluntary contributions: Yes

Transfer of experience—total: Mandatory

Transfer of experience—partial: Optional

KANSAS

Coverage

Employers with one employee working: 20 weeks

Alternative conditions: Quarterly payroll of $1,500

Exclusions

Insurance agents on commission: Yes

Real estate agents on commission: No

Casual labor: No

Student nurses and interns in employ of a hospital: No

Students working for schools: Yes

Contributions

Taxable wage base: $6,000

Standard tax rate: 2.52% agriculture, forestry and fisheries; 2.91% contract construction; 2.27% manufacturing; 1.94% all others

Minimum tax rate: 0.06%

Maximum tax rate: 4.3%

Tax year: Calendar year

Qualification for experience rating: Benefits chargeable for 24 months ending June 30

Experience Rating Provisions

Method: Reserve ratio formula

Voluntary contributions: Yes

Transfer of experience—total: Mandatory

Transfer of experience—partial: Optional

KENTUCKY

Coverage

Employers with one employee working: 20 weeks

Alternative conditions: Quarterly payroll of $1,500

Exclusions

Insurance agents on commission: Yes

Real estate agents on commission: Yes

Casual labor: Yes

Student nurses and interns in employ of a hospital: Yes

Students working for schools: Yes

Contributions

Taxable wage base: $6,000

Standard tax rate: 3.0%

Minimum tax rate: 1.3%

Maximum tax rate: 6.7%

Tax year: Calendar year

Qualification for experience rating: Benefits chargeable for 36 months ending Sept. 30

Experience Rating Provisions

Method: Reserve ratio formula

Voluntary contributions: Yes

Transfer of experience—total: Mandatory

Transfer of experience—partial: Optional

LOUISIANA

Coverage

Employers with one employee working: 20 weeks

Alternative conditions: Quarterly payroll of $1,500

Exclusions

Insurance agents on commission: Yes

Real estate agents on commission: Yes

Casual labor: Yes
Student nurses and interns in employ of a hospital: Yes
Students working for schools: Yes

Contributions
Taxable wage base: $6,000
Standard tax rate: 3.39108%
Minimum tax rate: 0.10276%
Maximum tax rate: 3.39108%
Tax year: Calendar year
Qualification for experience rating: Benefits chargeable for 36 months ending June 30

Experience Rating Provisions
Method: Reserve ratio formula
Voluntary contributions: Yes
Transfer of experience—total: Mandatory
Transfer of experience—partial: Optional

MAINE

Coverage
Employers with one employee working: 20 weeks
Alternative conditions: Quarterly payroll of $1,500

Exclusions
Insurance agents on commission: Yes
Real estate agents on commission: Yes
Casual labor: No
Student nurses and interns in employ of a hospital: Yes
Students working for schools: Yes

Contributions
Taxable wage base: $6,000
Standard tax rate: 3.0%
Minimum tax rate: 2.4%
Maximum tax rate: 5.0%
Tax year: Calendar year *
Qualification for experience rating: Benefits chargeable for 36 months ending Dec. 31

Experience Rating Provisions
Method: Reserve ratio formula
Voluntary contributions: Yes
Transfer of experience—total: Mandatory
Transfer of experience—partial: Not permitted

MARYLAND

Coverage
Employers with one employee working: Any time
Alternative conditions: Quarterly payroll of $1,500

Exclusions
Insurance agents on commission: Yes
Real estate agents on commission: Applicable only while exempt from FUTA
Casual labor: Yes
Student nurses and interns in employ of a hospital: Yes
Students working for schools: Yes

Contributions
Taxable wage base: $6,000
Standard tax rate: 2.3%
Minimum tax rate: 0.1%
Maximum tax rate: 5.0% **
Tax year: Fiscal year
Qualification for experience rating:

* Prior to Jan. 1, 1982 contributions rates were assigned on a fiscal year basis.
** A special rate is assigned an employer who locates in a federally designated "urban enterprise zone": 2.0% for employee residents of the zone; 2.7% for all other employees.

Benefits chargeable for one year ending Dec. 31. Contributions payable for 2 years ending Dec. 31 on annual payroll of at least $200.

Experience Rating Provisions

Method: Benefit ratio formula

Voluntary contributions: No

Transfer of experience—total: Mandatory

Transfer of experience—partial: Mandatory

MASSACHUSETTS

Coverage

Employers with one employee working: 13 weeks

Alternative conditions: Quarterly payroll of $1,500

Exclusions

Insurance agents on commission: Yes

Real estate agents on commission: Yes

Casual labor: Yes

Student nurses and interns in employ of a hospital: Yes

Students working for schools: Yes

Contributions

Taxable wage base: $6,000

Standard tax rate: 3.7% *

Minimum tax rate: 2.9%

Maximum tax rate: 6.7%

Tax year: Calendar year

Qualification for experience rating: Benefits chargeable for 12 months ending Sept. 30

Experience Rating Provisions

Method: Reserve ratio formula

Voluntary contributions: No

---

* New employer rate 3.0% if employer was never previously subject to the law.

Transfer of experience—total: Mandatory

Transfer of experience—partial: Not permitted

MICHIGAN

Coverage

Employers with one employee working: 20 weeks

Alternative conditions: Quarterly payroll of $1,000

Exclusions

Insurance agents on commission: Yes

Real estate agents on commission: Yes

Casual labor: No

Student nurses and interns in employ of a hospital: No

Students working for schools: Yes

Contributions

Taxable wage base: $6,000

Standard tax rate: 2.7% (certain construction contractors 4.0%)

Minimum tax rate: 1.0%

Maximum tax rate: 9.0%

Tax year: Calendar year

Qualification for experience rating: Contributions payable for up to June 30 in fourth consecutive year of liability

Experience Rating Provisions

Method: Benefit ratio plus reserve ratio formulas

Voluntary contributions: Yes

Transfer of experience—total: Mandatory

Transfer of experience—partial: Optional

MINNESOTA

Coverage

Employers with one employee working: 20 weeks

Alternative conditions: Quarterly payroll of $1,500

Exclusions

Insurance agents on commission: Yes

Real estate agents on commission: Yes

Casual labor: Yes

Student nurses and interns in employ of a hospital: Yes

Students working for schools: Yes

Contributions

Taxable wage base: $8,000

Standard tax rate: 2.1%

Minimum tax rate: 1.0%

Maximum tax rate: 7.5%

Tax year: Calendar year

Qualification for experience rating: Benefits chargeable for 12 months ending June 30

Experience Rating Provisions

Method: Benefit ratio formula

Voluntary contributions: Yes (Used to reduce the amount of benefits charged.)

Transfer of experience—total: Mandatory

Transfer of experience—partial: Optional

MISSISSIPPI

Coverage

Employers with one employee working: 20 weeks

Alternative conditions: Quarterly payroll of $1,500

Exclusions

Insurance agents on commission: Yes

Real estate agents on commission: No

Casual labor: Yes

Student nurses and interns in employ of a hospital: Yes

Students working for schools: Yes

Contributions

Taxable wage base: $6,000

Standard tax rate: 1.7%

Minimum tax rate: 1.7%

Maximum tax rate: 4.0%

Tax year: Calendar year

Qualification for experience rating: Benefits chargeable for 12 months ending June 30

Experience Rating Provisions

Method: Benefit ratio formula

Voluntary contributions: No

Transfer of experience—total: Mandatory

Transfer of experience—partial: Optional

MISSOURI

Coverage

Employers with one employee working: 20 weeks

Alternative conditions: Quarterly payroll of $1,500

Exclusions

Insurance agents on commission: Yes

Real estate agents on commission: Yes

Casual labor: No

Student nurses and interns in employ of a hospital: No

Students working for schools: Yes, if remuneration (exclusive of room, board, and tuition) does not exceed $50 per calendar quarter

Contributions

Taxable wage base: $6,600

Standard tax rate: Greater of 2.7% or average industry rate for assigned industrial classification

Minimum tax rate: 0.5%

Maximum tax rate: 4.9%

Tax year: Calendar year

Qualification for experience rating: Benefits chargeable for 36 months ending June 30; for 12 months end-June 30 if new employer

Experience Rating Provisions

Method: Reserve ratio formula

Voluntary contributions: Yes

Transfer of experience—total: Mandatory

Transfer of experience—partial: Under certain conditions

MONTANA

Coverage

Employers with payroll of: Over $500 in year

Alternative conditions: Quarterly payroll of $1,500

Exclusions

Insurance agents on commission: Yes

Real estate agents on commission: Yes

Casual labor: No

Student nurses and interns in employ of a hospital: No

Students working for schools: Yes

Contributions

Taxable wage base: $8,000

Standard tax rate: 3.7%

Minimum tax rate: 1.7%

Maximum tax rate: 4.4%

Tax year: Calendar year

Qualification for experience rating: Contributions payable for 3 years ending June 30

Experience Rating Provisions

Method: Reserve ratio formula

Voluntary contributions: No

Transfer of experience—total: Mandatory

Transfer of experience—partial: Mandatory

NEBRASKA

Coverage

Employers with one employee working: 20 weeks

Alternative conditions: Quarterly payroll of $1,500

Exclusions

Insurance agents on commission: Yes

Real estate agents on commission: Yes

Casual labor: Yes

Student nurses and interns in employ of a hospital: Yes

Students working for schools: Yes

Contributions

Taxable wage base: $6,000

Standard tax rate: 2.7%

Minimum tax rate: 0.1%

Maximum tax rate: 3.7%

Tax year: Calendar year

Qualification for experience rating: Benefits chargeable for one year ending Dec. 31. Contributions payable for 2 years ending Dec. 31.

Experience Rating Provisions

Method: Reserve ratio formula

Voluntary contributions: Yes

Transfer of experience—total: Mandatory

Transfer of experience—partial: Optional

NEVADA

Coverage

Employers with payroll of: $225 in quarter

Alternative conditions: Quarterly payroll of $1,500

Exclusions

Insurance agents on commission: No

Real estate agents on commission: Yes

Casual labor: No

Student nurses and interns in employ of a hospital: No

Students working for schools: Yes

Contributions

Taxable wage base: $9,300

Standard tax rate: 3.0%

Minimum tax rate: 0.3%

Maximum tax rate: 3.6%

Tax year: Calendar year

Qualification for experience rating: Benefits chargeable for 10 quarters ending June 30

Experience Rating Provisions

Method: Reserve ratio formula

Voluntary contributions: No

Transfer of experience—total: Optional

Transfer of experience—partial: Optional

NEW HAMPSHIRE

Coverage

Employers with one employee working: 20 weeks

Alternative conditions: Quarterly payroll of $1,500

Exclusions

Insurance agents on commission: Yes

Real estate agents on commission: Yes

Casual labor: Yes

Student nurses and interns in employ of a hospital: No

Students working for schools: Yes

Contributions

Taxable wage base: $6,000

Standard tax rate: 2.7%

Minimum tax rate: 0.01%

Maximum tax rate: 6.5%

Tax year: Quarterly

Qualification for experience rating: Benefits chargeable for 12 months ending Dec. 31

Experience Rating Provisions

Method: Reserve ratio formula

Voluntary contributions: No

Transfer of experience—total: Mandatory

Transfer of experience—partial: Optional

NEW JERSEY

Coverage

Employers with payroll of: $1,000 in year

Alternative conditions: Quarterly payroll of $1,500

Exclusions

Insurance agents on commission: Yes

Real estate agents on commission: Yes

Casual labor: No

Student nurses and interns in employ of a hospital: Yes

Students working for schools: Yes

Contributions

Taxable wage base: $8,200

Standard tax rate: 3.4%

Minimum tax rate: 1.2%

Maximum tax rate: 6.2%

Tax year: Fiscal year

Qualification for experience rating: Benefits chargeable for 3 years ending Dec. 31

Experience Rating Provisions

Method: Reserve ratio formula

Voluntary contributions: Yes

Transfer of experience—total: Optional

Transfer of experience—partial: Optional

NEW MEXICO

Coverage

Employers with one employee working: 20 weeks

Alternative conditions: Quarterly payroll of $450

Exclusions

Insurance agents on commission: Yes

Real estate agents on commission: Yes

Casual labor: No

Student nurses and interns in employ of a hospital: No

Students working for schools: No

Contributions

Taxable wage base: $8,500

Standard tax rate: 2.7%

Minimum tax rate: 0.6%

Maximum tax rate: 4.2%

Tax year: Calendar year

Qualification for experience rating: Benefits chargeable for 36 months ending June 30

Experience Rating Provisions

Method: Reserve ratio formula

Voluntary contributions: Yes

Transfer of experience—total: Optional

Transfer of experience—partial: Optional

NEW YORK

Coverage

Employers with payroll of: $300 in quarter

Alternative conditions: Quarterly payroll of $1,500

Exclusions

Insurance agents on commission: No

Real estate agents on commission: No

Casual labor: No

Student nurses and interns in employ of a hospital: No

Students working for schools: Yes

Contributions

Taxable wage base: $6,000

Standard tax rate: 3.7% (includes 1% subsidiary tax)

Minimum tax rate: 1.5%

Maximum tax rate: 5.2%

Tax year: Calendar year

Qualification for experience rating: Benefits chargeable for 4 quarters ending Dec. 31

Experience Rating Provisions

Method: Reserve ratio formula

Voluntary contributions: Yes

Transfer of experience—total: Mandatory

Transfer of experience—partial: Mandatory

NORTH CAROLINA

Coverage

Employers with one employee working: 20 weeks

Alternative conditions: Quarterly payroll of $1,500

Exclusions

Insurance agents on commission: Yes

Real estate agents on commission: Yes

Casual labor: Yes

Student nurses and interns in employ of a hospital: No

Students working for schools: Yes

Contributions

Taxable wage base: $6,000

Standard tax rate: 2.7%

Minimum tax rate: 0.1%

Maximum tax rate: 5.7%

Tax year: Calendar year

Qualification for experience rating: Benefits chargeable for over 13 months ending July 31

Experience Rating Provisions

Method: Reserve ratio formula

Voluntary contributions: Yes

Transfer of experience—total: Optional

Transfer of experience—partial: Optional

NORTH DAKOTA

Coverage

Employers with one employee working: 20 weeks

Alternative conditions: Quarterly payroll of $1,500

Exclusions

Insurance agents on commission: Yes

Real estate agents on commission: Yes

Casual labor: Yes

Student nurses and interns in employ of a hospital: No

Students working for schools: Yes

Contributions

Taxable wage base: $9,240

Standard tax rate: 1.0% min. to 5.0% max. (avg. industry rate)

Minimum tax rate: 0.5%

Maximum tax rate: 5.0%

Tax year: Calendar year

Qualification for experience rating: Benefits chargeable for 12 months ending Dec. 31

Experience Rating Provisions

Method: Reserve ratio formula

Voluntary contributions: Yes

Transfer of experience—total: Optional

Transfer of experience—partial: Not permitted

OHIO

Coverage

Employers with one employee working: 20 weeks

Alternative conditions: Quarterly payroll of $1,500

Exclusions

Insurance agents on commission: Yes

Real estate agents on commission: No

Casual labor: Yes

Student nurses and interns in employ of a hospital: Yes

Students working for schools: Yes

Contributions

Taxable wage base: $6,000

Standard tax rate: 3.0%

Minimum tax rate: 1.1%

Maximum tax rate: 4.8%

Tax year: Calendar year

Qualification for experience rating: Benefits chargeable for 4 quarters ending June 30

Experience Rating Provisions

Method: Reserve ratio formula

Voluntary contributions: Yes

Transfer of experience—total: Manda-

Transfer of experience—partial: Optional

tory

OKLAHOMA

Coverage

Employers with one employee working: 20 weeks

Alternative conditions: Quarterly payroll of $1,500

Exclusions

Insurance agents on commission: Yes

Real estate agents on commission: No

Casual labor: No

Student nurses and interns in employ of a hospital: Yes

Students working for schools: Yes

Contributions

Taxable wage base: $6,000

Standard tax rate: 3.1%

Minimum tax rate: 0.1%

Maximum tax rate: 3.1%

Tax year: Calendar year

Qualification for experience rating: Benefits chargeable for one year ending Dec. 31

Experience Rating Provisions

Method: Benefit-wage ratio formula

Voluntary contributions: No

Transfer of experience—total: Mandatory

Transfer of experience—partial: Optional

OREGON

Coverage

Employers with one employee working: 18 weeks

Alternative conditions: Quarterly payroll of $225

Exclusions

Insurance agents on commission: Yes

Real estate agents on commission: Yes

Casual labor: Yes

Student nurses and interns in employ of a hospital: Yes

Students working for schools: Yes

Contributions

Taxable wage base: $11,000

Standard tax rate: 3.4%

Minimum tax rate: 2.0%

Maximum tax rate: 3.8%

Tax year: Calendar year

Qualification for experience rating: Benefits chargeable for 12 months ending June 30

Experience Rating Provisions

Method: Benefit ratio formula

Voluntary contributions: No

Transfer of experience—total: Mandatory

Transfer of experience—partial: No provision

PENNSYLVANIA

Coverage

Employers with one employee working: Any time

Alternative conditions: Quarterly payroll of $1,500

Exclusions

Insurance agents on commission: Yes

Real estate agents on commission: Yes

Casual labor: Yes

Student nurses and interns in employ of a hospital: Yes

Students working for schools: Yes

Contributions

Taxable wage base: $6,600

Standard tax rate: 3.5% (6.5% for construction industry)

Minimum tax rate: 2.35%

Maximum tax rate: 6.45%

Tax year: Calendar year

Qualification for experience rating: Contributions payable for one or more of 4 quarters immediately preceding 12-month period before June 30

Experience Rating Provisions

Method: Reserve ratio plus benefit-ratio formulas

Voluntary contributions: Yes

Transfer of experience—total: Optional

Transfer of experience—partial: Optional

PUERTO RICO

Coverage

Employers with one employee working: Any time

Alternative conditions: Quarterly payroll of $1,500

Exclusions

Insurance agents on commission: No

Real estate agents on commission: No

Casual labor: Yes

Student nurses and interns in employ of a hospital: No

Students working for schools: Yes

Contributions

Taxable wage base: All wages

Standard tax rate: 2.95% (employers covered by FUTA); 3.45% (employers not covered by FUTA)

Minimum tax rate: 2.95%

Maximum tax rate: 2.95%

Tax year: Does not provide for experience rate. Tax rate is based on total wages.

Qualification for experience rating: No experience rating provisions

Experience Rating Provisions

Method: Not applicable

Voluntary contributions: Not applicable

Transfer of experience—total: Not applicable

Transfer of experience—partial: Not applicable

RHODE ISLAND

Coverage

Employers with one employee working: Any time

Alternative conditions: Quarterly payroll of $1,500

Exclusions

Insurance agents on commission: Yes

Real estate agents on commission: Yes

Casual labor: Yes

Student nurses and interns in employ of a hospital: No

Students working for schools: Yes

Contributions

Taxable wage base: $8,600

Standard tax rate: 4.2%

Minimum tax rate: 2.8%

Maximum tax rate: 6.0%

Tax year: Calendar year

Qualification for experience rating: Benefits chargeable for 12 months ending June 30. Contributions payable for 12 months ending June 30.

Experience Rating Provisions

Method: Reserve ratio formula

Voluntary contributions: No

Transfer of experience—total: Optional

Transfer of experience—partial: Optional

SOUTH CAROLINA

Coverage

Employers with one employee working: 20 weeks

Alternative conditions: Quarterly payroll of $1,500

Exclusions

Insurance agents on commission: Yes

Real estate agents on commission: Yes

Casual labor: Yes

Student nurses and interns in employ of a hospital: Yes

Students working for schools: Yes

Contributions

Taxable wage base: $6,000

Standard tax rate: 2.7%

Minimum tax rate: 1.3%

Maximum tax rate: 4.1%

Tax year: Calendar year

Qualification for experience rating: Contributions payable for 24 months

Experience Rating Provisions

Method: Reserve ratio formula

Voluntary contributions: Yes

Transfer of experience—total: Mandatory

Transfer of experience—partial: Optional

SOUTH DAKOTA

Coverage

Employers with one employee working: 20 weeks

Alternative conditions: Quarterly payroll of $1,500

Exclusions

Insurance agents on commission: Yes

Real estate agents on commission: No

Casual labor: No

Student nurses and interns in employ of a hospital: Yes

Students working for schools: Yes

Contributions

Taxable wage base: $6,000

Standard tax rate: If liable before April 1, 1981 2.9%; after April 1, 1981 3.3%

Minimum tax rate: 0.6% *

Maximum tax rate: 6.1% *

Tax year: Calendar year

Qualification for experience rating: Benefits chargeable for 24 months ending Sept. 30

* Rates for first quarter 1982 only; beginning second quarter 1982 minimum rate 0.2%, maximum rate 5.7%.

Experience Rating Provisions

Method: Reserve ratio formula

Voluntary contributions: Yes

Transfer of experience—total: Optional

Transfer of experience—partial: Optional

TENNESSEE

Coverage

Employers with one employee working: 20 weeks

Alternative conditions: Quarterly payroll of $1,500

Exclusions

Insurance agents on commission: Yes

Real estate agents on commission: Yes

Casual labor: No

Student nurses and interns in employ of a hospital: No

Students working for schools: Yes

Contributions

Taxable wage base: $6,000

Standard tax rate: 2.7%

Minimum tax rate: 0.75%

Maximum tax rate: 4.4%

Tax year: Fiscal year

Qualification for experience rating: Benefits chargeable for 36 months ending Dec. 31

Experience Rating Provisions

Method: Reserve ratio formula

Voluntary contributions: No

Transfer of experience—total: Optional

Transfer of experience—partial: Optional

TEXAS

Coverage

Employers with one employee working: 20 weeks

Alternative conditions: Quarterly payroll of $1,500

Exclusions

Insurance agents on commission: Yes
Real estate agents on commission: No
Casual labor: No
Student nurses and interns in employ of a hospital: Yes
Students working for schools: Yes

Contributions

Taxable wage base: $6,000
Standard tax rate: 2.7%
Minimum tax rate: 0.1%
Maximum tax rate: 4.0%
Tax year: Calendar year
Qualification for experience rating: Benefits chargeable for 4 quarters immediately preceding Oct. 1

Experience Rating Provisions

Method: Benefit ratio formula
Voluntary contributions: No
Transfer of experience—total: Optional
Transfer of experience—partial: Optional

UTAH

Coverage

Employers with payroll of: $140 in quarter
Alternative conditions: Quarterly payroll of $1,500

Exclusions

Insurance agents on commission: Yes
Real estate agents on commission: Yes
Casual labor: Yes
Student nurses and interns in employ of a hospital: No
Students working for schools: Yes

Contributions

Taxable wage base: $13,300
Standard tax rate: 2.7%
Minimum tax rate: 1.3%
Maximum tax rate: 2.8%
Tax year: Calendar year
Qualification for experience rating: Contributions payable for 3 years ending Dec. 31

Experience Rating Provisions

Method: Payroll-variation formula
Voluntary contributions: No
Transfer of experience—total: Mandatory
Transfer of experience—partial: Mandatory

VERMONT

Coverage

Employers with one employee working: 20 weeks
Alternative conditions: Quarterly payroll of $1,500

Exclusions

Insurance agents on commission: Yes
Real estate agents on commission: Yes
Casual labor: Yes
Student nurses and interns in employ of a hospital: No
Students working for schools: Yes

Contributions

Taxable wage base: $6,000
Standard tax rate: 3.2%
Minimum tax rate: 1.7%
Maximum tax rate: 6.0%
Tax year: Fiscal year
Qualification for experience rating: Benefits chargeable for 3 years ending Dec. 31

Experience Rating Provisions

Method: Benefit ratio formula
Voluntary contributions: No

Transfer of experience—total: Mandatory

Transfer of experience—partial: Not permitted

VIRGINIA

Coverage

Employers with one employee working: 20 weeks

Alternative conditions: Quarterly payroll of $1,500

Exclusions

Insurance agents on commission: Yes

Real estate agents on commission: Yes

Casual labor: Yes

Student nurses and interns in employ of a hospital: Yes

Students working for schools: Yes

Contributions

Taxable wage base: $6,000

Standard tax rate: 6.2%

Minimum tax rate: 0.8%

Maximum tax rate: 6.9%

Tax year: Calendar year

Qualification for experience rating: Benefits chargeable for 12 months ending June 30

Experience Rating Provisions

Method: Benefit ratio formula

Voluntary contributions: No

Transfer of experience—total: Optional

Transfer of experience—partial: Optional

WASHINGTON

Coverage

Employers with one employee working: Any time

Alternative conditions: Quarterly payroll of $1,500

Exclusions

Insurance agents on commission: Yes

Real estate agents on commission: Yes

Casual labor: Yes

Student nurses and interns in employ of a hospital: No

Students working for schools: Yes

Contributions

Taxable wage base: $10,800

Standard tax rate: 3.0% *

Minimum tax rate: 3.0% *

Maximum tax rate: 3.0% *

Tax year: Calendar year

Qualification for experience rating: Benefits chargeable for 36 months ending June 30

Experience Rating Provisions

Method: Payroll-decline plus benefit ratio

Voluntary contributions: No

Transfer of experience—total: Mandatory

Transfer of experience—partial: Mandatory

WEST VIRGINIA

Coverage

Employers with one employee working: 20 weeks

Alternative conditions: Quarterly payroll of $1,500

Exclusions

Insurance agents on commission: Yes

Real estate agents on commission: No

Casual labor: No

Student nurses and interns in employ of a hospital: No

Students working for schools: Yes

---

* Experience rating currently suspended.

Contributions

Taxable wage base: $8,000

Standard tax rate: 8.5% foreign corporation; 8.5% construction; all others 3.7%

Minimum tax rate: 2.5%

Maximum tax rate: 8.5%

Tax year: Calendar year

Qualification for experience rating: Benefits chargeable for 36 months before June 30

Experience Rating Provisions

Method: Reserve ratio formula

Voluntary contributions: Yes

Transfer of experience—total: Mandatory

Transfer of experience—partial: Not permitted

WISCONSIN

Coverage

Employers with one employee working: 20 weeks

Alternative conditions: Quarterly payroll of $1,500

Exclusions

Insurance agents on commission: Yes

Real estate agents on commission: Yes

Casual labor: No

Student nurses and interns in employ of a hospital: Yes

Students working for schools: Yes

Contributions

Taxable wage base: $6,000

Standard tax rate: 3.6%

Minimum tax rate: 0.0%

Maximum tax rate: 7.4%

Tax year: Calendar year

Qualification for experience rating: Benefits chargeable for 18 months before June 30

Experience Rating Provisions

Method: Reserve ratio formula

Voluntary contributions: Yes

Transfer of experience—total: Optional

Transfer of experience—partial: Optional

WYOMING

Coverage

Employers with payroll of: Over $500 in year

Alternative conditions: Quarterly payroll of $1,500

Exclusions

Insurance agents on commission: No

Real estate agents on commission: Yes

Casual labor: No

Student nurses and interns in employ of a hospital: No

Students working for schools: Yes

Contributions

Taxable wage base: $6,000

Standard tax rate: 3.08%

Minimum tax rate: 0.38%

Maximum tax rate: 3.08%

Tax year: Calendar year

Qualification for experience rating: Benefits chargeable for 36 months ending June 30

Experience Rating Provisions

Method: Benefit ratio formula

Voluntary contributions: No

Transfer of experience—total: Mandatory

Transfer of experience—partial: No provision

20

Death Benefits—Types of Plans

MICHAEL F. KLEIN, JR.
Price Waterhouse

INTRODUCTION

One important objective of comprehensive employee benefit planning is to provide a source of replacement income for dependents in the event of an employee's premature death. While an employee is active, the emphasis is on replacement income needs of the family unit. Beginning at retirement, the typical concern is for the needs of a surviving spouse.

Some sources of replacement income at death are government mandated: the Social Security system and workers' compensation laws, which cover death due to occupational causes. But for most employees, particularly at the higher compensation levels, the more important source is employer-sponsored private plans. Death benefits can be provided under group life insurance plans, under pension, profit-sharing, or thrift plans, and various other arrangements.

One of the more frequent failings in employee benefit plan design work is failure to take into account in designing a particular plan—a group life plan, for example—the magnitude of benefits payable under other employer-sponsored and government-mandated plans with respect to the same contingency—death in this case. The result can be costly benefit overlap.

After first analyzing government-mandated death benefits under the Social Security system, this chapter reviews the use of group term insurance, whole life insurance, and uninsured vehicles for delivering death benefit protection under various plan structures. Special legal and tax considerations relating to these insurance vehicles and plan structures are then analyzed. Financing considerations are reviewed in Chapter 21.

SOCIAL SECURITY DEATH BENEFITS

The Social Security system is a major source of family income replacement benefits in the event of death of active and retired employees.

The following material is a summary of the eligibility requirements and benefits that may be payable to the widow, widower, divorced wife, children, and dependent parents and grandchildren of a deceased worker or retiree.

Eligibility for all of these benefits depends on the deceased worker having been either 'fully" or "currently" insured. Since Social Security laws and regulations have changed many times over the years, special transitional rules and exceptions may apply to individuals who qualified for benefits in earlier years.

Widow's Benefits

Definition. The Social Security law contains highly detailed rules on what constitutes being a widow. A *widow* generally means a wife of an individual at the time of his death, but only if she was married to him for at least nine months (except in certain circumstances of accidental death) or if various other tests relating mainly to parent status with regard to his children are met.

Eligibility. Eligibility for full widow's benefits depends on five factors:

1. *Age.* Full benefits are available to the widow beginning at age 65. Reductions are made if payments begin between ages 65 and 60 (earliest age).
2. *Marital status.* A widow who remarries after she has attained age 60 will receive either her widow's benefits or the benefit to which she may be entitled through her new husband.
3. *Disability.* A widow who is so severely disabled as to be unable to engage in any gainful activity may be eligible for a reduced widow's benefit beginning at age 50. She must have become so disabled within seven years of the death of the husband on whom her benefits are based or the termination of her mother's benefits (as explained below) or within seven years of the termination of a previous period of entitlement to widow's disability benefits.
4. *Application for benefits.* Unless a widow was entitled to wife's benefits for the month before her husband died, she must make an application for widow's benefits.
5. *Fully insured status.* The deceased spouse must have been fully insured.

Determination of Benefit Amounts. The amount of benefits available depends on the deceased husband's earnings history. Generally, a widow who is age 65 or older when she first becomes eligible for widow's benefits will receive 100 percent of the primary insurance amount of her husband. However, if he had ever received an actuarially reduced benefit (because he collected benefits before age 65), the widow's benefits cannot exceed the greater of his actuarially reduced benefits or 82½ percent of his primary insurance amount. On the other hand, if the deceased husband had earned a delayed retirement income credit because he did not receive benefits between ages 65 and 72, the widow's benefit will be based on the increased benefit.

Example: A retires at age 65 and begins to receive a Social Security retirement benefit of $500 per month (his primary insurance amount). Upon attaining age 65, his spouse, *B*, begins to receive a spouse's benefit equal to one-half of his benefit, or $250 per month. Upon *A*'s death, *B*'s benefit will be adjusted to widow's benefit of $500 per month, i.e., the same amount *A* had been receiving.

Assume that *A* had instead retired at age 62 when his primary insurance amount was $430 per month. He chose to receive a reduced retirement benefit of $344, or 80 percent of his full benefit. Upon *A*'s death, his wife, *B*, who is age 66, will receive a widow's benefit of $355, because 82½ percent of *A*'s unreduced benefit is a larger amount than *A*'s reduced benefit had been.

Benefit Reductions. A widow's benefit is subject to reduction under certain circumstances:

- *Benefits between ages 60 to 65.* If a widow elects to begin receiving benefits between ages 60 to 65, her benefit is actuarially reduced by 19/40 of one percent for each month benefits are payable before age 65.
- *Disabled widow's benefits.* Benefits payable to a disabled widow (see above) are subject to an additional reduction of 43/240 of one percent for each month benefits are payable between the ages of 50 and 59. For example, if benefits begin at age 50, the reduction factor would be 50 percent.
- *Excess earnings.* If a widow under age 72 has earnings in excess of the retirement test, then her benefits are subject to reduction.
- *Public pension entitlement.* Beginning in December 1982, a widow's benefit will be reduced dollar for dollar by the amount of public retirement pension available to her as a result of her own employment, if that employment was not covered by Social Security. This applies only to those who filed applications for benefits in or after December 1977.

Benefits on Own Account. If a widow is entitled to equal or greater benefits on her own earnings history than she would be entitled to as a widow, she receives her own retirement benefits rather than a widow's benefit. If the widow's benefit is larger, the retirement benefit is paid separately and offset against the former.

Widow's Benefits for Surviving Divorced Wife. A woman who qualifies as a "surviving divorced wife" can receive a widow's benefit even though another woman is also entitled to widow's benefits with respect to the same man.

A woman must have been married to the deceased individual for at least ten years (twenty years before 1979). Benefits for a qualifying surviving divorced wife are determined in the same way as a widow's benefit and are subject to the same reductions because of age, earnings, etc. The deceased individual must have been fully insured.

A surviving divorced wife's benefits terminate if she remarries before age 60 or becomes entitled to a benefit under other provisions of the Social Security law that at least equals her deceased former husband's primary benefit.

Widower's Benefits

Prior to December 1977, a widower was required to prove that he had been a dependent of his wife in order to receive widower's benefits. In response to a Supreme Court ruling that the dependency test constituted sex-based discrimination, this provision was dropped.

A widower is entitled to receive the same benefit as a widow. The definition of a widower contains the same requirements as for a widow and the methods of benefit calculation are the same.

At present time, however, there is no benefit for a man comparable to the "surviving divorced wife" benefit.

Mother's or Father's Benefits

Even if under age 60, a widow, surviving divorced wife, or widower of an individual can be entitled to a benefit if he or she has a child *in care.* Having a child in care means that the parent:

- Exercises parental control and responsibility for the welfare and care of a child under 18 or a child over 18 who is mentally incompetent; or
- Performs personal services for a mentally competent disabled child age 18 or over. The requirements for a mother's or father's benefit are:
  —He or she has not remarried;
  —At the time of application he or she has in care a natural or legally adopted child of the deceased individual provided the child is entitled to child's benefits (see below) other than solely because of student status;
  —The deceased individual was either fully or currently insured.

Benefits continue provided the individual does not remarry and has such a child in care.

A mother's or father's benefit equals three-quarters of the deceased worker's primary insurance account. It is subject to the same reductions for excess earnings or receipt of public retirement benefits as a widow's benefit. It is not, however, subject to reduction because of the age of the recipient.

If an individual is entitled to a greater benefit on his or her own earning's record, then that benefit will be paid in place of the mother's or father's benefit. If the retirement benefit is smaller, it is paid separately and the mother's or father's benefit reduced accordingly.

Child's Benefits

The child of any deceased individual who dies while fully or currently insured is eligible for child's benefits. The benefit is three-quarters of the deceased individual's primary insurance amount.

The Social Security laws provide detailed definitions of a *child.* For purposes of the law, a child means:

- A natural or legally adopted child;
- A stepchild who has been a stepchild for one year before application for benefits is made (nine months if the individual is deceased);
- A grandchild or stepgrandchild of an individual or his spouse provided the child's parents were deceased or disabled at the time the grandparent became entitled to benefits or the child was legally adopted on the death of a grandparent by the grandparent's surviving spouse. Prior to age 18, the child must have been living with and receiving at least half of his support from the grandparent for at least one year prior to the grandparent's entitlement to benefits.

To be eligible for benefits, the child must be unmarried and under age 18, or under age 22 if he or she is a full-time student as defined under the law. A person who became disabled before age 22 may also receive benefits beyond age 18.

A child can qualify for benefits on the basis of either parent's earnings record, or in some circumstances on a grandparent's earnings record. Benefits are available to both natural and adopted children although special rules apply to a child adopted after the individual on whose record he would receive benefits has become entitled to old-age or disability benefits.

A child's benefits are not affected by the remarriage of his surviving parent or by the loss of mother's or father's benefits due to excess earnings.

A child is assumed to be a dependent of his natural or adopting parent unless the individual is not living with or contributing to the support of the child and the child is neither the legitimate nor the adopted child of such individual or the child has been adopted by someone else.

Subject to certain broader interpretations under the Social Security law, state law governs the determination of family status or relationships.

Parents' Benefits

The parent of an individual who dies while fully insured may be entitled to benefits on the individual's account.

Eligibility for parents' benefits require that the parent:

- Has reached age 62;
- Was receiving at least one-half of his or her support from the individual;
- Has not married since the worker's death; and
- Files application for benefits.

The parent benefit is 82½ percent of the primary insurance amount of the deceased worker, or 75 percent for each parent where there are two.

Maximum Family Benefits

Based on the previous discussion, it is evident that a number of individuals can simultaneously be receiving benefits on the account of the same deceased individual. For example, benefits could be payable to a widow, dependent children under age 18, a disabled dependent child over age 18, a surviving divorced wife, and to dependent parents.

The law does impose overall limits on the maximum benefits that can be paid to one family (excluding those paid to a surviving divorced wife). Prior to the 1977 indexing of Social Security benefits to changes in the cost of living it was easy to give dollar limits. The basic formula for determining family maximum benefits based on the worker's primary insurance amount (PIA) is now the following (for 1981):

150 percent of the first $248 +
272 percent of PIA over $248 through $358 +
134 percent of PIA over $358 through $467 +
175 percent of PIA over $467

Each year these formula breakpoints are adjusted to reflect the increase in the national average wage in the second preceding year.

Lump-Sum Death Benefits

A lump-sum death benefit of $255 is payable to the widow or widower of a worker who dies while fully or currently insured. The widow or widower must be residing in the same household as the deceased at the time of death.

If the benefit is not paid to a widow or widower, it can be paid to a funeral home or other person to be applied toward unpaid burial expenses.

In general, application for the lump-sum benefit must be made within two years of the death of the worker. However, no application is needed if the person entitled to the lump sum was entitled to a wife's or husband's benefits before the month in which the worker died.

Summary

The Social Security laws, which have been amended many times over the years, have become highly complex. The preceding summary is just that; it does not cover the many transitional and minimum benefit rules and special provisions that affect individuals who have already qualified for benefits. In addition, there are provisions that protect against loss of benefits in special situations.

Questions about an individual employee or beneficiary's benefits under Social Security should be discussed with the local Social Security office that has access to the necessary earnings records and eligibility documentation records.

GROUP INSURANCE

Term Life Insurance

Group term life insurance sponsored by employers is the primary source of protection against loss of income for the dependents of many workers.

The availability and the level of insurance protection sponsored depend on several factors:

- Legal requirements (discussed in detail later in this chapter)
- Insurance company underwriting rules

- Cost considerations
- Degree of employee cost sharing

Underwriting Rules. Insurance company underwriting rules (which incorporate the legal requirements) are the guidelines an insurer uses in deciding whether or not it wishes to assume the risk presented by a particular employee group and the terms under which it will assume the risk.

Underwriting rules are intended to assure that the risk involved is no greater than that assumed by the insurer when it sets its rate structure for a class of business. If the risk does not fit the norm, an additional premium must be charged.

The principal rules of insurers are concerned with the holder of the contract (usually the employer), the employee group covered, the individual employees in the group, and the amounts of insurance at risk.

1. *The contractholder.* The insurer is concerned that the contractholder is a legal entity entitled to enter into a contract and that it is a reputable and financially secure company or organization.

2. *The employee group.* The group of insureds as a whole is then evaluated. Does the nature of the work expose workers to unusual health risks? For example, miners, asbestos workers, and firemen have less favorable life expectancy than normal. Some companies will underwrite only standard or close to standard risks. Others will underwrite high-risk groups for a price.

3. *Minimum size requirements.* If employees pay part of the premium, have at least 75 percent of those eligible enrolled? The 75 percent enrollment requirement (which is a legal requirement in many states) is intended to prevent adverse selection against the insurer. In other words, if only those who are in poor health or only older workers enroll for insurance, the risk to the insurer would be increased. If coverage is noncontributory, all eligible employees must be covered to avoid discrimination or adverse selection.

4. *Classes of eligible employees.* Are the classes based on a condition pertaining to employment, as required by law? Are the definitions clear and well drawn so as to avoid administrative disputes and costly legal actions? Some examples of unacceptable and acceptable classifications of employees are shown in Figure 20.1.

5. *The individual employee.* By its nature, group insurance normally precludes the use of medical questionnaires or examinations. There is no "individual" underwriting. The primary underwriting rule for an individual is the actively-at-work rule. If an employee is not actively at work on the day coverage would otherwise be effective, coverage is postponed until he returns. If an employee declines coverage within thirty-one days of when first eligible, he may be required to submit evidence of insurability to be covered at a later date.

6. *Amount of insurance.* The amount of insurance provided for each class of insureds is possibly the most important underwriting rule. It is also

Unacceptable	*Problem*
Male employees and all female employees age 30 and over.	Discrimination based on age and sex. Not based on condition pertaining to employment.
Clerical and administrative employees other than management employees.	Not a clear definition. Are supervisors considered management?
Acceptable	*Advantage*
Employees covered by a collective bargaining agreement between the employer and Union Local XXX.	Definition based on bargaining unit definition.
Employees classified as nonexempt employees. Employees who are on the management monthly payroll.	Ties into classification required by federal law. Clear delineation of management.

Fig. 20.1 Unacceptable and Acceptable Classifications

the area of greatest variation among insurers, and even within the same insurance company as its policies and strategy change in response to market conditions.

Certain generalizations can be made. The larger the group, the higher the maximum amount of insurance permitted. The amount of insurance should bear some relationship to the need for income replacement. Since the need for insurance is very personal, this is usually accomplished by relating the amount of insurance to salary or job title. An exception is the typical union-negotiated contract which usually provides a flat dollar amount for all employees. The schedules in Figure 20.2 are merely illustrative. They are not meant to connote maximum amounts of coverage which could be available in particular cases.

For relatively small groups with 25 to 100 employees, schedules like those shown in Figure 20.2 should be generally available. As groups increase in size, coverage of up to four to five times salary, with a maximum of $250,000 or more, may be available. Groups with a favorable history of claims experience may be able to obtain higher coverage than those with poor or no experience.

In some circumstances, it may be possible to obtain higher maximum benefits than the group's size would otherwise warrant by submitting evidence of insurability. This practice, which is not prohibited for groups with ten or more employees, is most often found in trade associations or professional association plans. The insurance company will agree to provide a "guaranteed

Classification	*Amount of Insurance*
Corporate officers	$50,000
All other exempt employees	$25,000
All other employees	$12,500
All exempt employees	200 percent of annual base salary rounded to next highest $1,000, not to exceed $150,000.
All other employees	100 percent of annual base salary, rounded to next highest $1,000.
Annual salary:	Amount of insurance:
At least $9,000	$10,000
$10,000 but less than $12,000	$12,000
$12,000 but less than $15,000	$15,000
$15,000 but less than $20,000	$20,000
$20,000 but less than $30,000	$40,000
$30,000 but less than $50,000	$50,000
$50,000 and over	$75,000

Fig. 20.2 Amounts of Coverage

issue" amount to all otherwise eligible individuals with greater benefits available only on an individually underwritten basis. For example, a small employer may be offered the following choices under a trade association plan:

Schedule I	*Schedule II*
Life insurance equal to 100 percent of basic annual salary. Maximum benefit $75,000.	Life insurance equal to percent of basic annual salary. Maximum guaranteed issue amount of $100,000. With satisfactory evidence of insurability, maximum may be up to $200,000.

From the employees' point of view, schedules based on salary are most desirable since they adjust automatically to increased earnings. Schedules such as the third type in Figure 20.2, however, can be inequitable since a $1 difference in salary can change the amount of insurance by thousands.

Flat dollar schedules (such as $10,000 for every employee) were once fairly common but are now largely limited to union groups. Unions in general have not negotiated rich group term life programs.

Cost Considerations. The volume of insurance is, of course, a major determinant of the cost of coverage but what is more important is the age and sex of the employees in the group. As explained in Chapter 21, the cost of group term life is determined by measuring the exposure to risk by age and sex. The higher the average age of employees with high amounts of insurance, the higher the average cost. Conversely, the greater the distribution of risk on female employees, the lower the cost.

As long as an employee group has a relatively stable age and sex distribution, the average cost will remain stable. In a growing company with younger employees joining the group, the average rate may decrease. However, where the group is aging, the cost will increase, giving rise to the practice of decreasing the amount of insurance for employees over age 60 or 65.

At these later ages, an employee has often accumulated substantial balances under a profit-sharing plan or thrift plan, or (as discussed later in this chapter) may be entitled to survivor annuity protection under a pension plan. Under these circumstances, the need for group life insurance coverage can diminish.

Until the 1978 Amendments to the Age Discrimination in Employment Act of 1967 (ADEA), it was common to reduce coverage for older employees and to discontinue coverage at age 65. A typical schedule was to reduce coverage by 20 percent at age 60, with a full phaseout at age 65 which was usually the normal retirement age.

The law now generally prohibits involuntary termination of employment before age 70. Coverage cutbacks at earlier ages cannot be greater than justified by the increase in cost of coverage. Under existing regulations, three approaches to cutbacks are permitted:

1. *Year-by-year direct relationship between increased cost and reduction.* For example, if the cost of continuing an amount of insurance increases by 8 percent between ages 60 and 61, then the amount of insurance can be cut back 8 percent. In a schedule based on salary, the employee must still receive any increased benefit due to salary increases. The increased benefit can then be adjusted downward based on age.
2. *Five-year average.* The benefit reduction factor can be calculated on five-year average cost increases. For example, benefit reductions for employees between ages 60 and 65 can be based on the increase in the average cost for ages 60 to 65 as compared with ages 55 to 60.
3. *Benefit package approach.* Instead of cost-justifying age reductions on a benefit-plan-by-benefit-plan approach, an employer can (subject to some important limitations) cost-justify age-related adjustments with respect to the entire package of employee benefit plans that cover an employee. Within the package, one type of benefit (e.g., life insurance), can be cut back more than could be individually justified if another type of benefit (e.g., disability protection), is cut back commensurately less. The usefulness of the benefit package approach is, however, limited because of the following restrictions:

   —Retirement and pension plans cannot be included in the benefit package for this purpose.

—Health benefits cannot be cut back by an amount greater than could be justified on the benefit-by-benefit approach.

The existing regulations were promulgated by the Department of Labor. Responsibility for enforcement of the ADEA has been transferred to the Equal Employment Opportunity Commission (EEOC). The EEOC has indicated that it may not fully accept the present interpretive regulations. This area should be carefully monitored for further changes.

Employee Cost Sharing. It is quite common today, particularly in the case of collectively bargained plans, for employers to pay the entire cost of group term life insurance. But there are still many plans, referred to as contributory plans, where a portion of the premium is paid by employees, usually through payroll withholding. Here the cost of the plan is shared between the employer and the employees.

Aside from administrative simplicity, probably the most important advantage of employer-pay-all arrangements is the income tax advantage. Premiums paid by employers are tax deductible, whereas premiums paid by employees are not. And as explained later in this chapter, employees are not required to recognize any taxable income on the first $50,000 of employer-paid group term life insurance.

Aside from the obvious economic advantage to the employer of having employees absorb part of the cost of the benefit, the most significant advantage of contributory coverage is that employees who do not really need the insurance will tend not to take it. This avoids wasting employer premium dollars on unmarried employees without dependents or others who for various reasons do not need the coverage.

Where basic coverage is contributory, the contribution rate can be set at a uniform amount per thousand of coverage regardless of age, or the rate can be age related. The former arrangement is quite favorable for older employees and, conversely, no great bargain for younger workers. Use of the latter arrangement can be restricted, in the case of older employees, by state laws limiting the maximum amount an employee can be required to contribute. For example, under some state laws employees may not be required to contribute more than $.60 per $1,000 per month for coverage.

A growing trend is for the employer to provide at its cost a basic level of coverage—one to two times salary. Employees are given the opportunity to buy at their cost an additional one to two times salary of insurance. Generally, a minimum number of employees must enroll in order to meet underwriting requirements.

Conversion Privilege. By state law, retiring employees or other employees who lost all or part of their coverage may be able to convert the term coverage to an ordinary life insurance policy. The full conversion privilege is detailed in the discussion of legal requirements later in this chapter. They are summarized as follows:

The full amount of discontinued coverage can be converted if the employee ceases to be a member of an eligible class (i.e., promotion to foreman ends coverage under a collectively bargained plan) or terminates employment, including by retirement.

If the policy terminates, a more limited conversion privilege is available to employees who have been insured for at least five years.

The drawback of the conversion privilege for retiring employees, in particular, is cost. The ordinary life policy is issued without medical underwriting but at the full premium based on the employee's age. The cost of conversion is usually prohibitive for a retiring employee.

Since group term life has no cash values that can be used to buy paid-up coverage, the retired employee may lose all life insurance. In theory, the retired employee may have a lesser need for coverage. He may also have insurance from other sources. But for many employees, retirement brings an end to all substantial lump-sum death benefit protection. A retiree will, however, often have continued death benefit protection as a result of joint and survivor arrangements under a pension plan.

Accidental Death and Dismemberment

Accidental death and dismemberment insurance (AD&D) provides special benefits in the event of accidental death or loss of sight or use of a limb. Because the incidence of claims is fairly low, the cost is minimal—$.04 to $.06 per $1,000 of insurance per month.

The most common approach is for the amount of AD&D to equal the amount of group term life. In this, AD&D resembles a double indemnity provision in an ordinary life policy.

Because of the low premium, insurers will generally offer AD&D only to group life insurance policyholders. If the group is in a standard-risk industry, coverage is "twenty-four hour," that is, both on- and off-the-job accidents are covered. Where above-average occupational risks are known to be common in an industry, occupational accidents may be excluded. Such accidents are covered by workers' compensation laws.

Occupational AD&D coverage is available from most insurance companies at a higher premium, except for very hazardous occupations.

Excluded Risks. Because of the difficulties inherent in determining the degree of accident involved in certain instances, death or losses from the following are usually not covered:

- Suicide or attempted suicide while sane or insane;
- An act of war, police action, or participation in an act of insurrection or civil disobedience;

- Ptomaine poisoning or other infection or bacterial disease except when contracted as a result of an accidental injury;
- Participation in a felony;
- Mental or physical disease;
- Air travel on noncommercial flights;
- As noted previously, in some instances, job-related accidents are excluded.

Benefits. The losses incurred determine the amount of benefit paid. The usual schedule provides the following:

Loss	*Benefit*
Death	100 percent of principal amount
Loss of eye	50 percent
Loss of hand at or above wrist	50 percent
Loss of foot at or above ankle	50 percent
Multiple loss	100 percent

Business Travel Insurance. As an alternative to paying for airport flight insurance, many companies have arranged business travel insurance. Generally, any accident that occurs while an employee is involved in travel on company business is covered. In some cases, routine commuting is also covered.

In recent years, there has been a modest trend away from AD&D in favor of twenty-four-hour travel accident insurance, particularly among salaried employees.

The amounts of insurance are substantial—$200,000 or more per employee. An overall maximum limit on losses incurred by more than one employee is usually imposed.

In addition to the usual AD&D restrictions, travel in "war zones" may be excluded. Special restrictions may apply to company planes.

Underwriting Considerations. This type of coverage is similar to casualty insurance in that underwriting rules involve the numbers of individuals covered and the amount of business travel rather than the age and sex of the individuals. As in the case of group term life insurance, AD&D may be offered on an employee-contributory basis.

Group Paid-Up Insurance

As discussed previously, the one serious inadequacy of group term life insurance is the absence of a permanent insurance element to provide protection at termination of employment or retirement.

One approach, which insurance companies promoted in the 1950s and 1960s, is group paid-up. Because of the disadvantages indicated below, group paid-up has not been used extensively.

Essentially, group paid-up is similar to an ordinary life policy. A principal amount of coverage is specified. In the first year, the full amount is term insurance. Each year a portion of the premium buys a unit of paid-up coverage. As the paid-up coverage increases, the term portion decreases. The amount of paid-up coverage purchased each year depends on the age of the employee.

Because of Internal Revenue Service rules, the employer usually pays the term cost and the employee pays the premium for paid-up units. In theory, the employer's cost will decrease as more and more of an employee's coverage is paid up. The employee, on the other hand, has paid up permanent insurance when employment terminates. When the paid-up amount is less than $250, a cash-out is usually made in place of continuing the benefit.

Disadvantages. One significant disadvantage is the complexity and cost of administering this type of plan as opposed to term coverage. Dollars used for administration could be used for increased term coverage. The use of premium dollars to invest in paid-up insurance raises the same questions as term versus ordinary insurance arguments in individually purchased policies.

Another problem area is that older workers entering the group may not accumulate enough paid-up insurance. Employers may feel obligated to continue additional term coverage on retirees.

Tax Problems. The issuance in 1979 of the present IRS regulations pertaining to group life insurance (discussed later in this chapter) further discouraged traditional group permanent plans of the type described above. The regulations now prohibit including permanent insurance in a group term plan unless each employee has the right to decline the permanent coverage and if it is declined, the term coverage amount is not reduced.

Survivor Benefit Plans

Various sources of income replacement for an employee's family in the event of preretirement death have been discussed earlier in this chapter—Social Security, group life, and AD&D insurance. Other sources will be discussed later—including death benefits under qualified pension and profit-sharing plans.

While these programs may provide generous benefits, they have limitations for estate planning purposes:

1. Group life insurance, AD&D, and similar benefits are usually paid in a lump sum. The sudden acquisition of a large sum may produce a false sense of security in a family that is not used to handling more than a regular paycheck.
2. Group life insurance is generally related to compensation which does not necessarily correspond to the needs of the individual employee. Younger

employees who have the greatest need for insurance often have the lowest amount of coverage.

3. Benefits available from qualified pension and profit-sharing plans are to a large extent a function of years of service and are usually insignificant for younger employees.

While an employer cannot resolve each employee's individual estate planning problems, there are alternatives to traditional benefit design which can relate death benefits closer to survivor income protection needs.

Designing a Survivor Income Plan. The basic approach to designing a survivor income plan is the same that management uses in establishing benefit levels under its other income replacement plans—defined benefit pension plans and long-term disability programs. The following steps are necessary:

1. Estimate the level of income a family would need to maintain its standard of living.
2. Subtract Social Security and any other employer-provided survivor benefits.
3. Adjust for estimated taxes and job-related expenses. The remainder is the employee's survivor income needs to be provided in whole or in part through employer-sponsored programs.
4. Determine the portion of these needs that the employer wishes to meet through a survivor income plan.

In net effect, a survivor income plan operates to provide replacement income in somewhat the same manner as a long-term disability plan, except that the triggering event is death rather than disability.

Typical Benefits. Using as a guideline the typical long-term disability income replacement ratio of 50 to 60 percent of compensation, offset by Social Security, a plan might provide the following benefits:

Spouse's benefit of 40 to 50 percent of final pay for life or until remarriage or until the deceased employee would have reached normal retirement age. An additional 10 percent for each dependent child, with a maximum limit of an additional 20 to 30 percent. Additional benefits are paid for children if there is no spouse at the time of the employee's death, or the spouse subsequently dies while they remain dependent. Benefits would be offset by Social Security benefits as of the date they first become payable. Plan benefits are not adjusted for subsequent changes in Social Security benefits, thus providing a measure of inflation protection.

Many variations are possible. Benefits may be paid for limited periods, for example five or ten years.

Structuring the Program. A common vehicle for funding a survivor income program is an existing group life insurance policy. An employee can be given the option of converting a portion of his existing lump-sum benefits into a survivor income benefit which approximates the family's needs. Alternatively, the employee is offered the option of purchasing insurance equal to additional multiples of salary with benefits paid by the insurance company as a survivor annuity.

A survivor income program can also be structured on a stand-alone basis, as a replacement for or a supplement to the group life program. Under this approach the benefit schedule would be structured as described above without reference to a group life insurance principal amount.

The plan could be entirely employer-paid, or contributory. If the latter, the employee contribution rate could be structured as a flat percentage of pay, or related more precisely to the risk for each employee. Since the latter depends not only on the employee's age but on the spouse's age and the ages and number of children, this approach can be complex if applied precisely. Relating the contribution rate to the number of dependents, as is sometimes done with group health insurance, might be an acceptable compromise.

Tax Consequences. The employee incurs imputed taxable income in the same manner as under a group term life program, based on the group term insurance equivalent of the benefit provided. As proceeds of life insurance, a significant portion of the benefits paid to beneficiaries are exempt from income tax. These tax results could differ if the protection is furnished other than through a life insurance company, as more fully discussed later in this chapter.

Term Life Insurance Under Defined Contribution Plans

While it is not common, group term life insurance may be found as part of a qualified money purchase, profit-sharing or thrift plan. During a member's early years of participation in these defined contribution plans, the death benefits available from the plan (i.e., the participant's account balance) are often quite small. This benefit increases with time to a substantial level as the member approaches retirement. This growth of death benefits, however, is often opposite to an employee's need for protection. In general, most employees will have a greater need for death benefit protection when they are younger and are facing a number of financial obligations, than when they are older and many of their obligations have been met. Group term life insurance can provide a convenient solution to this problem of coordinating death benefits with the employee's need. It can be used to provide a substantial death benefit during the early years of plan membership and can be decreased or eliminated entirely as the death benefit available from the individual's account balance increases.

Internal Revenue Service Limitations. It is important when including any life insurance as part of a qualified retirement program not to exceed the

IRS's "incidental" benefit limitations. Under a defined contribution plan, the IRS requires that the cost of providing group term life insurance for any one individual cannot exceed 25 percent of the aggregate employer contributions and forfeitures allocated to his account. In a profit-sharing or thrift plan, this limitation applies to the portion of the account balance which has not been accumulated for the time span necessary for distribution (usually two years). No limit applies to funds that have been on deposit for the required time period nor does it apply to voluntary employee contributions used to purchase insurance. The 25 percent limitation also applies to money purchase plans but it applies to all accumulated funds, not just those that have been on deposit for less than two years.

Allocation of Costs. Where insurance is provided, the participants' accounts must be charged with the cost of the insurance. The simplest way of doing this is to charge each participant's account for the same premium per $1,000 of insurance. While this is the easiest way of allocating costs it is not the most equitable since the actual cost of providing life insurance increases with age. A more equitable, but more complex, arrangement would result in charges to accounts being based on a variable schedule that reflects the employee's age.

In situations where the group life insurance coverage is elective in whole or in part by the participant, an age- and sex-related premium schedule is essential to guard against adverse selection and to make it economically feasible for younger employees to elect the coverage. Consideration should usually be given to making the insurance coverage voluntary in whole or in part. In this way the employees who do not want or need the insurance will not have to see their account balances reduced for benefits they do not desire.

Disadvantages. In general, it is usually more advantageous to provide group term life insurance benefits separately from any qualified retirement programs because of the following factors:

Taxable income. The value of the first $50,000 of insurance is not considered taxable income to the employee when the benefit is provided separately from a qualified plan. When the insurance is provided as part of a qualified plan, the value of all insurance gives rise to taxable income.

Higher tax rates. The rates used to determine the value of the insurance usually are higher where the insurance is part of a qualified plan. For example, a 40-year-old employee who has a group term life insurance benefit of $75,000 through a qualified retirement plan has taxable income attributable to that benefit of $331.50 ($4.42 × 75). Were this same $75,000 group term life insurance benefit provided outside of the plan, it would generate taxable income of only $69 ($2.76 × (75 − 50)). The basis for these tax computations is explained later in this chapter.

Limited flexibility. Another disadvantage of including insurance in the retirement plan is limited flexibility. The limited flexibility is due to the 25 percent limitation previously mentioned and the general need to relate premiums on behalf of any participant to funds otherwise available under the plan. If the insurance were provided outside of the qualified plan, the amount of insurance could be based on more flexible criteria such as an individual's compensation, job classification, or age.

WHOLE LIFE INSURANCE

Use in Defined Benefit Pension Plans

While group term insurance as part of a qualified plan is not very common, whole life insurance is much more so. This is particularly true in defined benefit pension plans with only a few participants.

Whole life insurance provides a way for a pension plan to provide a substantial death benefit for employees immediately upon entering the plan. This may be particularly important if there are less than ten employees in the company, in view of the tax and other difficulties in arranging appropriate group term life coverage for less than ten lives.

Function of Policies. Where whole life insurance is part of a defined benefit plan, the benefits are funded through a combination of the insurance policies and a separate fund often referred to as a *side* or *auxiliary* fund. When the assets used to provide plan benefits are divided between the cash value in the insurance policies and a separate trust or investment fund the plan is often referred to as *split funded*. At retirement the benefit is provided by the purchase of an annuity from the insurance company. Sufficient assets are withdrawn from the side fund to convert the ordinary life insurance policies to annuities which will provide the promised pension benefits.

Guaranteed Rate. The amount of the assets necessary to convert the whole life insurance policy to an annuity is a function of the policy's cash value and the annuity conversion rate. This rate is guaranteed at the date the policy is issued. Thus, the maximum cost at retirement of the pension that is being funded, in part, by the insurance policy, is guaranteed when the policy is issued. Of course, as new policies are issued, the guaranteed annuity rate for these new policies may differ from the rate guaranteed in previous policies.

Amount of Insurance. The amount of the whole life insurance purchased for any individual is usually a function of his anticipated retirement benefit. The IRS requires that the insured death benefit in a defined benefit plan be *incidental.* Incidental is defined as a death benefit that does not exceed 100 times the participant's expected monthly retirement pension. Most split-funded plans will provide life insurance equal to this 100 times maximum limit.

Example: A plan provides for a normal retirement benefit of 50 percent of final compensation and provides a death benefit equal to 100 times the expected monthly pension. Employee Smith enters the plan at age 30 with annual compensation of $12,000. Thus Smith's expected retirement benefits are $6,000 per year or $500 per month. An insurance policy with a face amount of $50,000 would be issued on Smith's life. In addition to the policy premium, the employer would also make a contribution to the side fund on Smith's behalf. The contribution to the side fund would be actuarially determined to provide that the side fund accumulated at retirement age on behalf of Smith would be sufficient, when added to the cash value of the $50,000 insurance policy, to convert the insurance policy to an annuity providing a monthly benefit of $500. The following year Mr. Smith's salary increases 10 percent to $13,200. His new expected pension is now $6,600 per year or $550 per month. In order to maintain the death benefits at a level of 100 times the expected pension, a new insurance policy with a face amount of $5,000 has to be issued. An increased contribution to the side fund will also be required; the increase being the amount necessary to accumulate to a sum at retirement sufficient to convert the $5,000 insurance policy to an annuity providing a monthly pension of $50. Salary increases in subsequent years will lead to additional policies and additional increases to the annual side fund contribution so that at retirement, Mr. Smith will have several individual life insurance policies to be converted to annuities.

Advantages and Disadvantages. Substantial death benefits in the early years of plan membership, guaranteed cash values, and annuity purchase-rate guarantees are the major advantages of a split-funded plan. There are, however, substantial disadvantages in providing whole life insurance as part of a qualified plan.

Cost considerations. One of the major disadvantages is the relatively high initial cost of whole life insurance. Although the premium remains level for the life of the policy, the issuance expenses are charged primarily against the first few premiums. Commissions on ordinary life insurance are typically about 50 percent of a policy's first-year premium and a substantially smaller percentage of the premiums in later years. Since new policies are issued annually, not only for the new plan members but also for the previous members whose expected benefits have risen due to salary increases, the total commission payout can be substantial.

Expenses frontloaded. Charging the bulk of the commissions and other administrative expenses against the first few premiums means that the cash value of the insurance policy the first year or two after its issue is relatively small or, in some cases, nonexistent. This in turn leads to significant cost if there is substantial turnover of employees during their early years of plan membership or shortly after substantial policies have been purchased by the plan on their lives. While the money that has been deposited in the side fund on behalf of these terminated employees can be used to help provide the retirement benefits for the remaining plan members, the funds which have been used to pay the first premium or two on an insurance policy yield little or no cash-value return due to the high front-end charges.

To alleviate this factor, it is sometimes possible to arrange with the insurance company that if a policy must be cancelled within, e.g., one year of issuance, the excess of the actual premium paid over the one-year term insurance cost will be refunded to the plan.

Tax consideration. Another disadvantage of the use of ordinary life insurance is the taxable income that accrues to the employees. This so-called "P.S. 58" cost is the value of the pure insurance protection provided the employee (i.e., face amount of policy less cash value). The value for each $1,000 of pure insurance is based on the participant's age and is usually determined under tables established by the IRS, which are explained later in this chapter. This value is deemed to be taxable income to the employee covered by the insurance. Were the same amount of pure insurance provided outside the plan through a group term life insurance plan the employee's taxable income would be considerably reduced or even eliminated.

Investment inflexibility. One final disadvantage of using whole life insurance is the lack of investment flexibility that the trustees have with the plan assets that accumulate in the form of cash values. These funds are not as readily available for the trustees to take advantage of investment opportunities as are the assets in the side fund.

Retirement Income Policy—An Alternative. An alternative to the split-funded arrangement is the retirement income contract. Retirement income contracts are used as the sole means of accumulating assets for a retirement benefit. Thus, in plans that utilize these contracts there is no side fund in addition to the policies. The policy premiums are the only plan cost. Because of this, the policies must generate much higher cash values than ordinary life insurance contracts. The death benefit is equal to the greater of the policy's cash value or its face amount. In the later years the former will exceed the latter.

It is important to note when an insured death benefit is provided, whether through whole life insurance or retirement income policies, the "pure" insurance protection (face amount less cash value) is analagous to decreasing term insurance. This is particularly evident in a retirement income policy where due to the large savings element of the policy the cash values exceed the face amount of the policy some years prior to retirement. Thus, where insurance protection is a prime consideration, retirement income policies are not as advantageous as whole life insurance. Where insurance protection is not that important, however, retirement income policies offer the simplicity and annuity-rate guarantees found in split-funded plans, plus eliminating the effects of variable investment performance (favorable or unfavorable) which can occur with a side fund.

Use in Defined Contribution Plans

Whole life insurance may be purchased through defined contribution plans as well as defined benefit plans. While virtually all defined contribution plans provide a death benefit equal to the individual's account balance, this balance is relatively small in the early years of plan membership. As in the case of defined benefit plans, whole life insurance is a means of providing a substantial death benefit in the early years of plan membership.

Function of Policies. From the participant's viewpoint, there is a substantial difference between the use of whole life insurance in a defined benefit plan and its use in a defined contribution plan. Under a defined benefit plan the purchase of whole life insurance does not have an impact on the pension benefit promised under the plan. In a defined contribution plan, the benefit under the plan is whatever can be provided from the account balance. To the extent that assets are used to pay for premiums on life insurance policies the ultimate retirement benefit available from the plan will be reduced.

Because the purchase of life insurance has a direct impact on an individual's account balance and because the individuals covered by the plan will have varying needs for insurance, it would be advisable to make the purchase of any life insurance under the plan an option for each individual plan participant. Those who desire the insurance protection can obtain it and those who have no need for it do not have to have their account balances reduced to pay for it.

At retirement or other termination of employment, the cash surrender value of the policy will be reflected in the participant's account balance. Typically, the policy will be distributed to the terminated participant along with his vested interest in other plan assets. Unless the policy is converted to an annuity contract within sixty days after its distribution, its cash value will be taxable to the terminated participant in the year of receipt.

Amount of Insurance. As in defined benefit plans, the total amount of life insurance provided must be "incidental." In a defined contribution plan, this means no more than 50 percent of the accumulated contributions and forfeitures may be used to pay whole life insurance premiums.

Profit-Sharing Plans. In the case of profit-sharing plans, the 50 percent restriction applies only to those funds that have not been on deposit for the period of time required by the plan for distribution (the IRS requires that funds be on deposit for a minimum of two years). Funds that have been on deposit for the required time period may be used entirely for insurance premiums.

Money Purchase Pension Plans. The 50 percent restriction applies somewhat differently to money purchase pension plans. Under this type of defined contribution plan, the 50 percent limitation applies to all funds regardless of the length of time they have been on deposit.

Disadvantages. The same disadvantages associated with whole life insurance in a defined benefit plan—high issuance expense, higher taxable income to the employee, and investment losses on early cancellation of the policy—are also present when whole life insurance is purchased through a profit-sharing trust. Moreover, application of the 50 percent limitation can be tricky.

Assume that a participant enters the plan in a year when there is a substantial contribution and uses 50 percent of the amount allocated to his account to pay the initial premium on a whole life policy. Since the contributions to many profit-sharing plans are discretionary, a large contribution in one year may be followed by little or no contribution in the next year. If this occurs in the above described situation, the policy may have to be cancelled or adjusted since the second year's premium, when added to the first year's premium, could very easily be more than 50 percent of the accumulated contributions and forfeitures. Cancellation after one year would result in little, if any, cash value being returned.

Use in Supplemental Death Benefits for Executives

Outside of the qualified pension and profit-sharing area, whole life insurance is generally used only in programs designed to provide supplemental benefits for an executive group. There are various reasons for entering into these arrangements, but basically they come down to a desire to provide either or both of the following:

- Pre- and post-retirement death benefit coverage in excess of that available to the executive under group term life and other broad-based plans of the company.
- Additional retirement income in excess of that available to the executive under the company's broad-based retirement plans.

Only the first of these objectives will be focused on in the discussion that follows.

Structure of Plans. There are three structures under which whole life insurance can be used to provide death benefit protection for an executive's family:

- The policy is completely owned by the executive; employer pays all or part of premiums
- Split-dollar arrangement
- The policy is entirely owned by the company, as a means of financing the payment of death benefits by the employer to the executive's family

It should be obvious that for the same policy on a given executive, the pre-tax cost to the employer and the executive combined will be the same under all three structures. The differences lie in the sharing of the pre-tax cost by the employer and the executive, and in the tax effects.

Employer-Paid/Employee-Owned. Under the first structure, the portion of the premium paid by the employer is tax deductible to it, and its cost is the after-tax expense of the premium payments. Conversely, the executive must report as personal taxable income the portion of the premium paid by the company. The net effect of the arrangement is much the same as if the company had simply given the executive additional cash compensation, which he used to purchase personal life insurance. Thus, this arrangement is not frequently encountered.

Split-Dollar. The second structure, split-dollar arrangements, is quite frequently used. As the name implies, there is a sharing of ownership of and benefits under the policy, and often, of premium payments. The original split-dollar approach was that the company owned the cash surrender value of the policy and in the event of preretirement death was entitled to a share of the death benefits under the policy equal to the cash surrender value. The executive owned the remainder of the policy death benefit. The current trend is for the corporation's interest to equal its aggregate premium payments. Thus, in the event of the executive's preretirement death, the company would recover all of its outlays and its cost would have been the cost of money, i.e., loss of earnings on the premium outlays. If the executive lives until retirement, the usual approach is for the company to borrow out of the policy an amount equal to its aggregate premium outlays, and then to turn complete ownership of the policy over to the retiring executive subject to the loan.

As to the executive, split-dollar has somewhat the effect of declining term insurance until retirement, at which point he becomes the owner of a whole life policy subject to loans. The effect of a declining amount of coverage year by year is usually reduced or eliminated by applying dividends on the policy for the purchase of additional insurance.

Under split-dollar, the executive must report as taxable income any excess of the value of the protection he had in a given year (usually determined by applying P.S. 58 rates to his share of the death benefits) over his share, if any, of the premium payments. But the company is not entitled to any tax deductions with respect to P.S. 58 costs reported by the executive as taxable income.

Nevertheless, the executive's tax burden will usually be considerably less than under a structure whereby he would be the full owner of the policy, without sacrificing all that much in the way of insurance protection. Split-dollar is usually less expensive for the employer as well. These cost considerations are discussed more fully in Chapter 21.

Employer-Paid/Employer Owned. Under the third structure, life insurance is used essentially as a corporate investment vehicle for the purpose of producing a gain (excess of policy death benefits payable to the company over its net premium outlays) for the purpose of defraying the employer's costs of paying uninsured death benefits to the employee's beneficiary. Thus, under this structure what the beneficiary receives is not regarded as the proceeds of life insurance with the result that the tax treatment to the beneficiary is not nearly as favorable as under the other structures. However, the structure might be much more cost effective for the employer (on an after-tax basis) than the others, since its benefit outlays to the beneficiary should be tax deductible whereas the gain it realizes from the insurance policy it owns on the employee's life should be tax free.

These tax considerations are discussed in greater depth later in this chapter. The cost advantages and disadvantages to the employer of the various structures are explored in Chapter 21.

UNINSURED DEATH BENEFIT PROVISIONS—DEFINED BENEFIT PENSION PLANS

ERISA Joint and Survivor Requirements

At Retirement Age. ERISA requires that all plans that provide for the payment of benefits in the form of a life annuity must provide for the payment of these benefits in a form having the effect of a qualified joint and survivor annuity.

Definition. A *qualified joint and survivor annuity* is an annuity payable for the life of the participant, with payments continuing to his or her spouse upon the participant's death. The continuation to the surviving spouse cannot be less than 50 percent nor more than 100 percent of the annuity payable during the joint lives of the participant and the spouse.

Eligibility. This benefit is required for all participants who are eligible to receive retirement benefits as a result of being eligible for normal retirement. The plan must provide that benefits will be paid in the qualified joint and survivor annuity form to all participants who have been married to the same spouse throughout the one-year period ending on the date of the individual's death unless he elects otherwise.

Election. The participant must be given a reasonable period before the annuity starting date, after having received a written explanation of the terms and conditions of the joint and survivor annuity, in order to elect in writing not to receive benefits in this form.

It is usual for a defined benefit pension plan to define the normal retirement benefit in terms of a single life annuity and to provide that the benefit will be paid to a married participant in the form of an actuarially equivalent qualified joint and survivor annuity unless the participant elects otherwise (*election out*). Thus the cost of the post-retirement survivor benefit is borne by the participant. In some cases, the employer absorbs part or all of the cost by imposing less than an actuarial reduction or no reduction at all. Where there is no reduction, the joint and survivor benefit becomes the standard form of benefit and there is no need for an "election out" provision; however, this is rare.

Preretirement Joint and Survivor Option. A plan may also be required to provide surviving spouse protection for employees not yet eligible for normal retirement.

Eligibility. ERISA requires that if a plan allows for the payment of benefits prior to the normal retirement age (i.e., early retirement), it must also provide for pre-normal retirement age surviving spouse protection. As with benefits payable after normal retirement age, in such a plan the death benefit must be made available to all eligible participants who have been married to their spouses for at least one year. This benefit (the *early survivor annuity*) must be available beginning on the later of the earliest retirement date under the plan or the date ten years prior to the normal retirement age. Thus, in a plan where normal retirement is at age 65 and early retirement is possible at age 50, an early survivor annuity need not be provided prior to age 55.

Electing in. Unlike the post-normal retirement age death benefit, this benefit need not be automatic upon reaching the eligible age. An eligible employee must be given a reasonable amount of time to elect to receive the death benefit protection (*election in*). It should be noted that if a plan does not have an early retirement provision it need not offer the early survivor annuity.

If a participant (1) dies after his normal retirement age while still in active service or (2) terminates after having qualified for an early retirement benefit (provided it is within ten years of his normal retirement age), but dies before benefits begin, he is deemed to have retired the day before his death and his qualified spouse is automatically eligible for a survivor annuity.

Cost considerations. As is the case for the post-normal retirement age benefit, the employer need not bear the cost of providing an early survivor annuity. As an alternative, the employer may require a reduction in the benefits ultimately payable upon eventual retirement of the employee in order to pay for the value of the death benefit protection. For example, the plan could provide that for each month an early survivor annuity election is in effect, the retirement benefit the participant eventually receives (assuming he lives until retirement) will be reduced by one-tenth of one percent. This reduction factor, which is merely illustrative, should represent the equivalent of the term insurance cost of providing what is really preretirement life insurance protection in annuity form.

To avoid the complexities involved in administering a participant-paid elective early survivor annuity benefit and what might be perceived as adverse employee reaction to resulting pension reductions, some employers have opted to bear the cost of providing this benefit. Where that is the case, it is sensible to provide the benefit to all eligible participants automatically, rather than making it elective.

EXAMPLE 1: Year-by-Year Age Differentials—Percent of Normal Form—50% Joint & Survivor

Participant's Age	*Spouse's Age*									
	60	*61*	*62*	*63*	*64*	*65*	*66*	*67*	*68*	*69*
64	85.4	86.0	86.5	87.1	87.6	88.1	88.7	89.3	89.8	90.4
65	84.3	84.8	85.4	86.0	86.6	87.1	87.7	88.3	88.9	89.5
66	83.1	83.6	84.2	84.8	85.4	86.1	86.7	87.3	87.9	88.5

EXAMPLE 2: Five-Year Age Grouping for Spouse's Age—Percent of Normal Form

Participant's Age	*Years Younger 1–5*	*Years Older 0–4*
64	86.0	88.7
65	85.4	88.3
66	84.8	87.9

Based on 6 percent interest and 1971 Group Annuity Mortality Table—Male. (Female ages set back five years.)

Fig. 20.4 Age Differential Factors Used in Adjustment Tables

Actuarial Factors. The reduction factors that will be applied to determine joint and survivor annuity payments may be dependent on both the actuarial assumptions used to estimate plan costs as well as on the age difference between the participant and the spouse. A plan will generally contain tables of reduction factors to be applied or to merely specify that actuarial equivalencies based on plan assumptions may be used. However, spurred by Revenue Ruling 79-90, many plans now incorporate tables of adjustment factors in the plan document.

The adjustment tables, based on the age of the participant at the time of election, may provide different factors for each year of difference between the participant's and spouse's age or may provide factors only for different ranges of age difference. An example of both types of factors is provided in Figure 20.4.

The factors applied for the early survivor annuity benefit (if employee paid) are dependent on the length of time for which this death benefit protection is in effect. Where reduction factors are included in the plan, they are typically represented by a percentage reduction for each month the death benefit protection is in effect. Typically, if the benefit is in effect from age 55 to normal retirement age at 65, the total reduction in the normal retirement benefit is in the range of 5 to 10 percent.

Timing of Elections. Although ERISA itself merely requires that a "reasonable" period of time be provided for making the "election out" or the "election in," IRS regulations provide very rigidly defined time frames for making (or revoking) elections, which vary with particular plan circumstances. There are also very detailed rules on the type of information which must be provided to participants at stipulated times with respect to these elections and their effect on his benefits. A plan administrator must be conversant with these regulations [1] in order not to inadvertently run afoul of the stringent ERISA requirements in this area.

Other Uninsured Death Benefits

There is no prohibition against plans providing either pre- or post-retirement death benefits which are more generous than the ERISA qualified joint and survivor annuity rules would require.

Accrued Benefit. In the case of preretirement death, plans could provide (and some do) for a death benefit payment equal to the present value of the participant's accrued pension benefit at date of death. If desired, this benefit could be limited to only the vested portion of the accrued pension benefit.

---

[1] Treas. Reg. § 1.411(a)-11.

Internal Revenue Service Limitations. The plan could also provide for an uninsured death benefit in an amount exceeding the present value of the accrued pension benefit—subject only to observing IRS requirements that ancillary benefits in pension plans be limited to amounts regarded as "incidental" under its rules.

Contributory Plans. If employees contribute to a pension plan, it usually provides, at a minimum, for the return of the employee's contributions plus interest in the event of preretirement death.

Benefits From Other Sources. Many employers believe that preretirement death benefit protection can be furnished much more efficiently through group life insurance and other arrangements outside of the pension plan. Tax considerations are involved, but more importantly protection levels under group life insurance plans can be geared to perceived employee needs at various compensation levels, family status, or ages. Accrued pension benefits are not a particularly good measure of the need for death benefit protection.

Post-Retirement Death. It is not uncommon for plans to provide a period certain for pension payments. For example, a plan might provide that if a pensioner dies within ten years of retirement, pension payments will be continued for the balance of that ten-year period to a beneficiary. Annuity guarantees of this type must be coordinated with the ERISA-mandated joint and survivor annuity requirement. Where the guarantee is not provided for as a matter of course, it is often provided for as an option. In that case, the participant pays for the protection by accepting an actuarial reduction in his benefit.

If the plan is contributory on the part of employees, a provision guaranteeing that aggregate pension payments will at least equal accumulated employee contributions is common.

UNINSURED DEATH BENEFITS— TAX-QUALIFIED DEFINED CONTRIBUTION PLANS

Even where life insurance is not purchased as part of a defined contribution plan, virtually all of these plans provide death benefits.

Distribution of Account Balance

In the great majority of cases, the death benefit is equal to the value of the participant's account balance upon death. Some plans, however, limit the death benefit to the vested percentage of the participant's account. While it would be technically possible to provide for foreiture of even a vested account balance at preretirement death (except as the ERISA early survivor annuity provisions might otherwise require), this is rarely seen in practice.

Some defined contribution plans also provide for a *terminal share* upon the death of a participant. A terminal share is a final contribution made to a participant's account which is typically based on his yearly service or compensation from the beginning of the most recent plan year until his death.

Forms of Payment

Death benefits from defined contribution plans may be paid out in any number of optional forms—lump sums, installments, or annuities. It is important to consider the tax consequences of various types of distributions prior to electing a payout option.

Joint and Survivor Options. ERISA makes no explicit distinction between defined contribution plans and defined benefit plans with respect to the joint and survivor annuity requirements discussed above. While the application of these requirements to defined benefit pension plans is relatively straightforward, that is not the case with defined contribution plans. Prior to ERISA, it was common for defined contribution plans to offer an annuity contract as an optional form for distributing benefits. Under ERISA, the IRS issued a regulation that provides that in order for a defined contribution plan to be able to offer benefits in any life annuity form, a qualified joint and survivor annuity must become the standard form of benefit distribution under the plan, with the more conventional forms such as lump sum or installment payments becoming elective options.

To avoid administrative and other difficulties which this approach would entail, many plans simply eliminated life annuities as a form of benefit distribution, which could be an unfortunate result for plan participants.

Recently, the Tax Court has held that this regulation is invalid and that ERISA still permits a life annuity to be an optional form of benefit.[2] Only if a participant actually elects to receive an annuity would the qualified joint and survivor annuity requirements have to be observed. It remains to be seen whether IRS will accept this decision, or whether it will continue to litigate the issue.

The regulations do provide that a defined contribution plan need not provide a preretirement early survivor annuity election (as previously discussed) if it provides a survivor benefit at least equal in value to the vested portion of the participant's account balance at date of death.

Insured Benefits

Some plan sponsors feel that defined contribution plans do not provide adequate death benefits during the early years of a member's plan participa-

---

[2] BBS Assocs., Inc., 74 T.C. 1118 (1980).

tion when his account balance is particularly small. An alternative or supplement to the uninsured death benefit would be to provide for an insured death benefit through the plan. The advantages and disadvantages of this alternative were discussed earlier in this chapter.

OTHER UNINSURED EMPLOYER-FURNISHED DEATH BENEFITS

$5,000 Tax-Exempt Benefit

The tax laws have long permitted an employer to pay up to a $5,000 tax-free death benefit to the beneficiary or estate of a deceased employee. Although the benefit is tax free to the recipient, it is nonetheless tax deductible to the employer.

While the value of a $5,000 benefit has of course been significantly eroded by inflation since it was first introduced, it is still an important item to bear in mind in structuring a death benefit package.

Eligibility. The tax exclusion is available whether the benefit is paid in a lump sum or in installments, but there are two significant restrictions on its use:

- The tax exclusion is not available for any amount which the decedent had a nonforfeitable right to receive while living. Thus, for example, it would not be available for deferred compensation payments to a beneficiary who survives an employee, if the employee would have received the payments in all events had he lived.
- It is not available for the survivor annuity under a joint and survivor annuity arrangement.

Exception. There is an important exception to the first restriction, and it concerns lump-sum distributions from tax-qualified pension, profit-sharing or stock bonus plans, or tax-sheltered annuities.[3] Even though a deceased employee had a vested right to receive the qualified plan benefit if he had lived, the $5,000 exclusion is still available for a lump-sum distribution to his beneficiary if he dies.

Thus, in the case of employers sponsoring tax-qualified plans under which lump-sum distributions to beneficiaries are permitted and commonly used, it would be redundant from the tax viewpoint for the employer to provide an additional $5,000 death benefit outside the plan. The $5,000 tax-free amount can be used only once with respect to any decedent.

---

[3] I.R.C. § 403(b)

Additional Benefits

Uninsured death benefits in excess of $5,000 can be paid by an employer, but will almost always be treated as taxable income to the beneficiary. Benefits of this type can be made available to selected employees without regard to anti-discrimination rules of the type applicable to tax-qualified retirement plans, or the underwriting and tax rules applicable to group insurance. There are, however, a number of special tax considerations applicable to plans of this type which are discussed later in this chapter.

SPECIAL LEGAL CONSIDERATIONS

State Group Life Insurance Laws

Group life insurance programs must be designed within the dual framework of IRS requirements for favorable tax treatment of employer-paid premiums and benefits and the group insurance laws of the state in which the contract is written. (The District of Columbia and Puerto Rico also have group insurance laws and should be considered "states" for purposes of this discussion.)

The federal tax rules are discussed later in this chapter. The following is a brief summary of the most important areas in which the states exercise control over group life insurance. While there are some differences in the laws and regulations of the fifty-two jurisdictions, use of the model laws and contract language developed by the National Association of Insurance Commissioners has brought a high degree of standardization. Important state legal requirements include:

Jurisdiction. Generally, the laws of the state in which a contract is delivered govern, although some states such as New York also regulate all contracts which are issued by an insurance company which is domiciled in that state. The practical importance of determining jurisdiction is that an employer with operations in more than one state may be able to avoid restrictive laws by having the contract delivered in another state. This is done to avoid the limits a few states impose on the maximum amount of group term insurance that can be written. (See discussion below.)

Eligible Groups. State laws prescribe the kinds of groups that can buy coverage. These may include:

- *Employer group.* The employer who holds the contract may be a corporation, a partnership, or a sole proprietor. Employees of subsidiary, affiliated, and associated companies can be covered under the same contract.
- *Multiple-employer groups.* There are several types of multiple-employer groups which may hold a group contract. In most states, voluntary trade

associations of employers in the same or related industry (home builders, automobile dealers, etc.) may form a group. Benefits for members of unions that negotiate on an industry or area-wide basis usually are provided through joint union and employer trusts (frequently called Taft-Hartley trusts).

- *Associations.* Most states permit group insurance contracts to be issued to a wide variety of voluntary associations, including religious, fraternal, and social groups and professional societies (doctors, accountants, etc.).
- *Public employee groups.* In many states, political subdivisions can hold a contract on the same basis as any other employer. In others, a specific legislative authorization may be required.
- *Labor unions.* A labor union or employee association that pays for benefits with its own funds and/or member contributions may hold a group insurance contract.

Eligible Employees. Where inclusion in a group is based on the employer/employee relationship, the term *employee* is generally broadly defined to include common-law employees, partners, sole proprietors, retired employees, and in some states, directors. Under some circumstances, independent contractors, such as insurance agents, may also be covered as employees.

Minimum Group Size. For an employer-sponsored plan, state minimum size requirements require from two to ten employees. In some states, the minimum size for trade association and other voluntary association plans may be 100 or more participants.

Participation. Generally, noncontributory plans, i.e., those paid for fully by the employer or other plan sponsor, must cover 100 percent of all eligible employees. Contributory plans must cover 75 percent of eligible employees. Eligible employees are those included in the classes of employees covered by the contract. The definition of an eligible class must be based on a condition pertaining to employment. For example, eligibility can be based on completion of a minimum period of service, membership in a union, job classification or title.

An exception to the minimum participation rules can be made to exclude employees who have religious objections to being insured. An employer faced with this situation should consult with legal counsel on the desirability of having such employees sign a waiver of insurance. Insurance companies usually request evidence of such a waiver to protect themselves against a claim from the employee's estate or from a spouse who did not share the same religious convictions.

If the plan is contributory, employees must enroll within thirty-one days of first becoming eligible. If insurance is declined and the employee changes his mind, evidence of insurability is required. However, plans are allowed to offer open enrollment periods occasionally during which the evidence of insurability requirements can be waived. The purpose of the evidence of insurability rule is to protect the insurance company against adverse selection.

Amounts of Insurance. At one time, close to 50 percent of the jurisdictions limited the amount of group term life insurance which could be provided for any individual. These restrictions have gradually been removed. At the present time only three states retain any restrictions:

State	*Maximum*
California	$50,000, applicable only to *trusteed* employer-provided plans
Texas	$50,000, or if compensation is at least $25,000, 20 percent of compensation not to exceed $100,000
Wisconsin	$100,000

Since the restrictions apply generally to contracts delivered in these states, it is common practice for an employer to have the contract delivered in another state in which it maintains a place of business.

Beneficiary. With the exception of a prohibition against the employer being named the beneficiary, state laws do not restrict the right of an employee to name the beneficiary of group life insurance.

Generally, the contract does spell out in a "facility of payment" section, how the insurance will be paid if the named beneficiary is dead or cannot be located. The usual approach is to permit payment to the employee's spouse, children, parents, or brothers and sisters, or as a last resort, to the employee's estate.

Conversion Privilege. When an employee terminates his employment or ceases to be an eligible member of a covered class of employees, his coverage under a group term life policy terminates. Under state law, the employee is generally permitted to obtain an individual ordinary life insurance policy of an amount equal to the amount of his previous coverage. The policy must be issued without evidence of insurability or medical examination. The premium is based on the individual's age on the effective date of the policy which is thirty-one days after termination of the group policy.

The conversion privilege is also available for employees who have been insured for at least five years on termination of the group term policy. However, the maximum amount that can be converted is the lesser of: (a) $2,000 [4] or (b) the amount for which he had previously been insured, reduced by the amount of group life which he becomes eligible for from any other policy within thirty-one days. Should the employee die within the thirty-one-day period in which the conversion privilege is exercisable, his beneficiary is entitled to a benefit equal to the amount to which he would

---

[4] This $2,000 maximum is applied only in the event the group policy is cancelled.

have been entitled under an individual policy to which the employee was entitled to convert.

In some states, the employee has the right to buy a one-year term policy instead of the ordinary life policy. The purpose of the conversion privilege is to allow an employee to continue insurance between jobs or after retirement. The difficulty, however, is that the cost of an ordinary policy at older ages may be prohibitive.

The employer is charged under an experience-rated contract for each employee who uses the conversion privilege.

Assignment by the Insured. Until recently, insured employees were not permitted to assign ownership of their group life insurance. However, as the amounts of insurance available increased, so did interest in removing the death benefits from the employee's estate. In response to this interest and to favorable IRS rulings, assignments of incidents of ownership are now generally permitted. At present, only three jurisdictions (Alaska, Delaware, and the District of Columbia) have not passed legislation which either expressly permits such assignment or does not prohibit it. A discussion of the estate tax considerations in such an assignment is provided later in this chapter.

Assignment by the Group Policyholder. Generally, the group contract itself is not assignable. However, if a business is sold or changes its form of doing business (partnership to corporation, for example), the insurance contract will generally permit an assignment to the new entity, subject to the insurance company's express written agreement. If a new contract had to be written, the coverage might have to be provided at full rates, without the benefit of the group's experience credits, even though the insured employee group remained the same.

Insuring Agreements. The group contract generally must contain a provision stating that the group policy, including any riders or amendments, and the application submitted by the contractholder and insured individuals (if any) constitute the entire contract. In addition, the policy provides that only an officer of the insurance company is authorized to amend the policy.

Incontestability. Except in the case of nonpayment of premium, an insurance company is prohibited from contesting an employee's coverage under a group term policy after coverage has been in effect for one year. For example, if an employee is mistakenly allowed to enroll under a class of employees in which he is not eligible to be included, his coverage will not be contested after it has been in effect for one year.

The validity of the group policy itself cannot be contested after it has been in force for one year, except for nonpayment of premium.

Grace Period. As with most insurance policies, the employer has thirty-one days from the due date to pay each premium. As long as the premium is paid, any claims incurred during the grace period must be paid.

Certificate of Insurance. Each employee must receive a brief description of the most significant group policy provisions, a statement of the amount of his insurance, and a statement of any circumstances under which benefits may not be paid.

ERISA Requirements

Group life insurance plans are "welfare plans" under ERISA and are subject to the reporting and disclosure requirements of Title I. If the plan covers 100 or more employees, an annual filing (Form 5500) is due to the Department of Labor.

Employees must receive summary plan descriptions. This requirement is usually met by the certificate of insurance, supplemented by a booklet written in layman's language. (See Chapter 5 for a full discussion of ERISA disclosure requirements.)

SPECIAL TAX CONSIDERATIONS

Group Life Insurance—Income Taxes

Death Benefit Proceeds Exemption. Generally, as long as it can be established that death benefit proceeds are in the nature of life insurance, they will be wholly excludable from the beneficiary's gross income.[5] This exclusion will apply whether the beneficiary is a corporation, partnership, individual, or the insured's estate and regardless of who paid the premiums and who owned the policy. It will apply whether proceeds are paid from group permanent or group term. And, with regard to term insurance, it will apply whether the policy is provided under a Section 79 plan (as discussed below) or under a tax-qualified retirement plan such as a profit-sharing plan.

While the exclusion is clearly available for death benefits paid by the insurance company issuing a group life policy, it is not at all clear that it would be allowable for benefits paid from a self-insurance vehicle such as a Section 501(c)(9) trust (see the discussion later in this chapter).

Installment Payment. The exclusion does not apply to interest earned under an arrangement whereby policy proceeds are held by the insurer at interest subsequent to the death of the insured. But as discussed below, a surviving spouse can exclude up to $1,000 a year of the equivalent of interest

---

[5] I.R.C. § 101(a).

under an arrangement whereby policy proceeds are paid in installments or as an annuity.

In cases where proceeds are paid to a beneficiary in installments, the principal amount of insurance (usually total amount of the proceeds payable at insured's death) will be prorated over the payment period. The portion of each installment payment which is equal to the prorated amount will be excluded from the beneficiary's gross income as a return of principal. Any amount received in excess of such prorated amount is to be treated as interest and, therefore, taxable to the beneficiary as ordinary income. If, however, the beneficiary is the surviving spouse of the insured, such spouse is allowed to exclude as much as $1,000 of such interest each year in addition to the prorated principal amount. This $1,000 of interest may be excluded once a year for each insured no matter how many policies are in existence on the life of that insured.

Surviving Spouse Exclusion. The $1,000 exclusion for benefits paid to a surviving spouse may be illustrated by the following example.

Example: Upon the death of her husband, Mrs. *A* (surviving spouse) elects to receive the insurance proceeds with respect to her husband in ten annual installments based on a guaranteed interest rate. The life insurance proceeds amounted to $100,000. Each of the ten annual installments would be paid to Mrs. *A* in the amount of $11,200 (based on a guaranteed interest rate). The prorated amount is $10,000 ($100,000 ÷ 10). Due to earnings of the insurer in excess of those necessary to pay guaranteed installments, the second payment from the insurer amounted to $12,000. This exceeds the guaranteed payment by $800. The amount to be included in the gross income of the surviving spouse would be determined as follows:

Fixed payment (includes guaranteed interest)	$11,200
Excess interest	800
Total payment	12,000
Prorated amount	10,000
Excess over prorated amount	2,000
Annual excess over prorated amount, excludable by a surviving spouse	1,000
Amount includable in gross income	$ 1,000

Section 79 Rules (Taxation of Employees). The cost of group term life insurance protection provided to an employee prior to retirement by his employer will generally be tax exempt in amounts up to $50,000 of coverage.

Eligibility. This exemption is available to the employee only if:

- Coverage is on the life of the employee under a plan of group term life insurance, and is provided as compensation for services rendered by the insured in his capacity as an employee.
- The insurance is carried by the employer of the insured.

Aggregation of coverage. In cases where an employee holds more than one job, he must combine all group term coverage and may not exclude the cost of more than $50,000.

Employee contributions. If the employee's coverage is greater than $50,000, the excess will be taxable as personal services income. If, however, the employee has contributed toward the cost of the insurance, his entire contribution is permitted to be allocated to coverage in excess of $50,000. He may, therefore, subtract whatever he contributes from the amount he would otherwise be taxed on. Employees are not, however, permitted to carry over from year to year any portion of their contribution which is unused for this purpose.

Calculation of tax liability. The cost of coverage which is taxable to the employee is calculated on a monthly basis as follows:

- Determine total amount of group term life insurance coverage on the life of the employee in each calendar month of his taxable year (or average at beginning and end of a month in which a change occurs).
- Subtract $50,000 from each month's coverage.
- If there is any remainder, the appropriate rate, from the table below, is to be applied to such remainder for each month. (See Figure 20.5 below, for the monthly premium rates.)
- If there have been any employee contributions for the year, subtract the total of such contributions from the *sum* of monthly costs.

Example: B is an employee of Company *X*. He is thirty-two years old. Company *X* carries group term life insurance on the life of Employee *B*. *B* contributes $10 per month towards this coverage. The amount of the policy is $175,000. The beneficiary of the life insurance policy is Employee *B*'s wife. The amount that is taxable to *B* is computed as follows:

1. Total amount of group term life insurance coverage on the life of *B* in each calendar month of his taxable year	$175,000.00
2. Subtract allowable exclusion	50,000.00
3. Remainder	$125,000.00
4. Apply appropriate rate (in this case, $ .10 per 1,000) for monthly cost of excess amount	12.50

5. Multiply by 12 for annual cost		150.00
6. Subtract annual contribution by *B* ($10 × $12)		120.00
7. Amount taxable to *B*	$	30.00

Thus, the employee's taxable amount is determined according to the amount of coverage provided to such employee over his tax year. This determination does not depend upon whether or not premiums are actually paid by the employer during that taxable year, or how much those premiums were. Figure 20.5 below sets forth the rates to be used in calculating the cost of excess group term life insurance protection. For purposes of this calculation, apply the rate for the employee's attained age on the last day of his taxable year. In the case of an employee who has an attained age of over 64, use the rate applicable to those in the age 60 to 64 bracket.

Five-Year Age Bracket	*Cost of $1,000 of Protection for One-Month Period*
Under 30	$ .08
30 to 34	.10
35 to 39	.14
40 to 44	.23
45 to 49	.40
50 to 54	.68
55 to 59	1.10
60 to 64	1.63

Fig. 20.5 Uniform Premiums for $1,000 of Group Term Life Insurance Protection

Exception: the $50,000 exemption is not available in cases where group term life insurance is purchased under a qualified pension or profit-sharing plan. No part of such cost is permitted to be excluded from the employee's gross income.

Special exemptions. There are also certain cases where the cost of group term life insurance will be tax exempt to the employee even for amounts over $50,000. Exceptions to the $50,000 ceiling are:

- The employee has terminated employment with the employer and has attained retirement age or become permanently disabled.
- The employer is the beneficiary under the policy (unless employer is required to pay proceeds to beneficiary or estate of employee).
- The designated beneficiary is a charitable organization (in which case no charitable deduction is allowable for such designation).

The first exception is quite significant. In effect, the provision of continued group life insurance coverage after retirement never results in any taxable income to the employee. Consider two situations. Under one employer's plan, a particular class of employees is furnished with $150,000 of employer-paid group life insurance, which continues at that level until retirement and then terminates. Under another employer's plan, the arrangement is the same except that the insurance continues after retirement and thus, will eventually be paid to a beneficiary. At any age prior to retirement, employees under both plans report the same amount of taxable income, i.e., the Figure 20.5 rates applied to $100,000 ($150,000 – $50,000) of coverage. After retirement, neither reports any taxable income even though under the second plan the $150,000 of coverage continues until death.

Internal Revenue Service requirements. In order for an arrangement to qualify as a plan of group term life insurance within the meaning of Section 79 (thus qualifying for the income tax benefits explained above), a number of technical requirements must be met.

1. *Plan design.* The most significant is that the insurance must cover a group of employees, and that the amount of insurance furnished to each employee is determined under a formula which precludes individual selection. The formula must be based on factors such as age, compensation, years of service, or position, or in a contributory plan, it can be determined on a limited number of alternative schedules that are based on the amount each employee elects to contribute.
2. *State laws.* Another requirement is that Section 79 does not apply to any amount of insurance in excess of the limits under applicable state law on the amount of insurance that can be provided for an employee under a single contract of group term life insurance.
3. *No anti-discrimination rules.* Provided the prohibition against individual selection is observed, and provided that the covered group includes at least ten full-time employees, there are no anti-discrimination coverage requirements of the type applicable to tax-qualified retirement plans. Thus, for example, a plan could provide insurance of five times salary for the officer group, and one times salary (or no insurance) for all other employees. Or it could provide $250,000 of insurance for employees earning more than $40,000 and $25,000 of insurance for all other employees.
4. *Fewer than ten employees.* If the covered group includes fewer than ten full-time employees, special rules apply:

- All full-time employees of the employer must be covered, except those who cannot provide satisfactory evidence of insurability if the plan requires it.
- Evidence of insurability, if required for eligibility to participate or amount of insurance, must be limited to a medical questionnaire. A physical examination cannot be required.

- The amount of insurance must be computed either as a uniform percentage of compensation, or on the basis of coverage brackets under which no bracket may exceed two and one-half times the next lower bracket, and the lowest bracket must be at least 10 percent of the highest bracket. Exceptions are provided which permit reduced coverage for employees who cannot present satisfactory evidence of insurability (if required), and which permit separate brackets for employees over age 65.

An example of a coverage schedule that is acceptable for a less-than-ten-lives group is:

Compensation	*Amount of Insurance*
Less than $20,000	One times salary
$20,000 but less than $40,000	Two times salary
$40,000 and over	Three times salary

But in a recent ruling,[6] the IRS considered a schedule of the type illustrated above under circumstances where in fact there were no employees with salaries in the middle bracket range ($20,000 to $40,000), and there had not been any in recent years. The IRS held that under the circumstances there were in reality only two brackets: one times salary and three times salary. That was unacceptable, because the two and one-half times rule was violated.

5. *Adverse tax consequences.* If treatment under Section 79 is lost because of violation of this rule or any of the other rules summarized above, the tax effect on the covered employees is significant:

- The exemption for the first $50,000 of coverage would be lost;
- Taxable income inclusion would be based on the actual cost of the coverage, rather than the Figure 20.5 amount;
- Retired employees who retain coverage would have to recognize taxable income.

Plan With Permanent Benefit. Section 79 treatment applies only to group insurance that provides no *permanent benefit,* as that term is defined in the regulations.

Definition. A permanent benefit is an economic benefit that extends beyond one policy year, such as a paid-up or cash surrender value. But the term "permanent benefit" does not include:

- A right to convert or continue life insurance after group life coverage terminates;

---

[6] Rev. Rul. 80-220, 1980-2 C.B. 35.

- Any other feature that provides no economic benefit to the employee other than current insurance protection;
- A feature under which term life insurance is provided at a level premium for a period of five years or less.

Combination plans. Term insurance can be combined with insurance providing a permanent benefit under the same group policy or arrangement (such as group permanent insurance explained previously in this chapter), but only if the following conditions are met:

- The policy or the employer designates in writing the part of the death benefit that is group term life insurance.
- The part of the benefit designated as the group term life insurance benefit is not less than the difference between the total death benefit under the policy and the employee's "deemed death benefit" (see below) at the end of the policy year.
- Employees may elect to decline or drop the permanent benefit.
- The death benefit amount designated as the group term benefit that is provided to any employee is not reduced because of that employee's election to decline or drop the permanent benefit.

The term "deemed death benefit" (DDB) is defined in the regulations that provide the rules to be followed in allocating the premium paid under the policy between the permanent benefit and the group insurance benefit. Those highly technical rules are explained in Chapter 21.

Application of tax rules. The permanent benefit is not eligible for Section 79 treatment. Its cost is taxable to the employee to the extent paid by the employer. The group term life benefit is entitled to Section 79 treatment if the tests summarized above are met.

Example: Under a group plan, an employee is furnished with $70,000 of group term life insurance without charge. The employee is also permitted to purchase units of paid-up permanent life insurance at a cost specified in the arrangement. The amount of term insurance provided is not affected by whether or not the employee elects to take the permanent benefit. Assume that all of the conditions (summarized above) for permissible inclusion of a permanent benefit in a group life plan are met.

The employee is age 47, and elects to take the permanent benefit at a cost to him of $150. By applying the formula set forth in the regulations for allocating the premium for the entire coverage between the permanent and term elements, the cost of the permanent benefit is determined to be $350. The amount of taxable income required to be reported by the employee is determined as follows:

Cost of permanent benefit	$ 350	
Less: Amount paid by employee	150	
		$200
Term insurance coverage	$70,000	
Less: Excludable amount	50,000	
Taxable coverage	$20,000	
Amount includable at Fig. 20.5 rate (20 × $.40 × 12)		96
Total amount of reportable income		$296

Dependent Insurance. Section 79 benefits are available only for insurance on the life of the employee, and not for any dependent coverage under the group life arrangement. Thus, an employee is taxable on the cost of any dependent coverage to the extent paid for by the employer, unless the dependent coverage can be regarded as "incidental." The regulations provide that the cost of dependent coverage is considered incidental if the amount of insurance payable on the death of a spouse or child does not exceed $2,000.

Tax Rules and Survivor Benefit Plans. The same basic income tax rules applicable to conventional group life plans are also applicable to survivor benefit plans assuming Section 79 requirements are otherwise met. But special computations are required where the survivor benefit plan does not specify a principal amount of insurance.

As discussed earlier in this chapter, a typical survivor benefit plan might provide that in the event of an employee's death a stipulated percentage of the employee's compensation will be payable to a surviving spouse for life, or for a stipulated period of years. If there are one or more dependent children, an additional percentage may be payable until the children attain a certain age. Other contingent benefits or restrictions on the benefits may be provided.

Present value of benefits. The regulations [7] provide generally that the present value of the promised benefits must be determined year by year (more precisely, monthly) for each covered employee. That present value is equated to a principal amount of group term life coverage. Thus, for example, if the present value of a 43-year-old's survivor benefit coverage were determined to be $80,000, the Figure 20.5 rate for the 40 to 44-year-old age bracket would be applied to $30,000 ($80,000 – $50,000) to determine the amount includable in the employee's taxable income for that year. This assumes the employee has no other Section 79 insurance coverage which would absorb the $50,000 exemption.

The present value of the benefits can be computed based on conventional

[7] Treas. Reg. § 1.79-3(b).

actuarial techniques utilizing an interest discount and life contingency factors relating to the surviving spouse, children, and any other primary or contingent beneficiaries. The regulations require that the interest discount rate and mortality tables employed by the insurer be used for this purpose.

Similarly, in the event of the employee's death, the present value of the benefit streams must be determined to compute the amount of benefit payments that can be excluded from the beneficiaries' incomes as the proceeds of life insurance. As explained above, where tax-exempt life insurance proceeds are payable in installments, the principal amount is prorated over the expected period of payment. In addition, a surviving spouse receiving such payments is entitled to exclude from taxable income up to $1,000 per year of interest equivalent.

Example: Under a relatively simple plan, a surviving wife is entitled to receive $10,000 per year for life upon the death of her husband (the employee). At his death, the present value of the benefit stream is determined to be $140,000, and she has a life expectancy of twenty years. The amount includable in her taxable income each year is $2,000, computed as follows:

Annual payment	$10,000
Prorated principal amount ($140,000 ÷ 20)	(7,000)
Excludable interest equivalent	(1,000)
Taxable amount	$ 2,000

In more involved cases, where there is more than one beneficiary or there are contingent beneficiaries, or payments are guaranteed for some period of years, the determination of the present value (principal amount of insurance equivalent) is more complex, as is the computation of the proration of that principal amount among various beneficiaries and payment years. The regulations [8] provide detailed rules as to how the prorations are to be determined in complex cases.

Obviously, an employer sponsoring a survivor benefit plan must be prepared to furnish to employees and beneficiaries, or cause the insurer to furnish, the amounts necessary for the computation of their taxable incomes.

Group Life Insurance—Estate and Gift Taxes

Assignment to Remove From Gross Estate. The general rule is that group life insurance proceeds are includable, for federal estate tax purposes, in the gross estate of a deceased employee. That is true whether the death benefit proceeds are paid to the estate or to a named beneficiary.

[8] Treas. Reg. § 1.101-4(d).

But employees have an opportunity to keep the proceeds out of the gross estate by assigning all "incidents of ownership" in the insurance coverage to someone else. Since group term life proceeds are often a very major portion of an employee's potential estate, this possibility opens up a highly significant opportunity for tax saving through careful estate planning.[9]

Incidents of ownership. The phrase *incidents of ownership* is a term of art. Incidents of ownership include:

- The right to name or change the beneficiary;
- The right to assign the policy or revoke the assignment;
- The right to surrender or cancel the policy;
- The right to pledge the policy as security;
- The right to convert group term coverage to an individual policy upon termination of employment.

The above list is not necessarily all inclusive. This is a highly technical area in which details that might seem trivial can be all important. *Any* rights retained by an employee in group term coverage after an assignment is executed, no matter how inconsequential they may seem, will be sufficient to require inclusion of the insurance proceeds in the gross estate if the rights can be construed as an incident of ownership.

State laws. In order for an assignment of ownership of group term life insurance to be acceptable for estate tax purposes, the IRS requires that governing state law must permit assignment as most states now do.

Permitted by insurer. The insurance company must also permit assignment. Insurers have developed forms acceptable to them for making the assignments, which can be made available to employees.

Three-year rule. A very important estate tax rule provides that an assignment of ownership in a life insurance policy made within three years of death will not be effective to remove the policy proceeds from the gross estate of the assignor. Thus, only after three years have elapsed from the time an assignment of group life coverage is made can an employee be reasonably confident that this estate planning technique will be effective.

The term "reasonably confident" is used advisedly, since there are some remaining uncertainties, the outcome of which depends on the future attitudes of the IRS and the courts. One uncertainty is that an employee of necessity always retains the de facto ability to cancel group life coverage by terminating

---

[9] As a result of the enactment of an unlimited marital deduction for estate and gift tax purposes as part of the Economic Recovery Tax Act of 1981, the significance of the technique has been minimized where the beneficiary of the insurance is a surviving spouse.

employment. IRS has, however, ruled that this ability will not be construed as an incident of ownership.

Annual renewal. Another problem is that since group term life insurance policies normally extend for a one-year term and are then renewed, it had been feared that IRS might contend that each annual renewal is, in effect, a new assignment, with the result that it would never be possible to avoid the three years prior to date-of-death rule. In a recent ruling, the IRS held that annual renewal did not create a new assignment, reasoning that the net result of the arrangement was continuing life insurance rights and not the acquisition of a new policy each year.[10] It cited the employer's right of automatic renewal of the policy and the assignee's right to convert the group coverage to an individual policy.

Change in insurers. In a recent published ruling,[11] the IRS reversed its earlier adverse ruling in a situation in which, following the execution of an assignment, the employer switched its group life coverage to a new insurance company. The employee died within three years of the switch in insurers but more than three years subsequent to the execution of the original assignment. At the time of the original assignment, the employee had executed an agreement with his spouse that the assignment would vest in her not only all ownership rights under the present policy but also under any other group policy his employer may acquire.

The IRS has now ruled that a new assignment of ownership will not cause the policy proceeds to be included in the insured's estate if the new assignment was necessitated by a change in the employer's master insurance plan carrier and the new insurance arrangement is identical in all relevant aspects to the previous arrangements.

The ruling leaves unclear when IRS would consider a new assignment to have been "necessitated by a change in insurers." Also, it does not identify what terms of the new policy would have to be identical "in all relevant aspects." These issues may be addressed in subsequent rulings. Legal counsel should be consulted about the effect of a change in insurers on existing assignments of group term life insurance.

Assignment to spouse. The question of to whom a group life policy should be assigned is also quite important. Prior to the 1981 tax legislation, it was common practice for ownership to be assigned to the employee's spouse, who is also named as beneficiary. While this is a straightforward arrangement, it may serve only to defer rather than to eliminate an estate tax problem. Unless the policy proceeds are consumed by the surviving spouse, they will

---

10 Rev. Rul. 82-13, I.R.B. 1982-2.

11 Rev. Rul. 80-289, 1980-2 C.B. 270.

eventually be included in the spouse's gross estate, with significant estate tax liability potential.

Assignment to trust. A way of avoiding this result is to assign ownership of the policy to a trust which would also be named as beneficiary. The spouse can be given an income interest in the trust, the principal of which will ultimately pass to the couple's children or other heirs.

If properly structured, this arrangement can result in the insurance proceeds bypassing the spouse's gross estate as well. But use of a trust can result in gift tax problems, as discussed in the next section of this chapter.

Non-tax considerations. Non-tax considerations are also important in deciding on an assignment. For example, if an employee assigns all incidents of ownership to his spouse, is thereafter divorced, and then remarries, he may be precluded from providing group term life insurance protection for his new spouse because the former spouse retains ownership of the coverage.

While an assignment may be effective in removing policy proceeds from the employee's gross estate, it is likely, in most cases, that premiums paid within three years of the date of death will be included in the gross estate. This point is discussed in the section that follows.

Gift Tax Considerations. A gratuitous assignment of all incidents of ownership under a group life insurance policy is a gift subject to possible gift tax liability. But for gift tax purposes, life insurance is valued at its reserve value which is basically equivalent to cash surrender value. Since term life insurance has no cash surrender value, the assignment of group term life coverage normally does not result in any gift tax. At most, the value of the policy at date of assignment might be the amount of unearned premium, if any.

Premiums paid subsequent to assignment. Gift tax problems frequently arise with respect to subsequent premium payments on the coverage. If the group term coverage is entirely contributory (i.e., not employer-paid at all), and the assignee pays all premiums subsequent to the assignment, there is no problem. But that is the rare case.

More frequently, the coverage is either fully or partially employer paid. To the extent the coverage is contributory, the employee rather than the assignee continues to pay the premiums in some cases. Under these circumstances, gift tax complications can arise.

The IRS has ruled that where group term life coverage is employer paid, the employee continues to be subject to income taxation under Section 79 even though ownership of the policy rights has been assigned to another person.[12] It has further held that these premium payments by the employer

---

[12] Rev. Rul. 76-490, 1976-2 C.B. 300.

result in gifts by the employee to the assignee. And, of course, any direct payment of premiums by the employee is also a gift.

The IRS has not specified how the amount of the gift is to be determined where the premium is employer paid, but it seems reasonable to assume that the Figure 20.5 rates used for income tax purposes (as discussed above) should be acceptable.

Gift tax exclusion. To the extent that the gift amount that results is less than the $10,000 annual per donee gift tax exclusion amount, there is no particular problem. That, of course, assumes that the employee has not used all or part of the exclusion amount for other gifts to the assignee during the year. Although the $10,000 exclusion is only available for gifts of a "present interest" in property, and not for a "future interest," the IRS has held that the payment of premiums on an insurance policy owned by an individual is a gift of a present interest.

But if the policy is owned by a trust (which was suggested above as a possible estate planning device), the IRS will usually treat the premium payments as a gift of future interest. That means the payments would be taxable without regard to the $10,000 exclusion, although the availability of the unified credit against the gift tax liability could eliminate any actual tax liability for some period of time.

In an attempt to solve this problem, a technique has been developed where by inserting language in the trust agreement giving the beneficiaries the right to request distributions from the trust each year, a present interest might be created. While this approach has met with some success both in the courts and with the IRS, it is a rather artificial device in the usual case where in fact the trust has no assets out of which the payments to the beneficiaries could be made if they were demanded. Thus, ultimate acceptability of this approach should be regarded as an unsettled matter at present.

Retired life reserves. If assigned post-retirement coverage is funded by the employer through a retired life reserve technique (as discussed in Chapter 21), it is arguable that to the extent of the reserve a large taxable gift could arise at retirement when the employee's interest in the coverage usually becomes nonforfeitable. Some commentators have suggested that by incorporating noncomplete clauses and the like in the arrangement, it could be maintained that the employee's interest never becomes nonforfeitable, and thus, the large gift in a single year might be avoided. But the gift tax consequences of retired life reserve arrangements is an unsettled area, in which there are no authoritative pronouncements as yet.

It must be kept in mind that the fact that assignments of group life coverage may produce gift tax liabilities does not mean that the anticipated estate tax savings will not outweigh them.

Special Estate Tax Considerations. Where survivor benefit plans constitute a form of group life insurance, the same basic estate and gift tax considerations discussed above will apply to those plans as well. The structure of survivor benefit plans often is such that it can be contended that the employee never has any incidents of ownership in the coverage in the first place.

That contention can be made where the employee is automatically covered under the plan as a condition of employment and where the employee has no elections or discretion whatever as to the designation of beneficiaries or the amount and form of benefits they would receive. If the employee can successfully contend that he has no incidents of ownership, then no assignment is necessary to keep the value of the coverage out of his gross estate.

The courts have considered the incidents of ownership question with respect to the survivor benefit plan of a particular company under which employees had no discretion as to who the beneficiaries were or how much they were to receive, but could designate the time and manner of payment under some circumstances. The courts have split as to whether possession of that limited right constituted an incident of ownership sufficient to require inclusion of the value of the benefits in the gross estate.

Nevertheless, it seems possible through careful plan design to structure an arrangement that would result in employees having no incidents of ownership. Whether the potential tax saving is commensurate with the lack of flexibility which could result in an employee's ability to best determine how to structure protection for his particular family situation is a matter of judgment.

In summary, assignment of group life insurance coverage can result in significant estate tax savings for senior level employees with relatively large estates, but there are many difficult problem areas to be considered.

Whole Life Insurance

Benefits Paid From a Qualified Plan. Under qualified pension and profit-sharing plans an employee is generally not currently taxed on the employer's contributions to the plan. The employee pays no tax until such time as benefits are distributed or made available. However, if the plan provides for life insurance protection, the employee is deemed to have received a distribution each year equal to that part of the employer's contribution or trust earnings that has been applied during such year to provide insurance on his life.[13] He must, therefore, pay tax currently on the cost of that protection. This rule holds whether insurance is provided under a trusteed or nontrusteed annuity plan and whether or not it is provided under group permanent or individual cash value life insurance policies or term insurance.

The cost of life insurance coverage is taxable currently to the employee if, under the plan:

---

[13] I.R.C. § 72(m)(3).

1. Proceeds are payable to the employee's estate or beneficiary; or
2. Proceeds are payable to the trustee of the plan under an arrangement where the plan provides that the trustee must pay such proceeds to the employee's estate or beneficiary.

The participant is not taxed on the insurance cost in cases where the trustee has the right to retain any portion of the death proceeds.

Pure insurance protection. Where the plan owns whole life insurance policies (or retirement income policies), only the cost of the pure insurance protection is taxed to the participants on a current basis. The amount of taxable income is determined by use of the IRS's published *one-year term rates.* These rates are generally referred to as P.S. 58 rates and are set forth in Figure 20.6 below:

One-Year Term Premiums for $1,000 of Life Insurance Protection

Age	*Premium*	*Age*	*Premium*	*Age*	*Premium*
15	$1.27	37	$ 3.63	59	$ 19.08
16	1.38	38	3.87	60	20.73
17	1.48	39	4.14	61	22.53
18	1.52	40	4.42	62	24.50
19	1.56	41	4.73	63	26.63
20	1.61	42	5.07	64	28.98
21	1.67	43	5.44	65	31.51
22	1.73	44	5.85	66	34.28
23	1.79	45	6.30	67	37.31
24	1.86	46	6.78	68	40.59
25	1.93	47	7.32	69	44.17
26	2.02	48	7.89	70	48.06
27	2.11	49	8.53	71	52.29
28	2.20	50	9.22	72	56.89
29	2.31	51	9.97	73	61.89
30	2.43	52	10.79	74	67.33
31	2.57	53	11.69	75	73.23
32	2.70	54	12.67	76	79.63
33	2.86	55	13.74	77	86.57
34	3.02	56	14.91	78	94.09
35	3.21	57	16.18	79	102.23
36	3.41	58	17.56	80	111.04
				81	120.57

Fig. 20.6 "P.S. 58" Rates

Taxable income calculation. The calculation of cost is accomplished by applying the rate at the insured's age to an amount that is the difference between the policy's face amount and the cash surrender value at the close of the year. The rate to be used is that for the insured's age on his birthday nearest the beginning of the policy year. (Note: If consistently used, the IRS would probably allow use of the rate applicable for age attained at last birthday.) If, however, the insurance company's published premium rates for individual one-year term policies (initial issuance insurance) available to all standard risks are lower than the P.S. 58 rates, the lower rates may be used.

Example: A is a participant in a split-funded defined benefit pension plan under which he is covered by a whole life insurance policy providing a death benefit equal to 100 times his projected monthly retirement benefit. At the end of the year when *A* is age 43, the death benefit under the policy is $75,000 and its cash surrender value is $15,000. *A* must report taxable income determined by applying a term premium rate to $60,000 of coverage. At the P.S. 58 rate of $5.44 per $1,000 at age 43, the amount of income to be reported would be $326.40.

In cases where, subsequent to an employer's payment of the premium, an employee terminates service prior to the end of the year for which the premium was paid, he must include in gross income the annual term cost less the unearned premium credit which is reallocated to pay premiums for remaining participants.

Employee contributions. Where a plan provides for employee contributions, life insurance protection is deemed to have been paid first from employer contributions and trust earnings. Thus, unless the plan specifically provides that employee contributions are to be used to pay insurance costs, P.S. 58 costs are taxed to the employee.

P.S. 58 costs may, in some circumstances, be recovered tax free from the ultimate distribution of plan benefits. This point is discussed more fully hereinafter.

Taxation of Death Benefit Proceeds. When the employee dies prior to retirement and his beneficiary receives the policy death benefit in the form of a lump-sum cash payment, a portion of the proceeds will be income tax exempt as representing the proceeds of life insurance. The tax-exempt amount will be equal to the difference between the cash surrender value and the face amount of the policy. The cash surrender value amount will be regarded as a distribution from the plan, taxable in the same manner as uninsured death benefits from qualified plans (as explained hereinafter).

Example: Assume that *A* in the preceding example dies at the end of the year and the $75,000 death benefit under the policy is paid to his beneficiary. $60,000 will be exempt from income tax, and the $15,000 cash surrender value (along with any benefits distributable to the beneficiary from other plan assets) is subject to income tax under the rules applicable to uninsured death benefits from a qualified plan.

Installment distribution. If the life insurance policy proceeds are distributable to the beneficiary in annual installments rather than a lump sum, then each installment must initially be split between the portion attributable to the pure death benefit and the portion attributable to the cash surrender value. That is done in proportion to the division of the lump-sum value.

Taxation of the portion of the annual installment attributable to the pure death benefit is determined in the same manner as previously explained for group life insurance proceeds distributed in installments. Taxation of the remaining portion is determined in the same manner as for uninsured death benefits under qualified plans.

Example: Assume that in lieu of receiving the $75,000 of life insurance proceeds in the example above in a lump sum, the beneficiary (who is his surviving spouse) elects to receive the proceeds in ten annual installments of $10,000 each. $8,000 of each installment ($60,000/$75,000) is treated as attributable to the pure insurance protection and $2,000 is attributable to the cash surrender value. Of the $8,000 amount, $6,000 will be tax exempt as the proceeds of life insurance ($60,000 ÷ 10), and $1,000 will be exempt as the equivalent of interest payable to a surviving spouse. The remaining $1,000 will be taxable. The $2,000 attributable to the cash surrender value will be taxed in the same manner as uninsured death benefits from a qualified plan.

Eligibility. The exclusion for the pure death benefit element of the policy is available only where the premiums have been paid out of employee contributions or by employer contributions where the term insurance costs (P.S. 58 costs) were taxed to the participant. Thus, if under a noncontributory plan some portion of the insurance death benefit proceeds are to be retained by the trustee rather than distributed to the beneficiary (with the result that P.S. 58 costs are not taxed to the participant), then upon death no portion of the policy proceeds is excludable by the beneficiary.

Estate and Gift Tax Consequences. The estate tax treatment of the death benefit proceeds of a whole life insurance policy held by a qualified plan is determined in the same manner as for uninsured death benefits from a qualified plan. The fact that the source of the benefit is a life insurance policy, rather than other plan assets, does not result in any distinction for estate tax purposes.

Reference is made to the discussion of uninsured death benefits from a qualified plan for an explanation of the estate tax rules. The gift tax rules applicable to the designation of beneficiaries are discussed under this heading as well.

Uninsured Death Benefits Under Qualified Plans

Income Tax Treatment. Taxation of uninsured death benefits received by a beneficiary from a qualified plan is subject to basically the same rules applicable to benefits paid to a participant.

Thus, if the death benefits are received in the form of a qualifying lump-sum distribution, a beneficiary is entitled to essentially the same tax benefits (long-term capital gains treatment, ten-year averaging, tax-free rollover, exclusion of appreciation in value of employer securities) available to a participant. But the tax-free rollover provisions are available only to a beneficiary who is a surviving spouse. If the death benefits are paid in installments or as an annuity, the tax treatment is essentially the same as for a participant receiving benefits in that form.

As noted earlier in this chapter, a death benefit distributable in the form of life insurance proceeds is treated as an uninsured benefit to the extent of the cash surrender value of the policy.

There are, however, a number of special rules applicable only to a beneficiary. These are:

- $5,000 death benefit exclusion
- Recovery of P.S. 58 costs against death benefits
- Qualification of death benefit distribution for lump-sum treatment
- Interplay of lump-sum distribution rules and estate tax rules
- Income in respect of a decedent deduction

$5,000 death benefit exclusion. If the death benefit is distributed to the beneficiary in the form of a qualifying lump-sum distribution, it is eligible for the $5,000 death benefit exclusion which was explained earlier in this chapter. Thus, in determining the ten-year averaging tax (and long-term capital gain tax, if applicable), the $5,000 amount is treated as if it were an employee contribution to the plan. If, however, the beneficiaries of the deceased employee are also entitled to other employer-furnished death benefits that qualify for the $5,000 exclusion, it must be borne in mind that the $5,000 exclusion can be used only once. If more than one beneficiary is involved, it must be allocated among the beneficiaries pro rata to their benefit entitlements.

If the death benefit is distributable in a form other than a qualifying lump-sum distribution, the availability of the $5,000 exclusion depends upon whether, at the time of death, any of the participant's accrued benefits under the plan were forfeitable (i.e., not vested).

> *Example:* A profit-sharing plan has a ten-year cliff vesting schedule and Employee *A* dies after completing eight years of service with an account balance under the plan of $60,000. The plan provides that accounts are nonforfeitable in the event of termination of employment for death or

disability regardless of the ten-year vesting schedule applicable to termination for other causes. *A*'s beneficiary elects under the plan to receive the $60,000 in interest-bearing installments over a ten-year period. Since *A*'s benefits were forfeitable, the $5,000 death benefit exclusion is available and is treated as an employee contribution in determining the taxability of the installments to the beneficiary under the annuity rules discussed in Chapter 17.

If, on the other hand, *A* died after twelve years of service, when his account balance was fully vested, the $5,000 exclusion would not be available for death benefits paid in any form other than a qualifying lump-sum distribution.

Since benefits under qualified plans must be fully vested after the attainment of normal retirement age, this means that the $5,000 exclusion is available to the beneficiary of a deceased retired employee only if the death benefits are taken in the form of a qualifying lump-sum distribution.

Note that the $5,000 exclusion is available only with respect to deceased common-law employees and not self-employed persons. Thus, death benefits paid from a Keogh plan to the beneficiary of a deceased partner or sole proprietor are never eligible.

P.S. 58 costs. If an employee who dies prior to retirement was a participant in a qualified plan that provided death benefit protection via life insurance (such as a split-funded plan), the aggregate of the P.S. 58 costs included in the decedent's taxable income for all years can be deducted from the cash surrender value portion of the death benefit in determining the amount taxable to the beneficiary. The P.S. 58 costs are in effect treated as employee contributions.

If the participant dies after he has started to draw benefits under the plan, as for example in the case of a retiree with benefits in pay status, a beneficiary who is entitled to benefits upon the death of the retiree can exclude P.S. 58 costs only to the extent the retiree was able to exclude them in determining the taxability of his retirement benefits. In effect, the beneficiary can only step into the shoes of the retiree and continue to deduct any of the P.S. 58 costs that the retiree had not previously recovered if in fact he was entitled to recover them. See Chapter 17 for a discussion of the circumstances under which P.S. 58 costs can be treated as employee contributions in determining the taxability of retirement benefits.

P.S. 58 costs can never be treated as employee contributions with respect to an owner-employee under a Keogh plan.

Qualification of death benefits as a lump-sum distribution. The general rules for the characterization of a distribution from a plan as a qualifying lump-sum distribution (or a distribution eligible for rollover treatment) are discussed in Chapter 17. One special rule in the case of a death benefit is that if a retired or terminated participant has commenced to draw benefits in annuity or installment form, any remaining benefits payable to a beneficiary upon the death of the participant can nevertheless be treated as a qualifying lump-sum distribution if the beneficiary takes them in lump-sum form and the other tests for qualifying status are met.

Thus, for example, if *A* retires and starts to draw benefits from a profit-sharing plan in the form of installments payable for ten years and dies three years after retirement, his beneficiary will be eligible for qualifying lump-sum distribution treatment if she takes the value of the remaining installments in a lump sum.

If, however, the beneficiary's entitlement to death benefits is under an annuity contract that had previously been distributed from the plan to the retiree, rather than being an obligation of the plan itself, taking the death benefits under the annuity contract in lump-sum form will not qualify. Thus, if *A* in the previous example had elected to have the trustees of the plan purchase an annuity contract for him in lieu of receiving installment payments from the plan, the IRS takes the position that his beneficiary would never be eligible for qualifying lump-sum distribution treatment with respect to any survivor benefits she may have under the contract.

Interplay of lump-sum distribution and estate tax rules. As more fully discussed in the section that follows, any estate tax exemption that might otherwise be allowable for death benefits under a qualified plan is lost if the benefits are distributed in lump-sum form *and* the beneficiary elects to pay income tax on those benefits under the ten-year averaging or long-term capital gain provisions.

Income in respect of decedent (IRD) deduction. If all or a portion of the death benefit is included in the gross estate of the participant because of the above rule or for other reasons, the portion of the federal estate tax liability treated as attributable to the inclusion of the death benefits is allowable as an income tax deduction to the beneficiary. The IRD deduction rules are more fully explained later in this chapter in connection with the discussion of uninsured death benefits paid other than under qualified plans.

If the death benefit is taxed as a qualifying lump-sum distribution under the ten-year averaging or long-term capital gain provisions, any IRD deduction with respect to the benefit is not allowable against ordinary income. Rather, it must be subtracted from the lump-sum distribution amount in making the ten-year averaging or long-term capital gain computations.

The principles set forth in the preceding discussions are illustrated by the following example:

Example: *A* was a participant in a profit-sharing plan under which a portion of employer contributions were devoted to the purchase of whole life insurance on the participant's life. The plan permitted voluntary contributions and by the time of *A*'s preretirement death he had contributed an aggregate of $8,000 to the plan. He had paid tax on P.S. 58 costs over the years aggregating $3,000. He was covered by a $75,000 life insurance policy which had a cash surrender value of $18,000. His account balances representing his interest in the assets of the plan other than the life insurance policy totaled $60,000. *A*'s beneficiary elects to receive his total interest under the plan as a lump-sum cash distribution and to pay tax on it under the ten-year averaging/long-term capital gain rules. Accordingly, the entire value of *A*'s interest in the plan is included in his gross estate and the amount of federal estate tax treated as attributable to that inclusion is $6,000. The amount on which *A*'s beneficiary must pay tax under the ten-year averaging/long-term capital gain rules is $56,000, determined as follows:

Life insurance proceeds		$ 75,000
Account balance		60,000
		$135,000
Less: Pure death benefit under policy ($75,000 − 18,000)		57,000
Amount treated as distribution from plan		$ 78,000
Less:		
Employee contributions	$8,000	
P.S. 58 costs	3,000	
Death benefit exclusion	5,000	
IRD deduction	6,000	22,000
Taxable amount		$56,000

Estate and Gift Tax Treatment. Death benefits payable under a qualified plan are excludable from the gross estate of a participant if *all* of the following conditions are met:[14]

- The benefit is not payable to or for the benefit of the decedent's estate; i.e., the beneficiary is someone other than the estate.
- The benefit is attributable to employer, not employee, contributions to the plan.
- If the benefit is distributed in the form of a qualified lump-sum distribution, the recipient irrevocably elects not to determine the income tax on the benefit under the ten-year averaging or long-term capital gain provisions.

Not for the benefit of the estate. The benefit would be regarded as being "for the benefit of" the decedent's estate if the recipient were legally obligated to use the payment to pay taxes or debts of the estate. Payment to a trust,

[14] I.R.C. § 2039. The unlimited marital deduction makes the exemption moot if the beneficiary is the surviving spouse.

even a testamentary trust, is not regarded as payment to or for the benefit of the estate provided the trustee is not obligated to use the funds for the payment of debts or taxes of the estate, and does not in fact do so.

Employer/employee contributions. In cases where the death benefit is attributable to both employer and employee contributions, the amount that may be excluded is usually calculated according to an apportionment formula. The excludable amount is the amount that bears the same ratio to the total value of the death benefit as the employer's total contributions on behalf of the employee bear to the combination of employee and employer contributions. If, however, employer contributions are not readily ascertainable (as is often the case under a defined benefit pension plan), the value of all benefits payable at death (or, if earlier, at the date of the employee's retirement) less employee contributions will be considered the amount of the employer's contributions.

The IRS has held, however, that the apportionment formula is not to be applied in any case in which employee contributions and the earnings thereon are precisely determinable, as would be the case where they are held in a separate account. Under those circumstances, the separate account balance would be included in the gross estate and the balance of the death benefit, if any, excluded.

For these purposes, P.S. 58 costs are not treated as employee contributions. Contributions by self-employed persons are treated as employer contributions to the extent they were tax deductible.

Tax deferral possible. Although the beneficiary must forego ten-year averaging/capital gain treatment on a lump-sum distribution in order to permit an estate tax exemption that does not necessarily mean the beneficiary must pay an immediate tax. If the beneficiary is a surviving spouse, the distribution could be rolled over to an IRA, thus deferring the tax.

Difficulties can arise in cases where the beneficiaries of the estate and the recipient of the lump-sum distribution are different parties with diverse interests. Advance planning is necessary to avert a potential conflict of objectives. Under any circumstances, computations will be necessary to determine whether the estate tax exemption or the ten-year averaging/capital gain provisions produce the better tax result.

Gift tax considerations. As to gift taxes, the designation by a participant of a death benefit beneficiary under a qualified plan does not present any gift tax problem if the plan is entirely employer paid; i.e., noncontributory. If the plan is contributory, there is still no problem provided the designation is revocable, as would usually be the case. If the designation were irrevocable, the value of the survivor benefit at the date of the designation, to the extent attributable to employee contributions, would be a gift of future interest subject to gift tax.

Uninsured Death Benefits Under Nonqualified Plans or Arrangements

Income Tax Treatment. As a general rule, death benefits paid by an employer under a nonqualified plan are taxed to the beneficiary when received. These payments are normally regarded as in the nature of compensation for prior services rendered by the decedent.

$5,000 exclusion. Provided the deceased employee did not have a nonforfeitable right to receive the payments while living, the $5,000 death benefit exclusion from taxable income should be available to the beneficiary. If payments were due to the decedent during his lifetime under the contract, plan, or arrangement, the presence of any forfeiture provisions may suffice to permit the exclusion. For example, although deferred compensation is usually structured as essentially nonforfeitable after retirement, the agreement may call for forfeiture if the retired employee competes with or damages his former employer.

IRD deduction. If the value of the death benefits was included in the gross estate of the decedent (see discussion below), the beneficiary is allowed an income tax deduction for the estate tax attributable to the inclusion of the benefits in the gross estate. This deduction is referred to as the income in respect of a decedent (IRD) deduction.

The IRD deduction is determined by computing the estate tax differential with and without the value of the death benefit being included in the gross estate.[15]

> *Example:* Under a nonqualified plan, upon the death of *A* the employer will pay $10,000 a year for ten years to his beneficiary *B*. Upon *A*'s death, the present value of these benefits (determined to be $65,000) is included in his gross estate, which increases the estate tax by $4,000 from what it would otherwise be. The IRD deduction is $4,000. This amount represents 4 percent of the $100,000 aggregate death benefits to be paid. Each year $10,000 will be included in the beneficiary's income, and a $400 deduction (4 percent) will be allowed.

Gratuitous benefits. If death benefit payments are not made pursuant to a plan or contract but are decided upon gratuitously by the employer following an employee's death, it is possible to contend that the payments should not be taxable as compensation but should be tax free to the beneficiary as representing a gift. The IRS will invariably contest this contention. Its position is that any payments by a former employer with respect to a deceased employee are not a gift. The courts have split on the question, with

---

15 I.R.C. § 691(c). Because of the interplay with the unlimited marital deduction for estate tax purposes, there will normally be no IRD deduction where the beneficiary is a surviving spouse.

each case being decided on its particular facts. For example, if a widow were in destitute financial condition and that fact bore heavily on the employer's decision to make the payments, a gift might be indicated.

Generally, if the employer is a tax-paying organization it would not want to see the payments treated as a gift since it would lose its tax deduction. Even where the benefits are included in the taxable income of the beneficiary, a closely owned corporation may have trouble with its deduction if the deceased employee and/or the beneficiary is or was a significant stockholder. The IRS could contend that the deductions should be disallowed as representing unreasonable compensation or a dividend. Here too, the considerations are peculiarly factual. Significant facts include the magnitude of the payments and whether or not similar benefits are made available to the families of employees who are not major stockholders.

Estate and Gift Tax Considerations. As a general rule, the present value of death benefits payable to beneficiaries of a deceased employee under plans other than qualified plans is included in the gross estate.[16] There are two exceptions under which such death benefits might escape estate taxation:

- Gratuitous benefits; i.e., benefits not required to be paid under a plan or contractual arrangement, but unilaterally decided upon by the employer following the employee's death.
- Benefits under a death-benefit-only plan; i.e., a plan under which no payments can be made to the employee during his lifetime.

Gratuitous benefits. The considerations involved in judging whether gratuitous benefits can escape estate taxes are quite similar to those discussed above with regard to income taxes. In other words, if it can be successfully argued in a particular case that benefit payments represent a gift on the part of the employer, and hence are not subject to income taxes, it would follow that the payments also should not be included in the deceased employee's gross estate since they would not be property in which the decedent had an interest at the time of his death. But just as in the case of the income tax issue, the IRS can be expected to strongly resist any attempt to characterize benefits as gratuitous payments.

Death-benefit-only plans. It is not uncommon to find plans under which only beneficiaries who survive the employee can receive a benefit. No benefit is ever payable to the employee. But in determining whether benefits under such plans can escape estate taxation, the rule is that *all* plans of the employer (other than qualified pension, profit-sharing, or stock bonus plans) which provide for post-employment benefits must be considered together. If

---

[16] This inclusion in the gross estate will not normally result in a tax when the payment is to a surviving spouse.

under *any* such nonqualified plan the employee, had he lived, could have received a benefit, then no estate tax exclusions are allowable.

Under this rule, the IRS can be expected to point to any living benefit the decedent might have received, regardless of how remote, to deny an estate tax exclusion. For example, in the case of an active employee, the IRS will usually regard participation in a long-term disability plan as sufficient to deny an estate tax exclusion for benefits under a death-benefit-only plan. The record of the courts in supporting this IRS position has been mixed.

Even if the estate can prevail on this point, there are other grounds on which the IRS can seek to deny an estate tax exclusion; for example, if the decedent had retained the right to change or revoke a beneficiary designation or if coverage under the plan commenced within three years of death.

In short, it is quite difficult to avoid inclusion of death benefits under non-qualified plans in a deceased employee's estate. The rules are highly technical and complex and expert advice is essential if it is the employer's objective to structure a plan that can achieve this result.

Gift tax considerations. As to gift taxes, an irrevocable designation by an employee of a beneficiary who will receive death benefits under a nonqualified plan can result in a taxable gift.[17] Unless there is an objective of structuring a plan to exclude the death benefits from the employee's gross estate, there is no particular reason to make beneficiary designations irrevocable. Thus, the potential gift tax problem is easily avoided. But if the employer is trying to structure a plan that will avoid estate taxes, the gift tax ramifications of irrevocable beneficiary designations add one more dimension to the problems previously discussed.

Death Benefits Paid From Section 501(c)(9) Trusts

The use of Section 501(c)(9) trusts as a funding vehicle for nonqualified employee benefit plans, including death benefits, is discussed in Chapter 21. Where death benefits are paid from such trusts, the principal tax question is whether the benefits can be treated as the proceeds of life insurance (thus entitling the recipient to an income tax exemption), or whether they must be treated in the same manner as uninsured death benefits paid directly by the employer (as explained above). There is no direct authority on this question, although it is understood that the IRS has ruled privately in certain cases that life insurance treatment is appropriate where the actuarial basis for funding the trust is sufficiently similar to life insurance premiums and reserves. Moreover, some courts have accorded life insurance proceeds treatment to benefits paid from death benefit funds established by state and local governments, and there may be some analogy here with Section 501(c)(9) trusts.

At present, however, this question must be regarded as unsettled.

---

[17] There will be no gift tax liability where a spouse is the designated beneficiary.

Executive Supplemental Benefits

It was noted earlier in this chapter that there are three structures under which whole life insurance can be used as a vehicle for providing supplemental death benefits for executives under a nonqualified plan:

- Policy wholly owned by executive; corporation pays all or part of premium;
- Policy wholly owned by employer as funding vehicle for providing uninsured death benefit protection for executive;
- Split-dollar arrangement.

The tax considerations differ significantly under each structure. In fact, the differing tax results are usually the principal reason for preferring one structure over another.

Policy Wholly Owned by Executive. The tax results here are straightforward. Any portion of the premium paid by the employer is treated as additional compensation to the executive, taxable as such to him and deductible by the company.

The life insurance policy is subject to the normal tax rules applicable to personally owned life insurance. These are:

- Premium payments are not tax deductible.
- Dividends under the policy are not taxable until such time (if ever) that in the aggregate they exceed premiums paid. This rarely occurs unless the insured lives to an advanced age.
- Death benefits paid under the policy are received income tax free.
- If, however, the policy is cashed in prior to death, any excess of the cash surrender value over net premiums paid (gross premiums less dividends received in cash or used to reduce premiums) is taxable.
- Interest paid on loans against the policy (pursuant to a plan that contemplates systematic borrowing against increases in the cash surrender value) is tax deductible, provided the so-called "four out of seven" rule is observed. This rule requires that at least four out of the first seven premiums be paid from other than borrowed funds. For purposes of this rule, it is irrelevant whether funds are borrowed from the insurance company or from another source.

Under circumstances where premiums are paid by the employer and the executive borrows against the policy for the purpose of paying his income tax on the premium payments rather than paying the premiums themselves, it is arguable that the interest should be deductible without regard to the "four out of seven" rule. But there is no direct authority on that point, and the prudent course of action is always to observe the "four out of seven" rule.

Transfer of ownership. As in the case of group term life insurance coverage, an executive may be able to achieve significant estate planning objectives by assigning all incidents of ownership in the policy to someone else. The estate and gift tax considerations that were discussed earlier in this chapter with regard to assignments of term insurance are equally applicable here. But an important additional consideration is that, unlike a term policy, whole life insurance has a cash surrender value. The assignment of a whole life policy will result in a taxable gift in an amount approximating the cash surrender value at the time of the assignment. For this reason, it is usually preferable to assign the policy at an early stage, before the cash surrender value has built up to significant levels. But if all or a portion of the cash surrender value is borrowed out of the policy, the net value for gift tax purposes is decreased by the amount of the outstanding borrowings.

Policy Wholly Owned by Employer. Under this structure, the insurance policy is used essentially as a funding device for financing the payment of uninsured death benefits by the employer to a beneficiary.

Example: An employer enters into an agreement with an executive whereby upon his death, whether before or after retirement, the employer will pay $10,000 per year for ten years to his beneficiary. The company expects that its payments to the beneficiary will be tax deductible, and accordingly, views its total after-tax cost of the arrangement as being $50,000 (50 percent of $100,000 of total benefits). It further calculates that at the date of death, the present value of its obligation on an after-tax basis will be about $35,000.

To fund this obligation, the company purchases a $35,000 whole life insurance policy on the executive's life. The company has all rights of ownership in the policy, to which the executive has no preferred claim. The executive's beneficiary will be in the position of an uninsured creditor with regard to the death benefits promised under the agreement.

Although as an employee benefit planning matter the employer will typically view the entire arrangement as one plan, from a tax viewpoint it must be separated into two distinct elements:

- The ownership of a life insurance policy by the employer, subject to the tax rules regarding whole life insurance policies summarized above.
- A promise to pay an uninsured death benefit to an executive's beneficiary under a nonqualified plan. The tax rules applicable to such plans were explained earlier in this chapter.

From the executive's viewpoint, this second structure may be preferable to the first structure explained above, since he should not have to pay any personal income tax as a result of the arrangement during his lifetime. On the other hand, it will not be as favorable for his beneficiary, since the benefit payments will be subject to income tax rather than being tax-exempt life insurance proceeds.

Moreover, under this second structure, the executive does not have as much estate planning flexibility since he does not own a life insurance policy that he can assign. As explained earlier in this chapter, the likelihood is that the value of the benefits will be included in his gross estate.

Internal Revenue Service challenge to employer-paid benefits. It is not prudent to have the benefits payable by the employer to an executive and his beneficiary mirror precisely the benefits payable under the insurance contract owned by the company. In a recent court case [18] in which the employer-promised benefits (principally deferred compensation) were identical to those provided under the employer-owned insurance contract, the IRS contended that as a matter of substance the employee ought to be regarded as the beneficial owner of the insurance, and hence, taxable on the premium payments. Although the court rejected this approach, it did find that one net result of the arrangement was to provide the equivalent of life insurance protection for the employee, on which he should be taxed currently—presumably at P.S. 58 rates.

Split-Dollar Arrangements. From a tax viewpoint, these arrangements are perhaps the most complex. Part of the complexity results from the almost infinite variety of specific arrangements that can be structured under the broad concept of split-dollar plans.

General rule. In general, the concept contemplates that prior to retirement, ownership of the policy will be split between the employer and the executive. The employer will pay all or most of the premiums and will have an interest in the policy death benefit equal to (or more or less than) its total premium payments. The balance of the death benefit is payable to the executive's named beneficiary. Thus, if the executive dies prior to retirement, the company will recover a predesigned portion of (equal to, or more or less than) its premium outlays, and the beneficiary receives the balance of the proceeds.

At retirement. If the executive lives until retirement, there is a fork in the road, and two basic paths the arrangement can take. Following one path, the company borrows out of the policy (to the extent not previously borrowed) an amount equal to its predesigned portion of the premium outlays. It then turns over full ownership of the policy, subject to the loan, to the executive. From this point on, the arrangement is essentially the same as the first structure explained above.

---

[18] Goldsmith, 78-1 U.S.T.C. ¶ 83,702 (Ct. Cl. 1978).

Following the second path, the employer assumes full ownership of the policy and thereafter promises to pay an uninsured death benefit to the retired executive's heirs in an amount that the policy will fund. From this point on, the arrangement is essentially the same as the second structure explained above.

The basic tax rules applicable to owners of whole life insurance policies, previously described, are applicable to both employer and executive in their capacities as owners of all or a portion of the policy. Additional rules applicable to split-dollar arrangements are the following:

P.S. 58 cost. If all premiums are paid by the employer, the executive must report as taxable income an amount determined by applying a term rate to his share of the policy death benefit (total death benefit less portion payable to the employer). The term rates are usually taken from the P.S. 58 table, the use of which has been previously explained. If the executive pays a portion of the premiums personally, his payments are offset against the P.S. 58 income which would otherwise have to be reported.

It is the position of the IRS that the employer is not entitled to a tax deduction for the P.S. 58 income reported by the employee under a split-dollar arrangement. Since it is inherently inefficient as a tax matter for an employee to have to report taxable income under an arrangement that does not give the employer a deduction, a technique has evolved for curing this problem.

The approach is to have the employee pay a portion of the premium equal to the P.S. 58 cost, thereby eliminating any taxable income pickup by the employee. The employer pays the employee additional compensation in an amount approximating twice the employee's premium cost. Assuming a 50 percent personal tax rate, half of the additional compensation is used to pay the tax attributable to that compensation and the other half is used to reimburse the employee for the premium payment.

Provided the additional compensation is reasonable in amount when added to the employee's other compensation, the employer will be permitted a tax deduction for its payment. Assuming a 50 percent corporate tax rate, the additional compensation on an after-tax basis will approximate the amount by which the employer's share of the premium payment has been reduced.

Example:

Total premium	$ 8,000
Amount of insurance:	
Employer share	20,000
Employee share	180,000
Total	200,000
P.S. 58 cost:	
Executive age 43	980
Tax on P.S. 58 cost at 50 percent	$ 490

	Cash Flow	
	Company	*Executive*
Alternative A: Company pays entire premium:		
Premium payment	$(8,000)	
P.S. 58 tax		$ (490)
Alternative B: Additional compensation technique:		
Premium payment	(7,020)	(980)
Additional compensation	(1,960)	1,960
Tax effect	980	(980)
	$(8,000)	$ 0

Although the immediate cash-flow impact on the employer is similar under both alternatives, the second approach (Alternative B) may be more expensive in the long run. This point is considered in the discussion of financing alternatives in Chapter 21.

Transfer for value question. Although the general rule is that death benefit proceeds under life insurance policies are tax free to the beneficiary, there are some exceptions. One is where the policy is transferred for a valuable consideration. If the original owner of the policy transfers the policy or any interest therein to another person for valuable consideration, death benefits ultimately paid will be taxable to the beneficiary to the extent they exceed the total of:

- The consideration paid for the transfer; and
- Premiums and other amounts subsequently paid by the transferee.

Since split-dollar arrangements contemplate that at retirement one party's interest in the insurance policy will be transferred to the other, the "transfer for value" rule must be considered. Fortunately, the rule by its terms does not apply if the transfer is to the insured or to a corporation in which the insured is a shareholder or officer.

Thus, under the alternative where full ownership of the policy is transferred to the executive, the transfer for value rule does not apply. But if the alternative of transferring full ownership to the employer is followed, then the transfer for value rule could apply if the executive were neither an officer nor a shareholder of the employer. It could be contended that the employer's agreement to pay an uninsured death benefit to the executive's beneficiary represents valuable consideration for the transfer by the executive to the company of his preretirement interest in the policy.

Interest in cash value. Under the alternative where full ownership of the policy is eventually transferred to the executive, the question of possible taxability of net cash surrender value must be considered. Under many split-dollar arrangements, cash surrender value will exceed aggregate employer premium payments prior to retirement age. In an unpublished ruling,[19] the IRS held that net cash surrender value belonging to an employee under a split-dollar arrangement may be taxable to him at such time as the employee's interest in the cash value becomes nonforfeitable. The measure of the taxable amount is any excess of the cash value over any premium payments made by the employee with respect to his interest in the cash value.

The ruling makes it clear that any tax on cash surrender value buildups would be in addition to the usual P.S. 58 tax with respect to the pure death benefit protection afforded the employee under the arrangement.

Unfortunately, the ruling fails to make clear how the portion of premium attributable to the employee's interest in net cash surrender value should be determined. Presumably, if the employee is paying a portion of the total premium equal only to the P.S. 58 cost (i.e., a pure term cost), but is accruing a nonforfeitable interest in cash surrender value in addition to pure insurance protection, some measure of taxation would be indicated. But at present there are simply no authoritative pronouncements on the determination of the measurement or timing of any resultant tax liability.

---

[19] Ltr. Rul. 7916029 (Jan. 17, 1979).

21

Death Benefit Plans—Financial, Legal, and Tax Considerations

MICHAEL F. KLEIN, JR.
Price Waterhouse

FINANCING SOCIAL SECURITY BENEFITS

All Social Security benefits, including death and survivor benefits, are financed by payroll taxes imposed by the Federal Insurance Contributions Act (FICA) equally on employers and employees.

Structure of Social Security Taxes

Technically, there are two separate taxes:

- Social Security tax which funds retirement, death, survivor, and disability benefits
- Hospital insurance tax which funds Medicare—Part A

Legislated Tax Rates. The FICA tax rates are part of the Internal Revenue Code and can only be changed by an act of Congress. Because of the well-publicized financial problems of the Social Security system, the required level of contributions (taxes) has been increasing in recent years.

As of 1981, the scheduled tax rates for employers and employees (each), and the maximum amount of annual earnings taxable were as follows:[1]

Calendar Year	*Social Security Rate*	*Hospital Insurance Rate*	*Total FICA Rate*	*Maximum Taxable Wages*	*Maximum Tax—Paid By Employer and By Employee*
1980	5.08%	1.05%	6.13%	$25,900	$1,587.67
1981	5.35	1.30	6.65	29,700	1,975.05
1982–1984	5.40	1.30	6.70	?	?
1985	5.70	1.35	7.05	?	?
1986–1989	5.70	1.45	7.15	?	?
1990 and later	6.20	1.45	7.65	?	?

The Social Security tax rate for self-employed individuals is 75 percent of the combined employer and employee rate.

Allocation of Taxes. The Social Security tax is deposited in two funds—the federal Old Age and Survivors Insurance trust fund (OASI) and the Disability Insurance trust fund (DI). Social Security death and survivor benefits are paid out of the OASI fund.

Because of short-term insufficiency projected for the OASI fund, legislation approved in 1980 provides for temporary increases in the proportion of the Social Security tax allocated to that fund, with a commensurate decrease in the proportion allocated to the DI fund. For 1980 and 1981, the revised allocations are as follows:

	OASI	*DI*	*Total Tax*
1980	4.52%	0.56%	5.08%
1981	4.70%	0.65%	5.35%

Wages Subject to Social Security Taxes

Wage Base. Beginning with the calendar year 1982, the maximum annual taxable wages for any individual (the wage "base") will be subject to annual increases based on the automatic inflation adjustment features of the Social Security system. Wage base increases are geared to wage rate inflation, whereas adjustment of benefit payments is geared to changes in the Consumer Price Index. Wage base increases go into effect in the calendar year following any automatic increase in benefits which takes place the preceding June. The amount of the wage base increase is based on increases in the

[1] I.R.C. § 3101.

average of total wages reported for covered employment since the last adjustment. The amount of any wage base increase for a calendar year must be announced on or before the preceding November 1.

Maximum Wage Limitations. Special rules apply to the determination of maximum wages subject to Social Security tax in particular cases.

More than one employer. If an employee holds two or more jobs during a calendar year because he has changed jobs or is concurrently employed by more than one employer, each employer must apply the wage base limitation separately. Thus, it is possible for both the employee, and his employers in the aggregate, to pay more than the maximum per individual FICA tax to which each is subject (which was $1,975.05 for 1981).

Excess payments. The employee obtains relief for the excess payment by treating it as additional income taxes paid or withheld on the employee's personal income tax return. But the employers are not entitled to any refund.

> *Example:* During 1981, *X* is employed by Company *A* for the first six months and by Company *B* for the second six months. *X* is paid $20,000 by each employer, and each withholds Social Security and hospital insurance taxes of $1,330 (6.65 percent of $20,000) from *X*'s pay. Each employer also pays $1,330 of tax with respect to *X*.
>
> *X* will treat $684.95 ($1,330 × 2 − $1,975.05) as additional income taxes paid on his 1981 income tax return. But neither Company *A* nor Company *B* will be entitled to any refund.

Concurrent employers. Where a highly compensated individual is concurrently employed by two or more affiliated employers, payment of excess employer taxes can be avoided by employing a "common paymaster" procedure permitted by the Internal Revenue Code.[2] Essentially, one of the related corporations acts as the single employer for purposes of paying the employee and calculating payroll tax liabilities, but each corporation for which services are actively rendered bears its appropriate share of the wage and payroll tax costs. Use of the common paymaster procedures is subject to a number of detailed restrictions set forth in the Treasury regulations.

Successor employer. Another situation in which duplicative employer taxes can be avoided is that of the successor employer. If during a calendar year one employer acquires substantially all the property used in the trade or business of another, and the employees of the acquired business thereupon become employees of the acquiring employer, wages paid by the predecessor

---

[2] I.R.C. § 3121(s).

employer may be taken into account by the successor employer in applying the maximum wage limitation amount.[3]

Exclusions From Wages. While wages for FICA tax purposes are broadly defined, there are a number of significant exemptions. These include:

- Pension and retirement income payments or contributions to funds or insurance or annuity contracts for retirement purposes;
- Disability benefits and sick pay under plans meeting certain tests;
- Benefits or contributions under various other types of employee benefit plans, including death benefits, qualified group legal services and educational assistance programs;
- Deferred compensation payable after termination of employment, subject to certain tests.

Exempt Employment and Voluntary Coverage. While coverage of employment under the Social Security system is very broad, there are a number of exceptions. The principal ones are:

- Employees of the federal government and its various instrumentalities;
- Employees of state and local governments and most political subdivisions and instrumentalities thereof;
- Employment by a religious, charitable, scientific, educational, or other organization exempt from federal income taxes under Section 501(c)(3) of the Code.

Voluntary coverage. Employees of state and local governments and their exempt subdivisions and instrumentalities, and employees of Section 501 (c)(3) organizations, can be brought under the Social Security system by voluntary actions.

Employees of state and local governments, etc., can be covered by special agreements entered into between the governmental entities and the U.S. Department of Health and Human Services. These agreements permit wide-ranging coverage patterns as among employees of particular governmental entities and groups of employees within the same governmental entity. These are known as *coverage groups*. In some cases, coverage can only be extended by means of a referendum among the employees proposed to be covered.

Once a state or a political subdivision has been covered for at least five years, it can elect to withdraw from the system by giving two years advance notice. Once the entity withdraws, it cannot again join the Social Security system.

---

[3] I.R.C. § 3121(a)(1).

Election of coverage by nonprofit organizations. A Section 501(c)(3) organization may elect coverage by filing a waiver of its exemption from coverage pursuant to applicable provisions of the Code.[4] Once a waiver certificate is filed, all employees hired after the quarter in which the certificate was filed are automatically covered. Those individuals who were employees during the quarter in which the certificate was filed are covered only if they individually so elect ("concur in the waiver").

A Section 501(c)(3) organization that has elected coverage (waived its exemption) may withdraw from the system upon two years advance notice. Such advance notice may be given only after coverage has been in effect for at least eight years.

Because in the past a number of Section 501(c)(3) organizations mistakenly paid FICA taxes without ever filing a waiver certificate, there are a number of complex provisions dealing with constructive or deemed filings, late filings, back taxes, and the like.

Possible Future Developments

The combination of concern about the long-term financial stability of the Social Security system and questions about the adverse impact on the economy of increasing taxation of lower- and middle-income workers has led to discussions of financing the system at least partially through general tax revenues, directly or indirectly. Other solutions offered have been curtailment of future benefit increases under the automatic escalator provisions and lengthening of the retirement age.

Suggestions have also been made for expanding the tax base for Social Security by requiring all employees to be covered.

Many public employees can retire, with substantial pension, at relatively early ages. They can then seek employment covered by Social Security and earn coverage without having contributed to the system throughout their working lives. Federal employees, including the military, who can retire with twenty years of service, can in this way collect both a federal pension and Social Security. This so-called "double dipping" has generated much discussion but no change in the law to date.

GROUP LIFE INSURANCE

Premium Calculations

While the group life insurance rate for any one particular insured group is often represented as a single rate per $1,000 of insurance in force, it should be obvious that the actual cost of providing life insurance protection differs from individual to individual. The uniform rate per $1,000 is really a

---

4 I.R.C. § 3121(k).

composite of the actual insurance cost being charged for each of the individuals covered.

The rates initially charged an insured group are usually based upon a standard premium table. This rate table, developed by the New York State Insurance Department, represents required rates for group term insurance for all companies which are licensed to underwrite insurance in the state of New York. Companies that are not licensed to underwrite insurance in the state of New York often use lower rates, but since most major insurers are licensed in New York, new underwriting is quite often based on the New York rates.

The mortality table from which these standard premium rates were derived is the 1960 Commissioners Standard Group Table (CSG). Examples of some of the rates under this table are illustrated in Figure 21.1. The female rates represent 60 percent (40 percent discount) of the male rates. A discount from these initial rates is usually available based on the calculated monthly premium.

	Monthly Premium Per $1,000 of Insurance Coverage	
Age	*Males*	*Females*
20	$ .23	$ .14
25	.25	.15
30	.27	.16
35	.32	.19
40	.45	.27
45	.68	.41
55	1.65	.99
65	3.78	2.27
75	8.56	5.14

Fig. 21.1 Monthly Premium Rates Based on 1960 CSG

Below is a simplified example of how a rate per $1,000 of insurance coverage might be developed based on a composite of the rates at each different age. The example is based on a group of 100 lives, fifty males and fifty females, with $10,000 of life insurance each.

Males	*Number of Employees*	*Volume of Insurance (000s)*	*Rate per $1,000*	*Gross Monthly Premium*
Age 30	10	$ 100	.27	$ 27
35	10	100	.32	32
40	10	100	.45	45
45	10	100	.68	68
50	10	100	1.06	106

Females	*Number of Employees*	*Volume of Insurance (000s)*	*Rate per $1,000*	*Gross Monthly Premium*
Age 20	10	100	.14	14
25	10	100	.15	15
30	10	100	.16	16
35	10	100	.19	19
40	10	100	.27	27
Totals	100	$1,000		$369

Expense load:	Lesser of $.20 per $1,000 of insurance or $8	$ 8
Volume reduction:	5% if monthly premium is between $350 and $400	(19)
Net monthly premium		$358

Contributory Plans. In a contributory plan, all or a portion of the premium is paid by participating employees rather than by the employer. As explained in Chapter 20, employee contributions can be tax effective where coverage is in excess of $50,000, since the contributions will reduce or eliminate the taxable income the employees would otherwise have to recognize with respect to the excess coverage.

Contributory plans follow two basic patterns. Under one pattern, employees contribute toward the cost of all group life coverage. Under the second, a basic layer (perhaps one times salary) is provided at employer cost, and employees have the option of purchasing additional layers fully or partially at their own cost.

Where the first pattern is used, the employee contribution rate per $1,000 of coverage could be a flat rate regardless of age. This rate could be established by relating the desired employee sharing proportion to the net group premium rate charged by the insurance company. Thus, if the net premium cost for the group were $.40 per $1,000 per month and 50–50 sharing were the objective, the employee contribution rate would be set at $.20.

This approach in effect provides a subsidy for older employees at the expense of the younger employees. An alternative approach is to use age-related employee contribution rates. These rates could be developed on a precise basis by applying the cost-sharing objective to the age components of the group rate calculation as illustrated above. More commonly, standard term premium tables can be used.

Where employee contributions are used to purchase additional coverage on an optional basis, age-related contribution rates are essential to preclude bias in favor of elections of additional coverage predominately by the older employee group.

Cost of Conversion Privilege. Because those individuals who convert group life coverage to a permanent form tend to be uninsurable at standard rates, adverse selection against the insurance company results. The cost of this adverse selection is reflected initially in the experience of the insurance company's individual policy lines, but it is typically passed along to the group department in the form of a charge per $1,000 of insurance converted. The group department in turn must recover this charge by including it in the group term life premium structure.

Premium Renewal Rates

After the initial year of group term life insurance coverage, renewal premium rates need not be determined on the basis of 1960 CSG rates. Renewal premiums may be based on the experience of the group covered or the experience of a "pool" of policyholders.

Pooling. In general, a smaller case will have its experience "pooled" with the experience of a number of other relatively small policyholders. From these individual case experiences, a "pool" experience is developed which will serve as the basis for determining renewal premiums for all companies in the pool. Companies are pooled to allow insurance companies to make reasonable estimates as to the incidence of claims. Actuarial tables can be used to predict incidences of mortality with a fair degree of accuracy only when they are applied to sizeable populations. The smaller the population, the greater the margin for error. Thus, the insurance company may be able to predict with acceptable accuracy the incidence of claims for a 2,000-life company but not for a twenty-life company. By pooling small cases, the insurance company can develop a sufficiently large number of insureds to effectively apply actuarial estimates.

Experience Rated. When the insured group of a policyholder is large enough to allow for the effective application of actuarial estimating techniques, the case may be experience rated. Renewal rates for experience-rated cases are based, to some extent, on the actual experience of the covered group and in part on the experience of the entire class of policyholders. There are many different methods of determining which portion of a premium will be based on a group's own experience and which portion will be based on the experience of the entire class of insured groups, and these methods will differ from insurer to insurer. It is typical, however, that the weight given a group's actual experience will increase as the size of the group increases.

Fully Experience Rated. The largest insured groups are fully experience rated. Adverse experience will cause renewal premiums to increase and favorable experience will have the opposite effect. It should be noted here that the incidence and magnitude of claims are not the sole determinants in establishing the premium. As with any insurance premium, the insurance company's overhead, taxes, profits, and other expenses must be built into the rate structure.

A fully experience-rated group may, however, have an unexpectedly high level of claims in any one year which could cause a sudden large increase in the future premiums. In order to help stabilize the premiums for experience-rated cases, a number of different methods are employed.

Contingency reserves. One method is to establish contingency reserves that can be used to offset excessive claims in any particular year. This reserve, which may be accumulated from dividend margins, would be reestablished after any depletion by excess claims.

Excess amounts pooling. Another method used to avoid excessively large charges against a group's experience in any one year is known as *excess amounts pooling.* Under this method, claims above a certain level are rated on a pooled rather than an experience basis. The claim limits are typically set on an individual basis. That is, any single claim in the group's experience that exceeds the established limit will have the experience in excess of that limit charged to the pool of experience rather than to the covered group alone.

Loss limit method. One further method of achieving this experience/pooling ratio is called the *loss limit* method. Using this approach, a limit is set on the aggregate claims which may be charged against a group's experience in any one year. Aggregate claims in excess of this limit will be charged to the experience of the pool of insured cases. The loss limit is typically expressed as a percentage of the group's premium.

Financing Arrangements

Group life insurance premiums are calculated to provide for anticipated claims, expenses, taxes, retention and risk charges, and reserves. While the employer has no control over the level of claims, financing arrangements may be available to help reduce the cost of some of the other premium components.

Particular emphasis is often placed on cash flow, with the intention of altering the once prevalent pattern of a large conservatively determined premium due on the first day of the policy year, to be partially recouped more than a year later through a dividend. Emphasis is now commonly placed on minimizing the reserves held by the insurer for current protection, with the employer one way or another obligated to provide the insurance company with funds to meet claims on an as-needed basis.

Minimum Premium Plan. One type of arrangement is known as a *minimum premium plan.* Under this arrangement, the employer bears (as premium) claim costs up to a predetermined level (typically 80–90 percent of the regular premium) and pays a "risk premium" for claims above the level. After this level is reached, the insurance company will absorb further claims. Thus, the total premium paid is some percentage of what it would be normally, and the premium taxes are proportionately reduced.

Minimum premium plans are most commonly used with large experience-rated cases where the premium tax and cash-flow savings can be significant. Not all states have accepted the legal and tax status of these plans, however. In addition, a minimum premium plan is not as conveniently applied to life insurance as it is to health insurance due to the greater fluctuation of claims from year to year.

Retrospective Rating. Another financing arrangement that is sometimes used is called *retrospective rating.* Under this arrangement the employer pays a percentage of the otherwise determined premium. At the end of the policy year, the insurance company may then assess an additional charge to reflect the actual experience during the year. If the experience is particularly good, the employer may be entitled to a refund. A retrospective rating arrangement effectively allows the employer to retain a portion of the reserve that would otherwise have been paid out as premium during the year. While the employer may eventually have to pay these reserves, it has had the use of its money and could reduce costs to the extent that earnings on the reserve amounts exceed the earnings which would have been credited by the insurer. Like a minimum premium plan, however, retrospective rating arrangements are not commonly used with group life insurance due to the volatility of claims.

Allocation of Premium

In cases where group life insurance plans include some element of permanent coverage, the premium must be allocated between the term and permanent coverages in accordance with Treasury regulations. The reason for this allocation is that employees are taxable on the premium cost of any permanent coverage to the extent that premium is paid by the employer. But employees are not taxed on the actual premiums paid for the term coverage; rather (as was explained in Chapter 20) the amount includable in an employee's income is based on the application to the employee's coverage of the uniform premium table which appears in the regulations.

Allocation Formula. In applying these tax rules, the allocation of the actual premium between the permanent and term coverages is not left to the insurance company's discretion. The Treasury regulations [5] provide that the

[5] Treas. Reg. § 1.79-1(d).

premium cost of the permanent insurance for any employee for any policy year is determined by applying the net single premium rate for paid-up whole life insurance at the employee's attained age at the beginning of the year to the increase during that year of the "deemed death benefit" under the permanent coverage.

The *deemed death benefit* (DDB) at the end of any policy year is determined by dividing the cash value at that date of the employee's permanent insurance (or policy reserve, if greater) by the net single premium rate for paid-up insurance at the employee's attained age. Or in other words, how much paid-up insurance will the cash value or policy reserve support? This year-end DDB is then compared with the similarly determined benefit at the end of the preceding policy year, to determine the increase in the DDB which occurred in the policy year. The net single premium cost of this increase in the deemed paid-up benefit is the cost of the permanent coverage for that year.

This premium amount, less any portion thereof paid by the employee, is the amount included in the employee's income for tax purposes. In addition, as explained in Chapter 20, the employee is taxed on the term portion of the coverage (in excess of $50,000) based on the uniform term premium table contained in the regulations.

The net single premiums and the net level premium reserve in the above calculations are required to be computed using the 1958 CSG mortality table and a 4 percent interest rate.

Dividends. All or a portion of any dividends on a group life policy which provides a permanent benefit are includable in the employee's income for tax purposes to the extent the dividends are actually or constructively received by the employee. If the entire premium cost of the permanent insurance is paid by the employer, then any policy dividends received by the employee would be included in the employee's income for tax purposes. In other cases, the portion of any dividends received by the employee which must be included in his taxable income is determined by applying a formula set forth in the regulations. Essentially, this formula determines on a cumulative basis (considering the current and all prior policy years) the excess of total premium costs for the permanent coverage pursuant to the regulations, and total dividends received by the employee, over the portion of the premium costs paid by the employee and dividends included in the employee's income for prior policy years.

Differing Years. In cases where the policy year and the employee's taxable year do not coincide, the amount of income reportable by the employee (because of permanent benefits) is allocated between the taxable year in which the policy year begins, and that in which it ends, on the basis of the portion of the premium for permanent benefits which is paid in each taxable year.

Post-Retirement Group Term Coverage

In Chapter 20, the problems involved in continuing group term life insurance on retired employees were discussed. The cost of continuing large amounts of insurance can become substantial, particularly with an aging plan population.

Alternative Funding Approaches. Since death benefits for retirees are a guaranteed claim, employers can adopt a pay-as-you-go approach. Instead of paying premiums to an insurance company, the employer pays the death benefits as claims occur. In this way, the employer has the use of funds that would otherwise be held as a reserve for claims by an insurance company.

There are disadvantages to this approach:

- Since the benefit paid is not the proceeds of life insurance, the benefit may be taxable to the beneficiary, to the extent it exceeds the $5,000 employee death benefit exclusion. (See Chapter 20 for a full explanation of the taxation of employer death benefits.)
- Large lump-sum death benefits can cause a cash-flow problem for the employer since the timing of the claims is not fully predictable.

Where the benefits for retirees are modest, these factors may not be of consequence. However, where the benefits are substantial, alternatives should be considered.

Modified Pay-As-You-Go. One approach, which is feasible for large groups sponsored by financially solid employers, is to structure the pay-as-you-go arrangement as life insurance. That is, the retired employee's beneficiary receives the benefit from the life insurance company pursuant to a group life plan and policy that provides for continued coverage after retirement. The experience-rated premium arrangement is such that, in net effect, the employer pays the insurance company for each claim (in the form of premium) as it arises, plus expense and profit charges. Thus, the effect of pay-as-you-go financing is retained, but the beneficiary obtains the tax benefits associated with treatment as life insurance proceeds.

Of course, it is important that the experience-rating arrangement for determining the premium be such that some element of risk sharing with the insurance company is retained. Otherwise, it could be contended that as a tax matter the benefits should not be treated as life insurance. Risk sharing might take the form of insurance company responsibility for annual losses in excess of a maximum limit.

Retired Life Reserve. An alternative to pay-as-you-go is to pre-fund liability for post-retirement group life continuation through a retired lives reserve.

Example: Under a group life insurance plan, active employees are insured for two times salary. At retirement, an amount of insurance equal to one half the coverage in effect immediately prior to retirement is continued.

The employer pays an annual premium for the preretirement coverage, determined in the normal manner. It pays an additional premium each year for the purpose of establishing a reserve with the insurance company calculated to be sufficient, at the time of retirement, to fund the post-retirement continuation.

In effect, the retired life reserve is intended to accumulate an amount which, at retirement, will be sufficient to fund the equivalent of the single premium cost of paid-up life insurance. The insurance coverage, however, continues to be group term life which has no cash surrender value or other permanent feature which would afford the employee anything other than pure death benefit protection.

Internal Revenue Service position. The IRS has held that employer contributions (premiums) to a retired life reserve are deductible on a current basis, provided:

- The balance in the reserve is held by the insurance company solely for the purpose of providing insurance coverage on active or retired lives so long as any active or retired employee remains alive.
- The contract does not give the employer the right to recapture any portion of the reserve so long as any active or retired employee remains alive.
- The amount paid into the retired life reserve annually is not more than that which would be required, on an actuarial basis, to fairly allocate the cost of insurance coverage provided for retired employees over the working lives of such covered employees.[6]

It is implicit in these and other IRS rulings that the employer is not taxable on interest credited by the insurance company to the reserve.[7]

Funding levels. Funding a retired lives reserve is similar to pension funding. A level cost is determined for each covered employee sufficient to accumulate the necessary reserve by retirement age. Forfeitures due to termination of employment prior to retirement are applied to reduce the cost for the continuing employees; presumably forfeitures can or should be anticipated in advance through appropriate turnover assumptions.

---

[6] Rev. Ruls. 69-382, 1969-2 C.B. 28; 73-599 1973-2 C.B. 40.

[7] *Id.* See also Rev. Rul. 77-92, 1977-1 C.B. 41. At present, the IRS will not issue ruling letters on retired life reserve plans pending completion of a study of whether it should change any of its positions on the tax attributes and consequences of these plans. See Rev. Proc. 80-22, § 5.01. The present position of IRS is summarized in the text.

Upon the adoption of a new plan, the cost for the older employees can be spread over their remaining working lives. Alternatively, an initial past-service cost can be determined and amortized over a period of years similar to pension funding.

At retirement, there are two approaches:

- An amount is withdrawn from the retired lives reserve which the insurance company guarantees will be sufficient to cover the cost of providing the post-retirement continuation; or
- The insurance company withdraws from the reserve each year, for as long as the retired employee lives, amounts equivalent to annual term insurance premiums.

Under the first alternative the insurance company assumes the post-retirement mortality risk, whereas under the second arrangement that risk is retained by the employer. Again, these alternatives resemble pension funding, since they are similar to the distinction between purchasing annuities at retirement versus paying retirement benefits from a trust or other unallocated fund.

Trusteed retired life reserve. As an alternative to the retired lives fund being held by the insurer, the fund can be accumulated in an employee benefit trust. The advantages of a trust are that higher investment earnings might be realized than the interest credits an insurer would make, and state premium taxes and insurance company expense charges might be reduced.

One possibility in appropriate circumstances is to use a Section 501(c)(9) tax-exempt trust as the funding vehicle. These trusts are discussed later in this chapter. The IRS has ruled that contributions to a Section 501(c)(9) trust for the purpose of funding a retired lives reserve are tax deductible under the same rules (summarized above) which govern a reserve held by an insurer.[8]

Where a Section 501(c)(9) trust is not feasible, a taxable trust might be used. Although the trust earnings would be subject to income tax, tax-exempt bonds could be considered as a funding vehicle. Alternatively, the trust might invest in annuity contracts which could defer the tax pursuant to the annuity rules. But upon cashing in the contracts or the receipt of benefits thereunder, the tax incidence would have to be considered.

SURVIVOR'S BENEFIT PLANS—PREMIUMS

Insurers offer survivor income benefits on a group insurance basis. This insurance, which as described in Chapter 20 provides a continuing income

[8] Rev. Ruls. 69-478, 1969-2 C.B. 29; 73-599, 1973-2 C.B. 40.

to the survivor upon the death of the insured, is in many ways another form of term life insurance. It differs from typical life insurance in two important aspects. The most obvious of these is that the death benefit is paid in monthly installments rather than a lump sum. In addition, survivor's income benefits are usually payable only if qualified survivors, as defined by the insurance contract, are alive.

Benefits are usually paid over a specified period of time such as until the survivor reaches age 65 or for a fixed period such as ten or fifteen years. Benefits are also frequently payable to more than one survivor—usually a spouse and young children. Policies may also have a remarriage provision which discontinues benefits upon the remarriage of the surviving spouse.

Basis of Rates

The premium calculation for group survivor benefits is similar to the calculation for regular group life insurance except that joint life probabilities must be taken into account rather than single life probabilities. In addition, the probability of remarriage must also be considered where the benefit payment is affected by the remarriage of the surviving spouse.

Thus, as in the case of group term life insurance, the most significant factor in determining the group premium rate is the probability of death during the policy year of the employees at the various ages which comprise the group. But whereas these probability factors are applied to fixed death benefit amounts in determining term life premiums, in survivor benefit plans the probability factors are applied to the present value of the benefit stream payable to the survivor beneficiary or beneficiaries.

Development of Benefit Stream. The determination of the present value of the benefit stream requires the application of annuity valuation techniques quite similar to those involved in pension funding.

Example: Under a group survivor benefit plan, in the event of an employee's death a surviving spouse receives a benefit equal to one half the employee's final-average compensation. The benefit is payable for the spouse's life or until the date on which the employee would have attained normal retirement age, whichever is earlier.

Employee *A* is age 45, and normal retirement age is 65. In determining the group premium rate, the basic procedure with respect to *A* is to apply the probability of *A*'s death during the policy year to the present value of the benefit which his spouse would receive if he died. The present value of the benefit is the value of an annuity of *X* dollars payable monthly for twenty years, discounted by the probability of the death of *A*'s spouse during the twenty-year period. The amount of the monthly benefit is determined by reference to *A*'s final-average compensation, as defined in the plan.

Experience rating and reserves. Essentially the same considerations with respect to experience rating, premium financing techniques, and employee contributions apply to these plans as to group term life plans. An additional difference, however, is that unlike preretirement group term life a survivor benefit plan will develop significant reserves. That is, as deaths develop, the benefits are not immediately payable. Rather, the present value of the future benefit stream must be reserved—as in the case of a long-term disability (LTD) plan.

Thus, the reserve financing alternatives for LTD plans—Section 501(c)(9) trusts and the like—should also be considered for survivor benefit plans.

USE OF SECTION 501(c)(9) TRUSTS

Life Benefits Through Section 501(c)(9) Trusts

Among the types of benefits that may be provided by a Section 501(c)(9) trust are *life benefits*. A life benefit is defined in the Treasury regulations as a benefit payable by reason of the death of a member of the voluntary employee beneficiary association, or a dependent. The benefit can be paid directly by the trust to the beneficiary, or it may be provided through insurance.

Benefits That May Be Provided.[9] As a general rule, Section 501(c)(9) trusts are limited to providing current protection only, i.e., term insurance. There are, however, some exceptions:

- The association may provide a permanent benefit as defined in and subject to the restrictions of the regulations relating to group life insurance under Section 79. These definitions and restrictions were discussed in Chapter 20.
- The association may provide a right to convert to individual coverage on termination of eligibility for coverage through the trust.
- In the case of an association funded through employee contributions only, any life insurance contract may be utilized.

Although pension, annuity, and similar benefits may not be provided through a Section 501(c)(9) trust, a permissible life benefit may be settled in the form of an annuity to the beneficiary in lieu of a lump-sum death benefit. That is true regardless of whether the arrangement permits settlement in a lump sum. Thus, Section 501(c)(9) trusts are viable for funding survivor benefit plans.

---

9 Treas. Reg. § 1.501(c)(9)-3.

Insurance vs. Self-Insurance. A Section 501(c)(9) trust can pay benefits either directly to beneficiaries, or via group life insurance contracts where the trust is the contractholder.

Tax implications. The distinction can be more important to the beneficiaries from a tax viewpoint, than to the employer with respect to its funding arrangements. As noted in Chapter 20, there is substantial doubt that death benefits paid directly by a trust, without the involvement of a life insurance company, would qualify for income tax exclusion by the beneficiary as the proceeds of life insurance. Thus, the income tax position of the beneficiary is more secure if the death benefit proceeds are received from a life insurance company under a group insurance contract held by the trust.

Employer costs. From the viewpoint of the employer, its funding requirements under an arrangement that provides only current protection may not differ significantly as between an uninsured benefit and a fully experience-rated group insurance contract held by the trust. The insured arrangement will involve costs for state premium taxes and insurance company retentions which a self-insured trust may avoid or minimize. But essentially, the trust serves as a flow-through vehicle for premium dollars running from the employer to the insurance company. It is of course necessary, in the case of a self-insured trust, to be certain that state insurance or tax laws do not impose additional restrictions or costs with respect to this method of operating.

Reserve accumulations. Utilization of a Section 501(c)(9) trust can produce significant funding advantages in cases where the type of death benefit coverage requires the accumulation of reserves. This occurs where either protection is provided to retirees or is provided for employees under a survivor benefit type of plan. The trust rather than an insurance company can be used as the vehicle for accumulating reserves.

Investments of the reserve funds by the trust are controlled by its trustees who may be wholly or partially designated by the employer. Since the trust will be a welfare benefit plan within the meaning of ERISA, its investment policies will be subject to the ERISA prudent man rule and other fiduciary restrictions. Nevertheless, investment performance of a trust portfolio may be viewed as having greater potential than the interest credits on reserves an insurance company would make. Furthermore, the investment income of the trust is accumulated tax free provided it does not constitute unrelated business income.

Thus, it is impossible to structure arrangements whereby reserves are accumulated in the trust for eventual application to the payment of premiums to an insurance company under contracts providing continued group life insurance coverage for retirees. As noted earlier in this chapter, current tax deductions are allowed to the employer for periodic contributions to a retired lives reserve, whether that reserve is held by an insurance company or trust.

Internal Revenue Service Anti-Discrimination Rules. As noted in Chapter 20, Section 501(c)(9) trusts are subject to anti-discrimination rules.[10] Thus, death benefits may not be provided under such a trust if they are disproportionate in favor of officers, shareholders, or highly compensated employees. Furthermore, eligibility for benefits and the amounts thereof can be limited to or differentiated among various classifications of employees only on the basis of reasonable and objective nondiscriminatory standards.

Accordingly, a Section 501(c)(9) trust may not be a viable vehicle for providing death benefits solely to a relatively highly compensated group of employees, or under coverage schedules that provide death benefit amounts that are disproportionate to compensation levels. In particular, if post-retirement group life protection is provided in significant amounts only for officers or some other highly compensated classification of employees, with no or only a nominal amount of post-retirement protection for the other employees, a Section 501(c)(9) trust may not be a viable vehicle.

WHOLE LIFE INSURANCE—FINANCIAL CONSIDERATIONS

Basic Structure

Unlike term insurance, whole life insurance is designed to provide a level death benefit for the life of the insured at a level annual cost. The premium does not increase from year to year but is fixed at the issuance of the policy. Since the cost of providing life insurance protection increases with the age of the insured, the development of a level premium necessitates that in the early years of the policy's existence the premium be more than adequate to pay for the cost of the insurance protection provided. The excess of the premium over the actual cost can then be used to develop a reserve which can be used to offset the cost of the insurance coverage in the later years of the policy's existence when the premium alone is no longer sufficient to provide for the cost.

While the premium for whole life insurance is substantially greater in the early years of the policy than for an equivalent amount of term insurance coverage, the level premium becomes more competitive as the years pass and the term insurance rates increase. One of the principal reasons for this is the "overpayment" or excess of the premium over the cost of insurance in the early years of the policy. These overpayments create a surplus which is used to pay expenses and create a reserve. This reserve is invested to help offset the increasing cost of providing insurance protection as the insured ages. Another reason that whole life insurance premium becomes more competitive is that the amount of "pure" insurance is actually decreasing as the policy matures. The cash value of the policy (substantially equivalent

[10] Treas. Reg. §§ 1.501(c)(9)-2, 1.501(c)(9)-4(b).

to the reserve) is available to the owner of the policy at any time, not only upon the death of the insured. Thus, the true amount at risk or "pure" insurance is the face amount of the policy less the cash value. Since the face amount remains constant and the cash value increases, the amount of "pure" insurance provided decreases as the policy matures. This decrease in the amount at risk helps to offset the increased cost of providing insurance as the insured gets older.

Key Definitions.

- *Owner.* The person able to exercise all rights under the policy, including the right to name the beneficiary, borrow against the policy, assign or surrender it, and exercise dividend and settlement options.
- *Insured.* The person whose death is the contingency the policy insures against. The insured may or may not be the owner of the policy.
- *Beneficiary.* The person or legal entity entitled to the death benefit provided by the policy upon the death of the insured. The beneficiary may also be the owner of the policy.

Cash Surrender Value. Consider the following cash surrender value schedule for a $50,000 whole life policy issued on the life of a male age 40, with an annual premium of $900:

Policy Year	*Cash Surrender Value*	*Pure Insurance Protection* *
1	—	$50,000
2	—	50,000
3	$ 750	49,250
4	1,600	48,400
5	2,450	47,550
10	7,000	43,000
15	11,900	38,100
20	17,000	33,000

* Represents the excess of the $50,000 face amount of the policy over the cash surrender value.

The pattern displayed above leads some observers to conclude that a cash value life insurance policy can be viewed as a combination of declining term insurance and an accumulating savings account—the total of the two at any time equaling the death benefit under the policy.

Cost Analysis Fundamentals

Buy Term and Invest the Difference. This view leads to the "buy term and invest the difference" approach to analyzing the economic consequences of purchasing a cash value policy. For example, in years one and two an appropriate premium cost for $50,000 of term insurance at ages 40 and 41 respectively is subtracted from the $900 premium for the cash value policy, and the balance is considered invested at an assumed rate of return. In year three, the cost of $49,250 of term insurance at age 42 is subtracted from the $900 level premium, and the excess is considered added to the investment fund. The analysis is continued for as many years as one cares to go out, and comparison is made between the year-by-year cash value of the policy and the balance in the assumed investment fund.

The obvious point is that if the assumed investment fund shows the greater balances, an individual presumably could achieve the same level of protection and be better off financially if he were to buy only term insurance and invest the premium differential—if the assumed rate of investment return seems reasonably achievable. This approach, although perhaps simplistic, is fundamentally valid. A more precise determination would require that the differing tax consequences of cash life insurance and other investments be taken into account.

Objection is often raised to this approach on the basis that as a practical matter, many people are unlikely to have the self-discipline necessary to faithfully pursue a program of investing the difference. In other words, the argument is that cash value life insurance should be viewed rather like a bank's Christmas Club. While the point may be perfectly valid in terms of the realities of human behavior, it clearly has no relevance as a financial analysis matter—particularly in evaluating corporate controlled programs.

Rate of Return on Cash Values. A variation on the "buy term and invest the difference" approach is to use the technique to analyze the rate of return implicit in the policy's own cash values. For example, in the above illustration there is $47,550 of pure insurance protection in year five. If a term rate of $4.40 per $1,000 is assumed, then $210 of the total premium is buying current protection. The balance of $690 is going into the cash value.

By working with the opening and closing cash value balances each year and the "principal" input into the cash value thus determined, one can back into the effective net rate of interest being credited on the cash value each year (net, that is, of the insurance company's expense and profit retention). A judgment can then be reached whether the rate of return is acceptable in light of alternative investment opportunities.

These approaches produce results that are only as good as the assumption made as to what a reasonable term premium is for the current protection.

Imputed Cost of Current Protection. An alternative approach is to use an acceptable rate of investment return to back into the premium being paid for the current protection being provided by the whole life policy.

For example, if one assumes for the sake of analysis that 8 percent would be an acceptable rate of return on an alternative investment, then the cash value increases under the policy can be analyzed to determine how much of the premium must be applied to cash values to achieve an 8 percent return. The balance of the premium is regarded as going for current protection.

In the above illustration, the cash value increases from $1,600 at the beginning of year five to $2,450 at the end of that year—an increase of $850. Eight percent of the opening cash value is $128, so that the $722 balance of the increase can be regarded as coming out of the net premium payment. That leaves $178 of the premium for providing the $47,550 of current protection, which works out to $3.74 per $1,000. One can then judge whether, for a male age 44, that is an acceptable term cost.

Dividends

The analyses illustrated above assume a fixed level premium, which is the arrangement that prevails under a nonparticipating ("no par") policy. The analysis becomes more complex when participating policies are considered, i.e., policies on which dividends are paid.

Definition. A policy dividend is a partial return of premium. That is, as the insurance company's future experience with regard to the key factors of investment return, mortality, and expense charges are on balance more favorable to it than it originally assumed in fixing the premium, it is in a position to rebate a portion of the premiums in the form of dividends.

Participating vs. Nonparticipating. Initial premiums are higher for participating than for nonparticipating policies which are identical in other respects, but projected dividends are usually sufficient that in the long run the participating policy is likely to be cheaper.

Policies written by mutual life insurance companies (i.e., policyholder-owned) are of the participating type. Policies written by stock life insurance companies (i.e., investor-owned) can be either participating or nonparticipating.

Insurance companies publish dividend scales with respect to participating policies. These scales project the estimated dividends that will be paid on the policy year by year in the future, based on the company's current dividend practices. The scales typically project a dividend amount which starts out quite low but increases year by year as a dollar amount per $1,000 of face value.

No Guarantees. Dividend scales are not guaranteed and can be increased or decreased in the future at the insurance company's sole discretion. Thus, dividends actually received may differ from those projected at the time of policy issuance. Although experience differs from company to company, on balance the recent years' record of the insurance industry in maintaining and improving dividend scales has been excellent.

Dividend Payments. Dividends usually are payable as of the first day of each policy year. Many policies also provide for a terminal dividend, i.e., upon the death of the insured there is paid not only the face amount of the policy, but a pro rata portion of the dividend which would have been paid with respect to the policy year in which death occurs.

Dividend Options. At the option of the policy owner, dividends can be applied in a number of different ways. Typical alternatives include:

- Received in cash
- Offset against premium due
- Held by the insurance company with interest credited—can be drawn down by the policy owner at any time (similar to a savings account)
- Used to purchase additional protection in the form of paid-up additions, or term insurance
- Purchase a combination of term protection and paid-up additions—this is the so-called "fifth dividend option" used under certain "minimum deposit" insurance plans—as explained hereinafter

The first three alternatives are self-explanatory. A paid-up addition is in effect single premium cash value insurance. For example, if a dividend of $1,000 is payable on a policy insuring a male presently age 45, it might be used to purchase a paid-up addition of perhaps $3,000. The addition, which increases the death benefit (face amount) of the policy by $3,000, would have an initial cash surrender value approximately equal to the dividend. Although no further premiums are due with respect to the paid-up addition, its cash surrender value increases each year and dividends will be payable with respect to it. Thus, although the amount of a paid-up addition purchasable with a given dividend amount is obviously less than the amount of term protection which could be bought, paid-up additions have a compounding effect in generating additional future dividends and cash value increases (and hence borrowing capacity) on a policy. For that reason, they are particularly important in structuring minimum deposit plans, as discussed hereinafter.

Policy Loans

Cash value insurance policies provide borrowing privileges to the policy owner. Usually, the owner can borrow from the insurance company at any time an amount equal to or marginally less than the cash surrender value. There is no obligation ever to repay the loan. If the insured dies or the policy is surrendered at a time when there are outstanding loan obligations, the loan amount is simply deducted from the death benefit proceeds or cash surrender value payment.

The rate of interest payable on loans is fixed by the policy. In turn, the policy cannot provide for a greater rate of interest than that permitted by state insurance law. The most common rate permitted today is 8 percent, although pressure is now being exerted in the states to permit policy loan rates that will fluctuate with prevailing interest rates on some basis. If the necessary statutory changes are enacted to permit such rates, they can apply only to new policies. The loan rates built into existing policies cannot be changed.

At times when interest rates are extraordinarily high—for example, the 20 percent prime rate prevailing in early 1981—the ability to borrow at 8 percent is obviously a very significant advantage to a policyholder. Conversely, it is a financial drain on the insurance companies which could otherwise invest the funds at a much higher rate. Anything that adversely impacts the insurance company's investment yield obviously also adversely impacts its ability to maintain and improve dividend scales.

Premium Payment Variations

The basic form of whole life insurance provides for the payment of premiums for the life of the insured. Premium payments may be designed, however, to cover different periods of time in response to different needs. An individual may wish to coordinate his premium payments with the period of time which coincides with his greatest ability to pay.

Paid-Up Policy. An individual may wish to have his policy paid up by the time he reaches age 65, when he expects his annual income to drop substantially. Alternatively, he may wish to pay up the policy over a fixed number of years, for example, fifteen or twenty, to coordinate the premium payments with other financial responsibilities. Annual premiums are, of course, greater for the various paid-up policies than for a whole life arrangement.

Modified Life Policy. The policy may also be issued on a "modified life" basis rather than a level premium basis. Under the modified life approach, premiums are lower than the level premium in the initial years and higher in the later years. Again, the purpose of this approach is to tailor the premium payments to the insured's ability to pay. The increasing premium of a modified life payment schedule may appear similar to the schedule for a term insurance policy, but it should be clear that the initial premiums of a modified life policy are still greater than the premiums for an equivalent amount of term insurance. That is because, unlike term insurance, the modified life policy develops a cash value and reserve albeit more slowly than a level premium policy.

Risk Differentiation. Premiums may be modified for reasons other than to simply rearrange the payment schedule. They may also be modified to account for a specific risk or lack of one. The risk involved with insuring any one person differs from individual to individual, yet most individuals are classed in the same premium pricing structure. The reason for this is that the actuarial techniques used to establish premium rates are valid only when applied to sufficiently large populations. Thus, the actuaries will be able to predict with some accuracy the mortality experience of all the male insureds for example, but predicting the mortality experience for John Doe would be a matter of chance. There are, however, sufficiently large classes of individuals whose common characteristic(s) will make their mortality experience different from the experience of the population as a whole.

Preferred risks. Where an individual can qualify for a classification with a decided mortality advantage, many insurers will issue what are called "preferred risk" policies. These policies provide for a lower premium rate than the standard policies. An example of a risk category for which insurers are increasingly offering preferred risk policies is nonsmokers.

Substandard risks. It is more common, however, for insurers to identify groups that represent "substandard" risks. Some of the factors used in determining whether or not an individual is a substandard risk are medical history, physical build, and occupation. Individuals who are classed as substandard risks may have policies issued to them on a substandard ("rated") premium basis. The amount of increase over the standard premium depends on the degree of extra risk involved with the particular substandard classification.

Waiver of Premium. Premiums may also be adjusted for any ancillary benefits that may be provided by the policy. Virtually all insurers offer waiver of premium protection as part of their ordinary life insurance policies at a slight extra charge. This protection allows the insured to discontinue making premium payments during a period of disability, as defined in the contract. Should the insured become disabled, the policy would remain in full force with the same cash value and dividends that would develop if the insured were still paying the premium.

Termination of Premium Payments. There are alternatives to cashing in a policy in order to terminate the obligation to make premium payments. One is to convert the policy to a paid-up amount of permanent life insurance. The paid-up insurance amount will, of course, be a reduced amount compared to the policy's original face value. The insurance amount will be that appropriate to the single premium which the policy's reserve (cash value) at the time of conversion would support.

A second alternative is to convert the policy to extended term insurance for a period of years. The effect is to extend protection equal to the face amount of the policy for whatever period the reserve (cash value) of the policy at the date of conversion will support. Thereafter, the insurance completely terminates.

Net Cost Comparisons

Life insurance is not a regulated industry in the sense of regulation that results in a uniform price charged by all insurers for an identical product. Life insurance pricing is competitive among insurers, and there can be surprisingly wide variations.

It is not possible to compare costs by simply comparing the level premium charged by different companies for the same amount of coverage. On participating policies, comparative dividend scales are of critical importance. And on any policies, cash value buildup patterns can differ in situations where the premium is essentially the same.

Net Premium vs. Cash Values Method. At one time, it was common for those marketing insurance to compare net premiums (premiums less aggregate projected dividends) over, e.g., twenty years with the cash surrender value at that time. Because the cash value often would exceed aggregate net premiums after that period of time, it was claimed that the insurance was "no cost" or would produce a "profit."

Timing of cash flows is of critical importance in comparing policies. Obviously, the cost of the insurance protection obtained during the period (excess of face value over emerging cash values) was the interest or other investment return the policy owner could have earned during the period on the funds which were tied up in net premiums. Although the net premium method of cost comparison, illustrated above, has fallen into official disrepute because it gives no recognition to the time value of money, it is still encountered.

Interest-Adjusted Cost Index Method. The National Association of Insurance Commissioners has devised an interest-adjusted cost index method of comparison which the insurance laws of many states now require be disclosed to prospective insurance purchasers at time of sale.

The *payments index* is determined by first accumulating both the annual premium payments and projected dividends at an interest rate over the first ten years and twenty years after policy issuance. The future values of the net payment streams thus determined are then divided by the future value of an annuity due of $1 at the interest rate, to determine the net level dollar payments per annum that would produce the future values.

The *surrender index* continues the approach by subtracting the cash surrender value at the end of the ten- and twenty-year periods (and any termination dividends) from the future values of the payment streams. Again, these net future values are divided by the future value of an annuity due of $1 to determine the level annual payments which would produce the net future values.

> *Example:* A $1,000 participating policy requires a premium of $25. The future value of $25 accumulated for twenty years at 5 percent is $867.98. The year-by-year projected dividends accumulated for the twenty-year period at 5 percent produce a future value of $234.01. Thus, the net future value of the payments stream is $867.98 − $234.01, or $633.97. Dividing by the future value of an annuity due of $1 ($34.72) produces a payments index of 18.26. This simply means that $18.26 deposited each year for twenty years, accumulated at 5 percent interest, would yield $633.97 after twenty years.

If the cash surrender value after twenty years is $350, then the net cost of surrendering the policy after that period of time, on an interest-adjusted basis, is $283.97 ($633.97 − $350). This ignores any termination dividend. By dividing $283.97 by the future value of a $1 annuity due, a "surrender index" of 8.18 is determined. This simply means that $8.18 deposited each year for twenty years, accumulated at 5 percent interest, will produce the interest-adjusted cost of policy surrender at the end of that period.

Using the Indexes. These indexes are not particularly useful on a stand-alone basis. Their utility lies in comparing the indexes for the same policy issued by different insurance companies. The policy having the lowest indexes on a comparative basis may be potentially the lowest cost policy.

Nevertheless, the usefulness of these indexes is limited. They do not convey relative information for points of comparison other than precisely ten or twenty years out. And the interest rate used to compute the indexes (5 percent) is not representative of the level of interest rates (even an after-tax rate) prevailing in inflationary times. And of course, actual dividends may turn out to be different than the projections used in determining the indexes.

Nevertheless, the indexes may provide a quick indicator of relative costs which could be useful in selecting from an array of policies for further detailed analysis.

Representative Policy Values. Figures 21.2 and 21.3 convey information about comparative costs for a number of policies which were available in 1980. The figures are not intended to be a representative sample of all of the available products, but are merely intended to give the reader some feel for the range of individual cash value policy costs.

		Whole Life		Paid Up at Age 65	
Issue age		35	45	35	45
Annual level premium		$ 210	$ 307	$ 246	$ 403
Aggregate premiums	10 years	2,100	3,070	2,460	4,030
	20 years	4,200	6,140	4,920	8,060
Aggregate dividends	10 years	681	974	835	1,293
	20 years	2,018	2,910	2,435	3,761
Cash surrender value	10 years	1,289	1,826	1,515	2,579
	20 years	3,005	4,004	3,635	6,294
Net surrender cost	10 years	130	270	110	158
(gain)	20 years	(823)	(774)	(1,150)	(1,995)
Interest-adjusted indexes (5 percent)					
Payments index	10 years	14.81	21.92	17.03	28.51
	20 years	12.42	18.39	14.23	24.19
Surrender index	10 years	5.05	8.09	5.56	8.98
	20 years	3.76	6.86	3.76	6.06

Note: The above is based on 1980 dividend scale. Net surrender costs and interest-adjusted indexes would be lower for policy amounts greater than $10,000.

Source: Northwestern Mutual Life Ins. Co. from the 1980 edition of *Best's Flitcraft Compend.*

Fig. 21.2 Illustration of Costs. $10,000 of Insurance on a Male Life—Standard Risk

WHOLE LIFE INSURANCE—TAX CONSIDERATIONS

It was explained in Chapter 20 that individual cash value life insurance policies are typically utilized by employers to finance death and other benefits for executive groups. It was further explained that there are three basic structures for accomplishing this:

1. All rights to the policy are owned by the executive; the company pays all or a portion of the premium.
2. A split-dollar arrangement whereby ownership and benefits under the policy are split between the company and the executive until retirement. Thereafter, full ownership of the policy reverts to either the employer or the executive, and the arrangement becomes essentially the same as either (1) above or (3) below.
3. All rights under the policy are owned by the employer. Upon the death of the executive, whether before or after retirement, the company uses the

	Whole Life		*Paid Up at Age 65*	
Issue age	35	45	35	45
Annual level premiums				
Northwestern Mutual	$210	$307	$246	$403
Mutual Benefit (New Jersey)	236	332	279	440
National Life of Vermont	222	322	259	427
New England Life	180	264	216	335
Massachusetts Mutual	175	256	196	324
Payments index (5 percent)—10 years				
Northwestern Mutual	14.81	21.92	17.03	28.51
Mutual Benefit (New Jersey)	18.83	26.57	21.98	N/A
National Life of Vermont	19.85	27.65	22.72	35.66
New England Life	15.72	23.48	18.08	29.92
Massachusetts Mutual	15.16	21.97	17.14	25.21
Surrender index (5 percent)—10 years				
Northwestern Mutual	5.05	8.09	5.56	8.98
Mutual Benefit (New Jersey)	6.29	9.75	6.76	N/A
National Life of Vermont	7.20	11.01	7.47	12.12
New England Life	5.97	9.69	10.39	14.90
Massachusetts Mutual	5.42	8.18	5.66	7.88

Note: The above is based on 8 percent loan rate policies and 1980 dividend scales.

Source: 1980 edition of *Best's Flitcraft Compend.*

Fig. 21.3 Comparative Costs. $10,000 of Insurance on a Male Life—Standard Risk

policy proceeds to reimburse it for the cost of paying uninsured death or other benefits to the executive's beneficiary.

Implications for Employer

In structuring these arrangements, there are a number of basic tax rules with respect to the employer which must be borne in mind.

Deductibility of Premiums. The employer is not allowed any tax deduction for the payment of premiums on a life insurance policy of which it is directly or indirectly a beneficiary.[11] Thus, premiums paid by the employer under structures (2) and (3) are not tax deductible. Premiums paid under structure (1) are deductible, and are treated as a payment of compensation to the executive.

[11] I.R.C. § 264.

Thus, even though under structure (2) the executive must recognize some taxable income with regard to the death benefit protection he obtains under a split-dollar arrangement prior to retirement, the employer is not permitted a tax deduction for its premium payment which finances that death benefit protection.[12] To overcome this inequity, arrangements have been devised whereby a portion of the premium is paid by the executive, and he or she is reimbursed for that premium payment by the employer in the form of a bonus or other cash compensation payment. The result is that the employer obtains a tax deduction for the compensation payment, and its premium outlay which is a nondeductible expenditure is reduced by a like amount. Thus, the employer obtains its tax deduction. On the executive's side, the net after-tax position is essentially the same.

Dividends. Dividends paid under participating policies are not taxable to the policy owner to the extent that the dividends in the aggregate do not exceed the premiums previously paid. For tax purposes, a dividend is simply treated as a return of premium.

Sales presentations for cash value insurance products generally emphasize that dividends are not taxable. It is well to keep in mind that that is true only to the extent that the dividends do not in the aggregate exceed the premiums previously paid.[13]

Surrender of Policy. If a policy is surrendered for its cash surrender value, any excess of the amount received over net premiums previously paid (premiums less dividends received in cash or used to reduce premium) is taxable and is treated as ordinary income. Tax-free treatment of gains from holding life insurance policies is extended only to death benefit proceeds, not to surrender amounts.[14]

Death Benefits. Although the general rule is that death benefits received under a policy are tax free even though they exceed net premiums previously paid, there are exceptions such as under the transfer for value rule, which is discussed in Chapter 20. This rule must be watched under split-dollar structures, if full ownership of the policy reverts to the employer at retirement.

Interest on Policy Loans. As a general rule, interest on policy loans or on other borrowings for the purpose of paying premiums is tax deductible. There are, however, pitfalls.

Four-out-of-seven rule. This rule provides for the disallowance of any interest on indebtedness incurred or continued to purchase a life insurance, endowment, or annuity contract pursuant to a plan of purchase which con-

---

[12] Rev. Rul. 64-328, 1964-2 C.B. 11.
[13] I.R.C. § 72.
[14] *Id.*

templates the systematic direct or indirect borrowing of part of all of the increases in the cash value—unless no part of four of the first seven annual premiums on the policy is paid by means of indebtedness.[15] If this rule is violated, not only interest paid or incurred during the first seven years is disallowed, but subsequent interest payments as well.

While there are exceptions to the application of this rule, such as demonstrating successfully that the indebtedness was incurred in connection with the taxpayer's trade or business rather than for premium payment purposes, the only prudent course of action is to be certain that at least four of the first seven annual premiums are paid from a source other than borrowed funds. The following specific points should be noted:

- The rule applies not only to interest on policy loans, but to interest on borrowings from any lender for the purpose of carrying the policy.
- Any borrowings during the first seven years in excess of the premium for the year in which borrowed will be thrown back against earlier years. Thus, for example, if the first four premiums on a policy are paid other than from borrowed funds, but in the fifth year the taxpayer borrows an amount in excess of the premium for the fifth year, the excess will be thrown back to an earlier year resulting in that earlier year's premium also being regarded as paid in part with borrowed funds. Thus, the taxpayer would have to pay either the sixth- or seventh-year premium out of nonborrowed funds in order to comply with the test.
- The position of the IRS seems to be that this throwback rule does not apply after completion of the seven-year period. Thus, it is common under minimum deposit arrangements to borrow all of the cash values out of the policy in the eighth year, even though the amount borrowed exceeds the premium for the eighth year and is in effect a recoupment of some of the premiums paid during the first seven years.
- In the event of a substantial increase in any annual premium on a contract, a new seven-year period begins on the day such increased premium is paid. Because of this rule, it is not possible to borrow (on a tax-deductible basis) on modified life or graded premium plans, until such time as the premium reaches its ultimate level. At that point, the final seven-year period begins to run and borrowing can commence consistent with observing the four-out-of-seven rule during that final period.

Loan net of interest. When a policy loan is made, some insurance companies will deduct the first year's interest from the amount of the loan and remit the net proceeds to the contractholder. In the case of cash-basis taxpayers, the practice can cause the first year's interest deduction to be disallowed. The IRS follows the rule[16] that a taxpayer is not considered to have paid an amount of interest which is advanced by the maker of the loan to which the interest relates.

---

[15] I.R.C. § 264.
[16] Rev. Rul. 73-482, 1973-2 C.B. 44.

Single premium policies. No deduction is allowable for indebtedness incurred or continued to purchase a single premium life insurance, endowment, or annuity contract.[17] For purposes of this tax rule, the term "single premium" does not necessarily have the same meaning as for normal insurance purposes. A *single premium contract* is defined as one under which substantially all the premiums are paid within a period of four years from the date on which a contract is purchased, or where an amount is deposited with the insurer for payment of a substantial number of future premiums on the contract.

CASH VALUE LIFE INSURANCE IN EXECUTIVE SUPPLEMENTAL DEATH BENEFITS

The No-Cost Theme

The major feature of proposals for using cash value life insurance to fund plans providing death and other supplemental benefits for executive groups is that the arrangements are very often described as low cost or no cost. Whereas financing these benefits through group term life insurance or unfunded plans obviously results in a cost to the company, the use of cash value life insurance is usually structured in a manner claimed to result in the recoupment by the company of all or virtually all of its benefit costs.

These no-cost claims are particularly intriguing in view of the well-known characteristics of the front-end expense load in individual cash value life insurance policies. That is, quite typically the first-year premium is almost entirely absorbed by commissions and other policy issuance expenses, so that premium dollars do not really begin to work for the policyholder until the second year. By contrast, group life insurance arrangements involve a lower expense loading and, of course, uninsured plans involve no expense load other than any internal administrative costs the employer may incur.

Analysis of Funding Approaches

The key to understanding the low-cost phenomenon lies in appreciating the fundamental differences between the funding plans proposed when cash value life insurance policies are utilized, compared to the funding plans traditionally utilized for employee benefits. The distinction can best be grasped by considering the application of these fundamental differences to pension funding.

Annuity Concept. Pension plan funding is typically based on an annuity concept. That is, the objective is to determine an appropriate amount of

17 I.R.C. § 264.

annual contributions which, together with the earnings of the fund, will be sufficient to pay the promised pensions. The source of the pension payments is both the principal of the fund (i.e., the contributions) and its income.

A company usually perceives its pension costs to be only its contributions to the fund. These costs will be less than the actual pension benefits ultimately paid, the difference representing fund income. The company typically does not perceive that the fund income indicates an additional pension cost to it, although in reality, by pre-funding prior to the time the payments are actually due to retirees, the company has lost the earning power of the funds in the interim. In other words, the company has incurred a cost of money in addition to its recorded pension costs.

Endowment Concept. Conceptually, there is another way of funding a pension plan, which could be called the *endowment approach.* It simply means that much larger contributions would be made to the fund, with the objective that fund income alone could be sufficient to pay the promised pensions. Upon the completion of all pension payments, the principal of the fund would revert to the employer.

Under the endowment approach, the company could perceive that its contributions to the pension fund are not a cost at all but rather an asset in the nature of refundable non-interest-bearing advances. Its pension cost would be entirely a cost of money, i.e., the loss of earning power on the advances.

The endowment approach is never used in pension funding, if for no other reason than that it is not feasible from a tax viewpoint. But it is precisely the endowment approach, rather than the annuity approach, which is used in funding supplemental executive benefit plans utilizing cash value life insurance. The fundamental reason why these plans appear to be low cost or no cost is that it is the gain derived from holding life insurance policies as an investment which pays for the benefits. The premium dollars, which represent the amount invested, are eventually returned to the employer.

Implementing the Endowment Approach. How the endowment approach is utilized can be illustrated by a simple example. Assume that the company has promised an executive a $50,000 post-retirement death benefit. The company could insure that benefit by simply purchasing a $50,000 ordinary life insurance policy, which at date of death would pay the benefit to the executive's heirs. If that were done, the company would perceive its cost as being the net premiums paid for the policy, let us say $20,000. That would be the annuity approach, since both the net premium and the investment earnings implicit in the policy's death benefit would fund the payment.

The perceived $20,000 cost under the annuity approach can be changed to an approach perceived as no cost by the simple expedient of buying more life insurance. For example, the company could purchase $85,000 rather than $50,000 of insurance. The net premium would increase to about $34,000. But the proceeds of $85,000 would be sufficient to recoup both the net premium and the $50,000 cost of the death benefit paid to the executive's heirs.

That is the endowment approach, and its basic thrust is quite simple: purchase enough insurance to recover both the benefit cost and the premium cost. It should be apparent that under this endowment approach, the company's cost is the cost of money on the funds it has tied up in the net insurance premiums, until the death of the executive.

Cost of Money. Under most of these plans, the cost of money for the funds invested in premiums will represent mainly interest on anticipated policy loans from the insurance company, at an interest rate (typically 8 percent today) guaranteed in the policy. But in order to obtain tax deductions for the interest, the "four out of seven" tax rule must be observed, i.e., at least four of the first seven annual premium payments on a policy must be paid from sources other than borrowed funds.

Typically, in the eighth policy year the employer will borrow out the premiums not previously borrowed, and borrow all premiums thereafter.

Thus, the company's cost of money can consist of:

1. Interest paid on the policy loans;
2. Cost of money on initial premiums paid other than through policy loans, until the eighth year; and
3. Cost of money on benefits paid to executives or their heirs prior to the receipt of policy proceeds.

An example of the latter type of cost of money is when an executive is paid supplemental retirement benefits by the company for a period of years, but the company does not recover those payments until the retired executive dies.

Investment Return Analysis. Costs are incurred to finance an investment in a life insurance policy to produce a return sufficient to pay for the benefits provided to the executive or his heirs. Thus, it is important to compare the rate of return that can reasonably be expected from the investment, with the cost of money rate.

Analyzing a life insurance policy from an investment viewpoint requires some reorientation of conventional thinking about life insurance. Traditionally, the primary motive for purchasing cash value life insurance has been to obtain protection against the adverse financial consequences of premature death. The investment attributes, traditionally viewed as the cash value of the policy, have been regarded as secondary.

Similarly, the conventional view that cash value life insurance is a poor investment derives from comparisons of cash surrender value buildups with premium payments. But under these plans, cash surrender values are not viewed as having any particular importance other than as a measure of borrowing capacity under the policy. Usually there is no intention of cashing in the policy at any point. Rather the objective is to hold it until death, in order to obtain the much larger death benefit. Furthermore, the death benefit is received free of income tax, whereas cashing in a policy can result in taxable income. Thus, the investment analysis must compare the expected proceeds from the investment, which is the death benefit, with the amount invested, which is net premiums.

The Discount Bond Analogy. Viewed in this fashion, a life insurance policy is really a peculiar sort of discount bond. It has a fixed maturity value, i.e., the death benefit, but an uncertain maturity date. Furthermore, the purchase price is paid in installments, as annual premiums. If the premiums are payable on a whole life basis, even the total purchase price is uncertain. But many policies used in supplemental executive benefit plans are of the type which become paid up at age 65, or after some fixed period of years. Therefore, there is a ceiling on the total purchase price.

If dividends are taken in cash, the investment analysis should compare the death benefit with aggregate net premiums. Usually, however, because of the heavy borrowing against the policies, dividends are not used to reduce premiums until such time as the policy becomes paid up. In the interim, they are used to purchase additional insurance, usually paid-up additions which in effect represent annual purchases of single premium life insurance. The intention is that this additional insurance will offset the borrowing against the policy, so that the benefit payable upon death will still come close to the original face amount of the policy.

Where this occurs, the investment analysis should compare the total death benefits expected from the policy, including paid-up additions anticipated to be purchased with projected dividends, with aggregate premiums payable.

Example: A 40-year-old executive is promised a $150,000 death benefit if he stays with the company until retirement age 65.

It is proposed that these benefits be funded by having the company purchase a $113,500 paid-up-at-age-65, participating insurance policy on the executive's life. The annual premium is $3,450. The company will borrow all premium payments, subject to the "four out of seven" rule. The policy loan interest rate is 8 percent. Dividends will be used to buy paid-up additional insurance until age 65; thereafter, they will be taken in cash.

Based on dividend projections and an assumption that the executive will die at age 80, the following results are forecast (in $1,000s):

Proceeds (nontaxable)	
Death benefit	
Original	$113.5
Paid-up additions	70.8
Repay loans	(86.4)
Net	97.9
Dividends taken in cash	70.0
	167.9
Payments (tax deductible)	
Benefits paid executive	150.0
Interest on policy loans	190.0
	340.0
Tax saving at 50 percent	(170.0)
	$170.0

Thus, if the assumptions as to date of death, dividends, and effective tax rates turn out to be correct, the representation is that the $150,000 of benefits paid to the executive's beneficiary should cost the company virtually nothing.

Analyzing the Presentation. The preceding example jumbles together three different transactions:

1. Investing in a life insurance policy
2. Borrowing funds to finance the investment
3. Paying benefits to the executive's beneficiary

A meaningful analytical technique is to compute the anticipated rate of return on the investment, based on the assumptions, and to compare it with the cost of funds.

Looking at the anticipated investment results, we have the following:

Death benefit	
Original	$113.5
Paid-up additions	70.8
	184.3
Net premium invested	
Premiums	86.4
Dividends taken in cash	(70.0)
	16.4
Projected investment gain	$167.9

While the gain looks huge compared to net premiums invested, it actually represents a yield to maturity of about 4.1 percent. In other words, if annual premium payments (ages 40 to 65) and dividends (ages 66 to 80) were viewed as deposits to and withdrawals from a savings account, and the question asked was "what interest rate, compounded annually, is necessary for the balance in the savings account to be approximately $185,000 at age 80?," the answer would be: "approximately 4.1 percent."

That is an after-tax rate of return. If a 50 percent marginal tax rate is assumed, the return would appear to be about even with the 8 percent cost of funds on the policy loans. As such, the adequacy of the rate of return on the investment is obviously questionable.

Interpreting the Results. The example used above is intended to demonstrate a technique that can be used for financial analysis of the rate of return which might be anticipated from a cash value life insurance policy purchased as an investment. The 4.1 percent anticipated rate of return determined in the example should not be construed as a norm, since rate of return can vary markedly among different policies. As explained earlier in this chapter, the pricing and financial structure of cash value life insurance products is not uniform, and wide variations can be encountered. These product variations can significantly affect rate of return.

Uncertainty in assumptions. Rate of return is quite sensitive to the assumed date of death. For example, if in the above example death were assumed at age 75 or 70, the rate of return would improve to 4.4 percent and 4.8 percent respectively. On the other hand, if death occurs after age 80, the rate of return declines further.

There is also uncertainty as to the cost of funds. The 8 percent policy loan rate provides a ceiling, but if interest rates were to drop below 8 percent, policy loans could be refinanced. There are also financing requirements to be met other than through policy loans, namely four out of the first seven premiums, and any benefit disbursements prior to the collection of death benefit proceeds. Here the company is subject to the variability of market interest rates.

Importance of Mortality Experience. In the final analysis, both rate of return and (to a lesser degree) cost of funds is a gamble on how long the executive will live. Early death will produce a high rate of return, and minimize the cost of funds. Living to a ripe old age has the opposite result.

Where only a few key employees are involved in a program, actual mortality experience could vary significantly from what initial life expectancies might indicate. If a program covers a relatively large group, e.g., fifty or more individuals, more predictable mortality experience could reasonably be anticipated. Nevertheless, conventional mortality tables are based on the average experience of hundreds of thousands of individuals. Any presentation that attempts to project year-by-year cash flows for a relatively small group of covered individuals, based on assuming some predictable pattern of individual deaths, should be viewed skeptically.

Personal Tax Considerations

The example analyzed above illustrates one of the three structures that can be employed in utilizing cash value life insurance policies to provide death benefits for executives. It is the third structure, i.e., where the insurance is entirely owned by the company which will be the recipient of the tax-free insurance death benefit. From the personal tax viewpoint, a significant disadvantage of this structure is that the benefit paid by the employer represents taxable income to the beneficiary rather than income tax free proceeds of life insurance. Furthermore, in all likelihood the value of the benefit will be included in the executive's gross estate for estate tax purposes.

Group Term Life Cost Recoupment. One approach devised to combat this problem is to provide the death benefit under a group life insurance plan and to utilize the corporate-owned individual life insurance policy as a vehicle for recouping the premium cost that results to the company under an experience-rated group contract upon incurring the claim resulting from the executive's death. Since the group life insurance premium is deductible to the company in essentially the same manner as would be the payment of an uninsured death benefit, the corporation comes out much the same. But from the viewpoint of the beneficiary, the payment can represent the proceeds of life insurance rather than an uninsured death benefit.

Alternative for Financing Benefits. Whether the death benefit paid to a beneficiary takes the form of group life insurance or a direct (uninsured) payment from the employer, the bottom line question is whether the employer should:

1. Finance the payment by the purchase of an individual cash value life insurance policy.
2. Finance the payment by purchasing some other type of investment.
3. Not finance the payment at all, i.e., handle it on a pay-as-you-go basis.

The type of analysis suggested above for determining rate of return on investment in an individual life insurance policy should be helpful in reaching a decision on the financing question.

Split-Dollar Structure

Under structures (1) and (2) described previously, the death benefit for an executive's beneficiary is payable directly under the policy. Under structure (1), the policy is owned by the executive but the company pays all or a portion of the premiums. Structure (2) is a split-dollar arrangement. Although essentially the same policy could be used under either structure, the company's cost (and the executive's cost) will differ.

Example of Split-Dollar: Assume that a company wishes to provide $500,000 of permanent death benefit protection for a 50-year-old executive. It is considering a split-dollar proposal which would utilize a paid-up-at-age-65 participating life insurance policy having the following characteristics:

Face amount:	$670,000
Annual premium:	29,700
Policy loan rate:	8 percent

The proposal is that the executive pay a portion of the premium equal to the term cost for the current protection, and that the employer pay the balance of the premium.

Prior to the policy becoming paid up at age 65, dividends would be used to purchase additional insurance in the form of paid-up additions. After the policy becomes paid up, dividends can be taken in cash.

The purpose of using dividends to purchase paid-up additions is to maintain the net death benefit at an amount sufficient to provide the executive with $500,000 of coverage despite borrowing against the policy.

Premium payments would be split as follows (in $1,000s):

		Company		*Executive* *	
Year/Age		*Annual*	*Cumulative*	*Annual*	*Cumulative*
1	50	$26.7	$ 26.7	$ 3.0	$ 3.0
2	51	26.3	53.0	3.4	6.4
3	52	26.0	79.0	3.7	10.1
4	53	25.7	104.7	4.0	14.1
5	54	25.3	130.0	4.4	18.5
6	55	24.9	154.9	4.8	23.3
7	56	24.4	179.3	5.3	28.6
8	57	23.9	203.2	5.8	34.4
9	58	23.4	226.6	6.3	40.7
10	59	22.8	249.4	6.9	47.6
11	60	22.2	271.6	7.5	55.1
12	61	21.4	293.0	8.3	63.4
13	62	20.5	313.5	9.2	72.6
14	63	19.8	333.3	9.9	82.5
15	64	18.9	352.2	10.8	93.3

* The above is based on the insurer's published rates for a $500,000 one-year individual term policy, which are lower than the P.S. 58 table rates.

The company would borrow amounts equal to its premium payments, limited however in the early years by the four-out-of-seven rule. The pattern of borrowings and related interest costs would be as follows:

Year	Accumulated Premium Payments	Loan Outstanding	Net Unrecovered Premium	Annual Loan Interest Cost
1	26.7	—	26.7	—
2	53.0	—	53.0	—
3	79.0	—	79.0	—
4	104.7	—	104.7	—
5	130.0	25.3	104.7	2.0
6	154.9	50.2	104.7	4.0
7	179.3	74.6	104.7	6.0
8	203.2	203.2	—	16.2
9	226.6	226.6	—	18.1
10	249.4	249.4	—	20.0
11	271.6	271.6	—	21.7
12	293.0	293.0	—	23.4
13	313.5	313.5	—	25.1
14	333.3	333.3	—	26.7
15	352.2	352.2	—	28.2

The arrangement would provide that the company owns the excess of the total death benefit under the policy (including paid-up additions) over the $500,000 assigned to the executive. The excess of the company's share of the death benefit over its total borrowings under the policy is referred to as its net death benefit. The company's projected net death benefit position year by year can be compared to its net unrecovered premiums as follows:

Year	Net Death Benefit	Net Unrecovered Premiums
1	170.0	26.7
2	174.1	53.0
3	177.7	79.0
4	182.9	104.7
5	164.3	104.7
6	147.9	104.7
7	133.9	104.7
8	17.8	—
9	9.0	—
10	3.1	—
11	.3	—
12	.8	—
13	3.8	—
14	8.1	—
15	14.0	—

Thus, in the event of the executive's death prior to retirement, the company's share of the net death benefit should at any time be sufficient to at least recoup its unrecovered premiums, and the executive's beneficiary would receive $500,000 of insurance proceeds.

Net Cash Surrender Value. Cash surrender value less loans against the policy, referred to as net CSV, is projected to be as follows:

Year	*Net CSV*
1	$ 0
2	26.5
3	53.7
4	82.3
5	87.3
6	94.6
7	104.4
8	12.0
9	27.5
10	46.0
11	68.0
12	93.5
13	123.0
14	156.0
15	192.5

There are two ways in which the net CSV might be handled. Starting in the eighth year, the company could assign all of the net CSV to the executive. He would, however, then have to recognize some taxable income each year with respect to the net CSV buildup. Alternatively, the company could retain ownership of the net CSV until age 65, which would defer the recognition of taxable income by the executive. He would have to recognize that income at the time the paid-up policy is turned over to him.

Results at Retirement. At age 65, the company would turn over full ownership of the paid-up policy to the executive. At that time projected policy values would be as follows:

Gross death benefit	$866.2
Loans	352.2
Net death benefit	$514.0
Gross cash surrender value	544.7
Loans	352.2
Net CSV	$192.5

Although no further premiums are payable, the executive would be obligated to pay tax-deductible interest of $28,200 per year on the policy loans. He would, however, be entitled to the dividends on the policy, projected to be about $15,000 per year at age 65, increasing by about $500 per year thereafter. The interest would be tax deductible, but the dividends would not be taxable until such time, if ever, that aggregate dividends exceeded the total of premiums paid by the executive—and, arguably, taxable income recognized by the executive on net CSV. Thus, on a net of tax basis, the executive's carrying cost for the policy should not be significant. His exact position in this regard would depend on his post-retirement tax brackets.

It should be noted that net CSV would continue to increase by about $10,000 per year after age 65, and that the executive would have the right, if he chose, to borrow against net CSV or to cash in the policy.

Employer's Cost. Since the employer is expected to recoup all of its premium payments under the arrangement, its cost is a cost of money. It consists of the interest payments under the policy loan as scheduled above, plus an additional cost of money during the first seven years when the four-out-of-seven rule precludes it from full borrowing to pay premiums.

The executive's cost is his share of the premiums as illustrated above, plus whatever tax he may owe on the net CSV. Since his share of the premiums equals the cost of the current insurance protection which the arrangement affords him prior to retirement, he has no additional tax cost.

The company could offset the executive's cost by paying him additional compensation equal to approximately twice the amount of the executive's share of premiums. That, of course, would represent an additional cost to the company.

Policy Fully Owned by Executive

Under structure (1), as described previously, the very same policy could be owned outright by the executive from the beginning. The company could pay all of the premium cost ($29,700 per year) as compensation, with no future recoupment. In the early years of the arrangement, the company's level cost would be greater than its cost of money under the split-dollar approach illustrated above. In the years close to retirement, the cost of money approaches the premium cost.

Under this structure the executive would have to pay tax on $29,700 of compensation each year. That would be much more costly to him in the early years than his share of premium under the split-dollar approach. But in later years, the executive would be able to borrow on the policy in much the same manner as the company would have under the split-dollar approach, and still maintain at least $500,000 of insurance coverage. These loans could cover the executive's tax cost and his interest cost (net of tax benefit) on the borrowings.

Summary

As can be appreciated from the above discussion, there are a number of alternative structures for providing and financing death benefit protection for executives. There is no substitute for close attention to detail, intensive quantitative analysis, and careful screening of insurance products in selecting the most favorable arrangement from the viewpoint of both the executive and the company.

WHOLE LIFE INSURANCE IN SPLIT FUNDING DEFINED BENEFIT PLANS

The advantages and disadvantages of split funding defined benefit pension plans by using whole life insurance policies as a funding vehicle were discussed in Chapter 20, and will not be repeated here in any detail. An employer considering adopting a split-funded plan needs to ask itself the following questions:

- Is furnishing retirement benefits my sole objective, or do I wish to provide my employees with both retirement benefits and significant preretirement death benefit protection?
- If the latter, am I better off providing the death benefit protection under the retirement plan, or under a completely separate plan?

Cost of Split Funding

If it is not the employer's objective to provide significant preretirement death benefit protection, then there is usually no point in utilizing a split-funded plan. Comparisons will almost always show that the cost of delivering the retirement benefits under the split-funded plan are considerably higher than delivering the same benefits using other funding vehicles. The reason is quite simple. Under a split-funded plan, a portion of the contributions is devoted to providing the death benefit protection, rather than going to fund retirement benefits. Under alternative funding vehicles, all of the contributions are used to provide retirement benefits.

The quantitative analysis is straightforward. The annual cost for maintaining a given level of benefits under a split-funded plan is first determined by aggregating the premiums for the life insurance portion plus the required contribution to the side fund, using an interest rate assumption and the annuity conversion rates in the policy.

The cost for the same level of benefits, funded entirely through an unallocated investment fund arrangement, can then be determined by utilizing the same interest rate assumption as for the side fund, and representative annuity conversion rates.

The approach is necessarily somewhat simplistic. Cost projections for split-funded plans typically do not factor in either projected future salary increases, or employee turnover which can lead to forfeitures. Projections may also not take into account dividends which will be payable on the policies.

On the other hand, the projection of cost under an alternative funding plan would give consideration to all of the typical actuarial cost method and assumption variables which were discussed in Chapter 11, including salary projection and turnover.

Preretirement Death Benefits. If the employer's objective in adopting a plan is to provide a significant level of preretirement death benefit protection along with retirement benefits, the analysis needs to address whether the death benefits are more efficiently provided under the retirement plan (via split funding) or outside the plan. Providing the death benefits outside the plan can permit a greater amount of flexibility in designing benefit levels. If the death benefits are provided under the retirement plan, the strict anti-discrimination rules applicable to tax-qualified plans severely limit design flexibility. As a practical matter, the death benefit for any employee must be a uniform multiple of his retirement benefit—typically 100 times the projected monthly retirement benefit.

Group term life alternative. If the death benefits are provided outside of the tax-qualified retirement plan via group term life insurance, there is considerably more flexibility in designing the insurance levels. Typically, the levels will be more proportionate to current compensation than to projected retirement benefits. The design considerations and constraints applicable to group term life insurance plans are discussed in Chapter 20.

Individual whole life policies alternative. If the death benefit protection provided outside the retirement plan takes the form of individual whole life insurance policies, design flexibility is complete since the employer may select any employee it wishes for any amount of coverage it cares to provide.

Evaluating the Alternatives

From the employer's financial and tax viewpoint, the principal considerations are:

1. The relative costs of furnishing death benefits for employees utilizing whole life insurance versus term insurance—a subject which was discussed in detail earlier in this chapter; and
2. The differing tax considerations for the employer as regards the various vehicles.

Employer's Tax Considerations. Subject to ERISA limitations, discussed in Chapter 14, all of an employer's contributions to a qualified retirement plan are tax deductible on a current basis. That is true regardless of whether the contributions are used entirely to fund retirement benefits, or a portion of the contributions are used to fund death benefits under a split-funded plan. Similarly, if group term life insurance is used as the vehicle to deliver death benefit protection, all of the employer's premium dollars for the group term life insurance are also fully tax deductible.

On the other hand, if the death benefit protection is delivered via individual whole life insurance policies outside the qualified plan then the premium dollars paid by the employer are tax deductible only if the employer is not a beneficiary under the policy. In that event, the employer paid premiums are tax deductible since they are regarded as additional compensation and taxable as such to the employee. This point was discussed in greater detail earlier in this chapter.

Overall Comparison. From the employer's viewpoint, the cost of delivering both retirement and death benefits under a split-funded tax-qualified plan can be compared with the cost of delivering solely retirement benefits under the tax-qualified plan coupled with delivering the death benefit protection under group term life insurance. The technique simply takes the methodology for comparing split-funded plans with alternatively funded retirement plans, which was suggested above, and adds the cost of group term life insurance premiums to the required annual contribution under the alternatively funded retirement plan. The total of the two can then be compared to the annual contribution under the split-funded plan, so as to measure the employer's comparative cost for delivering essentially the same combination of benefits under two different plans and financing structures. Since the employer's contributions and premiums are fully tax deductible either way, the comparison can be made on a pre-tax basis.

UNINSURED DEATH BENEFITS IN DEFINED BENEFIT PLANS

ERISA—Mandated Survivor Benefits

The two forms of ERISA-mandated surviving spouse benefits are:

- Qualified joint and survivor annuity (post-retirement benefit)
- Early survivor annuity (preretirement benefit)

Post-Retirement Benefit

The post-retirement benefit requires generally that in the case of a married participant, the plan must provide to the spouse, if he or she survives the retired participant, a life annuity continuation not less than 50 percent or greater than 100 percent of the retirement annuity which was payable while both the participant and the spouse were living.

Financing. The overwhelmingly predominant practice is to pass the cost of the qualified joint and survivor annuity along to the participant via an actuarial reduction of the pension. Thus, usual practice is for the standard retirement benefit to be expressed as a single life annuity. If a married participant chooses (by not "electing out") to take a qualified joint and survivor annuity instead, his or her pension is reduced from what it would have been on a single life basis, to account actuarially for the cost of the survivor benefit.

Thus, if all of the actuarial assumptions made in computing the reduction factors are exactly realized, there is no cost to the plan sponsor. But as in the case of other actuarial assumptions, some deviation between the assumptions and ultimate experience is likely to emerge. The actuarial gains and losses which result will represent a cost or gain (as the case may be) to the plan sponsor, resulting from the qualified joint and survivor annuity feature. (Generally, there will be some loss. The reason is that the actuarial reduction factors are derived from average experience, but employees with less than average life expectancy are more likely to take the joint and survivor form. It is very difficult to guard effectively against such anti-selection.)

Typical qualified joint and survivor annuity reduction factors were illustrated in Chapter 20.

Preretirement Benefit

This ERISA provision, which affects only plans that offer early retirement benefits, requires that commencing at the earliest date at which a participant can retire under the plan (but not earlier than ten years prior to normal retirement age), the plan must permit a participant to elect to provide a survivor spouse benefit. The benefit is a life annuity for the spouse equal to the survivor annuity he or she would have had, under the qualified joint and survivor form described above, had the participant retired on the day before his death.

Financing. Practice varies with respect to financing the cost of the early survivor annuity. Some plans pass the cost along to those participants who elect the benefit. The predominant form of charging the participants is by means of an eventual reduction of the participant's retirement benefit if he lives until retirement.

Calculating the cost. The early survivor benefit is in substance a form of term insurance protection. It is essentially similar to the survivor benefit plans described earlier in this chapter as a subset of the broad category of group term life insurance plans. Thus, determining the cost of the ERISA-mandated early survivor benefit is similar to determining an appropriate premium for a group survivor benefit plan. In addition to the absolute amount of the monthly benefit, the two key factors are:

1. The age of the participant, which determines the probability of his death and hence, the incidence of a benefit claim.
2. The age of the spouse, which determines the probabilities of the period of time during which the benefit would be payable.

These age factors can be used actuarially to determine a premium rate per dollar of benefit. However, most plans that reduce a participant's pension to absorb the cost of providing the preretirement death benefit protection do so by expressing the reduction as a flat percentage for each month for which the protection was in effect. Sometimes the percentage varies by participant age brackets. For example, a representative charge (pension reduction) might be one-twenty-fourth of one percent for each month the early survivor benefit election is in effect for participants under age 60, and one-twelfth of one percent for each month after attainment of age 60.

In order to relate the charge more precisely to the risk presented by each electing participant, the age of the spouse should also be taken into account. But this refinement is infrequently seen in practice.

Alternative Employee Financing Arrangements. Although reduction of the pension is the most common form of enabling participants to pay for the protection, it is not the only way. The Treasury regulations [18] permit other arrangements—such as allowing the participant to pay a cash premium on a current basis—provided the plan also provides as an option a procedure whereby an out-of-pocket outlay by the participant is not required.

As in the case of the qualified joint and survivor annuity, actuarial gains or losses can require some part of the cost (or gain) from the preretirement elective coverage to be absorbed by the employer even though the basic thrust is that the benefit is participant paid. That is even more likely with respect to the preretirement coverage in view of the relatively imprecise way in which participant charges are typically determined.

Employer Financing. The alternative approach is to provide the early survivor annuity automatically under the plan, at employer cost. The cost and funding considerations in this approach are quite similar to those discussed immediately below, with respect to non-ERISA-mandated death benefits.

Other Death Benefits

Some plans provide death benefits greater than those required by ERISA. Where no insurance is involved the most common provision is to provide a death benefit equal to the present value of the retirement benefit accrued.[19]

---

[18] Treas. Reg. § 1.401(a)-11(e).

[19] Another type of benefit sometimes provided for is an annuity to the spouse equal to some percentage of the employee's accrued annuity.

Under this arrangement the death benefit during the early years of plan membership is usually quite small but increases, depending on the actuarial assumptions, to approximately 100 to 120 times the anticipated annual pension. The reasons for this dramatically increasing death benefit are twofold. First, the benefit accrued is often based on years of service or plan membership elapsed, both of which are typically minimal during the first few years of participation. As time passes, the accrued benefit, as a percentage of the final retirement pension, usually increases proportionately. In addition to this proportionate increase in the accrued benefit, the present value of each dollar of accrued benefit increases as the participant approaches retirement age. Thus, not only is the accrued benefit increasing each year, but the present value of each dollar of accrued benefit is also increasing.

Financing. Typically, where a plan provides for uninsured death benefits and the employer is paying for the benefit, the cost of the benefit is incorporated by the actuary into the overall cost of the plan. A portion of each year's plan cost represents an amount to fund not only a portion of the death benefit expected to be provided in that year but also a portion of the death benefits expected to be paid out in the future. Thus, the death benefits are pre-funded in the same manner as the retirement benefits are. On occasion, however, the costs for the uninsured death benefits are computed on a "term cost" basis. Using this method, the cost for the death benefits in any one year is the value of the death benefits expected to be paid out in that year. There is no pre-funding of the death benefits that will be paid out in future years. For any one individual, the term-costing approach usually results in an annually increasing cost. That is due to the fact that as an individual ages, the probability of death increases and the absolute amount of the benefit also tends to increase. In an aging population of employees, the term-costing method may lead to rapidly increasing term costs for death benefits.

Coordination With Other Plans

As previously pointed out, the death benefits under a retirement plan can reach substantial sums even when there is no insurance involved. When death benefits are also provided to employees through other programs, such as group life insurance, the benefits should be coordinated with those in the retirement plan. For example, a limit could be placed on the amount of group life insurance an individual receives when the death benefit offered under the retirement plan reaches a certain level. Another option might be to provide for a decreasing schedule of group life insurance which reflects the increasing death benefit under the retirement plan. Of course, it may be the employer's intention to provide a death benefit which increases rapidly. In this case, placing limits or restrictions on the group life insurance benefit would not be desirable. The point is that employers should be aware of the substantial death benefits which may be provided by their retirement plans and should take these benefits into account in their overall employee benefits planning.

Part IV

Protection Against Extraordinary or Catastrophic Costs

22

Health Cost Containment Strategies

DIANA CHAPMAN WALSH[1]

Director of Program Evaluation, Boston University Health Policy Institute

THE EMPLOYER'S PERSPECTIVE ON HEALTH CARE COSTS

Most general managers know considerably more today about the dynamics of the health care system than they did ten or even five years ago. Much of

[1] Thanks are owed to Richard Logan of the Health Services Council in Philadelphia for a substantial contribution to the section on health planning and resource allocation

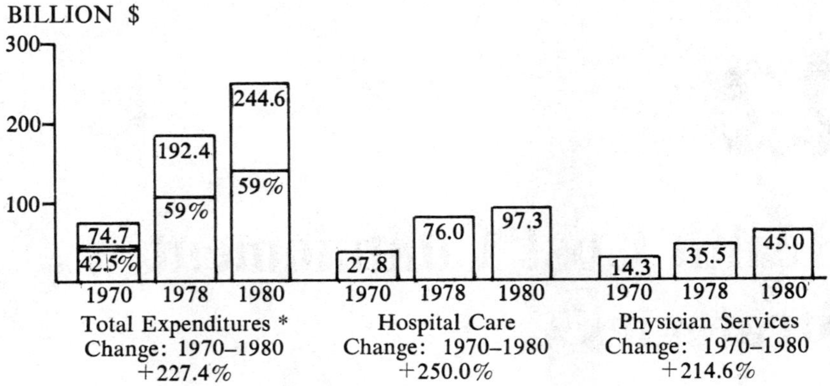

* Percentages referred to in "Total Expenditures" indicate proportion of total costs paid by private payments, includes direct payments, private third-party payments, and philanthrophy.

Fig. 22.1 Some Key Indicators of the Rise in Health Care Costs [2]

what management knows comes filtered through risk and benefit managers, many of whom have become quite sophisticated about the economics of medical care. The statistics on rising health care costs are available and widely quoted; Figure 22.1 includes the major indicators of rising costs. Other indicators include:

- Total health expenditures rose from 7.6 percent of the Gross National Product in 1970 to 9.1 percent in 1978 and are expected to reach 9.5 percent in 1980.[3]
- Total health expenditures rose 12.5 percent annually compared with 10 percent annual rise in GNP.[4]
- Per capita expenditures rose from $359 in 1970 to $863 in 1978 and are projected to reach $1,078 by 1980—an increase of approximately 200 percent.[5]
- Health insurance premiums in the United States rose from $26.2 billion in 1972 to $51.9 billion in 1977—an increase of approximately 98 percent.[6]
- The number of active physicians rose from 318,955 in 1970 to 410,341 in 1978 and is projected to reach 437,269 in 1980—an annual increase of 3.2

---

and, with John English of his staff, for assistance with an early draft of other parts of the chapter. Susan Kelleher of the Center for Industry and Health Care in Boston helped with the research.

[2] Health Care Financing Admin., 1 Health Care Financing Rev. 1–18 (No. 3 Winter 1980).

[3] Cameron & Kirkland, Jr., "Five Burdens That Make a Rich U.S. Feel Poor," Fortune 72–79 (Jan. 14, 1980).

[4] Note 2 *supra.*

[5] *Id.*

[6] Health Insurance Inst., *Source Book of Health Insurance Data, 1978-79* at 6 (1979).

percent compared with total population increase of 0.9 percent during the same period. From 634 Americans per physician in 1970, the ratio is expected to fall to 410 persons per physician in 1990 and 375 in 2000.[7]

Cost containment in health is a relatively new policy; access and quality used to take precedence, accompanied routinely by a somewhat perfunctory acknowledgment of the importance of trying to stay within the lowest reasonable costs. Now that costs have emerged as the highest priority, knowledge is lacking on how they can be stabilized, because there has been little controlled experimentation. Specific cost containment programs tend to rest on logic and judgment rather than on thorough analysis of which proposed approach should be effective. This chapter catalogs, describes, and briefly assesses the diverse programs and strategies that companies are developing to stabilize their health care costs.

Diagnosis of the problem of rising health care costs assigns employers a central role in finding a solution. There are two reasons for this. First, it is costing them a lot of money; second, it is intertwined with the employee benefit package. Since the end of World War II, steady growth of employer-financed health insurance coverage has involved employers even more directly in the problem of rising costs. Most large companies are now routinely seeing annual increases of from 8 to 15 percent (and sometimes much more) in the cost of the health insurance premium, with no major change in the scope of coverage of the benefit package. These increases typically reflect a combination of inflation and stepped-up use of health services.

Employer-paid health insurance dulls consumer consciousness of the costs of care, permits hospitals and other segments of the health care industry to constantly refine and expand their "product" (the mix, level, and technological complexity of the services offered), and raises consumer expectations. The acceleration to the present level of expectation is a virtually irreversible process that creates a vicious circle: more extensive third-party coverage feeds cost escalation which, in turn, increases the need for yet more extensive coverage. With or without a national health insurance plan, one can safely predict that employers will continue, directly or indirectly, to pay a substantial share of the nation's health care bill. Cost containment is undoubtedly here to stay, and managers will be challenged to sort through the various available options to identify those best suited to their particular companies and local circumstances and to finally arrive at a cohesive, constructive, and cost-effective strategy for providing adequate employee health care protection.

---

[7] Note 2 *supra*; *Payer, Provider, Consumer: Industry Confronts Health Care Costs* 39 (Industry and Health Care Series No. 1) (R. Egdahl & D. Walsh, Eds., 1977).

Need for a Comprehensive Corporate Health Strategy

Although cost stabilization programs are changing constantly, this chapter tries to provide a succinct but thorough review of current approaches. The organization of subject matter is summarized in Figure 22.2.

Short Range (Direct)	*Middle Range*	*Long Range (Indirect)*
Reduce Premium:	Restructure the System:	Shift Focus to Prevention:
• Administrative costs • Volume of use • Charges for services	• Competition health maintenance organizations (HMOs) and/or • Resource allocation (HSAs)	• Protect environment • Promote health and mental health

Fig. 22.2 Summary of Industry's Options for Stabilizing Health Care Costs

Cost containment options available to industry are categorized chronologically from (1) "short-range" and direct efforts to stabilize the costs of next year's health insurance premium to (2) "middle-range" experiments to restructure the health care system in order to affect aggregate costs to all payers including industry, and finally to (3) a long-range and more remote (but possibly more important) focus to prevent illness in the first place, thereby avoiding or diminishing the costs of treatment. Using the long-range strategy is sensible but it is difficult to relate it convincingly to such factors as the cost of employee health benefits, absenteeism, disability, workers' compensation, or productivity.

The complexity of the long-range options also reflects their more ambiguous place within the corporation. Where the short-range activities fall unequivocally within the domain of benefits, finance, and risk managers, the long-range opportunities may involve the medical, industrial hygiene, and industrial relations departments, plant managers who sit on local hospital boards, public affairs departments and corporate contributions committees, and other functional units often unaccustomed to the kind of collective action that may be necessary to develop and carry out a consistent and effective corporate health policy.

Ideally the three options should be combined in a comprehensive corporate health strategy that cuts across functional lines and serves as a basis for making specific short-term decisions as they arise. It has been said that when corporations make business decisions in the absence of a strategic framework, the decisions tend to ordain the strategy rather than the other way around.[8] In the case of health care, it can be argued that piecemeal decisions in public and private sectors over the years have accelerated health care costs and indeed have shaped present goals—containing runaway costs. In pursuit of that mission, companies will do well to develop a policy framework for their many health-related involvements and expenditures.

SHORT-RANGE OPTIONS FOR STABILIZING COSTS

Although many factors affect the costs of health services, the premium costs for an employee health benefit package can be divided into three component parts:

1. Charges for administering the insurance plan;
2. Frequency and intensity with which covered services are used;
3. Unit costs of that use.

Effective cost containment approaches have to reckon with all three elements because the health care system is known for its "Chinese pillow" characteristics i.e., downward pressure at one point causes ballooning out at another. But for purposes of analysis, the cost containment strategies initiated by companies can be grouped in those three categories, elaborated in Figure 22.3. As a primary orientation, each addresses either administrative costs, utilization levels, or charges by physicians, hospitals, and other suppliers.

Administrative Costs

Administrative costs should be considered in terms of alterations in the funding and administrative vehicles for the plan. Considering these changes raises the question of what services the administrative fee is buying and what bearing these services have on costs. This section first considers funding alternatives and then examines the claims review and control mechanisms that have traditionally fallen within the realm of the carrier's or administrator's routine services.

Financial Alternatives. Faced with steady inflation in health insurance costs, financial and benefits managers have sought (and for the most part have found) ways to assure the highest possible proportion of health services (that is, paid claims) out of the total premium paid the insurer. Most large firms have worked with their carriers, brokers, consultants, or through in-house efforts, to shrink health premium expenses relating only indirectly, if at all, to claims filed against the plan.

---

[8] Tregoe & Zimmerman, "Strategic Thinking: Key to Corporate Survival," 68 *A.M.A. Mgm't Rev.* 9–14 (Feb. 1979).

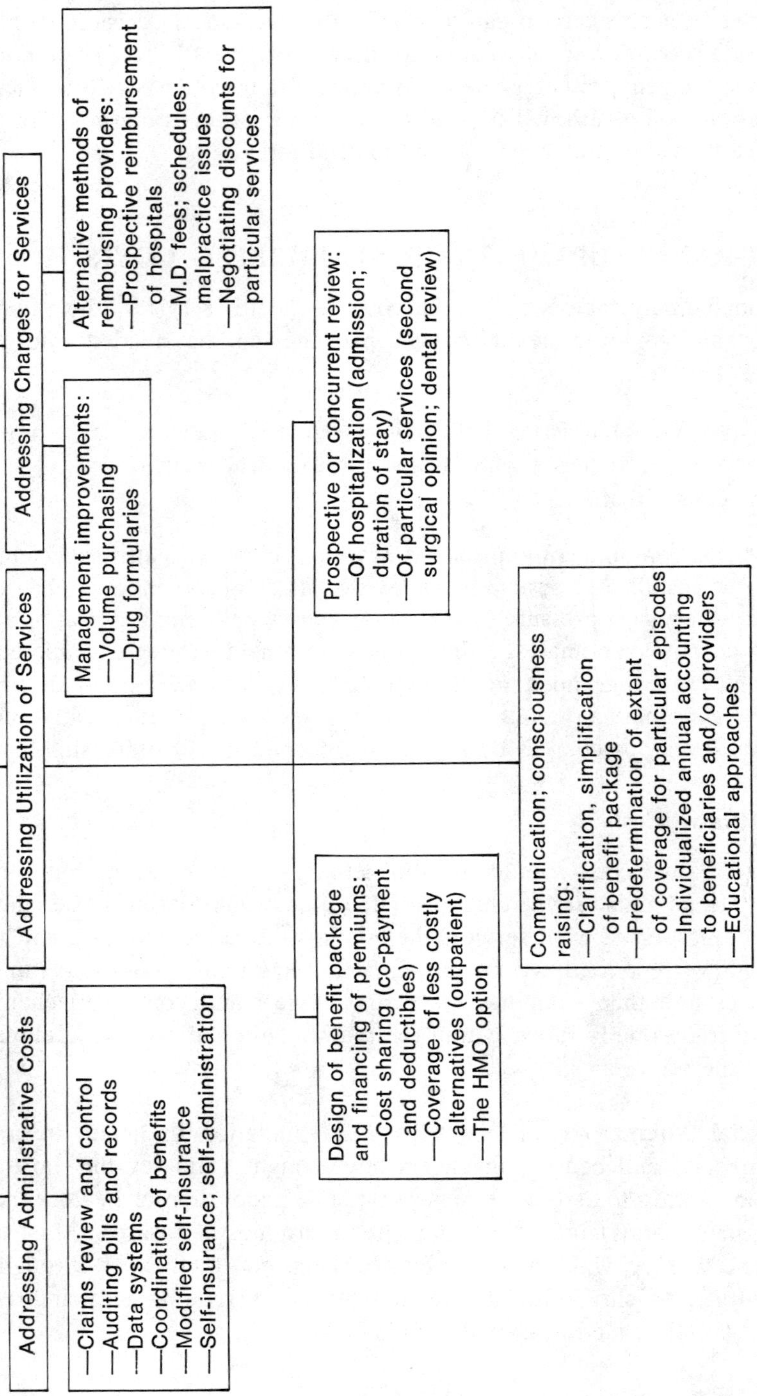

Source: Payer, Provider, Consumer: Industry Confronts Health Care Costs 24 (Egdahl & Walsh, Eds., 1977).

Fig. 22.3 Cost Containment Activities

Funding alternatives began to attract attention after 1964, which saw the advent of the minimum premium plan. Originally developed chiefly as a means of reducing state premium taxes by shifting to the policyholder a portion of the claims liability, this arrangement maintained the insurance carrier in the role of underwriter, claims processor, and administrator, still providing enrollment, documentation, communication, legal, and actuarial services. Subsequent refinements enabled employers to assume responsibility for various administrative tasks and for a growing share of the risk in order to cut costs. Fiscal arrangements that were nearly universal twenty years ago—conventional insurance coverage with the carrier holding full reserves and administering the plan—have given way to a wide range of financing alternatives.

The term "self-insurance," often used in this context, is a misnomer here, because full "self-insurance" technically no longer involves "insurance," and is a highly ambiguous term, applied indiscriminately to self-funding, self-administration, and even at times to minimum premium situations. For clarity, it helps to classify the major funding options within four broad categories along a spectrum from greatest insurance company involvement to least.[9]

Conventional full insurance. The carrier collects a premium (usually experience-rated), underwrites the risk of unexpected fluctuations in claims, and provides administrative services including enrolling employees, filling out government forms, producing summary plan descriptions and other communication vehicles, providing actuarial and legal services, and related activities. The premium includes an actuarially determined amount earmarked for claim payments plus a retention to cover the insurance company's cost of doing business; state premium taxes (typically about 2 percent of the premium); administrative charges; risk charges (protection for the carrier against termination of the contract); brokers' commissions; and reserves against fluctuations in claims.

Minimum premium plan. Developed principally to reduce state premium taxes, which it does in most but not all states, this arrangement retains the carrier in much the same role as in a conventionally insured plan, except for an amendment to the contract in which the carrier and the policyholder each agree to assume a specified share of the claims liability. Typically, the policyholder's "maximum dollar limit," above which the insurer will pay, is set as a percentage (often 90 percent) of claims expected in relation to previous years' experience.

Self-funding with an Administrative Services Only contract. Not a financing mechanism, but a device for administering a self-funded plan, an Ad-

---

[9] *Containing Health Benefit Costs: The Self-Insurance Option* 12–18 (Industry and Health Care Series No. 6) R. Egdahl & D. Walsh, Eds. (1979).

ministrative Services Only (ASO) contract involves no assumption of risk by a third-party insurer; the employer establishes reserves independently or through a Section 501(c)(9) trust. The plan is "self-insured," or, to be more precise, "self-funded." States neither tax uninsured health benefit plans nor require filing of contracts with state insurance commissioners giving a large multistate employer considerably more flexibility in the design (and redesign) of diverse benefit plans offered. Review of claims, data collection, plan design, and other administrative duties are contracted out to a third party, often an insurance carrier or a contract administrator, or sometimes are done partly in-house or with a consultant. Stop-loss coverage is sometimes purchased in conjunction with claims administration to protect the otherwise self-insured policyholder against excessive claims.

Self-funding and self-administration. This represents the other end of the spectrum from conventional coverage. With or without a Section 501(c)(9) trust, the employer or multiemployer trust takes on all the administrative functions associated with the health benefit. Some degree of self-funding of the risk, through such devices as lag periods, interim accounting, minimum premium, or ASO arrangements, is now nearly universal among companies with 500 or more employees. Complete self-administration of the employee health benefit plan is much less widespread.

Economies of scale play a part in the decision to self-administer; firms incurring $1 million or more in annual claims appear most likely to seriously consider this option, although very small firms with fairly simple benefit plans can also achieve savings through self-administration. Given the somewhat specialized nature of the administrative tasks involved, self-administration is usually approached with caution and an attempt is made to assess realistically the company's in-house capabilities to perform these tasks as effectively and efficiently as insurance carriers or third-party administrators.

Self-administration has been said to reduce by about half the total administrative costs—to about 2.5 to 3 percent of claims paid.[10] Money managers debate the amount saved by bringing the reserves and the risk in-house, but there is near-unanimity on a general conclusion of far greater import. It is foolish to focus efforts on shaving percentage points off the 5, 10, or possibly even 15 cents of the premium dollar represented by administrative costs—the tip of the iceberg of total health care expenditures—if the employer does not recognize the problem of the escalating cost of paying for the claims. On the other hand, if self-insurance gives the employer a better handle on data—as is frequently asserted—then it can open the way to a generally more systematic and more effective approach to containing health care costs.[11]

---

[10] American Health Mgm't and Consulting Corp. (hereinafter cited as AHMAC), *An Assessment of the Opportunities for Effective Health Care Cost Containment* 2-21 (Dec. 1978) (unpublished report prepared for The Sun Co. Radnor, Pa.).

[11] Id. at 2–16.

The need for comprehensive data. Recognizing the need for more comprehensive data represents a major shift over the past few years in the thinking of benefits and risk managers. Having made most of the refinements possible in the realm of administrative savings, some large policyholders are making new demands on their carriers and some insurance firms are adopting new marketing postures. More comprehensive data is being requested and in some cases being produced for more effective management of benefits. Data includes information not just on claims paid and their costs, as before, but on utilization of services by geographical area and/or hospital and by major diagnostic or procedural category. This request demonstrates a desire to understand and ultimately to redress imbalances and irrationalities thought to exist in patterns of health care delivery in the United States. Companies possessing this kind of information are in the minority and still fewer actually use it, but the situation is changing rapidly.

Retrospective and Prospective Claims Review. Retrospective claims review in some degree is a routine administrative service; the scope and intensity of the review, however, and the manner of follow-up can vary widely. Claims are analyzed for less than full liability of the benefit plan owing to:

- Ineligibility of the claimant;
- Lack of coverage for the service;
- Duplicate reimbursement through overlapping coverage;
- Discrepancies between the services claimed and those delivered;
- Excessive charges for the services rendered.

These analyses have centered on hospital services. The review is normally conducted by a claims clerk, employed by the plan administrator (whether carrier, third party, or the employer himself), with backup support from nurses and physicians to resolve cases involving medical judgments or disputes. Often the claim is reviewed not only for eligibility but also for the appropriateness of the procedures carried out vis-à-vis the diagnosis reported. The billed charges are compared to regional norms and attention is paid to the possibilities for coordinating benefits with another insurance plan or subrogating the case to a third-party tort feasor.

The more aggressive claims review programs are computerized and produce detailed management reports. Some measure the appropriateness of the care and the charges claimed against model treatment profiles, broken down by major diagnostic category. Procedures falling outside of statistical norms are flagged by the computer and a claims clerk then assesses the appropriateness of the claim. The review, whether manual or computerized, results in one of the following: (1) denial; (2) modification; (3) payment of the claim; or (4) its return to the provider for additional documentation.

Coordination of benefits (COB) prevents duplicate reimbursement for a given service covered under more than one policy. A look at the results from

COB alone suggests the range of rigor with which third parties perform various administrative tasks. Against an average national return through COB of 2 to 4 percent, John Hancock Mutual Life reports a 7.5 percent return using its HANSTAR system and United States Administrators, a third-party administrative firm in California, reports COB returns of 11 percent. Other dramatic savings have been attributed to COB. Bruce F. Spencer, who reported savings of over 14 percent achieved by Borden, Inc., feels that it was unusual: "probably about as far as you'll ever see anybody go, and a lot farther than most will go." [12]

United States Administrators goes further than this by attending not only to the appropriateness of claims but much more closely to the appropriateness of *care*. United States Administrators' approach is aggressive and has in some cases reduced the client's health benefit costs by one-third,[13] not, one presumes, without arousing some antipathy among physicians, hospitals, and possibly employees, athough a concerted effort is made to hold the patient harmless for unwarranted charges. This approach is described below in the section on utilization review because it goes beyond retrospective claims analysis into prospective review of use of health-care services.

As long as the claims review is retrospective, it remains administrative and largely unrelated to the volume of use except to the extent that it may alert providers and patients to the fact that claims are checked. Once the utilization review program becomes concurrent or prospective—evaluating the need for a planned hospitalization or treatment while decisions can still be influenced—it aims at the level and type of health-care service used.

Utilization of Services

The second short-range option for cost containment addresses the volume of health service use and takes two basic directions:

- Modifications in the design or scope of the benefit package, seeking to alter the incentives; or
- Professional review programs aiming to identify and either forestall or disallow payment for services deemed inappropriate.

Both have a strong educational thrust; whether tacit or explicit, an underlying goal is to heighten the cost consciousness of consumers and providers of health services. Their prime goal, usually, is to shift use away from inpatient hospital-based care which represents both the largest and the fastest growing share of health care expenditures.

Restructuring the Benefit Package. Changing the benefit package is a nearly universal strategy among large-scale payers for medical insurance.

---

[12] Note 9 *supra,* at 33.
[13] Note 10 *supra,* at 2–31.

Restructuring the package replaces the faulty incentives blamed for cost escalation with a benefit package that promotes less costly alternatives—usually care requiring fewer hospital days or avoiding the hospital altogether. Justified on grounds that more utilization of medical care is often not "better" and can indeed be "worse" for the patient, the most obvious benefit modification—cost sharing by employees—is introduced through co-insurance and deductibles.

Cost Sharing. Cost sharing reintroduces an element of personal financial responsibility for health care, thus discouraging excess utilization. Costs may be shared in three ways. Employees can pay a portion of the monthly premium (a *co-insurance rate*) and perhaps gain an appreciation for trade-offs involved in plan options; or they may be required to share the costs at the point of service through co-payments or deductibles. A *co-payment* scheme requires the insured to share costs with the employer according to a fixed ratio (e.g., 20:80 or 40:60 respectively, sometimes 50:50) and usually only up to a maximum out-of-pocket cost. *Deductibles* are borne by the beneficiary before the plan begins to pay benefits for covered expenses and are often scaled to the employee's salary range, while co-payment provisions tend to apply across the board. Many plans combine both features with a ceiling above which the employee is fully covered. The cost-sharing provision in both cases is applied to a specific benefit: hospitalization, physicians' services, dental or vision care, for example.

Co-payments and deductibles are frequently found in major medical insurance policies, the fastest growing type of policy since its introduction in 1951 in response to a demand for protection against large, unpredictable expenses. Deductibles presuppose that the insured can budget for routine medical expenses and, thus, fit logically with the concept of insurance against major episodes of illness. They reduce the administrative costs of processing a lot of small claims.

Practical difficulties. Collectively bargained plans have led the movement away from cost sharing, and unions have been predictably opposed to retrenchment in this area. They have seen it as forcing beneficiaries to limit their use of health services, causing some, for lack of funds, to get less medical care than they need and subverting the goals of prevention, early detection, and treatment. A study of cost sharing under public health insurance in Canada did find that the burden fell disproportionately on lower income beneficiaries.[14] A California study found that the introduction of co-insurance in a prepaid plan diminished the plan's ability to enroll lower income subscribers.[15] Fine tuning of the co-payment and deductible provisions (for

---

[14] Beck, "The Effects of Copayment on the Poor," 11 *J. Human Resources* 129 (Winter 1974).

[15] Scitovsky & Snyder, "Effect of Coinsurance on the Use of Physician Services," Social Security Bull. 3–12 (June 1972); Scitovsky & McCall, "Coinsurance and the

example, scaling them to income) may be a way to mitigate, but probably not obviate, problems of access to needed care. Cost sharing is expensive to administer if finely tuned, but potentially inequitable if not. The impact of cost sharing on use is difficult for an employer to isolate in part because the "experiment" is usually contaminated by other modifications to the benefit package, made to soften the blow of newly instituted cost sharing.

One economist argues that practical difficulties (union opposition and the availability of supplementary insurance) would probably thwart wide-scale implementation of cost-sharing measures, and that, furthermore, "co-payment may involve greater costs than benefits and is not a good solution." [16]

A physician summarized his 1978 literature review on an equally pessimistic note:

> Where [policy manipulation of cost-sharing] might be effective, that is, in direct application to hospital insurance, it is likely to be unacceptable; where it is likely to be acceptable, that is, in reducing cost-sharing in ambulatory care, it is likely to be ineffective.[17]

Current cost-sharing efforts. Opposition and ambiguity notwithstanding, many employers have taken or are seriously considering steps away from fully paid premiums and first-dollar coverage toward increased or more selective cost sharing. Standard Oil of California, for example, has negotiated a health benefit that offers employees a choice of four different levels of coverage, the lower two involving sizeable co-insurance and deductibles, the higher amounting to first-dollar coverage but requiring substantial employee sharing of the premium cost ($96/month for the highest option).[18] Altering the proportion of premium and claims borne by employer and employee on the front end can reduce the employer's premium while (presumably) restoring more appropriate incentives. Although offering a range of alternatives as Standard Oil has done may be unwieldy administratively, it provides employers an opportunity to educate employees and to experiment with the impact of cost sharing and other plan modifications without trying to sell an across-the-board change while lacking adequate information on its effect.[19]

This type of comprehensive benefits planning involves weighing a number of variables. The research evidence points out that cost-sharing arrangements are affected by level of payment, population subgroup, duration and

---

Demand for Physician Services: Four Years Later," Social Security Bull. 19–27 (May 1977).

[16] Klarman, "The Financing of Health Care," 106 *Daedalus* 266 (Winter 1977).

[17] Chassin, "The Containment of Hospital Costs: A Strategic Assessment," 16 Med. Care 12 (Supp. Oct. 1978).

[18] Note 10 *supra,* at 2-2.

[19] DiPrete, "Cost Containment Through Benefit Plan Design," in *Background Papers on Industry's Changing Role in Health Care Delivery,* 117–133 (Industry and Health Care Series No. 3 1977).

communication of the provision, and type of service. Hospital care is nearly always found to be least, and ambulatory services most, sensitive to cost-sharing requirements.[20] In short, evidence is lacking on how to achieve desired results through cost sharing, although the option is attracting increased attention. The Rand Corporation is conducting a major social experiment designed to address, among other questions, the effects of cost sharing. Preliminary results about the use of services indicate that persons fully covered for medical services spend about 50 percent more than do similar persons with income-related catastrophe insurance. Both ambulatory services and hospital admissions increased although expenditures per admission did not differ significantly.[21]

Coverage of Less Costly Alternatives. As the first health services to be insured, hospitalization and inpatient surgery remain the most fully covered categories of care. Physicians' services rendered in the hospital are now well covered too, as are x-ray and laboratory tests irrespective of setting. Coverage is least complete for office visits to physicians, ambulatory clinic visits, home care—the categories of personal health service with the lowest unit costs and presumably the greatest likelihood of facilitating prevention, early diagnosis, and treatment of conditions that could become serious.

Hospital charges account for the largest and fastest growing share of national and corporate health expenditures. In hopes of reducing excessive use of inpatient services, many employers have broadened their benefit packages to cover alternatives such as preadmission testing, ambulatory surgery, skilled and intermediate nursing home care, home health care and hospice services. Where hospital costs are high, it stands to reason that these non-hospital coverages—if they become alternatives to inpatient care—should reduce costs. But the qualifiers in that statement do present a problem. Although financial incentives can be built into the plan to encourage the use of alternatives, no effective way has been found to insure their exclusive or even predominant use as substitutes for the use of hospitals. Where ambulatory coverage is increased without other changes, hospitalization rates usually increase and seldom if ever decrease. The results of covering ambulatory services as alternatives have been disappointing or mixed, but the evidence is not all in yet.

For example, a study of the use of these cost-shifting techniques by thirty-three companies in the greater Philadelphia area showed diversity of approach

---

[20] Note 17 *supra.*

[21] Phelps & Newhouse, *The Effects of Coinsurance on the Demand for Physician Services* (The Rand Corp. 1972); Phelps & Newhouse, *Coinsurance and the Demand for Medical Services* (The Rand Corp. 1973); Keeler, Newhouse & Phelps, *Deductibles and the Demand for Medical Services: The Theory of a Consumer Facing a Variable Price Schedule Under Uncertainty* (The Rand Corp. 1974); Newhouse, "Some Interim Results from a Controlled Trial of Cost Sharing in Health Insurance," 305 New England J. Med. 1501–1507 (Dec. 17, 1981).

and uncertain impact.[22] Outpatient services and preadmission testing were normally covered through the major medical components of these companies' plans; few reported benefit descriptions that specified short procedure units or preadmission testing, but all appeared to include indirect coverage of these services. Home care programs were rarely reported covered, although the national trend is toward greater emphasis here. Skilled or intermediate nursing care facilities were covered in about one-third of the companies studied, typically equating a day of such care to half a day of hospital care in order to apply benefit period limits.

Preadmission testing. Preadmission testing has yet to demonstrate important cost savings, despite strong underlying logic. Candidates for elective surgery are usually admitted to the hospital a day or more in advance of the scheduled procedure to allow ample time for laboratory tests. Insurance programs have reinforced this practice by limiting coverage of laboratory tests partially or exclusively to those performed on inpatients. By covering outpatient preoperative tests, preadmission testing programs should reduce the length and cost of hospitalization for elective surgery and should also reduce the number of days an employee is absent from work.

But several recent studies have failed to document savings. Even when covered by insurance, the tests are often not done prior to admission, or are repeated when the patient enters the hospital. The schedules of some hospitals are not flexible enough to enable this program to be coordinated with established admission protocols. Moreover, the economic incentives on hospital administrators, for whom ancillary service revenues are often critical and on physicians, for whom the hospital is convenient, work strongly against their striving to make preadmission testing programs succeed.

Although there are isolated accounts of savings achieved through preadmission testing, for example a $278,000 annual savings tallied by Public Service Electric and Gas of New Jersey,[23] the evidence is unclear. However, a company that is willing to go beyond merely paying for the innovation, and to engage actively with local physicians and hospital staffs in a concerted effort to make the program work, may find the results worth the effort.

Ambulatory surgery. Surgical procedures performed outside of the usual hospital setting apparently result in some cost savings. Coverage for simple surgical procedures (such as dilation and currettage, tubal ligation, hernia repair, and excision of skin lesions) performed in freestanding surgical centers, ambulatory units within hospitals, or surgeons' offices instead of the hospital operating room is easily added to the benefit plan. It should save the costs of hospital room charges, reduce laboratory fees, and shorten the

---

[22] The Penjerdel Council, Greater Philadelphia Chamber of Commerce, and Health Services Council, *Cost Effective Management of Health Benefit Programs,* (1979) (a project of the Joint Health Cost Containment Comm., Philadelphia, Pa.).

[23] Note 10 *supra,* at 2–4.

nursing and staff time expended on each case. Extensive evaluations have not been conducted on corporate experiences with this innovation and there is some concern that freestanding surgical centers represent additional rather than shifted costs. But employers have felt that the coverage does save some money; approximately a day's worth of hospital confinement is averted each time an employee elects the option of ambulatory surgery.

Auxiliary nursing and health services. Nursing home services, home health, and hospice care are other benefit provisions that seem capable of reducing costs. But inadequate reimbursement for these lower levels of service has been shown in both government and private programs to prevent transfer of patients who no longer need the technology- and labor-intensive services of a hospital. Again, the evidence on use of nursing home and home care is sketchy, but suggests savings.

Health Maintenance Organization (HMO). The HMO option is a special case. HMOs are prepaid health plans in which providers contract to deliver a specified package of services to a defined population. Combining a financing vehicle and a comprehensive benefits delivery system, HMOs have served as the standard bearer for the "pro-competition" forces in the national health policy debate. As such, HMOs are more than just another benefit plan modification—although they are that as well. This section deals with HMOs within the context of benefit design, leaving for a later section the political and philosophical aspects of private industry's position on HMOs.

Well before the federal government enacted the Health Maintenance Organization Act of 1973, (under the provisions of which an HMO may solicit the employees of a company with twenty-five or more workers in a given location that is serviced by an HMO, and offer them HMO membership as an alternative to indemnity insurance), segments of private industry were offering membership in a prepaid plan as an option under employee health insurance, and some firms and unions were deeply involved in the development of prepaid plans. For example, a May 1975 study (conducted before the promulgation of the dual-choice regulations) found that 19 percent of the 300 large corporations surveyed already offered a dual option and another 3 percent were "working on it." [24] The original federal statute mandated employer provision of a dual option under certain circumstances for federally qualified HMOs, but set such unrealistic criteria for qualification as to impede the HMO movement. These were revised in 1976 amendments. The mandatory dual-option clause has been controversial and relatively ineffectual, since a concerted educational effort may be needed before a prepaid plan wili penetrate a new market. An enthusiastic employer can assist in the educational process, but a reluctant one can satisfy the letter of the dual-

[24] Seubold, "HMOs: The View from the Program," 90 Public Health Rep. 99–103 (1975).

option requirement while stimulating very little employee interest in the plan. Most HMOs view mandatory dual choice as a final resort, and even then probably futile in the absence of an appealing benefits package. HMOs emphasize coordinated care, budgetable expenses, "one-stop-shopping," often more comprehensive benefits than the traditional insurance option, and better continuity of care for nearly equivalent premiums. Programs with monthly family premiums more than $10 or $15 higher than the alternative benefit package seldom achieve significant penetration, with or without mandatory dual choice.

Insurance carriers and consultants, corporations and unions have developed rules of thumb and checklists to guide employers in assessing an HMO. Because federal qualification cannot guarantee uniformly high-quality service, employers are counseled to assess the options being offered their employees.

Employer enthusiasm reflects a blend of philosophical and pecuniary motives. Philosophically it is a statement in favor of the beneficiary's freedom to choose and an endorsement of the long-range potential of HMOs as a private sector mechanism to reduce overutilization and perhaps to moderate costs. The minority of employers have enough employees enrolled in HMOs to affect materially the total costs of their benefit plans. But a succession of studies spanning over a decade has strongly suggested that HMOs do care for their patients less expensively than traditional medical services, largely through reductions in hospitalization rates for medical and surgical services.[25]

In 1976 HMOs nationally increased their rates only 19 percent, while many third-party payers introduced rate hikes of 30 to 40 percent. A 1979 survey conducted by the National Association of Employers on Health Maintenance Organizations (NAEHMO) found that responding companies offering an HMO option experienced a slower increase (10.3 percent) in health care costs from 1977 to 1978 than companies not offering HMOs (12 percent). At 8.9 percent, the increases in HMO costs were also more moderate than were the increases in overall health benefit costs. The average hospitalization rates for employees opting for HMO membership were reported by these same companies at 346 days per 1,000, compared with 801 days per 1,000 for their employees covered by indemnity insurance. However, the 144 responding companies expressed less confidence in HMOs as a cost containment strategy than in other programs such as self-insurance, disability claims review, chemical dependency programs and COB. Only 61 percent of respondents considered HMOs effective in containing costs.[26]

Many large corporations now offer scores of HMOs across the country. A few firms, such as AT&T, are conducting careful evaluations of their experiences.[27] The final word—for now—is that HMOs belong as one ele-

---

[25] Luft, *Health Maintenance Organizations* (1981).

[26] National Assoc. of Employers on Health Maintenance Organizations, *NAEHMO Overview of Annual Survey of HMOs* (1978).

[27] Mitchell & Dunn, "Comparative Absence Experience Among Employees Covered

ment in a company's cost containment portfolio, but for the short range are no panacea. An important question raised by the HMO experience is whether one or more of their cost-containing features can be transferred into non-HMO programs.

Utilization Review and Control. An HMO is, among other things, a closed financial system. It is not clear as yet whether or not the incentives created by this feature are essential to the reductions in utilization which some prepaid plans have achieved; however programs are being developed to clarify at least part of this question by applying the strong peer review procedures characteristic of some HMOs to the unstructured fee-for-service system.

From the routine retrospective claims review conducted principally to screen out ineligible or invalid claims, it is, in theory, a reasonably short step to more aggressive claims review focusing on utilization. Two basic methods are used, alone or in combination: (1) retrospective review, very much like the earlier generation of claims review, but with a new emphasis on the appropriateness of the care; and (2) precertification or concurrent review, designed to monitor hospitalizations in progress for the necessity of the admission and the reasonableness of the length of stay. Common to both are two underlying needs: (1) data and (2) an action arm. This section briefly describes the two types of utilization control program, and some of the available action arms. Data issues were discussed, above, at the conclusion of the section on Financing Alternatives.

Retrospective utilization review. This program usually involves elaborate computer operations; Blue Shield of California, for example, uses a system with 11,500 edits and audits.[28] The computer program typically uses rigid decision rules, developed from statistical distributions of regional practice norms, with advice and consultation from area physicians and sometimes from consumers. These standards of practice are specific to groups of medical diagnoses, for example United States Administrators has model treatment screens for 3,400 different diagnoses grouped by International Classification of Diseases Adapted (ICDA) codes. The computer program makes all routine checks on eligibility conducted in conventional claims review, checks fees against computerized fee profiles and also assesses whether the treatment ordered is standard for the diagnosis recorded. This is the first stage of review. At the second stage a non-physician claims clerk takes the pended claim, and goes back to the original record for coding errors or other possible explanations for the anomaly. If none is found, the case moves on to the third and final level of review by an expert professional committee.

---

by a Prepaid or a Blue Cross/Blue Shield Health Insurance Program," 20 *J. Occupational Med.* 797–800 (1978).

[28] *Employee Benefit Plan Review Research Report,* (hereinafter cited as EBPRRR) "Medical Policy Integrated with Computerized Claims Payment: Blue Shield of California Saves $82,593,332," 335.0–9 (Feb. 1979).

Programs vary in how rigid their decision rules are and in what proportion of claims they deal with at the three levels. Computer algorithms at the first stage should be the system's workhorse; the more effective they are at catching problems—and real problems—the higher the program's yield and efficiency in husbanding expensive physician review time. From 10 to 35 percent of hospital days and ancillary services are said to be unnecessary, although perhaps half of this "misuse" lies beyond the immediate control of providers in administrative problems such as difficulty in finding needed nursing home beds or home care services.[29] For the most part, the decision rules that have to date been developed are not highly refined and tend to set their thresholds high rather than run the risk of holding up and incurring costs in review of claims that will ultimately pass muster.

In an excellent "strategic assessment" of the literature on hospital cost containment, Dr. Mark R. Chassin points out that "the medical profession does not really know how many hospital days are required to treat most illnesses," and offers a specific example in support of this contention:

> The current standard treatment for an uncomplicated myocardial infarction is 14 days hospitalization. This was established by a well-designed, randomized trial that compared outcomes of such patients hospitalized for 14 as opposed to 21 days, and found no benefit to the additional 7 days. This, however, does not establish that 14 days is optimum. Is the optimum between 14 and 21? Is 10 days or even 7 days better? A recent non-randomized study suggests that there is a group of patients for whom a 7-day stay is entirely appropriate. There is even data strongly suggesting that some patients with myocardial infarctions do better at home.[30]

Despite imponderables of this sort, some utilization control programs are reporting savings. Blue Shield of California, for example, was billed $4.1 billion for the contracts it covered in 1977 and paid out $3.2 billion. The remainder was saved through administrative controls ($304 million), charge controls on government programs ($556 million), and medical review ($54 million).[31] United States Administrators reports savings in the neighborhood of 10 to 30 percent.[32]

Prospective and concurrent utilization review. The chief distinction between retrospective claims review and prospective or concurrent utilization review is the time at which the review is conducted. Many utilization review programs combine all three techniques. Prospective review programs include preadmission screening for hospitalization or for certain specified procedures, second opinion programs prior to elective surgery, or, prior to dental pro-

---

[29] Gertman & Restuccia, "The Appropriateness Valuation Protocol: A Technique for Assessing Unnecessary Days of Hospital Care," 19 *Med. Care* 855-871 (1981).

[30] Note 17 *supra,* at 13.

[31] Note 28 *supra.*

[32] Note 9 *supra,* at 41.

cedures and the like, provisions to enable employees to determine in advance of undergoing a particular treatment the extent to which it will be covered.

Concurrent utilization review usually refers to in-hospital programs where a nurse or some other health professional certifies the appropriateness of a hospital admission and monitors the length of stay based on established criteria that take into account the patient's age, sex, and diagnosis. These programs typically have a multilevel review mechanism through which the attending physician can appeal the program's ruling to other physicians in the hospital and then to regional and state physician committees. In theory, conducting the review while a decision is being made to render a medical service allows the time to intervene and to prevent an inappropriate choice.

Available action arms. The organizations capable of acting on information concerning inappropriate utilization include HMOs, insurance carriers, and third-party administrators. In the last analysis, though, it is physicians' behavior that must change and utilization or "peer" review has classically been considered the nearly exclusive domain of physician-dominated *professional standards review organizations* (PSROs), created as part of the 1972 amendments to the Social Security Act.[33] The purpose of the PSRO legislation was to establish a means of insuring that the services financed through government programs are medically necessary, in accord with professionally recognized standards, and appropriately provided in the most economical setting. Independent of the medical facilities they evaluate, PSROs develop and use local standards of appropriate hospital admission, length of stay, and course of treatment and institute programs of preadmission certification, concurrent review, and retrospective medical audit. PSROs are responsible for reviewing care directly or monitoring the performance of a facility's medical staff utilization review committee, which is delegated the review function. Many PSROs are creatures of county medical societies or derivative foundations for medical care (FMCs).

Controversy has accompanied the PSRO program, which had a very slow start. The most fundamental criticism is the "fox guarding the henhouse" analogy which questions the wisdom of asking the medical profession to police itself. There has also been considerable debate over the primary mission of PSROs and what they can reasonably hope to accomplish. One complaint that frequently comes from outside the medical profession is that the PSRO program fails to take into account the patient's perception of what constitutes quality in health care. Within the profession, some say that PSROs' focus on cost has interfered with their effectiveness in assessing quality—that they ought to be released from the demands of accounting for costs to work exclusively on assuring quality care. Others worry that PSROs may actually elevate costs in some circumstances by raising a community's

[33] Pub. L. No. 92–603, 1972 amendments to the Social Security Act.

standards of care, or that they cost more to administer than they repay in savings.

PSROs have been subjected to repeated evaluations. A 1976 analysis conducted by the Institute of Medicine of the National Academy of Sciences concluded from surveying eighteen programs that it was too early to say that hospital concurrent review programs are effective because even where changes in utilization had been documented, the reasons behind them were not fully understood.[34] Early federal evaluations of PSROs uncovered no difference in hospitalization rates, comparing PSRO and non-PSRO areas between 1974 and 1976, but were unable to make inferences from these findings, owing to methodological deficiencies. Repeated evaluations have produced equivocal evidence of aggregate cost savings. One question is whether the program has merely induced hospitals to shift costs from one to another category of payer. A second question is whether the costs of maintaining the program are defrayed by any savings it can legitimately claim.[35] For these reasons, the program has suffered.

With federal encouragement, PSROs have extended the boundaries of their quality assurance and utilization reviews to take in privately financed patients. Insurance carriers, including Blue Cross and Blue Shield plans, business, and some labor unions have been arranging for and financing concurrent peer review of beneficiaries' use of hospitalization, surgery, and the newer benefit programs thought especially susceptible to overuse, for example, dental and vision care and hearing aid coverage. As of mid-1978, forty-two PSROs were conducting some form of private review.

PSROs and FMCs have each formed national umbrella organizations and have joined together in the creation of Private Review Network, Inc., which specializes in conducting peer review for private insurance carriers and employers through subcontracts with local PSROs and foundations for medical care.

One such unit is the Maricopa Foundation for Medical Care in Arizona, which reported 1975 and 1976 statistics for enrollees in its review program at 420 and 500 hospital days per 1,000 compared to 610 and 680 for a large insurance carrier in the same region. In the second year of the contract with the Maricopa Foundation, Motorola experienced a decrease in average length of stay from 7.5 to 5.8 days.[36] Caterpillar Tractor Company in Peoria and Deere and Company in Moline have contracted for private review with the Mid-State FMC, an Illinois PSRO, and both report reductions in average length of hospital stay.[37]

---

[34] Institute of Medicine, *Assessing Quality in Health Care: An Evaluation* (Nat'l Academy of Sciences, 1976).

[35] Schwartz, "The Regulation Strategy for Controlling Hospital Costs," New England J. Med. 305 (21) 1249–1255 (1981).

[36] Note 10 *supra,* at 2–26.

[37] EBPRRR "Professional Standards Reviewing Organizations (PSROs): Most Local Areas Have Begun Review Activities," 335.0-1 (June 1979).

Second surgical opinion. This option lies on the boundary between a benefit plan modification and a utilization review program. It enables a patient recommended for elective surgery to seek an independent consultation, usually but not always with a board-certified specialist, to determine whether the operation should be performed. If the second opinion conflicts with the first, a third may also be paid for. In most programs the second consultation is voluntary, i.e., the patient initiates it; sometimes the consultation is mandatory, although proponents of the program are emphatic that the patient decide which advice to follow and be enabled to seek a third opinion if the first two conflict. Second opinion programs normally have an administrative structure with intake officers to make arrangements with a panel of consulting surgeons who have agreed to accept a specified fee for the consultation and not to perform the surgery, if it is needed. Many of these programs have a research orientation which includes provisions to follow the patient's progress for at least a year or two after the episode.

A research-oriented second surgical opinion program developed in 1972 at the Cornell Medical School in collaboration with several large unions in New York City is probably the best-known, if not the first, such program. Dr. Eugene McCarthy, who developed the Cornell program, says that elective surgery represents about 40 percent of hospital admissions for the population under age 65 and "is the heavyweight component in major medical coverage."[38] He speaks of "a veritable epidemic in elective surgery in the United States," and in 1977 cited as evidence a 23 percent increase in elective surgery over the previous five years, a rate four times the growth of the population, causing 5 million additional surgical procedures to be financed by the medical care premium dollar.[39] Significant regional variations in the incidence of certain procedures[40] suggest that many surgical procedures may be unwarranted. The problem is attributed in part to an oversupply of surgeons, and of general physicians many who perform surgery without specialized training.

In Dr. McCarthy's research with both voluntary and mandatory second opinion programs, over one-quarter of the cases (27.6 percent) resulted in nonconfirmation of the original recommendation in favor of elective surgery, and the great bulk of nonconfirmations occurred in orthopedics and gynecology. Most patients followed the consultant's advice, and the limited longer term data available (a four-year follow-up of 392 patients) found stability in this pattern; of those not confirmed for surgery, 84 percent of patients in the voluntary program and 70 percent in the mandatory one still had not undergone surgery.[41]

Many employers have instituted this program, only to find that very few

---

[38] R. Egdahl & D. Walsh, note 7 *supra,* at 37.

[39] *Id.*

[40] Wennberg & Gittelshon, "Small Area Variation in Health Care Delivery," 182 Science 1102–1108 (Dec. 14, 1973).

[41] Note 10 *supra.*

of their employees seek the second opinion. Several large insurance carriers are experimenting with second opinion programs, and the preliminary evidence suggests savings on the order of $15 for every $1 spent. Numerous empirical questions remain to be answered especially with regard to the long-term experiences of participants in the program. They may forego the surgery and carry a heavier burden of disease, or postpone the procedure for a period of time but ultimately undergo it. On the available evidence it is argued that these programs restrain costs and curtail unwarranted surgery, increase benefits rather than cut back and may improve the information available to consumers, bringing them back into deciding on an important matter related to their health. In addition, they may create a sentinel effect which could serve to raise the general standards of care in the medical communities in which they are instituted. Like all of the innovations described here, second opinion programs are far more effective if they are part of a thoughtful and cohesive effort to present employees with a wider range of choices and better information with which to weigh them.

The Educational Element. For a company carefully structuring the incentives in its benefit plan to encourage cost-conscious behavior, it will obviously be important to describe these features of the plan as clearly as possible. Although one of the effects of the Employee Retirement Income Security Act of 1974 (ERISA) has been the escalation of administrative costs, it may also foster better communication in the area of cost control, by spelling out for employees how they can be prudent consumers of health care.[42]

Specific techniques are also being tried to supplement traditional communication approaches. These include individualized annual accounting to employees of the specific costs they have incurred against their insurance coverage, or the opportunity to determine the extent of coverage in advance of seeking a particular treatment. Little evidence is available on the effects of these efforts, which are exceedingly difficult to isolate and measure.

In summary, it is evident that the design of cost-effective benefit packages, together with an effective communication program, promises substantially better cost control than either technique alone. While some evidence suggests that employee education may result in greater cost escalation, this effect is more likely related to their specific content than to the existence of educational programs. An educational program clarifying a company's benefits without stressing their proper use could lead to such a result, just as an expansion of outpatient coverage, if unaccompanied by effective communication, can elevate costs. But even with the best of coordination and preplanning, cost containment approaches with regard to the use of services still interact with inflationary incentives created by prevailing reimbursement methods.

---

[42] Stokes, "ERISA: An Opportunity for Better Communication of Employee Health Benefit Plans," *Health Services and Health Hazards: The Employee's Need to Know*, 128–133 (Industry and Health Care Series No. 4) (R. Egdahl & D. Walsh, Eds., 1978).

Charges for Services

The third group of short-range cost containment approaches—those altering the methods by which suppliers are paid—seeks to rectify the problem of inflationary incentives. Of the three groups of options open to employers, this third is the least commonly used and the least fully developed. Blue Cross organizations, private insurers, and some companies are tightening their methods for paying hospitals and other facilities, pharmacists, opticians, and occasionally physicians. For example, purchasing items in volume, such as pharmaceuticals, and blood donor programs sponsored by some companies and unions fall within the broad category of alternative payment methods.

That the concept of alternative reimbursement is still in an embryonic stage is not due to lack of interest. To the contrary, rare unanimity exists among those who have studied the effects of current retrospective cost-based reimbursement methods: they are inflationary. How to resolve this problem without creating others as serious is another question entirely.

Incentive Reimbursement of Hospitals

In the mid-1960s, the Medicare and Medicaid programs established the practice of reimbursing hospitals for the actual "reasonable costs" incurred in caring for patients, plus a share of depreciation and interest. Many Blue Cross plans followed suit. The inflationary impact of this reimbursement approach soon became evident; retrospective cost reimbursement creates a system driven by the antithesis of cost consciousness—where a hospital grows and prospers in direct proportion to the sums of money it can spend. Third-party payers (especially the government) then adopted one type of self-protective measure—elaborate regulations—excluding certain classes of costs (for example, bad debts and research) from allowable charges and establishing mechanisms to prevent fraud and abuse. Next came attempts by the federal government to place ceilings on reimbursement levels, through wage and price controls, limits on Medicare payments, and the Carter administration's proposed cost containment legislation.

In a radical departure from cost reimbursement, Blue Cross plans and state governments experimented in the late 1960s with various kinds of prospective hospital reimbursement programs or rate-setting methods using complex retrospective adjustments. Extraordinarily complex and diverse, these programs were defined and catalogued differently by nearly every analyst. A 1978 review defined "incentive reimbursement" broadly and identified four basic forms, only one of which—prospective reimbursement—was found to have real potential.[43]

Prospective rate-setting programs are attempts by an external authority to control in advance the amount of future reimbursement hospitals will

[43] Note 17 *supra,* at 41.

receive for specific units of service.[44] In her definitive review of rate-setting programs, Katherine Bauer sounds a cautionary note:

> The methodology for implementing a task of this delicacy is still at a primitive stage, and expectations of cost containment through most of the types of rate setting programs currently in operation should be kept modest . . . rate setting per se is just a highly complicated tinkering operation, plugging up leaks in one small section of a rudderless ship that is cracking at the seams.[45]

HEW's (now called Health and Human Services Department) PSRO evaluations for 1978 and 1979 observed *increased* hospital utilization for Medicare beneficiaries in states with hospital rate-setting programs. The Health Care Financing Administration (HCFA) is conducting a sophisticated evaluation of hospital rate-setting commissions but "preliminary findings using crude measures cause concern as to the eventual results." [46] HCFA is also supporting experiments in New Jersey and elsewhere in reimbursing hospitals by the case rather than by the day. Fee schedules are set for over 300 different diagnosis-related groups (DRGs) and these permit hospitals with a more complex mix of cases to collect higher fees.

Physicians' Fees. Hospitalization has been the priority on the health care cost agenda, but physician costs are taking on new prominence. The share of physicians' charges financed by third parties is approaching two-thirds and the rate of inflation in physicians' fees was reported in a 1978 report of the President's Council on Wage and Price Stability for nearly three decades to have "consistently outpaced overall inflation except during the 1971-74 period of wage and price controls." [47] The Council blamed organized medicine's anti-competitive practices during the first half of the century for the early inflation in fees but traced the phenomenon after the mid-1960s largely to the growth of private and public health insurance coverage and changes in the methods of third-party payment. The problem was captured succinctly in a *Newsweek* guest editorial: "Somehow or other, a system of physician compensation has developed in this country so that the less a doctor talks to you and the more he does to you, the more he is paid." [48]

UCR system. With the enactment of Medicare in 1966, the traditional use of benefit schedules gave way to a fee screening system, called UCR for "usual, customary, and reasonable." Medicare's UCR system flys under a different banner (CPR for "customary, prevailing, and reasonable) but is

---

[44] Bauer, "Hospital Rate Setting—This Way to Salvation?" 55 Milbank Memorial Fund Q./Health & Soc'y 117–158 (Winter 1977).

[45] *Id.* at 153.

[46] Note 35 *supra.*

[47] Dyckman, *A Study of Physician's Fees,* (U.S. Gov't Printing Office 1978) (staff report for the Council on Wage and Price Stability, Exec. Office of the President).

[48] Fox, "Why People Are Mad at Doctors," Newsweek 4 (Jan. 10, 1977).

otherwise basically the same. Only the United States uses such a system.

UCR is also sometimes called a *profile system,* because it is based on data profiles of a physician's charging patterns over a period of time. Under UCR the third party will pay the lesser of actual charges, or one of three levels of the fee screen:

1. "Usual" (generally the median charge of the individual physician);
2. "Customary" (usually some percentile, such as the seventy-fifth, of the average charges of all physicians in a geographic area for the service in question);
3. "Reasonable" (definitions vary but generally include fees that are above the usual or customary levels if they can be justified by a review committee).

The UCR system is criticized for the imbalances and inequities it seems to foster or at least perpetuate. Self-employed clinicians, for example, averaged 1976 earnings of $63,000, compared with $138,000 and $122,000 for hospital-based radiologists and pathologists.[49] Gross geographical disparities in fees are not explained by differences in cost-of-living, malpractice premiums, or other professional expenses, quality of care or supply of or demand for services. Ralph Nader's Health Research Group concluded the following:

> In fact, they appear to result from a payment system which allows physicians in local reimbursement areas to substantially determine their own fees without regard to any of these factors. Thus the system both preserves completely arbitrary regional differences which preexisted Medicare and contains an inherently inflationary bias.[50]

Inflationary pressures. The inflationary pressures have caused physicians' earnings to jump from something under twice those of a broad group of technicians and professionals in 1939 to four times as much in 1975. The pressures work as follows: with future reimbursement levels depending on current charges, physicians are encouraged to submit ever higher bills to raise their "usual" charge levels. As the community's physicians follow this pattern, the customary charge increases.

Various administrative controls are being suggested or tried by third-party payers to counter this inflationary impact; for example: the setting of ceilings on yearly increases or tying the allowable rates of change to an index of general economic trends; lowering the definition of customary charges in an

---

[49] Carter, "Doctor's Fees—Free From the Law of Supply and Demand," 200 Science 30 (No. 7 April 1978); see also Kirchner, "Fees: Are They Getting Out of Hand?" Med. Econ. 167–192 (Oct. 16, 1978).

[50] Bogue, "Why Not the Most: A Physician's Guide to Locating in Cities with the Most Excessive Medicare Fees in the Country and an HEW Guide to Stopping This Waste of a Billion Dollars," (Feb. 1977) (staff report of the Health Research Group, Wash. D.C.).

area (perhaps from the seventy-fifth to the sixtieth percentile) or reducing the frequency with which charge profiles are updated (e.g., from twelve to eighteen months). Also the government has threatened to prohibit from dominating the governing boards of third-party insurers provider groups (such as physicians and hospital administrators) with a financial interest in the health care system. Another proposal has been made to require disclosure of communitywide customary fees—now a well-guarded secret. The thought is that this might stimulate public debate, open up professional competition and perhaps ultimately restrain costs. But these are viewed as minor adjustments, pending more thorough reform. The HCFA has commissioned several studies of alternative methods of reimbursing physicians.

Maximum benefit and relative value schedules. There is increasing interest in a fee schedule or *maximum benefit schedule* as a major alternative. This system is used in Canada and throughout most of Europe. The schedule sets a relatively fixed payment for a service and applies it uniformly, irrespective of the physician's individual characteristics. In the past thirty-five years, these schedules have evolved from many simple schedules to a few comprehensive ones. A relative value scale (RVS) expresses the relationship between services in units of value rather than in dollars. Benefit schedules then apply conversion factors of the relative value to obtain dollar amounts. The California Medical Society publishes the most widely used relative value schedule, not to set fees, the Society contends, but to provide a uniform nomenclature and standardized coding system, and relative values within specialty sections. This California RVS has come under attack by the Federal Trade Commission on the allegation that the publication of a relative value schedule by a professional society gives the appearance of price-fixing and is illegal. The Federal Trade Commission appears not to object to third-party carriers developing their own schedules but small private insurance companies generally lack the requisite claims experience.

Relative value schedules are criticized for at least three defects:

1. They are believed to create incentives to provide certain types of service because they are procedure-oriented and reward physicians for providing more technical services, such as surgery, and fewer consultative or preventive services.
2. The number of services included in the schedules has proliferated over time. In an attempt to define services precisely there have been progressive subdivisions of services and procedures into ever finer components, with increasing levels of complexity and value. The physician decides which level of service he has supplied and can be expected to bill for the higher valued service.
3. The conversion factors may be negotiated among the parties, mandated by the third party, or arrived at by some other method, but the primary consideration has been what the market will bear in the level of insurance premiums.

The government's thought of moving to a fee schedule supposes some method of negotiating with physicians. Blue Shield of Delaware has for the last three years been negotiating a percent limit on increases in physicians fees and estimates savings over the three years at close to $1 million; the program was possible because Blue Shield is the dominant carrier in Delaware and has contracts with 97 percent of the state's physicians. The United Storeworkers Union Security Trust maintains a panel of physicians who have agreed in advance to accept the plan's fee schedule. A list of these physicians is circulated to plan members, who are at liberty to go elsewhere for care—knowing that the decision may involve out-of-pocket expenses.

Questions of physician reimbursement raise the related issue of the number and location of physicians. Some economists contend that imbalances in certain specialties and locations can be redressed by altering the incentives in the reimbursement scheme. "Supply and distribution" problems confound many of the short-range cost containment options catalogued here. If there are too many surgeons, as it appears there are or soon will be, ambulatory surgery centers could simply beget more surgery rather than transfer of cases from the hospital. Hospital utilization review may be fighting overwhelming odds in situations where excess hospital beds create powerful incentives on hospital staffs to keep them filled and financed. Dilemmas such as these belong in the area here designated the "middle range," where the focus is the health care delivery system and methods to restructure and rationalize it to stabilize overall costs.

MIDDLE-RANGE EFFORTS TO REALIGN THE SYSTEM

Most of the short-range options discussed above make their diagnoses in narrow and concrete terms: if the premium seems too high, cut the carrier's retention; if hospital costs seem excessive, reduce utilization or change the payment formula; if physicians' fees appear high, negotiate them down . . . and so on.

Middle-range approaches to cost containment trace the problem to a more fundamental understanding of what has gone awry. Utilization of health services remains the bottom line in terms of payoff, but the problem of imbalances in use is viewed in terms of market failure—a whole economic sector functioning poorly for a number of reasons, including weak or perverse incentives that face both providers and consumers, a lack of price competition on the supply side, and distortions and consumer ignorance on the demand side.

Now the focus is on the question of public policy and how to correct a defective market. It is far easier to diagnose market failure than to fashion an adequate strategy either to repair or to replace the defective market forces in a $180 billion-a-year + "cottage industry." The diagnosis of market failure is a relatively clean theoretical construct but politics and ideology confound the choice of remedy, in part because of ambiguity concerning the best means to the end (greater efficiency). More importantly, there is dissent concerning the end itself and the essential function of a health care system in an affluent modern society.

Competition vs. Central Planning

Two different mechanisms for correcting market defects in health are posed: competition vs. central planning or regulation. Competition has been largely a code word for the development of "alternative delivery systems," that is, HMOs. The proponents of competition argue for informed consumer choice among competing alternative systems. They view decentralized price competition as the most efficient and socially desirable means of allocating scarce resources. Regulation is, by contrast, centralized, whether in government-regulated programs backed by sanctions, or quasi-regulatory communitywide health planning, in which business has long played a central role in some parts of the country. Health planning and resource-allocation programs seek to rationalize the supply and distribution of health care providers and facilities, thus reducing or adjusting provider-stimulated demand for services.

Neither regulation and planning nor competition is being advocated in a pure form. Charles Lindblom, the political scientist, points out that although centralized planning is on the increase in the Western world, to assume that this necessarily vitiates the market is like implying that the decline of swimming results from the growing popularity of jogging. The fallacy is to assume that both planning and regulation cannot go on simultaneously.[51] That regulation can and often does take the form of steering or guiding the market is evident in the New York Stock Exchange—the symbol of free enterprise in the West—which operates with an integration of pro-competitive regulatory rules and sanctions.

The question of what kind of regulation is needed to accomplish what ends and how has been receiving growing attention. Performance regulations of various kinds are being discussed as an alternative or supplement to what Charles Schultze [52] has called "command and control regulation" and others, more pejoratively, "omnibus tinkering."

Industry's cost containment options in the middle range can be separated into two conventional categories: (1) regulatory strategies, including health planning and resource allocation; and (2) efforts to develop competitive health systems. These are discussed very briefly here, to demonstrate their place in a thorough understanding of cost containment possibilities. Industry has a voice and a role in these public policy deliberations—and a stake nearly as great as that of the other major payer, government. But in this

---

[51] Lindblom, *Politics and Markets* (1977).
[52] Schultze, *The Public Use of Private Interest* (1977).

arena companies lack the flexibility to act more or less unilaterally (subject to the constraints of collective bargaining and pertinent regulations) as they do in the design and administration of the employee health benefit package.

Regulation, Health Planning, and Resource Allocation

Regulation, by definition, is a government pursuit. Corporate managers come closest to being health care regulators when they emulate and complement the government's short-term regulatory approaches, e.g., by contracting with PSROs, or where they participate in the health planning process, whose only real levers are regulatory sanctions. Yet health planning began and has remained chiefly in the private sector, although business involvement has fluctuated over the years, with congressional specification of the ground rules.

The Hospital Survey and Construction Act of 1946 (the "Hill-Burton" program) established a framework within which area-wide planning could be coordinated with state planning. The Act made funds available for the construction of hospitals in areas of need, as demonstrated in state-formulated plans. In time, states came to depend on area-wide planning agencies, which had sprung up on a voluntary basis, for technical assistance and most of the more than eighty voluntary area-wide health facilities planning agencies in operation by the mid-1960s had been fostered by local businesses, often with support from health insurers and hospitals.

When Congress passed the Comprehensive Health Planning Act (CHP), during the mid-1960s-era of social legislation, it set the stage for federal domination of area-wide health planning by providing matching funds for those area-wide planning agencies subjecting themselves to substantial federal control. The business involvement that had previously been a prominent feature of the area-wide health facilities planning agencies soon disappeared as a result of governmental requirements that the new CHP agencies represent all socioeconomic levels within a given community and allow a degree of provider participation, which soon dominated.

National Health Planning and Resources Development Act. Seven years later Congress passed the National Health Planning and Resources Development Act of 1974 replacing the CHP agencies with *health systems agencies* (HSAs). This legislation sought to correct problems that had developed under the CHP program because of ambiguities concerning its mission and the measurement of success. The law and subsequent regulations have appreciably improved the planning process, in which a formal role is now viewed for business firms as "major purchasers of care." Government spokesmen have increasingly stressed their concern that business interests be prominently involved in the activities of the health planning agencies, and that participation has increased.

But many bureaucratic problems nevertheless remain. Of the 203 HSAs, 178 are private, nonprofit agencies and the remaining twenty-five are sponsored by local governments. Though nominally private, the agencies must adhere to highly formalistic government-specified requirements for processes and documentation. Like the predecessor CHP agencies, HSAs are obliged to represent all socioeconomic levels as well as a broad array of "providers," defined as those who derive their incomes from providing health care services. The impact of the latter requirement varies from area to area but can stifle consumer (that is, nonprovider) participation when consumers feel incompetent to debate technical health policy issues with professionals in the field. This situation calls for education of consumers to understand their responsibilities as representatives of entire geographic areas and the technical aspects of health planning. Not all HSAs have been able to meet this challenge. Business participants often find the decision-making process frustrating because of the many fragmented constituencies that must be represented in health systems agencies.

The hope that areawide health planning will, in time, stabilize health care costs encourages business participation. Results to date are inconclusive. After surveying the literature on the health planning agencies' effects on costs and finding little persuasive evidence of cost decreases, a committee of the Institute of Medicine cautioned against prematurely holding the planning effort to expectations it cannot meet:

> The committee recommends that the limitations of HSAs in reducing health care expenditures be recognized, because unrealistic expectations are likely to lead to the conclusion that the program has not succeeded. In lieu of that limited approach, the committee recommends that the planning agencies be judged according to a broad set of measures including measures of improvement in access, quality, and equality, not only in cost moderation. The broad strategy is more suited to their statutory mandate.[53]

Business, Health Systems Agencies, and Health Planning. The essential function of an area-wide planning process, according to the committee, is to allocate finite resources which means choosing among competing priorities. Whatever their effect on costs and with or without a business voice, HSAs or state planning authorities will play some part in the allocation of local resources through their certification-of-need authority which purportedly gives them direct access to health facilities' major capital investment decisions. The task of business therefore is to stimulate HSAs to become more cost conscious in their decision-making. This requires an organized effort on the part of the local business community with several aims in mind:

☐ To obtain participation in HSAs by knowledgeable business representatives committed to cost containment. No easy task in light of the extraordinary demands on time made by public groups of this nature, this effort is crucial if the voice of business is to be heard at all. Business can participate

---

[53] Institute of Medicine, *Health Planning in the United States: Issues in Guideline Development* 27 (Nat'l Academy of Sciences 1980).

directly through membership on HSA boards and sub-area councils, or indirectly through community action projects, at least sixteen of which are currently operating across the country.[54] Some broadly represent diverse community interests, others limit their membership to business. Acting individually or through business coalitions, some companies have underlined the importance of an informed voice in area-wide health planning by sponsoring special educational seminars for employees holding volunteer positions on HSA, hospital, or community health agency boards.

☐ To monitor, on behalf of the business community, the results of area-wide health planning with an eye to the overall thrust of many seemingly unrelated decisions. HSAs in large metropolitan areas consider dozens of projects at a single meeting; distinctions among them can blur with the sheer volume of detail. Lacking uniform criteria for judging projects, many HSAs reach inconsistent decisions on similar cases because subjective or political factors intervene. When a watchdog group representing business interests serves as an effective counterbalance to these tendencies, it not only serves its own interests, but upgrades the overall process. Health planning is that rare forum in which management and labor can sit side by side with common interests as payers for and consumers of health services.

☐ To influence and reinforce, through traditional philanthropic activities, the goals and decisions emanating from the area-wide planning process. Although hospitals finance most of their major capital improvements through debt issues, high interest rates often oblige them to raise substantial sums for front-end financing. For most hospitals this entails fairly large-scale fund raising, aimed principally at business firms with a history of support for such activities. Companies with an interest in cost containment are finding it to their advantage to question hospitals regarding the costs and benefits to be expected from major capital improvements and to lean heavily on the findings of the HSA staffs regarding the overall usefulness of such projects. Well-staffed watchdog groups representing business interests have sometimes served as a clearinghouse for member companies, evaluating the specific funding requests they receive from institutional providers of health care.

Companies can appropriately question whether a commitment to area-wide planning will repay the expenditure and effort required. The answer is not immediately clear and will differ depending on the company's objectives and perspectives. For some, the lack of direct control they have over the costs of health care—other than the influence they can wield in the planning process—will militate for an aggressive role in planning. Others may find compelling the view taken by the Institute of Medicine's committee that the planning network is not the cure-all to rising health costs but is an important

---

[54] Government Research Corp., *A Report on Coalitions to Contain Health Care Costs* (Oct. 1977).

and "unusual example of democracy at work in American society." [55] Still others will remain unconvinced and will search for better alternatives.

Competition and Consumer Choice

One alternative to area-wide planning that has a following is creating an effective market for health services by encouraging the growth of many different alternative systems of care that will compete head-to-head on the basis of costs, quality, and patient satisfaction.[56] Prepaid health plans, or HMOs of various sorts, are the only tested models of such alternative systems.

Health Maintenance Organizations. HMOs circumscribe within a fixed budget the traditional open-ended relationship between providers, patients, and payers. As defined earlier, HMOs are based on the concept that providers contract to deliver a specified package of services to a defined population for a fixed premium, established on the basis of actuarial projections. The consumer, in deciding to enroll, also locks himself in. He now has to pay out-of-pocket expenses should he choose to go outside of the HMO for a health care service available through the plan. With the sky no longer the limit on health care spending in this closed financing system, incentives can be introduced to encourage providers and consumers to conserve finite resources.

HMO proponents contend that if several such plans operate within a single geographical area, each HMO will be forced to compete for members (patients) on the basis of product and price. The self-discipline that is likely to result is illustrated by the Minneapolis experience, where about 15 percent of the population belongs to one of seven competing HMOs, and enrollment continues to grow at the rate of 30 percent a year.

Background and growth. The present value of prepaid health plans is demonstrated by their record. A few prototypes emerged well before the turn of the century. Their first sign of growth occurred in the 1930s; in the 1970s they became an instrument of national health policy, based on persuasive evidence of their capacity, under the right circumstances, to provide medical care at lower cost than the traditional unstructured system. A few studies have shown that successful mature plans, such as Kaiser Permanente in California, have cut costs by 10 to 40 percent. Many more studies indicate that various types of prepaid plans make considerably less use of the hospital, with no evidence of compromised quality, as compared with the traditional system. Since hospital costs account for a major share of health care costs, this finding explains most of the demonstrated savings of the well-established

---

[55] Note 53 *supra*, at 25.

[56] Enthoven, "Consumer-Choice Health Plan," 298 *New England J. Med.* 650–658, 709–720 (1978).

plans and suggests that prepaid plans should have significant potential for controlling costs.

Despite their popularity in political circles, prepaid health plans have taken hold less rapidly than was hoped when, in 1971, their development was espoused as national policy. As of June 30, 1981, 10.3 million people were enrolled in 242 HMOs, up 13.2 percent from the 9.1 million in 236 plans as of June 30, 1980.[57] Many plans were started during the early 1970s, and that growth has continued. Between 1976 and 1977, the number of operating HMOs increased by almost 15 percent. Still, the older plans account for almost three-quarters of total HMO enrollment, and the rate of increase in membership has fallen short of expectations. There are various explanations for the disappointing growth rate; one is that HMOs are difficult to start because they necessitate major changes in the behavior of physicians and patients. An important question for industry, then, is when is the effort justified? This is a question that several large industrial firms are now investigating.

Health maintenance organization industry relationship. What is the relationship of HMOs to industry? This question can be answered in two parts. First, what can HMOs do for industry to ease the burden of paying for employees' health care without taking away benefits or compromising the quality of care? Second, what can industry do for the HMO "movement," to realign the incentives in health care, foster competition, and thereby build private sector solutions to the dilemma of rising costs?

Industry's involvement with prepaid health care antedates the "HMO movement." From the outset, architects of the movement have viewed employee groups as a major source of potential HMO members. We have already discussed the dual-choice provision of the 1973 Health Maintenance Act, and the challenge of marketing HMOs to employee groups accustomed to traditional third-party health insurance.

The government has now moved beyond the dual-choice requirement and has called on industry to do more for HMOs than merely serve as a hospitable, but relatively passive, conduit of marketing information to employees. That call to action was symbolized by the HMO Conference convened by what was then the Department of Health, Education, and Welfare in March 1978. The conference seemed to reflect the hope that industry might strengthen the mildly anemic HMO movement if large corporations would use their prestige and resources to sponsor, or at least spark, the development of HMOs for their employees. This was the government's answer to the second half of the question. Industry's answer to that same question—the extent to which corporations will choose to become actively involved in HMO sponsorship—remains clouded. Like any lasting partnership, the association between industry and HMOs will work well only if it involves an identifiable

[57] "Number of HMO Enrollees Hits New High of 10.3 Million," Business Insurance (Nov. 2, 1981).

quid pro quo. Several firms have been assessing the advantages to be gained in return for the risks associated with sponsoring their own HMOs.

Attempts to define and classify. The first hurdle in this assessment is arriving at definitions and applicable models. The generic term "HMO" is questioned on grounds that prepaid plans do not really "maintain health" but rather introduce management rigors. If an HMO is federally qualified, it is defined in one way. But some plans never seek qualification and even the largest and most famous—the Kaiser plans—only recently sought federal qualification. Definitions obscure facts—how many HMOs exist, how many people they serve, at what rate they are growing, and why some plans fail.

A relatively simple and convenient conceptual framework divides HMOs into two broad categories reflecting the way they organize and pay participating physicians: *closed-panel salaried group plans* and *open-panel fee-for-service plans.* The two HMO classifications subdivide into the other models depicted in Figure 22.4. Hybrid forms are also beginning to evolve, as efforts are made to preserve the best of both species.

Meanwhile there are several bills before Congress to stimulate expansion of HMOs and reforms to foster consumer choice, mostly through changes in the tax laws including exemptions, credits, and subsidies for individuals and/or businesses. Where alternative systems already exist, there is merit to proposals that will create incentives for employers to offer and employees to join them. However, federal legislation proposed along these lines seems unlikely to have a major impact unless or until there is dramatic growth in the availability of competing alternatives.

The Voluntary Effort

The Voluntary Effort (VE), a nationwide coalition of representatives of the hospital industry, the medical profession, the major insurers, the business community, and organized consumer groups, represents another solution—voluntary private sector self-regulation. Initiated in December 1977 to forestall the Carter administration's bill to cap hospital revenues, the VE set and met specific targets for stabilizing the rate of inflation in hospital expenditures in 1978 and 1979, working entirely through the voluntary cooperation of the many institutions involved. By 1980, however, perhaps because the visible threat of the revenue-capping legislation had receded, the inflation in expenditures resumed and hit unprecedented levels. With the effectiveness of the broad-based VE now in doubt, some local areas have seen the beginnings of vigorous activity on the part of private-sector payers. Individual corporations and business coalitions, sometimes allied with other prominent local interests (health providers, state or local government agencies, insurers, PSROs, and so on), are beginning to take part in negotiating rates, reviewing utilization, redesigning benefit coverage, and other activities aimed at containing expenditures.

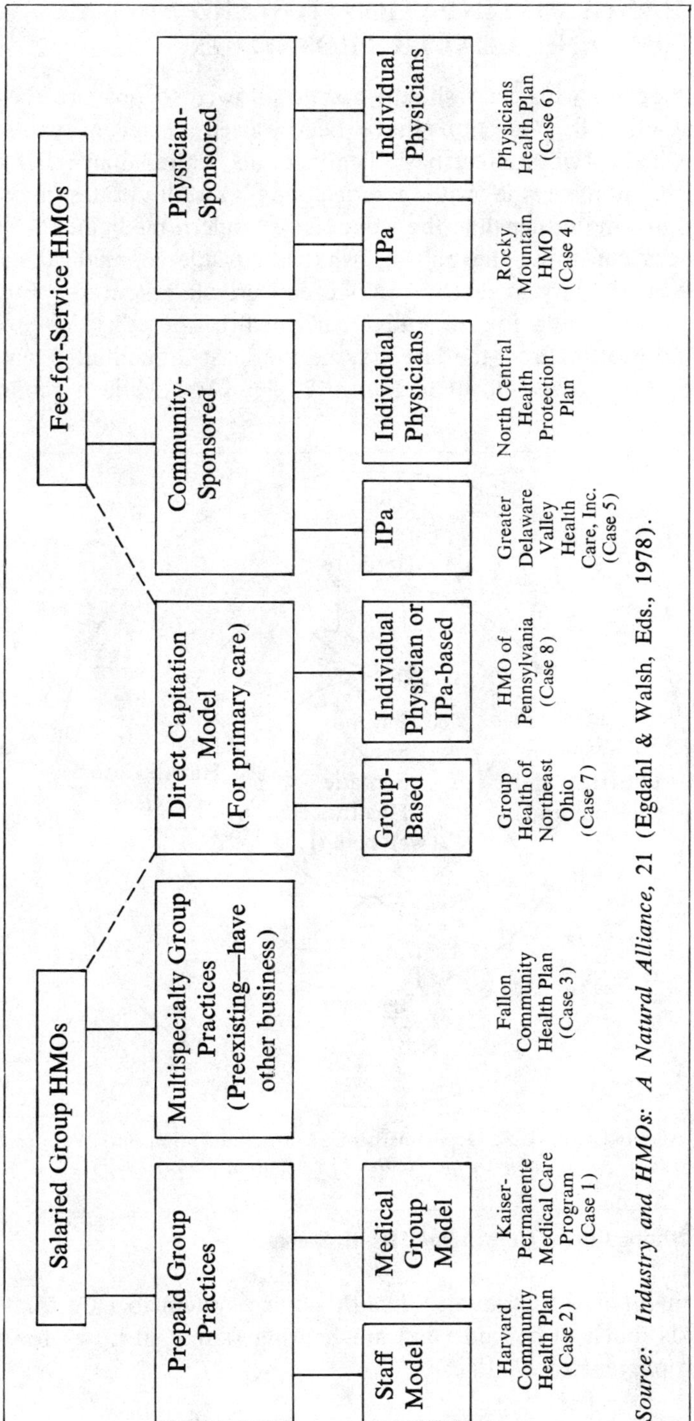

Source: Industry and HMOs: A Natural Alliance, 21 (Egdahl & Walsh, Eds., 1978).

Fig. 22.4 HMO Classification

A LONG-RANGE ORIENTATION TOWARD PREVENTION AND HEALTH PROMOTION

A preoccupation with costs should not be allowed to obscure the fundamental goal—health. Questions have been raised in recent years about whether medical services affect basic health at all, rather than relief of pain and suffering, in the same way that declining mortality rates may reflect gains in real income rather than the wonders of modern medicine.[58] Personal health services constitute the bulk of what is considered medical care and consume by far the largest share of public and private resources. But of the four factors responsible for an individual's health—heredity, environment, behavior, and health care—the last may be the least influential (signified by the width of the arrows shown in Figure 22.5). And while it remains important to maintain a high-quality health service system to care for those in need, there is much to be said (and much being said right now) for shifting the focus to prevention of illness.

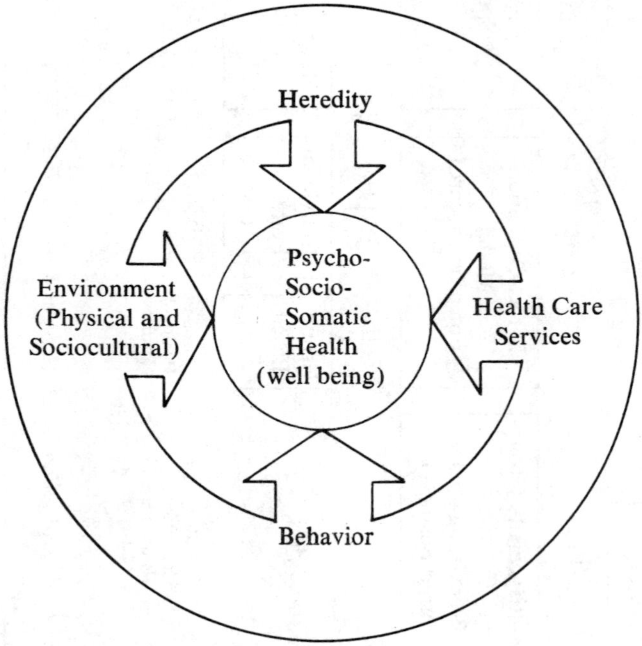

Source: Adapted from U.S. Department of Health, Education and Welfare, *Conditions for Change in the Health Care System* (Sept. 1977).

Fig. 22.5 Major Forces Influencing Health Status

[58] See Fuchs, *Who Shall Live?* (1974).

The concept of prevention, in terms of industry's role, has two parts. The more basic one, primary prevention or health protection, has been a traditional function of occupational medicine and industrial hygiene. This is a first-order issue for industry as a social responsibility and under the general-duty clause of the 1970 Occupational Safety and Health Act, requiring employers to furnish a workplace "free of recognized hazards." A second-order of prevention attracting increased attention is the influence on health of behavioral factors (lifestyle) and the "health promotion" program defined to modify them. Both relate remotely, if at all, to the direct costs of this year's insurance premiums. Health protection and health promotion efforts are increasingly being undertaken by the government and by business in the hope of eventually influencing costs. They are considered briefly here in that light.

Health Protection

Environmental exposures within the workplace and outside are thought to be responsible for many, if not most, of the ills plaguing modern man. Recognizing this, the general public and agencies of government have tried to hold business firms accountable for negative effects they may have unleashed on the environment in and around work-sites. A government task force attributes to environmental toxins six important categories of health problems:

1. Reproductive and developmental toxicity;
2. Mutagenesis;
3. Carcinogenesis;
4. Chronic degenerative diseases (cardiovascular, respiratory, and others);
5. Neurologic and behavioral toxicity;
6. Immunologic diseases.[59]

Potential sources of exposure include air, water, food, drugs, motor vehicles, guns, and physical hazards. Controls in occupational settings can be instituted through engineering or administrative changes or by employee requirement to wear protective devices such as earplugs or respirators. The specific details of this task are beyond our scope here, but within the context of cost containment, the following pressures should be recognized:

- A changing legal climate is broadening the legal liability of employers for the effects of work on health;

---

[59] U.S. Dep't of Health, Education, & Welfare, Public Health Servs., Office of the Ass't Sec'y for Health, Departmental Task Force on Prevention, *Disease Prevention and Health Promotion: Federal Programs and Prospects* 66 (U.S. Gov't Printing Office [No. 017-001-00418-9] Sept. 1979).

- Changes in retirement policy and expansion of health benefits to include coverage for retirees as a supplemental to government insurance will continue to extend employers' financial incentives to protect the health of their employees;
- Expanded scientific information is abetting the assignment of legal liability by finding associations that were previously unknown or unsuspected (for example, the recent finding from the Framingham heart study that, among women workers, those doing clerical work experience higher cardiovascular risk);
- The proliferation of chemicals in the workplace creates an imperative to set reasonable policy with insufficient scientific knowledge;
- The complications and escalating demands of evolving social policy (the Pregnancy Disability Act [60] and the Rehabilitation Act are two recent examples) bring new and sometimes conflicting pressures on management attention.

A corporate health strategy should deal early and thoroughly with these issues of health protection—that is, the question of what work is doing to and for employees' health. A cost containment strategy will typically begin within the area of employee benefits, but benefits specialists should remember that their best-laid plans will be flawed unless the company's health protection program is efficient.

Health Promotion

Lifestyle has been identified as an important contributor to premature mortality and chronic disability. Alcohol, cigarettes, motor vehicles, firearms, obesity, and stress greatly contribute to or cause deaths and disabling injuries or diseases that young and middle-aged people contract.[61] For this reason, discussions of health policy now include health education and promotion of healthful living and since many Americans spend most of their day on the job, the workplace is the logical place to implement health promotion strategies.[62] Very little is currently known, however, about how to modify people's habits. Nevertheless, industry is clearly in a position to take a leadership role.

Controlling Health Risks. The features of a health promotion program in industry vary widely. Identification and control of health risks underlie

---

[60] See *Women, Work and Health: Challenges to Corporate Policy,* (Industry and Health Care Series No. 8) (R. Egdahl & D. Walsh, Eds., 1980).

[61] U.S. Dep't of Health, Education, & Welfare, *Healthy People: The Surgeon General's Report on Health Promotion and Disease Prevention* (U.S. Gov't Printing Office [No. 017-001-0041602] 1979).

[62] See U.S. Dep't of Health, Education, & Welfare, *Proceedings of the National Conference on Health Promotion Programs in Occupational Setting* (U.S. Gov't Printing Office [No. 603-389-2562] 1979).

most programs; this helps maximize the cost effectiveness of specific interventions. A reduction in risk often measures the intervention's impact on health.

Heart and blood vessel disease is the leading cause of death in the United States; heart disease, alone is the leading cause of premature death, measured in years of potential life lost, assuming an average lifespan of seventy-five years. Cardiovascular disease is said to account for about 20 to 30 percent of national health care expenditures. The causes of cardiovascular disease are not fully understood, but epidemiological data points to certain associations, termed *primary risk factors*. These include hypertension (high blood pressure), hypercholesterolemia (high levels of cholesterol in the blood), cigarette smoking, and personality characteristics. Some approaches such as programs for discontinuance of smoking and anti-hypertensive medication can be instituted directly; other approaches require indirect interventions on several levels. For example, nutrition is considered important for reducing daily cholesterol intake and for controlling obesity, which some investigators feel add to the risk of cardiovascular problems. Physical activity may also help reduce risk, and stress management programs may or may not influence the personality traits associated with risk.

A decrease in mortality rates that can be attained by avoiding known risks is yet to be demonstrated conclusively. Nor is there unanimity on the most effective interventions. Health promotion programs are therefore initiated with a leap of faith, and one of the important contributions needed from companies taking that leap is a commitment to measurement and documentation in order to fill gaps in knowledge.

Other programs often included in health promotion are, like cardiovascular risk reduction, based on an appreciation of the magnitude of the particular problem being addressed and an intuitive sense that taking some action is preferrable to doing nothing.

- Smoking control programs, either as part of a comprehensive cardiovascular fitness effort or alone, seem to make sense in light of the Surgeon General's 1975 report calling cigarette smoking "the single largest preventable cause of illness and early disease; [63]
- Hypertension screening and control, an intervention that has been studied more than most, is said, if done well, to produce measurable reductions in absenteeism and hospital days; [64]
- Substance-abuse programs focusing on drugs and/or alcohol have been effective; the latter is a major problem in its own right and a principal cause

---

[63] See Center for Disease Control, *The Health Consequences of Smoking* (Dep't of Health, Education, & Welfare, Jan. 1978).

[64] Alderman, Green, & Flynn, "Hypertension Control Programs in Occupational Settings," 95 Public Health Reps. 158–163 (March-April 1980); Hanna & Graham, "A Cost-Benefit Study of a Hypertension Screening and Treatment Program at the Work Setting," 15 Inquiry 345–358 (Dec. 1978).

of automobile accidents and cirrhosis of the liver—two of the ten leading causes of death in the United States;

- Accident prevention programs often build on established in-plant safety programs and emphasize safety on the highways and at home. Highway accidents were the third leading cause of death based on years of potential life lost among Americans ages 1 to 74 in 1975;
- Nutrition and weight control programs are less common and little evidence is available by which to judge them. As part of an overall effort to upgrade health awareness, some companies are offering nutritionally preferred foods on their cafeteria and dining room menus and in vending machines;
- Cancer risk reduction through screening and health education may make sense to the extent that early detection does, but evidence to date suggests a targeted and parsimonious use of cancer screening dollars;
- Fitness and exercise programs are proliferating. As a job perquisite riding the crest of the current jogging and physical fitness wave, they are easy to justify and there is mounting evidence "that the relation between exercise and good health is more than circumstantial." [65] As part of a systematic program targeted to high risk individuals, exercise programs probably do pay off.
- Employee assistance programs (EAPs) are often separated administratively and conceptually from other health promotion activities, with the exception of alcohol and substance-abuse control, one of the traditional roots of EAPs. They involve counseling and referral for emotional problems that are interfering with job performance. A quarter of the population is said to be suffering at any given time from mild to moderate depression, and direct treatment for mental illness was estimated at about 12 percent of total health care expenditures in 1976. It is generally conceded now that occupationally based mental health programs, which help people cope with personal problems, have potential advantages including accessibility, early case findings, the threat of dismissing an employee who refuses to confront a drinking problem, and the opportunity to monitor the patient's progress. Some EAPs have reported reductions of absenteeism and/or medical care costs.[66]

In each of these program areas, there is a diversity of approach and little definitive evidence to help choose one over another. In conclusion, industry cost containment activities show considerable ingenuity. Some of the efforts appear promising, although few have produced irrefutable evidence of effectiveness. Little is known about overlapping effects they may have or about unintended side effects within the health system or beyond. For example, the gains in systemwide efficiency of closing down a community hospital may result in unemployment. Most of the cost containment strategies developed to date have ardent supporters and equally convinced detractors. And

---

[65] Pafenbarger & Hyde, "Exercise as Protection Against Heart Attack," 302(18) New England J. Med. 1027 (1980).

[66] *Mental Wellness Programs for Employees,* (Industry and Health Care Series No. 9) (W. Goldbeck, Ed., R. Egdahl & D. Walsh, Series Eds., 1980).

most appear to either require a major commitment of time and energy, which will have to be sustained over a period of years before results can reasonably be expected, or promise a quick but relatively minor payoff. The challenge will be to sort through the possibilities, to identify those best suited to local circumstances, and to arrive at a comprehensive and well-thought-out approach that makes sense for the company, its employees, and the broader community.

23

Medical and Dental Plans

STEVEN SIEVERTS

Vice-President, Blue Cross and Blue Shield of Greater New York

DANIEL ROSENBERG

Marketing Analyst, Blue Cross and Blue Shield of Greater New York

INTRODUCTION

Year by year, employers and employees alike have witnessed rising hospital and medical care costs. This phenomenon is reflected in the increased cost to employers of providing health insurance programs and in employees' demands for more benefits and lower out-of-pocket medical care costs. These conditions make it mandatory that both employers and carriers strive to provide the best benefits package with the most responsive administration at the lowest possible cost. In addition to this important consideration, which requires careful study and decision-making, an employer selecting a carrier and designing a program to provide health care insurance for its employees must investigate and select from an often bewildering number of possibilities.

Choosing the insurance carrier is probably the single most important decision in designing a health benefits program. The differences among carriers in providing customer services, in financing arrangements, in true administrative charges, and in achieving economies in costs of claims are significant factors for the employer to consider. Balancing these considerations must be assurance of quality health care for employees and efficient and sensitive processing of claims (particularly preserving patients' rights of privacy).

The procedure for selecting a carrier should also involve a company's analysis of the insurance plan it has been using—or, if this is the first time the company has offered health insurance to its employees, it should analyze the claims data of programs offered by similar sized companies in its locality. This effort should be combined with study of medical and hospital costs (and cost trends) in the localities where the company's employees live.

A company's funds for providing employee health insurance are always limited, so selection of what benefits to provide at a cost the company can afford is the next important decision in designing a health benefits program that focuses on protecting employees' families from the high costs of treating illness and injury. Such a program not only provides security for present employees but also helps the employer to compete effectively in attracting and keeping new employees.

There are three general types of medical care insurance programs: basic health insurance, major medical insurance, and health maintenance organizations.

BASIC HEALTH INSURANCE

Basic health insurance generally provides for first-dollar coverage (no deductibles) on a paid-in-full "service benefits" basis or, less commonly, a fixed-dollar indemnity schedule. Service benefits are expressed in terms of services covered rather than in terms of dollar limits. Indemnity benefits pay in full for each service, up to the limits set by the coverage for each such service.

The two major categories are basic hospitalization (including outpatient services) and basic medical/surgical (physician coverage) programs.

Basic Hospitalization

Inpatient Benefit Programs. Hospital service plans such as Blue Cross usually limit coverage to care in licensed contracting (or member) hospitals. Commercial carriers generally do not contract with hospitals, so licensure is usually the only requirement.

Basic hospital programs always cover inpatient diagnosis and/or treatment of an injury or illness—that is, they cover an individual who may require both diagnosis and treatment, or only treatment, of a covered condition, and in either case the program will cover his hospitalization costs.

A *service hospitalization program* provides coverage for a set maximum number of days (e.g., 30, 90, 180, or 365 days), on a paid-in-full basis. Daily room, board, and nursing care costs (usually in a semi-private room) are covered, as well as the cost of all covered ancillary services, such as the use of the operating room, drugs, x-rays, laboratory tests, and radiation therapy. An *indemnity hospitalization program* provides for a fixed payment per day for daily room, board, and nursing care costs, for a set maximum number of days of hospitalization. In addition, a maximum dollar indemnity for covered ancillary charges (usually a set multiple of the room indemnity allowance for one day) is provided. For example, a *low-level indemnity program* might provide up to $50 per day for room and board for up to 120 days, plus up to $1,000 for covered ancillary services. A *high-level indemnity program* might double or triple that.

With either a service or an indemnity hospitalization insurance program, it is important to decide under what conditions a new period of covered hospital days becomes available once an individual's initial coverage is exhausted. A number of options are available: a new maximum benefit might begin for each separate cause of hospitalization, for each renewal year for the insurance program, for each calendar year, or for each hospital stay that follows the previous covered stay by more than a set number of days (e.g., 90, or 180 days).

Benefit Limitations. All hospitalization programs specify limits as to what will be covered, usually in an effort to provide coverage only for services related to acute illness or injury, rather than long-term sickness or disability.

Mental disorders. Coverage of treatment for mental disorders is frequently limited to fewer days of hospital benefits than are provided for other conditions. Furthermore, benefits are sometimes provided only for psychiatric care in general or nonspecialty hospitals (i.e., care in psychiatric specialty hospitals or other long-term-stay institutions is excluded), and frequently care in public psychiatric facilities is not covered at all.

Diagnostic admissions. Basic hospitalization programs usually do not provide coverage for diagnostic hospital admissions when only diagnosis but no treatment is involved, unless this type of coverage is specifically included in the contract.

Unnecessary or inappropriate care. It is common in basic hospitalization insurance programs to find clauses denying coverage for medically inappropriate or unnecessary care. However, the carriers vary considerably in their ability to detect and deal with situations in which services are delivered that are not medically indicated—or in which no useful services at all are rendered. This is a consideration in choosing a carrier.

Alcoholism treatment and drug abuse treatment. Basic hospitalization programs often limit coverage for alcoholism to a specified number of days for detoxification, with little or no coverage for actual rehabilitation. Coverage for drug abuse is frequently similarly limited or is even excluded entirely except for the medical complications of drug overdoses, in part because of professional misgivings about whether hospital care is the best way to treat patients with addictive disorders.

Services by hospital-based physicians. Coverage of services provided by hospital-based physicians (e.g., radiology, laboratory medicine, anesthesia, and physical medicine/rehabilitation) can vary depending on how the services are administratively organized at the hospital to which the patient is admitted. Often the hospitals in a region will have regional patterns as to how the physician components of such services are compensated.

Outpatient Programs. Basic hospitalization programs also cover certain services of hospital outpatient departments and sometimes selected services of non-hospital ambulatory care facilities that do not require overnight stays in hospitals.

Accidental injury. Almost all basic health insurance programs provide full benefits for visits to hospital emergency rooms, including all services and supplies. The outpatient visit must take place within a set period of time (e.g., 24, 48, or 72 hours) following the accident that caused the treated injury.

Emergency involving sudden and serious illness. Coverage for hospital care of sudden and serious illness treated on an outpatient basis also is common. It generally offers the same benefits as for accidental injury and requires that the necessary services be performed at the hospital within twelve or twenty-four hours of the onset of the condition.

Additional Outpatient Benefits. Beyond emergency care, outpatient benefits can vary widely among carriers. Some outpatient services have been shown to actually save dollars if they reduce the amount of inpatient care used.

Outpatient surgery. The services of hospital outpatient surgery departments and, where available, free-standing ambulatory surgery centers and specialty facilities such as abortion centers are usually covered by basic hospitalization programs. As a substitute for inpatient care, services in such programs can be safe and cost effective, provided that adequate standards for appropriate use and quality care are enforced by the facility and monitored by the carrier.

Preadmission testing. The first day or two of an individual's hospitalization for elective surgery are usually taken up with laboratory tests and radiologic and other diagnostic studies. A preadmission testing benefit covers these tests through the basic hospitalization program if the tests are provided prior to the actual inpatient stay. Until fairly recently, preadmission testing service, either provided by hospitals or as a health insurance benefit, was uncommon. Because changed practice by patients, physicians, and hospitals is required, it is a challenge for carriers to get preadmission testing benefits accepted and used.

Home care. Many basic hospitalization programs provide coverage for services delivered in the patient's home following hospitalization. Covered care can include nursing, physical therapy, home health aide services, and other services delivered through a certified home health agency, which can be a hospital or a nursing agency.

Diagnostic services. Some basic hospitalization programs cover diagnostic tests provided through and by contracting hospitals. Because these are services used with some frequency by many people, they can be quite costly from an insurance standpoint. This benefit can be very popular with employees, especially with respect to expensive tests such as gallbladder studies and electroencephalograms.

Basic Medical/Surgical Coverage

Basic medical/surgical coverage pays for selected services of both medical and osteopathic physicians and sometimes nonphysician practitioners such as podiatrists and psychologists. Typically, surgical procedures are covered wherever performed, and all physician services are covered during hospitalizations.

Physician Compensation. Physicians generally are compensated on a fee-for-service basis, fees varying with the types of services performed. Several different methods of determining insurance coverage for physicians' services have evolved.

Indemnity schedules. This form of coverage provides a fixed payment for each specific service rendered, applied to whatever charge a practitioner actually makes for the service. The carrier prepares a schedule of these indemnities, usually with consistent internal relative values so that a roughly similar proportion of the typical fee is covered regardless of which service is rendered. However, since each carrier writes its own schedule, schedules with identical maximum indemnities may vary significantly from carrier to carrier. The differences may be mathematical only; that is, the schedules may have set different relative values for various services. Alternatively, they may reflect actual differences in coverage. For example, when more than one surgical procedure is performed at one time, some carriers provide less coverage than they would provide if each procedure were done separately. Other carriers simply count each procedure independently. In addition, a carrier may establish a maximum limit for coverage of all procedures performed on a patient by a physician on the same date, and some carriers limit the total dollars provided for one disability or one hospital stay. These differences among programs should be examined carefully because they can have real significance to the value of coverage.

Relative value units. The first *relative value* study was performed by the California Blue Shield plan in the early 1960s. This and later analyses lead to the promulgation of relative value schedules which are used to establish fees. In practice, these schedules are frequently revised. This approach establishes a standardized nomenclature for each service performed by doctors, and sets an appropriate relationship among medical procedures. A routine hospital visit by an internist is usually set up as one unit, to which all other procedures are related. By applying a dollar factor to these units, a fee schedule results. For example, with a physician hospital visit worth one unit, an appendectomy might be worth forty units, and a tonsillectomy ten units. If a factor of $20 were applied in the resulting schedule, allowances would be $20 for a physician hospital visit, $800 for an appendectomy, and $200 for a tonsillectomy. Relative value schedules can be used to establish consistent fee schedules with different dollar factors that reflect the cost of medical care in different regions of the country. (Relative value schedules have also been used by some organized medical groups to establish desired compensation results, but recent court rulings cast doubts on the legality of this practice from an antitrust standpoint. As an action taken unilaterally by a carrier to establish coverage, however, it seems to be entirely legal.)

Usual, customary, and reasonable (UCR) fees. UCR basic medical/surgical programs were developed to meet a demand for basic in-full coverage for physician services. In essence, UCR is an effort to establish a fair maximum payment for specific procedures in specific regions. Programs developed by some Blue Shield plans, commercial insurance companies, and the federal Medicare program use a variety of definitions for terms such as *usual, customary,* and *reasonable.* Usual may be defined as the most common charge made by an individual physician for a particular service. Customary may be defined as the most common charge physicians with similar training, within a particular geographical area, make for the given service. Reasonable may be defined as a charge that meets the test of general acceptability as to the particular procedure, time requirements, or complexity. UCR programs, underwritten by many local Blue Shield plans, utilize a computerized system that records physicians' charges for each procedure, and arrays all the charges to establish profiles for the region. It then finds the level at which a fixed proportion of physicians' fees will be at or below the UCR limits, which then becomes a screen and reveals a customary charge.

In some Blue Shield and similar plans, contracts with participating physicians assure that no covered patient will be billed in excess of the UCR maximum. In most areas, however, physicians who charge more than the UCR fees are free to try to collect the uninsured balances from their patients.

Specific Services. The following services may or may not be covered in basic medical/surgical programs in various areas of the country.

Anesthesia. The cost of anesthesiologists' services may be covered through the basic hospitalization program or may be part of the basic medical/surgical program. The latter may provide a fixed percentage (25 percent or 50 percent for example) to the anesthesiologist of the indemnities provided for the surgeons, payment on a UCR basis for anesthesiology fees, or payment through a relative value schedule for specific anesthesiology services.

Diagnostic x-ray. Radiology also may be covered under the basic hospitalization program or the basic medical/surgical program. X-ray benefits provided by the various carriers have to be closely examined, as coverages vary. Services may be provided, for example, only in the inpatient hospital, or permitted in the hospital outpatient department, or in a radiologist's office as well. When coverage is provided through a basic medical/surgical program, physician compensation may be on a UCR, relative value schedule, or fixed-indemnity basis. Frequently the coverage of radiologists' services in hospitals is only for the physician's service; the costs of the films, equipment and technicians are institutional and thus covered under the basic hospital program.

Radiation therapy. When provided, coverage of radiation therapy benefits for inpatients is usually similar to diagnostic x-ray coverage. Outpatient benefits, however, may be handled differently: sometimes the benefit is restricted to cancer care, and there may be an overall annual limit on these benefits.

Laboratory tests and services. For inpatients, all diagnostic laboratory tests are usually covered under the basic hospitalization program. Certain professional services of pathologists may be covered, however, similar to the way diagnostic x-rays are covered under the basic medical/surgical program. Outpatient laboratory tests are often not covered under basic hospitalization programs, although this also varies by region.

In-hospital specialist consultation. When provided under basic medical/surgical programs, coverage for this service is usually restricted to either one consultation per hospital admission or one consultation *per specialty* per hospital admission. (In the administration of these limits, exceptions are made by some carriers in cases with serious illness and multiple diagnoses.)

Home and office physician visits. These services are usually not covered under a basic medical/surgical program because patients' use of these services and the medical necessity for them are difficult to measure in terms of appropriate need and compensation. Moreover, it is rather costly to administer a program with a relatively high volume of relatively low-fee services.

Preventive health care. Preventive health care services, aimed at maintaining health and preventing illness rather than diagnosing and treating sickness and injury, are clearly important, but there is considerable skepticism about whether most such services are cost effective. Annual physical examinations and extensive multiphasic screening, for example, are expensive and generally regarded as having little preventive value. On the other hand, both basic immunizations for children and regular dental visits are reasonable in cost and have substantial preventive consequences.

It may be that health insurance, in its traditional forms, is not the best way to finance the various types of preventive health care services. The following preventive services are sometimes covered by basic medical/surgical programs.

Well baby care. This benefit is well defined and provides for physician care of infants and very young children. Coverage may specify that the services include basic immunizations and monitoring of the baby's early development, or may be limited to services only for newborns while still in the hospital.

Diagnostic screening. Some carriers now directly furnish or arrange diagnostic screening services, usually at the work-site rather than through the traditional insurance mechanism. These programs generally are limited to a few disease categories, such as high blood pressure, one or more categories of cancer, and/or diabetes. They should include a vigorous effort to refer patients to their physicians if the screening suggests possible disease because finding possible disease is pointless if it does not result in medical attention.

MAJOR MEDICAL INSURANCE

This form of coverage is based on reimbursing the insured person for out-of-pocket expenses incurred for covered services, less fixed amounts as front-end deductibles and co-insurance payments. Major medical coverage can either supplement basic insurances, picking up where the basic coverage ends for particular services and providing coverage for services not in the basic program, or it can be the whole insurance program, with no first-dollar basic coverage at all.

Benefits and Services Provided

Typical major medical programs cover a significantly wider range of benefits than do basic hospitalization and medical/surgical programs, especially with respect to out-of-hospital services. Most types of medical expenses are routinely covered, except for dental care, long-term institutional care, and the services of certain nonphysician practitioners such as chiropractors and naturopaths. Hospital daily charges, hospital ancillary expenses, and physicians' charges not fully covered by basic programs (if any) are covered under the major medical program. In addition, expenses *not* covered under basic programs (e.g., physician out-of-hospital charges, prescription drugs, medical equipment and appliances, private duty nursing, and ambulance service) are usually covered. Also covered are the fees of licensed professionals, such as physicians (including doctors of osteopathy), clinical psychologists, physiotherapists, podiatrists, optometrists, and speech therapists. Occasionally, the services of Christian Science practitioners, licensed social workers, nurse-midwives, and other health care professionals are also covered.

Although *dentists' fees* may be paid when specified surgical services (e.g., removal of a cyst from a patient's tongue) are performed, most dental services (e.g., fillings and making dental appliances) are not usually covered, except when treatment follows an accident. On the other hand, in-hospital *oral surgery* is usually covered by both basic medical/surgical programs and major medical programs.

Similarly, the services of *podiatrists* are usually covered when fractured feet or toes are treated, but not when minor office procedures (e.g., the removal of corns, calluses, or bunions) are performed. *Chiropractic services* may be covered, particularly if the state where the covered individual lives has enacted laws requiring that carriers include such coverage in their programs.

In-hospital care major medical *benefits for treatment of mental disorders* are sometimes provided on the same basis as for other conditions and sometimes have lower limits similar to those found in basic hospitalization programs. Provision of benefits for outpatient treatment of psychiatric and psychological conditions, however, probably varies more widely than any other major medical benefit. Covered services may be limited to physician care or may include the services of clinical psychologists and sometimes psychiatric social workers and other licensed counselors. Because of the especially voluntary nature of the demand for such services, insuring then can become disproportionately costly.

These benefits may be integrated with other major medical program benefits, or they may have separate dollar, deductible, or co-payment limits of their own.

Other services not usually covered under major medical programs are: most dental care, routinely prescribed hearing tests and hearing aids, optometric examinations, eyeglasses, contact lenses, nonprescription drugs, travel for medical care, marriage counseling, physical checkups unrelated to the diagnosis of illness or injury and nursing home care.

Types of Major Medical Programs

Supplemental Programs. This type of program is added to a plan offering both basic hospitalization and medical/surgical benefits. A *corridor deductible* (see discussion below) is applied when this coverage is used before the major medical coverage can become effective. The covered individual must pay a set cash amount for covered services, whether or not benefits have been used. The program then reimburses the insured person for a percentage of the eligible expenses of specified covered services.

Wrap-Around Programs. A wrap-around major medical program is sometimes added to a plan of basic hospitalization benefits in lieu of basic medical/surgical benefits, thus providing the advantages of first-dollar coverage and service benefits for necessary expensive institutional health services. This kind of coverage also uses a corridor deductible.

Comprehensive Programs. A comprehensive major medical program provides an alternative to programs combining basic hospitalization and medical/surgical coverage. Usually all covered benefits in a comprehensive program are melded into a single package, with one set of deductibles and co-insurances. There is no first-dollar coverage in this kind of program.

Major Medical Deductibles

The ostensible purpose of deductibles is to deter marginal demands for covered services and to encourage price consciousness on the part of patients. Recent inflationary trends, however, have sharply reduced the impact of fixed deductibles, and there is considerable controversy as to whether any deductibles other than very large ones have these effects. Recently, some major medical programs have put in escalator deductibles, that rise automatically as the index of medical prices goes up.

Corridor vs. Integrated Deductibles. Most supplemental and wrap-around major medical deductibles in use today are *corridor deductibles*. This means that the dollar deductible is applied after the basic hospitalization and medical/surgical program benefits are rendered for those items covered under the basic programs. Corridor deductibles for supplemental and wrap-around major medical programs range from $50 to $500. Occasionally they vary according to employee salary levels. Usually the deductible is expressed on a per-individual/per-year basis, with a combined maximum per-family deductible.

The much rarer *integrated deductibles* are generally associated with deductibles per defined cause and call for a dollar deductible (e.g., $500 or $1,000) to be applied before the major medical program will cover expenses, regardless of whether or not the basic hospitalization and/or medical/surgical program covered those expenses. For example, if a covered individual had $1,000 or expenses fully covered by his basic program(s), the $1,000 major medical deductible would be satisfied.

The deductible may be applied on one of the following bases:

- *Per calendar year.* This means that deductibles are applied only once, no matter how many conditions are involved, during January 1 to December

31 of each year. The calendar year is the most common and easiest to understand approach taken in newly written major medical programs. For employees, it has the extra advantage of coinciding with the tax year.

- *Per fiscal or contract year.* On this basis, the deductibles are applied once per fiscal or contract year, no matter how many conditions are involved. The twelve-month period constituting the fiscal or contract year may begin on any date but is usually the anniversary date of the insurance contract or the start of the employer's accounting period.
- *Per cause.* This approach to deductibles is becoming rare (except for coverage of long-term conditions, in which patients with total disabilities may have no annual renewals of deductibles). It means that each separate disability or condition has a new deductible applied to it.

Liberalizations in Deductibles

Last Quarter Carry-Over. This common liberalization of the per-year deductible applies to covered expenses incurred during October, November, and December, to which that year's deductible would otherwise be applied because the covered individual has not used the programs, and so not incurred the deductible, earlier in the year. This feature allows those expenses to be credited towards the next year's deductible instead. In this way, situations are avoided in which, because additional covered expenses occur early in the next year, an individual would have the deductible applied twice in a short period of time.

Prior Carrier Carry-Over. Frequently, when a company changes from one major medical program carrier to another, the new carrier will provide a carry-over feature whereby unreimbursed expenses incurred in the last ninety days of the prior program can be credited towards the deductible of the new carrier.

Common Accident Clause. Many major medical programs contain a clause that liberalizes the application of deductibles when more than one member of a covered family is involved in a single (common) accident. This clause guarantees that no more than one deductible is applied to all the covered members of the family in such cases.

Family Deductible. There are two types of this common feature of deductibles:

- Applying no more than two or perhaps three deductibles per family per year, irrespective of family size;
- Applying no more than a set dollar sum (e.g., $200, $250, or $300) per family per year.

There is a subtle but significant difference in these two approaches to the family deductible. For example, if a program has a $100 deductible per person per year, applying no more than two deductibles for a covered family would not mean a $200 maximum deductible for the family; instead, it would mean that at least two members of the family must each meet the $100 deductible before no more deductibles are applied to the remaining members of the family. Thus, if six members of a covered family incurred $80 of major medical expense each, there would be no major medical payment of any of these claims, since no member met the $100 deductible.

Fixing a set dollar sum as the maximum family deductible, in contrast (e.g., $200), means that once any or all members of the covered family have accumulated $200 of major medical expenses and paid them to satisfy the deductible, no more deductibles would be applied for the balance of the year. Under this plan, if six members of a covered family each incurred $80 of major medical expenses during the year, for a total family expense of $480, the insured individual would pay only the $200 deductible and the major medical program would cover the remaining $280, less the co-insurance portion that the individual must pay.

Benefit Periods

A *benefit period* is the period of time for which major medical benefits are extended. Commonly, when the deductible is on a per-year basis, the benefit period extends to December 31 of each year. This is by far the simplest form to administer, and is more easily understood by all of those affected.

However, when the deductible is expressed on a *per cause basis,* the benefit period may be separately extended for the specific condition or disability, as defined in the major medical contract. These individual benefit periods often have a maximum limit of two or three years. The benefit period ends when the covered person does not incur any expense for the condition or disability over a sixty-day, ninety-day, or six-month period. In addition, there are other minor variations concerning how benefit periods are figured under this approach, which is used less and less in major medical programs.

Co-Insurance

Co-insurance, the sharing of covered expenses between the carrier and the insured patient, is applied after a deductible has been met. Co-insurance is believed by some authorities to hold down the use of marginally beneficial medical services, because the insured bears part of the cost. With the exception of primary physician visits, however, there is little hard evidence to show that co-insurance reduces utilization. In fact, because it enables the consumer to purchase expensive services for only 20 percent or 25 percent of the total cost (see Typical Co-insurance, below), co-insurance actually may have the effect of stimulating increased use of the services. In any case, it probably has little effect on the incidence of hospitalization and visits for emergency care, which are perceived by patients as being medically required regardless of cost, but which make up the largest part of total medical expense.

In any event, because co-insurance does transfer a sizeable fraction of medical expense to the insured person, it does have the effect of lowering the premiums for a given set of benefits, or it permits a given premium level to purchase a somewhat greater range of benefits.

Typical Co-Insurance. Eighty percent coverage of medical expenses, with the patient liable for the other 20 percent, is the most common form of major medical co-insurance. Less often, 75 percent, 85 percent, or 90 percent coverage is offered.

Split Co-Insurance. For some major medical programs, the co-insurance is "split." For example, a plan might provide 80 percent coverage on expenses that supplement basic program benefits (e.g., charges for hospitalization or surgery), and 85 percent or 90 percent coverage for other types of expenses (e.g., physician home and office visits, prescription drugs, and appliances).

Co-Insurance Followed by 100 Percent Coverage. An increasingly common feature today is major medical payment of 80 percent of covered expenses up to a certain dollar amount, followed by paid-in-full benefits. For example, a calendar-year major medical plan might cover 80 percent of the first $2,000 of covered expenses in a calendar year and then provide 100 percent coverage for the balance of the year. Similarly, a "per cause" major medical plan might provide 80 percent of the first $2,000 of expenses for the specific condition either for the balance of the benefit period or the lifetime of the patient.

Out-of-Hospital Mental Care. In a major medical program, out-of-hospital treatment of mental disorders may be covered according to the same co-insurance factor as other conditions. More typically, however, when coverage for this service is provided, it is on a 50 percent co-insured basis, with stated maximum limits.

Maximums

Most major medical programs have *maximum pay-out* features. That is, beyond a specified level of expenses the insurance no longer provides coverage.

Application. Maximum dollar amounts may be applied to a benefit period or year; to a specific condition (per cause); to total disability; to a covered individual's lifetime; or to combinations of these (for example, a dollar maximum per calendar year with a much higher dollar maximum covering the person's lifetime under the program).

Separate Inside Limits. *Inside limits* may be included in major medical programs for specific conditions and/or services. There may be special dollar limits on hospitalizations and out-of-hospital visits for mental disorders, as well as limits established for such benefits as private duty nursing care or ambulance services.

Maximum Dollar Limits. Dollar limits for major medical coverage vary from $5,000 to $1 million to no limit at all. The dollar amount may be expressed as both a yearly maximum and a lifetime maximum (e.g., benefits covered up to $50,000 per year, with a lifetime maximum of $100,000).

Renewability of dollar limit maximums. Often a major medical program will provide for renewability of the maximum. This may be accomplished by a *health statement* or through an automatic renewal after a period of time. Under a health statement provision, the insured individual obtains a medical statement from the physician (on a form furnished by the insurance carrier) that says that he is now in good health. The carrier, using its own discretion, may then renew the maximum. Depending on the program, these health statements may be submitted after $5,000 or some other amount of covered expense has been reached, or after the entire lifetime maximum has been expended.

Some programs have an automatic annual renewal provision that provides for the restoration each year of up to or some amount of the total maximum.

SPECIAL RIDERS

Broader Coverage

Some basic hospitalization programs and some standardized major medical programs (as compared to those especially planned for large groups) leave uncovered certain elements of medical expense for which an employer may wish to provide coverage. These benefits can often be purchased as *riders* to either or both basic hospitalization and major medical contracts. The riders can be either for a kind of expense (e.g., vision care, alcoholism rehabilitation, or hospitalization in psychiatric specialty hospitals) or for the purpose of broadening a type of coverage (e.g., adding to a maximum number of hospital days, or covering purely diagnostic hospital admissions, or upgrading the payment levels for physicians' services).

Dread Disease Riders

A variety of *dread disease riders* are written by some commercial insurance carriers. These usually provide for payment up to $5,000, $10,000, or some other limit for expenses associated with a specific disease or condition. With the increased enrollment in and comprehensiveness of health insurance programs, these riders have decreased in popularity and are under increasing criticism from public regulatory agencies. One reason for this is the fact that these benefits are sometimes written to cover polio, diptheria, or typhoid—conditions that are now very rare. More often today such a rider is written to cover a category of disease, such as heart condition or cancer.

Dread disease riders make little sense from an economic standpoint, since comprehensive basic hospitalization and major medical programs can cover the same conditions at far lower insurance cost and with a much higher likelihood of meaningful protection for people. To have a separately administered and underwritten program for a comparatively low-incidence condition inflates the premiums needed to provide the coverage and cover administrative costs.

HEALTH MAINTENANCE ORGANIZATIONS

Health maintenance organizations (HMOs) are planned alternatives to the traditional ways in which people get medical services. A person or family may choose to join an HMO instead of being on its own in the marketplace of local, privately practicing physicians and competing hospitals. The decision to join an HMO presents a trade-off: in return for agreeing to restrict all non-emergency covered services to only those physicians and facilities provided by the HMO, the subscriber gets a broader set of benefits than a typical basic hospitalization/major medical plan would provide, usually at considerably lower out-of-pocket costs.

HMOs are entities that have two distinct functions: to *insure* the costs of the care needed by their subscribing members and to *provide* most of that care, either directly through physician group practice clinics or through contractual arrangements with local physicians and hospitals. For fixed monthly payments, the provider of care assures provision of services, with few arbitrary limits. Partly because HMOs attempt to exercise fairly vigorous professional controls over the use of hospital care, which ordinarily consumes well over half of U.S. health benefits dollars, significantly lower hospitalization incidence is generally found in HMO populations than in comparable populations covered under traditional programs.

Dual or Multiple Choice

Employees usually have a choice, when they begin work, between the employer's regular package of health insurance benefits or an HMO—if they live in the limited service area of an HMO that has executed an agreement with the employer. If the HMO is not selected initially, the option to do so may be offered to employees during a two-week period, once or twice a year, at their place of employment. To finance the HMO plan, the employer usually contributes the same amount paid toward the regular insurance coverage, and the employee pays any additional premiums due each month through payroll deductions. Some metropolitan areas now have two or more HMOs in competition with the traditional medical care delivery system, so employers sometimes offer more than one HMO alternative, in addition to a traditionally structured health insurance plan, for their employees to choose among.

Federal Qualification

About two-thirds of HMOs are qualified under the federal Health Maintenance Organization Act (HMOA), in addition to whatever licensures are required under state law for the insuring entity and the care-providing entity of the HMO. Federal qualification mandates that employers (other than some that are government agencies or operating under certain labor agreements) make dual choice available to employees if there are at least twenty-five employees living in the HMO's service area. An HMO qualified under the HMOA may have been established with the aid of federal planning grants and/or interest-bearing federal loans for initial capitalization and start-up costs.

The absence of federal qualification is not in itself any indication that an HMO is unsound, nor is federal qualification any guarantee that an HMO is adequately administered, either fiscally or from a medical care standpoint. HMOs that are not federally qualified may simply not have had any need for public monies. Both federally qualified HMOs and those that are not are usually regulated by state government. In some jurisdictions (e.g., New York and Illinois), state HMO laws provide special regulation similar to the provisions of the HMOA.

Forms of HMOs

The two basic types of HMOs are group models and individual practice associations (IPAs). Both are structured on essentially the same principle: a group of physicians or an entity that employs or contracts with physicians, accepts responsibility for both the medical care for enrolled HMO subscribers and the financing of that medical care on a prepaid basis. The two HMO types differ importantly, however, in how they are organized and in the way most doctors who participated are compensated.

Some HMOs, particularly those with several sites where patients come for care, establish one legal entity for the insurance aspects of their program and one or more additional separate contracting entities to provide the actual care. Examples of such HMOs, each with several care-providing clinics or agencies, are Kaiser Permanente on the West Coast and elsewhere, the Health Insurance Plan of Greater New York, and a number of Blue Cross and Blue Shield HMOs across the country.

Group Practice Model HMOs. In the group model HMO, a group of physicians, representing multiple specialties, is formally organized to practice as a single entity. Usually they care for patients at a single location, sharing facilities and personnel. Commonly, a comprehensive centralized health care facility is used to house the HMO. Subscribers to the HMO constitute most of these physicians' practice. The group may be organized as a private partnership, as a practice corporation, or as employees of a nonprofit corporation, or as employees of the HMO itself. (If the physician group members are employees of the HMO, the group model is called a *staff model*. Many of the relatively small group practice HMOs established under the HMOA in the late 1970s and early 1980s are staff models.)

In the group model, HMO subscribers are able to get most outpatient services at a single location from members of the physician group and their staff, although certain specialty services are sometimes purchased on a fee-for-service basis from physicians in the community. Typically, group model HMOs make extensive use of nonphysician personnel, including specially trained nurses, to supplement the physicians' care. A few HMOs (notably, most of the Kaiser Permanente plans) own their own hospitals, but the usual pattern is for the group physicians to obtain privileges at local hospitals, sometimes on a planned basis. At one time, many medical societies and conservative physicians opposed group model HMOs and tried to block group practice physicians from receiving hospital medical staff appointments, but this is no longer a common problem in most regions.

Individual Practice HMOs. In an Individual Practice Association (IPA), in contrast to the group practice model, the members of the group of physicians organized in the HMO continue to practice out of their private offices, and HMO members form only a part of their total practice. The participating physicians are compensated on a fee-for-service basis governed by complex contractual risk-sharing arrangements that assure that the total amount of money spent in providing care does not exceed the total amount of revenues from HMO members. The key to the IPA is the association that the involved physicians form and are committed to. The association must exercise professional and administrative control over the physicians' practices in serving the HMO members. Quality of care must be controlled, and the association seeks to assure that neither hospital care nor physicians' services are overutilized.

The *principal advantages* of the IPA model are that (1) HMO subscribers are not limited to receiving care from relatively few designated physicians in a single location, but rather may select from a larger number of physicians; and (2) the start-up costs and operating overhead of the IPA are significantly lower than in the group practice model, with its requirement of a fairly elaborate centralized facility. The *principal disadvantages* of the IPA model are that (1) inevitably the internal peer controls are not as strong as those in the group practice model, which often leads to higher rates of use of both physician services and institutional care; and (2) the risk-sharing by the IPA physicians may result in their having to accept less than their usual fees for serving HMO patients, which in turn may stimulate some physicians to drop out of the HMO's service program.

Problems of HMO Insolvency. A particular problem in the early 1980s has been the fiscal collapse of several small federally qualified HMOs. The causes of these insolvencies are too complex to be detailed here, but two general causes can be described: (1) adherence to monthly premiums that were too far below actual costs of the care given and (2) HMO management that seemed unable to control administrative and patient care costs adequately. The presence of a substantial line of federal credit may have lulled HMO managements and the federal bureaucracy into failure to identify the financial problems until they were out of control.

With few exceptions, most efforts to enable insolvent HMOs to survive before or after entering formal bankruptcy have been successful, often by attracting new ownership, and sometimes through write-offs of all or most of the multimillion dollar loan by the federal office of HMOs in the Department of Health and Human Services.

Employers are rightly concerned about whether their employees will be protected in the event of actions by hospitals and other providers that were not paid for covered services prior to an HMO's collapse. The possibility of insolvency is remote in the case of large multi-unit HMOs, HMOs affiliated with Blue Cross and Blue Shield, and HMOs operated by large corporations, such as INA and Prudential. Small independent HMOs, however, ought to be able to demonstrate sufficient reserve capacity to assure that their subscribers will not risk collection actions by unpaid providers in the event of financial difficulty. Such reserves often involve reinsurance, often through underwriting relationships with the local Blue Cross plan. For example, the HMO may provide protection to its members by purchasing insured coverage for hospitalization from Blue Cross under an experience-rated premium structure. (See discussion below on rating mechanisms.)

DENTAL PROGRAMS

Dental health insurance is the most rapidly growing aspect of employee health benefits programs. In part because many regular health insurance programs are already very comprehensive in their coverage, employers and workers who wish to offer still broader benefits have turned to dental coverages. This kind of insurance is clearly popular with employees and their families, because dental expenses, even for "routine" care, can become a burden.

Covered Services

A uniform code of dental nomenclature issued by the American Dental Association is used by most health insurance carriers to specify covered procedures within service categories. Each carrier's program should be examined to determine whether all the following service categories are included and whether there are any categorical exclusions or limits:

1. Diagnostic services (examinations, x-rays, and tests)
2. Preventive services (prophylactic treatment, such as flouride treatments, teeth cleaning, and training in dental hygiene)
3. Restorative services (fillings, inlays, crowns)
4. Endodontics (root canal therapy, apicoectomy)
5. Periodontics (gum disease therapies)
6. Removable prosthodontics (partial and complete dentures)
7. Fixed prosthodontics (bridges, crowns)
8. Oral surgery (tongue surgery, incisions for impaction, treatment of fractures)
9. Orthodontics (straightening teeth)
10. Adjunctive services (miscellaneous services such as anesthesia, drugs, consultation)

Each carrier selects from these ten areas of service and groups its selections into its own categories. For example, a basic dental insurance program might cover only diagnostic and preventive services, or might also cover restorative services, endodontics, and oral surgery. Many dental programs stress—and therefore cover—preventive dental care, which, unlike much preventive medical care, has a clear effect on the incidence of dental pathology and therefore on dental costs.

New dental plans tend to have a high initial cost, as subscribers obtain treatment of accumulated dental problems (sometimes neglected for years). It should be noted, however, that many persons resist non-emergency dental care, even if it is cost free.

Limitations

Each dental program has its own set of limitations and exclusions. The following are some examples:

Diagnostic X-Rays. Bite-wing x-rays and full-mouth x-rays may have limitations—no more than one set of full mouth x-rays may be covered per year.

Selected Restorative Services. It is common for a dental insurance plan to cover silver amalgam fillings in full, while requiring some form of co-insurance for the more costly gold inlays or crowns. Restorations required as a consequence of accidental injury may have special higher limitations, while restorations that are primarily cosmetic may have lower limits or be excluded entirely.

Prosthodontics. Replacement or repair of removable dentures and bridges may be limited to one every three or five years. Under some plans, replacement of artificial teeth is not covered unless it is to replace teeth lost since the start of the coverage.

Orthodontics. Most dental plans do not cover orthodontics or the straightening of teeth. When provided, orthodontic services may be restricted to dependents, dependents under a certain age, or anyone under a specific age. In addition, orthodontics is usually not covered by the same type of indemnity schedule or co-insurance provided for other types of coverage in most programs. Orthodontics coverage almost always specifies a yearly and a lifetime dollar maximum.

Duplication of Benefits

Most dental programs contain a duplication of certain procedures also covered under basic medical/surgical programs, such as excision of oral cysts, treatment of fractures of facial bones, and surgery in the facial area. Major medical programs also may provide coverage for some services covered by dental insurance if the service is provided by a physician or oral surgeon rather than a dentist. (Hospitalization for dental services is virtually never covered under dental insurance, but is provided by basic hospitalization programs.) These duplications are for services that have a low incidence in a large population, so it is not unusual for there to be no formal mechanism to avert double claims from the insured. The informal mechanisms are generally sufficient to prevent this from being a major concern.

Types of Dental Programs

Free-Standing Programs. Free-standing dental programs are generally administered with little or no reference to other coverages. They usually pay dentists and oral surgeons through (1) a dollar indemnity schedule, with or without deductibles and co-insurance; or (2) a UCR payment system similar to medical/surgical UCR, with or without deductibles or co-insurance (as defined previously). In addition, a free-standing dental insurance plan may set overall yearly dollar maximums for the dental program as a whole and may set yearly and lifetime dollar maximums for specific areas of benefits, such as orthodontics or prosthetics.

Free-standing programs are provided through commercial insurance companies or nonprofit service plans such as Blue Cross and Blue Shield and

Delta Dental corporations. Each of these carriers may provide indemnity or UCR compensation structures. Some service plans may provide greater benefits for subscribers who use participating dentists (see Dental Cost Control, Participating Dentists, below) as an effort toward cost and quality control.

Integration Within Major Medical Programs. A number of major medical programs have expanded benefits to cover dental expenses. The principal feature is a common deductible for medical and dental expenses. In keeping with the nature of major medical programs, dental expenses usually are covered on a UCR basis and employ the same co-insurance factor as the medical part of the coverage. There may, however, be inside limits for specific dental areas, such as orthodontics.

Per Capita Plans. In several regions of the country, experimentation is under way to provide dental insurance by paying dentists (singly or in groups) on a monthly per capita basis rather than on a fee-for-service basis, in return for provision of total primary dental care as needed by the subscribers who choose the option. It is too soon to judge the effectiveness of this approach.

Dental Cost Control

Four effective types of dental cost control are: (1) incentive co-insurance, (2) prior authorization, (3) utilization review, and (4) participation agreements with dentists.

Incentive Co-Insurance. Complex, expensive dental procedures are almost always the result of neglect in primary and preventive dental care. Under incentive co-insurance, a greater percentage of benefits (e.g., moving from 70 percent in the first year to 80 percent, 90 percent, and 100 percent in the following years) is provided if the individual does not fail to visit his or her dentist at least once each year. The intended effect of incentive co-insurance is to accent preventive and basic dentistry in order to minimize later extensive and costly dental care.

Prior Authorization. This requirement is sometimes labeled "precertification" or "predetermination." When an extensive procedure is indicated, the dentist submits a treatment plan to the insurance carrier and obtains prior authorization to qualify for coverage, before starting the patient's treatment. Some carriers require prior authorization if the cost of treatment will exceed a fixed amount, usually $100; other carriers apply this requirement only to certain elective services in categories such as prosthetics, periodontics, and oral surgery. Prior authorization enables both patients and dentist to know in advance what benefits will be provided after the dental plan's own dental consultants review the proposed course of treatment. This is important, since dentistry often has several alternate and equally valid methods of treatment of a given condition, and prior authorization can aid in steering patients to less costly approaches. In addition, the fact that a consultant will review the case may cause some dentists to be more conservative in proposing costly treatments with only marginal benefits.

Utilization Review. Utilization review provides both cost and quality controls. A carrier that employs computerized screens to select cases for professional review can uncover questionable care and aberrant practice patterns and can identify potential over-chargers and over-utilizers as well as poor quality and inappropriateness of care. The professional review of possibly questionable care is done by competent dental specialists, aided by trained paraprofessionals.

Participating Dentists. Some nonprofit dental service plans have contracts with participating dentists under which the practitioners agree to take payment from the plan and not to make additional charges for covered services. Frequently these plans also have extensive utilization review and quality assurance stipulations.

VISION CARE PROGRAMS

Definition

Most health insurance programs provide some coverage of ophthalmological care, in the sense that hospitalization and surgery for diseases and injuries of the eye are covered. Vision care coverage applies to items not normally provided for in basic and major medical health insurance programs, such as routine eye examinations, refractions, eyeglass lenses, contact lenses, and the purchase and fitting of frames. Vision care plans are not yet common, except in some industries where labor management funds provide special health benefits, but they are growing in popularity.

Types of Programs

Similar to dental coverage, there are three general types of vision care programs.

Free-Standing Programs. Free-standing vision care programs almost always have a fixed indemnity schedule of compensation and a strictly limited range of benefits, such as one refraction and one pair of eyeglasses per year per individual.

Integration Within Major Medical Programs. Sometimes vision care is covered as an adjunct to a major medical program, with the same deductibles and the same co-insurance arrangements. However, the benefit is almost always based on a fixed amount for each specific covered service, rather than a UCR schedule.

Vision Service Plans. In some areas, optometric offices with optical dispensaries have been established that provide refractions and eyeglasses at low cost. Some of these offices have relationships with carriers, employers, or welfare funds to provide defined vision care services for employees and dependents on a prepaid basis. Another method is to provide an indemnity coverage program for provision of similar services by community optometrists and opticians.

Limitations

Vision Examinations. Generally, no more than one vision examination per year by an ophthalmologist or optometrist is covered.

Eyeglass Frames. Frames are usually limited to one set per two-year period (or some other period) and usually coverage is only for the value of a basic set, not costly designer sets or gold rims.

Eyeglass Lenses. Usually a pair of lenses once a year is covered. The coverage schedule for lenses takes into account the various types: single-vision, bifocals, trifocals, and lenticular.

Contact Lenses. Contact lenses generally are covered only if the patient has a medical condition requiring them. Otherwise, if contact lenses are substituted for a regular pair of eyeglass lenses and frames, the program might make payment limited to the cost of a regular pair of lenses and frames, or not cover the cost at all.

Sunglass and Eyeglass Replacement. Most programs do not cover sunglasses or replacement of lost or broken frames or lenses.

PRESCRIPTION DRUG PROGRAMS

Background

From their earliest development, most major medical programs have included prescription drugs as a covered service. (This may have had the effect of slowing down the development of free-standing prescription drug programs.) In any case, it is not uncommon for employers to obtain a separate basic prescription drug program as part of a comprehensive health benefits package. As a major medical program benefit, coverage of prescription drugs presents problems of administrative control over claims submission and processing because most prescriptions are low-cost items, with little documentation. Some of these programs rely on contracts between a prepayment plan and individual retail pharmacies, specifying the reimbursement rate, which is usually lower than the usual retail charges. For example, the plan may cover the pharmacy's acquisition cost plus a flat $3 processing charge. Plans of this kind use computers to process claims and control costs. They may work on an insured basis, or they may provide administrative services only, so that the employer pays the full direct costs of the programs. Insurers and self-insured companies may or may not utilize outside administrators for the purpose of conducting a prescription drug coverage program.

Deductibles

Most prescription drug programs have a per prescription deductible, such as $1 or $2. Many programs, particularly in Blue Cross and Blue Shield plans, encourage the use of a participating pharmacy by increasing the deductible or introducing a co-insurance percentage (e.g., 75 percent or 80 percent) when a nonparticipating pharmacy is utilized. It can be to the advantage of retail pharmacies to participate, because the program may attract volume business and assure rapid and sure payment.

The drugs covered are limited to those legally requiring a prescription written by a licensed physician or dentist. Depending upon the program, oral contraceptives are sometimes excluded, unless they are being prescribed to remedy a medical condition. Generally drug programs will not cover drugs dispensed to a patient in a hospital, nursing home, or other institution; also usually excluded are therapeutic devices, hypodermic needles and other devices, as well as the costs of administering or injecting prescription drugs.

SPECIAL TOPICS

Employee Eligibility Standards

A survey of hospitalization protection conducted by the U.S. Department of Labor in 1974 showed that health benefits coverage was granted by employers to new employees: at once, 38 percent of the time; after a one-month wait, 28 percent of the time; after a two-month wait, 8 percent of the time; after a three-month wait, 16 percent of the time; after a four-month wait, 11 percent of the time. Most programs did not cover temporary and part-time workers. For the most part, benefits in addition to hospitalization used the same eligibility standards as for hospital coverage.

The current situation is one of gradually more liberal standards for eligibility, especially among large employers.

Dependent Coverage and Limitations

Most programs cover dependents as well as employees. Some employers pay the full cost of dependent coverage; others require a payroll deduction for all or a portion of the costs, but may give the employee the option of not having his or her dependents covered (for example, because they are covered under a spouse's employment).

Dependents must be clearly defined. Usually the term is confined to spouses and to children under a specified age when living at home or at school or college. (Questions as to the coverage of the children of divorced or widowed parents are complex and variable.) Children are usually considered to be dependents from birth (although some programs may cover children only after fourteen or fifteen days of age) up to age 19. Sometimes newborn nursery costs for well infants are excluded. An increasing number of programs, however, are covering children to a later age, such as 21, 23, or 25, sometimes only if they are full-time students. Some Blue Cross and Blue Shield plans and others provide programs that cover disabled children living at home, regardless of age.

Under commercial group health insurance programs, employees are covered when first eligible only if on that date they are actively at work. If an employee is hospitalized on the date that coverage becomes effective, the hospitalization would not be covered for a period of time because of such an "at work" requirement. In addition, under many commercial health insurance programs, an employee's dependents are not covered if, on the date of the employee's eligibility, a dependent is hospitalized. In such a case, coverage for the individual is deferred until discharge from the hospital.

Most Blue Cross and Blue Shield plans do not have either an employee "at work" clause or an exclusion of dependents who happen to be hospitalized on their effective date of coverage.

Program Limitations

Many programs have clauses excluding coverage for services related to health conditions that existed prior to the date of eligibility, until after specified waiting periods have elapsed. Under certain conditions, this limitation is sometimes waived by the insurer.

Legislation and Regulation

In recent years there has been an acceleration in federal and state regulation of group health benefits through legislation and administrative interpretations emanating from government agencies. The purpose of these interventions is usually to mandate broader coverages or to assure consumer protection. Among other circumstances, these regulations have affected the following:

- "Preexisting condition" exclusions and/or limitations
- Availability of maternity benefits
- Discrimination in rates and benefits because of race, sex, or age
- Home care benefits
- Emergency care benefits in outpatient departments of hospitals
- Duplication of Medicare and Medicaid benefits
- Duplication of Worker's Compensation benefits
- Duplication of automobile "no fault" benefits
- The application of "coordination of benefits" clauses
- Coverage of handicapped, unmarried dependent children who are incapable of self-support
- Compulsory dual-choice (or multiple choice) options to include HMOs when they are operational in service areas where a percentage of employees reside.

Federal Legislation. The following laws are samples of recent federal legislation affecting regulation of group health benefits:

- The *Pregnancy Discrimination Act* of October, 1978, requires that health insurance plans provide the same benefits for maternity coverage as are provided for all other medical conditions.
- The *Voluntary Wage Guidelines* of the late 1970s, in arriving at the "voluntary" ceiling of 8 percent for annual compensation increases, counted fringe benefits, including health insurance, as part of an individual's wage package.
- The *HMO Act* of 1973 deals with employers' obligations to federally qualified HMOs.
- The *Employee Retirement Income Security Act of 1974* (*ERISA*) laid out rules regarding equity in giving fringe benefits to employees.

New York State Legislation. Insurance legislation passed by New York State is second in importance and influence only to federal legislation, since a large number of national corporations have headquarters in New York State. Furthermore, because the New York State Department of Insurance is widely regarded as perhaps the most professional of these departments nationwide, it is common for other states to adopt regulations similar to, if not based upon, New York's.

New York State minimum standards. On December 1, 1972, New York State established minimum standards for health insurance. *Basic hospital insurance, basic medical/surgical insurance,* and *major medical insurance* were defined. Any program not meeting the defined standards cannot legally use the defined terms. In addition, New York State requires health insurance program disclosure whereby literature, advertising, and certificates must contain (1) a statement concerning whether they meet these state standards; (2) a statement of whether or not the programs meet certain specified criteria of itemized benefits; and (3) the anticipated ratio of benefits to premium rates (*loss ratios*). In addition, New York State has established rules for the application of non-duplication provisions; the non-application of *pre-existing condition* clauses when an employer is replacing one carrier with another; employee and/or dependent conversion rights as well as minimum coverages for such converted contracts; and several similar matters.

New York State mandated benefits. Through a series of laws and regulatory interpretations, New York State mandates that benefits, such as the following, be provided under group health coverages:

- Conversion rights of former spouses
- Children covered from birth
- Maternity coverage
- Preadmission diagnostic testing prior to surgery
- Emergency care
- Non-exclusion of certain types of reconstructive surgery
- Second surgical opinions as part of medical/surgical programs
- Home health care as part of basic hospitalization programs

In addition, discrimination in group health plans against medical services provided by dentists, physical therapists, clinical psychologists, and certified social workers is prohibited in certain instances. Also, coverage must be offered (or available) for such services as in-hospital short-term treatment of mental disorders; home health care; ambulatory care in hospitals, and emergency care in physicians' offices.

Other State Regulations. Sometimes following New York's lead, most other states have also passed statutes and issued regulations requiring various benefits, conversion rights, and so forth in group health care plans. In general, when a state promulgates a rule requiring a specific service to be covered by health insurance programs, it does so in response to effective lobbying by the particular health professionals or institutions that will receive direct benefits from the new coverage. In contrast, state rules requiring expanded rights and privileges for insured persons usually stem from various consumer-oriented efforts, sometimes stimulated by legislative hearings or media exposès demonstrating inequities or abuses. There is now a welter of state regulation regarding health insurance benefits. For example, as of January 1978, state mandates had been issued regarding:

- Treatment of alcoholism and drug abuse (eighteen states)
- Dependent coverage (sixteen states)
- Newborn coverage (thirty-nine states)
- Treatment of mental conditions (seventeen states)
- Out-of-hospital care (fourteen states)

Anti-Duplication Clauses

Anti-duplication clauses guard against claims in excess of actual medical costs, resulting from dual coverages for particular services. It is widely believed that a patient who can expect to receive greater reimbursement for medical services than the sum of his or her total costs for care has an incentive to run up the number and cost of medical services. Whether or not this belief is valid, mechanisms to prevent duplicate payment may have real effects on health insurance premium levels.

Coordination of Benefits. The most frequently found and commonly administered anti-duplication mechanism is coordination of benefits (COB), which is a specific clause in most group health insurance contracts. COB provisions are applied when more than one group coverage is applicable to a patient's claims: the clause provides an orderly process to determine which coverage is "primary"—that is, which group contract pays its full benefits before the second group coverage is called upon to pay any uncovered balances. Non-group coverages are generally exempt from COB provisions.

In December, 1970, the National Association of Insurance Commissioners (NAIC) adopted COB guidelines. These guidelines were based on COB practices developed in the early 1960s by Blue Cross and the commercial insurance industry. In the guidelines, the NAIC has defined COB terminology and established the recommended order in which benefits are to be determined.

"Allowable expense." The NAIC has defined *allowable expense* as including "all services covered in whole or in part under any of the 'Plans' involved except where benefit design and local conditions, particularly those relating to service benefit organizations, are deemed to permit a different definition." In simple terms, this means that in no case can an insured person who files valid claims get less benefits for a service covered under either of the group contracts than he or she would have gotten if only one or the other of the contracts had been in effect; and it means that if any service is covered by contracts, the insured person will be fully reimbursed for his or her costs for that service, but not in excess of those costs.

Order of benefit determination. When a patient is covered by two or more plans, the first (primary) payer is determined by the following rules:

1. If one of the contracts does not have a COB provision, it automatically becomes the primary or first payer.
2. The group contract covering the patient in his or her own name rather than as a dependent becomes primary.
3. For a child covered as a dependent by both parents, the contract of the father becomes primary.

If none of the above rules applies, the contract covering the patient for the longer period of time becomes primary.

Subrogation. Subrogation requires an insured person to turn over to the health insurance carrier medical expenses recovered from someone else. For example, a person who wins a lawsuit for damages from an accidental injury in a store or theater, when the damages include compensation for medical expenses already covered by group health insurance, would have to reimburse the health insurer.

Implementing subrogation is a complex, costly matter. It is not permitted in New York State, but outside of New York State, subrogation in health insurance is commonly available.

"No-Fault" Automobile Insurance. Twenty-one states as of 1980 had "no-fault" insurance, which contains "medical payments" provisions, usually with an upper limit, for injuries suffered as a result of auto accidents. "No-fault" auto insurance is sometimes considered primary and thus pays first, with group health insurance being secondary in the payment of medical claims. In other states, however, the situation may be mixed or even the reverse.

Retirees

Since 1966, most Americans over the age of 64 have been covered by Medicare. This massive federal social insurance program now covers most individuals who reach age 65 (retired or not); individuals receiving federal disability payments for twenty-four consecutive months; and individuals with permanent kidney failure or end stage renal disease after the first three months. Most employee health insurance programs provide *carve-out* benefits for active employees who are eligible for Medicare, whether under or over age 64. A carve-out program is one where the employee or covered dependent receives the same benefits as any other employee—except that any portion of those benefits that are also covered through Medicare are deducted from what he would otherwise receive. Recent federal legislation requires implementation of a carve-out approach for "active" employees over age 65 by companies who employ fifteen or more.

While still in the minority, the number of companies continuing health benefits for retirees (under and over age 65) is increasing. There are many variations as to the type and amount of health insurance benefits given to retirees, but predominantly, the pattern is emerging of providing the same benefits as received by active employees, with, of course, a carve-out for those over age 65 or otherwise eligible for Medicare.

Health Insurance Rating

In health insurance, the establishment of premium rates is called *rating*. There are three approaches to rating.

Community Rating. This rating mechanism establishes premiums for uniform benefit programs based on the average cost of care for all subscribers in a broad geographical area, without taking into account any specific group's anticipated claim experience or age, sex, income, or industry classification. Costs and risks are thus spread evenly across the entire community covered by the program.

Experience Rating. With this mechanism, premiums are established for either standard or specially designed benefit programs based on the anticipated or actual cost of care for a specific insured group. The rating is based on the group's prior claim history (if any) and/or factors such as geographical distribution; age, sex, and industrial classification; and, in some instances, job status, educational level, other general classifications.

Experience rating can be done prospectively or retrospectively. A prospective rate utilizes the group's past claims experience in calculating the rate for the coming contract period. A retrospective rate is adjusted after the fact to reflect actual claims costs, if they are lower than expected. In the eventuality of a good claims experience, a retrospective rate contract provides for a refund or dividend at the end of the contract period, which retroactively produces a lower net for that contract period.

Class Rating. Uniform benefit premiums established under this rating are based on the anticipated claims experience for each category of groups. The specific category may comprise companies in a particular industry, companies of particular sizes (e.g., companies with between fifty and 100 employees), or companies located in specific areas.

Historically, Blue Cross and Blue Shield plans, as well as the few "non-Blue" service benefit plans, were community-rated while commercial insurance programs were experience- or class-rated. Modern competitive pressure forced altering of the "Blue" approach, because commercial health insurers were able to provide experience rating to low-risk groups at premiums below the community rates. There are still strong elements of community rating in most Blue Cross and Blue Shield plans, however, especially for small groups, while larger groups (especially those that are multiregional) are now generally experience rated. Most Blue Cross and Blue Shield plans attempt to place small surcharges on their experience rating to subsidize the higher risk sectors of the small-group and direct-paying population enrolled under community rates.

Retention and Reserves

Retention is the amount of money retained by the carrier beyond the cost of claims, in order to cover the costs of administration, reserves to cover risk, profits (for commercial carriers), and the like. Premiums are thus a combination of the claims costs and the retention. Some insurance buyers may look at *retention percentage* as the primary means of measuring the cost of a health insurance program. This is not a wise approach, because differences in the percentages of retention of competing carriers are sometimes dwarfed by the large differences in the claims costs among those carriers. Moreover, percentage of retention is frequently a misleading term. The terms *percentage of retention* and *retention* have to be defined carefully and uniformly before any comparison among carriers' proposals is made. Retention as a percentage of premium may have various denominators such as initial annual premium; net annual premium (i.e., after a dividend is issued); total claims; or even claims plus one or more of the elements of retention (e.g., claims plus the cost of administering claims). The most useful basis for calculation would seem to be the total costs of claims, so that the retention can be calculated clearly as the additional costs retained by the carrier.

The term retention itself also needs detailed definition, because some carriers expect the employer to perform certain services which other carriers would expect to do for the employer. Conversely, there are employers that prefer to do certain of the tasks that would ordinarily be done by the carrier. Among the items that may or may not be included in a carrier's retention are:

- Reserves for unpaid claims
- Premium taxes
- Other taxes or governmental charges
- Claims administration costs
- Cost control expenditures
- Confirmation of employee eligibility
- Statistical information and reports
- Professional consultation (actuarial, legal, etc.) health insurance
- Employee and dependent identification cards
- Employee literature
- Employee health education
- Risk charges

As to the items of service covered by the retention, attention must be given not to the cost alone but also to the quality and efficiency of those services. For example, if a lower retention is associated with slow, error-prone claims payments, the employer may be plagued by employee complaints far out of proportion to the initial cost savings.

In experience-rated group contracts, fiscal reserves must be set up as part of the insurance function, due to the inevitable lapse in time between when employees incur claims and the time of final submission, clearance, and payment of those claims. The reserves are established for outstanding claims that are still unreported, or reported but not yet approved and paid. Carriers are accountable for the ultimate accuracy of the calculations of these reserves.

In addition to the charges for services, taxes, and reserves, retention also contains a *risk charge* which reflects the *credibility* of a group. Credibility is a mathematical relationship involving predictability and stability of the number and dollar amounts of claims, compared to the size of the group. Generally, the larger the group, the more probable it is that the aggregate of claims will be stable and predictable, with a resultant lower risk charge. That is to say, if a group is sizeable enough, its aggregate experience will not be greatly affected by the occasional low-frequency extremely expensive case, such as a very sick newborn infant or a seriously burned accident victim. For a smaller experienced-ruled group, on the other hand, one or two such very costly cases could have devastating effects.

Insured Programs vs. Self-Insurance

There are three principal functions performed by a carrier in a fully insured program:

- Administration and payment of claims, including dealing with employees, dependents, and the providers of care
- Calculation assumption of financial risk
- Cost containment and health care quality assurance

Self-Insurance. An employer may decide that he can provide one or more of the above carrier functions, in whole or in part, at less cost or with more efficiency and effectiveness than any carrier. If an employer decides to become his own health insurer, he must also decide whether he will handle everything himself or obtain outside assistance and advice to perform some of the insurance functions.

A decision whether or not to choose any alternative to a fully insured program should be strongly influenced by consideration of whether the savings projected will actually materialize, and whether any small, one-time gains in cash flow may be offset by administrative costs added over time.

A low availability of cash, together with high interest rates, often promotes employer concerns about the management of cash flow. Cash flow is a particular factor in group health insurance, because of the time lags between the payment of premiums, the incurrence of claims, and final payment of claims. An employer's concern with self-insurance may also be directed towards eliminating or reducing certain elements of retention costs (e.g., administrative charges, risk assumption, and/or state premium taxes), or even toward finding ways to reduce the cost of claims.

Only a very large employer should consider structuring a health benefits program that is fully self-insured and self-administered. A host of complex issues, over and above true net costs, are involved, including the impact on personnel morale; the rights of employees and their dependents to privacy with respect to their medical care; the high likelihood of eventual strict federal and state regulation of self-insured programs; and the probable difficulty of converting a self-insured program back to a carrier-run program. Concerning this last point, employers should consider the relative ease of switching carriers because of concerns about costs or service, compared to the trauma of eliminating employee positions that have been created to administer a health benefits program.

Certain alternative funding arrangements can be made with carriers that pay premium taxes (as most Blue Cross and Blue Shield plans do not). This may be advantageous for an employer if they result in a reduction in retention charges attributable to state premium taxes (which are usually about 2 percent of total premiums) paid by commercial insurers.

Insured programs. Based on their years of experience, insurance carriers reasonably maintain that they are professionally and technically competent in the handling of claims; in providing actuarial, legal, and risk services; and in holding down health care utilization and costs. They are prepared to compete on just those points.

Insurance carriers, in addition, can provide employers with improved cash flow through the adoption of special fiscal arrangements. The essential feature calls for comparatively low initial interim monthly payments, with the employer held responsible for the full annual premium after the end of the fiscal year. If the group's experience has been advantageous, the employer may be called upon to add a minimal (or no) payment to the lower monthly payments that have already been made; if claims costs were higher than anticipated, up to the full premium would be owed. This system improves the employer's cash position while providing the insurance carrier with the assurance of receiving the full annual premium, at the point when (and if) it is needed. These fiscal systems are known by a variety of names, such as "advanced deposit," "deferred premium," and "payment of charges." They are usually accompanied by somewhat higher retention rates to offset the carrier's loss of interest on the held funds.

Cost Containment and Provider Relationships

In recent years, growing attention has properly been focused by employers on the spiraling costs of providing health benefits. The causes of the rising costs are complex and often poorly understood. What is quite clear is that whether or not the rate of per capita increase in personal health services expenditures exceeds a given year's increase in the Consumer Price Index, or a given year's unadjusted growth in the Gross National Product, the upward forces in the economics of health care are extraordinarily complex and difficult to control. (Chapter 22 discusses in detail health cost containment strategies.)

Co-insurance and cost-sharing arrangements are currently receiving attention as means of deterring patients from demanding medical care services. There is some evidence that this approach can affect the rates of utilization of relatively low-cost health care services of the sort that people exercise a good deal of personal discretion about, such as primary dental visits, well-child pediatric visits, physician visits for minor illnesses, and the like. These high-volume services represent, however, only a tiny fraction of health care costs, of which considerably more than half are incurred with respect to services requiring hospitalization. Furthermore, decisions such as whether a patient should undergo surgery or extensive diagnostic tests, or be hospitalized, are primarily physicians' decisions, rather than choices by consumers, and thus not very much influenced by cost-sharing arrangements.

For this reason, as well as the fact that cost sharing is generally unpopular among consumers, health care cost containment efforts are being more and more directed toward finding ways to alter patterns of physician practice with regard to utilization of costly services, without in any way damaging the quality of care.

Central Role of Provider. The organization that administers a health benefits program is in a good position to influence how medical care is actually delivered, and therefore to develop a meaningful cost containment system. An important requirement is that the organization have the respect and cooperation of the care providers. This is more readily achieved if the organization represents a significantly large sector of the health benefits buyers in the community.

Development of sophisticated data bases is an important component in dealing with providers effectively to hold down the quantity and price of services, while promoting quality care. Practical cost containment programs must be able to pinpoint individual hospitals, doctors, and categories of medical conditions that represent problems of high costs and services of questionable value to patients, in comparison to regional and national standards and norms. A feature unique to many Blue Cross and Blue Shield plans is establishment of contractual arrangements with hospitals and physicians, under which significant cost savings can be achieved. Aggressive claims administration can show some effective results, however, even without provider contracts.

Plans with institutional reimbursement arrangements based on calculations derived from the actual cost of care, rather than on prices set unilaterally by the institutions, can show cost savings because the payment rates are well below those prices.

Forecasting Group Costs. With respect to actual costs to specific employers of providing health care benefits, no one can accurately foretell future group experience. Proposed rates and estimated retentions are based on actuarial assumptions as well as on historical data. Some actuaries may be more conservative than others in promulgating rates, but this has no effect on long-term costs. What finally matters is the actual costs incurred by the employer for the coverage.

In order to evaluate carriers' probable ability to deal with the problems of costs over the long run, the employer should obtain information relating to the specific steps taken by carriers to control the various factors of health care cost increases: inflation in prices, increased utilization, and fraud and abuse. The employer should ask questions in the following areas:

Price inflation. What does the carrier do to deal with the year-by-year rise in the prices of hospital and medical services? Does the carrier cover provider bills on the basis of the "retail" posted prices, or according to lower, "wholesale" or "discounted" rates? Are hospital costs and utilization audited and reviewed? Are there controls on physician fee payments?

Increased utilization of services. What specific steps does the carrier take to control the tendency for year-by-year rise in the utilization of hospital services, both inpatient and outpatient? What controls are in place regarding non-hospital provider services, especially physician services? Do the carrier's programs provide positive incentives to provide for implementing less costly alternatives? And to patients to utilize such services? Does the carrier develop and use professional standards for the uses of particularly costly services, ranging from inpatient days to "high technology" diagnostic studies?

Program fraud and abuse. How well organized and experienced is the carrier in dealing independently with the intricate problems of detecting and investigating, as well as preventing, fraudulent and abusive claims and other practices by patients, employees, and institutional, professional, and non-professional providers? The level of business ethics in the hospital field and among physicians is remarkably high, but the problem of fraud and abuse remains. In most areas of the country, losses due to fraud are probably very low, due to the professionalism and ethical standards of the field. The preventive programs of major carriers are probably a contributing factor to this phenomenon, however.

Checking fraud and abuse requires perceptive claims administration and careful study of accumulated statistics about medical care prices and utilization, since fraud and abuse can often be detected only through studies of cost and utilization patterns. In addition, skilled professional review by trained professionals with technical expertise in law, auditing, contract interpretation, and investigatory methods aids in detection and prevention of fraud and abuse. The carrier investigating fraud and abuse must also be prepared to work with licensing and law enforcement agencies in circumstances where laws have been violated. At the same time, however, care must be taken to assure careful handling of information so that patients' right to privacy is protected.

24

Group Legal Services and Group Auto Plans

Qualified Group Legal Services Plans

LEON E. IRISH

Caplin & Drysdale, Chartered

INTRODUCTION

Beginning in 1977 special tax benefits have been available on a temporary basis for prepaid group legal services plans provided for employees by their employers. As part of the Economic Recovery Tax Act of 1981, Congress extended until the end of 1985 the rules of Sections 120 and 501(c)(20) of the Internal Revenue Code that give favorable tax treatment to qualified group legal services benefits. Once the study and report by the Secretaries of Labor and Treasury called for by the Tax Reform Act of 1976 have been filed, and final regulations have appeared, it is likely that Congress will make these provisions permanent features of the Code. In the process it may clarify or correct any problems remaining after the final regulations have appeared.

Experience to date demonstrates that qualified group legal services plans involve minimal loss of tax revenues but can provide effective legal services at modest cost to groups of working Americans who do not currently use and cannot afford legal services in other forms. Major labor unions may make qualified group legal services a prominent item on the bargaining table in coming years. Employers who have established these plans have found that they are widely used and appreciated, but that the cost of them is far lower than the cost of, say, medical or dental plans. Major insurance companies intend to begin widescale marketing of legal services plan insurance. The result is expected to be continued growth of qualified group legal services plans for both union and non-union workers. This article surveys the development of these plans, delineates the legal requirements applicable to them, and points out practical possibilities and potential pitfalls for such plans.

Overview of Tax Rules

Section 120 of the Code excludes from gross income amounts contributed by an employer to, and the value of personal legal services provided under, a qualified group legal services plan. Section 501(c)(20) provides tax-exempt status for a trust or organization whose exclusive function is to form part of a qualified group legal services plan or plans. Finally, employer contributions to a group legal services plan are deductible as business expenses if they satisfy the ordinary and necessary test of Section 162. This trio of tax benefits—exclusion from income, nontaxability of funds set aside, and employer deductions—makes qualified group legal services plans highly attractive fringe benefits.

Individuals have long been able to deduct the cost of legal services rendered in connection with a trade or business, or investment property, or in connection with the determination, collection, or refund of any tax. For legal services provided to employees on a prepaid basis through employer-funded plans, the new provisions of the Code provide comparable tax benefits for nondeductible personal legal services, such as those rendered in connection with divorce or family law, consumer problems, workers' compensation, tort litigation, personal bankruptcy, wills and trusts, and the purchase and sale of personal residences.

Basic Concepts and Distinctions

There are many kinds of group legal services plans. Although the tax benefits under Sections 120 and 501(c)(20) are limited to the employment context, the kinds of plans are not. In order to understand how group legal services plans work, it is useful to explain at the outset some basic concepts and distinctions.

Group. Almost any group can form a legal services plan, for example, employees of a particular company, members of a particular union, participants in a consumers cooperative, students at a university, members of a tenants organization, an automobile club, or of a religious, professional, or social group, and so forth.[1] The fundamental attraction of a group plan is that it offers economies of scale and risk shifting. Thus, a particular legal service (e.g., drafting a simple will or trust) may be rendered more efficiently if done frequently under centralized control. Also, a group may be able to spread among its members the risk that any one of them may incur legal expenses of a particular type, (e.g., a tort lawsuit or bankruptcy).

By providing a stable client base, a group may also enable a lawyer or group of lawyers to commit to providing legal services of a kind that might not be practicable on an individual basis. For example, it might be feasible to practice Social Security law only with the assurance of a large and stable client base that frequently had such problems. Finally, group legal services plans may be able to develop specialized legal services for a particular kind of client. For example, lawyers for a teachers' group might specialize in teacher tenure, accreditation, and promotion issues.

Prepaid. By definition, a *prepaid plan* calls for advance funding, through insurance premiums, contributions to a trust, or advance payments to the providers of legal services. In participant-sponsored plans, the prepayment arrangement may call for a fixed monthly or yearly fee, for example,

---

[1] For a systematic analysis of the possible components and configurations of legal services plans, see Pfennigstorf & Kimball, "Legal Services Plans: A Typology," 2 Am. B. Foundation Research J. 411 (1976).

$75-$100 per year for coverage on a wide range of personal legal problems. In employer-sponsored or union-sponsored plans, the employer or union member will be called upon to make periodic contributions according to premium schedules or projected utilization rates, or pursuant to agreement (e.g., $.05 per hour).

Insured vs. Noninsured. A prepaid plan funded through insurance may call for premiums under a fixed schedule, and the insurance company may provide or pay for the legal services, or reimburse participants for legal expenses. A noninsured prepaid plan may provide for contributions to a trust fund, with legal services provided or paid for out of that fund. In the case of an insurance arrangement or prepayments to service providers, the insurance company or service providers will in almost all cases bear the risk that the premiums or prepayments will be insufficient to cover claims or the cost of providing services. Under trusteed arrangements, however, it could happen that, for lack of funds, a participant with a covered claim will get no legal services, unless specific provision is made to prevent this.

Automatic vs. Voluntary Enrollment. In an *automatic enrollment plan,* all members of a particular group (e.g., members of a certain union or employees of a particular company) are entitled automatically to coverage under the plan. In a *voluntary enrollment plan,* members of a specific group (e.g., members of a consumers group or religious society) may decide on an individual basis whether or not to participate. Because those who are most likely to use legal services are most apt to enroll in a voluntary plan, the utilization rate per member is generally much higher in voluntary enrollment plans than in automatic enrollment plans. This factor may require membership fees or contributions to be much higher in voluntary plans, or even threaten their solvency. Automatic enrollment is typical of employer- and union-sponsored plans, and voluntary enrollment of nonemployment-related plans.

Coverage. In practice, very few, if any, plans offer unlimited coverage, and fewer and fewer plans are limited to rendering only one kind of legal service.[2] The trend is towards broad coverage with specified exceptions (e.g., felony representation) and utilization limits (e.g., no more than one will every three years, no more than fifty hours of legal services per year in connection with litigation). An excellent example of the kinds and range of legal services available under the emerging generation of group legal services plans, together with the applicable limitations, is provided by the UAW Legal Services Plan for Chrysler hourly workers. This plan is reproduced in Appendix 24-1 at the end of this chapter.

---

[2] A conspicuous continuing example, however, is provided by the legal services offered to automobile club members, which typically are limited to automobile-related legal problems.

Closed vs. Open Panel. The sponsors of a *closed panel plan* select and limit the attorneys who may provide services to participants. The *staff closed panel plan* employs its own lawyers as salaried employees. The arrangement, similar to the HMO model for delivery of medical services, permits the maximum degree of control by the plan over the nature, quality, and cost of services rendered. The prospects of making significant advances in efficient delivery of quality legal services are probably greatest in this kind of plan.

The *retained closed panel plan* retains one or more private attorneys or law firms. Retained attorneys may be paid at a negotiated rate per capita, per matter, or, more typically, per hour. The arrangement may call for minimum and/or maximum dollar amounts per year. A large plan may use both staff and retained closed panel arrangements. For example, the UAW Legal Services Plan currently employs about sixty staff attorneys and retains about 600 attorneys on contract to provide legal services to the more than 100,000 Chrysler hourly workers, retirees, and their dependents in forty-six different states.

Under an *open panel plan,* participants may choose their own attorney, who is then fully or partially reimbursed for his services under the benefits schedule maintained by the plan. This model, which is similar to the delivery of medical services under a Blue Cross or Blue Shield plan, more nearly preserves the traditional procedure under which a client selects his own attorney. Under a *modified open panel plan* attorneys must agree in advance not to exceed certain fee or rate schedules, and to follow other rules. For example, the attorneys might have to agree to provide a one-half hour consultation for $15, to pay the first $10 of each fee to the plan, and to charge no more than $50 an hour for subsequent work, with various maximum dollar limits for particular jobs, which may be subject to waiver in extraordinary circumstances. Any qualified lawyer willing to agree to these terms is enrolled, and a participant covered by the plan may select any enrolled attorney. Alternatively, an insurance company that is sponsoring a modified open panel system may provide a fixed indemnity schedule under which fees of nonparticipating attorneys are paid, while offering full fee payments on covered matters for participating attorneys.

Unions and consumers groups generally favor staff closed or retained closed panel systems, whereas bar associations generally favor open panel systems.

DEVELOPMENT OF PREPAID GROUP LEGAL SERVICES PLANS

Although large scale and widespread use of group legal services is a relatively new phenomenon, physicians in Fort Wayne, Indiana formed an organization to provide legal services for suits against them as early as 1899.

In Europe, legal expense insurance has generally been accepted and extensively used for more than fifty years. In this country, however, legal expense insurance and group legal services have been slow in coming. Among the principal reasons for this have been various rules of legal ethics administered by bar organizations that have in effect forbidden attorneys from practicing in corporate form or as employees. In addition, various group legal services arrangements have been treated as violating rules against advertising or conflicts of interest.

Inadequate Availability of Legal Services for the Middle Class

The consequences for the utilization of legal services of these historical facts have been dramatic. According to a study funded by the American Bar Association, one-third of the American public has never used the services of an attorney and another third has had only one experience in their lifetimes with an attorney. In addition, 62 percent think that legal fees are too high, and 69 percent feel that they are unable to determine whether an attorney is competent to handle their affairs.[3]

These facts paint a picture of the utilization of legal services that is greatly at odds with that of medical services. It may well be that people do not need legal services as frequently as they need medical services, and that it would be undesirable on both an individual and a societal level if people resorted to lawyers too frequently. If it is only people with large incomes who currently can afford private attorneys, and only the truly indigent who can qualify for legal assistance from neighborhood legal clinics or legal aid programs, then the problem of inadequate delivery of legal services is indeed a problem of the middle class. The middle class as well as the rich and the poor may face divorce, need to buy or sell a house, be sued, face bankruptcy, or confront any of a hundred possible different legal circumstances where the services of a lawyer would help to avoid harm or litigation or see that the individual's interests were more fully protected or vindicated. The growing availability of prepaid group legal services programs may provide at least a partial solution.

Milestones

First Amendment Breakthrough. In the early 1960s there were only a handful of group legal services plans, principally retained closed panel plans maintained by unions or employee associations to handle particular kinds of cases. For example, the United Mine Workers sponsored legal services plans to provide members with representation in connection with unemployment compensation and workers' compensation cases, and some teachers' associa-

---

[3] B. Curran, *The Legal Needs of the Public: The Final Report of A National Survey of the Special Committee to Survey Legal Needs of the American Bar Association,* (American Bar Foundation 1977).

tions maintained plans to provide legal services for job-related matters, such as tenure, accreditation, and termination. Bar associations throughout the country sought to limit or outlaw practice on a group basis, and the resulting litigation resulted in four significant decisions by the Supreme Court.[4] In *United Transportation Union v. State Bar of Michigan,* the Supreme Court summarized the important First Amendment values that are at stake: "The common thread running through our decisions . . . is that collective activity undertaken to obtain meaningful access to the courts is a fundamental right within the protection of the First Amendment." [5]

Taft-Hartley Amendment. The decisions of the Supreme Court recognizing that group legal services plans have protected status under the First Amendment provided a spur to a series of legislative developments that eliminated the principal legal barriers to group legal services plans. The first of these was the addition in 1973 of an exemption from the prohibitions of Section 302 of the Labor and Management Relations Act. This amendment permits trusts that are jointly administered by employers and union officials to receive employer contributions and use them to provide prepaid group legal services.[6] This change in effect removed any labor law impediment to collective bargaining for prepaid group legal services plans.

Employee Retirement Income Security Act of 1974 (ERISA). Notwithstanding the decisions of the Supreme Court and the amendment of the Taft-Hartley Act, in 1974 there were still a variety of state law impediments to prepaid group legal services plans. Some states passed laws strictly regulating prepaid plans as a form of insurance or mandating open panels. The National Association of Insurance Commissioners had drafted a Model Act under which state insurance commissioners would have regulatory authority over all legal services plans. In other states bar associations continued to hamstring efforts to develop group legal services plans. In response, a group of unions and consumers groups succeeded in having prepaid group legal services plans included in the definition of *employee welfare benefit plan* in ERISA.

The principal significance of regulation of legal services plans by ERISA is that Section 514 of ERISA specifically preempts "any and all State laws insofar as they may now or hereafter relate to any employee benefit plans" covered by ERISA. Although Section 514(2)(A) of ERISA saves state insurance laws from preemption, Section 514(2)(B) of ERISA provides

---

[4] NAACP v. Button, 371 U.S. 415 (1963); Brotherhood of Ry. Trainmen v. Virginia *ex rel.* Virginia State Bar, 377 U.S. 1 (1964); United Mine Workers v. Illinois State Bar Ass'n, 389 U.S. 217 (1967); United Transp. Union v. The State Bar of Michigan, 401 U.S. 576 (1971). See Zimroth, "Group Legal Services and the Constitution," 76 Yale L.J. 966 (1967).

[5] 401 U.S. at 585.

[6] Pub. L. No. 93-95; 29 U.S.C. § 186(c)(8).

that no employee benefit plan or related trust may be deemed to be an insurance company or engaged in the business of insurance. This presumably precludes a state from regulating or limiting the provision of benefits under a group legal services plan even if the plan is funded through insurance, although the purely insurance aspects may be regulated.

As demonstrated by a colloquy on the floor of the Senate between the two principal sponsors of ERISA, a similar result was intended for state bar rules of professional responsibility.[7] Thus, although bar organizations cannot use ethical rules indirectly to bar closed panel plans or the use of financial intermediaries to pay legal fees, professional responsibility rules are not wholly preempted. Attorneys in a prepaid group legal services plan, like other attorneys, may be required, for example, to meet reasonable licensing requirements and to respond exclusively to the interests and needs of their clients. ERISA, of course, does not preempt state insurance or other laws with respect to nonemployee group legal services plans, such as plans for automobile club members, university students, or members of consumers or other groups.

Revision of ABA Ethics Rules. In response to the pressure from Supreme Court decisions, bar groups, consumers groups, unions, and others, the American Bar Association (ABA), and many state and local bar associations as well, have substantially liberalized their rules applicable to group legal services plans. In response to the decisions of the Supreme Court, the ABA in 1969 revised the Code of Professional Responsibility to permit group legal services plans, "but only in those instances and to the extent that controlling constitutional interpretation at the time of the rendition of the services requires the allowance of such legal service activities." [8] As part of the infamous "Houston Amendments," this restrictive provision was deleted in 1974, but only at the price of adopting provisions that would in effect permit group legal services to be rendered only by open panel plans. A year later this restriction was quietly revoked and language was substituted that would generally permit a lawyer to work with a group legal services plan if there were no interference with the exercise of his independent professional judgment on behalf of his client. The conditions that must be met under the ABA Code of Professionability can be summarized as follows:

- The organization must derive no profit from the services of the lawyer.
- The lawyer must not have initiated the organization for his personal benefit.
- The organization must not be operated for the purpose of procuring outside legal employment for the lawyer.
- The member or beneficiary must be recognized as the lawyer's client.

---

[7] See discussion between Sen. Javits and Sen. Williams, 120 Cong. Rec. S15757-S15758 (Aug. 22, 1974).

[8] American Bar Foundation, *Annotated Code of Professional Responsibility* 72 (1979).

- The member or beneficiary must retain the right to select other counsel than that furnished by the organization, and some procedure must be provided to meet the situation where the counsel selected cannot ethically serve.
- The lawyer must not know or have cause to know that the organization is operating in violation of applicable rules and regulations.
- The organization must file an annual report with the appropriate bar authority.

Changes in Advertising Rules. The liberalization of bar rules with respect to group practice—which is of crucial importance to group legal services plans not covered by the preemption provision of ERISA—is mirrored in recent changes in bar rules relating to advertising. Once again, the bar has followed the lead of the Supreme Court. In *Bates v. State Bar,*[9] the Supreme Court struck down, as violative of the First Amendment, a state bar rule prohibiting attorneys from publicizing themselves as lawyers through newspaper, radio, or television advertisments or other means of commercial publicity. Emphasizing that it was not addressing itself to the issue of advertising, the quality of legal services or the question of personal solicitation, the Court held 5–4 that lawyers have a constitutional right to advertise the prices at which routine legal services will be furnished. The Court stated, however, that false, misleading, and deceptive advertising may be prohibited and that reasonable restraints may be placed on the time, place, and manner of advertising.

The question of solicitation was addressed by the Supreme Court in two cases in the year following the *Bates* decision. In *Ohralik v. Ohio State Bar Ass'n,*[10] it held that a state may constitutionally restrict in-person solicitation of accident victims who were in the hospital. In *Matter of Primus,*[11] the Court held that the First Amendment protected a solicitation letter from an American Civil Liberties Union lawyer who sought to represent for free a woman who had been sterilized as a condition for receiving Medicaid. The Court said that *Primus* involved more than commercial speech, for the attorney was exercising her freedom of association by urging collective activity to obtain meaningful access to the courts.

In the recent case of *In re R.M.J.,*[12] the Supreme Court struck down as violative of the First and Fourteenth Amendments provisions of the ethical rules of the Supreme Court of Missouri that (1) required an attorney to list his fields of law according to precise listings of areas set forth by rule; (2) prohibited an attorney from identifying the jurisdictions in which he is licensed to practice; and (3) forbade an attorney from mailing cards announcing the opening of his office to people other than lawyers, clients, former clients, personal friends, and relatives. The Court ruled that states

---

[9] 433 U.S. 350 (1977).
[10] 436 U.S. 447 (1978).
[11] 436 U.S. 412 (1978).
[12] 50 U.S.L.W. 4185 (U.S., Jan. 25, 1982) (No. 80-1431).

may prohibit "inherently misleading" advertising or advertising that is shown in fact to be misleading, but that restrictions may be "no broader than reasonably necessary to prevent the deception." The states may also regulate communications that are not misleading, but only if and to the extent that doing so serves a substantial state interest.

Thus, the Supreme Court has laid down a broad area of presumptive protection for professional advertising by attorneys, casting upon the states the affirmative burden of showing that such commercial speech is misleading or that its regulation otherwise serves some substantial state interest. Of particular importance is the fact that the Court struck down a prohibition on the use of general letters of solicitation. This aspect of the decision may make it possible for group legal services plans to send general mailings in an effort to solicit larger membership. The precise scope of the constitutional rule that has been laid down by the Court, however, will become clear only as it is applied on a case-by-case basis.[13]

ERISA Requirements

At the same time that ERISA preempted state laws insofar as they might seek to regulate or limit employee prepaid group legal services plans for employees or union members, ERISA imposed some significant federal requirements. Along with other welfare plans, group legal services plans are free of the participation, vesting, and funding requirements of Parts 2 and 3 of Title I of ERISA. However, they are subject to the reporting requirements of Part 1, the fiduciary responsibility requirements of Part 4, and the remedial provisions of Part 5. Like other welfare plans, ERISA requires each covered prepaid legal services plan to be written and, if it has assets, to have them held in trust.[14] No trust is required, however, if the plan is funded through insurance contracts.[15] Annual reports must be filed with the Department of Labor on each covered prepaid legal services plan,[16] and a summary plan description, as well as a summary annual report, must be given to each plan participant.[17]

Fiduciary Responsibility. The fiduciary responsibility provisions of ERISA apply to ERISA prepaid legal services plans just as they do to other welfare plans. These rules require that each fiduciary discharge his duties solely in the interest of participants and beneficiaries and for the exclusive purpose of

[13] See slip op. at 11–12 and n.16. For other relevant decisions on commercial free speech, see also Bigelow v. Virginia, 421 U.S. 809 (1975); Virginia State Bd. of Pharmacy v. Virginia Citizens Consumer Council, 425 U.S. 748 (1976); Central Hudson Gas & Elec. Corp. v. Public Serv. Comm'n, 447 U.S. 557 (1980).

[14] ERISA §§ 402(a)(1), 403(a).

[15] ERISA § 403(b)(1).

[16] ERISA § 104(a)(1).

[17] ERISA §§ 102(a)(1), 104(b)(3). A limited exception is made for certain small welfare plans. DOL Reg. § 2520.104-20.

providing benefits to participants and their beneficiaries and defraying reasonable expenses of administering the plan.[18] The fiduciary must act with the care, skill, prudence, and diligence under the circumstances that a prudent man acting in a like capacity and familiar with such matters would use in the conduct of an enterprise of a like character and with like aims.[19] If the plan is funded, the trustee or investment manager must diversify the investments of the plan so as to minimize the risk of large losses.[20] Complex prohibited transaction rules also apply.[21]

There are numerous statutory exemptions to the fiduciary provisions,[22] and individual exemptions may also be sought.[23] If there is a breach of any of the duties imposed by ERISA, a plan participant, fiduciary, or the Department of Labor may sue to correct the situation.[24] Fiduciaries who cause loss to a plan are personally liable and may be removed.[25]

Special problems for legal services plans. Among the difficult questions that arise for legal services plans under the fiduciary responsibility and prohibited transaction rules of ERISA are whether attorneys that provide services to the employer or union associated with the plan may provide services under it and, if so, how they may be compensated without inpropriety.

The areas in which ERISA imposes no requirements are as significant as the areas in which it does. Thus, ERISA establishes no standards for the benefits that are to be provided under a prepaid group legal services plan. Furthermore, as welfare plans, legal services plans are exempt from ERISA's standards for funding or insuring financial soundness. Finally, ERISA establishes no quality controls over the services provided under such plans, and does not proscribe or limit discrimination in favor of highly compensated employees. Thus, a corporation might comply fully with the requirements of ERISA if it established an insured prepaid group legal services plan to provide investment or tax counseling and representation to employees who earned $50,000 or more per year. Such a plan might fully meet the requirements of ERISA, and, because it is subject to ERISA, it would not be subject to regulation by state laws. Although the benefits under such a plan would constitute additional income to participants, they would be entitled to offsetting deductions under Section 212 of the Code.

---

[18] ERISA § 404(a)(1)(A).
[19] ERISA § 404(a)(1)(B).
[20] ERISA § 404(a)(1)(C).
[21] ERISA § 406.
[22] ERISA § 408(b).
[23] ERISA § 408(a).
[24] ERISA § 502.
[25] ERISA § 409.

ANTITRUST REQUIREMENTS

An important set of laws that is not preempted by ERISA—and thus is potentially applicable to all group legal services plans—are the federal antitrust laws.

Sherman Act Implications

Section 1 of the Sherman Act prohibits restraints on interstate commerce. In *Goldfarb v. Virginia State Bar,*[26] legal services rendered under a county bar association minimum fee schedule for real estate title examinations were held to have a sufficient effect upon interstate commerce to be subject to the Sherman Act's ban on price fixing: "Where, as a matter of law or practical necessity, legal services are an integral part of an interstate transaction, a restraint on these services may substantially affect commerce for Sherman Act purposes." [27]

In *Goldfarb* the trial court had made no finding that the transaction before it had actually involved interstate commerce. The court had merely found that purchases of real property in the county in question (Fairfax, Virginia) frequently involved substantial amounts of money from out of state.[28] Thus, the Supreme Court apparently held that the Sherman Act is applicable to contracts to provide legal services whether or not they involve interstate commerce, so long as the class of legal services to which they belong involves or may affect interstate commerce. In short, the Court laid down a rule that probably subjects all legal services to the Sherman Act, for it is difficult to imagine any class of legal services that does not sometimes affect interstate commerce.

The applicability of the antitrust laws to group legal services plans is further complicated by the uncertainties surrounding the "state action" doctrine of *Parker v. Brown,*[29] under which the antitrust laws are held not to apply to activities engaged in pursuant to a state regulatory scheme. In *Goldfarb* it was argued that the minimum fee schedule promulgated by the county bar association made fees charged under it immune to the antitrust laws. The Court disagreed, pointing out that the state had not *required* the anticompetitive activity in question:

> [A]lthough the [Virginia] Supreme Court's ethical codes mention advisory fee schedules they do not direct either respondent [the state and county bar associations] to supply them, or require the type of price floor which arose from respondents' activities. . . . It is not enough that, as the County Bar puts it, anticompetitive conduct is "prompted" by state action; rather, anticompetitive activities must be compelled by direction of the State acting as sovereign.[30]

---

[26] 421 U.S. 773 (1975).
[27] *Id.* at 785.
[28] 355 F. Supp. 491, 494, 497 (E.D. Va. 1973).
[29] 317 U.S. 341 (1943).
[30] 421 U.S. at 790.

In short, *Goldfarb* made it relatively clear that price-fixing efforts by bar associations, even if carried out under the mantel of state authority, will not be immune from attack under the antitrust laws. Since it is unlikely that particular fees will ever be compelled by state or local bar associations, *Goldfarb* seems to have thrown the door wide open to scrutinizing lawyers' fee schedules under the antitrust laws.

Vulnerability of Open Panel Plans

Open panel legal services plans are perhaps most prone to attack under the antitrust laws. Certainly, if a bar association or a group of lawyers sets the fees to be charged, this would seem to be price fixing, which is a per se violation of the Sherman Act. Even if all the schedule did was to set maximum prices to be charged for various services, it would seem to be subject to challenge under the well-established prohibition on maximum price fixing.[31] On the other hand, if the plan merely specifies that it will not pay more than specified amounts for particular services, leaving the lawyer and the client free to arrange for larger payments, this would seem analagous to the typical pattern under medical Blue Cross and Blue Shield plans, and may be considerably safer from antitrust challenge.

Although the theoretical basis for it is not entirely clear, the Justice Department apparently has taken the position that a fee schedule for an open panel legal services plan will not violate the antitrust laws if the fee schedule is alterable by non-lawyers rather than lawyers.

Closed Panel Plans

There would appear to be fewer antitrust concerns with closed panel plans, at least to the extent that the panel attorneys are employees of the legal services plan. However, under the doctrine of *Royal Drug*[32] large closed panel plans may come into question under the antitrust laws, even if they are operated through insurance companies. Although the McCarran-Ferguson Act exempts the "business of insurance" from the antitrust laws, the Supreme Court held in *Royal Drug* that this exemption does not extend to the "business of insurers." In the particular case this meant that a "providers contract" under which Blue Shield of Texas, in order to minimize costs and maximize profits, purchased drugs and pharmaceuticals only from participating pharmacies, was not exempt under McCarran-Ferguson and constituted illegal price-fixing under the antitrust laws. Although the reach of *Royal Drug* is not fully settled, it seems probable that sizeable closed panel group legal services plans, whether staff or retained, and whether insured or not, may be

---

[31] Albrecht v. Herald Co., 390 U.S. 145 (1968); Kiefer-Stewart Co. v. Joseph E. Seagram & Sons, Inc., 340 U.S. 211 (1951).

[32] Group Life & Health Ins. Co. v. Royal Drug Co., 440 U.S. 205 (1979).

subject to being sued for price fixing under the antitrust laws by nonparticipating attorneys who believe that business is being diverted from them, or even by participating attorneys who feel that their fees are insufficient. This question is apt to become increasingly important as group legal services plans grow and proliferate.

TAX DEVELOPMENTS

Disincentive Nature of Tax Laws

Most working Americans do not need legal services for the purposes for which they have long been deductible—trade or business expenses or investments. Rather, they need them for the whole range of personal problems, such as divorce, buying and selling a home, or personal injuries. The cost of most personal legal services, however, is not deductible. And, if legal services for such purposes were provided by an employer, the traditional tax result would be to trigger additional taxable income to the employee equal to the value of the services provided. Moreover, legal expense insurance has largely been unavailable in this country until recent years, and income earned on funds set aside to provide legal services for a group other than through insurance would be taxable. For these reasons, and despite the deductibility to the employer of any amounts paid for legal services for employees that do not constitute unreasonable compensation, the tax laws have traditionally provided a substantial disincentive to the establishment of prepaid group legal services plans for employees.

Membership Plans. Comparable tax disincentives apply with respect to group legal services plans not funded by employers. If members of a consumers group or students at a university put up $50 each to fund group legal services for themselves, although such amounts are neither deductible nor do they trigger additional income, their contributions come out of after-tax dollars. In the case of union members who earmark part of their union dues for use in a prepaid group legal services plan, the earmarked portion may be deductible as union dues. Since there is a long and venerable history of unions providing legal services for their members in connection with job-related matters, union dues paid for such purposes are probably deductible. Legal services provided under such a plan, like other benefits provided by a union for members, would presumably not be income.

This result points toward the proper answer to the next question, which is whether investment income on amounts set aside for a member-funded group legal services plan is taxable or not. To the extent that such amounts are merely investment income earned by a tax-exempt entity, such as a union, or a university, the answer is that the income is not taxable. If a separate trust is set up to hold the money, however, or if the organization maintaining the fund is taxable, then any income earned on the invested funds would be taxable. Finally, if a member who paid $50 to the plan received $1,000 worth of legal services in a particular year, the traditional position of the IRS would appear to be that he would not be taxed on $950, though the theoretical basis for this conclusion is not entirely clear.

Struggle for Tax-Exempt Status

Initial efforts to achieve tax treatment for legal services comparable to that afforded for medical services focused on achieving tax-exempt status for trusts set up to hold the funds of a prepaid group legal services plan. In the early 1970s tax-exempt status under Section 501(c)(3) of the Code was granted to the Shreveport Laborers Legal Services plan, an experimental prepaid group legal services plan sponsored jointly by the Laborers Union and the ABA in an effort to determine the viability and desirability of prepaid plans. It is understood that the ground for this exemption was the scientific and experimental nature of the plan, and that only one other plan, also set up on an experimental basis for a temporary period, has been afforded similar treatment. If a prepaid legal services plan is set up for the express purpose of helping the poor, however, or some segment of it, such as a disadvantaged minority, and the funds do not come principally or exclusively from fees or dues paid by those covered by the plan, there would seem to be no sound reason why such a plan should not be given tax-exempt status under Section 501(c)(3) of the Code.

In the early 1970s a concentrated effort was made by major law firms to obtain exempt status under Section 501(c)(4) for group legal services plans. It was argued that status as a social welfare organization under Section 501(c)(4) should be granted because such status is enjoyed by Blue Cross and Blue Shield plans. Although a few district offices initially were favorable, the national office of the IRS, without convincing rationale, refused.

Attention was then focused on Section 501(c)(9), which confers exempt status on employees' associations that provide for the payment of "life, sick, accident, or other benefits. . . ." The IRS, however, took the position that the phrase "other benefits" includes only benefits similar to "life, sick, and accident benefits" in the sense that they are intended to safeguard or improve the health of the employee or to protect against a contingency that interrupts earning power. This view has been confirmed by the recently issued final regulations under Section 501(c)(9).[33] Although the final regulations under Section 501(c)(9) do not permit legal services benefits to be paid out of such plans, they do permit funds to be transferred from a Section 501(c)(9) trust to a Section 501(c)(20) trust, where they can be used to provide legal services benefits.[34]

---

[33] Treas. Reg. § 1.501(c)(9)-3(d).
[34] Treas. Reg. § 1.501(c)(9)-3(c).

The Tax Reform Act of 1976

New Sections 120 and 501(c)(20) of the Code were enacted as part of the Tax Reform Act of 1976 over strong opposition from the leadership and staffs of the tax-writing committees as well as from the Treasury. Their enactment was due to the determined efforts of Senator Packwood and the strong support of a coalition of major unions, the ABA, large insurance companies, and teachers and consumers organizations. Unlike Sections 104 and 105 (dealing with medical benefits and sick pay), Section 120 provides for exclusion from gross income only for the value of legal services benefits that meet certain standards for qualification.

Qualification Requirements. The exclusion of Section 120 is limited to plans sponsored by an employer for the exclusive benefit of his employees or their spouses or dependents.[35] A plan may, however, be maintained for the employees of several employers, either pursuant to a collective bargaining agreement or otherwise.[36] There is no exclusion from gross income under Section 120, though, for the value of legal services provided by legal aid plans, neighborhood legal services clinics for the poor, bar referral, military, university, credit union, or automobile club legal services plans, or for membership plans sponsored by consumers cooperative, religious societies, unions, etc. Whether the receipt of such benefits constitutes income must be determined under general principles of tax law.

Defined Terms. *Dependent* under Section 120 has the same meaning as it does under Section 152. The term *employee* includes retired, disabled, or laid-off employees, or those on leave. The term *spouse* includes a surviving spouse,[37] and the term "dependent" includes those who were dependents at the employee's death and are under 21 at the time the legal services are rendered. The exclusion also extends to sole proprietors and partners. A qualified plan may also provide services to the estate or personal representative of a deceased employee, spouse, or dependent.

Formal Requirements. There must be a *separate written plan of an employer.* A collectively bargained agreement will satisfy this requirement, as will multiple documents, such as an agreement, a plan, and a trust. The

---

[35] The IRS has ruled that a plan is not for the exclusive benefit of employees if participants are entitled to unlimited hours of benefits of legal representation so long as that representation is for the ultimate benefit of the employer corporation. Ltr. Rul. 8018046 (Feb. 6, 1980).

[36] In determining whether a multiple-employer plan meets the exclusive benefit test, the employees of any employer that maintains the plan are to be considered the employees of each employer who maintains the plan. Prop. Reg. § 1.120-2(d)(2).

[37] A legal service provided to a former spouse after divorce, annulment, or separate maintenance qualifies only if it relates to the divorce, annulment, or separate maintenance.

proposed regulations take the position that, although the employer may reserve the right to change or terminate the plan or discontinue contributions to it, the plan must be a permanent rather than a temporary program.

What Constitutes Personal Legal Services. A qualified plan must be limited to providing *personal legal services*. This term is not clearly defined in the Code or the legislative history. It is undisputed that if an employee would have been entitled to a trade or business deduction under Section 162 if he had paid for the legal services himself, then the services are not "personal" in the required sense. Legal services in connection with the determination, collection, or refund of taxes, the fees for which would be deductible under Section 212(3), may be provided under a qualified group legal services plan. However, the proposed regulations take the position that legal services fees that would have been deductible under Sections 212(1) or 212(2) if paid for by the employee (i.e., legal services for the production or collection of income or for the management, conservation, or maintenance of property held for the production of income) are not "personal" legal services and therefore may not be provided under a qualified plan. This point is disputed, and exclusion of such legal services cannot be justified on revenue grounds. Investment-oriented legal services provided to employees on a nonqualified basis would be deductible by both the employer and the employee. If they could instead be provided through qualified plans, the tax result would be the same. The employer again gets a deduction, and employees come out the same by reason of the Section 120 exclusion, but the services must at least be provided on a nondiscriminatory basis. This issue may be clarified in the final regulations or by Congress.

It seems undisputed that the following kinds of legal services benefits can be provided by a qualified group legal services plan:

- Divorce, child support, and other family law matters
- Wills, trusts, and estate planning
- Probate of estates and gift and estate taxation
- Personal bankruptcy, debt, or garnishment matters
- Personal criminal matters
- Personal injuries, including workers' compensation
- Personal insurance and contract matters
- Personal property matters, including damage claims
- Sale, purchase, or other transactions involving personal residences
- Consumer complaints and litigation
- Personal landlord and tenant matters
- Tax return preparation, audits, and litigation

A related issue concerns the question of what constitutes *legal services*. Under the proposed regulations any services performed by a lawyer that constitute the practice of law, and fees for summonses, transcripts, filing fees, government agency filing fees (but not taxes), and similar fees are legal services. The proposed regulations also take the position that a qualified plan may provide a service performed by a person who is not a lawyer if the service is performed under the direction or control of a lawyer, in connection with a legal service performed by a lawyer, and the fee for the service is included in the legal fee of the lawyer. For example, a plan may, under these conditions, provide the services of an accountant, a researcher, a paralegal, a law clerk, an investigator, or a title searcher.

Employer Prepayment. To be qualified a plan must provide "through prepayment of, or provision in advance for, legal fees in whole or in part by the employer." It is clear that a plan satisfies this requirement if all payments under it are provided by employer contributions to a funded Section 501(c)(20) trust, through premium payments to an insurance company, or as prepayments to providers of legal services.[38] This requirement may also be satisfied by employer funding for a group legal services plan at the option of employees participating in a cafeteria plan under Section 125, under which qualified legal services benefits are one option. Direct employer payments to employees are not allowed, however, nor would a pure pay-as-you-go plan satisfy this requirement of the statute.

Major disputed questions are whether a qualified legal services plan may provide for employee contributions, and whether insured legal services plans may provide for a deductible amount or employee co-payment. Although Section 120(b) seems to require only funding "in whole or in part by the employer," the proposed regulations generally take the position that a qualified plan must be funded entirely by the employer,[39] though traditional tax analysis might be that any plan that is funded primarily by the employer, i.e., more than 50 percent, would be an employer plan. Provision for employee co-payments or deductibles would not in any event seem to contradict the requirement of employer funding. If this matter is not clarified in the final regulations, which are expected to be promulgated soon, there is a good chance that the issue will be addressed legislatively. Of course, if an arrangement were permitted that called for no, or virtually no, funding by an employer or an employee organization, a serious question would arise whether such a plan would be an employee welfare benefit plan under ERISA. If not, it would not get the benefit of the ERISA preemption of various state insurance or bar ethics rules.

---

[38] Prepayments or premiums are to be made on or before the tenth day of the month during which the legal services to which they relate may reasonably be expected to be rendered.

[39] Minor exceptions are provided for surviving spouses, surviving dependents, and short-hour workers under certain collectively bargained plans. Prop. Reg. §§ 1.120-2(h)(2), 1.120-2(h)(3).

Anti-Discrimination Rules. To be qualified a group legal services plan must meet certain anti-discrimination rules. The general standard is like that in the area of pension, profit-sharing, and stock bonus plans (i.e., contributions and benefits under a qualified group legal services plan must not discriminate in favor of employees who are officers, shareholders, self-employed individuals, or highly compensated employees). Further, classification of the employees who are eligible for participation in a plan must be found by the IRS not to be discriminatory in favor of this prohibited group.[40] However, union members who have bargained for legal services may be excluded in testing for discrimination in eligibility.

Limitation group. In addition to these general rules, Section 120(d)(3) provides that not more than 25 percent of the amounts contributed under a plan during the year may be provided for the class of individuals who are shareholders or owners, or their spouses or dependents, each of whom on any day of the year owns more than 5 percent of the stock or of the capital or profits interest in the employer (the *limitation group*). Since a group legal services plan does not provide individual accounts for participants, but is in the nature of a defined benefit plan rather than a defined contribution plan, this statutory test prohibiting more than 25 percent of the contributions in any year from going to the limitation group does not make obvious sense. The proposed regulations, however, would transmute it into a rule that is at least intelligible by providing that, if the same benefits are made available to each participant, the percentage of contributions deemed contributed on behalf of the limitation group for the year is the same as the percentage that the members of the prohibited group constitute of all covered employees. This rule should mean that no sizeable legal services benefits plan with a single benefit structure for all members will run afoul of the 25 percent rule. Special rules are provided, however, where the benefits under the plan are not equally available to all or where premiums are determined on the basis of individual circumstances.[41] In an apparent attempt to mitigate the annual contributions test in the statute, the proposed regulations provide that a plan will in all events be disqualified for the next year if during the past three years more than 25 percent of the benefits under the plan were paid or provided to members of the limitation group.

Establishing Qualified Status. In order for a group legal services plan to be qualified, it must give notice to the IRS that it is applying for recognition of its status as a qualified plan. The notice for recognition should be filed with the key district director on IRS Form 1024, together with an accompany-

---

[40] A plan for officers or management only is discriminatory.

[41] A plan will in all events satisfy the 25 percent rule if it provides, and is operated, so that no legal services will be provided or reimbursed if to do so would cause the fair market value of legal services or benefits provided or reimbursed to members of the limitation group under the plan to date during that plan year to exceed 25 percent.

ing Schedule L. The filing should be made by the employer sponsoring the plan or the person administering it.

In the case of a group legal services plan maintained by several employers but not pursuant to a collective bargaining agreement, such as one for the salaried employees of a controlled group of corporations, a separate filing must be made by each adopting employer.[42] In the case of multiple employer plans maintained pursuant to a collective bargaining agreement, however, only one application is required and the Schedule L for it need only include information with respect to employers who have adopted the plan at the time of the filing of the notice for recognition. No filing is required for employers who subsequently join the plan. If the IRS issues a favorable ruling or determination on a group legal services plan, that plan will be treated as qualified with respect to the adopting employer as of the date of its adoption if the application with respect to it was filed before the end of the first plan year, or the end of the plan year within which the employer adopts the plan.[43] Transition rules are provided for plans in existence prior to June 4, 1976.

Qualified Legal Services Trust Requirements. Section 120 of the Code contemplates that the funding for a qualified group legal services plan will be provided by advance premiums paid to an insurance company, prepayments to service providers, or through contributions to an organization or trust exempt under Section 501(c)(20). In order to be exempt under that provision, an organization or trust must be one created or organized in the United States the exclusive function of which is to form part of a qualified group legal services plan or plans under Section 120.

Advertising and Promotion. Increasingly, qualified group legal services are being provided by organizations set up for that purpose. The special conditions laid down by the IRS for ruling favorably on such organizations has already been noted. One of the questions that has arisen in connection with such organizations is the extent to which they may use their funds to advertise and promote their services. The IRS has recently issued a letter ruling that is favorable on this issue.[44]

In this letter ruling, a nonprofit corporation had been established to provide qualified group legal services under Section 120, and it had obtained a ruling that it was tax exempt under Section 501(c)(20). It sought per-

---

[42] The IRS has made favorable rulings for prepaid group legal services plans that are not trusteed or insured conditioned upon the requirement that they do not provide services under any legal services plans that are not qualified. Practically, this means that law firms or clinics that seek I.R.C. § 120 status must render services only to the covered employees of employers that file qualifying Schedule Ls with the IRS.

[43] For example, IRS approval of a plan by letter dated November 18, 1980, related back and covered all plan years beginning after 1976.

[44] Ltr. Rul. 8121087 (Feb. 26, 1981).

mission to use surplus funds in an amount equal to 25 percent of its reserves, which amount was not actuarially required in order to provide the benefits for which the corporation was already committed, for advertising and promotion. It proposed to spend some of the money on informational materials and the rest on part-time independent contractors who would promote the adoption of the plan by selected collective bargaining units. In these circumstances, the IRS ruled that these expenditures would not jeopardize the Section 501(c)(20) status of the organization nor its classification as a Section 120 plan.

It is not clear the extent to which the position taken in this ruling represents the considered judgment of the IRS as to the general standards to be applied with respect to the use of legal services funds for the purpose of advertising and promotion, so caution is warranted.

Disqualification. If a plan receives a favorable ruling or determination letter but thereafter fails to comply with one or more of the rules for qualification, the result required by the statute is disqualification of the plan. The apparent effect of disqualification is to tax all participants on the value of legal services benefits received during the period of disqualification and to tax the trust on all income during that same period. There would be no loss of employer deductions unless the benefits constituted "unreasonable" compensation or otherwise failed to meet the "ordinary and necessary" test of Section 162.

Retroactive disqualification seems wholly inequitable when the defect in the plan has come about accidentally or through inadvertance. For example, if one rank-and-file person quits during the last days of a plan year, thereby causing more than 25 percent of contributions for that year to be allocable to the limitation group, without there being sufficient time for any corrective action to be taken, disqualification seems a disproportionate and inappropriate penalty. Similarly, if a plan administrator provides legal services to a participant to purchase a house not realizing the house is being purchased for business or investment purposes rather than personal use, disqualification seems a harsh and misdirected remedy.

Since most serious qualification defects in group legal services plans will involve discrimination, one possible alternative to disqualification would be to preserve the exempt status of the trust and the exclusion from income for rank-and-file employees, but to tax prohibited or limitation group members, as appropriate, and to deny employer deductions to the same extent. Another possibility would be to require correction of all defects and to impose an excise tax as an inducement for running plans correctly from the outset. Merely requiring prospective correction, however, without imposing some sanction for past defects, might induce some to operate plans in defiance of Code requirements until they were caught. Whatever the proper remedy, however, it seems clear that disqualification is inappropriate and that Congress should devise a more appropriate alternative sanction system.

APPENDIX 24-1. UAW Legal Services Plan for Chrysler Hourly Workers

"Except as otherwise limited, reasonable and necessary services will be provided at no charge to Participants to cover the following named benefits:

"1. *Matters Where Full Legal Services, Including Litigation, Are Covered Benefits.* All legal services, and any costs of litigation, required in connection with the following matters are covered:

(a) Defense of collection action on personal or family debts;
(b) Defense of garnishment;
(c) Repossession and replevin;
(d) Personal bankruptcy;
(e) Consumer complaints and warranty;
(f) Contracts;
(g) Insurance claims or loss of coverage;
(h) Real estate closings on principal family or personal residences.

"Appeals where appropriate are also included for the matters set out above. There are no time limitations or maximums on the benefits in this Paragraph.

"2. *Matters Where Office Work Only Is A Covered Benefit.* In matters not included in Paragraph 1 and not excluded in Paragraph 4, work by an attorney in his or her office is a covered benefit. The types of office work which may be provided under this Paragraph include the following:

Legal drafting—Preparation of wills, leases for tenants, and other legal documents
Legal research
Factual evaluations
Document review
Telephone calls
Correspondence
Self-help counseling, where appropriate

"3. *Referrals.* When legal services not available as a covered benefit under the Plan are required, the Plan will seek to provide a referral to an attorney with whom the Plan has an agreement providing, among other things, for a specific and reasonable fee to be paid by the person to the attorney. A person referred to a Cooperating Attorney shall be entitled nonetheless to consult with a Plan attorney concerning the matter and such Plan attorney shall be entitled to discuss the matter with the Cooperating Attorney when requested by the person referred.

"4. *Exclusions From Coverage.* The coverage of Paragraph 2 does not include preparation of tax returns, matters where representation on a contingent fee basis is available, or matters where litigation is pending.

"The coverage of Paragraph 1 does not include plaintiff actions on claims of $300 or less or tort actions.

"The following are excluded from all coverages:

(a) Any proceeding directed against Chrysler Corporation or any of its officers or agents or subsidiaries;
(b) Any proceeding directed against UAW, any of its subordinate or affiliated bodies, or the officers or agents of UAW;
(c) Any proceeding where the UAW itself would be prohibited from defraying the costs of such legal services by the provisions of the Labor-Management Reporting and Disclosure Act of 1959;
(d) Fines and penalties, whether civil or criminal;
(e) Any judgment for civil damages, whether compensatory, punitive, or both;
(f) Any proceeding pending on January 1, 1979, or such earlier date that benefits were available to a Participant, where the Participant has previously retained an attorney;
(g) Legal services which are not personal legal services within the meaning of Section 120 of the Internal Revenue Code of 1954, as amended;
(h) Legal services which are deductible on tax returns as a business expense or which are predominantly related to income producing property;
(i) Mortgage, or title insurance, survey expenses, and other non-legal costs attendant to the purchase or sale of real estate;
(j) Litigation involving elections, election laws, or warrant to any civil office;
(k) Workers Compensation or Unemployment Compensation matters, but only where Chrysler is a party to the dispute, or otherwise involved;
(l) Any dispute involving the terms, benefits or coverage of this Plan;
(m) Any dispute as to a participant's right or benefits under the UAW-Chrysler Agreement, such as hospitalization/health benefits."

Group Automobile Insurance

RUSSELL F. SCHUCK
Manager, Employee Benefits Planning, International Business Machines Corporation

MICHAEL J. MCGEE
Manager, Mass Merchandising Department, Kemper Insurance

INTRODUCTION

Employer Sponsorship

Car owners are finding it increasingly difficult to secure automobile insurance and to afford the premiums when this insurance is available. Some employers try to ease these problems for their employees by sponsoring a method of purchasing automobile insurance as a group. Such group purchasing plans are generally referred to in the insurance industry as *mass merchandising*. Figure 24.1 below lists insurance companies or groups that were writing mass merchandising programs for employee groups in 1981.

Sponsorship of a mass merchandising plan for automobile insurance provides a service for employees at very low cost to the employer. The employer provides time and space for on-premises counseling, utilizes in-house publications and internal mail for regular promotions of the program, and arranges for premiums to be paid through payroll deductions.

Sponsorship places an obligation on the employer to select a stable insur-

Company	*Franchise Group*	*True Group*
Aetna Insurance Group, Hartford, Conn.	No	Yes
AIU Insurance Company, Manchester, Vt.	Yes	Yes
Bankers Life of Iowa, Des Moines, Iowa	Yes	No
California Casualty Insurance Co., San Mateo, Cal.	Yes	No
Kemper Group, Long Grove, Ill.	Yes	Yes
Metropolitan Property & Liability Ins. Co., Warwick, R.I.	Yes	Yes
National General Insurance Co., Columbus, Ohio	Yes	No
Provident General Ins. Co., Chatanooga, Tenn.	Yes	Yes
Prudential Property & Casualty Ins. Co., Holmdel, N.J.	No	Yes
Travelers Insurance Companies, Hartford, Conn.	Yes	Yes
Wasau Insurance Companies, St. Louis, Mo.	Yes	Yes

Fig. 24.1 Insurance Companies That Write Mass Merchandising Programs

ance carrier with a workable program, and to choose a reliable insurance agent or broker to handle the counseling and enrollment.

Types of Programs

Mass merchandising programs generally fall into two categories: *franchise group programs* and *true group programs.*

Franchise Group. Franchise group auto, more commonly known by the generic name, mass merchandising, is the type of automobile insurance that is most generally available today. In a franchise group program each employee is individually underwritten by the insurance company, each continues to pay individual premium rates, and each receives an individual insurance policy. Most insurance companies apply a premium that is discounted from the company's usual rate. Some do not.

Since the employee is individually underwritten, not all employees are acceptable to the carrier, and premiums vary because the price for each employee is based upon driving experience and upon the carrier's rates for that experience. Some individuals, therefore, will not benefit from the program, and can find a lower price by shopping around.

A franchise group auto program usually enrolls about 10 percent to 15 percent of eligible employees in the first year and plateaus at 25 percent to 40 percent after two or three years. The percentage of participation, or penetration, is factored by many variables, the most important of which appear to be the amount of time spent on the sales effort by the insurance counselor, the amount of promotional effort expended by the sponsor, and the rate being charged to the employee.

Some employers contribute toward the employee's premium in a franchise program, but this is rare. In most instances, the employer contributes toward the premium only if the employee uses his car for company business (e.g., personal cars used by outside salesmen, inspectors, or area managers). Employer contributions towards automobile insurance premium are currently considered by the IRS to be ordinary income to the employee and are taxable as such.

True Group. True group auto is characterized by the same features as other group employee benefit plans.

Eligibility and coverage. Eligibility is based upon conditions relating to employment without individual underwriting. The employer selects uniform benefits that provide coverage for all participants. The insurance carrier issues a master group contract to the employer and booklet/certificates are issued to the employees.

Premium rate classifications. Premium rates are based upon the characteristics of the group, and, in general, all members of the group pay the same rate. In practice, there may be a small number of broad rate classifications with all participants in a class paying the same rate. Depending upon the carrier, these broad rate classifications may be determined by any combination of the following variables: the number of cars in the family, the number of inexperienced drivers, the territory in which the cars are garaged, or the number of accidents.

Because the rates are averaged among a broad spectrum of employees, the rate for some of the employees will be higher and for the others will be lower than they had been paying on the open market. But to attract the proper cross-section of participants the group rate must be attractive to almost everyone, particularly the good risks. As with group life, the group auto rate is attractive only if there is an employer contribution.

Employer contribution. The minimum level of employer contribution varies from group to group, but it is generally expected to be in the neighborhood of 50 percent of the premium. The employer contribution may be a specific dollar amount, or a percentage of the total premium, or a percentage of a specific coverage (e.g., 100 percent of the liability coverage).

The portion of the premium which is paid by the employee is paid through payroll deduction.

Calculating the group rate. If the group is large enough, the total premium may be developed through *experience rating.* In this case, past loss experience of the group is used in projecting future needs for payment of losses, expenses, commission and profit.

Smaller groups, however, would be subject to extreme fluctuations during bad loss years. Therefore they are usually *pool rated.* That is, losses are pooled either with all groups of similar size or with all of the insurance company's automobile experience in that territory or state. The individual rate charged to each employee is then an average or composite that, when multiplied by the number in the group, will yield the total premium required.

Legislative Background

State Laws. From the 1920s to the 1960s sponsorship of group automobile insurance was discouraged by the belief in some quarters that to provide a lower rate for specified groups, even though warranted, would constitute unfair discrimination against those outside the groups. During that period the majority of states developed a restrictive regulatory atmosphere with regard to mass merchandising automobile insurance. Through statutes, regulations or administrative rulings, the states implemented prohibitions which effectively inhibited growth.

In the late 1960s support for this type of legislation began to erode. Many regulators, supported by (or perhaps prodded by) court decisions, the rise of consumerism, and the real or imagined threat of federal intervention rejected the discrimination arguments. The National Association of Insurance Commissioners went so far as to promulgate model legislation in an attempt to liberalize controls and to clarify regulatory inconsistencies among the states. Insurance carriers found that they could write franchise group programs in some states with specific legislative approval. In others, programs could be developed either through a subsidiary company or through a special policy that differed from that sold by the insurer on the open market.

The end result has been that the existing regulations concerning mass merchandising now have little, if any, effect on the sale of franchise group plans. However, it is a different story for true group plans.

Problems with true group plans. At the state level, several types of laws and regulations affect the marketing of true group auto plans—the so-called "fictitious group" laws, the unfair rate discrimination laws, and in some states, specific "enabling" legislation designed to control group auto.

At the time of this writing, it is difficult to assert definitely which states will permit and which will not permit the writing of true group auto plans. The pertinent laws are still being tested, but the insurance departments of the following states are generally considered to have either the official attitude or the necessary regulations to permit writing true group auto programs for employee groups.

Arizona
California
Colorado
Connecticut
Georgia
Hawaii
Illinois
Maine
Massachusetts
Michigan
Minnesota
Nebraska
Nevada
New Jersey
New Mexico
New York
North Dakota
Pennsylvania
Rhode Island
Washington
West Virginia
Wisconsin

The following states have a regulatory climate or insurance department attitude that would appear to almost certainly preclude writing true group auto:

Alabama
Alaska
Arkansas
Idaho
Iowa
Kansas
Kentucky
Maryland
Montana
New Hampshire
North Carolina
Ohio
Oklahoma
South Carolina
South Dakota
Tennessee
Texas
Vermont
Virginia
Wyoming

In the remaining states there is enough doubt regarding the regulations or administrative interpretation to leave the question open either way. Note that these lists should be used with caution. The inclusion of states on each list is a matter of opinion, is subject to change, and should be verified with a qualified agent or broker.

Federal Laws. At the federal level there are no laws that directly affect mass merchandised auto insurance either positively or negatively. All regulation of automobile insurance is maintained at the state level. There has been some interest in federal legislation mandating state approval of franchise group and true group programs, but none of the proposed methods has found acceptance.

The most positive way to support automobile insurance programs through federal legislation would be to change some provisions of the Federal Labor Code and the Internal Revenue Code. The former controls labor bargaining while the latter controls the tax treatment of employee benefits.

The Taft-Hartley provisions of the Federal Labor Code set up procedures for the handling of employer contributions toward union-negotiated employee benefits. It stipulates the specific benefits for which employer contributions may be funneled through the so-called Taft-Hartley Fund. Since employer contributions for group automobile plans are not specifically stipulated in the Federal Labor Code, they cannot be processed through the Fund. However, there is nothing to prevent the contributions from being sent directly to the carrier.

Similarly, the Internal Revenue Code names specific employee benefits towards which the employer contributes and the contributions to which are not considered as taxable income to the employee. Since group automobile is not specifically mentioned as exempt in the Internal Revenue Code, employer contributions toward the premium are considered as taxable income to the employee.

There is nothing in the Internal Revenue Code to prevent an employer from making a contribution toward an employee's automobile insurance. However, a change in the Code to remove the contribution from the employee's taxable income would certainly make the contribution a more desirable and more popular employee benefit.

ASSESSMENT

In making the decision to institute a group automobile insurance program, management must first choose between the franchise and true group plan, with full knowledge of the advantages and disadvantages of each in relation to the benefits derived by the employees. The following analysis gives the general advantages and disadvantages of each type of program.

Franchise Group: Advantages and Disadvantages

The franchise group program's advantages to employees can be summed up as follows:

- Possible reduction in costs
- Convenience of payroll deductions
- Good service from carrier
- Objective advice from agent
- Easy access to counseling and information

Management finds it a desirable program because it demonstrates its interest in employees at relatively little cost, it is available in virtually all states, and it may reduce time lost from work by employees who might have otherwise been uninsured.

On the other hand, the franchise group plan does not appeal to many employees. Since the policy for every employee is written separately, cost savings are not assured. In addition, the payroll deduction that is instituted to cover the employee's contribution seemingly reduces take-home pay. Management may foresee additional problems, such as:

- Pressure by employees for other payroll deduction items
- Possible pressure to subsidize the premiums
- Some administrative cost in setting up program and entering monthly changes to payroll system
- Some loss of productivity if counseling is permitted on premises during work hours
- Administrative expense in promoting program

True Group: Advantages and Disadvantages

A true group program has many of the advantages of the franchise type, with the addition of the following:

- Cost savings for almost all employees is assured
- Program will involve 75 percent to 90 percent of employees
- Administration is simplified and the program is readily communicated to employees
- Issuance and continuation of coverage for all eligible employees is guaranteed

The true group has many of the disadvantages of the franchise type, with the following additional problems:

- In addition to administrative expenses, the employer must make a substantial subsidy toward the cost of the premiums
- Premium cost and amount of the subsidy will continue to rise along with other benefit costs

ADMINISTRATION

The administration of the franchise group plan is generally handled by the insurance company or by the agent. The employer becomes involved in the distribution of promotional material and payroll deductions. The insurance company or agent handles the sign-up of employees, claims reporting, and changes in coverage and/or premium. Automobile insurance involves more changes in payroll deductions than do contributory life and health programs.

True group programs differ from franchise in that the usual group enrollment procedures and administration are used. Normally the employer will handle administration. A well-designed program reduces paperwork to a minimum. Because the group approach calls for a premium guarantee for one year, mid-term changes in premium should be eliminated. Claims should be reported directly to the carrier.

Billings

The insurance company will use either a *negative billing* system or a *positive billing* system in administering a franchise group plan. With the former, the insurance agent calculates deductions and sends an individual payroll deduction notice to the payroll department for each new policy and for each change in premium. A second copy of these changes goes to the insurance company, which accumulates them in its system and at the end of the month sends a list billing to payroll for the amounts that should have been taken during the month.

In a positive billing system the insurance company calculates all deductions (usually in an automated system) and sends a list billing before the start of each month. This type of billing is an advance billing that tells the payroll department the deduction amounts to be taken in the upcoming month.

In either of these systems the bill may be in the form of hard copy (paper), punched cards, or magnetic tape. Transmittal back to the insurance carrier can take either of the same forms. The form used will depend upon the sophistication of the insurance company's system and the employer's payroll system.

With any of the methods, the insurance company should be able to adapt to the employer's payroll frequency, or even to more than one payroll frequency. Some insurance companies require a minimum number of people on payroll to qualify. This minimum may vary from ten to 1,000 depending upon the company, or upon the influence the agent or broker has with that company.

True group billing systems not only should keep accurate track of the detail billing of each payroll deduction but also should bill accurately for the employer subsidy for each employee—preferably on a monthly basis.

Costs

It is impossible to predict the exact costs involved in franchise or true group auto programs. However, the following factors should be considered in an attempt to calculate these costs. Many of these procedures are optional and may be eliminated if the costs are excessive or do not aid the program significantly.

Introducing the Program. The following are employer costs related to introducing the franchise or true group auto program:

- Distribution of the announcement, to the employees. The cost of printing and material is normally borne by the insurance company.
- Inclusion of the announcement in the in-house employee newsletter or publication.
- Scheduling meetings to explain the program to management and supervisory staff or to all employees. One hour of meeting time will be required per session for franchise; two hours for true group.
- Handling of written reply cards from employees expressing interest or lack of interest in franchise program. 60 percent response is a reasonable estimate.
- Handling sign-up applications for true group. One-quarter to one-half hour per application will be required depending upon the need for follow-up to complete the forms.
- Arranging for counseling space with telephone for the franchise plan.
- Programming time to incorporate new deduction into payroll system.

Ongoing Activities. The following are employer costs related to the on-going activities of the franchise or true group auto program:

- Employer subsidy. For a true group plan, employer subsidy will be the most substantial cost. This cost would vary by type of program and the carrier's plan. A general approximation of the required subsidy would be one-half of the annual premium for full coverage on a middle-age driver with no accidents or violations, driving a mid-price new Ford or Chevrolet for pleasure only, in the territory where the program would be installed.
- Productivity loss during counseling sessions. A reasonable estimate of the time required for counseling is one-half day per week per 1,000 employees off the job during the first two years, reducing to one-quarter after that time.
- Entry of employee deductions to payroll system. Costs should approximate 10 percent spread over the first three years, and 10 percent per month for charges.
- End-of-month reconcilement. This procedure may take from one to ten hours depending upon the sophistication of the employer's payroll system and upon how much manual reconcilement may be requested by the insurance company.

- Time spent by the personnel and payroll departments in answering complaints about service. This cost is difficult to estimate, but the time spent will be in an inverse ratio to the care spent in selecting the insurance agent and the carrier.
- Publicity costs
  —Placement of articles or reminders about the program in the in-house publication, three to four times per year.
  —Three or four distributions per year of promotional material provided by the insurance company.
  —Placing posters on bulletin boards and changing posters three or four times per year.

Management may choose to incorporate safety education features into its automobile insurance program. An ongoing safety program can reduce costs to some degree. Such savings would probably result in lower premium increases rather than in price decreases.

OUTLOOK

Franchise group auto plans are available through many carriers and in virtually every state. At the present time, approximately one percent of all automobile insurance is written through franchise programs.

Interest in employer-sponsored franchise programs has stabilized. The major impetus for providing programs comes from employers that have made it a practice to search out services and benefits that will meet an employee need and/or promote good will at relatively low cost. Employee credit unions have also made franchise programs available to their memberships as part of their overall service-oriented offerings. Labor unions have little interest in promoting franchise programs because all members would not be eligible and because employer subsidies typically are not involved.

A very limited number of true group automobile programs exist today—probably no more than twenty in the entire country. There are so few plans, not because of a lack of interest but because a true group program is not possible without a substantial employer subsidy, a subsidy that the IRS considers taxable income to the employee. Strong efforts are needed to bring about changes in the Code whereby employer subsidies for automobile insurance premiums would be treated in the same way as employer subsidies for group life and health premiums.

These changes may come about, according to current predictions, in anywhere from three to fifteen years. If employee/consumer concerns regarding the availability and affordability of auto insurance continue to grow and be heard, a favorable environment for true group insurance—with tax exemptions on employer subsidies—will begin to emerge. There are, however, two major inhibitors. First, given the general economic climate, the federal government is reluctant to adopt an approach that would result in the loss of significant, potential tax revenues, and the prognosis for pending legislation is not favorable. Second, from the employer's point of view, the relatively high cost of the subsidies involved is likely to work against the true group concept when its cost is balanced against the price of other personnel priorities and business interests.

Part V

Specialized Plans

25

Flexible/Cafeteria Plans

Thomas H. Paine
Hewitt Associates

INTRODUCTION

Flexibility in compensation or benefits is a system under which each employee has some choice as to the form in which compensation is paid. Such a program may be restricted to employee benefits, in which case the individual can choose among various benefit options. Another approach is to provide choices among employee benefit coverages and cash, thereby enlarging the scope of flexibility to direct compensation as well as benefits. However, the heart of flexible programs is the system of non-cash choices provided.

Historical Development

Approaches to Flexibility. Flexibility in various forms has existed in benefit programs for many years.

Employee-paid coverages. One form has been totally employee-paid coverages provided in addition to a basic program paid by the employer—optional life insurance is an example. The employer is providing the advantages of group purchasing power and availability of protection on a group basis regardless of the individual's health.

Supplemental coverage. A second form of flexibility is supplemental coverage available in addition to a basic program, with the cost of the supplement shared by employer and employee. For example, a company may provide basic medical care and offer major medical with the employee and the company splitting the cost. A savings plan may permit an employee to save voluntarily from one percent to 6 percent of his salary, with the company contributing $.50 for each $1 the employees deposit. In this type of flexible arrangement, additional compensation is offered to employees who choose supplementary coverage but is not available to those who do not choose to participate. In this sense, additional compensation is provided on a conditional basis.

Choice of supplemental compensation. A third type of flexibility involves a choice as to the form in which supplemental compensation is provided by the organization. For example, in some profit-sharing plans the employee can choose whether to defer his entire allocation or defer only part and receive the balance in cash. Another illustration is a choice between taking a fourth week of vacation and receiving cash in lieu thereof. The distinguishing characteristic of this type of arrangement is that the employee will receive equivalent value in one form or another.

Modern approach. This last approach to flexibility is the type of flexible or cafeteria program being developed today. Basic levels of compensation and benefits are applicable to all employees, and a supplemental allowance is made available to each participant by the employer. The individual chooses how to allocate this supplement. Unlike earlier types of programs in which few choices were offered, the new emerging programs of flexible benefits provide considerably wider choice.

Early Experimentation. There was little interest in flexibility until around 1970. Prior to that time, most organizations were concerned with developing benefit programs with adequate coverage in each major area of economic risk including death, disability, retirement, and incurrence of medical expenses. It made little sense to talk about providing employees with a choice of coverages until all of their basic security needs were met to a reasonable degree. However, once basic needs were met, some employers began to permit their employees to tailor some benefit expenditures to meet their personal preferences. For example, when both a husband and a wife work at companies that have good medical coverage, can the couple achieve greater satisfaction if one of them is allowed to allocate some money for other purposes? A few organizations began to move towards flexibility on the basis of this logic.

Effect of Recent Legislation

When the Employee Retirement Income Security Act (ERISA) was passed in 1974, Section 2006 banned the further spread of cafeteria programs, which included any choices faxed to employees as currently taxable income. This prohibition stemmed from a concern that cafeteria plans were somewhat akin to salary reduction arrangements, which the government felt were primarily helping highly paid persons. ERISA also directed the Internal Revenue Service to recommend permanent rules for such programs to Congress. In the meantime, existing plans could continue, but no new ones could be developed.

In the interim, interest in flexibility kept rising because more organizations had developed their benefit programs to meet all basic security needs. Prohibited from providing programs that offered choices between taxable and nontaxable items, some employers turned toward flexible programs under which all choices were limited to nontaxable benefits. Not until the passage of the Revenue Act of 1978 was choice between taxable and nontaxable items again permitted. This law unleased considerable pent-up interest in flexibility. Many organizations are now examining the feasibility of this approach and some are developing programs that will become operational in the early 1980s.

FLEXIBLE PROGRAM STRUCTURES

Different structures can be created for a flexible program, depending on the desired items of choices and the combinations acceptable under present law. Theoretically, a program can offer unlimited choice among nontaxable retirement and welfare benefits, taxable benefits, time off, and cash compensation. If an individual chooses to take his value in taxable forms, taxable income has been realized in the current year. The issue is whether an individual choosing items not currently taxable also realizes taxable income because he is in *constructive receipt* of the entire amount subject to choice. This doctrine of constructive receipt states that if choice is available between value received now or later, it will be taxed as if it were received now. Similarly, if a person can choose between one item that is taxable and another that is not, he will be taxed regardless of which choice is made.

Under certain circumstances, the IRS is willing to allow some choice without considering the entire allowance to be constructively received. In these cases, each individual is taxed on the basis of the options actually selected rather than on the value of the allowance available. Following are some of the ways in which flexible programs can be structured within present government rules.

Welfare/Cash Structure

Section 125 of the Internal Revenue Code added by the Revenue Act of 1978 provides that no amount shall be included in the gross income of a participant in a *cafeteria plan* solely because under the plan the participant may choose among various benefits. The term cafeteria plan means a written plan under which all participants are employees and each may choose among two or more benefits. These benefits can be nontaxable benefits or cash, property, or other taxable benefits. However, the term cafeteria plan does not include any program that provides for deferred compensation, except a plan that is qualified under Section 401(k) of the Code applying to cash-deferred profit-sharing programs.

To qualify as a cafeteria plan, the program must cover a nondiscriminatory group of employees, using the same definitions as applied to qualified retirement plans. Also, no employee can be required to complete more than three years of employment as a condition for participation. In addition, the plan must meet certain tests that prevent the plan from favoring the highly compensated by giving them greater benefits or contributions than are allocable to lower paid participants. (These nondiscrimination provisions are discussed later in this chapter.)

In the following example of a cafeteria plan, Employer *A* maintains a medical program that provides noncontributory hospital and surgical benefits for all participants. It offers major medical protection for a cost of $25 a month and dental coverage for $15 a month. The cafeteria program gives each participant an allowance of $40 a month. He may select either or both medical coverages or he may choose neither. Any amount of the $40 allowance not spent for benefits is payable in cash, subject to withholding tax.

Profit-Sharing/Cash Structure

A second approach permits employees to choose between deferring the employer allocation in a qualified profit-sharing trust or taking cash. New Section 401(k), added to the Code by the Revenue Act of 1978, provides revised rules under which these programs operate. So long as the pattern of deferment does not discriminate in favor of the highly paid, this structure results in no current tax on deferred amounts, while allowances taken in cash are currently taxable income and subject to withholding tax.

To be considered a *qualified cash-or-deferred arrangement,* all optionally deferred amounts must be fully vested. The plan must provide that employer contributions deferred by employee election may not be distributed until retirement, death, disability, or separation from service or until hardship or the attainment of age 59½. The plan may not provide for distribution solely upon completion of a stated period of participation or the lapse of a fixed number of years since the contribution was made.

This structure permits a trade-off between current cash and long-term savings, with taxes on both the savings and investment yield deferred until time of distribution. The plan must qualify as a deferred profit-sharing plan by providing that the contribution must be made from current corporate earnings or earned surplus. The contribution does not have to be determined by a formula related to current profitability but could be a specified dollar amount or percent of pay.

Employer *B* takes this approach in the following example. In addition to a noncontributory pension plan, *B* contributes 5 percent of compensation on behalf of each participant to a profit-sharing plan. Each employee may decide whether none, part, or all of his 5 percent allocation is to be deferred or taken in cash. So long as the pattern of actual allocations into the deferred trust are not discriminatory in favor of the highly compensated, this flexible structure provides a trade-off between current cash and tax-deferred savings.

Benefits-Only Structure

Another structure is to offer choices among nontaxable benefits, with no option for cash or currently taxable benefits. Since no income can be constructively received under any option, the existence of choice does not produce currently taxable income. Employees can choose between welfare benefits and deferred compensation, a structure not available under either a cafeteria plan or a cash-deferred profit-sharing arrangement.

For example, assume that Employer *C* maintains a basic noncontributory program providing life insurance, disability, medical, and pension benefits. In addition, he provides a supplemental allowance of $40 plus 5 percent of compensation that the individual can use to purchase supplemental life insurance (up to $50,000), major medical and dental coverage, added long-term disability benefits, and tax-deferred savings. So long as the pattern of savings does not discriminate in favor of the highly compensated, this structure does not produce currently taxable income for any participant.

Three-Way Structure

In 1980, legislation was passed that permits a plan to provide options simultaneously in welfare benefits, deferred compensation, and cash. This combination can be accomplished by adopting a cafeteria plan under Section 125 of the Code and including a cash-deferred profit-sharing plan qualifying under Section 401(k) of the Code.

EMPLOYER MOTIVATIONS FOR FLEXIBLE PROGRAMS

An organization may have various motivations to consider flexibility in compensation and benefits. These reasons may be classified into four categories:

- Make compensation more useful to employees
- Maximize perceived value
- Contain costs
- Manage compensation more effectively

Making Compensation More Useful to Employees

Companies may wish to permit individuals to meet their specific needs and preferences. No matter how extensive a benefit program is, it cannot meet the particular needs of every employee. The young breadwinner with a large family may feel he needs significant life insurance protection and extensive medical coverage. Another employee whose spouse works at a company that provides extensive employee benefits may feel little need for medical and death benefits but have great interest in savings and additional time off. A person close to retirement may value pension benefits higher than other coverages.

As a generalization, the typical nonflexible benefit program has been developed for the male employee who has a nonworking wife at home caring for minor children. However, in 1980 only 15 percent of American households consisted of this family pattern. More predominant are families with two income earners, some with children and others without. The increasing proportion of women in the labor force suggests greater diversity in benefit needs. Flexibility is seen by many employers as a way to provide enough choices to meet these highly varying needs without wasting money by providing extensive coverage for those who do not need it.

Experience indicates that when a group of employees is given an opportunity to tailor plans to meet personal preferences, most participants change from their present coverages. In one instance, with a fairly narrow set of choices being offered, 22 percent of participants elected options that restored their pre-flexible coverage while 78 percent made changes. In another case, with a wider number of choices, only 8 percent opted to restore their program to its pre-flexible level while 92 percent found other combinations of benefits more to their satisfaction.

A related motivation for flexibility is to permit an employee to alter benefit coverages as needs change over a career. A single employee who is hired at age 25 may undergo various events during a career of working for the organization that change needs for benefit protection and preference for cash. These may include: getting married, buying a house, raising a family, sending children to college, changing locations, increasing savings, and finally retiring. A flexible program with an annual election permits the individual to change coverages as needs change.

Benefit programs can be made more useful to employees by maximizing the tax effectiveness to participants of the organization's benefit expenditures. In the normal benefit program, optional coverages are purchased with employees' after-tax dollars. Under a flexible program, there is no currently taxable income if the employer's allowance is allocated to nontaxable benefits. Only if the employee wants optional coverages beyond what the employer-provided allowance will purchase does he resort to making after-tax contributions through payroll deductions.

Could it be said that tax effectiveness is the underlying theme in developing flexible programs? Probably not, because flexibility makes no more effective use of tax dollars than completely noncontributory nonflexible programs. More accurately, tax effectiveness is a result individuals can achieve, but it is not a primary motive for most organizations.

Maximizing Perceived Value

Many employers try to make employees more aware of the value of total compensation. Often the value of the "hidden paycheck" is clearly explained with good communications materials. An additional step is the benefit statement that shows each participant the amounts of his individual benefits and sometimes the value of them as well. A motive for flexibility is to make employees even more aware of the value of non-cash compensation by giving them annual elections to spend an allowance of employer-provided dollars. What could bring home the message of value more clearly than a chance to spend those dollars for one's own purposes?

Perhaps the most common motivation for flexible programs is to create greater satisfaction with a given level of employer expenditure. This is more than getting credit with employees for amounts spent on non-cash compensation items. It involves the ability of a flexible program to please participants by making the program more useful to them. Perceived value is higher if a given level of company expense is spent in a flexible way. It is also a way for the organization to demonstrate that the individual is important. It underlines the message that "this is a good place to work."

A flexible structure also lets the employer provide more forms of pay and benefits than the organization alone can afford. As benefits expand to new areas, the typical nonflexible program is faced with paying most or all the cost for each added item to be perceived favorably by employees and to avoid adverse selection. In a flexible structure, the employer can add to the options offered without having to add correspondingly to the amount of the flexible allowance. This system divorces decisions on items of benefits offered and the source of funds to purchase them. It can raise perceived value by sponsoring a wider group of options for the same employer price tag than can a nonflexible program.

Containing Employer Costs

When a flexible program is introduced, the company is not likely to save money. The employer is trying to change the employee's outlook from "what have you done for me lately?" to "how best can I use the money available to me?" This message is not likely to get across if the employee perceives that the flexible allowance is too small to satisfy needs or to restore the pre-flexible level of benefits. Thus, initial cost savings is unlikely to be achieved.

However, flexibility may operate to contain cost increases in the future. New coverages may be added without increasing employer cost to the full extent of the price of each new coverage, nor is the employer committed to increase the flexible allowance to keep pace with the rising prices of optional coverages. In addition, since employees know that higher claims experience will be reflected in higher option prices in future years, overuse of optional benefits will be discouraged.

To what extent can an organization hold back on the growth of flexible allowances when the price of options keeps rising with increases in compensation levels and medical costs?

There is probably some limit beyond which the employee will feel squeezed, and the employer will no longer achieve his goal of maximizing satisfaction. However, the benefits ball park is a big one, and employees are not apt to measure precisely the value of their employer's contributions to the noncash compensation system compared to that of other organizations. There can be a gap between actual cost and perceived value. A flexible system may maximize perceived value for a given level of employer cost. This difference between actual cost and perceived value supplies the potential for cost containment.

Managing Compensation More Effectively

Some organizations have circumstances that permit flexibility to attain additional goals. One company had many programs of welfare and pension benefits for different groups within their employee population. Flexibility makes it possible to sponsor fewer separate programs, since the core and options can be identical and only flexible allowances vary. In another instance, the company operates in various industries, some of which have high benefit levels and others have low ones. Faced with the dilemma of maintaining a uniform program that is too costly for the low profit margin division or sponsoring a plethora of plans, flexibility makes possible the same benefit coverages for all groups; the only difference is the size of the flexible allowance.

Some organizations feel that flexibiliity will help emphasize total compensation decisions. When a wage or salary increase is given, there is an automatic increase in non-cash compensation levels and costs. The employee does not see the hidden increase and tends to think of the paycheck as total compensation. As flexibility develops, the employer may be able to grant an increase in total compensation and permit the employee to select how to allocate that total increase among cash and non-cash compensation items.

Another important issue in some organizations is the relationship between unionized hourly employees and the non-unionized salaried group. Frequently a pattern develops that changes are implemented first for the union group through collective bargaining. Employers fear that increases granted to salaried people first will become a target for the union to secure in negotiations. In this situation, salaried benefit changes usually come after the union settles and the changes partially or totally follow the union pattern. Flexibility may give an employer a chance to break this lock-step between hourly and salaried groups by adopting a flexible program for salaried people. The amount of the flexible allowance and the timing of increases is related to the annual election cycle and not to the union bargaining calendar. The separation of decision between offering new choices and increasing the employer-provided flexible allowance makes the flexible program noncomparable to the hourly one.

APPROACHES TO FLEXIBILITY

There are four approaches that organizations are taking to cafeteria programs now being developed. There are also various combinations of these methods, and there are probably other types that will emerge.

The "Add On" Plan

Prior to considering flexibility, the employer has an existing program of benefits. The levels are lower than what the employer wants them to be, and he is willing to add money to the program. However, instead of making decisions as to what benefit improvements each employee should be given, the employer wishes to establish an allowance for each employee and let each person choose how to spend that money among a series of optional coverages. The "add on" type of cafeteria plan is characterized by no diminution in existing benefits at the time the program is established.

The new plan works in this way: Prior to the start of each year, each participant selects what benefit coverages he wants from a list of optional choices. The price for each choice has been set by the employer to correspond to the expected cost of that coverage to that employee for that year. The employer provides an allowance, often termed *flexible credits,* which is allocated among participants on a nondiscriminatory basis. If the individual wishes more optional coverages than his allowance will purchase, he signs up for payroll deductions to fund the difference. If a person wants less optional coverage than his allowances are able to purchase, the difference is payable as additional cash compensation during the year. These cash payments, of course, are taxable income subject to withholding.

The "Opt Up or Down" Plan

Another employer wants to start a flexible program but does not wish to increase his expenditures for employee benefits. He wants to offer individuals some choice as to how the money now being spent on their behalf is allocated among various benefits. For each area in which choice is desired, the employer establishes various levels of coverage, some lower and some higher than the existing level of coverage. There is no specific allowance developed for each employee, but each can develop his own allowance by opting for coverages that are less costly than those in the pre-flexible program.

Prior to the start of each year, the individual elects the coverages he wishes for the following year. Each variation from the pre-flexible coverage has a price tag attached to it, with prices determined on the basis of expected value to each participant. Reductions from pre-flexible coverage frees money to be spent some other place, and additions require more money spent. If in aggregate the individual chooses coverages that are of less value than the standard package, the difference is payable as cash compensation throughout the year. If he wants coverages that are in aggregate of greater value than the standard package, he must authorize payroll deductions to pay for the difference.

The "Core Plus Options" Plan

This employer has a generous program of benefits in effect. He believes that some of the levels are higher than many employees require, especially those who have no dependents and those with working spouses. The employer separates his existing program into two parts. The first is a series of core benefits lower than existing benefit levels that the employer feels must apply to every employee. There is no flexibility with respect to these core coverages. The other portion of the program is a series of benefit choices within each area of coverage from which the individual may choose the coverage he wants. An allowance is provided by the employer equal to the difference in value between the pre-flexible program and the new core level of nonflexible benefits. This amount is allocated among participants on a nondiscriminatory basis. (The employer may choose to spend additional money in the form of added credits but this is not required to establish the "core plus options" plan.)

Prior to the start of each year, a participant elects the coverages he wishes for the following year. Each option has a price tag attached to it equal to the expected cost of that coverage for those who select it. If in aggregate the employee chooses coverages of greater value than the available allowance, the difference is funded by payroll deductions. If the individual chooses in aggregate coverage that has less value than the amount of the allowance, the difference is paid as cash compensation during the year.

The "core plus options" plan can arrive at the same structure as the "opt up or down" type if the core level of benefits corresponds to the lowest set of optional choices under the "opt up or down" approach and if the range of optional coverages and their prices are set identically. However, the two approaches operate very differently in the way they are expressed and the mechanics of election.

The "Total Compensation" Plan

Like the "add on" program, the "total compensation" approach starts with an existing level of benefits and does not reduce them. However, in this case the source of funds to purchase optional additional coverages comes from foregone cash compensation increases. The employer does not add to his cost of benefits. Instead, he gives each individual a choice as to whether increases in total compensation are to be paid in used cash or applied to purchase benefits.

The employer schedules 5 percent of pay (or some other percentage of pay or flat dollar amounts) for each employee to become an allowance for choosing optional coverages. Each year employees elect how to allocate that 5 percent among optional benefit coverages and additional cash compensation. The employee may also use payroll deductions to pay for additional benefits.

SOME PROBLEMS WITH FLEXIBLE PROGRAMS

There are a number of issues in designing and administering flexible programs that are either unique to this type of program or more serious in a flexible program than in other types of benefit plans. Four of them are worth particular mention:

1. Applying the nondiscrimination provision of the Internal Revenue Code to cafeteria and cash-deferred profit-sharing plans,
2. Minimizing the impact of adverse selection,
3. Dealing with the consequences of employees making poor choices, and
4. Handling the increased administrative costs in installing and maintaining a flexible program.

Applying Nondiscrimination Provisions

Both the qualified cash-or-deferred profit-sharing plans and the cafeteria plans have special rules to be sure that tax advantages do not accrue solely to the highly paid. The principle involved in both cases is that the highly compensated will have currently taxable income if the nondiscrimination standard is not met, while other employees will experience no adverse effect. The way discrimination is avoided differs in the two types of plans.

Qualified Cash-or-Deferred Profit-Sharing Arrangements. Section 401(k) of the Code defines the term *actual deferred percentage* (ADP). This is a ratio of employer contributions elected to be deferred into the trust divided by the total compensation of the eligible group of participants. For example, if the flexible allowance were 5 percent of compensation for a group and the aggregate amount deferred were 60 percent of that allocation, the ADP would be 3 percent. Separate ADP figures are calculated for two groups: the highest paid one-third of employees and the remaining two-thirds.

The plan is judged to be nondiscriminatory if the ADP for the highest paid one-third is not more than 1½ times the ADP of the other group. An alternate test is that the plan is nondiscriminatory if the excess of the ADP for the group of highly compensated employees over that of the other group is not more than 3 percentage points, provided also that the ADP for the highly compensated is not more than the ADP of the other group multiplied by 2½. For example, if the ADP for the lower paid group is one percent of compensation, the limit for the higher paid group is 2½ percent. If the ADP for the lower paid group is 4 percent, the higher paid group can be 7 percent. If the lower paid group's ADP is 10 percent, the higher paid group can be 15 percent.

Cafeteria Plans. Two different tests are applied in Section 125 of the Code to determine if a cafeteria plan is nondiscriminatory. One is applied if health benefits are not included. The plan is nondiscriminatory if nontaxable benefits and total benefits (or employer contributions allocable to nontaxable benefits and total benefits) do not discriminate in favor of the highly paid. Since this test is conditioned on the results of the actual election, the nondiscrimination test has to be applied in actual practice after the elections have taken place. It is not possible to design a plan with both taxable and nontaxable choices that is guaranteed to pass the test.

If health benefits are included, a cafeteria plan is considered nondiscriminatory if contributions for the health benefits either equal 100 percent of the cost of the coverage selected by a majority of highly paid persons who are similarly situated or equal at least 75 percent of the cost of the highest available coverage for any participant similarly situated. Contributions or benefits in excess of those for health benefits must be a uniform percentage of pay. Applying the first of these two tests again depends on results of actual elections. The second test can be passed when the plan is designed. For example, assume that nonflexible medical coverage costs $360 per employee per year and the highest priced medical option costs $200. Employer contributions must be 75 percent of the cost of the highest option or $420 per employee. Since the employer pays $360 for nonflexible coverage, at least $60 must be added in the flexible allowance. The formula for allocating flexible credits among participants might be $60 plus *X* percent of pay.

Minimizing Adverse Selection

If choices are made available to employees for a set price, won't those with a greater chance of incurring that risk select the option, while those with a lesser chance will spend their money elsewhere? If so, this will drive up the cost of the option to employees or cause the employer to subsidize the option. This problem of potential adverse selection applies to risk coverages such as death benefits, medical benefits and disability protection.

There is no one way to assure that adverse selection will not raise the costs in a flexible program. However, there are a number of steps that can be considered to minimize its impact.

Placing Certain Coverages in Nonflexible Core. Some coverages cannot be written as separate options without involving adverse selection. For example, it is not feasible to isolate maternity benefits as a separate coverage, since many employees can clearly classify themselves as potential users or nonusers of this benefit. Vision care benefits is another example. As a solution, those types of coverages should either be included in the nonflexible portion of the program or several options might be lumped together to make them more attractive to a larger group.

Offering Some Options on an Individual Basis. Some coverages are better provided on an individual basis. For example, the employee can be given an opportunity to build retirement income through an individual savings account rather than through purchasing pension units. Vision care benefits might be handled on this basis, charging employees who select the option the expected cost of the benefit, assuming that each person who elects the benefit will utilize the service.

Offering Price Options Tailored to Value of the Coverage. The plan can charge prices directly related to the amount on an individual's risk. For example, life insurance coverage can relate prices to attained age. This encourages young people to join the plan. The results should be greater participation and less adverse selection.

Subsidizing Coverages to Attract More Participants. Some coverages may stand by themselves better if they are subsidized. Dental care may be a good example. Perhaps 40 percent of a group will be attracted to dental benefits if offered at a price intended to sustain expected claims. However, if the price is reduced through employer subsidy of the option, a higher degree of participation can be secured and the impact of adverse selection lessened.

Providing Some Limits on Choice. Some benefits may be more supportable at the offered price if employees must sign up for two or three years rather than just one. Dental care is a good example. For life insurance, an employee may be required to show evidence of insurability if he wishes to increase the amount of coverage.

None of these approaches will totally eliminate adverse selection. However, judicious design and the incorporation of some limitations will help to limit its impact.

Avoiding the Consequences of Employees Making Poor Choices

How does the employer protect against the employee making poor choices when spending his flexible credits? The first line of defense is to create a nonflexible core of basic benefits, providing levels of coverage that prevent the organization from being embarrassed if the individual does not opt for any more coverage. This core concept reduces the organization's concern for the consequences of employee choice.

There are some additional things that an organization can do to help employees make smart choices. Prior to the establishment of the program, a random sample of employees can be drawn and small study groups created to assist in designing the flexible options. By knowing which choices appeal to employees and which are understandable, the program can be developed to help employees make better selections.

It is also helpful for the entire employee group to go through a simulation prior to the first real election. This helps employees understand how the system works and gives them the training to handle the first election with less concern for making mistakes. This simulation also provides good data on which the insurance company can base its prices for options. This data can also be used to test whether enrollment is likely to meet IRS nondiscrimination rules.

The election process can provide another mechanism for increasing the likelihood that employees know what choices they have made. The initial election form is a turn-around document that the employee fills in and returns. His entries are keypunched into the computer, which produces a copy of the same form with the employee's choices filled in. It is then returned to the employee, asking him to review it again and sign a statement that these are the choices he wants for the next year and that he authorizes any necessary payroll deductions. This process assures that the employee has made choices with due consideration. It also constitutes protection for the organization in event of later suit by the employee or a dependent that he was not aware of the consequences of the choices he made.

Above all, one needs to communicate clearly and repeatedly if employees are to make smart choices under a flexible program. Good communications can help employees understand the concepts involved and how each of the options works.

An analysis of elections made by employees in various organizations indicates that individuals are able to take this responsibility and exercise it well. At least this is true where communications have been ample and where the benefit programs themselves have been simplified to the point where understanding can be created. Perhaps this should not be too surprising, since most employees manage complicated personal transactions in a satisfactory way.

Handling Administrative Requirements

Another set of issues involves the additional costs associated with administering a flexible program. Unquestionably, administrative tasks are more complicated. There are higher start-up costs associated with an involved design process, a complicated set of approvals needed from government agencies, a need to develop underwriting safeguards, the necessity of building a computer system to handle the election process, and the need for good communications in getting the new approach launched. Also needed are reports for management and the insurers that will provide financial controls.

Higher Start-Up Costs. The amount of start-up cost varies significantly among organizations, depending on the complexity of the program and the extent of their internal resources, primarily data processing. A program with a dozen choices being offered to a group of 1,000 or more employees requires sophisticated computer programming to operate the election process. There must be a good data base from which to draw the necessary information. The election module must make the necessary computations, produce the election form, check the correctness of employee entries and produce the necessary reports for management, cost accounting, insurance companies, and employee records. Whether this work is performed internally or purchased outside, it is likely that the development of the administrative system will cost upwards of $100,000. When the other costs of communicating, enrolling, training the administrators, securing legal approvals, and negotiating insurance arrangements are added, the cost of installing a flexible program may well run $500,000 or more.

Additional On-Going Costs. Once installed, a flexible program is likely to cost more to administer than a nonflexible one. If most administrative tasks are performed by computer, the number of additional people required for ongoing administration will be limited. In each location some individual must be a resource to answer questions (but not counsel). The central administration burden may also require additional personnel. The total additional burden should be expected to be less than one per 1,000 employees. Of course, the larger the group covered, the smaller the ratio.

Measured against these additional administrative costs are the advantages the organization wishes to achieve with flexibility—involving employees, maximizing satisfaction, using employer dollars better, and enhancing the perception that this is a good place to work. One must measure what added costs are appropriate to achieve these goals.

More Complex Tasks. Once established, the flexible program also has more complicated administrative tasks. There is greater effort in enrolling employees. Changes in marital status may trigger revised elections. Communications activities on a regular basis must be good enough so the employer can avoid counseling on an individual basis with employees. However, some personnel representatives must still be available to counsel on how to make the elections and what individual rights exist under the program.

For organizations that are already providing a significant number of options, the administrative tasks may not seem much more complex. For a company that runs a noncontributory basic set of employee benefits, moving to a flexible structure may cause significant enlargement of administrative tasks.

THE FUTURE FOR FLEXIBILITY

It seems likely that flexible compensation and benefit systems will spread in the future. Our work forces are becoming more diverse and the value systems among employees are changing. The cost for non-cash compensation keeps rising, and employers are looking for ways to maximize satisfaction among employees from the money spent on benefits. Employees want more say about conditions affecting their jobs and how they are paid. The concept of flexibility fits well with both employer and employee objectives.

Probably large organizations with greater sophistication in data processing and higher levels of current benefit expenditures will lead the way. They have lower overhead costs per covered participant to install and maintain a flexible system. Gradually, flexibility will be extended to smaller groups of employees. Whether flexibility will ever spread to employee groups represented by unions cannot be easily predicted. The needs of another entity, the union, will also have to be met if flexibility is to become attractive.

26

Multiemployer Plans

PAUL S. BERGER[1]
Arnold & Porter

K. PETER SCHMIDT
Arnold & Porter

[1] The authors wish to acknowledge the valuable assistance of Douglas W. Ell in the preparation of this chapter.

INTRODUCTION

A multiemployer plan is an employee benefit plan to which more than one employer is required to contribute, which is maintained pursuant to one or more collective bargaining agreements.[2] Although rules relating specifically to such plans were included in the Employee Retirement Income Security Act of 1974 (ERISA) from its inception, the number of such rules increased dramatically on September 26, 1980 with enactment of the Multiemployer Pension Plan Amendments Act of 1980 (MPPAA). This new legislation completely rewrote the termination insurance provisions (Title IV) of ERISA as they applied to multiemployer pension plans.

Development of Multiemployer Plans

Multiemployer plans originally developed to benefit workers in industries in which job changes are frequent and there is little continuity in the employer-employee relationship. Such conditions would not generally permit a worker to qualify for a pension or other benefit under a single-employer plan. In the construction industry, for example, employees are frequently hired only for a specific project. In other industries, fierce competition, frequent business failure, or recurring layoffs may prevent the establishment of stable employer-employee relationships. Millions of workers are, however, currently participating in multiemployer plans, and earning pension and other benefits.

Concept of Combined Service

Multiemployer plans receive contributions from many employers and credit benefits on the basis of a worker's combined service with all contributing employers. Thus, in the case of a multiemployer pension plan, a worker

---

[2] ERISA § 3(37); I.R.C. § 414(f). See also ERISA § 4001(a)(3). The Secretary of Labor may create other requirements which a plan must satisfy to be a multiemployer plan but as of this writing had not done so. Prior to MPPAA, a plan was not within the definition of a multiemployer plan if any one employer contributed more than 50 percent of total contributions. Plans which now fall within the definition of a multiemployer plan but which did not prior to MPPAA may elect not to be treated as a multiemployer plan. ERISA § 3(37)(E); I.R.C. § 414(f)(5). Such plans are referred to as "multiple-employer plans."

who is employed during his career by a number of employers who contribute to the plan will earn pension and vesting credit for all such service. Some plans, through reciprocal agreements, even award credit for service covered under another plan.

Contributing Employers

The employers contributing to a multiemployer plan generally include all employers who employ members of a particular national or local union. For example, a typical plan might cover all union garment workers in the United States or all carpenters in northern New Jersey.

Administration

Multiemployer plans are established and governed by collective bargaining agreements. Multiemployer plans are generally administered by a joint board of employer and union trustees. This joint board usually establishes benefit levels and attempts to operate within the budget established by the collective bargaining agreement.

Statutory Rules Prior to ERISA

Prior to ERISA there were no special statutory rules for multiemployer plans. Technically these plans were viewed as a number of separate plans adopted by each contributing employer, and the discrimination and deduction rules were applicable on an employer-by-employer basis. However, in practice, collectively bargained plans were administratively treated on a unitary basis.[3]

Scope of Chapter

The revolutionary impact of ERISA in numerous areas has been described in previous chapters. For example, ERISA added important provisions relating to administration, reporting, fiduciary responsibility, enforcement, and, for pension plans, relating to participation, vesting, funding, and termination insurance, to name only a few.

In general, the provisions and accompanying requirements of ERISA, as amended, apply to multiemployer plans in the same manner as to single-employer plans. This chapter does not restate the features of ERISA applicable to both single-employer and multiemployer plans. Instead, the discussion focuses on the special rules for and problems of multiemployer plans.[4]

---

[3] For a discussion of multiemployer plans prior to ERISA and the effect of ERISA on multiemployer plans, see Berger & Hester, "Effect of ERISA on Multiemployer Plans" (Pts. 1–2), 42 J. Taxation 82, 138 (1975).

[4] Preliminarily, it is of interest that ERISA explicitly provided that collectively bargained multiemployer plans should be treated as a single plan in most cases. For

SPECIAL ADJUSTMENTS FOR MULTIEMPLOYER PLANS

This discussion covers the special adjustments which have been made to interpret and apply the general rules of ERISA, as amended, in the context of a multiemployer plan. Later parts discuss special rules relating to termination insurance for a multiemployer pension plan, mergers and transfers of multiemployer pension plans, and multiemployer welfare plans.

Participation and Vesting

ERISA's requirements generally with respect to participation, vesting of benefits, and accrual of benefits are described in Chapter 14. Under Section 210 of ERISA and Section 413 of the Internal Revenue Code, these requirements apply to multiemployer plans as if all employers contributing to the plan constituted a single employer.[5] For example, covered service with different participating employers must be aggregated to determine an employee's eligibility to participate.

Noncovered Service. Under Department of Labor regulations, a plan to which more than one employer contributes is not required to grant participation or vesting credit for service with a participating employer when that service is "noncovered" service, i.e., service for which no contributions are required, unless the noncovered service precedes or follows covered service, and no "quit, discharge, or retirement" occurs between the covered and noncovered service.[6] Thus, for example, if a company participates in a multiemployer plan, but only with respect to certain categories of employees in Florida, an employee who transfers directly from employment with that company in New York to a covered position with the same company in Florida would receive credit, for purposes of participation and vesting, for his years of service with the company in New York. On the other hand, if an employee with prior years of service for the company in New York should enter into covered service with an employer in Florida unrelated to his previous employer or return to employment in Florida with the first employer after a period of service with another employer, the prior service with the first employer in New York need not be counted for purposes of vesting or eligibility to participate.

Withdrawal and Termination. A multiemployer pension plan is not required to take into account, for purposes of determining a participant's vested percentage in accrued benefits, service after either (1) the par-

---

example, as discussed later in this chapter, all participants and contributing employers are generally aggregated in determining compliance with the rules relating to participation, vesting, funding, and discrimination, among others.

[5] ERISA § 210(a), I.R.C. § 413(b).

[6] DOL Reg. § 2530.210(c).

ticipant's employer completely withdraws from the plan, or (2) the plan terminates. In the case of a partial withdrawal resulting from a "bargaining unit withdrawal," as described above, subsequent service in the withdrawn unit may be disregarded to the extent of regulations to be adopted by the Treasury.[7]

Accrual of Benefits

Benefits Only Accrued for Covered Service. For purposes of benefit accruals, as opposed to vesting credit, a multiemployer plan is only required to take covered service into account. Thus, an employer who works in covered service with employers *A* and *B* would accrue benefits from his service with both employers. However, an employee who engages in covered service with employer *A* and then transfers to noncovered service with employer *A* (for example, a factory worker who is promoted to management or who transfers to a unit not covered by the plan) would not accrue further benefits after the transfer, although he would continue to receive further credit for purposes of participation and vesting.

Past-Service Credit. To encourage new employers to enter into the plan, many multiemployer plans award pension credit for service with a participating employer prior to the time that employer began contributing to the plan. Some multiemployer plans award full "past-service credit" instantly upon a new employer's entry into the plan, while others limit the maximum past-service credit an employee may receive according to that employee's service following the entrance of the new employer into the plan.

Cancellation of past-service credit. One of the fundamental principles of ERISA is that pension rights, once "vested," cannot be lost. However, multiemployer plans may provide for the cancellation of past-service credit with respect to the employees of an employer that subsequently withdraws from the plan.[8] The underlying rationale is to prevent multiemployer plans from being burdened with pension liabilities for which no corresponding contributions were received, and to prevent employers from temporarily joining a multiemployer plan merely to gain past-service credit for employees.

Multilevel Plans. Some multiemployer pension plans allow contributing employees to agree to contribute at one of several rates. Correspondingly higher benefit credit is earned by participants whose employers bargain for the higher contribution rates. For example, Company *A* might agree to contribute $.50 per hour of service, so that its employees would be eligible for a maximum pension benefit of $300 per month, whereas Company *B* might

---

[7] I.R.C. § 411(a)(4)(G).
[8] See I.R.C. § 411(a)(3)(E); Treas. Reg. § 1.414(f)-1(b)(2)(i).

agree to contribute $1 per hour of service, so that its employees would be eligible for a maximum pension benefit of $600 per month.

In the situation described above, a participant who switched from Company *A* to Company *B* would generally accrue benefits at twice his former rate. Since all contributing employers are treated as one employer for purposes of ERISA's accrual rules, this situation might be thought to violate the anti-backloading provisions of the three statutory benefit accrual tests.[9] However, the relevant Treasury regulations make clear that plans may satisfy different methods with respect to different classifications of employees, or separately satisfy one method with respect to each such classification, provided that the plan is not structured to evade the benefit accrual requirements.[10]

Nonstandard Accrual Formulas. Many multiemployer plans do not use a participant's years of service or years of participation to compute accrued benefits. Instead, these plans may calculate the accrued benefit as a set amount per hour, day, or month, or as a set percent of contributions received or gross pay. Plans are permitted to use any of these formulas provided it is reasonable and consistent and takes into account all covered service during the employee's participation in the plan that is required to be taken into account for benefit accrual purposes.[11]

Funding

Contribution Shortfalls. Employer contributions to a multiemployer plan are established by one or more collective bargaining agreements, and are generally calculated as a set amount per *base unit* (which could be hours worked, tons of production, dollars of compensation, etc.). Those rates cannot easily be adjusted during the term of a collective bargaining agreement. Accordingly, an event such as a strike or layoff, or even general economic deterioration, could lead to an unexpected decline in the number of base units and an unintentional funding shortfall.

Congress recognized this problem when ERISA was originally enacted. The legislative history of ERISA indicates that multiemployer plans should be allowed to receive contributions at collectively bargained rates throughout the period of the collective bargaining agreement without incurring a funding deficiency, provided that the rate of contributions was reasonable when set.[12]

Election of shortfall method. The Treasury has published regulations that generally permit pension plans receiving contributions at a rate specified in

---

[9] I.e., the "3 percent" test, the "133⅓ percent" test, and the "fractional" test. See ERISA § 204; I.R.C. § 411(b).

[10] Treas. Reg. § 1.411(b)-1(a). See also 120 Cong. Rec. H8701 (daily ed. Aug. 20, 1974) (statement of Representative Dent, floor manager of ERISA in the House).

[11] DOL Reg. § 2530.204-3.

[12] See H.R. Rep. No. 1280, 93d Cong., 2d Sess. 285 (1974).

a collective bargaining agreement to elect the *shortfall method* of complying with the funding requirements of ERISA.[13] Simply stated, under the shortfall method the funding standard account is charged not with the actual costs for that year, but rather with an artificial *net shortfall charge*. The net shortfall charge is meant to approximate the product of (1) the funding charge that would normally apply, and (2) the ratio of actual base units to estimated base units. Thus, if only 50 percent of the covered hours expected is actually worked, the funding charge for that year would be approximately 50 percent lower than under the general funding requirements. Any discrepancy between this charge and the funding charge otherwise applicable must be amortized in succeeding plan years.[14]

Multiemployer Pension Plan Amendments Act Changes. MPPAA amended the funding rules pertaining to multiemployer pension plans in several ways. For example, all pension plans are required to amortize certain items such as increases or decreases in unfunded past-service liabilities, experience gains or losses, and gains or losses resulting from changes in actuarial assumptions.[15] Multiemployer plans are now required to use the same amortization periods for these items as single-employer plans, with respect to such amounts arising after 1980. For example, a multiemployer pension plan must now amortize past-service charges arising after 1980 over thirty years, not forty as previously required.

The MPPAA also created special funding requirements for plans in reorganization. These requirements are briefly described in the section on reorganization in this chapter.

Credit for Uncollectible Contributions. The Internal Revenue Service has taken the position that a defined benefit multiemployer plan must award credit for hours of covered service, regardless of whether the participant's employer actually makes the required contribution. This requirement creates problems, since someone must ultimately pay for all credit the plan grants. Defined benefit multiemployer plans may have some flexibility in this area since they can take account of uncollected contributions in the actuarial calculations used to determine the supportable level of benefits.

Problems posed for individual account plans. However, in several cases, the IRS has taken a similar position regarding individual account plans. That is, such plans would be required to credit participants' accounts with amounts that employers are required to contribute, whether or not contributions are actually made. Individual account plans do not have the flexibility

---

13 Treas. Reg. §§ 1.412(c)(1)-1, 1.412(c)(1)-2.

14 The explanation set forth above is necessarily oversimplified, and thus not totally accurate. Moreover, the final shortfall regulations did not resolve all problems of multiemployer plans in this regard.

15 I.R.C. § 412(b).

described above regarding actuarial assumptions and do not have a supplemental source of funds with which to credit participants' accounts. For this reason, the practice of individual account plans has generally been to credit the account of a participant only for contributions actually received. As of this writing, efforts were underway to reverse the initial position of the IRS.

Record-keeping, Notification, and Disclosure

Recognition of Record-keeping Burdens. Many multiemployer plans lack complete records of participants' years of service or accrued benefits. When ERISA was enacted in 1974, Congress recognized the tremendous record-keeping burdens faced by many multiemployer plans.[16] Such plans often utilize information maintained by the government, such as Social Security records, to determine eligibility for benefits. Section 209 of ERISA therefore provides that multiemployer plans are only required to maintain records sufficient to determine the benefits due or which may become due to employees "in accordance with regulations prescribed by the Secretary [of Labor]." As of the date of this writing, regulations governing individual benefit reporting and record-keeping had been proposed, but there is no indication as to when such regulations might be finalized.

Additional Communications Complexities. The principles and concerns relating to benefit communications, described in Chapter 6, are generally applicable to multiemployer plans, although there may be additional complexities resulting from the size and nature of certain multiemployer plans. For example, where notice is required to all "interested parties" to the plan, as in the case of a determination regarding plan qualification, it may be impractical to mail notice to all participants, and publication in union newspapers is sometimes sufficient. Also, multiemployer plans often have large numbers of non-English-speaking participants, and are required to make assistance in understanding rights and obligations under the plan available to such persons.[17] Multiemployer plans with different benefits for different classes of participants may elect to prepare and distribute separate plan summaries for each class.[18]

Disclosure Requirements. In general, every plan administrator, or employer who maintains an employee pension benefit plan, must file, on Form 5500, annual reports with the Department of Labor and the Treasury. For multiemployer plans, however, contributing employers need not file.

---

16 See 120 Cong. Rec. H8701 (daily ed. Aug. 20, 1974) (remarks of Rep. Dent); 120 Cong. Rec. S15739-40 (daily ed. Aug. 22, 1974) (remarks of Sen. Williams).

17 DOL Reg. § 2520.102-2(c).

18 DOL Reg. § 2520.102-4.

Discrimination

Any employee benefit plan will not qualify for tax-exempt status if contributions to or benefits from the plan discriminate in favor of officers, shareholders, or highly compensated employers. This requirement is applied to participants of a multiemployer plan as if all participants who are subject to the same benefit computation formula were employed by a single employer.[19]

The Exclusive Benefit Rule

In some cases the administrator of a multiemployer plan may determine that an employer has mistakenly made excess contributions or payments of withdrawal liability. The exclusive benefit rule is not violated by the return of any such overpayments to the employer, provided the money is returned within six months from the date the existence of an overpayment is determined.[20] In determining whether the exclusive benefit test is met for a multiemployer plan all plan participants are considered to be the employees of each employer.[21]

Deduction Limitations

Section 404(a) of the Internal Revenue Code limits the maximum federal income tax deduction which may be claimed by an employer for contributions to a pension plan. This limitation is satisfied for employer contributions to a multiemployer pension plan if all *anticipated* contributions do not exceed such limitation.[22]

Accounting Rules

Generally the accounting rules currently applicable to single-employer plans apply with equal force to multiemployer plans. For defined benefit multiemployer pension plans, however, two additional points are noteworthy.

Implications of New Funding Requirements. MPPAA established new funding requirements and obligations for employers participating in multiemployer plans. Shortly after the enactment of this legislation, the staff of the Financial Accounting Standards Board, the principal rule-making body for the accounting profession, issued an advisory bulletin discussing the accounting implications this new law would have on participating employers.[23] This bulletin was not intended to set forth new accounting prin-

---

19 I.R.C. § 413(b)(2).
20 I.R.C. § 401(a)(2).
21 I.R.C. § 413(b)(3).
22 I.R.C. § 413(b)(7).
23 See FASB Technical Bulletin, No. 81-3, Multiemployer Pension Plan Amendments Act of 1980 (1981).

ciples relating specifically to multiemployer plan sponsors, but rather to offer guidance concerning the application of existing accounting principles to employers covered by the new provisions. Accordingly, the main point stressed by this bulletin is that existing accounting principles require disclosure of the "nature and effect" of the new funding requirements and obligations for employers that participate in multiemployer pension plans. The bulletin does not specify either the form or content of such disclosures, leaving the task of interpreting and complying with this requirement to participating employers and their accountants.

Exception to General Disclosure Requirements. All employers sponsoring pension plans are required to make disclosures in their financial statements, or notes thereto, relating to the present value of vested and nonvested accumulated plan benefits, the amount of net plan assets available for benefits, the assumed rate of return used in calculating the present value of accumulated benefits, and the date as of which this information was determined. *No* such disclosures, however, need be made by an employer participating in a multiemployer plan if the particular employer's "relative position and undertakings" of the items noted above is not ascertainable.[24] In such a situation, all that is required is disclosure of the circumstances concerning the individual multiemployer plan sponsor's inability to determine its "relative position and undertakings" of such items.

PENSION TERMINATION INSURANCE

This discussion covers the numerous important changes made by MPPAA in the termination insurance provisions (Title IV) of ERISA applicable to multiemployer plans. For example, it is now plan insolvency, not plan termination, that is the insurable event triggering financial assistance by the Pension Benefit Guaranty Corporation (PBGC). Terminated multiemployer plans are now "frozen" rather than liquidated. Certain financially distressed plans are now deemed to be in "reorganization," and may be forced to reduce benefits (but not below the level guaranteed by the PBGC) and to increase employer contributions. MPPAA also increased the insurance premiums paid to the PBGC, and permitted the partition of certain multiemployer plans in the event a major contributing employer goes bankrupt. Despite these and a variety of other changes, the provisions of Title IV of greatest interest to multiemployer pension plans and contributing employers are the new sections relating to withdrawal liability.

---

[24] FASB Statement No. 36, Para. 9. The Statement does not define what is meant by the "relative position and undertakings" of a participating employer. This Statement was issued prior to the enactment of MPPAA, and does not expressly refer to an employer's "share" of unfunded liabilities for withdrawal or termination liability purposes. Nonetheless, this "share" may arguably correspond to a particular employer's "relative position and undertakings."

Withdrawal Liability

Background. Among the most important provisions of Title IV with special applicability to multiemployer pension plans are those that can impose liability upon the withdrawal of an employer from such a plan. These provisions, and the reason for their recent addition to ERISA, are discussed below.

Incentive for employer withdrawal. Under ERISA as originally enacted, the withdrawal of an employer from a multiemployer pension plan did not generally give rise to liability, although the withdrawal of a "substantial employer" required that a bond or escrow be posted to protect against later plan termination. Liability was imposed only upon plan termination, and then only upon those employers who had participated in the plan in any portion of the five years preceding termination. This liability, calculated to represent an allocation of the plan's unfunded, guaranteed benefits, could be as much as 30 percent of the employer's net worth.

The possibility of future liability created, particularly in multiemployer pension plans with substantial unfunded liabilities, a significant incentive for employers to get out of the plan before it terminated. Employers who might otherwise have stayed with the plan had to consider the awareness of other employers of this incentive and their consequent withdrawal or possible withdrawal. Although there would be no liability if the plan did not terminate, large numbers of withdrawals (whether motivated by fear of contingent liability or not) would diminish the plan's contribution base, and make plan termination more likely. The fear of contingent liability threatened to become a self-fulfilling prophecy. No one wanted to be "the last man out," the one left holding the bag if the plan did terminate. Moreover, as fewer and fewer employers were left, the larger would be the fraction of the plan's unfunded liabilities for which each remaining employer was responsible.

Finally, if large numbers of employers did withdraw, there could well be an incentive for the remaining employers voluntarily to terminate the plan so as to impose liability on the withdrawn employers.

The problem described above was a uniquely multiemployer-plan problem since the withdrawal of an employer without plan termination and the consequent imposition of contingent employer liability, could only occur in such plans. In a single-employer, partially funded plan, the "withdrawal" of the only contributing employer would necessarily result in termination of the plan.

Imposition of liability upon withdrawals. The new legislation seeks to deal with this problem by imposing liability upon withdrawals after April 28, 1980, the general effective date of the withdrawal liability provisions. In effect, employers have to pay their share of the plan's unfunded liabilities whether they stay with the plan or not. Employers who stay with the plan continue contributions, and have the advantage of accruing additional benefits for their employees. Employers who leave the plan must pay through withdrawal liability, and thus no longer have an incentive to withdraw in order to avoid paying this share. Moreover, because the shares of withdrawing employers must be borne by them, and are not imposed on the employers remaining with the plan, employers who remain need not worry about being responsible for an ever-increasing share of the plan's liabilities.[25]

Responsibility of the Plan Sponsor. Under the new law, whenever an employer "withdraws" from a multiemployer pension plan, the plan sponsor[26] is required to (1) determine the amount of the employer's withdrawal liability, (2) notify the employer of this amount, and (3) collect this amount from the employer.[27]

Determining When a Withdrawal Occurs. An employer's withdrawal from a multiemployer pension plan may be either *complete* or *partial*. In general, a complete withdrawal is defined to occur whenever an employer either permanently ceases to have an obligation to contribute to the plan, or permanently ceases to have operations covered under the plan.[28] The date that the employer ceased to have an obligation to contribute, or ceased to employ persons covered by the plan, is deemed to be the date of withdrawal.[29]

Construction industry definition. A special definition of withdrawal applies to the construction industry.[30] The reasons for this special definition, and a detailed explanation of the special rule, are set forth below.

Frequently, a construction contractor comes into a plan's jurisdiction in order to work on a specific project, e.g., the construction of a subway system. When the project is completed, the contractor may move on to work in other jurisdictions, and "permanently ceases to have an obligation to contribute under the plan" within the meaning of the general definition of withdrawal. However, if the contractor's employees have been local workers, they are likely to remain in the plan's jurisdiction and work for other participating employers. To this extent there will have been no dilution of the plan's contribution base, and the plan will not suffer from the employer's "withdrawal." To the extent the contractor's employees came into the plan's jurisdiction

---

[25] The imposition of this liability on withdrawing employers has already resulted in numerous constitutional challenges to the new legislation. See, e.g., Johnson Motor Lines, Inc. v. Central States, Southeast, and Southwest Areas Pension Fund, No. 81-C-3703 (N.D. Ill. July 1, 1981) (temporary restraining order issued preventing collection of withdrawal liability); Peick v. PBGC, No. 81-C-1911 (N.D. Ill., filed April 6, 1981).

[26] The "plan sponsor" is defined in Section 4001(a)(10) of ERISA as, with respect to a multiemployer plan, the plan's joint board of trustees or, if there is no such board, the plan administrator.

[27] ERISA § 4202. See also ERISA § 4219(b)(1).

[28] ERISA § 4203(a).

[29] ERISA § 4203(e).

[30] ERISA § 4203(b).

only for the particular project involved and leave after completion of the project, they are not likely to have enough covered service to have earned a nonforfeitable benefit. The plan should thus have a substantial net inflow from contributions attributable to such employees, and again the plan will suffer no damage. For these reasons, the main threat to multiemployer pension plans in the construction industry is from employers who continue to work in the jurisdiction, but cease contributions, i.e., go non-union, rather than from employers who go out of business or leave the plan's jurisdiction.

Because of these characteristics, an employer does not generally "withdraw," within the meaning of the statute, from a construction industry plan unless the employer ceases to have an obligation to contribute *and* continues to do similar work in the jurisdiction of the collective bargaining agreement which previously called for contributions.[31] In this regard, resumption of such work in the jurisdiction of the plan within five years—three in the case of a mass withdrawal of all employers [32]—has the same effect as the continuation of work.[33]

The construction industry definition of withdrawal is not applicable to an employer who has a contribution obligation to the plan on behalf of non-construction employees unless substantially all of its employees are in fact performing work in the construction industry.[34] Also, the definition is applicable only to plans that primarily cover employees in the building and construction industry, unless a plan elects to apply this definition only for its construction industry employers.[35]

Other special withdrawal definitions. A rule virtually identical to that set forth above for the construction industry is applicable to entertainment industry plans.[36] An entertainment industry plan may nonetheless be amended to adopt the general withdrawal rule, and the PBGC may require the use of the general withdrawal rule if necessary to protect the interest of plan participants and beneficiaries or to prevent a significant risk of loss to the PBGC.

There is also a special withdrawal definition applicable to multiemployer pension plans if "substantially all" [37] of the contributions to the plan are made by employers primarily engaged in the long and short haul trucking industry, the household goods moving industry, or the public warehousing

---

31 ERISA § 4203(b)(2).
32 ERISA § 4203(b)(3).
33 ERISA § 4203(b)(2)(B)(ii).
34 ERISA § 4203(b)(1)(A).
35 ERISA § 4203(b)(1)(B).
36 ERISA § 4203(c).
37 Legislative history suggests that "substantially all" in this context means at least 85 percent. 126 Cong. Rec. H7900 (daily ed. Aug. 26, 1980) (statement by Rep. Thompson, floor manager of MPPAA in the House). But see the post-enactment statement of Sen. Durenberger, one of the principal proponents of a special trucking-industry rule, to the effect that "substantially all" means anything over 50 percent. 126 Cong. Rec. S14725 (daily ed. Nov. 19, 1980).

industry.[38] Under this definition, withdrawal occurs only where the employer either permanently ceases to have an obligation to make contributions or permanently ceases all covered operations, does not continue to perform work within the jurisdiction of the plan, *and* either the PBGC determines that this cessation has caused substantial damage to the plan's contribution base, or the employer fails to post a bond or escrow in an amount equal to 50 percent of the employer's withdrawal liability.[39] If the PBGC determines within five years that the employer's cessation resulted in damage to the contribution base of the plan, the employer is treated as having withdrawn on the date his contribution obligation or operations ceased, and the bond or escrow is forfeited to the plan. However, the amount of liability is not limited to the bond or escrow.

The trucking industry rule is thus similar to the construction/entertainment rule in that it imposes liability on employers who, in effect, go non-union. The primary distinction is that, under the trucking industry rule, liability for employers who do not go non-union generally depends on whether, as determined by the PBGC, the plan has suffered substantial damage to its contribution base; this test does not exist in the construction/entertainment industry rule.

Extension of the construction entertainment rule. The PBGC is permitted under the new legislation to adopt regulations extending the special withdrawal rule applicable to the construction and entertainment industries to multiemployer pension plans in other industries.[40] The PBGC may extend this rule only to industries where the characteristics that would make the construction rule appropriate are clearly shown, and only where the PBGC determines there will be no significant risk to the PBGC because of its benefit guarantees.[41]

Special sale of assets rule. The sale of the assets of a corporation that had been contributing to a multiemployer pension plan will generally constitute a withdrawal, since the corporation will no longer have operations covered under the plan.[42] However, under certain conditions an employer may, in a bona fide, arm's-length transaction with an unrelated party, sell its assets without incurring withdrawal liability.[43] Generally stated, the conditions are

---

38 ERISA § 4203(d).

39 ERISA § 4203(d)(3).

40 ERISA § 4203(f)(1). See also 46 Fed. Reg. 53685 (Oct. 30, 1981).

41 ERISA § 4203(f)(2). See also Joint Explanation of the Senate Comms. of Labor and Human Resources and Finance, 126 Cong. Rec. S10116 (daily ed. July 29, 1980); Report of the House Comm. on Education and Labor, H.R. Rep. No. 96-869 Pt. I, 96th Cong., 2d Sess. 75-76 (1980); 126 Cong. Rec. H7900 (daily ed. Aug. 26, 1980) (remarks of Rep. Thompson, floor manager of MPPAA in the House).

42 Note that a sale of the company's stock rather than its assets will not, of itself, constitute a withdrawal.

43 ERISA § 4204.

as follows: First, the purchaser must be obligated to contribute to the plan for substantially the same number of contribution base units for which the seller was obligated to contribute. Second, the purchasing employer must post for five years a bond or escrow in an amount generally equal to the last year's contributions by the selling employer. Finally, the sale contract must provide that, in the event any withdrawal liability of the purchasing employer is not paid, the selling employer is secondarily liable for any withdrawal liability it would have had but for this section.[44] The PBGC has been given authority to vary, by regulation or exemption, the second and third of these conditions.[45]

If the above conditions are satisfied, and the selling employer is then liquidated or all or substantially all of its assets are distributed during this five-year period, the selling employer must post a bond or escrow in the amount of the withdrawal liability it would have absent the "sale of assets" provision.[46] The seller's bond or escrow is forfeited if the purchaser withdraws from the plan within five years after the sale of assets and does not pay its withdrawal liability at any time thereafter.[47]

"Free look" option. If certain conditions are satisfied, a multiemployer pension plan may be amended to permit employers to participate for as many as six consecutive plan years (but no more than the number of years required for vesting under the plan), and then to withdraw without liability.[48] The purpose of this option is to allow plans to attract new employers with a "free look" lasting as long as two collective bargaining cycles. The underlying rationale is that since participation for a period less than that required to earn a vested benefit is unlikely to generate significant liabilities in the plan,

---

[44] ERISA § 4204(a)(1). As of the date of this writing the PBGC has issued a procedural regulation in this area which describes the process of applying for an individual or class waiver or exemption. 46 Fed. Reg. 46127 (1981). However, regardless of whether the seller is exempted from the requirement in Section 4204(a)(1)(C) of ERISA that the contract of sale provide for secondary liability of the seller, the seller remains secondarily liable under Section 4204(a)(2) of ERISA. See note 47.

[45] ERISA § 4204(c).

[46] ERISA § 4204(a)(3)(A).

[47] ERISA § 4204(a)(2). The PBGC has taken the position that it does not have authority to waive this requirement for a seller's bond, or to waive the seller's secondary liability under Section 4204(a)(2) of ERISA. However, the PBGC has determined that a waiver would be appropriate under certain circumstances. On July 1, 1981, the PBGC issued a bulletin in which it interpreted Section 4224 of ERISA—which authorizes multiemployer plans to adopt plan rules providing for terms and conditions for the satisfaction of an employer's withdrawal liability—to permit plans to adopt a rule allowing for modification or waiver of the requirements of the seller's bond or escrow, and the contingent liability of the seller, in certain circumstances. For example, the PBGC noted that a waiver of the seller's bond or escrow might be appropriate if the requirement "would frustrate a transaction under which an ongoing, solvent purchaser would purchase the assets and assume the contribution requirement of a seller that is a Debtor under the Bankruptcy Code," or if "the purchaser's financial condition indicates that the seller's bond is not necessary to protect the plan."

[48] ERISA § 4210.

and since the employer will be making contributions throughout this entire period, the plan is unlikely to be harmed even if the employer does withdraw.

The conditions under which this option is available are as follows:

1. It is available only if the employer was first obligated to contribute to the plan after September 26, 1980.
2. It is not available to multiemployer pension plans that primarily cover employees in the construction industry.
3. The employer's required contributions for each year of participation must be less than 2 percent of all employer contributions made to the plan for such year.
4. An employer may use this option only once with respect to a given plan; that is, an employer is eligible for only one "free look" per plan.
5. The plan must have had, in the plan year preceding the employer's entry, a ratio of plan assets to benefit payments made of at least eight to one.
6. The plan must provide for the cutback in past-service credit permitted under Section 411(a)(3) of the Code.

Partial withdrawals. Although the discussion to this point has concerned only "complete" withdrawals, the new legislation also creates liability for certain "partial" withdrawals. Without such liability, employers could avoid withdrawal liability altogether by maintaining a token operation solely for that purpose. The partial withdrawal rules have been structured however, to avoid triggering liability when temporary fluctuations in employment, e.g., seasonal or industrywide declines, cause a drop in employer contributions or covered personnel. In general, a *partial* withdrawal occurs when there is either a severe shrinkage of an employer's contributions to the plan, a "bargaining unit withdrawal," or a "facility withdrawal." [49] The partial withdrawal rules are discussed in more detail below.

☐ *Severe shrinkage.* A partial withdrawal because of severe shrinkage—referred to technically as a "70 percent contribution decline"—occurs if, in any three consecutive plan years, the number of contribution base units for which the employer must contribute, i.e., covered hours, compensation or output, or whatever else, contributions are based on, is less than 30 percent of the number of contribution base units for the "high base year." [50] This latter number is computed as the average number of contribution base units for the two highest of the five years preceding the three-consecutive-year period.[51]

---

[49] ERISA § 4205(a).

[50] ERISA § 4205(b)(1).

[51] ERISA § 4205(b)(1)(B)(ii). To avoid the imposition of liability for withdrawals which began prior to the general effective date of MPPAA, all three years in the test period must commence after April 28, 1981, and reductions in contributions in plan years ending before April 29, 1980 are disregarded. MPPAA §§ 108(d)(1), 108(d)(3). See also ERISA § 4206(a)(1)(B).

☐ *Bargaining unit withdrawal.* A partial withdrawal because of a "bargaining unit withdrawal" occurs if an employer who is required to contribute to a multiemployer pension plan under two or more collective bargaining agreements ceases to have an obligation to contribute under at least one (but less than all) of the agreements, and either (1) continues to perform work in the jurisdiction of the collective bargaining agreement of the type for which contributions were previously required, or (2) transfers such work to another location. For example, an employer contributing, under two different collective bargaining agreements, to a single multiemployer pension plan for factories in New York and New Jersey would have a partial withdrawal if the New Jersey factory went non-union or if the work done at the New Jersey factory was transferred outside the jurisdiction of the plan.

☐ *Facility withdrawal.* A partial withdrawal because of a "facility withdrawal" occurs when an employer permanently ceases to participate with respect to work performed at one or more but fewer than all of its facilities, but continues to perform work at the facility of the type for which the obligation to contribute ceased.[52] In the example above this would occur if contributions to the plan on behalf of the New York and New Jersey factories were made under the same collective bargaining agreement, and the New Jersey factory went non-union.

A partial withdrawal does not occur solely because one collective bargaining agreement that requires contributions to a multiemployer pension plan has been substituted for another agreement which requires contributions to the same plan.[53] Also, special definitions of partial withdrawal may apply to multiemployer pension plans in the construction industry,[54] the entertainment industry,[55] the retail food industry,[56] the Great Lakes shipping industry,[57] and to the so-called "1950s Mineworkers plans" (as defined in Section 404(c) of the Code.[58]

Abatement of withdrawal liability. A renewal of or increase in an employer's contributions to a multiemployer pension plan may result in the reduction or waiver of liability for a prior withdrawal. In effect, the employer is forgiven to some extent, although it cannot recover past payments of withdrawal liability. The circumstances in which this may occur following a complete withdrawal are to be set forth in future PBGC regulations.[59]

---

52 ERISA § 4205(b)(2)(A)(ii).
53 ERISA § 4205(b)(2)(B).
54 ERISA § 4208(d)(1). See also 126 Cong. Rec. H7900-01 (daily ed. August 26, 1980) (remarks of Rep. Thompson, floor manager of MPPAA in the House).
55 ERISA § 4208(d)(2).
56 ERISA § 4205(c).
57 MPPAA § 108(c)(2). It is believed that this provision applies to only one employer.
58 ERISA § 4205(d).
59 ERISA § 4207.

There are, by contrast, detailed statutory provisions governing when an employer's partial withdrawal liability may be reduced in whole or in part. These rules only apply where partial liability arises from a "severe shrinkage," i.e., a 70 percent decline in the number of contribution base units.[60] In general, partial liability for a severe shrinkage may be reduced or waived if there is:

1. A two-year 90 percent restoration of the previous level of the employer's contribution base;
2. A restoration of the employer's contribution base to at least 30 percent of its high at a time when the plan's overall contribution base is at least 90 percent of the level in the partial withdrawal year; or
3. An increase of 10 percent or more in the employer's contribution base.

The PBGC may issue regulations governing other circumstances in which an employer's partial withdrawal liability may be abated, or regulations governing a plan's authority to adopt amendments eliminating partial withdrawal liability.[61]

Transactions to evade or avoid liability. If a principal purpose of any transaction is to evade or avoid withdrawal liability, withdrawal liability is to be determined and collected "without regard to such transaction."[62] This provision protects multiemployer pension plans against manipulation of the form of a transaction in order to avoid liability. For example, a contributing construction employer that "goes out of business" in a jurisdiction only to reappear immediately in the guise of a noncontributing alter ego could be held, under this provision, to have withdrawn from the plan. The legislative history suggests that the withdrawal liability provisions should be applied according to the substance and not the form of the transaction, and that liability should be imposed whenever "evasion of liability is a principal purpose of a transaction, whether or not the transaction has other purposes as well."[63]

Events that are not withdrawals. Provided the change causes no interruption in employer contributions or in the obligation to contribute, an employer does not "withdraw" from a multiemployer pension plan solely because of

---

[60] The Joint Explanation of the Senate Comms. of Labor and Human Resources and Finance states that if a partial withdrawal arises because of both a severe shrinkage and another type of partial withdrawal, the abatement rules nevertheless apply. 126 Cong. Rec. S10116 (daily ed. July 29, 1980). The abatement of partial withdrawal liability rules do not apply to a retail food industry plan which has adopted the modified definition of partial withdrawal in ERISA § 4205(c).

[61] ERISA § 4208(e).

[62] ERISA § 4212(c).

[63] 126 Cong. Rec. H7898 (daily ed. Aug. 26, 1980) (remarks of Rep. Thompson, floor manager of MPPAA in the House).

a change in business form. Thus, a withdrawal does not occur solely because the employer ceases to exist by reason of:

1. A corporate reorganization involving a mere change in identity, form, or place of organization;
2. A liquidation into a parent corporation;
3. A merger, consolidation, or division; or
4. A change to an unincorporated form of business enterprise.[64]

In these situations the resulting entity is considered the original employer.

A withdrawal also does not occur if the employer suspends contributions during a labor dispute involving its employees.[65] However, the legislative history states that if subsequent events "indicate that contributions have ceased permanently—for example, all employees covered under the plan have been permanently replaced or the facility has been closed—the fact that the cessation of any contribution obligation was preceded by a labor dispute does not mean that no withdrawal has taken place." [66]

Computation of Withdrawal Liability. The plan sponsor of a multiemployer pension plan is required to calculate and send notice of withdrawal liability to any employer who withdraws from the plan.[67]

Initial calculation complete withdrawal. The first step in the calculation of withdrawal liability is to calculate the employer's "share" [68] of the plan's unfunded vested benefits.[69] A plan's unfunded vested benefits are equal to the excess of the value of all nonforfeitable benefits accrued by participants over the value of plan assets.

The statute provides for alternatives that plans may choose in allocating liability, but all methods have at least one feature in common. Each attempts to allocate all or nearly all of the plan's unfunded, nonforfeitable liabilities to employers currently participating in the plan. Thus, a withdrawal of all employers should theoretically result in aggregate withdrawal liability approximately equal to the plan's total unfunded vested liabilities.

---

[64] ERISA §§ 4062(d), 4218(1).

[65] ERISA § 4218(2).

[66] 126 Cong. Rec. H7898 (daily ed. Aug. 26, 1980) (remarks of Rep. Thompson, floor manager of MPPAA in the House).

[67] ERISA §§ 4202, 4219(b)(1).

[68] Since most plans have liabilities attributable to employers no longer participating in the plan, and since the withdrawal liability provisions are meant to allocate all the plan's unfunded vested benefits, each employer's share will usually include liabilities that are not attributable to its participation in the plan.

[69] As discussed within, employers are not generally required to pay this withdrawal liability in a lump sum. Rather, annual payments, calculated not by reference to total liability but rather by reference to the employer's historic contribution levels, must be made for the number of years (but not more than twenty) required to amortize the total liability.

Section 4211 of ERISA sets forth four alternative methods of determining an employer's share of unfunded vested benefits. Plans must choose one method for all employers. These methods are generally referred to as the

- Attributable method
- Rolling-5 method
- Modified presumptive method
- Presumptive method

Plans may, subject to PBGC approval, adopt allocation methods of their own creation. They may also make certain modifications to the four statutory methods without PBGC approval. Plans which do not adopt a particular method of allocation are required to use the presumptive method, except for the so-called "1950s Mineworkers plans." [70]

The actual mechanics of the four methods of computing withdrawal liability are extremely complicated. The effect of each method, however, is as follows.

☐ *Attributable method.* Under the "attributable" method, each employer is allocated the unfunded liabilities attributable to its participation in the plan plus a share of the unfunded, "unattributable" liabilities, i.e., those attributable to the participation of employers no longer connected with the plan.

☐ *Rolling-5 method.* Under the rolling-5 method, all the unfunded liabilities of the plan are allocated in proportion to contributions made by current employers during the five years preceding withdrawal.

☐ *Modified presumptive method.* Under the "modified presumptive" method, the plan's unfunded liabilities at the time the new legislation was enacted are allocated in proportion to the contributions the employers then made in the plan during the preceding five years. Any additional unfunded liabilities are allocated in proportion to current employers' contributions in the five years preceding withdrawal.

☐ *Presumptive method.* Under the "presumptive" method, which applies in the absence of an election by the plan to use a different method, unfunded liabilities at the time the new legislation was enacted are allocated as under the "modified presumptive" method. Any additional unfunded liabilities, however, are allocated, year by year, in proportion to employer contributions in the five years preceding the year in which the unfunding was deemed to accrue.

Plans may, by amendment, adopt any other method for determining withdrawal liability, subject to PBGC approval.[71] Before approving such a

---

[70] ERISA §§ 4211(b)(1), 4211(d)(1).

[71] ERISA § 4211(c)(5)(A). A construction industry plan must use the presumptive rule with respect to employers in the construction industry. ERISA § 4211(c)(1).

method the PBGC must determine that adoption of the method "would not significantly increase the risk of loss to plan participants and beneficiaries," or to the PBGC. Any such alternative method must provide for the allocation of substantially all of the plan's unfunded, vested liabilities among all employers who have an obligation to contribute to the plan.[72]

The PBGC has also set forth standard modifications to the four statutory methods which may be adopted without PBGC approval prior to May 1, 1983. These modifications recognize that some plans may lack adequate records to perform the computations necessary under the statutory methods, and are designed to ease administrative burdens.[73]

Initial calculation—partial withdrawals. Partial withdrawal liability is determined as a prorated share of the liability the employer would have had for a complete withdrawal.[74] The complete withdrawal liability is calculated as of the date of the facility or bargaining unit withdrawal, or, in the case of a partial withdrawal through severe shrinkage, as of the end of the first of the three consecutive plan years during which that shrinkage is measured.[75] The prorated share is determined by multiplying the complete withdrawal liability by a fraction, the numerator of which is the number of contribution base units by which the total of the employer's contribution base units has declined (measured as of the plan year following the year in which the partial withdrawal occurred). The denominator of this fraction is the average of the employer's contribution base units in the five preceding plan years (in the case of a severe shrinkage, the five years preceding the three consecutive years exhibiting the decline).[76]

ERISA also provides that the amount of any partial withdrawal liability in any plan year shall be applied as a credit against liability for a partial or complete withdrawal in a subsequent year.[77] The PBGC has regulation authority to provide for appropriate adjustments in this credit.[78]

Reduction of liability for transfer of plan liabilities. After the initial calculation of withdrawal liability, a variety of adjustments may be required. One circumstance requiring an adjustment to withdrawal liability is the transfer of liabilities, incident to an employer's withdrawal, to another plan. In this situation the employer's withdrawal liability is reduced by the value of the plan liabilities so transferred.[79]

In general, a plan need not consent to transfer liabilities to another plan, thus reducing the employer's withdrawal liability. However, a special rule

---

[72] ERISA § 4211(c)(5)(B); PBGC Interim Reg. § 262.164.
[73] See 46 Fed. Reg. 4894 (1981).
[74] ERISA § 4206(a).
[75] ERISA § 4206(a)(1).
[76] ERISA § 4206(a)(2).
[77] ERISA § 4206(b)(1).
[78] ERISA § 4206(b)(2).
[79] ERISA § 4211(e).

exists where an employer has withdrawn as a result of a change of collective bargaining representative occurring after April 28, 1980, pursuant to which participants of the old plan have or will become participants of a new multiemployer pension plan. In such cases the withdrawing employer can generally compel the transfer of assets and liabilities to the new plan, and the new plan must generally accept the transfer.

This provision is intended to protect employers. A change in bargaining agent generally occurs as a result of one union organizing employees that had previously been represented by another union. Representation decisions belong, in theory at least, totally to the employees, and the employer may in fact have little or no influence in this decision. If the new collective bargaining agreement requires the employer to make contributions only to a plan associated with the new union, the employer will thereby withdraw from the old plan.

In order to avoid imposing two separate but continuing liabilities on the employer, ERISA provides for a transfer of assets and liabilities:

- *Liabilities.* The liabilities transferred are the vested benefits of the employees who, as a result of the change in bargaining representative, are no longer working in service covered by the old plan.
- *Assets.* The amount of assets transferred, if any, is equal to the excess of the liabilities transferred over the employer's withdrawal liability to the old plan, computed without regard to the transfer of assets and liabilities.

If the liabilities transferred are less than the employer's withdrawal liability, no assets are transferred, and the employer has withdrawal liability to the old plan offset by the amount of liabilities transferred.[80]

To prevent an employer who withdraws from the new plan shortly thereafter from escaping withdrawal liability altogether, the employer's withdrawal liability to the new plan is calculated as the greater of (1) what it would otherwise be under the new plan, and (2) the amount of withdrawal liability to the old plan that was offset by the transfer, reduced by 5 percent for every year following the transfer.[81]

Special rules for withdrawal following plan mergers. If a withdrawal occurs in the first plan year following a merger of multiemployer pension plans, liability is computed as if each plan had remained a separate plan. In other cases in which a withdrawal follows a merger of multiemployer pension plans the amount of withdrawal liability is to be computed pursuant to

---

80 ERISA §§ 4211(e), 4235(c).

81 ERISA § 4235(f)(2). Because the withdrawal liability computations are based in large part on the proportion of the plan's total contributions made by the withdrawing employer during the preceding five years, the employer's immediate withdrawal from the new plan, to which it would then have made little or no contribution, might otherwise result in a loophole for avoiding withdrawal liability altogether.

PBGC regulations, which as of the date of this writing have not yet been finalized.[82]

De minimis reduction. Certain amounts of withdrawal liability are considered "de minimis" and are excused.[83] Unless a plan is amended to provide for a higher amount, this includes amounts of $50,000 or less. In order to prevent a "cliff," where a liability of $50,000 would be totally forgiven but a liability of $50,001 would not be excused at all, the statute provides that the $50,000 de minimis amount is a vanishing deductible. That is, $50,000 is subtracted from any withdrawal liability which does not exceed $100,000. For each dollar that the liability exceeds $100,000, the de minimis deductible is reduced one dollar. Thus, at $150,000 the deductible is completely phased out.

A plan may be amended to increase the de minimis deductible up to $100,000. If a plan is so amended, the deductible begins to "vanish" for liability in excess of $150,000. However, for any multiemployer pension plan, whether amended or not, the de minimis deductible may not exceed three-fourths of one percent of the plan's unfunded vested benefits.

The de minimis deductible is not applicable in certain situations where substantially all employers withdraw from the plan, or if the employer withdraws pursuant to an arrangement or agreement to withdraw among substantially all of the plan's employers.[84]

Other limitations on withdrawal liability. There are limitations on withdrawal liability with respect to an employer that sells substantially all of its assets, or an insolvent employer undergoing liquidation. Certain assets of the employer may be exempt from withdrawal liability.

☐ *Sale of substantially all assets.* In the case of a bona fide sale of all or substantially all of the employer's assets in an arm's-length transaction with an unrelated party, withdrawal liability may not exceed a portion of the liquidation or dissolution value of the employer (determined without regard to any withdrawal liability) after such sale.[85] The portion, which depends on the amount of such liquidation or dissolution value, is 30 percent for liquidation values of $2 million or less, and approaches 80 percent for higher values.

☐ *Insolvency.* Where an insolvent employer [86] is undergoing liquidation or dissolution, withdrawal liability is limited to 50 percent of what it would

---

[82] ERISA § 4211(f).

[83] ERISA § 4209.

[84] ERISA §§ 4209(c), 4209(d).

[85] ERISA § 4225(a).

[86] An employer is insolvent for these purposes if its liabilities exclusive of withdrawal liability exceed its assets (determined as of the commencement of the liquidation or dissolution). ERISA § 4225(d)(1).

otherwise be, plus any remainder of the liability that can be recouped from the liquidation or dissolution value of the employer.[87] In effect, this provision gives half the withdrawal liability a bankruptcy priority on a par with general creditors, and half a priority below that of general creditors. In the common situation where an insolvent employer's liabilities exceed its liquidation or dissolution value, a multiemployer pension plan will be forced to write off at least half the amount it might otherwise hope to collect.

☐ *Employers who are individuals.* Certain relief is provided to employers who are individuals, i.e., sole proprietors or partners. In these cases the employer's personal assets that would be exempt under bankruptcy law are shielded from withdrawal liability.[88]

Application of plan amendments. To elect some of the options offered to plans by MPPAA, e.g., one of the alternative withdrawal liability computation methods, plan amendment is required. Also, plans are permitted to adopt, by amendment, alternative rules governing the satisfaction of an employer's withdrawal liability, if those rules are consistent with MPPAA and the PBGC's regulations.[89] However, plan rules or amendments adopted after January 31, 1981 may not be applied to determine the withdrawal liability of any employer who withdraws before the date on which the rule or amendment was adopted, unless the employer consents.[90] All plan rules and amendments relating to withdrawal liability must be applied uniformly, except that the creditworthiness of particular employers may be taken into account. Notice of plan amendments must be given to all participating employers and employee organizations.[91]

Most plan amendments relating to withdrawal liability adopted after September 26, 1983 do not become effective unless the PBGC either approves the amendment or fails to disapprove the amendment within ninety days after receiving notice of such amendment.[92] The PBGC is directed to disapprove such an amendment only if it determines that the amendment creates an unreasonable risk of loss either to plan participants and beneficiaries or to the PBGC.

The Collection of Withdrawal Liability.

Procedures for collection and disputes. The initial procedures for the collection of withdrawal liability are set forth in Section 4219 of ERISA.

---

[87] ERISA § 4225(b).
[88] ERISA § 4225(c).
[89] ERISA §§ 4219(c)(7), 4224.
[90] ERISA § 4214(a).
[91] ERISA § 4214(b).
[92] ERISA § 4220. This provision applies to amendments authorized by Sections 4201 through 4219 of ERISA except for amendments permitted by ERISA § 4211(c)(5) (alternative allocation methods requiring PBGC approval), and therefore includes most amendments relating to the calculation or collection of withdrawal liability.

☐ *Notification and demand for payment.* "As soon as practicable" after an employer's complete or partial withdrawal, the plan's sponsor must notify the employer of the amount of the liability and the schedule for payment, and demand payment in accordance with the schedule.[93] The plan's sponsor is not given any discretion in this matter; theoretically, failure to notify the employer may even be punishable by fines.[94] If necessary to enable the plan to compute withdrawal liability, the plan sponsor may request information from the employer and the employer must furnish such information within thirty days after receiving a written request.[95] An employer, regardless of whether it has withdrawn, may at any time request from the plan *general* information, i.e., information not unique to that employer, relating to existing or potential withdrawal liability.[96]

☐ *Informal review.* After receiving the notice and demand of withdrawal liability, an employer may seek informal review by the plan. The employer has ninety days to ask the plan sponsor to review any matter related to the determination of withdrawal liability and the schedule of payments, to identify inaccuracies in the calculations, and to furnish additional relevant information. After a "reasonable review" of any matter raised, the plan sponsor must notify the employer of its decision, and the basis for that decision.

☐ *Arbitration.* If the parties are unable to agree at this point, the next step is intended to be arbitration.[97] Either party acting alone may initiate arbitration within a sixty-day period after the earlier of (1) the plan's notification to the employer of its determination as to an employer-requested review, or (2) 120 days after the date of the employer's request for review. The parties may jointly initiate arbitration within a 180-day period commencing with the plan's initial demand for payment.

Arbitration proceedings are to be conducted "in accordance with fair and equitable procedures to be promulgated" by the PBGC. The PBGC has not yet suggested any such procedures, but has announced that it will do so shortly.[98]

☐ *Collection action.* If no arbitration proceeding is initiated within the time periods previously noted, the plan's sponsor may bring a collection

---

93 ERISA § 4219(b)(1).

94 Cf. ERISA § 4302.

95 ERISA § 4219(a).

96 ERISA § 4221(e).

97 Interestingly, MPPAA specifies arbitration only to resolve disputes concerning determinations under Sections 4201 through 4219 of ERISA. ERISA § 4221(a)(1). Thus, for example, there appears to be no mandate for arbitration of disputes surrounding the sale of assets and insolvency limitations of Section 4225 of ERISA.

98 46 Fed. Reg. 53693 (1981). The statute itself provides that, to the extent consistent with Title IV of ERISA, arbitrations are to be conducted in the same manner as provided in Title 9 of the U.S. Code. ERISA § 4221(b)(3).

action in state or federal court.[99] The statute and the relevant legislative history suggest that arbitration is compulsory,[100] but it is not yet clear that a court would preclude an employer that has not participated in arbitration from raising a substantive defense in any such collection action.

A legal action relating to withdrawal liability may be brought in the U.S. district court in the district where the plan is administered or where a defendant resides or does business. A fiduciary of a multiemployer pension plan is also permitted to bring an action to collect withdrawal liability in any state court of competent jurisdiction.[101]

In any action brought by a multiemployer pension plan to compel an employer to pay withdrawal liability, any failure of the employer to make any withdrawal liability payment when due is treated in the same manner as a deliniquent contribution within the meaning of Section 515 of ERISA.[102] The primary significance of this provision is that, if the plan prevails, it is entitled to

1. The unpaid withdrawal liability,
2. Interest on the unpaid withdrawal liability,
3. An amount equal to the greater of (a) interest on the unpaid withdrawal liability or (b) liquidated damages as determined under the plan (but not to exceed 20 percent unless permitted under federal or state law),
4. Reasonable attorney's fees and costs, and
5. Such other legal or equitable relief as the court deems proper.[103]

The legislative history of the new legislation suggests that a multiemployer plan is permitted to enter into a settlement with an employer to resolve disputed withdrawal liability.[104]

Presumptions. Any determination made by a plan sponsor under ERISA Sections 4201 through 4219 or under ERISA Section 4225—virtually all determinations relating to the calculation and assessment of withdrawal liability—"is presumed correct unless the party contesting the determination shows by a preponderance of the evidence that the determination was unreasonable or clearly erroneous." [105] The actuarial computation of unfunded

---

99 ERISA § 4221(b)(1).

100 See, e.g., Joint Explanation of the Senate Comms. of Labor and Human Resources and Finance, 126 Cong. Rec. S10120 (daily ed. July 29, 1980).

101 ERISA § 4301(c).

102 ERISA § 4301(b).

103 ERISA § 502(d). Actions brought pursuant to Section 515 of ERISA may have to be commenced in federal district court. ERISA § 502(e)(1). Thus, liquidated damages may not be available for collection actions in state court.

104 Joint Explanation of the Senate Comms. of Labor and Human Resources and Finance, 126 Cong. Rec. S10119 (daily ed. July 29, 1980); 126 Cong. Rec. S11673 (daily ed. Aug. 26, 1980) (remarks of Sen. Williams, floor manager of MPPAA in the Senate).

105 ERISA § 4221(a)(3)(A).

vested benefits for a given plan year is specifically presumed correct unless it is shown by a preponderance of the evidence that (1) the actuarial assumptions and methods used were, in the aggregate, unreasonable, or (2) the plan's actuary made a "significant error" in applying those assumptions and methods.[106] Finally, if an arbitrator's decision is appealed, "there shall be a presumption, rebuttable only by a clear preponderance of the evidence, that the findings of fact made by the arbitrator were correct." [107]

Controlled-group definition of employer. Section 4001(b)(1) of ERISA provides that all trades or businesses (whether or not incorporated) that are under common control shall be treated as a single employer. Thus, if one member of a controlled group withdraws from a multiemployer pension plan, all members of the group will be responsible for any liability.[108] By the same token, however, no complete withdrawal is deemed to occur if any member of the controlled group continues to have both a contribution obligation and operations covered under the plan.

Payment. The statute requires that payments of withdrawal liability begin no later than sixty days after the plan sponsor's initial demand for payment.[109] An employer may prepay the outstanding withdrawal liability at any time in whole or in part without penalty.[110]

If liability is not prepaid, the required annual payment is determined by reference not to the total liability, but rather to the employer's previous contributions. Generally, the annual payment is equal to the annual average contribution base units for the three highest plan years in the ten years ending with the year of withdrawal, multiplied by the employer's highest contribution rate during the same period.[111] Annual payments are payable in four equal quarterly installments, or at other intervals specified by plan rules.[112]

After the annual payment is determined, the period over which payments must be made is calculated as the number of years necessary, using assumptions from the plan's most recent actuarial valuation, to amortize the total withdrawal liability.[113] If this period exceeds twenty years, the employer's liability is usually limited to the first twenty annual payments.[114] This "twenty-year cap" does not apply if there is a "mass withdrawal," which

---

106 ERISA § 4221(a)(3)(B).

107 ERISA § 4221(c).

108 PBGC v. Ouimet Corp., 470 F. Supp. 945 (D. Mass. 1979), *aff'd*, 630 F.2d 4 (1st Cir. 1980), *cert. denied* 450 U.S. 914 (1981). See also 126 Cong. Rec. S11672 (daily ed. Aug. 26, 1980) (remarks of Sen. Williams, floor manager of MPPAA in the Senate).

109 ERISA § 4219(c)(2).

110 ERISA § 4219(c)(4).

111 ERISA § 4219(c)(1)(C).

112 ERISA § 4219(c)(3).

113 ERISA § 4219(c)(1)(A).

114 ERISA § 4219(c)(1)(B).

occurs when all employers withdraw from the plan, or substantially all the employers withdraw pursuant to an agreement or arrangement to withdraw.

The annual payment for a partial withdrawal is calculated as described above and prorated to take account of the fact that the withdrawal was only partial.[115] Interest accrues, at prevailing market rates, on delinquent payments.[116]

Plans may adopt rules for other terms and conditions for satisfaction of liability if they are consistent with MPPAA and PBGC regulations.[117]

Acceleration of withdrawal liability. One of the most interesting and significant questions posed by MPPAA is under what circumstances a plan may accelerate an employer's withdrawal liability, so as to demand payment of, and, if necessary, bring suit for the entire amount of liability. Acceleration is permitted under Section 4219(c)(5) of ERISA if a "default" occurs. Default is defined as either an employer's failure to make a payment of withdrawal liability within sixty days after being notified that such payment is overdue, or any other event defined in plan rules "which indicates a substantial likelihood that the employer will be unable to pay its withdrawal liability."

Inasmuch as default, and the consequent acceleration of liability, is likely to be a powerful collection weapon which plans will generally strive to utilize, and which employers will generally seek to avoid, its precise definition and application are likely to be the subject of future litigation. As discussed below, the statute contains some ambiguities in this regard.

There is no language in the statute itself that would preclude acceleration during the dispute resolution process. However, the Joint Explanation of the Senate Labor and Finance Committees twice specifically states that withdrawal liability may not be accelerated because of a default occurring while an employer is challenging a plan's determination of withdrawal liability.[118]

The only guidance as to which events might properly be considered to indicate a substantial likelihood that the employer will be unable to pay is set forth in a Committee Print prepared by the Senate Committee on Labor and Human Resources, which states that a plan's definition should be "commercially reasonable." [119]

---

[115] ERISA § 4219(c)(1)(E).

[116] ERISA §§ 4219(c)(3), 4219(c)(6).

[117] ERISA §§ 4219(c)(7), 4224.

[118] 126 Cong. Rec. S10119, S10120 (daily ed. July 29, 1980). An earlier report of the Senate Comm. on Labor and Human Resources stated that the default provision was intended to apply to partial, complete, and interim withdrawal liability. S.1076—Senate Comm. on Labor and Human Resources, *The Multiemployer Pension Plan Amendments Act of 1980: Summary and Analysis of Consideration,* 96th Cong., 2d Sess. 21 (Comm. Print 1980).

[119] S.1076—Senate Comm. on Labor and Human Resources, *The Multiemployer Pension Plan Amendments Act of 1980: Summary and Analysis of Consideration,* 96th Cong., 2d Sess. 21 (Comm. Print 1980).

Insurance against uncollectible withdrawal liability. Multiemployer pension plans may be unable to collect certain amounts of withdrawal liability because of rules such as the de minimis provision, the twenty-year cap, or because the amounts are simply uncollectible. Moreover, plans may wish to establish a mechanism for insuring, in effect, advance funding of, the "unattributable" portion of an employer's withdrawal liability.[120]

☐ *Self insurance: supertrusts.* Plans may insure themselves with respect to these items by establishing and participating in "withdrawal liability payment funds," known as "supertrusts." [121] Supertrusts are voluntary funds that are established by plan sponsors, are tax exempt under a newly established section of the Code,[122] are funded by premiums paid by plans, and are administered by a board of trustees on which employers and employees are equally represented.

☐ *PBGC supplemental insurance.* MPPAA also requires the PBGC to establish, by May 1, 1982, a voluntary program to reimburse multiemployer pension plans for withdrawal liability payments which are uncollectible because of bankruptcy or similar proceedings involving an employer. However, because of budget problems, it is unlikely that the PBGC will meet this deadline. Plans electing PBGC supplemental insurance will pay additional premiums to the PBGC. Congress intended that PBGC regulations governing both such supplemental payment funds and supertrusts would not "be designed for the purpose of providing either of the arrangements a competitive advantage over the other.[123]

Pension Benefit Guaranty Corporation Guaranteed Benefits

The PBGC guarantees a portion of the pension benefit of participants in defined benefit multiemployer pension plans.[124] The portion guaranteed is referred to as the participant's basic benefit.[125] In most cases it is equal to 100 percent of the first $5 of monthly benefits per year of service plus 75 percent of the next $15 of monthly benefit per year of service. Benefits in excess of $20 per year of service are generally not guaranteed.[126] Thus, a

---

[120] Although supertrusts may also pay the attributable portion of such liability, the supertrust must be subrogated to the plan's claim therefor.

[121] ERISA § 4223.

[122] I.R.C. § 501(c)(22).

[123] Joint Explanation of the Senate Comms. of Labor and Human Resources and Finance, 126 Cong. Rec. S10120 (daily ed. July 29, 1980).

[124] For a discussion of the difference between a defined benefit and defined contribution plan, see Connally v. PBGC, 581 F.2d 729 (9th Cir. 1978), *cert. denied* 440 U.S. 935 (1979).

[125] ERISA § 4001(a)(6).

[126] A special transition rule provides that for persons receiving benefits as of July 29, 1980 and for persons with vested benefits who are, as of July 29, 1980, within three years of retirement, benefits in effect on that date are guaranteed to the same extent as single-employer plan benefits, i.e., generally 100 percent. ERISA § 4022A(h).

participant who had accrued \$25 of monthly benefit for each of thirty years of service (for a total accrued benefit of \$750 per month) would have a guaranteed benefit of \$487.50 per month, calculated as $(\$5 \times 30) + (\$15 \times 30 \times .75) = \$487.50$.

A benefit is not guaranteed unless it has been in effect for five years. Also, if the plan did not meet certain pre-ERISA funding rules, the 75 percent guarantee for benefits between \$5 and \$20 per month is reduced to 65 percent.

Pension Benefit Guaranty Corporation Insurance Premiums

To support its multiemployer activities and to provide funds for financial assistance, the PBGC collects premiums from multiemployer pension plans. The present premium is \$1.40 per participant per year. Current law provides that this figure will be increased in steps to \$2.60 per participant per year for plan years beginning after September 26, 1988. The PBGC may accelerate the increases up to that level if necessary to provide assistance to plans, or if the assets of the PBGC's multiemployer guarantee funds are not equal to at least twice the amount of financial assistance paid by the PBGC in the preceding year.[127]

Reorganization

The reorganization provisions are designed to identify plans in financial trouble so that additional funding may be provided, and, within specific permitted limits, accrued benefits may be reduced. A multiemployer pension plan is automatically deemed to be "in reorganization" if the annual amount required to amortize vested benefits in pay status over ten years and all other vested benefits over twenty-five years exceeds the minimum annual funding required by the general funding rules of ERISA. This test tends to identify plans where either the percentage of the plan's total accrued benefits that are nonforfeitable is high or the ratio of retirees to active workers is high. A plan in reorganization must so notify participating employers and unions.

Reduction of Benefits. Notwithstanding the general ERISA prohibition on retroactive reduction of accrued benefits, a plan in reorganization may eliminate accrued benefits attributable to a benefit increase adopted after March 26, 1980 that has not been in effect for five years.[128] A plan must notify participants before making such a reduction.

Increasing Employer Contributions. Plans in reorganization must also attack their problems by increasing employer contributions to comply with

---

127 ERISA § 4006; PBGC Reg. § 2610.
128 ERISA § 4244A(a)(1).

special funding rules. Amounts contributed to such plans must satisfy the "minimum contribution requirement," which generally results in a higher rate of employer contributions. However, the reorganization provisions themselves will generally not require a contributions increase of more than 7 percent over the level required in the preceding year.[129]

Overburden Credit. A special provision is designed to mitigate the funding burden of employers in certain situations, such as those in so-called "declining industries," where technological or other innovation has produced a long-term decline in the number of people working in employment covered by industry plans.[130] If a plan in reorganization has more pensioners than active employees, an "overburden credit" is permitted. For such plans the funding requirement is reduced by the excess of pensioners over active participants, multiplied by one half of the average guaranteed benefit paid by the plan.

Termination

The Multiemployer Act made important changes in both the definition of termination and the consequences resulting from termination. Previously, a plan could terminate solely by decision of the trustees. Further, termination triggered both the PBGC guarantee of benefits and the contingent liability of participating employers.

As discussed above, employer liability is no longer dependent on plan termination, and it is now plan insolvency, and not plan termination, which triggers the PBGC benefit guarantees. Further, the entire concept of plan termination has been fundamentally altered. "Terminated" multiemployer plans are "frozen" rather than liquidated; the plans stay in existence to pay benefits as due, and, unless fully funded, to collect the contributions (or withdrawal liability payments) for which employers remain liable.

Definition and Date of Termination. Under Section 4041A of ERISA, a multiemployer plan terminates upon the happening of any of three events:

1. The withdrawal of every employer from the plan, or the cessation of the obligation of all employers to contribute under the plan;[131]
2. Adoption of an amendment providing that no further plan credit of any type is to accrue for continued service with participating employers; or
3. Adoption of an amendment causing the plan to become an individual account plan.[132]

---

[129] ERISA § 4243(d)(1)(A).

[130] ERISA § 4244.

[131] ERISA § 4041A(a). Because of the special definitions of withdrawal for the construction, entertainment, and trucking industries, all employers may cease to contribute to the plan even though no employer has technically withdrawn.

[132] The PBGC may also institute proceedings to terminate any pension plan whenever it determines either (1) the plan has not met certain minimum funding standards,

A plan that terminates by mass withdrawal or the cessation of all contribution obligations is deemed to terminate on the earlier of (1) the date on which the last employer withdraws, or (2) the first day of the first plan year for which no contributions are required[133] A plan that terminates by amendment (either to "freeze" the plan or to convert it to an individual account plan) is deemed to terminate on the date on which the amendment is adopted, or, if later, the date on which it is effective.[134]

Effect of Termination. In plans terminated other than by a mass withdrawal or cessation of all contribution obligations, employers must continue making contributions until the PBGC finds that the plan is or soon will be fully funded.[135] Such contributions are generally to be at a rate at least as great as the highest rate at which the employer was obligated during the five years preceding plan termination, although the PBGC may approve a reduction in rate for plans that will soon be fully funded.

A plan terminated by a mass withdrawal or cessation of all contribution obligations, for which the value of plan assets is less than the value of vested benefits, is required to pay only benefits vested as of the date of plan termination, and may be required to reduce benefits. Benefits are to be reduced to the extent necessary to ensure that the plan's assets are sufficient, but may not be reduced below the level of basic benefits guaranteed by the PBGC. If the plan becomes insolvent it may apply to the PBGC for financial assistance.[136] Unless assets are distributed in full satisfaction of all vested benefits, benefits attributable to employer contributions (other than death benefits) must generally be paid in the form of an annuity.[137]

Insolvency

Insolvency and not plan termination is now the insurable event triggering the PBGC guarantee. A multiemployer plan is "insolvent" in a plan year if its available resources are not sufficient to pay full benefits under the plan.[138]

Reduction of Benefits. An insolvent multiemployer pension plan is required to reduce benefits to the highest level which may be paid out of the plan's available resources. However, benefits may not be reduced below

---

(2) the plan is not able to pay benefits when due, (3) a plan which has unfunded vested benefits makes a large payment to a substantial owner, or (4) the risk of loss to the PBGC may be expected to "increase unreasonably" if the plan is not terminated. ERISA § 4042(a).

133 ERISA § 4041A(b)(2).

134 ERISA § 4041A(b)(1).

135 ERISA § 4041A(e).

136 ERISA §§ 4281(d), 4261(a).

137 ERISA § 4041A(c)(2).

138 ERISA § 4245(b). A similar definition of insolvency for terminated plans is contained in ERISA § 4281(d)(2).

the level of "basic benefits," which are the level of benefits guaranteed by the PBGC. If the PBGC has developed a procedure which guarantees a higher level of benefits than the "basic benefits," the insolvent plan must reduce benefits only to such higher level.[139]

Funding Relief. There is also funding relief for employers contributing to an insolvent plan. Once a plan in reorganization becomes insolvent, employers are protected against a further decline in the number of base units for which contributions are made to the plan. In effect, the plan is allowed to use the number of base units just before it became insolvent to calculate the required contribution rate.[140]

Financial Assistance. Insolvent plans remain in existence, and must apply to the PBGC for financial assistance. If the PBGC verifies that the plan is or will be unable to pay basic benefits when due, the PBGC must provide assistance to enable the plan to provide basic benefits. PBGC financial assistance is legally a loan to the plan, which the plan is theoretically obligated to repay.[141]

Partition

A bankrupt employer may threaten the solvency of a multiemployer pension plan. However, such a plan might be financially sound if it could disregard this employer and its employees. In this situation the PBGC may partition the plan, and transfer the vested benefits directly attributable to service with that employer, and an equitable share of assets, to a newly created plan.[142] The newly created plan is eligible for the benefit guaranties of the PBGC, and is treated as a terminated multiemployer plan to which the bankrupt employer has withdrawal liability. The joint statement of the Senate Labor and Finance Committees states that partition should be ordered only when "it is very clear that the failure to partition will result in the insolvency of the multiemployer plan." [143]

MERGERS AND TRANSFERS

The limitations on plan mergers and transfers set forth in Section 208 of ERISA as originally passed were specifically inapplicable to multiemployer plans. The new legislation added provisions governing mergers and transfers between multiemployer pension plans, and mergers and transfers between a

---

[139] ERISA §§ 4245(a), 4022A(g)(5).
[140] ERISA §§ 4243(b)(2), 4243(c)(2)(B).
[141] ERISA § 4261(b)(2).
[142] ERISA § 4233.
[143] 126 Cong. Rec. S10121 (daily ed. July 29, 1980).

multiemployer pension plan and a single-employer pension plan. These provisions are intended to protect plan participants and the PBGC.

Four requirements must be satisfied before a multiemployer pension plan can merge with, or transfer assets or liabilities to, another multiemployer pension plan.

1. The plan sponsor must notify the PBGC of the merger or transfer at least 120 days before the effective date of the transfer.
2. No participant's or beneficiary's accrued benefit may be reduced by the transfer.
3. The benefits of participant and benefieciaries must not be reasonably expected to be suspended because of a plan insolvency.
4. Each plan involved in the merger or transfer must have had a recent actuarial valuation of its assets and liabilities.[144]

Where the PBGC determines that these conditions are satisfied, the merger or transfer will not violate the prohibited transaction rules.

Mergers and transfers between a multiemployer pension plan and a single-employer pension plan must satisfy the requirement that no participant's or beneficiary's accrued benefit may be reduced as a result of the merger or transfer.[145] Under certain circumstances a multiemployer pension plan which transfers liabilities to a single-employer pension plan may be liable to the PBGC if the single-employer plan terminates within five years of the transfer.[146]

Transfers of assets from a multiemployer plan to another plan must be in accordance with plan rules and Section 4234 of ERISA. However, Section 4234 does not apply to transfers pursuant to written reciprocity agreements.[147]

MULTIEMPLOYER WELFARE PLANS

Section 501(c)(9) of the Code creates an exemption from income tax for qualified voluntary employees' beneficiary associations providing life, sick, accident, and other benefits. Generally, the tax status of multiemployer plans providing nonpension benefits is governed by this provision of the Code. Plans of this type, often referred to as "welfare plans," are generally taxed in the same manner and subject to the same restrictions regardless of whether the plan is a multiemployer plan or a single-employer plan.[148]

---

144 ERISA § 4231(b).
145 ERISA § 4232(b).
146 ERISA § 4232(c).
147 ERISA § 4234(c).
148 See Chapters 18 and 20.

Internal Revenue Service Restrictions on Membership

The IRS' recent regulations governing welfare plans impose restrictions on membership that are of particular interest to multiemployer welfare plans. The regulations require that benefits be provided only to participants (including dependents and designated beneficiaries), and further restrict eligibility for membership to individuals having an "employment-related common bond." [149] The regulations list as typical examples of acceptable membership groups those defined by reference "to coverage under one or more collective bargaining agreements (with respect to benefits provided by reason of such agreement(s)), to membership in a labor union, or to membership in one or more locals of a national or international labor union." The final regulations also clarify that

1. Employees of a labor union will be considered to share an employment-related common bond with union members,
2. Employees of a plan will be considered to share such a bond with plan members, and
3. Persons who in the normal course of employment are employed intermittently by different employers in the same industry are eligible for coverage as long as this pattern of employment is typical of their industry.

The regulations suggest, and the sources confirm, that two or more unrelated welfare plans may cooperate in providing benefits to members, including the sharing of costs and services.[150]

---

149 Treas. Reg. § 1.501(c)(9)-2(a)(1).

150 See, e.g., Technical Advice Memorandum issued to Local 443, Transportation Health Services and Insurance Plan, in March 1981.

27

Tax-Deferred Annuities

RICHARD REICHLER

Ernst & Whinney

INTRODUCTION

Tax-deferred annuities provide a retirement income program for employees of certain tax-exempt organizations. The amounts saved can build up tax free and often will enjoy preferred estate tax advantages. The earnings, however, do not escape tax forever. When the amounts are paid the annuitant will have ordinary income but the individual's tax rate should be lower at that time. Such income may be subject to state law maximum rates that apply to personal service income.

Advantages of Tax-Deferred Annuities

The tax-deferred annuity is a method of accomplishing the objective of tax deferral. In many instances, it is an easy, flexible and low-cost means of achieving this goal. For tax-exempt organizations, it has the following advantages:

- A tax-sheltered annuity program, unlike a tax-qualified plan, does not require a formal plan and trust indenture, Internal Revenue Service approval and costly legal fees.
- Unlike tax-qualified retirement plans, there is no requirement that tax-sheltered annuities be made available to a nondiscriminatory group of employees. Rather, individual employees may choose whether to seek the benefit of this savings vehicle.
- Tax-sheltered annuities are flexible in that each employee can choose, subject to certain maximums, the amount he wishes to put into the program and may select the payment options that are most suitable to his situation. The ability to select deferred-payment obligations, as stated, can also have favorable estate tax consequences.

For *employees* of tax-exempt organizations, the tax-deferred annuity is also advantageous:

- Tax-sheltered annuities are portable. If the employee changes his position and his new employer is willing to pay a portion of his compensation to such an annuity, that employee can continue his tax-sheltered annuity program without loss or added expense.

Eligibility

Tax-deferred annuities were available under the 1939 Internal Revenue Code to employees of charitable, religious, educational, literary, and scientific organizations exempt from income tax under Section 101(6) of the Code (the predecessor to the Section 501(c)(3) exemption for charitable organizations). Because of the desirability of having a vested untaxed fund, many highly taxed employees utilized this vehicle. For example, a wealthy individual who was active in a charitable foundation that he created would arrange to receive his entire pay this way. Similarly, a doctor who was a part-time employee of a hospital would take his entire pay in the form of a tax-sheltered annuity.

To end this practice, in 1958 Congress amended the law to limit the amount that an employee could exclude from his income in a tax year. This limit, known as the *exclusion allowance,* also reversed a restrictive IRS position that a tax-deferred annuity contract qualified only if it was a supplement to past or current compensation and that an employee could not agree to forego an increase in current compensation to which he otherwise might be entitled in order to have his employer agree to buy a tax-deferred annuity for him.

In addition to these modifications, Congress also extended to tax-deferred annuities certain benefits then only available to participants in tax-qualified plans. The rationale was that by providing the exclusion allowance rule it had, in effect, established a substitute in regard to educational, charitable, and religious organizations for the qualification required of industrial plans. The additional tax benefits were (1) the income tax exclusion for up to $5,000 of the amounts attributable to the employer's contributions within the exclusion allowance, even if such amounts would not otherwise qualify for this death benefit exclusion because the employee's interest was vested prior to his death; (2) an estate tax exclusion for the portion of the annuity purchased by employer contributions within the exclusion allowance; and (3) a gift tax exclusion for the provision of survivor benefits purchased by employer contributions within the exclusion allowance.

After the 1958 amendments were enacted, the IRS ruled that employees of public schools were not exempt under Section 501(a) of the Code and therefore were not entitled to the benefits of tax-sheltered annuities. In 1961, Congress changed the law to correct this problem. The Senate Finance Committee amendment provided that amounts paid to purchase annuity contracts for employees of public school systems qualify for the exclusion from gross income in the same manner and to the same extent as amounts used to purchase contracts for employees of private organizations described in Section 501(c)(3) of the Code, including private schools. This amendment[1] was made applicable to taxable years beginning after December 31, 1957, the same effective date as the 1958 amendments to Section 403(b).

Although employees of public school systems are eligible to participate in tax-sheltered annuity programs, employees of other organizations of state and local government generally are not. State and local governmental organizations that do not perform functions integral to state or local government but whose functions resemble those of Section 501(c)(3) organizations may be eligible. State, county, and city hospitals are examples of such organizations.

Accordingly, those who perform services as employees directly or indirectly for a public educational institution are eligible. Employees who perform services involving the operation or direction of an education program of a state or political subdivision are employees performing services indirectly for such institution.

Applicability of ERISA Title I

Certain tax-deferred annuity plans are covered by Title I of ERISA and are subject to regulation by the Labor Department; others are not. A tax-deferred annuity plan is generally considered a "plan" under Section 3(2) of Title I and therefore subject to Title I requirements unless it is specifically

[1] Pub. L. No. 87-370, 75 Stat. 796, (1961).

exempted because the plan is one entered into pursuant to a salary reduction agreement or an agreement to forego a salary increase and meets other requirements set forth in Treasury Regulations § 2510.3-2(f). In addition, governmental and church plans are exempt from Title I.

OPERATION OF TAX-DEFERRED ANNUITY PROGRAM

Source of Annuity Premiums

The annuity contract must be purchased for the employee by the employer and the amounts paid must be paid or contributed by the employer. This does not mean, however, that the economic cost of the tax-sheltered annuity must be borne by the employer. The IRS no longer takes the position that the purchase of the tax-deferred annuity has to be a supplement to the past or current compensation of the employee and that an employee may not agree to forego an increase in salary or to take a reduction in salary in exchange for the tax-deferred annuity. Consequently, the entire economic cost of the tax-deferred annuity can now safely be borne by the employee without fear of tax disqualification.

Agreements between employer and employee with respect to salary reduction or increase in salary must apply only to amounts that the employee may earn after the effective date of the agreement and are legally binding and irrevocable with respect to amounts the employee earns while the agreement is in effect. Although the employee cannot make more than one agreement a year with the same employer, he can terminate the entire agreement with respect to amounts he has not yet earned. Consequently, if the employee agrees to a salary reduction of $2,500 for 1982 and incurs unforeseen expenses in the summer of 1982, he can terminate his salary reduction agreement with regard to the remaining 1982 earnings. If at the end of 1982, the employee again is in a position to forego the immediate use of a portion of his salary, he can elect again with respect to 1982 to have up to 20 percent of his includable·compensation paid for a tax-sheltered annuity. The employee's election should be made *before* the beginning of each year in order to have the exclusion allowance apply to the entire year's salary. A change in the amounts of contributions resulting from a change in salary under an agreement specifying a percentage of compensation does not constitute a new salary reduction agreement, nor does a change in insurance carrier.

Funding Media

Originally, the only investment that could be used to fund a tax-sheltered annuity was an annuity contract that provided no insurance protection. In 1962, the passage of H.R. 10 permitted the use of two additional investment media: insurance company contracts that provide incidental life insurance protection, such as a typical retirement income policy, and an investment contract called a face-amount certificate.

The Pension Reform Act permitted contributions to custodial accounts that invest the contributions in open-end shares (mutual funds) of a regulated investment company. The Tax Reform Act of 1976 added closed-end investment company shares to the investment media. The Revenue Act of 1978 amended Section 403(b)(7) of the Code to provide that if contributions are invested in any regulated investment company stock, the amounts invested may not be distributed except upon death, disability, separation from service, attainment of age 59½ or financial hardship.

A contract issued after December 31, 1962 will not qualify as an "annuity contract" for the purpose of Section 403(b) unless it is "nonforfeitable." A contract is transferable for this purpose "if the owner can sell, assign, discount, or pledge as collateral for a loan or as security for the performance of an obligation or for any other purpose his interest in the . . . contract to any person other than the issuer thereof."

LIMITATIONS ON CONTRIBUTIONS

The extent of a tax-deferred annuity program is limited by two major tax considerations: (1) the exclusion allowance, which limits the amount that can be contributed without tax under such a program; and (2) the limitations on employer contributions under the tax-qualified arrangements contained in Section 415 of the Code. There is, of course, a further practical factor that affects the ability of an employee to utilize the exclusion allowance—his ability to save a portion of his current income.

Tax Exclusion Allowance

Computing the Allowance. The exclusion allowance is a limitation or ceiling on the amount that may be set aside without current tax on the employee. In general, without regard to past service, this "exclusion allowance" is 20 percent of the employee's compensation, figured without the amount that is to be excluded (or 16⅔ percent of the gross compensation before reduction for the contribution). The result, expressed as a dollar amount, is then multiplied by the total number of years of the employee's service for that employer less the amount, if any, contributed by the employer for annuity contracts and certain other benefits for the employee in the past that were excludable from his gross income.

The following example illustrates the first step of this computation. An employee earning $12,000 per year could pay as an annuity premium up to $2,000 in the taxable year (20 percent of the reduced amount ($12,000 − $2,000 or $10,000) = $2,000). Furthermore, if this employee had past service with his present employer, he might possibly have been paid by his employer an additional amount for each year of past service.

The exclusion allowance is the maximum contribution that may be designated without tax consequences. Of course, less than the maximum amount may be set aside. For example, an employee earning $12,000 per year could choose to have any amount up to $2,000 paid as the premium for the annuity contract and that amount would be excluded from his gross income. Although there is no minimum amount required by the law, many insurance companies require a minimum annual annuity premium of $1,000 on any annuity contract they write; mutual fund users do not have such a limit.

Section 403(b)(2) of the Code requires that the exclusion allowance or limitation for the taxable year be computed taking into consideration the employee's past service and the aggregate of the amounts contributed by the employer for annuity contracts and excludable from the gross income of the employee for any prior taxable year. Substantially similar language is found in the report of the Senate Finance Committee that approved this legislative change in 1958.

In 1964, the IRS promulgated regulations that provided the maximum exclusion allowance (20 percent of includable compensation times the number of years of service) be reduced not only by the aggregate of the excludable amounts contributed by the employer for annuity contracts in prior years but also by all contributions made by the employer for the benefit of the employee's benefit, which under Section 402(a) were excludable from the employee's gross income for prior years (contributions to an exempt pension trust, as well as by certain other contributions made by the employer).

Putting aside the question of the validity of the IRS "interpretation" of the exclusion allowance provision, conformity with its requirement reduces the amount that can be put into the tax-deferred annuity because both the pension contributions made by the employer in prior years and the amount of annuity premium paid in the preceding year or years must be subtracted from the top line of the formula. In some cases the employee will be able to determine exactly how much his employer contributes to a retirement program. (This will be true under profit-sharing or money purchase plans in which the employer contributes a fixed percentage of compensation with the amount contributed being used to purchase a retirement annuity of undetermined amount.) Generally, however, retirement programs provide for retirement annuities of a determined or determinable amount and the employer is required to make contributions in an amount that, based upon actuarial principles, will be sufficient at retirement to provide the retirement annuity. In these cases, the employee must refer to a formula devised by the IRS. If during a single taxable year amounts are contributed for annuity contracts for the employee by two or more qualified employers, a separate exclusion allowance is computed with respect to each employer.

Includable Compensation. An employee's includable compensation for purposes of determining the exclusion allowance is the amount that an employee earns during the most recent period (ending not later than the close of the taxable year) that is equal to a year of service. Generally, if income is included in gross income, and if it comes from the employer providing the benefit, it is includable compensation. However, sick pay is included in income for this purpose, and foreign income and the cost of incidental life insurance protection, even though included in gross income, have been excluded from includable compensation.

Years of Service. In the case of an organization described in Section 501(c)(3) of the Code, only service for the present employer is counted, and then only during the period in which the employer met the test of being an organization so described. In the case of service with a state, a state political subdivision, or an agency or instrumentality of a state or its subdivision, only service with the same employer and service as employee of an educational institution is counted. Qualifying prior service with the latter category of employers, even that before 1958, appeals to be includable, even though the Code was first amended in 1961, effective from 1958, to cover employees of such organizations.

A significant provision in the regulations states that in determining years of service the employer's annual work period, not the employee's taxable year, is the standard of measurement. Consequently, an employee who works an academic year could have service from January 1 to June 30 and if he worked the next academic year for the same employer he would have service from September 1 to December 31. This would constitute a full year of service. If, however, that employee worked the second academic year for a different employer, he would have had six-tenths of a year of service for his first employer and four-tenths of a year of service for his second employer. Although the regulations are silent on the question of computing service where, for instance, a fall semester usually starts on September 10, it would appear that as more than half a month is involved the entire month may be considered whereas if less than a half a month is involved that month should be ignored.

If at the close of a taxable year the employee has a period of service of less than one year, he is considered to have one year of service for purposes of computing his exclusion allowance for that year. However, this short period must be used to determine his includable compensation for that year without tacking on compensation from any earlier period to make up twelve full months.

Part-Time Employees. A tax-sheltered annuity may be purchased for a part-time employee, who is interested in such a program. In determining the maximum contribution permitted, the exclusion allowance formula, of course, is related to his compensation for those part-time rather than full-time services, and certain adjustments must therefore be made in its computation. In determining whether an individual is a full- or part-time employee, the amount of work that he is required to perform should be compared with the amount of work normally required of individuals holding the same position with the same employer and who generally derive the major portion of their personal service income from this position.

This comparison may be made under any method that reasonably reflects the amount of work required. In the case of the number of hours of classroom instruction required, for example, a full year of service is determined with reference to the usual annual work period of instructors employed full-time. In a university where the usual annual work period consists of the fall and spring semesters, an instructor who teaches a full schedule during these semesters is deemed to have worked a full year.

Section 415 Limits

Even if the amount contributed on an employee's behalf falls within the amount permitted by the exclusion allowance it must still meet the requirements of Section 415 of the Code relating to the overall limits on contributions on tax-deferred retirement savings. Under Section 415, a tax-deferred retirement plan is treated as a defined contribution plan.

As a general rule, the maximum annual addition that can be made to the account of a participant for the limitation year that ends with or within the taxable year is limited to: (1) the lesser of $25,000 as adjusted for cost of living increases from 1975 or; (2) 25 percent of the participants compensation for the taxable year. Contributions in a year in excess of the applicable limitation, besides being includable in gross income, reduce the Section 403(b) exclusion allowance dollar for dollar. (The limitation year for the purpose of the Section 415 calculation is the calendar year. However, the employee may change the year to another twelve-month period by attaching a statement to his return, unless the tax-sheltered annuity plan has to be taken into account in computing the limits applicable to another plan.)

To determine the limit on other plans in which the employee covered by a Section 403(b) plan is a participant, the individual is considered to have provided the annuity under a plan of a business that he controls.[2] Thus, if a doctor is covered under a plan of a professional corporation of which he is the owner and a tax-sheltered annuity plan of a hospital at which he works, both such plans must be aggregated in determining whether the Section 415 limits are exceeded.

Catch-Up Exceptions. There are exceptions to the basic contribution limit of Section 415 described above. These exceptions reflect a congressional response to the desire of participants in tax-sheltered annuity programs to maximize their contributions in the latter years of their service with qualifying institutions when their income is higher and their retirement more imminent.

---

[2] I.R.C. § 415(e)(5).

Eligible employees. The exceptions to the basic defined contribution plan limit in Section 415(b), which is applicable to tax-deferred annuities, are commonly known as the *catch-up* exceptions. They apply *only* to those employed by educational institutions, hospitals, and home health service agencies. For this purpose, educational institutions include primary and secondary schools, colleges, universities, normal schools, technical schools, mechanical schools, and similar institutions. The term does not include noneducational institutions, on-the-job training, correspondence schools, night schools, etc.

Possible elections. Only one of the three following catch-up exceptions may be elected by the eligible employee, and that election is irrevocable.

1. In the year an employee separates from the service, he may make a contribution equal to the lesser of (1) amounts that could have been contributed (but were not) during the employee's last ten years or less of service ending on the date of service separation or (2) the limit under Section 415. This section can be used only once.
   The following formula describes the first catch-up exception if the contribution is derived from a salary reduction agreement.

$$X = \frac{(M + C)\,L - 5E}{5 + L} - C$$

X = Maximum single contribution

M = Annual compensation received and receivable by and credited to the employee during his or her final taxable year of employment from and by the employer;

a. After excluding any contribution (in addition to cash compensation) made by the employer in the employee's final taxable year of employment for any other Section 403(b) plan and any other type of tax-deferred annuity contracts already in effect,

b. Before excluding the single contribution made by the employer in his or her final taxable year of employment as a result of a salary reduction for the new Section 403(b) plan being arranged (i.e., X).

L = Years of past service from the date of employment or from a date ten years prior to the date of the employee's termination of employment, whichever date is later, to the end of his or her final taxable year of employment, taken to the last complete month.

E = Aggregate of all contributions made by his or her employer in all years prior to the final taxable year of employment, not exceeding ten, for all Section 403(b) plans and other tax-deferred annuity contracts already in effect.

C = Aggregate of all contributions (in addition to his or her cash compensation) made by the employer in the employee's final taxable year of employment for any other Section 403(b) plans and any other tax-deferred annuity contracts already in effect.

2. An employee may elect to have the defined contribution maximum of Section 415 apply.
3. An employee, each year, may contribute the least of: (1) the amount of the exclusion allowance under Section 403(b)(2); (2) $4,000 plus 25 percent of his salary; or (3) $15,000. The employee may elect this exception for any one or more of his taxable years. The Section 415 maximum is not relevant since the maximum contribution that can be generated is $15,000. Subject to these limits, the following formula may be used to determine the maximum salary reduction for a level premium contract under the regular exclusion allowance.

$$\text{Maximum level premium} = \frac{SY - 5(B + AF + QN)}{Y + 5F}$$

S = Current includable compensation without reduction for the proposed tax-sheltered annuity but after salary reduction for qualified plan, state teachers' retirement system or eligible state deferred compensation plan.

B = Sum of (1) employer contributions excluded from taxable income in previous years for a tax-sheltered annuity and/or qualified pension plan (or state teachers' retirement system), (2) excludable contributions to an eligible state-deferred compensation plan by any employer (whether or not the one providing the annuity) in any previous tax year counted as a year of service, and (3) in tax years beginning after January 24, 1980, contributions in excess of the Section 415 "overall limits" made in prior tax years beginning after January 24, 1980.

A = Excludable employer contributions for a tax-sheltered annuity previously started and to be continued

Q = Excludable employer contributions for a qualified pension plan (or state teachers' retirement system) previously started and to be continued

Employee Plans (Nonqualified)

Y = Total number of years' service from start of employment to retirement (or to end of year in which last premium is to be paid, if earlier)

N = Number of annual excludable contributions Q to be made (current year plus future years) but not including any contribution to be made in the final year premium is to be paid

F = Current year plus future years in which premium is to be paid

This formula is based on the assumption that, as to contributions to plans other than tax-sheltered annuities, only contributions made in *prior* years reduce the exclusion allowance.[3] Thus, in the final year in which contributions are made to both a tax-sheltered annuity and a pension plan, the pension plan contribution never becomes a prior contribution and thus does not reduce the exclusion allowance. This formula assumes that all plans involved are co-terminous or that employer pension contributions cease the year before

---

[3] Rev. Rul. 70-243, 1970-1 C.B. 107 and Treas. Reg. § 1.403(b)-1(d)(3).

the last contribution under the tax-sheltered annuity. Many insurers use a more conservative formula which reduces the exclusion allowance by the amount of the current contribution to the pension plan, as follows:

$$\text{Maximum level premium} = \frac{SY - 5(B + AF + QF)}{Y + 5F}$$

Excise Tax for Excess Contributions

There is an excise tax of 6 percent on contributions in excess of the limits that are made to a custodial account (see below). This excise tax does not apply to contributions in excess of the limits that are made under an annuity contract.

The excise tax is deductible, and is paid on the amount contributed over the lesser of the exclusion allowance or the limitation on employer contributions.

FEDERAL TAX CONSIDERATIONS FOR EMPLOYEES

Amounts Received Under Annuity Contracts

A tax-deferred annuity merely serves to postpone reporting of the monies paid for the annuity, not to avoid the tax. Consequently, it is provided in Section 403(b)(1) of the Code that the employee shall include in his gross income the amounts received under the annuity contract for the year received as provided in Section 72 (relating to annuities).

Investment in the Contract. If the employee lives to retirement age and begins to receive the annuity payments due him under the contract, if no contributions have been made in excess of the exclusion allowance, he will have to pay taxes in the year of receipt for the full amount paid under the annuity contract. This is because he has not previously paid taxes on the full amount of the consideration paid for the annuity contract, and the earnings on those amounts, and he accordingly has no "cost" for the annuity contract. To the extent that amounts have been paid in excess of the exclusion ratio, they were taxed to the employee when paid and represent his investment in the contract that is recoverable tax free. Included in the investment in the contract would be the cost of any life insurance protection provided under the plan. Also included would be the charge (if any) for premium waiver and, in certain cases, for dividends paid on participating contracts.

Dividends Distributed Prior to Retirement. Those annuity contracts purchased for the employee that participate in dividends paid by the insurance company before the retirement date can cause tax problems. Generally speaking, before retirement any dividends apportioned are payable at the end of contract years. Various dividend options are available and the selection of a particular option seems to have an effect on the tax consequences. The employee, as the owner of the annuity contract, is the person entitled to the dividend and to elect one of the several options:

1. Purchase of paid-up additions;
2. Application of the dividends toward the annual premium;
3. Taking a cash payment; or
4. Accumulating the dividends at interest.

If the employee elects to purchase paid-up additions to the maturity value, since the exclusion from income is predicated on the exclusion allowance computed with reference to the original premium paid, it would appear that the full amount of the premium paid has been paid for the annuity contract and should be excluded from the employee's income. If the employee elects to have the dividend applied toward the next annual premium, there is a problem that as the employee is entitled to the dividend it is not being paid by the employer for the annuity contract, a requirement of Section 403(b). However, the prevalent view is that the reduction in premium does not result in current tax liability. Rather, the exclusion allowance would be measured against the net premium paid. Nevertheless, there are serious administrative problems in amending a salary reduction agreement each year to reflect the dividend of the preceding year. Clearly, if the employee chooses to withdraw the dividend in cash, the IRS will consider the dividend as current taxable income. An election to accumulate the dividends at interest should produce the same result as the election to purchase paid-up additions. However, as interest is credited each year to the accumulated dividends, the IRS may contend that this interest is taxable currently to the employee. The option that offers the least troublesome result from a tax and practical point of view is the election to have the dividends purchase paid-up additions to the maturity value.

Dividends After Retirement. The problem of dividends after retirement is not as great. These dividends are generally paid with the regular income payments and will represent additional ordinary income taxable at that time.

Realizing Cash Value Before Retirement. One advantage to the employee under a tax-sheltered annuity program is that if he is in need of money he can surrender his annuity contract in whole or in part and realize cash value. Of course, to the extent that he realizes such value, he will have taxable income in that year. Where under the terms of the annuity contract the employee can borrow against the cash value prior to the annuity starting date, the tax result is less clear. The IRS has ruled that amounts are taxable currently as ordinary income.[4] However, the U.S. Tax Court held in *Minnis v. Comm'r* [5] that such a transaction should be treated as a loan. Subsequently, the IRS stated that it will not follow the decision in *Minnis* and will continue to treat policy loans as the receipt of taxable income.[6]

Tax-Free Rollover

The Revenue Act of 1978 amended the Code to permit a tax-free rollover of a distribution from a Section 403(b) annuity contract to an IRA or to another Section 403(b) annuity contract. In order to qualify, the distribution must be one that would constitute a lump-sum distribution under Section 402(e)(4)(A) if lump-sum tax treatment were available to a Section 403(b) annuity. Thus, in order to qualify, the employee must receive a total distribution of his interest in one taxable year because of separation from service or after reaching age 59½. The usual rules relating to rollovers apply, except that the distribution may not be rolled over to a qualified plan. For rollover purposes, all annuity contracts purchased by the employer for the employee are treated as a single contract. Therefore, if more than one tax-sheltered annuity has been purchased for the employee, the employee's interest in all such contracts must be distributed before a distribution will qualify as a "total distribution."

A partial rollover is permitted. If only a part of the total distribution is rolled over, the balance is subject to tax as ordinary income.

Employment Taxes

To the extent the annual premium is within the employee's exclusion allowance, it is not considered wages for withholding purposes. However, premium payments in excess of the exclusion allowance are "wages" subject to withholding.

Even though such premiums paid that do not exceed the exclusion allowance are not taxable income, they are considered wages for Social Security tax and benefit purposes where the plan is established on a salary reduction basis.[7] However, if the tax-deferred annuity plan is in addition to the covered employee's regular salary, the annuity premiums are not "wages" for Social Security purposes.[8]

---

[4] Rev. Rul. 67-258, 1967-2 C.B. 68.
[5] 71 T.C. 94 (1979).
[6] Rev. Rul. 81-126, 1981-17 C.B. 6.
[7] Rev. Rul. 65-208, 1965-2 C.B. 383.
[8] Rev. Rul. 53-181 1953-2 C.B. 111.

TAX TREATMENT IN THE EVENT OF DEATH

Favored vs. Non-Favored Organizations

The tax treatment of death benefits under a tax-deferred annuity plan differs depending upon the type of employer. The tax rules applicable to Section 501(c)(3) organizations operating in the areas of religion, education, or charity, which also fall within the definition of Sections 170(b)(1)(A)(ii) or 170(b)(1)(A)(vi) are different from the rules applicable to other Section 501(c)(3) organizations. The former organizations are frequently referred to as *favored institutions*. While only private educational institutions are favored by Section 170(b)(1)(A)(ii), the Tax Court has held in *Estate of Leslie Johnson*[9] that the favored treatment extended to public school employees. The Commissioner has acquiesced in that adverse decision.[10]

The recipient of death benefits paid under a tax-deferred annuity plan (assuming no life insurance) who is the survivor of an employee of a favored institution is entitled to a $5,000 death benefit. If the employee was not employed by a favored institution, no such exclusion would be available with respect to his nonforfeitable rights under the plan.

In the case of a retirement income insurance contract, the pure insurance proceeds (total proceeds less cash value) paid to any beneficiary are exempt from tax under Section 101(a). The cash value portion of the payment is taxed in the manner discussed above (subject to the $5,000 exclusion where available).

Certain lump-sum distributions made to the spouse of an employee under a tax-sheltered annuity are subject to rollover contribution rules.

Federal Estate Tax Exemptions

Death benefits paid to a named beneficiary (other than the executor) of a deceased employee of a favored institution of the type referred to above (including public school employees) are not subject to federal estate tax to the extent such benefits are attributable to employer contributions excluded from gross income. The cost of any life insurance protection is not excluded from the employee's gross income.[11] If a portion of employer contributions is not excluded from the employee's gross income, the amount exempt from estate tax is determined as follows:

$$\frac{\text{Excludable Amount}}{\text{Total Employer Contributions}} \times \text{Death Benefit} = \text{Exempt Portion}$$

---

[9] 56 T.C. 944 (1971).

[10] See 1973-2 C.B. 2.

[11] Memo from IRS national office to district director, Philadelphia, Pa. (April 27, 1966).

No taxable gift occurs if a favored Section 501(c)(3) organization employee designates a beneficiary or survivor in a manner which makes such designation irrevocable during his lifetime.

In all other tax-deferred annuity plans, such a designation produces a taxable gift of the entire interest transferred. In all cases, the amount attributable to employee contributions is a taxable gift.

28

Special Benefits and Services

RUSSELL F. SCHUCK

Manager, Employee Benefits Planning, International Business Machines Corporation

GROWTH OF SPECIAL BENEFITS AND SERVICES

To job seekers in the past, *employee benefits* signified retirement pay and protection against some of life's more pernicious hazards. Today however, they have come to mean a myriad of other things, and many observers, particularly those in large companies, are convinced that the evolution of employee benefits still has a long course to run. While the standard benefits package continues to change its shape and character, there is an expanding layer of benefits to be found on the outer perimeter of many programs—the so-called fringe benefits. Some of the fringes are designed to help employees meet certain expenses that relate, at least indirectly, to the employer's own interests. Others, however, are benefits conceived to demonstrate the added value and even the uniqueness of working for a particular employer.

Fortune 500 Survey

The extent of these special benefits is clearly demonstrated in the findings of a recent Warren, Gorham & Lamont survey of Fortune 500 companies. As indicated in Figure 28.1, one out of four respondents offers employees a choice of work hours. Organized sports and recreation activities appear to be fixed elements in the large company environment; and service recognition programs have become the norm. Financial assistance for employee education in one form or another is nearly universal.

Clearly, employers are striving to develop creative programs to meet the needs of employees and their dependents in and beyond the workplace. And, the trend can only be expected to grow.

EDUCATIONAL SUPPORT PROGRAMS

There are several reasons why employers have a major interest in offering a variety of educational support programs:

- Educational assistance generally is highly visible, socially desirable, and relatively low cost.
- Certain continuing education programs enable many employees to stay abreast of the knowledge explosion, enhance their professionalism, and add to their job skills and career development.
- General educational enhancement improves the quality of the work force, enriches employees' lives, and is a powerful attraction to upwardly mobile new employees.
- Management development programs attract and prepare future company leaders.

Employee Programs

Within the framework of special benefits and employee services it is appropriate to limit the discussion that follows to those programs that appeal to the general employee population. Consequently, management development and other forms of direct company education programs will not be discussed.

Because of their "benefits appeal" and inherent merits, many companies have instituted tuition assistance programs for employees and grant or loan programs for dependents. A relatively new arrival is the concept of financial assistance for courses taken in preparation for retirement.

Tuition Assistance. Most companies provide tuition assistance for educational course expenses incurred by employees when the course is related to the employee's current job or future career development. Courses also qualify that will lead to an academic degree related to the employee's current job or career, or that will help him attain a high school diploma.

Limits. For reasons of budgetary control and to prevent the employee from over-extending himself, a firm may decide to establish a maximum expenditure per year per semester. If the firm limits the number of credits (e.g., four or eight per semester) for which the employee may enroll, instead of limiting the dollar expenditure, it may avoid the necessity of annual inflation adjustments. For example, one employer reimburses employees up to eight credit hours per term, provided the courses are job-related. Dollar limits may, however, be established for non-job-related courses. Such limitations range from $150 per course to the $1,200 to $1,500 that is the current cost of eight college credits.

Program or Service	*Percentage of Respondents Offering*	*Comments*
Credit union	56%	Of those companies with credit unions, the majority reported participation by 50% or more of their employees. Range of employee participation: 10 to 100%.
Flexible work hours	26	Companies reporting flexible work hours had programs staggered between 7:30 AM and 9:00 PM; a few reported summer schedules of 4½-day or 4-day weeks.
Recreation Facilities/programs Sports activities	50	Almost 75% of the respondents indicated they had some kind of sports/recreation program for their employees.
Other recreational and social events	68	Most companies sponsoring sports activities provided uniforms and/or fees for use of facilities. A few also gave paid time off or provided transportation to and from practice and games. The company picnic was the most popular recreational event.
Length-of-service award	85	The typical length-of-service award was given at 5-year intervals. Jewelry is the usual gift. After 25 years, most companies made the award at a dinner or luncheon in the employee's honor.
Paid time off: Military Jury duty Marriage	 77 98 17	Almost all responding companies granted paid time off for jury duty. Some reimbursed employees for the difference between military or jury pay and their regular salary.
Food and refreshment: Cafeteria Vending machines Coffee/snack wagon Free coffee/tea	 62 82 21 60	Companies with subsidized cafeterias served a large range of employees—from 66 at a single location to 400,000 at many locations in a multinational firm. Thirty-seven firms with cafeterias reported running them at a loss, while 9 reported breaking even. Only 4 reported a profit-making operation. Of the respondent companies that furnish vending machines, most provide only cold drinks and/or candy/snack food. Coffee/snack wagons are usually run at a loss. Companies offering free coffee and tea generally did not limit quantities.
Employee discounts	43	Companies that have employee discount programs on consumer products reported a range of product discounts from 10 to 60% from retail price.
Employee suggestion awards	28	Most companies that compensate employees for usable suggestions offered cash

Program or Service	*Percentage of Respondents Offering*	*Comments*
		awards, usually a percentage of the money saved during the first year of implementation. Awards ranged from $25 to $100,000 per suggestion in one company with an active program.
Educational support:		Almost every company responding offered some form of educational subsidy for employees. Most refunded part or all of tuition for job-related courses upon satisfactory completion of the course. Of those companies with matching grant programs, half contributed only to their employees' alma maters, with half requiring only that the donee be an accredited institution.
Tuition refunds	98	
Matching grants	58	
Scholarship programs	59	
Other amenities/ services/programs	20	Among the reported benefits not covered in the survey were the following: • Child adoption assistance program • Special care for handicapped children • Full-service gym supervised by physical therapist • Free physical examinations • Blood pressure checks • Education to quit smoking • Weight-control classes • Lunch-time exercise program • Education for coping with stress • First Aid/CPR instruction • Free tickets to entertainment activities

Source: Based on 102 responses to an informal survey conducted in 1981 by Warren, Gorham & Lamont.

Fig. 28.1 Special Benefits—Fortune 500 Companies

Tuition reimbursement. Almost all tuition assistance is in the form of tuition reimbursement. This means that the employee pays all tuition and fees for his courses initially, and the employer usually reimburses the employee "upon satisfactory completion" of the course. Employers may consider loans or advances to employees who find it difficult to make initial tuition payments. In most companies such loans are exceptions rather than policy. Experience shows that more than 90 percent of participants satisfactorily complete their courses.

Amount of reimbursement. Some of the earlier plans reimbursed only 50 percent of the employee's tuition expenses. Today, most industrial firms reimburse from 75 percent to 100 percent of tuition costs upon satisfactory completion of the course. Most financial institutions and many service companies reimburse 100 percent of tuition, and some also reimburse for books or other required materials. A small and declining number of companies vary reimbursement according to the student's grade achievement.

Administration. The tuition assistance program should include a formal approval procedure that involves both local management and the personnel department; the eligibility of the course and the accreditation of the institution under the reimbursement program should be predetermined. Complete records of an employee's participation in the educational program should be maintained in his or her personnel file to assist management in assessing the employee's potential growth in the business. Summary records permit the company to make judgments about the utilization and value of the tuition assistance program.

Preparation for Retirement. A relatively new approach in the world of education assistance combines the concept of helping employees make a smooth transition to retirement and the practical value of tuition refund for external education courses.

In 1976, IBM adopted the "Retirement Education Assistance Plan," a forerunner of this approach. The plan is designed to help the employee and spouse prepare for an active and enjoyable retirement. The company helps pay the cost of tuition and registration fees for instruction in such courses as:

- Real estate
- TV/radio repair
- Interior decorating
- Creative writing
- Musical instruction
- Carpentry
- Hotel/motel management
- Photography
- Tax accounting
- Art and ceramics

Participation can begin as early as age 52 for employees who will have fifteen years of service by age 55 or three years prior to their thirtieth service anniversary. The spouse becomes eligible once the employee meets the eligibility requirements. Eligibility can continue until two years after the actual date of the employee's retirement. The employee and spouse are eligible to receive a maximum total assistance of $2,500 per individual.

The plan covers courses offered by nationally accredited colleges as well as many adult education courses.

Tax Aspects. Before 1979, education costs picked up by employers counted as additional compensation for employees, unless the courses taken were necessary to satisfy company requirements and retain salary, employment, or status or to maintain or improve skills in order for the employee to properly perform his duties. Even then, costs might still be considered compensation if the courses were part of a program leading to qualification for a different trade or profession.

Now, through 1983, the law has been liberalized: companies can implement and adjust educational assistance plans without creating tax problems for employees. Under a qualified plan, benefits are excluded from the employee's gross income and can still be deducted as business expenses by the company. A plan qualifies if:

- There is a written plan set up for the exclusive benefit of employees with the intention of providing them with educational assistance.
- The plan does not discriminate in favor of officers, owners, or highly compensated employees or their spouses and/or dependents.
- Employees are not given a choice between educational assistance or additional salary or other benefits.
- Eligible employees are given reasonable notification of the terms and availability of the plan.

Employee Dependents

A number of larger organizations have established scholarship and loan programs for the post-secondary education of the children of active or retired employees.

Scholarships. Generally, firms supply the financial wherewithal for scholarship programs, but they leave the actual administration and election of scholarship recipients to nationally known selection agencies. A typical plan works as follows: Eligible high school juniors take a national qualifying test, the Preliminary Scholastic Aptitude Text/National Merit Scholarship Qualifying Test (PSAT/NMSQT). The National Merit Scholarship Corporation (NMSC) selects candidates from the highest scoring eligible candidates and awards scholarships on the basis of academic record, leadership qualities, extracurricular accomplishments, etc. The amount of the award varies with family needs.

In addition to a merit scholarship program using the services of NMSC, an employer can arrange with College Scholarship Service (CSS) to administer a scholarship program for children of employees. A statement of scholarship program policy at Cummins Engine Co., Inc. is reproduced in Figure 28.2.

Student Loans. Some companies also make student loans available to assist employees' children in obtaining college educations. Usually these programs parallel the state-run guaranteed student loan programs established by the U.S. Higher Education Act of 1965 for those employee dependents who do not qualify for the government-supported loans.

Eligible students apply for loans at participating banks. The loans are guaranteed by a third party such as the United Students Aid Fund

Sons and Daughters Scholarship Program

Eligibility

Applications will be accepted only from high school seniors, college freshmen and high school graduates who have been out of school for no more than four years and who have not yet started college. Only those who ranked in the top 20% of their respective classes may apply. Eligible for consideration are sons or daughters of any company employee, including employees in regional offices or participating subsidiaries, provided the parent has (or had at the time of death or retirement) one or more years' seniority prior to the time of application. Sons and daughters of officers of the company are excluded and the Foundation annually establishes financial guidelines. The applicant must be planning study toward a bachelor's degree in the arts, sciences or a profession normally requiring four or more years of training. Scholarships will be awarded only to students who enroll in regionally accredited four-year institutions.

Selection

Scholarships will be awarded by an impartial committee comprised of non-Cummins persons. Selections will be made primarily on the basis of promise, as determined through an evaluation of academic records, references, a written application, a 200 word essay, and an interview, and only secondarily on the basis of financial need.

How To Apply

Application forms are available through the Cummins Engine Foundation and at several announced locations throughout Cummins Engine Company. They include a personal information sheet and an essay to be completed by the applicant, three character references to be completed by teachers, employers, or other adults well acquainted with, but not related to, the applicant, and instructions for providing transcript reports and test scores. Applicants must submit a Financial Aid Form to the College Scholarship Service, stipulating that a copy of the results be sent to the Cummins Engine Foundation. Financial Aid Forms should be available through high school or college financial aid or placement offices, or directly from the College Scholarship Service, 888 Seventh Avenue, New York, New York, 10019. The form should be submitted to the College Scholarship Service no later than January 15. The Cummins Identification Number 7206 should be shown in Item 44 of the Financial Aid Form.

Completed applications, together with all supporting documents, must be returned to Cummins Engine Foundation, Inc., 1000 Fifth Street, Columbus, Indiana 47201 no later than February 1.

Amount

Scholarships may range up to a maximum of $1500 per year. The number of awards each year varies depending on the total number of applications received and is governed by rules published by the Internal Revenue Service of the U.S. Treasury Department.

Payment of Award

After the scholar has been admitted to the college or university of his/her choice, the award will be deposited with the school in his/her name.

Source: Cummins Engine Co., Inc.

Fig. 28.2 Scholarship Program

(USAFund), a private nonprofit organization that is supported by corporate contributions. Loan amounts, terms, and interest rates are all similar to those of the higher education loan programs. In considering the implementation of a company-sponsored loan program, firms must assess the implications of the changing student eligibility requirements of the federal program. The limited availability of student loans through the government program may result in extensive use and increased costs to private corporations that offer this benefit to the children of employees.

Matching Gifts

In addition to tuition refund, scholarships, and loans, many companies offer another form of educational assistance that does not directly benefit employees or dependents but rather the learning institutions. This program matches any employee contribution (gift) to eligible institutions of higher education. Normally a company places an upper limit on the aggregate of gifts it will match for any individual employee. The matching gift program enables the corporation to demonstrate its role as a good corporate citizen in the community; at the same time, the employee participates in the total contribution, which is usually more than he might be able to afford as an individual. Figure 28.3 is a matching gifts form for use by company personnel in transmitting contributions to donee institutions.

SOCIAL-RECREATIONAL PROGRAMS

Many companies find that a balanced program of specialized recreational activities yields positive results in employee productivity and morale. Accordingly, companies frequently sponsor recreational and social clubs and activities that correspond to their employees' varied interests.

Sports Activities

Company-sponsored or subsidized sports activities are becoming increasingly popular. These activities are often arranged and run by the employees, who have a stake in their management and the opportunity for valuable leadership experience. Various forms of employees' activities associations have been established to conduct not only sports, but social and recreational activities in an organized manner. Every employee is eligible to be a member of the association, which is managed by a board of directors who appropriate funds for each budgeted activity. The association's activities funds may be subsidized by an annual company contribution for each employee, with the employees paying the remainder of the cost of the activities. As shown in Figure 28.1, 50 percent of the companies polled in a recent survey of large firms had some kind of sports program, with softball the leading

THE
SQUIBB CORPORATION
MATCHING GIFTS PLAN

INSTRUCTIONS:

(1) The employee, officer or director should fill out PART A and transmit the entire form with his or her contribution to the institution.

(2) Upon receipt of the contribution, the institution should fill out and execute PART B, and then return this entire form to the Office of the Treasurer, address shown below:

(3) See reverse side for provisions of this plan.

SC2 REV. 2/80

PART A *(To be filled in by SQUIBB CORPORATION employee, officer or director)*

Enclosed is my personal contribution to:
(Name & address of institution, alumni fund, foundation or association)

DATE

☐ CASH ☐ CHECK

AMOUNT

$

I hereby authorize the institution named above to report this gift to SQUIBB CORPORATION for the purpose of qualifying for a contribution from that Corporation in accordance with the provisions of its plan for matching gifts.

(SIGNATURE)

PRINT NAME (First, Middle, Last)	PLANT OR OFFICE
HOME ADDRESS	DIVISION
CITY & STATE	DATE EMPLOYED OR ELECTED

YOUR RELATIONSHIP TO INSTITUTION: ☐ ALUMNUS ☐ PARENT ☐ FRIEND ☐ OTHER

PART B *(To be filled in by a financial officer of the institution)*

I hereby certify that the contribution described above was received by:
(Name & address of institution, alumni fund, foundation or association)

on ____ / ____ / ____ from ________
Name of employee

and that the organization qualifies under the provisions of this plan to receive a grant from SQUIBB CORPORATION.

(Signature of Financial Officer)

NAME AND ADDRESS OF INSTITUTION	PRINT NAME OF FINANCIAL OFFICER
	TITLE
	DATE CERTIFICATION IS MAILED

ADDRESS ALL CORRESPONDENCE TO :

TREASURER
SQUIBB CORPORATION
40 WEST 57th STREET
NEW YORK, NEW YORK 10019

(NOTE: SEE REVERSE SIDE FOR PROVISIONS OF PLAN)

Fig. 28.3 Matching Gifts Transmittal Form

team sport. One firm reported a program of six team sports and three individual-participation sports.

On-Site Recreational Activities

In addition to the company-sponsored or subsidized clubs and teams, some larger firms at major locations provide on-site recreational facilities,

[*Reverse side*]

THE
SQUIBB CORPORATION
MATCHING GIFTS PLAN

Educational institutions and voluntary hospitals in this country find themselves in an increasingly difficult predicament as costs continue to escalate.

To encourage Squibb Corporation employees, officers, directors and retirees to make financial contributions to schools and voluntary hospitals of their choice, Squibb Corporation has established a plan to match their gifts to eligible institutions.

NAME OF THE PLAN

The name of the plan is "The Squibb Corporation Matching Gifts Plan."

LIMITS ON AMOUNTS TO BE MATCHED

Any gift or gifts to colleges, universities, secondary schools, and voluntary hospitals from a minimum of $25 to a maximum of $3,000 per eligible donor in any calendar year, will be matched by Squibb Corporation at the rate of two dollars for each dollar contributed. Contributions may be divided among different institutions not to exceed the maximum indicated above provided that each gift is $25 or more. The gift must represent an actual personal contribution (not merely a pledge) by the eligible donor or his or her personal foundation. Payments of tuition and other fees are not regarded as contributions, nor are dues payable to national or local alumni groups, or insurance premium payments on policies under which the institution is a beneficiary. No carryover into succeeding years will be permitted should gifts exceed the annual maximum. Forms covering gifts within the limitation, however, may still be honored if received by April 30 of the following year.

ELIGIBLE DONOR

Any regular, full-time employee, any officer or director, or any retiree of Squibb Corporation, or its participating components, is eligible to participate in the plan provided that he or she has been in the employ, or an officer or director, of the company for at least one year.

ELIGIBLE INSTITUTIONS

To be eligible, the institution must be recognized by the U.S. Internal Revenue Service as an organization to which tax-deductible contributions may be made and be in one of the two following categories:

1. All non-proprietary colleges or universities listed in the Educational Directory, Part 3, Higher Education published by the U.S. Office of Education and privately supported, non-profit secondary schools are considered eligible for matching gifts if located in the United States or its possessions.
2. All non-profit, non-proprietary voluntary hospitals located in the United States or its possessions, which are accredited by an appropriate regional or professional accrediting association.

DURATION OF THE PLAN

It is contemplated that this will be a continuing plan. Squibb Corporation, however, reserves the right to suspend, amend, revoke, or terminate this plan at any time and to fix, from time to time, an overall ceiling on the aggregate amount of its contributions in any calendar year.

HOW THE PLAN WORKS

1. An eligible donor making a gift to a qualified institution will fill in Part A of the form on the reverse side of this sheet, sending this entire sheet to the institution together with his or her contribution (pledges as such will not be matched).
2. Part B of the form must be executed by a financial officer of the institution. The signatures of officers of alumni funds, foundations, or associations will not be accepted. Both Parts A and B of the form must be returned by the instituion to the Treasurer, Squibb Corporation, 40 West 57th Street, New York, New York 10019.
3. After verification that the gift qualifies, a check will be forwarded to the institution by Squibb Corporation.
4. Notification will be given to each donor after the matching grant has been made by Squibb Corporation.

ADMINISTRATION

Any questions regarding the Plan should be directed to the Treasurer's Office of Squibb Corporation. The administration, interpretation, and application of the provisions of this Plan shall be entirely within the discretion of Squibb Corporation and all decisions of Squibb Corporation shall be final.

SC2 REV. 2/80

Source: Squibb Corporation

such as a gymnasium, running track, or physical fitness course. A few major industrial firms offer company-owned country club facilities to their employees at nominal cost. Small and medium-sized firms, on the other hand, are often approached by private recreational organizations who, through the company, offer memberships at discount rates to employees.

A company should consider the following factors in connection with the proposed construction of a company recreational facility:

- Population size, age/sex mix, and interests of employees
- Existing company facilities
- Accessible community facilities
- Community acceptance
- Impact on company employees at other locations
- Climate and terrain

Announcements regarding company-operated or subsidized recreational facilities should clearly state that members of both sexes are eligible to participate in each activity.

Other Recreational Programs

Other popular recreational activities include discount tickets to sports events, recreational parks, theatres, and movies. The company picnic and Christmas party, to which families are invited, are perennially popular events. Special service anniversary recognition events such as a dinner/dance for employees and spouses may be long anticipated and remembered. Large companies with many subsidiaries may celebrate these occasions on a branch or divisional level.

TIME OFF WITH PAY

This benefit, as the name implies, refers to payment for time that is not spent in actual employment, and generally refers to the following categories:

- Vacations
- Holidays
- Individual needs

Paid holidays and vacations are now universally provided in all industries, and represent one of the most costly employee benefits. The 1979 Chamber of Commerce Survey of employee benefits indicated that holidays and vacations combined averaged 7.9 percent of payroll for all companies. Although paid holidays and vacations *per se* have long been regarded as basic benefits, they are discussed here for convenience and also because certain employee options now associated with them in some companies may indeed be considered "special" benefits.

Vacations

Duration. Opportunities for change of environment and relaxation are considered a necessity for all employees and are generally granted in accordance with length of service. Figure 28.4 shows the amounts of vacation commonly provided in private industry in 1979. Note that the schedule provides a formula for some vacation for the first calendar year of employment, and ranges from two weeks for one to nine years of service to five weeks for twenty-five years or more of employment. Vacation in the year of hire may be accrued on a prorated basis, such as one day per month up to a certain cut-off date. Another approach is to have an alternative vacation schedule based on age so that more experienced people can qualify for three or four weeks of vacation, for example, rather than starting afresh with a more limited vacation allowance as a new hire.

Service	*Weeks of Vacation*
6 months	1
1-9 years	2
10-14 years	3
15-24 years	4
25 and over	5

Source: U.S. Department of Labor, Bureau of Labor Statistics, Report No. 615, July 1980.

Fig. 28.4 Typical Private Industry Vacation Schedule—1979

Scheduling by Employee. Insofar as practical, many companies permit employees to schedule vacations in accordance with their personal preferences and/or length of service. However, vacation scheduling practices vary from industry to industry and supervisory approval on timing is always necessary to see that offices and plants are adequately staffed.

Liberalization. There are inevitable pressures on companies to liberalize their vacation schedules by adding more time off or lowering service requirements for current entitlements. Benefit planning research may indicate that increased vacation would be a good way to reward long service, recruit new employees, remain competitive with other companies, and generally improve morale. However, management will want to carefully consider costs of additional time off and its effects on productivity.

Special Features. Some vacation plans have special features to make them more flexible and appealing to employees. These include:

Day at a time. Vacation may be taken a day at a time, or in half days.

Prorating. Instead of giving increased vacation at five- or ten-year intervals, employees accrue vacation in shorter increments (e.g., one additional day per year of service). Such a plan provides increasing time off sooner but does lose the advantage of milestone recognition, and could be more costly than the traditional approach.

Banking. Employees are allowed to carry over a limited amount of vacation from year to year subject to management approval. Banking allows employees to save time for extended vacations, and if deferral is also permitted to retirement age this may assist them to retire early, or cash out the time to supplement retirement. In times of low workload, the vacation bank can help preserve jobs if employees use some of their accrued vacation time.

Pay in lieu of vacation. Allowing employees to cash out part of their vacation can provide extra cash to those who want to enjoy vacation, and to those who cannot take all their vacation because of business needs or other reasons. In a high workload situation it might also be advantageous to the company to have employees take pay instead of time off. Companies considering this alternative must weigh these advantages against additional costs and the possibility that having employees take cash instead of time off could be contrary to the needs of the business and the basic intent of the vacation plan.

Anniversary year bonus. Employees are given extra vacation at significant service anniversaries (e.g., double vacation in the twenty-fifth year and every five years thereafter).

Extended vacations. Large blocks of time off may be provided periodically. Such a plan has been negotiated by the steelworkers in the basic steel industry with the intent of increasing job security. In this plan, the work force is divided in half by seniority, with the senior group receiving thirteen weeks vacation every five years (fourteen weeks after twenty-five years), and the junior group receiving four weeks every five years in addition to regular vacation. There has been no trend in other industries to adopt this approach.

Vacation bonus. Cash is given in addition to regular vacation pay—a rare but popular benefit.

Holidays

Paid holidays now amount to ten or more days in most industries. Companies generally close on traditional national holidays known as the "Basic 6": (New Year's Day, Memorial Day, Fourth of July, Labor Day, Thanksgiving, and Christmas). Other holidays may be designated by the company, or provided as personal holidays taken at the employee's option. Generally, holidays are designated by companies on either a companywide or local basis, because they meet one or more of the following criteria:

- Are recognized holidays such as Washington's Birthday or Columbus Day.
- Commemorate traditional cultural or historical events such as Patriot's Day in Boston.
- Add a holiday to a weekend or fill in Friday or Monday when major holidays fall on Thursday or Tuesday.
- Balance the distribution of holidays throughout the year.
- Agree with holiday practices of other companies in the local area.

Personally selected holidays enable employees to select days off that are most meaningful to them. For example, these days could be used for observation of religious or commemorative events, recreation, birthdays, or anniversaries. Personal holidays could be especially useful to new hires and short-service employees who have relatively less vacation time. They could also facilitate accommodation to customer needs for certain sales and service employees. In a manufacturing environment, however, scheduled days may be seen as less disruptive to production schedules.

Individual Needs

Most companies' current personnel programs also provide employees with time off for specified individual situations. These include civic service such as jury duty, military reserve commitments, and voting in public elections, as well as personal reasons such as family bereavement.

Jury Duty. Statutory payments for jury duty vary from state to state and from court to court, and are relatively low. To protect employees from loss of income while serving on a jury, companies generally pay the difference between jury duty pay and regular salary. Because the jury pay is low, some companies pay full salary for jury duty.

Military Service. In typical plans, leaves of absence of a year or more are granted to employees serving one tour of active military duty. When the volunteer army approach is utilized in lieu of a draft system, military leave experience among large employers is extremely low. Summer reserve duties require shorter absences and often are compensated in the same way as jury duty. Employees subject to such duty are paid the difference between their base salary and their military pay for up to one tour per year. Civil emergencies may be handled similarly, to a limit such as thirty days a year.

Elections. Employees are generally allowed reasonable time off to vote in specified elections. Usually this applies to major general elections, either at the state or federal level, or to district and presidential primaries. The time off might be specified (e.g., a half day) or might be given on an "if needed" basis. Some states require that employees be given time off to vote if they cannot do so outside normal working hours.

Personal Reasons. It is customary to allow necessary time off with pay (usually three consecutively scheduled work days) for absence due to the death of a member of an employee's immediate family. (Immediate family usually includes parents, spouse, child, in-laws, grandparents, brother or sister, or any member of employee's household.)

Personal time off with pay may also be given at management discretion for other reasons. These might include family illness, religious observance, marriage, medical and dental appointments, and other personal business that cannot be handled outside regular working hours.

Such time off might range from a few hours to a week or more. Such factors as the employee's work record, prior requests for time off, loss of production, and expense to the company would be considered in granting an employee's request for personal time off.

DEPARTURES FROM STANDARD WORK SCHEDULES

Flexible Work Schedules

The major objective of any flexible work schedule system is to serve the interests of both employees and management. The operational needs of the organization must come first, but they can frequently be made compatible with employees' desires. To be successful, the entire concept must have the cooperation of all concerned and must be supported and endorsed by top management and backed by all levels of supervision.

Flexible work schedule systems vary, but generally allow individuals to select their daily work hours between a set period of time (e.g., from 8 AM to 5 PM) and require that all employees be present during "core time" (e.g., from 9 AM to 4 PM). Thus, the system permits increased individual employee flexibility, without disrupting the firm's work flow or service.

Variations. Some variations on the flexible work schedule concept are as follows:

Variable daily schedules. Employees may choose to vary daily arrival time within the limits established by local management (for example, up to thirty minutes before or thirty minutes after normal start time). Departure time would vary by the same amount so that total working hours for the day would be the same.

Staggered schedules. Employees select from two or more start times predetermined by management. Business conditions may sometimes require that the employee's manager make the selection.

Customized work schedules. Unique business or personal situations may sometimes require that managers work individually with employees to establish a special schedule for a specific time period. For example, a manager may customize the starting or stopping time for an employee to match public transportation timetables.

Fixed work schedules. Fixed work schedules are usually found when there is a high degree of interdependence with preceding or succeeding operations. Sometimes a fixed work schedule will be required when there is only a single employee involved. This arrangement will be found where a uniform starting time is required, but where the manager is able to accommodate the preferences of employees in establishing the schedule.

Pre-Implementation Planning. It is important for local management to carefully consider the various alternatives that will provide the right balance in meeting employee needs and the needs of the business. Some guidelines follow:

1. *Allow sufficient time for detailed planning.* Lead time is the key element to consider in planning the introduction of flexible work schedules to individual departments. Allow sufficient time to assess all aspects of implementation before committing to an implementation date.
2. *Review department objectives.* Before deciding the applicability of flexible work schedules, review the overall objectives of the department and the degree to which they are being attained.
3. *Review specific job requirements.* Review the requirements of each job and its relationship to the accomplishment of department objectives. A review of the following items will be helpful in determining which alternative work schedule arrangement best satisfies those objectives.

- *Nature, frequency, and timing of external contacts:*
  —Telephone contacts
  —Personal contacts
  —Alternative method of handling
  —Controlled by employee
  —Minimum staffing requirements
- *Internal contacts:*
  —Type
  —Relationship to start/stop time
  —Changeability
  —Interdependence with other departments
  —Back-up support available

- *Specific work performed:*
  —Relationship to other jobs (i.e., manufacturing assembly line, administrative stand-alone)
  —Process-dependent
  —Shift-dependent
- *Employee control of work performed:*
  —Self-paced
  —Work scheduled or assigned by others
  —Customer driven
- *Safety/security requirements:*
  —Work-alone restrictions
  —Proprietary information handling

4. *Apply "best fit" test.* When the review of job responsibilities is completed, several or all of the alternative arrangements should be tested against each job to determine which ones can apply and which are clearly not suited to the particular job being reviewed.
5. *Involve employees.* Having determined which alternatives will apply, meet individually with each employee to discuss personal preference. Seek employees' opinions and be receptive to ideas that may enhance the schedule selection process. These conversations should result in mutually acceptable schedules. Consider a pilot test before general implementation.
6. *Review exclusions.* When the review of job requirements results in the conclusion that no flexibility beyond the existing work schedule can be provided, be prepared to explain why the flexible alternatives are impractical. Are the reasons evident? Are they understandable to employees in terms of peak periods, shift or process dependencies, or special interface requirements?

Accountability and Control. Along with flexibility comes the need for control and accountability, as well as a reliable and unbiased record of the hours each employee works. There are several "accountability" approaches to consider, ranging from the honor system to electronic timekeeping systems.

Assessment. A flexible work schedule system may not be appropriate for some companies. For example, the nature or size of the business may be such that flexible work schedules would disrupt customer service. However, under optimum conditions it can pay dividends in improved employee moral and commuting time and decreased rates of absenteeism and lateness.

Four-Day Week

As industrial society develops a leisure orientation and demands additional time for personal pursuits, the four-day workweek is being increasingly discussed.

Operation. Under a typical system, employees agree with their manager on the day to be taken off, and work from 8 AM to 6 PM, less lunch and breaks, spending, for example, a total of thirty-seven hours actually on the job, thus satisfying the standard work-hour norm. The day off chosen—usually Friday or Monday—remains constant.

A Mixed Blessing. Despite some success stories, not all workers appreciate this fringe benefit and many companies would find it a distinct disadvantage.

- While some employees may adapt easily and respond favorably to the four-day week, other employees who are accustomed to traditional weekends may find the longer workday onerous and the adjustment difficult. If, for example, transportation extends the workday by another hour on each end, the resulting twelve hour day may not be feasible.
- For some employees who have personal needs (e.g., child care, care of an elderly parent, attendance at night school, participation in recreational activities) the "stretched out" day under a four-day workweek may not be desirable.
- Management may find in some instances that the extra two hours per day are not used productively and that work quality suffers.
- Like flexible work schedules, the four-day week may pose problems for some companies in which production depends on the standard workweek, and for service organizations whose customers expect service during conventional hours on a five-day week basis. Careful management and application of resources may resolve these problems.

A workable compromise may be to schedule work hours from 8 AM to 5 PM in exchange for a half day off, (e.g., Friday afternoon). Some companies have adopted this practice for the summer months. The variations from the "standard" work schedules are many and the selection of the appropriate arrangement must be based on compatability with business objectives and employee needs.

DAY CARE

Between 1960 and 1979, the number of married working women with children under age 6 increased 26 percent, and experts predict that between now and 1990, one million women with children will be entering the work force each year. This demographic shift has raised a question among employers as to whether they will continue to attract and retain the quality employees necessary to run the business with or without company assistance for day care for children of current and prospective employees.

The various types of day care centers may be classified as:

- Community—Nonprofit
- Public—Nonprofit
- Industry—Nonprofit
- Private—For profit

Companies considering involvement in day care assistance may want to weigh the following options:

1. Centers can be owned and operated by employers.
2. Centers can be financially sponsored or subsidized by employers.
3. Employers may reimburse a portion of employee expenses or make direct payments to service vendors.
4. Employers may contribute financial support directly to local nonprofit centers, or through United Way funds.

Advantages

There are several arguments in support of company-assisted day care programs:

- Replace potentially higher cost of private nursery schools.
- Company-sponsored or company-operated centers may provide more flexible hours than private facilities.
- May assist recruitment and attainment of equal employment opportunity objectives.
- May help retain skilled labor, otherwise lost through attrition of employees with child care needs.
- Well-organized centers can assist a child in his/her preschool education and development.

Disadvantages

On the other hand, there are arguments for not establishing direct day care assistance programs:

- High cost for an employer to run a day care center and/or provide a reimbursement program (see below); the greater the number of company offices and plants, the greater the implications of cost and administration.
- Possible tendency of employees at all salary levels to use center as a "nursery," rather than as a means of meeting real economic need; to correct this an employer could require employees to submit to a financial "needs" test. However, this may be administratively burdensome and not palatable from an employee relations viewpoint.
- Pressure for assistance in other areas when an employee incurs personal expenses related to continuance of employment (e.g., care of elderly parents).
- Relative poor track record of some centers sponsored by employers, (e.g., no reduction in employee absenteeism and/or turnover).

Costs

It has been estimated that the annual cost of sending a child to a day care center five days a week is approximately $3,000. Even at a 50 percent reimbursement level the liability for direct day care assistance is considerable. Although the Economic Recovery Tax Act of 1981 has made day care expense reimbursement tax exempt for employees, the cost to employers is high. To build, operate and maintain company facilities can be a great deal more expensive on a per capita basis. However, it should be noted that tax legislation designed to encourage employer-sponsored day care facilities can reduce capital expenditures via amortization of construction and service installation costs.

Employers will have to continue to monitor the prospects of day care and measure their individual business needs and capabilities to attract and retain quality employees. In addition, the role of the employer as a corporate citizen may indicate that financial support to day care to meet a social need may be appropriate even if the company's needs per se do not require direct assistance to employees.

EMPLOYEE CREDIT UNIONS

Employee credit unions are nonprofit, member-directed organizations that provide certain financial services to their members, such as savings and loans at relatively attractive interest rates and perhaps other peripheral services (e.g., certain group insurance plans).

An employee credit union elects its own officers and establishes policy in accordance with guidelines issued by the Bureau of Federal Credit Unions or individual state Leagues of Credit Unions. A credit union formed by company employees operates independently of the company; by law an employer cannot form a credit union or prevent the creation of one by employees.

Companies find that a credit union serves several purposes:

- Provides attractive and convenient financial services for members (relatively low cost loans, savings dividends, etc.),
- Can help to reduce employees' financial concerns,
- Decreases the need for granting employees financial aid in the form of pay advances and loans,
- May offer certain group employee-pay-all benefits that the company does not wish to currently sponsor,
- Gives employees serving in executive credit union positions practical experience with financial matters.

Employers can support and encourage the growth and success of credit unions by supplying them with needed office space and related facilities and supplies as well as access to the company's payroll deduction system. An employer may also choose to encourage personnel in related areas, such as auditing and accounting, to serve as advisors or committee members, and to publicize credit union efforts through their newsletters or brochures. It must be clear however, that financial and operational activities are the responsibility of the employee credit union and are independent of the company.

COMPANY FOOD SERVICES

Company Cafeterias

Major corporations today provide their employees with a comfortable, often attractive, dining facility with food at affordable rates. Although this service requires considerable resources on the part of the employer, who usually runs this facility at cost or even a loss, it is often a must for companies that have moved to the suburbs or to areas where there are few if any outside dining facilities. Even in urban locations, many firms find that internal eating facilities promote productivity due to the tighter administration of the lunchtime period.

The general view is that employees have a personal responsibility for paying for their lunches. However, with food prices steadily escalating most employers view cafeteria operations as a major tangible personnel service. In addition to space, firms usually provide equipment, utilities and sometimes labor. Since free meals may be construed by the IRS as taxable income, few companies completely subsidize employee meals.

Concessionaire Approach

If a firm believes that it is advantageous to have food on the premises, but does not have the expertise or the desire to assume the full burden of a cafeteria operation, a popular alternative is to use the services of one or more of the numerous food service companies who specialize in operating cafeterias for companies and institutions. The service company can very likely provide quality food at costs substantially lower than employees would normally pay at outside facilities.

Vending Operations

Machine-dispensed coffee, tea, hot chocolate, juices, soft drinks, and other food items offered by employers at cost are also regarded as a meaningful convenience for employees.

SERVICE AWARDS

Many employers want to demonstrate appreciation to employees who have spent a good portion of their working careers with the company.

Service awards are usually emblems, accessories, or other forms of recognition after five years or ten years of service. Some companies emphasize significant milestones such as twenty-five years of service. A statement of service awards policy of RCA is reproduced in Figure 28.5.

RCA
Industrial Relations Policy

Number: P-502
Approved: 9/15/81
Supersedes: 6/16/81
Subject: SERVICE AWARD PROGRAM
Page: 1

POLICY

I. The RCA Service Award Program gives recognition to employees who have substantial periods of continuous service with the Company and its predecessor companies. The Program consists of:

A. Emblem and accessory jewelry awards for 10, 15, 20, 25, 30, 35, 40, 45 and 50 years of continuous service.

B. Special Recognition Awards for 25 and 40 years of continuous service.

II. PRESENTATION OF AWARDS

A. Presentation of the award emblems and accessory jewelry should be made, if possible, on the employee's service anniversary date. It is recommended that the presentation ceremony for anniversaries of 15 years through 50 years include an informal luncheon.

B. Presentation of the 25 year and 40 year special recognition awards will be made at location annual awards ceremonies between September 1 and the last day of December of the applicable year at dinner or luncheon ceremonies.

III. ATTENDANCE AT ANNUAL AWARD CEREMONIES

A. Attendance at the annual award ceremonies will include 25 and 40 year award recipients, active employees marking their 30th and 35th service anniversaries and active employees with over 40 years of service.

B. Attendance may be expanded to include all active employees with 25 years of service or more where the number of long-service employees does not present a critical accommodation problem.

IV. Continuous service credit will be accumulated in accordance with Industrial Relations Policy E-205, Service Credit.

RESPONSIBILITY

V. Major Operating Units

Each Major Operating Unit will arrange for procurement and delivery of service awards through the local Purchasing activities.

VI. RCA Staff

A. The Manager, Business Programs and Employee Services will:

1. Determine standard basic designs of Service Awards.

2. Designate vendors for supplying Service Awards in cooperation with RCA Staff Purchasing.

3. Provide interpretation of this Policy.

Source: RCA

Fig. 28.5 Statement of Service Award Policy

Regular and part-time employees who complete twenty-five years of service often get special recognition and become members of such groups as IBM's Quarter Century Club, who receive honor certificates, a monetary award, a choice of insignias and gifts, and are invited to a special luncheon or dinner at company expense. Some firms, on a specific employee service anniversary, allow the spouse to select a gift from a specified list.

In considering the implementation of a service award program, the frequency of service recognition should be measured against the company's objectives, the diversity of skills and professions in the firm, and current employee attitudes regarding the type of award such as service emblems. Existing programs should also be reviewed periodically to determine if they continue to be appropriate and appreciated.

PURCHASE DISCOUNTS

A company may choose to offer its employees several types of purchase discounts:

1. *Discounts on company items and work-related merchandise.* Companies that manufacture consumer goods often provide these items to their employees at substantial savings. This practice enables the company to reduce its inventory of old stock, and promote its merchandise, while granting a tangible employee benefit. Companies may also arrange for employees to purchase at a discount work-related items from local vendors. Non-company items such as major appliances may also be available for sale at considerable savings.
2. *Subsidized shopping facilities.* Some employers may allow individual vendors to come on company property to sell their merchandise to employees at competitive prices.
3. *Department and discount stores.* By special arrangements, local stores may provide special discounts for employees of major companies.
4. *Department store employee discounts.* Many department stores supply their employees with discount passes that can be used in all departments. Discounts typically range from 10 percent to 25 percent depending on the item being purchased.

In the companies surveyed in Figure 28.1, product discounts on company products ranged from 10 percent to 60 percent from retail price.

There are several factors to consider in making a decision on offering purchase discounts to employees. On the plus side, there is the potential goodwill that may result from employee savings, convenience and the availability of desirable items at a discount, such as safety-related products. On the other hand, there can be dissatisfaction among local businesses that sell the same or comparable products; employees may not be satisfied with the size of the discount as compared to sale prices elsewhere; if a non-company product is offered at a discount there can be employee interest in discounts on other goods and services beyond the original intent of the employer.

One practice to consider is to keep unsolicited discount information on file with the company-employee social club, if one exists, for interested employees to refer to.

RELOCATION ASSISTANCE

A relocation assistance program provides various forms of expense reimbursement when an employee is transferred to a different work location. Relocation assistance plays an important role when the mission of a particular work location or division changes and significant numbers of personnel must be permanently transferred.

Covered Expenses

The forms of relocation assistance have changed considerably over the years. The following types of expenses are appropriate for consideration in developing or amending a relocation assistance program.

Assistance in Sale of Present Home. If an employee independently sells his or her present residence, the employer may reimburse:

- Licensed real estate brokerage fees up to a stated percentage of the gross selling price such as 6 percent
- Statutory costs imposed on the seller by federal, state, or local law
- Attorney fees, mortgage fees, title search, title insurance up to a maximum amount
- Advertising costs

An employer may choose to engage one or more "relocation firms" in order to expedite the sale of an employee's present home. The general sequence of events may be as follows:

- The relocation firm contacts the employee to explain its services.
- The employee is asked to choose one or more qualified appraisers to estimate the "fair market value" of the residence, based on average of the appraisals.
- The relocation firm offers to purchase the home at the fair market value.
- The employee has the choice of accepting the offer within a stated period of time such as two to three months or he may choose to sell the home independently to obtain a better offer.

Carrying Two Homes. An employee who is transferred may purchase a new home prior to the sale of his present residence. In these cases the employer may cover certain duplicate carrying charges on the older residence such as:

- Property taxes
- Heat, electricity, water, and maintenance costs
- Insurance premiums
- Interest on approved loans

Temporary Quarters. The employer will normally pay all reasonable travel expenses for the employee and family to move to the new location by the most direct route. Upon arrival, it is customary to reimburse:

- Basic living expenses such as hotel and food expenses within a specified period, such as one or two months.
- Reasonable house hunting expenses during the same period.

Moving Personal Belongings. Typically, the employer will cover the cost of packing, moving, and unpacking most belongings transported from the old location to the new location. Covered items usually include household furnishings, appliances, automobiles, clothing, tools, pets, and other reasonable items. The employer will usually insure household and personal property while in transit and in storage if necessary.

Assistance in Purchasing New Home. The employer will normally reimburse statutory costs imposed directly on the employee by federal, state, and local law in connection with the purchase of a new home. Additional assistance may be provided to cover a variety of expenses including:

- Mortgage discount fees charged by a commercial lending institution
- Title insurance or guarantee
- Tax and title search
- Attorney's fees
- Survey fees, pest inspection fees, etc.

These expenses can be limited to a flat dollar amount or a percentage of the purchase price of the new home (e.g., up to 3 percent or 4 percent).

Mortgage interest rate differential. A relatively new form of assistance is called the *mortgage interest rate differential* (MIRD). The idea is to assist the employee who is asked to transfer at a time when the mortgage rate at the new location significantly exceeds the rate at the present location. The arrangement is usually temporary in nature so as to serve as a useful tool only during periods of inflationary mortgage rates. Formulas for providing MIRD are varied and can be somewhat complex. Generally, the payment is made in a lump sum covering two to three years of interest assistance.

Equity loan. Employers may also choose to provide an *equity loan,* interest free, up to the amount of the equity in the employee's present home (or a modification of the equity value) for a variety of costs related to a home purchase including the down payment, land purchase, construction costs, etc.

The key to the design of a relocation assistance plan is the business need to transfer the employee. Employers must also recognize that two-career families (both spouses working) now exceed 50 percent of the U.S. marriages; this will have a significant impact on an employee's ability or willingness to relocate. In any event, relocation assistance is a true blending of the changing needs of the business and human resource needs; the cost/benefit ratio must be carefully measured and monitored to assure an appropriate balance of these needs on a continuous basis.

SUGGESTION PLAN AWARDS

Under a suggestion plan system, management encourages employees to submit suggestions in writing that will result in improved productivity, products, or working conditions. Employees are rewarded, usually through a specified schedule of monetary awards, for suggestions that are adopted and implemented.

According to the National Association of Suggestion Systems (NASS), the current popularity of these systems, first formally instituted in this country in 1896, is borne out by the fact that there are in the United States an estimated 6,000 formal suggestion systems and possibly an equal number of semi-formal ones. The 600 current corporate members of NASS, representing more than 10 million employees, report that over 1,300,000 suggestions were received in 1979, of which almost 317,200 were accepted and implemented—an adoption rate of 24 percent.

Suggestion plan procedures must be tailored to each company's individual needs, and must be carefully planned and monitored. The system can backfire and cause employee disappointment and frustration if management does not clearly pinpoint:

- Its objectives;
- Which groups of employees are eligible;
- The categories in which ideas will be welcomed and the types of suggestions that are eligible for awards;
- The procedures that must be followed;
- Whether or not the employee's identity should be known at various stages of the evaluation process;
- The evaluation procedures that will be instituted, and
- The types and amounts of awards that are attainable.

Objectives

Suggestion plan systems are generally instituted to increase productivity through the creativity of employees; the plan also provides the employer with the opportunity to increase employee morale through tangible, public recognition of constructive ideas.

Eligibility

Typically, all employees are encouraged to submit suggestions but not all employees are eligible to receive monetary awards. Employees in management positions are often not eligible for awards; "eligible" employees generally do not qualify for awards when the idea is related to their regular duties and job responsibilities.

Acceptable Suggestions

Under the broad umbrella of improved productivity, the idea or suggestion should have one or more of the following effects:

- Save material, time, or money
- Improve product quality or reliability
- Enhance customer service
- Improve safety, health, or security
- Result in a new approach, method or design

In spelling out the intent of a suggestion plan and the categories of ideas eligible for awards, it is equally important to communicate those subjects or areas that are *not* eligible for awards, such as employee benefits, corrections to protect material, routine maintenance, and ideas already under consideration by the company. Each employer's list of ineligible items will vary with the company's type of business and attitude on what constitutes a creative idea that warrants recognition.

Administrative Procedures

In a typically well-run plan, suggestions are written up by the employee according to detailed instructions on a form supplied by management and deposited in a centrally located depository. (Each form should contain one suggestion, which then becomes the property of the company.) Collected forms are numbered, if contributions are to be judged anonymously, and designated a priority listing according to the date of submission. Receipt of a suggestion is acknowledged promptly. Designated reviewers evaluate each suggestion and decide if it merits acceptance and a cash award. If the suggestion is rejected, the employee is notified in writing with an explanation.

In managing such a plan, it is essential that these procedures be thoroughly understood by employees. Prompt response and acknowledgement is essential. The employee should have the opportunity to appeal, within a suitable time frame, the results of the evaluation if the suggestion is not accepted. In short, if a suggestion system is to be successful, employees must believe that their ideas are being thoughtfully and honestly evaluated and that due credit will be given them if their suggestions are adopted.

Awards

The minimum award is usually in the $20 to $25 range; maximum can range from $25,000 to $100,000 or more. Awards are often based on the principle of providing the employee with a percentage, e.g., 25 percent, of the net savings during the first year after installation, as estimated by the department responsible for determining such costs, in cooperation with the suggestion administrator. Some employers also award a percentage of the second year's savings.

Awards are made at the time a suggestion is put into effect. It should be noted that the IRS regards suggestion awards as part of company compensation to employees, and the awards are subject to normal withholding taxes.

BENEFITS FOR HANDICAPPED CHILDREN

Introduction

Parents of a mentally retarded, emotionally disturbed, or physically handicapped child can be faced with a severe financial burden because of the costs of necessary special care for the child. While some of these costs are covered under many group medical benefit plans, most of them are not.

Employer programs, specifically designed to defray a significant portion of expenses related to the care of a handicapped child, are rare in U.S. industry today. This chapter will acquaint the reader with the workings of an approach to a formalized program for special care of handicapped children.

The intention of a special care program is to help free parents from a portion of their financial worries by providing some additional assistance towards the cost of required care and treatment of handicapped children if they are in qualified residential or outpatient care facilities or if they are getting certain kinds of treatment by qualified health professionals.

While all employees would be eligible for these benefits, only a small portion would actually utilize such a program (e.g., five employees per thousand). But, for parents of a handicapped child, a special care program is extremely meaningful, and all indications are that the assistance—available in the event of need—would be well regarded by all employees.

Legislative Situation

Several states grant state benefits for the education and care of handicapped children. A state may base the receipt of benefits on economic hardship or ability of the recipient to pay. In the determination of a recipient's economic hardship or ability to pay, a state may consider the recipient's company benefits or insurance plan benefits, depending upon the wording of the plan and of applicable state laws.

If the employer intends that all benefits from federal and state sources should first be applied before calculating the company's reimbursement to the employee, the language of the plan and the administrative procedure must explicitly specify that benefits are contingent on the employee first receiving full government benefits without regard to the existence of the company plan.

Special Care for Children Assistance Plan

An assistance plan for the special care for children is a program designed to assist employees in meeting certain expenses outside the scope of the basic medical plans that they may incur for the care of a mentally, emotionally, or physically handicapped child. This assistance would be provided only after the child has received all assistance otherwise available from federal, state, and other sources.

If the child has a disability and is being treated in a clinic or special day or residential care facility, or by an independent practitioner (e.g., a speech pathologist or audiologist) under the direction of a physician, the employee may be entitled to benefits.

Under such a program, each situation would be individually reviewed by a company panel to determine eligibility for assistance, and if approved, reimbursement would be provided for a portion of the required charges incurred up to a predetermined maximum dollar benefit per individual child.

Eligible charges may be determined by multiplying the approved charges by preestablished percentages and dollar deductibles, as shown in the following example:

- 75 percent of the approved charges of a day or residential care or day care facility
- 100 percent of the approved charges of an outpatient facility, clinic or charges for a special eligible device

An annual family deductible would then be applied after the calculation of the appropriate percentage formula, and the employee reimbursed for a percentage (e.g., 80 percent) of the remaining eligible charges (see Figure 28.6). By first excluding 25 percent of the approved day care or residential care charges, the company takes into account the room and/or meal charges that all parents generally incur.

Funding. Outside assistance is generally funded by tax revenues to which both employees and employers contribute. Therefore, the objective of a plan is to provide a supplemental benefit after the employee has received

Example A—Residential

Assume an employee's expense is $7,500 and he applies for outside aid and receives $2,500:

Authorized charge	$7,500
Less: Outside aid (equals or exceeds 25%)	−2,500
Employee expense	5,000
Less: Deductible	−150
	$4,850
Reimbursement rate	80%
Reimbursement	$3,880

Where the assistance equals or exceeds the initial percentage reduction in the assistance formula (25%), the assistance will be used to reduce the authorized charges and the initial percentage reduction will not be applied.

Example B—Day Care

Assume an employee's expense is $2,800 and he receives no outside assistance:

Authorized charge	$2,800
Initial percentage reduction	25%
	$2,100
Less: Deductible	−150
	$1,950
Reimbursement rate	80%
Reimbursement	$1,560

Where there is no assistance, or the assistance is less than the initial percentage reduction, the assistance will not be used in the assistance formula and the initial percentage reduction will be applied to the entire amount of covered charges.

Example C—Clinic

Since the assistance formula for clinics does not provide any initial percentage reduction, any outside assistance received would be deducted:

Authorized charge	$1,100
Less: Assistance	−200
Employee's expense	900
Less: Deductible	−150
	$ 750
Reimbursement rate	80%
Reimbursement	$ 600

Fig. 28.6 Special Care Coverage

all other assistance to which he or she is already entitled. In applying for such assistance, company benefits should not be included by the providing authority in calculating the amount to be paid by the employee. Eligible charges, incurred at a public or private facility, would be reimbursable under the plan only if those charges are payable by the individual irrespective of the existence of the plan.

Plan Provisions

Eligible Children. Generally, the plan would consider a handicapped child to be a child who is mentally retarded, emotionally disturbed, or physically handicapped and is under the care of a physician. The definition of eligible children, with respect to age, dependency, etc., would be the same definition used under the company's regular medical benefit plans.

Eligible Institutions. *Eligible institutions* may be defined as: a residential care facility (child resides at facility), or a day school (child attends facility full-time), or a clinic or other outpatient facility (child visits frequently).

The charges for treatment would be considered eligible for reimbursement if the facility:

- Is operated under the supervision of physicians;
- Has a planned program for medical treatment, rehabilitation, or custodial care of the child's condition, which has been reviewed, approved, and is supervised by physicians;
- Furnishes education only as an adjunct to the medical treatment, rehabilitation, or custodial care of the child;
- Has the approval of, or meets minimum standards of, applicable professional associations (e.g., American Medical Association, American Psychiatric Association);
- Is licensed or certified by, or has specific approval of applicable governmental agencies (e.g., State or Federal Department of Health and/or Mental Hygiene).

Treatment by Speech Pathologists and Audiologists. When an employee's child has a bona fide functional speech or hearing disability and receives necessary care and treatment from an independent speech pathologist or independent audiologist (i.e., services rendered outside an approved special care facility such as a clinic), the charges incurred may be reviewed for reimbursement under the special care plan if they are not eligible under the company's basic medical plan. The speech pathologist or audiologist should hold a certificate of clinical competence in speech therapy or audiology or be eligible for such certification, and meet certain other professional and educational requirements.

Hearing Aids and Special Eyeglasses. If the handicapped child's hearing and/or sight is impaired and the child requires a hearing aid or special vision aids, the charges incurred may be reviewed for reimbursement under the plan. For example, one hearing aid device would be provided within a thirty-six-month period for an eligible child. Charges for glasses that are prescribed for the correction of nearsightedness, farsightedness, or astigmatism would not be eligible, but charges for required special vision aids, such as prisms, for severe loss or impairment of sight would be eligible.

Parental Counseling. Under certain conditions, charges for parental counseling may fall within the intent of the plan. If charges are incurred by the parent for counseling that is an integral part of the treatment being rendered to the child, these charges may be considered for eligibility under the special care plan.

Administration

Applying for Assistance. To obtain benefits, an employee would be required to submit a claim, and might be asked to include the following: a statement from the child's physician or psychiatrist, a statement of the special facility (when applicable), and a statement of the independent practitioner (when applicable).

The completed forms, with itemized bills, would be forwarded through the local benefits administrator to a special care review panel, which would include a medical director and a panel administrator. The panel would review each case and determine eligibility under the plan. A copy of the panel's letter of approval would be forwarded to the employee's work location for reimbursement.

Subsequent claims. Once the panel has reviewed and approved the first claim, subsequent claims would be submitted directly to the location claims processor if the charges were not in excess of the authorized amounts and if there were no change in the facility or practitioner rendering treatment.

Utilization

The types of facilities utilized under a special care plan might range as follows:

Special Care Facility	*Typical Annual Charge*	*Percent of Claims Submitted*
Residential	$7,500	20%
Day Care	2,800	20%
Clinic	1,100	60%

Outlook

There has not been any visible industry movement toward formal, published employer benefit programs designed to absorb expenses for the unique care of handicapped children. The IBM Special Care for Children Assistance plan, and Eastman Kodak's Extended Care plan, which are comparable in intent and purpose, are examples of two formalized programs. There may be other unpublished programs where individual cases are considered as the need arises. In any event, there appears to be room in the future for the implementation of additional employer programs designed to assist employee-parents of handicapped children with their special care expenses.

ADOPTION ASSISTANCE

Introduction

An adoption assistance plan is intended to provide financial assistance toward the expenses of adopting children, and may cover adoptions through an agency, private adoptions, or spouse adoptions (children of prior marriages).

Such a plan is intended to cover some portion of the expenses incurred by an employee in adopting a child, just as health care benefits assist in the coverage of medical expenses associated with childbirth.

The plan will generally be utilized by a relatively small percentage of the total employee population. However, it can provide meaningful assistance, as well as a degree of equity. All indications are that where such a program exists, it is well received by all employees.

Existing Programs

There are relatively few adoption assistance programs in the United States today; such programs were unheard of prior to the 1970s. One of the earliest was the IBM Adoption Assistance program, which was introduced in December, 1972. Other companies that have introduced adoption assistance plans include G.D. Searle (Chicago, Ill.), S.C. Johnson (Racine, Wis.), Digital Equipment (Maynard, Mass.), Xerox (Stamford, Conn.), Hallmark (Kansas City, Mo.), and Pitney Bowes (Stamford, Conn.).

While provisions of the few existing programs vary in detail, the following brief description will provide a general picture of the structure of an adoption assistance plan.

Eligible charges include adoption agency fees, placement fees, attorney's fees, and other required legal fees, medical charges for prospective parents when physical examinations are required by the adoption source, maternity fees of the child's natural mother and temporary foster care charges (immediately preceding placement of the child with the adopting family).

Cost Considerations

In considering implementation of an adoption assistance program, a variety of potential costs and related items must be studied and a decision reached on eligibility of charges and the structure of the plan.

Adoption Agency Fees. Agency fees may be a flat adoption fee or a sliding scale fee based on the applicant's earnings. Such fees may include application and placement charges, home and completion study fees (investigation of the adopting household done by the agency to determine its suitability) and foster care fees.

Some adoption agencies request that the adopting family make a voluntary contribution or donation to the agency. An employer designing an adoption assistance plan would have to ask the question: Can reimbursement of unstructured, voluntary contributions be administered equitably within the intent of the program and without affecting other benefit plans, such as medical plans, where evidence of eligible fees or charges are required?

Other agencies will require a donation or gift of a certain amount as a part of the adoptive process. It may be determined that such a required donation is, in fact, an agency fee for the services rendered and as such, may be considered for reimbursement.

Legal Fees. Many adoptions are arranged directly through an attorney; sometimes an agency fee will also be included in addition to the attorney's costs. Legal fees incurred in the process of adoption include a retainer fee, charges for law library research, and charges incurred in obtaining such documents as the child's birth certificate.

Court or docket fees that may be incurred include filing charges, order of adoption, court clerk fees, service of summons, transcript fees, etc. Other official charges that may be incurred are Department of Public Health fees, county or state clerical fees, taxation costs, investigation fees, etc.

Consideration must be given to whether or not the plan design should include coverage of the legal fees when an individual adopts the child or children by a previous marriage and legally changes their surname. Part of the consideration will be the intent of the plan, costs, and the ability to distinguish between types of adoptions in determining benefits eligibility.

Hospital Charges and Physical Examination Fees. In the case of private adoption, the maternity expense for the natural mother is usually incurred by the adoptive parent. The adoptive parent may also incur medical expenses for physical examination fees, when required by the adoption agency.

Publication Expense. Publication expense may be incurred in order to notify the child's natural father, in the event that he cannot be located.

Children of Foreign Origin. If the child being adopted is of foreign origin, certain expenses unique to this situation will be incurred. Among them are immigration, naturalization, passport and photo expense for the child, translation charges, telegram fees, State Department processing fees, and orphans court fees, if specifically related to the foreign adoption.

A question to be considered is whether or not the employer chooses to cover, in addition to these expenses, the transportation expenses associated with the adoption of a child from a foreign country. The answer will vary, depending upon the company's philosophy or practice regarding transportation expenses in general and what precedent, if any, will be established for coverage of a variety of transportation expenses under existing medical benefit plans (e.g., transportation expense for a major surgical procedure to be performed in a distant city or another country).

Other Charges. Other charges that may be incurred by the adoptive parent and are not generally covered under existing adoption assistance plans, include (1) charges incurred by the parents in the process of adoption, such as travel and accommodation expenses and telephone calls; (2) charges for the changes to wills in order to include the newly adopted child in such wills; (3) legal fees incurred to obtain guardianship or custody of own child; and (4) clothing costs for the child.

Administration

Audit of Application. Each application should be reviewed to determine eligibility of the charges being submitted and to insure benefits have not been paid previously for any of the eligible charges.

An employer may decide to permit the processing of adoption charges prior to the completion of the adoption and the full amount of the expenses to be incurred. In such cases, an accurate and current accounting of charges and benefits-to-date must be maintained to insure that the maximum benefit is not exceeded in the processing of subsequent charges for the same adoption.

Coordination of Benefits. Situations may arise periodically where the question of coordination of benefits for adoption expense reimbursement will become an issue when both husband and wife are employed. Such cases, however, will be relatively rare, due to the uniqueness of adoption assistance plans in industry.

Tax Status. Benefits received under an adoption assistance plan are considered taxable income, subject to federal, state, and local income tax withholding and FICA.

Several bills have been proposed in Congress in the past to allow deductions for adoption expense in the same manner as medical expenses that, if enacted, would allow companies to pursue exemption of company benefits received by employees from taxable income. However, to date, such proposals to alter tax legislation in this regard has not been favorably acted upon.[1]

Utilization

Participation in an adoption assistance plan can be expected to be about three or four employees per thousand.

The distribution of various types of adoptions that may be experienced under an adoption assistance plan is roughly as follows:

Type	*Percentage of Total*
Agency expense only	15%
Agency plus legal expense	5% to 10%
Agency plus legal and medical expense	1%
Legal expense only	40%
Adoption of spouse's child/Legal expense	20% to 25%
Private (non-agency) legal and medical expense	5%
Foreign	5%

Outlook

Although still relatively uncommon in industry, adoption assistance programs are being studied as a viable, relatively low cost benefit by more and more major corporations. A change in tax regulations to provide a more favorable treatment of company-paid coverage of adoption expenses would no doubt increase interest in adoption assistance programs.

---

[1] Since 1975, at least fifty bills relating to deductibility of adoption benefits have been introduced. S.1479, introduced in July, 1981, would exclude from the income of an employee certain adoption expenses paid by an employer.

Suggested Reading

PART I Benefits Principles and Administration

AICPA. *Fringe Benefits: A Proposal for the Future.* New York: AICPA, 1979.

AICPA, *Illustrations of Accounting for Employee Benefits.* Financial Report Survey: No. 14. New York: AICPA, 1977.

Coffin, Richard M., and Shaw, Michael S. *Effective Communication of Employee Benefits.* New York: American Management Association, Inc., 1971.

Gilbert, Geoffrey M., et al. *Accounting and Auditing for Employee Benefit Plans.* Boston: Warren, Gorham & Lamont, Inc., 1978.

Jost, Lee R., and Sutherland, C. Bruce. *Guide to Professional Benefit Plan Management and Administration.* Brookfield, Wis.: International Foundation of Employment Benefit Plans, 1980.

Lawson, J.W., and Smith, Ballard. *Management's Complete Guide to Employee Benefits.* Chicago: Dartnell Corp., 1980.

Lindsay, Fred. *Employee Benefits: Nineteen Eighty.* U.S. Chamber of Commerce, 1981.

Mamorsky, Jeffrey D. *Employee Benefits Law—ERISA and Beyond.* New York: Law Journal Seminars Press, 1980.

McCaffery, Robert M. *Managing the Employee Benefits Program.* New York: American Management Association, 1972.

Meyer, Mitchell, *Women and Employee Benefits.* Report Series No. 752. New York: The Conference Board, Inc., 1978.

Miller, Ned A. *The Complete Guide to Employee Benefit Plans.* Rockville Center, New York: Farnsworth Publishing Co., 1977.

Rosenbloom, Jerry S., and Hallman, G. Victor. *Employee Benefit Planning.* Englewood Cliffs, N.J.: Prentice-Hall, Inc., 1981.

Snider, H. Wayne, ed. *Employee Benefits Management.* New York: The Risk and Insurance Management Society, 1980.

Weeks, David A., ed. *Rethinking Employee Benefit Assumptions.* Report Series No. 739. The Conference Board, Inc., 1978.

PART II Replacement Income—Retirement

Albright, Robert L. "Deferred Compensation Payments—The Revenue Rulings Don't Tell the Whole Story About FICA and FUTA." *The Compensation Planning Journal* TMCJ 80-2 February 1980, pp. 5–6.

Allen, Everett T., Jr.; Melone, Joseph J.; and Rosenbloom, Jerry S. *Pension Planning.* 3d ed. Homewood, Ill.: Richard D. Irwin, Inc., 1976.

Ball, Robert M. *Social Security Today and Tomorrow.* New York: Columbia University Press, 1979.

Bernetich, John D. "Deferred Compensation: The Present Status of Income Tax and Estate Tax Consequences." *Taxes—The Tax Magazine,* 57, No. 3 March 1979, pp. 153-158.

Blackman, Irving. "Choosing Pension or Profit Sharing Plans: What to Look for When Selecting Plans for a Client." *Taxation for Accountants* 15 (1975): 148.

CCH Editorial Staff. *Life Insurance as Estate Planning Tool for Close Corporations Stockholders.* Tax Angles and Tax Savings Series. Chicago, Ill.: Commerce Clearing House, Inc., 1978.

CCH Staff. *Guidebook to Pension Planning.* Chicago, Ill.: Commerce Clearing House, Inc. 1977.

Dankner, Harold D. "A Second Look at ESOPs, Options and Similar Arrangements." N.Y.U. Institute on Federal Taxation 37 (1979): 32-1.

Eckstein, Otto, ed. *Studies in the Economics of Income Maintenance.* Brookings Institution Studies of Government Finance. Westport, Conn.: Greenwood Press, 1977.

Fingal, Charles V., Jr. "1978 Changes Affecting The Taxation of Deferred Compensation, Retirement Plans, and Fringe Benefits." *The Tax Adviser* 10, No. 4 April 1979, pp. 196–205.

Hill, Stanfield, and McKay, Joseph T. "The Flowering of Financed Life Insurance." *Trusts & Estates,* 118, No. 1 January 1979, pp. 59–63.

Hodges, Leo C. "Nonqualified Deferred Compensation After the Revenue Act of 1978." *The Compensation Planning Journal,* TMCJ 79-10 October 1979, pp. 3–12.

Kroll, Arthur H. "Deferred Compensation Arrangements.' *Tax Management Portfolios* (No. 385). Edited by Leonard L. Silverstein. Washington, D.C.: Tax Management Inc., a division of the Bureau of National Affairs, Inc., 1978.

Kroll, Arthur H., and Tauber, Yale D. *Employee Benefits and ERISA Case Law Service.* Boston: Warren, Gorham & Lamont, Inc. 1979.

McGill, Dan M., ed. *Social Security and Private Pension Plans: Competitive or Complementary?* Homewood, Ill.: Richard D. Irwin, Inc., 1977.

McGill, Dan M. *Fundamentals of Private Pensions.* (Published for the Pension Research Council) Homewood, Ill.: Richard D. Irwin, Inc., 1979.

McGinn, Daniel F. *Joint Trust Pension Plans.* Pension Research Council. Homewood, Ill.: Richard D. Irwin, Inc., 1978.

Menke, John D. "ESOPs, New Look Under the Final Regulations." *Journal of Pension Planning and Compliance* 5 May 1979, p. 213.

Mezzullo, Louis A. "Analyzing the ESOP Loan Regs.: Scope of Exemption, Use of Proceeds, Right of First Refusal." *Journal of Taxation,* 48 February 1978, p. 115.

Myers, Robert J. *Social Security.* Homewood, Ill.: Richard D. Irwin, Inc., 1981.

Peish, C. Frederick. "Avoid Taxation of Pension Death Benefits." *Trust and Estates* 119, No. 2 (1980): 53.

Richter, Anthony B. "Supplementing Executive Pensions With Corporate-Owned Life Insurance." *Financial Executive,* XLVII, No. 10 October 1979, pp. 18–20.

Robinson, Joseph S. "Employers Buying More Whole Life on Executives." *Business Insurance,* 13, No. 9 April 30, 1979, pp. 93–94.

Rothman, David C., ed. *Pension and Profit-Sharing Plans* (a series of folios) Philadelphia, Pa.: ALI-ABA Committee on Continuing Professional Education, 1979.

Sacher, Charles P. "How and When a Rollover IRA Should Be Used to Receive a Lump Sum Distribution," *Taxation for Lawyers* 24 (1980): 82.

Smith, Carlton J. "Key-Man Uses on Life and Health Insurance." Chapter 47 of *Life and Health Insurance Handbook.* 2d ed. Edited by Davis W. Gregg. Homewood, Ill.: Richard D. Irwin, Inc., 619–630.

Stein, Bruno. *Social Security and Pensions in Transition: Understanding the American Retirement System.* New York: The Free Press, 1980.

Stein, Bruno. *Social Security and the Private Pension System.* New York: Industrial Relations Counselors, Inc. 1979.

Sullivan, James J. "Deferred Cash Compensation—The Other Side of the Coin." *Compensation Review,* Second Quarter 1979, pp. 38–42.

Tax Research Institute of America, Inc. *Executive Compensation & Taxation Coordinator.* New York: The Research Institute of America, Inc., 1980.

Taylor, Samuel A.L., Jr. "Measuring the Adequacy of Retirement Income." *Financial Executive,* XLVII, No. 12 December 1979 pp. 16–21.

Walsh, William F., and Mamorsky, Jeffrey D. "FICA Taxation on Nonqualified Deferred Compensation Under Individual Agreements." *Pension World,* 16, No. 3 March 1980, pp. 49–53.

Wangard, Robert E. "Selecting a Qualified Plan After ERISA: The Alternatives, Problems and Costs." 43 *Journal of Taxation* 43 (1975): 145.

Weinberg, Bernard. "Opportunities and Methods for Insurance Purchases Using Corporate Dollars—An Overview." *CLU Journal*, XXXIV, No. 2 April 1980, pp. 10–26.

Wyatt, Arthur R.; Dieter, Richard; Stewart, John E. "Accounting For Deferred Compensation." *Tax Management Portfolios* (No. 393). Edited by Leonard L. Silverstein. Washington, D.C.: Tax Management, Inc., a division of the Bureau of National Affairs, Inc., 1978.

Zalutsky, Morton H., "Considerations in Planning Distributions from Qualified Plans." *ALI-ABA Course Materials Journal* 3, No. 1 (1978) 9.

PART III Replacement Income—Disability, Unemployment, and Death

Becker, Joseph M. *Experience Rating in Unemployment Insurance: An Experiment in Competitive Socialism*. Baltimore, Md.: The Johns Hopkins University Press, 1972.

Becker, Joseph M. *Unemployment Benefits: Should There Be a Compulsory Federal Standard?* Washington, D.C.: American Enterprise Institute for Public Policy Research, 1980.

Blaustein, Saul J. and Kozlowski, Paul J. *Interstate Differences in Unemployment Insurance Benefit Costs: A Cross-section Study*. Kalamazoo, Mich.: Upjohn, W.E. Institute for Employment Research, 1978.

Consumers Union Report on Life Insurance. Mount Vernon, N.Y.: 1980.

Eilers, Robert D., and Crowe, Robert M., ed., *Group Insurance Handbook*. Homewood, Ill.: Richard D. Irwin, Inc., 1965.

Gregg, Davis, and Lucas, Vane B. *Life and Health Insurance Handbook*. 3d ed. New York: Dow Jones-Irwin, 1973.

Halpin, Terrence C. "The Effect of Unemployment Insurance on Seasonal Fluctuations in Employment," *Industrial and Labor Relations Review*, 32, No. 3 (1979).

Hamermesh, Daniel S. *Unemployment Insurance and the Older American*. Kalamazoo, Mich.: Upjohn Institute, 1980.

Howards, Irving, et al. *Disability Benefits*. New York: Praeger Publishers, 1979.

Huebner, S.S., and Black, K. *Life Insurance*. 9th ed. Englewood Cliffs, N.J.: Prentice-Hall, 1976.

Klock, David R. "Group Insurance Planning and the Role of the Professional Life Underwriter." *CLU Journal*, 33 July 1979.

Krass, Stephen J. "Employer-Provided Group-Term Life Requires Coordinated Income, Gift, Estate Tax Planning." *Taxation for Lawyers,* 9 November/December 1980, pp. 146–149.

Life Insurance Planning. (updated looseleaf service). Englewood Cliffs, N.J.: Institute for Business Planning.

Mackin, Paul J. *Benefit Financing in Unemployment Insurance: A Problem of Balancing Responsibilities.* Kalamazoo, Mich.: Upjohn Institute, 1978.

McCaffree, Kenneth M., and Malhotra, Suresh. *Unemployment, Eligibility Rules and the Loss of Health Insurance Benefits.* Brookfield, Wis.: International Foundation of Employment Benefit Plans, 1977.

McGill, Daniel M. *Life Insurance.* Homewood, Ill.: Richard D. Irwin, Inc., 1967.

Roberts, James E. *Federal Income, Estate & Gift Taxation of Group Life Insurance.* Rockville Center, N.Y.: Farnsworth Publishing Co., 1976.

Tax Facts on Life Insurance. Cincinnati, Ohio: National Underwriters Co. (published annually).

PART IV Protection Against Extraordinary or Catastrophic Costs

Ashford, Nicholas A. *Crisis in the Workplace: Occupational Disease and Injury.* Cambridge, Mass.: MIT Press, 1976.

Bacow, Lawrence C. *Bargaining for Job Safety and Health.* Cambridge, Mass.: MIT Press, 1980.

Bell, Donald R. "Dental and Vision Care Benefits in Health Insurance Plans." *Monthly Labor Review,* 103, June 1980, pp. 22–26.

Chassin, Mark R. "The Containing of Hospital Costs: A Strategic Assessment." *Medical Care* (supplement) 16 October 1978, pp. 1–55.

DeMent, Sandy, "Prepaid Legal Service Plans: Past Developments, Present Status, and Future Prospects," *Pension World,* 14, No. 7 July 1978, p. 17.

Egdahl, Richard H., and Walsh, Diana Chapman, eds. *Payer, Provider, Consumer: Industry Confronts Health Care Costs. A Business Persepctive on Industry and Health Care. Background Papers on Industry's Changing Role in Health Care Delivery. Health Services and Health Hazards: The Employee's Need to Know. Industry and HMOs: A Natural Alliance. Containing Health Benefit Costs: The Self-Insurance Option. Industry's Voice in Health Policy. Women, Work, and Health: Challenges to Corporate Policy. Mental Wellness Programs for Employees.* Series on Industry and Health Care, vols. 1–9. New York: Springer-Verlag New York, Inc., 1977–1980. (available from Boston University Center for Industry and Health Care, 53 Bay State Road, Boston, Mass. 02215).

"For Prepaid Legal, A Day in Court is on the Docket." *Business Insurance,* 15, No. 13 March 30, 1981, p. 3.

Gaines, Sidney. "How Prepaid Legal Plans Work." *Risk Management,* 28, No. 8 August 1981, pp. 28–31.

Langstraat, Craig J. "Medical Reimbursement Plans—Changes for the 1980's." *Taxes,* 58 April 1980, pp. 276–278.

National Academy of Sciences, Institute of Medicine. *Assessing Quality in Health Care: An Evaluation.* Washington, D.C.: IOM Publication 76–04, November 1976.

National Academy of Sciences, Institute of Medicine. *Health Planning in the United States: Issues in Guideline Development.* Washington, D.C.: IOM Publications 80-01, March 1980.

National Chamber Foundation. *A National Health Care Strategy.* Washington, D.C.: 1978.

"Prepaid Group Legal Plans." *Segal Company Newsletter,* 25, No. 2 Summer 1981.

Spencer, Bruce. *Group Benefits in a Changing Society.* rev. ed. Chicago: Charles D. Spencer & Assocs., 1978.

U.S. Department of Health, Education, and Welfare, Health Care Financing Administration, Office of Research, Demonstrations, and Statistics. *Health Care Financing Review* 1 Winter 1980.

U.S. Department of Health, Education and Welfare, Public Health Service, Office of the Assistant Secretary for Health and Surgeon General. *Healthy People, The Surgeon General's Report on Health Promotion and Disease Prevention,* no. 79-55071, (Washington, D.C.: Government Printing Office, 1979).

U.S. Department of Health, Education and Welfare, Public Health Service, Office of the Assistant Secretary for Health. *Proceedings of the National Conference on Health Promotion Programs in Occupational Settings, January 17-19, 1979,* (Washington, D.C.: Government Printing Office, 1979).

U.S. Public Health Service. "Health Promotion Programs in Occupational Settings—A Special Section." *Public Health Reports* 95 March–April 1980, pp. 99–200.

PART V Specialized Plans

"Adoption Benefits." *Hewitt Associates Research Report,* October 1980.

"Auto Insurance May Catch On This Time." *Wall Street Journal*, January 7, 1981, p. 25.

"American Can Expands Its Flexible Benefits Program." *Employee Benefits Plan Review Research Reports,* 28, No. 8 February 22, 1980, p. .007-7.

Beadle, Carson E. "Cafeteria Benefits Need Careful Planning." *IF Employee Benefits Journal,* September 1981.

"Blue Book Quiz on Multiemployer Pension Plan Amendments Act" *Kwasha Lipton Special Report,* July 1981.

Cooper, Robert W., and McFadden, John J. "Cafeteria Compensation Plans: The Revenue Act of 1978—The New Ground Rules and Some New Issues" *CLU Journal,* 34, No. 2 April 1980, pp. 29–39.

"Deferred Compensation Added to Cafeteria Choices." *Hewitt Associates Special Report*. December 19, 1980.

"Employers Lend Hand in Day Care," *Business Insurance,* 15, No. 11 March 16, 1981, p. 3.

Golembiewski, Robert T.; Fox, Ronald G.; and Proehl, Carl W., Jr. "Flexitime, the Supervisors' Verdict." *The Wharton Magazine,* 4, No. 4 Summer 1980.

"Low Cost, Employee Goodwill Persuades Employers to Introduce a Variety of Adoption Benefits." *Employee Benefit Plan Review,* 35, No. 8 February 1981.

Multiemployer Pension Plan Arbitration Rules. Brookfield, Wis.: International Foundation of Employer Benefit Plans, 1981.

O'Brien, Dorothy. *Flexitime™—The Emerging Employee Benefit*. Verona, N.J.: Personnel Research Assocs., 1981.

Petersen, Donald J. "Flexitime in the United States—The Lessons of Experience." *Personnel*, 57, No. 1 January-February 1980, pp. 21–31.

Werther, William B., Jr., and Cone, James R. "Implementing Flexible Fringe Benefits Through Variable Incentive Plans." *CLU Journal,* 33, No. 1 January 1979, pp. 37–43.

Yoder, Dale, and Eneman, Herbert G., Jr. *ASPA Handbook of Personnel and Industrial Relations*. Washington, D.C.: Bureau of National Affairs, 1979.

PERIODICALS

BNA Pension Reporter [weekly]
Bureau of National Affairs
1231 25th Street, N.W.
Washington, D.C. 20037

CLU Journal [quarterly]
American Society of CLU
270 Bryn Mawr Avenue
Bryn Mawr, Pa. 19010

Compensation Review [quarterly]
AMACOM
Box 319
Saranac Lake, N.Y. 12983

EBPR Research Reports [weekly]
Charles D. Spencer & Assocs.
222 West Adams Street
Chicago, Ill. 60606

Employee Benefit Plan Review [monthly]
Charles D. Spencer & Assocs.
222 West Adams Street
Chicago, Ill. 60606

Employee Benefit Research Institute [periodic report]
1800 M Street, N.W. Suite 275
Washington, D.C. 20036

Employer's HMO Newsletter [monthly]
Personnel Research Associates
49 Oakridge Road
Verona, N.J. 07044

Executive Compensation and Employee Benefits Report [monthly]
210 South Street
Boston, Mass. 02111

ESOP Quarterly [quarterly]
ESOP Council of America
11661 San Vicente Boulevard
Suite 901
Los Angeles, Cal. 90049

Health Services Information [weekly]
HealthCare Publications
1080 National Press Building
Washington, D.C. 20045

IF Employee Benefits Journal [quarterly]
International Foundation Employee Benefit Plans
P.O. Box 69
Brookfield, Wis. 53005

Internal Revenue Bulletin [weekly]
Superintendent of Documents
U.S. Government Printing Office
Washington, D.C. 20402

Journal of Pension Planning & Compliance [quarterly]
Panel Publishers
14 Plaza Road
Greenvale, N.Y. 11548

Pension Actuary [monthly]
American Society Pension Actuaries
1700 K Street, N.W.
Washington, D.C. 20006

Pension & Profit Sharing Report [monthly]
Prentice-Hall, Inc.
Sylvan Avenue
Englewood Cliffs, N.J. 07632

Pensions & Investments [biweekly]
Crain Communications
740 Rush Street
Chicago, Ill. 60611

Pension World [monthly]
Communication Channels, Inc.
6285 Barfield Road
Atlanta, Ga. 30328

Tax Adviser [monthly]
American Institute of CPAs
1211 Avenue of the Americas
New York, N.Y. 10036

Taxation for Accountants [monthly]
210 South Street
Boston, Mass. 02111

Taxation for Lawyers [bimonthly]
210 South Street
Boston, Mass. 02111

Taxes [monthly]
Commerce Clearing House
4025 West Peterson Avenue
Chicago, Ill. 60646

Trusts & Estates [monthly]
Communications Channels Inc.
6285 Barfield Road
Atlanta, Ga. 30328

U.S. Department of Labor News [weekly]
U.S. Department of Labor
Office of Information
Washington, D.C. 20210

Index

D

J

K

L

O